Our Promise

Our Promise

Achieving Educational Equality for America's Children

Selected Essays and Articles

Maurice R. Dyson
Thomas Jefferson School of Law

Daniel B. Weddle
University of Missouri-Kansas City School of Law

Carolina Academic Press
Durham, North Carolina

Library of Congress Cataloging-in-Publication Data

Our promise : achieving educational equality for America's children / edited by Maurice R. Dyson and Daniel Weddle.
    p. cm.
 Includes bibliographical references and index.
 ISBN 978-1-59460-127-9 (alk. paper)
1. Educational equalization—United States. 2. Discrimination in education—United States. 3. United States. No Child Left Behind Act of 2001. I. Dyson, Maurice R. II. Weddle, Daniel. III. Title.

LC213.2.O88 2008
379.2'6—dc22

                        2008043652

Carolina Academic Press
700 Kent Street
Durham, North Carolina 27701
Telephone (919) 489-7486
Fax (919) 493-5668
www.cap-press.com

Printed in the United States of America

Dedicated to the loving memory of MaryAnne Lee
MRD

To Jenny
DW

Contents

VI Creating Learner-Centered Communities

Foreword

Philip T.K. Daniel, J.D., Ed.D.
WILLIAM AND MARIE FLESHER PROFESSOR OF EDUCATIONAL ADMINISTRATION
ADJUNCT PROFESSOR OF LAW
THE OHIO STATE UNIVERSITY
COLUMBUS, OHIO
JULY 2009

American education holds the promise of equal opportunity and of providing a path toward social mobility. Numerous inequities in our educational system, however, continue to hinder disadvantaged groups from participating on a level playing field as they navigate the route toward academic advancement. Further, these populations continue to find themselves limited in their prospects for improvement due to ongoing discrimination and societal stratification.

Indeed, as achievements have been made toward greater equity in education the sense of urgency has been replaced by more relaxed approaches by educational decision makers and legislative policy makers as regards fairness and justice. The reality, nonetheless, is that our institutions must continue to be vigilant in monitoring and seeking educational equality particularly since overcoming bias is still territory that students must navigate.

As evidenced by this enlightening collection of essays and articles, scholars are continuing to refocus the educational conversation toward issues of equity and equality against the backdrop of accountability. Their research communicates that equality and equitable treatment for every population in education is still a very relevant conversation that has implications for all aspects of the pedagogical experience from elementary and secondary education to higher education. These scholars press for further research and the ongoing reassessment of policy to continue to refine systems that have been put in place to create a more balanced and fair educational environment. Further, they add to both the historical and current perspectives relating to achieving equality in our educational systems. Their articles serve to increase our understanding about the fulfillment of hope in the quest toward attainment of educational advancement. The book, hence, represents an assessment of the educational possibilities in our country.

The authors elevate discussion through their research in advocating for increased attention to educational access, school alternatives and choice, school finance, and availability of resources. Further, these scholars show that although there has been legislative and judicial activity addressing the concept of educational equity, there are still major discrepancies and imbalances when comparing schools, districts, and opportunities for different student groups in our nation's educational institutions.

This edited volume provides a thought-provoking collection of papers by expert legal scholars and serves as a reminder of the extensive work that is yet to be accomplished in the evaluation of educational policy. The authors encourage us to take a second look at the research surrounding the topics of equality in education and urge us to examine the benchmarks of progress so as to gauge next steps and possible new directions in educational achievement.

In the chapters, the authors supply poignant insights about the promotion of success in the creation of the American educational enterprise by following the miasmatic denial of human dignity in the landmark case of *Plessy v. Ferguson*, 163 U.S. 537 (1896), to the feasibility of educational equality through the landmark case of *Brown v. Board of Education*, 347 U.S. 483 (1954). Likewise, they address more contemporary legal activity in *Grutter v. Bollinger*, 539 U.S. 306 (2003) and *Parents Involved in Community Schools v. Seattle School District No. 1*, 127 S.Ct. 2738 (2007), cases that serve to illuminate the struggles surrounding attempts to maintain ground and further achieve parity in schools for all students.

The text is divided into six sections that render perspectives on the occurrences of educational success through the educational pipeline stretching from K–12 through higher education and serve to communicate that there are many factors that influence educational progress and access to educational opportunities. Further, these collective works provide awareness into the issues of educational adequacy and accountability through a look at No Child Left Behind, 20 U.S.C.A. §§ 6301 et seq. (2002), the federally based accountability policy of the day, and the issues that have resulted from its enactment. The book also includes critiques and discussion of the emergence of charter schools as models of choice, autonomy, and accountability. Issues of race, gender, and language are also examined as authors explore perspectives and research that surrounds the experiences of divergent student populations. This section evidences educational gaps and challenges that exist for many in an educational system whose platform is anything but remedial. Further, the linkages of disability and delinquency are explored to highlight often neglected areas of difference in the discourse of educational equality. Finally, the promise of improved educational experiences as a result of federal and local policies is explored in the section on creating learner-centered communities by examining educational programs designed to improve student success for various student groups.

In a sense this is a compilation of works that serve as a reminder that the nation's growth, and its history will be measured not by its crepuscular and steganographic support of educating a select few in education, but, instead, by establishing the bright light of accountability and our commitment to every student by advocating for the full embodiment of equality in education.

Acknowledgments

I would like to thank Dean Rudy Hasl, the Faculty and Staff of the Thomas Jefferson School of Law, Professor Adrien Wing, Professor Michael Olivas, and Professor Philip T.K. Daniel.

Maurice R. Dyson

I would like to thank my UMKC colleagues for their invaluable help and support in making this book a reality: Ellen Suni, Nancy Levit, Allen Rostron, Lawrence MacLachlan, Kathleen Hall, Phill Johnson, Rick Thomas, and Debra Banister.

Daniel Weddle

Introduction

Maurice R. Dyson and Daniel Weddle

July 2009

For decision makers and policy makers, a true roadmap for educational reform must begin with an intellectually honest dialogue that critiques both law and policy with a view to serving the most vulnerable of our children. Formidable obstacles remain in the path of realizing a quality public education for all children, and if we are to overcome those obstacles, those of us in legal, educational and other disciplines must work together in the search for powerful ways to advance true equity in our educational system. This book brings together voices from multiple disciplines to examine the difficulties facing the nation's schools and to propose observations and recommendations for future reform.

From the reauthorization of the No Child Left Behind Act to the Supreme Court's recent education decisions involving race in K–12 education and higher education to the mounting concerns regarding school finance and testing, this compendium of works represents the first conscious effort to explore educational law through the interrelated fields of critical race theory, educational philosophy, sociology, civil rights, pedagogical theory and law. Our objective in this book has been threefold. In the first instance, we seek to clearly define and reconceptualize fundamental doctrine and the very ways in which it arranges legal relationships and policy in the debate to reform public education. Second, we have attempted to explore the continuum of social, economic and political influence in the law and the means by which it has affected substantive legal rules and standards governing the allocation of educational opportunity. We explore the seemingly intractable issues in educational equality such as school finance, special education, affirmative action, desegregation, curricular reform and bilingual education, just to name a few. Through the prisms of race, ethnicity, language, disability, socioeconomic status, sex and gender orientation, we explore the landscape of educational law and policy in the hope of gaining new insights for achieving greater educational equity and corrective justice. Finally, by exploring different aspects of educational policy through a variety of analytical frameworks, we hope to reach scholarly audiences, reformists, advocates and policy makers who reside beyond the academic domain and to begin a broader discussion that includes voices from all corners of our society.

That broader discussion is critically important, but until now it has been either lacking or muted. We have noticed that those arguing education cases in the nation's courts are often seeking remedies that nearly anyone outside the legal world would find ill-advised. Social science data (although still often contentious) and existing best practices do not support many of the remedies that attorneys have long advocated and which are, in many cases, detrimental to the very remedial goals sought. Likewise, as educators we have witnessed school districts crippled by the fear of liability, make—in the midst of that fear—the most rudimentary errors that eventually expose them to enormous liability. We must build bridge to connect the world of educators, policy makers and lawyers.

It occurred to us then that if educators, lawyers and decision makers alike knew that the law provides a map that contains ample room for discretion in the choice of roads to effective reform, they would be more likely to use that discretion more powerfully and competently. Importantly, the law is not a roadmap so much as a map of landmines and pitfalls to avoid; it gives very little guidance about what is actually best for our public education system and our nation's children. Therefore, a more nuanced interdisciplinary discussion is crucial to successful reform.

Accordingly, our work has attempted to delineate not only where the law ends but where educational discretion begins. In this regard, we are fortunate to be joined by a very talented group of distinguished contributors who hail from law, education, sociology, civil rights and other disciplines to offer important insights and to move us closer to achieving the promise our nation has made to its children. That promise is central to the American dream, central to our nation's health, and paramount to our moral obligation to one another. We invite you to partake in this important dialogue and trust you will be both edified and inspired by *Our Promise: Achieving Educational Equality for America's Children.*

I
Desegregation, Diversity and Discrimination

1

Desegregation and the Struggle for Equal Schooling: Rolling the Rock of Sisyphus

Molly Townes O'Brien

In the ancient Greek myth, Sisyphus is sentenced by the gods to roll a tremendous, heavy stone up toward the top of a mountain every day throughout eternity. At the end of each day, just before he reaches the top, Sisyphus watches, exhausted, as the stone tumbles back down to the bottom of the mountain.

Like Sisyphus, school reformers have struggled mightily to push American education toward the ideals of equal opportunity and equal access, only to see their progress roll like Sisyphus' stone back to the bottom of the mountain, time and again. The problem, of course, is that the reformers must push the stone up a mountain made steep by the self-interest of those who are privileged in an unequal system. Although almost everyone endorses egalitarian ideals in the abstract, no one likes to give up a real advantage or privilege. People are especially loathe to give up an advantage or even a potential advantage that may accrue to their own children. So the stone is a heavy one and the mountain exhaustingly steep. Nevertheless, closing the gap between the egalitarian rhetoric and the discriminatory reality of public schooling has been the target of school reform for decades and a major goal of the civil rights movement.

This chapter recounts the Sisyphean effort to achieve equal educational opportunity for African Americans through school desegregation. It is a task that has endured for more than a century and that has occupied the energies of some of America's greatest lawyers, activists, scholars and school reformers. Further, in spite of countless setbacks, the labor continues. It is important to note as an initial matter exactly what is at stake in school desegregation. Simply mixing people of different races together is not what school desegregation is all about. Equality, opportunity, and access, rather than assimilation, are the goals of school desegregation. Robert Carter, one of the lawyers who litigated *Brown v. Board of Education*,[1] commented, "While we fashioned *Brown* on the theory that equal education and integrated education were one and the same, the goal was not integration but equal educational opportunity."[2] Educational opportunity, in turn, was to provide economic and social uplift for an oppressed black community.

---

1. 347 U.S. 483 (1954) (holding that in public education the doctrine of "separate but equal" has no place).
2. Robert L. Carter, *A Reassessment of Brown v. Board* 25, in Shades of Brown: New Perspectives on School Desegregation (Derrick Bell, ed., 1980).

The Mismatch of Ideals and Reality

Americans have always placed special importance on public schooling.[3] Benjamin Rush proclaimed in 1786, "The business of education has acquired a new complexion by the independence of our country … The form of government we have assumed has created a new class of duties to every American."[4] Self-government created citizen-rulers who must be educated to direct the affairs of the republic, and the founders of the nation viewed education as crucial to the experiment in self-government. Moreover, as public education expanded, it was touted as more than a tool for effective government. Horace Mann, Secretary of the State Board of Education in Massachusetts in 1837 and the most articulate public voice of the movement for universal free schooling, contended that the common school, if properly developed and justly administered, could become a virtual panacea for all of society's ills, slaying the vices of "intemperance, avarice, war, slavery, bigotry, the woes of want and the wickedness of waste."[5] The mission of the school was not merely to ensure that each child received the rudiments of academic knowledge but also to reform society by bringing children together to be educated in shared values, morality, and discipline.

Early school activists believed that bringing children together in a common school would develop not only affinity among citizens but also true equality. In theory, at least, education would bring about citizen equality by distributing knowledge and nurturing individual merit and ingenuity in all classes of children. Children in America, born into differing economic circumstances, would have equality of *opportunity* because of the publicly supported school system. The government would not redistribute wealth or capital. The government would, however, freely distribute *education*. By diffusing civilization's accumulated wealth of knowledge to all children, the school would counteract the "tendency to the domination of capital and the servility of labor."[6] Universal education would allow for social mobility and encourage ingenuity and progress.

Horace Mann declared the school to be the "the great equalizer of the conditions of men— the balance wheel of the social machinery":[7]

> If one class possesses all the wealth and the education, while the residue of society is ignorant and poor, it matters not by what name the relation between them may be called; the latter, in fact and in truth, will be the servile dependents and subjects of the former. But if education be equably diffused, it will draw property after it, by the strongest of all attractions; for such a thing never did happen, and never can happen, as that an intelligent and practical body of men should be permanently poor.[8]

---

3. Parts of the following pages are adapted from the author's article *Brown on the Ground: A Journey of Faith in Common Schooling*, 35 Toledo L. Rev. 813–839 (2004).

4. Lawrence A. Cremin, American Education, The National Experience, 1783–1876, 116 (1980) (quoting Benjamin Rush).

5. Horace Mann, *Twelfth Annual Report of the Board of Education, Together with the Twelfth Annual Report of the Secretary of the Board* (1848), reprinted in Lawrence A. Cremin, ed., The Republic and the School: Horace Mann on the Education of Free Men (1957), 79–80, 84–97.

6. *Id.* at 86.

7. *Id.* at 87.

8. *Id.* at 86–87.

Ralph Waldo Emerson described American free public schooling as the most radical of revolutions:

> The poor man, whom the law does not allow to take an ear of corn when starving, nor a pair of shoes for his freezing feet, is allowed to put his hand into the pocket of the rich, and say, You shall educate me, not as you will, but as I will: not alone in the elements, but, by further provision, in the languages, in sciences, in the useful and in elegant arts.[9]

Thus, economic integration and citizen equality have been core ideals of American public schooling since its founding. The egalitarian ideals of free schooling, however, have never matched public school reality. According to Professor Carl Kaestle, the ideology that promoted the common school system, "in all its variants, featured a belief in the racial superiority of whites."[10] White society considered blacks to be "unassimilable" and therefore not worthy of acculturation in a common school.[11] Therefore, although early school advocates spoke of the need for universal, free public schooling, the public schools established in nineteenth-century America were almost universally segregated by race.[12] The public education that was offered to black children in the Northeast, Midwest, and West, was not only segregated by race but was also inferior in resources, materials, pedagogy, and curricula.[13] In the South, slaves typically received no schooling and were forbidden by law to learn to read.

American public schools have historically segregated, failed to educate, or miseducated poor children, Native American children, non-English speakers, disabled children and black Americans. Rather than serving as an avenue of social mobility, the school system has worked, in the words of the famous educator, John Dewey, as "a vast filtering system … unaware of its own biases" to perpetuate the existing social order.[14] Although opportunity, equality, and social mobility have always been core rhetorical ideals of American public schooling, the reality of public schooling has been segregation, inequality and perpetuation of the status quo.

---

9. Ralph Waldo Emerson, *Education*, in Educational Ideas In America: A Documentary History 176 (1974).

10. Carl F. Kaestle, Pillars Of The Republic 172–180 (1983).

11. Lawrence A. Cremin, American Education: The Metropolitan Experience 1876–1980, 242 (1988). For many years, Native American children were also considered unassimilable. They faced a public program of extermination or removal rather than education and assimilation. *Id.;* Kaestle, Pillars Of The Republic, *supra* note 10, at 180. Further, many Catholic families did not *want* to be assimilated. Inasmuch as common schooling sought to inculcate shared values, it encountered conflict whenever the values of the school were not in fact shared by the families and cultures of the children being taught. *See generally,* Rosemary Salomone, Visions Of Schooling: Conscience, Community And Common Education (2000); Kaestle, Pillars Of The Republic, *supra* note 10, at 167–170 (describing Catholic conflict with the common school crusade) and at 179–180 (describing various groups who were left out or dissented against the common school ideology).

12. Kaestle, Pillars Of The Republic, *supra* note 10, at 173–174 (1983). There were a few exceptions. Schools in Lowell, Nantucket, New Bedford and Worcester, Massachusetts, for example, integrated before 1850. *Id.* at 177.

13. *Id.* at 172–180.

14. David Tyack, One Best System: A History Of American Urban Education 198 (1974) (quoting John Dewey, *Individuality, Equality, and Superiority,* 33 The New Republic 61, 62 (December 13, 1922).

The Legal Foundations of Segregation and Inequality

The African American struggle to gain access to high-quality public education began more than 150 years ago. In the South, where whites feared that educating blacks might upset white authority or lead to slave revolt, the slave community developed a "fundamental belief in universal education as a necessary basis for freedom and citizenship."[15] Following the Civil War, black Southerners enthusiastically joined in efforts to establish public schools. For former slaves, education meant liberation.[16] They were among the first native Southerners to campaign for universal, state-supported public education.[17] With newly elected black members, reconstruction legislatures across the South drafted new state constitutional provisions for public schooling.

During the nineteenth century, African Americans and their white allies formed local and ad hoc organizations to pool their resources and fund lawsuits seeking an end to racial discrimination in schooling.[18] At least eighty-two cases challenging race discrimination in schools were filed between 1834 and 1903 in twenty states and the District of Columbia.[19] Although many of these cases achieved some success on a local level, victories were often short-lived.[20] Then, at the end of the nineteenth century, the black struggle for equal schooling was dealt two devastating blows.

First, in *Plessy v. Ferguson*,[21] the Supreme Court upheld a Louisiana statute requiring racial segregation in "separate but equal" railroad cars. *Plessy* validated racial segregation laws, finding no violation of the Fourteenth Amendment where the law required travelers to be seated according to their race in "separate but equal" railroad cars. Three years later, the Supreme Court delivered a second devastating blow to the black quest for equal

---

15. JAMES D. ANDERSON, THE EDUCATION OF BLACKS IN THE SOUTH, 1860–1935, 281 (1988).

16. ADAM FAIRCLOUGH, TEACHING EQUALITY: BLACK SCHOOLS IN THE AGE OF JIM CROW 3 (2001).

17. ANDERSON, *supra* note 15, at 4 (1988).

18. *See, e.g.,* J. Morgan Kousser, *Separate But Not Equal: The Supreme Court's First Decision on Racial Discrimination in Schools,* 46 J. S. HIST. 17, 22–23 (1980) (describing how lawyers were hired to contest the closing of Ware High School in Richmond County, Georgia). During the late nineteenth century several civil rights organizations adopted litigation agendas. These included the Afro-American Council, led by Booker T. Washington, the Niagara Movement, whose founders included W. E. B. Du Bois, and the Constitution League, founded by industrialist John Milholland. Susan D. Carle, *Race, Class and Legal Ethics in the Early NAACP (1919–1920),* 20 LAW & HIST. REV. 97, 101–103 (2002).

19. J. MORGAN KOUSSER, DEAD END: THE DEVELOPMENT OF NINETEENTH-CENTURY LITIGATION ON RACIAL DISCRIMINATION IN SCHOOLS (1986). *See also* RICHARD KLUGER, SIMPLE JUSTICE 170 (1975) (describing the results of litigation challenging segregated schools in twenty-nine states before 1935).

20. Professor J. Morgan Kousser asserts that court decision favored the plaintiffs in a majority of the suits seeking racial integration during the nineteenth century. He notes, however, that because local judges' terms were often short and because of white resistance to integration, victories in the court did not always translate into changes in the schools. KOUSSER, *supra* note 19, at 8–10, n. 23. Nineteenth-century suits seeking school integration suffered famous defeats in court as well. *See, e.g., Roberts v. City of Boston,* 5 CUSHING REPORTS 198 (1849) (upholding race segregation in Boston's public schools); *Ohio ex rel. Directors of Eastern and Western School Districts of Cincinnati v. City of Cincinnati,* 19 Ohio 178 (1850) (upholding race segregation in Cincinnati's public schools).

21. 163 U.S. 537 (1896).

schooling when it declined to enforce the "equal" aspect of "separate but equal" in the case of *Cumming v. Richmond County*.[22]

Cumming v. Richmond County was the first challenge to separate and unequal schooling to reach the U.S. Supreme Court. The controversy began in 1897 when the all-white Richmond County Board of Education closed Ware High School, a black public high school in Augusta, Georgia.[23] During the Reconstruction era, black citizens in Augusta had made great strides toward the creation of a black middle class. Black Augustans had established one of the first colleges for black students. They had also established the only high school for black students in Georgia. When the board closed the school, members of the small and elite black middle class came together to resist the board's decision. First they petitioned the board to keep the school open. They pointed out that the board supported a public high school for white girls, and a Baptist high school for white boys and girls. They pointed out that new state appropriations provided enough to support schools for both races and that the law required separate but equal schools.

The board rejected the petition, claiming that the money saved by closing the high school was needed to hire elementary school teachers for black children. Meanwhile, the board continued its support of a public high school for white girls and a Baptist high school for white boys and girls and spent three to four times as much money on each white student in the county as it did on each black student.[24]

Black parents then brought suit seeking to enjoin collection of taxes for the white high schools until the black high school was reinstated. The suit was initially successful in the local Superior Court, but was overturned by the Georgia Supreme Court. In their appeal to the U.S. Supreme Court, plaintiffs did not challenge the constitutionality of the Georgia law that required separate school facilities for the races, but asked that tax collection be enjoined until equal facilities were made available to both races. Justice Harlan, who three years earlier in *Plessy v. Ferguson* had argued in an eloquent dissenting opinion that a color-blind Constitution did not permit the separation of the races in train accommodations, wrote the opinion for a unanimous court, declaring that

> in [the Court's] opinion, it is impracticable to distribute taxes equally. The appropriation of a portion of the taxes for a white girls' high school is not more discrimination against these colored plaintiffs than it is against many white people in the county. A taxpayer who has boys and no girls of a school age has as much right to complain of the unequal distribution of the taxes to a girls' high school as have these plaintiffs.[25]

Justice Harlan went on to credit the board's explanation of their reasons for closing the school, and declined to exercise federal judicial power to require state officials to spend tax money equally for black and white education. Together, the *Plessy* and *Cumming* decisions tacitly validated separate and unequal schooling, gave the states "a green light to heighten discrimination in publicly funded activities[,] and discouraged black litigants from seeking redress in the federal courts."[26]

---

22. 175 U.S. 528 (1899).
23. Kousser, *supra* note 18, at 25 (1980).
24. *Id.* at 24–25.
25. 175 U.S. 528, 543 (1899).
26. Kousser, *supra* note 18, at 42.

In the years that followed *Plessy* and *Cumming*, public schooling expanded and gained more importance across the nation, but schooling for African Americans was separate and profoundly unequal. In a district where white children rode on a bus to a brick school building equipped with a cafeteria, a library, indoor plumbing and heat and a janitorial staff, black children walked to a school that was a one-room wooden structure without a library or even indoor plumbing. Black teachers were paid less than white teachers. Black children were given the cast-off books from the white schools. Every aspect of the separate schooling system was unequal. In some places, schooling for African American students was not merely separate and unequal; it was separate and nonexistent. For example, no public high school for black students was established in Richmond County to replace Ware High School until 1945.[27]

Across the nation—North and South—many black children lacked access to basic education.[28] For the few black children who received a high-quality primary education, opportunities to advance to higher education were extremely limited. In the South, states had established separate colleges for black students, but provided only a limited number of degree options. The doors of the state flagship institutions, which offered doctoral programs in the arts and sciences and training in medicine and law, were firmly closed to black students. Their doors were open to whites only. Only whites had access to the most prestigious education, knowledge and degrees.

Pushing the Stone:
The NAACP Quest for Equal Schooling

With the founding of the National Association for the Advancement of Colored People (NAACP) in 1909, the black struggle for civil rights gained national coordination.[29] The NAACP's National Legal Committee charter defined the committee's work as "dealing with injustice in the courts as it affects the Negro" and as having a "national scope."[30] The goal of NAACP legal activity, however, was not merely to vindicate the rights of individual plaintiffs in court. Rather, the goal was to change the society. Early NAACP leaders recognized that African Americans "are confronted every day of their lives with the most galling conditions; ... subjected to insult ... refused service and courteous treatment ... even in places where they are guaranteed absolute equality with their white brethren by legal statutes."[31] The National Legal Committee goal would be "an organized attack on the whole system of discrimination in places of public accommodation."[32]

---

27. *Id.* at 61.
28. Some excellent black schools did exist during the segregationist era. Many of these schools were established and funded through the private efforts of black parents and philanthropic institutions. *See, generally*, Vanessa Siddle Walker, THEIR HIGHEST POTENTIAL: AN AFRICAN AMERICAN SCHOOL COMMUNITY IN THE SEGREGATED SOUTH (1996).
29. The story of the early NAACP is told in several sources. *See, e.g.*, CHARLES FLINT KELLOGG, NAACP: A HISTORY OF THE NATIONAL ASSOCIATION FOR THE ADVANCEMENT OF COLORED PEOPLE (1967).
30. Susan D. Carle, *supra* note 18.
31. *Id.* at 115 (quoting Joel Springarn).
32. *Id.* at 116 (quoting Joel Springarn).

In 1922, an $800,000 donation from Charles Garland, given to support "liberal and radical causes,"[33] was used to set up the American Fund for Public Service, commonly known as the Garland Fund. The Garland Fund was administered by a group of liberal activists, who in 1929 formed a committee to consider "Negro work practices and problems."[34] Under the leadership of James Weldon Johnson, a former general secretary of the NAACP,[35] the committee recommended that the Garland Fund finance "a large-scale, widespread, dramatic campaign to give the Southern Negro his constitutional rights, his political and civil equality." In 1930 the Garland Fund gave the NAACP a $100,000 grant for the purpose of launching a "coordinated campaign of litigation against Jim Crow laws in transportation, education, voting and jury service."[36]

With the receipt of the Garland Fund grant, the NAACP had, for the first time, enough money to develop a long-term, sustainable litigation plan.[37] Armed with a long-term litigation strategy carefully planned "to secure decisions, rulings and public opinion on the broad principle instead of being devoted to merely miscellaneous cases,"[38] the NAACP embarked on a campaign to eliminate discrimination in housing, education and employment.

Under the leadership of Charles Hamilton Houston and his successor Thurgood Marshall, the NAACP spearheaded a nationwide effort to bring cases before the courts challenging discrimination against blacks. The NAACP already had a nationwide constituency; now it began to build a network of lawyers who would handle cases to advance the cause.[39] Early victories of the legal campaign came in cases challenging separate wage scales for black and white teachers[40] and in cases challenging segregation in higher education.[41] The plan to undermine the "separate but equal" doctrine was to begin without challenging the legal requirement of racial segregation. The cases brought asked the courts to enforce the requirement that the facilities provided to the races be "equal." Further, the NAACP selected cases involving graduate students, to avoid inciting the white community's fear of general race-mixing in the public schools.

The NAACP's litigating arm, the Legal Defense Fund (NAACP/LDF), adhered to its long-term plan, pursuing graduate school cases and winning Supreme Court victories in *Sipuel*

---

33. Kluger, *supra* note 19, at 132 (1977).

34. *Id.* at 132.

35. *Id.* at 132.

36. Mark V. Tushnet, Making Civil Rights Law: Thurgood Marshall and the Supreme Court, 1936–61, 12 (1994); Kluger *supra* note 19, at 132.

37. Kluger, *supra* note 19, at 133.

38. Oliver Houck, *With Charity for All*, 93 Yale L.J. 1415, 1457 (1984) at 1440–41; Kluger, *supra* note 19, at 133. *See, generally,* Mark V. Tushnet, The NAACP's Legal Strategy against Segregated Education, 1925–1950 (1987).

39. The ACLU pioneered the concept of working with a network of cooperating lawyers around the country. Charles R. Epp, The Rights Revolution 49–50 (1998). The NAACP also maintained a national network of affiliated lawyers, but because of early negative experiences with local counsel, the NAACP carefully selected cases and maintained control of its own litigation agenda. *See* Kellogg, *supra* note 29, at 203 (describing how local counsel failed to create a positive record for appeal in the trial of *McCabe v. Atchison Topeka and Santa Fe*).

40. More than thirty teacher salary equalization cases were brought between 1930 and 1950. Most were successful. Robert A. Margo, Race and Schooling in the South 1880–1950, 64–65 (1990).

41. *Pearson v. Murray*, 169 Md. 478, 182 A. 590 (1936) (ordering Maryland Law School to admit qualified black resident because no separate alternative placement provided equal treatment under the law).

v. Board of Regents,[42] *Sweatt v. Painter*[43] and *McLaurin v. Oklahoma State Regents*.[44] Each victory opened the door to higher education to one black student. Where the opportunities provided by the states to black college students were shown to be separate and unequal, the Supreme Court was now willing to step in to invalidate the exclusion of black students from state universities. Each victory eroded the legitimacy of the "separate but equal" doctrine.

Each victory also sparked fear in the white establishment. Some state administrators recognized that if separate schools for black elementary and secondary students continued to be uniformly and patently unequal, a general challenge to the separation of races would eventually win. This realization sparked a wave of school equalization campaigns during the 1940s. These campaigns generally improved black education but never came close to establishing equal schooling for black students. By the 1940s, the chasm between black and white education was so large that only a massive infusion of new funds for black education could have brought it up to a minimally adequate level.[45]

Meanwhile, the white reaction to the NAACP court victories included not only some level of defensive school equalization but also bitter retaliation. Plaintiffs in civil rights cases were fired from their jobs, threatened, burned out of their homes, denied credit, arrested on trumped up charges, or beaten.[46] Thurgood Marshall himself was threatened, chased, and arrested on false charges.[47] Traveling in the segregated South, where black lawyers were either a rarity or completely unheard of, Marshall and his colleagues often encountered hostility from judges who cut short their presentations and sustained every objection against them.[48] In spite of the hardships, however, Marshall and the other lawyers at the NAACP/LDF persisted in trying cases, filing appeals, and winning favorable precedents. Gradually, they chipped away at the legal and logical underpinnings of the separate but equal doctrine until it lacked any tenable supporting rationale. After a string of victories in cases seeking to enforce the "equal" aspect of the "separate but equal" doctrine, it was time for a frontal attack on the legal separation of the races.

The decision to push ahead for racial integration of public elementary and secondary schools was controversial, even within the black community.[49] Many within the black

---

42. 332 U.S. 631, *mandamus denied sub nom.*, *Fisher v. Hurst*, 333 U.S. 147 (1948).

43. 339 U.S. 629, *reh'g denied*, 340 U.S. 946 (1950).

44. 339 U.S. 637 (1950). Following these decisions, state and federal courts ordered black students admitted to graduate programs in five more states. U.S. Comm'n on Civil Rights, Equal Protection of the Laws in Public Higher Education 34 (1960) (Virginia); *State ex rel. Toliver v. Board of Educ.*, 230 S.W.2d 724 (Mo.1950) (Missouri); *Wilson v. Board of Supervisors*, 92 F.Supp. 986 (E.D.La.1950), aff'd, 340 U.S. 909 (1951) (Louisiana); *McKissick v. Carmichael*, 187 F.2d 949 (4th Cir.1951), cert. denied, 341 U.S. 951 (1951) (North Carolina); *Gray v. University of Tenn.*, 342 U.S. 517 (1952) (Tennessee).

45. See, *e.g.*, Benjamin Mays, *Why an Atlanta School Suit?* 5 New South 1, 2 (1950) (arguing that the enormous gulf between black and white schools made the cost of bringing black schools up to the level of white schools so high as to make it unlikely that true equalization might ever occur).

46. See, *e.g.*, Kluger, *supra* note 19, at 3.

47. *Id.* at 224–226.

48. *Id.* at 223.

49. *Id.* at 165–66 (describing W. E. B. Du Bois's concern that pursuing desegregation would undermine rather than build black pride and status); Jack Greenberg, Crusaders in the Courts: Legal Battles of the Civil Rights Movement 59–60 (2004) (explaining the view that desegregation was misguided because black children would be received with hostility in the white schools.) *See also,* Molly Townes O'Brien, *Brown on the Ground: A Journey of Faith in Public Schooling*, 35 Toledo L. Rev. 813, 819–830 (2004) (discussing the reasons for choosing schools as the vehicle for reform).

community, including W. E. B. Du Bois, believed that black children would be mistreated and miseducated in white schools. The decision to challenge segregation was, however, a decision that Robert Carter, a leading NAACP lawyer, would later describe as the only possibility.

> Blatant, open, raw racism, churlish and uncivilized, was a fact of life in the South, and we were told that the South's outrageously demeaning race relations mores would never change. In the South black children were openly short-changed in per capita pupil allocations and in every other educational resource. We knew of no publicly financed segregated black school that could conceivably be considered the equivalent of its white counter-part. It seemed self-evident that segregation was the malfunction in the system that relegated blacks to inferior educational status and that integration was the only tool that could accomplish the necessary adjustment.[50]

In theory, if white children and black children attended the *same* schools, they would necessarily receive the *same* education. It was evident that white parents valued education highly enough to make sure that their children received a high-quality education. And black parents and activists knew that quality education was "an indispensable need" if poor black families were to "have any chance or hope of escaping the depressing fate of their forebears."[51] Equal educational opportunity—in the form of integrated educational opportunity—was to provide equal access to the social and economic opportunity structure.

The watershed victory came in the consolidated appeal of four cases challenging segregation in elementary education, *Brown v. Board of Education*.[52] In the 1954 landmark decision, the Supreme Court invalidated "separate but equal" education. Justice Warren, writing for a unanimous court, held,

> In these days it is doubtful that any child may reasonably be expected to succeed in life if he is denied the opportunity of an education. Such an opportunity, where the state has undertaken to provide it, is a right which must be made available to all on equal terms.... We conclude that in the field of public education the doctrine of separate but equal has no place. Separate educational facilities are inherently unequal.[53]

With the announcement of the *Brown* decision, it appeared that a new era in public schooling might be within reach. The task of pushing the public school toward its ideals of equal opportunity now had a new champion, the federal courts. Perhaps Sisyphus' stone would reach the top of the mountain at last. When the decision was announced, many within the black community were optimistic that white society would comply with the ruling in good faith. In an optimistic moment, NAACP leader Thurgood Marshall predicted that segregation in schools would be eliminated within five years and that all forms of racial segregation would be stamped out by the hundredth anniversary of the Emancipation Proclamation.[54]

---

50. Robert L. Carter, *A Reassessment of Brown v. Board,* in Shades of Brown: New Perspectives on School Desegregation, Derrick Bell, ed. 22 (1980).

51. *Id.* at 24 (discussing, specifically, unskilled black Southerners who migrated to Northern urban communities and suffered from "unemployment, underemployment and unemployability").

52. 347 U.S. 483 (1954).

53. *Id.*

54. Kluger, *supra* note 19, at 714.

The Stone Rolls Back: Lack of Clarity in the Courts and White Resistance to *Brown* Thwart the Movement toward Equal Schooling

The 1954 *Brown* decision (*Brown I*) struck down state-imposed racial segregation in the public schools but, unfortunately, provided no guidance for how to proceed with the task of moving from a dual system of race-segregated schools to a unitary system of race-integrated schools. *Brown II*,[55] the implementing decision that in 1955 followed on the heels of *Brown I*, returned the cases to the district courts for desegregation plans to be developed with "all deliberate speed."[56] Meanwhile, a complex blend of traditional and institutional racism, fear of change, and resentment of federal "meddling" with the Southern "way of life" fed a movement that called for "massive resistance" against the Supreme Court's *Brown* decisions.[57] White resistance to desegregation took many forms. Southern legislatures passed resolutions vowing to resist the "Second Reconstruction" of the South. Georgia, Virginia, Mississippi, Arkansas and Alabama passed laws requiring all schools to close in the event of a court desegregation order. In some states, tuition grant laws were enacted to enable white families to leave public schools to attend private schools.[58]

When the four consolidated cases that made up the *Brown* case were returned to the district courts, the judges called on local school authorities to set up plans for the transition to unitary school systems. The local school authorities were, of course, the same white school authorities who had supported school segregation and who had opposed the *Brown* litigation. Indeed, they did face a dilemma: in their view, white children could not reasonably be asked to leave their high-quality all-white schools to attend the underfunded and inadequate all-black schools. The parents would never allow their children to do that. Further, not enough room existed in the white schools for both the white students and all of the black students. Society had not made a sufficient economic commitment to education to support high-quality schools for all of the children. Now school authorities shied away from the prospect of stripping white children of the privilege of attending superior, all-white schools. Some feared that desegregation could destroy public support for public education and thus destroy the public schools. Rather than move to implement *Brown,* they delayed and avoided the legal requirement for change. They presented the district courts with plans that would effect the least possible change to the existing educational system. The district court judges—all white, male leaders in their communities who had been raised in the segregated system—faced tremendous anti-*Brown* sentiment and may also have feared doing damage to the existing educational institutions.[59] The district courts thus endorsed school attendance plans that had only

---

55. 349 U.S. 294 (1955).

56. *Id.* at 301.

57. *See* Numan v. Bartley, The Rise of Massive Resistance: Race and Politics in the South During the 1950s (1969); Earl Black, Southern Governors And Civil Rights: Racial Segregation as a Campaign Issue in the Second Reconstruction (1976); J. W. Ely, Crisis in Conservative Virginia (1976); N. R. McMillen, The Citizens' Council: Organized Resistance to the Second Reconstruction, 1954–1964 (1971).

58. Molly Townes O'Brien, *Private School Tuition Vouchers and the Realities of Racial Politics,* 64 Tenn. L. Rev. 359, 386 (1997).

59. *See, generally,* J. W. Peltason, Fifty-Eight Lonely Men: Southern Federal Judges and School Desegregation (1971).

modest aspirations for change. In *Briggs v. Elliott*,[60] the District Court in South Carolina wrote,

> Nothing in the Constitution or in the decision of the Supreme Court takes away from the people freedom to choose the schools they attend. The Constitution, in other words, does not require integration. It merely forbids discrimination. It does not forbid such segregation as occurs as the result of voluntary action. It merely forbids the use of governmental power to enforce segregation.[61]

Relying on this interpretation of *Brown*, several states set up "freedom of choice" plans which purported to allow black students to attend formerly white schools, but which resulted in little or no racial integration in the schools. The most effective strategies to avoid actual desegregation, however, employed administrative manipulation and legal delay. By gerrymandering school districts, creating difficult administrative procedures for student transfer, and skillfully delaying court action, whites were able to delay any meaningful implementation of *Brown* for more than a decade.[62]

Meanwhile, other resistance to *Brown* was aimed directly at the NAACP and its litigating arm, the LDF. In the years following *Brown*, the very existence of the NAACP/LDF was challenged. Southern states "passed laws and started legislative investigations, criminal prosecutions, suits for injunction, and disbarment proceedings against lawyers to put the NAACP and LDF out of business."[63] The NAACP/LDF fought on, winning before the Supreme Court and establishing in *NAACP v. Button*[64] the principle that organizing for the purpose of bringing public interest litigation is a First Amendment right.

Between 1954 and 1964, very little racial desegregation occurred. In 1957 in Little Rock, Arkansas, the National Guard had to be called out to support the token integration of Central High School.[65] In 1961 in Atlanta, Georgia, a few black students peacefully desegregated formerly all-white Grady High School. Meanwhile, school systems throughout the South still operated with separate and identifiable "Negro schools" and "white schools." Across the nation, schooling was still separate and unequal. Orders of the federal court were ineffective in achieving any real progress toward integrated education.

Pushing the Stone Upward:
The Affirmative Duty to Eliminate Dual Systems

Before change could take place in the schools, change had to take place in society. During the 1960s the civil rights movement and television coverage of that movement began

---

60. 132 F. Supp. 776 (D.C.S.C. 1955).

61. *Id*. at 777.

62. Gary Orfield and John T. Yun, *Resegregation in American Schools*, figure 1 (titled Percentage of Black Students Attending Majority White Schools in the South 1954–1996) (June 1999), www.civilrightsproject.harvard.edu/research/deseg/Resegregation_American_ Schools99 (showing that almost no desegregation took place between 1954 and 1964 and that substantial desegregation began only after the passage of the 1964 Civil Rights Act).

63. GREENBERG, CRUSADERS, *supra* note 49, at 217. *See also*, *NAACP v. Button* 371 U.S. 415 (1963); *NAACP v. Alabama* 377 U.S. 288 (1964) (reversing a decision restraining the NAACP from doing business in Alabama).

64. *NAACP v. Button*, 371 U.S. 415 (1963).

65. *See, generally*, EILEEN LUCAS, CRACKING THE WALL: THE STRUGGLES OF THE LITTLE ROCK NINE (1997) (following the stories of the nine black students who integrated Little Rock High School).

to change the way mainstream whites thought about segregation laws. Mainstream America watched on television as nonviolent black protesters were beaten by police, pushed back with the spray of fire hoses, and attacked by police dogs. Dr. Martin Luther King Jr., and other civil rights leaders pressed white Americans to take seriously the ideals of equality and justice and encouraged black Americans to face the persecution of white mobs with the Christian attitude of loving one's enemies. As the civil rights movement successfully captured the moral high ground and began to sway political opinion against overt and violent racism, the political branches of government began to respond.

The first effective governmental assistance in implementing school desegregation came from Congress with the passage of the 1964 Civil Rights Act, which made federal funding for schools contingent on ending racial discrimination. Enforcement of the act marked an important governmental shift from declaring rights to taking action. The Johnson administration endorsed the idea that it was not enough simply to outlaw segregation laws; affirmative action would be necessary to dismantle the system of race segregation and discrimination. In a speech delivered at Howard University in 1965, Lyndon Johnson praised the passage of the 1964 Civil Rights Act and other federal legislation designed to remove the legal barriers to equality. The barriers to freedom, he said, are "tumbling down,"

> but freedom is not enough. You do not wipe away the scars of centuries by saying: Now you are free to go where you want, and do as you desire, and choose the leaders you please.
>
> You do not take a person who, for years, has been hobbled by chains and liberate him, bring him up to the starting line of a race and then say, "you are free to compete with all the others," and still justly believe that you have been completely fair.
>
> Thus it is not enough just to open the gates of opportunity. All our citizens must have the ability to walk through those gates.
>
> This is the next and the more profound stage of the battle for civil rights. We seek not just freedom but opportunity. We seek not just legal equity but human ability, not just equality as a right and a theory but equality as a fact and equality as a result.[66]

With the Johnson administration firmly behind enforcement of the nondiscrimination provisions of the Civil Rights Act of 1964, progress began to be made toward school desegregation.[67] Meanwhile, the NAACP continued to pursue school desegregation cases in court and won a string of legal victories that promised enforcement of *Brown*. In *Green v. County School Board of New Kent County*,[68] the Supreme Court held that instituting a "freedom of choice" did not satisfy the school district's duty to dismantle the dual system of education. The court pointed out that in spite of the "freedom of choice" plan, the district's two schools remained racially identifiable.

> Racial identification of the system's schools was complete, extending not just to the composition of student bodies at the two schools but to every facet of school

---

66. Lyndon B. Johnson, Commencement Address at Howard University, June 4, 1965, Lyndon Baines Johnson Library and Museum, National Archives and Records Administration, available at www.lbjlib.utexas.edu/johnson/archives.hom/speeches.hom/650604.asp.

67. Orfield and Yun, *supra* note 62 at figure 1; *see also* Gary Orfield and Susan Eaton, DISMANTLING DESEGREGATION: THE QUIET REVERSAL OF *BROWN V. BOARD OF EDUCATION* (1996) (describing the Johnson administration's enforcement of the 1964 Civil Rights Act); STEPHEN C. HALPERN, ON THE LIMITS OF THE LAW (1995).

68. 391 U.S. 430 (1968).

operations—faculty, staff, transportation, extracurricular activities and facilities. In short, the State, acting through the local school board and school officials, organized and operated a dual system, part "white" and part "Negro."[69]

Compliance with *Brown* would require more than allowing a few courageous black children to attend previously all-white schools. In *Green,* the Supreme Court held that *Brown* charged school authorities with an "affirmative duty to take whatever steps might be necessary to convert [from a dual system of segregated schools] to a unitary system in which racial discrimination would be eliminated root and branch."[70] Further, the Court would not tolerate more delay in implementing conversion plans. In *Alexander v. Holmes County Board of Education,*[71] the Supreme Court decided that the time for "deliberate speed" had ended. The Board of Education was required to begin a reasonable program of desegregation "now." School administrators facing the prospect of both desegregation litigation and the threat of loss of federal funding, began to make plans for more than token desegregation. Under the watchful eye of the federal district courts, school districts began to put plans in place to create unitary school systems—that is, systems that were not racially identifiable in any of the major facets identified in the *Green* decision: faculty, staff, transportation, extracurricular activities or facilities.

Further, because the elimination of the segregated systems of attendance would not be achieved by voluntary choice, school authorities began to put in place mandatory student assignment plans. In *Swann v. City of Charlotte Mecklenberg,*[72] the Supreme Court upheld a desegregation plan that redrew attendance zones and used busing to effect racial integration. The decisions of the Supreme Court in *Swann* and *Green,* together with the enforcement of the Civil Rights Act of 1964, brought about a substantial degree of racial integration. Local school authorities tried a variety of methods, singly or in combination, to desegregate schools. These included mandatory busing, school pairing, magnet schools, majority to minority transfer programs (M-to-M transfer), open enrollment and voluntary transfer programs. Progress toward the elimination of racially identifiable schools was particularly notable in the South, where the federal government focused its enforcement actions because of the history of state-mandated systems of racial segregation. In 1964, only 2.3 percent of African American students in the South attended majority white schools. By 1967, that number had increased to 13.9 percent. African American children attending majority white schools increased to increased to 23.4 percent in 1968, and to 37.6 percent in 1976.[73]

The Stone Rolls Back: Supreme Court Retrenchment

For a brief moment, it seemed that the stone was moving easily toward the top of the mountain. With support from both the Supreme Court and the executive branches of gov-

---

69. 391 U.S. at 435.

70. *Id.* at 438.

71. 396 U.S. 19 (1969).

72. 402 U.S. 1 (1971).

73. Gary Orfield, The Civil Rights Project, Harvard University, Schools More Separate: Consequences of a Decade of Resegregation (2001), available at www.civilrightsproject.harvard.edu/ research/deseg/Schools_More_Separate.pdf.

ernment, achieving racial integration in public schooling looked possible. But public sentiment continued to disfavor school desegregation. The problems of unequal buildings, facilities and teaching staffs did not disappear. White parents did not want their children to spend an hour every day on the bus to travel to an inferior school across town. Moreover, racial tensions in schools and discrimination against black students within newly integrated schools prevented integrated schools from delivering the promised equal opportunity.

As political support for school integration eroded, both the Supreme Court and the executive backed away from enforcing equal schooling. With the retirement of liberal Supreme Court Justice Earl Warren in 1969 and the addition of two new conservative members to the Supreme Court shortly thereafter, the Supreme Court began a long, slow retrenchment from *Green* and *Swann*. Although the process of desegregation continued (and achieved increasing levels of racial integration through about 1988), the notable turning point in Supreme Court precedent came in 1974 in a case called *Milliken v. Bradley*.[74] The case involved segregated schools in Detroit, where a majority of the students in the entire school system were African American. To effect racial integration, the District Court had ordered school desegregation of both the city of Detroit and the adjoining white suburbs.[75]

The Supreme Court invalidated the metropolitan-wide approach to desegregation, holding that the federal courts could not order an interdistrict remedy in the absence of evidence of an interdistrict violation of the Constitution.[76] In so holding, the Supreme Court decision effectively foreclosed the possibility of achieving racial desegregation in many Northern and Western cities. It also encouraged white flight from inner cities and the establishment of racial and economic segregation in schools based on residential patterns. After *Milliken*, families who could buy a home in a wealthy or all-white district could effectively insulate their children from having to attend school with poor or minority children.[77]

In the years that followed the *Milliken* decision, desegregation cases continued to flow into the federal courts; the federal courts continued to find racial discrimination in violation of the Constitution; and desegregation orders were implemented. In those areas where no effective racial integration was possible within district boundaries, the courts ordered "compensatory education" programs to compensate the victims of discrimination.[78] These programs generally increased financial resources available to racially isolated schools. It is difficult to assess the relative merits or achievements of desegregation or compensatory education programs in making progress toward equal educational opportunity, but substantial research demonstrates that racial integration in schools had positive benefits on the "life chances" of minority students.[79] Nevertheless, desegregation reached its high-water mark in 1988 as school districts began to come back into court asking to be released from desegregation orders. In a series of three decisions, the Supreme Court established guidelines for releasing school systems from federal court supervision and "not so gently urged the courts to begin the process of dismantling desegregation decrees."[80]

---

74. 418 U.S. 717 (1974).

75. *Id.* at 734–35.

76. *Id.* at 748–49.

77. In those states where school finance is based on local property taxes, the cumulative effect of the residential choices of wealthy parents also contributes to the disparity between poor (primarily inner-city and rural) districts and wealthy suburban districts.

78. See, *e.g.*, *Milliken v. Bradley*, 433 U.S. 267 (1977) and *Missouri v. Jenkins*, 515 U.S. 70 (1995).

79. See James Ryan, *Schools, Race and Money,* 100 YALE L.J. 249, 297–307 (1999) (reviewing the research results of studies of the benefits of racial integration).

80. *Id.* at 265 (referring to *Missouri v. Jenkins*, 515 U.S. 70 (1995); *Freeman v. Pitts*, 503 U.S. 467 (1992); and *Board of Educ. v. Dowell*, 498 U.S. 237 (1991)).

Pushing the Stone in a Postdesegregation Era

The experience of school desegregation in DeKalb County, Georgia, presents a good illustration of how quickly the stone rolls back to the bottom of the hill. Within two months of the Supreme Court's ruling in *Green*, a group of black parents, represented by the NAACP, filed suit challenging DeKalb County's freedom of choice plan.[81] On June 12, 1969, the federal district court entered an order that abolished the district's freedom of choice plan and required the DeKalb County School System to eliminate the vestiges of its dual system.[82] The school authorities then closed all of the black schools and reassigned the black students to the previously all-white schools near their residences.[83] Attendance zones were drawn to allow for neighborhood schools; in the residential reshuffling that occurred during the succeeding years, racially identifiable schools reemerged. Schools were racially identifiable not only by the race of their students but also by the race of their faculty, staff and administrators.[84] Moreover, the predominantly white schools were staffed by teachers with higher levels of experience, and more money was spent per pupil in the predominantly white schools.[85]

Following further court action by black parents, a Majority to Minority (M-to-M) student transfer program was implemented in 1976 to allow students to move from a school where their race was a majority to a school where their race was in the minority.[86] Although the M-to-M transfer program was ostensibly race-neutral—that is, a student of any race could voluntarily move to a school where his race was in the minority—the program was used almost exclusively by black students to gain access to predominantly white schools.[87] Other programs put into effect to "combat segregation" included teacher and administrator reassignment plans; magnet schools for the performing arts, science and foreign languages; and occupational centers. A court-appointed biracial committee was established to review proposed boundary line changes, school openings and closings and the M-to-M program.[88] During this era, black plaintiffs put constant pressure on school officials to desegregate the schools and improve the quality of education being offered to black children in the county. Robert Freeman, school superintendent from 1980 to 1996, remarked that the time and energy he devoted to responding to the lawsuit was enormous. He told an Atlanta newspaper, "My snooze alarm didn't play music. It said, 'Will the defendant please rise.'"[89]

In 1986, the DeKalb County School System went back to court, seeking an order for final dismissal of the litigation.[90] School officials sought an order declaring that the school system had achieved unitary status as required by *Green*, in spite of the continuing racial identifiability of schools in the county. The District Court agreed that the schools had reached unitary status in several of the *Green* factors—student assignments, transportation, physical facilities and extracurricular activities—and cited the long-standing efforts

---

81. *Freeman v. Pitts*, 503 U.S. 467, 472 (1992).

82. *Pitts v. Freeman*, 887 F.2d 1438, 1442 (11th Cir. 1989).

83. 503 U.S. at 472.

84. 887 F2d. at 1441–43.

85. *Id.*

86. *Id.* at 473.

87. *Id.* at 1438, 1441.

88. *Id.*

89. Bill Torpy, "Bitter Lessons: Dekalb schools' 30-year struggle for racial balance has led to resegregation, and the question: What was gained?" ATLANTA CONSTITUTION (September 30, 1999).

90. 503 U.S. at 473.

and good faith of the school officials. The District Court attributed remaining segregation to voluntary demographic changes for which the DeKalb County Schools were not responsible. Although the schools had never reached unitary status in all of the *Green* factors simultaneously, the District Court ordered that the schools be released from federal court supervision in the areas where unitary status had been achieved.

The Eleventh Circuit Court reversed, saying that the system of de jure segregation could not be said to be eliminated until all facets of the school achieved unitary status simultaneously. The Court of Appeals summarized the status of race segregation in the system as follows:

> The DeKalb County School System ("DCSS") serves 79,991 students in more than 90 schools. Black students constitute 47 percent of the DCSS population. Despite the system's racial balance, 50 percent of the black students attend schools with black populations of more than 90 percent. Similarly, 27 percent of the DCSS's white students attend schools with white populations of more than 90 percent. The DCSS operates a segregated school system.[91]

The Eleventh Circuit went on to point out that black teachers, staff and administrators remained concentrated in identifiably black schools; that teachers in the identifiably black schools had, on average, less experience; and that less money was spent per pupil in the predominantly black schools.[92] The Eleventh Circuit refused to release the school district from federal court supervision in incremental stages.[93] The Supreme Court reversed, holding that the district need not meet all of the *Green* factors simultaneously to be declared unitary.[94]

Following the Supreme Court decision, the case was remanded to the District Court for a factual determination on the issue of unitary status given the new Supreme Court standard. In 1996, the District Court found that the DeKalb County Schools were unitary and released them from federal supervision.[95]

For two years following the court's determination that the schools were unitary, DeKalb County continued to operate its voluntary M-to-M program.[96] The program had broad support in the community and provided a continuing opportunity to achieve some degree of racial integration across the boundaries of school attendance zones.[97] In February 1999, however, a conservative interest group delivered an ultimatum to the DeKalb County School Board: end the M-to-M program for the 1999–2000 school year or face a lawsuit.[98] The Southeastern Legal Foundation (SLF), a "public interest" law firm opposed to all forms of affirmative action, argued that the M-to-M program benefited black students at the expense of white students and was constitutionally invalid.[99] Taking account of a student's race in making attendance decisions, the SLF argued, unconstitutionally discriminates on the basis of race;[100] after a school is declared to have abolished its de jure

---

91. 887 F.2d 1438, 1441.

92. *Id.* at 1442.

93. 503 U.S. at 484–85.

94. *Id.* at 490–91, 500.

95. *Mills v. Freeman*, 942 F. Supp 1449, 1464 (N.D. Ga. 1996).

96. Diane Loupe, "School Watch; Lawsuit Threatened Over M-to-M Transfers," ATLANTA CONSTITUTION (February 18, 1999).

97. Diane Loupe, "DeKalb County will end its $6 million busing program," ATLANTA CONSTITUTION (May 11, 1999).

98. *Id.*

99. Loupe, "School Watch," *supra* note 96.

100. *Id.*

segregation system, the school authorities may no longer use race as a basis for any decision making. All of the programs designed to minimize or eliminate race discrimination, put in place after long years of struggle by black plaintiffs—and which had been required by court order since at least 1976—were now suddenly unconstitutional, according to the SLF.[101]

In response to the threatened lawsuit, the DeKalb County School Board abandoned its M-to-M program and its race-conscious placement system in magnet schools without a fight. Indeed, the county not only abandoned its efforts to desegregate without a fight, it actually paid the SLF $5,000 in attorneys' fees.[102] A few years later, in 2004, Southwest DeKalb High School, which had been racially mixed (about 50 percent white students and 50 percent black students) in the 1970s, graduated a class of 300 black students. Most of the students had never had a white classmate.[103]

The Demise of Voluntary Integration Plans

The outcome in the DeKalb County School System was not a local aberration, but instead was an arguably logical result of a line of Supreme Court jurisprudence that limits the ability of governments to make race-based decisions, even as part of a program designed to even the playing field for minority groups. In 1989, in a case involving race-based affirmative action in governmental construction contracts, the Supreme Court held that "the standard of review under the Equal Protection Clause is not dependent on the race of those burdened or benefitted by a particular classification,"[104] and that the courts should strictly scrutinize all governmental racial classifications, permitting only those that are narrowly tailored to remedy past constitutional violations or to serve a compelling governmental interest.[105] On this basis, racial preferences in governmental contracting programs were held invalid. Other programs in which the government favored minority applicants for jobs or other benefits were similarly held to be unconstitutional.[106] Following these precedents, governments are responsible only for their own acts of racial discrimination and may not enact racial quotas or set-aside programs to counterbalance private racism or general societal discrimination. Voluntary desegregation plans are therefore constitutionally suspect.

After a school system has been declared to be "unitary," programs designed to promote racial integration can no longer be justified as a remedy for past discrimination. Voluntary racial integration programs are thus treated by the courts like any measure that discriminates based on race.[107] In light of the Supreme Court's dictum in *Freeman v. Pitts* that

---

101. Diane Loupe, "DeKalb County," *supre* note 97.

102. Ben Smith III, "Dekalb votes to end racial busing," Atlanta Constitution (December 7, 1999).

103. Dahleen Glanton, "South sees integration gains slip into past; From white to mixed to black," Chicago Tribune (May 17, 2004).

104. *City of Richmond v. J.A. Croson Co.*, 488 U.S. 469, 493–94 (1989).

105. *Id.*; Adarand v. Pena, 515 U.S. 200, 222–24 (1995).

106. See, *e.g. Regents of University of California v. Bakke*, 438 U.S. 265 (1978) (invalidating the University of California Medical School admissions policy).

107. *But see Parents Involved in Community Schools v. Seattle District Schools*, 551 U.S. ___, 127 S.Ct. 2738, 2815 (2007) (Breyer, J., arguing in dissent that voluntary integration measures should not be treated as indistinguishable from segregation measures that discriminated against the minority race).

"racial balance is not to be achieved for its own sake,"[108] even voluntary measures designed to eliminate racial segregation would fail constitutional scrutiny unless they are narrowly tailored to meet a compelling state interest.

But what governmental interest may be considered to be compelling enough to support race-conscious student placement decisions in public schooling?[109] In the decade following *Freeman v. Pitts,* this question was an open one. Nevertheless, race-conscious placement programs were infrequently upheld. In *Tuttle v. Arlington School Board,*[110] the Fourth Circuit Court invalidated a public school admission policy designed to "promote racial, ethnic, and socioeconomic diversity" on the grounds that the policy was not "narrowly tailored" to achieve the stated goal.[111] Similarly, in *Eisenberg v. Montgomery County Public Schools,*[112] the Fourth Circuit invalidated a voluntary transfer and magnet program designed to avoid racial isolation and promote student diversity on the grounds that the program was not "narrowly tailored."[113] In both cases, the court avoided deciding explicitly whether avoiding racial isolation or achieving racial diversity could be considered to be a compelling governmental interest. Taking a different approach, the Second Circuit arrived at a similar result in *Brewer v. West Irondequoit Central School District.*[114] There, the court considered the constitutional validity of a program that allowed minority students to voluntarily transfer to suburban schools. The stated goal of the program was to "reduce, prevent and eliminate minority group isolation."[115] The Second Circuit held that reducing racial isolation is a compelling state interest, but remanded the case to the district court for further consideration of whether the program was sufficiently narrowly tailored.[116]

In 2003, however, the Supreme Court considered whether "diversity" may be considered to be a compelling interest in higher education admissions.[117] In *Grutter v. Bollinger* the Supreme Court examined the admissions policy of the University of Michigan Law School and held that the law school has a compelling interest in assembling a diverse student body.[118] The Court emphasized the law school's mission and highlighted the importance of "diffusion of knowledge and opportunity through public institutions of higher education ... to all individuals regardless of race or ethnicity."[119] The Court further noted the benefits that a diverse student body brings to the law school, including increasing cross-racial understanding, stimulating positive educational outcomes and laying the groundwork for success in an "increasingly diverse workforce and society."[120]

The admissions plan used by the University of Michigan Law School was also held to be sufficiently narrowly tailored to serve its compelling state interest. The Supreme Court mapped out restrictive boundaries for the law school's use of race as a factor in admis-

---

108. *Freeman v. Pitts* 503 U.S. 467, 469 (1992).
109. *See id.* at 469.
110. 195 F.3d 698 (4th Cir. 1999).
111. *Id.* at 705.
112. 197 F.3d 123 (4th Cir. 1999), *cert. denied, Montgomery County Pub. Schs. v. Eisenberg,* 529 U.S. 1019 (2000).
113. *Id.* at 131.
114. 212 F.3d 738 (2nd Cir. 2000).
115. *Id.* at 741–42.
116. *Id.* at 753.
117. *Grutter v. Bollinger,* 539 U.S. 306 (2003).
118. *Id.* at 327–28.
119. *Id.* at 332.
120. *Id.* at 330.

sions: to be sufficiently narrowly tailored, the admissions process must not set a racial quota; it further must not be "mechanical or conclusive" but must allow for flexibility and individualized consideration in the admissions decision.[121] Before adopting a race-conscious policy, serious consideration must have been given to race-neutral alternatives.[122] The policy must also minimize the adverse impact on nonpreferred group members and have a definitive end date.[123] The University of Michigan Law School's admissions process satisfied all of these requirements and was upheld.[124]

Following the *Grutter* decision, race-conscious admissions policies in K–12 education were upheld in several cases, including *Comfort v. Lynn School Committee.*[125] The First Circuit Court of Appeals upheld a program in which students were assigned to a neighborhood school, but could request a transfer to a non-neighborhood school. The requests would be considered in light of the racial balance of the assigned and requested schools. In upholding the conscious use of the student's race as a factor in making the attendance decision, the First Circuit wrote:

> The goal of the Lynn plan — to achieve the educational and civic benefits of exposing youngsters to those of different races — is not unlawful; the attack is upon the means. Yet given the goal, it is not easy to see how it can be achieved in a community like Lynn without using race as a touchstone. The problem is that in Lynn, as in many other cities, minorities and whites often live in different neighborhoods. Lynn's aim is to preserve local schools as an option without having the housing pattern of de facto segregation projected into the school system. The choice is between openly using race as a criterion or concealing it through some clumsier proxy device (e.g., transfer restrictions based upon family income).[126]

The Court decided that the transfers did not unduly deprive any child of a comparable quality education and sensibly achieved its goal of improving the racial balance of schools district-wide.[127]

In its most recent pronouncement on the subject, the Supreme Court all but closed the door to voluntary measures designed to achieve racial balance. In *Parents Involved in Community Schools v. Seattle School District*[128] a divided Supreme Court invalidated race-conscious student assignment schemes in Seattle, Washington, and Louisville, Kentucky. Each school district had created a student assignment system that took race into account and attempted to achieve racial attendance levels that roughly reflected district demographics. Both school districts allowed substantial student or parent choice in school attendance and used race as a preference, tiebreaker or limiting constraint on transfer. The programs could fairly be characterized as modest efforts to minimize racial segregation in schools. The racial constraints affected only a small minority of the total student population and resulted in only a small number of students attending a different school than

---

121. *Id.* at 336–37.

122. *Id.* at 339.

123. *Id.* at 342.

124. In a companion case, *Gratz v. Bollinger*, 539 U.S. 244, 271–74 (2003), the University of Michigan's undergraduate affirmative action admission policy, which assigned a certain number of points to applications based on minority status and did not provide for individualized consideration of each application, was invalidated as insufficiently narrowly tailored.

125. 418 F.3d 1 (1st Cir. 2005).

126. *Id.* at 28–29.

127. *Id.*

128. 551 U.S. ___, 127 S.Ct. 2738 (2007).

they would have otherwise chosen. Neither Seattle nor Louisville school districts were under court order to desegregate at the time the lawsuit was commenced.[129]

Writing for the plurality, Chief Justice Roberts found that the districts had failed to demonstrate any compelling state interest in their student assignment programs and had further failed to narrowly tailor the programs to meet the interest stated. In Roberts's view, "The way to stop discrimination on the basis of race is to stop discriminating on the basis of race."[130] Justice Thomas took an even dimmer view of the districts' racial balance goals, saying, "The school boards have no interest in remedying the sundry consequences of prior segregation unrelated to schooling."[131]

In a dissent joined by Justices Stevens, Souter and Ginsburg, Justice Breyer wrote that the constitution permits state action aimed at reducing and eventually eliminating school segregation. Emphasizing that the basic goal of the Fourteenth Amendment was to secure civil rights for African Americans, he wrote,

> There is reason to believe that those who drafted an Amendment with this basic purpose in mind would have understood the legal and practical difference between the use of race-conscious criteria in defiance of that purpose, namely to keep the races apart, and the use of race-conscious criteria to further that purpose, namely to bring the races together.[132]

The deciding vote was cast by Justice Kennedy, who concluded that avoiding racial isolation may serve as a compelling state interest, but nevertheless concurred in the judgment that the school districts had not narrowly tailored their programs. Explaining the flaw in the districts' plans, Justice Kennedy wrote,

> This Nation has a moral and ethical obligation to fulfill its historic commitment to creating an integrated society that ensures equal opportunity for all of its children. A compelling interest exists in avoiding racial isolation, an interest that a school district, in its discretion and expertise, may choose to pursue. Likewise, a district may consider it a compelling interest to achieve a diverse student population. Race may be one component of that diversity, but other demographic factors, plus special talents and needs, should also be considered. What the government is not permitted to do, absent a showing of necessity not made here, is to classify every student on the basis of race and to assign each of them to schools based on that classification. Crude measures of this sort threaten to reduce children to racial chits valued and traded according to one school's supply and another's demand.[133]

Justice Kennedy attempted to leave the door open for future plans to achieve educational equity and racial integration, but emphasized that any such plan must not resort to "widespread governmental allocation of benefits and burdens on the basis of racial classifications."[134] Given the modest goals and means of the Seattle and Louisville plans, which Kennedy deemed to be too crude to meet the constitution's narrow tailoring requirement, it is difficult to envision the administrative specifics of a desegregation program that would receive the approval of the Supreme Court.

---

129. *Id.* at 2738–51.
130. *Id.* at 2768.
131. *Id.* at 2775 (Thomas, J. concurring).
132. *Id.* at 2815 (Breyer, J., dissenting).
133. *Id.* at 2797 (Kennedy, J., concurring in the judgment).
134. *Id.*

Continuing to Push the Stone

The trend in education law and policy is away from measures that directly advance racial integration as a method for achieving greater equality in public schooling. Some say this trend is appropriate because school desegregation has failed black children miserably.[135] Other scholars contend that it is "too early to abandon concerted efforts to achieve greater integration" because of evidence that race integration bestows benefits that school finance reform and other school reforms cannot achieve.[136] Given the short duration of federal enforcement of desegregation measures and the success of resistance to racial integration, it could aptly be pointed out that school desegregation has not yet been tried. Meanwhile, parents, school reformers and school authorities frequently acknowledge the value of integrated school programs and actively seek to offer them. Because of the strict scrutiny applied to any race-conscious measure and the difficulty of meeting the narrow tailoring requirement, however, school districts are now abandoning even modest measures that would provide some degree of racial integration.

In spite of more than a century of activism seeking equal schooling for African American children, America's schools remain substantially segregated and unequal. Lyndon Johnson's aspiration of "equality as a fact and as a result" has not occurred. The fiftieth anniversary of *Brown* was celebrated in the context of an education system that is still separate and unequal. Segregation in elementary and secondary schools—which decreased dramatically between 1968 and 1986—is once again on the rise. Statistics on school segregation between 1986 and 2002 show that the percentage of African American students attending majority white schools has decreased every year.[137] Between 1986 (the high water mark of school's integration) and 1999, the percentage of African American students attending school where the student body is 90 percent or more African American rose from 62.9 percent to 70.2 percent.[138] Similarly, the "achievement gap" between black and white students, which narrowed during the 1980s, is also beginning to widen again.[139] Even where black students and white students attend the same schools, students are often separated into "tracks" or special programs where their own race is the majority.[140] Further, the schools with the greatest concentration of racial minorities also tend to have high numbers of students who live in poverty, a condition that increases the educational burden those schools must bear and impairs the educational and employment chances of the students who attend those schools.[141] Once again, the stone is rolling back down the hill.

Allowing the stone to roll back cannot be an option. Education is the national currency of social mobility. To get a good job, as the saying goes, get a good education. In

---

135. Derrick A. Bell Jr., *The Unintended Lessons in Brown v. Board of Education*, 49 N.Y. Law Rev. 1053, 1062 (2004–2005) (discussing tracking, disparate discipline, white flight and other humiliations faced by black children in desegregated schools).

136. *See, e.g.,* Ryan, *supra* note 79, at 315.

137. Gary Orfield and Chungmei Lee, *Brown at 50: King's Dream or Plessy's Nightmare?* The Civil Rights Project at Harvard University (2004); Chungmei Lee, *Is Resegregation Real?*, The Civil Rights Project at Harvard University (2004).

138. *Id.*

139. Jaekyung Lee, *Racial and Ethnic Achievement Gap Trends: Reversing the Progress Toward Equity?* 31(1) Educational Researcher 3–12 (2002).

140. Jeannie Oakes, Keeping Track: How Schools Structure Inequality (1985).

141. Gary Orfield and Chungmei Lee, *Why Segregation Matters: Poverty and Educational Inequality*, The Civil Rights Project of Harvard University (2005).

general, Americans feel comfortable relying on education to fulfill its most important so-cial aspirations because most Americans believe that education is the foundation of mer-itocracy. A meritocracy based on educational achievement is fair only to the extent that education is a community resource that can be freely and equally distributed to all chil-dren who would take advantage of it. Thus, school reformers struggle on with the Sisyphean task of providing each child access to a high-quality education. Of course, as Albert Camus pointed out, "The struggle itself toward the heights is enough to fill a man's heart. One must imagine Sisyphus happy."[142]

---

142. Albert Camus, The Myth of Sisyphus and Other Essays (1955).

2

When Government Is a Passive Participant in Private Discrimination: A Critical Look at White Privilege and the Tacit Return to Interposition in *PICS v. Seattle School District*

Maurice R. Dyson*

I. Introduction

This chapter disputes Samuel Estreicher's nonpreference neutrality theory regarding the Supreme Court's approach to tiebreaker cases.[1] Estreicher's theory is that the Court is con-

* Associate Professor of Law, Thomas Jefferson School of Law; J.D., Columbia University School of Law; A.B., Columbia College, Columbia University; Association of American Law Schools Section on Education Law National Chair, 2005-06; Order of the Barristers, Member; Roothbert Fund Fellow; Lester A. and Stella Porter Russell Endowment Recipient. Special thanks to Dean Rudy Hasl and the faculty of Thomas Jefferson School of Law. This chapter is dedicated to the loving memory of my mother MaryAnne Lee, whose life lessons have enduringly inspired my compassionate love for social justice.

1. The term "tiebreaker cases" in this chapter refers the consolidated case of *Parents Involved in Community Schools v. Seattle School District No. 1* (*PICS*), 127 S.Ct. 2738 (2007), resolving the issue of racial tiebreakers used in the Seattle school district in *PICS v. Seattle School District No. 1*, 426 F.3d 1162 (9th Cir. 2005), and the Louisville school system in *Meredith v. Jefferson County Board of Education*, 416 F.3d 513 (6th Cir. 2005).

In Seattle, the school district adopted a plan that allowed ninth-graders to choose which high school within the school district they would like to attend. *PICS*, 127 S.Ct. at 2747. When too many students selected a particular school as their first choice, the school district used a system of tiebreakers to decide which students would be admitted to that school. *Id.* The most contentious tiebreaker was a racial factor intended to maintain racial diversity within an oversubscribed school by using a predetermined number of percentage points that reflected the composition of Seattle's total student population. *Id.* These targets were approximately 40 percent white and 60 percent nonwhite; when these percentage parameters were threatened, the racial tiebreaker took effect. *Id.* At a particular school, either whites or non-whites could be favored for admission depending on which race would bring the racial balance closer to the percentage goal. *Id.* In effect, the racial factor became a tiebreaker as to which student, based on

cerned merely with the neutral distribution—and withholding—of governmental benefits on the basis of race and ethnicity.[2] This chapter argues that the Court's narrow tailoring analysis is intellectually dishonest. Instead, this chapter proffers a competing theory of jurisprudential interposition to explain the Court's current approach to race-based remedies in pupil assignments. Under this theory, the Court's approach to tiebreaker cases is tacitly and metaphorically guided by the invisible hand of the repudiated doctrine of interposition,[3] thus judicially protecting white privilege.

In support of this proposition, this chapter demonstrates that whether the Supreme Court will find a racial remedy constitutional can be predicted by considering whether a remedy offends the prerogative of white privilege under the "unduly burdensome" requirement of narrow-tailoring analysis. This fundamentally undermines the nonpreference theory. In *Parents Involved in Community Schools v. Seattle School District No. 1* (*PICS*),[4] *Milliken v. Bradley* (*Milliken I*),[5] and similar cases, the Court accomplishes this by two

---

the district-wide racial demographics, would gain admission to the school. *Id.*

Similarly, in Louisville, Kentucky, a school system established an enrollment plan designed to achieve substantial racial integration through school choice. *Id.* at 2749. In the instance when schools could not accommodate all of the students, student enrollment was decided on the basis of several factors, including place of residence, school capacity, and random chance, as well as race. *Id.* No school, however, was allowed to have an enrollment of black students less than 15 percent or greater than 50 percent of its student population. *Id.*

2. According to Estreicher, "Where the state acts through racially neutral means, there is no preferential allocation of government goods and services on the basis of one's race. There is no racial division of the spoils, no basis for constitutional concern when a 'magnet school' is created in a minority-dense neighborhood; the top 10 percent of every high school class is automatically granted admission to the state university system; or active recruiting for students takes place in economically disadvantaged neighborhoods—as long as the opportunity is not allocated on the basis of race and is available on equal terms to all races." Samuel Estreicher, *The Non-Preferment Principle and the 'Racial Tiebreaker' Cases*, 2007 CATO SUP. CT. REV. 239, 250 (2007), *available at* http://www.cato.org/pubs/scr/2007/estreicher.pdf.

3. The doctrine of interposition is "an official act on the part of a State government to question the constitutionality of a policy established by the central government." FELIX MORLEY, FREEDOM AND FEDERALISM 240 (1981). As a response to the politically unpopular Alien and Sedition Acts, founding fathers Thomas Jefferson and James Madison, through the Kentucky and Virginia Resolutions respectively, asserted that the U.S. Constitution limited the authority of the federal government, stating that "in case of deliberate, palpable, and dangerous exercise of other powers not granted by the said compact, ... the States who are parties thereto, have the right and are in duty bound to interpose for arresting the progress of evil." JAMES McCLELLAN, LIBERTY, ORDER AND JUSTICE: AN INTRODUCTION TO THE CONSTITUTIONAL PRINCIPLES OF AMERICAN GOVERNMENT 493 (3d ed. 2000) (quoting Va. Res. of 1798 ¶ 2 (1798)). As the argument goes, because states are independent co-parties and signatories to the Constitution, if the federal government breaches the covenant, the doctrine of interposition holds that each state has an unqualified right to determine a breach of the covenant exists. *Id.* The Kentucky resolution asserted that the federal government would "stop nothing short of despotism; since the discretion of those who administer the government, and not the constitution, would be the measure of their powers." Ky. Res. of 1799 ¶ 4 (1799).

The doctrine of interposition was revisited in the aftermath of the U.S. Supreme Court's landmark ruling in *Brown v. Bd. of Educ.*, 347 U.S. 483 (1954), which declared that de jure segregation of public schools for black and white students denied black children of the equal protection of the law. *Id.* at 495. Opponents of school integration used the doctrine of interposition to argue that the state could "interpose" between an unconstitutional federal mandate of integration and local authorities based on state sovereignty. For instance, James Jackson Kilpatrick, editor of the *Richmond News Leader*, criticized the Court decisions to end segregation through advocating the revival of the doctrine of interposition. *See generally* JAMES KILPATRICK, THE SOUTHERN CASE FOR SCHOOL SEGREGATION (1962); JAMES KILPATRICK, THE SOVEREIGN STATES: NOTES OF A CITIZEN OF VIRGINIA (1957).

4. *PICS*, 127 S.Ct. at 2738.

5. *Milliken v. Bradley*, 418 U.S. 717 (1974).

methods. The first is by judicial fiat. The second method consists of "carve outs" designed to exempt, justify, and immunize white discriminatory preferences and white flight from liability without similarly subjecting such blatantly defiant behavior to strict scrutiny or narrow tailoring. This chapter demonstrates that this immunization from liability and protection of white social advantage, relative to the discriminatory use of public goods like high-demand schools, is tantamount to validating exclusionary prerogatives. These prerogatives, as seen in *PICS* and *Milliken I*, comport with definitional notions of white privilege and largely explain the failure of desegregation efforts.

As the premise of this chapter makes clear, narrow tailoring—which appears to use race to benefit people of color—seems to threaten the notion of white privilege when used consistently. Therefore, it is easier for the Court to rhetorically argue that whites will be unduly burdened by such racial schemes. But more often, the Court's contempt for race-based remedies is disguised in a rhetorical focus on the unfair treatment and inferior typing of minorities, rather than the real adverse impact on white communities.[6] In this way, the Court's rhetorical focus may serve to obscure the real animating reason for its holding and rationale. Conceivably, the *PICS* Court may have sympathetically sided with the plaintiffs because of the adverse impact on white students and families, rather than because of any individual racial stereotyping of minority students as the majority asserted.[7] Indeed, one may be compelled to ask why else the Court would obscure the impact of the racial tiebreaker as minimal when, in reality, the facts in the record revealed it had a more substantial adverse impact on white students and families.[8]

The reasons the Court may obscure its rhetoric can be subject to infinite speculation. Perhaps for the Court, it is more palatable to discuss the impact of a racial tiebreaker on minority groups than to confess to siding with a complaining white community that already enjoys disproportionate influence as the political and social majority. Using rhetoric to conceal that a racial tiebreaker is encroaching on a prerogative of white families who already enjoy many societal benefits may ultimately disguise the Court's uneven-handed approach to the equal protection clause, which was designed to protect politically impotent, discrete, and insular racial minority groups.

One might speculate that the Court made the decision for the "appearance" of a preference-neutral principle to mask the reality that the Court metaphorically "interposed" itself between Seattle's tiebreaker and white *PICS* plaintiffs under the guise of saving minorities from unfair racial stereotypes. While the Court's opinion appears to be couched in terms of a neutral principle, the opinion is a disservice to civil rights advocates because it disguises the real animating reasoning behind the Court's holding and rationale. Consequently, masking the Court's reasoning in the tiebreaker cases on the neutrality principle will result in misguided litigation efforts in the future. Future litigation may be directed at addressing the pretext of neutrality rather than the real concern of preserving

---

6. *See, e.g., Adarand Constructors Inc. v. Pena*, 515 U.S. 200, 241 (1995) (Thomas, J., concurring in part and concurring in judgment) (arguing that affirmative action programs "stamp minorities with a badge of inferiority"); *City of Richmond v. J.A. Croson Co.* (*Croson*), 488 U.S. 469, 493 (1989) (asserting that racial classifications may promote notions of racial inferiority); *Regents of Univ. of Cal. v. Bakke*, 438 U.S. 265, 298 (1978) (citing racial preferences as further reinforcement of racial inferiority).

7. *PICS*, 127 S.Ct. at 2738 ("Even when it comes to race, the plans here employ only a limited notion of diversity, viewing race exclusively in white/nonwhite terms in Seattle and black/'other' terms in Jefferson County.").

8. *See infra* fig.1.

local racialized preferences for majoritarian white communities with which the Court appears to be more concerned. Thus, if the latter rationale is a more reliable predictor of how the Court will address these racial remedial questions in the future, civil rights advocates should be mindful of the political and social concerns of white communities masked in the Court's invocation of the neutrality principle.

In particular, this chapter proposes a theoretical model of passive participant discrimination, rooted in *City of Richmond v. J.A. Croson Co.* (*Croson*),[9] that could justify Seattle's use of targeted race-conscious measures to remedy private discrimination as a compelling governmental interest. Under Supreme Court jurisprudence, generalized private societal discrimination is not legally cognizable as a compelling state interest justifying remedial intervention on the basis of race.[10] In contrast to this approach, under the theoretical model of passive participant discrimination, private racialized preferences in neighborhoods that exclude and segregate students of color from the enjoyment of a public good such as education become permissible targets for race-based intervention.[11] Under this passive participant model, the government must act to counter the adverse consequences of private discriminatory preferences if these preferences result in a racially discriminatory allocation of public goods such as education. Failure to do so would make the government a passive participant in private discrimination.

In this regard, this chapter emphasizes the critical missteps of *PICS* respondents by failing to explicitly argue the remedial justification based on private discriminatory preferences as grounded in *Croson*, and also failing to assert with sufficient specificity that the respondent school district possessed evidence that its own spending practices and resource allocations exacerbated a pattern of prior discrimination before it employed race-conscious relief. Furthermore, the *PICS* respondents' failure to argue that the district's expenditures effectively engendered racial segregation in schools and neighborhoods was unfortunate for two principal reasons. First, the Seattle School District missed an important opportunity to demonstrate to the Court it was correcting its own spending allocation patterns that directly led to racially imbalanced student enrollments. Conceivably, correcting one's own discriminatory conduct may have been a permissible remedial justification to use the racial tiebreaker in the precise way the school district employed it.

Second, by failing to argue that its own unequal spending allocation patterns led to discriminatory participation in educational programs it financed throughout the district, the respondents left themselves open to another potential attack. This potential empirical attack, often seen in school finance cases, is that increased expenditures do not always raise student performance. Thus, the school district failed to show that the racial tiebreaker was connected to bona fide pedagogical goals related to improving minority student achievement, which may have been adversely impacted by its own spending allocation patterns throughout the district.

Part II of this chapter lays out the nonpreference principle and its shortcomings in light of the phenomenon of white privilege and the Court's willingness to assert a stewardship role of judicial protection of this privilege. Part III examines the Court's narrow tailoring test requirement that a compelling state interest must not pose an undue burden on nonbeneficiaries. This test amounts to the legal enshrinement of the protection

---

9. *Croson*, 488 U.S. at 469.
10. *See Wygant v. Jackson Bd. of Educ.*, 476 U.S. 267, 274 (1986).
11. *See id.*

of white privilege. Part IV makes a closer examination of the prerogative of white privilege and how the Court's approach accomplishes the intended effect of the repudiated doctrine of interposition. Finally, Part V lays out the theoretical construct for three remedial justifications and remedies based on the suggestion in *Croson* that in discrete cases, government may in fact be able to rectify private discrimination.

II. The Fallacy of the Nonpreference Principle

Strict scrutiny is the most stringent standard of review used by federal courts; courts use it when a compelling state interest is asserted in two basic contexts. First, strict scrutiny applies when a "fundamental" right is infringed, such as those enumerated in the Bill of Rights, including those the Court has deemed protected by the liberty provision of the Fourteenth Amendment.[12] Second, strict scrutiny applies whenever a challenged government action involves the use of a suspect classification, such as race or national origin, that implicates the equal protection clause of the Fourteenth Amendment.[13] Thus, whenever a racial classification such as the tiebreaker in *PICS* is employed, the Court applies strict scrutiny analysis.

The strict scrutiny analysis has two prongs.[14] First, the Court inquires whether there is a sufficiently compelling state interest to justify the racial classification.[15] In *Grutter v. Bollinger*, the Supreme Court made clear that the state interest of achieving racial diversity in the classroom is such an interest.[16]

Under the second prong, the Court essentially examines whether the racial classification is narrowly tailored to use the least restrictive means possible.[17] Where the governmental action employs a racial tiebreaker for instance, it seems there cannot be a less restrictive way to effectively achieve the compelling government interest of racial diversity that neither encompasses too much impermissible racial discrimination (overinclusive) or fails to address essential aspects of the compelling interest (underinclusive). But

---

12. *See Bakke*, 438 U.S. at 357 (Brennan, J., concurring in part and dissenting in part).

13. The strict scrutiny standard of review finds its origins in the famous note 4 in *United States v. Carolene Products Co.*, 304 U.S. 144, 152 n.4 (1938). It states:

> There may be narrower scope for operation of the presumption of constitutionality when legislation appears on its face to be within a specific prohibition of the Constitution, such as those of the first ten amendments, which are deemed equally specific when held to be embraced within the Fourteenth.
>
> It is unnecessary to consider now whether legislation which restricts those political processes which can ordinarily be expected to bring about repeal of undesirable legislation, is to be subjected to more exacting judicial scrutiny under the general prohibitions of the Fourteenth Amendment than are most other types of legislation. On restrictions upon the right to vote, on restraints upon the dissemination of information, on interferences with political organizations, as to prohibition of peaceable assembly.
>
> Nor need we enquire whether similar considerations enter into the review of statutes directed at particular religious, or national, or racial minorities: whether prejudice against discrete and insular minorities may be a special condition, which tends seriously to curtail the operation of those political processes ordinarily to be relied upon to protect minorities, and which may call for a correspondingly more searching judicial inquiry.

Id. (citations omitted).

14. *Grutter v. Bollinger*, 539 U.S. 306, 327 (2003).

15. *Id.*

16. *Id.* at 333.

17. *Id.*

in reality, strict scrutiny's requirement that the use of race must be narrowly tailored rests substantively on the government's ability to effectuate its goals in a way that is not unduly burdensome to nonbeneficiaries.[18]

Samuel Estreicher and other commentators have noted this prong of strict scrutiny analysis is not concerned merely with the distribution of governmental benefits but also with the withholding of such benefits on the basis of race and ethnicity.[19] Accordingly, the government serves as the provider of public goods such as education, law enforcement, and municipal services, and the Court is the ultimate arbiter of the administration of public goods in accordance with this view of equal protection.[20] Estreicher refers to this approach as the nonpreference principle.[21] Under this principle, he concludes that the vast body of jurisprudence in the arena of racial diversity and racial remedies is best explained in the following fashion:

> Where the state acts through racially neutral means, there is no preferential allocation of government goods and services on the basis of one's race. There is no racial division of the spoils, no basis for constitutional concern when a "magnet school" is created in a minority-dense neighborhood; the top ten percent of every high school class is automatically granted admission to the state university system; or active recruiting for students takes place in economically disadvantaged neighborhoods—as long as the opportunity is not allocated on the basis of race and is available on equal terms to all races.[22] According to this view, so long as government does not pick winners and losers, it properly discharges its responsibility to provide and allocate resources consistently with the Equal Protection Clause.[23]

Under the nonpreference principle, the Court plays its most vital role under the Fourteenth Amendment as referee by requiring the provision and allocation of governmental benefits in race-neutral terms.[24] Estreicher's assertion that the Court adheres to the nonpreference principle is not new. To argue that the Court follows a nonpreference principle is to say that the Court adheres to color-blind jurisprudence,[25] an idea long promoted before critical race scholarship divulged its problematic assumptions.[26]

---

18. *See United States v. Paradise*, 480 U.S. 149, 183 (1987) (holding that a race-conscious decree "does not disproportionately harm the interests, or unnecessarily trammel the rights, of innocent individuals"). *See also Adarand Constructors, Inc. v. Pena*, 515 U.S. 200, 276 (1995) (Ginsburg, J., dissenting) ("Court review can ensure that preferences are not so large as to trammel unduly upon the opportunities of others or interfere too harshly with legitimate expectations of persons in once-preferred groups."); *Fullilove v. Klutznick*, 448 U.S. 448, 484 (1980) ("'[A] sharing of the burden' by innocent parties is not impermissible.") (citation omitted). *Cf. United Steelworkers v. Weber*, 443 U.S. 193, 208 (1979) (discussing whether use of race "does not unnecessarily trammel the interests" of third parties).

19. *See* Estreicher, *supra* note 2, at 244.

20. *See Metro Broad., Inc. v. FCC*, 497 U.S. 547, 637 (1990) (Kennedy, J., dissenting) (describing the Court as a "case-by-case arbiter of when it is desirable and benign for the Government to disfavor some citizens and favor others"), *overruled by Adarand*, 515 U.S. at 227.

21. Estreicher, *supra* note 2, at 244.

22. *Id.* at 250.

23. *See id.*

24. *See id.*

25. The term "color-blind" comes from Justice Harlan's famous dissent in *Plessy v. Ferguson*, 163 U.S. 537, 559 (1896) (Harlan, J., dissenting). *See also Adarand*, 515 U.S. at 227 (Scalia, J., concurring) ("Government may treat people differently because of their race only for the most compelling reasons.").

26. *See* Michael Omi & Howard Winant, Racial Formation in the United States: From the 1960s to the 1980s, at 60 (1986) ("Despite periodic calls ... for us to ignore race and adopt 'color blind' racial attitudes, skin color 'differences' continue to rationalize distinct treatment of racially identified individuals and groups."); Maurice R. Dyson, *Multiracial Identity, Monoracial Authenticity & Racial Privacy: Towards an Adequate Theory of Multiracial Resistance*, 9 Mich. J. Race & L. 387, 396 (2004) ("'Being color blind will not eliminate the racism and prejudice that exists within our society.'")

Critical race theory, an opposing viewpoint, is a way of looking at racial relations, particularly within the United States, by examining laws, assumptions, and interactions, and then finding the racial components within them.[27] This theory can help advance the cause of racial equality through greater awareness, perhaps more than a sometimes simplistic "color-blind" approach.[28] In this regard, one of the more interesting recent developments in critical race theory is a questioning of the normative acceptance of whiteness and how it does and does not account for the Court's jurisprudence in the arena of racial remedies in equal protection analysis.[29] Following critical race theory, and contrary to Estreicher's assertion, this chapter asserts that the nonpreference principle fails to account for the Court's protection of the majoritarian society's values in ways that call the principle into question.[30]

Indeed, in cases where states use tiebreakers to remedy racial disparities in school districts, it becomes clear that the nonpreference principle provides only a superficial explanation for the Court's current approach. When race is used in an outcome-determinative fashion, one could not credibly controvert that such governmental schemes do not operate in a way that effectively creates winners and losers.[31] In this regard, the mechanics of the integration tiebreakers in *PICS* are instructive.[32]

In *PICS*, a series of four tiebreakers were sequentially triggered when a high-demand school had been deemed "integration positive."[33] When applying the first tiebreaker, the school district gave preference to students with siblings already attending the requested school.[34] According to the school district, during the 2000–2001 academic year, this tiebreaker accounted for somewhere between 15 percent and 20 percent of high school assignments.[35] If the district still failed to meet numerical targets (first within 10 percent and then 15 percent of the population), the second tiebreaker was triggered and student assignments were based entirely on race.[36] This racial tiebreaker was triggered if attendance would help bring the school closer to the district-wide average of 41 percent white and 49 percent minority.[37] If an oversubscribed school was racially balanced, then a third tiebreaker assigned students based on geographical distance.[38] The distance between students' homes and the school to which they sought admission would break the tie, with those who lived closest admitted first.[39] Distance was orig-

---

(quoting Meeting of the Board of Supervisors, Santa Clara Public Health Dep't, Agenda Item A: Oppose Racial Privacy Initiative (Mar. 11, 2003)); Neil Gotanda, *A Critique of "Our Constitution Is Color Blind,"* 44 STAN. L. REV. 1, 53–55 (1991) (discussing the problems of nonrecognition of race by the government).

27. *See* Mari J. Matsuda, *Voices of America: Accent, Antidiscrimination Law, and a Jurisprudence for the Last Reconstruction*, 100 YALE L.J. 1329, 1331 n.7 (1991).

28. *See* Robert L. Hayman Jr., *The Color of Tradition: Critical Race Theory and Postmodern Constitutional Traditionalism*, 30 HARV. C.R.-C.L. L. REV. 57, 76 (1995).

29. *See* Cheryl I. Harris, *Whiteness as Property*, 106 HARV. L. REV. 1707, 1766 (1993) ("The assumption that whiteness is a property interest entitled to protection is an idea born of systematic white supremacy and nurtured over the years, not only by the law of slavery and 'Jim Crow,' but also by the more recent decisions and rationales of the Supreme Court concerning affirmative action.").

30. *See* OMI & WINANT, *supra* note 26, at 60; Gotanda, *supra* note 26, at 53–55.

31. *See, e.g., Grutter v. Bollinger*, 539 U.S. 306, 339 (2003) (stating that whenever race is used as a factor in a school admissions policy, "race is likely outcome determinative for many members of minority groups").

32. *See PICS v. Seattle Sch. Dist. No. 1*, 127 S. Ct. 2738, 2747 (2007).

33. *Id.*

34. *Id.*

35. *Id.* at 2806.

36. *Id.* at 2747.

37. *Id.*

38. *Id.*

39. *Id.*

inally used as the second tiebreaker, but it was ineffective at halting resegregation.[40] The last tiebreaker, a random lottery, was rarely used.[41]

Under this scheme, Seattle played a role in creating winners and losers in the struggle for access to the city's academic excellence programs and top schools.[42] The scheme created winners in the African American students hailing from minority neighborhood schools in southern Seattle, where the curriculum paled in comparison to that offered in the northern, high-demand, predominantly white public schools.[43] Arguably, the scheme created losers when viewed from the perspective of white privilege because it meant whites were no longer assured that there would be no incursions on the geographical scope of privileged schools, even when buying into a desirable school district ZIP code.[44]

As the Seattle plan demonstrates, the interference of racial remedies with privilege, even if relatively small, becomes magnified when the remedies restrict white prerogative.[45] Indeed, this best explains how suburban factions have historically diminished the impact of such reforms with exclusionary zoning practices[46] and private home ownership covenants[47] that collectively operate as type-signaling and screening mechanisms.[48] The primary effect of these tactics is to cartelize the housing market, in turn granting select students greater educational opportunities than they would receive in a noncartelized suburban school market without an integration tiebreaker.[49] Absent such race-based remedies, "selectivity in suburban school markets is then reinforced through the strategic use of educational policies that serve as locking and sorting devices to block access by perceived "undesirables.""[50]

---

40. *Id.* at 2805 (Breyer, J., dissenting).

41. *PICS v. Seattle Sch. Dist. No. 1* (*PICS II*), 426 F.3d 1162, 1171 (9th Cir. 2005).

42. *See* Deborah N. Archer, *Moving beyond Strict Scrutiny: The Need for a More Nuanced Standard of Equal Protection Analysis for K through 12 Integration Programs*, 9 U. Pa. J. Const. L. 629, 652–53 (2007).

43. *See* Archer, *supra* note 42, at 630 n.3 (noting that a "desegregated educational experience opens opportunity networks in areas of higher education and employment").

44. *See* Lee Anne Fennell, *Homes Rule*, 112 Yale L.J. 617, 623 (2002) (reviewing William A. Fischel, The Homevoter Hypothesis: How Home Values Influence Local Government Taxation, School Finance, and Land-Use Policies 213 (2001)).

45. *See id.* at 642 n.105.

46. *See* Fischel, *supra* note 44, at 213; Charles M. Haar, Land-Use Planning: A Casebook on the Use, Misuse, and Re-Use of Urban Land 185–86 (3d ed. 1976); Fennell, *supra* note 44, at 624 n.29 (noting that exclusionary zoning practices were sweeping the country in the era following 1910). *See also* Richard C. Schragger, *The Limits of Localism*, 100 Mich. L. Rev. 371, 418–19 (2001) (discussing the holding in *Warth v. Seldin*, 422 U.S. 490 (1975), that city residents lacked standing to challenge suburb's exclusionary decision).

47. *See* Robert H. Nelson, *Zoning by Private Contract, in* The Fall and Rise of Freedom of Contract 157, 159–66 (F.H. Buckley ed., 1999) (discussing neighborhood association enforcement of covenants); Gregory S. Alexander, *Dilemmas of Group Autonomy: Residential Associations and Community*, 75 Cornell L. Rev. 1, 16 (1989) (discussing residential association restrictions in the form of covenants); Christopher Berry, *Land Use Regulation and Residential Segregation: Does Zoning Matter?*, 3 Am. L. & Econ. Rev. 251, 260 (2001) (discussing how Houston controls neighborhood development without zoning through restrictive covenants); Clayton P. Gillette, *Courts, Covenants, and Communities*, 61 U. Chi. L. Rev. 1375, 1382–83 (1994) (discussing residential association control through covenants).

48. As a general matter, a signal can be defined as a behavior or phenotype produced by one individual (the signaler) that serves to influence the behavior of a second individual (the signal receiver) by transmitting information. *See* Alex M. Johnson, *How Race and Poverty Intersect to Prevent Integration: Destabilizing Race as a Vehicle to Integrate Neighborhoods*, 143 U. Pa. L. Rev. 1595, 1646 (1995).

49. *See* Fennell, *supra* note 44, at 635.

50. Maurice R. Dyson, *Playing Games with Equality: A Game Theoretic Critique of Educational Sanctions, Remedies, and Strategic Noncompliance*, 77 Temple L. Rev. 577, 584 (2004). A "locking" device is one that locks out or effectively blocks minorities from inclusion or equal participation in quality educational programs and desirable communities and can include zoning rules, high property

The ultimate goals of a white suburban cartel are to protect white privilege in neighborhood schooling and to protect suburbanites' single largest undiversified asset—their home—from "uninsurable drops in value."[51] Too often, these cartelistic restraints, designed to reinforce white privilege rather than educational policy, determine who gets what, when, and how much of the best in life that quality education can offer.[52]

Significantly, to be classified as "cartelistic," a restraint—whether at the Supreme Court level of narrow tailoring analysis or at the community or school level—does not require "a classic, overt agreement to suppress competition."[53] Furthermore, the "cartelistic" concept should be "understood broadly to encompass the full range of naked restraints—ones that limit or eliminate competition within some aspect of the production or distribution of educational quality."[54] By definition, cartelistic restraints "operate to create, allocate, or exploit economic power on the part of one or more participants in the agreement."[55] Therefore, the Court strengthens cartelistic control when it upholds majoritarian values and white privilege in cases where race-based remedies threaten "to pick winners or losers in" a manner inconsistent with the settled expectations of the majority.[56]

Accordingly, the Supreme Court's narrow tailoring approach in contemporary educational race-based remedy cases reinforces the cartelistic notion of white privilege in neighborhood schools.[57] The Court's approach ensures that any race-based remedy does not unduly burden nonbeneficiaries as to threaten the status quo of white privilege embodied in a desirable school ZIP code.[58] One example of this is the Court's treatment of open-choice programs. Open-choice programs, such as those adopted in Seattle and Louisville, are school assignment plans that "promote racially integrated and more equitable schools and ... try to reflect the racial diversity of the community at large."[59] In tiebreaker cases, the Court views open choice as contentious because there is in fact real choice, unlike other programs that purport to increase access to education.[60] Open-choice programs at the most selective schools in cities em-

---

taxes, restrictive covenants, and high tuition rates. *See* Lee Anne Fennell, *Beyond Exit and Voice: User Participation in the Production of Local Public Goods*, 80 TEX. L. REV. 1, 46 (2001). A "sorting" device is one that filters and categorizes students in ways that marginalize equal educational opportunity and can include such measures as academic tracking, which groups students within classes based on perceived ability, or discriminatory admissions practices. *See* Jon Hanson & David Yosifon, *The Situational Character: A Critical Realist Perspective on the Human Animal*, 93 GEO. L.J. 1, 59 (2004).

51. *See* Dyson, *supra* note 50, at 617. *See also* Robert C. Ellickson, *Property in Land*, 102 YALE L.J. 1315, 1353 (1993) (noting that "more than seventy-five percent of wealth takes the form of human capital").

52. Fennell, *supra* note 44, at 628–29.

53. Dyson, *supra* note 50, at 585.

54. *Id.*

55. *Id.*

56. *See Grutter v. Bollinger*, 539 U.S. 306, 369 (2003) (Thomas, J., concurring in part and dissenting in part).

57. Michael J. Kaufman, *(Still) Constitutional School De-Segregation Strategies: Teaching Racial Literacy to Secondary School Students and Preferencing Racially-Literate Applicants to Higher Education*, 13 MICH. J. RACE & L. 147, 161–62 (2007).

58. *Id.*

59. *See* Suzanne E. Eckes, *Public School Integration and the 'Cruel Irony' of the Decision in Parents Involved in Community Schools v. Seattle School District No. 1*, EDUC. L. REP., Apr. 3, 2008, at 1, 1.

60. *See* James E. Ryan & Michael Heise, *The Political Economy of School Choice*, 111 YALE L.J. 2043, 2100 (2002).

ploying race-based remedies fundamentally threaten the status quo.[61] This sociopolitical context may best explain the Court's approach to the racial tiebreaker cases, particularly in *PICS*.

The *PICS* case provides a marked example of the Court upholding majoritarian values. In 1977, Seattle voluntarily addressed racial segregation to head off a lawsuit by adopting a large-scale busing program.[62] Despite its efforts, patterns of racial segregation in school enrollment persisted.[63] In 1988, the school board adopted a less intrusive "controlled-choice" plan that allowed families to choose schools within groupings based on race, geography, and other factors.[64] Seattle's race-neutral approach, however, remained ineffectual at breaking up the monopoly of white privilege and minority disadvantage for ten years.[65] Only in 1998, after extensive study, including public surveys, did the school district adopt the open-choice policy at issue.[66] The new policy applied to high schools for the 1999–2000 school year.[67] Despite the school district's extensive studies and surveys, the Supreme Court in *PICS* did not fully acknowledge that the school district had employed a race-neutral plan for ten years and had considered other race-neutral alternatives before finally deciding on its current pupil assignment plan.[68]

Adopting the narrow tailoring analysis of the lower courts, which followed *Grutter v. Bollinger*[69] and *Gratz v. Bollinger*,[70] the Supreme Court found that the school district's policy violated all but one of the narrow tailoring analytical elements.[71] The Court held that the assignment policy's racial tiebreaker broke the cardinal rule of *Gratz*, which requires individualized consideration of each applicant and avoids the use of a racial quota.[72] The Court concluded that the racial tiebreaker made race paramount as the "defining feature of [a student's] application" with automatic race-based admission through the use of an impermissible racial quota.[73]

---

61. *See* Eckes, *supra* note 59, at 8. This differs from open choice under the No Child Left Behind Act because, unlike the No Child Left Behind Act, all the schools in the open-choice program were attractive options. Transfer policies out of schools failing to meet academic benchmarks are meaningless when most of the surrounding schools are also unattractive options.

62. *PICS v. Seattle Sch. Dist. No. 1*, 127 S. Ct. 2738, 2804 (2007) (Stevens, J., dissenting).

63. *See* Alexandra Villarreal O'Rourke, *Picking up the Pieces after* PICS: *Evaluating Current Efforts to Narrow the Education Gap*, 11 Harv. Latino L. Rev. 263, 265 (2008).

64. Goodwin Liu, *Seattle and Louisville*, 95 Cal. L. Rev. 277, 313 (2007).

65. *Id.*

66. *Id.*

67. *Id.* at 314.

68. *See PICS*, 127 S.Ct. at 2766. The opinion reached by the court of appeals prior to the *PICS* decision criticized the district for failing to "earnestly appraise" the adoption of a randomized lottery, which the court recognized "would necessarily produce levels of school diversity statistically comparable to (and perhaps even more proportional than) the [d]istrict's racial tiebreaker." The court noted that the reasons for rejecting consideration of a lottery in *Grutter* did not exist in this case because student assignments did not consider merit and there was accordingly "absolutely no possibility that a lottery would diminish the quality of admitted students." The court also faulted the district for not considering the "adopt[ion] a diversity-oriented policy that [did] not rely exclusively on race, but which instead account[ed] for the wider array of characteristics that comprise the kind of true diversity lauded by Justice Powell in *Bakke* and by the Court in *Grutter*." The court further suggested that the district should have given more consideration to proposals to use English proficiency or eligibility for free or reduced lunch as an alternative tiebreaker. Lisa J. Holmes, Comment, *After* Grutter: *Ensuring Diversity in K–12 Schools*, 52 UCLA L. Rev. 563, 585 n.159 (2004) (citations omitted).

69. *Grutter v. Bollinger*, 539 U.S. 306 (2003).

70. *Gratz v. Bollinger*, 539 U.S. 244 (2003).

71. *PICS v. Seattle Sch. Dist. No. 1 (PICS III)*, 377 F.3d 949, 976 n.32 (9th Cir. 2004).

72. *Gratz*, 539 U.S. at 293.

73. *PICS III*, 377 F.3d at 969 (quoting *Grutter*, 539 U.S. at 337).

III. White Privilege and the Tiebreaker that Became a Deal Breaker

In contrast to Estreicher's nonpreference principle, another view of the Court's approach exists that better harmonizes its confusing and sometimes apparently contradictory jurisprudence in this area. Specifically, the Court's narrow tailoring test — requiring that a compelling state interest not pose an undue burden on nonbeneficiaries — amounts to the legal enshrinement of the protection of white privilege.[74]

By definition, white privilege means the ability to exercise white prerogative free of intrusion or encroachment.[75] This prerogative can include the unqualified belief that one should have the right to attend a predominantly white-populated neighborhood school with academically enriched programs to the exclusion of students of color.[76] White privilege may also "authorize or license a white person to do what is forbidden or wrong for non-whites," such as justifying blatant racial discrimination.[77] For instance, it can justify or excuse truculent noncompliance with a burden that should be borne by all, whether it is the equal protection clause, a desegregation mandate, or the application of a racial tiebreaker designed to more evenly allocate quality educational opportunity.[78] In this way, white privilege consists of unquestioned assumptions, social advantages, and benefits that inure to the benefit of those who have traditionally dominated American society politically, economically, and socially.[79]

In cases where race remedies challenged the fundamental status quo of white privilege, the Berger, Rehnquist, and Roberts Courts have been more inclined to limit, undermine, narrow, or declare the remedial measures unconstitutional.[80] On the other

---

74. *See Naser Jewelers, Inc. v. City of Concord*, 513 F.3d 27, 33–34 (1st Cir. 2008).

75. *See* CRITICAL WHITE STUDIES: LOOKING BEHIND THE MIRROR 273–75, 291–99, 306–9, 315–18, 323–26, 331–32, 619–25, 654–57 (Richard Delgado & Jean Stefancic eds., 1997).

76. *See* Defining "White Privilege," http://academic.udayton.edu/Race/01race/Whiteness00.htm (last visited Oct. 16, 2008).

77. *Id.*

78. *See id.*

79. *See* Peggy McIntosh, *White Privilege and Male Privilege: A Personal Account of Coming to See Correspondences through Work in Women's Studies* 5 (Wellsey Coll. Ctr. for Research on Women, Working Paper No. 189, 1998), *available at* http://eric.ed.gov/ERICWebPortal/contentdelivery/servlet/ERIC Servlet?accno=ED335262.

80. *See, e.g., Gratz v. Bollinger*, 539 U.S. 244, 244 (2003) (striking down use of race as a factor in university admissions where a white applicant is denied admission); *Grutter v. Bollinger*, 539 U.S. 306, 343 (2003) (suggesting a twenty-five-year limit on affirmative action that adversely impacts white applicants); *Missouri v. Jenkins*, 515 U.S. 70, 99–100 (1995) (limiting continued state duty to fund desegregation plans to attract whites to black neighborhoods while limiting black school from funding to address educational vestiges of racial discrimination); *Freeman v. Pitts*, 503 U.S. 467, 489 (1992) (approving incremental implementation of a desegregation decree and partial declaration of unitary status); *Bd. of Educ. v. Dowell*, 498 U.S. 237, 248 (1991) (holding a duty to eliminate the effects of segregation was required just to the extent practicable, abandoning the comprehensive root-and-branch approach); *Wygant v. Jackson Bd. of Educ.*, 476 U.S. 267, 267 (1986) (prohibiting a lay-off of white and nonminority teachers to achieve desegregation); *Crawford v. Bd. of Educ.*, 458 U.S. 527, 528 (1982) (finding that California's amended constitution to limit desegregation mandates was constitutional); *Regents of Univ. of Cal. v. Bakke*, 438 U.S. 265, 311–12 (1978) (restraining the university's use of race as a factor in admissions process where a white applicant was denied admission); *Dayton v. Brinkman*, 433 U.S. 406, 420 (1977) (finding several discriminatory actions by the state school board an inadequate violation to justify desegregation remedy that would impact white neighborhoods); *Pasadena v. Spangler*, 427 U.S. 424, 439–40 (1976) (narrowing the court's authority to remedy resegregative effects after a desegregation mandate); *Milliken v. Bradley*, 418 U.S. 717, 745–46

hand, race remedies that only marginally accommodated but did not fundamentally foreclose white privilege have withstood judicial scrutiny.[81] In instances where privilege centers around scarce resources like academic excellence programs—including those in the *PICS* litigation[82] and Louisville, Kentucky, litigation[83]—the Court's ju-

---

(1974) (rendering an impermissible and ineffective interdistrict remedy that would include white suburbs notwithstanding finding of a state violation).

81. *See, e.g., Grutter v. Bollinger,* 539 U.S. 306, 341 (2003) (concluding "that in the context of its individualized inquiry into the possible diversity contributions of all applicants, the Law School's race-conscious admissions program does not unduly harm nonminority applicants"); *Adarand Constructors, Inc. v. Pena,* 515 U.S. 200, 276 (1995) (Ginsburg, J., dissenting) ("Court review can ensure that preferences are not so large as to trammel unduly upon the opportunities of others or interfere too harshly with legitimate expectations of persons in once-preferred groups.") (citation omitted); *United States v. Paradise,* 480 U.S. 149, 183 (1987) (stating that a race-conscious decree "does not disproportionately harm the interests, or unnecessarily trammel the rights, of innocent individuals"). *Cf. Fullilove v. Klutznick,* 448 U.S. 448, 484 (1980) ("It is not a constitutional defect in this program that it may disappoint the expectations of nonminority firms. When effectuating a limited and properly tailored remedy to cure the effects of prior discrimination, such 'a sharing of the burden' by innocent parties is not impermissible.") (citation omitted); *United Steelworkers v. Weber,* 443 U.S. 193, 208 (1979) (upholding voluntary affirmative action plan as it "does not unnecessarily trammel the interests" of third parties).

82. *See* Petitioner's Brief at 19–21, *PICS v. Seattle Sch. Dist. No. 1,* 127 S.Ct. 2738 (2007) (No. 05-908). Parents filed this suit under 42 U.S.C. § 1983, asserting violations of the equal protection clause and Title VI of the Civil Rights Act, 42 U.S.C. 9 § 2000d, as well as state law claims. On cross motions, the district court granted summary judgment in favor of the district, so there were no findings of fact. The judge found no violation of state law, the equal protection clause, or the federal Civil Rights Act. On appeal to the Ninth Circuit, a three-judge panel unanimously found for parents on the state law claim and enjoined the use of the race preference. The panel later withdrew that decision, vacated the injunction, and certified the state law issues to the Washington Supreme Court, which decided those issues in favor of the district.

While the federal claims were still pending, this Court decided *Grutter* and *Gratz.* The parties rebriefed and reargued parents' equal protection claim in light of those decisions. The panel decided in favor of parents, holding that the district's plan was not narrowly tailored because it is indistinguishable from a "pure racial quota" and "fails virtually every one of the narrow tailoring requirements." One judge dissented.

A rehearing en banc resulted in a decision in favor of the district by a vote of seven (including one concurrence) to four. The en banc majority, relying on the observation in *Grutter* that "context matters," extended the reasoning in that decision to hold that racial diversity can be a compelling governmental interest for high schools. The majority also held that much of the narrow tailoring analysis of *Grutter* and *Gratz* does not apply in the high school context so that, inter alia, a mechanical racial preference can satisfy the narrow tailoring prong of strict scrutiny when implemented to achieve a predetermined white-nonwhite ratio. In reaching this conclusion, the majority deferred to the judgment of the school board regarding the need for a racial preference. It also held that a racial classification does not "unduly harm any students" so long as it does not "uniformly benefit any race or group of individuals to the detriment of another." One judge concurred in the judgment, advocating adoption of a "rational basis" standard of review.

Four judges dissented. They rejected the majority's "relaxed," "deferential" standard of review; its deference to the school board; and its group rights theory of the equal protection clause. The dissent concluded that when strict scrutiny is applied, the district's racial preference is unconstitutional because it seeks to accomplish only a predetermined white-nonwhite ratio (not "genuine" diversity); because the plan operates as a quota; and because it is not narrowly tailored as required by *Grutter* and *Gratz. Id.* (citations omitted).

83. *See Meredith v. Jefferson County Bd. of Educ.,* 547 U.S. 1178 (2006), consolidated with *PICS* on grant of certiorari. *Meredith* concerned the Jefferson County Board of Education's operation of public schools in Louisville, Kentucky. *See PICS,* 127 S.Ct. at 2749.

In 1973 a federal court found that Jefferson County had maintained a segregated school system, and in 1975 the District Court entered a desegregation decree. Jefferson County operated under this decree until 2000, when the District Court dissolved the decree after finding that the district had

risprudence is even more finely attuned to detect small yet distinct threats to white privilege.[84]

Given the scarcity of quality, high-demand local schools, courts do not view an integration tiebreaker that threatens white privilege, no matter how discrete, as inconsequential by nonbeneficiaries.[85] This is true even if other equally good alternatives exist.[86] Forcing white parents to send their children to more racially integrated schools violates narrow tailoring analysis because it unduly impinges on white privilege.[87]

A. The *PICS* Case and White Privilege

The *PICS* case illustrates the principle that the Court will declare unconstitutional a racial remedy that challenges the status quo of white privilege. In Seattle, due to the extraordinarily high demand for assignment to Ballard High School, many residents of the adjacent predominantly white Queen Anne and Magnolia areas were considerably unhappy about the effect of the integration tiebreaker.[88] Some perceived that the integration tiebreaker prevented white students in those neighborhoods from exercising white prerogative; the tiebreaker meant that many white students could not access Ballard's then brand-new building or were not assigned to Nathan Hale High School, which had recently become popular due to innovative academic programs.[89]

Families from these neighborhoods could have sent their children to Franklin High School, which the *PICS* record demonstrates is a "very impressive" school, or they could have sought assignment to Garfield High School, regarded by many as Seattle's most prestigious high school, which was integration-neutral at the time.[90] White privilege, however, does not always comport with the perceived notion that whites will exercise their prerogative to select a quality or high-demand school. Rather, the essence of white privilege is the prerogative to select a particular school, even if excellent alternatives exist, without interference from the government.[91] The privilege exists even if the government seeks the laudable ends of preventing resegregation.[92] Thus, it matters not for equal protection analysis that Franklin and Garfield, two excellent schools, were available to white students.

When viewed in this fashion, the "cognizable harm" of the open-choice plan under the narrow tailoring analysis was not that residents of Queen Anne and Magnolia were

---

achieved unitary status by eliminating "to the greatest extent practicable" the vestiges of its prior policy of segregation.

In 2001, after the decree had been dissolved, Jefferson County adopted the voluntary student assignment plan at issue in this case. Approximately 34 percent of the district's 97,000 students are black; most of the remaining 66 percent are white. The plan requires all nonmagnet schools to maintain a minimum black enrollment of 15 percent, and a maximum black enrollment of 50 percent. *Id.* (citations omitted).

84. *See PICS,* 127 S.Ct. at 2805.

85. *See* Lawrence F. Rossow, Lori Connery, & Nanette Schmitt, *Limitations on Voluntary School Desegregation Plans: The Seattle and Louisville Cases,* EDUC. L. REP., Nov. 9, 2007, at 21, 40.

86. *Id.*

87. *See id.*

88. *PICS,* 127 S.Ct. at 2747–48.

89. Brief for Respondents at 6, *PICS v. Seattle Sch. Dist. No. 1,* 127 S.Ct. 2738 (2007) (No. 05-908).

90. *Id.*

91. *See* Brief for Nat'l Lawyers Guild as Amicus Curiae Supporting Respondents at 11, *PICS,* 127 S.Ct. 2738 (No. 05-908).

92. *See id.*

cut off from other excellent schools.[93] The notion that these other schools were harmful is somewhat laughable. Instead, the harm under the narrow tailoring analysis is that the school district's plan fundamentally interfered with white prerogative by preventing white students from attending their first-choice schools. To see this, it is worth recounting some of the specific facts surrounding the exercise of that prerogative in *PICS*.

In 2000, Jill Kurfirst began considering which Seattle-area high schools her teenage son, Andy Meeks, should attend.[94] Andy had attention deficit disorder and dyslexia, but he learned well in environments that involved hands-on training.[95] Ballard was Andy's first choice because it offered a special Biotech Career Academy.[96] He met the prerequisites, applied, and was accepted into the program.[97] The school district, however, did not assign Andy, who is white, to Ballard.[98] Ballard was one of several schools where the Seattle Public School District gave preference to minorities because the number of applicants exceeded the available spots and the district considered the school racially imbalanced.[99] Instead, Andy was placed at Ingraham High, a school that lacked special academic programs and college preparatory classes.[100] Additionally, the district did not run school buses to Ingraham from the North Seattle neighborhood where Andy lived.[101] As a result, the Kurfirst family decided to move to a new school district.[102]

The Court's opinion, however, appears not to recognize the adverse impact that the tiebreaker had on the Kurfist family. Indeed, the majority opinion in *PICS* characterized the integration tiebreaker as follows:" While we do not suggest that *greater* use of race would be preferable, the minimal impact of the districts' racial classifications on school enrollment casts doubt on the necessity of using such classifications."[103]

Chief Justice Roberts's characterization, however, is neither accurate nor innocuous. Indeed, it strategically obscures two important elements. First, by characterizing the tiebreaker as having only marginal effect, the Court could conveniently argue that the tiebreaker was not necessary to achieve the desired ends of diversity.[104] Second, it elides the fact that the tiebreaker had more substantial impact on integration than the Court appeared willing to admit.[105] The reluctance of the Court and the tiebreaker's critics to ac-

---

93. *See* Brief for NAACP Legal Defense & Educ. Fund as Amicus Curiae Supporting Respondents at 2, *PICS*, 127 S.Ct. 2738 (No. 05-908).

94. *PICS v. Seattle Sch. Dist. No. 1*, 127 S.Ct. 2738, 2748 (2007).

95. *Id.*

96. *Id.*

97. *See id.*

98. *See* Rebekah Denn, *Parents File Suit over Race Policy*, SEATTLE POST-INTELLIGENCER (Wash.), July 19, 2000, at B1.

99. *See PICS*, 127 S.Ct. at 2747. The school district's open-choice policy did not apply only to schools in which white students were above a certain percentage of students. At another school, Franklin High, the district used the same racial tiebreaker to admit white students to a school with a larger minority population. *Id.* at 2747–48.

100. *See id.*

101. Brief of Petitioner at 8–9, *PICS*, 127 S.Ct. 2738 (No. 05-908). *But see* Brief of Respondent at 46, *PICS*, 127 S.Ct. 2738 (No. 05-908) (noting that Ingraham was "ranked in the same category for academic rigor as Ballard, Franklin, and Garfield" and that "Petitioner's claim that bus service was not available from Queen Anne and Magnolia was incorrect").

102. Brief of Petitioner at 9, *PICS*, 127 S.Ct. 2738 (No. 05-908).

103. *PICS*, 127 S.Ct. at 2760.

104. *See id.* at 2756.

105. *Compare id.* ("When the actual racial breakdown is considered, enrolling students without regard to their race yields a substantially diverse student body under any definition of diversity."), *with* Respondent's Brief in Opposition at 5, *PICS*, 127 S Ct. 2738 (No. 05-908) (charting the differ-

knowledge the more-than-modest effect of the tiebreaker might be due in part to an effort to obscure the fact that the tiebreaker was by no means excessive, but still substantial enough to interfere with white privilege.[106]

By characterizing the tiebreaker as having marginal effect, the Court could argue that the tiebreaker was not necessary to achieve diversity.[107] Roberts was quick to point out that the school district did not need to use the tiebreaker because the number of students actually admitted under the tiebreaker was marginal at best.[108] This characterization, however, warrants closer examination, not only for its accuracy in the *PICS* case but because it also profoundly misstates the Court's previous pronouncements on narrow tailoring analysis[109] and establishes a logical and practical inconsistency that is virtually impossible for a school district not to offend.

Indeed, an integration tiebreaker with a marginal effect on minorities would seem likely to meet the narrow-tailoring requirement of strict scrutiny. Narrow tailoring analysis requires the Court to consider the potential adverse effect of any race-based remedy to determine whether the measure unduly burdens nonbeneficiaries.[110] This is a significant consideration. In fact, the potential adverse effect was of vital importance in *Gratz*; it was the pivotal consideration in the Court's decision to strike down the University of Michigan's undergraduate admission scheme.[111] Michigan's mechanistic addition of twenty points to a candidate's admission score because of their race was constitutionally repugnant because it adversely impacted the ability of white students to gain admission to the university's undergraduate college.[112]

If the additional points in *Gratz* constituted an undue burden on white applicants, then *PICS* warrants an examination to determine whether and to what extent the integration tiebreaker might adversely affect the white students seeking admission to Seattle's high-demand white schools.[113] Under this consideration, one might have thought that an integration tiebreaker with a marginal effect on minorities would concomitantly be less burdensome on white nonbeneficiaries and successfully survive the narrow tailoring requirement.

If Chief Justice Roberts's characterization is accurate and the integration tiebreaker produced only negligible effects, then what accounts for the Court's conclusion that the tiebreaker was not narrowly tailored?[114] One way to understand the Court's reasoning is to understand that race remedies that survive strict scrutiny must be neither too burdensome nor too inconsequential.[115] On one hand, a remedy that overly burdens non-

---

ence between how diverse the entering ninth-grade classes at the Seattle high schools would be with the tiebreaker compared to without the tiebreaker).

106. *See PICS*, 127 S.Ct. at 2760.

107. *See id.* at 2756 ("The extreme measure of relying on race in assignments is unnecessary to achieve the stated goals.").

108. *Id.* at 2760.

109. *See Grutter v. Bollinger*, 539 U.S. 306, 341 (2003) ("To be narrowly tailored, a race-conscious admissions program must not 'unduly burden individuals who are not members of the favored racial and ethnic groups.'") (quoting *Metro Broad., Inc. v. FCC*, 497 U.S. 547, 630 (1990) (O'Connor, J., dissenting)).

110. *See id.*

111. *Gratz v. Bollinger*, 539 U.S. 244, 270–76 (2003).

112. *See id.* at 270.

113. *See PICS v. Seattle Sch. Dist. No. 1*, 127 S.Ct. 2738, 2759–60 (2007).

114. *See id.*

115. *See, e.g., PICS*, 127 S.Ct. at 2760 (noting that "the minimal impact of the districts' racial classifications on school enrollment casts doubt on the necessity of using such classifications"); *Regents of Univ. of Cal. v. Bakke*, 438 U.S. 265, 315 (1978) (finding that a quota system is too burdensome be-

beneficiaries will not survive judicial scrutiny under narrow tailoring.[116] On the other hand, if a remedy produces only a marginal effect, a school district will not meet its heavy evidentiary burden under the other strict scrutiny requirement that the remedy be necessary to achieve the perceived educational benefit.[117]

On its face, most observers will likely accept this reasoning because of its consistency with the measured, balanced, and objective posture that the majority in *PICS* purports to couch its plurality decision.[118] This approach also works harmoniously with Estreicher's nonpreference principle of Fourteenth Amendment constitutional jurisprudence.[119] Keeping an ostensibly middle ground on the employment of race constitutes the quintessential preference neutrality the nonpreference principle espouses.[120] As already suggested, however, scrutinizing the Court's treatment of race-based remedies, including its approach to the *PICS* admissions scheme, under the guise of objectivity and nonpreference is inaccurate and incomplete. As suggested, the racial tiebreaker was more effective than the Court opinion may have led on.

As Figure 2.1 demonstrates, contrary to Chief Justice Roberts's characterization of the tiebreaker,[121] its use led to more than what could be accurately characterized as marginal outcomes. The figure below shows that the percentages of minority students in Seattle's most desirable schools, such as Ballard and Nathan, were significantly impacted by the tiebreaker:

Figure 2.1 Racial Tiebreaker Operation[122]

School	9th-Grade Class Percentage of Students of Color with Integration Tiebreaker	9th-Grade Class Percentage of Students of Color without Integration Tiebreaker
Franklin (South)	59.5	79.2
Hale (North)	40.6	30.5
Ballard (North)	54.2	33.0
Roosevelt (North)	55.3	41.1

For example, in Ballard, as the figure illustrates, it can hardly be said that the increase of over 21 percent in students of color in one of the city's most high-demand, predominantly white schools did not threaten the status quo privilege that white families deemed

---

cause it "insulat[es] each category of applicants with certain desired qualifications from competition with all other applicants").

116. *See Bakke*, 438 U.S. at 307.
117. *See PICS*, 127 S.Ct at 2760.
118. *See id.* at 2760–61.
119. *See* Estreicher, *supra* note 2, at 242–43.
120. *See id.* at 246–49 (comparing the Court's holding in *Grutter* with its holding in *PICS*).
121. *See PICS*, 127 S.Ct. at 2760.
122. *See* Respondent's Brief in Opposition at 5, *PICS*, 127 S.Ct. 2738 (No. 05-908).

an entitlement, whether by race, proximity, or buy-in to the local property tax base.[123] The same would apply, albeit to a lesser extent, at Roosevelt and Hale at more than 14 percent and 10 percent, respectively.[124]

By underplaying the efficacy of the tiebreaker, the Court falsely concluded that the remedy was not necessary.[125] The Court's inaccurate portrayal of the tiebreaker's operation also obscures the fact that because of its significant impact, the tiebreaker fundamentally threatened white privilege, exemplified here by the exercise of white suburban prerogative to select the most desirable schools.[126] The Court also focused on the unfair treatment and typing of minorities,[127] which may have served to mask the real reason the suit was brought and the Court sympathetically sided with the *PICS* plaintiffs—that is, the adverse impact on white students and families. Why else would the Court characterize the racial tiebreaker's impact as minimal when it actually had a more substantial impact?

One might speculate that the Court reached its conclusion in *PICS* for the "appearance" of a nonpreference principle when, in reality, the Court was metaphorically interposing itself between Seattle's tiebreaker and the sympathetic white *PICS* plaintiffs under the guise of saving minorities from unfair stereotypes.[128] The nonpreference front is a disservice to civil rights advocates and will frustrate future litigation efforts by obscuring the Court's real methods to address racial remedial questions.

Unlike the Supreme Court, the lower court in *PICS* concluded that the racial tiebreaker had more than a minimal impact on third-party nonminorities,[129] and ultimately amounted to an "unadulterated pursuit of racial proportionality."[130] Accordingly, the court struck down the open-choice plan.[131] As the lower court's decision demonstrates, Seattle's open-choice program may have been held unconstitutional in part because of its significant usurpation of white privilege and white families' assumed entitlement that their children may attend the school of their choice.[132] White privilege, from this vantage point, not only provides immunity from transfer to minority neighborhood schools, it also guards against any impingement on the geographical scope of the privilege that is assured by buying into a desirable school district.[133]

---

123. Brief of Petitioner at 4, *PICS*, 127 S.Ct. 2738 (No. 05-908) (explaining that Ballard is one of the most selected schools by students).

124. *Id.* (explaining that Roosevelt and Hale are only selected by 18 percent of the students).

125. *PICS v. Seattle Sch. Dist. No. 1*, 127 S.Ct. 2738, 2818–19 (2007) (Stevens, J., dissenting).

126. *See* McIntosh, *supra* note 79, at 5.

127. *PICS*, 127 S.Ct. at 2755–56.

128. *Id.* at 2768 ("The way to stop discrimination on the basis of race is to stop discriminating on the basis of race.").

129. *See PICS v. Seattle Sch. Dist. No. 1 (PICS III)*, 377 F.3d 949, 975 (9th Cir. 2004). The court concluded that "the extent to which [the district] use[d] race [was] not calibrated to the benefits sought. Over time, 'the band'... ranged from as much as +/-25 percent to as little as +/-10 percent, and ... +/-15 percent" at the time of litigation. *Id.* (citation omitted). The court found that such variance did not represent "the measure of tailored proportionality. Instead, it represent[ed] a stubborn adherence to the use of race for race's sake, with the effect that some non-preferred student applicants [would] be displaced solely because of their racial and ethnic identities—to no benefit at all." *Id.*

130. *Id.* at 976.

131. *Id.*

132. *See PICS*, 127 S.Ct. at 2738.

133. *See* Defining "White Privilege," *supra* note 76.

B. The Effect of White Privilege in the Plaintiffs' Decision-Making Process in *PICS*

In analyzing the *PICS* decision, it is important to see how white privilege may have played into the plaintiffs' decision-making process. White privilege, a collective assortment of various conceptual definitions, includes:

1. (a) [a] right, advantage, or immunity granted to or enjoyed by white persons beyond the common advantage of all others; an exemption in many particular cases from certain burdens or liabilities[;] (b) [a] special advantage or benefit of white persons; with reference to divine dispensations, natural advantages, gifts of fortune, genetic endowments, social relations, etc.[;]

2. [a] privileged position ... [or] advantage white persons enjoy over non-white persons[;]

3. (a) the special right or immunity attaching to white persons as a social relation [exercising] prerogative[;] ... [;]

4. (a) to invest white persons with a privilege or privileges; to grant to white persons a particular right or immunity; to benefit or favor specially white persons; ... [;]

5. to authorize or license of white person or persons what is forbidden or wrong for non-whites; to justify, [or] excuse[; and]

6. to give to white persons special freedom or immunity *from* some liability or burden to which non-white persons are subject; to exempt.[134]

1. White Privilege as an Implicit Right

Under the first definitional category, the plaintiffs may have believed they had an implicit right to go to the school of their choosing. For example, Jill Kurfirst believed Andy had a right to attend Ballard, his first-choice school, because he met the prerequisites, applied, and was accepted into the program.[135]

2. White Privilege as a Privileged Position over Nonwhites

Under the second definitional category, where white privilege is regarded as the possession of an advantage that white persons enjoy over nonwhite persons, the plaintiffs may have perceived Seattle's tiebreaker as effectively placing white students in a subordinate position relative to African Americans admitted to Ballard under the racial tiebreaker.[136] To suggest that a white child generally does not possess an advantage over nonwhites to attend a perceived superior school affronts white privilege.[137]

Just as indignant to the notion of white privilege is the relative inability of a parent, if she so desires, to isolate her child from racial interaction, even if other excellent alternative schools may exist with fine college preparatory programs. In her notable paper, *White Privilege and Male Privilege: A Personal Account of Coming to See Correspondences through Work*

---

134. *Id.*

135. Brief of Petitioner at 7, *PICS v. Seattle Sch. Dist. No. 1*, 127 S.Ct. 2738 (2007) (No. 05-908).

136. *See* Defining "White Privilege," *supra* note 76.

137. *Id.*

in Women's Studies, Peggy McIntosh explored this very notion of white privilege, manifested in a series of unquestioned assumptions, social advantages, and benefits.[138] She includes the following list of advantages that persist because of white privilege:

1. I can if I wish arrange to be in the company of people of my race most of the time.

2. I can avoid spending time with people whom I was trained to mistrust and who have learned to mistrust my kind or me.

3. If I should need to move, I can be pretty sure of renting or purchasing housing in an area which [I] can afford and in which I would want to live.

4. I can be pretty sure that my neighbors in such a location will be neutral or pleasant to me. ...

5. I can be sure that my children will be given curricular materials that testify to the existence of their race. ...

6. I can be pretty sure of having my voice heard in a group in which I am the only member of my race. ...

7. I can arrange to protect my children most of the time from people who might not like them.

8. I do not have to educate my children to be aware of systemic racism for their own daily physical protection.

9. I can be pretty sure that my children's teachers and employers will tolerate them if they fit school and workplace norms; my chief worries about them do not concern others' attitudes toward their race. ...

10. I can remain oblivious of the language and customs of persons of color who constitute the world's majority without feeling in my culture any penalty for such oblivion. ...

11. My culture gives me little fear about ignoring the perspectives and powers of people of other races. ...

12. I can easily find academic courses and institutions which give attention only to people of my race. ...

13. I will feel welcomed and "normal" in the usual walks of public life, institutional and social.[139]

Arguably, attendance at a predominantly white school like Ballard in a predominantly white neighborhood would further each of these manifestations of white privilege.[140] A jurisprudence that permits the operation of private racial preferences in the allocation of a public good like education should be repugnant to the nonpreference principle of equal protection analysis. That it is not can hardly be overlooked.

3. White Privilege as a Special Right

Analyzing the *PICS* case under the third and fourth definitions of white privilege—where the privilege is regarded as the special right attaching to white persons—the plaintiffs in *PICS* might have been motivated in part to bring suit despite the existence of vi-

---

138. *See* McIntosh, *supra* note 79, at 5–9, 17.

139. *Id.*

140. *See id.*

able alternative schooling because it was their ultimate prerogative to attend a more predominantly white-populated school with special programs.[141] Narrow tailoring analysis obliged white students to exercise that privilege without any interference by the school district.[142] In effect, the Court does not have to explicitly pick winners and losers, for it accomplishes that by simply supporting noninterference with the wholesale operation of unspoken white privilege.

The Court's tacit, unacknowledged adherence to the enforcement of this special right—the unspoken claim to white privilege—enforces the guise of American society as a meritocracy, rather than as a way to maintain white privilege. The fallacy of an open meritocratic society is furthered underscored by the Court's silent support of white privilege, which obscures the unequalizing effect of private discriminatory preferences on public school resources.[143] As McIntosh stated:

> It seems to me that obliviousness about white advantage ... is kept strongly inculturated in the United States so as to maintain the myth of meritocracy, the myth that democratic choice is equally available to all. Keeping most people unaware that freedom of confident action is there for just a small number of people props up those in power, and serves to keep power in the hands of the same groups that have most of it already.[144]

Thus, narrow tailoring analysis serves as a naked restraint on equal-protection analysis, protecting the cartelistic operation of white privilege in local schooling without having to fully acknowledge its existence.[145]

4. *White Privilege as an Immunity from Wrong*

Under the fifth and sixth definitional categories, white privilege authorizes or licenses a white person to do what is forbidden or wrong for nonwhites.[146] It can justify or excuse truculent noncompliance with a burden that should be borne by all.[147] White privilege is the special freedom or immunity *from* some liability or burden to which nonwhite persons are subject.[148] In this regard, it is significant that the *PICS* tiebreaker did not just require students of color to attend white schools that were deemed "integration positive" but also required white students to attend schools with higher concentrations of minorities.[149] In refusing to submit to the school district's pupil assignment plan, the white plaintiffs' actions are an authentic claim of exemption from the normal operation of the district's rules.

Furthermore, it is significant that middle-class black plaintiffs attending Garfield seeking admission to Ballard could have just as easily brought this suit. Presumably, parents

---

141. *See PICS v. Seattle Sch. Dist. No. 1*, 127 S.Ct. 2738, 2748 (2007) (noting that although accepted into a selective program more conducive to the needs of a nonwhite ADHD student, that student's assignment into the program by the school was eventually denied due to use of a racial tiebreaker).

142. *See id.*

143. *See id.*

144. McIntosh, *supra* note 79, at 18–19.

145. *Id.* at 18 ("Most talk by whites about equal opportunity seems to me now to be about equal opportunity to try to get into a position of dominance while denying that *systems* of dominance exist.").

146. *See* Defining "White Privilege," *supra* note 76.

147. *See id.*

148. *See* McIntosh, *supra* note 79, at 12 ("Whiteness protected me from many kinds of hostility, distress and violence, which I was being subtly trained to visit, in turn, upon people of color.").

149. *PICS*, 127 S.Ct. at 2747–48.

of the black students who applied and were admitted to Ballard had similar motivations to those of white parents. In the zero-sum game of picking winners and losers, however, we look to white privilege to delineate the winners and losers before a court intercedes. We then look to the constitutional jurisprudence of narrow tailoring analysis to explain how that objective is achieved using the full force and effect of the law.[150] Equal protection analysis recognizes winners and losers by encapsulating within narrow tailoring the avoidance of an adverse impact on nonbeneficiaries.[151] This places a naked restraint on the ability of school districts to break up monopolies of white privilege or even monopolies of racial isolation and concentrated poverty.

C. Beneficial Remedial Purposes and the Court's Application of Strict Scrutiny

When courts apply strict scrutiny for beneficial remedial purposes, some observers will quickly point out that strict scrutiny also applies when the classification is used for a purported invidious purpose.[152] This line of argument is socially disingenuous if not intellectually dishonest. White privilege is fundamentally threatened to a greater degree when race is used to give an advantage to minorities under a beneficial remedial purpose, thereby interfering with the born prerogative of white residents.[153] Permitting interference with white prerogative encroaches on white privilege much more than the mere removal of formalistic legal handicaps to racial equality, like the repeal of Jim Crow laws.[154] Removing formal racial barriers poses no real competitive threat to quality schooling without a racial tiebreaker.[155]

Additionally, strict scrutiny analysis has been roundly criticized for failing to make a distinction between remedial and harmful uses of race.[156] Justice O'Connor's opinion in *Croson*, however, illustrates the Court's reasons for subjecting racially sensitive admissions programs designed for a remedial purpose, like Seattle's, to strict scrutiny.[157] Justice O'Connor asserted that identifying all uses of race as suspicious and subjecting them to strict scrutiny allows judges to "smoke out" illegitimate uses of race that masquerade as helpful to disadvantaged groups.[158] "Absent searching judicial inquiry into the justification for such race-based measures," O'Connor stated, "there is simply no way of determining what classifications are 'benign' or 'remedial' and what classifications are in fact motivated by illegitimate notions of racial inferiority or simple racial politics."[159]

---

150. *See Grutter v. Bollinger*, 539 U.S. 306, 341 (2003).

151. *See id.*

152. *PICS v. Seattle Sch. Dist. No. 1*, 127 S.Ct. 2738, 2774 (2007) (Thomas, J., concurring).

153. *Id.* at 2775 (arguing that each use of race to afford equality actually excludes someone based on his or her race).

154. *Id.* at 2836 (Breyer, J., dissenting).

155. *See id.*

156. *See, e.g., PICS v. Seattle Sch. Dist. No. 1 (PICS II)*, 426 F.3d 2263, 1193 (9th Cir. 2005) (Kozinski, J., concurring) (noting that the use of race in pupil assignments was "certainly more benign than laws that favor or disfavor one race, segregate by race, or create quotas for or against a racial group"); *Comfort v. Lynn School Comm.*, 418 F. 3d 1, 28–29 (1st Cir. 2005) (Boudin, C.J., concurring) (stating that race-based criteria are "far from the original evils at which the Fourteenth Amendment was addressed").

157. *City of Richmond v. J.A. Croson Co. (Croson)*, 488 U.S. 469, 493 (1989).

158. *Id.*

159. *Id.*

A nuanced analysis that tries to meaningfully distinguish a remedial purpose from an invidious one requires a rigorous examination of the interest asserted and the purpose for which race is being used.[160] If a court finds a legitimate remedial beneficial purpose, then it should relax its narrow tailoring analysis.[161] Although O'Connor explicitly resisted such an approach in *Croson*,[162] she appears to have retreated from that position in *Grutter v. Bollinger*.[163]

Perhaps what best explains O'Connor's more deferential brand of strict scrutiny in *Grutter*, notwithstanding an ostensibly larger burden placed on nonbeneficiaries there than in *PICS*, is the pivotal importance of education.[164] O'Connor may have applied strict scrutiny to the diversity rationale in *Grutter*, but then relaxed that burden with regard to the narrow tailoring requirement so as to mitigate the adverse effects of white privilege on minority disadvantage in university admissions.[165] Seeing education as an all-too-important path to leadership, O'Connor may have realized the educational context warranted this approach over the "fatal in fact" approach that the *PICS* Court applied.[166]

IV. White Privilege and the Metaphorical Return to Interposition: The Supremacy of Interposition over the Supremacy Clause

Many early opponents of integration and the *Brown v. Board of Education* ruling subscribed to the doctrine of interposition.[167] Under this doctrine, state sovereignty permits a state to "interpose" itself between an unconstitutional federal mandate and local authorities.[168] The Virginia legislature adopted the interposition doctrine as a direct response to the *Brown* decision when it passed the Interposition Resolution in 1956.[169] The doctrine largely developed from the editorials written in 1955–56 by James J. Kilpatrick, then editor of the *Richmond News Leader*.[170] Kilpatrick used the historical writings of Thomas

---

160. *Id.* at 494–95.

161. *Id.* at 495.

162. *Id.* at 494–95. In *Croson*, O'Connor stated:

> Under the standard proposed by Justice Marshall's dissent, "race-conscious classifications designed to further remedial goals," are forthwith subject to a relaxed standard of review. How the dissent arrives at the legal conclusion that a racial classification is "designed to further remedial goals," without first engaging in an examination of the factual basis for its enactment and the nexus between its scope and that factual basis, we are not told. However, once the "remedial" conclusion is reached, the dissent's standard is singularly deferential, and bears little resemblance to the close examination of legislative purpose we have engaged in when reviewing classifications based either on race or gender.

Id. (citation omitted).

163. *Grutter v. Bollinger*, 539 U.S. 306, 337–38 (2003).

164. *Id.* at 330.

165. *Id.* at 337–38.

166. Justice Brennan argued that the Court's "review under the Fourteenth Amendment should be strict not 'strict' in theory and fatal in fact." *Regents of Univ. of Cal. v. Bakke*, 438 U.S. 265, 361–62 (1978) (internal quotations omitted).

167. *E.g.*, 1956 Extra Session, Virginia General Assembly 1–3 (1956) [hereafter 1956 Extra Session], *available at* http://mars.gmu.edu/dspace/bitstream/1920/2340/2/mann_43_05_02B.pdf.

168. *Id.*

169. *Id.* at 3.

170. Television News of The Civil Rights Era: 1950–1970, Primary Documents, http://www.vcdh.virginia.edu/civilrightstv/documents/leg_007.html (last visited June 18, 2008).

Jefferson and James Madison to revive and develop the doctrine of interposition to attack the federal courts that purported to rest on constitutional and historical justifications for desegregation orders.[171]

The Virginia Senate Committee for Courts of Justice detailed a constitutional history for interposition aimed at preventing integration in schools as follows:

> The right of a State to interpose its sovereign powers against encroachment by the Federal Government rests upon certain basic assumptions in history and law. These are:
>
> First, that when the colonies dissolved the political bands that had connected them with Great Britain, they became precisely what they declared themselves to be: Free and Independent States.
>
> Second, that in uniting under the Articles of Confederation, and later under the Constitution of 1787, the States acted as separate, individual States.
>
> Third, that the people of the States, in agreeing to the constitutional compact, have delegated only certain enumerated powers to the general government, and have reserved all other powers to their States or to themselves.
>
> Fourth, that when the general government usurps powers not delegated, the States have an inalienable right to interpose their sovereign powers so as to arrest the progress of the evil.
>
> Fifth, that the question of such encroachment cannot be properly decided by an agency of the general government itself, but can only be decided by the States themselves as parties to the compact.[172]

Though the Supreme Court repudiated this doctrine as a fundamental violation of the supremacy clause of the Constitution,[173] a similar version of the doctrine exists in the Supreme Court's recent jurisprudence. Although distinguishable on many bases, one can hardly contradict that the metaphorical and practical effect of the Court's jurisprudence, when it comes to race, leads to the same result as the doctrine of interposition. The Court's current jurisprudence ensures no undue burden on whites exists with regard to racial integration mandates, whether through a court order or the operation of a tiebreaker.[174] The Court does this by essentially returning power from the federal government to the individual localities of suburbs, as the doctrine of interposition did for states.[175]

Today, states themselves do not need to use the doctrine of interposition; they need not actively interpose themselves between the federal government and a perceived unjust mandate.[176] Instead, the federal courts themselves have taken up that role on behalf of

---

171. *Id.*

172. Comm. for Courts of Justice, Senate of Va., The Doctrine of Interposition: Its History and Application, A Report on Senate Joint Resolution 3, General Assembly of Virginia 1956 and Related Matters, S. Doc. No. 21, at 4 (1957), *available at* http://www.lva.lib.va.us/whoweare/exhibits/brown/doctrine_interposition.htm (last visited June 15, 2008).

173. *See Cooper v. Aaron*, 358 U.S. 1, 17 (1958).

174. *See* Dr. J. Kenneth Moreland et al., Separate but Not Equal: Race, Education, and Prince Edward County, Virginia (July 1963) (unpublished manuscript prepared for the U.S. Commission on Civil Rights on file with the University of Toledo Law Review), *available at* http://www.library.vcu.edu/jbc/speccoll/pec03a.html.

175. *Id.*

176. *See id.*

states' rights.[177] The seamless and invisible changing of the guard from states to federal courts has concealed the continued operation of interposition. As Kendall Clark observes:

> In studying historical examples and theories of oppression, it becomes clear that social (in)visibility is an important strategy. Early feminists make this point over and over. If men and women equally believe, for example, that women are *by their very nature* subordinate to men, then gender oppression seems natural, inevitable, timeless. If you can design structures of oppression which are invisible, which seem *natural*, they will be more effective than structures which are visible. If you can convince everyone, but especially members of the oppressed group itself, that the way things are is natural or inevitable or unavoidable [or neutral], people will be less likely to challenge the way things are.[178]

In this fashion, racial integration mandates that appear to violate the unspoken usurpation of white privilege inevitably appear constitutionally invalid under the fatal in fact scrutiny of racial remedies.[179] Thus, the invisible hand of interposition in the *PICS* approach and others like it remains unmasked.

By a proxy of nomenclature, narrow tailoring analysis steps in for its invisible brother, interposition, to safeguard white privilege by ensuring that the path to selectivity and exclusivity will not be obstructed or interfered with by notions of racial fairness or the operation of federal or state integration laws and racial remedies.[180] To see this, one need only supplant the word "state" in Virginia's 1956 resolution with "white suburb" and the argument begins to look like the hands-off-suburbia stance that the Court has adamantly defended and championed over the past three decades.[181] Thus, in its tacit legal form today, interposition's invisible presence is undeniably felt in the narrow tailoring construct. It takes the form of inevitability that race will be declared judicially (if not socially) irrelevant, as recent precedent[182] and Justice O'Connor's twenty-five-year deadline for affirmative action in *Grutter* ominously portends.[183]

In effect, instead of a Governor Faubus standing in the doorway obstructing access to nine Little Rock African American children[184] or a university that represents the bastion and citadel of Southern exclusivity denying access to James Meredith,[185] the Court has taken that role itself. The Court appears obliged to accomplish the same obstruc-

---

177. *See id.*

178. *See* Defining "White Privilege," *supra* note 76.

179. *See Regents of Univ. of Cal. v. Bakke*, 438 U.S. 265, 361–62 (1978) (supporting that strict scrutiny is often "fatal in fact").

180. *See* Estreicher, *supra* note 19, at 241–42 (discussing the narrow tailoring analysis in *PICS*).

181. *See* 1956 EXTRA SESSION, *supra* note 167, at 1–3.

182. The Court has explicitly attempted to move the country to the equal protection clause's "'ultimate goal' of 'eliminat[ing] entirely from governmental decision-making such irrelevant factors as a human being's race.'" *City of Richmond v. J.A. Croson Co.* (*Croson*), 488 U.S. 469, 495 (1989) (Stevens, J., dissenting) (quoting *Wygant v. Jackson Bd. of Educ.*, 476 U.S. 267, 320 (1986) (alteration in original)).

183. *Grutter v. Bollinger*, 539 U.S. 306, 343 (2003). The Court noted that it "take[s] the Law School at its word that it would 'like nothing better than to find a race-neutral admissions formula' and will terminate its race-conscious admissions program as soon as practicable. The Court expect[s] that 25 years from now, the use of racial preferences will no longer be necessary to further the interest approved today." *Id.*

184. JACK GREENBERG, CRUSADES IN THE COURT: HOW A DEDICATED BAND OF LAWYERS FOUGHT FOR THE CIVIL RIGHTS REVOLUTION 228–32 (1994).

185. JUAN WILLIAMS, EYES ON THE PRIZE: AMERICA'S CIVIL RIGHTS YEARS 1954–1965 at 213–18 (1987).

tive purpose through the narrow tailoring requirement—a requirement virtually impossible not to offend without coincidentally also offending notions of white privilege.

When viewed in this manner, it is possible to reconcile the Court's apparently contradictory approach to strict scrutiny in the majority of its post-*Brown* race-based cases and in its racial tiebreaker cases. On one hand, the Court has respected the political integrity and autonomy of the local municipal decision-making process by allowing city organs and school districts to flout or water down the *Brown* mandate.[186] On the other hand, the Court recently appears to wholly disregard the autonomous decision-making of school districts and boards of education. In *PICS*, for instance, the Court did not respect the board of education and the Seattle school district's decision making process or their ability to implement policy pursuant to a democratic and educational process after the board and district reviewed decades of failed desegregation policy.[187] This implicit double standard approach cannot be effectively explained by Estreicher's nonpreference principle, but rather by the spirit of interposition. This spirit arises wherever the white privilege prerogative is offended and has found its way to the highest bench, where the locus of conservative power has migrated from local municipalities to guard that privilege.[188]

The pivotal case of *Milliken I* also illustrates that narrow tailoring has become the de facto legal successor of the doctrine of interposition.[189] Shortly after Governor William Milliken executed Michigan Act 48 into law, suspending a voluntary 1970 desegregation plan by the Detroit Board of Education, a strategy of political retribution intended to undermine any desegregation progress began.[190] Detroit School Board members who voted for the desegregation plan were removed from office by recall.[191] After their removal, the new board proposed a magnet plan that would have essentially continued the segregated pupil assignment.[192] In response, the NAACP sued to enjoin the enforcement of Act 48 and called for the reinstatement of the suspended voluntary desegregation plan.[193]

The late Judge Stephen Roth of the U.S. District Court for the Eastern District of Michigan presided over the trial.[194] The NAACP petitioned for a temporary restraining order and preliminary injunction, but Judge Roth denied both.[195] The plaintiffs appealed to the U.S. Court of Appeals for the Sixth Circuit, which found in their favor, holding that Act 48 was

---

186. *Freeman v. Pitts*, 503 U.S. 467, 490 (1992) (noting that "the school district and all state entities participating with it in operating the schools" can be "held accountable to the citizenry [and] to the political process"). *See also Milliken v. Bradley*, 418 U.S. 717, 742 (1974) (holding that *Brown's* remedial mandate did not extend to suburbs and stating that "local control over the educational process affords citizens an opportunity to participate in decision making, permits the structuring of school programs to fit local needs, and encourages 'experimentation, innovation, and a healthy competition for educational excellence'") (quoting *San Antonio Indep. Sch. Dist. v. Rodriguez*, 411 U.S. 1, 50 (1973)).

187. *See PICS v. Seattle Sch. Dist. No. 1,* 127 S.Ct. 2738 2766 (2007).

188. *See* Estreicher, *supra* note 19, at 249.

189. *See Milliken v. Bradley*, 418 U.S 717, 722–23 (1974).

190. *Id.* at 722.

191. PAUL R. DIMOND, BEYOND BUSING: INSIDE THE CHALLENGES TO URBAN SEGREGATION 27 (1985).

192. *Id.* at 35.

193. *Milliken*, 418 U.S. at 723.

194. *See* DIMOND, *supra* note 191, at 31.

195. *Id.* at 31–32.

unconstitutional because the equal protection clause required compliance with *Brown*.[196] The case was remanded and during the forty-one-day trial, Judge Roth's opinion of the matter changed.[197] In 1971, Judge Roth held what many had long known: school segregation and housing segregation are interdependent phenomena, and any remedy must address both.[198]

With regard to the need for interdistrict relief, the court held that the only constitutionally sufficient plan would have to cross the boundaries between the city and suburban school districts.[199] This meant implementing an interdistrict plan free from the geographical boundaries of racial segregation, such as district boundary lines created by the school district.[200] In its five-to-four decision, the Supreme Court affirmed with respect to the findings of intradistrict segregation, but reversed the portion of the holding dealing with the interdistrict remedy.[201] Chief Justice Warren Burger declared, "We conclude that the relief … was based upon an erroneous standard and was unsupported by record evidence that acts of the outlying districts effected the discrimination found to exist in the schools of Detroit."[202]

The ruling set forth the proposition that state control over public education falls second to local control when no state violation exists.[203] The rationale of the decision, however, is tenuous in the sense that the de jure segregation was legalized through a state law enacted by state legislatures.[204] Furthermore, neither the Constitution nor the Fourteenth Amendment make such a distinction between the state and a local school district.[205] Thus, *Milliken I* imports a constrained analysis in constitutional law to preserve the predominantly white suburban interests and the privilege to be free from interference from the courts and minority student enrollment.[206]

There was no doubt that the plaintiffs in *Milliken I* had shown sufficient purposeful discrimination in the Detroit school system to establish a violation of their constitutional rights.[207] Indeed, this determination went uncontested in the Supreme Court.[208] The only question was what the state of Michigan—whose powers had been

---

196. *Id*. at 74.

197. On remand, Judge Roth again refused to grant a preliminary injunction, *Bradley v. Milliken* (*Bradley II*), 338 F. Supp. 582, 592 (E.D. Mich. 1971), and the Sixth Circuit court affirmed, again directing a trial on the merits. *Bradley v. Milliken* (*Bradley III*), 484 F.2d 215, 258 (6th Cir. 1973).

198. *Bradley II*, 338 F. Supp. at 593. Judge Roth's findings included an explicit finding that both the state of Michigan and the Detroit board had committed "acts which have been causal factors in the segregated condition of the public schools of the City of Detroit." *Id*. at 592.

199. *Bradley III*, 484 F.2d at 249.

200. *Id*.

201. *Milliken v. Bradley*, 418 U.S. 717, 752–53 (1974).

202. *Id*. at 752. The Court held the district court had no equitable power to include in its remedial decree any school district whose racial composition had not been shown to be the product of de jure segregation. The defendants did not, however, challenge the district court's finding of de jure segregation within the city of Detroit. Accordingly, the Court remanded the case for formulation of a Detroit-only remedial decree. *Id*. at 752–53.

203. *See id*. at 748–49.

204. *Id*. at 750–51.

205. *See* U.S. Const. amend. XIV.

206. *See* Leonard P. Strickman, *School Desegregation at the Crossroads*, 70 Nw. U. L. Rev. 725, 754 (1975).

207. *Id*.

208. *Id*.

used to violate the right—and its subsidiary school boards were going to do about it.[209] By the time of *Milliken I*, it was clear that absent proof of a formal racial classification, a finding of purposeful discrimination was necessary to establish an equal protection violation in school cases.[210] The *Milliken I* decision effectively severed the school-residential segregation nexus, making future efforts to integrate in a vacuum formidable, isolated, and practically impossible.[211] The decision did, however, accomplish one important objective by permitting suits to go forward against segregated single districts.[212]

After the trial court ruled on an intradistrict remedy, the case wound its way through the courts back to the Supreme Court in *Milliken II*.[213] This time the issue before the Court was whether Michigan was liable for the costs of the remedial measures based on a finding that the state had intentionally discriminated.[214] The Court was not persuaded by the state's Eleventh Amendment immunity argument, and held that it could be directed to pay the cost of remedying the dual system.[215] The holding extended to underwriting the cost of ancillary educational relief.[216] Thus, Michigan had to pay half of the costs, approximately $5.8 million, for vocational programs such as reading programs and "in-service training of teachers, testing, and counselors."[217]

Undoubtedly, without *Milliken II*, states would continue to remain unaccountable under the guise of state immunity, leaving the costs of remedial programs for black children without funding throughout the nation.[218] Also true, however, is that the Court in *Milliken I* struck a severe blow to *Brown* with its interdistrict remedy holding, as circumscribed as it was to suit the modern temperament of white suburbia.[219] Even where they provide remedies, courts have found interdistrict remedies improper in all but a handful of cases.[220] A dissenting Justice Douglas declared: "When we rule against the met-

---

209. *Milliken*, 418 U.S. at 800 n.19 (Marshall, J., dissenting). *See also* Strickman, *supra* note 206, at 753 ("While *Milliken* is on its face a remedy case, Chief Justice Burger's opinion considerably reduces the underlying rights by limiting judicial cognizance of the injury suffered.").

210. *See, e.g., Washington v. Davis*, 426 U.S. 229, 239–43 (1976) (distinguishing between invidious discriminatory purpose and disproportionate impact); *Keyes v. Sch. Dist. No. 1*, 413 U.S. 189, 198 (1973) ("Plaintiffs must prove not only that segregated schooling exists but also that it was brought about or maintained by intentional state action.").

211. *See Milliken v. Bradley*, 418 U.S. 717, 745 (1974).

212. *See, e.g., Dayton Bd. of Educ. v. Brinkman*, 443 U.S. 526, 529 (1979) (upholding the desegregation of Dayton, Ohio's school district); *Columbus Bd. of Educ. v. Penick*, 443 U.S. 449, 458 (1979) (allowing students of the Columbus, Ohio, school district to challenge the district's dual school system and holding that the district has a duty to dismantle the segregated school system); *Reed v. Rhodes*, 607 F.2d 714, 716 (6th Cir. 1979), *cert. denied*, 445 U.S. 935 (1980) (holding the Cleveland School District liable for the constitutional violations related to the school district's segregation of students).

213. *Milliken v. Bradley (Milliken II)*, 433 U.S. 267, 269 (1977).

214. *Id.*

215. *Id.* at 290.

216. *Id.*

217. *Id.* at 293–94 (Powell, J., concurring).

218. *See United States v. Bd. of Sch. Comm'rs*, 677 F.2d 1185, 1187–88 (7th Cir. 1982).

219. *See* Norman Amaker, Milliken v. Bradley: *The Meaning of the Constitution in School Desegregation Cases*, 2 Hastings Const. L.Q. 349, 352 (1975) (arguing that "the quarrel [is not one of remedy,] but really exposes a fundamental difference in the view taken of the nature of the constitutional right of the present day black descendants of slaves who attend the nation's public schools").

220. *See* Bradley W. Joondeph, *A Second Redemption?*, 56 Wash. & Lee L. Rev. 169, 183 n.96 (1999) (reviewing Gary Orfield et al., Dismantling Desegregation: The Quiet Reversal of Brown v. Board of Education (1996)). Joondeph noted that "courts have ordered interdistrict de-

ropolitan area remedy we take a step that will likely put the problems of the blacks and our society back to the period that antedated the 'separate-but-equal regime' of *Plessy v. Ferguson*."[221]

For school districts that want to stem the tide of eroding race-based remedies in the face of increasing racial inequality in public schooling, the voluntary use of racial balancing and race-conscious admissions has become more prominent and contentious in recent years.[222] *Milliken I* fell short in holding that outlying suburban school districts could not be included in a desegregation decree if they did not violate the equal protection clause.[223] Indeed, commentators have sharply criticized *Milliken I* on this ground alone as being too narrow a construction by the Court.[224]

Another critique may also explain the Court's modern jurisprudential approach. In keeping with the definitional concepts of white privilege discussed thus far, one can see how the Court concerns itself with the protection of this prerogative to have local white neighborhood schools.[225] Whites have the prerogative to enjoy an exemption free from liability.[226] We see this in the way suburbs form, in part, as a result of white flight from desegregation mandates.[227] A white community formed to evade the consequences of de-

---

segregation remedies based on a finding of significant interdistrict segregative effects for only the following four school systems: Indianapolis, Little Rock, Louisville, and Wilmington." *Id. See also Little Rock Sch. Dist. v. Pulaski County Special Sch. Dist.*, 778 F.2d 404, 433–34 (8th Cir. 1985), *cert. denied*, 476 U.S. 1186 (1986) (holding that "the interdistrict violations by the defendants justify interdistrict relief to [a certain extent]"); *United States v. Bd. of Sch. Comm'rs*, 637 F.2d 1101, 1113–14 (7th Cir. 1980), *cert. denied*, 449 U.S. 838 (1980) (upholding the district court's interdistrict transfer remedy); *Newburg Area Council v. Bd. of Educ.*, 510 F.2d 1358, 1361 (6th Cir. 1974), *cert. denied*, 421 U.S. 931 (1975) (declaring the district court's interdistrict remedy appropriate with some modifications); *Evans v. Buchanan*, 447 F. Supp. 982, 999–1000, 1040 (D. Del. 1978), *aff'd*, 582 F.2d 750 (3d Cir. 1978), *cert. denied*, 446 U.S. 923 (1980) (implementing an interdistrict desegregation plan in Wilmington, Delaware). Joondeph further noted that "federal courts have approved settlement agreements in St. Louis and Milwaukee involving voluntary interdistrict student transfer programs." Joondeph, *supra*, at 183 n.96.

221. *Milliken v. Bradley*, 418 U.S. 717, 759 (1974) (Douglas, J., dissenting) (citation omitted).

222. *See, e.g., Gratz v. Bollinger*, 539 U.S. 244, 249–51 (2003) (declaring the University of Michigan's use of race preference in admissions violates the equal protection clause of the Fourteenth Amendment).

223. *See Milliken*, 418 U.S. at 745.

224. *See* Mark C. Rahdert, *Obstacles and Wrong Turns on the Road from* Brown: Milliken v. Bradley *and the Quest for Racial Diversity in Education*, 13 TEMPLE POL. & CIV. RTS. L. REV. 785, 786 (2004) ("If there is one single case that marks the point where the Court started to abandon its quest to integrate American public education, in my view that case is *Milliken v. Bradley*."). *See also* Michael Heise, *Litigated Learning and the Limits of the Law*, 57 VAND. L. REV. 2417, 2430–31 (2004) ("The *Milliken* decision effectively brought [racial integration] to a close.").

225. *See* James E. Ryan, *Schools, Race, and Money*, 109 YALE L.J. 249, 282 (1999) (discussing *Milliken* and recognizing the Court's "refusal to include the suburbs in busing plans, in turn, protected white suburbs and thus gave middle-class whites a place to go").

226. *See* Ronald Turner, *The Voluntary School Integration Cases and the Contextual Equal Protection Clause*, 51 HOWARD L.J. 251, 285 (2008) (stating that as a result of *Milliken*, "the participants in and the beneficiaries of white flight to suburban (and more affluent) school districts were now effectively insulated from metropolitan-wide desegregation remedies and integration efforts") (citations omitted).

227. *See* John Charles Boger, *Education's "Perfect Storm"? Racial Resegregation, High Stakes Testing, and School Resource Inequities: The Case of North Carolina*, 81 N.C. L. REV. 1375, 1392 (2003). *But see* Ryan, *supra* note 225, at 282 (questioning whether desegregation led to white flight).

segregation mandates[228] is not subject to heightened judicial scrutiny, nor strict scrutiny's narrow tailoring, despite its blatant evasion of the mandate.[229]

Judicial protection of white privilege may explain why segregation has prevailed even though many districts today still operate under court-ordered desegregation.[230] Though the statistical portrait clearly varies somewhat, conservative estimates place the total number of these districts somewhere in the hundreds,[231] including many of the largest districts in the country.[232] One author reports that "approximately 400 school districts in the United States are still under court order from desegregation cases."[233] Another researcher observed that "almost 700 school districts nationwide have formal desegregation plans, and the majority of these plans are either court-ordered or mandated by a state or federal agency.... About 60 percent of our largest 150 school districts have desegregation plans of some type."[234]

Although the exact number of school districts under desegregation supervision remains undetermined, it is clear that there is a limited window of opportunity for millions of students, many in the nation's largest school districts where students of color are concentrated,[235] to seek race-based remedies in an effort to close the achieve-

---

228. For literature discussing these consequences, see generally GLENN C. LOURY, THE ANATOMY OF RACIAL INEQUALITY (2002); DOUGLAS S. MASSEY & NANCY A. DENTON, AMERICAN APARTHEID: SEGREGATION AND THE MAKING OF THE UNDERCLASS (1993); MELVIN OLIVER & THOMAS M. SHAPIRO, BLACK WEALTH/WHITE WEALTH: A NEW PERSPECTIVE ON RACIAL INEQUALITY (1995); GARY ORFIELD & CAROLE ASHKINAZE, CLOSING DOOR: CONSERVATIVE POLICY AND BLACK OPPORTUNITY (1991); MYRON ORFIELD, METRO-POLITICS: A REGIONAL AGENDA FOR COMMUNITY & STABILITY (1998); DAVID RUSK, CITIES WITHOUT SUBURBS (1993); WILLIAM JULIUS WILSON, THE TRULY DISADVANTAGED (1987).

229. See City of Richmond v. J.A. Croson Co. (Croson), 488 U.S. 469, 510 (1989) (citing Wygant v. Jackson Bd. of Educ., 476 U.S. 267, 276 (1986)); Grutter v. Bollinger, 539 U.S. 306, 339–43 (2003).

230. See Roger Clegg, The Destructiveness of Continuing Desegregation Orders: What Happens When the School You Go to Depends on the Color of Your Skin, FINDLAW.COM, Sept. 5, 2002, http://writ.news.findlaw.com/commentary/20020905_clegg.html.

231. See RICHARD D. KAHLENBERG, ALL TOGETHER NOW: CREATING MIDDLE-CLASS SCHOOLS THROUGH PUBLIC CHOICE 305 n.60 (2001) (estimating that "about three hundred ... school districts are still under federal supervision"); Nick Lewin, The No Child Left Behind Act of 2001: The Triumph of School Choice over Racial Desegregation, 12 GEO. J. POVERTY L. & POL'Y 95, 111 n.119 (2005) (citing David S. Tatel, Desegregation versus School Reform: Resolving the Conflict, 4 STAN L. & POL'Y REV. 61, 63 (1992)) ("According to one study, more than 960 districts underwent desegregation from 1968 to 1986. The Office for Civil Rights of the Department of Education lists 256 districts with combined enrollments of over two million students, forty-six percent of whom are minority, currently operating under court supervision in cases brought by the Justice Department.").

232. See Brief Amici Curiae of the Council of Great City Schools, the American Association of School Administrators and the National Association of Secondary School Principals at 1–3, Bd. of Educ. v. Dowell, 498 U.S. 237 (1991) (No. 89-1080); Tatel, supra note 231, at 63.

233. Clegg, supra note 230.

234. Lewin, supra note 231, at 112 (quoting KHALENBERG, supra note 232, at 305).

235. See Michael Heise, Brown v. Board of Education, Footnote 11, and Multidisciplinarity, 90 CORNELL L. REV. 279, 285 tbl.1 (2005). The percentage of residential white non-Hispanics compared to the percentage of school district white non-Hispanics in New York City was 35 percent to 15.3 percent; in Los Angeles, 29.7 percent to 9.9 percent; in Chicago, 31.3 percent to 9.6 percent; in Dade County, Fla., 41.3 percent to 11.3 percent; in Broward County, Fla., 58.0 percent to 41.2 percent; in Clark County, Nev., 60.2 percent to 49.9 percent; in Houston, 30.8 percent to 10.0 percent; in Philadelphia, 42.5 percent to 16.7 percent; in Hillsborough County, Fla., 63.3 percent to 51.8 percent; in Detroit, 10.5 percent to 3.7 percent. Id. at 285. "As of 1995 all of the students in East St. Louis, Illinois, and Compton, California, were minority. http://web2.westlaw.com/result/documenttext. aspx?cnt=DOC&rs=LAWS2.0&fn=_top&query=%22BROWN+V.+BOARD+OF+EDUCATION%22+%2

ment gap.[236] This opportunity must not be squandered while a court order remains in effect. To be sure, the migration of white families with school-aged children from urban to nonurban areas is a function of many factors in addition to white privilege.[237] The fact that voluntary desegregation efforts constitute one such factor contributing to this migration, however, suggests that white communities act defensively to protect their relative advantage and exclusivity by deliberately evading court orders.[238]

If, as the Supreme Court stated in *Milliken I*, the scope of the desegregation remedy must match the scope of the equal protection violation, it seems inconsistent to hold as a matter of law that a statewide violation of the equal protection clause could be found, but that the suburbs, which are a political subdivision of the state, could escape the purview of a desegregation consent decree altogether.[239] Thus, *Milliken I* highlights the Court's protection of white suburbs formed to subvert the efficacy of integration mandates.[240] Today, such a nuanced analysis cannot fit within the permissible strictures of the Fourteenth Amendment, but the judicial protection of white privilege may explain this result.

Estreicher's nonpreference principle should have no application where private actors are engaging in racial preference patterns to the exclusion of students of color.[241] If the nonpreference principle did apply, it would seriously question the presumed neutrality of law that gives effect to enforcing privatized discriminatory preferences.[242] Viewed in this way, the *Milliken I* decision can be seen as the judicial embodiment of the notion of interposition. There, the Court in *Milliken I* acted as the intervenor, interposing itself between the school district governmental unit and the local hands-off

---

6+%22FREEMAN+V.+PITTS%22&ss=CNT&cfid=1&blinkedcitelist=False&sv=Split&rlt=CLID_QRYRLT 454811&sskey=CLID_SSSA434811&mt=LawSchoolPractitioner&origin=Search&method=TNC&rp=%2fs earch%2fdefault.wl&db=JLR&vr=2.0&n=17&scxt=WL&cxt=RL&service=Search&eq=search&docsample= False&dups=False&rltdb=CLID_DB5128811&fcl=False"\l"FN;F18#FN;F18". Close to all (between 93 percent and 96 percent) of the students in Detroit, Washington, D.C., Hartford, New Orleans, San Antonio, Camden, Oakland, and Atlanta were minority. In Richmond, Virginia and Newark, New Jersey, over 90 percent of the students were minority." *Id.* at 284. *See also* Erica Frankenberg et al., A Multiracial Society with Segregated Schools: Are We Losing the Dream? (2003) ("The nation's largest school systems account for a shrinking share of the total enrollment and are, almost without exception, overwhelmingly nonwhite and increasingly segregated internally."), *available at* http://www.civilrightsproject.ucla.edu/research/reseg03/resegregation03.php; Peter Irons, Jim Crow's Children: The Broken Promise of the *Brown* Decision 338 (2002) ("There has not been a single year in American history in which at least half of the nation's black children attended schools that were largely white."); Gary Orfield & John T. Yun, Resegregation in American Schools 9 tbl.4 (1999) (discussing the enrollment of the largest central city school districts by race and ethnicity for 1996 through 1997), *available at* http://sitemaker.umich.edu/356.meili/the_crisis; Craig D. Jerald & Bridget K. Curran, *By the Numbers: The Urban Picture*, Educ. Wk., Jan. 8, 1998, at 56 (comparing educational achievement in urban school districts with nonurban school districts).

236. *See* Orfield & Yun, *supra* note 230, at 6.

237. *See* Bradley W. Joondeph, *Skepticism and School Desegregation*, 76 Wash. U. L.Q. 161, 163 (1998) (citing various factors for white migration including "declining white birth rates and white out-migration attributable primarily to increasing crime rates and fears related to an increasing percentage of minority residents").

238. *See* David J. Armor, Forced Justice: School Desegregation and the Law 208–13 (1995).

239. *See Milliken v. Bradley*, 418 U.S. 717, 744–45 (1974).

240. *Id.* at 745–47.

241. *See* Estreicher, *supra* note 2, at 242–46.

242. *See City of Richmond v. J.A. Croson Co.* (*Croson*), 488 U.S. 469, 518–19 (1989) (Kennedy, J., concurring); Ian Ayres & Frederick E. Vars, *When Does Private Discrimination Justify Public Affirmative Action?*, 98 Colum. L. Rev. 1577, 1604 (1998).

sovereignty of white communities, free to exercise their prerogative unencumbered by the Fourteenth Amendment.[243]

V. A Theoretical Construct to Combat the Interposition of White Privilege: Racial Remedies When Government Is a Passive Participant in Private Discrimination

Although redressing general societal discrimination is not legally permissible to justify race-based remedial measures,[244] private racial preferences that are furthered by public spending are a legitimate remedial justification. Through the allocation of resources, the government contributes to the effects of private discriminatory actions, leading to the segregation of people of different races and the exclusion of people of color from the enjoyment of public education.[245] Failure to act makes the government complicit in the privatized preferences exercised by white privilege.[246] Of course, this is contrary to Justice Thomas's conception of private choices.[247] As Justice Thomas stated in his concurrence in *Missouri v. Jenkins*:

> Neutral policies, such as local school assignments,[248] do not offend the Constitution when individual private choices concerning work or residence produce schools with high black populations. The Constitution does not prevent individuals from choosing to live together, to work together, or to send their children to school together, so long as the State does not interfere with their choices on the basis of race.[249]

Justice Thomas finds nothing problematic with racial imbalance and thus by extension he concludes in *PICS* that racial balancing fails to constitute a compelling state interest.[250]

---

243. *See Milliken*, 418 U.S. at 752.

244. *See Croson*, 488 U.S. at 498.

245. *See* Gary Orfield, *Why Segregation Is Inherently Unequal: The Abandonment of* Brown *and the Continuing Failure of* Plessy, 49 N.Y.L. Sch. L. Rev. 1041, 1042 (2005). *See also* Tresa Baldas, *Saying Goodbye to Desegregation Plans*, Nat'l L.J., June 16, 2003, at 4 ("Harvard researcher Gary Orfield ... [stated] 'We're going back to a kind of *Plessy* separate-but-equal world. I blame the courts. Because the courts are responsible for the resegregation of the South.'").

246. *See* Tanya K. Hernandez, *An Exploration of the Efficacy of Class-Based Approaches to Racial Justice: The Cuban Context*, 33 U.C. Davis L. Rev. 1135, 1165 (2000). In that scenario, the Court places its imprimatur on private racialized preferences when it permits those preferences to continue by excluding remedial measures designed to mitigate their adverse effects. James A. Kushner, *New Urbanism: Urban Development and Ethnic Integration in Europe and the United States*, 5 U. Md. L.J. Race, Religion, Gender & Class 27, 27 n.1 (2005).

247. *See* Jill Goldenziel, *Administratively Quirky, Constitutionally Murky: The Bush Faith-Based Initiative*, 8 N.Y.U. J. Legis. & Pub. Pol'y 359, 369 (2005).

248. If one were to assume that it was not "neutral policies" that led to segregation in housing patterns but rather intentional discrimination in housing, this makes racial balancing provisions more unfair to African Americans. If that is the case, the racist housing policies of the majority results in African Americans' increased difficulty or inability to create charter schools near their own homes that are reflective of the district as a whole.

249. *Missouri v. Jenkins*, 515 U.S. 70, 121 (1995) (Thomas, J., concurring) (internal citation omitted).

250. *PICS v. Seattle Sch. Dist. No. 1*, 127 S.Ct. 2738, 2768 (Thomas, J., concurring).

Justice Thomas's opinion is an incomplete analysis, however, because it overlooks language in *Croson* that justifies public affirmative action remedies used to ameliorate the effects of private discrimination.[251] As Justice O'Connor noted in *Croson*:

> While the States and their subdivisions may take remedial action when they possess evidence that their own spending practices are exacerbating a pattern of prior discrimination, they must identify that discrimination, public or private, with some specificity before they may use race-conscious relief.[252]

Therefore, following *Croson*, it is conceivable that public affirmative action may be used to remedy private discrimination in limited circumstances.[253] In *PICS*, the Court noted that in Seattle there was never a finding of racial discrimination, nor was the district court under any desegregation order.[254]

A. Passive Participation through Private Racial Preferences

To begin with, it is necessary to reexamine the common assumption in *PICS* that, beyond creating diversity, government affirmative action can be used only to remedy government discrimination.[255] Presumably this proposition comes from Justice Powell's plurality opinion in *Wygant v. Jackson Board of Education*, which noted that the Supreme Court "has insisted upon some showing of prior discrimination by the governmental unit involved before allowing limited use of racial classifications in order to remedy such discrimination."[256] Despite the fact that *Croson* overturned *Wygant* by holding that remedying private discrimination is a compelling governmental interest,[257] several federal circuits have insistently remained steadfast to the principle that governmental units can only use affirmative action to remedy their own discrimination.[258] Other federal courts, however, correctly took note that the *Croson* holding supplanted *Wygant*.[259]

---

251. *See City of Richmond v. J.A. Croson Co.* (*Croson*), 488 U.S. 469, 489 (1989).

252. *Id.* at 504.

253. *See id.*

254. *PICS*, 127 S.Ct. at 2747. Likewise, in Louisville, Kentucky, the Court concluded that because the desegregation decree was lifted in 2000, the use of racial remedies was prohibited to address segregation. *Id.* at 2749.

255. *Id.* at 2751–53.

256. *Wygant v. Jackson Bd. of Educ.*, 476 U.S. 267, 274 (1986). *See also Croson*, 488 U.S. at 485 ("'Findings of *societal* discrimination will not suffice; the findings must concern prior discrimination *by the government unit involved*.'") (quoting *J.A. Croson Co. v. City of Richmond*, 822 F.2d 1355, 1358 (4th Cir. 1987)).

257. *Croson*, 488 U.S. at 485.

258. *See Messer v. Meno*, 130 F.3d 130, 136 (5th Cir. 1997); *Aiken v. City of Memphis*, 37 F.3d 1155, 1162 (6th Cir. 1994); *In re Birmingham Reverse Discrimination Employment Litig.*, 20 F.3d 1525, 1540 (11th Cir. 1994); *Contractors Ass'n v. City of Philadelphia*, 6 F.3d 990, 1002 n.10 (3d Cir. 1993); *Billish v. City of Chicago*, 962 F.2d 1269, 1280 (7th Cir. 1992); *Coral Constr. Co. v. King County*, 941 F.2d 910, 916 n.6 (9th Cir. 1991); *Hiller v. County of Suffolk*, 977 F. Supp. 202, 206 (E.D.N.Y. 1997); *McLaughlin v. Boston Sch. Comm.*, 938 F. Supp. 1001, 1008 (D. Mass. 1996); *Koski v. Gainer*, No. 92C3293, 1995 U.S. Dist. LEXIS 14604, at *40 (N.D. Ill. 1995); *Mallory v. Harkness*, 895 F. Supp. 1556, 1559 (S.D. Fla. 1995); *Shuford v. Ala. State Bd. of Educ.*, 846 F. Supp. 1511, 1521 (M.D. Ala. 1994); *Concrete Gen., Inc. v. Wash. Suburban Sanitary Comm'n*, 779 F. Supp. 370, 378 (D. Md. 1991).

259. *E.g.*, *Concrete Works of Colo., Inc. v. City and County of Denver*, 36 F.3d 1513, 1529 (10th Cir. 1994); *O'Donnell Constr. Co. v. District of Columbia*, 963 F.2d 420, 429 (D.C. Cir. 1992) (Ginsburg, J., concurring); *Tennessee Asphalt Co. v. Farris*, 942 F.2d 969, 974 (6th Cir. 1991).

In *Croson*, Justice O'Connor suggested that the discriminatory exclusion of eligible minority-owned businesses from professional trade associations sufficed as a compelling state interest.[260] But what evidence of private discrimination might be used to validate an affirmative action program? Is there a causal justification for affirmative action based on the government's compelling interest in ensuring that its spending does not cause private discrimination? Indeed, the causal justification was implicitly embraced by *Croson*'s "passive participant" discussion:

> If the city could show that it had essentially become a "passive participant" in a system of racial exclusion practiced by elements of the local construction industry, we think it clear that the city could take affirmative steps to dismantle such a system. It is beyond dispute that any public entity, state or federal, has a compelling interest in assuring that public dollars, drawn from the tax contributions of all citizens, do not serve to finance the evil of private prejudice.[261]

The causal justification applies to the facts in *PICS*. In *PICS*, schools in northern Seattle were located in predominantly white neighborhoods and composed of white students, whereas the schools in the southern part of Seattle were located in predominantly minority neighborhoods and composed of minority students.[262] The Seattle school district, as a political subdivision of the state, may have exacerbated racial segregation in public schooling through the use of taxpayer dollars by locating these schools in such a fashion or by passively endorsing such racial segregation through the segregated use of its public facilities.[263]

The *PICS* saga reveals that the racially identifiable enrollments in Seattle were often the result of (1) widely perceived differences in the quality of a given school; (2) local convenience of a neighborhood school without the provision of district transportation; or (3) the private racial preferences of families and students.[264] An adequate remedial justification, then, would have effectively captured these underlying reasons as a lawful basis for racial remedial intervention.[265]

In this regard, it is no coincidence that the lines of racial segregation in Seattle often, but not always, mirror the line between high-demand schools with majority white student populations and low-demand schools with predominantly minority student populations. High demand mainly correlates with the racial demographics of the school.[266] Similarly, when high-demand innovative programs are cordoned off to predominantly white schools, it follows that white students can and will take the most advantage of such programs.[267] In such cases, the government should be able to implement affirmative action on behalf of the affected neighborhood students. The government participates in private discrimination because its location of schools, special academic programs, and

---

260. *City of Richmond v. J.A. Croson Co.* (*Croson*), 488 U.S. 469, 503 (1989) ("In such a case, the city would have a compelling interest in preventing its tax dollars from assisting these organizations in maintaining a racially segregated construction market.").

261. *Id.* at 492.

262. *See* Brief of Respondents at 4, *PICS v. Seattle Sch. Dist. No. 1*, 127 S.Ct. 2738 (2007) (No. 05-908).

263. *See Croson*, 488 U.S. at 492.

264. *See* Brief of Petitioner at 7–9, *PICS v. Seattle Sch. Dist. No. 1*, 127 S.Ct. 2738 (2007) (No. 05-908).

265. *See Grutter v. Bollinger*, 539 U.S. 306, 337 (2003).

266. *See* Brief of Petitioner at 5, *PICS v. Seattle Sch. Dist. No. 1*, 127 S.Ct. 2738 (2007) (No. 05-908).

267. *See id.*

resources can facilitate private discrimination in the neighborhoods' racial residential patterns.[268]

In *PICS*, the Seattle school district made the passive participant argument (albeit de-linked from the *Croson* rationale) by showing that the district's plan was reactive to the private choices of families instead of an attempt to work backward to achieve a particular result.[269] The Court may not have fully appreciated the fact that the school board and district administrators employed the integration tiebreaker based on the operation of families' private choices.[270] The district sought to correct any racial distortion or disparities resulting from such choices.[271] Because the tiebreaker was a tiebreaker, and nothing more, it did not purport at the outset to dictate where students must attend school.[272]

The district used the tiebreaker only where there was a failure in the private individual decisions of families and students, and the district phased out the tiebreaker as needed.[273] Reacting to the racially discriminatory preferences that led to skewed student body demographics, the Seattle school district used the tiebreaker to correct the private-market failure of choice that could lead to the perpetuation and facilitation of racial discrimination in public schools supported by public taxpayer dollars.[274] Without correction, the school district would have become a passive participant in such private discrimination because of its location of schools throughout a segregated school district. If, as was the case in Seattle, high-quality schools are located in predominantly white neighborhoods and inferior schools in predominantly minority neighborhoods, the government may have an obligation to correct this pattern if it leads to racialized enrollments.[275]

Certainly, the schools in the Seattle school districts varied widely in many measures of school quality, as the *PICS* petitioners were apt to point out:

> Families and the school board use various objective criteria to evaluate school quality: scores on standardized tests, numbers of college preparatory and Advanced Placement ("AP") courses offered, percentage of students who take AP courses and SAT tests, percentage of graduates who attend college, *Seattle Times* college-preparedness rankings, University of Washington rankings, and disciplinary statistics. The oversubscribed schools score better than the others on these measures of quality.[276]

The segregated schools also varied in the levels of perceived quality depending on the district's allocation of resources, as evidenced by the special academic programs offered in predominantly white neighborhoods.[277] For example, the plaintiffs noted that "Ballard offers a Biotech Academy, with separate admissions prerequisites, and Hale offers a 'Ninth

---

268. *See PICS v. Seattle Sch. Dist. No. 1*, 127 S.Ct. 2738, 2802 (2007) (Breyer, J., dissenting).

269. *See* Brief of Respondent at 2, *PICS*, 127 S.Ct. 2738 (No. 05-908).

270. *See PICS*, 127 S.Ct. at 2796.

271. *See* Brief of Respondent at 7, *PICS*, 127 S.Ct. 2738 (No. 05-908).

272. *See id.*

273. *See id.* at 47–48.

274. *See* Gary Orfield, *Metropolitan School Desegregation: Impacts on Metropolitan Society*, *in* In Pursuit of a Dream Deferred: Linking Housing and Education Policy 121, 136 (John A. Powell et al. eds., 2001).

275. *See* Brief of Petitioner at 4 n.1, *PICS*, 127 S.Ct. 2738 (No. 05-908) ("Oversubscribed schools were more prestigious, 'competition for assignment to those schools is keen,' and 'students denied their choice of schools are deprived of curriculum advantages not necessarily available at other schools.'") (citations omitted).

276. *Id.* at 4.

277. *See id.*

Grade Academy' and an 'Integrated Studies' program."[278] The presence of these programs in predominantly white schools may suggest discriminatory use of the district's spending power in ways that exacerbate racial discrimination. That three of the oversubscribed schools (Ballard, Hale, and Roosevelt) are located north of downtown where the majority of district students are white, further suggests that the district's allocation of resources is tracked along racially segregated enrollment demographics.[279] Of the five under-subscribed schools, three are located in predominantly minority neighborhoods south of downtown.[280]

The fact that the district, when making assignments for the 2000–2001 school year, did not run school buses to Ingraham, one of the undersubscribed schools in the north, from the Queen Anne or Magnolia neighborhoods, where the plaintiff Ms. Kurfirst lived, made Ingraham a less desirable option for families in those neighborhoods.[281] Distantly located superior schools and programs without adequate transportation from neighborhoods that are predominately composed of one race might also lead to racially imbalanced action.[282] Thus, lack of adequate transportation may also serve as a basis for impermissible state action, and the government may have a duty to remediate the discriminatory impact of its resource allocation decisions.[283] Furthermore, inadequate school transportation may suffice to show that the racial demographics of enrollment are not (solely) the consequence of constitutionally unactionable societal discrimination, but rather are a result of the school district's allocation of resources.[284]

B. Passive Participation under Section 8 Housing Subsidies

In addition to the foregoing, a second method conceivably exists to establish the government as a passive participant in private discrimination.[285] Under this approach, the government becomes a passive participant when it does not modify or recalibrate its affirmative action objective to account for reduced minority access to quality public schooling as a result of private discrimination.[286] In this fashion, *Croson* instructs that, should a private association refuse to accredit minority businesses, the government would act as a passive participant in the association's private discrimination, provided that the government looked to the association's membership status to determine bidder eligibility.[287] As *Cro-*

---

278. *Id.*

279. *See id.*

280. *Id.* at 5. The exceptions are in the north, where there is the Ingraham School, and in the west, where there is the West Seattle School. *Id.*

281. *Id.* at 8–9.

282. *Id.* at 22.

283. *See Wygant v. Jackson Bd. of Educ.*, 476 U.S. 267, 274 (1986). For example, "attendance at Ingraham would have required some children to take three city buses to get to school, leading to a round-trip commute of over four hours." Petitioner's Brief at 9, *PICS v. Seattle Sch. Dist. No. 1*, 127 S.Ct. 2738 (2007) (No. 05-908). Enrollment at Ingraham would have required each of the plaintiffs to leave home at 5:30 a.m. and return at 8 or 9 p.m., often alone or in the dark. *Id.*

284. *See City of Richmond v. J.A. Croson Co.* (*Croson*), 488 U.S. 469, 498–99 (1989) (stating that remedying effects of past societal discrimination is too amorphous and unlimited to constitute a justification for race-based decisions by government).

285. *See id.* at 504.

286. *See id.*

287. *See id.* at 503.

son illustrates, "in such a case, the city would have a compelling interest in preventing its tax dollars from assisting these organizations in maintaining a racially segregated construction market."[288]

Now, for example, consider a situation in which neighborhoods are formed through racially discriminatory bank redlining practices whereby minority families are steered into predominantly minority neighborhoods.[289] Additionally, what happens if landlords in predominantly white neighborhoods discriminate against recipients of federal housing vouchers by denying them the opportunity to rent? What if a school relies on such neighborhood demographics to base its admissions policy? Under this approach, if the Seattle school district were to solely rely on the geographical proximity to the school, as it did in the third tiebreaker (without the employment of the integration tiebreaker), it would become a passive participant in racial discrimination.[290]

U.S. Department of Housing and Urban Development section 8 housing subsidies provide another example of government passive participation in private discrimination. Along with the increase in popularity of section 8 subsidies, recipients of these vouchers face increased opposition from suburban communities seeking to maintain their white privilege, that is, favorable schooling, zoning exclusivity, municipal services, and the preservation of their property tax values.[291] Not surprisingly, a high concentration of voucher recipients live in only a few neighborhoods, despite the earmarking of more than $17 billion in public taxpayer dollars for federal housing and community development.[292] This phenomenon is understandable when one considers the administration of federal subsidies under the law.

Even though section 8 housing was created with the aim of addressing social segregation, the law has not afforded the protections of civil rights antidiscrimination principles in section 8 vouchers.[293] As Paul Boudreau observes:

> Although the Fair Housing Act prohibits owners of apartment buildings from discriminating on the basis of race, religion, sex or national origin, federal law does not prevent discrimination against housing-subsidy recipients. While lenders of

---

288. *Id.*

289. Redlining was an "insidious tool of private bankers to limit lending to certain (minority) neighborhoods." Alex M. Johnson, *How Race and Poverty Intersect to Prevent Integration: Destabilizing Race as a Vehicle to Integrate Neighborhoods*, 143 U. Pa. L. Rev. 1595, 1612 (1995). The Home Owners' Loan Corporation (HOLC), a federal program designed to encourage home ownership, set up a rating system to "evaluate the risks associated with loans made to particular urban neighborhoods." *Id.* at 1613. The system consisted of four ratings, each represented by a color. *Id.* Red represented the least desirable of these four ratings, and any homeowner within the neighborhoods marked with red rarely received HOLC loans. *Id.* While many of the white suburban neighborhoods received favorable ratings from the HOLC, the inner-city, predominantly black neighborhoods received the least desirable red rating. *See id. See also* U.S. Fed. Hous. Admin., Underwriting Manual: Underwriting and Valuation Procedure under Title II of the National Housing Act Part II, §.9 (1938) (expressing concern with "inharmonious racial or nationality groups" and stating that "if a neighborhood is to retain stability, it is necessary that properties shall continue to be occupied by the same social and racial classes").

290. *See Croson*, 488 U.S. at 503.

291. *See* Fredrick Kunkle, *Housing Vouchers No Magic Key; Rising Rents, Dwindling Choices Thwart Low-Income Residents*, Wash. Post., Aug. 5, 2002, at A1.

292. *See* U.S. Dep't of Housing and Urban Development, Fiscal Year 2003 Budget Summary 7 (2002) (containing HUD budget allocations), *available at* http://www.hud.gov/about/budget/fy03/bugsum.pdf.

293. Paul Boudreaux, *Vouchers, Buses & Flats: The Persistence of Social Segregation*, 49 Vill. L. Rev. 55, 74 (2004).

credit may not discriminate on this basis, there is no such restriction in housing law. Accordingly, landlords may refuse to rent to voucher recipients, either because of concerns over their worthiness as renters or because they do not want to integrate their building with persons of a poor social class.[294]

Without a federal prohibition preventing discrimination against section 8 voucher recipients, racially segregated neighborhoods will likely persist.[295] A strong argument exists that the government acts as a passive participant in private discrimination in this scenario because its failure to explicitly prohibit discrimination may have directly led to discriminatory patterns in housing.[296] In other words, but for the government's failure to prohibit discrimination against section 8 voucher recipients, more diverse neighborhoods would exist and more minority students would have access to better schools. Thus, although the government did not cause the private discrimination, the government can (and should) constitutionally take action to ensure that its school admissions process is not distorted by private residential discrimination.[297]

Aside from the integration tiebreaker approach, a proposal for future affirmative action reform under this "but for" rationale might require that federal housing subsidies explicitly take race and ethnicity into account.[298] Without protections like those in the Fair Housing Act, federal tax dollars actually further discriminatory preferences and exclusionary white privilege rather than abate them.[299] If the objective of the section 8 program was to ameliorate residential segregation, then it has utterly failed.

When federal tax dollars are used to further private discriminatory racial preferences that lead to segregated housing patterns, it is logical, prudent, and necessary to use race-based antidiscrimination principles to counteract such private preferences. Returning to a theme discussed earlier in this chapter, the government must create public affirmative action and race-based remedies. The failure to take such action implicitly makes the government a complicit passive coparticipant in private discriminatory matters[300] by allowing private actors to discriminate against housing recipients of federal subsidies, in turn impacting the racial demographics of a school district.[301]

When examined in this context, it is clear that the Supreme Court's protection of white privilege, found in its narrow tailoring analysis in *PICS* and in the rest of its body of racial remedy jurisprudence, along with similar treatment in federal housing subsidies, created a "perfect storm."[302] Both Supreme Court precedent and the administration of housing subsidies appear to suggest time and again that advocates should not unduly impinge on the white suburban prerogative.[303]

In this context, the nonpreference principle is neither neutral nor principled. To the contrary, the principle appears to be outcome determinative on the basis of race by working to reach a specific result and contorting principles of equality to justify the preserva-

294. *Id.* at 72–73.

295. *See id.* at 74.

296. *See City of Richmond v. J.A. Croson Co. (Croson),* 488 U.S. 469, 503 (1989).

297. *See id.*

298. Boudreaux, *supra* note 293, at 75.

299. *See* Brian S. Prestes, Comment, *Application of the Equal Credit Opportunity Act to Housing Leases,* 67 U. Chi. L. Rev. 865, 865 (2000).

300. *See* Ayres & Vars, *supra* note 242, at 1585–86.

301. Ian Ayres, *Narrow Tailoring,* 43 UCLA L. Rev. 1781, 1800–16 (1996).

302. *See* Boger, *supra* note 227, at 1375.

303. *See* Myron Orfield, *Racial Integration and Community Revitalization: Applying the Fair Housing Act to the Low Income Housing Tax Credit,* 58 Vand. L. Rev. 1747, 1802–3 (2005).

tion of white privilege.[304] The answer cannot be merely to capitulate to this exercise of suburban white privilege, but must instead be to challenge it.[305] Some advocates have seen limited victories. In *Hills v. Gautreaux*, for instance, the Court upheld a district court order directing the HUD and Chicago public housing authorities to "engage in remedial efforts in the metropolitan area outside the city limits of Chicago."[306] The prerogative of white privilege, however, has led to dramatic and bitter battles to avoid the placement of predominantly black public housing facilities in predominantly white neighborhoods.[307] These battles often result in a surrounding segregated school system that the government, in its allocation and spending of tax dollars, facilitates as a passive participant.[308]

The government could alleviate some of the housing problems by exercising its spending powers to purchase affordable housing in socioeconomically diverse neighborhoods.[309] By purchasing housing in predominantly white neighborhoods, the government could offset the current problem of placing too many affordable housing units in predominantly poor minority communities, which exacerbates racial segregation in public schooling.[310] Where private discriminatory housing preferences go unchecked, minority access to local quality schooling becomes distorted.[311]

C. Causal and But-For Theories for Race-Based Affirmative Action

The two approaches discussed previously are consistent with the model articulated by Ian Ayres and Frederick Vars in their discussion of theoretical remedies that *Croson* might authorize with respect to minority contractors.[312] Ayres and Vars discuss three private discrimination rationales that would buttress Seattle's use of race to address de facto segregation consistent with *Croson* and Kennedy's concurring opinion in *PICS*.[313] Although they raise these rationales in the context of minority contractors, the rationales are nonetheless a helpful guidepost to mention in support of the contentions previously provided.[314] They are to:

(1) ensure that government spending on public schools does not directly or indirectly facilitate private discrimination (the "causal" justification);

(2) correct for the depressive effect of private discrimination on the capacity of minority Section Eight recipients (the "but-for" justification); and

(3) compensate for shortfalls in private sales caused by purely private discrimination by buying subsidized affordable housing for Section 8 recipients in discrete

---

304. *See* James G. Wilson, *Justice Diffused: A Comparison of Edmund Burke's Conservatism with the Views of Five Conservative Academic Judges*, 40 U. Miami L. Rev. 913, 965–66 (1986) (discussing Scalia's view on affirmative action and explaining that it is anything but neutral).

305. *See Boudreaux, supra* note 293, at 70 n.95 (discussing commentary on exclusionary zoning).

306. *See Hills v. Gautreaux*, 425 U.S. 284, 306–07 (1976).

307. *See Boudreaux, supra* note 293, at 72 (citing *United States v. Yonkers Bd. of Educ.*, 837 F.2d 1181, 1185 (2d Cir. 1987)).

308. *See Yonkers*, 837 F.2d at 1236–37.

309. *City of Richmond v. J.A. Croson Co.* (*Croson*), 488 U.S. 469, 492 (1989).

310. Ayres & Vars, *supra* note 242, at 1613.

311. *Id.*

312. *Id.* at 1604.

313. *Id.* at 1577.

314. *Id.*

amounts sufficiently diffused so as not to offend white privilege, so long as the scope of the government remedy is restricted to that particular market (the "single-market" justification).[315]

Although both the causal and but-for theories for race-based affirmative action remedies are predicated on both private discrimination and public spending, they are not redundant premises.[316] While the causal justification is based on public spending that leads to private discrimination (as with locating high-demand public schools and programs in racially white neighborhoods and inferior schools in minority neighborhoods),[317] a different basis exists for the but-for justification.[318] The latter revolves around the question of whether private discrimination causes otherwise neutral public purchasing criteria to have a discriminatory effect (as with section 8 vouchers).[319] In the absence of affirmative action, according to Ayres and Vars, either of these causal relationships would make the government a "passive participant" in the private discrimination.[320]

Croson's remedial justification may even extend beyond these two bases. Under their single-market justification, Ayres and Vars assert that "government should be able to use affirmative action in procurement not just to correct shortfalls in government purchasing caused by private discrimination, but also to correct shortfalls in private purchasing caused by private discrimination."[321] This remedial purpose might justify using affirmative action for governmental purchasing of affordable housing in areas where section 8 recipients would otherwise be shut out.[322]

There is, however, at least one limitation to this justification. According to Ayres and Vars, "this principle suggests that government cannot use affirmative action in one market to remedy discrimination in another."[323] This remedial principle would preclude the school district from using its purchasing power to acquire affordable housing in residential suburbs.[324] The principle thus presents a similar obstacle raised by the limited remedial scope in *Milliken I*, in that suburbs cannot be included in corrective actions where they were not involved in the scope of the violation.[325] The limitation does not preclude the school district from working in collaborative conjunction with other organs of government to remediate discriminatory housing patterns. Nor does the limitation preclude the ability of a school district, under the first two justifications, to take similar action as

---

315. *Id.* at 1585–87.

316. *Id.* at 1610.

317. *See Seattle Sch. Dist. No. 1 v. Washington*, 473 F. Supp. 996, 1007 (W.D. Wash. 1979), *aff'd in part, rev'd in part*, 633 F.2d 1338 (9th Cir. 1980), *aff'd sub nom., Washington v. Seattle Sch. Dist. No. 1*, 458 U.S. 457 (1982) ("Segregated housing patterns exist in the City of Seattle. These segregated housing patterns result in racially imbalanced schools when a neighborhood school assignment policy is implemented."); *PICS v. Seattle Sch. Dist. No. 1*, 72 P.3d 151, 153 (2003) ("Because of racially segregating housing patterns, mandatory assignment to neighborhood schools would result in largely segregated schools."). *See also* Brief of Respondent at 2 n.2, *PICS v. Seattle Sch. Dist. No. 1*, 127 S.Ct. 2738 (2007) (No. 05-908) ("Due to Seattle's racial diversity and its racially imbalanced housing patterns, if Seattle's children were simply assigned to the high schools nearest their homes, the high schools would become segregated in fact ("*de facto*" segregated).") (citations omitted).

318. Ayres & Vars, *supra* note 242, at 1604–5.

319. Brief of Respondent at 2, *PICS*, 127 S.Ct. 2738 (No. 05-908).

320. Ayres & Vars, *supra* note 242, at 1585–86.

321. *Id.* at 1587.

322. *Id.*

323. *Id.* at 1619.

324. *See id.*

325. *Milliken v. Bradley*, 418 U.S. 717, 745 (1974).

Seattle did by using a tiebreaker method based on more nuanced, race-conscious, and facially-neutral factors.

Future advocacy approaches must adopt a modified litigation strategy that focuses on the discriminatory allocation of educational resources in a racially disparate manner in schools rather than in neighborhood housing. In *PICS*, the Seattle school district may have contributed to the segregated character of the schools by the concentrated allocation of specialized and attractive resources in high-demand schools.[326] But because Seattle did not justify its remedial authority on the basis of correcting its own spending decisions and discriminatory resource allocation patterns (the *Croson* justification), it failed to effectively counter the argument that "racial balancing was not being achieved for its own [sake]."[327] Had the district shown that its past disparate allocation of resources led to a de facto segregation in its schools, it would have established its duty to use remedial measures.

VI. Conclusion

It is both revealing and ironic that if the Seattle school district had waited for the NAACP to a file a formal lawsuit (after the NAACP filed a civil rights complaint) before engaging in its voluntary desegregation efforts, the district might have had greater legal cover and a cognizable, discernible basis to argue that it was correcting its own discriminatory spending and resource allocation patterns.[328] The Court's current approach to

---

326. *PICS v. Seattle Sch. Dist. No. 1*, 127 S.Ct. 2738, 2828 (2007).

327. The Seattle school district made a number of mistakes in *PICS* that weakened its position in the case. Despite experimenting with geographical, sibling, and lottery interventions, district officials testified that they did not consider using race-neutral alternative. *PICS*, 127 S.Ct. at 2766. Also, when asked whether the district gave "any serious consideration to the adoption of a plan ... that did not use racial balancing as a factor or a goal," the superintendent testified, "I *think the general answer to the question is no* ... I mean it's possible informally [*sic*] ideas were floated here or there, but I don't remember any significant staff work being done." Brief of Petitioner at 17, *PICS*, 127 S.Ct. 2738 (No. 05-908). This unfortunate utterance was exacerbated by the plaintiff's expert, Dr. David Armor, who testified that the district's report was not supported by the evidence the district cited and, further, was based on subjective measures that did not even specifically relate to the Seattle school district. *Id.* at 15. In wholly failing to show that they were correcting their own discriminatory behavior in the disparate allocation of resources throughout the district's schools, which could be persuasively shown to have a nexus to the de facto segregation that resulted, the *PICS* respondents missed a critical opportunity to garner Justice Kennedy's vital swing vote. *See PICS*, 127 S.Ct. at 2792 (Kennedy, J., concurring). As the Supreme Court explained in *Freeman v. Pitts*: "Racial balance is not to be achieved for its own sake. It is to be pursued when racial imbalance has been caused by a constitutional violation." *Freeman v. Pitts*, 503 U.S. 467, 494 (1992).

328. In 1963, Seattle's voluntary majority-to-minority pupil assignment plan did not achieve racial integration. By 1971, the Board of Education decided to implement a mandatory middle school assignment plan. *See Seattle Sch. Dist. No. 1 v. Washington*, 473 F. Supp. 996, 1002, 1006 (W.D. Wash. 1979), *aff'd*, 663 F.2d 1338 (9th Cir. 1980), *aff'd*, 458 U.S. 457 (1982). This effort resulted in initial litigation and the board narrowly survived a recall initiative. The court also upheld the board's plan in *Citizens Against Mandatory Bussing v. Brooks*, 495 P.2d 657 (Wash. 1972) (en banc). However, in 1977, the ACLU, NAACP, and Church Council of Greater Seattle threatened suit at that time when the NAACP filed a complaint with the Office for Civil Rights of the Department of Health, Education and Welfare. *PICS*, 127 S.Ct. at 2804 (Breyer, J., dissenting). *See also* 45 C.F.R. § 80.7(c) (2006) (requiring an official to "make a prompt investigation whenever a ... complaint ... indicates a possible failure to comply with [nondiscriminatory standards]"). That complaint alleged that the district was purposely maintaining segregated schools. *See Seattle Sch. Dist. No. 1*, 473 F. Supp. at 1005–6. In an effort to avoid litigation, the presidents of the local Chamber of Commerce, Municipal League,

race-based remedies may create a perverse incentive against school districts taking any reactive or proactive efforts to correct their own behavior, because these efforts might lead to litigation.

In forcing deference to the courts before undertaking voluntary efforts, the Court's plurality jurists may implicitly see the courts, rather than the school districts, as best able to judge how school districts should allocate their resources.[329] Although this flies in the face of typical conservative rallying calls for judicial restraint and respect for the principles of federalism, separation of powers, and local control of schools,[330] the Court is presumably willing to turn each of these on its head so that it may judicially protect white privilege. In effect, by waiting for a lawsuit, a remedial question is transformed from a matter of administrative discretion to a judicial question that then falls under the guardianship of a conservative court.[331]

Estreicher's nonpreference neutrality theory of the Supreme Court's approach to the tiebreaker cases is both incomplete and inaccurate. The theory's faults lie in the idea that the Court concerns itself only with the neutral distribution and withholding of governmental benefits. A closer review of the Court's narrow tailoring analysis refutes this idea.

The Court's narrow tailoring analysis appears guided by the metaphorical return to jurisprudential interposition to accomplish the judicial protection of white privilege. If one can better predict the constitutionality of a racial remedy by considering whether it offends the prerogative of white privilege instead of by proper review under the "unduly burdensome" requirement of narrow tailoring, it not only fundamentally undermines the nonpreference theory but also calls for a new theory of remedial justification and remedy. The three remedial justifications explored here in the context of the *PICS* decision may plausibly survive strict scrutiny according to the Court's previous announcements, while reframing racial remedies in the context of correction rather than diversity, where they rightfully belong.

Urban League, and Seattle's mayor lobbied the district to abide in the elimination of racially isolated schools. *See id.* at 1007.

329. *See PICS*, 127 S.Ct. at 2833 (Breyer, J., dissenting).

330. *See id.* at 2798 (Breyer, J., dissenting) ("I do not understand why this Court's cases, which rest the significance of a 'unitary' finding in part upon the wisdom and desirability of returning schools to local control, should deprive those local officials of legal permission to use means they once found necessary to combat persisting injustices."). *See also id.* at 2785 n.23 (Breyer, J., dissenting) ("The Court is ... dealing with thousands of local school districts and schools. Is each to be the subject of litigation in the District Courts? ... The delicate nature of the problem of segregation and the paramount interest of the [State] in preserving the internal peace and tranquility of its people indicates that this is a question which can best be solved on the local level, at least until Congress declares otherwise." (citations omitted)).

331. *PICS*, 127 S.Ct. at 2771 n.4 (Thomas, J., concurring).

3

De Facto Segregation and Group Blindness: Proposals for Narrow Tailoring under a New Viable State Interest in *PICS v. Seattle School District*

Maurice R. Dyson[*]

Introduction

In this chapter, Professor Dyson proposes a remedial justification predicated on a new viable state interest and remedial theory of targeted race-conscious intervention. He advocates utilizing federal mandates and state constitutions to justify race-explicit and race-conscious remedies based on factors that indirectly target what he terms "race-at risk." In this regard, Dyson also raises a salient critique of the individual versus group rights debate that centers around the question of race-based remedies and persuasively argues that whereas conservative approaches to remedies evade racial accountability by resorting to the familiar refrain that the Fourteenth Amendment only protects individuals rather than groups, more progressive remedial approaches also accomplish the same by focusing too broadly on racial groups as a way to diminish individualist racial accountability. As a result, students of color are often caught in the middle of an individual color-blind approach on the one hand and what he terms as a "thin diversity-group blind" approach on the other. He points to the current regulatory administration of No Child Left Behind (NCLB) and affirmative action in higher education to support this proposition. Moreover, Professor Dyson argues that the NCLB's current approach of allowing states to exempt certain groups

---

[*] Associate Professor of Law, Thomas Jefferson School of Law; J.D., Columbia University School of Law; A.B., Columbia College, Columbia University; Association of American Law Schools Section on Education Law National Chair, 2005–2006; Order of the Barristers, Member; Roothbert Fund Fellow; Lester A. and Stella Porter Russell Endowment Recipient. Special thanks to Dean Rudy Hasl and the faculty of Thomas Jefferson School of Law. This chapter is dedicated to the loving memory of my mother, MaryAnne Lee, whose life lessons have enduringly inspired my compassionate love for social justice.

students of color from academic accountability constitutes a group-blind approach which violates Kennedy's prohibition of treating exempted students in a different fashion solely on the basis of systematic, individual typing by race, particularly whenever that typing exacerbates unequal educational opportunity. As Dyson observes, the census multicategorical movement, the Grutter *and* Gratz *decisions, as well as the* Seattle *and* Louisville *cases all powerfully suggests the nation is and must continue move toward a more contextualized view of race and ethnicity. The author is also able to effectively show how his proposed "race-at risk" theoretical conception of facially neutral and race-conscious intervention overcomes his conception of the thin diversity-group blind approach, as well as the pigmentation thin diversity critique of Parents Involved in Community Schools (PICS) petitioners and the Roberts court criticism that Seattle's race tie breaker leads to less diverse races based on a limited binary racialized paradigm of diversity. As Dyson notes, there are three distinct and competing notions of diversity at issue in PICS based on Seattle's definition, Justice Roberts multirace conception and Justice Kennedy's PICS/Grutter hybrid diversity. He suggests that any proposed plan will only be constitutionally sound only if it takes into account both Roberts's and Kennedy's notion of diversity and is narrowly tailored in ways to make clear that race will not be unqualifiedly used to threaten white privilege. This is not an insignificant concern because herein lies another missed opportunity to garner Kennedy's swing vote as evidenced by his offense to what he perceived as "Seattle's crude racial categories of 'white and non-white' as the basis for student assignments" when one considers the district was "composed of a diversity of races, with fewer than half of the students classified as 'white.'" Finally, the author proposes specific factors (both race-explicit and facially neutral) as well as legislative reforms for NCLB's reauthorization as an alternative to the tiebreaker approach that overcomes both group-blind evasive compliance as well as the structural barriers and disincentives for student transfers to higher performing districts in a targeted facially neutral fashion consistent with Kennedy's concurrence. In this manner, Professor Dyson is able to show how his more nuanced NCLB revised approach authorizes a broader interdistrict remedial scope not possible in* Milliken *and which includes the kind of educational remedies struck down in* Missouri v. Jenkins. *It also more closely locates the remedial justification in the higher education diversity rationale to establish the proposition that affirmative action cannot be principally dismantled without first achieving racial accountability in the K–12 pipeline.*

Overview

Part I locates the debate of individual rights and group blindness within the PICS varying notions of diversity. It also lays out a new viable state interest based on closing the achievement gap. Part II propounds a new remedial approach to the woes of the NCLB when Title I is congressionally reauthorized. Part III proposes a new multifactoral analysis that can provide nationwide guidance to school districts on ways to engage in lawful narrow tailoring of race conscious remedies, targeted interventions and resource allocation patterns that might have been unlawful in *Missouri v. Jenkins.* Part IV lays out a new theoretical approach to NCLB interdistrict remedies that introduces competition and structural incentives to overcome the barriers and disincentives of interdistrict transfers that might not have otherwise been possible in *Milliken v. Bradley* and which, in tandem with targeted intervention, is consistent with the rationale of PICS.

Part I

It is significant that in the drawn-out saga of the race-based remedies in Seattle and Louisville[1] were challenged under the Fourteenth Amendment which announced that "no State shall ... deny to any person within its jurisdiction the equal protection of the laws."[2] With a fair amount of regularity conservative critics of racial remedies are quick to point out that the Equal Protection Clause, by its terms, does not admit to racial classifications or protect group rights based on race, only individual rights.[3] The argument typically goes something like this: Government has no business engaging in racial profiling and should not be basing remedies on the basis of group identity or giving an unfair advantage to racial groups. Indeed, this was the impetus behind Washington state's Initiative 200 that PICS also challenged the racial tie breaker.[4] Ward Connerly, who also unsuc-

---

1. See Pet. S. Ct. Brief, *Parents Involved in Cmty. Sch. v. Seattle Sch. Dist. No. 1*, 127 S. Ct. 2738(2007) ("Parents filed this suit under 42 U.S.C. § 1983, asserting violations of the Equal Protection Clause and Title VI of the Civil Rights Act, 42 U.S.C. 9 2000d, as well as state law claims. JA 3 1. On cross motions, the district court granted summary judgment in favor of the District. Pet. App. 269–303. The judge found no violation of state law, the Equal Protection Clause, or the federal Civil Rights Act. On appeal to the Ninth Circuit, a three-judge panel unanimously found for Parents on the state law claim and enjoined the use of the race preference. The panel later withdrew that decision, vacated the injunction, and certified the state law issues to the Washington Supreme Court, which decided those issues in favor of the District. While the federal claims were still pending, this Court decided Grutter and Gratz. The parties rebriefed and reargued Parents' Equal Protection claim in light of those decisions. The panel decided in favor of Parents, holding that the District's plan was not narrowly tailored because it is indistinguishable from a "pure racial quota" and "fails virtually every one of the narrow tailoring requirements." Pet. App. 165. One judge dissented. Pet. App. 21 1–68. A rehearing en banc resulted in a decision in favor of the District by a vote of seven (including one concurrence) to four. Pet. App. 1–128. The en banc majority, relying on the observation in Grutter that "context matters," extended the reasoning in that decision to hold that racial diversity can be a compelling governmental interest for high schools. E.g., Pet. App. 33. The majority also held that much of the narrow tailoring analysis of Grutter and Gratz does not apply in the high school context, e.g., Pet. App. 42, 47–8, so that, inter alia, a mechanical racial preference can satisfy the narrow tailoring prong of strict scrutiny when implemented to achieve a pre-determined white-nonnwhite ratio. In reaching this conclusion, the majority deferred to the judgment of the school board regarding the need for a racial preference. E.g., Pet. App. 51–52, 57–58. It also held that a racial classification does not "unduly harm any students" so long as it does not "uniformly benefit any race or group of individuals to the detriment of another." Pet. App. 59–60. One judge concurred in the judgment, advocating adoption of a "rational basis" standard of review. Pet. App. 63–70. Four judges dissented. Pet. App. 71–128. They rejected the majority's "relaxed," "deferential" standard of review, Pet. App. 72, 77; its deference to the school board, Pet. App. 95, 98–99, 112–13; and its group rights theory of the Equal Protection Clause, Pet. App. 115–19. The dissent concluded that, when strict scrutiny is applied, the District's racial preference is unconstitutional because it seeks to accomplish only a predetermined white-nonwhite ratio (not "genuine" diversity), e.g., Pet. App. 84–86, 100, 125–26; because the plan operates as a quota, Pet. App. 108–1 1 ; and because it is not narrowly tailored as required by Grutter and Gratz, Pet. App. 101, 111–15, 119–25.").

2. See U.S. Const. amend. XIV, § 1.

3. See *Rutan v. Republican Party of Ill.*, 497 U.S. 62, 96, 110 (1990) (Scalia, J., dissenting) ("The Fourteenth Amendment's requirement of 'equal protection of the laws,' combined with the Thirteenth Amendment's abolition of the institution of black slavery, leaves no room for doubt that laws treating people differently because of their race are invalid.").

4. Initiative 200 provides, in pertinent part, as follows: "The state shall not discriminate against, or grant preferential treatment to, any individual or group on the basis of race, sex, color, ethnicity, or national origin in the operation of public employment, public education, or public contracting." Wash. Rev. Code §49.60.400(1) (2006).

cessfully initiated the Racial Privacy Initiative, goes one step further.[5] He states that since the races are mixing, it no longer makes sense to use racial classifications and that one's race is their own private matter.[6] A great deal has already been said how this narrow construction of the Equal Protection Clause ignores that the real nature of discrimination which is not against an individual, but rather that because that individual's perceived membership in a particular racial group.[7] With all the problematic issues this raises for racial accountability for government,[8] it is nonetheless clear from the census multicategorical movement,[9] the *Grutter*[10] and *Gratz*[11] decisions, and the *Seattle* and *Louisville* cases suggests the nation must move toward a more contextualized view of race and ethnicity. As I have suggested elsewhere, this is not necessarily a negative development so long as recognition of multiracial groups is predicated on need and concerns of equity.

There appears to be three distinct and competing notions of diversity at issue in PICS that must first be carefully parsed out. The first is based on Seattle's definition which essentially equates a binary paradigm of white-nonwhite integration as tantamount to racial diversity or "thin diversity-group blindness" as I call it which is hardly diversity at all that it understandably offended the Court's plurality interpretation of narrow tailoring.[12] This "thin diversity, group blind" approach stands in stark contrast to Justice Roberts multirace conception of diversity. Under this view it is insufficient to examine solely the white-nonwhite binary character of racial classifications but rather a constitutional consideration that turns on an inclusion of different races. In comparison, Justice Kennedy's "PICS/Grutter hybrid diversity" as I refer to it, adopts the PICS's critique of Roberts's opinion but also goes further to look to the particular and special talents and needs of individual students that comes closer to the notion of diversity as envisaged in *Grutter* where a child's student assignment plan is not solely predicated on the basis of is or her race (even if there are multiple races), but which is also predicated on some modified individualized consideration of talents and needs, combined with demographic factors, that is appropriately tailored to the K–12 context.[13] Accordingly, I suggests that any proposed plan can only be constitutionally sound if it takes into account both Roberts's and Kennedy's notion of diversity. The question of whether Seattle's plan achieved true diversity, therefore, is not

---

5. See generally Edwin Garcia, Initiative Splits GOP Leaders Looking at Effort To Ban Data on Race, *San Jose Mercury News*, Feb. 22, 2003, at A1. Ward Connerly is no stranger to the conservative attack on racial classification and affirmative action. He authored Proposition 209, which prohibits state entities from discriminating against or giving preferential treatment to any individual or group in public employment, public education, or public contracting on the basis of race, sex, color, ethnicity, or national origin. California Civil Rights Initiative (Proposition 209), Cal. Const. art. I, §31 (1996).

6. I have questioned whether Connerly's proposition that race, an observable phenomenon in many cases based on physical phenotype can always be fairly regarded as a "private" matter for the perpetrator of discrimination, see generally Maurice R. Dyson, Multiracial Identity, Monoracial Authenticity & Racial Privacy: Towards an Adequate Theory of Multiracial Resistance, 9 *Mich. J. of Race & L.* 387 (2004).

7. Id.

8. Id.

9. Reginald Leamon Robinson, The Shifting Race-Consciousness Matrix and the Multiracial Category Movement: A Critical Reply to Professor Hernandez, 20 *B.C. Third World L.J.* 231, 238 (2000).

10. 123 S. Ct. 2325 (2003).

11. 123 S. Ct. 2411 (2003).

12. 127 S. Ct. at 2738 (Roberts, C.J.) ("Even when it comes to race, the plans here employ only a limited notion of diversity, viewing race exclusively in white/nonwhite terms in Seattle and black/"other" terms in Jefferson County.").

13. *Parents Involved in Cmty. Sch. v. Seattle Sch. Dist. No. 1*, 127 S. Ct. at 2797 (Kennedy, J., concurring in part and concurring in the judgment).

Figure 1. Binary Diversity Scenario under Seattle Tie-Breaker Plan*

Integration v. Diversity

Does the Seattle Plan Achieve Meaningful Diversity?

> **School A =**
> 50% Asian American, 50% White
> No African Americans, Latinos, Native Americans =
> racially balanced under Seattle Plan

> **School B =**
> 30% Asian, 25% African American,
> 25% Latino, 20% White = not racially balanced
> under Seattle plan

  * This figure represents only a hypothetical scenario based on the structure of the Seattle tie breaker rather than the actual operation of the Seattle Plan in practice. This figure is adapted from language found in Justice Roberts's majority opinion, see 127 S. Ct. at 2738(Roberts, C.J.).

an insignificant concern because therein lied another missed opportunity for PICS respondents to garner Kennedy's swing vote as evidenced by his offense to what he perceived as "Seattle's crude racial categories of 'white and non-white' as the basis for student assignments" when in a "district composed of a diversity of races, with fewer than half of the students classified as 'white.'"[14] In this regard, it is revealing to consider the Roberts plurality characterization of the tiebreaker's limited conception of diversity (see Figure 1).

As the foregoing illustrates, the Seattle plan theoretically leads to skewed demographics in the School A scenario above not only because it does not tie racial remedy to either true diversity[15] (whether diversity is defined to be (1) binary-racial integration in the Seattle District's conception;[16] (2) multiple racial groups as Justice Roberts appears to employ, or PICS/Grutter hybrid diversity that also looks to individual student talents, needs, abilities, interests, demographic factors, and race as Justice Kennedy appears to apply).[17] The reader may recognize the similar outspoken critical race critique this author has raised elsewhere with respect to a monolithic, essentialist thin conception of diversity in

---

14. 127 S. Ct. at 2791.

15. Of course, this does not mean that there is lack of diversity in the Asian community as a monolithic view might suggest. In actuality, Southeast Asian Americans are more similar to those of African Americans than to white Americans with respect to their socioeconomic status, see Note, Perpetuating the Exclusion of Asian Americans from the Affirmative Action Debate: An Oversight of the Diversity Rationale in *Grutter v. Bollinger*, 38 *U.C. Davis L. Rev.* 545 (2005). Further, a critical distinction needs to be made between foreign born versus American born Asians, the latter enjoying a greater educational advantage, see Asian Pacific American Legal Center of Southern California, Asian Law Caucus & National Asian Pacific American Legal Consortium, The Diverse Face of Asians and Pacific Islanders in California, Asian & Pacific Islander Demographic Profile (2005), available at www.apalc.org/CA_Report_feb_%202_05.pdf.

16. Seattle removed from its web site which described "emphasizing individualism as opposed to a more collective ideology" as a form of "cultural racism," and now provides it has no intention "to hold onto unsuccessful concepts such as [a] ... colorblind mentality." Harrell, School Web Site Removed: Examples of Racism Sparked Controversy, *Seattle Post-Intelligencer*, June 2, 2006, pp. B1, B5.

17. *Parents Involved in Cmty. Sch. v. Seattle Sch. Dist. No. 1*, 127 S. Ct. at 2797 (Kennedy, J., concurring in part and concurring in the judgment).

higher education affirmative action that categorically favors certain minorities to the whole exclusions of others to distort racial accountability based on group blindness.[18]

But educational lawyers and policy makers should be concerned about this black/white binary paradigm of diversity for another critical reason. Seattle's approach wholly de-links it student assignment plan from academic need. This suggest a need for a theoretical remedial justification predicated on new viable state interest and a novel remedial theory of targeted race-conscious intervention by utilizing the No Child Left Behind Act (NCLB) to justify race-explicit and race-conscious remedies based on factors that indirectly target what I term "race-at risk." This "race-at risk" theoretical conception of intervention properly puts the focus where it should be—on race and ethnicity factors that implicates the greatest academic need for all learners. Moreover, this proposed approach overcomes the pigmentation diversity critique of PICS petitioners and the Roberts court criticism that Seattle's race tie breaker leads to less diverse races based on a limited binary racial paradigm of diversity. While the author has also proposed this new theory well before the PICS decision,[19] it must be remembered that respondents and amici would still not prevail using this new theory with such a thin conception of diversity in its student assignment plan. This is because such "thin diversity" as I refer to appears to be somewhat at odds with the asserted compelling interests in support of the School District's race-based student enrollment system. Those interests include:

> "(1) Educational benefits such as promoting student discussion of racial and ethnic issues and adding different viewpoints to class discussion;
>
> (2) Social benefits such as increasing the likelihood of socializing with people of different races, preparing students for citizenship in a multi-cultural and multiethnic world, fostering racial and cultural understanding, and increasing integration later in life; and
>
> (3) Avoiding racially concentrated schools which are separate and unequal in that they have more poverty, lower achievement, less qualified teachers, and fewer advanced courses."[20]

Of course, other remedial justifications have proffered beyond these.[21] But what the foregoing fails to make clear is that there may be a viable state interest (under a closing the achievement gap rationale between the lowest-highest performers with race-conscious but facially neutral criterion) or a compelling state interest (in closing the "racial" achievement gap under race-explicit factoral considerations) as I have previously suggested.[22] Under a theoretical approach that instead favors students of color in accordance with the greatest academic need based on closing this achievement gap, one can then see that the composition of School B in the scenario above also happens to come closer to the kind of conception of diversity (multiple races) that the Roberts court applies and the PICS/Grutter individualized notion of diversity as Kennedy envisions. Viewed in this way,

---

18. See generally Maurice R. Dyson, Racial Free-Riding The Coattails of a Dream Deferred: Can I Borrow Your Social Capital? 13 *William and Mary Bill of Rts J.* 967 (2005).

19. See Maurice R. Dyson, In Search of the Talented Tenth: Diversity, Affirmative Access, and University-Driven Reform, 6 *Harv. Latino L. Rev.* 41 (2003).

20. Pet. App. 20a–21a (Board Statement Reaffirming Diversity Rationale); id. at 23a–24a, 27a–28a; See also Brief for Center for Individual Rights, at 6.

21. See generally Maurice R. Dyson, When Government Is a Passive Participant in Private Discrimination: A Critical Look at White Privilege & The Tacit Return to Interposition in *PICS v. Seattle School District,* 40 *U. of Tol. L. Rev* 145 (2008).

22. See Maurice R. Dyson, In Search of the Talented Tenth: Diversity, Affirmative Access, and University-Driven Reform, 6 *Harv. Latino L. Rev.* 41 (2003).

Figure 2. Academically Gifted Program Enrollment by Race*

What percentage of students, by ethnic group, are enrolled in programs that serve students who are academically highly gifted and academically gifted?					
	Asian	African Am.	Latino	Native Am.	White
APP					
2003–2004	22%	4%	3%	1%	71%
2004–2005	21%	4%	3%	1%	70%
Spectrum					
2003–2004	19%	8%	5%	2%	66%
2004–2005	19%	9%	5%	2%	67%
District Population	23%	22%	11%	2%	41%

* This chart is reproduced in its entirety from Seattle schools' web site, see www.seattle schools.org/demographics.

School A is not only problematic for the reasons the PICS courts alludes to, but principally because the composition of School A may not be tied to the fact that Asians and whites representing the total racial demographics are the two racial constituencies that are in the least at-risk and therefore the least in need of remedial intervention.

Thus, a new theoretical approach to target race and ethnicity is warranted than the binary, acontextualized approach utilized in Seattle. This next section contemplates the contours, benefits, and limitations of a new targeted theory of remedial intervention that not only defines a viable state interest, but also lays outs in detail multifactorial analysis that demonstrates an appropriate fit between this asserted interest and the means in which that interest may be lawfully accomplished. Under this approach, the focus is not merely on racial balancing of students, but rather targeted race-conscious balancing of school resources tied to effective intervention strategies which are specifically designed for an at-risk student population. In fact, as Figure 2 demonstrates, School A's composition becomes principally problematic because in Seattle Asians and whites are concentrated more heavily in the academically gifted category.

Similarly, the number of Asian and white students that may be found eligible for academically gifted student populations in the Seattle district also make the racial composition of School A problematic as Figure 3 reveals.

Likewise, if we were to focus on School A's demographics in Seattle, we do a critical disservice to the academic needs of a diverse constituency both within the Asian community and beyond.

As the linguistic breakdown in Figure 4 illustrates, a more nuanced view of race and ethnicity that is tied to specific academic need is warranted and in alignment with individualized consideration mandated in PICS and the *Bollinger* cases.

Based on the foregoing illustration, conceivably a focus on placing Korean students in Ballard based on favorable test scores might do a significant disservice to Chinese and Vietnamese students that are perhaps in greater need of bilingual education services, enriched curricula, and targeted intervention to close the achievement gap. Justice Kennedy would thus likely find this more nuanced approach constitutionally sound. Likewise, a focus on race without regard to national origin of Somalians and others not tied to educational

Figure 3. Academically Gifted Program Eligibility by Race*

What percentage of students, by ethnic group, have been nominated for advanced learning eligibility testing and found eligible?

	Asian	African Am.	Latino	Native Am.	White
2003–2004					
Nominated	25%	12%	6%	1%	56%
Eligible					
•Academically Highly Gifted	8%	4%	6%	1%	13%
•Academically Gifted	31%	17%	30%	27%	41%
2004–2005					
Nominated	23%	9%	4%	1%	63%
Eligible					
•Academically Highly Gifted	7%	4%	8%	0%	8%
•Academically Gifted	28%	15%	28%	32%	34%
District Population	23%	22%	11%	2%	41%

* This chart is reproduced in its entirety from Seattle schools' web site, see www.seattle schools.org/demographics.

Figure 4. Bilingual Education Program Eligibility by Ethnicity*

What are the primary languages and grade levels of those receiving bilingual services as of October 2005?

% of Students Served Speaking Languages per Grade Level

	Elementary	Middle	High
Amharic	2%	2%	4%
Cambodian	3%	4%	3%
Chinese	13%	9%	14%
Korean	1%	0%	0%
Laotian	4%	3%	3%
Oromo	2%	1%	4%
Somalian	10%	8%	12%
Spanish	34%	36%	29%
Tagalog	6%	9%	8%
Tigrigna	2%	2%	2%
Vietnamese	18%	17%	12%
Other	6%	6%	8%

* This chart is reproduced in its entirety from Seattle schools' web site, see www.seattle schools.org/demographics.

needs may be counterproductive to closing the achievement gap. But to say that race may never be used in remedial measures as the PICS plaintiffs contended, represents a gross misreading of the *Grutter* rationale. As stated in *Grutter,* context matters when reviewing race-based government action:

> Generalizations ... must not be applied out of context in disregard of variant controlling facts.... Not every decision influenced by race is equally objectionable and strict scrutiny is designed to provide a framework for carefully examining the importance and the sincerity of the reasons advanced by the governmental decision maker for the use of race in that particular context.[23]

That all use of race is prohibited under strict scrutiny analysis is also inconsistent with Justice Kennedy's approach. In fact, in Kennedy's view, government can be legitimately concerned with preventing "de facto resegregation" of the public schools and is "free to devise race conscious measures to address the problem in a general way and without treating each student in a different fashion solely on the basis of a systematic, individual typing by race."[24]

In addition, Justice Kennedy in his concurring opinion states that race-conscious remedies may be appropriately used to avoid strict scrutiny. The various means of achieving race conscious remedies include (1) strategic site selection of new schools; (2) allocating resources for special programs; (3) recruiting students and faculty in a targeted fashion; and, (4) tracking enrollments, performance, and other statistics by race. As Justice Kennedy stated: "These mechanisms are race conscious but do not lead to different treatment based on a classification that tells each student he or she is to be defined by race, so it is unlikely that any of them would demand strict scrutiny to be found permissible."[25]

Closing the achievement gap remains the central and key area where a state interest may be the most forcefully stated for a new interventionist strategy.[26] Whereas President Bush has frequently referenced this racial "achievement gap"[27] and the necessity of eliminating the "de facto educational apartheid"[28] that exist and the President Bush's commitment to eradicating the "soft bigotry of low expectations"[29] that accompany it, the need for re-

---

23. *Grutter v. Bollinger,* 539 U.S. at 327.

24. *Parents Involved in Cmty. Sch. v. Seattle Sch. Dist. No. 1,* 127 S. Ct. 2738, 2792 (2007) (Kennedy, J., concurring in part and concurring in the judgment).

25. *Parents Involved in Cmty. Sch. v. Seattle Sch. Dist. No. 1,* 127 S. Ct. 2738, 2792 (2007).

26. See Dr. Rod Paige, U.S. Sec'y of Educ., Remarks at the Kennedy Sch. of Gov't, "Fifty Years After *Brown v. Board of Education*: What Has Been Accomplished and What Remains to Be Done?" (Apr. 22, 2004).

27. See, e.g., "Remarks by President Bush on No Child Left Behind." (Oct. 5, 2006), available at Standard News, www.standardnewswire.com/index.php?module=release&task=view&releaseID=119 ("There's an achievement gap in America that's not good for the future of this country.").

28. Dr. Rod Paige, U.S. Sec'y of Educ., Remarks at the Kennedy Sch. of Gov't, "Fifty Years After *Brown v. Board of Education*: What Has Been Accomplished and What Remains to Be Done?" (Apr. 22, 2004).

29. See Pres. Bush, Remarks in a Discussion at the Nat'l Inst. of Health, 40 Weekly Comp. Pres. Doc. 870, 874 (May 12, 2004) ("As part of the new accountability system, the No Child Left Behind Act, we break out based upon race. It's really essential we do that. It's really important. If you don't do that, you're likely to leave people behind. And that's not right. There's ... an achievement gap in America that will be closed. It must be closed, and will be closed. It won't be closed unless you're honest about the achievement gap, unless you're able to see clearly who needs help"); Pres. Bush, Remarks at Hyde Park Elementary Sch., 39 Weekly Comp. Pres. Doc. 1178, 1181 (Sept. 9, 2003) ("we want to know ... whether or not the African American students are learning").

calibrated remedies to meet this widening gap is manifest.[30] Congress has also eloquently spoken on the need to close the achievement gap with urgency and transparency.[31] It responded with congressional action in the form of the No Child Left Behind Act (NCLB).

It is instructive that the NCLB mandates that each state's plan for educational accountability include, *inter alia*, "separate measurable annual objectives for continuous and substantial improvement for ... [t]he achievement of ... students from major racial and ethnic groups."[32] Moreover, the federal statute itself employs race-conscious federal accountability in mandating accountability reporting on the basis of race.[33] Moreover, that the NCLB requires that student test results are disaggregated by race at both the school and district levels to be quantified against the annual objectives of each state's plan[34] and that it further purports to holds states accountable for raising the academic performance for discrete racially identifiable clusters of students suggest there is a viable and valid state interest for closing the achievement gap.[35] Furthermore, this interest is not merely intended to be symbolic, but an interest that attaches significant penalties where states fail to live up to its commitment to close this gap.[36] Thus, the NCLB provides a remedial justification for a new viable state interest.

Part II: Closing the Achievement Gap, Group-Blind Accountability, and the NCLB

Another troubling aspect of the group-blind dynamic is the wholesale lumping of students together. But rather than being motivated in an effort to eradicate racial inequity as a tie-breaker, group blindness by some progressive legislative agendas act in ways that are sure to exacerbate it. In fact, here, the recognition of the racial group is not to counteract the individualist, textualist color-blind approach to the equal protection clause that often characterizes conservative critiques. Often, group blindness, in contrast, explicitly recognizes racial groups as distinct but creates the scenario where race and color are used

---

30. See e.g., Pres. Bush, Remarks to the Nat'l Urban League Conference, 39 Weekly Comp. Pres. Doc. 984, 987 (July 28, 2003) ("Equal education is one of the most pressing civil rights of our day. Nearly half a century after Brown..., there's still an achievement gap in America.").

31. See, e.g., 147 Cong. Rec. S13322, S13324 (Dec. 17, 2001) (Sen. Kennedy's comments) ("One of the major goals [of the NCLB] ... is to lessen ... the educational achievement gap between ... minority and nonminority students."); 147 Cong. Rec. S4125, S4133 (May 2, 2001) (Sen. Frist's comments) ("We have all talked a lot about the achievement gap which has not narrowed but in fact gotten wider over time."); 147 Cong. Rec. H10082, H10103 (Dec. 13, 2001) (Rep. Miller's comments) ("My colleagues said they wanted accountability for closing the achievement gap, and we have provided that.... We believe that because an individual is a minority does not mean they cannot learn. And the evidence is overwhelming that we are right."); 147 Cong. Rec. S3774, S3775 (Apr. 23, 2001) (Sen. Gregg's comments) (discussing reasons why "we are going to say for different ethnic groups, different racial groups ... explain whether or not those kids are learning").

32. See § 6311(b)(2)(C)(v)(II)(bb).

33. The NCLB mandates that each state's plan include, *inter alia*, "separate measurable annual objectives for continuous and substantial improvement for ... [t]he achievement of ... students from major racial and ethnic groups." Id.

34. See 20 U.S.C. § 6311(b)(3)(C)(xiii).

35. See id. §§ 6311(b)(2)(B), 6311(b)(2)(C)(v)(II)(bb).

36. The sanctions for failure to meet academic benchmarks of accountability referred to as academic yearly progress or AYP includes the dissolution of the school or the abolishment of the district as a unit of local government. See id. §§ 6316(b)(7)(C)(iv), (8)(B); id. §§ 6316(c)(7)(A), (10)(c).

to lower standards of racial accountability. In higher education affirmative action, this often takes the form of grouping Africans, African Americans, Caribbeans, and biracial persons under the generic rubric of "black" to cosmetically satisfy diversity thin notions of affirmative action compliance.[37] The effect of the group-blind approach results in often bestowing the benefits of racial remedies on one specific nationality without a closer critical examination as to whether the benefits are fairly distributed within the racial nomenclature as a whole. Thus, it is not surprising to see Africans and Caribbeans derive greater benefit from affirmative action programs over African Americans when university administrators only look to color rather than national origin, ethnicity, under-representation or the greatest academic need.[38]

However, in the K–12 context, it is the accountability framework of the NCLB that becomes the basis for incentivizing group blindness on the generic nomenclature of "minority" to exclude Latinos and African Americans in disturbingly large numbers. In this regard, it is helpful to see how the NCLB categorically lumps students of color together to often systematically exclude them from racial accountability of providing a quality education that meets rising academic benchmarks set under the NCLB. Increasingly, at an alarming rate, for instance, many schools in the nation are failing to meet academic benchmarks under the NCLB from approximately six thousand to nine thousand high poverty schools or approximately 50 percent.[39] Not coincidentally, the adverse consequences of the NCLB accountability framework are felt even more profoundly on schools serving predominantly minority student populations that may engage in documented practices such suspending bilingual education students, retaining students of color in grade, or fudging drop out rates in the specific years school districts are expected to give NCLB-mandated assessments.[40] Given the troubling history of testing as a means to bring about racially discriminatory impact on students of color, this correlation between the NCLB and students of color is even more suspect.[41] Thus, if race-conscious remedies are to be effective, must not only target students of color, but must attempt to beneficially concentrate resources through the use of race-conscious remedies to students of color in a more nuanced fashion that the PICS decision calls for. This chapter proposes that the PICS notion of diversity can best be met by examining race-conscious academic need for the most at risk students in order to narrowly tailor and targeted race-conscious reme-

---

37. See generally Maurice R. Dyson, Racial Free-Riding The Coattails of a Dream Deferred: Can I Borrow Your Social Capital? 13 *William and Mary Bill of Rts J.* 967 (2005).

38. See id at 967–69.

39. Diana Jean Schemo, 20 States Ask for Flexibility in School Law, *N.Y. Times*, Feb. 22, 2006.

40. Gail L. Sunderman, The Civil Rights Project, Harvard University, The Unraveling of No Child Left Behind: How Negotiated Changes Transform the Law 14 (2006), available at www.civil rightsproject.harvard.edu/research/esea/nclb_unraveling.php; see also Stephen A. Rosenbaum, Aligning or Maligning? Getting Inside a New Idea, Getting Behind No Child Left Behind and Getting Outside of it All, 15 *Hastings Women's L.J.* 1, 26 (2004).

41. Leon J. Kamin, The Science and Politics of IQ 5–30 (1974); Daria Roithmayr, Deconstructing the Distinction Between Bias and Merit, 85 *Cal. L. Rev.* 1449, 1486–91 (1997) (discussing the advent of testing prompted by discriminatory intent); Maurice R. Dyson, Leave No Child Behind: Normative Proposals to Link Educational Adequacy Claims and High Stakes Assessment Due Process Challenges, 7 *Texas J. C.L.-C.R. F.* 1 (2002); Jay P. Heubert & and Robert M. Hauser, High Stakes: Testing for Tracking, Promotion, and Graduation (1999); *GI Forum Image de Tejas v. Texas Educ. Agency*, 87 F. Supp. 2d 667 (W.D. Tex. 2000); *Georgia Conference of NAACPs v. Georgia*, 775 F.2d 1403 (11th Cir. 1985); Milbrey W. McLaughlin & Lorrie E. Shepard, Improving Education Through Standards-Based Reform 7–17 (1995); Darling-Hammond & Falk, Using Standards and Assessments to Support Student Learning, Phi Delta Kappan, Nov. 1997, at 190–99; Wolk, Education's High-Stakes Gamble, Educ. Wk., Dec. 9, 1998, at 48; Taylor, Standards, Tests, and Civil Rights, Educ. Wk., Nov. 15, 2000.

dies in a pedagogically sound fashion.[42] The most sound approach may be target the most at-risk students of color under a familiar but newly asserted state interest—closing the achievement gap for the lowest achievers.[43]

In this regard, it is significant that the No Child Left Behind Act, as contentious as its enforcement has become, nonetheless is useful in establishing the proposition that a national priority has been set in educational policy to close the achievement gap.[44] In doing so, it sets requirements for state definitions of adequate yearly progress, which is the progress that schools and districts must show in educating all students to grade-level standards, as reflected in student assessments. In terms of targeted racial remedies, the NCLB theoretically already sets up a paradigm for subgroup accountability: English language learners, students with disabilities, economically disadvantaged youth, and break-outs by race and ethnicity.[45] NCLB sets a goal for proficiency for all students and each subgroup by the end of the 2013–14 school year. The Secretary of Education approves and monitors each state's accountability plan, ensuring that it meets the NCLB minimum requirements.

Although a new state interest would not be dependent on the NCLB, the federal mandate provides a starting point to argue that schools have a legitimate state interest to close the achievement gap between its lowest achievers and the highest performers since the predicate of the NCLB is that all children can learn if properly supported.[46] Such a legitimate state interest may become a sufficient basis to lawfully engage either in race-based remedies (closing the racial achievement gap) or more generally under the generic rationale (closing the achievement gap between highest and lowest achievers) but with greater focus on race-conscious targeted interventions and remedies. Under this lesser judicial level of scrutiny, this approach may rest on more solid constitutional ground. This is because if rational basis review applies to a new conception of a state interest, it is easier to overcome the hostile approach to race-explicit classifications and is also entitled to greater judicial deference. Greater judicial deference is appropriate since focusing on lowest end of academic achievers is a legitimate way to effectuate the general educational interest to leave no child behind. Moreover, this remedial focus would represent paradigmatic educational policy expertise that is entitled to heightened deference under strict scrutiny.[47]

Under this new state interest consistent with *Grutter*, courts would be basing its race-conscious remedies on the purported benefit of closing the achievement gap. Further, if this approach is used to grant further targeted aid and intervention rather than employing sanctions, punitive consequences, and burdensome oversight, we could see more local

---

42. See Maurice R. Dyson, In Search of the Talented Tenth: Diversity, Affirmative Access, and University-Driven Reform, 6 *Harv. Latino L. Rev.* 41 (2003) (advocating race-conscious outreach and remedies based on NCLB and empirical support of University of Texas effective race-conscious outreach efforts); see also *GI Forum v. Tex. Educ. Agency*, 87 F. Supp. 2d 667, 674 (W.D. Tex. 2000) (finding targeted intervention a mitigating factor to uphold test validity).

43. See generally Maurice R. Dyson, In Search of the Talented Tenth, supra note 42.

44. No Child Left Behind Act of 2001, 107 Pub. L. No. 110, §1111 (b)(2)(H)(i), (iii), 115 Stat. 1425, 1448 (2002).

45. 20 U.S.C. §§6311(b)(2)(C)(v)(II), (b)(3)(C)(xiii) (2006).

46. That all children can learn when held to high expectations is reflected in congressional findings supporting the 1994 Title I amendments wherein Congress noted that all children can master challenging content and complex problem-solving skills. Congress explicitly acknowledged that "research clearly shows that children, including low-achieving children can succeed when expectations are high and all children are given an opportunity to learn challenging material." 20 U.S.C.A.§6301(c)(1) (West Supp. 1997).

47. See 127 S. Ct. at 2797.

school district willingness to comply with this mandate in exchange for greater autonomy. This approach, however, would require a return to benchmarking state progress on
the National Association of Educational Progress (a nationalized educational standard)
as originally envisioned under the NCLB, but which was later abandoned so as to prevent
state watering down of standards.[48] This rationale might stand in stark contrast to the
Seattle plan because as Roberts noted, the school districts there were "working backward
to achieve a particular type of racial balance, rather than working forward from some
demonstration of the level of diversity that provides the purported benefits."[49] The challenged plans were constitutionally flawed because they sought, at bottom, to achieve racial
balance rather than pedagogic diversity.

Under this achievement gap rationale, transfers to a majority-white school may be justified because majority-black schools continue to suffer the greatest academically, which
is easier to sustain under conservative constitutional jurisprudence than claiming the minority black school is so because of the effects of prior official segregation. Further, this
approach has the more direct route rationale to achieving racial equality because it does
not purport to ground its remedies based on prior de facto segregation or the perceived
benefits of diversity, of which the court is likely to be the most skeptical.

A school district can presumptively justify transferring students from the minority south
end of Seattle where the lowest performers are the most heavily concentrated to Ballard, Hale,
and other northern Seattle schools that are performing well. This is because the basis of race-
conscious transfers of at-risk students to well-performing schools is the most expedient
and direct way to quickly close the achievement gap between the city's lowest academic
performers and its higher performing ones. This rationale can also justify targeted race-
conscious interventions, targeted funding, the provision of higher paying teachers, and
special programs that might have otherwise been problematic under a desegregation context.[50]

Under an asserted new state interest that simply proposes to close the achievement
gap, it is hard to overcome the argument that higher teacher compensation, greater selectivity of quality teachers, and more highly enriched curriculum and programs in schools
that have the lowest academic achievers that are the most at-risk of academic failure is not
rationally related to closing the achievement gap.[51] Here again, it matters that the NCLB
mandates schools and states to address this concern, although the asserted interest should
not rest on the statute alone. This is because the new state interest would be wholly dependent on the NCLB statute itself, which might be just as easily repealed under political pressure or administratively watered down through enforcement, thereby jeopardizing
the asserted interest itself and the efficacy of racial remedies.[52] This is particularly a concern where approximately two dozen states have petitioned the U.S. Department of Ed-

---

48. Goodwin Liu, Interstate Equality in Educational Opportunity, 81 *N.Y.U. L. Rev.* 2044, 2107–08
(Dec. 2006).
49. See 127 S. Ct. at 2797.
50. See generally *Missouri v. Jenkins*, 515 U. S. 70 (1995) (holding that raising teacher's salaries exceeded remedial scope of desegregation mandate).
51. Transcript of Nixon's Statement on School Busing, *N.Y. Times*, Mar. 17, 1972, at 22 ("It is
time for us to make a national commitment to see that the schools in the central cities are upgraded
so that the children who go there will have just as good a chance to get quality education as do the
children who go to school in the suburbs.").
52. AP, No Child Loophole Misses Millions of Scores, April 18, 2006, available at
www.cnn.com/2006.EDUCATION/04/18/no.child.loophole.ap/index.html (discussing the relaxation
of reporting requirements by race); Gregg Topo, Report: NEA Pays Opponents of NCLB, *USA Today*,
July 10, 2006, available at www.usatoday.com/news/education/2006-07-10-nea-nochild_x.htm.

ucation for exemptions under the NCLB reporting mandates to exclude larger numbers of students in racial subgroups, thus permitting relaxed racial accountability by subgroup breakdowns for approximately two million students nationwide even where fifty students of a given race in a testing population exist and which are up to seven times more likely to have their scores excluded.[53] According to Gail Sunderman of the Harvard Civil Rights Project, while less than 2 percent of white children's scores remain excluded from a separate category, blacks and Latino have approximately 10 percent of their scores excluded.[54] Therefore, while the NCLB provides the justification for race-conscious tracking of student progress, a true race-conscious interventionist approach advocated under this asserted state interest proposed above will help address these troubling developments in the enforcement of the NCLB mandate. States can still look generally to the NCLB justification of closing the achievement gap as a general one that is also located in a whole host of federal, state, and local accountability mandates and even state educational adequacy constitutional mandates.[55] As the Washington Supreme Court noted:

> Admittedly, we have never explicitly held that the state constitution requires racial integration. We have, however, been unwavering in holding that chapter IX imposes upon the State the paramount duty to provide an ample, general, and uniform basic education to all children. Therefore, if it is determined that in a contemporary setting *de facto* segregated schools cannot provide children with the educational opportunities necessary to equip them for their role as citizens, then the state constitution would most certainly mandate integrated schools.[56]

Although the Washington Supreme Court suggested that the state constitution might indirectly justify correcting the de facto segregation, it was not the first to do so. In *Sheff v. O'Neill*, Connecticut (based on its constitutional language) was the only state to use its constitutional provision to find de facto racial isolation unconstitutional.[57] Similarly, the federal Magnet Schools Assistance Program (MSAP) also provides that "it is in the best interests of the United States to continue the Federal Government's support of local educational agencies that are voluntarily seeking to foster meaningful interaction among students of different racial and ethnic backgrounds, beginning at the earliest stages of such students' education."[58] The MSAP "to assist in the desegregation of schools ... by providing financial assistance to eligible local educational agencies for ... the elimination, reduction, or prevention of minority group isolation in elementary schools and secondary schools."[59]

Further, Justice Kennedy has also suggested in PICS that the court may use race in some general way to address the educational effect of de facto segregation.[60] However,

---

53. Id.

54. Gail L. Sunderman, The Civil Rights Project, Harvard University, The Unraveling of No Child Left Behind: How Negotiated Changes Transform the Law 14 (2006), available at www.civilrightsproject. harvard.edu/research/esea/nclb_unraveling.php.

55. These are state constitutional provisions requiring states to provide an adequate education to the children of the state, see generally Maurice R. Dyson, Leave No Child Behind: Normative Proposals to Link Educational Adequacy Claims and High Stakes Assessment Due Process Challenges, 7 Tex. J C.L.-C.R. F. 1 (2002).

56. See *Parents Involved in Cmty. Sch. v. Seattle Sch. Dist. No. 1*, 149 Wash. 2d 660, 682 72 P. 3d 151, 162–63 (2003).

57. See *Sheff v. O'Neill*, 733 A.2d 925 (1999).

58. See 20 U.S.C. §7231(a)(4)(A).

59. Id. at §7231(b)(1).

60. See *Parents Involved in Cmty. Sch. v. Seattle Sch. Dist. No. 1*, 127 S. Ct. at 2797.

Justice Kennedy's suggestion appears to be fundamentally at odds with the Court's approach on question concerning the ability of schools to correct de facto segregation. For instance, in *Missouri v. Jenkins*, the Supreme Court stated in a five to four holding that overturned a district court ruling that the lower court exceeded their authority in ordering measures such as across-the-board state-funded salary increases, and in the order to fund continued quality education programs to correct de facto racial inequality.[61]

In June 1985, the District Court issued its first remedial order and established as its goal the "elimination of all vestiges of state imposed segregation."[62] The District Court determined that "segregation ha[d] caused a system wide *reduction* in student achievement in the schools of the KCMSD."[63] The District Court made no particularized findings regarding the extent that student achievement had been reduced or what portion of that reduction was attributable to segregation. The District Court also identified twenty-five schools within the KCMSD that had enrollments of 90 percent or more black students.[64]

The District Court mandated programs to expand educational opportunities for all KCMSD students: full-day kindergarten; expanded summer school; before and after school tutoring; and an early childhood development program.[65] Finally, the District Court implemented a state-funded "effective schools" program that consisted of substantial yearly cash grants to each of the schools within the KCMSD.[66] Under the "effective schools" program, the state was required to fund programs at both the twenty-five racially identifiable schools as well as the forty-three other schools within the KCMSD.

In addition, prompted by the desire to "provide a greater educational opportunity to *all* KCMSD students," the District Court approved a comprehensive magnet school and capital improvements plan and held the state and the KCMSD jointly and severally liable for its funding.[67] Under the District Court's plan, every senior high school, every middle school, and one half of the elementary schools were converted into magnet schools.

Likewise, the Court of Appeals relied on statements made by the District Court during a May 28, 1992, hearing:

> The Court's goal was to integrate the Kansas City, Missouri, School District to the *maximum degree possible*, and all these other matters were elements to be used to try to integrate the Kansas City, Missouri, schools so the goal is integration. That's the goal. And a high standard of quality education. The magnet schools, the summer school program and all these programs are tied to that goal, and until such time as that goal has been reached, then we have not reached the goal.... The goal is to integrate the Kansas City, Missouri, School district. So I think we are wasting our time. (2 App. 482; emphasis added).[68]

Both the district court and appeals court decisions reveal an implicit belief that the goals of integration are best achieved by making efforts to improve the quality of public schooling. However, the U.S. Supreme Court did not agree. But this link between integration goals and quality schooling did not appear to animate the Supreme Court's opposition

---

61. *Missouri v. Jenkins*, 515 U.S. 70 (1995).
62. *Jenkins v. Missouri*, 639 F. Supp. 19, 23 (WD Mo. 1985).
63. Id. at 24.
64. Id. at 36.
65. Id. at 30–33.
66. Id. at 33–34.
67. Id.
68. See 11 F. 3d, at 761.

to the lower courts approach as it was concerned about the substantial fiscal expenditures:

> As a result, the desegregation costs have escalated and now are approaching an annual cost of $200 million. These massive expenditures have financed "high schools in which every classroom will have air conditioning, an alarm system, and 15 microcomputers; a 2,000 square foot planetarium; green houses and vivariums; a 25 acre farm with an air conditioned meeting room for 104 people; a Model United Nations wired for language translation; broadcast capable radio and television studios with an editing and animation lab; a temperature controlled art gallery; movie editing and screening rooms; a 3,500 square foot dust free diesel mechanics room; 1,875 square foot elementary school animal rooms for use in a zoo project; swimming pools; and numerous other facilities."[69]

The Supreme Court found these educational remedies to exceed the scope of the desegregation mandate.[70] However, in contrast to *Jenkins*, this new state interest will lawfully justify race-conscious remedies such as the placement of the most effective teachers in the district in low-performing black and Latino schools, the transfers of at-risk black and Latino students into predominantly white selective neighborhood schools, the strategic construction of new blue ribbon math and science programs as well as magnet schools in mixed minority locations. But it is not accurate to say that race cannot be taken into account at all. To effectively use racial classifications on sound legal ground, it is also paramount to identify facially neutral factors that are not merely race-conscious but also have a purported connection to closing unequal educational opportunity under achievement gap to ensure the means employed fit this asserted state interest. As Justice Kennedy made clear in his concurrence:

> If school authorities are concerned that the student-body compositions of certain schools interfere with the objectives of offering an equal educational opportunity to all of their students, they are free to devise race-conscious measures to address the problem in a general way and without treating each student in a different fashion solely on the basis of systematic, individual typing by race.[71]

In thinking about some of the ways school districts and states could lawfully achieve such a race-conscious targeted approach, it is also important that district show that the race-conscious targeted approach is consistent with the rationale of closing the achievement gap between the lowest academic achievers and higher performing ones. One way to do this is to base race-conscious factors in academic need, at-risk factors for academic failure and in characteristics that are designed not merely to target students of color, but the students of color most in need of targeted intervention, which often may include black and Latino students as opposed to American-born Asian or upper class minorities that tend to perform higher on national academic indicators. This also helps achieve racial diversity in the Roberts and Kennedy vein.

What the above discussion makes clear is that an asserted diversity plan is not sufficient if it does not comport with both Roberts's and Kennedy's notion of diversity. But what is also equally clear is that asserted rational or compelling state interest to close the achievement gap is also insufficient by itself if it fails to take into account these varying notions of diversity. Interestingly, the Court did not specifically disavow this rationale of closing the achievement gap as a compelling state interest any more than it did address

---

69. *Jenkins II*, 495 U. S., at 77 (Kennedy, J., concurring in part and concurring in judgment).
70. Id.
71. 127 S. Ct. at 2797.

the open question of whether the educational and social benefits asserted flow from racial diversity may be compelling. What Kennedy suggested was that racial isolation and the need to achieve a racially diverse student population in which race is one component are compelling interests.

Part III: A Viable Multifactoral Proposals for Narrow Tailoring: A Look at Novel Race-Conscious Factors

This chapter has now laid out a viable remedial justification under the Court's precedent. Thus, there are no shortages of compelling state interests one might to justify the use of race. But it is precisely the form and fashion that becomes critical for narrow tailoring purposes that is often the sticking point. Indeed the three parts of the PICS holding that actually garnered five votes confirms this observation, which can be summarized as follows: that the case was not moot (Part II); that the plans could not be justified based on the remedial interests or intellectual diversity (Part III-A); and that the plans were not narrowly tailored (Part III-C). Thus a remedial justification that grounds the state interest in using race must inform how the use of race may be narrowly tailored.

However, as the premise of this chapter makes clear, narrow tailoring that appears to use race to benefit people of color in an unqualified way threatens the notion of white privilege, which makes it easier to rhetorically argue and legally hold that whites will be unduly burdened by such racial schemes. As Part I suggests, the fact that the Court focuses on the unfair treatment and typing of minorities may serve to obscure the real animating reason why the suit was brought and why the Court may have sympathetically sided with the PICS plaintiffs—that is, the adverse impact on Caucasian students and families. Why else would the Court obscure the impact of racial tie breaker as minimal when it had more substantial impact? Certainly, it was for the "appearance" of a preference-neutral principle, when in reality the court was interposing itself between the Seattle's tie breaker and white PICS plaintiffs under the guise it was saving minorities from being unfairly racially stereotyped.[72]

In light of this, what is clear is that the details of the remedial plans must align with their purported remedial justifications where race must be qualified in its use and must be narrowly tailored in a more "nuanced" fashion so as not to offend white privilege. How might this be achieved? Justice Kennedy's ambiguous answer is as follows:

> "If schools could have achieved their stated ends through different means. These include the facially neutral means ... or if necessary, a more nuanced, individual evaluation of the school needs and characteristics that might include race as a component. The latter approach would be informed by Grutter, though of course the criteria relevant to student placement would differ based on the age of the students, the needs of the parents and the role of the schools."[73]

---

72. See 127 S. Ct. at 2797; see also *Metro Broadcasting, Inc. v. FCC*, 497 U. S. 547, 610 (1990) ("We are a Nation not of black and white alone, but one teeming with divergent communities knitted together with various traditions and carried forth, above all, by individuals") (O'Connor, J., dissenting).

73. 127 S. Ct. at 2797.

Just what nuanced means Justice Kennedy is referring to he did not make clear other than the resource allocation suggestions in the location of schools; drawing and national advocates are left with little guidance as to how to achieve diversity in a narrowly tailored fashion. He also does not make clear what factors a court might consider that is informed by *Grutter* relative to the K–12 context. Accordingly, I have taken to suggesting below some novel but relevant factors a state or school district can justifiably use to capture the relevant racial population under the four remedial justifications I have proffered in this chapter or which were argued in the PICS case. These factors can be used by school districts across the nation to achieve the desired integration, diversity, and racial accountability in a way that is consistent with narrow tailoring analysis as well as the pedagogical concerns raised herein. They are as follows.

Proposals for Viable Multifactoral Considerations: Factors for Race-Conscious Targeted Intervention, Resource Allocation, and Pupil/Teacher Assignments under Narrow Tailoring

(1) The student's performance on standardized tests and NCLB in comparison with those of other students from similar socioeconomic backgrounds disaggregated on the basis of race and ethnicity;[74]

(2) Whether the student's school has received a waiver or exemption by the U.S. Department of Education to NCLB reporting requirements that excludes a significant percentage of students of color from accountability reporting requirement under the NCLB;[75]

(3)(a) Whether the student's school demographics, absent remedial intervention on the basis of race, will remain or become racially isolated;[76]

(3)(b) Whether the student attended at any time a school which was previously under a court-ordered desegregation plan;[77]

---

74. This factor is race-conscious may adequately capture race and academic need simultaneously, see generally Maurice R. Dyson, Leave No Child Behind: Normative Proposals to Link Educational Adequacy Claims and High Stakes Assessment Due Process Challenges, 7 *Tex. J C.L.-C.R. F.* 1 (2002); *GI Forum Image de Tejas v. Texas Educ. Agency*, 87 F. Supp. 2d 667 (W.D. Tex. 2000); *Larry P. v. Riles*, 793 F.2d 969, 980 (9th Cir. 1984); *Georgia Conference of NAACPs v. Georgia*, 775 F.2d 1403 (11th Cir. 1985). Forgan, Teachers Don't Want to Be Labeled, Phi Delta Kappan, Sept. 1973; Leon J. Kamin, The Science and Politics of IQ 5–30 (1974); Milbrey W. McLaughlin & Lorrie E. Shepard, Improving Education through Standards-Based Reform 7–17 (1995).

75. See AP, No Child Loophole Misses Millions of Scores, April 18, 2006, available at www.cnn.com/2006.EDUCATION/04/18/no.child.loophole.ap/index.html (discussing the relaxation of reporting requirements by race); Gregg Topo, Report: NEA Pays Opponents of NCLB, *USA Today*, July 10, 2006, available at www.usatoday.com/news/education/2006-07-10-nea-nochild_x.htm.

76. In his concurrence Justice Kennedy noted that "avoiding racial isolation" and to achieve a "diverse student population" in which race is one component are compelling interests, see *Parents Involved in Cmty. Sch. v. Seattle Sch. Dist. No. 1*, 127 S. Ct. at 2797 ("The Nation has a moral and ethical obligation to fulfill its historic commitment to creating an integrated society in avoiding racial isolation, an interest that a school district, in its discretion and expertise, may choose to pursue.").

77. This factor is race-conscious in that many cities under a desegregation plan (whether currently or in the past) fairly tracks racially isolated minority neighborhoods despite integration efforts that were flouted by white flight and the Court's protection of white privilege to leave fleeing whites out of any integration remedy as demonstrated herein. Despite the Court's decision invalidating de jure school segregation, many school boards either refused to comply with *Brown* or significantly delayed its implementation. One year after the original *Brown* decision, the Court mandated school desegregation with "all deliberate speed" and required "good faith compliance at the earliest practicable date." *Brown v. Board of Educ.*, 349 U.S. 294, 300–01 (1955); see also *Watson v. City of Memphis*, 373 U.S. 526 (1963); *Calhoun v. Latimer*, 377 U.S. 263 (1964); *Griffin v. County Sch. Bd.*, 377 U.S. 218 (1964). But for nearly twenty years following *Brown*, school districts obstinately defied man-

(4) Whether the student's school demographics is substantially in need of bilingual education compared to other district schools;[78]

(5) Whether the student's school has a pattern or practice of ability grouping or tracking of students that is substantially identifiable by race or by traditional at risk factors that increase academic failure or drop out;[79]

(6) Whether the student's school has a high identification, referral, and placement into special education students substantially identifiable by race or by traditional risk factors for academic failure or drop out;[80]

---

dates to desegregate their once de jure segregated schools. See also Michael Heise, *Brown v. Board of Education*, note 11, and Multidisciplinarity, CORNELL L. REV. 279 (2005). Since educational remedies designed to close the achievement gap were specifically foreclosed in *Milliken* and *Jenkins*, a school district could legitimately attempt to address the educational vestiges of segregation under the auspices of the rational basis new state interest of closing the achievement gap. Further, given the impact of desegregation on student drop out, see Effects of Desegregation on Minority Student Dropout Rates, available at www.eric.ed.gov/ERICWebPortal/recordDetail?accno=EJ174865-19k (last visited Jan. 10, 2008), this factor may become a legitimate basis for targeted race-conscious academic remedies.

78. This factor is race-conscious insofar as it has been recognized that language has served as a proxy for race, ethnicity, and immigrant status, see generally Kevin R. Johnson & George Martinez, Discrimination By Proxy: The Case of Proposition 227 and the Ban on Bilingual Education, 33 *U.C. Davis L. Rev.* 1227 (2000); Lynn Olson, Mixed Needs of Immigrants Pose Challenges for Schools, EDUC. WK., Sept. 27, 2000; CRP Report, What Works for the Children? What We Know and Don't Know About Bilingual Education (2002); Susan Baker & Kenji Hakuta, Bilingual Education and Latino Civil Rights (Stanford University); *Plyler v. Doe*, 457 U.S. 202 (1982); *Lau v. Nichols*, 414 U.S. 563 (1974); *Keyes v. Sch. Dist. No. 1*, 575 F. Supp. 1503 (D. Colo. 1983); Peter West, Indians Work to Save a Language and Their Heritage, EDUC. WK., Sept. 30, 1992; Mary Ann Zehr, Prop. 227 Makes Instruction Less Consistent, Study Says, EDUC. WK., May 3, 2000; Sack, Riley Endorses Dual Immersion Programs, EDUC. WK., Mar. 22, 2000, at 34; Gold, Legal Settlement in Bilingual Case Hailed as Model, EDUC. WK., Jan. 11, 1989, at 1, 12; Cummins, Empowering Minority Students: a Framework for Intervention, HARV. EDUC. REV. 56(1): 18 (Feb. 1986); *Castenada v. Pickard*, 648F.2d989 [5th Cir. 1981]) (establishing a three-part test for determining whether a school district "has taken appropriate action to overcome language barriers."). It requires that the school district's program (1) be based on sound educational theories, (2) effectively implement the education theories, and (3) produce results showing that language barriers are being overcome. Given the state of social science research, implementing strict one-year English immersion programs as Ron Unz has funded in California or mandating three-year time limits on bilingual education instruction would likely violate the rights of many children granted under the Equal Educational Opportunities Act which condified *Castenada's* tripartite test. This factor could be used for targeted intervention as opposed to transfers as well.

79. Ability grouping and tracking is a common practice that may sufficiently serve as a proxy for historically underrepresented minorities that remain disproportionately placed into lower tracks, see CHARLES T. CLOTFELTER, AFTER BROWN 137–46 (2004); This factor captures race indirectly based on the prevalent racially identifiable character of schools, see generally JEANNIE OAKES, KEEPING TRACK: HOW SCHOOLS STRUCTURE INEQUALITY (1985). Of course, those who conclude that ability grouping is harmful to students in lower-level groups or tracks and that it should therefore be abandoned makes the sometimes unsupportable assumption that the same students would receive superior instruction in more heterogeneous groups or classrooms. However, there is sufficient empirical evidence that even in heterogeneous, mixed-ability classrooms, low-achieving minority students may still receive inferior instruction or treatment. See Thomas Good, Two decades of research on teacher expectations: Findings and future directions. *Journal of Teacher Education*, 38, 32–47 (1987). Thus the need for intra-class accountability becomes pivotal under this proposed framework to ensure proper teaching and to eschew cheating or grade inflation.

80. For many states, this factor is a proxy for targeting race given its race-conscious dimension that students of color in general and African American students in particular are frequently the most impacted by the placement and referral of students into special education, see e.g., Daniel J. Losen and Kevin G. Welner, Disabling Discrimination in our Public Schools: Comprehensive Legal Challenges to Inappropriate

(7) Whether the student's school has a high incidence, pattern, or practice of student discipline, suspensions, or expulsions identifiable by race or traditional at risk factors for academic failure or drop out;[81]

(8) Whether the student's school and/or neighborhood is characterized as persistently dangerous in character as defined under the NCLB or state definitions;[82]

(9) Whether the student possesses athletic, cultural, or artistic talents, interests, and needs or personal adversity, family hardship, or community service that add to or enhance the diversity of the school;[83]

(10) Whether the student's school has a high percentage of parental noninvolvement and other socioeconomic factors that may increase the risk of academic failure or drop out;[84]

(11) Whether the student has been deprived of prenatal care and formative intensive literacy intervention that may increase the risk of academic failure or drop out;[85]

---

and Inadequate Special Education Services for Minority Children, 36 Harv. C.R.-C.L. L. Rev. 407, 434 (2001); *Hobson v. Hansen*, 269 F.Supp. 401 (D.D.C. 1967), aff'd sub. nom. *Smuck v. Hobson*, 408 F.2d 175 (D.C.Cir. 1969 (en banc); U.S. Dept. of Education, "IDEA Final Regulations: Major Issues" (Mar. 1999); *Bd. of Educ. v. Rowley*, 458 U.S. 176 (1982); *Irving Indep. Sch. Dist. v. Tatro*, 104 S. Ct. 3371 (summary); *Zobrest v. Catalina Foothills Sch. Dist.*, 113 S. Ct. 2462 (1993); U.S. Dept. of Education, "IDEA Topic Brief 10: Parentally Placed Children in Private Schools" (Mar. 1999); *Florence County Sch. Dist. Four v. Carter*, 114 S. Ct. 361 (1993) (summary); *Honig v. Doe*, 484 U.S. 305 (1988) (summary); U.S. Dept. of Education, "IDEA Final Regulations: Discipline for Children with Disabilities" (Mar. 1999); A Rising Tide of Disabilities, Educ. Wk., Nov. 29, 2000, at 25; Steinberg, supra note 128; Focusing on Minorities in Special Education, supra note 128; Merrow, What's So Special About Special Education?, Educ. Wk., May 8, 1996, at 48, 38; Webb, With New Court Decisions Backing Them, Advocates See Inclusion as a Question of Values, Harv. Educ. Letter (X)(4): 1–4 (July/Aug. 1994); Krantz, Separate Is Not Equal, Educ. Wk., June 21, 1993, at 38, 40; Cohen, Inclusion Should Not Include Deaf Students, Educ. Wk., Apr. 20, 1994, at 35; Fine, More Disabled Students Graduating, Ed. Dept. Report Says, Educ. Wk., Dec. 6, 2000, at 26; Diplomas and Disabilities, Educ. Wk., Dec. 6, 2000, at 26; U.S. Dept. of Education, "Questions and Answers About Provisions in the IDEA Related to Students with Disabilities and State and District-wide Assessments" (Aug. 24, 2000); John O'Neil, A Better IDEA, *N.Y. Times*, Apr. 14, 2002, at A17.

81. This factor traces race based on the high incidence of student discipline in schools under the auspices of zero tolerance policies that have a disproportionate adverse impact on students of color. See generally Zero Tolerance Policies: An Issue Brief, available at www.ednews.org/chapters/1609/1/ZERO-TOLERANCE-POLICIES-AN-ISSUE-BRIEF/Page1.html (last visited Jan. 5, 2008); Augustina Reyes, Discipline, Achievement and Race: Is Zero Tolerance the Answer? available at www.eric.ed.gov/ERICWebPortal/recordDetail?accno=ED491258-24k.html (last visited Jan. 5, 2008).

82. This factor is already accounted for as an authorized basis for student transfers under the NCLB that also tracks race fairly accurately given the context that academically at risk black and Latino students nationwide reside in high-crime neighborhoods. See Press Release, 27 Schools Named As "Persistently Dangerous" Under NCLB available at www.emsc.nysed.gov/irts/violence-data/2007/DangerousSchoolsRelease8-21-07.htm-80k (last visited Jan. 5, 2008).

83. Tracking enrollment based on athletic, cultural, or artistic talents, interests, and needs can be used in a race-conscious manner that is constitutionally permissible, see *Parents Involved in Cmty. Sch. v. Seattle Sch. Dist. No. 1*, 127 S. Ct. at 2797; see also *Grutter*, 539 U. S., at 338.

84. This factor is race-conscious, when combined with other factors, effectively captures minority student demographics frequently located in high poverty schools that face lack of parental involvement. See Christopher Edley, et al., Achieving Higher Educational Standards For All; Conference Summary, available at books.google.com/books?id=IRRgTMZIkVYC&pg=PA193&lpg=PA193&dq=transfer+bad+teachers+(Kahlenberg,+2001).&source=web&ots=-Dm3qr6xW5&sig=w_m1suFZX6gwo-SDN1nz6RjZnaE (last visited Jan. 9, 2008).

85. See generally Valerie Lee, David T. Burkham, Inequality at the Starting Gate (2002) (noting that before even entering kindergarten, the average cognitive score of children in the highest socioeconomic grouping are 60 percent higher than the scores of the lowest counterpart participating in the study. More-

(12) The financial status and funding of the applicant's school district[86] and the student's family income;[87]

(13) Whether the student's school has a high teacher turnover rate, absentee teacher rate, high percentage of auxiliary substitute instructors employed, or un-certified teachers teaching out of field one or more classes per day;[88]

(14) The percent and number of teachers with a college major or minor (or other equivalent formal training) in the field of work for which they are responsible for the major portion of the school day;[89]

(15) Whether student's school alumni are disproportionately underrepresented or overrepresented in math/sciences profession or in higher education generally;[90]

---

over, this factor fairly traces race insofar as average math achievement is 21 percent lower for black than for whites, and 19 percent lower for Hispanics. This is because race and ethnicity are associated with SES insofar as 34 percent of black children and 29 percent of Hispanic children are in the lowest quintile of SES compared with only 9 percent of white children, aee Maurice R. Dyson, Leave No Child Behind: Normative Proposals to Link Educational Adequacy Claims To High Stakes Due Process Assessment Challenges, 1 *Tex. C.L.-C.R. F.* 1 (2002).

86. See e.g., Jonathon Kozol, Savage Inequalities: Children in America's Schools 99–101 (1992); Council of the Great City Schools, Adequate State Financing of Urban Schools: An Analysis of State Funding of the New York City Public Schools 40–43 (2000), available at www.cgcs.org/pdfs/NYCAdequateFinance Report.pdf; Council of the Great City Schools, Adequate State Financing of Urban Schools: An Analysis of State Funding of the Philadelphia Public Schools 30–33 (1998), available at www.cgcs.org/pdfs/PhiladelphiaAdequateReport.pdf.

87. Coleman and colleagues found that a child's socioeconomic background was significant in predicting a student's academic performance, see generally JAMES C. COLEMAN, EQUALITY OF EDUCATIONAL OPPORTUNITY (Dept. of Health, Education and Welfare 1966).

88. This factor is race-conscious, when combined with other factors, effectively captures minority student demographics frequently located in high-poverty schools that face high teacher turnover, high teacher absenteeism, or large percentage of substitute teachers. See Charles Clotfelter, Helen Ladd, & Jacob Vigdor, Who Teaches Whom? Race and the Distribution of Novice Teachers, 24 *Econ. Educ. Rev.* 377 (2005); Catherine Freeman, Benjamin Scafidi, & David Sjoquist, Racial Segregation in Georgia Public Schools, 1994–2001: Trends, Causes and Impact on Teacher Quality, in School Resegregation: Must the South Turn Back 154 (John Charles Boger & Gary Orfield eds., 2005). See Christopher Edley, et al., Achieving Higher Educational Standards For All; Conference Summary, available at books.google.com/books?id=IRRgTMZIkVYC&pg=PA193&lpg=PA193&dq=transfer+bad+teachers+(Kahlenberg,+2001).&source=web&ots=-Dm3qr6xW5&sig=w_m1suFZX6gwo-SDN1nz6RjZnaE (last visited Jan. 9, 2008) ("High poverty schools have high tach turnover, teachers teaching out of subject, less parental involvement in school affairs, less able to ensure high standards, and less likely to pressure administrators to fire or transfer bad teachers."). According to the research done for Quality Counts 2003, 56 percent of teachers in high-poverty schools agree that student disrespect is a moderate or serious problem; 80 percent said students are unprepared to learn; 75 percent found that the lack of parent involvement is a moderate or serious problem. Larger percentages of teachers in these schools, compared to low-poverty schools, also said student and teacher absenteeism and student apathy is a moderate to serious problem. Teachers in high-poverty schools or high-minority schools were not satisfied with their salaries, did not receive a great deal of support from parents or cooperative efforts among staff members, and lacked necessary materials to teach. See generally To Close the Gap, Quality Counts, available at dese.mo.gov/divimprove/instrtech/newsletters/february03.html-146k (last visited Jan. 10, 2008).

89. This factor fairly accurately tracks race insofar schools where predominantly students of color are educated nationwide typically have fewer teachers in their college major or trained field, see Erica Frankenberg et al., Charter schools and race: A lost opportunity for Integrated education, 11 EDUC. POL'Y ANALYSIS ARCHIVES 28 (2005).

90. This factor is designed to target a demographic focused on at risk students of color rather than merely looking to racial minority status that might include Asians and other minorities in less need of targeted academic intervention. See e.g., Figures of Academically Gifted Student Eligibility, infra.

(16) Whether, based on other risk factors, the student would be at risk of drop out, grade retention, or who may be the first generation of his or her family to attend or graduate from high school;[91]

(17) Whether the student's school composition, programming, resources, tends to confirm or perpetuate stereotypes or encourage prejudice reduction;[92]

(18) Whether the student's school has a high student/teacher ratio and class size in core academic subjects;[93]

(19) The school's total expenditures on full-time teacher training, recruitment, retention;[94]

(20) The availability or lack thereof of academic excellence and support programs, e.g., homework online, supplemental tutorial services, programs for gifted and talented students, advancement placement courses;[95]

(21) The availability or lack thereof of special instructional methodologies, e.g., accelerated learning, curriculum compacting, and multigrade grouping;[96]

(22) The availability or lack thereof of lab opportunities, e.g., computer, language, science, etc;[97]

---

91. Drop out rates also fairly capture minority at risk demographics to serve as a useful factor for targeted race-conscious interventions, see Dropout Rates for Minority Students Keep Rising in Cities, available at query.nytimes.com/gst/fullpage.html? res=9C02E7DF113AF93BA1575AC0A962958260-48k (last visited Jan. 10, 2008).

92. Promoting prejudice reduction in elementary and secondary education may fairly track race because racial prejudices and implicit biases are developed early in school life and can become entrenched over time as to undermine academic success, social cohesion, and community stability. see Frances E. Aboud, Children and Prejudice (1988); Andrew Scott Baron & Mahzarin H. Banaji, The Development of Implicit Attitudes: Evidence of Race Evaluations from Ages 6 and 10 and Adulthood, 17 *Psychol. Sci.* 53 (2006); See, e.g., Thomas F. Pettigrew & Linda R. Tropp, A Meta-Analytic Test of Intergroup Contact Theory, 90 *J. Personality & Soc. Psychol.* 751 (2006); Thomas F. Pettigrew, Intergroup Contact Theory, 49 *Ann. Rev. Psychol.* 65 (1998). Heidi Mc-Glothlin & Melanie Killen, Intergroup Attitudes of European American Children Attending Ethnically Homogeneous Schools, 77 *Child Dev.* 1375 (2006); Heidi McGlothlin et al., European-American Children's Intergroup Attitudes About Peer Relationships, 23 *Brit. J. Developmental Psychol.* 227 (2005) (discussing bias among white students); Nancy Geyelin Margie et al., Minority Children's Intergroup Attitudes About Peer Relationships, 23 Brit. J. Developmental Psychol. 251 (2005) (discussing bias among minority students).

93. See Frederick Mosteller, The Tennessee Study of Class Size in the Early School Grades, 5 *The Future of Children* 113 (1995); William S. Koski & Henry Levin, Twenty-Five Years After *Rodriguez*: What Have We Learned? 102 Tchrs. C. Rec. 3, 480–513 (2000).

94. See Hidden Teacher Spending Gaps: A Tale of Two Schools, available at www.hiddengap.org/resources/TechnicalAppendixHiddenGapII.pdf (last visited Jan. 9, 2008).

95. See Roslyn Arlin Mickelson, The Academic Consequences of Desegregation and Segregation: Evidence from the Charlotte-Mecklenburg Schools, 81 *N.C. L. Rev.* 1513, 1547–48 (2003) (finding that racially identifiable black schools had deficiencies in fewer Advanced Placement courses, and fewer services for gifted and talented students); See also John T. Yun & Jose F. Moreno, College Access, K–12 Concentrated Disadvantage, and the Next 25 Years of Education Research, 35 *Educ. Researcher* 12, 15–16 (2006).

96. Such programs may be serve as an effective targeted remedy for high-poverty schools with high concentrations of race, see e.g., William H. Clune, Accelerated Education as a Remedy for High Poverty Schools, 28 *U. Mich. J.L. Reform* 655, 667–69 (1995).

97. See Mickelson, The Academic Consequences of Desegregation and Segregation, 81 *N.C. L. Rev.* at 1547–48.

(23) The availability or lack thereof of extracurricular performance activities including those that are curriculum and attendance supporting;[98]

(24) The availability or lack thereof of air conditioning/heating, cleanliness of facility, total acreage of school site, condition and quality of facilities, school campus, classrooms, media center, hallways, etc;[99]

(25) Whether the school's administrative policies, practices, public releases, local press coverage, or fiscal expenditures (including those cited in these factors) negatively impacts the school district's racial enrollments patterns or the allocation of educational resources in a racially identifiable manner;[100]

(26) Whether the school's surrounding neighborhood has a high incidence of racial gentrification, commercial loan redlining practices, or a pattern of racial or socioeconomic discrimination against Section 8 housing subsidy recipients that negatively impacts the school district's racial enrollments patterns or the allocation of educational resources in a racially identifiable manner.[101]

Once again, these factors are not exhaustive but may reflect a starting point for states to convey their values of inclusion, academic excellence, and good citizenship by utilizing group blind approaches in K–12 education that target race and for positive interventionist strategies.[102] These factors suggests schools and community stakeholders may lawfully engage and advocate race-conscious remedies that have a rationale nexus to closing the achievement gap that would have no problem surviving rational basis review with the incidental benefit of preparing students for a multiracial society.[103] Empirically, the use of these factors in Seattle could presumably address race, ethnicity, and income in ways that could target at-risk students in Seattle. The previous overview of Seattle's demographics bears this out. Furthermore, there are enormous legal, policy, and tactical advantages of this approach that grounds race-conscious remedies under the closing the achievement gap state interest. There are also significant advantages in using the factors I have suggested above as well. Collectively, these advantages may be summarized as follows.

(1) Race could be used as one factor among many targeted race-conscious factors based on a prioritization of academic need to close the racial achievement gap;

(2) Incentive-based school transfers could justifiably place minority students in high demand schools meeting or exceeding adequate yearly progress goals or just schools with higher SES standing as the most effective or expedient way to close the racial achievement gap under state accountability statutes and NCLB;

---

98. NCES, Extracurricular Participation and Student Engagement, available at nces.ed.gov/pubs95/web/95741.asp (last visited Jan. 9, 2008).

99. These resources inequities also fairly accurately track race, see Jonathon Kozol, Savage Inequalities: Children in America's Schools 99–101 (1992).

100. See discussion on Croson remedial justification, infra.

101. Paul Boudreaux, Vouchers, Buses & Flats: The Persistence of Social Segregation, 49 *Vill. L. Rev.* 55 72, 73 (2004).

102. See *Plyler v. Doe*, 457 U.S. 202, 221 (1982) (noting that public schools are "the primary vehicle for transmitting the values on which our society rests.").

103. See *Spangler v. Pasadena City Bd. of Educ.*, 611 F.2d 1239, 1242 (9th Cir. 1979) (Kennedy, J., concurring) ("One purpose of education is to prepare children for living in our society, which is a multiracial society."); *Wash. v. Seattle Sch. Dist. No. 1*, 458 U.S. 457, 473 (1982) ("preparing minority children for citizenship in our pluralistic society" and "teaching members of the racial majority to live in harmony and mutual respect with children of minority heritage.").

(3) Use of race statistics under NCLB would not be working backward to achieve a particular type of racial balance, but rather work forward from some demonstration of academic need to close the achievement gap per the school district's expertise which need not trigger strict scrutiny;

(4) Greater emphasis on these factors in K–12 pipeline may lead to greater minority student readiness for college and retention of students of color in higher education and underrepresented professional programs. This would of course better ground this state interest well within the constitutional construct of affirmative upheld in *Grutter* since it follows that as long as the persistent gap in minority student achievement remains in the K–12 context, the diversity interest in *Grutter* cannot be sunsetted. As it was observed in *Grutter*:

> As lower school education in minority communities improves, an increase in the number of [qualified minority] students may be anticipated. From today's vantage point, one may hope ... that over the next generation's span, progress toward nondiscrimination and genuinely equal opportunity will make it safe to sunset affirmative action.[104]

(5)(a) Consistent with Chief Justice Roberts's analysis, there is "individualized consideration"[105] in student reassignments based on that student's individual performance on academic state assessments and holistic review would be based not on viewpoint diversity but a holistic totality of the circumstances that each proposed factor could be used to inform what targeted intervention is most appropriate;

(5)(b) Moreover, this holistic review of the individual student and his or her learning environment in devising targeted strategies to close the academic achievement gap falls well within the purview of a school district's legitimate authority, experimental expertise, and paradigmatic judgment on educational policy matters that justify heightened judicial deference that Justice Kennedy recognizes apply to school districts in devising racial remedies;[106]

(5)(c) Not only would greater judicial deference be entitled based on a school district's educational policy expertise in closing the achievement gap, but ju-

---

104. See *Grutter*, 539 U.S. at 346.

105. Incidentally, it appears a rather misguided to import part and parcel the notion of "individualized consideration" from *Grutter* without first some critical assessment of the K–12 context. The requirement of "individualized holistic review" was relevant to the law school's interest in *Grutter* to encourage "'the robust exchange of ideas' fostered by viewpoint diversity," see *Grutter*, 539 U.S. at 324, which is distinct from a compelling interest is in racial integration, where "the only relevant criterion, ... is a student's race; individualized consideration beyond that is irrelevant to the compelling interest," see *Comfort v. Lynn Sch. Comm.*, 418 F.3d 1, 18 (1st Cir. 2005); See *Brewer v. W. Irondequoit Cent. Sch. Dist.*, 212 F.3d 738, 752 (2d Cir. 2000) ("If reducing racial isolation is standing alone a constitutionally permissible goal..., then there is no more effective means of achieving that goal than to base decisions on race."); PICS, 426 F.3d at 1191 ("The logic is self-evident: When racial diversity is a principal element of the school district's compelling interest, then a narrowly tailored plan may explicitly take race into account."). Indeed, it is bizarre to suggest individualized consideration of kindergartners, or elementary students viewpoint diversity would enhance a elementary or middle school.

106. See 127 S.Ct. at 2797; *San Antonio Indep. Sch. Dist. v. Rodriguez*, 411 U.S. 1, 43 (1973) ("the judiciary is well advised to refrain from imposing on the States inflexible constitutional restraints that could circumscribe or handicap the continued research and experimentation so vital to finding even partial solutions to educational problems and to keeping abreast of ever-changing conditions"); *Milliken v. Bradley*, 418 U.S. 717, 741 (1974) ("no single tradition in public education is more deeply rooted than local control over the operation of schools").

dicial deference would also be entitled based on first amendment rights to academic freedom under the First Amendment. Although it has been suggested that the justification offered for deference to college and graduate school administrators' "academic freedom" guaranteed by the First Amendment does not support deference to local school board members,[107] this ignores the fact students rights under the first amendment do not vanish in the schoolhouse gates.[108] Therefore, it follows that if students have a limited First Amendment right in K–12, it suggest that K–12 institutions have an obligation to inculcate responsible appreciation for first amendment rights, to educate students on how to exercise those first amendment rights responsibly in the K–12 context, and to devise learning environments and programs that are related to facilitating such purposes as it deems appropriate in the exercise of its academic freedom, albeit it may be more circumscribed in the K–12 context;[109]

(6) Consistent with Justice Kennedy's concurring opinion, this approach could also have the added benefit of legitimately justifying the prevention of "de facto resegregation" of the public schools and is "free to devise race conscious measures to address the problem in a general way and without treating each student in a different fashion solely on the basis of a systematic, individual typing by race";

(7) Notwithstanding the above, the benefits that flow from diversity because attendance as a higher performing school is presumptively regarded under the NCLB as matter of right and is supported by ample social science evidence. Even absent NCLB, exposure to a high-performing school or school with less race-conscious at risk factors is rationally related to closing achievement gap;

(8) This more nuanced NCLB revised approach authorizes a broader interdistrict remedial scope not possible in *Milliken*. It also more closely locates the remedial justification in the higher education diversity rationale to establish the proposition that affirmative action cannot be principally dismantled without first achieving racial accountability in the K–12 pipeline. The NCLB and similar accountability mandates provides a justifiable and common sense nexus such that it follows that affirmative action in higher education cannot be principally dismantled without first achieving racial accountability in the K–12 pipeline;

(9) The interest in closing the achievement gap avoids the judicial concerns of impermissible racial integration remedies such as increasing teacher salaries, funding quality education programs, specialized schools, and programs designed

---

107. See Jay P. Lecher, Learning from Experience: Why Racial Diversity Cannot Be a Legally Compelling Interest in Elementary and Secondary Education, 32 *S.W.U.L. Rev.* 201, 215 (2003). A university's academic freedom includes the rights "to determine for itself on academic grounds who may teach, what may be taught, how it shall be taught, and who may be admitted to study." *Bakke*, 438 U.S. at 312 (Powell, J., concurring); see also *Keyshian v. Board of Regents*, 385 U.S. 589 (1967); *Sweezy v. New Hampshire*, 354 U.S. 234 (1957). ·

108. However, since students rights under the first amendment do not vanish once students enter the schoolhouse gates, see *Tinker v. Des Moines Schl. Dist.*, 393 U.S. 503 (1969) this necessarily suggest that K–12 institutions have an obligation to educate students on how to exercise those first amendment rights, see *Chandler v. McMinville Schl. Dist.* 978 F2d 524 (9th Cir. 1992). In so doing, it enjoys academic freedom, the scope of which is more limited, but which still legitimately exists to ensure those rights are responsibly exercised, see *Hazelwood Schl. Dist. v. Kuhlmeier*, 484 U.S. 260 (1988).

109. See *Bethel Sch. Dist. No. 403 v. Fraser*, 478 U.S. 675, 683 (1986) ("The process of educating our youth for citizenship in public schools is not confined to books, the curriculum, and the civics class; schools must teach by example the shared values of a civilized social order.").

to achieve "desegregative attractiveness" through these educational remedies like those struck down in *Missouri v. Jenkins* that would be considered too far removed from an acceptable implementation of a permissible means to remedy previous legally mandated segregation. Under a mandate to close the achievement gap between the strongest and weakest performers (implicitly closing the racial achievement gap), a district will have more leeway to experiment[110] with such educational policies in accordance with local needs to eradicate the educational vestiges of segregation that went left unredressed despite Milliken II's mandate to remove such vestiges;[111]

(10) Even if the NCLB accountability scheme is underfunded or its assessment criteria are flawed, using such assessments for the beneficial purpose of minority student placement in high-demand schools rather than attaching adverse high-stakes consequences, is consistent with psychometric testing principles and is proper under Title VI of the Civil Rights Act.

While the foregoing provides a novel way for school districts to exercise greater discretion to exercise targeted race-conscious remedies for resource allocation, school siting, and student transfers to close the achievement gap, it is imperative to understand the structural impediments under the NCLB that have diminished the promise of its school choice remedies. It is also just as important to provide normative proposals that not only remove these impediments, but which provide a positive incentive for school districts and students alike to engage in effective, meaningful school choice transfer options and educational remedies.

However, because the act's benchmarks require the reporting of test scores, on a disaggregated basis for minority and ethnic subgroups where academic achievement gap is the most pronounced, it may also have the unintended effect of harming charter schools' ability to recruit and retain high-quality teachers called for under the act. This is because teachers will be held accountable by any prospective school employer for academic results. These teachers presumably would be discouraged from accepting employment with a black school student body that consist of a majority of academically challenged charter school students. Thus, instead of rewarding at-risk and/or predominantly minority charter schools for their valiant efforts to serve this historically marginalized community, they may be unfairly punished for these laudable efforts and face possible closure.

Fourth, for similar reasons, there appears to be a great reluctance in promoting transfers of special needs minority students to high-performing schools who would normally have a right to transfer out of a failing school designated as "in need of improvement." This is because the receiving school districts presumably have an incentive to discourage at-risk minority students transfers to omit them from their own school's accountability profile. Fifth, even assuming a student would be allowed to transfer successfully, the adequacy of school capacity to receive the overwhelming number of students who do qualify for the transfer is severely limited even as the law mandates that lack of school capacity is not an excuse for noncompliance with its mandate. While school districts could es-

---

110. Courts should "allow citizens to participate in decisionmaking" and to "allow innovation so that school programs can fit local needs." *Bd. of Educ. v. Dowell*, 498 U.S. 237, 248 (1991); See Pitts, 503 U.S. at 490 ("It must be acknowledged that the potential for discrimination and racial hostility is still present in our country, and its manifestations may emerge in new and subtle forms after the effects of de jure segregation have been eliminated. It is the duty of the State and its subdivisions to ensure that such forces do not shape or control the policies of its school systems. Where control lies, so too does responsibility.").

111. See *Milliken v. Bradley* [Milliken II], 433 U.S. at 280–82.

tablish a cooperative agreement with other school districts for transfers under this mandate, this still does not remove the disincentives it creates for schools to avoid accepting these students. Sixth, this disincentive lies with not only receiving school districts but sending school districts as well. This is because, under the act, transferring schools may essentially view the transfer options, which become triggered when the school fails to meet academic benchmarks for two consecutive years, as a badge of shame. As a result, they often do notoriously very little to educate parents and students about transfer opportunities even though they are required by law to do so. Finally, it should not be assumed that families of color have no concern or grievance against busing their children on long daily commutes to schools that may be miles away from the familiarity of their home neighborhoods.

One novel and new way to effectively overcome these considerations is to provide an incentive for receiving school districts to enjoy greater autonomy by more relaxed accountability reporting and benchmark compliance under NCLB in exchange for more targeted accountability and reporting for at-risk students showing continued and steady progress for these students the receiving school district accepts. Under this scenario, for instance, Ballard then would not need to show lockstep progress on increased benchmarks from year to year until 2014 for 95 percent of its entire student body so long as it can be shown that it has made steady progress biannually for all of its students generally and that it has substantially closed the achievement gap from at risk students transferring from southern Seattle neighborhood schools specifically that are floundering on AYP benchmarks.

Part IV: A New Theoretical Model for NCLB Accountability[112]

Theoretically, a relaxed reporting and compliance model that looks at progress every two years for its general student population based on its own state standards is conceivable so long as there still remains a discernible standard by which to benchmark the progress of at risk students accepted into that student population focused on the NAEP progress (along with other student portfolio assessment tools. Instead of focusing on all students in its accountability framework, the NCLB will ensure it leaves no child behind by focusing on the most vulnerable student demographic that is most threatened to be left behind. In exchange for more leeway in NCLB regulatory oversight, a school district receiving at-risk students would need to show substantial progress for this at-risk student population and would received increased lockstep funding jumps tied to the NAEP progress of at risk students. This approach would essentially authorize the U.S. Department of Education to grant waivers and exemptions for non–at-risk students in exchange for greater accountability to minority at risk students rather than the current status quo, which currently grants exemptions that excludes racial minorities from the accountability picture.

---

112. I have made this theoretical proposal in various talks throughout the nation. These suggested are predicated on changes to an accountability framework that would be benchmarked to the NAEP as originally proposed, see generally Maurice R. Dyson, Leave No Child Behind: Normative Proposals to Link Educational Adequacy Claims and High Stakes Assessment Due Process Challenges, 7 *Texas J. C.L.-C.R. F.* 1 (2002).

In this way, schools accepting a certain percentage of at-risk students may enjoy more leeway in NCLB regulatory oversight for its non–at-risk student population in exchange for greater annual accountability compliance with respect to its at-risk student population. This provides an incentive for schools to target resources for students who are in the greatest need of those resources. A school does not ignore the rest of its student population merely because there are more targeted resources for at-risk students. Presumably, with more relaxed accountability comes greater flexibility to introduce enriched curricula for all, but with targeted intervention strategies focused on students of color in the greatest academic need.

While School District A accepts a percentage of at-risk students under this proposal, it must not introduce tracking, sorting, or segregative practices that exclude those students from the rest of the general student body (much like mandated inclusion of special education students in a least restrict environment under the IDEA); they can however introduce additional remedial contexts to supplement, but not supplant the general education context of all its students. In this way, we may see greater exercise of the transfer option when there are real options like Ballard, Hale, or Roosevelt for parents that make the exercise of that choice an attractive one that is supported by the transportation costs and increased lockstep funding increases tied to increased NAEP performance for at risk students.

Under this model, the accountability of the student follows a growth model of accountability that I have previously proposed elsewhere.[113] Here we look at the progress of the student from grade to grade based on the overall performance of the individual student over the entire course of his or her educational career. This approach becomes the epitome of "individualized consideration" for targeted intervention that comports with PICS and the *Bollinger* case rationales. School District B would also have the same benefit of a growth model of accountability under the NAEP and would have the same benefit to compete for increased funding incentive rewards for showing progress for at risk students. To boost School District B's ability to compete for federal fiscal NAEP incentive rewards, it would also receive increased foundational funding in recognition that School District B may have a higher percentage of at-risk students than School District A. Funding would also reflect costs of educating students based on an education cost index (ECI) that takes into account the costs of technology, linguistic, and special needs of at-risk students.[114]

However, funding would also follow the student from the sending School District B to the receiving School District A. Further, much like accountability would follow the student, so too would it follow each individual teacher with greater compensation and special monetary and on the job benefits for teachers who show progress for at-risk student populations. In addition, the closer monitoring explicitly called for under

---

113. Maurice R. Dyson, In Search of the Talented Tenth: Diversity, Affirmative Access, and University-Driven Reform, 6 *Harv. Latino L. Rev.* 41 (2003).

114. Price adjustments are often part of horizontal equity analyses because they are meant to adjust the nominal dollars to reflect differences in prices of constant quality inputs across districts. Student weights are used in vertical equity analyses to reflect differences in costs of educating pupils. See Equity and Adequacy in Education Finance: Issues and Perspectives, Commission on Behavioral and Social Sciences and Education, available at books.nap.edu/openbook.php?record_id= 6166&page=261 (last visited Jan. 9, 2008) ("Thus, a focus on performance is inevitably unfair unless it can somehow account for the impact on performance of factors that are outside the control of school officials. Without such an accounting, some schools get credit for favorable conditions that were not of their making and other schools get blamed for unfavorable conditions over which they have no control. In order to be fair, school report cards and performance-based state aid systems must distinguish between poor performance based on external factors and poor performance based on school inefficiency.").

this targeted approach for at-risk students would help alleviate concerns that there remains no cheating or intentional distortion of academic outcomes with strict penalties attaching where such evidence may exist for both school, teacher, and student impropriety, whichever the case may be.[115] Pursuant to this state interest that is readily more than capable of surviving judicial scrutiny, school districts and courts could have the legitimacy and justification needed to bring about the educational remedies that were struck down in *Milliken v. Bradley, Missouri v. Jenkins,* and *PICS v. Seattle* designed implicitly to close the racial achievement gap. At long last, there is viable path to achieving the goals of integration, diversity, and even more significantly racial equality through access to academic quality programs that is appropriately based on academic need.

However, in addition to transfers, magnet schools, and competitive programs that are strategically located in racially mixed neighborhoods could yield positive results for students of color where there is also significant socioeconomic diversity as well.[116] Wrap around programs, which are programs designed to address family and student's personal and educational needs, may also be targeted to minority neighborhood schools.[117] Under this proposal, there is no problem in fixing income or geographical quotas or "critical mass targets" of low SES students for admission seats in a high SES K–12 school. The critical mass targets would be specifically tied to socioeconomic race-consciousness, but not race-explicit classifications. These at risk student factors for academic failure may be legitimately pursued so long as they are rationally related to further the academic goal of closing the achievement gap generally for the lowest student performers (as opposed to the racial achievement gap; pursuing racial integration or racial diversity per se).

These targets will also help ensure that the student enrollment demographics need not be adversely affected by increased gentrification and rising property values in a surrounding neighborhood because it will keep seats reserved for the most academically at-risk students supported by transportation costs where necessary. But just as there is a need for a critical mass of at risk students, there must also be critical mass targets for non–at-risk students to ensure the kind of socioeconomic diversity needed for the optimal educational benefits to flow. This approach, however more susceptible it may be to empirical attacks notwithstanding the strong evidence in support of it, allows targets to be tied to a forward-looking goal of achieving optimal educational benefits in the classroom.[118]

Although as noted above that Justice Thomas finds nothing problematic with racial balancing and thus by extension he concludes that it is not a compelling state interest, it is worth nothing that Justice Kennedy did not joint Parts III-B of this opinion. Moreover, while in *Freeman v. Pitts,* the Court stated plainly that "once the racial imbalance due to the *de jure* violation has been remedied, the school district is under no duty to remedy

---

115. See How States Inflate Their Educational Progress Under NCLB, available at www.education sector.org/usr_doc/Hot_Air_NCLB.pdf (last visited Jan. 10, 2008); see also Brian A. Jacob, In Rotten Apples: An Investigation of the Prevalence and Predictors of Teacher Cheating (NBER Working Paper No. 9413).

116. See Coleman Report, supra note 87.

117. See James Comer School Development Program, available at cecp.air.org/resources/success/ school_development_program.asp (last visited Jan. 9, 2008).

118. Cf. *Gratz v. Bollinger,* 539 U.S. 244, 262 (2003); *Northeastern Fla. Chapter of the Associated Gen. Contractors of America v. City of Jacksonville, Florida,* 508 U.S. 656, 666 (1993).

imbalance that is caused by demographic factors,"[119] this does not comport with the Croson justification as illustrated above where the remedial justification can be properly rooted in state action. Nor does racial balancing offend *Milliken* where the court noted that "the Constitution is not violated by racial imbalance in the schools, *without more*"[120] (emphasis added). Presumably the four remedial justifications proffered in this chapter are the additional basis for intervention. Nonetheless, the characteristics of this proposed approach is significant because this scheme does not work backward to achieve racial balancing per se that is not adequately grounded in pedagogical theory and practice. Nonetheless, in this model of SES academic at risk enrollment, it is very imperative that even though rational basis review would apply, states and school districts should fully document its research findings on SES demographic mixing that would then become the basis for justifying "critical mass" targets for at-risk students that are identifiable by race.

Conclusion

It may be disingenuous to suggest other proxies for race as Justice Kennedy has to target that which might be impermissible to do directly. As was noted in *Grutter*: "If honesty is the best policy, surely Michigan's accurately described, fully disclosed College affirmative action program is preferable to achieving similar numbers through winks, nods, and disguises."[121] In this vein, if it is impermissible to consider race openly then, the argument goes, there is no reason to believe that any backdoor surrogate purposefully designed to take account of race would be any less objectionable.[122] However, compounding this problem of transparency is the legal proposition that although socioeconomic status and income do not trigger strict scrutiny, it also lacks the legal protection theoretically accorded to race in constitutional law which is subject to the most exacting standard of scrutiny.[123] Further, notwithstanding the foregoing, the use of race will nonetheless remain palpably relevant both in both K–12 education and in higher education if the goal remains to close the achievement gap. It follows that unless and until the mandate to close the achievement gap in K–12 education occurs, then affirmative action in higher education cannot in principle be dismantled. To effectively combat these trends, it is imperative that a more contextualized approach that fundamentally rethinks the paradigm of targeted but holistic remedial intervention as Justice Kennedy suggests is the glimmer of hope in an otherwise intractable problem and rigid constitutional jurisprudence. Nothing less will suffice to achieve the true spirit of *Brown's* unmet mandate: racial equality predicated on equal access to quality, desirable educational choice, and opportunity.

---

119. 503 U.S. at 494.

120. See *Milliken v. Bradley*, 433 U.S. 267, 280 n.14 (1977).

121. See id.; See also PICS, 426 F.3d at 1189 ("We do not require the District to conceal its compelling interest of achieving racial diversity and avoiding racial concentration or isolation through the use of 'some clumsier proxy device' such as poverty," quoting Comfort, 418 F.3d at 29 (Boudin, C.J., concurring)).

122. See *Gratz v. Bollinger*, 539 U.S. 244, 305 (2003) (Ginsburg, J., dissenting).

123. See *Edwards v. California*, 314 U.S. 160, 184–85 (1941) (Jackson, J., concurring) (stating poverty can never be basis for legal discrimination); *San Antonio Indep. Sch. Dist. v. Rodriguez*, 411 U.S. 1, 23 (1973).

II
The Pipeline: K–12 and the Higher Educational Opportunity Nexus

4

Fiscal Inequity and Resegregation: Two Pressing Mutual Concerns of K–12 Education and Higher Education

William A. Kaplin*

I. Introduction

A. Focus and Purpose of This Chapter

Many legal and policy developments involving K–12 education (elementary/secondary education) in the United States also have important repercussions for higher education. Problems that develop at the K–12 level and resist satisfactory resolution there may sooner or later be transformed into problems at the level of higher education; challenges and opportunities that arise in K–12 education may sooner or later be transformed into challenges and opportunities for higher education. These cycles can also operate in reverse.

Two areas of interconnection between K–12 education and higher education have particularly significant policy and legal implications, both current and long-range. The first area concerns *fiscal inequities* affecting the quality of K–12 education and the availability of a college education, particularly for students of low socioeconomic status and minority students. The second area concerns racial and ethnic *resegregation* of K–12 education, its effects on the quality of K–12 education for minority students, and its effects on the racial diversity and racial climate of colleges and universities.

Fiscal inequity and racial segregation are two branches of what has been a protracted struggle for equal educational opportunity in the United States that began before *Brown v. Board of Education* in 1954 and continues to the present day. The struggle has often been manifested by litigation. "Decades ago race and school desegregation litigation forged the initial modern understanding of equal opportunity. More recently, school finance lit-

---

* Research Professor of Law, The Catholic University of America; Distinguished Professorial Lecturer and Sr. Fellow, Center for Excellence in Higher Ed. Law and Policy, Stetson University College of Law.

igation displaced desegregation litigation as the major instrument for enhancing equal educational opportunity."[1] Now desegregation (or more pointedly resegregation) issues have reemerged to resume their position alongside fiscal equity issues, prompted both by worrisome data on the increasing racial identifiability of K–12 schools[2] and by the U.S. Supreme Court's 2007 decision in the *Seattle School District* case.[3]

After addressing the growing interconnections between K–12 and higher education, this chapter explores developments regarding fiscal inequity and resegregation, suggesting challenges to which leaders at both levels might direct their attentions. The chapter then addresses how structures and processes of governance for both K–12 education and higher education may inhibit the capacities of both levels to collaborate on matters of mutual interest, thus prompting a need to reform governance structures. Last, the chapter provides various examples of initiatives that are now under way to address concerns and challenges of the type the discussion has identified.

Educators and policy makers at each level of education, K–12 and higher, must become much more concerned about the other level's performance and problems, and they must channel that heightened concern into new initiatives based on mutuality of interests and new mechanisms for collaboration between the two levels. Fiscal inequity and resegregation represent two critically important problem areas that cry out for such heightened concern and collaboration. Our future demands it.

B. Examples of Interconnections between K–12 Education and Higher Education

Interconnections between the two levels of education are not particularly difficult to find if one looks for them. Here are some common examples.

(1) *Students with Disabilities*. In 1975, Congress passed the Education of All Handicapped Children Act, which later became (and remains) the Individuals with Disabilities Education Act (IDEA),[4] a statute that provides funds for services for K–12 students with disabilities and establishes guidelines for such services. On implementation of the new law, local school districts began developing and expanding services for students with disabilities, and the numbers of students identified as disabled began to increase sharply. In due time, these students graduated from high school—prepared to enter college and expecting special services from the institutions in which they enrolled.[5] The huge increases in disabled students applying to and enrolling in college created problems for higher education, as well as a historic opportunity—and both the problems and opportunities are made more difficult because IDEA does not apply to colleges and universities and therefore does not trigger the funding and programmatic guidance for colleges that the federal government provides to K–12 education.

---

1. Michael Heise, *Educational Adequacy as Legal Theory: Implications from Equal Educational Opportunity Doctrine*, Cornell Law School Legal Studies Research Paper Series, Paper 37, March 8, 2006, available at lsr.nellco.org/cornell//srp/papers/37.

2. *See, e.g.*, Erica Frankenberg, et al., A Multi-Racial Society with Segregated Schools: Are We Losing the Dream? (Civil Rights Center at Harvard, Jan. 2003), available at www.civilrightsproject.ucla.edu/research/reseg03/reseg03_.full.php.

3. *Parents Involved in Community Schools v. Seattle School District No. 1*, 127 S.Ct. 2738 (2007). See part III of this chapter for an in-depth discussion of the case.

4. 20 U.S.C. 1400 *et seq.*

5. *See* Laura Rothstein, *Disability Law and Higher Education: A Road Map for Where We've Been and Where We May be Heading*, 63 Md. L. Rev. 122, 123–131 (2004).

(2) *Female Student Athletes.* In 1972, Congress passed the Title IX statute prohibiting sex discrimination by educational institutions that receive federal funds.[6] The implementing regulations cover sex discrimination in physical education classes, intramural athletics, and interscholastic/intercollegiate athletics.[7] As a result of these new requirements, the athletic interests and skill levels of female elementary school and secondary school students gradually increased. In due time, greatly increased numbers of these students graduated from high school and entered college prepared to and expecting to participate in intercollegiate and intramural sports programs in a variety of sports, some of which had been restricted to male students. Equitably accommodating all of these diverse interests created numerous problems for higher education and presented a substantial (and continuing) challenge, especially regarding intercollegiate athletics.[8]

(3) *College Readiness: Underprepared Students.* Colleges and universities have long been interested in the academic preparedness or readiness of high school students for a college education. Although preparation is primarily the responsibility of the elementary and secondary schools, their successes and failures in performing this responsibility may affect higher education in numerous ways. When high school graduation rates decline or remain stagnant, as has occurred in recent years,[9] colleges and universities may need to reconsider and perhaps lower their admissions standards to maintain class size; alternatively, they may need to reconsider and perhaps supplement their operating budgets. When substantial percentages of high school graduates are deficient in English, math, or science, colleges and universities may need to institute or expand remedial education programs—an action that may affect not only admissions and budgeting but also curriculum and student advisement. Thus, responding to inadequacies or (as will be seen shortly) inequities in K–12 education's performance may create a variety of problems and challenges for higher education.

(4) *Accountability.* Accountability, with its lesser included concepts of assessment and transparency, seems to be the primary watchword in contemporary education reform. The push for more accountability is not new, but it has new force and emphasis as a result of Congress's passage of the No Child Left Behind Act (NCLB) in 2001.[10] NCLB applies only to K–12 education and has been implemented primarily with respect to elementary education. Its focus is on setting standards of achievement, tracking students' progress and individual schools' progress through standardized testing, and providing interventions to assist students and schools that are not "measuring up."

Apparently stimulated by this emphasis on accountability in K–12 education, there has been discussion in federal government circles of developing governmental accountability requirements for colleges and universities, including the possible use of standardized tests for assessment purposes—thus providing another major example of developments in K–12 education that create problems or challenges for higher education as well.[11]

---

6. 20 U.S.C. 1681 *et seq.*

7. 34 C.F.R. Part 106.

8. *See* William Kaplin & Barbara Lee, THE LAW OF HIGHER EDUCATION: A COMPREHENSIVE GUIDE TO LEGAL IMPLICATIONS OF ADMINISTRATIVE DECISION MAKING, 4th ed. (Jossey-Bass, 2006), sec. 10.4.6.

9. *See, e.g.,* Jay Green, *Public High School Graduation and College Readiness Rates: 1991–2002* (Manhattan Institute, 2005), available at www.manhattan-institute.org/html/ewp_08.htm.

10. 20 U.S.C. 6301 *et seq. See* Paul Peterson & Martin West (eds.), NO CHILD LEFT BEHIND? THE POLITICS AND PRACTICE OF SCHOOL ACCOUNTABILITY (2003).

11. *See, e.g., No College Left Behind?,* INSIDE HIGHER ED, February 15, 2006, available at inside-highered.com/news/2006/02/15/testing.

In 2005–2006, the discussion about accountability in higher education was expanded and highlighted as a result of the deliberations of the U.S. Secretary of Education's Commission on the Future of Higher Education (known as the Spellings Commission). In its final report, *A Test of Leadership: Charting the Future of U.S. Higher Education,* the commission stopped short of recommending federally mandated academic standards or federally mandated assessment tests for higher education. But the report did contain key findings and recommendations on the lack of accountability and the need to create "a robust culture of accountability and transparency throughout higher education."[12] The commission also turned its attention to secondary education, recommending accountability initiatives that would require "state assessments in high school to ensure that diplomas mean students are prepared to enter college or the workforce"[13]—initiatives that would likely require the cooperation of higher education and, if successfully implemented, would likely increase pressures for similar initiatives in higher education.

C. Barriers to Cooperation between K–12 Education and Higher Education

Just as it is not difficult to find areas of interconnection between K–12 education and higher education, it is not difficult to perceive why there are such interconnections. The two levels are, after all, two halves of a total education experience that now reaches from preschool education to advanced postdoctorate education. Neither level could perform its assigned and evolving roles if the other level did not exist or did not remain a going concern.

Nevertheless, the law and policy interconnections between K–12 and higher education for the most part have not been major concerns in the day-to-day functioning of the educators (or legal counsel) that serve colleges and universities or local school districts, nor have they been a priority of policy makers. In large part, this lack of concern has existed because, both historically and presently, the two levels of education have been operated and governed separately from each other to a remarkable degree. State governments, as well as the federal government, have maintained clear boundaries separating policy making and funding for each level from that for the other. As a result, education leaders at the two levels have not recognized or worked together on matters of mutual interest to anywhere near the extent that researchers and other outside observers might claim to be in the best interests of the total education enterprise.

Another factor that has apparently inhibited greater awareness and collaboration between the two levels has been the relative lack of data and analysis that unearths the subtleties of the law and policy interconnections or identifies and measures particular negative effects that policies and practices at one level may have on the other. Similarly, and partly because of the lack of data and analysis, there have been relatively few proven methods for resolving particular problems that arise when developments in K–12 education have negative effects on higher education or vice versa.

Fortunately, all of these factors inhibiting interaction between the two levels of education have been changing, quite rapidly, since the turn of the century. Various founda-

---

12. A Test of Leadership: Charting the Future of U.S. Higher Education, at 14, 18, 21 (U.S. Dept. of Education, 2006), available at ed.gov/about/bdscomm/list/hiedfuture/reports/final-report.pdf.
  13. *Id.* at p. 18.

tions, think tanks, governmental and nonprofit commissions, advocacy organizations, and some higher education institutions have conducted or sponsored research on matters of mutual concern to the two levels of education. Some of these same groups, as well as state agencies in various states, have undertaken demonstration projects and other initiatives to facilitate cooperation between the two levels. A number of the reports, papers, books, and policy statements that have resulted are cited and relied on in the remainder of this chapter.

II. Fiscal Inequities

Equity issues in higher education may be divided into three categories: equity in preparedness for college, equity in access to college, and equity in progressing through and completing college.[14] For K–12 education, a similar division may be made: equity in preparedness for elementary school or high school;[15] equity in access to particular schools, programs, or classes—for example, advanced placement courses;[16] and equity in progressing through the grade levels and the testing requirements that culminate in high school graduation. For each category, the focus is usually on students from racial and ethnic minority groups and, increasingly, on students from families of low socioeconomic status.[17]

Various recent studies have indicated that as a nation, we are not doing well in promoting equity for these groups in either K–12 or higher education. "Gauging Student Learning," a report issued by the Editorial Projects in Education Research Center in January 2007, surveys inequities in K–12 education.[18] A report issued by the Education Trust in August 2006, *Promise Abandoned*, uses national data sets to survey inequities in higher education.[19] This report paints a disturbing picture, concluding that "Instead of expand-

---

14. *See generally* Thomas Bailey & Vanessa Morest (eds.), Defending the Community College Equity Agenda (Johns Hopkins University, 2006).

15. One of the main factors regarding preparedness for elementary school is inequity in access to preschool (or pre-K) education. This factor has become increasingly important and is attracting considerable attention. *See, e.g.,* Comn. for Economic Development, The Economic Promise of Investing in High Quality Preschool: Using Early Education to Improve Economic Growth and the Fiscal Sustainability of States and the Nation (2006), available at www.ced.org/docs/report/report_prek_econpromise.pdf.

16. The Washington Post prepares an annual "Post Challenge Index" that compares high schools across the United States on the basis of student participation in AP and IB (International Baccalaureate) tests. The index shows substantial variances among schools in student participation—variances that suggest substantial inequities in access to these courses and tests. To see the 2005, 2006, and 2007 Challenge Indexes, go to projects.washingtonpost.com/challengeindex/local/.

17. *See, e.g.,* William Bowen, Martin Kurzweil, & Eugene Tobin, Equity and Excellence in American Higher Education (U. Va. Press, 2005).

18. *Gauging Student Learning*, Quality Counts 2007: From Cradle to Career (Education Week, 2007), available at www.edweek.org/go/qc07. *See also* Peter Sacks, Tearing Down The Gates: Confronting The Class Divide in American Education (U. Cal. Press, 2007).

19. Kati Haycock, Promise Abandoned: How Policy Choices and Institutional Practices Restrict College Opportunities (Education Trust, 2006) 1–20, available at www2.edtrust.org/EdTrust/Promise+Abandoned+Report.htm; quoted below with permission. *See also Gated Communities of Higher Education*, in Postsecondary Education Opportunity, March 2007; Indicators of Opportunity in Higher Education: 2005 Status Report (Pell Institute, 2005), available at www.pellinstitute.org/files/6_Indicators.pdf; Timpane & Hauptman, *Improving the Academic Preparation and Performance of Low-Income Students in American Higher Education*, in Richard Kahlenberg

ing and equalizing opportunity in our country, much of higher education has simply become another agent of stratification."[20]

Various findings in the report support this conclusion, including these:

- "Only about one-half of all '*college-qualified*' students from low-income families enter a four-year college, compared to over 80 percent of similarly qualified students from high-income families."[21]

- "Among the *best-prepared* students in the country ... more than 20 percent of those from low-income families don't go directly on to college. Among high achievers from high-income families, only 3 percent don't enter college right away."[22]

- "From 1995 to 2003 ... the portion of institutional aid awarded to low-income students shrunk from 56 percent to 35 percent in public colleges and from 44 percent to 27 percent in private colleges."[23]

- "College costs rapidly escalate without the commensurate increases in student aid necessary to help low-income families pay those costs."[24]

- "Through a set of practices known as enrollment management, leaders in both public and private four-year colleges increasingly are choosing to use their resources to compete with each other for high-end, high-scoring students instead of providing a chance for college-qualified students from low-income families who cannot attend college without adequate financial support."[25]

- "For the low-income, minority, and first-generation students who do get into four-year colleges and universities, frequent institutional indifference to their success has a similar effect on how many of them actually get a college degree. Yes, some colleges work at eliminating unnecessary obstacles to timely graduation. For far too many colleges, though, institutional responsibility stops at giving students access to college, and student success is often left up to the students themselves."[26]

- "By age 24, 75 percent of students from the top income quartile receive Bachelor's degrees. For students growing up in low-income families, on the other hand, ... fewer than 9 percent ... will earn a bachelor's degree by 24."[27]

- "Only about 40 percent of African-American *freshmen* and 47 percent of Latino *freshmen* obtain bachelor's degrees within six years, compared to 59 percent of White *freshmen* and 66 percent of Asian *freshmen*." "African-Americans between 25 and 29 attain ... bachelor's degrees at nearly one-half—and Latinos at one-third—the rate of Whites."[28]

- "Instead of gradually getting better, most of these gaps are getting worse."[29]

(ed.), AMERICA'S UNTAPPED RESOURCE: LOW-INCOME STUDENTS IN HIGHER EDUCATION (Century Foundation Press, 2004).

20. PROMISE ABANDONED, p. 1.
21. *Id.*, p. 8 (emphasis added).
22. *Id.*, p. 3 (emphasis added).
23. *Id.*, p. 8.
24. *Id.*, p. 2.
25. *Id.*
26. *Id.*
27. *Id.*
28. *Id.*, pp. 2, 10 (emphasis added).
29. *Id.*, p. 2. The material quoted in the text accompanying notes 20–29 is quoted with the permission of the copyright holder, The Education Trust; *see supra* note 19 and accompanying text.

Various factors contribute to these inequities, including some that may affect students even before their formal schooling begins.[30] Some of these factors derive from inequities in K–12 education, whose effects are then passed on to higher education. For K–12 education, the factor that usually receives the most attention is government funding for education. If government spends less money (on an average dollars per student basis) on schools with concentrations of low-income students or of minority students, it is argued, then these students have less opportunity to progress academically, compared with students in better funded schools that do not have such concentrations of low-income or minority students.

The available data demonstrates that there are such disparities in funding—often called "funding gaps"—that serve to disadvantage low-income[31] and minority students in many schools and school districts nationwide. According to *Funding Gaps 2006*, the sixth in a series of annual funding reports by the Education Trust,

> Even as we've extended a free public education to all children, we've rigged the system against the success of some of our most vulnerable children. How do we do that? By taking the children who arrive at school with the greatest needs and giving them less in school. Our low-income and minority students, in particular, get less of what matters most; these students get the fewest experienced and well-educated teachers, the least rigorous curriculum, and the lowest quality facilities.
>
> At the core of these inequities is a set of school finance policy choices that systematically shortchange low-income and minority students and the schools and districts that serve them.[32]

As *Funding Gaps 2006* demonstrates, in K–12 education there are inequities on three levels. At the state level, some states are poorer than others, with less money to spend on education but greater concentrations of low-income students ("interstate inequities"). At the local school district level, in many states, districts with the greatest concentrations of low-income students or minority students have less money available for education than districts with the smallest concentrations of low-income or minority students ("interdistrict inequities"). At the level of individual schools, in many districts, less money is allocated to schools with concentrations of low-income or minority students than to schools without such concentrations ("intra-district inequities"). In addition, there are funding inequities evident in many of the largest urban areas in the United States ("metropolitan inequities"), where central city school districts with high concentrations of low-

---

30. *See, e.g.,* Valerie Lee & David Burkam, Inequality at the Starting Gate: Social Background Differences in Achievement as Children Begin School (Economic Policy Institute, 2002), available at www.epinet.org/books/starting_gate.html; and *see generally* C. Michael Henry (ed.), Race, Poverty, and Domestic Policy (Yale Univ. Press, 2004).

31. Commentators and researchers sometimes use the term "low-income" rather than "low socioeconomic status" to describe the class of students that is subjected to fiscal and other inequities in education. "Low income" is more easily quantifiable than "low socioeconomic status" and is thus often used in data studies such as the one that is discussed next. But "low socioeconomic status" is more descriptive than "low income," since the disadvantages affecting this class of students are not solely the result of the family's low income. *See, e.g.,* Bowen, Kurzweil, & Tobin, note 17 *supra,* at 77–79, 90, 226, 228, 251. This chapter generally uses the term "low socioeconomic status" but switches to the term "low income" when discussing a study using that term.

32. Liu, Wiener, Pristoop, & Roza, Funding Gaps 2006 (Education Trust, 2006), p. 1, available at www.edtrust.org. *See also* Jonathan Kozol, The Shame of the Nation (Three Rivers Press, 2005), pp. 244–248.

income and minority students have substantially less funding per student than the sur-rounding suburban school districts.[33]

Such funding inequities have been evident and a source of controversy for many years. In the late 1960s, concerned interest groups and parents began challenging these inequities in court—in particular the inequities among local school districts that are created or perpetuated by a state's system of public school finance. Evidence of glaring inter-district inequities was introduced in these lawsuits, along with various legal theories for finding these inequities to be unconstitutional.[34] This litigation has continued into the twenty-first century. State courts have found many state systems to be unconstitutional under their state constitutions, which has necessitated state legislation to "fix" the unconstitutional school finance system, which in turn has led to future lawsuits challenging the new leg-islation.[35] Along the way, a dichotomy developed between genuine "equity" lawsuits, whose goal was to equalize, across school districts, the financial resources available for K–12 ed-ucation, and "adequacy" lawsuits, whose goal was to ensure that all districts had suffi-cient resources to provide an "adequate" education to each student in the district.[36] Over time, and increasingly through the "adequacy" approach, improvements have been made in the state school finance systems.[37] Despite this long-running saga of interrelated judi-cial and legislative activity, however, serious and widespread inequities remain.[38]

The *Funding Gaps 2006* report summarizes the school finance data and conclusions based on the data, as follows:

> In 26 of the 49 states studied, the highest poverty school districts receive fewer resources than the lowest poverty school districts.... [A]cross the country [in the aggregate] state and local funds provide $825 per student less in the highest poverty districts than in the most affluent districts.... [S]tates ... that allow fund-ing gaps to persist ... are compounding the disadvantages that low-income stu-dents face outside of school and undercutting public education's ability to act as an engine of social mobility.
>
> In 28 states, high-minority districts receive less state and local money for each child than low-minority districts. Across the country [in the aggregate] $908 less per student is spent on students in the districts educating the most students of color, as compared to the districts educating the fewest students of color.[39]

33. *See* Kozol, *supra* note 32 at 321–325 (appendix).

34. *See, e.g., San Antonio Indep. School District v. Rodriquez*, 411 U.S. 1 (1973); *Serrano v. Priest*; 487 P.2d 1241 (Cal. 1971) ("Serrano I").

35. *See generally* Paula Lundberg, *State Courts and School Funding: A Fifty State Analysis*, 63 Alb. L. Rev. 1101 (2000).

36. Compare *Serrano v. Priest*, *supra* note 34, with *Robinson v. Cahill*, 303 A.2d 273 (N.J. 1973) ("Robinson I"); and *see generally* Michael Heise, *Equal Educational Opportunity, Hollow Victories, and the Demise of School Finance Equity Theory*, 32 Ga. L. Rev. 543 (1998).

37. For an illustrative case study, focusing on New Jersey, *see* Catherine Gewertz, *A Level Playing Field*, in Quality Counts 2005: No Small Change, Education Week, Jan. 6, 2005, vol. 24, issue 17, p. 41. *See also*, regarding New York State, Brian Nickerson & Gerard Deehihan, *From Equity to Ade-quacy: The Legal Battle for Increased State Funding of Poor School Districts in New York*, 30 Fordham Urban L. J. 1341 (2003).

38. In addition to the data that follow on inter-district fiscal inequalities, a variety of other data, much of it broken down by state, can be found in Quality Counts 2005, *supra* note 37, Education Week, Jan. 6, 2005, vol. 24, issue17. *See generally*, Koski & Reich, *When "Adequate" Isn't: The Retreat from Equality in Law and Policy and Why It Matters*, 56 Emory L. J. 545 (2006).

39. Funding Gaps 2006, *supra* note 32, at 1–6. Carmen Arroyo, FUNDING GAP 2007 (Educa-tion Trust, 2008), also available on the Education Trust's web site, indicates improvements in some states and backsliding in others.

Why should colleges and universities care about these inequities in K–12 education? The most obvious reason is because their effects carry over into higher education and may be perpetuated there. Data from the *Promise Abandoned* report support this conclusion with respect to a range of effects.[40] Moreover, the inequities fostered at the K–12 level may be exacerbated at the higher education level, or new inequities may be created, with effects more pronounced than would have been the case had there not been substantial inequities in K–12 education. A clear example is the current systems for providing and allocating student financial aid, which create inequity in access to college.[41]

For higher education leaders, therefore, pressing questions arise concerning how they can avoid perpetuating inequities that arise from K–12 education and how they can desist from fostering any new inequities. Such questions implicate the recruitment functions, the admissions functions, the financial aid functions, the academic and social support functions, and perhaps other functions of individual colleges and universities. At the same time, fiscal inequity issues at both levels of education raise broader public policy questions, for K–12 education and higher education policy makers in state governments and the federal government, concerning how to alleviate fiscal inequities throughout this nation's educational system and how K–12 and higher education might collaborate in this crucial endeavor.

III. Resegregation

A. Segregation, Resegregation, and Affirmative Action

Just as recent studies indicate that, as a nation, we are not doing well in promoting fiscal equity in our educational systems (see part II), other recent studies suggest that we are backsliding in our promotion of racial and ethnic integration or diversity. As one recent report put the matter,

> the trends shown in this report are those of increasing isolation and profound inequality [in the nation's public schools]. The consequences become larger each year because of the growing number and percentage of nonwhite and impoverished students and the dramatic relationships between educational attainment and economic success in a globalized economy.[42]

---

40. Promise Abandoned, *supra* notes 19–29. *See also* Danette Gerald & Kati Haycock, Engines of Inequality: Diminishing Equity in the Nation's Premier Public Universities (Education Trust, 2006); National Center for Education Statistics, Placing College Graduation Rates in Context: How 4-Year College Graduation Rates Vary with Selectivity and the Size of Low-Income Enrollment (U.S. Department of Education, 2006); and *see generally* Bowen, et al., *supra* note 17.

41. *See, e.g.*, Advisory Committee on Student Financial Assistance, Mortgaging Our Future: How Financial Barriers to College Undercut America's Global Competitiveness (2006), available at www.ed.gov/acsfa; Edward St. John, et al., Expanding College Access: The Impact of State Finance Strategies (Lumina Foundation, 2004), available at www.luminafoundation.org; Lawrence Gladieux, *Low-Income Students and Affordability of Higher Education*, in Kahlenberg, *supra* note 19.

42. Gary Orfield & Chungmei Lee, Historic Reversals, Accelerating Resegregation, and the Need for New Integration Strategies (Civil Rights Project, UCLA, Aug. 2007), pp. 3–4, available at www.civilrightsproject.ucla.edu/research/deseg/reversals_reseg-need.pdf. The data documenting these trends are on pp. 13–45 of the report. Recommendations for alleviating racial isolation and resegregation in the schools are on pp. 49–50.

This problem in K–12 education manifests itself primarily through the phenomenon of "resegregation" of schools and school districts previously desegregated by court decree or by voluntary action. In higher education, the problem manifests itself primarily in a retreat, sometimes legally compelled, from affirmative action plans for admissions and financial aid that explicitly take race into account to foster student body diversity.

In general, racial segregation in education occurs when the racial composition of the student population of a particular public school (or school program) diverges substantially from the overall student racial composition of the district's schools. When the divergence is particularly great—as, for example, when a school has a black student population of 90 percent even though the total student population of the district's schools is only 10 percent black, the school is often called a "racially isolated" school. Colleges and universities (and individual programs) may also be racially segregated, but the segregation may be measured in a different way.

Not all racial segregation in education is unlawful. Ever since *Brown v. Board of Education* in 1954, courts have distinguished between de jure segregation—which is mandated or purposefully facilitated by government—and de facto segregation—which is caused by private forces such as families' voluntary private choices of where to live or, in higher education, students' voluntary private choices of what college to attend. When a court finds segregation to be de jure, the school district (or college) must take affirmative steps to dismantle the present effects of the segregation it has caused. When the segregation is de facto, however, government has no legal duty to undo it, at least not under the federal Constitution and federal law.

That de facto racial segregation in education is generally not unlawful, however, does not mean that it is desirable or beneficial, either in terms of education policy or of public policy.[43] Educators, policy analysts, and public policy makers have therefore often argued that public school districts, and colleges and universities, should take affirmative steps to alleviate de facto segregation and its negative effects. In this context, questions have often arisen concerning whether government may voluntarily choose to take actions that would alleviate the de facto segregation or increase student diversity in a particular school district, college, or university. Plans for doing so, sometimes called "voluntary affirmative action plans," may assign or select students partly on the basis of race (sometimes called "reverse discrimination"). In such circumstances, contentious legal and policy issues frequently arise.[44] Beginning around the end of the 1990s, these issues have taken

---

43. "Socioeconomic segregation," that is, segregation of students by family income or socioeconomic status, may also occur in public school districts. Such segregation is generally de facto and not unlawful but, as with de facto racial segregation, may nevertheless be undesirable as a matter of policy. For this reason, some school districts have recently adopted school assignment plans that take family income and related factors into account, with the goal of facilitating socioeconomic diversity of student bodies. School boards may expect that such plans will also foster racial diversity, but that is not necessarily the case. *See* Jonathan Glater & Alan Finder, *Diversity Plans Based on Income Leave Some Schools Segregated*, New York Times, July 15, 2007, at A-24.

44. Due to such controversies regarding race-based affirmative action, some colleges and universities recently have adopted or are considering admissions plans that take socioeconomic status into account in lieu of race (class-based affirmative action). The reasoning is usually that race and low income are sufficiently correlated that increasing socioeconomic diversity will at the same time increase racial diversity. (For examples regarding K–12 education, see *supra* note 43; for examples regarding higher education, see Kathleen Sullivan, *After Affirmative Action*, 59 Ohio State L. J. 1039 (1998)). Although promotion of socioeconomic diversity would likely have some positive effect on racial and ethnic diversity as well, the effect is likely to be considerably less than what would result from a plan that explicitly takes race into account. See Bowen, et al., *supra* note 17, at 183–85, 361 n. 67.

on new force and urgency as a result of data demonstrating that across much of the nation, public schools that had been desegregated by court decree in the post–*Brown v. Board of Education* era are becoming resegregated, arguably by forces that would be considered de facto.

Higher education cases on voluntary affirmative action in admissions reached the U.S. Supreme Court before K–12 cases on student assignment plans. An early (now classic) case is the *Bakke* case decided in 1978,[45] which invalidated an admissions plan of the University of California–Davis medical school and, through the various opinions of the justices, set the legal parameters for the ensuing debate. Similar issues returned to the Court twenty-five years later in *Grutter v. Bollinger*[46] and *Gratz v. Bollinger*,[47] companion cases involving two affirmative action admissions plans used at the University of Michigan. In upholding the law school plan and invalidating the undergraduate plan, the Court set out the law on voluntary, race-conscious plans for admissions.[48]

Most recently, in the 2007 case of *Parents Involved in Community Schools v. Seattle School District No. 1*,[49] the Court decided its first major case on student assignment plans in K–12 education, using basically the same principles it had used for voluntary affirmative action plans. The case concerned race-conscious student assignment plans used by two school districts (one in Seattle, Washington, and one in Louisville [Jefferson County], Kentucky) as a means for achieving racial diversity in K–12 education. By a vote of five to four, the Court held that these plans used racial classifications in way that violated the Fourteenth Amendment's equal protection clause in the U.S. Constitution.

B. The *Seattle School District* Case

To understand the *Seattle School District* case, it is necessary to understand the divisions within the Court. There were five opinions issued in the case. The lead opinion by Chief Justice Roberts contains four parts and various subparts, some of which speak for a majority of five justices, and others of which speak for a plurality of four justices. Justice Kennedy provided the fifth vote for the parts that speak for a majority and declined to support the parts that speak only for a plurality. In addition to the Roberts opinion, there are concurring opinions by Justice Kennedy (for himself alone) and Justice Thomas (for himself alone) and dissenting opinions by Justice Breyer (for four justices) and Justice Stevens (for himself alone).

The case's legal significance can be uncovered and elucidated by comparing and contrasting the Roberts, Kennedy, and Breyer opinions. One can discern two areas of great significance: (1) the case reaffirms the *Grutter* and *Gratz* requirements that colleges and universities must meet for a valid race-based admissions plan—but at the same time tightens up these requirements, thus signaling that courts should strictly enforce them in future cases; (2) the case makes it exceedingly difficult for K–12 school districts to justify any consideration of race in a voluntary plan for assigning students to schools (or programs) so as to alleviate de facto segregation or resegregation. This part of the chap-

---

45. *Regents of the University of California v. Bakke*, 438 U.S. 265 (1978).
46. 539 U.S. 306 (2003).
47. 539 U.S. 244 (2003)
48. *See generally* Kaplin & Lee, *supra* note 8, sec. 8.2.5.
49. 127 S.Ct. 2738 (2007).

ter focuses primarily on the second aspect of the case.[50] The emphasis is on how the Court's ruling serves to interconnect K–12 and higher education with respect to their mutual interest in racial diversity.

Chief Justice Roberts's opinion in the *Seattle School District* case emphasizes the strictness of the "strict scrutiny review" applicable to K–12 student assignment plans that employ racial classifications and indicates that courts are not to accord any deference to a school district's judgments about the importance of racial diversity to its educational mission. According to the chief justice, the two plans before the Court both failed strict scrutiny review — in part because the school districts' alleged interests were essentially interests in racial balancing or racial proportionality, which are not "compelling" interests, and in part because the plans' provisions were not "narrowly tailored" to the achievement of any compelling interest.

In particular, the Roberts opinion emphasizes the importance of the requirement that school districts identify and consider race-neutral alternatives before employing any racial classification in a student assignment plan. This requirement, in fact, was central to the Court's holding that the two student assignment plans at issue in the case both violated the equal protection clause. The Seattle School District had rejected race-neutral alternatives "with little or no consideration"; and Jefferson County had "failed to present any evidence that it considered alternatives." The Roberts opinion also emphasizes that school districts have the burden of proving that "the way in which they have employed individual racial classifications is necessary to achieve their stated ends"; and that the use of racial classifications must be "indispensable" to achieving the school district's diversity objectives and may be used only "as 'a last resort.'"[51] (Justice Kennedy used the same quoted language to make this same point in his concurring opinion in the *Seattle School District* case.[52])

Because Justice Kennedy provided the fifth vote for some, but not all, of Chief Justice Roberts's opinion, Kennedy's separate concurring opinion assumes particular importance. The Roberts opinion — its reasoning and the implications of its reasoning — may be considered law and an authoritative guide to what the courts will do in future cases, only to the extent that Justice Kennedy agrees with this reasoning and its implications. It is critical, then, to determine how Justice Kennedy's analysis differs from that of Chief Justice Roberts.

Justice Kennedy's opinion is consistent with the Roberts opinion in insisting on a vigorous "strict scrutiny review" for student assignment plans that employ racial classifications. But within this strict scrutiny framework, Justice Kennedy, unlike Chief Justice Roberts, takes pains to carve out some room for the permissible use of race-conscious measures. According to Justice Kennedy,

> Parts of the opinion by THE CHIEF JUSTICE imply an all-too-unyielding insistence that race cannot be a factor in instances when, in my view, it may be taken into account. The [Roberts] opinion is too dismissive of the legitimate interest government has in ensuring all people have equal opportunity regardless of their race.[53]

---

50. For analysis of the first aspect of the case, see W. Kaplin & B. Lee, The Law of Higher Education, 4th ed. (Jossey-Bass, 2006), Sec. 8.2.5 update, available at www.nacua.org/publications/lohe/Updates/Updates082707.doc.

51. 127 S.Ct. at 2759–61 (Roberts, C.J., for the majority), quoting *Richmond v. Croson*, 488 U.S. at 519 (Kennedy, J., concurring).

52. 127 S.Ct. at 2792.

53. 127 S.Ct. at 2791 (Kennedy, J., concurring).

In explanation, the Kennedy opinion then emphasizes that the concept of a "color-blind" Constitution is "an aspiration [that] must command our assent," but that "in the real world, it is regrettable to say, it cannot be a universal constitutional principle."[54]

Justice Kennedy's differences with Chief Justice Roberts manifest themselves in the "compelling interest" analysis that is one component of strict scrutiny review. (The other component, "narrow tailoring" analysis, is discussed shortly.) Justice Kennedy is more amenable than the chief justice to finding compelling interests sufficient to support race-conscious plans. Whereas the chief justice rejected the school districts' compelling interest claims, Justice Kennedy did not. Instead, Justice Kennedy determined that for K–12 education, a "compelling interest exists in avoiding racial isolation [of students]" and that it is "a compelling interest to achieve a diverse student population," with "race [being] one component of that diversity."[55] In these respects, Justice Kennedy is aligned with the four dissenting justices rather than with the four justices joining in the Roberts opinion, thus making the Kennedy view the majority view.

Regarding the other component of strict scrutiny review, "narrow-tailoring," the Kennedy opinion is consistent with the Roberts opinion. For his part, Justice Kennedy asserts that to comply with narrow tailoring, a school "must establish, *in detail*, how decisions based on an individual student's race are made," including "who makes the decisions; what if any oversight is employed; [and] the *precise* circumstances in which" race will be used in making decisions.[56] The four justices joining the Roberts opinion would apparently agree with these requirements, making them the majority view.

Of broader significance, Justice Kennedy's opinion emphasizes that in his view, there are other "race conscious measures," beyond using racial classifications in student assignment plans, that "school boards may [use to] pursue the goal of bringing together students of diverse backgrounds and races." Examples that Justice Kennedy used include "strategic site selection of new schools; drawing attendance zones with general recognition of the demographics of neighborhoods; allocating resources for special programs; [and] recruiting students and faculty in a targeted fashion." According to the Kennedy opinion: "These mechanisms are race conscious but do not lead to different treatment based on a classification that tells each student he or she is to be defined by race, so it is unlikely any of them would demand strict scrutiny to be found permissible."[57]

The Roberts opinion makes a similar point that may be supportive of at least part of Justice Kennedy's position. Chief Justice Roberts suggested that there may be "other means for achieving greater racial diversity in schools" that are not precluded by the *Seattle School District* ruling and could be constitutional. The examples Roberts used include "set[ting] measurable objectives to track the achievement of students from major racial and ethnic groups," as well as decisions on "where to construct new schools, how to allocate resources among schools, and which academic offerings to provide to attract students to certain schools." The first example, Roberts said, "has nothing to do with the pertinent issues" in the *Seattle School District* case; the other examples "implicate different considerations than the explicit racial classifications at issue" in the case.[58] Taking account of the character of these examples, Chief Justice Roberts's suggestion seems to be that some race-conscious planning and some race-conscious programs could be permissible when race is

54. 127 S.Ct. at 2791–92 (Kennedy, J., concurring).
55. 127 S.Ct. at 2797 (Kennedy, J. concurring).
56. 127 S. Ct. at 2789–90 (emphasis added).
57. 127 S.Ct. at 2792 (Kennedy, J. concurring).
58. 127 S.Ct. at 2766 (Roberts, C.J., for a plurality).

not used as a criterion for making decisions about particular individuals. To the extent that the Kennedy reasoning is consistent with this Roberts reasoning, the Kennedy reasoning becomes a majority view (indeed, a view that all the dissenters would apparently accept as well).

C. Longer Term Implications of the *Seattle School District* Case

The growth of resegregation of the nation's public schools is a well-documented phenomenon.[59] Dissenting in the *Seattle School District* case, Justice Breyer reviewed the data on resegregation. He explained that despite gains in desegregating schools in the 1970s and 1980s, "progress has stalled" since then. In the 1990s, the percentage of children attending segregated schools "reversed direction," with the percentages rising rather than falling. For example, "between 1968 and 1980, the number of black children attending school where minority children constituted more than half of the school fell from 77% to 63% in the Nation," but by 2000 the figure had risen "from 63% to 72% in the Nation." Similarly, between 1968 and 1980, the number of black children attending schools that were "more than 90% minority fell from 64% to 33% in the Nation" but by 2000 had risen from 33 percent to 37 percent.[60]

Justice Breyer then asserted (for four justices) that, given the current conditions depicted by the data, school districts have a "compelling interest" in "continuing to combat the remnants of segregation caused in whole or in part by ... school-related policies, which have often affected not only schools, but also housing patterns, employment practices, economic conditions, and social attitudes." This interest, Breyer claimed, "has its roots in preventing what gradually may become the *de facto* resegregation of America's public schools." Similarly, according to Justice Breyer, school districts have "an interest in overcoming the adverse educational effects produced by and associated with highly segregated schools."[61] Justice Kennedy, in his separate concurring opinion, appears to agree with some of the reasoning and sentiments in these parts of the Breyer dissenting opinion.[62]

In contrast to Justice Breyer's dissent, Chief Justice Roberts's opinion in the *Seattle School District* case rejects the premise that the school district interests identified by Justice Breyer are "compelling" interests in the context of this case and asserts that even if these interests were compelling, the school districts' student assignment plans would still fail strict scrutiny review because they are not "narrowly tailored" to accomplish these interests. (Justice Kennedy did not join this part of the Roberts opinion.)

What effect would the Roberts opinion's reasoning have on K–12 public education in the future? Justice Breyer's answer to this question is clear: "The Court's decision today

---

59. *See, e.g.,* Gary Orfield & Chungmei Lee, *Racial Transformation and the Changing Nature of Segregation* (Civ. Rts. Project at Harvard, 2006), available at www.civilrightsproject.ucla.edu/research/deseg/deseg06.php; Frankenberg, et al., *supra* note 2.

60. 127 S.Ct. at 2801–02 (Breyer, J., dissenting); see also 127 S.Ct. at 2833, 2837–39 (Breyer, J., dissenting). For comparable data cited in the 2003 *Grutter* and *Gratz* cases, see 539 U.S. at 345 (Ginsburg, J., concurring in *Grutter*); 539 U.S. at 298–301 (Ginsburg, J., dissenting in *Gratz*).

61. 127 S.Ct. at 2801–02 (Breyer, J. dissenting).

62. *See supra* note 55 and accompanying text. *See also* 127 S.Ct. at 2789, 2791 (Kennedy, J. concurring).

slows down and sets back the work of local school boards to bring about racially diverse schools." It "will obstruct efforts by state and local governments to deal effectively with the growing resegregation of public schools," and it "undermines *Brown* [*v. Board of Education*'s] promise of integrated primary and secondary education that local communities have sought to make a reality."[63] Justice Breyer's conclusions are supported by the fact that many hundreds of school districts had used or were then using student assignment plans that took the student's race into account.[64]

Such negative effects flowing from the *Seattle School District* case would be most apparent if future courts follow the reasoning of the four justices that join all parts of the Roberts opinion. If later courts instead follow the reasoning of the Kennedy opinion, the potential negative effects would be alleviated to some significant extent.

From this understanding of the *Seattle School District* case and its potential effect on initiatives to combat resegregation in K–12 education, we can also perceive the potential, longer range effects of the case on higher education. In the *Grutter* and *Gratz* higher education cases, the many *amicus curiae* briefs filed in the cases made clear that colleges and universities are strong proponents of racial and ethnic diversity. The prevailing view is that racial and ethnic diversity has educational benefits for higher education, as well as civic benefits for the nation, and realizing such benefits is an important part of the mission of most institutions. This view was adopted by the Court in the *Grutter* case.[65] How institutions approach issues of diversity, however, and how hard they have to work to achieve diversity objectives, depends in large part on the extent of racial diversity in the nation's elementary and secondary schools.

To the extent that large numbers of K–12 schools become or remain racially isolated, for example, these schools will be hindered in doing the work of "promoting 'cross-racial understanding,'... break[ing] down racial stereotypes, and enabl[ing] students to better understand persons of different races.'"[66] Consequently, the burden of playing "catch up" with this important work would fall on higher education. Similarly, if racially isolated K–12 schools tend to be environments that are less amenable to learning and that disproportionately place minority students at risk,[67] then these schools will graduate fewer minority students qualified and prepared for higher education. Consequently, the applicant pools for higher educational institutions would not become more diverse over time, and could become less diverse, making it more difficult for institutions to achieve racial and ethnic diversity of their student bodies. Some institutions may lower their expectations and settle for less diversity. Other institutions may be led to admit students who are to some extent unqualified and then cure these deficits through offering remedial courses. Either way, there could be substantial negative effects on the institution.

---

63. 127 S.Ct. at 2835, 2800.

64. *See* 127 S.Ct. at 2831–33 (Breyer, J., dissenting); *see also* Brief of [State Attorney Generals] as Amici Curiae, at 3–10, filed in the *Seattle School District* case, available at naacpldf.org/volint/add-docs/volint-school-amicus.html.

65. 539 U.S. at 330–33 (Justice O'Connor for the majority).

66. *Id.* at 330.

67. *See* 127 S.Ct. at 2820–21 (Breyer, J., dissenting); *see also* Brief of the American Education Research Ass'n as Amicus Curiae, Brief for Amici Curiae The American Psychological Ass'n and The Washington State Psychological Ass'n, and Brief of 553 Social Scientists as Amici Curiae, all filed in the *Seattle School District* case, available at naacpldf.org/volint/add-docs/volint-school-amicus.html. In addition, *see generally* Erica Frankenberg & Gary Orfield (eds.), LESSONS IN INTEGRATION: REALIZING THE PROMISE OF RACIAL DIVERSITY IN AMERICAN SCHOOLS (U. Va. Press, 2007).

Here is how one college president and recognized expert on race relations put the matter in an interview conducted shortly after the U.S. Supreme Court had issued its decision in the *Seattle School District* case:

> For [Beverly Daniel] Tatum, the Spelman [College] president, the decision ... [has] all sorts of implications.... By making it more difficult for school districts to desegregate, or to promote diverse student bodies in areas that are racially segregated in terms of housing, Tatum said, more students are going to grow up without meaningful interaction with students from other racial and ethnic groups.

> "What this means is that their views are going to be based on stereotypes," she said, and ... that leads to all kinds of insensitivities and incidents on college campuses.

> Tatum ... said that colleges are going to need to do "remedial work" with students who don't know how to interact with those who are different from themselves....

> So too, she said, [the decision will hurt] the low-income, minority students whose reality isn't reflected by the Supreme Court's talk of a race-neutral society...."There is so much at risk now to students of color in K–12 who are concentrated in low-income areas."[68]

IV. K–12/Higher Education Collaboration and the Role of Governance

Historically and presently, the states have had the primary role in establishing, overseeing, and funding education. The states have generally proceeded along two tracks, one for K–12 (elementary/secondary) education and one for higher education. There are typically two state agencies responsible for education in each state: a state board of education for K–12 education, and a state board of higher education (sometimes along with a state community college board) for higher education. The state legislatures typically have different oversight committees or subcommittees, and appropriations committees or subcommittees, for K–12 education and higher education. The federal government, which entered this picture much later, has also generally treated the two levels of education separately, setting the tone in 1965 when Congress passed the Elementary and Secondary Education Act, followed by a separate Higher Education Act.

Because the missions and clienteles of the two levels of education are different from one another, the separation of governance structures has enabled policy makers at each level to implement the particular mission and serve the particular clientele of the level that they represent. The reasons for maintaining this bifurcated system have begun to break down, however, in a world in which competitiveness in a global economy and mastery of technology are key considerations, and in which college degrees become ever more important to individuals, and a college-educated workforce becomes ever more important to the nation. In such a world, education becomes more a continuum than a series

---

68. Scott Jaschik, *Mixed Messages on Affirmative Action*, Inside Higher Ed (June 29, 2007) at 4; available at insidehighered.com/layout/set/print/news/2007/06/29/affirm; *See generally*, Brief of Amici Curiae American Council on Education and 20 other Higher Education Organizations, filed in the *Seattle School District* case, available at naacpldf.org/volint/add-docs/volint-school-amicus.html.

of separate stages, and the two levels of education become more invested in each other's missions.[69]

The issue of college readiness or academic preparedness (see part I) provides an instructive example of how interdependence between higher education and K–12 education is increasing, and how existing governance structures inhibit actions that would harness this interdependence and foster collaboration. The Spellings Commission Report (see part I) included various findings and recommendations on "access and achievement gaps" between high school and college and their effect on higher education. One key finding was that "ample evidence demonstrates that a key component of our national achievement problem is insufficient alignment between K–12 and higher education"—that is, alignment of standards, assessments, and curriculum.[70] This finding is paired with a recommendation that "higher education must assume responsibility for working with the K–12 system to ensure that teachers are adequately trained, curricula are aligned and entrance standards are clear," the goal being a "seamless integration between high school and college."[71] Responding to this report, the American Council on Education and five other national associations agreed that college unpreparedness is "a systemic problem of breadth and depth that warrants focused and sustained attention by all parties invested in K–12 education, including the higher education community"; and that "one key to solving this problem is to better align high school curricula and graduation requirements with college-readiness standards."[72]

To deal effectively with this national problem of unpreparedness, especially as it disproportionately affects low-socioeconomic status students and minority students, it may become necessary to modify the bifurcated system of educational governance. In an issue paper prepared for the Spellings Commission, two authors argued that the "issues of ... disjuncture between K–12 and higher education and college readiness lack an immediate audience or constituency, and ... fall between the cracks of separate governance and policy systems.... The educational needs of students demand changes in the fundamental policies that created and now reinforce the chasm between K–12 and postsecondary education."[73] Similarly, in a 2005 report, "An Action Agenda for Improving America's High Schools," the national Governors' Association and Achieve, Inc., asserted that "the public education system [must] be made to function more cohesively." Specifically, at a minimum, states should set up a permanent statewide commission or roundtable to frame a common education agenda and track progress. Alternatively, states could develop a sin-

---

69. See generally Peter Schmidt, *Powerful Forces Draw Academe into the Fray*, CHRONICLE OF HIGHER EDUCATION (March 10, 2006) at B4; TOUGH CHOICES OR TOUGH TIMES: THE REPORT OF THE NEW COMMISSION ON THE SKILLS OF THE AMERICAN WORKFORCE (Jossey-Bass, 2006); COMM. FOR ECONOMIC DEVELOPMENT, *supra* note 15. See also, for data indicating that the United States' competitiveness, in terms of educating its workforce, is slipping, EDUCATION AT A GLANCE 2007 (Org. for Eco. Co-op and Devel., 2007), available at www.orcd.org/dataoecd/4/55/393/3286.pdf.

70. A TEST OF LEADERSHIP, *supra* note 12, at 8–9.

71. *Id.* at 17.

72. *Addressing the Challenges Facing American Undergraduate Education: A Letter to Our Members*, at 4–5 (Sept. 21, 2006), available at www.acenet.edu, under "2006 Press Releases." *See Looking Through a Wider Lens*, in QUALITY COUNTS 2007: FROM CRADLE TO CAREER (Education Week 2007), available at www.edweek.org/go/qc07; Christopher Swanson, CITIES IN CRISIS: A SPECIAL ANALYTIC REPORT ON HIGH SCHOOL GRADUATION (EPE Research Center, 2008), available at www.edweek.org/rc/articles/2008/04/01/cities_in_crisis.html.

73. Michael Kirst & Andrea Venezia, *Improving College Readiness and Success for All Students: A Joint Responsibility Between K–12 and Postsecondary Education* at 3–4 (2006), available at www.ed.gov/about/bdscomm/list/hiedfuture/reports/kirst_venezia.pdf.

gle education governing board and state education agency with authority over early child-hood, elementary, secondary, and postsecondary education.[74]

Numerous questions thus arise for state and federal policymakers for both K–12 education and higher education, as well as for national education associations and individual colleges and universities and school districts. What structures, for instance, would best facilitate cooperation between the two levels of education in resolving the college unpreparedness problem? What structures would best facilitate resolving the pressing problems concerning fiscal inequities and resegregation, in which the two levels have strong mutual interests? Do states need to formally "integrate governance structures across the education sectors," as suggested in the issue paper quoted? What role should the federal government play in the reform of governance structures? What role should the education associations play? What can individual colleges and universities and school districts do, working together in their localities, to improve governance structures at the local or regional level?

V. Examples of Current Cooperative Efforts

The growing interconnections between K–12 education and higher education, and the resultant problems and challenges that arise, have by no means escaped the attentions of all education leaders and policy analysts. There are many "pockets of progress" — important ongoing efforts, large and small — that provide a base on which other colleges and universities, school districts, and education associations can build. This part of the chapter lists examples of such efforts. It is not a comprehensive list.

- UCLA partners with local K–12 schools through the Teach LA Urban Internships program that provides and supports teachers for the L.A. public schools.[75]

- Various universities and researchers are collaborating with local K–12 schools to develop alternative models for teacher education, or for preservice and in-service teacher training, that emphasize cross-cultural learning and preparation for cross-cultural teaching in racially diverse or low-income urban schools. Some universities involved in such efforts also have degree programs emphasizing the recruitment and preparation of teachers of color.[76]

- The University of Southern California, through its Center for Higher Education Policy Analysis, operates a mentoring program (Increasing Access via Mentoring, or I AM) for graduating seniors in nine Los Angeles public high schools, focusing particularly on first-in-family, minority, and low-income students.[77]

- Coppin State University in Baltimore, Maryland, operates a public elementary school and a public high school, the former adjacent to the university's campus and the latter on the campus, with the goal of serving low-income and minority students and preparing them for college.[78]

---

74. The Action Agenda is available at www.achieve.org/files/actionagenda2005.pdf. See *id.* at 20 for the governance recommendations.

75. *See* centerx.gseis.ucla.edu/TLA.

76. *See, e.g.,* Christine Sleeter, *Preparing Teachers for Multiracial and Historically Underserved Schools,* in Lessons in Integration, *supra* note 67, at 171–89 (note especially 177–80 and 185–86).

77. *See* www.usc.edu/dept/chepa.

78. *See* "Growing the Talent Pool," Inside Higher Ed. (December 19, 2006).

- Arizona State University has established the "ASU Advantage" program and the "Sun Devil Promise" to pay college costs for Arizona students from low-income families and to provide related parent education programs, partnerships with elementary and secondary schools, and support programs for students entering college.[79]

- Philadelphia Futures, a nonprofit organization, operates a "Sponsor-A-Scholar" program that brings together selected urban neighborhood schools, their teachers and counselors, and area colleges and universities in a partnership to assist economically disadvantaged students to obtain a college education. The program provides promising students with an adult mentor, academic support, and guidance on college selection during high school, as well as financial assistance, academic support, and guidance during college.[80]

- Sinclair Community College in Dayton, Ohio; Mott Community College in Flint, Michigan; and other institutions provide college learning and career counseling for high school students under the auspices of the American Youth Policy Forum.[81]

- As part of a movement called "early college high schools," various colleges are partnering with local high schools to provide college-level classes, along with tutoring and other support, to disadvantaged and at-risk high school students.[82]

- Various universities, through their law schools, are participating in the Wingspread P20 Leadership Pipeline Consortium. The consortium's purpose, according to its mission statement, is to work "across the educational continuum to improve the participation, persistence, and success of diverse students in high school and college, with the goal of enhancing their aspirations and capacity to move into positions in the legal profession and in leadership of the nation."[83]

- Various states have adopted programs to support the education of low-income students by providing help in preparing for college and paying for college. Indiana, for example, has a Twenty-first Century Scholars Program, established in 1990, that provides financial and other support for selected low-income students from seventh grade through college.[84]

- With encouragement from the Education Trust and others, state higher education and K–12 leaders in various states have joined with state governors and business and community leaders to create state-level "K–16 initiatives" or "P-16 initiatives" that are developing strategies for cooperation and joint action between

79. *See* www.asu.edu/promise.

80. *See* philadelphiafutures.org.sas. Another example of such a partnership program is "Boston Connects," in which Boston College is a partner. *See* Alvin Sanoff, *Boston College Reaches Out to Students and Teachers in the City's Public Schools,* Chronicle of Higher Education, March 10, 2006, at B26.

81. *See* www.aypf.org. *See also Secondary–Postsecondary Learning Options: Mott Middle College and Miami Valley Tech Prep: A Forum,* available at www.aypf.org/forumbriefs/2006/fb092906.htm; Jennifer Brown Lerner & Betsy Brand, *The College Ladder: Linking Secondary and Postsecondary Education for Success for All Students,* AYPF 2006, an AYPF compendium describing and evaluating various other secondary–postsecondary learning options (SPLOs).

82. *See, e.g.,* M. A.Chandler, *A New Tack to Help High-Schoolers at Risk: College,* Washington Post, November 11, 2006, at A4:1. For a study of the positive effects of such "dual enrollment" programs, see Karp, Calcagno, Hughes, Jeong, & Baily, The Postsecondary Achievement of Participants in Dual Enrollment: An Analysis of Student Outcomes in Two States (Nat'l Research Center for Career and Technical Education 2007).

83. *See* www.mcgeorge.edu/government_law_and_policy/education_law/index.htm.

84. *See* www.jcsc.org/21st%20Century/Actual/home.html.

colleges and universities and K–12 schools. A related development is the "P-16 Council" movement that is spawning state, regional, and local councils whose task is to better align high school and college academic standards. Spinning off from or sometimes preceding these developments, individual colleges and universities have established local "K–16 partnerships" with schools or school districts in their vicinity.[85]

• Congress has created two new grant programs that supplement the TRIO programs originated in 1965 and the GEAR UP program originated in 1998. The new programs, the Academic Competitiveness Grant Program and the SMART Grant Program (National Science and Mathematics Access to Retain Talent) are designed to facilitate college access for low-income high school students.[86]

There is clearly a need for increased support, financial and otherwise, for such pockets of progress. There is a need for increased collaboration and coordination among the leaders of such efforts. There is a need for further evaluation of such efforts and expansion or replication of the most successful efforts. There is a need for additional, new types of initiatives that maintain a clear focus on assisting low-income and minority students— in particular initiatives that challenge the systemic features of American education that serve to create or perpetuate the types of inequities addressed in this chapter.

---

85. *See, e.g., State and Local K–16 Initiatives* at www.edtrust.org. *See generally* Peter Schmidt, *A Tough Task for the States: Efforts to Get Schools and Colleges to Cooperate Yield Both Fixes and Frustration,* Chronicle of Higher Education, March 10, 2006, at B6.

86. These programs, however, were not well received by the higher education community when they were being implemented. *See, e.g., Education Department Rebuffs Colleges on Rules,* Inside Higher Ed, November 2, 2006, available at insidehighered.com.

5

The NCLB, Race, Ethnicity, Class and Diversity: Promoting a High School to Law/Graduate School Pipeline for Under-Represented Students

Jodie Roure*

Introduction

The crisis faced by students of color and poor students attending New York City high schools and other similarly situated high schools in the United States cannot be properly addressed with the continued emphasis on standardized testing and accountability mechanisms promoted through legislation such as the NCLB. These heavy quantitative standardized assessments are ineffective in measuring the true problems faced by the groups which are labeled as "failing," groups that predominately consist of students of color, low-income students and English language learners.

This chapter examines how race, ethnicity, class and diversity are factors in assessing how the No Child Left Behind Act (NCLB) has failed students in the United States, with emphasis on New York City schools, and proposes a national high school to law/graduate

* Jodie Roure, B.A., Rutgers University, Douglass College; J.D., Western New England College School of Law; Ph.D., State University of New York, University of Buffalo; Assistant Professor of John Jay College of Criminal Justice, Puerto Rican/Latin American Studies Department, City University of New York; Project Investigator of the New York City Human Rights High School Curriculum Research Project and the John Jay College Ronald H. Brown Summer Law School Prep Program for College Students Research Project, the John Jay College satellite of the overall program, which is directed by St. John's University School of Law Professor Leonard Baynes. For valuable comments on earlier drafts, I am grateful to Jonathan Scott Beane, Jon Rafael Roure, Dr. Ezra Matthias and Jamie Nicole Roure. For helpful answers to data requests, I thank Professor Leonard Baynes, Dean Jose Luis Morin and Jon Rafael Roure. Woorahm Sean Yoo, Rachel Pierre, Howard Caro-Lopez and Valter Ulaj provided excellent research assistance. Professor Luis Barrios and Scott Kessler provided incredible overall support.

school pipeline model to effect change and improvement for all students. The New York City Human Rights High School Curriculum Research Project (NYCHRHSCRP), a high school to law/graduate school pipeline research initiative, can serve as a model for policy makers and legislators to develop more meaningful and effective approaches to their process of improving, repairing and rebuilding the United States high school education system.

This pilot research project presents more effective ways of increasing learning, retention and promotion of higher education for most students. It works with students of color and first-generation college students from low-income backgrounds. Both of these student groups include English language learners and recent immigrants. The pilot project aims to provide an intensive college-based support system for both teachers and students at two inner-city high schools that have high populations of "at-risk" students; the project's goal is to ensure that most of the project's students graduate from high school and gain admission to college. The program's students would be pipelined into an existing program in the Puerto Rican/Latin American Studies Department at John Jay College of Criminal Justice, City University of New York, titled the Ronald H. Brown Summer Law School Prep Program for College Students.[1]

The Ronald H. Brown Summer Law School Prep Program for College Students is a two-year program designed to expose to the study of law low income and first-generation college students or members of groups typically under-represented in law schools — such as Latinos, African Americans and Native Americans. On completion of the first year of the Ronald H. Brown Program, some of the John Jay College participants are successfully admitted to the John Jay College B.A./M.A. program, which allows students to obtain master's degrees while simultaneously completing their bachelor's degrees by adding one more year to their academic studies at John Jay College. The Puerto Rican/Latin American Studies Department/John Jay College component of the Ronald H. Brown Summer Law School Prep Program received full funding for 2007–2008 from the CUNY Black Male Initiative, directed by Elliott Dawes. This funding provided vital student support services which have helped facilitate the law school admissions of four John Jay College students. Many of these students have received partial and full tuition scholarships. To date, the overall program has eleven students that have been accepted to law schools throughout the country. NYCHRHSCRP is based on the success of this program and extends its reach to high school students in an effort to further their basic human right to a quality education and, simultaneously, create better citizens.

Such programs are sorely needed. The American Bar Association (ABA) Commission on Racial and Ethnic Diversity in the Profession reports that in 1999 only 5.7 percent of all those enrolled in law school nationwide were Latino, 7.4 percent African American, 6.3 percent Asian and less than 1 percent Native American.[2] For 1998, people of color made

---

1. This program is offered through a collaboration among St. John's University School of Law and John Jay College of Criminal Justice, Medgar Evers College/CUNY, York College/CUNY, and St. John's University undergraduate. *See* Leonard Baynes, Memorandum (describing the successes of the Ronald H. Brown Program) (July 30, 2007) (on file with author).

2. Elizabeth Chambliss, Miles to Go 2000: Progress of Minorities in the Legal Profession 3 (2000) (discussing the under-represented minorities' representation in the legal field to report to the ABA Commission on Racial and Ethnic Diversity).

up only 7 percent of all lawyers and only 3 percent of all partners in law firms.[3] Although the United States Census Bureau reports that Latinos have become the "largest minority community" in the United States, surpassing African Americans in total numbers,[4] Latinos are still extremely under-represented in the legal profession.[5] The scarcity of people of color is so acute that even the ABA concedes that the legal profession has one of the lowest levels of representation of people of color among all professions:

> Minority representation among lawyers lags well behind minority representation in most other professions. In 1998, African Americans and Hispanics made up 12.5 percent of all professionals, including 14.3 percent of accountants, 9.7 percent of physicians, 9.4 percent of college and university teachers, and 7.9 percent of engineers—but only 7 percent of lawyers. The professions with lower levels of minority representation were dentists (4.8 percent) and natural scientists (6.9 percent).[6]

In a recent study sponsored by the Puerto Rican Legal Defense and Education Fund, Angelo Falcón reported that the degree of Latino under-representation in the judiciary is extraordinarily high, and projected an almost insurmountable gap for the future, given the ever-increasing Latino population.[7] Raising grave concerns about fairness in the judicial system, Falcón warns that if current trends persist an even larger disparity would result, with the percentage of judges only growing slightly over time.[8] "By the year 2050 (when the Census conservatively projects the Hispanic-American population to reach 24.3 percent of the total population), the number of Hispanic-American judges would have grown to 4.7 percent in the federal courts and 5.3 percent in the state courts."[9]

The Utility of Human Rights as the Foundation of a High School Curriculum

The right to education is an internationally recognized fundamental human right and makes possible other fundamental human rights such as the right to self-determination, just and favorable conditions of work and the right to a healthy environment. The right to an education is a fundamental right that is found in most international and regional human rights instruments, including the Universal Declaration of Human Rights (Article Twenty-Six);[10] the Convention on the Elimination of All Forms of Discrimination

---

3. *Id.*

4. Press Release, U.S. Bureau of the Census, *Hispanic Population Reaches All-time High of 38.8 Million, New Census Estimates Show* (June 18, 2003), www.census.gov/Press-Release/www/2003/cb03-100.html; D'Vera Cohn, *Hispanics Declared Largest Minority; Blacks Overtaken in* Census, WASH. POST, June 19, 2003, at A1.

5. *See supra* note 2.

6. *See id.* at 2.

7. ANGELO FALCÓN, OPENING THE COURTHOUSE DOORS: THE NEED FOR MORE HISPANIC JUDGES 2 (2002).

8. *Id.* at 4.

9. *Id.*

10. Universal Declaration of Human Rights, G.A. Res. 217A, at 71, U.N. GAOR, 3d Sess., 1st plen. Mtg., U.N. Doc A/810 (Dec. 12, 1948).

Against Women (Articles Ten and Fourteen);[11] the Convention on the Rights of the Child (Articles Twenty-Eight, Twenty-Nine and Forty);[12] the American Declaration on the Rights and Duties of Man (Article Twelve);[13] and the Committee on the Elimination of Racial Discrimination (Article Five).[14] Article Thirteen of the International Covenant on Economic, Social and Cultural Rights (ICESCR) recognizes

> the right of everyone to education ... that education shall be directed to the full development of the human personality and the sense of its dignity, and ... that education shall enable all persons to participate effectively in a free society, promote understanding, tolerance and friendship among all nations and all racial, ethnic or religious groups, and further the activities of the United Nations for the maintenance of peace.[15]

In addition, according to Article Fourteen of ICESCR, compulsory primary education should be offered free of charge.[16]

In the U.S. educational system, however, deep inequalities in education persist despite human rights standards requiring that governments guarantee the right to education to all persons.[17] The wealthy receive a high level of quality education, and most poor students and students of color are barely afforded fundamental literacy proficiency.[18] Many local-

---

11. U.N. Convention on the Elimination of All Forms of Discrimination Against Women, opened for signature Mar. 1, 1980, 1249 U.N.T.S. 13 (entered into force Sept. 3, 1981).

12. Convention on the Rights of the Child, *opened for signature* Jan. 26, 1990, G.A. Res. 44/25, U.N. GAOR 61st. plen. mtg. at 166, U.N. Doc. A/44/736 (1989), *reprinted in* 28 I.L.M. 1448 (1989) with corrections at 29 I.L.M. 1340 (1990).

13. O.A.S. Res. XXX, adopted by the Ninth International Conference of American States, Bogotá, Colombia, Mar. 30–May 2, 1948, OEA/Ser. L./V/II.23/doc. 2 rev. 6 (English 1979), *reprinted in* RICHARD B. LILLICH, INTERNATIONAL HUMAN RIGHTS INSTRUMENTS 430.1–430.10 (2d ed. 1990).

14. Convention on the Elimination of Racial Discrimination, *opened for signature* March 7, 1966, 660 U.N.T.S. 195 (entered into force Jan. 4, 1969; adopted by the United States Nov. 20, 1994).

15. International Covenant on Economic, Social and Cultural Rights, G.A. res. 2200A (XXI), 21 U.N.GAOR Supp. (No. 16) at 49, U.N. Doc. A/6316 (1966), 993 U.N.T.S. 3 (entered into force Jan. 3, 1976).

16. *See id.*

17. For detailed information regarding the inequalities, see generally Goodwin Liu, *Interstate Inequality Educational Opportunity*, 81 N.Y.U. L. REV. 2044 (2006) (discussing educational inequalities with a focus on interstate disparities); Frank I. Michaelman, *Foreword: On Protecting the Poor Through the Fourteenth Amendment*, 83 HARV. L. REV. 7, 52 (1969) ("education is terribly important and no convincing reason appears for tolerating the apparent injustice of wealth-determined inequality, while ... there does exist a persuasive justification for place-determined inequality."); Sharon E. Rush, *Lessons From and For "Disabled" Students*, 8 J. GENDER RACE & JUST. 75 (2004) (discussing the various educational inequalities, such as sexual orientation inequality, racial inequality and gender inequality faced in U.S. education).

18. *See Serrano v. Priest*, 487 P.2d 1241, 1251–52 (Cal. 1971) ("affluent districts can have their cake and eat it too; they can provide a high quality education for their children while paying lower taxes. Poor districts, by contrast, have no cake at all"). *See generally Bd. of Educ. v. Nyquist*, 408 N.Y.S.2d 606, 634 (1978) ("Effective programs to remedy or alleviate the problems of severe underachievement and failure cost much more money per pupil than the regular educational program because they require substantial numbers of additional personnel."); John I. Goodlad, *Common Schools for the Common Weal: Reconciling Self-Interest With the Common Good, in* ACCESS TO KNOWLEDGE — AN AGENDA FOR OUR NATIONS SCHOOLS 1, 4 (John I. Goodlad & Pamela Keating eds., 1990) (hereinafter ACCESS). *See also* Linda Darling-Hammond & Joslyn Green, *Teacher Quality & Equality, in* ACCESS, at 239 ("Because the distribution of teacher quality is skewed toward those students who attend affluent, well-endowed schools, poor and minority students are chronically and disproportionately exposed to teachers with less training and experience."). *See also* William J. Mathis, *No Child Left Behind: Costs and Benefits*, 84 PHI DELTA KAPPAN 679, *1 (2003), *available at* www.pdkintl.org/kappan/k0305mat.htm.

ities continue to allow mistreatment of children in poor and minority schools. In New York state's big five urban districts—New York City, Buffalo, Rochester, Syracuse and Yonkers,[19] which contain 83 percent of the state's failing schools—public arrests and the imposition of zero tolerance policies serve to push children out of the educational system and into the correctional system.[20] Furthermore, the standardization of test taking and state accountability through federal policies actually undermines the human right to education for U.S. children because they fail to ensure the reciprocal accountability of the students and schools to succeed and of the states to provide them with the means to do so.

A prime example is the NCLB, which has theoretically created accountability for children and schools; in actuality, it does not mirror the accountability of the government to those children to provide the wherewithal they need to be successful.[21] In addition, impediments to accessing education continue to multiply in contravention of international human rights law. Many high school students are being prevented from pursuing a college education because they do not receive a quality-based education.

The high school and college models proposed in this chapter are constructed to address this issue as a prevention measure and not a reactionary measure. Schools are pressured to teach to the test, a pressure that results in a lack of a quality education where basic principles of synthesis, analysis, comprehension and writing are ignored to obtain the numbers needed for a school to be considered "passing" under NCLB.[22] Students such as English language learners are more likely to be retained in English as a second language (ESL) and are forced to take fewer academic courses as a result.[23]

The facade provided to parents in the so-called guides to NCLB compromises the rights of parents and communities to participate in ensuring the right education in their local

---

The greater and more insidious danger, however, is the disparity in achievement within the United States. International test data tell us that we have the greatest inequities between our highest—and lowest-scoring students of any nation. In a UNICEF follow-up study, the gap between our average scorers and our low scorers gives the United States an abysmal ranking of twenty-first out of twenty-four industrialized nations in educational equality. *Id.*

19. David Hursh & Camille Anne Martina, *Neoliberalism and Schooling in the U.S. How State and Federal Government Education Policies Perpetuate Inequality*, JOURNAL FOR CRITICAL EDUC. POLICY, Oct. 2003, www.jceps.com/print.php?articleID=12.

20. John W. Sipple et al., *Adoption and Adaptation: School District Responses to State Imposed Learning and Graduation Requirements*, 26 EDUC. EVALUATION AND POLICY ANALYSIS 143, 143–44 (2004).

21. Nicholas L. Townsend, *Framing a Ceiling as a Floor: The Changing Definition of Learning Disabilities and the Conflicting Trends in Legislation Affecting Learning Disabled Students*, 40 CREIGHTON L. REV. 229, 249 (2007) ("No Child Left Behind's underlying assumptions about the homogeneity of learning are problematic because the imposition of universal standards sacrifices individualized education for a false sense of equality that ignores actual differences between students"). Various scholars have also been critical of relying heavily on standardized tests for accountability, which is the centerpiece of No Child Left Behind. *See, e.g.,* William Firestone, *Teaching to the Test in New Jersey: The Good, the Bad and the Ugly*, CEPA NEWSLETTER (Center for Education Policy Analysis, New Brunswick, N.J.) May 2001, at 1, www.CEPA.gse.rutgers.edu/CEPA_SPOINEWS.pdf (discussing the increase in the use of "drill and kill" test preparation practices in high-poverty districts, narrowing the overall curriculum); Daniel J. Losen, *Silent Segregation in Our Nation's Schools*, 34 HARV. C.R.-C.L. REV. 517, 517–18 (1999) (stating the negative effects of remedial education, including a narrowing of the curriculum offered to students tracked into lower levels).

22. *See generally* DAVID T. CONLEY, TOWARD A MORE COMPREHENSIVE CONCEPTION OF COLLEGE READINESS (2007) (discussing the problems of educational system focusing on standardized testing leading to lack of students' ability to think and analyze critically. The author states that this fundamental lack of critical thinking make students unprepared for college).

23. *See* Hursh & Martina, *supra* note 19.

schools and deprives schools of the salutary effects of such participation in creating curricula and approaches tailored to the particular needs of the communities' students. Parents are misled to believe that there is accuracy in reporting mechanisms of their children's progress under NCLB. The *Parents' Guide to No Child Left Behind* states that NCLB will give them objective data through standardized testing.[24] No proof exists that standardized testing increases fairness and objectivity. To the contrary, there is a history of inaccuracies in standardized testing, including testing biases that in fact demote poor students and students of color that are subject to them.[25]

This ineffective and penal approach toward "improving" education in the United States is further worsened by insufficient federal governmental funding. If the federal government would refrain from cuts in the education budgets and support equitable distribution of existing resources, the development of programs to support effective student learning could ensue. The creation of federal programs can be successful if they work toward the development of highly trained, diverse faculties and administrations for low-performing schools. This training must include the concepts adopted by international and national human rights documents that afford understanding and sensitivity toward the groups most in need. In the case of New York City, students of color, poor students and English language learners would be the groups most in need of attention throughout this developmental process. Moreover, there must exist a retention program within federally created programs to retain these highly trained, diverse faculties. Inadequate funding contravenes all of these crucial measures.

Some hope remains, fortunately, as cases are filed in the U.S. courts.[26] Courts are finding that local systems of funding for education are unequal and are inadequate and that these failings violate respective state constitutional rights to education.[27] Nevertheless, the Project Investigator for NYCHRHSCRP has found that the standards imposed by NCLB and New York City which focus on test-taking skills and passing standardized tests like the Regents Examination foster the most resistance from high school administrators and teachers, whose natural inclinations would be to foster the goals of the project but whose jobs depend on NCLB results.

---

24. *See* U.S. Dept. of Educ., No Child Left Behind—A Parent's Guide 5–8 (2003) (discussing the advantages of having a uniform compilation of datas across the board). *See generally* U.S. Dept. of Educ., Stronger Accountability: Questions and Answers on No Child Left Behind (describing data collection methods for school reports cards), available at www.ed.gov/nclb/accountability/schools/accountability.html.

25. *See* Julie Washington, *Early Literacy Skills in African-American Children: Research Considerations*, 16 Learning Disabilities 213, 213–21 (2001); Dara Wakefield, *NCLB Keeps Some Great Teaching Candidates Out Forever*, 72 Educ. Digest 51, 51–57 (2007); Anne C. Lewis, *Undoable Goals?*, 69 Educ. Digest 68, 68–69 (2004).

26. *See, e.g., Campaign for Fiscal Equity, Inc. v. State of New York*, 8 N.Y.3d 14 (2006) (holding that the state's estimated cost to a sound basic education at $1.93 billion in 2004 dollars is reasonable). Before further appeal, it was noted that "of those New York City ninth graders who do not transfer to another school system, only 50 percent graduate in four years, and 30 percent do not graduate or receive a general equivalency degree (GED) by the age of 21, when they cease to be eligible for free public education." *Campaign for Fiscal Equity, Inc. v. State of New York*, 100 N.Y.2d 893, 914 (N.Y. 2003), *aff'd*, 8 N.Y.3d 14 (2006). *See also Hancock v. Comm'r of Educ.*, 443 Mass. 428 (2005) (stating that the Commonwealth constitution's education clause imposes an enforceable duty on the magistrates and legislatures of Commonwealth to provide education in the public schools for the children there enrolled, whether they be rich or poor and without regard to the fiscal capacity of the community or district in which such children live).

27. *Hancock*, 443 Mass., at 481.

The Negative Effects of NCLB

At its inception, NCLB existed to make schools, administrators and teachers accountable for student achievement. The law provides that if a state receives NCLB funding, every child in that state must achieve state-developed academic proficiency standards.[28] States and schools that accept grants and assistance from the federal government must abide by mandates to hire highly qualified teachers in the classrooms and raise all students' achievement.[29] NCLB also seeks to strengthen the performance among low-income students, racial and ethnic minorities, students with limited English proficiency and disabled students.[30] Schools, according to NCLB, are regarded as the problem and can no longer overlook the low performance of individual children.

A number of components affect what constitutes efficiency and proficiency in student achievement. Each state is required by law to ensure that by 2014, all children are at grade-level "proficiency" in reading and math.[31] Each state, however, determines its own academic standards, the courses taught, the standardized tests used and the cutoff scores that define a student as proficient.[32] Although preliminary studies by researchers show that student achievement is improving, critics see otherwise:

> Embarrassing schools by labeling them as failing and threatening them with additional sanctions has not induced them to significantly improve student learning. To the contrary, the primary responses to the threat of sanctions have not been major improvements in teaching and learning, but widespread manipulations of test standards, scores and schedules to produce artificial compliance with AYP and postpone sanctions as long as possible.[33]

Furthermore, to meet Adequate Yearly Progress (AYP), schools may change benchmarks, lowering overall standards and compromising educational quality.[34]

As a result, a number of other unintended consequences have surfaced. Students, teachers, and administrators within the system may not be prepared to handle such a policy approach due to stress at all levels of the public education system created by NCLB.[35] State education departments have lost 50 percent of their employees in the last ten years due to the lack of necessary resources to handle the evaluation process.[36] Daly and Chrispeels have examined the psychological effects of NCLB and argue that as a result of the act's requirements, unintended consequences such as the inability to teach or learn and to solve problems creatively, the lack of self-efficacy, or the reduction of volunteerism and lack

---

28. 20 U.S.C. § 6311.

29. Barbara Mantel, *No Child Left Behind,* 15 CQ Researcher 469, 471 (2005).

30. *Id.* at 469.

31. 20 U.S.C. § 6311(b)(2)(F).

32. § 6311(b)(2)(A) (Supp. I 2001); § 6311(b)(2)(G)(ii)(iii) (Supp. I 2001).

33. Gershon M. Ratner, *Why the No Child Left Behind Act Needs to be Restructured to Accomplish its Goals and How to Do It,* 9 U.D.C.L. Rev 1, 14 (2007).

34. *Id. See also* David K. Cohen & Susan L. Moffitt, *Title I: Politics, Poverty, and Knowledge* 77–79, *in* The Future of the Federal Role in Elementary & Secondary Education (Center on Education Policy ed. 2001), http://www.ctredpol.org/pubs/booklets.html.

35. Alan J. Daly & Janet Chrispeels, *From Problem to Possibility: Leadership for Implementing and Deepening the Process of Effective Schools,* 4 Journal For Effective Sch. 7, 8–10 (2005).

36. *See* Mantel, *supra* note 29, at 481.

of cooperation have become manifested in school environments.[37] NCLB's approach and conceptual framework, therefore, promote a climate of failure, straining educational systems across the nation.[38]

Building a climate of success requires a change in attitude and perspective in contemporary schooling that cannot be underpinned by a "deficit-oriented" approach.[39] Public education should instead pursue more strength-based models.[40] If NCLB continues to follow its current course, by 2014, a number of schools, according to researchers and state departments, will be labeled "failing."[41] Again, these failing schools in New York State are located primarily in the big five urban districts: New York City, Buffalo, Rochester, Syracuse, and Yonkers.[42]

NYC Human Rights High School Curriculum Research Project

Major Questions Guiding the Project

NYCHRHSCRP is aimed at securing a successful transition from high school to law/graduate school for first-generation, low-income and minority students attending public high schools. The NYC pilot project is intended to serve as a national model for pipeline education. This pilot operates out of the Puerto Rican/Latin American Studies Department at John Jay College of Criminal Justice and is being implemented in two New York City high schools.

The first high school is a single-sex, seventh through twelfth grade education institution, The Young Women's Leadership School of East Harlem (TYWLS).[43] The total enrollment

---

37. *See generally* Daly & Chrispeels, *supra* note 35 (discussing how the system under NCLB creates a unique stress which threatens creative approaches necessary for education, and to rather, instill a strength-based approach).

38. *See* Alan J. Daly, Rigid Response in an Age of Accountability: The Potential of Leadership and Trust, at 3–12 (2006), eds.ucsd.edu/courses/eds288a%20S/August10/DalyRigid ResponseTrust.pdf.

39. Lance F. Fusarelli, *The Potential Impact of the No Child Left Behind Act on Equity and Diversity in American Education*, 18 Educ. Policy 71, 79–80 (2004) ("NCLB explicitly assumes that the state-mandated tests are aligned to the curriculum. Unfortunately, studies demonstrate that state tests are seldom aligned with the actual curriculum in use ... the quality of a school consists of more than test scores and includes such things as level of parental and student satisfaction ... Some fear that the focus on testing and accountability will harm students who learn differently, including *culturally and linguistically diverse learners*") (emphasis added). *See also* Daly & Chrispeels, *supra* note 35.

40. *See* Daly & Chrispeels, *supra* note 35.

41. Mark Goldberg, *Test Mess 2: Are We Doing Better a Year Later?*, 86 Phi Delta Kappan 389, 389 (2005) ("Approximately 26,000 of the nation's 91,400 public schools failed to make AYP in the 2002–03 school year."); Gerald W. Bracey, *The 14th Bracey Report on the Condition of Public Education*, 86 Phi Delta Kappan 139, 139 (2004) (showing a study indicating that 99 percent of public schools will be considered a "failure" by 2014 in California); Associated Press, *Study: 9 Out of 10 Schools Won't Meet Federal Standards in a Decade*, Hartford Courant 1 (May 28, 2004).

42. David Hursh & Camille Anne Martina, *Neoliberalism and Schooling in the U.S. How State and Federal Government Education Policies Perpetuate Inequality*, Journal for Critical Education Policy, Oct. 2003, www.jceps.com/print.php?articleID=12.

43. Young Women's Leadership Foundation Network Schools, www.ywlfoundation.org/ network_schl_harl.htm (last visited Oct. 20, 2007). Please note that these statistics are subject to change after October 31, 2007, when high schools are required to submit official statistics and demographics for the year.

is 422 students;[44] and the student profile consists of 33 percent African American, 66 percent Hispanic, 1 percent other.[45] Eighty-five percent of the students at this school qualify for reduced or free lunch.[46]

The second high school is a coed institution located in the South Bronx—Health Opportunities Secondary School (HOSS).[47] HOSS contains grade levels nine through twelve,[48] with a total enrollment of 615 students.[49] The student profile is 39 percent African American, 56 percent Hispanic, 1 percent white, 1 percent Asian and 3 percent other.[50] Fifty-seven percent of the students at this high school qualify for reduced or free lunch.[51]

This high school to law/graduate school pipeline research program develops critical thinking skills and effective citizenship through a human rights curriculum, and serves as a precollege intervention measure aimed at improving overall student performance and achievement by providing students early on with the tools needed to compete for the opportunity to attend law/graduate school. It examines and critically challenges the underlying assumptions of educational policies and their impact on disadvantaged groups, the impact and interplay of NCLB and other educational policies versus their intended purpose, and the need for mentorship and other retention measures.

The rationale behind this project is based on the fact that current federal and state approaches to education since the enactment of the NCLB are subpar and have not fulfilled state's responsibilities to prepare the youth to be active, productive and invested citizens. Therefore, the project is intended to address several questions: (1) what obstacles disadvantaged high school students in NYC face in accessing higher education and how they can be overcome; (2) whether human rights education can assist students to obtain access to law or graduate school while making them better citizens; (3) how students can prepare to pass the NYC Regents Examination while simultaneously developing the necessary skills to compete and successfully participate in college, graduate and professional education; (4) what measures need to be taken to retain these students at all levels of higher education; and (5) what role mentoring should play in the program and its effect on the successful graduation of these students. The NYCHRHSCRP implements teacher development via college faculty and community resources such as the promotion of training partnerships with the Justice Resource Center, directed by Debra Lesser, as a means to obtain student success while alleviating the institutions' stresses of compliance with NCLB—it offers a hands-on, teacher-oriented approach focusing on pedagogy and mentoring. The program later encourages teachers and students to participate in the Daly Model, which is a cooperative model[52] that promotes trust and social capital, self- and collective efficacy, positive psychology and positive organizational scholarship.[53]

The pipeline program is also designed to prepare young people to be effective citizens. An educated population ensures that individuals have the necessary intellectual tools to

---

44. *Id.*
45. *Id.*
46. *Id.*
47. Young Women's Leadership School, http://www.ywlfoundation.org/CB_schools2.htm#4 (last visited Oct. 20, 2007). Please note that these statistics are subject to change after October 31, 2007, when high schools are required to submit official statistics and demographics for the year.
48. *Id.*
49. *Id.*
50. *Id.*
51. *Id.*
52. Daly & Chrispeels, *supra* note 35, at 11–20.
53. *Id.*

engage in effective decision making in a democratic state.[54] The importance of the relationship between education and democratic citizenship goes as far back as Aristotle, who argued for public education as a means to ensure stability in democratic states.[55] Aristotle argued that a government is compelled to mold people to its form of government and develop a common interest among its citizenry—a process best accomplished through a public education system.[56] Alexis De Tocqueville also noted this relationship in his writings on American society, where he attributed the successful development of democratic principles in the United States to a citizenry with a strong political education.[57] American democracy succeeded because people were educated to become part of public life and not private life, according to Tocqueville.[58] Contemporary political scholars have continued to identify education as a key factor for democratic stability,[59] civic empowerment and optimism[60] and voter participation in democratic states.[61]

The United States' understanding of the connection between education and democratic citizenship, however, has focused almost exclusively on obligations specific to the nation-state. Economic globalization, human migration and cultural diffusion all make the idea of nationally oriented citizenship education difficult to sustain, since most aspects of public life in modern states are shaped by phenomena taking place beyond nation-state borders.[62] Specifically, citizenship must move away from a notion of rights based on membership in a national group toward one based on (1) rights and responsibilities; (2)

---

54. *See, e.g., Brown v. Bd. of Educ.*, 347 U.S. 483, 493 (1954) ("Today, education is perhaps the most important function of state and local governments.... Compulsory school attendance laws and the great expenditures for education both demonstrate our recognition of the importance of education to our democratic society. It is required in the performance of our most basic public responsibilities.... It is the very foundation of good citizenship. Today it is a principal instrument in awakening the child to cultural values, in preparing him for later professional training, and in helping him to adjust normally to his environment.").

55. For polity or constitutional government may be described generally as a fusion of oligarchy and democracy; but the term is usually applied to those forms of government which incline toward democracy, and the term *aristocracy* to those which incline toward oligarchy, because birth and education are commonly the accompaniments of wealth. THE POLITICS OF ARISTOTLE, bk. IV, at 98 (Benjamin Jowett trans., Colonial Press, rev. ed. 1900).

56. *See id.*

57. Roger Boesche, THE STRANGE LIBERALISM OF ALEXIS DE TOCQUEVILLE 85–87 (1987) (describing the concern that wealth would cause individuals to abandon public pursuits). *See also id.* at 128 (arguing that associations serve public needs in addition to private interests); 2 Alexis de Tocqueville, DEMOCRACY IN AMERICAN 387 (Henry Reeve trans., Shocken 1st ed. 1961) (1974).

58. *See id.*

59. Seymour Martin Lipset, *Some Social Requisites of Democracy: Economic Development and Political Legitimacy*, 53 AM. POL. SCI. REV. 69, 69–105 (1959); Adam Przeworski & Fernando Limongi, *Modernization: Theory and Facts*, 49 WORLD POL. 155, 156 (1997).

60. *See, e.g.,* Robert D. Putnam, BOWLING ALONE: THE COLLAPSE AND REVIVAL OF AMERICAN COMMUNITY 63 (2000) (showing social trends and changes in everyday American life to encourage a renewal of civic empowerment); Robert D. Putnam, *The Strange Disappearance of Civic America*, 24 AM. PROSPECT 34, 34–36 (1996) (stating the declining membership in social and community groups).

61. *See* David B. Magleby, *Let the Voters Decide? An Assessment of the Initiative and Referendum Process*, 66 U. COLO. L. REV. 13, 32 (1995) (those who vote are "better educated"); David B. Magleby, DIRECT LEGISLATION: VOTING ON BALLOT PROPOSITIONS IN THE UNITED STATES 108–10, 118–19, 138–43 (1984) (finding that understanding ballot measures in some states requires a reading comprehension level equal to that of a third-year college student and discussing the fact that poorer citizens are likely to vote on propositions).

62. For example, the economy of Mexico can be seen to be immensely affected by movements of the North American Free Trade Agreement (NAFTA).

access; (3) belonging; and (4) acceptance of multiple identities.[63] Civic education should emphasize some sort of "world citizenship" by taking into account the interconnected nature of the modern state system and the international legal and political structures that have emerged as a consequence of our increasingly interconnected world.[64]

In light of the transnational and multicultural character of modern states, the pipeline program places a greater emphasis on human rights curriculum as part of public education curricula. By studying the nature and role of human rights in today's world, students will understand the historical factors that have shaped today's emergent global society. They will also understand the international legal framework that can help them effectively engage in civic action to help create a cosmopolitan or world citizenship as well as immediate local change. As historian Michael Ignatieff argues, a focus on human rights can be an effective tool for rearticulating a new citizenship by providing a rights system that recognizes the validity of national identities and cultural practices, but which also ensures the right of individuals and groups to choose whether to align themselves with specific national identities and cultural norms.[65]

Furthermore, the fact that human rights are voluntarily incorporated by individual states into their legal frameworks makes it necessary for young people to understand how human rights affect their rights as citizens. The purpose of human rights education, as discussed by David Suarez,[66] is to (a) strengthen respect for human rights and fundamental freedoms; (b) foster the full development of the human personality and its sense of dignity; (c) promote tolerance, equality and friendship among all gender, sexual orientation, disability, racial, national, ethnic, religious and linguistic groups; (d) enable all persons to participate effectively in a free and democratic society governed by the rule of law; (e) build and maintain peace; and (f) promote people-centered, sustainable development and social justice.[67]

NYCHRHSCRP aims at increasing students' reading and math skills by superimposing a human rights curriculum over the Regents Examinations in two NYC high schools. It provides teachers with curriculum training and development. Students are provided human rights education aimed at increasing human rights awareness and violence reduction and prevention. Students are paired as mentees of John Jay College students who are in the Ronald H. Brown Summer Law School Prep Program, an existing college to

---

63. *See* Jeremy Waldon, *Teaching Cosmopolitan Right, in* CITIZENSHIP AND EDUCATION IN LIBERAL DEMOCRATIC SOCIETIES: TEACHING FOR COSMOPOLITAN VALUES AND COLLECTIVE IDENTITIES 23–56 (Kevin McDonough & Walter Feinberg eds., Oxford University Press, 2003).

64. *Id.*

65. For more information regarding Michael Ignatieff and his theory, see Michael Ignatieff with K. Anthony Appiah et al., HUMAN RIGHTS AS POLITICS AND IDOLATRY (Amy Gutmann ed., 2001); Michael Ignatieff, VIRTUAL WAR: KOSOVO AND BEYOND (2000); Michael Ignatieff, THE WARRIOR'S HONOR: ETHNIC WAR AND THE MODERN CONSCIENCE (1998); Michael Ignatieff, THE NEEDS OF STRANGERS (1984). *See also infra* note 66 and accompanying text.

66. David Suarez, *Education Professionals and the Construction of Human Rights Education*, 51 COMPARATIVE EDUC. REV. 48, 49–54 (2007).

67. *Id.* at 48. *See also* United Nations, General Assembly, United Nations Decade for Human Rights Education (1995–2004). Dr. Howard Gardner has constantly argued that various types of intelligence exist, that individuals display varying levels of different types of intelligence and that any specific type of intelligence should not be singled out arbitrarily or viewed as more favorable. *See* Howard Gardner, MULTIPLE INTELLIGENCES: NEW HORIZONS 5, 7, 20–21, 56 (2d ed. 2006). *See generally* Howard Gardner, FRAMES OF MIND: THE THEORY OF MULTIPLE INTELLIGENCES (1983); Howard Gardner, MULTIPLE INTELLIGENCES: THE THEORY INTO PRACTICE (1993); Howard Gardner, INTELLIGENCE REFRAMED: MULTIPLE INTELLIGENCES FOR THE 21ST CENTURY (1999).

law school pipeline program, and will receive mentoring and tutoring from these students in a college atmosphere. The goal is to foster the idea that higher education is not only necessary for the students' futures but also accessible to them.[68] Students gain analytical and critical thinking skills which are aimed at improving their standardized test taking capacities. Teachers gain professional development while assisting the high schools in attaining higher success rates.

The pipeline project also addresses a series of specific questions beyond those listed earlier in this chapter. (1) Can this human rights curriculum improve the probability of admission to higher levels of education? (2) How does the superimposition of a human rights curriculum work to raise standardized testing scores? (3) What is the impact of the curriculum on student development such as increased student participation, academic motivation and retention? (4) How does the human rights curriculum help increase civic participation (volunteerism, activism, student government/leadership)? (5) In turn, does this increase in participation positively impact on student performance in the classroom and on standardized tests? (6) How can the program best successfully graduate students in the pipeline? By examining these questions, the project researchers can develop effective tools for changing and improving the nation's educational system.

To assess the overall impact of human rights curriculum on academic performance, the project will employ a series of statistical measures. First, the project will conduct a comparative analysis of academic performance prior to and after the implementation of the human rights curriculum for each participating school. In addition, the study will examine the use of statistical indicators such as student grade point average, Regents Examination scores and SAT, GRE and LSAT scores. It will employ multivariate analysis to determine (a) the impact of the human rights curriculum on the probability of admission to different levels of higher education (two-year college, four-year college, graduate and professional school), (b) the impact of the curriculum on classroom skills (student participation, academic motivation), and (c) the effect of human rights curriculum on civic participation (volunteerism, activism, leadership and participation in student government).

The statistical analysis also controls for selected demographic variables such as age, sex, race, ethnicity and national origin and household socioeconomic status. Among other variables the project will examine are parental participation and institutional resources. To assess the overall impact of the curriculum on student performance, statistical analysis will be complemented with a series of qualitative approaches, such as student journals, focus groups and in-depth interviews with students and teachers. These interviews will examine elements such as student motivation, critical thinking and organizational skills.

The project ultimately attempts to pipeline NYC high school students to John Jay College of Criminal Justice, which is currently one of the largest Hispanic-serving institutions in the Northeast,[69] and from there to law/graduate school. Those participants who are admitted to John Jay College of Criminal Justice will begin preparation for law school/graduate school in their first year. English language learners, for example, can be pipelined in to the English language learner courses, called the EAP Learning Community courses, directed by Kate Szur, where they can receive the skill sets necessary for mastering college and professional-level English.

---

68. This is an increasingly important element of the program, especially for potential CUNY students given the "phasing out" of the associates degree programs at many CUNY colleges.

69. See Top 100 Colleges Awarding Degrees to Hispanics, 2006, http://www.hispanicoutlook.com/top100_fo cus.htm?section=b (last visited Oct. 16, 2007).

During their sophomore year, students can enroll in the Ronald H. Brown Summer Law School Prep Program. This program plays two important roles for high school participants. First, it provides the preintervention support that high school students need by creating access, overall support and interactive exposure to college. Second, it serves as a feeder program for students interested in attending law school and graduate school.

The Ronald H. Brown Summer Law School Prep Program at John Jay College

The Ronald H. Brown Summer Law School Prep Program for college sophomores, directed by Professor Leonard Baynes, exposes to the study of law, undergraduate students who are either low-income and first-generation college students or members of a group underrepresented in law schools, such as Latinos, African Americans and Native Americans.[70] The Puerto Rican/Latin American Studies Department/John Jay College portion of this program provides qualified John Jay College students with outreach and coordination of recruitment activities; presummer orientation, supervision and summer and academic year advisement; programmatic and curriculum support during the summer and academic semester sessions; and postsummer program student support activities for all John Jay students who have participated in the summer program (since its inception in 2005 to present) until they graduate from John Jay College. It also provides support to its graduates attending law and graduate schools. It provides program evaluation, improvements and outcomes assessment; creation of a student referral system for internship/externship placements; and model program training for feeder schools.[71]

The overall program was created to improve the diversity recruitment strategies for attracting under-represented students to the study of law and to graduate school. The Puerto Rican/Latin American Studies Department/John Jay College of Criminal Justice portion of this program provides mentoring of these students through writing-intensive learning communities, which have been shown to improve the retention of this group of students and has seen some of its students gain admission to top thirty U.S. law schools and other top graduate programs. It introduces the students to careers in education and law through clinical experiences and through other experiences such as community fieldwork and externships and mentoring programs with students currently attending law or graduate school. Through its rigorous simulated law school curriculum and through the writing-intensive Puerto Rican/Latin American Studies Department courses, this program promotes strategies that encourage program participants' interest in graduate school and professional school. It has been proven to effectively prepare them for competitive admissions processes, and it has increased their chances of gaining admission and successfully enrolling in graduate and professional schools. The success and reputation of the students seem also to have resulted in increased numbers of John Jay College students

---

70. This program is a collaborative initiative between the Puerto Rican/Latin American Studies Department John Jay College of Criminal Justice and the Ronald H. Brown Center for Civil Rights and Economic Development at the St. John's University School of Law, Medgar Evers College/CUNY, York College/CUNY, and St. John's University undergraduate.

71. As the project investigator of the John Jay College portion of this program, I focus the main points of discussion in this chapter on my work at John Jay College, although I reference to the overall program.

overall finding their way into conditional law school acceptance programs in New York City and other parts of the United States. Partial and full scholarships have also been awarded to many of the entering law students that have graduated from the program.

Throughout the academic year, college students that are enrolled in Puerto Rican/Latin American Studies Department courses work with at-risk inner-city high school students that are potential CUNY applicants via the NYCHRHSCRP. Through these efforts, the program improves the identification and recruitment of potential students who have fallen out of the traditional K–12 educational pipeline to college and who will not likely be reached by more traditional recruitment efforts. The college students work with the teachers on retention efforts for participating high school students.

The Puerto Rican/Latin American Studies Department of John Jay College of Criminal Justice is uniquely qualified for a project of this kind because it is situated in a college where the majority of the undergraduate student body consists of students of color and largely first-generation and low-income college students. The typical entering class at John Jay College of Criminal Justice over the last five years has included a student body that is approximately 53 percent Latino and African American in the baccalaureate degree program and 63 percent Latino and African American in the associate degree program. The college's Latino undergraduate population runs at between 33 and 45 percent of the college undergraduate population (A.A./B.A.).[72] The Puerto Rican/Latin American Studies Department is a department that offers courses in ethnic studies as part of the college's core requirements, as well as courses in Latin American and Latino studies; therefore, the department is well situated to reach large segments of the student body that are likely to be eligible for this program.

The Ronald H. Brown Summer Law School Prep Program has partnered with minority bar associations such as the Hispanic National Bar Association and the Black Bar Association to create mentor relationships and postprogram internship and externship opportunities for its students. In addition, students are mentored by the Latino/a Law Student Association, the Black Law Students Association and other multicultural law student associations at many NYC law schools, including St. John's.

The program is a two-year program that begins during the student's sophomore year. Each participating college selects ten students for the program, for a total of forty students. To qualify, the students must have completed between forty-five to seventy-five credits and be either low-income and first-generation college students or members of groups underrepresented in law schools. The students must have at least a 3.0 GPA and a genuine interest in attending law school. Over the past three years, the program has enrolled a racially and ethnically diverse class of students,[73] with an average GPA ranging from 3.0 to 3.9. The Puerto Rican/Latin American Studies Department/John Jay College application process includes a personal statement section and an interview utilizing the Socratic method, during which students analyze a fact pattern based closely on current issues.

---

72. Gail Hauss, Fall 2004 Fact Book, John Jay College of Criminal Justice 26 (2005).

73. *See supra* note 1. The students are ethnically and racially diverse. They include Asian Americans, Latinos(as) African Americans, and people of Caribbean ancestry, biracial individuals, Italian-Americans, and Albanians. Many of the students are from economically challenged circumstances — one worked as a home health aide and another was a single mother of three who currently receives public assistance and resides in public assistance housing in the South Bronx; several were former recipients of public assistance; several have grown up in homes receiving public assistance; many are first generation immigrants or children of immigrants to the United States; many grew up in homes in which English was not spoken; and many grew up in single parent households. Ages cover all ranges.

Accepted students are provided with a preorientation program, which includes the creation of a learning community that utilizes the concept of study groups to prepare the students for the assignments they will encounter during the summer. Students meet for at least one week at the Puerto Rican/Latin American Studies Department prior to the program start date to prepare for dealing with the law school materials. They are taught how to brief cases, are given *Black's Law Dictionaries* and taught how to use them, and are taught how to analyze and think critically about legal cases and the legal system. The program simulates real law school classes, and students read hundreds of pages over the course of the summer and more during the semester. Outcome assessments are also conducted by the Puerto Rican/Latin American Studies Department. Oral interviews are conducted along with assessment tests before and after the program, including the use of LSAT diagnostic test.

The sophomores selected to participate in 2007 received two weeks of law school classes taught by St. John's law faculty in the areas of business organizations, civil procedure, child advocacy, criminal law, constitutional law, international law, an internship seminar, immigration law, federal income tax, legal ethics, legal writing, race/racism and the law and torts. Law student tutors assist the sophomores with their homework assignments in briefing cases and doing legal analysis during mandatory homework hours. Law student teaching assistants also assist students after class and in the dormitories during mandatory study periods. As part of the internship seminar, the students prepare a written assignment, which provides them with greater insight to the law school experience.

The sophomores also spend one week shadowing state court judges in Queens, are given an overview of the LSAT, take a diagnostic LSAT exam, take field trips to law firm offices and spend five weeks interning in the Brooklyn and Queens district attorneys' offices. These additional experiences give the students opportunities to see what lawyers actually do. During their time in the district attorneys' offices, the students are assigned real work such as conducting intakes in the Domestic Violence Unit or, for those who are bilingual, translating documents or interviewing complaining parties and police officers.

Throughout the summer, the project investigator supervises the students both at the law school and in their internships with judges and the district attorneys' offices. She provides them with academic advising, career development and the overall academic and emotional support needed for such a rigorous program. Students may choose to receive seven academic credits from John Jay College of Criminal Justice for their participation in the sophomore program, and the program continues throughout the year as they work with the project investigator in many capacities, including their mentoring of NYC high school and first-year college students at John Jay College.

The second year of the program is open only to those who successfully complete the program the prior year. They apply and are interviewed by the Ronald H. Brown Center at St. John's. During the summer 2007 program, some juniors increased their scores by up to twenty points (on average ten points) based on Princeton Review Diagnostic Test Scores. To qualify for the second year, the students must have attended one of four undergraduate colleges: John Jay College of Criminal Justice/CUNY, Medgar Evers College/CUNY, St. John's University, or York College/CUNY. They must have maintained their 3.0 GPA and must have completed eighty-five college credits. In addition, their transcripts and résumés are reviewed, and the students undergo a program interview at the law school.

The project investigator assists the students in preparing for this process by reviewing their applications and working with students to write résumés and personal statements to be included with the written application. Based on the Ronald H. Brown Center's review, students are either accepted into or rejected from the junior program.[74] The project investigator, however, continues to work with all John Jay College/Ronald H. Brown students year-round to help them develop and work toward their career goals. Through the Puerto Rican/Latin American Studies Department, they receive the needed support after the sophomore year summer program, as do students who were admitted into the junior program. No student is abandoned.

The juniors spend ten intensive weeks learning how to take the LSAT. Based on their performances on the first diagnostic exam, they are divided into two groups, each class consisting of approximately ten students. Princeton Review runs this aspect of the program, using a master instructor who has experience teaching diverse students. During the ten weeks, the juniors take six diagnostic LSAT tests.

Three law school students serve as tutors during the LSAT program, assisting the juniors with homework and conducting drills until the date of the LSAT examination. Two of the tutors are assigned to the students who did not score well on the first diagnostic exam. The juniors are walked through the law school admissions process and receive tips on writing personal statements and on how to apply online through the LSDAS process. The project investigator then assists students with the overall completion of the entire law school application process. The juniors also receive ten group counseling sessions from certified psychotherapists to help them work through any test anxiety, and they attend a one-day efficacy training workshop to help them work through stereotype threat issues.[75] They complete a daily journal and other writing assignments, which the project investigator utilizes to assist the students with the law school application process.

Both sophomores and juniors complete an assessment of their learning styles so they can identify the best times and locations in which they are able to learn. This step is crucial for them to maximize their performances when they return to their undergraduate colleges and take the LSAT.

Over the course of the summer, prominent lawyers in the community talk to the both sophomores and juniors about the lawyers' practices and their experiences attending law school. Some of the speakers have included New York State Supreme Court Justice Patricia Satterfield; Melinda Molina, an associate at Sullivan and Cromwell; Lance Ogiste, counsel to the Brooklyn District Attorney; Lillian Llambelis of the New York State Attorney General's Office; Timothy Porter, counsel at Proskauer Rose; and Melissa Woods, assistant counsel, NAACP Legal Defense Fund. The sophomores and juniors also learn "How to be Successful" from an all-star panel of some of the highest ranking officials at the four undergraduate colleges.

For the summer of 2007, St. John's University made dorm space available to the sophomores and returning juniors at a deeply discounted rate. In 2006, 58 percent of the sophomores and juniors decided to stay in the dorms. An esprit de corps developed among the students and, as a result, has helped break down some of the barriers that existed among students from the four undergraduate colleges.[76] In addition, having dorm space available has proved to be a significant benefit for those students who live in the Bronx, Brooklyn

---

74. Some students opt out of the junior year for a variety of reasons such as family commitments, immigration issues, work responsibilities or other opportunities.

75. For more information, see Claude M. Steele & Joshua Aronson, *Stereotype Threat and the Intellectual Test Performance of African Americans*, 69 JOURNAL OF PERSONALITY AND SOCIAL PSYCHOLOGY 797, 797–811 (1995).

76. *See* Baynes, *supra* note 1.

and Washington Heights sections of Manhattan, for whom a one-way commute to the St. John's campus could be an almost two-hour ordeal.[77]

Conclusion

From a public policy standpoint, the utility of these programs as a nationwide model is vital, given the significant changes many colleges and universities such as CUNY are undergoing. Many CUNY schools are removing the associate degree programs from four-year colleges and relocating them to the local community colleges. Despite the "campus presence" that ultimately may result from a small four-year college representation at the community colleges' campuses, the bachelor's degree college atmosphere cannot be fully re-created on those campuses, especially given the distance and the logistics of the community colleges. This "phasing out" of associate degree programs at four-year colleges, coupled with an increase in college standards at CUNY and other colleges and universities, will ultimately result in a change of the diversity of the students for which colleges such as CUNY were commissioned to serve.

Pipeline models are becoming key factors in reconstructing high school education in the United States while maintaining access to higher education for under-represented students, and NYCHRHSCRP offers an especially effective model. The comprehensive approach of teaching critical and analytical thinking through the use of a human rights curriculum superimposed on the skills necessary to pass standardized tests such as those imposed by NCLB and the NYC Regents Examinations is an approach that addresses both of the most pressing expectations placed on secondary educational institutions: high schools can effectively prepare their students for high-stakes standardized tests without compromising the quality of the students' education. The pipelining aspect of NYCHRHSCRP provides the needed teacher development, especially in the area of human rights, addresses many of the inadequacies of the NCLB and its universal standards, and provides high school students with mentoring programs and exposure to college environments.

But for programs such as NYCHRHSCRP, the majority of the students being left behind under NCLB would never seriously consider higher education as an option. NYCHRHSCRP provides through its pre-intervention measures some of the basic skills necessary for students to compete successfully in the remedial and nonremedial courses they will face in college.

Moreover, the retention of both high school and college students is one of the most valuable outcomes of this pipeline concept; the pairing of students coming from similar backgrounds and similar educational experiences serves to promote responsibility, solidarity and security for all participants. The high school student has a role model with whom she can empathize on many levels and to whom she can look for practical academic guidance as well as social support. The college student gains an understanding of community fieldwork, a strengthened sense of community service and reaffirmation of her role in society as a stepping stone for the future leaders of the world. The NYCHRHSCRP fosters avenues for youth to discuss effective social change and facilitates the production of good citizens by ensuring our children—of all colors and backgrounds—will have the necessary tools to engage genuinely and effectively in the processes that are the lifeblood of a democratic state.

---

77. *See id.* at 3.

6

The Black Divide on Affirmative Action

Angela Onwuachi-Willig*

Introduction

In 2003, the U.S. Supreme Court held in *Grutter v. Bollinger*[1] that the University of Michigan Law School had a compelling state interest in attaining a diverse student body and that the institution's use of race in its individualized admissions process was narrowly tailored to further that interest.[2] The decision in *Grutter* was welcomed by academic institutions across the country, as it ensured, at least for twenty-five more years,[3] a means of maintaining diverse student bodies in institutions of higher education.

At the same time, *Grutter* and its companion case *Gratz v. Bollinger*[4] reopened the question, "Who should be the beneficiaries of affirmative action in higher education?" Opponents of affirmative action[5] again posed the well-known hypothetical concerning the debate of class versus race privilege—the inevitable question of whether the black neurosurgeon's son or daughter should receive any preference over the son or daughter of a poor white sanitation worker.[6] Additionally, scholars continued to raise the important question of how the model minority myth, in particular the view of Asian Americans as a monolithic group,

---

* Parts of this chapter were previously published in volume 60 of the VANDERBILT LAW REVIEW.

1. 539 U.S. 306 (2003).

2. *Id.* at 328–33.

3. *Id.* at 343; *see generally* Kevin R. Johnson, *The Last Twenty-Five Years of Affirmative Action?*, 21 CONST. COMMENT. 171, 179–90 (2004) (exploring the reality of a twenty-five-year limit on affirmative action).

4. 539 U.S. 244 (2003).

5. By "affirmative action," I refer to the act of considering the race of underrepresented racial minorities as a plus factor in admissions decisions and the expansion of the merits standards that are traditionally used to admit people into educational programs. *See* Angela Onwuachi-Willig, *Using the Master's Tool to Dismantle His House: Why Justice Clarence Thomas Makes the Case for Affirmative Action*, 47 ARIZ. L. REV. 113, 114 n.2 (2005); Anupam Chander, *Minorities, Shareholders, and Otherwise*, 113 YALE L.J. 119, 120 n.3 (2003); Martha S. West, *The Historical Roots of Affirmative Action*, 10 BERKELEY LA RAZA L.J. 607, 614 (1998).

6. *See* Sumi Cho, *Multiple Consciousness and the Diversity Dilemma*, 68 U. COLO. L. REV. 1035, 1037 (1997) [hereafter Cho, *Multiple Consciousness*] ("In rhetorical defense of such a compromise, stark juxtapositions are often made of the proverbial black 'son of the Pittsburgh neurosurgeon' to the 'son of the white sanitation worker.'"); *see also* Deborah C. Malamud, *Affirmative Action: Diversity of Opinion: Affirmative Action, Diversity, and the Black Middle Class*, 68 U. COLO. L. REV. 939,

may work to negatively impact Asian American students, especially those who are of Cambodian, Hmong, Laotian, and Vietnamese descent, under affirmative action policies.[7]

More recently, similar questions of inclusion and exclusion in affirmative programs have been raised about certain segments of the black community, not just about class—the upper middle-class black student versus the working-class or poor black student[8]—but about culture, background, and history. Much like students of Asian descent, black students in the United States are not, ethnically speaking, a monolithic group. As one *New York Times* article inquired, "Top colleges [may] take more Blacks, but which ones?"[9] The answer, some would say, is too many Blacks[10] who do not descend from slaves in the United States.[11]

967–97 (1997) (describing the disparities between black and white middle-class students).

7. *See* Harvey Gee, *From* Bakke *to* Grutter *and Beyond: Asian Americans and Diversity in America*, 9 Tex. J. C.L. & C.R. 129, 149–58 (2004); Sumi Cho, *Misconceptions Harm Asian Americans*, Chi. Trib., Apr. 30, 2004 (analyzing how Asian Americans are harmed by "stereotypes that characterize Asian Americans as an overeducated, overachieving 'model minority' group that does not suffer discrimination or does not deserve affirmative action"); Victoria Choy, Note, *Perpetuating the Exclusion of Asian-Americans from the Affirmative Action Debate: An Oversight of the Diversity Rationale in* Grutter v. Bollinger, 38 U.C. Davis L. Rev. 545, 569 (2005) ("Thus, courts, including the United States Supreme Court, erroneously view Asian Americans as a uniform, successful group. If judges and courts do not distinguish between the 'overrepresented' and underrepresented' Asian Americans, they may continue overlooking the needs of Asian Americans in equal protection jurisprudence.").

8. *See, e.g.*, Lani Guinier, *Our Preference for the Privileged*, B. Globe, July 9, 2004, at A13 [hereafter Guinier, *Our Preference*] (describing how current admissions criteria advantage the wealthy); Jason B. Johnson, *Shades of Gray in Black Enrollment; Immigrants' Rising Numbers a Concern to Some Activists*, S.F. Chron., Feb. 22, 2005, at A1 (quoting Ward Connerly as asserting that "affirmative action programs … have not really benefited low-income blacks, those who were descendants of slaves" but have instead "benefited middle and upper-income blacks"); *see also* Richard Delgado, *Ten Arguments Against Affirmative Action—How Valid?*, 50 Ala. L. Rev. 135, 140–41 (1998) (noting that race is more indicative of disadvantage than class).

9. Sarah Rimer & Karen W. Arenson, *Top Colleges Take More Blacks, But Which Ones?*, N.Y. Times, Jun. 24, 2004, at A1. Of course, race does not play a role in the admissions decisions of all black students, but for the sake of simplicity, I speak in broad terms.

10. Throughout this chapter, I capitalize the word "Black" or "White" when used as a noun to describe a racialized group.

As a general matter, when I am speaking of the entire community of people who may identify as black in the United States, citizen or noncitizen, I use the term "Blacks" instead of the term "African Americans." I refer to people who may identify as black and for whom all four grandparents were born in the United States as "African-Americans" or "the descendants." *See infra* text accompanying note 20. Collectively, I refer to black persons who are first generation in the United States (born outside of the United States) and who are second generation (born in the United States but have at least one parent who was born in another country) as "first and second generation" Blacks or black students or "students of direct Caribbean/African heritage." *See* Xue Lan Rong & Frank Brown, *The Effects of Immigrant Generation and Ethnicity on Educational Attainment Among Young African and Caribbean Blacks in the United States*, 71 Harv. Educ. Rev. 536, 537, 546 (2001); Matthijs Kalmijn, *The Socioeconomic Assimilation of Caribbean American Blacks*, 74 Social Forces 911, 915 (1996); *cf.* Elizabeth Chacko, *Identity and Assimilation Among Young Ethiopian Immigrants in Metropolitan Washington*, 93 Geographical Rev. 491, 491 (2005) (defining "persons who immigrated with their parents to the United States when they were less than twelve years of age" as the 1.5 generation). At times, I refer to first-generation Blacks who immigrated to the United States to establish a new residence and attended primary and/or secondary school in the United States as "resident black immigrants" or "immigrant Blacks." *Cf.* Diane L. Wolf, *There's No Place Like "Home": Emotional Transnationalism and the Struggles of Second-Generation Filipinos*, *in* Peggy Levitt & Mary C. Waters, The Changing Face of Home: The Transnational Lives of the Second Generation 255 (2002) ("Children of immigrants, or 'second-generation' youth, are defined as children born here to immigrant parents and children born abroad who have emigrated at a very early age."). I also use the phrase "West Indians" to refer to first- and second-generation Blacks from the Caribbean who are not Spanish-speaking. Although I make these distinctions between Blacks throughout the chapter, I do so only because they are necessary to the discussion, not for any other reason.

11. Rimer & Arenson, *supra* note 9, at A1.

As recent studies have revealed, a rising number of black students enrolled at elite colleges and universities are either black immigrant students who grew up and attended primary or secondary school in the United States or the American-born and -raised children of black immigrants.[12] For example, in a broad study of twenty-eight elite colleges and universities,[13] scholars at Princeton University and the University of Pennsylvania found that 41 percent of the black students on those campuses—which included schools such as Columbia, Howard, Oberlin, Swarthmore, and Yale—identified themselves as first or second generation Blacks.[14] Indeed, a *San Francisco Times* article described exactly this phenomenon at an elite public institution, the University of California–Berkeley, with black students such as Obi Amajoyi, who was born in the United States but whose parents are from Nigeria, making up a significant percentage of that school's black population.[15]

In a more directed study of students at Harvard College, Aisha Cecilia Haynie, an African American Harvard College graduate, discovered that out of all the black students who make up 8 percent of the undergraduate college's population, more than 60 percent of those students were either West Indian or African immigrants who attended primary or secondary school in the United States, the American-born children of black immigrants, or mixed-race individuals.[16] Specifically, Haynie found that black students of direct Caribbean heritage comprised 22.94 percent of black noninternational students at Harvard College while biracial students and students of direct African heritage constituted 25.88 percent and 12.35 percent, respectively, of the black noninternational student population at Harvard College.[17] She also discovered that African American students at Harvard College were proportionately outnumbered at the university, relative to first- and second-generation black students from the Caribbean and Africa. First- and second-generation Blacks constituted over 35 percent of the black students at Harvard College, even though they as a whole made up less than 10 percent of the total black population in the United States.[18] Only 37.65 percent, slightly more than one third of the black stu-

---

12. *See, e.g.*, Aisha Cecilia Haynie, *Not 'Just Black' Policy Considerations: The Influence of Ethnicity on Pathways to Academic Success Amongst Black Undergraduates at Harvard University*, 13 Pub. Int'l Affairs 40, 43 (2002).

13. The following schools (in alphabetical order) were included in the study: Barnard College, Bryn Mawr College, Columbia University, Denison University, Duke University, Emory University, Georgetown University, Howard University, Kenyon College, Miami University–Oxford, Northwestern University, Oberlin College, Pennsylvania State University, Princeton University, Rice University, Smith College, Stanford University, Swarthmore College, Tufts University, Tulane University, the University of California–Berkeley, the University of Michigan, the University of North Carolina, the University of Notre Dame, the University of Pennsylvania, Washington University–St. Louis, Williams College, and Yale University. Douglas S. Massey et. al, The Source of the River: The Social Origins of Freshmen at America's Selective Colleges and Universities 40–41, Tbl 2.5 (2003). When I refer to elite colleges, I am referring to these colleges and universities and other comparable schools.

14. *See* Massey et al., *supra* note 13, at 40–41; Johnson, *supra* note 8, at A1.

15. Johnson, *supra* note 8, at A1.

16. Haynie, *supra* note 12, at 43. Haynie's study involved more than 170 *noninternational* black students who attended Harvard College during the 1999–2000 academic year. According to Haynie, this group of subjects constituted a 71.4 percent response rate. *Id.* at 40, 42.

17. *Id.* at 43.

18. *Haynie*, supra note 12, at 43. Specifically, first-generation Blacks at Harvard comprised 8 percent of the black population at the school and 6.1 percent of the black population in the United States in 2000; second-generation Blacks at Harvard made up 41 percent of the black population at the school and 3.3 percent of the black population in the United States. *Id.*; *see also* Kalmijn, *supra* note 10, at 915 ("About 6 percent of the black community 16 years or older is Caribbean American. Caribbean blacks come from a large number of islands but a few countries make up the bulk of the

dents at Harvard College, were from families in which all four grandparents were born in the United States and were the descendants of American slaves.[19] Indeed, the absence of black American students with long-term generational roots in the United States on both sides of their families was so noticeable that such black students began to refer to themselves as "the descendants."[20]

For many of those concerned about how affirmative action advances social justice,[21] the rising number of first- and second-generation black students has become a cause for concern. To these individuals, these increasing numbers indicate that affirmative action programs are failing to reach those who were the original targets of the policy. Asserting that affirmative action was created as a means of overcoming the effects of slavery and the history of rampant discrimination against Blacks for more than 100 years thereafter, these

---

immigration flow: Jamaica (29 percent), Haiti (18 percent), the Dominican Republic (8 percent), and Trinidad-Tobago (8 percent)."); *see* Rong & Brown, *supra* note 10, at 537 (acknowledging that Jamaicans and Haitians make up the largest number of the 1.6 million foreign-born people of African origin living in the United States and that, while Nigerians and Ethiopians constitute the largest groups from Africa, "no large ethnic community of Black immigrants from African nations currently exists in the United States").

19. Haynie, *supra* note 12, at 43. Of course, many black Caribbeans descend from slaves in their own countries. *See* Camille A. Nelson, *Carriers of Globalization: Loss of Home and Self Within the African Diaspora*, 55 Fla. L. Rev. 539, 573–74 (2003) (noting the slavery in colonial Jamaica); Leonard M. Baynes, *Who Is Black Enough for You: The Story of One Black Man and His Family's Pursuit of the American Dream*, 11 Geo. Immigr. L.J. 97, 128 (1996) "('The only difference is that our [black Caribbeans'] slavery did not occur in the United States."); *cf.* Hope Lewis, *Lionheart Gals Facing the Dragon: The Human Rights of Inter/National Black Women in the United States*, 76 Or. L. Rev. 567, 619 (1997) ("The impact of that history, along with the related histories of global imperialism and neo-colonialism, continues to plague modern-day Blacks whether they are descended from slaves in the United States, Latin America.").

20. Rimer & Arenson, *supra* note 9, at A1.

21. The Supreme Court has rejected the use of affirmative action as a means of remedying societal discrimination. Nevertheless, it is important to discuss and analyze the social justice rationale for affirmative action; while social justice is not an accepted legal basis for the policy, it certainly drives supporters' perceptions about the need for affirmative action. *See* Transcript, *Who Gets In?: The Quest for Diversity After* Grutter, 52 Buff. L. Rev. 531, 553 (2004) [hereafter *Who Gets In*] (quoting David Chambers as stressing "the need for a broader vision of social justice" in affirmative action); Malamud, *supra* note 6, at 946 ("A judge will be more likely to read precedent as permitting a broader range of action if the judge is personally convinced there are good reasons to do so, even if those good reasons are reasons (like societal discrimination) that must go unstated. Thus, a justice faced with the question whether diversity as a justification for affirmative action survives strict scrutiny might well be influenced by her (unstated) views about why diversity cannot be achieved without affirmative action — which might well turn on the effects of societal discrimination."). For example, underlying Justice O'Connor's opinion in *Grutter* is the notion that affirmative action is still needed for many schools to achieve the goal of diversity — that because of past and present disadvantages, diversity cannot be fully achieved without affirmative action. If this idea were not central to the opinion, Justice O'Connor would not have needed to discuss a potential twenty-five-year limit on affirmative action, as the benefits of diversity are forever. *See* Johnson, *supra* note 3, at 184 ("However, time limits are normally associated with affirmative action programs designed to remedy past discrimination, not those aimed at ensuring a diverse student body.... Thus, the Court's suggestion of a 25 year time limit seems peculiar because it justified the University of Michigan's affirmative action program on a diversity rationale, not as a way of remedying past discrimination by the University of Michigan. If a diverse student body is the justification for affirmative action, it is uncertain why the law would require a time limit. Durational limits on a university's affirmative action program make sense to any affirmative action program only if one believes, as many proponents do, that remedying past discrimination really is the true justification for affirmative action, notwithstanding the claim of public universities that they seek a diverse student body.").

critics argue that participation of first- and second-generation Blacks in affirmative action programs does not truly further the goals of the policy. For example, the Reverend Jesse Jackson once proclaimed, "Universities have to give weight to the African American experience because that is for whom affirmative action was aimed in the first place. That intent must be honored."[22]

Others, such as Professors Lani Guinier and Henry Louis Gates, assert that the rising number of first- and second-generation Blacks reveals a flaw in the criteria that are generally used to determine merit during the admissions process at elite colleges and universities.[23] According to Guinier, current merit-based criteria reward and advantage those who are most privileged in society by failing to acknowledge the class and race privileges that may enable certain people to achieve high traditional academic success on grades and test scores.[24] As a consequence, she argues, many colleges and universities fail to recognize the merit in the work of those who are socioeconomically and racially disadvantaged but lack the access to privileges that could enable them to make it to the top of the admissions game.[25]

To some extent, one could argue that first- and second-generation Blacks fall into this category of privilege in that they tend to be more advantaged than African Americans in the admissions process and even on the job market. The claim is that acculturation into American society is easier for first- and second-generation Blacks because of positive images of them as hard-working immigrants, which stand in contrast to stereotypes of lazy black Americans. In addition, the claim is that first- and second-generation Blacks may have advantages over African Americans because of the psychological benefits of being a voluntary immigrant.[26]

---

22. Tom McNamee, *Who Really Benefits from Colleges' Affirmative Action?; Studies Show Many Are Immigrants, Biracial Students*, CHI. SUN-TIMES, Jul. 19, 2004, at 10 (quoting Jackson); *see also* Russ Mitchell & Randall Pinkston, College Admissions Criteria Favor Wealthy (CBS News: Evening News, July 3, 2004) ("We owe a debt, an obligation, to native born American blacks who can trace their history back to slavery and Jim Crow and continuing discrimination.").

23. Professor Guinier, who herself is of Jamaican-Caribbean ancestry, asserted that Haynie's discovery is "a window into the way 'meritocracy' has been destroyed by privilege and cumulative advantage. White students are also disproportionately privileged. It's about wealth, education, disposable assets, intergenerational wealth transfer." *"Roots" and Race*, HARV. MAG., Sept.–Oct. 2004, at 70 [hereafter *Roots*]; *see also* Rimer & Arenson, *supra* note 9, at A1 (describing discussions surrounding the make-up of the black college student population at elite schools).

24. *See* Stephen Carter, REFLECTIONS OF AN AFFIRMATIVE ACTION BABY 80 (1992) (asserting that the real winners in admissions programs are "the country's economically and educationally privileged"); *see also* Tomiko Brown-Nagin, *Elites, Social Movements, and the Law: The Case of Affirmative Action*, 105 COLUM. L. REV. 1436, 1476–77 (2005) ("Parental income, education, and occupational status are the primary positive indicators of whether a student is likely to attend quality elementary and secondary schools and thus a selective university, or any institution of higher education, for that matter.").

25. Lani Guinier, *Admissions Rituals as Political Acts: Guardians at the Gates of Our Democratic Ideals*, 117 HARV. L. REV. 113, 145–50 (2003); Guinier, *Our Preference, supra* note 8, at A13.

26. A voluntary immigrant is one who was not forced to come to the United States, *e.g.*, one who was not fleeing war and persecution. African Americans who were brought to colonial America as part of the slave trade, and their descendants are not voluntary immigrants, of course; as the late Professor John Ogbu explained, refugees are also not voluntary minorities. "*Immigrant or voluntary minorities* are people who have moved more or less voluntarily to the United States or to any other society because they believe that this would lead to more economic well-being, better overall opportunities, and/or greater political freedom." John U. Ogbu, *Differences in Cultural Frame of Reference*, 16 INT'L J. BEHAVIORAL DEVELOPMENT 483, 484 (1993). Of course, there is the question of whether the immigration of "voluntary immigrants" is truly voluntary when based on a desire to leave impoverished countries in hope of economic betterment.

For those in the camp of Professors Gates and Guinier, however, the problem is not the inclusion of first- and second-generation Blacks in affirmative action programs. Rather, the trouble lies in the way in which Blacks with long historical roots in the United States are being left behind, due in part to the failures of colleges and universities to find and recruit "the descendants" who can succeed at elite colleges and universities but are not finding their way to such institutions.[27]

One fact is clear: elite colleges and universities must begin to examine more closely the growing exclusion of the descendants on their campuses. These institutions must ask: to what extent, if any, should ancestral heritage play a role in the implementation of our affirmative action policies? If ancestral heritage is relevant, how should it be considered? For example, should ancestral heritage be evaluated in a way that may work to exclude first- and second-generation Blacks completely from affirmative action programs?

This chapter explores this very question concerning who should be the beneficiaries of affirmative action and specifically tackles the issue of whether affirmative action programs should exclude first- and second-generation black students.[28] Overall, this chapter argues that the inclusion of both first- and second-generation Blacks furthers the goals of affirmative action, in particular both the social justice and diversity rationales for the policy.[29] More important, this chapter contends that this debate about whether first- and second-generation Blacks should be eligible for affirmative action exposes the flaws of an admissions system that focuses solely on the endpoint of students in their academic careers rather than measuring the distance between where the students started their lives in terms of (dis)advantage and where they were able to climb in their academic journeys. In so doing, this chapter also stresses the importance of reevaluating traditional admissions standards at elite colleges and universities; such a reevaluation can aid schools in placing into their hallways more descendants and other disadvantaged students.

Before delving into this argument, however, Part I of this chapter highlights the importance of maintaining a social justice component to affirmative action programs, a contextual component that has slowly been dismantled at institutions of higher education,[30] and stresses the need for redoubled efforts in working to ensure that "the descendants" are not left behind on the road to college. In making this argument, Part I details and explores the various ethnic, cultural, and economic differences that may explain the disproportionate percentage of first- and second-generation Blacks in institutions of higher education across the United States. Part II argues that these differences should not work to exclude first- and second-generation black students from affirmative action programs. In making that argument, Part II analyzes the various purposes of affirmative action and then justifies the inclusion of first- and second-generation Blacks under both

---

27. *See* Haynie, *supra* note 12, at 43–53.

28. Although biracial students of African descent are also disproportionately underrepresented in elite institutions of higher education, they are not a primary focus in this discussion of race and inclusion in affirmative action programs, in part because many of them descend from people who were enslaved in the United States.

29. This chapter does not address the remedial justification for affirmative action because that rationale is limited to remedying only the discrimination of any particular institution in question. *See Wygant v. Jackson Bd. of Educ.*, 476 U.S. 267, 277–78 (1986). Given the disincentives of any school to admit its past discrimination, difficulties exist in receiving "compensation" for even African Americans or the descendants.

30. *Cf.* Guinier, *Our Preference*, *supra* note 8, at A13 ("Gone is the larger role of higher education in correcting for historical injustice, reaching out to those who are materially disadvantaged, encouraging publicly spirited innovators, or training a representative group of future leaders of all races.").

the social justice rationale and the diversity rationale as detailed in *Grutter*. Finally, this chapter concludes with a reiteration of the need to expand traditional views of merit in the admissions process at institutions of higher education.

I. Up from Slavery?

Since the creation of affirmative action in 1965,[31] scholars and activists have articulated numerous goals and reasons for the policy.[32] The most recently proclaimed rationale for affirmative action is diversity, which was upheld by the U.S. Supreme Court in *Grutter*.[33] Under this rationale, the enrollment of people from diverse racial and ethnic groups at colleges and universities campuses is critical to the learning process because such diversity helps increase understanding and tolerance among students and prepare them for work and leadership in an increasingly global market and economy.[34] Diversity is also viewed as a necessary component to the process of eliminating racial and gender stereotypes about which jobs, roles, or viewpoints are held by or are appropriate for members of any particular racial group.[35]

Given this rationale, it is difficult to argue in favor of excluding first- and second-generation Blacks from affirmative action programs because their presence, especially in an educational setting, helps prove that Blacks in the United States are not monolithic. Additionally, because of the way in which one's experiences often influence one's view or perspective on political and social matters, including first- and second-generation blacks increases the possibility of varying views among Blacks in any given institution. As a result, the learning experience for all is enhanced. Furthermore, the inclusion of a broad group of Blacks, including by ethnicity, helps create a critical mass of students of color on campuses that allows for an environment in which students of color will not feel as if they are speaking for their race on majority campuses.[36] As one African American student at Northwestern University in Chicago explained about the benefits of intraracial diversity among black students on her campus,

> The rich ethnic mix among black students — with all their differing points of view — gives me a sense of greater intellectual freedom. When I make a point in a classroom discussion, I don't worry as much that it might be taken as "the black ideal or black statement."[37]

From a social justice standpoint, however, the inclusion of first- and second-generation Blacks in affirmative action programs becomes more complicated. The basis of the

---

31. *See* Exec. Order No. 11,246, 30 Fed. Reg. 12,319 (Sept. 24, 1965); Onwuachi-Willig, *supra* note 5, at 125.

32. *See* Onwuachi-Willig, *supra* note 5, at 129; *see also* McNamee, *supra* note 22, at 10 ("Affirmative action has multiple goals, and I don't think that's stressed enough.").

33. *Grutter v. Bollinger*, 539 U.S. 306 (2003).

34. *Grutter*, 539 U.S. at 330–32; Onwuachi-Willig, *supra* note 5, at 128.

35. Onwuachi-Willig, *supra* note 5, at 128; Edward M. Chen, *The Judiciary, Diversity, and Justice for All*, 10 ASIAN L.J. 127, 134 (2003) (asserting that "[a] further harm of segregation and underrepresentation is the perpetuation of detrimental stereotypes, continuing the myth that certain groups are inherently incapable of attaining certain accomplishments or performing certain jobs").

36. *Grutter*, 539 U.S. at 320 (declaring that one benefit of diversity is the way in which it shows that there is no "'minority viewpoint' but rather a variety of viewpoints among" minorities).

37. McNamee, *supra* note 22, at 10 (quoting the student).

social justice rationale was most eloquently stated by President Lyndon B. Johnson in a speech to the graduating class of Howard University in 1965:

> You do not wipe away the scars of centuries by saying: "Now, you are free to go where you want, do as you desire, and choose the leaders you please." You do not take a man who for years has been hobbled by chains, liberate him, bring him to the starting line of a race, saying, 'you are free to compete with all the others,' and still justly believe you have been completely fair. Thus it is not enough just to open the gates of opportunity. All our citizens must have the ability to walk through those gates. This is the next and more profound stage of the battle for civil rights. We seek not just freedom but opportunity—not just legal equity but human ability—not just equality as a right and a theory, but equality as a fact and as a result.[38]

As described by President Johnson then, affirmative action was intended to assist a people who because of their race had been severely disadvantaged in schools and the job market to overcome the devastating effects of slavery, Jim Crow segregation, and contemporary racism in the United States.[39] Additionally, affirmative action was to produce benefits such as a greater number of role models for young children from disadvantaged racial groups and the donation of services to the underprivileged communities by those who had benefited from affirmative action.[40]

On this understanding of the social justice rationale, some race scholars contend that elite colleges and universities have failed to satisfy the goals of affirmative action because they have not focused their efforts on the recruitment and retention of "the descendants."[41] For example, one scholar has suggested that this understanding of the social justice rationale may be reason for limiting the participation of first- and second-generation Blacks in affirmative action programs so that energies can be refocused on the descendants.[42]

Concerns about the make-up of the current black population at many elite colleges and universities should be heeded. After all, admissions to colleges and universities should

---

38. Lyndon B. Johnson, *Commencement Address at Howard University, June 4, 1965: "To Fulfill These Rights,"* in Lee Rainwater & William L. Yancey, THE MOYNIHAN REPORT AND THE POLITICS OF CONTROVERSY (1967), at 126.

39. *Id.* at 125–29; Harry Holzer, *Affirmative Action After* Grutter: *Still Worth Preserving?*, 14 GEO. MASON U. CIV. RTS. L.J. 217, 219 (2004).

40. Paul Brest & Miranda Oshige, *Affirmative Action for Whom?*, 47 STAN. L. REV. 855, 865–73 (1995) (analyzing corrective justice as a rationale for affirmative action); *see also* Paul Brest, *Some Comments on* Grutter v. Bollinger, 51 DRAKE L. REV. 683, 683–86 (2003) (stating that individuals tend to give to organizations that support "groups with which they identify on the basis of characteristics such as race, ethnicity, and religion").

41. *See Roots, supra* note 23, at 70 (quoting Guinier, who has criticized the failure to reach native Blacks with long-term roots in the United States); *cf.* Bill Ong Hing, *Immigration Policies: Messages of Exclusion to African Americans*, 37 HOW. L.J. 237, 278–79 (1994) ("Those who are skeptical about this nation's commitment to addressing the plight of unemployed African Americans could look at the Immigration Act of 1990 and conclude that the nation is now beginning to use immigration to avoid improving the situation of native unemployed and under-skilled workers. A reasonable conclusion is that United States' leaders are either deliberately or subconsciously searching for a way to continue to avoid repairing the desperate situation of people whom they and the rest of the power structure have abandoned.").

42. Haynie, *supra* note 12, at 55 (arguing that "because all black students applying to [elite] schools are in essence competing for the same limited number of places," colleges and universities should begin to take the ethnic heritages of each of their black applicants into account).

not be just about creating "an aesthetic student body"[43] that looks racially diverse; rather, they should be about creating an environment in which students from differing backgrounds can genuinely learn from and gain from each other's experiences and expanding opportunities for education to people of all backgrounds. In the same way that many scholars have highlighted the advantages that white students from high socioeconomic classes may have in the admissions process, others have pinpointed various privileges that can enable first- and second-generation Blacks to have greater access to elite institutions of higher education. For example, some scholars have shown how immigration laws that favored educated and highly skilled black immigrants[44] have made it more likely for first- and second-generation Blacks, especially those of British Caribbean descent, to have higher incomes and educational backgrounds than African Americans or "the descendants" and thus more likely that their children will be enrolled at elite institutions.[45]

Additionally, they have pointed out how the same factors make it more likely for first- and second-generation Blacks to be employed as professionals than African Americans, another factor that increases the likelihood their children will enroll at elite institutions.[46] For example, in her study of Harvard College, Haynie found that 29.09 percent of the fathers of black Caribbean students had a college degree as compared to 14.86 percent of the fathers of African American students.[47] Although Haynie found that a greater percentage of fathers of African American students, 45.95 percent, possessed graduate or professional degrees than the fathers of black Caribbean students, of whom 41.82 percent had advanced degrees, she also found that 90.91 percent of African fathers with children at Harvard possessed graduate or professional degrees.[48] With respect to professions,

---

43. *Grutter*, 539 U.S. at 369–70 (Thomas, J., concurring in part and dissenting in part). Dean Frank Wu has explained that one danger of diversity is that a school can create a racially diverse classroom without achieving full integration or addressing the issues that face poor minorities, especially poor Blacks, in the educational pipeline. For example, he asserted, "We could have diversity by admitting a large number of Caribbean students, Haitians, Africans, and others who would not identify themselves nor perhaps be identified by others, as African-Americans." *Who Gets In*, *supra* note 21, at 533.

44. *See* Angela Onwuachi-Willig, *The Admission of Legacy Blacks*, 60 Vand. L. Rev. 101, 113 nn.38–39 (2007) (discussing how immigrations laws favored minority immigrants who were educated). Professor Bill Hing has written the following about the disproportionate percentage of Africans who entered the United States under an occupational preference:

> Of the 7614 Africans who immigrated in 1990 in other relative and occupational categories subject to quotas, thirty percent entered in an occupational preference. By way of comparison, the total quota immigrants from Mexico, 19,986, mainland China, 19,795, the Philippines, 19,588, India, 19,157, Korea, 18,624, and Vietnam, 8829, each outnumbered the sum of quota immigrants from the entire continent of Africa. The highest proportion of occupational visas in any of those countries was 17.1 percent for Korea. Mexico was under ten percent.

37 How. L.J. at 242.

45. Haynie, *supra* note 12, at 47.

46. *See generally* Barry R. Chiswick, *Sons of Immigrants: Are They at an Earnings Disadvantage?*, 67 Am. Econ Rev. 376 (1977). At the same time, scholars have found either that this income gap between black Caribbeans and African Americans is closing or does not exist. *See* Kalmijn, *supra* note 10, at 912, 928 (noting that the gap between Caribbean and African Americans has narrowed, is limited to the British Caribbean, and "the British advantage is limited to the occupational domain and is not as spectacular in magnitude as is commonly believed"); Kristin I. Butcher, *Black Immigrants to the United States: A Comparison with Native Blacks and Other Immigrants*, 47 Indus. Labor Relations Rev. 265 (1994) (finding that Caribbean immigrants were more likely to be employed in professional or managerial positions but finding no differences in earnings).

47. Haynie, *supra* note 12, at 48, Tbl. 5.

48. *Id.*

Haynie discovered that only 65.67 percent of fathers of African American students were occupied in managerial, administrative, professional, or paraprofessional occupations, as opposed to 76.47 percent of Caribbean fathers and 100 percent of African fathers.[49]

Scholars have also argued that in addition to higher education and income, first- and second-generation Blacks possess other advantages as a result of their immigrant status that may enable them to succeed in schools at greater rates. For example, the late Professor John Ogbu has explained that unlike involuntary immigrants such as the descendants, voluntary immigrants, which would include some first- and second-generation Blacks, generally are able to take advantage of educational opportunities because they, unlike African Americans, have not formed an oppositional culture that, as a means of resistance, rejects characteristics that are deemed "white."[50] According to the theory of oppositional culture, involuntary immigrants, such as African Americans, may view participation in the dominant culture as a threat to their identity; consequently, rather than viewing conformity that can lead to traditional success as a laudable goal, involuntary immigrants may view it as a betrayal of the group.[51]

For example, among high school students, black students in integrated environments who perform well academically, use standard English, or have primarily white friends may often be referred to by their peers as "acting white" or as "Oreos."[52] On the other hand, voluntary immigrants are more likely to view cultural differences from the dominant group as mere obstacles that they must overcome rather than ideas and practices they must resist.[53] To that end, first- and second generation Blacks are more likely to believe that it is possible to achieve the American dream if they work hard enough. Indeed, instead of comparing themselves to members of the dominant culture in terms of advantage and disadvantage, voluntary immigrants tend to compare themselves to the citizens in their own countries of origin; as a result, voluntary im-

---

49. *Id.* at 48, Tbl. 6; *see also* Malcolm Gladwell, *Black Like Them*, New Yorker, Apr. 29, 1996, available at www.gladwell.com/1996/1996_04_29_a_black.htm (describing the phenomenon in which West Indians in New York make more money than American Blacks).

50. Rong & Brown, *supra* note 10, at 540 (analyzing Ogbu's theories); *see also* Christopher Jencks, Rethinking Social Policy 129 (1992) ("In order to become fully assimilated into white America blacks must to some extent identify with people who have humiliated and oppressed them for three hundred years. Under these circumstances 'assimilation' is likely to be extraordinarily difficult."). Ogbu's theories are highly contested. *See* Prudence L. Carter, Keepin' It Real: School Success Beyond Black and White 53, 58 (2005) (explaining that "resistance to 'acting white' for many African American students is about maintaining cultural identity, not about embracing or rejecting the dominant standards of achievement"); Theresa Perry, Claude Steele, & Asa G. Hilliard III, Young, Gifted, and Black: Promoting High Achievement Among African-American Students 62–63 (2003) [hereinafter Young, Gifted, and Black] (critiquing Ogbu's theories).

51. *See also* Massey et al., *supra* note 13, at 8 (describing Ogbu's theories); Rong & Brown, *supra* note 18, at 540 (same).

52. *See also* Massey et al., *supra* note 13, at 8. An "Oreo" is defined as one who is black on the outside but white on the inside. *See* Kimberly Jade Norwood, *The Virulence of Blackthink and How Its Threat of Ostracism Threatens Those Not Deemed Black Enough*, 93 Ky. L.J. 143, 148 n.10 (2005). Some critics point to the successes of Caribbean Blacks to contend that the poor situation of many African Americans is a result of black American culture, not racism. However, as the experience of black Caribbeans in Canada, who have the same status in Canada as African Americans do in the United States, and of second-plus generation descendants of black Caribbeans in the United States demonstrates, much more is at work here than culture; much of it is racism. *See infra* Part II.

53. Massey et al., *supra* note 13, at 8; Gladwell, *supra* note 49; *see also* Lolita K. Buckner Inniss, *Tricky Magic: Blacks as Immigrants and the Paradox of Foreignness*, 49 DePaul L. Rev. 85, 123 (1999) (asserting that West Indians' "hopefulness ... fueled a move into the middle class").

migrants tend view themselves as more privileged than their compatriots in their home countries.[54]

Furthermore, as some scholars contend, unlike African Americans who are a distinct minority in the United States, many first-generation Blacks, although also a minority in this country, come from majority black countries where they are more frequently exposed to same-race role models of high achievement.[55] Exposure to same-race role models is a distinct advantage because the availability of role models can critically affect the success rates of young individuals. As some scholars have explained, young children from socially disadvantaged groups are more likely to have low career aspirations because they do not often see in positions of high achievement people who look like them and share their backgrounds.[56] Thus, to the extent that first- and second-generation Blacks (especially first-generation Blacks) have or have had visible models of success before them and the descendants have not, one would expect first- and second-generation black students to be in a better position to convince themselves that educational and occupational success in America is attainable.[57] For example, one Jamaican immigrant who worked as a teacher explained the differences she sees between West Indians and African Americans and the importance of seeing black leaders as a young child:

> I grew up seeing blacks in charge; that was my experience so I expect to be in charge. That's my frame of reference. American blacks, because of what was done to them, they don't quite see it like that. Those who see it like that are those who have escaped and have been educated, but even though they have been educated, something was done to them.[58]

As this woman's observations suggest, then, access to same-race role models presents a benefit to first- and second-generation Blacks not only because such models can show a person what he or she can become but also because such models can create an expectation in a person that he or she will achieve the same standard of success.

Additionally, as some studies hint, Whites often perceive first- and second-generation Blacks, in particular those of black Caribbean descent, more favorably than African Americans. In this sense, one could argue that first- and second-generation Blacks do not suffer the same racial stigma and disadvantage that the descendants have endured for generations.[59] For example, studies have shown that, in the employment context, immi-

---

54. Massey et al., *supra* note 13, at 8; *see also* John A. Garcia, *Caribbean Migration to the Mainland: A Review of Adaptive Experiences*, 487 Immigr. & Amer. Pub. Pol'y 114, 123 (1986) ("West Indians ... see life in the United States as better than in their homeland.").

55. Rong & Brown, *supra* note 10, at 555–56; Kalmijn, *supra* note 10, at 914; Mary C. Waters, *The Role of Lineage in Identity Formation Among Black Americans*, 14 Qualitative Sociology 57, 69–73 (1991).

56. *See, e.g.*, Brest & Oshige, *supra* note 40, at 869 (stating that young members of an intractably disadvantaged group often come to believe that "regardless of their efforts, group members simply cannot succeed"). Prior to the civil rights era, the problem of role modeling was not as dramatic because residential segregation ensured that poor black Americans also lived next to middle-class and upper-class black Americans, resulting in the availability of role models for poor as well as privileged black children within their own communities. *See* Olati Johnson, Book Note, *Integrating the "Underclass": Confronting America's Enduring Apartheid*, 47 Stan. L. Rev. 787, 807–08 (1995).

57. Sarah Stroud, *The Aim of Affirmative Action*, 25 Social Theory & Practice 385, 386–92 (1999) (describing the importance of same-race role models).

58. Mary C. Waters, Black Identities: West Indian Immigrant Dreams and American Realities 71 (1999).

59. Inniss, *supra* note 53, at 125 (referring to this phenomenon as the "Colin Powell Syndrome"). Professor Lani Guinier has claimed that "those from abroad 'have a different understanding of what

grant Blacks are identified as the "good Blacks" when compared to African Americans.[60] In particular, West Indian immigrants are often described by employers who hire a significant number of black workers as hard-working and reliable.[61] In comparing West Indian Blacks to African Americans, one white manager explained what he saw as the differences between the two groups:

> They [Caribbeans] tend to shy away from doing all of the illegal things because they have such strict rules down in their countries and jails. And they're nothing like here [African Americans]. So like, they're really paranoid to do something wrong. They seem to be very, very conscious of it. No matter what they have to do, if they have to try and work three jobs, they do. They won't go into drugs or anything like that.[62]

In fact, the tale of Caribbean success is so widely accepted as a story of the model black minority that the successes of first- and second-generation Blacks are often used to argue that African Americans have only themselves to blame for any educational and occupational failures.[63] Specifically, commentators point to Caribbean success as proof that it is not racism but instead black American culture that has created the plight of African Americans in this country.[64] As one author astutely noted, "The implication is that the key factor in understanding racial prejudice is not the behavior and attitudes of whites but the behavior and attitudes of blacks — not white discrimination but black culture."[65]

Finally, to the extent that there are positive stereotypes about black immigrants, such perceptions may transform into psychological benefits that can enable a certain kind of psychic freedom from the racial stigma and disadvantage — a psychic freedom that African Americans may have a harder time obtaining because of pervasive negative stereotypes about African Americans. In fact, some first- and second-generation Blacks work hard to ensure that distinctions are made between them and African Americans to avoid the full stigma and disadvantages of American blackness.[66] For example, one woman of Jamaican

---

it means to be black" and "they are less vulnerable to being viewed through the lens of a negative stereotype." *Roots, supra* note 23, at 70. Nathan Hare, founder of the very first ethnic studies program, which was at San Francisco State University, proclaimed,

> I have nothing against immigrants, but there are sociological realities we have to look at.... They don't have the stereotypes of them being lazy and so on.... We [African Americans] are the ex-slaves and inhabitants of the slums. They (immigrants) are coming in without that (baggage).

Johnson, *supra* note 8, at A1.

60. WATERS, *supra* note 58, at 116–23.

61. Suzanne Model, *West Indian Prosperity: Fact or Fiction?*, 42 SOCIAL PROBS. 535, 537 (1995).

62. Gladwell, *supra* note 49 (citing a study by Professor Mary Waters of Harvard University).

63. Gladwell, *supra* note 49 ("The example of West Indians as 'good' blacks makes the old blanket prejudice against American blacks all the easier to express."); Thomas Sowell, *Three Black Histories, in* ESSAYS AND DATA ON AMERICAN ETHNIC GROUPS 49 (1978) (arguing that the relative success of Caribbeans in the United States "undermines the explanatory power of current white discrimination as a cause of current black poverty").

64. *See* Sowell, *supra* note 63, at 43–49.

65. Gladwell, *supra* note 49.

66. *See* WATERS, *supra* note 58, at 5, 64–76; Gladwell, *supra* note 49 ("Their advantage depends on their remaining outsiders, on remaining unfamiliar, on being distinct by custom, culture, and language from the American blacks they would otherwise resemble."); *see also* Fernandez-Kelly and Suzanne Model, *West Indian Prosperity: Fact or Fiction?*, 42 SOCIAL PROBS. 535, 538 (1995) (noting that the success of study subjects, including second-generation black students with roots in Haiti, was "rooted in deliberate attempts [by the students] to disassociate themselves from the stigma imposed upon black populations in the United States through an affirmation of their national identity and their religious fervor"). Malcolm Gladwell has explained that "West Indians cannot escape the fact

descent, who believed that Whites would treat her better if they knew that she was not a native black American, had her mother teach her a Jamaican accent to use when she applied for jobs or places of residence.[67]

In the end, regardless of what findings are made in the future about first- and second-generation black students, it will be important for elite colleges and universities to reconsider their admissions policies and goals if they want to correct the increasing disappearance of African Americans from their hallways. If affirmative action is not fulfilling its corrective justice purposes in allowing for opportunities at and access to institutions of higher education for black students of all backgrounds, then schools with affirmative action programs have an obligation to reevaluate their admissions systems, and they should do so with an eye toward answering questions regarding the disproportionately low number of African American students or descendants on their campuses. As Professor Martha Biondi of Northwestern University asserted, "It's about being creative and looking for those uncut diamonds."[68] Schools should ask themselves, "Are we really making the effort to find those students who have shown, through the obstacles they have overcome and their drive for success, that they will contribute greatly to our school and succeed within our hallways?"

II. The Goals of Black Folks

While colleges and universities should be careful not to organize their programs to exclude African Americans or the descendants in a way that undermines the goals of affirmative action, they should also work to ensure that such efforts do not transform, change, or push the nation away from the various goals of affirmative action, including the goal of achieving social justice through affirmative action. When viewed through a race, class, or discrimination lens, however, the inclusion of first- and second-generation Blacks in affirmative action programs furthers both the diversity and social justice rationales for the policy.

A. Enhancing Diversity

The ways in which including first- and second-generation Blacks in affirmative action programs advances the diversity rationale of affirmative action are clear. The Supreme

---

that their success has come, to some extent, at the expense of American blacks, and that as they have noisily differentiated themselves from African-Americans—promoting the stereotype of themselves as the good blacks—they have made it easier for whites to join in." Gladwell, *supra* note 49; *see also* Chacko, *supra* note 10, at 494, 499 (noting that "first-generation Black immigrants overwhelmingly emphasized their ethnic identities and national origins, underplaying the more generic identification as Black"); M. Patricia Fernandez-Kelly & Richard Schauffler, *Divided Fates: Immigrant Children in a Restructured U.S. Economy*, 28 Int'l Migration Rev. 662, 682 (1994) (noting the same actions among Nicaraguan students who hold fast to their separate immigrant collective identity to protect themselves from negative stereotypes of other Latino groups). As Professor Mary Waters of Harvard University asserted, in some instances, it is immigrant Blacks who "voice some of the worst stereotypes and negative perceptions of American blacks imaginable." Waters, *supra* note 55, at 69; *see also* Waters, *supra* note 58, at 64–76 (quoting a series of negative comments about African-Americans by West Indians in New York).

67. Waters, *supra* note 55, at 70; *see also* F. Nii-Amoo Dodoo, *Assimilation Differences Among Africans in America*, 76 Soc. Forces 527, 531 (1997) (noting that "there is evidence that black immigrants emphasize their foreign origins because they perceive that it conveys an advantage").

68. McNamee, *supra* note 22, at 10.

Court first recognized the benefits of racial diversity on college campuses in its decision *Regents of University of California v. Bakke.*[69] Through Justice Powell's opinion, the Court acknowledged that schools could use race to ensure diversity as a means of enhancing the educational environment.[70]

Twenty-five years later in *Grutter*, the Supreme Court, in an opinion written by Justice O'Connor, endorsed Justice Powell's pronouncements about the many benefits of diversity. The Court explained that "just as growing up in a particular region or having particular professional experience is likely to affect an individual's views, so too is one's own, unique, experience of being a racial minority in a society ... in which race unfortunately still matters."[71] The Court then highlighted the various ways in which a university may benefit from having a racially diverse student body, such as enhanced learning among participants of differing backgrounds through exposure to diverse perspectives, an increased ability of students to work and live with people from different cultures, and the destruction of racial stereotypes regarding the intellectual capacity and viewpoints of both minority and majority members.[72]

According to the Court, diversity in classrooms is an integral part of promoting understanding across racial lines because it helps ensure meaningful representation of people who may bring perspectives that persons outside of their group may not hold.[73] Diversity also increases the possibility that all students will learn to appreciate their similarities with and differences from others and learn to communicate and work across racial boundaries.[74] Finally, in addition to improving cross-racial understanding, meaningful diversity assists in breaking down racial stereotypes because it forces people to learn that there is no "'minority viewpoint' but rather a variety of viewpoints among" minorities.[75]

The enrollment of first- and second-generation black students at colleges and universities advances all of these goals. First, having a population of first- and second-generation black students in institutions of higher education helps ensure that an often-overlooked minority group, Blacks, maintains some representation within the campus community. It also helps enrich the environment of any school with the host of experiences of first- and second-generation black students, students whose experiences in life may in some ways be similar to those of monoracial African Americans but may also differ in many respects. Second, the presence of a critical mass of first- and second-generation Blacks on college and university campuses enhances the possibility not only of majority members' learning to appreciate their similarities to and differences from Blacks as a whole but also to appreciate the various differences among Blacks themselves, culturally, socially, and personally.

In addition, the continuing existence of a critical mass of first- and second-generation Blacks at schools will enable better understanding and feelings between blacks of direct

---

69. 438 U.S. 265 (1978).

70. *Id.* at 314–15.

71. *Grutter v. Bollinger*, 539 U.S. 306, 333 (2003).

72. *Id.* at 329–36.

73. *Id.* at 319–20, 29–33; *see also* Devon W. Carbado & Mitu Gulati, *What Exactly Is Racial Diversity?*, 91 Cal. L. Rev. 1149, 1158–51 (2003) (detailing how a person's viewpoint is influenced by racial identity and how diversity may shape the content of discussions).

74. *See Grutter*, 539 U.S. at 329–36; *see also* Brest & Oshige, *supra* note 40, at 862 (exploring the rationales for affirmative action and how they apply to different racial groups).

75. *Grutter*, 539 U.S. 319–20 (quoting Dean Kent Syverud of Washington University in St. Louis School of Law).

Caribbean and African heritage and African Americans. Often, black students on predominantly white campuses form strong bonds to each other simply because of their low numbers. As one student at the University of California–Berkeley explained, "Because our numbers are so low, just being black on campus brings you together. The first thing is you're black."[76] In this sense, to the extent that a greater number or critical mass of Blacks on campus helps to alleviate feelings of alienation and isolation, then the presence of first- and second-generation black students on campus arguably helps increase the chances of retention for all black students, including the descendants, at these colleges and universities.

Finally, the inclusion of a minority group within one minority—specifically, first- and second-generation Blacks within the larger group of Blacks in the United States—makes it all the more likely that there will be a diverse range of views among that larger minority group throughout the entire campus community. Just as being a black American who descends from slaves in North Carolina may influence the perspective or views of a student, so too does being a second-generation Black American who descends from Caribbean slaves and grew up in New York City with the task of navigating his way between two very different worlds, such as a world of a strong Jamaican culture and another of urban African American culture.

The fact is that there is no all-encompassing black reality. Campuses will be better off in the long run if they work to ensure the inclusion of differing representations of black realities rather than exclude groups such as first- and second-generation Blacks from affirmative action programs. Such exclusion could have a deleterious effect on Blacks' entire representation on campus by taking away from the critical mass of students that helps combat declining retention rates of black students. In short, including first- and second-generation black students in affirmative action programs at colleges and universities powerfully advances the goals encompassed by the diversity rationale.

B. Reaching Social Justice

What is less obvious is how the consideration of first- and second-generation Blacks as part of affirmative action programs furthers the social justice component of the policy. Over the years, the meaning of social justice through affirmative action has become distorted. For example, in efforts to prohibit the use of affirmative action across the country, opponents of affirmative action have manipulated the social justice component of affirmative action by focusing many of their criticisms on class and arguing that the policy largely benefits the black middle class.[77] In so doing, they have essentially ignored the fact that affirmative action was never designed to specifically address disadvantages due to class, but those due to race.[78] Although both class and race disparities overlap in many

---

76. Johnson, *supra* note 8, at A1.

77. Frederick A. Morton Jr., Note, *Class-Based Affirmative Action: Another Illustration of America Denying the Impact of Race*, 45 RUTGERS L. REV. 1089, 1092, 1118 (1993); *see, e.g.*, Antonin Scalia, *The Disease As Cure: "In Order to Get Beyond Racism, We Must First Take Account of Race,"* 1979 WASH. U. L. Q. 147, 153–54 ("I am not willing to prefer the son of a prosperous and well-educated black doctor or lawyer—solely because of his race—to the son of a recent refugee of Eastern Europe who is working as a manual laborer to get his family ahead.").

78. Morton, *supra* note 77, at 1123–25 ("There is nothing in the history of affirmative action, however, that would suggest that race was used as a proxy or that class was originally the basis for such programs.... Rather, it was designed to equalize access to areas from which blacks were traditionally excluded.").

instances and colleges certainly need to address the way in which the admissions process generally advantages those from higher socioeconomic classes,[79] it is important to remember that the original policy focused on race and the need to overcome disadvantages due to racism. When one keeps that focus in mind, it becomes clear that having first- and second-generation Blacks in schools' affirmative action programs is a necessary and important part of advancing the social justice goals behind the policy. To argue that first- and second-generation Blacks should be excluded from affirmative action programs or that their participation should be severely limited in such programs because they may be in some instances more advantaged than African Americans misses the very point of affirmative action. As noted, affirmative action was instituted to address the disadvantages of being a racial minority, in particular a black person, in the United States; key among these disadvantages is being perceived as inferior simply because of one's skin color and suffering the effects of such perceptions on one's opportunities in life.[80] As Lee Bollinger, president of Columbia University, asserted, "The issue is not origin, but social practices. It matters in American society whether you grow up black or white. It's that differential effect that really is the basis for affirmative action."[81]

Just as many of the descendants understand that being light-skinned or middle class does not exempt any African Americans from the disadvantages of blackness and racism,[82] nor does being a first- or second-generation black American allow one to escape the harms of racial discrimination.[83] In most instances, white Americans simply do not distinguish between native Blacks with long-term roots in the United States and those with shorter roots in the country. As Professor Mary Waters of Harvard University has explained, "Society generally classifies [black people] according to the color of their skin," and the white community has generally been oblivious to the immigrant component of the black community.[84]

Although some studies indicate that within the employment context, West Indians are often viewed more favorably than African Americans, the fact remains that West Indians and first- and second-generation Blacks from other parts of the African diaspora still suffer from stigmas and disadvantages that are attached to their blackness. Such disadvantages accrue to those who identify as black, or rather to those who are identified as black in the United States, regardless of their or their parents' national origins.[85]

---

79. *See* William Julius Wilson, THE TRULY DISADVANTAGED 115, 163–64 (1987) (arguing that minorities from the most advantaged families are likely to be disproportionately represented in programs of preferential treatment).

80. *See generally* Angela Onwuachi-Willig & Mario L. Barnes, *By Any Other Name? On Being "Regarded As" Black, and Why Title VII Should Apply Even If Lakisha and Jamal Are White*, 2005 WISC. L. REV. 1283.

81. Rimer & Arenson, *supra* note 9, at A1.

82. Morton, *supra* note 77, at 1132 (stating that "it is a grave mistake … to [think] that because of a middle class background, [a] black child has not been victimized by past and present racial discrimination"); *see also* Camille Nelson, *Breaking the Camel's Back: A Consideration of Mitigatory Defenses and Racism-Related Mental Illness*, 9 MICH. J. RACE & L. 77, 84 (2003) ("Discrimination is not limited to low-income or uneducated Blacks, but is also reported by Black middle-class professionals.").

83. *See* Derrick Bell, FACES AT THE BOTTOM OF THE WELL: THE PERMANENCE OF RACISM 3 (1993) ("Despite undeniable progress for many, no African-Americans are insulated from incidents of racial discrimination. Our careers, even our lives, are threatened because of our color. Even the most successful of us are haunted by the plight of our less fortunate brethren who struggle for existence in what some social scientists call the 'underclass.'").

84. Waters, *supra* note 55, at 61.

85. Rong & Brown, *supra* note 10, at 556 ("Racism and discrimination prevent many Black immigrants from being incorporated into mainstream America.").

As Professor Devon Carbado has detailed, for many black immigrants to the United States, they become "Americanized" by the experience of racism in this country regardless of whether they desire to be so "naturalized" or not.[86] Describing his own experience as a Jamaican British immigrant to the United States, Professor Carbado explained that he did not initially wish to be perceived as a black American, with all of its attendant socially ascribed negative stereotypes,[87] but he had no choice about how he would be perceived. People imposed negative stereotypes that had developed about Blacks in the United States on him simply because of his phenotype. Professor Carbado eloquently explained,

> I became a black American long before I acquired American citizenship. *Unlike citizenship, black racial naturalization was always available to me, even as I tried to make myself unavailable for that particular Americanization process.* Given the negative images of black Americans on 1970s British television and the intra-racial tensions between blacks in the U.K. and blacks in America, I was not eager, upon my arrival to the United States, to assert a black American identity....
>
> *But I became a black American anyway.* Before I freely embraced that identity it was ascribed to me. This ascription is part of a broader social practice wherein all of us are made intelligible via racial categorization. My intelligibility was skin deep. More particularly, it was linked to the social construction of blackness, a social construction whose phenotypic reach I could not escape. Whether I liked it or not, my everyday social encounters were going to reflect standard racial scripts about black American life.
>
> And in fact they did. I was closely followed or completely ignored when I visited department stores. Women clutched their purses upon encountering me in elevators. People crossed the street to avoid me. The seat beside me on the bus was almost always racially available for another black person. Already I wanted to be a black American no more. But that racial desire was at odds with my racial destiny. *There was nothing I could do to prevent myself from increasingly becoming a black American.*[88]

In sum, the disadvantage of being black in the United States applies to all those who are perceived as belonging to that group, regardless of their more recent ancestry.[89]

---

86. Devon Carbado, *(E)racing the Fourth Amendment*, 100 MICH. L. REV. 946, 947–50 (2002).

87. *See* Michele Goodwin, *Race As Proxy: An Introduction*, 53 DEPAUL L. REV. 931, 933 (2004) ("Color is linked with laziness, incompetence, and hostility, as well as disfavored viewpoints, such as a lack of patriotism and disloyalty to the United States.").

88. *Id.* (emphasis added); *see also* Baynes, *supra* note 19, at 125 ("I am 'Black' in the American context, I stay Black, and (even if I wanted to, which I do not) I am physically unable to lose my racial identity."); Inniss, *supra* note 53, at 125–26 (describing the claim about the effect of American racism by Jamaican immigrant Colin Ferguson, who shot commuters on a subway in New York). A young Ethiopian immigrant student detailed similar feelings about discovering she was black through American racism. He stated:
> During the first couple of years [after arriving in the United States], I considered myself only Ethiopian. Then I started thinking of myself as African. As time passed ... I interacted more with [native] Blacks and other Americans. This country made me more aware of my race. *I was Blacker than I thought I was!*

Chacko, *supra* note 10, at 498 (emphasis added).

89. *See* Carbado, *supra* note 86, at 947–50; *see also* Kevin R. Johnson, *Immigration and Latino Identity*, 19 CHICANO-LATINO L. REV. 197, 206 (1998) (noting that "racism doesn't recognize the distinctions between Mexican-Americans and Mexican immigrants" because "to dominant society, a 'foreigner' is a 'foreigner'").

Several studies indicate that it is the racial stigma and disadvantages of blackness, and not the country from which one's grandparents or great-grandparents came, that negatively impacts the educational performance and opportunities of Blacks in the United States. Were it a simple matter of not having descended from slaves in this country, one would expect that the relative advantages of voluntary immigrant status would accrue to future generations of immigrant Blacks, much as it has done with certain Asian American groups who have the image of the "model minority"[90] attached to them.[91] Such an effect would seem consistent with assimilation theory, which contends that "national origin groups gradually become more similar to the members of the host society."[92] As immigrant Blacks and their children become more and more like their host community of native African Americans, however, the disadvantages suffered by that host community attach to the newcomers. While some "second-generation youth respond ... by joining with their parents in embracing the national identity of their countries of origin," those "second-generation youth who are racialized as black ... take on a black American identity," and "the adoption of this identity ... constitutes a rejection of white mainstream culture and values that, through processes linked to race and class, marginalize black youth."[93]

Normally, such acculturation and assimilation into one's host group would lead to "upward progress with each succeeding generation" as it has proven with certain groups of Asian descent,[94] but because the generations that follow first-generation Blacks and their children eventually come to resemble their host group African Americans, who are severely disadvantaged both economically and socially, these later generations do not continue to "benefit" from their more recent immigrant status.[95] Rather, cultural assimilation for these generations means that they "lose some of the advantages that their immigrant parents had over African-Americans, and that their race becomes a handicap in the status attainment process."[96]

As Professor Lolita Buckner Inniss has asserted, "The general failure of assimilation has made the black American experience unique among immigrant experiences in that

---

90. "The model minority stereotype posits Asian-Americans as uniquely successful among minority groups. They work hard, save money, and achieve material success, while their children study equally hard and earn high marks in school." Jean Shin, *The Asian American Closet*, 11 Asian L. J. 1, 3 (2004); *see also* Frank Wu, *Changing America, Three Arguments About Asian Americans and the Law*, 45 Am. U. L. Rev. 811, 813–14 (1996) (challenging the myth of the model minority). The image of the "model minority," however, has also proven to be damaging in other respects.

91. Chacko, *supra* note 10, at 493 (noting studies that show that some groups such as Eastern European and Russian Jews and some Asians, such as the Chinese and Korean, follow "a path of upward mobility and assimilation into the White middle class").

92. Kalmijn, *supra* note 10, at 912; *see also* Model, *supra* note 61, at 548 ("West Indians assimilate economically to the black population, not the white.").

93. George E. Fouron & Nina Glick-Schiller, *The Generation of Identity: Redefining the Second Generation Within a Transnational Social Field*, in Levitt & Waters, *supra* note 10, at 175.

94. *See* Rong & Brown, *supra* note 10, at 538–39; *see also* Waters, *supra* note 58, at 5 (noting that "when West Indians lose their distinctiveness as immigrants or ethnics they become not just Americans, but black Americans" and "given the ongoing prejudice and discrimination in American society, this represents downward mobility for immigrants and their children").

95. Rong & Brown, *supra* note 10, at 556 ("For many Black immigrants, assimilation to the culture of inner-city native Blacks may lead to permanent subordination and disadvantage."); Kalmijn, *supra* note 10, at 927 (same).

96. Kalmijn, *supra* note 10, at 912, 915 ("Caribbean blacks thus represent a case where cultural assimilation may hamper rather than improve their socioeconomic achievement."); *see also* Rong & Brown, *supra* note 10, at 541, 556 ("This process of racial socialization into oppositional culture among second-generation immigrants may disrupt the plans for intergenerational upward mobility of many first-generation parents who are moving ahead economically.").

it is an unremitting immigrant experience — an experience of continued exclusion."[97] The result is that, as future generations stemming from immigrant Blacks come to identify as part of their African American host group, they are more likely to associate with oppositional culture and tend to do less well in school and on the job market.[98] Thus, not only do second- and later-generation Blacks lose any benefit that their parents may have had in growing up and experiencing life and potentially more favorable race relations in their home countries, they also begin to lose the self-confidence and cultural distinctiveness that certain scholars have argued aided their ancestors in succeeding in the United States.[99] As Professor Mary Waters explained, the second generation or the children of immigrant Blacks begin to "use American, not Caribbean [or immigrant] yardsticks to measure how good a [situation] is."[100]

Studies demonstrate that for second-generation Blacks, lower self-esteem is associated with being born in the United States, not with being born, for example, in the West Indies.[101] Waters further noted that

> the experiences of West Indians show that even "good culture" is no match for racial discrimination. Over the course of one generation the structural realities of American race relations and the American economy undermine the cultures of the West Indian immigrants and create responses among the immigrants, and especially their children, that resemble the cultural responses of African Americans to long histories of exclusion and discrimination.[102]

In the end, the drop off rates for school and occupational attainment for third- and later-generation Blacks are often significant. Though even some white ethnics experience a drop-off in school attainment between the second and third generations, the differences are much larger for black populations, with Caribbeans having a 0.54 difference (more than half a year) in the number of years of school completed and Africans and Whites having a difference of 0.41 and 0.29, respectively.[103] Indeed, one study showed that by the third-plus generation, the percentage of students of Caribbean descent graduating from high school had fallen from 63.9 percent in the second generation to 50.2 percent in the third generation.[104] For the third generation of Blacks of more direct African descent, the high school graduation rate fell from 60.3 percent in the second generation to 51.4 percent in the third generation.[105] This trend remained the same for the completion of college, with the percentages falling again for those of Caribbean descent from 21.5 percent to 11.3 percent and those of African descent from 10.9 percent to 4.9 per-

---

97. Inniss, *supra* note 53, at 85–86.

98. Rong & Brown, *supra* note 10, at 543; Model, *supra* note 61, at 536–37; *see also* Ruben G. Rumbaut, *The Crucible Within: Ethnic Identity, Self-Esteem, and Segmented Assimilation Among Children of Immigrants*, 28 INT'L MIGRATION REV. 748 (1994) (noting that although Jamaicans often sustain a national origin identity into the second generation, that percentage "drops from 63 percent among those born in Jamaica to 23 percent among those born in the United States").

99. Kalmijn, *supra* note 10, at 914; *see also* Gladwell, *supra* note 49 (describing racism against West Indian Blacks in Canada as partially due to the fact that, unlike West Indian Americans, black Canadians do not have a group such as African Americans to keep them from being perceived as the bottom).

100. Waters, *supra* note 58, at 7.

101. Rumbaut, *supra* note 98, at 783.

102. Waters, *supra* note 58, at 8.

103. Rong & Brown, *supra* note 10, at 548.

104. *Id.* at 549–51, Tbl. 3.

105. *Id.* at 549–51, Tbl. 3. For third and later generations of persons of European descent, the high school graduation rate fell from 65.7 percent to 60.4 percent. *Id.*

cent.[106] In sum, after one generation, the benefits of immigrant status among first- and second-generation Blacks begin to disappear as those Blacks become a part of their host group and are forced to overcome the many disadvantages that stem from simply being black in America.[107]

Additionally, to argue for the exclusion of first- and second-generation Blacks based on their relative advantages to African Americans ignores the fact that first- and second-generation black Americans themselves are not a monolithic group. Much as there are differences in the socioeconomic status among Japanese, Chinese, and Korean Americans and Laotian, Cambodian, Vietnamese, and Hmong Americans, many of whom are severely poor,[108] there are vast differences among first- and second-generation Blacks from various countries.

For example, British Caribbean Blacks, who themselves are a diverse group, tend to be in a far better socioeconomic position than French- or Spanish-speaking Caribbean Blacks,[109] who are generally worse off than African Americans.[110] Although British Caribbeans complete slightly more years of schooling and are more likely to receive a college degree than African Americans, French- and Spanish-speaking Caribbeans are even less educated than African Americans.[111] According to data from one study, British Caribbeans complete an average of 12.1 years of schooling while African Americans complete an average of 12 years of schooling; French-speaking Caribbeans complete an average of 10.9 years of schooling; and Spanish-speaking Caribbeans complete an average of 10.3 years of schooling.[112] Likewise, although British Caribbeans may have an advantage over African Americans in terms of socioeconomic differences and occupational attainment—with 9 percent higher occupational status and 12 percent higher earnings than African Americans—French- and Spanish-speaking Caribbeans, when compared to African Americans, have 5 percent and 10 percent lower occupational status and 11 percent and 10 percent lower earnings, respectively.[113]

Such differences among ethnic groups of first- and second-generation Blacks are due in part to language, that is, the relative mastery of English and the positive images of those who are thought to have British accents.[114] Even social capital—consisting of reinforcing networks through churches and other ethnic community organizations—plays a significant role in determining who is advantaged by immigrant status among first- and second-generation Blacks. For example, unlike those of recent Caribbean descent who often have large communities and strong ethnic networks in the Northeast, many African immigrants, who lack a ready-made community in the United States because of signifi-

---

106. *Id.*

107. Waters, *supra* note 58, at 8 (noting that over time "the distinct elements of West Indian culture the immigrants are most proud of—a willingness to work, a lack of attention to racialism, a high value on education, and strong interests in saving for the future—are undermined by the realities of life in the United States").

108. John O. Calmore, *Racialized Space and the Culture of Segregation: "Hewing a Stone of Hope From a Mountain of Despair,* 143 U. Pa. L. Rev. 1233, 1247 (1995) (noting that 67.2 percent of Laotians, 65.5 percent of the Hmong, 46.2 percent of Cambodians, and 33.5 percent of Vietnamese live in poverty in the United States).

109. *See* Kalmijn, *supra* note 10, at 917.

110. *Id.* at 918–20.

111. *Id.* at 918.

112. *Id.* at 919, Tbl. 1 & 928 (also noting that Hispanic Caribbeans may face double discrimination because they are both black and Hispanic).

113. *Id.* at 920–22, Tbl. 2.

114. *Id.* at 918–22; *cf.* Chacko, *supra* note 10, at 502 (acknowledging how "[l]anguage proficiency [of English] assists Ethiopian immigrants to assimilate more rapidly than their peers from non-English-speaking countries").

cantly smaller numbers, "face more difficulties in distinguishing themselves culturally, socially, and psychologically from native Black Americans and may accordingly assimilate into popular youth culture or oppositional culture at a faster rate."[115] Likewise, those Caribbeans outside of the extensive network of islanders on the East Coast, face more difficulties in succeeding by traditional standards due to a lack of social capital.

Most important, the fact that some first- and second-generation Blacks may have some relative advantages, educationally and socioeconomically, over African Americans does not mean that they are generally advantaged in society. When compared to Whites, many first- and second-generation Blacks, even British Caribbeans, are still significantly disadvantaged.[116] Studies show that black families in general, including those of first- and second-generation Blacks, are behind white families in terms of education level, income, wealth, home ownership and value, and exposure to neighborhood violence.[117] Even the words of employers in various studies about black Caribbeans' advantage over African Americans indicate that employers only prefer black Caribbeans to African Americans, not black Caribbeans generally.[118]

Finally, we cannot ignore the fact that many first- and second-generation Blacks face double discrimination—traditional racism and xenophobia on the part of both by Whites and African Americans.[119] As one scholar noted, "Those from African countries suffer from negative stereotypes, often [being] considered unpolished, lacking in social graces, or unsophisticated. *The negative images are portrayed by American blacks no less than whites.*"[120] For example, one second generation Haitian student in secondary school described the double xenophobia she has experienced:

> It may be true that whites discriminate, but I have no complaints [about them] because I don't know many [whites] ... but blacks, they're trouble; they make fun of the way we [Haitians] speak.... They call us stupid and backwards and try to beat us up. I was always scared, so I [tried] to do well in school and that's how I ended [in a magnet school]. There I don't stand out as much and I can feel good about being Haitian.[121]

Studies have shown that part of the reason why first- and second-generation Blacks wish to form identities separate from African Americans or the descendants is the negative social treatment that they may have experienced from African Americans, which can

---

115. Rong & Brown, *supra* note 10, at 557; *see also* Haynie, *supra* note 12, at 45–46 (describing networks that have enabled Caribbean black students to participate in high school preparatory programs in the Northeast which feed students to elite Northeast colleges and universities such as Harvard).

116. Kalmijn, *supra* note 10, at 913.

117. *See* Onwuachi-Willig, *supra* note 44, at 150–55 (discussing and comparing numbers in each of these categories).

118. For example, as one white male manager asserted, "If I had one position open and *it was a West Indian versus an American black, I'd go with the West Indian* ... their reliability, their willingness to do the job ... *they have a different drive than American blacks.*" Model, *supra* note 61, at 535 (emphasis added).

119. Rong & Brown, *supra* note 10, at 544; *see also* Fernandez-Kelly and Schauffler, *supra* note 66, at 675, 684 (finding in a study of second-generation students that "when Haitian children speak of discrimination, they are often thinking of the verbal and physical abuses they experience at the hands of native black Americans in their neighborhoods and schools").

120. Inniss, *supra* note 53, at 132 (emphasis added).

121. Fernandez-Kelly and Schauffler, *supra* note 66, at 684. In a strange way, this negative treatment by African Americans of first- and second-generation Blacks can work to the advantage of first- and second-generation Blacks because it prevents, as we see in the quote above, their full integration into their host group.

include taunting because of accents and family dress.[122] As the data indicate, immigrant Blacks often experience deeper hurt as a result of such criticisms from African Americans than Whites.[123] Indeed, one could argue that first- and second-generation black Americans suffer a double disability that many African Americans do not have to endure, both the disadvantages of blackness in a racist American society and the disadvantages of foreignness in a nationalist society.[124] The simple fact is this: the black immigrant experience is rather complex. In the United States, non-native Blacks have been and are greeted by a variety of reactions — "a curious mixture of fear and admiration, distaste and awe,"[125] and much like the descendants, never inclusion.

Conclusion

Those of us entrenched in college and university life must begin to grapple with the increasing and disproportionate rate at which first- and second-generation Blacks are outpacing and outrunning African Americans on the pathways to our country's finest colleges and universities. The disproportionately low percentages of African Americans at the elite institutions of higher education should be of serious concern to schools that have race-based affirmative action programs and that express a commitment to both diversity and social justice. At the same time, however, these colleges and universities must be careful not to scapegoat certain segments of the black community — in particular first- and second-generation Blacks — in their efforts to ensure inclusion, opportunity, and diversity within their doors. In fact, Blacks themselves must be careful not to fight each other over one very tiny sliver of a pie that should be expanded and opened to all. After all, regardless of ancestral heritage, all Blacks endure discrimination in a society that negatively stereotypes, stigmatizes, and disadvantages blackness.

In the end, one critical step in reaching a broader level of inclusion among different groups is to reevaluate the traditional standards that colleges and universities use in deciding to whom they will open their doors and examine more closely the reasons more

---

122. Chacko, *supra* note 10, at 498. One young Ethiopian student described taunts from native American Blacks, asserting, "When you spoke, they would act like they didn't understand. They'd say, 'Speak English, man.'" *Id.* One immigrant described resentment and discrimination she felt from African Americans, noting,

> [When I came to this country] I thought that [black Americans] were going to be very much like me, that they were going to accept me as one of them. But I found that was not so at all. They felt that they were above us. The few that I had to deal with even insulted me at times, and they were not as willing to help you as a white person would. Those are the simple things that at that level of my mixing with people I met, I found that the black [Americans] were standoffish and didn't like us very much.

Waters, *supra* note 55, at 70.

123. Chacko, *supra* note 10, at 498 ("When native Blacks were vocally critically of them, young Ethiopian immigrants reported being more upset and offended than if the comments had been made by Whites.").

124. *See* Roy Simon Bryce-Laporte, *Black Immigrants: The Experience of Invisibility and Inequality*, 3 J. BLACK STUDS. 29 (1972) (arguing that Caribbean American Blacks face the double burden of xenophobia and racism on the labor market); *see also* Kalmijn, *supra* note 10, at 923 (noting that "immigrants typically face some disadvantages in the labor market upon arrival in American society due to a lack of information on jobs and possibly a shortage of social capital to support the status attainment process as well").

125. Inniss, *supra* note 53, at 88.

African Americans are not finding their way to elite colleges and universities. Indeed, such considerations are central to fulfilling not only the social justice rationale for affirmative action but also our interest in diversity. As the Supreme Court noted in *Grutter*, greater diversity, both interracially and intraracially, can only enhance institutions of higher education by bringing a wider range of voices, perspectives, and understanding to those places. Instead of creating and widening the black divide on the use of affirmative action, we should be joining together to ensure that all of these goals of affirmative action are fulfilled.

III
Educational Adequacy and Accountability

7

The No Child Left Behind Act and the Birth of Race-Conscious School Finance Litigation

Preston C. Green III,[*] Bruce D. Baker,[**] and
Joseph O. Oluwole[***]

Key Terms

Vertical Equity: Refers to the idea that particular categories of students and districts may have dramatically different needs that require different levels of resources.

Horizontal Equity: Refers to the idea that all districts should have relative equality of spending inputs to schooling regardless of property wealth.

Introduction

Minority plaintiffs have primarily pursued two types of legal arguments to attain equal educational opportunities: school desegregation and school finance.[1] The goal of school desegregation litigation is to remove the barriers that prevent minority students from attending public schools with white students.[2] The goal of school finance litigation is "to increase the amount and equalize the distribution of academic opportunities and performance of students disadvantaged by existing finance schemes."[3] However, since the Supreme

---

   * Associate Professor of Education and Law, Dickinson School of Law; College of Education,; Pennsylvania State University.
   ** Associate Professor, Department of Teaching and Leadership, University of Kansas.
   *** Assistant Professor of Education Law, Department of Counseling, Human Development and Educational Leadership, Montclair State University.
   1. Bruce D. Baker & Preston C. Green III, *Tricks of the Trade: State Legislative Actions in School Finance Policy That Perpetuate Racial Disparities in the Post-Brown Era*, 111 AM. J. OF EDUC. 372, 377 (2005).
   2. James Ryan, *Schools, Race, and Money*, 109 YALE L. J. 249, 252 (1999).
   3. *Id.*

Court has dramatically curtailed the scope of the school desegregation option,[4] the school finance litigation option may be the more viable option available to African-Americans to attain equal educational opportunities.

The goals of this chapter are to (1) examine the relationship between school finance litigation and levels of funding for high-minority school districts; (2) discuss the ways in which plaintiffs from high-minority school districts may more effectively use school finance litigation to attain equal educational opportunity; and (3) analyze the role that the No Child Left Behind Act (NCLB) may play in this quest.

The first section provides an overview of school finance litigation during the separate but equal era. We explain that courts adopted three standards during this period. Early court cases employed what has been characterized as a "nominal equality" standard. In the 1940s, federal courts applied a "racial neutrality" standard to uphold ostensibly racially neutral policies, which were in reality enacted to perpetuate inequities caused by overtly racially discriminatory funding policies. Near the end of the separate but equal era, a few courts employed a more searching "real equality" standard, which required a comparison of the facilities, curriculum, and teacher quality provided by white and colored schools.

The second section analyzes modern state and federal equal protection school finance litigation. We discuss how equal protection litigation sought to build on the logic of *Brown v. Board of Education*[5] and other desegregation cases. We also explain how one federal district court in *Hobson v. Hansen*[6] developed a separate but equal doctrine for de facto segregated public schools that was similar to the real equality standard at the end of the separate but equal era. Additionally, this section explains how the Supreme Court in *San Antonio Independent School District v. Rodriguez*[7] adopted the racial neutrality standard of the separate but equal era to permit racial funding disparities caused by local property taxation. Finally, this section explains how the Supreme Court in *Papasan v. Allain*[8] applied the racial neutrality standard to racial funding disparities caused by state distribution policies.

The third section examines the impact of school finance litigation on the resources provided to high-minority school districts. We point out that the courts' application of the racial neutrality standard pursuant to federal and state equal protection clauses may have enabled states to enact unequal distribution policies that have had a disparate impact on high-minority communities. We explain that a school finance system that truly addresses the needs of high-minority districts must take into account the fact that they may need more resources to attain equal educational opportunity. This is the case because high-minority school districts may need more funding to attain comparable resources (horizontal equity) and may require more resources to attain a certain level of educational outcomes (vertical equity).

---

4. *See Milliken v. Bradley*, 418 U.S. 717 (1974) (finding that suburban school districts may not be included in a metropolitan remedy unless the districts had committed de jure segregation); *Board of Educ. of Okla. City v. Dowell*, 498 U.S. 237 (1991) (finding that a federal district court may dissolve a desegregation decree and allow a school district to return to one-race schools if the segregation was caused by demographic changes); *Freeman v. Pitts*, 503 U.S. 467 (1992) (finding that a district court may withdraw incrementally from supervising a desegregation decree before the district had achieved full compliance); *Missouri v. Jenkins*, 515 U.S. 70 (1995) (finding that a comprehensive desegregation plan, designed to improve the school district's ability to attract nonminority students not enrolled in the school district, violated the equal protection clause).

5. 347 U.S. 483 (1954).

6. 269 F. Supp. 401 (D.D.C. 1967).

7. 411 U.S. 1 (1973).

8. *Papasan v. Allain*, 478 U.S. 265 (1986).

The fourth section observes that the equality standard adopted at the end of the separate but equal era and in the *Hobson* case may actually be better suited than the present neutrality and adequacy standards to address the need of high-minority school districts. This section also explains the role that NCLB may play in encouraging courts to adopt the "real equality" standard. Although NCLB may not be used to compel states to provide high-minority districts with horizontal and vertical equity, it may encourage courts to uphold race-based state education clause and due process clause challenges.

The final section explains the impact of *Parents Involved in Community Schools v. Seattle*[9] on our analysis. In this case, the Supreme Court examined the constitutionality of voluntary, race-conscious student assignment plans. We pay particular attention to Justice Anthony Kennedy's concurring opinion because he was the swing vote in the *Parents Involved* decision. We conclude that a majority of the Court could be persuaded that race-conscious funding measures do not violate the equal protection clause.

I: School Finance Litigation During the Separate but Equal Era

It might be surprising to some that this chapter starts with an analysis of the separate but equal era. We maintain that an understanding of the separate but equal era is important because racial funding disparities in certain states (e.g., Alabama and Kansas) are traceable to the period prior to *Brown v. Board of Education*.[10] Additionally, although it is generally accepted that the school finance litigation movement started in the 1960s,[11] many of the legal attempts to improve the quality of education provided to colored schools were based on school finance litigation concepts. Further, as will become clear in our analysis, the judiciary's adoption of the rational basis standard pursuant to equal protection challenges to school funding disparities was first established during the separate but equal era. In this section we discuss the methods that Southern and border states used to create racial funding disparities during this period. We also examine the equality standards that courts used to analyze challenges to inequitable funding practices.

A. Methods for Creating Racial Funding Disparities

During the period of the separate but equal doctrine, which the Supreme Court found constitutional in *Plessy v. Ferguson*,[12] and applied to public, elementary, and secondary education in *Cumming v. Richmond County Board of Education*[13] and *Gong Lum v. Rice*,[14] the resources that were available to racially segregated schools were by no means "equal":

---

9. 127 S. Ct. 2738 (2007).

10. Baker & Green, *supra* note 1.

11. Peter Enrich, *Leaving Equality Behind: New Directions in School Finance Reform*, 48 Vand. L. Rev. 101, 117 (1995); Michael Heise, *State Constitutions, School Finance Litigation, and the "Third Wave": From Equity to Adequacy*, 68 Temp. L. Rev. 1151 (2004).

12. 163 U.S. 537 (1896).

13. 175 U.S. 528 (1899).

14. 275 U.S. 78 (1927).

black schools received considerably less funding than white schools.[15] Southern and border states employed a variety of strategies to create this inequality. At the beginning of the twentieth century, state aid was usually distributed to counties according to total school-age population. County school boards were then given complete discretion to disburse such aid to school districts.[16] Boards then used this discretion to fund black and white schools inequitably.[17]

Southern and border states also created racial funding inequity by using dual salary schedules, which explicitly paid black teachers less than whites.[18] In the mid-1930s, the average black teacher's pay was only 61 percent of the average white teacher's.[19] Although school authorities justified this practice on the ground that they were not as well trained as white teachers, 80 percent of this salary difference was caused by wage discrimination.[20] The dual salary schedule also enabled Southern school districts to save millions—$26 million in 1941 alone.[21]

B. Equality Standards

1. Nominal Equality Standard

During the first four decades following the *Plessy* and *Cumming* decisions, courts upheld the constitutionality of racially segregated schools pursuant to the equal protection clause, as long as the facilities provided to both white and "colored" schools were substantially equal. Robert Leflar and Wylie Davis have characterized the equality standard during this period as one of "nominal equality";[22] indeed, during this period, courts permitted state practices that resulted in extreme funding disparities between white and colored schools. For example, in *Jones v. Board of Education of City of Muskogee*,[23] a black student challenged the constitutionality of a state statute that required district boards of education to prepare separate budgets funded through taxation for schools serving whites and children of color. He contended that because taxes were not proportionately distributed in accordance with the number of children in the city, the funding structure constituted a taking of property in violation of due process.[24] The plaintiff also asserted that the funding structure denied black taxpayers their right to due process and equal protection.[25] As a remedy, the student sought funding from the white schools in the district after funding for the colored schools had been exhausted.[26]

---

15. Robert A. Margo, Disenfranchisement and Segregated Schools, 1890–1910 (Garland, 1985).

16. *Id.*

17. *See* Horace M. Bond, The Education of the Negro in the American Social Order (Octagon, 1970); Margo, *supra* note 15.

18. Scott Baker, *Testing Equality: The National Teacher Examination and the NAACP's Legal Campaign to Equalize Teachers' Salaries*, 35 Hist. of Educ. Q. 49, 50 (1995).

19. *Id.*

20. *Id.*

21. *Id.* at 51.

22. Robert A. Leflar & Wylie H. Davis, *Segregation in the Public Schools—1953*, 67 Harv. L. Rev. 377, 388 (1954).

23. 217 P. 400 (Okla. 1923).

24. *Id.* at 403.

25. *Id.*

26. *Id.* at 402.

The Supreme Court of Oklahoma found "it was quite obvious from reading the agreed statement of facts in this case that the separate or colored schools have been shamefully discriminated against" in violation of the state constitution.[27] Although there were one-third more black students in the district, the value of the property on which the black school was located was one-ninth of that of the white schools.[28] The difference in curricula between the two sets of schools was "so unfair, unjust, and unreasonable as to amount to unmistakable discrimination."[29]

Despite these considerable differences, the court refused to find that the different funding methods for colored schools violated the federal constitution. The court so held because the plaintiff did not demonstrate that these methods failed to provide sufficient funds "to support and maintain both schools with equal accommodations and for terms of equal length."[30] In the absence of a holding that the funding statute unconstitutionally discriminated against colored schools, the court found that funds for white schools could not be used to support the maintenance of colored schools once funds set aside for such purposes had been exhausted.[31]

2. Racial Neutrality

In the mid-1930s, the National Association for the Advancement of Colored People (NAACP) embarked on a legal strategy that was designed to dismantle the system of racially segregated schooling by forcing school systems to equalize the quality of education offered to both colored and white schools. This practice would "raise the costs of operating segregated schools to such an extent that the South would be forced to abandon them."[32] This strategy drew from the ideas of NAACP Special Counsel Nathan Margold, who believed that desegregation could be achieved by challenging segregated schooling as actually administered.[33]

The first stage of this new approach was to challenge the racially discriminatory salary schedules that were common throughout the South. Thurgood Marshall, who was appointed assistant special counsel, led the effort.[34] Marshall achieved his first significant victory in *Mills v. Board of Education of Anne Arundel County*.[35] In this case, a district court declared that the salary schedule employed by a Maryland county board of education violated the equal protection clause because the "very substantial differential" between the salaries of the county's black and white teachers was due to racial discrimination.[36] Similarly, in *Alston v. School Board of City of Norfolk*,[37] Marshall convinced the Fourth Circuit that a Virginia city school board's salary schedule violated the equal protection clause because it paid black teachers less than white teachers with equal qualifications and experiences.

However, these cases did not require school boards to pay black teachers the same as white teachers. As the district court observed in *Mills*, "the Board has full discretion in

27. *Id.*
28. *Id.*
29. *Id.*
30. *Id.* at 403.
31. *Id.* at 403–04.
32. S. Baker, *supra* note 18, at 51.
33. *Id.*
34. *Id.*
35. 30 F. Supp. 245 (D.C.Md 1939).
36. *Id.* at 249.
37. 112 F.2d 992 (4th Cir. 1940).

its judgment to pay more than the minimum [state standard] to any white or colored teacher provided the discrimination is not solely on account of race or color."[38] School districts responded to this opening by basing salary schedules on scores attained on a standardized test, the National Teachers Examination (NTE).[39] Although the NTE was designed to help select teachers, Ben Wood, the designer of examination, told Southern school leaders that the NTE could also be used to determine salaries.[40] Wood also exhorted school authorities to fight the NAACP's equalization campaign by adopting a merit-based salary system.[41] Southern school leaders became convinced that the NTE could be the foundation of a merit-based system, once they found out that on a previous administration of the test, "the average score of blacks was 'at the lower fifth percentile' of whites."[42]

Federal courts consistently upheld these new racially unequal salary systems because they were based on objective criteria.[43] South Carolina's successful adoption of the NTE is illustrative. Prior to the NAACP's legal attack on teacher salaries, South Carolina operated a racially discriminatory salary system. After the Fourth Circuit declared this practice unconstitutional in *Alston*, the state legislature appointed a committee to examine the salary system, and that work was continued by the state board of education.[44] In 1944, the state board produced a report recommending the adoption of a unitary pay system based on NTE scores.[45] The legislature followed this recommendation in 1945.[46] At the time the legislature acted, it had access to the results of the November 1944 administration of the NTE, which indicated that 32 percent of the white candidates would obtain the highest certification credentials, whereas only 2 percent of black candidates would have obtained that classification.[47]

In *Thompson v. Gibbes*, a federal district court upheld the constitutionality of the new system. The court concluded that the NTE was the "proper yardstick" for measuring salaries because the results would be graded by a national board, which was unaware of the race of each test taker.[48] It also declared immaterial the assertion that many black teachers would fail or get very low scores on the NTE because of their inadequate preparation. The court believed its task was not to determine "whether this is a good method for the whites or a good method for the negroes."[49] Rather, the court believed that its purpose was to determine whether the new classification illegally used race as a basis for determining salaries.[50]

---

38. *Mills*, 30 F. Supp. at 249.

39. S. Baker, *supra* note 18, at 52.

40. *Id.* at 55.

41. *Id.*

42. *Id.*

43. *See Reynolds v. Board of Pub. Instruction for Dade County, Fla.*, 148 F.2d 754, 757 (5th Cir. 1945) (holding that salary scale that permitted teachers dissatisfied with pay to take tests prepared by the National Committee on Teacher Examinations was constitutional); *Thompson v. Gibbes*, 60 F. Supp. 872, 876 (D.C.S.C. 1945) (holding that state system of examination and certification was constitutional); *Turner v. Keefe*, 50 F. Supp. 647, 649 (D.C.Fla. 1943) (holding that teacher salary schedule based on "physical health, personality and character; scholarship and attitude; instructional skill and performance" was constitutional).

44. *United States v. South Carolina*, 445 F. Supp. 1094, 1105 (D.S.C. 1977).

45. *Id.*

46. *Id.*

47. *Id.*

48. *Thompson*, 60 F. Supp. at 876.

49. *Id.*

50. *Id.*

3. Real Equality

Beginning in the 1950s, a few courts applied an equality standard to racially segregated public schools that was more searching than the nominal and race-neutrality standards that were used earlier in the separate but equal era.[51] The impetus for this "real equality" standard was a line of Supreme Court cases in higher education that dealt with the admission of black plaintiffs to graduate and professional schools.[52] In these cases, courts compared a number of educational inputs, including curriculum, accreditation, and faculty. The most pertinent of these cases was *Sweatt v. Painter*. In this case, a black applicant was denied admission into the University of Texas Law School on racial grounds. A state trial court found that the denial of the applicant on racial grounds violated the equal protection clause.[53] The court did not order the school to admit the applicant but instead granted the state six months to build substantially equal facilities.[54] The trial court subsequently found that the educational opportunities provided by the white and black law schools were substantially equal.[55]

The Supreme Court reversed, finding that the two racially segregated schools violated the equal protection clause. The Court found that there was no substantial equality in terms of the educational resources provided by those two schools. It observed that the University of Texas Law School had sixteen full-time and three part-time faculty and a library that contained 65,000 volumes.[56] Further, the white school provided its students with "a law review, moot court facilities, scholarship funds, and Order of the Coif affiliation."[57] By contrast, the black law school had five full-time faculty, 16,500 volumes in its library, a practice court, and a legal aid association.[58] Additionally, the Court found that the two schools were not substantially equal in terms of academic outcomes: whereas the alumni of the University of Texas Law School "occup[ied] the most distinguished positions in the private practice of the law and in public life of the state," the black law school had only one alumnus become a member of the bar.[59]

The Court further distinguished the educational opportunities offered by the white and black law schools in the following manner:

> We cannot find substantial equality in the educational opportunities offered white and Negro law students by the state. In terms of number of the faculty, variety of courses and opportunity for specialization, size of the student body, scope of the library, availability of law review and similar activities, the University of Texas Law School is superior. What is more important the University of Texas Law School possesses to a far greater degree those qualities which are in-

---

51. Leflar & Davis, *supra* note 22, at 388.

52. *Missouri ex rel. Gaines v. Canada*, 305 U.S. 337 (1938) (finding that state of Missouri must provide black law student with an education "substantially equal" to that of white students); *Sipuel v. Board of Regents of Univ. of Okla.*, 332 U.S. 631 (1948) (finding that state must provide black law student with an education conforming with the equal protection clause); *Sweatt v. Painter*, 339 U.S. 629 (1950) (finding that separate school for black law students did not comply with the equal protection clause); *McLaurin v. Oklahoma State Regents*, 339 U.S. 637 (1950) (finding that the provision of a segregated education to a black student within a white law school violated the equal protection clause).

53. *Sweatt*, 339 U.S. at 631.

54. *Id.* at 632.

55. *Id.*

56. *Id.* at 632.

57. *Id.* at 632–33.

58. *Id.* at 633.

59. *Id.*

capable of objective measurement but which make for greatness in a law school. Such qualities, to name but a few, include reputation of the faculty, experience of the administration, position and influence of the alumni, standing in the community, traditions and prestige.[60]

Two courts applied to K–12 education the more rigorous equality standard used in *Sweatt*. In *State v. Board of Education of City of St. Louis*,[61] the Supreme Court of Missouri found a violation of the equal protection clause where a white high school in a school district offered a course in aeromechanics that was not offered by the black high school. The court acknowledged that the substantial equality standard did not require that "every subject taught in one school be offered in all others."[62] However, the court took notice of the fact that the aeromechanics course was taught three hours per day for five semesters.[63] Thus, a substantial inequality existed because only white students in the district had the opportunity to prepare for a career as an airplane mechanic.[64] As a remedy, the court ordered the white high school to enroll the black student.[65]

In *Gebhart v. Belton*,[66] two sets of black plaintiffs who attended segregated schools alleged that these schools were substantially unequal to the white schools. The Supreme Court of Delaware compared the black and white schools in terms of public funding, buildings, sites, accreditation, curriculum, faculty, libraries, physical and mental health services, extracurricular activities, and travel.[67] With respect to the first set of plaintiffs, the court found that the physical plant and the site of the black school were substantially inferior to those of the white school.[68] Substantial inequality also existed with respect to the class sizes in the physical education classes.[69] Additionally, substantial inequality existed with respect to the transportation because the school district provided transportation to students in the white school while refusing to provide transportation to the black plaintiffs.[70]

With regard to the second set of the black plaintiffs, the court found substantial inequality in the allocation of public funds.[71] As a result of this unequal distribution, which extended to teacher salaries, teachers in the white schools had superior formal training compared with teachers in the black school.[72] Further, the court found substantial inequality in the building and the site of the black and white school.[73] As was the case with the first set of plaintiffs, the court found that the refusal to provide transportation to the black schools constituted substantial inequality.[74] The court held that both sets of plaintiffs were enti-

---

60. *Id.* at 634.

61. 233 S.W.2d 697 (Mo. 1950).

62. *Id.* at 698.

63. *Id.* at 699.

64. *Id.*

65. *Id.*

66. 144 A.2d 137 (Del. 1952). *Gelton* was overturned by the Supreme Court in *Brown v. Board of Education.*

67. *Id.* at 142–52.

68. *Id.* at 145.

69. *Id.* at 146.

70. *Id.* at 147.

71. *Id.* at 150.

72. *Id.* at 151–52.

73. *Id.* at 150.

74. *Id.* at 152.

tled to an immediate cessation of the discrimination and to a decree ordering their enrollment in the white schools.[75]

II: Modern Equal Protection Clause Litigation

Beginning in the 1960s, civil rights advocates began to mount equal protection clause challenges to school funding disparities between rich and poor school districts. This line of litigation sought to build on *Brown* and its progeny.[76] In *Brown*, the Court spoke of the importance of education in impassioned terms:

> Today, education is perhaps the most important function of state and local governments. Compulsory school attendance laws and the great expenditures for education both demonstrate our recognition of the importance of education to our democratic society. It is required in the performance of our most basic public responsibilities, even service in the armed forces. It is the very foundation of good citizenship. Today it is a principal instrument in awakening the child to cultural values, in preparing him for later professional training, and in helping him to adjust normally to his environment. In these days, it is doubtful that any child may reasonably be expected to succeed in life if he is denied the opportunity of an education. Such an opportunity, where the state has undertaken to provide it, is a right which must be made available to all on equal terms.[77]

Because of the description of the importance of education, it was reasonable for contemporary observers to assume that the fundamental importance of education was part of the rationale for the Court's decision in *Brown*, and that the Court would be open to equal protection clause challenges in educational contexts outside the realm of de jure segregation.[78]

Despite an assumed connection between school funding disparities and the racial composition of school districts, most school finance challenges during this period did not address disparities based on race. This was due in large part to the fact that school finance litigation "is not targeted to assist only minority students, but rather is designed to assist all 'poor' students."[79] Thus, "school finance litigation is often depicted as a means of moving beyond race as a salient issue in education reform and as an effective way to achieve educational equity and adequacy for disadvantaged students from all racial and ethnic backgrounds."[80]

The one notable exception was *Hobson v. Hansen*. In *Hobson*, a federal district court applied the real neutrality standard to declare unconstitutional the de facto racial funding disparities in the District of Columbia school system. However, in *San Antonio Independent School District v. Rodriguez* and *Papasan v. Allain*, the Supreme Court rejected

---

75. *Id.*
76. Enrich, *supra* note 11, at 117.
77. *Brown*, 347 U.S. at 493 (1954).
78. Enrich, *supra* note 11, at 117.
79. Ryan, *supra* note 2, at 252.
80. *Id.*

Hobson by adopting the separate but equal era's racial neutrality standard. The remainder of this section discusses these three cases.

A. *Hobson v. Hansen*: Real Equality Standard as Applied to De Facto Segregation

In *Hobson*, the district court examined whether the District of Columbia was in compliance with *Bolling v. Sharpe*,[81] a companion case to *Brown*. The court found that the distribution of resources between black and white elementary schools was considerably unequal. The typical school building in the black ghettos was almost sixty years old, which was twenty years older than the median age of other school buildings in the city.[82] Black schools operated at 115 percent of capacity, whereas white schools generally operated at 77 percent capacity.[83] Teachers in the black schools had much less teaching experience and were twice as likely to have only temporary licenses.[84] By contrast, white schools had a large number of teachers with graduate degrees, a feature that was atypical of predominantly black schools.[85] Median per-pupil expenditures for black schools were $100 fewer than those of white schools.[86] All students attending predominantly white schools had the chance to attend kindergarten, while many students attending predominantly black schools did not have this opportunity.[87]

Although the disparities between black and white schools were not caused by intentional discrimination but by the indifference of school administrators,[88] the court still held that the District of Columbia denied students attending predominantly black schools of equal protection under the law.[89] In reaching this decision, the court fashioned a new separate but equal doctrine to address inequalities caused by de facto segregation.[90] As the court explained, "it should be clear that if whites and Negroes, or rich and poor, are to be consigned to separate schools pursuant to whatever policy, the minimum the Constitution will require and guarantee is that for their objectively measurable aspects these schools should be run on the basis of real equality, at least unless any inequalities are adequately justified."[91] The court justified this assertion by explaining, "Whatever the law was once, it is a testament to our maturing concept of equality that, with the help of Supreme Court decisions in the last decade, we now firmly recognize that the arbitrary quality of thoughtlessness can be as disastrous and unfair to private rights and the public interest as the perversity of a willful scheme."[92]

---

81. 347 U.S. 497 (1954) (holding that racially segregated schools in Washington, D.C., violated the due process clause).
82. *Hobson*, 269 F. Supp. at 495.
83. *Id.*
84. *Id.*
85. *Id.* at 495–96.
86. *Id.*
87. *Id.*
88. *Id.* at 442.
89. *Id.* at 496. This case was decided under the due process clause of the Fifth Amendment, which the Supreme Court held contains an equal protection component. *Bolling*, 347 U.S. at 498.
90. *Hobson*, 269 F. Supp. at 496.
91. *Id.*
92. *Id.* at 497.

B. *San Antonio Independent School District v. Rodriguez*: The Neutrality Standard Applied to Local Property Taxation

In *Rodriguez*, however, the Supreme Court adopted the racial neutrality approach to analyze school funding disparities under the equal protection clause. The *Rodriguez* Court held that existing disparities in funding between school districts that resulted from Texas's reliance on local property taxation were permissible. The Court rejected the claim that the school finance system should be subject to strict scrutiny because the plaintiffs were members of a suspect classification based on wealth.[93] The Court also rejected the notion that strict scrutiny was applicable because education was a fundamental interest under the Constitution.[94]

Instead of strict scrutiny, the Court found that the rational basis test was the appropriate form of analysis.[95] The Court then concluded that the use of local property taxation was rationally related to encouraging local control of the public schools. By becoming involved in educational decisions at the local level, community members demonstrated their depth of commitment to public education.[96] Local control also provided each locality with the means for participating "in the decision making process of determining how local tax dollars will be spent."[97] Moreover, local control enabled school districts "to tailor local plans for local needs" and encouraged "experimentation, innovation, and a healthy competition for educational excellence."[98]

Although the equal protection clause challenge in *Rodriguez* was based on wealth disparities, it is important to observe that the case served as an implicit rejection of the equality standard used in *Hobson v. Hansen*. Indeed, Taunya Lovell Banks observes that "race, in the broadest sense, was the elephant in the courtroom."[99] She further points out that the plaintiffs in *Rodriguez*, who were "characterized as poor and Mexican-American, seemed to be arguing that state educational funding determinations based on wealth not only impair a fundamental right, but also are suspect under the equal protection clause ... when these decisions disproportionately impact racialized groups."[100] The Supreme Court removed all doubt about the validity of *Hobson* in *Washington v. Davis*[101] by holding that a statute or official practice was not rendered unconstitutional by having an adverse disparate impact on minority groups. As the Court explained,

> Various Courts of Appeals have held in several contexts ... that the substantially disproportionate racial impact of a statute or official practice standing alone and without regard to discriminatory purpose, suffices to prove racial discrimination violating the equal protection clause ... To the extent that those cases rested

---

93. *Rodriguez*, 411 U.S. at 19–29.

94. *Id.* at 29–39.

95. *Id.* at 40.

96. *Id.* at 49.

97. *Id.* at 50.

98. *Id.* at 51.

99. Taunya Lovell Banks, *Brown at 50: Reconstructing Brown's Promise*, 44 Washburn L.J. 31, 59 (2004).

100. *Id.*

101. 426 U.S. 229 (1976) (finding that a police department's use of employment test for hiring purposes did not violate equal protection clause).

on or expressed the view that proof of discriminatory racial purpose is unnecessary in making out an equal protection violation, we are in disagreement.[102]

After the Supreme Court's ruling in *Rodriguez*, plaintiffs responded by bringing challenges through state equal protection clauses. However, courts have generally found that (1) rational basis analysis was applicable; and (2) the use of local property taxation was rationally related to the goal of maintaining local control.[103] For example, in *Board of Education, Levittown Union Free School Dist. v. Nyquist*, a case upholding New York's school finance system against a state equal protection challenge, the Court of Appeals of New York explained: "It is the willingness of the taxpayers of many districts to pay for and to provide enriched educational services and facilities beyond what the basic per pupil expenditure figures will permit that creates differentials in services and facilities. Justification for a system which allows for such willingness was recognized by the Supreme Court of the United States in *San Antonio School Dist. v. Rodriguez*."[104]

C. *Papasan v. Allain*: The Equality Standard Applied to State Distribution Policies

In *Papasan v. Allain*, the Supreme Court addressed the equality standard that would be applied to disparities caused by state distribution policies. The *Papasan* Court held that *Rodriguez* did not foreclose equal protection clause challenges to funding disparities caused by state distribution policies. In *Papasan*, plaintiffs alleged that Mississippi's unequal distribution of educational funds from "Sixteenth Section or Lieu Lands" violated the equal protection clause. The Fifth Circuit Court of Appeals held that *Rodriguez* was controlling and dismissed the complaint.[105] The Supreme Court vacated the judgment and remanded the case to the federal district court. While the Court agreed with the Fifth Circuit's holding that the rational basis test should be applied to the plaintiffs' claim, it found that the Fifth Circuit incorrectly concluded that *Rodriguez* was controlling.[106] As the Court explained, *Rodriguez* applied only to school funding disparities that were caused by local property taxation but did not address the constitutionality of state decisions "to divide state resources differently among school districts."[107]

---

102. *Id.* at 244–45.

103. These states are as follows: (1) Arizona: *Shofstall v. Hollins*, 515 P.2d 590 (Ariz. 1973); (2) Colorado: *Lujan v. Colorado St. Bd. of Educ.*, 649 P.2d 1005 (Colo. 1982); (3) Georgia: *McDaniel v. Thomas*, 285 S.E.2d 156 (Ga. 1981); (4) Idaho: *Thompson v. Engelking*, 537 P.2d 635 (Idaho 1975); (5) Illinois: *Committee for Educ. Rights v. Edgar*, 672 N.E.2d 1178 (Ill. 1996); (6) Maryland: *Hornbeck v. Somerset County Bd. of Educ.*, 458 A.2d 758 (Md. 1983); (7) New York: *Board of Educ., v. Nyquist*, 439 N.E.2d 359 (N.Y. 1982); (8) Ohio: *Board of Educ. v. Walter*, 390 N.E.2d 813 (Ohio 1979); (9) Oklahoma; *Fair Sch. Finance Council v. State*, 746 P.2d 1135 (Okla. 1987); (10) Rhode Island: *City of Pawtucket v. Sundlun*, 662 A.2d 40 (R.I. 1995); (11) Wisconsin: *Kukor v. Grover*, 436 N.W.2d 568 (Wisc. 1989). The three states that have held that reliance on local taxation fails the rational basis test are as follows: (1) Alabama: *Alabama Coalition for Equity v. Hunt* (Ala. Circ. Ct. 1993) (published as Appendix to Opinion of the Justices, 624 So.2d 107, 110 (Ala. 1993)); Arkansas: *Dupree v. Alma Sch. Dist. No. 30*, 651 S.W.2d 90 (Ark. 1983); (3) Tennessee: *Tennessee Small Sch. Sys. v. McWherter*, 851 S.W.2d 139 (Tenn. 1993).

104. *Nyquist*, 439 N.E.2d at 367.

105. 756 F.2d 1087 (5th Cir. 1985).

106. *Papasan*, 478 U.S. at 286–87.

107. *Id.* at 288.

The major limitation to *Papasan*-based litigation is the Supreme Court's conclusion that rational basis analysis would apply to such claims. When considered in tandem with *Washington v. Davis*, it is safe to conclude that policies that have a racially disparate impact would be analyzed under rational basis if states can articulate race-neutral justifications for these classifications. *Montoy v. Kansas*, a Kansas school finance case, is illustrative. In this case, a state trial court ruled that Kansas's funding disparities had an unconstitutional disparate impact on minority, disabled, and non–English speaking students in violation of the state and federal equal protection clauses. According to the court, the appropriate test for disparate impact claims was whether the disparate funding was rationally related to the state educational clause's guarantee of providing each child with an equal educational opportunity.[108] There was no justification for the disparities in educational funding in light of the fact that (1) minority and disadvantaged students were performing so poorly on the state's assessment system and (2) increases in educational funding would enable schools to employ strategies designed to raise their students' educational performance, such as reducing class sizes and hiring better trained teachers.[109]

However, the Kansas Supreme Court reversed the lower court's finding that the school finance system violated state and federal equal protection provisions.[110] Although the state high court agreed that the rational basis analysis was appropriate, it found that the lower court misapplied the test.[111] Rather, the funding differentials were permissible under the equal protection clause because they were all rationally related to legitimate purposes.[112] Further, the Kansas Supreme Court reversed the lower court's holding that the school finance formula had an unconstitutional disparate impact on minorities.[113] "In order to establish an equal protection claim on [the] basis of disparate impact," the court observed that "one must show not only that there is a disparate impact, but also that the impact can be traced to a discriminatory purpose."[114] The court rejected the racial disparity claim because plaintiffs did not show discriminatory purpose.[115]

III: *Rodriguez*, Race, and Equal Educational Opportunity

A. Assertion: *Rodriguez*'s Approval of Local Property Taxation Is the Principal Cause of Racial Funding Disparities

A number of scholars have asserted that the *Rodriguez* decision has led to widespread disparate funding between black and white school districts by permitting disparities caused

---

108. *Montoy v. State*, 2003 WL 22902963, at *21 (Kan. Dist. Ct. Dec. 2, 2003).
109. *Id.* at *47–48.
110. 120 P.3d 306 (Kan. 2005).
111. *Id.* at 308.
112. *Id.*
113. *Id.*
114. *Id.*
115. *Id.*

by local property taxation.[116] Erwin Chemerinsky also makes this assertion in the following passage:

> By the 1970s, it was also clear that there were substantial disparities in school funding. In 1972, education expert Christopher Jencks estimated that, on average, each white child received fifteen to twenty percent more in education funding than each black child. This trend continues throughout the country. For example, in the school year 1988–89, the Chicago public schools spent $5,265 for each student's education; but in the Niles school system, just north of the city, $9,371 was spent on each student's schooling. That same year, Camden, New Jersey spent $3,538 on each pupil; but Princeton, New Jersey spent $7,725. These disparities also correspond to race. For example, in Chicago, 45.4 percent of the students were white and 39.1 percent were African American; in Niles Township, the schools were 91.6 percent white and 0.4 percent black.
>
> There is, of course, a simple explanation for [racial funding] disparities in school funding. In most states, education is substantially funded by local property taxes. Wealthier suburbs have significantly larger tax bases than poor inner cities. The result is that suburbs can tax at a low rate and still have a great deal to spend on education. Cities must tax at a higher rate and nonetheless have less to spend.
>
> The Court had the opportunity to remedy this inequality in education in *San Antonio Independent School District v. Rodriguez*. But the Court profoundly failed by concluding that the inequalities in funding did not deny equal protection. *Rodriguez* involved a challenge to the Texas system of funding public schools largely through local property taxes. Texas' financing system meant that poor areas had to tax at a high rate, but had little to spend on education. In contrast wealthier areas could tax at low rates, but still maintained more funding for education.[117]

B. Problems with This Common Understanding

The relationship between racial funding disparities and school finance policies is more complicated than is commonly believed. First, the assertions that predominantly black school districts spend less per pupil on average nationally and that black-white spending disparities are the norm have been questioned in recent work. For example, Robert Bifulco finds that the average black students' funding is approximately 8.5 percent higher than the average white student funding, with no adjustments applied. When resources are adjusted for poverty, economies of scale and regional labor market variation — vertical equity factors — Bifulco finds that the average black student's district has from 3.2 percent to 15.8 percent less funding than the average white student's district.[118]

These national averages conceal important differences in black-white spending disparities across school districts within states and within major metropolitan areas. Bruce

---

116. Banks, *supra* note 99; Erwin Chemerinsky, *Separate and Unequal: American Public Education Today*, 52 Am. U. L. Rev. 1461 (2003); Lisa M. Fairfax, *The Silent Resurrection of* Plessy: *The Supreme Court's Acquiescence in the Resegregation of America's Schools*, 9 Temp. Pol. & Civ. Rts. L. Rev. 1, 3 (1998).

117. Chemerinsky, *supra* note 116, at 1470–71.

118. Robert Bifulco, *District Black-White Funding Disparities in the United States 1987–2002*, 31 J. of Educ. Fin. 172, 187 (2005).

Baker has found that in some locations such as Minneapolis, Boston, Kansas City, and Atlanta, urban core and urban fringe high percent black districts outspend in nominal dollars per pupil majority white school districts in the same state and/or metropolitan area.[119] However, in others such as Philadelphia and Chicago, urban core districts lag well behind in per pupil spending—far greater than 15 percent.[120] Similar, even more nuanced patterns occur across inner urban fringe districts in these and other metropolitan areas.[121]

Chicago public schools, used by Chemerinsky to provide anecdotal support for the stereotypical conditions of the poor, black urban core district, is a particularly intriguing case. First, Bruce Baker shows that Chicago public schools are among the only urban core districts that continue to spend well bellow the average for their core based statistical area. Second, Chicago public schools, while serving the largest number of black students in the metropolitan area, are only 49.7 percent black, compared to numerous other Cook county and Chicago metro area districts (seventeen districts in the Chicago metro alone) that exceed 80 percent black. Further, Chicago public schools rank sixty-second lowest (low but not at the bottom) of the 267 districts in the Chicago metro area in taxable property wealth per pupil at $141,980 in 2005, compared to predominantly black urban fringe districts with much lower taxable property wealth at $49,542 in Harvey (84 percent black), and $62,369 in Dolton (97.5 percent black).[122] Finally, Illinois remains among the most dependent, among states, on local property taxation for schools.[123] The Education Trust's Funding Gap report also consistently identifies Illinois as having among the greatest racial disparities in financing.[124] That is, while the Chicago example supports Chemerinsky's view, the Chicago example is not representative of national norms.

Chemerinsky's choice to contrast Camden and Princeton, New Jersey, is more peculiar, because on average in the state of New Jersey, from 1992 on, the statistical relationship between current spending per pupil and percent black enrollment among districts within the same labor markets in New Jersey has been positive. That is, despite Chemerinsky's anecdotal comparison of Camden and Princeton, New Jersey districts with higher black concentration spend more per pupil than New Jersey districts with lower black concentration each year from 1992 to 2005.[125]

Second, the role of property taxation in the creation of racial funding disparities is more complicated than one might suspect. For instance, local property taxation is no longer the dominant source of revenue for annual operations of public schools. By

---

119. Bruce D. Baker, *Black-White Funding Disparities in America's Major Metropolitan Areas* (on file with authors).

120. *Id.*

121. *Id.*

122. Analysis by Bruce D. Baker using Illinois state school finance data from 2004–05, provided by the Chicago Reporter while providing pro bono analytical support for *Chicago Matters* 2006 (Chicago Public Radio).

123. Illinois ranks sixteenth in total share of resources for schools generated from local tax sources in 2004–05 (U.S. Census Fiscal Survey of Local Governments, Elementary and Secondary Education Finances). However, this is somewhat deceptive because many states above Illinois in use of local resources actually rely on local tax revenues to enhance rather than erode equity (as in the Texas *Robin-Hood* plan, Chapter 41 of the Foundation School Plan, no longer in effect).

124. The Education Trust, *The Funding Gap 2005: Low-Income and Minority Students Shortchanged by Most States*, www2.edtrust.org/NR/rdonlyres/31D276EF-72E1-458A-8C71-E3D262A4C91E/0/FundingGap2005.pdf (visited Sep. 14, 2007).

125. Based on analysis by Bruce D. Baker of data from the U.S. Census Bureau's Fiscal Survey of Local Governments, Elementary and Secondary Education Finance, from 1989–90 to 2004–05. Demographic data compiled from the National Center for Education Statistics Common Core of Data, Public School Universe File.

2004–05, local shares of total revenue for public schools exceeded 50 percent in only ten to fifteen states.[126] Also, local property taxation may be used to level up resources across districts and in a few limited cases, revenue-sharing provisions have been applied to property taxation to improve equity.[127]

Third, urban core districts are not necessarily the most disadvantaged by reliance on property taxation, because in many cases these districts have relatively strong tax bases. Recall the comparisons of the city of Chicago and neighboring poor urban fringe districts above. Indeed the city of Chicago ranks low in its metropolitan area in taxable property wealth per pupil, sixty-second from bottom of 267 districts in 2004–05. But the city of Chicago still has greater than twice the taxable property wealth per pupil than poor urban fringe districts with much higher black population shares. In Missouri, the state average equalized assessed property value per pupil was $79,220 in 2004–05. For the Kansas City core based statistical area, average property wealth per pupil was $76,190, and for the St. Louis area, $100,032. In Kansas City (71 percent black), the taxable property wealth per pupil was $81,122 and St. Louis City (81 percent black) was $83,874. Though St. Louis city fell below the average for its metropolitan area, Kansas City did not.[128] However, as in the Chicago metro area, poor urban fringe districts with much higher black population shares had much lower taxable property wealth. These patterns exist because the urban fringe is typically predominantly residential, with high-density housing and little or commercial and/or industrial nonresidential tax base.

Fourth, urban center districts do not necessarily continue to serve the largest shares of black children. Nationally, by 2004–05 just under 50 million children attended unified public school districts with over 100 pupils, just over 7.5 million of whom were black.[129] Using the National Center for Education Statistics Locale Code system, just over 2.1 million of these students attended school districts in large central cities. A nearly equal number attended school districts on the fringe of large central cities (nearly 2.0 million) and another 1.4 million attended school districts in midsized cities (many of which lie within or just outside major urban fringe areas, such as Trenton and Camden, NJ).

C. Another Possible Culprit for Racial Funding Disparities: State Distribution Policies

Thus far, we have shown that (1) racial funding disparities in nominal spending per pupil are not consistent across states and metropolitan areas and national averages mask important differences; (2) the role of local revenues and property taxation is not as simple as we might expect, with property taxes playing a redistributive role in some cases and property taxation providing opportunities for greater school spending in some minority communities; (3) urban core school districts are not necessarily the most disadvantaged by reliance on property taxation because in many cases these districts have

---

126. *Public Education Finances 2005*, U.S. Census Bureau, ftp2.census.gov/govs/school/ 05f33pub.pdf (visited Sep. 14, 2007).

127. Bruce D. Baker et al., Financing Education Systems (Prentice Hall, 2007).

128. Analysis by Bruce D. Baker, using data from the Missouri Department of Elementary and Secondary Education on the state's 449 K12 unified school districts in 2004–05. Data available at Missouri Department of Elementary and Secondary Education, www.dese.mo.gov/schooldata/ ftp-data.html.

129. *Common Core of Data, Public School Universe 2004–05*, National Center for Education Statistics, www.nces.ed.gov/ccd (visited Sep. 20, 2007). Calculations by Bruce Baker.

relatively strong tax bases; and (4) urban center districts do not necessarily continue to serve the largest shares of black children. Obviously these last two realities are somewhat counterbalancing, still leading us to the finding that many predominantly minority school districts are still significantly disadvantaged under state school finance policies. Even while some are disadvantaged by virtue of the role of the property tax, perhaps as many are disadvantaged by direct function of state aid allocation policy.

School finance formulas typically contain cost adjustments designed to promote vertical equity. Vertical equity refers to the idea that particular categories of students and districts may have dramatically different needs that require different levels of resources.[130] School finance formulas provide supplemental funding to two groups of students: (1) students with disabilities as classified under the Individuals with Disabilities Education Act (IDEA);[131] and (2) fringe populations, or populations statistically in the minority who have been marginalized by the core curriculum, but who are not consistently protected statutorily across states.[132] Examples of fringe populations include at-risk, limited English proficient (LEP), and gifted and talented students.[133] Some school finance formulas also provide additional resources for school- and district-based characteristics.[134] State aid adjustments for school size can occur in several aid programs: basic operating aid, transportation aid, facilities, and categorical aid programs for rural districts.[135] A number of school finance formulas provide supplemental aid for geographic variations in the cost of teachers and other personnel.[136]

The most common assumption is that funding disparities between white and minority school districts may be "primarily a function of the overall level of commitment of state legislators to spend on public schools.... For example, that when less aid is allocated, poorer districts that serve more minority children simply fare less well."[137] In some states, representatives of nonurban, lower poverty districts have been politically effective at attaining more funding per pupil than high-poverty, high-minority districts.[138] Bruce Baker and William Duncombe show how the balance of cost and need adjustments in state school finance formulas is more likely to represent the balance of state population distribution and political power as much as (if not more than) the balance of actual costs and needs.[139] Among the methods of choice are adjustments for district size and geographic location.[140] Economies of scale adjustments tend to benefit small rural districts, which are most often

---

130. Bruce D. Baker, *Living on the Edges of School Finance Policy: The Plight of At Risk, Limited English Proficient and Gifted Children*, 15 Educ. Pol'y 699, 702 (2001).

131. Thomas Parrish et al., *State Special Education Finance Systems, 1999–2000*, Center for Education Finance: The Special Education Expenditure Project, 64.233.169.104/search?q=cache:H91nNWLOIdIJ:www.csef-air.org/publications/csef/state/statpart1.pdf+%-22State+Special+Education+Finance+Systems,+1999-2000%22&hl=en&ct=clnk&cd=2&gl=us (visited Sep. 14, 2007).

132. Baker, *supra* note 130, at 699.

133. *Id.*

134. Committee on Education Finance, National Research Council, Making Money Matter: Financing America's Schools 29 (National Academy Press, 1999).

135. *Id.*

136. *See* Preston C. Green & Bruce D. Baker, *Circumventing* Rodriguez: *Can Plaintiffs Use the equal protection clause to Challenge School Finance Disparities Caused by Inequitable State Distribution Policies?*, 7 Tex. F. on C.L. & C.R. 141, 153 (2002).

137. *Id.* at 375.

138. *See* Baker & Green, *supra* note 1, at 388–89 (discussing how the Kansas legislature adopted cost adjustments that benefited suburban school districts.

139. Bruce D. Baker & William D. Duncombe, *Balancing District Needs and Student Needs: The Role of Economies of Scale Adjustments and Pupil Need Weights in School Finance Formulas*, 29 J. of Educ. Fin. 195 (2004) [hereinafter Baker & Duncombe].

140. *Id.*

predominantly white.[141] Geographic adjustments are easily manipulated to benefit suburban school districts.[142] The political clout of suburban districts often allows them to obtain cost adjustments to more than offset the adjustments that advantage poor districts.[143]

Occasionally, racial funding inequality may be the result of ostensibly race-neutral policies designed to maintain the disparities of the separate but equal era.[144] Alabama's school finance formula demonstrates how racial school funding disparities in some states developed in the era of de jure segregation. Bruce Baker and Preston Green have found that on average, Alabama districts serving higher percentages of black children had systematically lower nominal funding per pupil.[145] Furthermore, Baker and Green demonstrate that state aid was actually allocated to county school districts in lower nominal amounts where black population shares were higher, after controlling for fiscal capacity and cost factors.[146] As a result, Alabama's aid formula provides systematically lower state aid per pupil to districts with higher black shares. This disparity results from the State Minimum Salary Schedule, which distributes teacher units and allocates costs on the basis of the education and experience level of teachers.[147] Alabama's purpose in adopting the present salary schedule may have been to perpetuate racial disparities through racially neutral means. In 1927, the State Board of Education implemented a teacher pay scale that paid black teachers 50 percent of what it paid white teachers.[148] It is unclear when Alabama stopped using an overtly race-based teacher pay policy, but it is possible that the state continued to employ such a policy until the late 1960s when the state legislature removed the authority from the state school boards to set teacher unit costs.[149]

D. Race, Funding, and Equal Educational Opportunity: Is Funding Equality Enough?

Educational equality takes many forms and is measured in many ways. In general, equity in school finance is conceptualized in terms of horizontal equity — the equal treatment

---

141. *Id.* at 218.
142. *Id.* at 213.
143. *Id.*
144. Baker & Green, *supra* note 1, at 377.
145. *Id.* at 380.
146. *Id.* at 379.
147. *Id.*
148. *Id.* at 385.
149. *Id.* at 410, note 9. Baker and Green provide the following explanation for reaching this conclusion:

> Other than the reference to the 1927 Equalization Fund program, we have found no reference to Alabama's use of race-based teacher salary schedules. Further, state school finance officials did not respond to our query as to when Alabama stopped this practice. We base our conclusion that the race-based teacher unit policy lasted until the late 1960s on the history of school desegregation in the state. We discussed earlier in this chapter that Alabama employed a number of organizational practices that were designed to circumvent school desegregation decrees. In 1957, the state legislature also enacted a statute that authorized local boards to close public schools and provide students with tuition grants to be used at private schools. A federal district struck down the tuition statute in *Lee v. Macon County Board of Education* (1967). The fact that Alabama could go so far as to close down public schools and provide tuition grants in order to avoid desegregation suggests that the state department of education would have no problem maintaining its race-based teacher unit cost schedule during this period.

of equals—and vertical equity—the appropriately different treatment of individuals with different educational needs or in different educational settings.[150] Under the conception of horizontal equity, equality is most often been measured in recent decades in terms of per pupil revenues or expenditures across school districts, with occasional though inconsistent consideration for differences in the purchasing power of educational expenditures.[151] Cases such as *Rodriguez* and subsequent state equal protection cases sought to disrupt the relationship between educational expenditures and school district taxable property wealth per pupil. That is, these cases sought to achieve a combination of fiscal neutrality—spending unrelated to district wealth—and horizontal equity—or relative equality of spending inputs to schooling across districts regardless of property wealth.[152]

Unfortunately, it is increasingly well understood that achieving equal dollar inputs is generally insufficient as a strategy even for providing equal quality of educational services across settings and children. One might argue, for example, that central to providing equal quality education across children is providing access to an equal quantity of teachers of equal qualifications. That is, regardless of where a child lives and attends school, he or she should have access to similar class size (teacher quantity) and to teachers with comparable educational preparation, professional training, and experience. However, it is increasingly well understood that working conditions including student population demographics as well as current levels of student performance influence strongly teachers' choices of where to work. In a study of Texas public elementary schools, Eric Hanushek and colleagues find that their research indicates that "a school with 10 percent more black students would require about 10 percent higher salaries in order to neutralize the increased probability of [nonminority female teachers] leaving."[153] That is, all else equal, it would cost more simply to provide comparable teaching quality in predominantly black schools. Pursuing policies of equal financial inputs might actually inhibit predominantly black school districts from being able to recruit and retain sufficient numbers of high-quality teachers.[154]

Furthermore, simply equalizing the quality of educational inputs is likely insufficient for closing achievement gaps. Closing achievement gaps, or providing black and white children equal opportunity to achieve specific outcome levels, will likely require providing substantially different quantities and qualities of educational inputs to predominantly black versus predominantly white schools.[155] Again, we emphasize a necessity for not only poverty- or socioeconomic-based differences but also race-based differences. As with teacher behavior on the teacher labor market, student outcomes and outcome gaps continue to have a strong black-white racial component not entirely explained by socioeconomic factors. Black-white differences in student achievement are a function of both individual students' race and by racial composition of the student's classroom level peer group.

Eric Hanushek and Steven Rivkin, using student-level data from Texas, find the uneven distribution of blacks across school districts can explain a significant portion of the

---

150. Baker et al., *supra* note 127.

151. *Id.*

152. William S. Koski, *Achieving "Adequacy" in the Classroom*, 27 B.C. Third World L.J. 13, 20 (2007).

153. Eric A. Hanushek et al., *Why Public Schools Lose Teachers*, 39 J. Hum. Resources 326, 350 (2004).

154. Jennifer Imazeki & Andrew Reschovsky, *Is No Child Left Behind and Un (or Under) Funded Federal Mandate? Evidence from Texas*, 57 Nat'l Tax J. 571 (2004).

155. Preston C. Green et al., *Race-Conscious Funding Strategies and School Finance Litigation*, 16 B.U. Pub. Int. L.J. 39, 42 (2006).

black-white achievement gap within the state.[156] Hanushek and Rivkin go further to discuss the interplay between race and peer group effect, with other factors tied to racial composition of schools. Using data from the state of Texas, and data on students in third through eighth grades from a recent national survey, Hanushek and Rivkin conclude,

> The substantial contribution of changes in achievement gaps between schools is consistent with an important role for schools, and we find that the imbalanced racial distribution of specific characteristics of teachers and peers—ones previously found to have significant effects on achievement—can account for all of the growth in the achievement gap following third grade.[157]

This recent work in particular highlights how the intersection of peer group effects and teacher quality distribution serve to simultaneously and substantially disadvantage black children attending racially isolated black schools.

Further, educational reform strategies that have been leveraged to improve achievement, such as class size reduction, have been shown to have differential effects on students' outcomes by race as well as socioeconomic status.[158] That is, all else equal, black children tend to benefit more than white children from certain educational interventions, including class size reduction. Capitalizing on the different marginal effects by race found in the Tennessee Class Size studies, Alan Krueger and Diane Whitmore simulate the extent to which class size reduction in particular might be leveraged for closing black-white achievement gaps.[159] Krueger and Whitmore find that "while students are in small classes, average test scores increase by 7 to 10 percentile points for black students and by 3 to 4 percentile points for white students."[160] Further, Krueger and Whitmore "find that having attended a small class compared to a regular-size class raises the likelihood that black students take the ACT or SAT college entrance exam from 31.8 to 41.3 percent, and raises the likelihood that white students take one of the exams from 44.7 to 46.4 percent. *As a consequence, if all students were assigned to a small class, the black-white gap in taking a college entrance exam would fall by an estimated 60 percent.*"[161] Henry Levin and colleagues make a similar case about the long-term economic value of investing in reforms targeted at African American males.[162]

---

156. Eric A. Hanushek & Steven G. Rivkin, *School Quality and the Black-White Achievement Gap*, www.stanford.edu/group/hebls/HanushekSchool.pdf (visited Sep. 1, 2007). Caroline Hoxby and Gretchen Weingarth instead suggest that average peer group performance and not race itself is the primary influence on individual performance. Caroline M. Hoxby & Gretchen Weingarth, *Taking Race out of the Equation: School Reassignment and the Structure of Peer Effects*, www.economics.harvard.edu/faculty/hoxby/papers/hoxby_weingarth_taking_race.pdf (visited Sep. 14, 2007). This perspective, however, brushes aside the underlying reality that the race of individual students in the peer group is associated with peer group performance.

157. Hanushek & Rivkin, *supra* note 156, at 28.

158. *See* Jeremy D. Finn & Charles M. Achilles, *Tennessee's Class Size Study: Findings, Implication, Misconceptions*, 21 EDUC. EVALUATION & POL'Y ANALYSIS 97 (1999); Jeremy D. Finn et al; *Small Classes in the Early Grades, Academic Achievement, and Graduating from High School*, 97 J. OF EEDUC. PSYCHOL. 214 (2005).

159. Alan B. Krueger & Diane M. Whitmore, *Would Smaller Classes Help Close the Black-White Achievement Gap*, Princeton University Industrial Relations Center, www.irs.princeton.edu/pubs/pdfs/ 451.pdf (visited Sep. 2, 2007).

160. *Id.* at 1.

161. *Id.* (emphasis added).

162. Henry M. Levin et al., *The Public Returns to Public Educational Investment in African-American Males*, Center for Benefit-Cost Studies of Education at Teachers College, Columbia University, www.cbcse.org/media/download_gallery/Public%20Returns%20Feb07.pdf (visited Sep. 2, 2007).

E. Horizontal Equity, Vertical Equity, and Cost Studies

Despite the evidence that high-minority districts may need additional resources to achieve horizontal and vertical equity, there is scant evidence of the use of racial indicators in the design of district cost studies.[163] The scarcity of race variables may be caused by researchers' hesitance to confront the political and legal repercussions that may derive from the conclusion that high-minority districts made need additional resources because of their racial composition.[164] However, researchers appear to have become less uneasy about considering race variables in computing school district educational costs. Using an approach known as cost function analysis, Jennifer Imazeki and Andrew Reschovsky found that there was a positive and statistically significant correlation between percentage of black and Hispanic students and the costs of achieving outcome levels required by NCLB.[165]

Cost function analysis is a statistical method which determines the costs associated with attaining a particular set of outcomes given district and student characteristics.[166] A cost function can predict the costs of achieving a specific set of outcomes in a district with average characteristics.[167] Additionally, a cost function analysis can create a cost index for each school district that indicates the relative cost of achieving the desired outcomes in each school district.[168] For example, the developer of a cost index would likely conclude that the per pupil costs of achieving the desired outcomes are higher than average in small, rural communities and that costs are higher in school districts with high percentages of economically disadvantaged students than in district with high percentages of children from more advantageous backgrounds.[169]

Building on Imazeki and Reschovsky's point that race can be used in the design of an education cost function, we analyzed in an article published in *Boston University Public Interest Law Journal* the costs associated with providing equal educational opportunities to high-minority districts in Missouri.[170] Our analysis examined the costs necessary to achieve a number of student outcome standards, including measures of proficiency in math and reading under the state assessment system and percentage of students matriculating to two- and four-year colleges.[171] To determine the effect that black population concentration may have on the costs of attaining specific sets of outcomes, our analysis estimated two models—one including and one excluding a percent black measure.[172] We found that "the percent black variable in the cost model drives cost per pupil much higher in ... racially isolated districts."[173] Further, we found that the Welston school district would $9,000 per pupil under our analysis when race was excluded, and $15,000 when race was included.[174]

· · ·

---

163. Green et al., *supra* note 154, at 50.
164. *Id.*
165. Imazeki & Reschovsky, *supra* note 154.
166. Lori L. Taylor et al., *Documentation for the NCES Comparable Wage Index Data File (May 2006)*, National Center for Educational Statistics, nces.ed.gov/pubs2006/2006865.pdf#search=%22%22Documentation%20for%20the%20NCES%20Comparable%20Wage%20Index%20Data%20File%22%22 (visited Aug. 29, 2006).
167. *Id.* at 6.
168. *Id.*
169. *Id.*
170. Green et al., *supra* note 154, at 54–63.
171. *Id.* at 55.
172. *Id.*
173. *Id.* at 58.
174. *Id.*

In summary, labor market analyses like those by Eric Hanushek and colleagues explain why race-based funding is required merely to achieve horizontal and vertical equity for black children. Where horizontal equity is measured in terms of equal access to teaching quality rather than dollar inputs, wage premiums based on school racial composition may be required. Alternative policies might include either redistributing children based on their race so as to eliminate the existing labor market behavior, or establishing statewide teacher assignment policies to ensure that each child in the state has access to comparable quality teachers. Krueger and Whitmore's simulations suggest the need for race-based vertical equity adjustment to advance the closure of achievement gaps. That is, schools and districts with higher black concentrations require greater quantities of at least comparable-quality teachers.

IV: Alternative Legal Arguments for Obtaining Vertical and Horizontal Equity for High-Minority Districts

A. The Need for New "Separate but Equal" Legal Approaches

Thus far, we have pointed out that students from high-minority school districts have used two types of legal approaches to attain equal educational opportunity: school desegregation and school finance. We have also observed that because students from many high-minority school districts do not have the opportunity to attend desegregated schools, they may have to focus on developing legal arguments that will help them obtain the resources necessary to obtain equal educational opportunity. The principal legal roadblock for these plaintiffs is the Supreme Court's acceptance of the racial neutrality jurisprudence under the equal protection clause, which has its origins during the separate but equal era: so long as governmental entities can articulate a race-neutral reason for their funding classifications, then the lenient rational basis test applies. Therefore, states may employ distribution policies that have a negative disparate impact on high-minority districts with little fear of an equal protection clause challenge. Another complication for plaintiffs from high-minority school districts is that such districts may need additional resources to achieve the school finance goals of horizontal and vertical equity.

Ironically, at the end of the separate but equal era, the Supreme Court developed an equality standard in *Sweatt* that might have effectively addressed the resource plight of high-minority districts. Recall that in *Sweatt*, the Court applied an equality standard that looked at the educational inputs (e.g., faculty quality and library holdings) and educational outcomes (passage of the bar and success in the profession) to determine that Texas's black law school was substantially inferior to the University of Texas. Also recall that courts applied *Sweatt*'s analysis of educational resources and educational outcomes to public elementary and secondary education; this analysis was later used in *Hobson* to strike down funding inequality in de facto segregated public schools.

We believe that the equality standard developed in *Sweatt* and *Hobson* may effectively address the resource woes of high-minority districts. First, as *Hobson* demonstrates, this approach could be used to strike down state distribution policies that "thoughtlessly" create funding inequality between low-minority and high-minority schools. Second, *Hobson*'s and *Sweatt*'s comparison of educational resources and outcomes may call for funding remedies designed to attain vertical and horizontal equity for high-minority school districts. We realize that in these cases, the courts' remedy was school desegregation. An alternative remedy may be to provide educational resources designed to (1) provide high-minority districts with the funding to attain resources necessary to attain equal educational opportunity (e.g., high-quality teachers), and (2) implement educational programming designed to raise the educational outcomes of students attending schools in high-minority districts (e.g., class size reduction).

In the next section, we explain the role that NCLB may play in helping high-minority districts attain horizontal and vertical equity. We also explore two possible arguments that students attending high-minority school districts can make to address state distribution policies that create racial funding disparities and to attain horizontal and vertical equity. These arguments are based on state education clauses and the due process clause.

B. The Role of NCLB

In 2002, Congress enacted NCLB, which requires all states to create accountability systems that apply to public schools.[175] A major goal of NCLB is to close "the achievement gap between high- and low-performing children, especially the achievement gaps between minority and nonminority students, and between disadvantaged children and their more advantaged peers."[176] NCLB requires all states to bring all students to levels of proficiency on state-developed tests by 2013–14.[177] NCLB also requires all students to make adequate yearly progress (AYP) on all specified state standards, including economically disadvantaged, racial and ethnic minorities; students with disabilities; and limited English proficient students.[178]

If a school fails to make AYP for two consecutive years, it will have to develop a plan for improvement and notify parents of the status.[179] Students attending schools that have failed to make AYP for three consecutive years must be provided supplemental services such as tutoring in addition to being allowed to transfer to another school.[180] A fourth consecutive failure to achieve AYP must result in the implementation of corrective action to improve the school, such as replacing staff or offering public school choice.[181] After a fifth year of failure, school restructuring must take place, such as conversion to a charter school, state takeover, or staff restructuring.[182] It is also possible for school districts to lose federal funding.[183]

By requiring states to disaggregate the academic outcomes data of minority students, NCLB has forced many state accountability systems to attempt to remedy racial achieve-

---

175. 20 U.S.C. §§ 6301 *et seq.* (2005).
176. *Id.* § 6301(3).
177. *Id.* § 6311(b)(2)(F).
178. *Id.* § 6311(b)(2)(C); Joseph O. Oluwole & Preston C. Green, *Charter Schools Under the NCLB: Choice and Equal Educational Opportunity*, 22 St. John's J. Legal Comment. 165 (2007).
179. *Id.* § 6316(b)(3)(A).
180. *Id.* § 6316(b)(5).
181. *Id.* § 6316(b)(7).
182. *Id.* § 6316(b)(8).
183. *Id.* § 6311(g)(2).

ment gaps for the first time. During the 1999–2000 school year, only six out of thirty-three states with accountability systems used narrowing the achievement gap as at least one criterion for determining AYP.[184] Consequently, many "successful" schools under state accountability systems had substantial racial achievement gaps.[185] The reason for this phenomenon was that many state accountability systems enacted before NCLB were based on average school-wide test scores. Thus, white students were able to raise the overall average in a number of schools to acceptable levels.[186]

It is doubtful that NCLB creates an implied right of action or a 42 U.S.C. § 1983 action to compel states to adopt race-conscious funding approaches. In *Association of Community Organizations for Reform Now v. New York City Department of Education*, a federal district court held that the text and structure of NCLB did not demonstrate a congressional intent to create individual enforceable rights under the statute.[187] Because the statute did not evince clear congressional intention to create individual rights, the court also ruled that NCLB may not be enforced under § 1983.[188]

Nevertheless, NCLB may still serve as the impetus for courts to hold that school finance formulas that fail to address the educational needs of high-minority districts violates state educational clauses and the due process clause. The next section explains how plaintiffs from high-minority school districts may mount education clause and due process clause challenges to obtain increased funding to reduce racial achievement gaps.

C. Education Clauses

Specifically, plaintiffs from high-minority school districts could argue that (1) the states' duty to provide a constitutionally education requires inclusion of standards of accountability, (2) high-minority districts have additional education costs that may affect their ability to attain the standards of accountability, and (3) state school finance systems have violated education clauses by failing to take into account the additional costs of high-minority school districts. With respect to the first prong, "it is ... widely accepted that establishing standards of accountability is part of the State's duty to provide a constitutionally adequate education."[189] The Supreme Court of New Hampshire has explained that "accountability means that the State must provide a definition of a

---

184. Margaret E. Goertz et al., *Assessment and Accountability Systems in the 50 States: 1999–2000*, Consortium for Policy Research in Education, www.cpre.org/Publications/rr46.pdf (visited Feb. 28, 2006).

185. Daria Hall et al., *What New "AYP" Information Tells Us About Schools, States, and Public Education*, The Education Trust, www2.edtrust.org/NR/rdonlyres/4B9BF8DE-987A-4063-B750-6D67607E7205/0/NewAYP.pdf (visited March 6, 2006); Lance D. Fusarelli, *The Potential Impact of the No Child Left Behind Act on Equity and Diversity in American Education*, 18 EDUC. POL'Y 71, 74–75 (2004).

186. Hall et al., *supra* note 185; Fusarelli, *supra* note 185, at 74–75.

187. *Association of Cmty. Organizations for Reform Now v. New York City Dep't of Educ.*, 269 F. Supp. 2d 338, 344 (S.D.N.Y. 2003).

188. *Id.*

189. *Claremont Sch. Dist. v. Governor*, 794 A.2d 744, 751 (N.H. 2002). *See also DeRolph v. State*, 728 N.E.2d 993, 1019 (Ohio 2000) (state's constitutional duty to provide adequate education requires "statewide standards that are fully developed, clearly stated, and understood by educators, students, and parents."); *Abbott v. Burke*, 693 A.2d 417, 427 (N.J. 1997) ("comprehensive statutory and administrative system for public education founded on standards that define the substantive meaning of education and that provide for measures of educational performance and achievement are consistent with the Constitution's education clause"); 120 P.3d 306 (Kan. 2005) (finding that the state leg-

constitutionally adequate education, the definition must have standards, and the standards must be subject to meaningful application so that it is possible to determine whether in delegating its obligation to provide a constitutionally adequate education, the State has fulfilled its duty."[190] The court went on to emphasize that the standards established within the accountability system are enforceable: "If the State cannot be held accountable for fulfilling its duty, the duty creates no obligation and is no longer a duty."[191]

With respect to the second prong, James Ryan and Thomas Saunders observe that "a handful of courts have displayed a halting but noticeable willingness to interpret state constitutions as mandating vertical equity."[192] Indeed, four state supreme courts have held that their education clauses require school finance systems to adopt vertical equity principles to meet the educational needs of disadvantaged students.[193] For example, in *Campbell County School District v. State*, the Wyoming Supreme Court observed that the state education clause's mandate for an equal opportunity for an education "necessarily contemplates the playing field to be leveled so each child has an equal chance for educational success."[194] The court also noted that "children with an impaired readiness to learn do not have the same equal opportunity for a quality education as do those children not impacted by personal or social ills simply because they do not have the same starting point in learning."[195] Thus, a school finance system that distributed funding without regard for the need to level the playing field failed to provide an equal opportunity for a quality education as required by the state education clause.[196]

In *Abbott v. Burke*,[197] the Supreme Court of New Jersey used vertical equity principles to hold that the Comprehensive Educational Improvement and Financing Act of 1996 (CEIFA) violated the state education clause's mandate of providing a thorough and efficient education. The CEIFA defined a thorough and efficient education in terms of core curriculum content standards, set achievement goals for these standards, and developed an improvement statewide assessment program for determining whether the state was meeting these standards.[198] CEIFA also developed educational funding standards that were correlated with the content standards.[199] The funding scheme was based on a model

---

islature had failed to satisfy its own definition of adequacy, which was based on state accreditation standards and student academic performance measures).

190. *Claremont Sch. Dist.*, 794 A.2d at 752.

191. *Id.*

192. James E. Ryan & Thomas Saunders, *Foreward to Symposium on School Finance Litigation: Emerging Trends of New Dead Ends*, 22 Yale L. & Pol'y Rev. 463, 465 (2004).

193. *Montoy*, 120 P.3d 306 (Kan. 2005) (finding that school finance system was unconstitutional because it was based on political compromise, thus distorting the weighting factors used for low enrollment, special education, vocational, bilingual education, and at-risk students); *Abbott v. Burke*, 575 A.2d 359, 385 (N.J. 1990) (*Abbott II*) (finding that the state's education clause requires the legislature to provide special needs districts (SNDs) with funding that was substantially equal to that of affluent districts, and educational programming that would address their "extreme disadvantages"); *Hoke County Bd. of Educ. v. State*, 599 S.E.2d 365, 393 (N.C. 2004) (finding that state had failed to meet educational needs of at-risk students in violation of education clause); *Campbell County Sch. Dist. v. State*, 907 P.2d 1238, 1278 (Wyo. 1995) (finding that education clause's mandate for an equal opportunity for an education "necessarily contemplates the playing field to be leveled so each child has an equal chance for educational success").

194. *Campbell County Sch. Dist.*, 907 P.2d at 1278.

195. *Id.*

196. *Id.* at 1278–79.

197. 693 A.2d 417 (N.J. 1997).

198. *Id.* at 425.

199. *Id.* at 426.

school district consisting of an elementary school of 500 pupils, a middle school of 675 pupils, a high school of 900 pupils, and a central office.[200]

Further, CEIFA provided supplemental aid for the special needs of disadvantaged students through two programs: Demonstrably Effective Program Aid (DEPA), and Early Childhood Program Aid (ECPA). DEPA provided aid for "instructional, school governance, and health and social welfare programs to benefit students enrolled in schools in which the concentration of low-income pupils is greater than 20 percent of total enrollment."[201] ECPA provided aid for childhood programs and services, such as full-day kindergarten and preschool.[202]

The New Jersey Supreme Court ruled that CEIFA's adoption of content and performance standards were a facially adequate definition of a thorough and efficient education.[203] However, the court ruled that the CEIFA's use of hypothetical model school district to determine the appropriate level of funding was unconstitutional because it failed to incorporate the needs and characteristics of SNDs. For instance, the model district did not take into consideration that facilities in SNDs were much older and needed more maintenance than other school districts.[204] Moreover, the model district failed to provide SNDs with the special educational programming that they would need to take advantage of educational opportunity.[205] Plaintiffs could establish the additional need of high-minority districts through education production and cost function studies, such as the ones discussed in section IV. Because of NCLB's focus on racial achievement gaps, the judiciary may be amenable to race-based vertical equity challenges.

Montoy v. State, a Kansas school finance case is illustrative. A trial court held that the School District Finance and Quality Performance Act of 1992 violated the education clause.[206] The court rejected the defendants' argument that the state's high national ranking on a variety of achievement tests proved that the state was providing an adequate education. "When these broad averages are disaggregated," the trial court pointed out, "it becomes clear that many categories of Kansas students (*minorities*, the poor, the disabled, and the limited English) are failing at alarming rates."[207] The court also found that increases in educational funding would enable districts to employ strategies, such as reducing class sizes and hiring better trained teachers, which could raise the academic performance of minority and disadvantaged students.[208] The state supreme court affirmed the trial court decision with respect to the education clause, finding that "the SDFQPA fails to provide adequate funding for a suitable education for students of their and other similarly situated districts, i.e., middle- and large-sized districts with a high proportion of minority and/or at-risk and special education students."[209]

With respect to the third prong, plaintiffs could demonstrate that the school finance system was not designed to provide for their educational needs, through an analysis of the legislative history surrounding the school finance formulas. In *Montoy*, for example, the Supreme Court of Kansas held that the SDFQPA violated the education clause because it

---

200. *Id.*
201. *Id.* at 435 (internal quotations omitted).
202. *Id.*
203. *Id.* at 428.
204. *Id.* at 431.
205. *Id.*
206. *Montoy v. State*, 2003 WL 22902963, at *43 (Kan. Dist. Ct. Dec. 2, 2003).
207. *Id.* at *42.
208. *Id.* at *47–48.
209. *Montoy*, 102 P.3d at 1164.

was based on former spending levels and political compromise instead of the actual costs of achieving a constitutionally adequate education.[210] This failure to determine the actual cost of an education distorted the weighting factors that the SDFQPA used for low enrollment, special education, vocational, bilingual education, and at-risk students.[211]

D. Due Process Clause

Further, plaintiffs from high-minority school districts may assert that school finance formulas that fail to provide them with the benefits of their accountability systems violate their substantive due process rights pursuant to the due process clause of the Fourteenth Amendment. The due process clause provides that no state shall "deprive any person of life, liberty or property, without due process of law."[212] Due process has two components. Procedural due process requires that before government deprives a person of a protected interest, it must provide that person with notice and an opportunity to be heard.[213] Substantive due process guards against "certain government actions regardless of the fairness of the procedures used to implement them."[214]

Plaintiffs from high-minority districts may argue that the failure to provide them with funding that meets their educational needs violates their property right to a constitutionally adequate education. For substantive due process, two requirements must be met: (1) it must be shown that the state has infringed on a property or liberty interest; and (2) the state's policy is not rationally related to achieving the governmental interest. With respect to property rights, in *Board of Regents v. Roth*,[215] the Supreme Court held that property interests are created by existing rules, such as state law, that create certain benefits and entitlements to those benefits. Recall that several state supreme courts have found that their state constitutions require states to provide students with vertical equity. These rulings would appear to establish a property right, as defined by state law, to an education that meets the additional needs of underprivileged students. Having established a property interest to vertical equity, plaintiffs from high-minority districts would then argue that a funding system that does not take race into account would not be rationally related to that property interest.

This chapter has shown that racial composition is a significant factor in the estimation of education costs and allocation of aid. This chapter has also shown that in many circumstances, funding to high minority districts may be based on political concerns or historical racial animus. Thus, such funding formulas would not be rationally related to the property interest of enabling students in high-minority districts to achieve an education that meets their educational needs.

The major drawback of substantive due process litigation (and education clause litigation for that matter) is that state accountability standards may be set so low as to be rendered meaningless. In 1976, Arthur Wise presciently identified this possibility, noting:

> From the beginning, some said that school finance lawsuits should not be argued on the basis of equal protection but on the basis of substantive due process.

---

210. *Id.*

211. *Id.*

212. U.S. Const. amend. XIV, § 1.

213. Richard B. Saphire & Paul Moke, *Litigating Bush v. Gore in the States: Dual Voting Systems and the Fourteenth Amendment*, 51 Vill. L. Rev. 229, 269 (2006).

214. *Daniels v. Williams*, 474 U.S. 327, 331 (1986).

215. 408 U.S. 564 (1972).

Such an approach implies that the cases would be concerned with minimum levels of protection to be afforded to children in the schools. The equal protection clause is much more encompassing, creating a demand for the equal treatment of equals. A substantive due process interpretation would mean only that protection needs to be provided up to a certain level.[216]

Indeed, in response to NCLB, several states have lowered the standards of their accountability systems.[217] It is important to note that excessively low standards may be in violation of state education clauses. Courts may be forced to strike down such standards.[218]

V: Parents Involved and the Future of Race-Conscious Funding

This section briefly examines the future of race-conscious funding after *Parents Involved in Community Schools v. Seattle School District No. 1*.[219] *Parents Involved* was a consolidation of two cases, *Parents Involved in Community Schools v. Seattle School District No. 1*[220] and *Meredith v. Jefferson County Board of Education*,[221] appealed to the U.S. Supreme Court. Both cases involved school districts' voluntary adoption of race-based student assignment plans to ensure racial balance in the various schools in the school districts— Seattle School District No. 1 and Jefferson County Public Schools. The plans were challenged as violations of the equal protection clause. In a five-to-four judgment, the Court held that the use of racial classifications to achieve racial balancing is unconstitutional under the equal protection clause.

Chief Justice Roberts wrote the Court and plurality opinions. Justice Kennedy, the swing vote in the case, joined the five-to-four judgment and wrote a separate concurrence. In the post-Justice O'Connor Court, he could be the pivotal vote in the event of a constitutional challenge to race-conscious funding. If Justice Kennedy votes with the dissenting Justices in *Parents Involved*—Justices Breyer, Ginsburg, Souter, and Stevens— that would be adequate to uphold race-conscious funding against constitutional challenge. While the plurality of Justices Alito, Scalia, Thomas, and Chief Justice Roberts would apply traditional strict scrutiny to all race-based classifications, even the plurality opinion does not foreclose all future uses of race. In this respect, Chief Justice Roberts specifically stated,

> other means — *e.g., where to construct new schools, how to allocate *resources among schools*, and which academic offerings, to provide to attract students to certain schools*—implicate different considerations than the explicit racial clas-

---

216. Arthur E. Wise, *Minimum Educational Adequacy: Beyond School Finance Reform*, 1 J. OF EDUC. FIN. 468, 477 (1976).

217. Tico A. Almeida, *Refocusing School Finance Litigation on At-Risk Children:* Leandro V. State of North Carolina, 22 YALE L. & POL'Y REV. 525, 546 (2004).

218. *Id.*

219. 127 S.Ct. 2738 (2007) (*Parents Involved*). For a more extensive analysis of the *Parents Involved* decision and its implications for race-conscious measures, see Joseph O. Oluwole & Preston C. Green, *Parents Involved and Race-conscious Measures: A Cause for Optimism*, 26 BUFF. PUB. INT. L.J. (forthcoming).

220. 137 F. Supp. 2d 1224 (W.D. Wash. 2001).

221. 330 F. Supp. 2d 834 (W.D.Ky. 2004).

sifications at issue in these cases, and we express no opinion on their validity—not even in dicta. Rather, we employ the familiar and well-established approach of strict scrutiny to evaluate the plans at issue today.[222]

Given that school funding is an archetype of resource allocation, this language suggests that race-conscious funding strategies could still have a positive future with Chief Justice Roberts or maybe even the plurality of justices, with the likely exception of Justice Thomas, who subscribes to the view that the Constitution is color-blind, precluding all uses of racial classifications.[223]

In his concurrence, Justice Kennedy stated that school districts can constitutionally pursue an interest in providing equal educational opportunity.[224] This suggests he would be amenable to race-conscious funding strategies designed to achieve equal educational opportunity. Justice Kennedy also noted that "if school authorities are concerned that the student-body compositions of certain schools interfere with the objective of offering an equal educational opportunity to all of their students, they are *free to devise race-conscious measures* to address the problem in a general way."[225] An indication of his willingness to permit race-conscious measures is also evident in his following statements:

> School boards may pursue the goal of bringing together students of diverse backgrounds and races through other means, including strategic site selection of new schools; drawing attendance zones with general recognition of the demographics of neighborhoods; allocating resources for special programs; recruiting students and faculty in a targeted fashion; and tracking enrollments, performance, and other statistics by race. These mechanisms are race conscious but do not lead to different treatment based on a classification that tells each student he or she is to be defined by race, so it is unlikely any of them would demand strict scrutiny to be found permissible.[226]

The dissenting justices are in favor of race-conscious measures as long as they serve inclusionary purposes as opposed to exclusionary purposes.[227] According to the Justices, "a longstanding and unbroken line of legal authority tell us that the equal protection clause permits local school boards to use race-conscious criteria to achieve positive race-related

---

222. *Parents Involved*, 127 S.Ct. at 2766 (emphasis added).

223. *Id.* at 2768, 2782; *see also Grutter*, 539 U.S. at 378 (Thomas, J., concurring in part and dissenting in part). The view that the Constitution is color-blind was first articulated by Justice John Marshall Harlan in *Plessy*, 163 U.S. 559 (Harlan, J., dissenting). Justice Kennedy believes this colorblind view is merely an aspiration and "cannot be a universal constitutional principle" in the real world. *Id.* at 2792. Justice Thomas is thus against both inclusionary and exclusionary uses of race.

224. *Id.* at 2792.

225. *Id.* (emphasis added).

226. *Id.*

227. *See id.* at 2815 ("a well-established legal view of the Fourteenth Amendment. That view understands the basic objective of those who wrote the equal protection clause as forbidding practices that lead to racial exclusion ... There is reason to believe that those who drafted an Amendment with this basic purpose in mind would have understood the legal and practical difference between the use of race-conscious criteria in defiance of that purpose, namely to keep the races apart, and the use of race-conscious criteria to further that purpose, namely to bring the races together ... Although the Constitution almost always forbids the former, it is significantly more lenient in respect to the latter") (internal quotes and citations omitted). *See also id.* ("Sometimes Members of this Court have disagreed about the degree of leniency that the Clause affords to programs designed to include ... But I can find no case in which this Court has followed Justice Thomas' colorblind approach. And I have found no case that otherwise repudiated this constitutional asymmetry between that which seeks to *exclude* and that which seeks to *include* members of minority races") (emphasis in original) (internal quotes and citations omitted).

goals, even when the Constitution does not compel it."[228] Under this same broad discretionary umbrella where the dissenting justices placed the race-based plans in *Parents Involved*, finding them constitutional would fell race-conscious measures such as race-conscious funding, as the language ostensibly indicates. Additionally, the dissenting justices would not apply traditional strict scrutiny to benign race-conscious measures, in order to enhance the chances of such measures surviving judicial scrutiny.[229]

The synopsis of this discussion is that *Parents Involved* suggests that the dissenting Justices would be in favor of race-conscious funding. The underlying position of the dissenting justices is that the Constitution should be interpreted "as affording the people, acting through their elected representatives, freedom to select the use of race-conscious criteria from among their available options."[230] Optimism might be taken from Chief Justice Roberts's statement that *Parents Involved* was not adjudication that race-conscious measures other than racial balancing plans are unconstitutional.[231] Furthermore, Justice Kennedy, the likely swing vote, seems receptive to race-conscious measures. This might supply the five-to-four vote upholding race-conscious funding or even six-to-three, should Chief Justice Roberts be persuaded.

Conclusion

Because the Supreme Court has limited the scope of school desegregation litigation, minority plaintiffs will have to focus on school finance litigation to obtain equal educational opportunity. This chapter has shown that the Supreme Court's racial neutrality jurisprudence has been a major barrier for minority plaintiffs in this quest. However, we disagree with the prevalent view that most high-minority school districts are harmed by a reliance on local property taxation. Instead, they are harmed by race-neutral distribution policies that tend to favor low-minority districts.

This chapter has also shown that the real equality standard applied in *Sweatt* and *Hobson* would have been ideal in helping minority students attain equal educational opportunity. This is because the legal analyses in these cases were amenable to race-conscious horizontal and vertical equity remedies. Although NCLB probably does not support a private right of action, its focus on racial educational performance may encourage courts to rule favorably on race-based challenges pursuant to state education clauses and the due process clause. Finally, the *Parents Involved* case suggests that a majority of the Supreme Court may find race-conscious school finance remedies permissible under the equal protection clause.

---

228. *Parents Involved*, 127 S.Ct. at 2811. Similarly, the dissenting justices stated that it is a constitutional valid legal principle "that the government may voluntarily adopt race-conscious measures to improve conditions of race even when it is not under a constitutional obligation to do so. That principle has been accepted by every branch of government and is rooted in the history of the equal protection clause itself." *Id.* at 2814. This would favor race-conscious funding.

229. *Id.* at 2816–18.

230. *Id.* at 2834.

231. *Id.* at 2766.

8

School Finance Litigation: Beyond Equality

Victoria J. Dodd

Introduction and Summary

In the early twenty-first century, public school finance litigation has become quite diffuse and fragmented, from both a legal and a policy viewpoint, but it has not brought with it the equitable school financing that eluded earlier reformers. The earliest cases on both the state[1] and federal[2] levels generally sought "equal" per pupil expenditures in public school districts throughout a state. By the 1990s, however, such litigation focused as well on the "adequacy" of educational results, and the former emphasis on money evolved into a much more complicated investigation of curricula, educational practices, and even testing results.

Much of this change in focus stemmed from the result in *San Antonio School District v. Rodriguez*,[3] in which the U.S. Supreme Court ruled that education is not a fundamental right, nor is poverty a suspect class. Because federal constitutional rights were no longer a fertile source of educational guarantees, state court judges began to probe their state constitutions to find analogous state protections, sometimes successfully and sometimes not. Over time, the search for an equally funded education therefore became much more than a search for equal distribution of funding: it became a search for an equitable or adequate education, an entirely different proposition.

Freed from a purely monetary focus, however, courts nevertheless hesitate to move strongly toward guaranteeing educational quality, particularly when the educational goals being sought are more than minimum competencies. At the same time, the "plain vanilla" simple property tax rate scheme of *Rodriguez* has been replaced in many states with funding formulas that only an economist could understand. To some extent the educational process has now been turned away from the loci of teachers, children, and parents, and instead has been put into the hands of "experts" and other bureaucrats.

Because of these and other frustrations, the Supreme Court should overrule *Rodriguez* and establish a universal, fundamental right to an adequate public education. Only then

---

1. *See generally Serrano v. Priest*, 5 Cal. 3d 584, 487 P.2d 1241, 96 Cal. Rptr. 601 (1971).
2. *See generally San Antonio Sch. Dist. v. Rodriguez*, 411 U.S. 1 (1973).
3. *Id.*

can the promises to America's children of an equitable and challenging education and life be fulfilled.

This chapter explores the legal transitions in school finance litigation over the past thirty years, with an eye toward explaining both what has happened and what should happen in the years to come. Sections concerning other early and later state educational funding cases follow.

The *Rodriguez* Case

The most important case in the American public school funding legal saga is *San Antonio Independent School District v. Rodriguez*.[4] This case was a challenge to the method of funding public schools in Texas by the local property tax, the typical method of financing American public schools. As in other states, relying on local property taxes, given widely varying property values, yielded in Texas very disparate per-pupil expenditures. In the Edgewood District, for instance, a predominately Hispanic area, per-pupil expenditures were $356;[5] while in affluent, Anglo Alamo Heights, per-pupil spending was $594.[6] These extreme funding differences between and among local school districts in Texas caused the U.S. District Court in Texas in the *Rodriguez* case to hold that this funding system violated the equal protection rights of Texas citizens.[7] Amazingly, the court concluded both that education was a "fundamental" interest and wealth a "suspect" classification.[8]

The result in the District Court in Texas was what commentators had expected, based on earlier state and federal cases. In California, for instance, the 1971 case of *Serrano v. Priest*[9] had held that a similar California school financing scheme violated the federal equal protection clause.[10] On the federal level, such earlier Supreme Court cases as *Shapiro v. Thompson*[11] had also given advocates hope that education would be deemed a fundamental right. The *Shapiro* court held that a one-year state waiting period to receive welfare benefits violated the federal equal protection clause.[12] Before the *Rodriguez* case there indeed was a genuine belief among many legal commentators that the Supreme Court, much like many European nations, might find various necessities of life, such as employment, housing,[13] education, and health care, to be "fundamental."

Such hopes were dashed when the Supreme Court issued its ruling in the *Rodriguez* case. In a five-to-four opinion, Justice Lewis Powell for the majority held that no suspect class was burdened by the Texas system;[14] and in addition, the U.S. Constitution was found to harbor no fundamental right to an education.[15]

---

4. 411 U.S. 1 (1973).

5. *Id.* at 12.

6. *Id.* at 13.

7. *Id.* at 16.

8. *Id.*

9. 5 Cal. 3d 584, 487 P.2d 1241, 96 Cal. Rptr. 601 (1971). *See infra* notes 33–51 and accompanying text.

10. 5 Cal. 3d at 605, 487 P.2d at 1252, 96 Cal. Rptr. at 615.

11. *Shapiro v. Thompson*, 394 U.S. 618 (1969).

12. *Id.* at 638.

13. *But see Lindsey v. Normet*, 405 U.S. 56 (1972) (no fundamental right to adequate housing for low-income people).

14. 411 U.S. at 28.

15. *See generally id.* at 29–40.

Justice Powell spent many pages of the majority opinion explaining the latter issue. Indeed, his very positive comments about the importance of public education were almost an argument against the outcome of the case:

> Nothing this Court holds today in any way detracts from our historic dedication to public education. We are in complete agreement with the conclusion of the three judge panel below that "the grave significance of education both to the individual and to our society" cannot be doubted. But the importance of a service performed by the state does not determine whether it must be regarded as fundamental for purposes of examination under the Equal Protection Clause.[16]... the key to discovering whether education is "fundamental" is not to be found in comparisons of the relative societal significance of education as opposed to subsistence or housing. Nor is it to be found by weighing whether education is as important as the right to travel. Rather, the answer lies in assessing whether there is a right to education explicitly or implicitly guaranteed by the Constitution.[17]... It is appellees' contention, however, that education is distinguishable from other services and benefits provided by the state because it bears a peculiarly close relationship to other rights and liberties accorded protection under the Constitution.[18]

Justice Powell then cautioned that "this Court's lack of specialized knowledge and experience counsels against premature interference with the informed judgments made at the state and local levels."[19] Hence, the Court found that a rational basis test sustained the local property taxation system, even with its "conceded imperfections."[20]

Justices White, Brennan, and Marshall wrote dissenting opinions, but Justice Marshall's contribution has achieved iconic status. Having himself argued before the Supreme Court the case of *Brown v. Board of Education*[21] and its various important precursors,[22] Justice Marshall focused on "discrimination on the basis of group wealth"[23] and the inability of impoverished children to enhance the tax basis of their school districts.[24] Because education "directly affects the ability of a child to exercise his First Amendment rights,"[25] and is "the dominant factor affecting political consciousness and participation,"[26] Justice Marshall concluded that there existed an "intimate relationship between [this] particular personal interest and specific constitutional guarantees." In Justice Marshall's mind, this sort of connection had in the past caused the Court to recognize fundamental rights and to use higher levels of constitutional scrutiny. Thus, Justice Marshall used "careful judicial scrutiny"[27] to analyze whether a state educational system that was based on or discriminated on the basis of district/group wealth was sustainable. He found that "any substantial degree of scrutiny of the operation of the Texas financing scheme reveals that

---

16. *Id.* at 30.
17. *Id.* at 33–34.
18. *Id.* at 35.
19. *Id.* at 42.
20. *Id.* at 44.
21. *Brown v. Bd. of Educ.*, 347 U.S. 483 (1954).
22. *E.g., Sweatt v. Painter*, 339 U.S. 629 (1950); *McLaurin v. Oklahoma State Regents*, 339 U.S. 637 (1950).
23. 411 U.S. at 122.
24. *Id.* at 123–124.
25. *Id.* at 112.
26. *Id.* at 113.
27. *Id.* at 124.

the State has selected means wholly inappropriate to secure its purported interest in assuring its school districts local fiscal control."[28]

Referring to the Texas scheme's discriminatory effects, Justice Marshall concluded that

> in this case we have been presented with an instance of such discrimination, in a particularly invidious form, against an individual interest of large constitutional and practical importance. To support the demonstrated discrimination in the provision of educational opportunity the State has offered a justification which, on analysis, takes on at least an ephemeral character. Thus, I believe that the wide disparities in taxable district property wealth inherent in the local property tax element of the Texas financing scheme render that scheme violative of the Equal Protection Clause.[29]

Early State School Financing Cases

As explained,[30] the California Supreme Court in the 1971 case of *Serrano v. Priest*[31] held that the state method of funding public schools primarily through local property taxes violated the equal protection clause of the Fourteenth Amendment of the U.S. Constitution.[32] This was so because as in the *Rodriguez* case,[33] the use of the local property tax system led to significant funding level differences among different school districts. Indeed, the per-pupil funding disparities in California in 1969–70 ranged from as little as $103 per child to $952 per child.[34] Echoing the reasoning of Justice Marshall in the later *Rodriguez* case,[35] the California Supreme Court found that

> this funding scheme invidiously discriminates against the poor because it makes the quality of a child's education a function of the wealth of his parents and neighbors. Recognizing as we must that the right to an education in our public schools is a fundamental interest which cannot be conditioned on wealth, we can discern no compelling state purpose necessitating the present method of financing. We have concluded, therefore, that such a system cannot withstand constitutional challenge and must fall before the equal protection clause.[36]

The court found it "irrefutable"[37] that the system was a classification based on wealth, and that "discrimination on the basis of district wealth"[38] was just as pernicious as dis-

---

28. *Id.* at 129.

29. *Id.* at 133.

30. *See supra* notes 9–10 and accompanying text.

31. *Serrano v. Priest*, 5 Cal. 3d 584, 487 P.2d 1241, 96 Cal. Rptr. 610 (1971).

32. *Id.* at 589.

33. *See supra* notes 4–8 and accompanying text.

34. 5 Cal. 3d at 592. As a student teacher at Beverly Hills High School in 1971, I observed a full-service media/TV studio; an observatory/planetarium; a full-time detective employed only to ferret out students who were attending the school but who did not actually legally reside within the district; and school rules that prevented students from eating lunch on the front lawn so as to deter kidnappings for ransom. As explained in the *Serrano* case, in 1968–69 the per-pupil expenditures in Beverly Hills were $1,231.72. *Id.* at 594, n.8.

35. *See infra* notes 21–29 and surrounding text.

36. 5 Cal. 3d. at 589.

37. *Id.* at 597.

38. *Id.* at 601.

crimination against individual wealth. Education was also found by the California court to be a fundamental interest, again just as Justice Marshall later argued in *Rodriguez*.[39] The *Serrano* Court based its ruling on

> the indispensable role which education plays in the modern industrial state. This role, we believe, has two significant aspects: first, education is a major determinant of an individual's chances for economic and social success in our competitive society; second, education is a unique influence on a child's development as a citizen and his participation in political and community life.[40]

Citing Horace Mann,[41] the father of modern education, the Court reversed the lower court's dismissal of the original complaint on a demurrer and remanded the case for the defendants' answer.

During the subsequent trial of the *Serrano* case, the Supreme Court made its ruling in *Rodriguez*, holding that federal equal protection was not violated by local property tax funding schemes.[42] The California trial court then held in the remanded *Serrano* case that California state equal protection guarantees were still violated,[43] even though the original *Serrano* decision was based primarily on a discussion of federal equal protection precedents. Despite changes then made in public school financing laws by the state legislature, an appeal was again brought to the state supreme court in *Serrano II*,[44] which became the foundational state equal protection case in California.

Although the state legislature in response to *Serrano I* had significantly increased state "foundation aid" in 1973–74 to $765 per elementary school child from $355, and to $950 per high school student from $488,[45] the California Supreme Court in *Serrano II* ruled that state equal protection was violated nonetheless. The primary reason for the decision was that "substantial disparities in expenditures per pupil resulting from differences in local taxable wealth will continue to exist."[46] Emphasizing the principle that the California state constitution may always give more protections than the federal constitution,[47] the court reaffirmed its *Serrano I* holding, even finding support in Justice Powell's language in *Rodriguez* concerning the federal courts' lack of "expertise and familiarity with local problems of school financing."[48] The state public school financing revolution had now begun in earnest, and the idea that local property tax funding of public schools might violate a state constitution's equal protection clause began to spread across the country.[49]

---

39. *See infra* notes 27–28 and surrounding text.

40. 5 Cal. 3d. at 605.

41. Horace Mann introduced the first state compulsory education scheme in Massachusetts as its commissioner of Education in 1837. He supported the "absolute right to an education of every human being that comes into the world and which, of course, proves the correlative duty of every government to see that the means of that education are provided for all." *Id.* at 619.

42. *Serrano v. Priest (Serrano II)*, 18 Cal. 3d 728, 557 P.2d 929, 135 Cal. Rptr. 345 (1976); *see infra* notes 14–20 and accompanying text.

43. 18 Cal. 3d. at 728.

44. *Serrano v. Priest (Serrano II)*, 18 Cal. 3d 728, 557 P.2d 929, 135 Cal. Rptr. 345 (1976).

45. 18 Cal. 3d at 742.

46. *Id.* at 746.

47. *Id.* at 764–65.

48. *Id.* at 766.

49. A few earlier state cases had, however, ruled on a state equal protection theory. *Sweetwater County v. Henkle*, 491 P. 2d 1234 (Wyo. 1971); *Milliken v. Green*, 390 Mich. 389, 212 N.W.2d 711 (1973) (financing violates state equal protection under rational basis test or strict scrutiny test); *Shofstall v. Hollins*, 110 Ariz. 88, 515 P.2d 590 (1973) (no violation of state equal protection).

Many other state supreme courts after *Serrano II* began to parse their state constitutions for violations of equal protection in the public school funding arena. Although a number of these plaintiffs failed to prevail under state equal protection theories,[50] in 1977 plaintiffs prevailed in a particularly instructive and foundational Connecticut case, *Horton v. Meskill*.[51] The *Horton* court understood that a great wave of potential reform was sweeping the nation: "The questions presented are not only of great importance but of considerable complexity, and it is of small comfort to note that members of the judiciary throughout the country are also being faced with same or similar complex questions."[52] In Connecticut at the time, 70 percent of all public school funding derived from the local level, as compared with a national figure of 50 percent.[53] Taxable property values varied from $20,000 per student to $170,000 per student,[54] and "mill" rates varied as well,[55] with poorer districts having to tax at much higher rates than wealthier districts.

The *Horton* court found that the Connecticut system for funding public schools was littered with disparities, even though, unlike the disparities in *Rodriguez* and *Serrano*, the district wealth differentials in Connecticut were considered to be "relative rather than absolute."[56] Unlike many preceding cases on the issue, the *Horton* plaintiffs were not representatives of extremely low-income districts.[57] But the relative district wealth disparities led to significant differences throughout the state in terms of curricular offerings, facilities, availability of counseling services, and teacher salaries,[58] all of which were sufficient to violate the state constitution's guarantee of equal protection. With the court's reasoning in *Horton v. Meskill*, virtually any state in the union could be subject to a similar ruling.[59]

At the same time that the theories of state equal protection were being developed in *Serrano I* and *II* and *Horton v. Meskill*, a parallel development was occurring—a state-based jurisprudence based not on equal protection guarantees, but on a so-called state education article. This approach was born in the 1973 case of *Robinson v. Cahill*.[60]

Robinson v. Cahill concerned the funding of public schools in New Jersey, and it was decided before the *Serrano II* decision was rendered. Indeed, the opinion was in the process of being written when the U.S. Supreme Court released the *Rodriguez* decision.[61] Perhaps because of the unexpected ruling in *Rodriguez*, the *Robinson* court was extremely reluctant to base its decision on the equal protection clause of the state constitution, even declaring that "we will not pursue the equal protection issue in the limited context of public education."[62] Instead the Robinson court turned to other language in New Jersey's constitution requiring that "the legislature ... provide for the maintenance and support of a

---

50. *E.g., McDaniel v. Thomas*, 248 Ga. 632, 285 S.E.2d 156 (1981); *Danson v. Casey*, 484 Pa. 415, 399 A.2d 360 (1979).

51. *Horton v. Meskill*, 172 Conn. 615, 376 A.2d 359 (1977).

52. *Id.* at 618.

53. *Id.* at 629.

54. *Id.* at 630.

55. *Id.*

56. *Id.* at 645.

57. Indeed, the father of the Horton child is an extremely highly respected appellate attorney in Connecticut who was also a lead counsel in *Sheff v. O'Neill*, 238 Conn. 1, 678 A.2d 1267 (1996), as well as representing the City of New London in *Kelo v. City of New London*, 545 U.S.469(2005).

58. 172 Conn. at 633.

59. *See* Victoria Dodd, Practical Education Law for the Twenty-First Century, 118 (2003).

60. *Robinson v. Cahill*, 62 N.J. 473, 303 A.2d 273 (1973), *cert. denied*, 414 U.S. 976 (1973).

61. See *supra* notes 4–20 and accompanying text.

62. 62 N.J. at 500.

thorough and efficient system of free public schools."[63] At the time of the case, the state of New Jersey provided only 28 percent of public school funding, less than even than that provided by Texas in the *Rodriguez* case.[64]

The *Robinson* court found that the foregoing language, which was added to the state constitution in 1875, meant that public education must be free, and that "the State must meet that obligation itself or if it chooses to enlist local government it must do so in terms which fulfill that obligation."[65] Providing only 28 percent of educational funding, the court stated, could never lead to "equal educational opportunity."[66] Thus, the key principle established by *Robinson* is that the state bears the burden of financing public schools and must ensure that it is done in an equitable fashion.

This approach allows more plaintiff activism because it is less dependent on the finding of large school funding disparities among school districts. Indeed, the later *Horton* court cited *Robinson* in its ruling on state equal protection, even though *Robinson* was solely based on the state education article theory.[67] After *Robinson*, therefore, state courts now had several theories on which to base their school funding cases, significantly increasing the plaintiffs' success rates in later school funding cases in the 1980s and 1990s.

Changing Approaches in Later State School Funding Cases

The state education article approach of *Robinson*[68] began to bear particular fruit in the 1980s. Beginning with such cases as *Pauley v. Kelly* in West Virginia,[69] courts used the language of state constitution education articles not merely to strike down state public school funding systems that yielded disparate revenues but also to begin to define the parameters of an effective education. Thus, concerns about equally funded schools began to evolve into broader notions of educational adequacy.

For instance, the state constitution of West Virginia required that "the legislature ... provide, by general law, for a thorough and efficient system of free schools."[70] The *Pauley* court directed the circuit court to intensively study the state's education system, including its structure, finances, roles of state education officials, and so on.[71] When the case returned to the West Virginia State Supreme Court in 1984,[72] the court validated the circuit court's approval of the defendants' Master Plan for Public Education, which the circuit court had concluded

> adopts a comprehensive description of standards for a high quality system of education, necessary to establish a foundation for learning in West Virginia schools, which may be considered as a recommendation to the Legislature as an exam-

---

63. N.J. Const. art. VIII, §4.
64. *See* Victoria Dodd, Practical Education for the Twenty-First Century 121, n.71. (2003).
65. 62 N.J. at 509.
66. *Id.* at 516.
67. 172 Conn. at 646.
68. *See supra* notes 62–69 and accompanying text.
69. *Pauley v. Kelly*, 162 W. Va. 672, 255 S.E.2d 859 (1979).
70. W. Va. Const. art. XII, §1.
71. 255 S.E.2d at 878–83.
72. *Pauley v. Bailey*, 174 W. Va. 167, 324 S.E.2d 128 (1984).

ple of a thorough and efficient system.... The plan is structured in a manner to address the critical deficiencies which require remedial action in, (1) establishing the standards of a high quality system of education, using as a guide the four (4) components of that system: curriculum, personnel, facilities, and materials and equipment; and (2) the financing of a thorough and efficient system of education.[73]

The merely unequal funding approaches of *Serrano*[74] and *Rodriguez*[75] had been superceded by a more active approach in the *Pauley* case, in which the court actually studied the elements of an effective educational scheme. In 1989, the Supreme Court of Kentucky carried this approach to its next level of refinement in *Rose v. Council for Better Education*.[76]

In *Rose*, the court was called on to decide whether the state legislature had complied with its state constitutional duty to "provide an efficient system of common schools throughout the state."[77] The court readily found that this state constitutional standard had been violated:

> The overall effect of appellant's evidence is a virtual concession that Kentucky's system of common schools is under funded and inadequate; is fraught with inequalities and inequities throughout the 177 local school districts; is ranked nationally in the lower 20–25 percent in virtually every category that is used to evaluate educational performance; and is not uniform among the districts in educational opportunities. When one considers the evidence presented by the appellants, there is little or no evidence to even begin to negate that of the appellees. The tidal wave of the appellees' evidence literally engulfs that of the appellants.[78]

Whereas earlier state courts had evinced some hesitation in striking down a state's educational system, including its financing, the *Rose* court was comfortable moving very deliberately. Presaging future educational standards movements, the court emphasized comparative statistics: Kentucky ranked fortieth in per-pupil spending; thirty-seventh in teacher salaries; forty-third in reliance on local property taxes; and only 68 percent of Kentucky's students graduated from high school.[79] Indeed, the court declared that all school districts' educational efforts in the entire state were "inadequate."[80]

Even more revolutionary was the court's leap to define the components of the "adequate" education required to be provided by the state legislature. Relying on *Pauley v. Kelly*,[81] the count enumerated the now-famous seven *Rose* factors:

> We concur with the trial court that an efficient system of education must have as its goal to provide each and every child with at least the seven following capacities: (i) sufficient oral and written communication skills to enable students to function in a complex and rapidly changing civilization; (ii) sufficient knowledge of economic, social, and political systems to enable the student to make informal choices; (iii) sufficient understanding of governmental processes to enable

---

73. *Id.* at 175.
74. *See supra* notes 33–50 and accompanying text.
75. *See supra* notes 4–29 and accompanying text.
76. 790 S.W.2d 186 (Ky. 1989).
77. Ky. Const. § 183.
78. 790 S.W.2d at 196–197.
79. *Id.* at 197.
80. *Id.* at 198.
81. *See supra* notes 71–75.

the student to understand the issues that affect his or her community, state, and nation; (iv) sufficient self-knowledge and knowledge of his or her mental and physical wellness; (v) sufficient grounding in the arts to enable each student to appreciate his or her cultural and historical heritage; (vi) sufficient trainings or preparation for advance training in either academic or vocational fields so as to enable each child to choose and pursue life work intelligently; and (vii) sufficient levels of academic or vocational skills to enable public school students to compete favorably with their counterparts in surrounding states, in academics or in the job market.[82]

Though some states, such as Kentucky in the *Rose* case, were making quantum leaps forward in education law jurisprudence, there was backtracking as well. In Oklahoma, for instance, the state supreme court in 1987[83] ruled that the state constitution did not require "a funding regime that provides equal expenditures per child."[84] The Oklahoma court found no allegations that children were denied an adequate education,[85] and relying on the reasoning of the *Rodriguez* case, found no violation of federal or state equal protection.[86] The Oklahoma state constitution merely provided that "the Legislature shall establish and maintain a system free public schools wherein all children of the State may be educated."[87] Thus, only a theory of basic equal protection had been brought forward by the plaintiffs in that Oklahoma case.

Just two years later, however, in the 1989 Texas *Edgewood* case, very different language in the state constitution of Texas was found to guarantee schoolchildren an "efficient" system of education.[88] The Texas state constitution provided:

A general diffusion of knowledge being essential to the preservation of the liberties and rights of the people, it shall be the duty of the legislature of the State to establish and make suitable provision for the support and maintenance of an efficient system of public free schools.[89]

Emphasizing the history of the state constitution clause, gross disparities in school district funding and district wealth, and the fact that nine states had ruled similarly,[90] the Texas Supreme Court found that the constitutional mandate had not been met and left it to the state legislature to remedy the situation.[91] The *Rodriguez* discussion was being left behind.

Deference to the state legislature remained the watchword in two significant state cases in 1993 challenging the funding of public schools in Tennessee and Massachusetts. The

---

82. 790 S.W.2d at 212.

83. *Fair School Finance Council of Okla. v. State*, 1987 Ok. 114, 746 P.2d 1135 (1987).

84. *Id.* at 1137.

85. *Id.* at 1150.

86. *Id. See also Lujan v. Colo. State Bd. of Educ.*, 649 P.2d 1005 (Colo. 1982); *Thompson v. Engelking*, 96 Idaho 793, 537 P.2d 635 (1975). *But see* note 115 and accompanying text.

87. Okla. Const. art. XIII § 1.

88. *Edgewood Indep. School Dist. v. Kirby*, 777 S.W.2d 391 (Tex. 1989).

89. Tex. Const. art. VII, § 1.

90. 777 S.W.2d at 398.

91. *Id.* at 399. Thus began an incredible saga of Texas school financing cases, continually challenging the revised school financing and taxing systems designed by the state legislature. *See generally* Yudof et al., EDUCATIONAL POLICY AND THE LAW, 800–804 (4th ed. 2002). The most recent case installments in this never-ending story are *West Orange-Cove Consol. Indep. Sch. Dist. v. Alanis*, 107 S.W.3d 558 (Tex. 2003) (holding lower courts erred in dismissing plaintiffs' complaint) and *Neeley v. West Orange—Cove Consol. Indep. Sch.Dist.*, 176 S.W. 3d 746 (Tex. 2005). *See also Neeley v. West Orange—Cove Consol. Indep. Sch. Dist.*, 228 S.W. 3d 864 (Tex.App.-Austin 2007) (attorney's fees).

Tennessee in *Tennessee Small School Systems v. McWhereter* found that the funding of public schools violated the state's equal protection guarantees,[92] but left it to the state legislature to establish a system that would provide substantially equal educational opportunities to all students. The Supreme Judicial Court in Massachusetts wrote an extremely elaborate, historically based opinion construing the education article of the Massachusetts state constitution to contain a fundamental right to an education, which was violated by the state administrative and financial educational apparatus.[93] Adopting the seven *Rose* factors[94] as a guide, and citing the *Edgewood* court's deference language, the Massachusetts court also left it to "the Commonwealth to take such steps as may be required in each instance effectively to devise a plan and sources of funds sufficient to meet the constitutional mandate."[95]

The Current State of State Educational Funding Litigation

The current state of public school financing litigation, nationwide, is now quite fragmented. More than forty states have entertained lawsuits arguing that state constitutional provisions are violated by underfunded and inadequate educational systems, and plaintiffs have prevailed in somewhat over half of those suits.[96] Yet the average percentage of a state's school budget funded at the local level in 2002–2003 was still 42.8 percent.[97] Per-pupil expenditures varied in 2002–2003 from a low of $5,792 in the state of Mississippi to a high of $12,568 in New Jersey.[98] School finance litigation continues in fits and starts, with new legal theories and defenses emerging and with outcomes frequently unpredictable in advance.

Some state courts have taken an abrupt about-face in their attitude in public school financing cases. In Arizona, for instance, the state court of appeals in 2003 held that lack of funding or disparite funding in public schools did not constitute a per se violation of the state constitution.[99] The court so held despite the fact that the Arizona Supreme Court had earlier ruled that "school financing systems which themselves create gross disparities are not general and uniform" and therefore violated the state's constitution.[100]

A number of other states have also held the line at some point in school finance reformation. Without signaling a full retreat, they very obviously refuse to proceed further. In Massachusetts, for instance, the state Supreme Judicial Court in 2005 refused to hold that continuing educational and financial deficiencies in the public schools constituted a violation of the state constitution's education article.[101] The Minnesota Supreme Court held

---

92. *Tenn. Small Sch. Systems v. McWherter*, 851 S.W.2d 139 (Tenn. 1993). The courts in Tennessee have entertained two subsequent related cases, the most recent being *Tenn. Small Sch. Systems v. McWherter*, 91 S.W.3d 232 (Tenn. 2002).
93. *McDuffy v. Sec. of Exec. Office of Educ.*, 415 Mass. 545, 615 N.E.2d 516 (1993).
94. *Id.* at 618.
95. *Id.* at 621.
96. Victoria Dodd, Practical Education for the Twenty-First Century, 116 (2003).
97. National Center for Educational Statistics, nces.ed.gov/ccd/stifis.asp (Table 2).
98. *Id.* at Table 5.
99. *Roosevelt Elem. v. State*, 205 Ariz. 584, 592, 74 P.3d 258, 266 (Ariz. Ct. App. 2003), *review denied*, 2004 Ariz. LEXIS 8 (Ariz., Jan. 7, 2004).
100. *Roosevelt Elem. v. State*, 179 Ariz. 233, 241, 877 P.2d 806, 814 (1994).
101. *Hancock v. Commissioner of Educ.*, 443 Mass. 428, 471, 822 N.E.2d 1134, 1164 (2005).

that the state of Minnesota adequately provided an education that met state constitutional standards, despite some lingering local financial disparities.[102] A similar result was reached in 2000 in Wisconsin.[103]

An emerging, although obvious, theory that has been used by some state courts to resist a plaintiff's public schools funding case is the doctrine of state separation of powers. In Alabama, for example, in the 2002 case of *Ex Parte James*,[104] the Alabama Supreme Court held the separation of powers doctrine required that the state funding lawsuit be dismissed.[105] Over vigorous concurrences and dissents, the majority held in *Ex Parte James* that because the state constitution requires that the legislature fund the public schools, it is up to the legislature, not the courts, to remedy any problems.[106] The case had been pending in the state court system since 1990. The Massachusetts state attorney general in the 2005 *Hancock* case, where the state prevailed, also emphasized separation of powers issues in his oral arguments for the Supreme Judicial Court.[107]

At the same time, the results and legal theories advanced in a few state public school funding cases have been highly successful. Although the Supreme Court in Montana in 2005 deferred to the state legislature to define what a "quality" public school education might comprise, the Montana court still held the current funding system to be constitutionally deficient.[108] The Supreme Court of Nevada in 2003 issued a writ of mandamus against the state legislature, compelling it to fund public education.[109] The Supreme Court of Idaho in 2004 found unconstitutional a state house bill that procedurally hampered the plaintiffs in the pending school funding litigation.[110]

Although some educational reform efforts have definitely stalled, an extremely hopeful development has also been a burgeoning interest in state-provided early childhood education. A leader in this area is the state of New Jersey. In the long-running *Abbott* litigation, the New Jersey Supreme Court in 1998 held in *Abbott V* that certain Abbott school districts had to provide half-day preschool programs for three- and four-year-old children; the state commissioner of education also had to "ensure" that the programs were adequately funded.[111] In *Abbott VI* the court clarified the programmatic requirements for the required preschool programs.[112]

Although the parties in New Jersey have continued to litigate the contours of "adequate" funding for these programs,[113] the *Abbott* decision has begun to exert some influence in other jurisdictions. In Massachusetts, although the state's highest court ultimately determined the state was not violating the state constitution, the earlier Superior Court master determined that early childhood education was a possible remedy for low-achiev-

---

102. *Skeen v. State*, 505 N.W.2d 299 (Minn. 1993).

103. *Vincent v. Voight*, 236 Wis. 2d 588, 632, 614 N.W.2d 388, 411 (2000).

104. *Ex Parte James*, 836 So.2d 813 (Ala. 2002).

105. *Id.* at 815.

106. *Id.*

107. *See* transcript of oral argument of the *Hancock* case before the Massachusetts Supreme Judicial Court, October 4, 2005. The author of this chapter was present at the oral arguments of the case.

108. *Columbia Falls Elem. Sch. Dist. No. 6 v. State*, 326 Mont. 304, 311 109 P.3d 257, 262 (Mont. 2005).

109. *Guinn v. Legislature of Nev.*, 119 Nev. 277, 71 P.3d 1269 (Nev. 2003), *cert. denied*, 2004 U.S. LEXIS 2335 (2004).

110. *Idaho Schools for Equal Ed'l. Opp. v. State*, 97 P.3d 453 (Idaho 2004).

111. *Abbott v. Burke*, 153 N.J. 480, 508, 710 A.2d 450 (1998) (*Abbott V*).

112. *Abbott v. Burke*, 170 N.J. 537, 540–41, 790 A.2d 842 (2002) (*Abbott VI*).

113. *See Bd. of Educ. of City of Millville v. New Jersey Dep't. of Educ.*, 872 A.2d 1052, 183 N.J. 264 (2005); *Bd. of Educ. of City of Passaic v. New Jersey Dep't of Educ.*, 872 A.2d 1062, 183 N.J. 281 (2005).

ing districts.[114] Since the later, negative *Hancock* decision, the Commonwealth of Massachusetts has voluntarily begun a push to develop a statutory scheme to provide early childhood education for all low-income children.[115] Similarly, the trial court in the principal North Carolina school funding case required the state to provide early childhood education, a decision that was reversed by the state supreme court in 2004.[116]

Despite these negative state supreme court rulings, however, according to the National Conference of State Legislators, eleven states in 2004 passed statutes relating to tax funding of prekindergarten programs.[117] In addition, thirty-two states in 2004 introduced legislation relating to early education proposals.[118] One can anticipate that enhanced early childhood education may become the next school finance litigation concern of the new millennium.

Various State Education Funding Models

As discussed,[119] significant financial disparities exist within and among the various states' public educational systems. In 2002–2003, for instance, the average state-funded component of a state's educational budget was 48.7 percent, varying from a low of 30.2 percent in Nevada to a high of 90.1 percent in Hawaii.[120] Yet state-based funding has been a significant component and goal of most of the state-based litigation discussed in this chapter. Federal support in 2002–2003 averaged 8.5 percent of a state's overall education budget.[121] Many state court decisions have also highlighted teachers' salaries as important indicators of educational health. Yet instructional expenditures per pupil in 2002–2003 ranged from $3,103 in Utah to $8,213 in New York.[122] Within states, too, the cases discussed in this chapter reveal that although gross funding disparities have lessened, funding differences remain.

A primary determinant of school financing uniformity within a state will be the exact funding model developed by the state legislature. In response to the litigation discussed in this chapter, a number of financial approaches have been devised to lower funding disparities between and among school districts. In Wisconsin, for example, state aid for education is comprised of equalization aid, categorical aid, and the school tax levy credit.[123] Equalization aid "provides each qualifying district with a guaranteed tax base, thereby minimizing differences in the ability of school districts to raise revenue through property tax."[124] The complexity of the equalization system is demonstrated by the fact that the amount of such aid is determined by five factors[125] and the aid itself applied at three different cost levels.[126] The exact amount of aid is determined by a complex, algebraic-type

---

114. finance1.doe.mass.edu/chapter70/McDuffy_report.pdf,364.

115. Mass. Gen. Laws ch. 15D, § 1–5 (2005).

116. *Hoke City Bd. of Educ. v. State*, 358 N.C. 605, 645, 599 S.E. 2d 365, 395 (2004).

117. Early Education in the States: A year in Review 2004, 12 (2004), www.ncsr.org/programs/educ/ed_finance/intro.htm.

118. *Id.* at 13.

119. *See supra* notes 101–3 and accompanying text.

120. National Center for Educational Statistics, nces.ed.gov/ccd/stifis.asp (Table 2). Hawaii contains only one school district, however. The next highest state is Minnesota at 73.8 percent. *Id.*

121. *Id.*

122. *Id.* (Table 5).

123. *Vincent v. Voight*, 614 N.W.2d 388, 396, 236 Wis. 2d 588, 602 (2000).

124. *Id.* at 603.

125. *Id.* at 604.

126. *Id.*

formula. Categorical aid is made up of twenty-five different programs, some of which are grants for which school districts need to apply, whereas others are "formula-driven."[127] The last part of the state aid program in Wisconsin is the school tax levy credit, which is allocated to cities, not local school districts.[128]

Another common approach used by many states, equally complex, is the "foundation aid" system. The continuing school finance litigation in Texas has taken extreme issue with the state's foundation aid program. That program, originally described in the *Rodriguez* case,[129] was originally designed to "have an equalizing influence on expenditures."[130] Struck down in 1989 by the Texas Supreme Court in *Edgewood I*[131] because it did not fund the most basic components of education, the foundation aid program was superceded by Texas Senate Bill I, Senate Bill 351, and Senate Bill 7.[132] Senate Bill I did not change the ability of wealthy school districts to raise vastly more funds than poorer school districts.[133] Senate Bill 351 consolidated school districts to create more uniform tax bases, but was also thought to be an unconstitutional tax, so it was in turn amended to Senate Bill 7. Senate Bill 7 required wealthier schools to recapture funds in an updated version of the original foundation aid program. At the end of 2005, a satisfactory Texas state funding statute had still not been finalized.[134] In 2006, however, the Texas legislature passed House Bill 1, which complied with a court-ordered deadline of June 1, 2006, to resolve the unconstitutionality of the state financing system for schools. It is sad that so much energy has been devoted to litigating the precise financing system, rather than to somehow working out a constitutional system in a more collaborative way many years earlier.

The foundation budget program in Massachusetts is also instructive. In the 2005 *Hancock* case, where the Supreme Judicial Court held that the state constitution education article was not being violated, Chief Justice Marshall discussed its impact:

> In sheer dollars, the total amount annually spent on kindergarten to grade twelve education rose from approximately $3.6 billion in fiscal year (FY) 1993, prior to the passage of the act, to $10.1 billion in FY 2002. Annual increase in school funding in that period averaged twelve percent. State aid, the great bulk of it from foundation budget funding, accounted for about thirty-nine percent of this annual spending. In all, from 1993 to 2003, the Commonwealth contributed about $31 billion to fund public education.... In the ten-year period following passage of the act, the gap in per pupil spending between high-property-value districts and low-property-value districts was cut by one-half, from thirty-eight percent in 1993 to approximately eighteen or nineteen percent in 2003.[135] In 2002, for example, public school funding per pupil in high poverty districts ($8,504) was four percent higher than spending in low poverty districts ($8,144).[136]

---

127. *Id.* at 605.

128. *Id.* at 608.

129. *San Antonio School Dist. v. Rodriguez,* 411 U.S. 1, 9 (1973).

130. *Id.* at 10.

131. *See supra* notes 90–93 and accompanying text.

132. *See generally West Orange-Cove Consol. v. Ananis,* 107 S.W.3d 558 (2003). *See* Yudof et al., Educational Policy and the Law, 800–804 (4th ed., 2002).

133. 107 S.W.3d at 567.

134. "Texas: No Resolution on School Financing," National Briefing, N.Y. Times Online, August 5, 2005, query.nytimes.com/gst/fullpage.html?res=9C04E4D8103EF933A1575BC0A9639C8B63.

135. 822 N.E.2d at 1147.

136. *Id.* at 1148, n. 22.

In 2002–2003, per-pupil expenditures in Massachusetts as expressed by another reporting agency were $10,460 versus $7,136 in Texas.[137] It appears that not only are disparities within a state relevant, so are the total amount of dollars spent per pupil as compared to other states.

A completely different financial methodology suggested in some states is the "cost-study" approach. Here, the calculus for determining state public school funding begins with a determination of the variables or components of an adequate education and then a "costing out" of those components. This approach therefore focuses first on educational quality and then dollars. Three states—New York, Massachusetts, and Kansas—have been proponents of this approach at some point.

In New York, the trial court in the long-running New York City school funding case required that the state ascertain the cost of a "sound basic education."[138] The reviewing court emphasized that "a sound basic education conveys not merely skills, but skills fashioned to meet a practical goal: meaningful civic participation in contemporary society."[139] The reviewing court accepted the trial court's requirement that the state "ascertain 'the actual costs of providing a sound basic education,'" except that it limited the study to only the New York City area, not statewide.[140] The cost-study approach therefore shifts the discussion away from only financial equality to educational equality and adequacy. Indeed, as the figures cited from Massachusetts demonstrate,[141] it may cost more per pupil to boost some low-income students to levels of academic performance parity than it costs per pupil to educate students in higher wealth districts.

Although ultimately overturned by the Massachusetts Supreme Judicial Court, the special master in the *Hancock* case also recommended an educational cost study, citing the New York case just discussed. In her 450-page report, she made the following recommendations:

> I recommend that the court follow the path that the New York Court of Appeals has recently chosen in a case concerning the adequacy of education provided in the New York City public schools. See *Campaign for Fiscal Equity, Inc. v. New York*, 100 N.Y. 2d 893, 928–932 (2003). Translated into this case, the relief would be an order directing the State defendants to: (1) ascertain the actual cost of providing the level of education in each of the focus school districts that permits *all* children in the district's public schools the opportunity to acquire the capabilities outlined in *McDuffy*—a directive that means, at present, the actual cost of implementing all seven of the Massachusetts curriculum frameworks in a manner appropriate for all the school district's children; (2) determine the costs associated with measures, to be carried out by the department working with the local school district administrators, that will provide meaningful improvement in the capacity of these local districts to carry out an effective implementation of the necessary educational program; and (3) implement whatever funding and administrative changes result from the determinations made in (1) and (2). This order would be directed to the State defendants to accomplish because *McDuffy*

---

137. *See supra* note 125, Table 5.

138. *Campaign for Fiscal Equity, Inc. v. State*, 801 N.E.2d 326, 329, 100 N.Y.893, 903, 769 N.Y.S.2d 106, 109 (2003); *modified by Campaign for Fiscal Equity, Inc. v. State*, 29 A.D.3d 175, 814 N.Y.S.2d 1(N.Y.App.Div.2006).

139. *Id.* at 330.

140. *Id.* at 348.

141. *See infra* notes 142–143 and surrounding text.

expressly holds that the Commonwealth, not the local districts, is ultimately responsible "to devise a plan and sources of funds sufficient to meet the constitutional mandate."... In the category of "should be considered" for a determination of cost, I recommend at least the following: (1) several categories presently included in the foundation budget—for example, teaching salaries, the low income factor, and the "bilingual education" factor—the question of course being whether these factors should be increased in the budget formula and, if so, by how much; (2) inclusion in the foundation budget of the various factors recommended by witnesses in this case (who were primarily witnesses for the defendants) such as a technology factor, teacher coaches, school leadership, etc.; (3) implementation of a class size system of under 20 for at least pre-kindergarten through third grade; (4) provision of adequately stocked, computer-equipped, and staffed school libraries; and (4) institution of regular, established (as opposed to episodic) remedial programs for children at risk of failing, such as remedial tutoring, extended day, extended year programs, or a combination of them.[142]

As discussed, the Massachusetts reviewing court held that because such substantial progress had been made by the state in increasing overall funding and decreasing funding disparities, the state was not constitutionally compelled to follow the special master's report.[143]

The Kansas Supreme Court has been particularly strict about the proper contours of a cost study that could form the basis or foundation of a state constitutionally sound school financing system. In January 2005, the court in *Montoy v. State* held that

in determining if the legislature has made suitable provision for the finance of public education, there are other factors to be considered in addition to whether students are provided a suitable education. Specifically, the district court found that the financing formula was not based upon actual costs to educate children but was instead based on former spending levels and political compromise. This failure to do any cost analysis distorted the low enrollment, special education, vocational, bilingual education, and the at-risk student weighting factors.[144]

Close followers of the Kansas situation were amazed when,[145] in June 2005, the Kansas Supreme Court again ruled that the state had not conducted a proper cost study to support its position: "This case is extraordinary, but the imperative remains that we decide it on the record before us. The A& M study, and the testimony supporting it, appear in the record in this case. The State cites no cost study or evidence to rebut the A & M study, instead offering conclusory affidavits from legislative leaders."[146] The cost-study approach appears to be a very viable tool for involving educators and financial analysts in determining school costs without being overly influenced by previous and outmoded state financing models.

Finally, the state of Vermont has developed a much-vaunted, as well as much-criticized, methodology of school funding, an example of what the public has called "Robin Hood" funding. In *Brigham v. State*,[147] the Vermont Supreme Court examined the constitutionality of the public school funding system in the state and strongly criticized the

---

142. finance1.doe.mass.edu/chapter70/McDuffy_report.pdf, 361–362, 365.

143. 443 Mass. at 457, 822 N.E.2d at 1155.

144. *Montoy v. State*, 278 Kan. 769, 774, 102 P.3d 1160, 1164 (2005).

145. I attended an education law symposium at Oxford University in July 2005, where educators from Kansas expressed pleasant surprise at the rulings of the Kansas Supreme Court.

146. *Montoy v. State*, 112 P.3d 923, 279 Kan. 817 (2005).

147. *Brigham v. State*, 166 Vt. 246, 692 A.2d 384 (1997).

foundation aid program: "From an equity standpoint, the major weakness of a foundation formula distribution system is that it equalizes capacity only to a level of a minimally adequate education program … a foundation-formula, state-aid program can boost the capacity of the poorest districts, but still leave substantial deficiencies in overall equity."[148] In response, the Vermont state legislature passed Act 60, which required that property-rich school districts redistribute some of their local property tax revenues to property-poor districts.[149] Despite much community protest from higher wealth districts, the Vermont Supreme Court has sustained the constitutionality of the state's new funding system.[150]

Other State and Federal Legal Approaches

This chapter has focused on state-based litigation as a primary driver of educational finance reform. A few other legal approaches have been utilized as well. At the state level, there have been several attempts to amend state constitutions regarding fundamental rights to an education or other educational funding issues; at the federal level, some interesting statutory and even federal constitutional remedies have been proposed.

In Florida in 1996,[151] the state Supreme Court was called on to determine whether the Florida constitution conferred a fundamental right to an education to citizens of Florida, and if so, whether that right was violated by the then-current system of funding Florida's public schools. The Florida constitution provided that "adequate provision … be made by law for a uniform system of free public schools and for the establishment, maintenance and operation of institutions of higher learning and other public education programs that the needs of people may require."[152] In construing the provision, the Florida Supreme Court held that the court's determining the meaning of "adequacy" would intrude on the domain of the legislature and that the legislature had been given great "discretion to determine what provision to make for an adequate and uniform system of free public schools."[153] Stymied by the court's ruling, advocates then proposed an amendment to the state's constitution that would state specific percentage amounts of overall state appropriations that must be allocated to public education.[154] The Florida Supreme Court then held that the amendment failed to comply with the "single-subject" requirement and therefore could not be put before the voters as written.[155]

In New Hampshire, state constitutional amendments have been promoted not to add rights in the area of education but to take them away, a unique response to state supreme court rulings. In a series of cases, called the *Claremont* litigation, the New Hampshire Supreme Court ruled that the state constitution education article required the state to

---

148. *Id.* at 253.

149. *See generally Anderson v. State*, 168 Vt. 641, 723 A.2d 1147 (1998) (no justiciable controversy).

150. *Stowe Citizens for Resp. Gov't. v. State*, 730 A.2d 573, 169 Vt. 559 (1999).

151. *Coalition for Adequacy and Fairness in School Funding, Inc. v. Chiles*, 680 So.2d 400 (Fla. 1996).

152. Fla. Const. Art. IX, § 1.

153. 680 So.2d at 408.

154. *See* Advisory Opinion to the Att'y Gen. re: Requirement for Adequate Public Educ. Funding, 703 So.2d 446 (Fla. 1997).

155. *Id.* at 450.

provide students with an adequate education.[156] Prior to this ruling, local school districts supplied about 90 percent of public school funding.

Although ultimately defeated by the state legislature, the proposed state constitutional amendment would have overruled the state's *Claremont* decisions by allowing the state to forgo funding public schools. It provided that the legislature shall have exclusive authority under this article to determine, either directly, or through a delegation of power to local school districts, or both, the content, extent, beneficiaries, and level and source of funding of public educational."[157] New Hampshire lacks a state income tax, so opponents of the *Claremont* decisions do not want the state to take on any additional state responsibilities.

Albeit not a state constitutional amendment approach, the state of Montana employed another novel approach in response to a Montana Supreme Court ruling finding the educational system inadequate and unconstitutional.[158] The legislature, required by the court to develop a new funding model, hired outside financial experts to analyze four different overall funding models, develop revised compensation systems, and survey district administrators. The legislature would then, in turn, draft new legislation based on the recommendations.[159]

On the federal level, in 2004 Senator Christopher Dodd[160] of Connecticut proposed Senate Bill 2428, "To provide for educational opportunities for all students in State public school systems, and for other purposes."[161] The short title of this law is the "Student Bill of Rights."[162] Some of the major findings of the bill are that

(1) A high-quality, highly competitive education for all students is imperative for the economic growth and productivity of the United States, for its effective national defense, and to achieve the historical aspiration to be one Nation of equal citizens. It is therefore necessary and proper to overcome the nationwide phenomenon of state public schools systems that do not meet the requirements of section 101(a), in which high-quality public schools typically serve high-income communities and poor-quality schools typically serve low-income, urban, rural, and minority communities.

(2) There exists in the States a significant educational opportunity gap for low-income, urban, rural, and minority students characterized by the following:

(A) Continuing disparities within states in students' access to the fundamentals of educational opportunity described in section 102.

(B) Highly differential educational expenditures (adjusted for cost and need) among school districts within states.

(C) Radically differential educational achievement among students in school districts within states as measured by the following:

(i) Achievement in mathematics, reading or language arts, and science on atate academic assessment required under section 1111(b)(3) of the Ele-

---

156. *Claremont Sch. Dist. v. Governor*, 142 N.H. 462, 703 A.2d 1353 (1997) (Claremont II).

157. *See* www.claremontlawsuit.org/constitutional_amendments.htm,5-6.

158. *Columbia Falls Elem. School Dist. No. 6 v. State*, 109 P.3d 257, 326 Mont. 304 (2005).

159. *See* "Final School Funding Report to be split in two," www.mtstandard.com/articles/2005/08/19/newstate/hjjebiajjehie.txt.

160. Senator Chris Dodd (D-Conn.) is not related to the author of this chapter.

161. S. 2428, 108th Cong., Preamble (2004).

162. *Id.* at § 1.

mentary and Secondary Education Act of 1965 (20 U.S.C. 6311(b)(3)) and on the National Assessment of Educational Progress.

(ii) Advanced placement courses taken.

(iii) SAT and ACT test scores.

(iv) Dropout rates and graduation rates.

(v) College-going and college-completion rates.

(vi) Job placement and retention rates and indices of job quality.

(3) As a consequence of this educational opportunity gap, the quality of a child's education depends largely upon where the child's family can afford to live, and the detriments of lower quality education are imposed particularly on—

(A) children from low-income families;

(B) children living in urban and rural areas; and

(C) minority children.

(4) Since 1785, Congress, exercising the power to admit new states under section 3 of article IV of the Constitution (and previously, the Congress of the Confederation of States under the Articles of Confederation), has imposed upon every state, as a fundamental condition of the state's admission, that the state provide for the establishment and maintenance of systems of public schools open to all children in such state.

(5) Over the years since the landmark ruling in Brown v. Board of Education, 347 U.S. 483, 493 (1954), when a unanimous Supreme court held that "the opportunity of an education…, where the state has undertaken to provide it, is a right which must be made available to all on equal terms," courts in 44 states have heard challenges to the establishment, maintenance, and operation of state public school systems that are separate and not educationally adequate.

(6) In 1970, the Presidential Commission on School Finance found that significant disparities in the distribution of educational resources existed among school districts within states because the states relied too significantly on local district financing for educational revenues, and that reforms in systems of school financing would increase the nation's ability to serve the educational needs of all children.

(7) In 1999, the National Research Council of the National Academy of Sciences published a report entitled "Making Money Matter, Financing America's Schools," which found that the concept of funding adequacy, which moves beyond the more traditional concepts of finance equity to focus attention on the sufficiency of funding for desired educational outcomes, is an important step in developing a fair and productive educational system….[163]

(8) The standards and accountability movement will succeed only if, in addition to standards and accountability, all schools have access to the educational resources necessary to enable students to achieve.[164]

The requirements of the act then provide that to receive federal education funding, each state must provide a quality education:

---

163. *Id.* at §3 (a)(1)–(7).
164. *Id.* at (11).

Each state receiving Federal financial assistance for elementary or secondary education shall ensure that the State's public school system provides all students within the State with an education that enables the students to acquire the knowledge and skills necessary for responsible citizenship in a diverse democracy, including the ability to participate fully in the political process through informed electoral choice to meet challenging student academic achievement standards, and to be able to compete and succeed in a global economy.[165]

The act spells out accountability systems, annual reporting requirements, the availability of a private right of action to enforce the act,[166] and so on. Creating, in essence, a federal state education article, the act could accomplish nationwide what the best of the state supreme court rulings have done at the state level.

A final federal proposal has been to amend the federal constitution to undo the results of the *Rodriguez* case. Congressman Jesse L. Jackson Jr. (D.-Ill.) proposed on March 2, 2005, the following constitutional amendment.

Joint Resolution

Proposing an amendment to the Constitution of the United States regarding the right of all citizens of the United States to a public education of equal high quality.

Resolved by the Senate and House of Representatives of the United States of American in Congress assembled (two-thirds of each House concurring therein), that the following article is proposed as an amendment to the Constitution of the United States, which shall be valid to all intents and purposes as part of the Constitution when ratified by the legislatures of three-fourths of the several States:

ARTICLE—

SECTION 1. All persons shall enjoy the right to a public education of equal high quality.

SECTION 2. The Congress shall have power to enforce and implement this article by appropriate legislation.[167]

In his press release, Jackson explained the rationale underlying his proposed amendment:

I believe every American has a human right to vote, to a public education and health care of equal high quality, to affordable housing, to a clean, safe and sustainable environment, to employment, and equal rights for women. I also believe the American people have a rational right to be taxed in a fair or progressive manner.

The 10th Amendment to the Constitution states: "The powers not delegated to the United States by the Constitution, nor prohibited by it to the State, are reserved to the States respectively, or to the people." For example, since the word "education" does not appear in the Constitution, education is a "state right." The word "slavery" never appeared in the Constitution, so the peculiar institution was protected by a states' right to own slaves—i.e., the 10th Amendment. The Emancipation Proclamation was a propaganda tool used in the Civil War. The

---

165. *Id.* at § 101(a).
166. *Id.* at § 131.
167. H.J. Res. 29, 109th Cong. 1st session (2005).

nation had to pass a 13th Amendment outlawing slavery in order to overcome the 10th Amendment's "states' right" to own slaves. Slavery is gone, but the 10th Amendment remains!

As a result, a "states' rights" educational system is structured to be "separate and unequal"—50 states, 3,067 counties, tens of thousands of cities, 15,000 school districts, and 85,000 schools—all "separate and unequal," each with varying degrees of opportunity, funding and quality. There's ONLY ONE WAY to legally guarantee "a public education of equal high quality" to every American and that is to add an education amendment to the Constitution! Yesterday I introduced H.J. Res. 29 to achieve that goal.

Most Americans believe the legal right to vote in our democracy is explicit (not just implicit) in our Constitution and laws. However, our Constitution only provides for nondiscrimination in voting on the basis of race, sex, and age in the 15th, 19th and 26th Amendments respectively. The U.S. Constitution contains no explicit right to vote! That's why I introduced H.J. Res. 28, a Voting Rights Amendment.

Impossible to pass constitutional amendments? We've already amended the Constitution 27 times. One amendment did take 202 years, but another took just years, but another took just 10 months, and one only 100 days. It all depends on the education and political consciousness of the American people. We need to prioritize H.J. Res. 28–30 and work on them one at a time, with emphasis on the voting, education and health care amendments.[168]

The Supreme Court Should Overrule the *Rodriguez* Case

This chapter began with a discussion of the fulcrum in this area of law, the case of *San Antonio Independent School District v. Rodriguez*.[169] Because the Supreme Court held in that case that wealth (poverty) was not a suspect class, nor was education a fundamental right,[170] the nation saw the explosion of state-based school financing litigation, which has been the primary focus of this chapter.

One might ask whether the Supreme Court should consider overruling the *Rodriguez* case. The Supreme Court could, and perhaps in the not-so-distant future will, supply important societal leadership by establishing a fundamental right to an adequate education.

The state cases could provide important guidance to the Court by supplying the legal and analytical foundation for the recognition of such a right and for developing its contours. Indeed, the states cases should guide the Court to establish a right not just to an equally funded education under equal protection theory, which was the goal of the plaintiffs in the *Rodriguez* case, but also to a high-level and multifaceted education as described

---

168. "Jackson Introduces Constitutional Amendments," press release, March 5, 2005, www.jessejacksonjr.org.

169. *See supra* notes 4–31 and surrounding text.

170. *See supra* notes 114–20 and surrounding text.

in many recent state cases. A fundamental right to an education at the federal level would also serve as a lodestar for future state legislation, especially in those states where no state-based right yet exists. In addition, a federal fundamental right to an adequate education would serve a similar useful purpose for drafters of federal legislation concerning educational adequacy.[171]

The Supreme Court's 2003 case *Lawrence v. Texas*[172] supplies some precedential hope that the Supreme Court could at some point in the future overrule the *Rodriguez* case. In *Lawrence*, the Court was deciding whether to overrule the 1986 case of *Bowers v. Hardwick*,[173] where the Supreme Court had held that there is no fundamental right of sexual orientation. In *Lawrence*, the Court concluded that it had overstated in *Bowers* an alleged historical tradition of criminalizing sodomy[174] and that many if not most states no longer prosecute the crime.[175] Justice Kennedy concluded the six-to-three majority opinion with this observation:

> Had those who drew and ratified the Due Process Clauses of the Fifth Amendment or the Fourteenth Amendment known the components of liberty in its manifold possibilities, they might have been more specific. They did not presume to have this insight. They knew times can blind us to certain truths and later generations can see that laws once thought necessary and proper in fact serve only to oppress. As the Constitution endures, persons in every generation can invoke its principles in their own search for greater freedom.[176]

There appears to be enough room in our evolving Constitution to include a fundamental right to an adequate education, under either substantive due process or equal protection theory.

Other Supreme Court precedents are relevant as well to establishing a fundamental right to an adequate education. In *Lawrence*, the Court relied on earlier statements in *Romer v. Evans*[177] and *Planned Parenthood of Southeastern Pa. v. Casey*[178] as casting doubt on the *Bowers* holding.[179] Similarly, the current Court could look to *Pierce v. Society of Sisters*,[180] *Meyer v. Nebraska*,[181] and *Plyler v. Doe*[182] for supportive statements regarding a fundamental right to an adequate public education. In *Pierce*, the Court held that requiring children to attend only public schools limited parents' liberty interest to "direct the upbringing and education of children under their control."[183] In *Meyer*, a state law that prohibited the teaching of foreign languages in public schools was held to interfere with "the natural duty of the parent to give his children education suitable to their station in life."[184] In *Plyler*, the refusal of school districts in Texas to educate the children of undocumented aliens was held to violate the equal protection clause under an interme-

---

171. *See, e.g.*, the discussion of Senator Dodd's proposed federal legislation in notes 160–66 and surrounding text.

172. *Lawrence v. Texas*, 539 U.S. 558 (2003).

173. *Bowers v. Hardwick*, 478 U.S. 186 (1986).

174. 539 U.S. at 559.

175. *Id.*

176. *Id.* at 578–79.

177. *Romer v. Evans*, 517 U.S. 620 (1996).

178. *Planned Parenthood of Southeaster Pa. v. Casey*, 505 U.S. 833 (1992).

179. 539 U.S. at 559–60.

180. *Pierce v. Society of Sisters*, 268 U.S. 510 (1925).

181. *Meyer v. Nebraska*, 262 U.S. 390 (1925).

182. *Plyler v. Doe*, 457 U.S. 202 (1982).

183. 268 U.S. at 534–35.

184. 262 U.S. at 400.

diate level of constitutional scrutiny.[185] Taken together, these holdings could supply fertile soil for an eventual fundamental right to an adequate education.

The state-based cases discussed in this chapter could themselves also supply grist for the Court's fundamental rights mill. In other areas of constitutional law, for instance in the area of criminal procedure, accepted state practice has been very relevant to the Court.[186] More than twenty state supreme courts have ruled that their state constitutions contain some sort of fundamental right to an education, under either an equal protection clause or education article. Over time, these favorable state court rulings may grow in number sufficient to influence a future U.S. Supreme Court ruling on the subject. In *Lawrence*, the Court, in considering current state practices, reasoned that "in our own constitutional system the deficiencies in *Bowers* became even more apparent in the years following its announcement. The 25 states with laws prohibiting the relevant conduct referenced in the Bowers decision are reduced now to 13, of which 4 enforce their laws only against homosexual conduct."[187] Even Texas, whose state law was at issue in *Bowers*, no longer prosecuted sodomy.[188]

A not dissimilar pattern of state practice exists currently concerning education rights. At the time of the *Rodriguez* case, it was mainly California courts that had found a fundamental right to an education, and it had done so pursuant to a federal, not state, theory of equal protection.[189] Now, more than twenty courts have found such a right in their own constitutions; ironically, even Texas, the state involved in the *Rodriguez* decision, has made such a ruling.[190] Perhaps sometime soon, the Supreme Court will reconsider its *Rodriguez* decision and align it with the nation's evolving consensus about the centrality of each child's right to an adequate education.

---

185. 457 U.S. at 230.
186. *See, e.g.*, *Duncan v. Louisiana*, 391 U.S. 145, 149–50 n. 14 (1968) (the fact that all states utilized jury trials in criminal matters influenced the Court's Sixth Amendment ruling).
187. 539 U.S. at 573.
188. *Id.*
189. *See supra* notes 33–51 and accompanying text.
190. *See supra* notes 90–93 and accompanying text.

9

Closing the Door on Public School Integration: *Parents Involved* and the Supreme Court's Continued Neglect of Adequacy Concerns

Osamudia R. James[*]

Introduction

Despite the Supreme Court's mandate to integrate schools, issued fifty-three years ago in *Brown v. Board of Education*,[1] American public education is moving further away from the integrative ideal. Integration gains resulting from the Court's 1954 decision were undermined when a change in the Court's jurisprudence during the 1990s permitted a return to neighborhood schools. The result has been the resegregation of students in American public schools,[2] with particularly deleterious consequences for black and Latino students.

In an effort to prevent resegregation of their public schools, the Seattle, Washington, and Jefferson County, Kentucky, school districts voluntarily implemented controlled-choice plans that factored race into school assignments when district schools became oversubscribed by students.[3] The plans were challenged by parents dissatisfied with their

* Copyright © 2007 by Osamudia R. James. William H. Hastie Fellow, University of Wisconsin Law School; B.A., University of Pennsylvania, 2001; J.D., Georgetown University Law Center, 2004. I am grateful to Michelle Adams and William Clune for their feedback on earlier drafts of this chapter, and to Sansun Yeh for her editing assistance. Finally, I thank my husband, Kamal James, who has never failed to support me in all my endeavors, professional or personal. An abridged version of this chapter previously appeared as an article in the *South Carolina Law Review*.

1. *Brown v. Bd. of Educ.*, 347 U.S. 483 (1954) (holding that separate state-sponsored public schools for white and black children were inherently unequal and violated the equal protection clause).

2. GARY ORFIELD & CHUNGMEI LEE, RACIAL TRANSFORMATION AND THE CHANGING NATURE OF SEGREGATION 4 (2006), *available* www.civilrightsproject.ucla.edu/research/deseg/Racial_Transformation. pdf.

3. Brief for Respondents at 4–11, *Parents Involved in Cmty. Sch. v. Seattle Sch. Dist.*, No. 1, 127 S. Ct. 2738 (U.S. 2007) (No. 05-908); Brief for Respondents at 4–9, *Parents Involved in Cmty. Sch. v. Seattle Sch. Dist.*, No. 1, 127 S. Ct. 2738 (No. 05-915).

school assignments and ultimately reached the Supreme Court. *Parents Involved in Community Schools v. Seattle School District No. 1*[4] and *Meredith v. Jefferson County Board of Education*[5] were the first cases to address (1) a school district's compelling interest in diversity, (2) a school board's license to use school assignments to facilitate diverse schools in a non-remedial context, and (3) the extent to which race may be a factor in making those assignments. In an opinion that consolidated both cases, the Court was unable to gather five votes to definitively address issues one and two. The Court did, however, garner sufficient votes to characterize the plans' use of race in school assignments as insufficiently narrowly tailored; as such, the plans violated the equal protection clause of the Fourteenth Amendment.[6] In his concurring opinion, joined by none of the other justices, Justice Kennedy stated that although educational equity was a compelling interest that could justify the consideration of race in school assignments, such consideration must be limited to "race-conscious" measures, as opposed to policies that take direct account of race.[7]

The Court's decision in *Parents Involved in Community Schools v. Seattle School District No. 1*[8] (*Parents Involved*) presents an opportunity to reconsider the necessity of racial integration in providing adequate education for children of color. Although adequacy is often conceptualized in monetary terms, this chapter suggests that adequately educating minority children requires the nonmonetary input of racial integration. Moreover, a school district's desire to reduce isolation through integration is a compelling interest that school districts are justified in pursuing through the consideration of race in school assignments. Part I considers school integration and school segregation as education inputs and canvasses social science research suggesting that school segregation results in the concentration of poverty in majority-minority schools,[9] and in the denial of political and social capital that integrated schools provide.[10] Part I also examines the relationship between the input of segregation and lower levels of academic achievement (output) for students in majority-minority schools. Part II revisits the Supreme Court precedents that have served as barriers to racial integration of primary and secondary schools.[11] These decisions reflect the Court's failure to recognize the necessity of integration in ensuring adequacy, and the Court's refusal to acknowledge the denial of equal education oppor-

---

4. *Parents Involved in Cmty. Sch. v. Seattle Sch. Dist., No. 1*, 426 F.3d 1162 (9th Cir. 2005), *cert. granted*, 126 S. Ct. 2351 (U.S. 2006).

5. *McFarland ex rel. McFarland v. Jefferson County Pub. Sch.*, 416 F.3d 513 (6th Cir. 2005), *cert. granted sub nom. Meredith v. Jefferson County Bd. of Educ.*, 126 S. Ct. 2351 (U.S. 2006).

6. *Parents Involved in Cmty. Sch. v. Seattle Sch. Dist., No. 1*, 127 S. Ct. 2738 (U.S. 2007).

7. *Id.* at 2788–97 (U.S. 2007) (Kennedy, J., concurring in part and concurring in the judgment).

8. *Parents Involved in Cmty. Sch. v. Seattle Sch. Dist., No. 1*, 127 S. Ct. 2738 (U.S. 2007).

9. Douglas Massey & Nancy Denton, American Apartheid: Segregation and the Making of the Underclass 118–25 (1993).

10. Impoverished schools negatively affect academic achievement and limit the employment networks to which students are exposed. Richard D. Kahlenberg, All Together Now: Creating Middle-Class Schools through Public School Choice 25 (2001). Moreover, concentrations of poverty can cultivate oppositional attitudes that devalue education. Massey & Denton, *supra* note 9, at 8.

11. *See e.g., Milliken v. Bradley*, 418 U.S. 717 (1974) (a federal court cannot impose an interdistrict remedy between a city and its surrounding suburbs to integrate city schools); *Bd. of Educ. v. Dowell*, 498 U.S. 237 (1991) (a school district can be released from desegregation orders, and be declared unitary, if the board complied in "good faith" with the orders and if vestiges of discrimination have been eliminated to the "extent practicable"); *Freeman v. Pitts*, 503 U.S. 467 (1992) (all indicators of desegregation do not have to be met simultaneously for a district to be declared unitary); *Missouri v. Jenkins*, 515 U.S. 70 (1995) (interdistrict remedies are not justified in the absence of interdistrict violations, and districts need not show correction of harms caused by segregation to be declared unitary).

tunity to students enrolled in majority-minority schools. Part III examines the Court's most recent integration decision in *Parents Involved*, which further undermined integration efforts by failing to decisively recognize a compelling interest in dismantling racial isolation, and in prohibiting school districts from considering the use of race in school assignments. The decision is particularly problematic because the case involved local, voluntary plans that were motivated by equity concerns and included race-neutral safeguards to prevent the misuse of race. In striking down the plans, the Court further entrenched unequal education for children of color, while closing the door on one of the few remaining options school districts could pursue to directly and efficiently integrate schools and provide adequate education for all students.

I. Segregation, Integration, and Adequacy

Educational adequacy is often pursued through school finance litigation, the goal of which has changed from obtaining equalized spending among school districts to recognizing the right of each student to an "adequate" education and sufficient monetary resources to obtain it.[12] These adequacy claims focus exclusively on state education clauses, which often impose affirmative obligations regarding states' educational duties.[13]

The pursuit of adequacy, however, is not limited to a financial context. Adequacy is fully defined as "the provision of a set of strategies, programs, curriculum, and instruction, with appropriate adjustments for special-needs students, districts, and schools, and their full financing, that is sufficient to teach students to *high* standards"(emphasis added).[14] As such, adequacy contemplates the relationship between educational input and educational output, and how the former affects academic achievement.[15] Integration and segregation are both educational strategies with the potential to not only impact other educational inputs but affect educational outcomes.

A. Segregation as an Input

In 2000, 65.2 percent of blacks in the United States would have had to relocate to achieve a residential pattern in which every neighborhood reflected the racial demographics of its region.[16] Although that figure dropped from 69.5 percent in 1990, it remains

---

12. James E. Ryan, *Schools, Race, and Money*, 109 YALE L.J. 249, 260, 268–69 (1999). For an in-depth discussion of the evolution of school finance litigation, as well as the advantages and disadvantages of both adequacy and equity, *see* Peter Enrich, *Leaving Equality Behind: New Directions in School Finance Reform*, 48 VAND. L. REV. 101 (1995); Michael Heise, *State Constitutions, School Finance Litigation, and the "Third Wave": From Equity to Adequacy*, 68 TEMP. L. REV. 1151 (1995).

13. Heise, *supra* note at 12, 1162; Ryan, *supra* note 12, at 268–69.

14. ALLAN R. ODDEN & LAWRENCE O. PICUS, SCHOOL FINANCE: A POLICY PERSPECTIVE 69 (2000).

15. *Id. See also* William H. Clune, *Accelerated Education as a Remedy for High-Poverty Schools*, 28 U. MICH. J.L. REFORM 655, 680 (1995) (arguing that adequacy responds to the needs of high-poverty schools by setting "appropriate, high expectations of performance, and … deliver[ing] the resources and governance necessary to reach those goals").

16. Edward L. Glaeser & Jacob L. Vigdor, *Racial Segregation: Promising News*, *in* REDEFINING URBAN & SUBURBAN AMERICA, EVIDENCE FROM CENSUS 2000 211, 220 (Bruce Katz & Robert E. Lang eds., 2003). 44.6 percent of Latinos in 2000 would have had to move to achieve racial integration. James E. Ryan & Michael Heise, *The Political Economy of School Choice*, 111 YALE L.J. 2043, 2094

in the hypersegregated range.[17] Because neighborhoods in most metropolitan areas across the country remain segregated by race and class, the nation's reliance on neighborhood schools has led to public schools that are segregated by race and class.

In the 2003–04 schoolyear, 73 percent of black students attended schools that were between 50 and 100 percent minority; 38 percent attended schools between 90 and 100 percent minority.[18] Similarly, 77 percent of Latinos attended schools between 50 and 100 percent minority, and 39 percent attended schools between 90 and 100 percent minority.[19] The average black student attended a school that was 53 percent black, even though blacks only constituted 17 percent of public school enrollment nationwide.[20] Latinos were similarly segregated, on average attending schools that were 55 percent Latino, despite accounting for only 19 percent of nationwide public school enrollment.[21] The average white student in 2003 attended schools that were 78 percent white, even though whites only constituted 58 percent of public school enrollment nationwide.[22]

Reliance on segregated neighborhood schools creates racially identifiable minority schools and classrooms that exert significant negative effects on the academic outcomes of black and white students enrolled therein.[23] Not only are racially identifiable minority schools more likely to be high-poverty schools, they are also more vulnerable to racist attitudes and behaviors that are still prevalent in our society. The results are depressed levels of achievement, lower graduation rates, and lower levels of college matriculation for students attending majority-minority schools.

1. Concentrations of Poverty

Segregation by race is systematically linked to segregation by socioeconomic status because racial minorities are more likely to be poor.[24] The result is that segregated minority schools are almost always high-poverty schools.[25] Generally, the percentage of poor students in a school increases as the percentage of minority students increases.[26] A common measure of poverty is student eligibility for free or reduced-price meals; a school is considered predominantly poor if more than 50 percent of students are eligi-

---

(2002). For additional discussion on the dissimilarity index, *see* MASSEY & DENTON, *supra* note 9, at 20, 74.

17. Glaeser & Vigdor, *supra* note 16, at 220. For additional discussion on hypersegregation, *see* MASSEY & DENTON, *supra* note 9, at 74–78.

18. ORFIELD & LEE, *supra* note 2, at 10 tbl. 3.

19. ORFIELD & LEE, *supra* note 2, at 11 tbl. 4. Because of their small share of total enrollments, Asians and American Indians are less likely to be segregated except in some areas of low-income Asian refugee communities and reservation schools. *Id.* at 11.

20. ORFIELD & LEE, *supra* note 2, at 8 tbl. 1, 9 tbl. 2.

21. ORFIELD & LEE, *supra* note 2, at 8 tbl. 1, 9 tbl. 2. In 2001, the average Asian student attended schools where only 22 percent of enrolled students were Asian. GARY ORFIELD & CHUNGMEI LEE, BROWN AT 50: KING'S DREAM OR PLESSY'S NIGHTMARE? 17 (2004), *available at* www.civilrightsproject.ucla.edu/research/reseg04/brown50.pdf.

22. ORFIELD & LEE, *supra* note 2, at 8 tbl. 1, 9 tbl. 2.

23. Roslyn Arlin Mickelson, *The Academic Consequences of Desegregation and Segregation: Evidence from the Charlotte-Mecklenburg Schools*, 81 N.C. L. REV. 1513, 1560 (2003).

24. GARY ORFIELD & CHUNGMEI LEE, WHY SEGREGATION MATTERS: POVERTY AND EDUCATIONAL INEQUALITY 14 (2005), *available at* www.civilrightsproject.ucla.edu/research/deseg/Why-_Segreg_Matters.pdf.

25. *Id.* at 8.

26. Ryan & Heise, *supra* note at 16, 2096.

ble.[27] In the 2001–02 school year, only 15 percent of intensely segregated white schools, or schools with less than one-tenth black and Latino students, were predominantly poor.[28] In contrast, 88 percent of intensely segregated minority schools had concentrated levels of poverty, where over half of the students qualified for free or reduced lunch.[29]

Lower socioeconomic status has been commonly understood to negatively impact student achievement on average,[30] a relationship that is not surprising considering the issues with which low-income families often struggle, including poor health care, inadequate housing, instability, and lack of quality early childhood education. The effect of poverty on school-wide student achievement seems to be nonlinear, with a "tipping point" or threshold at which the cumulative impact of poverty becomes much worse.[31] Most researchers have converged around the 50 percent mark, finding that the greatest decreases in student achievement occur as schools change from being majority middle-class schools to schools in which the percentage of students eligible for reduced-price meals is between 51 and 100 percent.[32] A 1997 study commissioned by the Department of Education showed that school poverty depresses the scores of all students if at least half the students are eligible for subsidized lunch; scores are seriously depressed when over 75 percent of students live in low-income housing.[33] Other research has similarly concluded that students in low-poverty schools typically score 50 to 75 percent higher on reading and math tests than students in high-poverty schools.[34] The disadvantages of attending high-poverty schools, however, are not limited to lower test scores. A 1980 study analyzed data on 26,425 tenth graders, then conducted follow-up interviews with the students two years later. The students who attended high-poverty schools had higher dropout and pregnancy rates than students of the same race and income who attended low-poverty schools.[35]

Unfortunately, the effects of concentrated poverty in schools are not readily addressed by compensatory measures. Although educators understand how to reach individual students from disadvantaged backgrounds, much less is known about how to alter educational outcomes in high-poverty schools full of disadvantaged students.[36] Furthermore, resource shortages are chronic at high-poverty schools, as the schools often have higher costs than wealthier schools. High-poverty schools typically spend more money on special needs

---

27. *Id.*

28. Orfield & Lee, *supra* note 21, at 21.

29. *Id.* at 21.

30. Researchers and policy makers have repeatedly affirmed the relationship between poverty and low academic achievement. *See e.g.* Orfield & Lee, *supra* note 24, at 6 ("Poverty is strongly related to everything from the child's physical development to the family's ability to stay in a neighborhood long enough so that a school might have an effect on the student."); RICHARD D. KAHLENBERG, ALL TOGETHER NOW: CREATING MIDDLE-CLASS SCHOOLS THROUGH PUBLIC SCHOOL CHOICE 50 (2001) ("Poor children come to school with about half the vocabulary of middle-class children of the same age.").

31. Kahlenberg, *supra* note 30, at 39.

32. *Id.* at 39–40.

33. MICHAEL J. PUMA ET AL., U.S. DEP'T OF EDUC., PROSPECTS: FINAL REPORT ON STUDENT OUTCOMES 12 (1997).

34. MICHAEL J. PUMA ET AL., U.S. DEP'T OF EDUC., PROSPECTS: THE CONGRESSIONALLY MANDATED STUDY OF EDUCATIONAL GROWTH AND OPPORTUNITY — INTERIM REPORT 18 (1993).

35. UNIV. OF N.C. CTR. FOR CIVIL RIGHTS, THE SOCIOECONOMIC COMPOSITION OF THE PUBLIC SCHOOLS: A CRUCIAL CONSIDERATION IN STUDENT ASSIGNMENT POLICY 2 (2005), www.law.unc.edu/PDFs/charlottereport.pdf.

36. *Id.* at 6.

education, including special education and bilingual services.[37] High-poverty schools also find it harder to attract and retain teachers, forcing the districts to provide higher economic incentives than their wealthier counterparts.[38] Urban districts with a high percentage of poor students also need to compensate for the high mobility of students, as well as for students suffering from untreated health problems, hunger, family disruption, and violence.[39] When compared to affluent suburban districts with more recent capital developments, high-poverty urban districts have higher security costs, and higher capital costs from buildings that are older and in more intense states of disrepair.[40] Addressing these additional costs becomes prohibitively expensive. As a result, even when high-poverty districts are given additional funding, the money spent on curriculum alone is often still less than the amount spent in wealthier districts. In the 1991–92 school year, for example, Hartford, Connecticut, was ranked the highest among all districts in its region for per-pupil expenditures. After subtracting expenditures for special needs programs, however, actual per-pupil spending on academic programming was lower than regional and state averages.[41]

Even when funding for high-poverty schools is increased, it is usually ineffective in improving educational outcomes without racial and economic desegregation. Arguments that there is no link between financial resources and educational outcomes have their roots in the 1966 Coleman report.[42] Although Coleman never concluded that the financial resources of a school don't matter, the report's findings were interpreted as indicating that schools, and their resources, have little influence on student achievement independent of family background and social context.[43] Richard Rothstein has since clarified the report's findings, explaining that the report did not suggest that schools don't influence achievement, but that "the quality of schools has little influence on *the difference* in average achievement" among students.[44] Put another way, although all students learn in school, schools have limited ability to affect differences in the rate of learning in children from different social classes.[45] Moreover, even the limited potential of resource in-

---

37. Molly S. McUsic, *The Future of* Brown v. Board of Education: *Economic Integration of the Public Schools*, 117 Harv. L. Rev. 1334, 1351 (2004).

38. *Id.* at 1351–52.

39. *Id.* at 1352.

40. *Id.* at 1351.

41. *Id.* at 1358–59.

42. James S. Coleman et al., U.S. Dep't of Health, Educ., & Welfare, Equality of Educational Opportunity (1966) (landmark national study of the effects and equality of educational opportunity in U.S. public schools). The "production-function" model on which the report's findings were based, and subsequent studies based on the same model, have been criticized as inadequate when applied to the education system. Methodological flaws in the specific research underlying the Coleman report have also led some researchers to characterize the report's findings a result of flawed analysis, and an inaccurate reflection of the "underlying behavioral reality." Kern Alexander & Richard G. Salmon, Public School Finance 356 tbl. 15.3, 360 (1995) (citing study by Hanushek and Kain). *But see* Richard Rothstein, Class and Schools: Using Social, Economic, and Educational Reform to Close the Black-White Achievement Gap 14 (2004) (explaining that scholarly efforts have consistently confirmed Coleman's findings, and that no analysis has been able to attribute less than two-thirds of the variations in student achievement to family characteristics of the student).

43. Alexander & Salmon, *supra* note 42, at 350–51.

44. Rothstein, *supra* note 42, at 15.

45. *Id.* Despite continuing debate as to the effect of school resources on student achievement, most studies have agreed on three points: (1) high levels of resources are associated with higher achievement in *some* cases; (2) the characteristics of schools that can produce higher achievement are difficult to identify; and (3) the presence or absence of resources is less consequential for academic achievement than the ways in which the resources are actually used. Adam Gamoran & Daniel A.

creases to positively affect academic outcomes is hindered without accompanying efforts to dismantle racial and economic isolation.[46] A telling example comes from the Hartford, Connecticut, school system, where millions of dollars were spent to fund the district at levels higher than surrounding suburbs for several years. The funding failed, however, to raise the test scores of its mostly poor and minority students to statewide and suburban averages. Fewer than 40 percent of ninth graders during the time period of increased funding graduated four years later.[47]

2. Peer Influence

The negative effect of poverty on schoolwide achievement is due in part to the effects of peer influence. In addition to its other findings, the Coleman report concluded that the socioeconomic status of one's peers exerts a significant influence on academic performance, and that the influence is greatest on students from disadvantaged backgrounds.[48] Similarly, one study of 20,000 students over three years found that for a large number of adolescents, peers—and not parents—were the chief determinants of how invested those adolescents were in school, and how committed they were to their educations.[49] There are several theories on why students can exert such a significant influence on each other. One theory suggests that children engage in behavior modeled by their friends, which affects not just the child's immediate behavior but also the child's perception of what is normal for his or her peer group.[50] Accordingly, a study of black children from low-income households headed by single mothers found that the children were more delinquent than children from middle-class two-parent households only if they lived and went to school in low-income neighborhoods. If they went to school in white middle-class neighborhoods, the levels of delinquency were comparable to their white peers.[51]

Peer influence can be negative or positive, helping create a school culture of success or a school culture of underachievement.[52] Signithia Fordham and John Ogbu theorize that, in reaction to the way they are treated in economic, political, social and psychological arenas, subordinated minorities can develop an oppositional sense of collective identity that rejects "white" American values.[53] Moreover, minorities are censured by members of

---

Long, *Equality of Educational Opportunity: A 40-Year Retrospective* 8 (Wis. Ctr. for Educ. Research, Working Paper No. 2006-9, 2006), *available at* www.wcer.wisc.edu/publications/workingPapers/ Working_Paper_No_2006_09.pdf.

46. Ryan, *supra* note 12, at 293.

47. Ryan, *supra* note 12, at 291; McUsic, *supra* note 37, at 1353 (also describing programs in Little Rock and Austin which, although designed to provide more money to high-poverty schools, similarly failed to raise test scores to the state average).

48. COLEMAN ET AL., *supra* note 42, at 34. In contrast to more advantaged students with stronger and more stable family backgrounds, disadvantaged students spend less time under adult supervision, making them more susceptible to peer influence. In addition, the disproportionate influence of school culture on disadvantaged students is also a result of "larger reservoirs of undeveloped talent," which are cultivated in high-achieving schools. KAHLENBERG, *supra* note 31, at 41.

49. KAHLENBERG, *supra* note 31, at 48 (referring to the research of Laurence Steinberg).

50. McUsic, *supra* note 37, at 1356–57.

51. McUsic, *supra* note 37, at 1357.

52. Russell W. Rumberger & Gregory J. Palardy, *Does Resegregation Matter?: The Impact of Social Composition on Academic Achievement in Southern High Schools, in* SCHOOL RESEGREGATION: MUST THE SOUTH TURN BACK? 127, 130 (John Charles Boger & Gary Orfield eds., 2005).

53. Signithia Fordham & John U. Ogbu, *Black Students' School Success: Coping with the "Burden of 'Acting White,'"* 18 URB. REV. 176, 181 (1986).

their community for crossing cultural boundaries by "acting white."[54] This phenomenon was replicated in their study of black public school students, where students were disparaged for "white" behavior, which included speaking standard English, studying in the library, and working diligently to get good grades.[55]

Fordham and Obgu's findings, however, are qualified by additional research. After controlling for class indicators, including parental income, mother's education, and family structure, researchers have concluded that black and white students have comparable dropout rates, put in comparable amounts of effort on homework, and have comparable levels of parental involvement.[56] As such, alienation from education may have more to do with class than with race. These findings are consistent with sociologist-documented tendencies that reflect a devaluation of education and resistance to middle-class values among members of lower classes.[57]

In addition, the research of economist Roland Fryer confirms the negative peer pressure among blacks associated with "acting white,"[58] but concludes that the "acting white" phenomenon is most intense in schools with less than 20 percent black student enrollment, and nonexistent in schools with more than 80 percent black student enrollment.[59] Fryer refers to the work of anthropologists who observe that efforts by members of social groups to preserve their identity accelerate when threats to internal cohesion intensify, particularly if the group stands to lose those successful members who enhance the power and cohesion of the group. Applying that observation to his data, Fryer rejects the theory of oppositional culture and instead explains that a student will necessarily experience a trade-off between academic success and rejection by his or her peers when that student comes from a traditionally low-achieving group fearful of losing one of their own, especially when that group comes in contact with more outsiders, as is the case in integrated schools.[60]

Both qualifying studies have implications for integrated schools. Findings that alienation from education is a function of class, in combination with evidence of the effects of peer influence, suggest that racial isolation should be disrupted, if only to reduce concentrations of poverty in schools and eliminate the potential of cultivating an anti-achievement culture. The increased incidence of the "acting white" phenomenon at integrated schools might be a compromise school districts make in the pursuit of equalized access to education. If, however, integrated schools are successful in cultivating higher academic achievement for minorities, that success may be instrumental in breaking down the perception among black students that they are part of a "traditionally low-achieving group," thus eliminating the fear that the academic success of one group member threatens the cohesion of the group.

---

54. *Id.* at 182.

55. *Id.* at 191.

56. Philip J. Cook & Jens Ludwig, *The Burden of "Acting White": Do Black Adolescents Disparage Academic Achievement?, in* THE BLACK-WHITE TEST SCORE GAP 375, 382–386 (Christopher Jencks & Meredith Phillips eds., 1998).

57. KAHLENBERG, *supra* note 31, at 52.

58. Roland G. Fryer, *"Acting White,"* 6 EDUC. NEXT 53, 56 (2006) (concluding that blacks and Latinos do experience decreases in popularity among their racial group as academic success increases, while high-achieving whites are "at the top of the popularity pyramid").

59. *Id.* at 53, 57; Roland G. Fryer Jr. & Paul Torelli, *An Empirical Analysis of 'Acting White'* 20 (Nat'l Bureau of Econ. Research, Working Paper No. 11334, 2005), *available at* www.nber.org/papers/w11334.

60. Fryer, *supra* note 58, at 53, 58.

3. Inferior Education

Majority-minority schools also encounter educational difficulties that have less to do with the effects of socioeconomic status on the students themselves, and more to do with the limited access of majority-minority schools to educational resources and materials. Several studies have agreed that (1) schools are incapable of improving the life outcomes of minorities without changing inefficiencies in expenditures for teacher experience and additional education; and (2) money is useful in producing higher test scores when it purchases teachers with strong literacy skills, reduces class size to eighteen students per teacher, retains experienced instructors, and increases the number of teachers with advanced degrees.[61] Teacher experience, test scores, and regular licensure all have positive effects on student achievement, with larger effects on math than reading.[62] In North Carolina, for example, the negative effect that a teacher with weak credentials has on student math achievement is generally comparable to the negative effect on student math achievement of having poorly educated parents.[63] Accordingly, the assignment of teachers with weak credentials to educationally disadvantaged students would "widen, rather than reduce, the already large achievement gaps associated with the socioeconomic differences that students bring to the classroom."[64]

Despite the understood relationship between teacher quality and student academic achievement, majority-minority schools are disproportionately assigned novice and less credentialed teachers. A 2004 U.S. Department of Education report found that schools with at least 75 percent low-income students employed three times as many uncertified or out-of-field teachers in English and science as schools with lower poverty rates.[65] In the Charlotte-Mecklenburg school district, the higher the percentage of black students in a school, the less likely that school's teachers were to be experienced or hold master's degrees.[66] In 2005, the Center for the Future of Teaching and Learning, in conjunction with California State University, issued a report noting that in the 2004–05 school year, 20 percent of teachers serving in California schools with minority populations between 91 and 100 percent were underprepared or novice teachers, as compared to only 11 percent of teachers serving in schools with few or no minorities.[67] Similarly, a 2005 study exploring the distribution of novice teachers in North Carolina revealed that black seventh graders across the state were 54 and 38 percent more likely to be assigned novice teachers in math and English, respectively, than their white peers.[68] Moreover, within districts,

---

61. ALEXANDER & SALMON, *supra* note 42, at 361–62. *See also* William H. Clune, *New Answers to Hard Questions Posed by Rodriguez: Ending the Separation of School Finance and Educational Policy by Bridging the Gap Between Wrong and Remedy,* 24 CONN. L. REV. 721, 725–26 (1992) (arguing that in well-conceived educational programs, additional financial input does produce substantial gains in student achievement).

62. Charles T. Clotfelter, Helen F. Ladd, & Jacob L. Vigdor, *How and Why Do Teacher Credentials Matter for Student Achievement?* 38 (Nat'l Bureau of Econ. Research, Working Paper No. 12828, 2007), *available at* www.nber.org/papers/w12828.

63. *Id.* at 31.

64. *Id.* at 31.

65. UNIV. OF N.C. CTR. FOR CIVIL RIGHTS, THE SOCIOECONOMIC COMPOSITION OF THE PUBLIC SCHOOLS: A CRUCIAL CONSIDERATION IN STUDENT ASSIGNMENT POLICY 4–5 (2005), www.law.unc.edu/PDFs/charlottereport.pdf.

66. Mickelson, *supra* note 23, at 1547.

67. CAMILLE E. ESCH ET AL., THE STATUS OF THE TEACHING PROFESSION 2005 70 (2005), *available at* www.hewlett.org/NR/rdonlyres/2DBD7358-5A34-4A96-ABBB-8B513F1874E9/0/CFTL StatusofTeaching2005.pdf.

68. Charles T. Clotfelter, Helen F. Ladd, & Jacob Vigdor, *Who Teaches Whom? Race and the Distribution of Novice Teachers,* 24 ECON. EDUC. REV. 377, 386, 391 (2005).

novice teachers were disproportionately assigned to schools, or classrooms within schools, that primarily served black students.[69] High-poverty and high-minority schools also report difficulties filling math and science positions. In 1996, 37 percent of principals in high-poverty schools and over 50 percent of principals in high-minority schools, reported difficulties finding qualified biology teachers; only 10 percent of principals in wealthy schools, and 15 percent of principals in majority-white schools reported the same.[70]

The disproportionate assignment of novice teachers to majority-minority schools and classrooms maintains white privilege. Interviews with secondary school principals in the Charlotte-Mecklenburg School System (CMS) resulted in admissions that although lower track students could have highly qualified teachers, higher-track students always do.[71] Although pedagogical reasons may exist to justify the near exclusive assignment of experienced teachers to higher-track students, evidence of racial tracking without regard to ability has been found to exist in the CMS system.[72] Accordingly, these admissions are disturbing indications of racial discrimination that is potentially replicated nationwide.[73]

High teacher turnover is also a problem in high-poverty majority-minority schools.[74] In California, for example, public schools with 90 to 100 percent minority enrollment are six times more likely than majority-white schools to have high teacher turnover.[75] High turnover is problematic because it creates continual hiring and instability. Not only are new teachers without mentors because so many of their colleagues are similarly inexperienced, but these schools must repeat basic training for a substantial number of new teachers year after year, which impedes school progress toward meeting pedagogical needs.[76]

The inability of majority-minority and/or high-poverty districts to recruit and retain experienced teachers occurs largely because talented teachers have numerous career options that do not present the challenges that racially and economically isolated schools do. Research suggests, however, that racial preference also influences teacher decisions to exit racially-identifiable schools. A study of Texas public school teachers spanning 1993 to 1996 found that high teacher mobility is positively correlated with higher black or Latino school enrollment, even after controlling for salaries, student test scores, class size, and school poverty.[77] A similar study of Georgia public elementary school teachers, spanning 1994 to 2001, found that nonblack teachers were more likely to exit schools with large

---

69. *Id.*

70. "High-minority schools" and "majority-white schools" are defined as schools with more than 90 percent minority and white populations, respectively. Gary Orfield, *The Growth of Segregation: African Americans, Latinos, and Unequal Education, in* Dismantling Desegregation: The Quiet Reversal of Brown v. Board of Education 53, 69 (Gary Orfield & Susan E. Eaton eds., 1996).

71. Mickelson, *supra* note 23, at 1547.

72. *See infra* notes 118–20 and accompanying text.

73. Pressure placed on administrators by parents and teachers has also been shown to influence assignment of novice teachers. The more power that parents of some students have to influence the decisions of school administrators, the more likely it is that other students will be assigned novice teachers. Similarly, the stronger the preferences of experienced teachers to work with "easy-to-educate" students, the more likely it is that other students will be assigned novice teachers. Clotfelter, Ladd, & Vigdor, *supra* note 68, at 391.

74. Orfield & Lee, *supra* note 24, at 17.

75. Goodwin Liu, *Seattle and Louisville*, 95 Cal. L. Rev. 277, 290 (2007).

76. Susanna Loeb, Linda Darling-Hammond, & John Luczak, *How Teaching Conditions Predict Teacher Turnover in California Schools*, 80 Peabody J. Educ. 44, 48 (2005).

77. Eric A. Hanushek, John F. Kain, & Steven G. Rivkin, *Why Public Schools Lose Teachers*, 39 J. Hum. Resources 326 (2004).

proportions of minority students.[78] Specifically, a one standard deviation increase in the proportion of black students in a school increased the probability that a nonblack teacher would exit in a particular year by more than 20 percent.[79] Moreover, changes in salary, poverty levels, or test scores led to insignificant changes in exit probability.[80] To the extent that relationships existed between likelihood of teacher exit and student test scores and poverty rates, the relationships were driven by the high correlation of test scores and poverty rates with the proportion of minority students in a school.[81] The study concluded that although nonblack teachers were more likely to exit high-poverty schools, this is so because they were more likely to leave a particular type of high-poverty school—one with a large proportion of minority students.[82]

Access to material resources, including media centers and current technology, are also negatively affected by increases in a school's minority student composition.[83] A 1988 National Association of Educational Progress study concluded that 16 percent of teachers in affluent schools reported a lack of materials and resources, as opposed to 59 percent of teachers in higher poverty schools,[84] which are more likely to be high-minority schools. Moreover, to the extent that high-minority or high-poverty schools offer precollege courses, insufficient student eligibility often leads to a watering down of the courses or course elimination.[85] As a result, low-income, high-minority urban schools often "do not offer the same range and level of courses as their more affluent suburban counterparts."[86] By high school, the differences are most pronounced; nationally, 34 percent of classes in low-minority high schools are high-ability classes, whereas in majority-minority high schools, only 11 percent of classes are similarly classified.[87] The differences in tracking and course offerings are only compounded by the teaching shortages with which high-minority and high-poverty schools grapple.

B. The Outputs of Segregation

The input of segregation yields patterns of low achievement among minority students attending majority-minority schools.[88] A study of 200,000 students attending more than 3,000 public elementary schools in Texas during the 1990s found a strong negative relationship between math achievement among black students and the percentage of black enrollment in each school.[89] Similarly, a 2004 study conducted by the University of Miami and the University of South Florida found that segregation was related to lower pass rates

---

78. Benjamin Scafidi, David L. Sjoquist, & Todd R. Stinebrickner, *Race, Poverty, and Teacher Mobility*, 26 Econ. Educ. Rev. 145, 151, 154 (2007).

79. *Id.* at 147, 151.

80. *Id.* at 147, 153–57.

81. *Id.* at 146–47.

82. *Id.* at 147. *But see* Loeb, Darling-Hammond & Luczak, *supra* note 76, at 44, 45 (concluding that the influence of student racial and socioeconomic status on teacher turnover is substantially reduced once certain working conditions, including facilities problems, large class sizes and lack of textbooks, are considered).

83. Mickelson, *supra* note 23, at 1547–48. *See also* Orfield, *supra* note 70, at 53, 67 (concluding that majority-minority schools suffer from inferior curriculums).

84. Orfield, *supra* note 70, at 53, 69.

85. *Id.* at 67.

86. *Id.* at 68.

87. "Low-minority" refers to schools that are less than 10 percent minority. "Majority-minority" refers to schools that are more than 90 percent minority. *Id.* at 68.

88. *Id.* at 65.

89. Liu, *supra* note 75, at 292–93.

on the state test for black students in racially isolated schools, even when the study controlled for expenditures, poverty levels, teaching quality, and size.[90]

The input of segregation also results in higher drop-out rates for students in majority-minority schools.[91] Despite gains made as a result of desegregation plans in the 1970s and 1980s,[92] the nationwide graduation rates for blacks and Latinos in 2001 were only 50 and 53 percent, respectively.[93] In contrast, the graduation rate for white and Asian students was 75 and 77 percent, respectively, far exceeding the national average of 68 percent.[94] The disparity is due to differences in school promoting power; in schools where more than half of the students come from minority backgrounds, promoting power is five times more likely to be weak than the promoting power of majority-white schools.[95] In 2002, almost one in three high schools that were more than 50 percent minority graduated less than half of their students;[96] among schools that were 90 percent or more white, only one in fifty schools had a similar record.[97] Although research suggests that a district's poverty level has the strongest independent effect on graduation rates among various district characteristics, segregation levels also exert a significant independent effect.[98] Accordingly, to the extent that minority students disproportionately attend majority-minority schools, they are less likely to graduate.

Finally, enrollment in majority-minority schools also negatively affects college matriculation for minorities. Data on admissions to state colleges and universities in California illustrate that the majority of blacks and Latinos who attend the UC system's most competitive institutions, including UC San Diego and UC Berkeley, graduated from majority-white schools.[99] When compared to students who attended majority-white or Asian schools, students attending black or Latino schools were less likely to apply, be admitted, or enroll in the UC system.[100]

---

90. Kathryn M. Borman et al., *Accountability in a Postdesegregation Era: The Continuing Significance of Racial Segregation in Florida's Schools*, 41 Am. Educ. Res. J. 605, 622 (2004). Evidence that segregation is related to lower academic achievement, even after controlling for poverty, is explained by research suggesting that income is an inexact proxy for the social class characteristics that differentiate minorities from whites with comparable income levels. For a more detailed discussion of social class differences between whites and minorities, and how those differences negatively impact achievement, see Rothstein, *supra* note 44, at 47–50.

91. *Id.* at 6.

92. *See* Jonathan Guryan, *Desegregation and Black Dropout Rates*, 94 Am. Econ. Rev. 919 (2004) (concluding that desegregation plans of the 1970s reduced high school dropout rates of blacks by two to three percentage points during the decade).

93. Christopher B. Swanson, *Sketching a Portrait of Public High School Graduation: Who Graduates? Who Doesn't?, in* Dropouts in America: Confronting the Graduation Rate Crisis 13, 22 (Gary Orfield ed., 2004).

94. *Id.*

95. "Promoting power" is a measure that compares the number of freshman at a high school to the number of seniors four years later. Although an ideal measure would compare the number of freshman to the number of graduates, data on the number of graduates at individual high schools are not available. Robert Balfanz & Nettie E. Legters, *Locating the Dropout Crisis: Which High Schools Produce the Nation's Dropouts?, in* Dropouts in America: Confronting the Graduation Rate Crisis 57, 58–59, 62 (Gary Orfield ed., 2004).

96. Orfield & Lee *supra* note 24, at 6.

97. *Id.*

98. Swanson, *supra* note 93, at 30.

99. Robert Teranishi & Tara L. Parker, Social Reproduction of Inequality: The Racial Composition of Feeder Schools to the University of California (2008) (manuscript under review, on file with author).

100. Robert Teranishi, Walter R. Allen, & Daniel G. Solórzano, *Opportunity at the Crossroads: Racial Inequality, School Segregation, and Higher Education in California*, 106 Tchrs. C. Rec. 2224, 2241 (2004).

C. Integration as an Input

In contrast to the negative effect of segregation on educational outcomes, enrollment in racially integrated schools has a generally positive effect on the educational outcomes of minority students. The benefits of integration occur, in large part, because integrated schools are more likely to be middle-class schools with specific characteristics that positively impact student academic achievement. Middle-class schools often benefit from high expectations and high standards among parents, teachers, and students.[101] Moreover, middle-class schools command ample resources, including curricular materials, highly qualified teachers, and small class size. The political and social capital afforded to middle- and high-income parents whose children attend middle-class schools also yields more accountability.[102] These characteristics stand in stark contrast to the concentrated poverty, culture of underachievement, and inferior educational resources that negatively affect minority outcomes in majority-minority schools. Richard Kahlenberg, an advocate of school integration by class, explains that the "best guarantee that a school will have what various individual reforms seek to achieve — high standards, qualified teachers, less crowded classes, and so on — is the presence of a critical mass of middle-class families to ensure that these things happen."[103]

One of the first studies to document the benefit of integrated schools to blacks was the Coleman report, which produced evidence that academic outcomes were better for black students who attended integrated schools than for those who attended segregated schools.[104] Further evidence surfaced during the 1970s and 1980s, when the gap between reading scores for black and white children was reduced by approximately half.[105] The gap in math scores decreased 25–40 percent, and the science gap decreased 15–25 percent during the same time.[106] The greatest gains for black student achievement occurred in the South, where desegregation was occurring for the first time.[107] Today, black students who attend integrated schools have higher test scores[108] and, when compared to black students who attend segregated schools, are more likely to attend and graduate from college, and to earn higher grades while there.[109]

Integrated schools also maximize learning opportunities. Cognitive psychologists have found that students in diverse environments learn more than students in homogeneous settings because diversity thwarts "automaticity," or the tendency to engage in groupthink.[110] Students in diverse classrooms benefit from the experience of incongruity, or

---

101. Goodwin Liu & William L. Taylor, *School Choice to Achieve Desegregation*, 74 FORDHAM L. REV. 791, 798 (2005).

102. *Id.*

103. KAHLENBERG, *supra* note 31, at 4.

104. COLEMAN ET AL., *supra* note 42, at 22.

105. Marshall S. Smith & Jennifer O'Day, *Educational Equality: 1966 and Now*, *in* SPHERES OF JUSTICE IN EDUCATION: THE 1990 AMERICAN EDUCATION FINANCE ASSOCIATION YEARBOOK 53, 80 (Deborah A. Verstegen & James Gordon Ward eds., 1991).

106. *Id.*

107. *Id.* at 81–82.

108. CATHERINE L. HORN & MICHAL KURLAENDER, THE END OF KEYES: RESEGREGATION TRENDS AND ACHIEVEMENT IN DENVER PUBLIC SCHOOLS 4 (2006), *available at* www.civilrightsproject. ucla.edu/research/deseg/denver-4_5_06.pdf.

109. Liu & Taylor, *supra* note 101, at 797 (citing Jomills Henry Braddock II, Robert L. Crain, & James M. McPartland, *A Long-Term View of School Desegregation: Some Recent Studies of Graduates as Adults*, 66 PHI DELTA KAPPAN 259, 263 (1984)).

110. Mickelson, *supra* note 23, at 1548.

dissonance, which encourages them to gather new information and create new thought patterns to understand their surroundings.[111] This experience enhances intellectual stimulation and leads to increased cognitive growth,[112] the absence of which undermines academic achievement in both white and majority-minority schools. Integrated schools also ensure that minority students get equal access to experienced and credentialed teachers because integrated schools do not encounter the same racial bias as racially identifiable majority-minority schools.

Disagreement has existed regarding the short-term effects of integration on academic outcomes. Critics of the conclusion that integration is linked to academic achievement point to inconsistent evidence regarding the benefit to blacks. Critics further argue that decreases in the racial achievement gap that occurred during the years of consistent desegregation were not a result of desegregation itself but of gains in African American upward social mobility over the past fifty years.[113] In an effort to separate the effects of school racial composition from the influence of social background on academic outcomes, Professor Roslyn Arlin Mickelson used data collected from the CMS.[114] The CMS system offered a unique set of data because, thirty-one years after the historic Supreme Court decision in *Swann v. Charlotte-Mecklenburg*[115] mandated the district's desegregation, the system was declared unitary in 2002 and immediately began to resegregate. Mickelson's research confirmed that racially identifiable black schools and classrooms exerted significant negative effects on both black and white students' academic outcomes.[116] In fact, both black and white students who experienced integrated schools and classrooms benefited academically in significant and substantive ways, even after controlling for individual and family background.[117]

Moreover, Mickelson's research suggested that ambiguous or conflicting conclusions regarding the academic benefits of desegregated schools are possibly the result of research that does not consider whether second-generation segregation or racial tracking undermines the benefits of school integration.[118] Tracking within integrated CMS schools maintained white privilege by disproportionately placing whites into higher tracks than their comparably able black peers, while disproportionately assigning black students to racially identifiable lower tracks with diminished access to superior learning opportunities.[119] These disparities persisted even after the study controlled for prior attendance in segregated black elementary schools, prior academic achievement, gender, attitudes, peer group, effort, and family background.[120] Potential gains to black students from desegregation can be similarly subverted nationwide. Accordingly, heterogeneous instructional strategies must be used to realize improved academic outcomes for minority students in integrated schools. Researchers also note that other factors, including desegregation at the earliest possible grades, a critical mass of students from various racial groups, diverse staff and desegregated extracurricular activities, also maximize the benefits of integration.[121]

---

111. Univ. of N.C. Ctr. for Civil Rights, *supra* note 65, at 14.

112. *Id.*

113. Mickelson, *supra* note 23, at 1517.

114. Mickelson, *supra* note 23.

115. *Swann v. Charlotte-Mecklenburg Bd. of Educ.*, 402 U.S. 1 (1971).

116. Mickelson, *supra* note 23, at 1560.

117. *Id.*

118. *Id.*

119. Ability was measured by prior achievement on standardized test scores. Mickelson, *supra* note 23, at 1530–34, 1548–56, 1560.

120. Mickelson, *supra* note 23, at 1554.

121. Horn & Kurlaender, *supra* note 108, at 5.

Less controversial is evidence of the long-term impact of integrated schools on students.[122] Integrated schooling is associated with higher educational and occupational aspirations for African Americans.[123] Studies that use longitudinal data to examine the social, psychological, academic, and systemic obstacles that affect career attainment for African Americans reveal that black male graduates from integrated high schools attained higher job status and higher incomes than their peers in segregated schools.[124] In addition, integration positively influences black males' occupational aspirations, even after controlling for family and individual characteristics.[125] Black and white students who graduate from integrated schools are also more likely to attend college, work, and live in desegregated settings,[126] thus dismantling the residential segregation that leads to segregated schools in the first place.

Research also suggests that minorities benefit psychologically from integrated settings. A study of student perceptions of safety and vulnerability in the sixth grade concluded that African American and Latino students in ethnically diverse classrooms felt safer and less lonely, while experiencing less peer harassment and developing higher levels of self-worth.[127] School-wide, increased ethnic diversity in middle schools was also associated with lower levels of vulnerability.[128] Authors of the study theorize that equalized power differentials in ethnically diverse schools may help decrease perceptions of vulnerability.[129] Researchers have also theorized that desegregated schools convey specific messages that shape minority expectations. Disadvantaged students tend to have an "external locus of control," or tendency to assume that nothing they do can affect their environment.[130] In contrast, advantaged students tend to have an "internal locus of control," or belief that their environment will respond if they are able enough to affect it.[131] Analysis from the Coleman report suggested that locus of control was one of the best predictors of student achievement among minority students.[132] Integrated schooling conveys to minority students that "many things are possible," and yields increases in the internality of control for black students in particular.[133] Increased internality of control generally encourages purposeful, achievement-oriented behavior, which can result in higher minority achievement.[134]

Finally, integration also positively influences civic and attitudinal outcomes in ways that are important for an increasingly diverse society. Students who attend integrated

---

122. Mickelson, *supra* note 23, at 1527–28 (noting that unlike disagreement regarding the short-term effects of desegregation on achievement, there is general agreement on the positive long-term effects of desegregation).

123. Horn & Kurlaender, *supra* note 108, at 4.

124. *Id.*, at 5.

125. *Id.*

126. Liu & Taylor, *supra* note 101, at 797.

127. Jaana Juvonen, Adrienne Nishina, & Sandra Graham, *Ethnic Diversity and Perceptions of Safety in Urban Middle Schools*, 17 Psychol. Sci. 393, 396–98 (2006).

128. *Id.* at 396–98.

129. *Id.* at 398. The authors also theorize that students with fewer classmates of the same ethnicity may be more likely to attribute harassment to the individual prejudices of others, while students with many same-ethnicity classmates may be more likely to blame themselves for their victimization. *Id.*

130. Rita E. Mahard & Robert L. Crain, *Research on Minority Achievement in Desegregated Schools*, *in* The Consequences of School Desegregation 103, 122 (Christine H. Rossell & Willis D. Hawley eds., 1983).

131. *Id.*

132. *Id.*

133. *Id.*

134. *Id.* at 122–23.

schools report higher comfort levels with members of racial groups other than their own,[135] and white students in integrated settings exhibit more racial tolerance and less fear of black peers over time than their counterparts in segregated settings.[136] The Harvard Civil Rights Project has conducted several surveys of high school students in integrated schools to document student experiences with racial and ethnic diversity. Seniors in Cambridge, Massachusetts, reported increases in their ability to understand diverse points of view, and enhanced desire to interact with people of different backgrounds.[137] One student in particular reported learning how to be respectful of other groups while staying committed to one's own beliefs and heritage.[138]

Integration is not a panacea. Even integrated, middle-class schools are limited in their ability to impact the educational outcomes of disadvantaged students because "if students come to school in unequal circumstances, they will … leave school with unequal skills and abilities."[139] Accordingly, efforts to eliminate disparities in educational outcomes must include large-scale reforms that address the societal problems that disproportionately affect the disadvantaged, including the income gap, a lack of affordable housing, and inadequate health care.[140] Nevertheless, high academic achievement of disadvantaged students is still more likely in middle-class schools, even considering the limited ability of schools to compensate for social background. A 1986 national assessment, for example, concluded that a disadvantaged student is twice as likely to fall into the bottom quartile of achievement when attending a high-poverty school than when attending a low-poverty school.[141] As such, exposing minority students to the social and political capital of middle-class schools, as well as to the culture of achievement more likely to be prevalent therein, is a positive first step in maximizing the opportunity for academic success among minority students.

D. A Compelling and Attainable Interest

Although integration has been resisted at times, many white and minority parents have described their children's experiences with integration positively.[142] Little evidence exists to suggest that the integration of majority white schools has any negative effect on white students,[143] prompting even opponents of forced integration to concede that "virtually all studies of desegregation and achievement have found little or no change in achievement or other educational outcomes for white students."[144] In addition, Americans of all backgrounds continue to express their belief in the importance of integrated education. In

---

135. HORN & KURLAENDER, *supra* note 108, at 5.

136. *Id.*

137. MICHAL KURLAENDER & JOHN T. YUN, THE IMPACT OF RACIAL AND ETHNIC DIVERSITY ON EDUCATIONAL OUTCOMES: CAMBRIDGE, MA SCHOOL DISTRICT 2 (2002), *available at* www.civilrightsproject.ucla.edu/research/diversity/cambridge_diversity.pdf.

138. *Id.* at 6.

139. ROTHSTEIN, *supra* note 44, at 129.

140. *Id.* at 129–47.

141. KAHLENBERG, *supra* note 31, at 26.

142. ORFIELD & LEE, *supra* note 2, at 5.

143. ORFIELD & LEE, *supra* note 24, at 42 (citing the research of Professor Willis Hawley).

144. DAVID J. ARMOR, FORCED JUSTICE: SCHOOL DESEGREGATION AND THE LAW 71 (1995). *See also* KAHLENBERG, *supra* note 31, at 38–39 (concluding that in response to integration, black student test scores increased while white student test scores did not decline, and quoting researchers Crain and Marhard as stating, "Virtually every writer on the subject has agreed that white test performance is unaffected by desegregation. We think it is safe to assume that this issue is settled.").

Boston, where one of America's most bitter conflicts over school desegregation took place, a large majority of the city's residents still want more to be done to integrate schools.[145]

Moreover, assertions that integration has never been successfully achieved, and thus cannot be successfully accomplished in the future, are unfounded. In 2004, the vast majority of black students in the Southern and border states attended schools far more integrated than was the case before the Supreme Court's decision in *Brown v. Board of Education*, even after accounting for recent regression in integration progress.[146] In addition, models of sustainable long-term integration do exist. Forty-eight years after the *Brown* decision, three of the four school districts implicated in the case still maintained substantial levels of integration.[147] One district, Wilmington, Delaware, was one of the nation's most integrated school districts in the 1980s, 1990s, and through the 2001–02 school year.[148]

The Supreme Court has characterized education as "perhaps the most important function of state and local governments,"[149] and has described public schools as "a most vital civic institution for the preservation of a democratic system of government."[150] The Court has also repeatedly recognized the role that education plays in "preparing [students] for later professional training,"[151] and in providing the "basic tools by which individuals might lead economically productive lives to the benefit of us all."[152] School districts that take their obligation to prepare all children for citizenship seriously should consider integration a necessary input for providing minority children with adequate education that can result in high academic achievement. The significant negative effect that enrollment in majority-minority schools has on academic achievement, high school graduation rates, and the educational and occupational aspirations of minority students makes a school district's desire to dismantle racially isolated public schools a compelling interest.

II. Supreme Court Jurisprudence and Adequacy

Unfortunately for minority students attending majority-minority schools, the Supreme Court has issued a string of decisions that have been hostile to integration efforts. Each opinion, from *Keyes v. School District No. 1*[153] to *Missouri v. Jenkins*,[154] incrementally eliminated options for effective and permanent integration.

---

145. ORFIELD & LEE, *supra* note 2, at 5.

146. ORFIELD & LEE, *supra* note 21, at 20.

147. *Id.* at 13.

148. *Id.* at 13. For more discussion about sustainable models of integration, *see* James E. Ryan & Michael Heise, *The Political Economy of School Choice*, 111 YALE L.J. 2043, 2124–35 (2002) (identifying school choice as a viable option in integrating schools, and suggesting incentives and strategies to make school choice programs more effective).

149. *Brown v. Bd. of Educ.*, 347 U.S. 483, 493 (1954).

150. *Plyler v. Doe*, 457 U.S. 202, 221 (1982).

151. *Brown*, 347 U.S. at 493; *Grutter v. Bollinger*, 539 U.S. 306, 331 (2003) ("We have repeatedly acknowledged the overriding importance of preparing students for work and citizenship, describing education as pivotal to 'sustaining our political and cultural heritage' with a fundamental role in maintaining the fabric of society. This Court has long recognized that 'education ... is the very foundation of good citizenship.'"(quoting *Plyler v. Doe*, 457 U.S. 202 (1982), *Brown v. Bd. of Educ.*, 347 U.S. 483 (1954)).

152. *Plyler v. Doe*, 457 U.S. 202, 221 (1982).

153. *Keyes v. Sch. Dist. No. 1, Denver, Colo.*, 413 U.S. 189 (1973).

154. *Missouri v. Jenkins*, 515 U.S. 70 (1995).

A. The Desegregation Cases

The attitude of recalcitrance with which the South met the Supreme Court's call for desegregation of public schools in *Brown*[155] changed when Title VI of the Civil Rights Act of 1964 was passed, giving teeth to integration mandates by prohibiting receipt of federal funds by any public institution engaged in discriminatory practices.[156] In addition, as the Court's impatience grew,[157] it finally began providing substantive guidance on desegregation by directly charging school districts with the duty to create unitary school systems,[158] providing targets for which districts should strive[159] and sanctioning specific tools, including busing and remedial alteration of school attendance zones, to achieve integration.[160] By the early 1970s, the South was more desegregated than any other region in the country.[161]

A change in the Court's jurisprudence, however, began to undermine the traction that integration had gained. The Court's 1973 decision in *Keyes v. School District No. 1*[162] was the first time the Court decided a school desegregation case from the North.[163] As was typical in the North, segregation in Denver, Colorado, public schools was a product of covert discriminatory policies, including strategic school selection and boundary changes, rather

---

155. When ruling on remedies in *Brown* II, the Court ordered states to desegregate and transition to a system of integrated public schools with "all deliberate speed." *Brown v. Bd. of Educ. of Topeka*, 349 U.S. 294, 301 (1955). The Court's failure to define either the term "desegregate" or the phrase "all deliberate speed" resulted in a vague enforcement order that could not overcome resistance from Southern political leaders willing to close public schools to prevent integration. In response to desegregation orders directly issued to Prince Edward County, Virginia, in *Brown v. Board of Education*, for example, the county closed all public schools and gave white families publicly funded vouchers to attend private schools. Between 1959 and 1964, there were no public schools in the County until the Supreme Court, in *Griffin v. County School Board*, forced their reopenings as virtually all-black institutions. ORFIELD & LEE, *supra* note 21, at 12.

156. 42 U.S.C. § 2000d (2007).

157. *See Cooper v. Aaron*, 358 U.S. 1, 16 (1958) (asserting, in response to the Little Rock, Arkansas, school board, which sought to delay a court-approved desegregation program because of the extreme racial hostility toward desegregation, that "constitutional rights ... are not to be sacrificed or yielded to the violence and disorder"); *Goss v. Bd. of Educ.*, 373 U.S. 683, 686 (1963) (noting that a school choice plan that allowed students who were part of the minority in their assigned school to transfer to schools where they were the majority was working toward the "perpetuation of segregation"); *Griffin v. County Sch. Bd.*, 377 U.S. 218, 229 (1964) (in striking down the Prince Edward County School Board's reaction to desegregation orders issued in *Brown* I, the Court observed, "There has been entirely too much deliberation and not enough speed."); *Alexander v. Holmes County Bd. of Ed.*, 396 U.S. 19, 20 (1969) (in vacating a stay of integration orders, the Court stated that "operation of segregated schools under a standard of allowing 'all deliberate speed' for desegregation is no longer constitutionally permissible. Under explicit holdings of this Court the obligation of every school district is to terminate dual school systems at once and to operate now and hereafter only unitary schools.").

158. A unitary system is a system that is not racially identifiable based on students, faculty, staff, transportation, extracurricular activities, or facilities. *Green v. County Sch. Bd.*, 391 U.S. 430, 435 (1968). These six factors have since become the most commonly used guidelines for determining whether a district is unitary.

159. The Court characterized mathematical ratios reflecting the racial composition of entire school systems as "useful starting point[s]" in setting desegregation goals. *Swann v. Charlotte-Mecklenburg Bd. of Educ.*, 402 U.S. 1, 25 (1971).

160. *Swann v. Charlotte-Mecklenburg Bd. of Educ.*, 402 U.S. 1, 28–31 (1971).

161. Gary Orfield, *Turning Back to Segregation, in* DISMANTLING DESEGREGATION: THE QUIET REVERSAL OF *BROWN V. BOARD OF EDUCATION* 1, 8 (Gary Orfield & Susan E. Eaton eds., 1996).

162. *Keyes v. Sch. Dist. No. 1, Denver, Colo.*, 413 U.S. 189 (1973).

163. Orfield, *supra* note 161, at 1, 8.

than overt laws openly mandating segregation.[164] Although past intentional segregation was easy to prove for the city's Park Hill area, it was difficult to prove for the core city schools. The district court declined to find constitutional violations based on intent, but decided that school board policies maintaining de facto[165] segregation in schools violated the equal protection clause when those policies resulted in unequal educational opportunities for students in the high-minority core city schools.[166] In response to testimony suggesting that compensatory financial measures would be unsuccessful without accompanying integration, the district court also ultimately ordered desegregation of the core city schools.[167]

The Supreme Court overturned the district court ruling, refusing to find that de facto segregation would amount to an equal protection violation.[168] Having declined three months earlier in a landmark school finance case, *San Antonio Independent School District v. Rodriguez*, to address whether there was a relationship between resources and quality of education,[169] the Court would not endorse the district court's compensatory monetary award.[170] Having also rejected the argument, in *Rodriguez*, that differences in the quality of education could constitute an equal protection violation,[171] the Court would not affirm the district court's holding that the Denver school district was liable for maintaining unequal educational opportunity for minorities.[172] Loathe to preserve Denver's segregated school system, however, the Court ignored equity and instead focused on de jure segregation, holding that proof of intentionally segregated actions in one part of the city could create a presumption of intent to create a dual system throughout the entire city.[173] In failing to recognize the equal protection violation inherent in even de facto segregation, the Court in *Keyes* created a practically insurmountable obstacle to obtaining judicial remedies to address government-sponsored segregation in the North.[174]

The Court's jurisprudence continued to shift in *Milliken v. Bradley*[175] and *Milliken v. Bradley* II.[176] At issue in *Milliken* was a desegregation plan that required integration between the predominantly black Detroit schools and the surrounding white suburban schools. Citing to the notion of local control of schools, the Court refused to order an interdistrict remedy in the absence of an interdistrict violation.[177] Accordingly, the district

---

164. Erwin Chemerinsky, *The Segregation and Resegregation of American Public Education: The Court's Role, in* School Resegregation: Must the South Turn Back? 29, 35 (John Charles Boger & Gary Orfield eds., 2005).

165. The distinction between de facto discrimination, meaning "existing in fact," and de jure discrimination, meaning "according to law," is a centerpiece of the Supreme Court's equal protection jurisprudence. Historically, racial segregation in schools has only been a violation of the equal protection clause when there is intent to segregate.

166. *Keyes v. Sch. Dist. No. 1, Denver, Colo.*, 313 F.Supp. 61, 83 (D. Colo. 1970).

167. *Keyes v. Sch. Dist. No. 1, Denver, Colo.*, 313 F.Supp. 90 (D. Colo. 1970).

168. *See generally Keyes v. Sch. Dist. No. 1, Denver, Colo.*, 413 U.S. 189 (1973).

169. The Court in *Rodriguez* suggested that the correlation between resources and educational equity was "assumed," and concluded that the question was both a "major source of controversy, and an "unsettled and disputed question." *San Antonio Indep. Sch. Dist. v. Rodriguez*, 411 U.S. 1, 23, 43 (1973).

170. Goodwin Liu, *The Parted Paths of School Desegregation and School Finance Litigation*, 24 Law & Ineq. 81, 94 (2006).

171. The Court in *Rodriguez* concluded that there was neither a suspect class nor a fundamental right implicated in the case. *San Antonio Indep. Sch. Dist. v. Rodriguez*, 411 U.S. 1, 23–29, 35 (1973).

172. Liu, *supra* note 170, at 81, 94–95.

173. *Keyes v. Sch. Dist. No. 1, Denver, Colo.*, 413 U.S. 189, 208 (1973).

174. Chemerinsky, *supra* note 164, at 35–36.

175. *Milliken v. Bradley*, 418 U.S. 717 (1974).

176. *Milliken v. Bradley*, 433 U.S. 267 (1977).

177. *Milliken v. Bradley*, 418 U.S. 717, 744–47 (1974).

court was prevented from ordering fifty-three suburban school districts to participate in the integration of Detroit schools,[178] even though it was otherwise impossible to integrate Detroit's majority black school district, itself the product of de jure segregation policies.[179] It was the first case to rationalize a segregated result where a constitutional violation of state-sponsored segregation had been found to exist.[180] Having foreclosed a remedy of integration in *Milliken*, the Court approved a desegregation plan in *Milliken* II that required the state to fund compensatory programs to address the harms of segregation.[181] Since *Milliken* II, the focus of desegregation cases involving urban districts in the North and West has shifted away from integrative remedies toward funding to improve educational quality.[182] As already discussed in detail, however, an influx of money does not necessarily address the obstacles that majority-minority schools must overcome.

Integration proponents consider the Court's next three desegregation decisions, *Board of Education of Oklahoma City Public Schools v. Dowell*,[183] *Freeman v. Pitts*,[184] and *Missouri v. Jenkins*,[185] a collective reversal of *Brown v. Board of Education*.[186] In *Dowell*, the Court sanctioned the termination of desegregation orders once school districts became unitary, even if the termination would lead to resegregation of district schools.[187] One year later, the Court went further, in *Freeman v. Pitts*, when it gave federal courts the authority to relinquish supervision or control of school districts in incremental stages, even if other desegregation orders for the same system remained in place.[188] As a result, students in affected districts never attend fully integrated school systems, especially if resegregation occurs as orders are lifted piecemeal. Such was the case in *Freeman*, where after having been released from desegregation orders regarding facilities, the DeKalb County, Georgia school system planned to construct a new building more likely to benefit whites than blacks.[189] The federal court was barred, however, from reviewing the discriminatory effects of the new construction because requirements in that part of the desegregation order had already been met.[190]

Three years later in 1995, the Court decided *Missouri v. Jenkins*.[191] Under federal court desegregation orders, and prevented from obtaining an integration remedy that would involve the suburbs under *Milliken*, the Kansas City Missouri School District (KCMSD) used compensatory funds for a desegregation order the district hoped would both lure white students from the suburbs and attract qualified teachers. Over $1 billion was spent to convert the city's public schools to first-rate magnet schools and in-

---

178. *Id.* at 745.

179. *Id.* at 717.

180. Laurence H. Tribe, American Constitutional Law 1495 (2d ed. 1988).

181. *Milliken v. Bradley*, 433 U.S. 267, 288–90 (1977).

182. Ryan, *supra* note 12, at 261–62.

183. *Bd. of Educ. v. Dowell*, 498 U.S. 237 (1991).

184. *Freeman v. Pitts*, 503 U.S. 467 (1992).

185. *Missouri v. Jenkins*, 515 U.S. 70 (1995).

186. Orfield, *supra* note 161, at 1, 1.

187. In determining whether unitary status had been achieved, district courts were to consider whether the school board "complied in good faith" with desegregation orders, and whether the "vestiges of past discrimination had been eliminated to the extent practicable." The latter could be determined by reference to the six factors outlined in *Green*. *Dowell*, 498 U.S. at 249–50.

188. *Freeman*, 503 U.S. at 485, 490–91.

189. Chemerinsky, *supra* note 164, at 39.

190. *Id.*

191. *Missouri v. Jenkins*, 515 U.S. 70 (1995).

crease teacher salaries across the district.[192] Furthermore, the district court ordered the state of Missouri to continue a quality education program until student achievement within the district reached national norms.[193] The plan led to considerable gains in integration. In 1983, twenty-five schools in the district had a minority enrollment rate of greater than 90 percent.[194] One decade later, no KCMSD elementary-school student attended a school with such a rate, and the percentage of middle and high school students attending schools with such a rate had declined from 45 to 22 percent.[195]

The Supreme Court acknowledged the district court's finding of a system-wide reduction in achievement due to segregation, but noted that the district court failed to identify the "incremental effect" of segregation on minority achievement.[196] Accordingly, the school district could be declared unitary, even if disparities in academic performance remained, as long as the school district complied with its desegregation orders.[197] The Court also ruled that the district court could not, as part of a desegregation order, mandate government expenditures for a plan that solicited even voluntary interdistrict integration in the absence of an interdistrict violation.[198] Finally, the Court emphasized a quick return to local control of the school system.[199] Without a court order guaranteeing state funding to the schools, white enrollment in KCMSD fell by 8 percent in September 1995, the largest yearly drop in a decade.[200]

B. The Failure of the Court's Jurisprudence

Professor Erwin Chemerinsky attributes the Court's problematic jurisprudence to the conservative political ideology of the majority of the justices who have sat on the Court since the 1970s.[201] Putting aside political leanings for a moment, the Court's jurisprudence also suggests a complete failure to recognize the necessity of integration in providing children of color with even minimally adequate educations.

---

192. Alison Morantz, *Money and Choice in Kansas City: Major Investments with Modest Returns,* in DISMANTLING DESEGREGATION: THE QUIET REVERSAL OF *BROWN V. BOARD OF EDUCATION* 241, 251, 254 (Gary Orfield & Susan E. Eaton eds., 1996).

193. *Jenkins,* 515 U.S. at 100.

194. Chemerinsky, *supra* note 164, at 39.

195. *Id.*

196. *Jenkins,* 515 U.S. at 101.

197. *Missouri v. Jenkins,* 515 U.S. 70, 101–02 (1995); Morantz, *supra* note 192, at 261–62; Chemerinsky, *supra* note 164, at 39.

198. *Jenkins,* 515 U.S. at 94–99.

199. *Jenkins,* 515 U.S. at 102.

200. Morantz, *supra* note 192, at 262.

201. Chemerinsky, *supra* note 164, at 41–42. Chemerinsky notes that *Milliken* I and *Rodriguez* were both five-to-four decisions, with the majority including four Nixon appointees. Similarly, the majority in each of the Court's early 1990s decisions were conservative Republican justices appointed by Reagan and George H. W. Bush, including former Chief Justice Rehnquist, former Justice Sandra Day O'Connor, and Justices Antonin Scalia, Anthony Kennedy, and Clarence Thomas. *But see* David J. Armor, *Rearguing* Brown v. Board of Education, TCHRS C. REC., Aug. 15, 2007, www.tcrecord.org/PrintContent.asp?ContentId=14584 (arguing that reducing the debate to liberal versus conservative ideology oversimplifies the issue, and that the Court's desegregation jurisprudence is split over three issues, including (1) de jure versus de facto segregation, (2) application of strict scrutiny analysis, and (3) the educational consequences of racial isolation).

The Court first failed in *Keyes*. If the Court had recognized then that racial and economic isolation are problematic, whether created with or without intent, the Court might have been moved to create a doctrine of education equity under which inequities in student allocation are impermissible equal protection violations.[202] Under such a doctrine, intent would not be required because school segregation is often the result of myriad local, state, and federal policies, including discriminatory residential policies, historical adherence to neighborhood schools, and "race-conscious" decisions by school boards, which, although hard to prove, are sometimes motivated by racial animus. Moreover, decisions that produce genuinely unintended racial consequences, however innocent, can often reflect unconscious bias traceable to the legacy of racial oppression with which our country has struggled since its inception. Most important, proving intent would not be required because the equal protection violation is not the segregation per se. Rather, the violation is the inequality in educational opportunity that results from the segregation. The harm of that inequality is identical, whether produced by de jure or de facto segregation, government action or government inaction.[203] In both cases, minority children bear the burden of that harm in violation of the spirit of the equal protection clause.

In *Milliken*, the Court undermined a district's ability to attain integration even in cases of de jure segregation. By preventing an interdistrict remedy absent an interdistrict violation, the Court limited right and remedy to the jurisdictional impact of the wrong. Although consistent with traditional doctrines of remedy, such an approach is disingenuous in the context of school desegregation because it forecloses the possibility of achieving genuine integration in Northern and Western metropolitan regions, where urban areas are majority-minority and school district boundaries are coterminous with municipal boundaries.[204] As a result, state governments responsible for de jure segregation in their cities, and potentially for actions that drove or incentivized whites to leave the city, are absolved of their crimes, even when it is within a state's ability to exercise authority over all state public schools to fashion the appropriate remedy. *Milliken* II did not ameliorate the effect of the Court's decision in *Milliken*, but highlighted the Court's misplaced faith in compensatory financial awards, the utility of which are limited in the absence of contemporaneous desegregation efforts.

Finally, the Court's trio of cases in the early 1990s significantly limited the ability of school districts to integrate schools for the long term. By allowing the termination of desegregation orders, even if it would result in resegregation, the Court in *Dowell* and *Freeman* transformed desegregation orders from tools used to create lasting equity to temporary punishments for historical wrongs. In doing so, the Court suggested that district courts are under no obligation to adopt remedies that ensure long-term integration and are free

---

202. The Court might have constructed the doctrine to also cover inequalities in resource allocation. Such a doctrine would have united school desegregation litigation with school finance litigation, two litigation strands that have rarely been pursued in tandem, but nevertheless share the common goal of eliminating educational inequality. For a more detailed discussion of the Court's missed opportunity to create a unified doctrine of equal educational opportunity, *see* Liu, *supra* note 170, at 81; James E. Ryan, *Schools, Race, and Money,* 109 YALE L.J. 249 (1999).

203. The Court recognized, in *Plyler v. Doe*, that "denial of education to some isolated group of children poses an affront to one of the goals of the Equal Protection Clause: the abolition of governmental barriers presenting unreasonable obstacles to advancement on the basis of individual merit." *Plyler v. Doe*, 457 U.S. 202, 221–22 (1982). Although *Plyler* addressed purposeful government action to deny education, the failure of districts to dismantle racially isolated schools that essentially deny equal education opportunity to minority children is arguably just as offensive to the goals of the equal protection clause.

204. Ryan, *supra* note 12, at 261.

to return to systems of their choice, however unequal, if they have complied with court orders for a period of time. In *Jenkins*, the Court further severed the connection between compliance with integration orders and the goal of achieving educational equity. By dismissing proof of remaining inequity in educational outcomes, the Court prioritized mere technical compliance with integration orders and a quick return to local control, over actual equal education opportunity for minority children.

Worse yet, *Dowell, Freeman,* and *Jenkins* collectively encouraged district courts around the country to release schools from desegregation orders.[205] The result has been a return to segregation. Between 1964 and 1970, when civil rights enforcement was at its greatest and the Court provided clear guidance on what was expected of school districts, the percent of black students enrolled in majority-white schools in the South increased more than fourteen-fold, from 2.3 percent to 33.1 percent.[206] The percentage continued to increase until reaching a peak in 1988 of approximately 44 percent.[207] Since the Court's decisions in the early 1990s, however, the percentage has steadily declined, reaching approximately 30 percent in 2001, a figure lower than percentages attained during the 1970s.[208]

Other regions of the country reflect similar patterns. In 1968, the percentage of black students in the border states attending schools with 50 to 100 percent black enrollment was 71.6.[209] That figure dropped to 59.3 percent in 1991, but crept back up to 67.9 percent by 2001.[210] In the Midwest, 1968 levels were at 77.3 percent, but dropped to 69.7 percent by 1991, only to rise to 72.9 percent in 2001.[211] Figures in the West started at 72.2 percent in 1968, and fell to 67.1 percent in 1988, only to rise to 75.8 percent in 2001.[212] In the Northeast, where significant levels of integration never occurred, the percentage has steadily risen from 66.8 percent in 1968 to 78.4 percent in 2001.[213] Even more troubling, the percentage of black students enrolled in Southern schools that were 90 to 100 percent minority in 1968 was 77.8 percent.[214] That figured dropped drastically to 24 percent in 1988, only to have risen back up to 31 percent by 2001.[215] Latinos, for whom attempts at integration have never been genuinely pursued,[216] are also experiencing increases in segregation.[217] The percent of Latino students enrolled in majority-minority schools in the West has almost doubled from 42 percent in 1968, to 80 percent in 2001.[218] The percentage of Latino students enrolled in 90 to 100 percent minority schools more than tripled during the same period, from 12 to 37 percent.[219]

205. Chemerinsky, *supra* note 164, at 40.

206. Orfield & Lee, *supra* note 21, at 18–19.

207. *Id.* at 18, 19 tbl. 7.

208. *Id.*

209. *Id.* at 19–20.

210. *Id.*

211. *Id.*

212. *Id.*

213. *Id.*

214. *Id.*

215. *Id.*

216. Orfield & Lee, *supra* note 2, at 4 (2006).

217. The increase is due, in part, to rapid growth in the Latino population in the Southwest and Florida. Enrollment increases of 50 percent or more in the past decade would have created increases in segregation, even if Latinos were distributed evenly across schools. Orfield & Lee, *supra* note 21, at 16.

218. *Id.* at 20.

219. *Id.*

III. *Parents Involved in Community Schools v. Seattle School District No. 1*

In light of the social science research that continually confirms the negative impact of segregation on minority students and the evidence of resegregation trends across the country, the Seattle, Washington, and Jefferson County, Kentucky, school districts took warranted steps to decrease racial isolation in their public schools. Despite the voluntary nature of the districts' integration plans and the compelling interest motivating the school boards, the Supreme Court struck down the plans. The decision in *Parents Involved in Community Schools v. Seattle School District No. 1* demonstrates that the Court's commitment to integration and equal education opportunity continues to wane.

A. The Voluntary Integration Plans in Seattle and Louisville

The Supreme Court's decision in *Parents Involved* consolidated two cases, one from Seattle, Washington, and one from Louisville, Kentucky. Fortunate enough to have sufficient members of various racial groups in the city to integrate, and no history of court-ordered desegregation, the Seattle School Board first took steps in the late 1970s to integrate their public schools.[220] The plan ultimately challenged in the Supreme Court was a controlled-choice plan that took effect in the ninth grade and asked parents to rank the city's high schools by enrollment preference.[221] School assignments were determined by choice unless and until a school became oversubscribed, at which point a series of tiebreakers was employed. The first tiebreaker favored students who had siblings already attending the school. The second tiebreaker favored students who lived closest to the school. When schools were oversubscribed by white or minority students, the second tiebreaker was subject to an integration tiebreaker.[222]

The plan required racial enrollment in each oversubscribed high school to fall within fifteen percentage points of white/nonwhite student enrollment district-wide.[223] Seattle is a multiracial community with blacks, Latinos, Native Americans, and Asians. Whites constitute about 40 percent of the city's residents.[224] Accordingly, the integration tiebreaker favored those students who would bring a school's racial composition within 25 and 55 percent white.[225] Although picked up by the Supreme Court as a sticking point, the plan's

---

220. Liu, *supra* note 75, at 313–14. Initial plans divided the district into zones that paired predominantly white and minority elementary schools, and then linked mandatory high school assignments to elementary school assignments. In response to resistance to the mandatory busing required by the plan, the district adopted a controlled-choice plan in 1988, according to which parents were asked to rank choices among a cluster of schools that met desegregation guidelines. *Id.*

221. Brief for Respondents at 5–6, *Parents Involved in Cmty. Sch. v. Seattle Sch. Dist., No. 1*, 127 S. Ct. 2738 (U.S. 2007) (No. 05-908).

222. Brief for Respondents at 6, *Parents Involved*, 127 S. Ct. 2738 (No. 05-908).

223. The Supreme Court, however, seemed to base their decision on Seattle's more restrictive plan operated prior to the 2001–02 school year, in which white enrollment of each school had to be within ten percentage points of white/nonwhite enrollment district-wide. *Parents Involved in Cmty. Sch. v. Seattle Sch. Dist., No. 1*, 127 S. Ct. 2738, 2747 (U.S. 2007).

224. Brief for Respondents at 1, *Parents Involved*, 127 S. Ct. 2738 (No. 05-908).

225. Brief for Respondents at 10, *Parents Involved*, 127 S. Ct. 2738 (No. 05-908).

white/nonwhite dichotomy accurately reflected segregation patterns in Seattle. Historically, the most pronounced segregation in the city has been between whites who live in the city's northern half and the minority groups who live in the city's southern half. In the 2000–01 school year, 66 percent of white students lived on the North side, while 84 percent of black students, 74 percent of Asian students, and 65 percent of Latino students lived on the South side.[226] As such, minority students lived in diverse neighborhoods and attended diverse schools, whereas white students in the city were racially isolated.[227] While the Seattle plan was in effect, twenty-four of thirty-six neighborhoods surrounding district elementary schools in the southern half of the city had populations that were more than 70 percent minority, and nine neighborhoods had populations that were 90 percent minority.[228] In the northern half of the city only two of twenty-five elementary school neighborhoods had populations that were more than 50 percent nonwhite.[229] In the 2001–02 school year, the race tiebreaker was used in only three out of the city's ten high schools.[230] In the 2000–01 school year, when the racial guidelines were narrower (between ten percentage points of the white/nonwhite enrollment district-wide), the tiebreaker was triggered in four out of ten schools, affecting just 300 students out of 3,000.[231]

In contrast to Seattle, the Jefferson County School District had a history of court-ordered desegregation.[232] The district is located in metropolitan Louisville and includes within its boundaries white suburbs where most of the district's white students attend school.[233] After achieving unitary status in 2000, the district adopted the voluntary student assignment plan ultimately challenged. The plan first created racially integrated "resides" areas that included clusters of schools within geographic attendance areas.[234] The district asked parents to rank resides schools, magnet schools, and optional programs by enrollment preference; the district made the initial assignment to a resides school if parents did not choose.[235] Students at all grade levels could apply for a transfer to any non-magnet school in the district if dissatisfied with their initial placement.[236] Elementary school transfer requests were granted or denied based on many factors, including family hardship, school capacity, program offerings, and race.[237]

Although less diverse than Seattle, the Jefferson County racial guidelines also considered the racial demographics of the area. About 34 percent of the district's students are black; the remaining 66 percent are almost exclusively white.[238] Although there has been

---

226. Liu, *supra* note 75, at 287.

227. *Id.*, at 288.

228. Brief for Respondents at 1–2, *Parents Involved in Cmty. Sch. v. Seattle Sch. Dist. No. 1*, 127 S. Ct. 2738 (U.S. 2007) (No. 05-908).

229. Brief for Respondents at 1–2, *Parents Involved*, 127 S. Ct. 2738 (No. 05-908).

230. Brief for Respondents at 10, *Parents Involved*, 127 S. Ct. 2738 (No. 05-908).

231. Brief for Respondents at 8–9, *Parents Involved*, 127 S. Ct. 2738 (No. 05-908).

232. Throughout the 1970s and 1980s, the district implemented court-ordered busing, school closings, gerrymandered attendance zones, magnet schools, school pairings, and clustering to achieve integration. The districted adopted a controlled-choice plan in 1984 to enhance stability, expand choice, and decrease the use of race in school assignments. Liu, *supra* note 75, at 314–15.

233. Brief for Respondents at 3–4, *Parents Involved in Cmty. Sch. v. Seattle Sch. Dist. No. 1*, 127 S. Ct. 2738 (U.S. 2007) (No. 05-915).

234. Brief for Respondents at 5–6, *Parents Involved*, 127 S. Ct. 2738 (No. 05-915).

235. Brief for Respondents at 6, *Parents Involved*, 127 S. Ct. 2738 (No. 05-915).

236. Brief for Respondents at 6–7, *Parents Involved*, 127 S. Ct. 2738 (No. 05-915).

237. Brief for Respondents at 7, *Parents Involved*, 127 S. Ct. 2738 (No. 05-915); *McFarland v. Jefferson County Pub. Sch.*, 330 F. Supp. 2d 834, 844 (W.D. Ky. 2004).

238. Brief for Respondents at 5, *Parents Involved in Cmty. Sch. v. Seattle Sch. Dist. No. 1*, 127 S. Ct. 2738 (U.S. 2007) (No. 05-915); Liu, *supra* note 75, at 286.

an increase in the presence of other ethnic minorities in Jefferson County, the area's residents are still largely black and white, a reality that led to racial classifications of "black" and "other" in the plan.[239] The plan required racial enrollment in each school to fall within 15 and 50 percent black.[240] In the 2002–03 school year, only 7 percent of students applied for transfers, most of which were granted. In the 2003–04 school year, most elementary students attended their initially assigned or first-choice school in their resides areas.[241]

Both programs were challenged and eventually reached the Supreme Court. The challenger from Seattle was Parents Involved in Community Schools, a nonprofit corporation comprised of parents whose children were, or might have been, denied assignment of their chosen high school because of race.[242] The challenger from Louisville was Crystal Meredith, a mother whose request for a transfer of her son to a school one mile from her home was denied because the transfer would have had adverse effects on desegregation efforts in the district.[243]

B. The Court's Holding

The Supreme Court issued a sharply divided majority/plurality opinion on June 28, 2007, in which it struck down both voluntary integration plans. A majority of the justices, including Chief Justice Roberts and Justices Scalia, Kennedy, Thomas, and Alito, subjected the plans to strict scrutiny and found that the districts did not have a compelling interest in using race to remedy the effects of past intentional discrimination; Seattle was never under court-ordered desegregation, and Jefferson County had been released from desegregation orders in 2000 when it achieved unitary status.[244] The use of race to address the compelling interest of diversity as conceptualized in higher education[245] was similarly inapplicable. In higher education, a candidate's ability to bring diversity to a campus was determined by several factors in addition to race or ethnicity, including having overcome personal hardship or possessing special talents.[246] Moreover, higher education institutions seek to cultivate viewpoint diversity through student exposure to different cultures, ideas, and people.[247] In contrast, the controlled-choice programs implemented in the school districts did not seek this sort of viewpoint diversity, instead making decisions on the basis of race alone—a point underscored by the binary "white/nonwhite" and "black/other" classifications utilized by the Seattle and Louisville plans.[248]

The same majority also noted that the assignment of students by race was an extreme approach that could only be justified by absolute necessity,[249] and that the limited impact of the plans on student assignment indicated that integration could have been effectively achieved in other ways.[250] Moreover, the districts failed to show that they considered meth-

---

239. Brief for Respondents at 5, *Parents Involved*, 127 S. Ct. 2738 (No. 05-915).

240. Brief for Respondents at 4–5, *Parents Involved*, 127 S. Ct. 2738 (No. 05-915).

241. Liu, *supra* note 75, at 315.

242. *Parents Involved in Cmty. Sch. v. Seattle Sch. Dist. No. 1*, 127 S. Ct. 2738, 2748 (U.S. 2007).

243. *Parents Involved in Cmty. Sch. v. Seattle Sch. Dist. No. 1*, 127 S. Ct. 2738, 2750 (U.S. 2007).

244. *Parents Involved*, 127 S. Ct. at 2752.

245. *Grutter v. Bollinger*, 539 U.S. 306, 328 (2003) (upholding the consideration of race in college and university admissions as long as race is just one of many factors considered in the effort to create a diverse student body).

246. *Parents Involved*, 127 S. Ct. at 2753.

247. *Id.*

248. *Parents Involved*, 127 S. Ct. at 2753–54.

249. *Parents Involved*, 127 S. Ct. at 2760.

250. *Parents Involved*, 127 S. Ct. at 2759–60.

ods other than explicit racial classifications to achieve integration goals.[251] As such, the plans were not narrowly tailored, according to the Court's strict scrutiny analysis.

Four of the justices, including Chief Justice Roberts and Justices Scalia, Thomas, and Alito, declined to even consider whether there was a compelling interest in using integration to address equity concerns. Even if equalizing educational opportunity was a compelling interest, the controlled-choice plans were insufficiently narrowly tailored to serve that interest.[252] Instead of basing the plans' integration goals on pedagogic theories about the levels of integration needed to obtain educational benefits, the goals were instead based on the racial demographics of the districts. Such a design is considered racial balancing and is patently illegitimate.[253]

Justice Kennedy filed a separate opinion, concurring in part and concurring in the judgment. Kennedy characterized the four justices in the plurality as too dismissive of a legitimate governmental interest in ensuring equal educational opportunity.[254] Nevertheless, individual racial classifications can only be used if they are a "last resort to achieve a compelling interest."[255] If districts are concerned that the racial composition of their schools interferes with equal educational opportunity, "absent some extraordinary showing not present [in *Parents Involved*],"[256] districts are only free to use race-conscious measures that take into account the problem but avoid assignment of students by race.[257]

C. The Court Fails Again

As discussed earlier, adequacy and the resulting equality in education opportunity is best achieved by eliminating racial isolation in public schools. This task does not require individual assessment of each student's diversity contribution but the even distribution of students by race. To be sure, cultivating viewpoint diversity and meaningful exchanges are important goals of integration. The primary goal of integration as an adequacy input, however, is not that black children attend school with students of different backgrounds, worldviews, or talents, each individually screened to assess unique contributions to diversity. Rather, the primary goal is to ensure that black children no longer attend racially isolated schools that concentrate poverty, aggregate negative peer influences, and fail to attract or retain high-quality teachers due to racial bias.

The Court's majority and plurality opinions, however, evince little understanding of this reality. Arguably, the majority's rejection of the use of race to address the compelling interest in cultivating diversity as conceptualized in higher education or in remedying past discrimination, is tenable. Unlike institutions of higher education, which are concerned with individually assessing the varied ways in which applicants will contribute to their academic community, school districts are concerned with overcoming the obstacles

---

251. *Parents Involved*, 127 S. Ct. at 2760.

252. *Parents Involved*, 127 S. Ct. at 2755.

253. *Parents Involved*, 127 S. Ct. at 2755–59.

254. *Parents Involved*, 127 S. Ct. at 2791 (Kennedy, J., concurring in part and concurring in the judgment).

255. *Parents Involved*, 127 S. Ct. at 2792 (Kennedy, J., concurring in part and concurring in the judgment).

256. *Parents Involved*, 127 S. Ct. at 2796 (Kennedy, J., concurring in part and concurring in the judgment).

257. *Parents Involved*, 127 S. Ct. at 2791–92 (Kennedy, J., concurring in part and concurring in the judgment).

that majority-minority schools face. Furthermore, even though the dissent correctly argues that the absence of a court finding does not necessarily mean that past de jure segregation has not occurred,[258] the goal of addressing racial isolation is distinct from remedying past segregation. The harm of racial isolation is not the segregation itself but the resulting negative effect on academic outcomes.

It is the plurality's consideration of race to address a third compelling interest in reducing racial isolation that is marred by a failure to appreciate the effects of segregation on educational outcomes. The plurality worked backward, citing insufficient narrow tailoring as a reason to avoid recognizing a compelling interest in reducing racial isolation. A school district's attempt to integrate K–12 public schools, however, is responsive to an obligation to equalize educational opportunity and provide *all* students with an adequate education. Recognition of this compelling interest was appropriate and necessary, even if the plurality ultimately decided that the plans were not narrowly tailored.

Recognition of the correct compelling interest might have prevented the plurality's flawed narrow tailoring analysis, which suggested that the plans' racial guidelines should have been based on pedagogic theories regarding the levels of integration necessary to secure achievement.[259] The plans' integration guidelines, however, were just that. As an abundance of research suggests, dismantling racial isolation and creating integrated schools more likely to be middle-class schools, addresses the concentration of poverty, culture of underachievement, and racial bias that negatively impact academic outcomes in racially and economically isolated schools. In using racial guidelines to eliminate or limit the number of majority-minority schools, both the Seattle and Louisville plans were effective.[260] Moreover, in light of the Court's previous decisions barring interdistrict remedies,[261] the very best any district with a significant number of blacks or Latinos can hope to achieve is congruence between districtwide demographics and enrollment patterns.

Although considered by advocates of integration to be the one bright spot in the Court's decision,[262] Justice Kennedy's concurrence is marked by a limited understanding of the practical limitations of integration efforts. Although Kennedy correctly identified a compelling interest in reducing racial isolation,[263] he declined to find an actual equal protection violation that would warrant the assignment of students by race.[264] As the result of de facto segregation, racial isolation could only be voluntarily addressed by race-conscious programs like strategic site selection of new schools, gerrymandered attendance zones, and fund allocation for special programs.[265] Some of these programs have already been tried

---

258. *Parents Involved*, 127 S. Ct. at 2810–11 (Breyer, J., dissenting).

259. *Parents Involved*, 127 S. Ct. at 2755–59.

260. *See supra* notes 225, 240, and accompanying text.

261. *Milliken v. Bradley*, 418 U.S. 717 (1974).

262. Charles Ogletree's applauded Justice Kennedy's concurrence, noting that "The hidden story in the decision today is that Justice Kennedy refused to follow the lead of the other four justices in eviscerating the legacy of *Brown*." Adam Liptak, *The Same Words, but Differing Views*, N.Y. Times, June 29, 2007, at A24. Similarly, Theodore M. Shaw, president of the NAACP Legal Defense Fund, highlighted Kennedy's break from the plurality, stating, "In some ways, considering what we anticipated, it's not as bad as it could have been." Robert Barnes, *Divided Court Limits Use of Race by School Districts*, Wash. Post, June 29, 2007, at A01.

263. *Parents Involved*, 127 S. Ct. at 2797 (Kennedy, J., concurring in part and concurring in the judgment) ("A compelling interest exists in avoiding racial isolation, an interest that a school district, in its discretion and expertise, may choose to pursue.").

264. *Parents Involved*, 127 S. Ct. at 2794–96 (Kennedy, J., concurring in part and concurring in the judgment).

265. *Parents Involved*, 127 S. Ct. at 2792–96 (Kennedy, J., concurring in part and concurring in the judgment).

and rejected by school districts for lack of community support.[266] The creation of attendance zones, for example, requires busing, which has repeatedly caused opposition and discontent throughout the history of desegregation. Busing is also expensive, and often disproportionately borne by African American students.[267] The creation of new schools, particularly in urban districts already struggling with scarce resources, is not feasible unless schools are placed on parcels in a region's least desirable area,[268] thus defeating the initial goal of attracting white, middle-class students. Furthermore, despite the creation of magnet schools and other special programs, parents still overwhelmingly choose neighborhood schools,[269] a pattern that undermines the success of special programming and underscores the need for controlled-choice programs to counter the trend.

Finally, Justice Kennedy's suggestion that school districts employ individualized review to create diverse schools[270] is impractical. Large school districts would have to individually assess tens of thousands of students and assign them to sometimes more than 100 schools.[271] School districts have neither the time nor the resources to devote to such a Herculean task. In addition, there are few factors, other than race, on which a school district can evaluate diversity in an elementary school-age child who has not yet had the opportunity to develop talents, special skills, or particular worldviews. As noted by Michael Casserly, executive director of the Council for the Great City Schools, "The strategies that [Kennedy] outlined have limited viability."[272] A better understanding of the limited efficacy of race-conscious measures might have prevented Justice Kennedy from joining the majority in characterizing the district plans as unnecessary, and therefore insufficiently narrowly tailored. The plans developed in Seattle and Louisville were realistic, practical, and effective.

The Court's decision in *Parents Involved* is also particularly problematic because of the nature of the programs struck down. Both the Seattle and Jefferson County plans were *voluntary* plans that specifically sought to address the very equity concerns outlined in this chapter.[273] As voluntary programs, the plans represented the educational judgments of locally elected officials who were responsive to their constituents.[274] As controlled-choice programs, the plans yielded increased parental buy-in and satisfaction.[275] Moreover, un-

---

266. The Seattle School District pursued their controlled-choice plans precisely because earlier plans, which involved mandatory busing and gerrymandered attendance zones, triggered white flight and community dissatisfaction. Liu, *supra* note 75, at 313.

267. Claire Smrekar, Commentary, *A Practical End to Racial Diversity in Schools*, Tchrs C. Rec., July 16, 2007, www.tcrecord.org/PrintContent.asp?ContentId=14549.

268. *Id.*

269. *Id.*

270. *Parents Involved*, 127 S. Ct. at 2793 (Kennedy, J., concurring in part and concurring in the judgment).

271. Smrekar, *supra* note 267.

272. Barnes, *supra* note 262, at A01.

273. Brief for Respondents at 28–31, *Parents Involved in Cmty. Sch. v. Seattle Sch. Dist. No. 1*, 127 S. Ct. 2738 (U.S. 2007) (No. 05-908); Brief for Respondents at 27–29, *Parents Involved in Cmty. Sch. v. Seattle Sch. Dist. No. 1*, 127 S. Ct. 2738 (U.S. 2007) (No. 05-915).

274. The Jefferson County School Board, for example, regularly polled students, graduates, parents, and the community at large to monitor attitudes about the district. Results indicated strong student, parent, and community support for a student assignment plan that provided choice while at the same time maintaining racially integrated schools. Brief for Respondents at 9, *Parents Involved*, 127 S. Ct. 2738 (No. 05-915).

275. Both school districts adopted their controlled-choice plans in part to reduce burdensome mandatory assignment plans that required busing, and to increase parental participation. Brief for Respondents at 4–6, *Parents Involved*, 127 S. Ct. 2738 (No. 05-908); Brief for Respondents at 22–24, *Parents Involved*, 127 S. Ct. 2738 (No. 05-915).

like the significant judicial effort required of the federal courts as they struggled with the implementation and remedial aftermath of *Brown* and its progeny,[276] these plans did not create a drain on judicial resources. As such, the plans presented the opportunity for deference to local control of education policy for which the Court has advocated in the past.[277]

In addition, both plans used race-neutral factors in their efforts to integrate schools, relying first on parent and student choice. The Seattle plan, for example, also considered sibling status and proximity to school when making assignments and used race only when necessary to prevent resegregation. Instead of adherence to strict racial guidelines, both plans used broad racial ranges to minimize consideration of race and avoid school assignments that merely mimicked district-wide racial demographics.[278] These features ensured that the plans were as narrowly tailored as possible, allowing the districts to consider race only as a last resort in a limited number of cases. As noted by the dissent, the use of race in these plans was more narrowly tailored than the use of race in the admissions plan upheld in *Grutter*, where race was considered in a large number of students' merit-based applications.[279] Although the district plans' occasional use of race meant that at some point race became determinative, it is impractical and disingenuous to prohibit any consideration of race after having identified racial isolation as a barrier to equalized education opportunity.

The controlled-choice plans utilized by the districts were among few options still available to school districts committed to providing integrated, high-quality education for all students. Districts were denied federal support for remedying de facto segregation in *Keyes*, and were prohibited, in *Milliken*, from implementing interdistrict remedies that would integrate majority-minority districts affected by de jure segregation. *Dowell, Freeman,* and *Jenkins* absolved states of federally imposed obligations to maintain integration long term. Voluntary controlled-choice plans are among the few alternatives for those diverse districts which, despite having achieved unitary status or having no history of legally sanctioned segregation, seek to promote long-term racial integration. The Court, however, has now eliminated even this option.

Although characterized as an effort to stop the racial discrimination outlawed in *Brown*,[280] the Court's decision actually furthers it by preventing school districts from addressing the educational input that arguably has the most significant impact on the quality of education for minorities. By denying school districts the opportunity to consider race in assignments, the Court sanctions educational inequity between white or integrated schools and majority-minority schools, while impeding district efforts to provide minority students with eq-

---

276. Heise, *supra* note 13, at 1156 (describing the Supreme Court's hesitancy, in *San Antonio v. Rodriguez*, to abrogate the national school finance system in light of the judicial effort spent on school desegregation issues). *See also* Michael Heise, *The Story of San Antonio Independent School Dist. v. Rodriguez: School Finance, Local Control, and Constitutional Limits* 14–15 (Cornell Law Sch. Legal Studies Research Paper Series, Paper No. 76, 2007), *available at* lsr.nellco.org/cornell/lsrp/papers/76 (citing the Court's concerns about federalism, unintended consequences, and practicality as reasons for the Court's refusal to restructure the national school finance system).

277. *Freeman v. Pitts*, 503 U.S. 467, 490 (1992) ("Local autonomy of school districts is a vital national tradition."); *Missouri v. Jenkins*, 515 U.S. 70, 99, 138 (1995) ("Our cases recognize that local autonomy of school districts is a vital national tradition.") ("Usurpation of the traditionally local control over education not only takes the judiciary beyond its proper sphere, it also deprives the States and their elected officials of their constitutional powers.") (Thomas, J., concurring).

278. *See supra* notes 225, 239, and accompanying text.

279. *Parents Involved in Cmty. Sch. v. Seattle Sch. Dist. No. 1*, 127 S. Ct. 2738, 2825 (U.S. 2007) (Breyer, J., dissenting).

280. "The way to stop discrimination on the basis of race is to stop discriminating on the basis of race." *Parents Involved*, 127 S. Ct. at 2768 (Roberts, J.).

uitable access to popular and highly sought-after schools. In Seattle, for example, the majority of the city's oversubscribed schools were located in predominantly white areas. Accordingly, school assignment plans based solely on geography and parental selection, with no consideration of race, disproportionately excluded nonwhite students from the schools of their choice.[281] The discrimination that the Court ironically perpetuates is a result of a continued unwillingness to distinguish between benign and invidious racial remedies, an insistent presumption against racial classifications no matter the purpose, and what can be increasingly characterized as willful ignorance of the necessity of integration to maximizing educational outcomes for all children so as to give legitimacy to *Brown*'s legacy of equality.

Conclusion

About 1,000 out of 15,000 school systems in the United States currently employ plans that consider race when making school assignments.[282] Accordingly, the impact of the Court's decision in *Parents Involved* is likely to be significant. Litigation has already begun,[283] validating Justice Breyer's prediction that the majority decision threatened to substitute disruptive race-related litigation for the present calm.[284] In addition to spurring litigation, the Court's decision created yet another obstacle to genuine and lasting integration necessary for the adequate education of all children. In light of social science data that elucidates the negative impact of segregation on the educational outcomes of minority students, the Court's decision has also rejected the genuine legacy of *Brown*—equal educational opportunity for minority students.[285]

Justice Kennedy's concurrence, however, may provide some hope for controlled-choice programs that explicitly consider race. Although he rejected the assignment of students by race, Justice Kennedy, like the dissenters, recognized a school district's compelling interest in preventing racial isolation, which creates educational inequity. Moreover, Kennedy's concurrence suggested that individual racial classifications might be permissible if dis-

---

281. Brief for Respondents at 33–34, *Parents Involved in Cmty. Sch. v. Seattle Sch. Dist. No. 1*, 127 S. Ct. 2738 (U.S. 2007) (No. 05-908).

282. Amit R. Paley & Brigid Schulte, *Court Ruling Likely to Further Segregate Schools, Educators Say*, Wash. Post, June 30, 2007, at A04.

283. Less than one month after the Court's decision, a couple in Madison, Wisconsin, sought an immediate court order to allow their child to transfer to a different school in the district. The request was previously denied under Wisconsin's Chapter 220 Integration Program because it would have increased racial imbalance in the originating school. Andy Hall, *Parents Ask Court for Change of Schools: They Want Their Daughter to Attend Kindergarten Near the School Where Mom Is a Teacher*, Wis. St. J., July 28, 2007, at B1.

284. *Parents Involved*, 127 S. Ct. at 2800 (Breyer, J., dissenting).

285. *Parents Involved*, 127 S. Ct. at 2800 (Breyer, J., dissenting). Nor is the warping of *Brown*'s legacy lost on the case's original litigators. In establishing support for the Court's position, Justice Roberts cited the *Brown* transcript and quoted one of the case's lawyers, Robert L. Carter, as stating, "No state has any authority under the equal protection clause of the Fourteenth Amendment to use race as a factor in affording educational opportunities among its citizens." Roberts characterized the statements as unambiguous. In reacting to the opinion, however, Carter challenged the interpretation, explaining that because race was used only to deny equal opportunity to blacks in the 1950s, Roberts's current use of the statement to strike down integration programs "stand[s] that argument on its head." Similarly, Jack Greenberg, who worked on *Brown* for the plaintiffs, characterized Roberts's interpretation as "preposterous," because *Brown* was concerned with the marginalization of black people. Adam Liptak, *The Same Words, but Differing Views*, N.Y. Times, June 29, 2007, at A24.

tricts can prove that such measures are a necessary last resort in response to the failure of race-conscious measures to achieve integration.[286] If a second case with a stronger factual record than *Parents Involved* provided the proof, Justice Kennedy might be swayed to join the four dissenters in upholding a controlled-choice plan similar to the two plans struck down. Litigators might also consider pursuing state adequacy suits that seek, as remedies, the straightforward consideration of race in school assignments. If the plans are motivated by equity concerns, include the race-neutral safeguards that were present in the Seattle and Louisville plans, and are based on strong factual records illustrating both the necessity of integration for adequate education and the limited efficacy of race-conscious efforts, they might be upheld by state supreme courts bound by state constitutions that obligate states to provide adequate educational services.[287] Although the plans would still be subject to ultimate review by the Supreme Court, Justice Kennedy might be persuaded to vote in their favor.

Alternately, socioeconomic integration has received renewed attention as a race-neutral plan that would be approved by the Court.[288] Because minorities are disproportionately poor, socioeconomic plans have the potential to address both the racial and economic isolation of majority-minority schools. Their success, however, depends on effective plan designs and district poverty rates low enough to facilitate the creation of middle-class schools. The latter makes the success of such programs less likely in high-poverty urban districts, unless the plans also incorporate the suburbs. The North Carolina Wake County Public School System, with a district-wide poverty rate of only 24 percent, has successfully created middle-class schools[289] that have improved student achievement.[290] In contrast, the Charlotte-Mecklenburg System implemented a transfer policy that allowed a low-income student to transfer to a middle-class school if he or she came from a low-poverty, low-achieving school,[291] but limits on seat availability have impeded the plan's success.[292] Moreover, socioeconomic integration plans do not necessarily create racially and ethnically diverse schools; the Seattle school board realized this when they considered substituting poverty for race in their plan.[293] As such, socioeconomic integration cannot

---

286. *Parents Involved*, 127 S. Ct. at 2792, 2796 (Kennedy, J., concurring in part and concurring in the judgment).

287. Litigators have already successfully obtained desegregation orders motivated by equity concerns by basing suits on state equal protection clauses. In *Sheff v. O'Neill*, 678 A.2d 1267 (Conn. 1996), the Connecticut supreme court concluded that the state failed to satisfy its obligation to provide equal educational opportunity by neglecting to remedy racial and ethnic isolation in the school system.

288. *See e.g.* Jonathan D. Glater & Alan Finder, *Diversity Plans Based on Income Leave Some Schools Segregated*, N.Y. Times, July 15, 2007, at A24; Smrekar, *supra* note 267 (analyzing the feasibility of integration by class).

289. The system assigns students so that no school has more than 40 percent low-income students, and no more than 25 percent low-achieving students . Susan Leigh Flinspach & Karen E. Banks, *Moving Beyond Race: Socioeconomic Diversity as a Race-Neutral Approach to Desegregation in the Wake County Schools, in* School Resegregation: Must the South Turn Back? 261, 270–76 (John Charles Boger & Gary Orfield eds., 2005).

290. The percent of black students in grades three to eight who scored at grade level on state reading tests rose from 40 percent in 1995 to 82 percent in 2006. Glater & Finder, *supra* note 288.

291. Glater & Finder, *supra* note 288.

292. *Id.*

293. The Seattle school board rejected economic disadvantage as a proxy for race, noting that "low-income white students in the north end [of the city] could fill all of the over-subscribed north end schools, and eliminate any opportunity for non-white students in the south end to attend those schools." Brief for Respondents at 41, *Parents Involved in Cmty. Sch. v. Seattle Sch. Dist. No. 1*, 127 S. Ct. 2738 (U.S. 2007) (No. 05-908). The same problem has surfaced in the San Francisco School District, where public schools are resegregating by race and ethnicity despite socioeconomic integration cannot

provide the civic and attitudinal benefits of racial integration, nor will it insulate racially identifiable majority-minority schools from racial bias.

Alternate options, however, are limited, and scholars may be right in suggesting that it is time to support race-neutral plans that are safe from the Court's review.[294] With its latest decision, the Court has maintained its problematic jurisprudence, ignoring the necessity of integration as an input for adequate education of black and Latino children, obstructing all practical efforts to achieve integration, and turning a blind eye to the racial inequity perpetuated by its decisions. For now, the U.S. Supreme Court has all but closed the door on public school integration.

School officials blame two issues for the resegregation: (1) students continue to apply to neighborhood schools, which do not recruit from students outside of their area; and (2) public school students in the city are relatively lower income overall, whatever their race or ethnicity, allowing for socioeconomic integration which does not necessarily produce racial integration. Glater & Finder, *supra* note 288.

294. *See, e.g.* Derrick Bell, *Desegregation's Demise*, CHRON. HIGHER EDUC. (Wash., D.C.), July 13, 2007, at B11(urging civil rights groups to "recognize and support" after-school and supplementary programs that are successfully eliciting academic success from students with poor educational outlooks, "not as a surrender of integration's goals, but as an acknowledgment that flexibility is needed in fulfilling the schooling needs of black and Latino children in today's conservative political landscape."); Eboni S. Nelson, *Parents Involved & Meredith: A Prediction Regarding the (Un)constitutionality of Race-Conscious Student Assignment Plans*, 84 DENV. U. L. REV. 293 (2006) (urging school officials, in light of the Supreme Court's desegregation jurisprudence, to consider race-neutral methods to achieve diversity).

10

No Child Left Behind: Creating and Sustaining a Two-Tiered System of Education for the Nation's Youth

Anita Kuykendall Stoll

The original intent of this essay was to explore some of the ways in which the No Child Left Behind Act (NCLB)[1] is helping address the inequalities in the American educational system. Unfortunately, the awful and embarrassing truth about NCLB is that it is not helping address the inequalities in the American educational system at all. In addition to attempting to bring all students to the same mediocre level of performance, NCLB is compounding the inequity in American schooling by creating a two-tiered system of education.

This system gives schools and those who run them the opportunity to perpetuate the reproduction of cultural inequality. Ironically, this is the same cultural and educational inequality that inspired lawmakers to create NCLB in the first place. NCLB could actually help seal the students it was intended to help in a world of inequality through the very education it seeks to provide. NCLB's intent is to ensure some students receive a functional knowledge of reading, writing and mathematics—basic education that will help them obtain basic, low-level jobs in the future. Other students who fall outside of the parameters of NCLB for whatever reason—attendance at higher-performing schools, for example—are eligible for a broad, in-depth education that will prepare them to be the future leaders. Students who attend lower-performing schools are denied access to an entire facet of their education—primarily the arts (by benevolent policy makers who know best how children learn and how to create a more educated and productive society)—to allow them to spend more time on the subjects that are measured by NCLB, namely, reading and math. With so much of their education neglected, even if these children manage to maintain an interest in education long enough to aspire to a college education, they will arrive at college to find themselves woefully underprepared. They will lack cultural capital—the forms of knowledge, skill, education and other advantages that give a person higher status in society—capital that is passed down in varying degrees from parents to their children and from teacher to student. This capital includes the attitudes and knowledge that makes the educational system a comfortable, familiar place

---

1. No Child Left Behind Act of 2001, 20 U.S.C. § 6301, et seq. (2008).

in which one can succeed easily.[2] They will lack the knowledge of art galleries and concert halls that is transmitted in ways that are not discussed in math problems.

In 2002 George W. Bush shared the secret of his Texas miracle with the rest of the nation. It contained the secret for making all students successful and college bound. It eventually became the blueprint for NCLB. NCLB promised to provide states with strategies and incentives to improve and strengthen the education provided by their public schools. It was heralded by many as the one thing that would bridge the "achievement gap" between black and white, rich and poor; it was presented as a way for all students, especially those in lower-performing schools to obtain a high-quality education. NCLB provided guidelines under which teachers and schools would be held accountable for the education of all of the students, just as similar laws did in the president's home state of Texas. It was not until much later that the nation discovered how unmiraculous NCLB truly was.

The goals of NCLB, to ensure "that all children have a fair and equal and significant opportunity to obtain a high-quality education and reach, at a minimum, proficiency on challenging State academic achievement standards and state academic assessments,"[3] seem reasonable at first glance. What thinking person would not want all students to have the opportunity to obtain a high-quality education? After all, were these not the goals espoused by the likes of Horace Mann, John Dewey and Eleanor Roosevelt? Among a well-educated populace, NCLB would truly be the great equalizer. Through NCLB, the post–"Texas miracle" public schools would be able to erase class boundaries, raise the poor out of the depths of their underachieving schools and place all students on an equal footing.

The measure of whether a school is doing well according to NCLB is called Adequate yearly progress (AYP). Each state determines the parameters of adequate yearly progress within the federal guidelines. Every school is judged on the basis of whether it meets the established benchmarks.

"Adequate yearly progress" shall be defined by the State in a manner that

(i) applies the same high standards of academic achievement to all public elementary school and secondary school students in the State;

(ii) is statistically valid and reliable;

(iii) results in continuous and substantial academic improvement for all students.[4]

This system of measuring improvement sounds so great that there is little wonder why so many people bought into it. AYP data are collected by the state and distributed to the schools for their use in improving the educational services they deliver. For data that will be used to determine the future of thousands of schoolchildren, teachers and administrators, however, they are collected in decidedly unreliable ways. The cohort scores are not compared to each other; one year's scores are compared to the next year. For example, sixth-

---

2. P. Bourdieu, *The Forms of Capital, in* HANDBOOK OF THEORY AND RESEARCH OF THE SOCIOLOGY OF EDUCATION 241(J.G. Richardson, ed. 1986).

3. 20 U.S.C. §9515 (a) (2) (A) (2008) (requiring the director of the Institute for Education Sciences to "identify topics that may require long-term research and topics that are focused on understanding and solving particular education problems and issues, including those associated with the goals and requirements of the Elementary and Secondary Education Act of 1965 (20 U.S.C. 6301 et seq.) [NCLB], the Individuals with Disabilities Education Act (20 U.S.C. 1400 et seq.), and the Higher Education Act of 1965 (20 U.S.C. 1001 et seq.).").

4. 20 U.S.C. §6311 (C) (2008).

grade data from 2007 is compared to sixth-grade data from 2006 and 2005. Such a comparison reveals how sixth-grade classes scored in these years, but these are different cohorts of students. AYP is based on the difference in scores (progress?) of different groups of students from year to year without actually measuring the progress the students themselves have made. If states really wanted to know how well the students were progressing, they would compare the scores of eighth graders in 2007 with their scores from seventh grade in 2006 and sixth grade in 2005. One is left to wonder what exactly NCLB is supposed to measure.

A further problem is that students can actually make progress but still not attain their district's arbitrarily set goal. Their schools are then still considered to be in trouble and must provide a further action plan even though the students have been making progress. School administrators often find themselves making desperate moves to save their schools and staff as well as push these students forward; as a result, even the very students who are making progress often denied access to courses in social studies, science and the visual and performing arts to give them more time to concentrate on reading and math.[5] In fact, however,

> the policy implications of the concept [more academic learning time] are by no means clear. Simply increasing the amount of time students spend in class or on homework may not necessarily translate into more learning. Students may not want to spend more time on schoolwork (or in this case these subjects) and may respond by dropping out or putting in less effort.[6]

The magic NCLB bullet was supposed to close the achievement gap, and this achievement gap could possibly be narrowing—the jury is still out. That magic bullet, however, may be widening the societal gap that occurs when children are denied access to the cultural capital that provides them social mobility and access to the social class privileges that students from higher-performing schools take for granted. Part of the difficulty is that achievement gaps are deeply affected by forces beyond the classroom:

> they are caused by powerful family characteristics that impact children long before they start school and continue to operate throughout their school years. It is possible that school programs can overcome family influences to close achievement gaps, but we have yet to discover how. A school staff cannot simply go to a shelf and find a set of classroom practices that are tested and proven.[7]

NCLB also promised fair and equal access to high quality education by "providing children an enriched and accelerated educational program ... [and] promoting schoolwide reform and ensuring the access of children to effective, scientifically based instructional strategies and challenging academic content."[8] Given this description, one might believe that an enriched program of study would include a curriculum filled with great music, art and opportunities to engage in risk taking through creative expression and hands-on activities. Even according to NCLB, the visual and performing arts are core subjects, courses that are integral to the education of all students and a necessary part of an accelerated and enriched educational program. Students who have the means to attend private schools and who do not have to live up to the NCLB standards are routinely provided with courses

---

5. John Wills, *Putting the Squeeze on Social Studies: Managing Teaching Dilemmas in Subject Areas Excluded from State Testing*, 109 Teachers College Record 1980 (Nov. 8, 2007).

6. Kevin Dougherty and Floyd M. Hammack, Education and Society: A Reader 336 (1990).

7. John B. Diamond & James Spillane, *High-Stakes Accountability in Urban Elementary Schools: Challenging or Reproducing Inequality?*, 106 Teachers College Record 1145 (2004).

8. 20 U.S.C. §6001 (8), (9).

in aesthetics, arts appreciation and performance that challenge them to be both creative risk takers and higher order thinkers.

These were the curricula of which the current policy makers were beneficiaries in their youth. Now, however, having so benefited, these same policy makers are quick to find those educational opportunities that served them so well to be outdated and irrelevant to students living in a modern world. For those students who attend schools that may be making progress but not living up to their district's NCLB goals, the focus on reading and math crowds out access to courses in the visual and performing arts, as well as science and social studies—key sources of the cultural capital policy makers themselves enjoyed.[9]

The race to produce acceptable NCLB test scores has left many public schools, especially those with high populations of low socioeconomic status and minority students who traditionally perform lower on these tests, doing a schizophrenic dance in which their desperation to achieve higher test scores has overcome their desire to provide all children with a comprehensive education. These districts are singing the praises of arts education on one hand, while systematically cutting the hours students are given access to the arts, science and social studies in elementary schools, and offering fewer aesthetic elective courses in middle schools. In some schools, the only electives that are available even to the high-performing students are subjects like double math and remedial reading. Aesthetic classes still appear on the books, but fewer and fewer students are actually granted access to them.

To make AYP, many schools seem to be under a constant barrage of academic remediation, an assault on the low test scores of students. They attack this low performance as if it were a cancer, but with so many different strategies that it might not be possible for any of them to take hold. Students who are reluctant readers are often deluged with more and more reading, in addition to propaganda and photos of famous people reading. Reading is good; but at some point, more reading is not necessarily better. In fact,

> the National Research Council's publication "Starting Out Right" warns that after several days of too many hours of reading every day, the reading experience might well start to become distasteful for a child.[10]

Nevertheless, extended day programs are used to provide after-school reading and math help. School day classes offer Corrective Reading, Read 180, double period algebra, math support pullout for students who almost get it,[11] extra reading time to instill a love of reading in the students, practice exams—given during the year but prior to the actual exam. Volumes of data, data, data are collected by teachers to be analyzed so they can structure their lessons to better accommodate their students' deficits.

Ironically, in this scatter shot style of remediation, the really needy kids, the kids who have little to no understanding of the content and who struggle in school, often do not receive sustained attention. Rather, it is "bubble" kids (students who score ten points lower or ten points higher than proficient on NCLB tests) who are targeted for the remedial help because "they have the best chances of gaining a few extra points that might put the school over the AYP mark."[12]

---

9. Wills, *supra* note 5, at 1980; Diamond & Spillane, *supra* note 7, at 1145.

10. Dee Hansen & Elaine Bernstorf, *Linking Music Learning to Reading Instruction*, MUSIC EDU-CATORS JOURNAL, March 2006, at 17.

11. Diamond & Spillane, *supra* note 7, at 1145.

12. Diamond & Spillane, *supra* note 7, at 1145.

One unintended consequence of NCLB is that everything that is not specifically tested is devalued, making the transmission of cultural capital from teachers to students almost nonexistent.

> Often schools use [additional] funds to acquire a model reading program. Research that supports some of these models finds that test scores have improved when students are provided more reading time and a lower teacher-pupil ratio. No one denies that these efforts are well intentioned; however, music educators (as well as art and physical education teachers) sometimes find that their instructional time is squeezed or even eliminated. Some arts educators have even been asked to teach reading or to have their students read texts that do not support the arts curriculum. As a result, the intensity of the reading instructions sometimes supersedes learning in other curriculum areas.[13]

Unfortunately, NCLB is creating a nation where students who have the misfortune to attend schools that do not meet the arbitrary AYP standards are further penalized by being denied access to courses in the arts that would go a long way in producing the cultural capital these students will need to succeed in college and in educated society.

One must ask, then, whether power and ideology are really the central theme of the achievement debate. Perhaps we should examine more closely the motives of those who advocate "success" in math and reading to the detriment of experiences that create valuable cultural capital. Countless issues of upscale magazines have chronicled the merits of providing children with instruction in music, as well as the connections between music instruction and mathematical knowledge. Policy makers who pretend to know what is best for students in low-performing schools are either not reading these articles or are pretending that isolating and marginalizing the students who achieve low scores on state mandated tests will somehow help these students accomplish much more.

In an interview with secretary of Education Spellings, the 2007 National Teacher of the Year Andrea Peterson (probably not so coincidentally a music teacher) spoke of the value of music education in helping uphold the standards of NCLB.[14] She gave the example of going to the Washington Symphony on Education Day and witnessing firsthand the teamwork, focus and concentration that was required of students who participate in ensemble music classes.[15] What she failed to mention is Symphony Day no more teaches children about how to create, perform and think about music than a day at the art museum teaches them how to paint. As one art professor has pointed out, "Children who have not learned how to see and mentally explore the various forms of arts and science will not be able to write, not because they cannot spell, but because they have nothing to say, nothing to reconstruct from sensory exploration of the environment."[16]

Art Day or Music Day or the International Festival and Family Science Night are not meant to replace an adequate program of studies in these areas. Symphony Day teaches students that other people work together to make music; unfortunately, the students will never be able to work together to make music; they will be too busy trying to make AYP.

It is true that one must be a good reader to be successful in many classes; but reading and math, although the most tested subjects, are not the only subjects one must know to

---

13. Hansen & Bernstorf, *supra* note 10, at 17.

14. Interview by U.S. Secretary of Education Margaret Spellings with Andrea Peterson, Teacher of the Year, May 2007, www.ed.gov/news/av/video/2007/ntoty.html (last visited March 22, 2008).

15. *Id.*

16. Hansen & Bernstorf, *supra* note 10, at 17.

be a contributing member of American society. Educational systems have a powerful ability to track students into high, medium and low tiers. That sort of tracking occurs through NCLB when students are denied access to some classes to provide them with more time to concentrate on subjects that are tested, as if the only knowledge that is ever transmitted in life comes from material that is measured and documented. If the children in the higher-performing or private schools are the only students who have access to information about music art and social studies, what kind of society are we creating? Should not every student, regardless of reading ability, have at least a nodding acquaintance with Mozart, Gauguin and Twyla Tharp? An education devoid of aesthetic value is a very dry education indeed.

When music programs are sacrificed to provide greater attention to reading, "students will be deprived of kinesthetic, aural, oral, visual and emotional experiences that can ultimately bring written texts to life."[17] Even if these children are finally able to access higher education as a result of their remedial training, they will still be at a distinct disadvantage in their adult lives because they heard Mozart only on "Symphony Day," and they never got to sing or draw at all. By blindly supporting NCLB without questioning the way impacts students in schools that do not make AYP, this nation is aiding and abetting the creation of a two-tiered society that will only compound the inequity that already exists.

---

17. Hansen & Bernstorf, *supra* note 10, at 17.

11

Accountability Charter Schools

Danielle Holley-Walker

Introduction

Charter schools will play an increasingly important role in the "New Accountability" reforms symbolized most prominently by the No Child Left Behind Act (NCLB). New Accountability is the basic premise that public schools in the United States where students are failing to meet expectations on standardized tests will be improved through structural changes. Those structural changes include removing local public schools from the control of a local school district to be managed by the state. NCLB provides that states should adopt accountability measures for public schools whose students fail to meet adequate yearly progress (AYP) on standardized tests toward the goal of students being proficient in both reading and math. The NCLB accountability measures include making supplemental educational services available to students, allowing student transfers, and even closing a failing public school to have it reopened as a charter school. My chapter argues that these New Accountability measures will lead to an increasing number of charter schools opening to replace failed traditional public schools.

As more states take over failing public schools from local school districts, the state will be have the daunting task of determining how to operate local public schools on a day-to-day basis. Faced with this challenge, some states will inevitably choose to rely on the charter school model. Charter schools are generally defined as public schools of choice operated under a (charter) contract issued by a public entity such as the state board of education or a local school board. These legally and fiscally autonomous schools are given public dollars per pupil, but have broad based autonomy including control over curriculum, school policy, and the hiring of teacher and administrators.

Charter schools acting as replacements for failed traditional public schools is already a reality in several school systems. For example, the Louisiana legislature passed the Recovery School District Act (RSDA) in 2003 to comply with NCLB Under the RSDA, a school failing to meet AYP for four years will be operated under the auspices of the state Recovery School District (RSD). Prior to Hurricane Katrina over 60 of the 116 public schools in New Orleans were taken over by the RSD. After Hurricane Katrina the Louisiana legislature expanded the jurisdiction of the RSD, leading to 107 of the 116 New Orleans public schools being operated by the state. In the new RSD-helmed New Orleans public school system, 60 percent of the fifty-seven reopened public schools are charter schools. These charter schools are a consequence of the aggressive RSDA accountability measures.

Though New Orleans is an extreme example due to the exceptional circumstances produced by Hurricane Katrina, "accountability charter schools" are emerging in other cities, such as Baltimore. The term "accountability charter schools" acknowledges that these new charter schools stray from the initial policy values underlying the charter school model. The original policy justifications for charter schools were to allow more choice for parents and students within the public school system. The autonomous nature of the charter school was intended to allow charter school operators to experiment with innovative educational methods.

Charter schools that are founded to take the place of failing public schools, like New Orleans's post–Hurricane Katrina charter schools, have a decidedly different purpose. The main purpose of these charter schools is to privatize a failing public school system. A state department of education is able to shift the responsibility for operating a failing public school into the hands of a charter operator and allow that charter operator the authority to improve the school.

This accountability charter school model shifts away from the initial charter school policy goals of choice and autonomy. Although there is the potential these charter schools will be able to create a fundamental paradigm shift for a struggling traditional public school system, there have also been serious questions raised as to the overall effectiveness of charter schools in improving student achievement.

I. New Accountability

New Accountability education reform policies are an outgrowth of standards-based education reform in which states or local school districts set forth what all students should know in certain subjects and utilize standardized tests to assess whether students are meeting those standards.[1] New Accountability reforms are those that reward or punish schools, teachers, and school boards based on student performance on these assessments.[2] Accountability measures include a variety of different actions, typically beginning with issuing reports to parents and the general public on the performance of schools on the yearly assessments, development of school improvement plans, and a series of escalating sanctions for schools that fail to meet performance targets. These sanctions include allowing student transfer, dismissal of teachers and administrators, state takeover, and school closure.[3]

The federal NCLB has become the most visible and arguably most significant of the New Accountability reforms. NCLB's stated purpose is to "ensure that all children have

---

1. *See* William Koski & Rob Reich, *When Adequate Isn't: The Retreat From Equity in Educational Law and Policy and Why It Matters*, 56 Emory L.J. 545, 577 (2006) (explaining the three primary elements in the standards-based reform strategy).

2. *See id.* at 578 (describing new accountability reforms including publishing school-wide performance on standards-based assessments, providing commendations to successful schools, offering failing schools technical assistance, and the option of state takeover or school closure for persistently failing schools).

3. *See* James S. Liebman & Charles F. Sabel, *The Federal No Child Left Behind Act and the Post-Desegregation Civil Rights Agenda*, 81 N. C. L. Rev. 1703, 1712–14 (2003) (detailing various New Accountability measures including reporting systems that publicize student outcomes on tests and disaggregate the data to highlight results for minority students and limited English proficiency students).

a fair, equal and significant opportunity to obtain a high-quality education."[4] Under NCLB all states are required to set academic content standards in reading, math, and eventually in science. States must then administer yearly assessments to determine whether students are meeting these academic standards.[5] NCLB further mandates state accountability measures to insure that students at each public school meet AYP toward the goal of all students being proficient in reading and math.[6]

NCLB requires states to designate schools where students fail to meet AYP as in need of "improvement, corrective action or restructuring."[7] A school that fails to meet AYP for two successive years is designated as in need of "improvement." After two additional failing years the schools is deemed to be in need of "corrective action." A school that fails to meet AYP for five successive years is marked for "restructuring." NCLB directs states to adopt escalating sanctions for each of these designations.[8] These sanctions include providing supplemental educational services for students, allowing students to transfer to other schools, replacing staff and administrators, state takeover, or reopening the school as a charter school.[9] Since the enactment of NCLB, it is estimated that over 2,000 schools have failed to make AYP for five years and are thus marked for restructuring.[10]

One consequence of NCLB and state New Accountability reforms is the shrinking power and autonomy of local school districts.[11] NCLB's requirement of statewide standards means less individualized curriculum across local school districts, and the pressure of yearly standardized testing results in more uniformity in the classroom because many educators begin to "teach to the test" to ensure student success on the yearly evaluations.[12] Also inherent in the concept of accountability is the fact that failing schools and school districts will be punished for failure.[13] As one observer has noted: "accountability sanctions are designed to curtail or eliminate local power. The ultimate sanction is disestab-

---

4. No Child Left Behind Act of 2001, 20 U.S.C. § 6301 (Supp. III 2003).

5. NCLB, 20 U.S.C. § 6301(1) (stating that the statute's goals will be met by "ensuring that high-quality academic assessments, accountability systems, teacher preparation and training, curriculum, and instructional materials are aligned with challenging State academic standards so that students, teachers, parents, and administrators can measure progress against common expectations for student achievement.").

6. *Id.* § 6311(b)(2)(A) (Supp. IV 2004) ("Each State plan shall demonstrate that the State has developed and is implementing a single, statewide, State accountability system that will be effective in ensuring that all local educational agencies, public elementary schools, and public secondary schools make adequate yearly progress as defined under this paragraph.").

7. Danielle Holley-Walker, *The Accountability Cycle: The Recovery School District Act and New Orleans' Charter Schools*, 40:1 Conn. L. Rev. 1, 15 (2007) [hereafter Holley-Walker, *Accountability Cycle*](citing 20 U.S.C. § 6316(b)(1)(D)).

8. *See* 20 U.S.C. § 6316(b)(1)(E)(I) (detailing the options for "improvement" schools); *id.* § 6316(b)(7)(C) (explaining the options for "corrective action" schools); *id.* § 6316(b)(8) (detailing the consequences for schools in need of "restructuring").

9. *See* Holley-Walker, *Accountability Cycle*, *supra* note 7, at 16 (noting that since NCLB states have adopted four major alternatives for schools restructuring: reopening the school as a charter school, replacing staff, entering into a contract for a private management company to operate the school, and takeover by the state educational agency).

10. *See* Claudia Wells & Sonja Steptoe, *How to Fix No Child Left Behind*, Time, May 27, 2007, at 10.

11. *See* Aaron Jay Saiger, *The Last Wave: The Rise of the Contingent School District*, 84 N. C. L. Rev. 857, 875 (2006) [hereafter Saiger, *The Last Wave*] (describing the way that NCLB restricts school district autonomy).

12. *See id.* at 876–77.

13. Aaron Jay Saiger, *Legislating Accountability: Standards, Sanctions, and School District Reform*, 46 Wm. & Mary L. Rev. 1655, 1659 (2005).

lishment: the school board and superintendent in a district failing persistently are unseated, and authority over all school matters reverts to the states."[14]

One direct challenge to local school district monopoly and power is the growing presence of charter schools. NCLB explicitly contemplates that one option for students in a failing traditional public schools is transfer to a public charter schools.[15] State boards of education faced with the reality of a growing number of failed traditional public schools may decide to allow the creation of more new charter schools, thus increasing the number of charter schools that are options for parents whose children attend failing or underperforming schools.

Some scholars argue that charter schools are a necessary and vital alternative to the traditional local school district oversight model. According to one observer, local school districts and traditional public schools have proven to be highly bureaucratized institutions that have failed to adequately serve poor children and stigmatized minorities and thus are in need of dramatic reforms, such as the charter school model.[16] Others have noted that the presence of charter schools destroys a school district's monopoly in the market of public education, and puts direct pressure on traditional public schools to improve student outcomes or face the desertion of students and state dollars to the growing number of charter schools.[17] These arguments make it clear that charter schools are an integral element of New Accountability reforms and the broader standards-based education reform movement.

II. The Charter School Model

A charter school is a public school that operates with greater autonomy than a traditional public school.[18] The charter school operator is granted a charter (contract) by a public entity with chartering authority, typically a state board of education, a local school board, or public university to operate for an initial period of typically three to five years with the option for renewal.[19] The theory of the charter school bargain is that the charter school operators are given more autonomy in exchange for greater accountability.[20] The charter school model is also defined by choice, the proposition that the school is opted into by administrators, teachers, and parents.

The first charter school legislation was passed in Minnesota in 1991.[21] Since that time, forty-one states have adopted charter school legislation and there are over 3,000 charter

---

14. *Id.*

15. *See* 20 U.S.C. § 6316(b)(1)(E)(I) (stating that any local school that fails to meet AYP for two years should provide all students enrolled in that school with the option of transfer to another public school including a "public charter school").

16. *See* Shavar D. Jeffries, *The Structural Inadequacy of Public Schools for Stigmatized Minorities: The Need for Institutional Remedies*, 34 Hastings Const. L. Q. 1, 5–6 (2006).

17. *See, e.g.,* Saiger, *The Last Wave, supra* note 11, at 883.

18. *See* Katherine E. Buckley & Priscilla Wohlstetter, *Introduction* to Taking Account of Charter Schools: What's Happened and What's Next? 1, 1 (Katherine E. Bulkley & Priscilla Wohlstetter eds., 2004).

19. *See id.*

20. *See generally,* William Haft, *Charter Schools and Nineteenth Century Corporation: A Match Made in the Public Interest*, 30 Ariz. St. L. J. 1023, 1035 (1998) (explaining that in exchange for greater independence charter school legislation typically requires evidence that students are meeting certain benchmarks).

21. Joe Nathan, *Minnesota and the Charter Public School Idea*, in The Charter School Landscape 17, 21 (Sandra Vergari ed., 2002).

schools in operation.[22] Although charter school legislation is created on a state-by-state basis, the federal government has provided financial support for charter schools since the passage of the federal Public Charter Schools Program Act in 1994.[23] The initial federal appropriation for charter schools was $6 million in 1994 and grew to $200 million by 2001.[24] The U.S. Department of Education strongly supports increasing the number of charter schools in operation.[25]

Since its inception, the charter school model has been evaluated and analyzed by legal scholars and education policy experts. These experts focus on several key values that underlie the charter school model: choice, autonomy, and accountability. Charter school legislation also emphasizes these values.[26] I discuss these values and themes to highlight in Part III some of the key differences in the accountability charter school model.

A. Choice

The charter school model is part of the larger school choice movement. School choice includes a variety of reforms such as publicly funded vouchers that fund parents sending their children to private schools, tax credits for private school tuition, and allowing parents to choose to enroll their students in public schools across school district lines.[27] Charter schools are perhaps the most popular of the school choice reforms and are supported across partisan lines and by communities of diverse racial and ethnic backgrounds.[28] In fact, some estimates are that charter schools are disproportionately attended by minority students.[29]

Many observers note that the element of choice may the greatest strength of the charter school model. Parents, teachers, and administrators are committed to the school in a collaborative process in which they have the common goal of successful student outcomes.[30] Also, some common complaints about traditional public schools, such as lack of parental involvement, are addressed directly in the charter school model. For example, many charter schools require parents to sign parental contracts in which they commit to ensuring student attendance, assisting with homework, and reading to their children outside of school hours.[31]

---

22. Walker Richmond, *Charter School Accountability: Rhetoric, Results, and Ramifications*, 12 VA. J. SOC. POL'Y & L. 330 (2004) [hereafter Richmond, *Charter School Accountability*].

23. Sandra Vergari, *Introduction* to THE CHARTER SCHOOL LANDSCAPE 1, 2 (Sandra Vergari ed., 2002) [hereafter Vergari, *Introduction*].

24. *Id.* at 2.

25. *See* Press Release, Dep't of Educ., No Child Left Behind and Charter Schools: Giving Parents Information and Options (May 2007), *available at* www.ed.gvo/print/nclb/choice/nclb-charter.html ("President Bush and Margaret Spellings are committed to charter schools open in every state.").

26. *See, e.g.,* La. Rev. Stat. Ann. § 17:3972(A) (stating that charter schools should be authorized to allow for the implementation of innovative educational programs and to determine whether these experiments produce positive results and should be replicated); Md. Educ. Code Ann. § 9-101 (stating that charter schools are intended to allow innovative learning opportunities and educational practices).

27. *See* Wendy Parker, *The Color of Choice: Race and Charter Schools*, 75 TUL. L. REV. 563, 564–65 (2001) [hereafter Parker, *The Color of Choice*].

28. *Id.* at 567.

29. *Id.* at 569.

30. *See* Richmond, *Charter School Accountability*, *supra* note 22, at 358–59 (documenting studies in which charter school parents, teachers, and administrators report greater input and satisfaction than the same groups in traditional public schools).

31. *Id.* at 359.

B. Autonomy

Charter schools have autonomy in most of the significant areas of school management. One question for charter schools has been whether this greater amount of independence actually improves instruction or student outcomes.[32] Educational policy experts point to three areas of charter school autonomy that are necessary for influencing instruction: budget, personnel, and educational issues such as curriculum.[33]

Priscilla Wohlstetter and Derrick Chau have studied the importance of budget autonomy to improved instruction in the charter school model. These authors point to studies that note that budget autonomy allows school administrators to identify the most important materials needed for instruction and to focus the school's resources on obtaining those materials.[34] Also, budgetary independence allows the charter school flexibility to redirect resources into the areas it is most needed.[35] When charter schools are able to raise money from external resources beyond the state provided per pupil spending the charter school operator is able to focus its fundraising efforts on specific instructional areas, such as purchasing computers for science and math instruction.[36]

Autonomy as to personnel may allow charter schools to hire teachers and administrators that do not have traditional teaching credentials, but provide expertise and skill sets thought to be crucial to instruction. Also, personnel in charter schools may be used to support student assessment outside of the yearly state testing.

Autonomy is thought to be key to the charter school model to allow charter schools to act as laboratories for innovative educational methodology and practices.[37] Many charter school advocates argue that successful innovations that originate in charter schools eventually may be adopted in traditional public schools.[38] Many charter school operators do take advantage of deregulation to implement innovative policies such as longer school days and Saturday school.[39] Charter schools may also pick a curricular focus, such as arts education as a theme to attract students and teachers to the schools. Finally, a segment of charter schools employ cultural focuses, such as an emphasis on African-American culture and history, in an effort to improve educational outcomes if their students are from a particular racial or cultural background.[40]

---

32. *See* Priscilla Wohlstetter & Derrick Chau, *Does Autonomy Matter? Implementing Research-Based Practices in Charter and Other Public Schools, in* Taking Account of Charter Schools: What's Happened and What's Next? 53, 54 (Katrina E. Bulkley & Priscilla Wohlstetter eds., 2004).

33. *Id.* at 55.

34. *See id.* at 65.

35. *See id.* at 66.

36. *Id.*

37. *See* Vergari, *Introduction, supra* note 23, at 2.

38. Sandra Vergari, *Conclusions* to The Charter School Landscape 253, 254–55 (Sandra Vergari ed., 2002).

39. *See, e.g.,* Martin Carnoy, et al., The Charter School Dust Up: Examining the Evidence On Achievement and Enrollment 51 (2005) [hereafter Carnoy, *The Charter School Dustup*] (describing the KIPP (Knowledge is Power program) charter school program including the longer school day and Saturday classes, and noting that KIPP is widely heralded as the most successful charter school model in the United States).

40. *See, e.g.,* John B. King Jr., *Fulfilling the Hope of* Brown v. Board of Education *Through Charter Schools, in* The Emancipatory Promise of Charter Schools: Towards a Progressive Politics of School Choice 55, 61–66 (Eric E. Rofes & Lisa M. Stulberg eds., 2004) (describing the success of Roxbury Preparatory Charter School, a majority African American charter school in Boston).

C. Accountability

As noted, the basic bargain of the charter school model is that charter school operators are given increased autonomy but are more accountable than the traditional public school. This bargain comes from the chartering process itself, which gives the charter school the ability to operate for an initial period of typically three to five years provided the school meets the requirements of its charter and applicable state law.[41] Most state charter statutes require a charter school operator applicant to set forth specific plans and goals regarding enrollment, personnel, and curriculum to have the charter application approved.[42] Most state charter statutes also provide for some annual review to ensure that charter operators are complying with the charter. These yearly reviews generally focus on budgetary matters and the state ensuring that the school has conducted the proper financial audits.[43] At the end of the initial three- or five-year chartering period, most states conduct a more thorough review of charter compliance, including assessing student performance and facility maintenance and reviewing any complaints against the charter school by teachers or parents.[44]

III. The Accountability Charter School Model

In this section I detail the emergence of what I term "accountability charter schools." Accountability charter schools are granted charters in an effort to replace failed traditional public schools. This phenomena is occurring because New Accountability reforms, such as NCLB, are forcing states to take over the day-to-day management of public schools from the local school districts. One way for state educational agencies to address this new burden is to approve more charter schools to assist in filling the void of the failed traditional public schools. The three major identifiers of accountability charter schools are (1) a local school district that has a significant number of failed traditional public schools under a New Accountability law; (2) the New Accountability statute puts a state board of education in control of filling the void for failed public schools in that school district; and (3) the state board of education approves charter school applications in greater numbers in the local area. This section provides three examples of emergence of accountability charter schools from California, New Orleans, and Baltimore. Part IV examines why this accountability charter school model differs significantly from the traditional charter school model detailed in Part II.

A. California

California provides an important example of a precursor to the accountability charter school model. California passed the second charter school statute in the United States

---

41. *See* Parker, *The Color of Choice, supra* note 27, at 576.

42. *See id.*

43. *See generally,* Judith Johnson & Alex Medler, *The Conceptual and Practical Development of Charter Schools,* 11 Stan. L. & Pol'y Rev. 291, 296 (2000) (discussing the various criteria on which charter schools are evaluated and concluding that school finances are the area most frequently subjected to external review).

44. *See generally id.* at 296 (noting that research on charter schools reveals that the review and renewal processes vary in many states and are unclear about the standards that should be applied).

in 1992.[45] The California legislation contemplates that charter schools may become a direct alternative to a traditional public school. The statute provides for a "conversion" charter school in which a traditional public school is converted to a charter school after a vote by a majority of the school administrators, teachers, and parents.[46] While the conversion charter school provision does not specify that a traditional public school may only be converted if that school is not meeting statewide student performance goals, in reality many of the California conversion charter schools are converted from underperforming traditional public schools. One defining feature of the California charter school law that makes it unlike the accountability charter school model I describe in New Orleans and Baltimore, is that generally local school districts, not the state department of education, are the chartering authority.[47] Despite this key distinction, the California conversion charter schools are an important example of the way that pressures on a traditional public schools system may lead to the proliferation of charter schools.

The *UCLA Charter School Study* documents the history and performance of charter schools in ten school districts in California.[48] The study includes information on charter schools in five large urban school districts.[49] The study notes that in these large urban school districts, such as the Mission Unified School District, many of the conversion charter schools were created in low-income areas where the schools serve mostly African American and Latino students.[50] Parents and educators involved in these conversion charter schools believe that shedding the traditional public school regulations will allow them to have more influence and input into the management of the school toward the goal of increasing student achievement.[51]

One of the most important findings of the *UCLA Charter School Study* is that the premise that charter schools will be more accountable than traditional public schools due to the charter authorization and review process is not a simple proposition.[52] The study found that accountability problems are especially prevalent in large urban school districts where the traditional public schools are underperforming on state assessments.[53] The study notes that poor student performance makes the local school district more politically vulnerable and susceptible to anti–public school ideology.[54] When the local school district is the chartering authority, these political pressures mean that a politically unpopular school district may be responsible for holding a more popular charter school accountable.[55] The community essentially tells the local school district to get out of the way of char-

---

45. Amy Stuart Wells, *Introduction* to Where Charter School Policy Fails: The Problems of Accountability and Equity 1, 21 (Amy Stuart Wells ed., 2002).

46. *See id.*

47. *See id.* (explaining that in the original California charter law only local school districts could grant charters, but even after various legislative amendments allowing the state board of education to become a chartering authority the vast number of charters are granted by local entities).

48. *Id.* at 18.

49. *See* Sibyll Carnochan, *Reinventing Government: What Urban School Districts can Learn From Charter Schools*, in Where Charter School Policy Fails: The Problems of Accountability and Equity 54, 58 (Amy Stuart Wells ed., 2002).

50. *See id.* at 59.

51. *See id.* at 62.

52. *See* Amy Stuart Wells et al., *The Politics of Accountability: California School Districts and Charter School Reform* in Where Charter School Policy Fails: The Problems of Accountability and Equity 29, 30–31 (Amy Stuart Wells ed., 2002).

53. *See id.* at 34.

54. *See id.* at 32–33.

55. *See id.* at 34.

ter school, because the charter school is a symbol of reform.[56] Local school district officials noted that political pressure made it difficult to deny a carter school application, even if the proposal is based on unsound educational policy, because the school board has no leverage to respond to community pressure to establish the new charter school.[57]

The example of the California conversion charter schools presents a few crucial insights into the interaction between New Accountability measures and charter schools. First, New Accountability policies, such as NCLB, that inform parents and the larger community about student performance on yearly statewide assessments may undermine the credibility and authority of a local school board if the school district is underperforming on assessments.[58] Thus, even if the underperformance doesn't result in extreme sanctions such as school closures or disestablishment of the local school district, accountability measures may erode confidence in the local school board.

Furthermore, in these school districts that are under attack, charter schools will be seen as positive alternatives. Even when the local school district is the chartering authority, the local school district and the charter schools may be seen by some members of the public as mutually exclusive educational alternatives. This scenario guarantees that charter schools will continue to be seen as a key component to educational reform.

The California charter school example also demonstrates that the notion of charter school accountability is not an objective, neutral concept. A chartering authority responsible for reviewing charter schools and holding them accountable may be subject to political pressure to allow the charter school to continue despite evidence of noncompliance with the charter or unsound educational practices. Of course, some of the worries about charter school accountability are answered by the fact that like other public schools charter schools are subject to the same NCLB-mandated statewide assessments and accountability measures.

B. New Orleans

New Orleans provides the paradigmatic example of the emergence of the accountability charter school model. In the wake of Hurricane Katrina, New Orleans has become the first majority charter school public school system in the United States. In the 2006–2007 school year thirty-two of the fifty-four schools open in New Orleans are charter schools.

Even prior to the hurricanes the New Orleans public schools were in crisis. Less than 25 percent of New Orleans's elementary schools had a majority of students who achieved basic proficiency in math and English.[59] These low levels of performance continued through high school, when only 35 percent of students taking the Graduate Exit Exam were found proficient in English and math.[60] Beyond these dismal student achievement statistics, the school system suffered rampant corruption and financial mismanagement. The public schools were $265 million in debt, seven schools were forced to close due to funding problems, and $52 million in additional revenue was needed just to bring the school buildings up to local building code standards.[61]

---

56. *See id.*

57. *See id.*

58. *See generally*, Saiger, *The Last Wave, supra* note 11, at 874–76 (describing the influence that New Accountability reforms have on a local school district's reputation).

59. Holley-Walker, *Accountability Cycle, supra* note 7, at 1.

60. *See id.*

61. *Id.* at 9.

In response to NCLB, the Louisiana legislature passed the Recovery School District Act (RSDA) in 2003.[62] Under the RSDA, any public school that fails to meet AYP for four consecutive years is subject to state take over; placed under the auspices of the Recovery School District (RSD).[63] After the hurricane the Orleans Parish school board said that they would be unable to reopen the New Orleans public schools for the 2005–2006 school year.[64] To give the state the authority to fill this void and operate the public schools the Louisiana legislature amended the RSDA.[65] The definition of a "failed" school was amended to include any school where a majority of students scored below the state average and were operated in school districts designated as being in "Academic Crisis."[66] As a result of this new definition, 107 of the 116 schools previously under the authority Orleans Parish School District were transferred to the RSD.[67]

The RSD stated that the hurricane presented "a once-in-a-lifetime opportunity to create a fundamentally better public education system in New Orleans."[68] Faced with the task of actually operating enough public schools to serve the needs of returning students, the RSD has relied heavily on charter schools.[69] At the beginning of the 2006–2007 school year there were only seventeen traditional public schools overseen by the RSD, in comparison to thirty-two charter schools.[70]

The most prevalent type of charter school currently operating in New Orleans is the Type 5 charter school.[71] Under the Louisiana charter school statute, a Type 5 charter is granted by the Louisiana State Board of Elementary and Secondary Education (BESE) and overseen by the RSD.[72] The RSDA states that once a failed traditional public school is controlled by the RSD, the school may be closed and reopened as a charter school.[73]

Though a Type 5 charter school is deregulated in much the same manner as other charter schools as to curriculum, personnel, and other educational policy, these charter schools do have additional restrictions.[74] For example, in Type 5 charter schools after two years there must be state-certified teacher in each core subject.[75] These additional restrictions indicate that the Type 5 charter schools that serve as replacements for traditional public schools are a distinctive charter school model.

C. Baltimore

Maryland enacted its first charter school legislation in 2003.[76] Similar to other states that have passed charter school laws, the Maryland statute states that the purpose of the

62. LA. REV. STAT. ANN. § 17:10.5(A) (2007).
63. LA. REV. STAT. ANN. § 17:10.5(A) (1) (d) (2007).
64. Holley-Walker, *Accountability Cycle, supra* note 7, at 10.
65. *Id.*
66. *Id.*
67. *Id.* at 11.
68. *Id.*
69. *Id.*
70. *Id.*
71. *Id.* at 13.
72. *Id.*
73. *Id.*
74. *Id.*
75. *Id.* at 13, note 89.
76. *See* MD. STATE DEP'T OF EDUCATION, AN EVALUATION OF THE MARYLAND CHARTER SCHOOL PROGRAM 3 (2006), *available at* www.marylandpublicschools.org/NR/rdonlyres/1CEB8910-211A-

charter schools is to "establish an alternative means within the existing public school system in order to provide innovative learning opportunities and creative educational approaches to improve the education of students."[77] Although the stated focus of the law is on innovation, in its first few years of implementation most of the charter schools in the state have opened in Baltimore, a city notorious for its struggling public school system. Of the twenty-three charter schools that have opened in Maryland since 2003, sixteen were opened in Baltimore.[78] There were an additional six charter schools opening in Baltimore in the 2007–2008 school year.[79]

Many of the Baltimore charter schools meet the definition of an accountability charter school. First, Baltimore has many traditional public schools that are in need of "restructuring" as defined by the Maryland accountability statute. As mandated by NCLB, Maryland's accountability statute, the Maryland School Improvement Program (MSIP), requires schools to meet annual targets in reading and math.[80] If these annual targets are not met, the MSIP has a five step accountability program.[81] If a school fails to meet its targets in the same subject for five years it is subject to "restructuring planning," and if the school fails for six consecutive years it is subject to "restructuring implementation."[82] Restructuring involves at least one of the following options: replacing all or most of the school staff, contracting with a management company to operate the school, reopening the school as a public charter school, and continuing to allow student transfer and supplemental education services.[83] As of the 2006–2007 school year there were forty-three Baltimore schools in need of restructuring.[84]

Due to these MSIP restructuring provisions, it is not surprising that Maryland charter schools have become an alternative to the failed traditional public schools. The Maryland charter school statute, like the California charter school law, allows for the creation of both new and "conversion" charter schools.[85] Conversion charter schools are defined as "any type of public school that existed prior to the charter school law and has since become a charter school."[86] Over half of the charter schools in Baltimore were converted from already existing public schools.[87]

47E0-909F-C452B3A76CAB/11238/CSProgramEval.pdf [hereafter An Evaluation of the Maryland Charter School Program].

77. *Id.* at 5.

78. *See* Md. State Dep't of Education, Maryland's Public Charter School Program: Providing High Quality Choices in Public Education 6 (2006), *available at* www.maryland publicschools.org [hereafter Maryland's Public Charter School Program].

79. *Id.* at 17.

80. *See* Md. State Dep't of Education, Schools in Improvement, Corrective Action, Restructuring: Fact Sheet 64 1 (2006), *available at* www.marylandpublicschools.org [hereafter Schools in Improvement].

81. *Id.* (schools failing to meet AYP are designated depending on the number of years of noncompliance as "school improvement year 1," "school improvement year 2," "corrective action," "restructuring planning," and "restructuring implementation.")

82. *Id.*

83. *Id.* at 2.

84. Md. State Dep't of Education, Title I Schools identified for Improvement, Corrective Action, Restructuring (in 2006–07 based on the data from 2005–06) (2007), *available at* www.marylandpublicschools.org/NR/rdonlyres/0146EDA2-5491-47DD [hereafter Schools Identified For Improvement].

85. Md. Educ. Code Ann. §9-102(4). The primary chartering authority is the county board of education. Md. Educ. Code Ann. §9-103.

86. Maryland's Public Charter School Program, *supra* note 78, at 6.

87. *Id.*

New Orleans and Baltimore represent two school systems where the application of New Accountability measures is resulting in a growing number of charter schools to replace failed traditional public schools. These accountability charter schools are an increasingly important element in the landscape of education reform.

IV. Evaluating Accountability Charter Schools

New Accountability reforms at the state level as mandated NCLB are causing a shift in some cities from a traditional charter school model to an accountability charter school model. The increasing numbers of charter schools that are created solely to ease the burden on states that must fill the void of failed traditional public schools previously managed by local school districts will have a significant impact on education reform in many cities.

A. Accountability Charter Schools and Student Achievement

There will likely be increasing pressure on these accountability charter schools to demonstrate gains in student achievement. One of the most robust debates surrounding charter schools is whether these schools are able to improve student outcomes. Some recent statistics raise serious doubts about the positive impact of charter schools on student performance on standardized tests. The National Center for Education Statistics gathers information on the national performance of charter school students based on the National Association of Educational Progress (NAEP) test results.[88] The 2004 and 2006 summaries of NAEP data reveal that fourth-graders in traditional public schools are performing better on reading and math standardized tests than students in charter schools.[89] Additionally, a group of educational policy experts who examined nineteen different studies from eleven states and the District of Columbia concluded that "there is no evidence that, on average, charter schools outperform regular schools. In fact, there is evidence that the average impact is negative."[90] This trend is also evident in the Maryland charter schools where only two public charter schools serving the third grade met or exceeded the state average for reading and math test scores.[91]

Some charter school advocates argue that these outcomes may be explained by the fact that charter schools serve more minority students and economically disadvantaged students than traditional public schools.[92] If the disparity in test scores between charter

---

88. Carnoy et al., *supra* note 39, at 9.

89. Nat'l Ctr. For Educ. Stat., A Closer Look At Charter Schools Using Hierarchical Linear Modeling, at vi (2006).

90. Carnoy et al., *supra* note 39, at 103.

91. Maryland's Public Charter School Program, *supra* note 78, at 12.

92. Carnoy et al., *supra* note 39, at 13–14. Carnoy and his coauthors examine this claim and dispute part of the conclusion, noting that although charter schools do include a disproportionately higher number of African American students, traditional public schools have a greater share of low-income students.

In Maryland, the students attending charter schools are mostly African American students and low income students. Seventy-seven percent of the Maryland students attending charter schools are African American, and 65 percent are eligible for free or reduced-priced meals. Maryland's Public Charter School Program, *supra* note 78, at 7.

schools and traditional public schools is due in part to the demographics of the charter school student population, these disparities are likely to continue in accountability charter schools. Accountability charter schools are filling the void created by failed traditional public schools, therefore there will likely be significant overlap in the student populations. For example, many of the students in New Orleans whose traditional public schools were closed under the requirements of the RSDA will begin to attend charter schools due to the fact that there are more charter schools available than traditional public schools. The accountability charter schools in New Orleans will be charged with bringing students from these failed schools up to proficiency level. Thus, accountability charter schools will likely inherit the struggles of the failed traditional public schools.

Charter schools are required to meet the same mandates as traditional public schools in taking yearly statewide assessments. If accountability charter school students are unable make AYP as required by state law, the charter schools will face the same accountability provisions that impact the traditional public schools. Also, because under many state charter school laws the chartering authority has the ability to revoke the charter for failure to meet specified levels of student achievement, these charter schools may face closure faster than a traditional public school would under the state's accountability provisions.[93] In upcoming years we may see an "accountability cycle" develop where charter schools replace failing traditional public schools only to absorb the failed traditional public school's students, suffer continuing underperformance on statewide assessments, and thus face closure or other less severe accountability measures.

There is emerging evidence that an "accountability cycle" may occur in some of the Maryland charter schools. In 2005–2006, thirteen Maryland charter schools administered the statewide test, and five charter schools failed to make AYP.[94] One charter school in Baltimore, Collington Square School, which was converted from a "restructuring" traditional public school, has not been able to make AYP and is now designated as in need of "restructuring implementation."[95] It is unclear what penalties the Maryland State Department of Education will impose on charter schools that are designated for restructuring.

B. Accountability Charter Schools at Odds with Core Charter School Values

Accountability charter schools may prove to be at odds with some core charter school values, such as school choice. In the basic charter school model, as explained in Part II, choice is a key value because educators, parents, and students all elect to be involved in the charter school, providing the school with a collaborative foundation. In cities like New Orleans and Baltimore, some charter schools are no longer premised on choice, but instead are instruments available to the state to privatize a struggling local school district. As charter schools begin to represent the value of privatization over the value of choice, many of the benefits derived from school choice may begin to fade. For example, in Baltimore the NCLB-mandated accountability measures are forcing the privatization of many

---

93. *See generally*, Suzanne E. Eckes et al., *Charter School Accountability: Legal Considerations Concerning Nonrenewal and Revocation Procedures*, 2006 B.Y.U. Educ. & L.J. 551, 551–52 (2006) (noting that almost 200 charters have been revoked and that more attention must be paid to the charter renewal and revocation process).

94. *See* Maryland's Public Charter School Program, *supra* note 78, at 8.

95. *Id.*

traditional public schools. Two of the main options for schools in need of restructuring are takeover by a private management company or conversion into a public charter school. Thus, more parents may find their former neighborhood school converted to a public charter school. The charter school will not be a meaningful choice for those parents and students; instead it will be a forced alternative.

Also, the pressure for accountability charter schools to meet AYP goals in reading and math may begin to suppress innovative curriculum, one of the key charter school values.[96] A school that previously focused on arts education or another theme may be forced to provide more concentrated instruction in reading and math to ensure the school's students perform well on statewide assessments. Parents and students who may have formerly elected a charter school program to receive innovative instruction and curriculum may find little difference in the accountability charter school program.

C. Accountability Charter Schools Provide a Critique of New Accountability Initiatives

Accountability charter schools may provide a powerful critique of New Accountability initiatives, especially NCLB. New Accountability statutes are premised on the notion that many of the problems in our public schools can be cured through structural reforms. The theory is that if we take away power from local school districts that preside over underperforming schools, the state will have more authority to institute educational reform policies. The emergence of accountability charter schools demonstrates that instead of states using accountability measures as an opportunity to institute education reform policy, the states are relying on private companies, such as charter school operators, to spearhead reform initiatives.

The NCLB mandate that forces states to measure school performance based solely on student standardized test scores may prove to be an obstacle for accountability charter schools that are intended to replace the failed traditional public schools. The inability of accountability charter schools to improve student standardized test scores may force Congress to consider amending NCLB to include multiple measures of student assessments, such as grades and teacher evaluations, to determine whether schools are meeting goals for student proficiency.

Conclusion

New Accountability education reforms and school choice reforms, like charter schools, are colliding. As the charter school model is transformed through its interaction with New Accountability measures, we will likely learn more about the efficacy of both types of reform. The charter school model must be reexamined based on its new role in New Accountability reform to determine whether educational benefits flow from charter schools whose central premise is privatization of failed traditional public schools.

---

96. *See generally,* Molly O'Brien, *Free at Last? Charter Schools and the "Deregulated" Curriculum,* 34 Akron L. Rev. 137, 159–163 (2000) (noting that standards based reforms and mandatory standardized testing may impede curriculum innovation in charter schools).

IV
Race, Gender and Language
Minority Status

12

Reform or Retrenchment? Single-Sex Education and the Construction of Race and Gender

Verna L. Williams[*]

Introduction

Desperate over the wasted lives of its young black men, Detroit is about to open the nation's first public schools for inner-city boys.... The plan is seen not as a fashionable education theory to be tested, but as an experiment with lives at stake, a last chance to save families and, ultimately, the city itself.... Opponents call the schools a discriminatory throwback. Race is not the issue, because 90 percent of Detroit's public school students are black.[1]

Desperate. Wasted. Last chance. These words signify crisis. Without question, the condition of urban school districts across the nation is dire.[2] With so few resources, so many

* Assistant Professor, University of Cincinnati College of Law; B.S., Georgetown University; J.D., Harvard Law School. I am grateful to Deborah Brake, Paul Butler, Martha Chamallas, Maurice Dyson, Rafael Gely, Joanna Grossman, Emily Houh, Deseriee Kennedy, Donna Nagy, and Wendy Parker for their helpful comments and support. I also thank the participants at faculty workshops at the University of Cincinnati College of Law and at the Northeast People of Color Legal Scholarship Conference in April 2003 where I presented earlier versions of this chapter. I am especially thankful for the excellent research assistance I received from the University of Cincinnati College of Law library staff and from my research assistants, James Fantetti, Heather Gomes, and Sayyid Majied-Muhammed. Thanks also go to Carolyn Murry for administrative support. Any omissions or errors are entirely my own. This piece is dedicated to the memory of my father, Sherman S. Williams.

1. Isabel Wilkerson, *Detroit's Boys-Only Schools Facing Bias Lawsuit*, N.Y. TIMES, Aug. 14, 1991, at A1.

2. For example, the New York Court of Appeals recently found that the state failed to provide New York City students—84 percent of whom are racial minorities—with a "sound basic education" as required under the state constitution. *Campaign for Fiscal Equity, Inc. v. State*, 801 N.E.2d 326, 329 (N.Y. 2003). The court found that significant disparities in per-pupil expenditures had resulted in "tens of thousands of students [being] placed in overcrowded classrooms, taught by unqualified teachers, and provided with inadequate facilities and equipment. The number of children in these straits is large enough to represent a systemic failure." *Id*. at 836; *see also* JONATHAN KOZOL, SAVAGE IN-

challenges, and so few prospects for meaningful reform, it is hardly surprising that parents are quick to grasp at anything that remotely promises to lead their children to college and careers rather than to the streets, prison, or the cemetery. It is hardly surprising that single-sex[3] education, which conjures up images of elite institutions such as Wellesley College and the success sure to follow, would seem to be a godsend. Why *not* try single-sex schools?

It's not about sex, it is about black men and black people [and] their right to self-determination.[4]

The Detroit Board of Education, with the support of many of the school district's parents, decided to try its hand at single-sex education, creating three all-male academies for students in grades six through eight.[5] These schools would be the balm for high dropout rates, low achievement, and hopelessness confronting their community.[6]

However, for Shawn Garrett, a Detroit mother and plaintiff in the *Garrett v. Board of Education* litigation, an important question was unanswered. What about her daughter, Crystal? Crystal, too, was part of a class that was more likely to quit school than graduate, more and more likely to be incarcerated or murdered.[7] Garrett wanted the board to help her daughter, too. But these new schools were for boys. For female students, three schools for pregnant girls were the only single-sex option.[8] Joined by another parent of a girl and the National Organization for Women Legal Defense and Education Fund, and represented by the American Civil Liberties Union (ACLU), Garrett sued the board to make this opportunity available to her daughter and other girls like her. These plaintiffs sought to block the all-male academies from opening.[9]

However, by the time the district court heard arguments on the motion for preliminary injunction, Garrett no longer was a party to the action.[10] Her decision to challenge the single-

---

EQUALITIES: CHILDREN IN AMERICA'S SCHOOLS 2–3 (1991) (discussing similar conditions in urban school districts throughout the nation).

3. In this chapter, "sex" refers to the biological categories of male and female; "gender" refers to the social construction of masculinity and femininity. *See, e.g.*, Katherine M. Franke, *The Central Mistake of Sex Discrimination Law: The Disaggregation of Sex From Gender*, 144 U. PA. L. REV. 1, 1 (1995) (explaining that the term "gender" refers to a "function of culture" and society assigned an individual, while "sex" refers to "a product of nature").

4. *Nightline: Detroit Black "Male Academies" Ruled Unfair* (ABC News television broadcast, Aug. 15, 1991) (transcript on file with author).

5. *See All-Girl Schools: Detroit Counters Lawsuit*, DAILY REPORT CARD, Aug. 8, 1991, *available at* LEXIS; *see also Garrett v. Bd. of Educ.*, 775 F. Supp. 1004, 1006 (E.D. Mich. 1991).

6. *See All-Girl Schools: Detroit Counters Lawsuit*, *supra* note 5; *see also Garrett*, 775 F. Supp. at 1007.

7. *See, e.g.*, PAULA C. JOHNSON, INNER LIVES: VOICES OF AFRICAN AMERICAN WOMEN IN PRISON 34 (2003) (noting that overall "women [are] the fastest-growing segment of the prison population ... African American women are the largest percentage of incarcerated women"); Joseph R. Biden Jr., *What About the Girls? The Role of the Federal Government in Addressing the Rise in Female Juvenile Offenders*, 14 STAN. L. & POL'Y REV. 29, 32, 34 (2003) (noting that between 1989 and 1998, the female juvenile delinquency rate rose 83 percent; that between 1989 and 1993, the arrest rate for female juveniles increased 55 percent compared to only 33 percent for males during that period; and that between 1988 and 1997, the number of cases in the juvenile justice system increased 106 percent for African American girls); Ossai Miazid, *The Gender Gap: Treatment of Girls in the United States Juvenile Justice System*, 10 HUM. RTS. BR. 10, 10 (2002) ("Between 1988 and 1997, girls' rate of detention increased more than twice that of boys.").

8. Laurel Shaper Walters, *The Plight of Black Male Schools*, CHRISTIAN SCI. MONITOR, Sept. 9, 1991, at 8.

9. *Garrett*, 775 F. Supp. at 1009.

10. *Id.* at 1005 n.1. In fact, Garrett dropped out of the litigation thirty minutes before the hear-

sex academies with two predominately white legal-advocacy organizations[11] was met with hostility and suspicion from the community.[12] After being the target of harassing and threatening phone calls, Garrett bowed out, leaving an anonymous plaintiff to proceed alone.[13]

The district court granted the preliminary injunction motion, ruling that the academies violated the Constitution's guarantee of equal protection[14] and Title IX,[15] the federal law prohibiting sex discrimination in education.[16] According to the district court, the plan was well intentioned but seriously flawed: while the Board created the academies to respond to "the crisis facing African-American males manifested by high homicide, unemployment, and drop-out rates.... [these justifications and the supporting data] fall short of demonstrating that excluding girls is substantially related to the achievement of the board's objectives."[17] The court noted that in creating the all-male academies, the board "ignor[ed] the plight of urban females, institutionalize[d] inequality and perpetuate[d] the myth that females are doing well in the current system."[18] The board ultimately opened the academies to female students, who enrolled over community objection and a boycott.[19] Initially, only a few girls signed up, but in the years that followed, many more became students of these schools.[20]

This case served as a cautionary tale, chilling the creation of new single-sex public schools[21] until 1996. In that year, the New York City Schools opened the Young Women's Leadership School (TYWLS) in East Harlem,[22] the legal status of which appears to be in limbo because of an administrative complaint pending at the Department of Education's Office for Civil Rights.[23] The Bush administration, seeking to lift the "legal cloud"[24] surrounding single-sex education, has signaled its intention to give TYWLS

---

ing began. *See id.*; *see also U.S. Judge Blocks Plan for All-Male Public Schools in Detroit*, N.Y. Times, Aug. 16, 1991, at A10.

11. While not a party to the litigation, the NAACP Legal Defense and Educational Fund made its voice heard on the issue, concluding that a similar Milwaukee plan represented "a threat to an integrated society... posed a real danger of racial resegregation... [and] undermined efforts to eliminate the pervasive isolation of black males." Rosemary C. Salomone, Same, Different, Equal: Rethinking Single-Sex Schooling 130–31 & n.28 (2003) (citing NAACP Legal Def. and Educ. Fund, Reflections on Proposals for Separate Schools for African-American Male Pupils 9 (1990)).

12. *Id.* at 134.

13. *Garrett*, 775 F. Supp. at 1005 nn.1–2.

14. *Id.* at 1008.

15. *Id.* Plaintiffs relied on Title IX of the Education Act Amendments of 1972 and its implementing regulations, which prohibit educational programs receiving federal funds from treating students differently based on sex. *Id.* (relying on 20 U.S.C. § 1681 (1990); 24 C.F.R. § 106 (1990)).

16. *Id.* at 1009–10.

17. *Id.* at 1007.

18. *Id.*

19. *See* Salomone, *supra* note 11, at 135.

20. *Id.* (noting that a balance of boys and girls now are enrolled in these academies).

21. *See id.* at 131.

22. Ann Rubenstein Tisch, a white philanthropist and former broadcaster, put this effort in motion working with Seymour Fleigel, a senior fellow at the Manhattan Institute, which is a conservative think tank. Somini Sengupta, *East Harlem District Is Considering an All-Boys Public School*, N.Y. Times, Dec. 12, 1996, at B9.

23. Like the Detroit schools, TYWLS also faced a legal challenge: this time by the New York Civil Liberties Union (NYCLU) and the National Organization for Women (NOW). But instead of filing suit in federal district court, these litigants went to the Department of Education's Office for Civil Rights, which has the authority to enforce Title IX and other civil rights laws. The NYCLU and NOW argued that TYWLS violated Title IX. *See Admin. Comp., NOW v. Bd. of Educ.*, (U.S. Dep't Educ. Off. Civil Rights Aug. 22, 1996) (on file with author). At this writing, the complaint is still pending.

24. *See* Diana Jean Schemo, *White House Proposes New View of Education Law to Encourage Single Sex Schools*, N.Y. Times, May 9, 2002, at A26 (quoting Tom Carroll, president of the Brighter

the green light and allow New York City and other school districts the flexibility to create single-sex schools.[25] For many educators and parents in urban schools, this news was like a tall glass of ice water after traversing the desert—a promise that, at long last, no child would be left behind.[26] But that optimism is premature.

The fact that so much of the discourse surrounding single-sex education is about Black[27] children in troubled urban school districts is cause for concern.[28] Put another way, there generally is no concomitant rush to segregate public schoolchildren based on sex in predominately White Grosse Pointe, Michigan, a suburb of Detroit, or Nebraska, for example.[29] If sex segregation were the silver bullet that its proponents suggest,[30] one might expect more school districts across the board to jump on the bandwagon. But that is not the case. Sex segregation appears to be the remedy for what ails public schools peopled for the most part by low-income students of color.[31]

Choice Foundation, which supports sex-segregated schools, praising the Bush proposal as representing the "first time we see the legal cloud lifted from single-sex schools").

25. *See infra* notes 84–106 and accompanying text.

26. The recent federal effort to promote single-sex schools, discussion *infra* Part I, is pursuant to the enactment of a provision in the No Child Left Behind Act of 2001 that allows schools districts to use certain federal monies to create single-sex schools. Pub. L. No. 107-110, § 1, 115 Stat. 1425 (Jan. 8, 2002) (codifying and amending 20 U.S.C.A. §§ 6301–7941 (West 2003)); *see also infra* notes 59–61 and accompanying text.

27. In this Article, I use the terms "Black" and "African American" to express that "Blacks like Asians, Latinos, and other 'minorities,' constitute a specific cultural group and, as such, require denotation as a proper noun." Kimberle Williams Crenshaw, *Race, Reform, and Retrenchment: Transformation and Legitimation in Antidiscrimination Law*, 101 HARV. L. REV. 1331, 1332 n.2 (1988).

28. It should noted that some research suggests that single-sex education benefits students of color. *See, e.g.*, Cornelius Riordan, *What Do We Know About the Effects of Single-Sex Schools in the Private Sector?: Implications for Public Schools, in* GENDER IN POLICY AND PRACTICE: PERSPECTIVES ON SINGLE-SEX AND COEDUCATIONAL SCHOOLING 10, 13 (Amanda Datnow & Lea Hubbard eds., 2002) (arguing that "the research is 'exceedingly persuasive' in demonstrating that single-sex schools are effective in terms of providing both greater equality and greater achievement, especially for low-income and working-class students, most particularly for African-American and Hispanic-American boys *and* girls"). However, even Riordan acknowledges that factors beyond the mere separation by sex account for the effectiveness of single-sex schooling. For example, smaller school size, an emphasis on academic subjects and achievement, and, significantly, the fact that parents and students alike choose such schooling because they want an enhanced educational experience all play a role. *Id.* at 18–19. For purposes of this chapter, however, I focus on the rhetoric concerning African American students and the attendant legal and social implications, recognizing, of course, that the issues and challenges identified may not apply wholesale to other students of color in urban schools.

29. *See, e.g.*, Judith Nygren, *Same-Sex Public Schools? Not Here*, OMAHA WORLD-HERALD, May 10, 2002, at 1A (noting that "single-gender schools have been, and are expected to remain, the domain of private education [and not public education] in Nebraska"). Notably, however, in the metropolitan Omaha area, single-sex schools have been proposed for African American boys "because that is what people in the community said was most needed." *Id.*

30. *See, e.g.*, Karen Stabiner, ALL GIRLS: SINGLE-SEX EDUCATION AND WHY IT MATTERS 315 (2002) ("Singe-sex schools got results, while cries for a general overhaul went begging.").

31. At this writing, there are twenty-five single-sex public schools in the nation, including five schools that have yet to open. Sixty-three other schools offer single-sex classrooms. *See* Nat'l Ass'n for Single Sex Pub. Educ., Single Sex Public Schools in the United States, *at* www.singlesexschools.org/schools.html (last visited Apr. 5, 2004) (on file with author). A few schools on the list, such as Baltimore's Western High School, have long histories of being single-sex institutions and only recently have become predominately minority. Most of the schools on this list were created within the last few years as part of the school reform movement. The vast majority of them primarily serve students of color.

Sex segregation has been deemed particularly necessary for African American males because they are an "endangered species ... target[ed] by this system for destruction and extermination."[32] In this connection, arguments for single-sex education focus on the myriad issues confronting Black male students, such as high rates of incarceration and homicide.[33] The rhetoric suggests that sex segregation addresses these problems because it compensates for the primary deficiency of many Black males: the fact that they are being raised in female-headed households. According to this argument, because Black males are surrounded by women, they lack appropriate role models[34] who "exemplify

School and Location	Percentage Minority Students
Charter School of San Diego	
San Diego, Cal. [Ed. Note: not on list]	60%
The San Francisco 49ers Academies	
Palo Alto, Cal.	87%
Fox Middle School	
Hartford, Conn. [Ed. Note: not on list]	90%
Philadelphia High School for Girls	
Philadelphia, Pa.	77%
Jefferson Leadership Academies	
Long Beach, Cal.	91%
Lincoln Elementary School	
Toledo, Ohio	98%
Mitchell Elementary School	
Denver, Colo.	98%
Moten Elementary School	
Washington, D.C.	100%
Paducah Middle School	
Paducah, Ky.	53%
Pepper George Middle School	
Philadelphia, Pa.	95%
Rhodes E. Washington Middle School	
Philadelphia, Pa.	99%
Southern Middle School	
Louisville, Ky.	55%
Stewart Elementary School	
Toledo, Ohio	99%
Thurgood Marshall Elementary	
Seattle, Wash.	94%
Western High School	
Baltimore, Md.	82%
Withrow High School	
Cincinnati, Ohio	91%
Young Women's Leadership Charter School	
Chicago, Ill.	87%
Young Women's Leadership High School	
New York, N.Y.	92%

Nat'l Center for Educ. Stat., *at* nces.ed/gov/schoolsearch/school_detail.asp? (last visited Aug. 1, 2003) (on file with author).

32. *Nightline*, *supra* note 4; *see also* Pamela J. Smith, Comment, *All-Male Black Schools and the Equal Protection Clause: A Step Forward Toward Education*, 66 Tul. L. Rev. 2003, 2004 (1992) (observing that African American males are endangered because of "'gang fights, vendettas, drug battles, accidents, drive-by shootings, ... malnutrition, poor education, drug or alcohol addition, the collapse of families, [and] series of medical problems linked to poverty, lifestyle, and heredity'") (citation omitted).

33. *See* Wilkerson, *supra* note 1, at A1.

34. *See, e.g.*, Dennis Kelly, *Detroit Academies Develop Black Males*, USA Today, Jan. 15, 1992, at 7A (quoting a Detroit fifth-grade teacher, who notes that "'many of the boys don't have a father at home'"); Richard Rothstein, *Single-Sex Schools: Why Ruin Good Experiments with Politics*, L.A. Times, Jan. 21,

the value of education,"[35] or who simply can teach them how to be men — that is, providers and husbands.[36] Providing these role models thus becomes an imperative, a way to "save families" and communities,[37] which places Black males at the center of the struggle for equal rights in education,[38] and makes Black mothers the locus of the many problems afflicting urban African American communities. This rhetoric echoes conclusions of long-discredited[39] social science theories propounded by former Senator Daniel Patrick Moynihan in *The Negro Family: The Case for National Action*,[40] which

---

1996, at 6 (suggesting that "elementary-school boys from low-income, single-parent homes in African American communities with few successful male role models require tough male-authority figures as teachers"); Smith, *supra* note 32, at 2031 (arguing that because "many African-American [single] mothers fail to develop their boys into men," boys need male role models); Wilkerson, *supra* note 1, at A1 ("Often having no fathers at home and seeing that the only men with any money in the neighborhood are drug dealers, the boys hunger for male direction.").

35. Nygren, *supra* note 29, at 1A.

36. Patrice M. Jones, *A Place All Their Own: Detroit Uses Special Academies to Help Black Boys Overcome Challenges*, Plain Dealer (Cleveland, Ohio), Apr. 23, 1996, at 1A (quoting a parent who believes "'this school will make my son into a provider, a responsible man'"); *Nightline*, *supra* note 4 (stating that the male academies mean that his "daughters will be able to have some positive African-American males to choose from when they get married").

37. *See* Wilkerson, *supra* note 1, at A1.

38. *See* Devon W. Carbado, *Men in Black*, 3 J. Gender Race & Just. 427, 434 (2000) (noting that "the social meaning of [Black male schools] is that, whatever the status of Black girls, it is Black boys, members of the first sex, who have the potential to become *strong Black men*, the potential to save themselves and thus the Black community").

39. *See, e.g.*, William Ryan, *Savage Discovery: The Moynihan Report*, in The Moynihan Report and the Politics of Controversy 457, 458 (Lee Rainwater & William L. Yancey eds., 1967). William Ryan, in an article originally published in *The Nation*, criticized the Moynihan Report because:

> [the Report] draws dangerously inexact conclusions from weak and insufficient data; encourages (no doubt unintentionally) a new form of subtle racism that might be termed "Savage Discovery," and seduces the reader into believing that it is not racism and discrimination but the weaknesses and defects of the Negro himself that account for the present status of inequality between Negro and white.

Id.

40. Daniel P. Moynihan, U.S. Dep't of Labor, The Negro Family: The Case for National Action (Greenwood Press 1981) (1965). The Moynihan Report sought to highlight the problems confronting African Americans to support strong enforcement of the Civil Rights Act of 1964. The Moynihan Report attempted to understand the issues and challenges confronting African Americans by examining their history. In this regard, the report identified several "pathologies" common among poor African American families: first and foremost among them was "matriarchy."

> The Negro community has been forced into a matriarchal structure which, because it is so out of line with the rest of the American society, seriously retards the progress of the group as a whole, and imposes a crushing burden on the Negro male and, in consequence, on a great many Negro women as well.
>
> There is, presumably, no special reason why a society in which males are dominant in family relationships is to be preferred to a matriarchal arrangement. However, it is clearly a disadvantage for a minority group to be operating on one principle, while the great majority of the population, and the one with the most advantages to begin with, is operating on another.

Id. at 29. Thus, according to the report, "'Negro husbands have unusually low power,'" unlike the majority of white families, which, the report claimed "'are equalitarian.'" *Id.* at 30–31.

Dominance of the wife in Black marriages was one of the fruits of slavery — a time when slaves were prohibited from marrying. *Id.* at 16. The Moynihan Report further argued that this pattern became entrenched during the post-Reconstruction era:

> When Jim Crow made its appearance towards the end of the 19th century, it may be speculated that it was the Negro male who was most humiliated thereby; the male was more likely to use public facilities, which rapidly became segregated once the process began, and just as important, segregation, and the submissiveness it exacts, is surely more destructive to the male than to the female personality. Keeping the Negro "in his place" can be trans-

attributed much of the "pathologies" affecting Black Americans to the shortcomings of the Black family, particularly the preponderance of female-headed households. Similarly, the overarching theme of today's discourse is that single-sex education is necessary to build Black men.

With respect to African American girls, the rhetoric focuses on preventing pregnancy. Specifically, advocates have argued that girls in a sex-segregated environment will be less distracted by boys and feel less pressure to become sexually active.[41] One commentator praised TYWLS as a place where girls could be "free from the social distractions and sexual pressures that too often reach *dangerous* proportions in urban public schools."[42] In fact, one of the touted virtues of TYWLS is that "pregnancy [among its students] is the stark exception."[43] In the same breath, this commentator observed that the benefit of a private, predominately white girls' school was that the girls "perceive themselves as more competent, more willing to pursue advanced work in fields such as math and science."[44] So much of the rhetoric regarding Black girls in education is about their sexuality,[45] suggesting that by just sitting in the same classroom with male students, there is a risk of pregnancy. Implicit in this discourse is a concern about single motherhood, which, as discussed, has been blamed for poverty, juvenile delinquency, and other problems.[46] This rhetoric reflects what some have identified as the devaluation of Black motherhood,[47] a related "deep suspicion of black women's sexuality and an intense desire to control their 'excessive' promis-

---

lated as keeping the Negro male in his place: the female was not a threat to anyone.

Unquestionably, these events worked against the emergence of a strong father figure. *Id.* In this respect, the Moynihan Report argued that slavery and the Jim Crow era enabled, indeed required, African American women to take the lead in family affairs. By modern times, Black women were the customary heads of households with their husbands playing a subservient role. The Moynihan Report suggested that this pattern of female dominance in the home perpetuated itself because of the tendency of African American females to attain higher levels of education than their male counterparts, which, in turn helped perpetuate the low achievement levels and high rates of delinquency and crime among Black youth, particularly the males. *See id.* at 31, 36–38.

41. *See* Nygren, *supra* note 29, at 1A.

42. Salomone, *supra* note 11, at 18 (emphasis added).

43. Karen Stabiner, *Boys Here, Girls There: Sure, if Equality Is the Goal*, Wash. Post, May 12, 2002, at B1; *see also* Alex Chadwick, *Morning Edition: Harlem All-Girls School Scrutinized after VMI Ruling* (NPR broadcast, Aug. 21, 1996), *available at* LEXIS ("These girls are moving on with their lives, they're taking charge of their lives—and it's not about having babies, it's not about getting stuck.").

44. Stabiner, *supra* note 43, at B1.

45. It should be noted that the suggestion that removing the other sex from the classroom eliminates sexual *distractions* is heterosexist in that it presumes that there are no gay, lesbian, or bisexual students who may be so distracted even without the other sex in the classroom.

46. *See supra* notes 34–40 and accompanying text; *see also* Martha Fineman, *Images of Mothers in Poverty Discourses*, 1991 Duke L.J. 274, 275. In this regard, the arguments supporting single-sex schools might be seen as an effort to reestablish patriarchy. The emphasis on the need for a male role model in the home asserts the primacy of the traditional family. This account is incomplete for several reasons. First, it fails to recognize that a father may indeed be present even if he is not married to the mother. *See* Fineman, *supra*, at 275. Additionally, such a focus presumes that married fathers are present in meaningful ways, which is not always the case. *See id.* Despite these shortcomings, these arguments are prominent and suggest that single-sex education policies promote the construct of the traditional nuclear family. Fineman argues that policymakers are drawn to this kind of policy because single motherhood is a "practice of resistance to patriarchal ideology, particularly because it represents a 'deliberate choice' in a world with birth control and abortion.... [Therefore, it] threatens the hold of the dominant [patriarchal] ideology." *See id.* at 290.

47. *See, e.g.*, Dorothy E. Roberts, *Racism and Patriarchy in the Meaning of Motherhood*, 1 Am. U. J. Gender & L. 1, 10–11 (1993). Roberts argues that patriarchy requires and rewards white motherhood, "but it denies to Black women even this modicum of value. Black women are deemed not even worthy of the dignity of childbearing." *Id.* at 11.

cuity and fecundity."[48] While it is certainly true that premature motherhood has serious implications for an uneducated teenager and her child, it is true for white teenagers as well as Black.[49] Yet such concerns typically have not arisen as justifications for all-female schools for white girls. The disparity suggests that underlying this concern is the desire to control Black female reproduction, which Dorothy Roberts has described as "a means of subordinating the entire race."[50]

Finally, the rhetoric regarding single-sex education for Black girls is unique in its emphasis on providing safety. For example, the principal of Philadelphia High School for Girls, which is almost 80 percent students of color,[51] has praised the school because there is "'less sexual harassment'" and more "'safety in an urban environment.'"[52] Similar comments have been made about other all-female schools in inner cities.[53] This rhetoric suggests that merely by removing Black males from the environment, these schools become safer even though they remain in urban settings where security is an issue for students and nonstudents alike.

The foregoing suggests that this effort is very much about race. But race is invisible when the players — students, parents, and educators — are people of color, which is the case here. Instead, the discourse centers on sex[54] and the presumably benign nature of

---

48. Regina Austin, *Sapphire Bound!*, 1989 WIS. L. REV. 539, 555. Austin criticizes the decision of the U.S. Court of Appeals for the Eighth Circuit in *Chambers v. Omaha Girls Club, Inc.*, 834 F.2d 697 (8th Cir. 1987), which affirmed the Girls Club's dismissal of an instructor because she was pregnant, unmarried, and therefore a negative role model for Black teenage girls. "The Club and the courts conceivably subscribe to a theory of reproduction, that can only be termed 'primitive,' which posits that simply seeing an unmarried pregnant woman can have such a powerful impact on adolescent females that they will be moved to imitate her by becoming pregnant themselves." *Id.* Similarly, advocates for single-sex schooling suggest that merely removing males from females in classes will prove to be an effective strategy against teenage pregnancy.

49. The United States has the highest rate of teen pregnancy in the industrialized world. Annie E. Casey Found., *When Kids Have Sex: Issues and Trends, at* www.aecf.org/kidscount/teen/ overview.htm (last visited Apr. 5, 2004) (on file with author). It should be noted that the rates of teen pregnancy in this nation have been on the decline for both white and Black females, with rates for Black teens diminishing at a greater rate than that of white teens. JACQUELINE E. DARROCH & SUSHEELA SINGH, WHY IS TEENAGE PREGNANCY DECLINING? THE ROLES OF ABSTINENCE, SEXUAL ACTIVITY, AND CONTRACEPTIVE USE 6–7 (Alan Guttmacher Inst., Occasional Rep. 1, Dec. 1999), *available at* www.guttmacher.org/pubs/or_teen_preg_decline.pdf (on file with author).

50. Roberts, *supra* note 47, at 11.

51. *See supra* note 31.

52. Ingrid Shaffer, *Single-sex Schools Are Proving Their Worth*, PATRIOT LEDGER (Boston, Mass.), June 5, 2002, at 11.

53. For example, Baltimore's Western High School is known "not only for its academic reputation but also for its physically safe environment." Salomone, *supra* note 11, at 32. Salomone also has described TYWLS as a "physically and emotionally safe haven for ... girls." *Id.* at 18.

54. *See, e.g.*, William Henry Hurd, *Gone with the Wind? VMI's Loss and the Future of Single-Sex Public Education*, 4 DUKE J. GENDER L. & POL'Y 27 (1997) (arguing that the Supreme Court decision in *United States v. Virginia*, 518 U.S. 515 (1996) (*VMI*), should not necessarily foreclose creation of single-sex schools); Nancy Levit, *Separating Equals: Educational Research and the Long-Term Consequences of Sex Segregation*, 67 GEO. WASH. L. REV. 451, 454 (1999) (examining "empirical evidence about single-sex schools in the larger context of sociological evidence regarding the construction of gender roles"); Denise C. Morgan, *Anti-Subordination Analysis after* United States v. Virginia: *Evaluating the Constitutionality of K–12 Single-Sex Public Schools*, 1999 U. CHI. LEGAL F. 381, 384 (identifying the "circumstances [under which single-sex public schools can] survive an anti-subordination challenge"); Amy H. Nemko, *Single-Sex Public Education After* VMI: *The Case for Women's Schools*, 21 HARV. WOMEN'S L.J. 19, 22 (1998) (single-sex public education is not per se unconstitutional); Carolyn B. Ramsey, *Subtracting Sexism from the Classroom: Law and Policy in the Debate Over All-Female Math and Science Classes in Public Schools*, 8 TEX. J. WOMEN & L. 1, 4 (1998) (arguing that all-female math and science classes do not presumptively violate the equal protection clause); Walteen Grady Truely & Martha F. Davis, *Public Education Programs for African-American Males: A Gender Equity Perspec-*

separating boys and girls in education,[55] which is not surprising because uttering *race* and *segregation* in the same breath is a combustible mix that evokes much higher scrutiny and greater skepticism. However, this single axis analysis focusing on sex alone is incomplete.

Because much of the effort to implement single-sex schooling centers on the nation's inner-city school systems, it has the potential to affect students of color greatly.[56] In addition, this nation's sad history with respect to educating students of color — particularly Black students — strongly counsels that any analysis of sex segregation must consider not only sex but also race at the very least,[57] to determine whether this reform strategy will liberate or subordinate Black children. Accordingly, this chapter argues that such an intersectional analysis[58] is essential to ensuring that current efforts to segregate students by sex actually effect reform and not retrenchment of discrimination.

Part I of this chapter examines the legal doctrine applicable to single-sex education and the Bush proposal to ease legal scrutiny of single-sex programming. Part II explores the overlapping histories of racial and sex-based segregation in education and the legal regime supporting it, as well as the concomitant raced and gendered hierarchy this system of education helped create. As a result, Part III concludes that any new effort to create single-sex schools or classes necessarily must be informed by an intersectional analysis and applies such a framework to *Garrett*.

---

tive, 21 N.Y.U. Rev. L. & Soc. Change 725, 728 (1995) (examining the Black all-male academies "from a women's educational equity perspective"); Valerie K. Vojdik, *Girls' Schools After* VMI: *Do They Make the Grade?*, 4 Duke J. Gender L. & Pol'y 69, 70 (1997) (arguing that all-girls schools are unconstitutional); Kristin S. Caplice, *The Case for Public Single-Sex Education*, 18 Harv. J.L. & Pub. Pol'y 227, 229 (1994) ("advocat[ing] public single-sex education as an alternative to coeducation"); Jennifer R. Cowan, *Distinguishing Private Women's Colleges from the* VMI *Decision*, 30 Colum. J.L. & Soc. Probs. 137, 138 (1996) (providing a "blueprint for defending [women's] colleges against [legal] challenges"). *But see* Jill Elaine Hasday, *The Principle and Practice of Women's "Full Citizenship": A Case Study of Sex-Segregated Public Education*, 101 Mich. L. Rev. 755, 758 (2002) (arguing that "'sex role confinement'" can occur in single-sex or coeducational schooling to perpetuate inequities based on sex, race, and class); Smith, *supra* note 32, at 2030 (arguing that sex segregation in predominantly Black schools should be subject to intermediate scrutiny).

55. *See, e.g.*, Neal Conan, *Talk of the Nation: Single-Sex Public Schools* (NPR broadcast, May 13, 2002), *available at* LEXIS (transcript on file with author) ("A lot of the single-sex schools we're talking about now ... are ones that clearly don't have their history in any kind of discriminatory path.").

56. This chapter takes no position on the efficacy of single-sex education for improving educational outcomes for students.

57. *See* Kimberle Crenshaw, *Demarginalizing the Intersection of Race and Sex: A Black Feminist Critique of Antidiscrimination Doctrine, Feminist Theory and Antiracist Politics*, 1989 U. Chi. Legal F. 139, 145 (stating that the failure to analyze such issues using a multiple axis "defeats efforts to restructure the distribution of opportunity and limits remedial relief to minor adjustments within an established hierarchy"); Angela P. Harris, *Race and Essentialism in Feminist Legal Theory*, 42 Stan. L. Rev. 581, 585 (1990) (criticizing feminist legal scholars for failing to consider how race intersects with sex).

58. *See supra* note 57; *see also* Dwight A. McBride, *Can the Queen Speak? Racial Essentialism, Sexuality, and the Problem of Authority*, *in* Black Men on Race, Gender, and Sexuality: A Critical Reader 253, 272 (Devon Carbado ed., 1999) (noting that "if I am thinking about race, I should already be thinking about gender, class, and sexuality"); Darren Lenard Hutchinson, *Identity Crisis: "Intersectionality," "Multidimensionality," and the Development of an Adequate Theory of Subordination*, 6 Mich. J. Race & L. 285, 297 (2001) (advocating an examination of the interactions between the myriad forms of oppression).

I. Legally Cloudy or Clear?:
The Law Regarding Single-Sex Education
and the Bush Proposal to Modify It

In the wake of the *Garrett* decision and the ambiguous status of TYWLS, interest has grown in making single-sex education an option for school districts, as has anxiety about the attendant risk of legal exposure. In this connection, the Bush administration has proposed new regulations meant to assist school districts' education reform efforts. Accordingly, a critical examination of sex segregation with an eye toward the students most likely to be affected is warranted. This part examines the current state of the law and the Bush administration proposal to modify it.

By signing into law the No Child Left Behind Act of 2001 (NCLBA),[59] President George W. Bush triggered a little known provision[60] that could lead to the proliferation of single-sex education throughout the nation's public schools. Namely, under the NCLB, local

---

59. Pub. L. No. 107-110, 115 Stat. 1425 (codifying and amending 20 U.S.C.A. §§ 6301–7941) (authorizing funding programs for schools serving low-income children and enacting provisions designed to hold schools accountable for student outcomes).

60. 20 U.S.C.A. § 7215(a)(23). This provision makes available federal funds for "innovative assistance programs," including those that would provide "same-gender schools and classrooms." *Id.* Senator Kay Bailey Hutchison (R-TX) sponsored the measure, joined by Senators Hillary Rodham Clinton (D-NY), Ted Kennedy (D-MA), and others. 147 Cong. Rec. S5943 (daily ed. June 7, 2001). Enactment of this provision culminated an effort started by former Senator John Danforth (R-MO) in 1993. Danforth proposed a measure that would have waived Title IX liability for a limited number of school districts to allow them to experiment with sex segregation without the threat of litigation. Such waivers were essential, according to Danforth, to provide school districts with the flexibility to innovate in this area.

> In school districts in Milwaukee and Detroit and Miami and Baltimore and Philadelphia, there have been at least some schools in those districts that have come to the conclusion that[,] for a least on a trial basis[,] they should have the opportunity[,] they should make the attempt to find out if for some of those kids, single-sex education works. However[,] the bad news is that they have been under the cloud of lawsuits when they have made that decision. They have been threatened and, in some cases, they have been sued....
>
> In the inner cities in particular, there have been attempts at same gender schooling in the form of classes to address the poor academic performance of the kids in those schools. However[,] legal opposition[,] particularly legal opposition that has been precipitated by the American Civil Liberties Union and by the National Organization of Women, have [*sic*] chilled those decisions.

140 Cong. Rec. S10,165 (daily ed. Aug. 1, 1994).

While Danforth saw the proposed exemptions to Title IX as lifting a cloud, others viewed his proposal as signaling a retrenchment in civil rights and a return to exclusionary educational policies. Kennedy opposed the measure because he was concerned about the precedent of waiving civil rights laws. Kennedy noted that the history of sex segregation was not entirely benign, which had troubling implications for the future: "we have seen in this country, when ... boys are in one area and the girls are in another, history has demonstrated time in and time out that [the girls] are the ones that have been left out and left behind." *Id.* at S10,170. The vast majority of senators disagreed, approving the measure by a strong margin of sixty-six to thirty-three. *Id.* at S10,163. When members of the Senate and the House of Representatives met to consider their respective versions of the Improving America's Schools Act (IASA), however, several members of the conference committee objected to the amendment because of "concerns about waiving civil rights laws to carry out the pilot programs." *See Conferees Inch Forward on Education Reauthorization Bill,* Congress Daily, Sept. 22, 1994. The provision ultimately was dropped from the final iteration of the IASA. *See* H.R. Rep. No. 103-761, at 649–50 (1994).

education agencies may dedicate certain funds to create single-sex schools and classes, provided that they do so "consistent with applicable law."[61] "Applicable law" in this area refers primarily to Title IX[62] and the Fourteenth Amendment of the Constitution.[63]

Title IX broadly prohibits sex discrimination in any federally funded education program or activity.[64] Importantly, it does not proscribe single-sex education outright.[65] For

---

61. 20 U.S.C.A. § 7215(a)(23).

62. 20 U.S.C. §§ 1681–1688 (2000).

63. U.S. CONST. amend. XIV. The Equal Educational Opportunities Act of 1974 (EEOA), Pub. L. No. 93-380, 88 Stat. 514 (codified at 20 U.S.C. §§ 1701–1758), and Title VI of the Civil Rights Act, 42 U.S.C. § 2000d, may have some applicability here, as well. The EEOA requires states to "remove the vestiges of a dual school system." 20 U.S.C. § 1703(b). The EEOA also outlaws assigning students to schools based on sex, among other categories, "if the assignment results in a greater degree of segregation ... than would result if such student were assigned to the school closest to his or her place of residence." *Id.* § 1703(c). Title VI, for its part, provides: "No person in the United States shall, on the ground of race, color, or national origin, be excluded from, denied the benefits of, or be subjected to discrimination under any program or activity receiving Federal financial assistance." 42 U.S.C. § 2000d. This chapter focuses primarily on the equal protection clause of the Fourteenth Amendment and Title IX, which are most commonly at issue with respect to single-sex schools.

64. Title IX states in relevant part: "No person in the United States shall, on the basis of sex, be excluded from participation in, be denied the benefits of, or be subjected to discrimination under any education program or activity receiving Federal financial assistance." 20 U.S.C. § 1681(a).

65. Congress never intended to outlaw single-sex education with the passage of Title IX. In fact, early versions of the statute explicitly exempted single-sex institutions, in part because they were not deemed to be discriminatory. *See* 117 CONG. REC. 39,252 (daily ed. Nov. 4, 1971). Other members sought to exclude single-sex colleges and universities so they would not be unduly burdened by integrating on the basis of sex. *Id.* at 39,251. Just as today, supporters of single-sex education cited diversity of educational offerings as a rationale for exempting such institutions from Title IX's coverage. *Id.* at 39,253. There also was considerable debate about whether single-sex education really was pedagogically sound. For example, in debates about the House version, lawmakers discussed the fact that single-sex colleges were on the decline and that there was a "legitimate controversy ... over the merits of single-sex versus coeducational institutions." *Id.* at 39,255. Ultimately, the version that passed in the House exempted undergraduate admissions. *Id.* at 39,364.

The Senate took a different approach. When former Senator Birch Bayh (D-IN) introduced his version of the Title IX in August 1971, this version provided a phase-in period for single-sex institutions. 117 CONG. REC. S30,399 (daily ed. Aug. 6, 1971). Under Bayh's amendment, VMI and the Citadel would have had to integrate based on sex, as would have women's colleges. *Id.* at S30,412. Other lawmakers who believed that colleges and universities should be free to determine the composition of their student body opposed this amendment. As one explained, some institutions may "feel that their own university ... would provide better educational opportunities ... if it kept that ratio [60 percent men to 40 percent women] than if it had a different mix." *Id.* at 30,406. This view prevailed and ultimately, Bayh's amendment failed.

The next year, Bayh offered a new version of his antidiscrimination measure, which exempted undergraduate admissions, as well as military academies from coverage. 118 CONG. REC. 5803 (daily ed. Feb. 28, 1972). Bayh justified these exceptions by asserting that coverage would "be disruptive both in terms of the academic program and in terms of psychological and financial alumni support." *Id.* at 5807. As for the military exception, Bayh explained candidly that it was intended to increase the odds of passage. He stated that "there are a few isolated instances where a girl might want to get into a military school." *Id.* at 5813. The amendment also exempted admissions at the elementary and secondary school level. *Id.* at 5812. But it would apply to admissions in vocational education, professional education, graduate education, and public undergraduate institutions. *Id.* at 5803.

Not satisfied with the balance Bayh tried to strike, former Senator Lloyd Bentsen (D-TX) offered an amendment that excluded historically single-sex colleges and universities from coverage under the bill. *Id.* at 5814. Four such institutions existed at the time, one of which was Texas Woman's University (TWU). *Id.* Bentsen argued that students should have the choice to attend a sex-segregated institution. *Id.* Former Senator John Tower (R-TX) supported this amendment, arguing that coeducational institutions were not preparing women adequately. He claimed that TWU "remed[ied] this oversight." *Id.* at 5814–15. Bayh agreed to this amendment based on his belief that women's institutions did not

example, Title IX does not apply to admissions in nonvocational elementary and secondary schools,[66] which are the very schools that are at issue. In addition, the statute does not apply to certain sex-segregated activities, such as "any Boys State conference, Boys Nation conference, Girls State conference or Girls Nation conference."[67] The statute does not apply to "father-son or mother-daughter activities at an educational institution."[68] Each of these activities may be sex segregated as long as "reasonably comparable activities" are provided for the excluded sex.[69] At present, Title IX's implementing regulations make clear that single-sex classes also are permissible in physical education classes "involv[ing] bodily contact" or in other classes dealing with "human sexuality."[70] Additionally, the regulations allow school districts to create single-sex classes for remedial or affirmative action purposes.[71]

The Constitution also allows for sex segregation in education under limited circumstances. Any effort to separate students based on sex is subject to heightened scrutiny, which places the burden on the state to provide an "'exceedingly persuasive justification'"[72] for classifying students based on sex. In *Mississippi University for Women v. Hogan*,[73] the Supreme Court explained that this "burden is met only by showing at least that the classification serves 'important governmental objectives and that the discriminatory means employed' are 'substantially related to the achievement of those objectives.'"[74] In other words, the stated rationale supporting sex-based admissions policies must be grounded in reality and not on fixed notions concerning the roles and abilities of males and females. Care must be taken in ascertaining whether the

---

contribute to discrimination against women in education. *Id.* at 5815. Bayh's measure passed with the amendment. 118 Cong. Rec. 6277 (daily ed. Mar. 1, 1972).

When members of the Senate and House convened to reconcile their respective bills, House sponsor Edith Green (D-OR) stated that she supported an exemption for single-sex schools because she feared that proponents of such schools would torpedo the bill without one. 118 Cong. Rec. S18, 437–38 (daily ed. May 23, 1972). As a matter of personal opinion, however, Green was equivocal, stating that she had not "resolved this in [her] own mind. But in those schools that do admit both men and women.... I think there ought to be an end to discrimination." *Id.* at S18,438. Green took a single-axis view of discrimination in this context, limiting her stated concern to bias confronting white women in education. Specifically, Green argued that "in many places women are required to have a higher grade point average and greater ability, but in terms of minority groups we lower the admission standards in order to have more numerically." *Id.* at S18,437. She added that "I just do not understand how the Congress, which has been concerned about minority groups not being in the apprenticeship program can let year after year go by with only token participation by girls." *Id.* at S18,438. Green thus not only accorded primacy to white women in the effort for gender equality in education, she established a *minorities versus white women* paradigm apparently as a strategic matter to promote passage of Title IX. By inserting race into the debate in this manner, Green suggested that deserving white women had been excluded from the regime of civil rights laws that existed at the time. In addition, her use of race ironically evoked the construction of white womanhood of requiring protection. *See infra* notes 181–86 and accompanying text.

66. 20 U.S.C. §1681(a)(1). *But see Garrett*, 775 F. Supp. at 1009 (holding that the exemption for elementary and secondary school admissions applies only to "historically pre-existing single sex schools; it is not viewed as authorization to establish new single sex schools"). To date, this is the only decision interpreting Title IX regulations in this manner.

67. 20 U.S.C. §1681(a)(7)(B).

68. *Id.* §1681(a)(8).

69. *Id.*

70. 34 C.F.R. §106.34(c), (e) (2003).

71. *Id.* §106.3.

72. *Pers. Adm'r of Mass. v. Feeney*, 442 U.S. 256, 273 (1979); *see also Miss. Univ. for Women v. Hogan*, 458 U.S. 718, 724 (1982) (quoting *Kirchberg v. Feenstra*, 450 U.S. 455, 461 (1981)).

73. 458 U.S. at 718.

74. *Id.* at 724 (citation omitted).

statutory objective itself reflects archaic and stereotypic notions. "Thus, if the statutory objective is to exclude or 'protect' members of one gender because they are presumed to suffer from an inherent handicap or to be innately inferior, the objective itself is illegitimate."[75]

The Court applied this test to the all-female admissions policy at the Mississippi University for Women School of Nursing, which had rejected the plaintiff's application because of his sex. According to the state, the admissions policy was necessary to "compensate for discrimination against women"; therefore, it was a form of "educational affirmative action."[76] The Court rejected this justification because the state failed to adduce evidence of historical barriers to nursing for women.[77] In so doing, the Court explained that a state may "evoke a compensatory purpose to justify an otherwise discriminatory classification only if members of the gender benefited by the classification actually suffer a disadvantage related to the classification."[78]

The Court further explicated the standard for sex-segregated education in *United States v. Virginia* (*VMI*).[79] In this case, the Court characterized the level of scrutiny to be applied as "skeptical,"[80] noting that such an analysis is the necessary "respon[se] to volumes of

---

75. *Id.* at 725 (citation omitted).

76. *Id.* at 727.

77. *Id.* at 729. However, it must be noted that the field of nursing has a raced and gendered hierarchy that has limited opportunities for women and men of color. *See* Evelyn Nakano Glenn, *From Servitude to Service Work: Historical Continuities in the Racial Division of Paid Reproductive Labor*, Signs: J. Women Culture & Soc. 1, 23 (1992). Registered nurses (RNs) are at the top of this hierarchy. They "perform medical tasks and patient care as delegated by physicians and enforc[e] hospital rules … [they] are overwhelming female and disproportionately white." *Id.* At the next level are licensed practical nurses (LPNs), whom the RNs supervise: they are "female but disproportionately women of color." *Id.* Further down the ladder are the "nurse's aides, predominantly women of color; and orderlies, … primarily men of color." *Id.* Access to the top positions means a higher salary, greater career options, and, as a result, potentially better quality of life:

> Unlike the lower ranks, registered nursing offers a career ladder. Starting as a staff nurse, a hospital RN can rise to head nurse, nursing supervisor, and finally, director of nursing. In 1980 [two years before the Court decided *Hogan*], whites were 86.7 percent of RNs even though they were only 76.7 percent of the population.... Racial-ethnic workers constituted 23.4 percent of LPNs, with Blacks, who were 11.7 percent of the population, making up fully 17.9 percent.... Among nurse's aides, 34.6 percent were minorities, with Blacks making up 27.0 percent of all aides.

Id. at 24. The underrepresentation of Blacks in nursing is directly related to discrimination. Specifically, "nursing schools in the South excluded Blacks altogether, while northern schools maintained strict quotas." *Id.* at 25. The few Blacks who were able to get training to become nurses were restricted to racially segregated courses that allowed them to treat only Black patients, even in the racially integrated Northern hospitals. *Id.* at 25–26. The social construction of Black women as immoral justified excluding them from this career path.

> [An administrator from Grady Hospital in Atlanta] declared that Negro women under her supervision had no morals: "They are such liars.... They shift responsibility whenever they can.... They quarrel constantly among themselves and will cut up each other's clothes for spite.... Unless they are constantly watched, they will steal anything in sight."

Id. at 26. Presented with a one-dimensional view of nursing—that is, one that examined only the gendered nature of the profession—the Supreme Court limited its analysis to the single axis of sex. *Hogan*, 458 U.S. at 729. However, had it been presented with an intersectional rendering of the justification for the admissions policy—assuming, of course, that the State actually was trying to remedy the historical exclusion of women and men of color—a different outcome might have resulted.

78. *Hogan*, 458 U.S. at 728.

79. 518 U.S. at 515.

80. *Id.* at 531. By invoking "skeptical scrutiny" and the phrase "'exceedingly persuasive justification,'" the Court prompted speculation as to whether it had increased the level of scrutiny afforded

history"[81] of discrimination against women. Notwithstanding its skepticism respecting sex-based classifications, however, the Court also reiterated that equal protection does not forbid all such classifications:

> Inherent differences between men and women, we have come to appreciate, remain cause for celebration, but not for denigration of the members of either sex or for artificial constraints on an individual's opportunity. Sex classifications may be used to compensate women for particular economic disabilities [they have] suffered to promote equal employment opportunity, to advance full development of the talent and capacities of our Nation's people. But such classifications may not be used, as they once were to create or perpetuate the legal, social, and economic inferiority of women.[82]

Thus, the Court held that single-sex education does not offend equal protection if it compensates for past discrimination or provides opportunities to overcome systemic subordination.[83]

Although Title IX and the Constitution already permit limited forms of sex segregation, the Bush administration is planning to amend Title IX's implementing regulations to create additional latitude for school districts to create such programming, according to a recently published Notice of Proposed Rulemaking.[84] This process[85] likely will result in a significant change in the Department of Education's policy on single-sex education and in Title IX's implementing regulations, which were promulgated almost thirty years ago.[86] The department has justified this shift by pointing to the progress that has been made respecting gender equality in education since Title IX's enactment:

> When Title IX was enacted in 1972 and when the current regulations were issued in 1975, discrimination against female students was widespread at all levels of education, including elementary and secondary education....
>
> Thus, at the time that the current regulations were issued, it was not unreasonable to base the regulations on a presumption that, if recipients were permitted to provide single-sex classes beyond the most limited of circumstances, discriminatory practices would likely continue.
>
> Over the past 30 years, the situation has changed dramatically.[87]

---

to sex-based classifications to something akin to strict scrutiny. *See id.*; *see also id.* at 574 (Scalia, J., dissenting) (asserting that the Court had "*de facto* abandon[ed] … intermediate scrutiny that has been our standard for sex-based classifications for some two decades"); Denise C. Morgan, *Anti-Subordination Analysis After* United States v. Virginia: *Evaluating the Constitutionality of K–12 Single-Sex Public Schools*, 1999 U. Chi. Legal F. 381, 383 (noting that the Court had not, in fact, increased the level of scrutiny).

81. *VMI*, 518 U.S. at 531.

82. *Id.* at 533–34 (citations omitted) (footnotes omitted) (quotations omitted).

83. *Id.*

84. Nondiscrimination on the Basis of Sex in Education Programs or Activities Receiving Federal Financial Assistance, 69 Fed. Reg. 11,276 (proposed Mar. 9, 2004) (to be codified at 34 C.F.R. pt. 106.34(b)(1)(i)). The department signaled its intention to regulate in this area in May 2002 in a Notice of Intent to Regulate (NOIR). *See* 67 Fed. Reg. 31,098 (May 8, 2002).

85. The NOIR was "intended to begin the process of public input on [this issue]," prior to the department's issuance of modified regulations. *Id.* at 31,098. Pursuant to the NOIR, the department received 170 comments. 69 Fed. Reg. at 11,277.

86. *See* 67 Fed. Reg. at 31,098 n.1 (observing that the existing regulations were issued after the department received and reviewed almost 10,000 comments from the public).

87. 69 Fed. Reg. at 11,276.

In this connection, the department has determined that the proposed regulations must meet school districts' need for "flexibility,"[88] suggesting that the progress toward gender equity in education, due in large part to Title IX, justifies relaxing the current regulatory scheme.

The proposed regulations would permit school districts to create single-sex classes[89] to fulfill an "important governmental [or educational] objective," which mirrors the constitutional standard.[90] In this context, the department has identified two such objectives: "provid[ing] a diversity of educational options to students and parents ... or ... meet[ing] the particular, identified educational needs of its students."[91] To be permissible under the proposed regulations, single-sex classes also must be "substantially related to meeting"[92] each of those goals. The proposed regulations further require that recipients provide "substantially equal"[93] op-

---

88. "Given the current environment, we believe that additional flexibility is warranted, and that this flexibility will not compromise equal educational opportunities for male and female students." *Id.* at 11,277.

89. The proposed amendments would not apply to classes in vocational schools. *Id.* at 11,278. The notice also reiterated that Title IX does not apply to admissions policies in nonvocational elementary and secondary schools. *Id.* at 11,281. The proposed regulations therefore would be inapplicable to such policies. *Id.*

90. *See, e.g., VMI*, 518 U.S. at 533.

91. 69 FED. REG. at 11,278.

92. *Id.*

93. *See id.* This proposed requirement departs from a suggestion made in the NOIR that such recipients need only provide "comparable" opportunities for the excluded sex, consistent with the existing regulations. 67 FED. REG. at 31,098–99. Rejecting that standard was appropriate.

An examination of *Vorchheimer v. Sch. Dist. of Philadelphia*, 400 F. Supp. 326, 334 (E.D. Pa. 1975), demonstrates not only the sheer inadequacy of the "comparability" standard but also how gendered presumptions can dominate the equality analysis of sex-segregated programming and, in so doing, reinforce subordination. In resolving the issue of whether all-male Central High School violated the equal protection clause, the district court concluded that the school was "comparable" to its all-female counterpart, Girls High. *Id.* at 329. But the facts suggested otherwise. *See id.* at 328–29.

Central, founded in 1836 as the first public high school in Philadelphia, boasted of illustrious alumni and prodigious resources. Its graduates included "many men who are currently prominent in the professional, political, and cultural life of [the] city and state ... [and the school] has a deserved reputation for training men who will become local and national leaders in all fields of endeavor." *Id.* at 328. The success of its graduates further was reflected in alumni contributions—tangible and intangible—that equaled those of college alumni. *Id.* at 329. Additionally, because of Central's history and tradition of excellence the school "attracted the attention of national leaders throughout [its] history," among them: former Presidents James Polk and Theodore Roosevelt, former Attorney General Robert Kennedy, and former Vice President Hubert Humphrey. *Id.* at 328–29. "The visits of the latter two ... were arranged through the auspices of the Barnwell Foundation, which was established by a Central alumnus." *Id.* at 329. Central had a "substantial private endowment," the only city high school to be so fortunate. *Id.*

In contrast, Girls High was founded in 1848 to train teachers—male and female alike—for the city's public schools. *Id.* at 328. The leaders among Girls High alumnae were neither as numerous nor as accomplished as were Central graduates. "Among the current community leaders who have graduated from Girls are three judges of the Court of Common Pleas of Philadelphia and the first vice-president of the American Medical Association." *Id.* at 329. Similarly, Girls High alumnae apparently had not demonstrated the same "dedication and loyalty" to their alma mater in terms of financial contributions, since no mention is made of such. Notwithstanding the reputation of the school, there apparently was no record of former presidents or Cabinet members visiting the campus to address students. However, despite all these disparities, the only difference the court observed between the two institutions was that the "scientific facilities" at Central were "superior." *Id.*

The fact that male students had access to greater resources, greater prestige, and greater opportunities to learn science was of no moment to the court because those were the students best able to make use of the social and economic advantages bound to follow from these experiences when they graduated. In other words, the disparity between Central and Girls High reflected the gender-based roles that male and female students would play on reaching adulthood, and therefore did not signal inequality. *See infra* notes 180–205 and accompanying text.

portunities to the excluded sex and that they provide single-sex opportunities in an "even-handed"[94] manner.

While the proposed regulations reflect the constitutional standard articulated in the Supreme Court's *VMI* decision, the proposed regulations depart from the antisubordination principles that animated the case in significant ways. For example, *VMI* noted that the Court's jurisprudence concerning gender-based classifications "reveals a strong presumption that [they] are invalid."[95] Instead, the department's regulations proceed from the premise that such skepticism is no longer necessary because "educational opportunities for young women and girls, and the commitment of educators to those opportunities have increased."[96] In addition, *VMI* made clear that sex-based classifications "must be genuine, not hypothesized or invented *post hoc* in response to litigation [nor] ... rely on overbroad generalizations about the different talents, capacities, or preferences of males and females."[97] In contrast, the proposed regulations would permit the creation of single-sex classes based on such ambiguous factors as "reliable information" and "sound educational judgment"[98] to "meet the particular, identified educational needs of the recipient's students."[99] In this regard, it should be noted that Virginia attempted to justify the all-female alternative to *VMI*, the Virginia Women's Institute for Leadership (VWIL) by relying on such rationales. For example, the fact that VWIL students neither received the same military training as *VMI* students nor "experience[d] the 'barracks' life 'crucial to the *VMI* experience,'"[100] was based on "pedagogical"[101] reasons—that is, the presumably sound educational judgment of a specially created task force that had determined that "a military model and, especially *VMI*'s adversative method, would be wholly inappropriate for educating and training *most women*."[102] By evoking the constitutional standard, but simultaneously providing recipients with the leeway to avoid their obligations, the proposed regulations very likely will lead to the very gender-based stereotyping Title IX was enacted to combat.

Skepticism concerning the department's approach is especially warranted given its conclusion that single-sex education is a beneficial pedagogical tool,[103] notwithstanding the long-standing and ongoing controversy regarding the merits or disadvantages of sex segregation.[104] Based on this determination, the proposed regulations do not require

---

While the U.S. Court of Appeals for the Third Circuit vacated the district court's decision, 532 F.2d 880 (3d Cir. 1976), and affirmed by an "equally divided" Supreme Court, 430 U.S. 703 (1977), a state court ultimately struck down the all-male policy as violative of its state constitution. *See generally Newberg v. Bd. of Pub. Educ.*, 26 Pa. D & C 3d. 682, 1983 Pa. D & C LEXIS 245 (C. P. Ct. 1983).

94. 67 Fed. Reg. at 31,098–99.

95. 518 U.S. at 532.

96. 69 Fed. Reg. at 11,276.

97. 518 U.S. at 533.

98. *Id.* at 11,279.

99. *Id.*

100. *VMI*, 518 U.S. at 548.

101. *Id.* at 549–50.

102. *Id.* at 550 (emphasis added).

103. "Educational research has suggested that in certain circumstances, single-sex education provides educational benefits for some students." 69 Fed. Reg. at 11,276. An accompanying footnote acknowledges that "there is presently a debate ... regarding the effectiveness of single sex education." *Id.* at 11,276 n.3. The fact that the department has deemed it necessary to promote single sex by modifying long-standing regulations suggests that department officials have determined that sex segregation is an educational policy worth pursuing irrespective of the ongoing debate.

104. *See, e.g., Levit, supra* note 54, at 451 (examining the conflicting empirical evidence regarding single-sex education); *see also* Patricia B. Campbell & Joe Sanders, *Challenging the System: Assumptions and Data Behind the Push for Single-Sex Schooling, in* Gender in Policy and Practice: Perspectives on Single-Sex and Coeducational Schooling 31, 32 (Amanda Datnow & Lea Hub-

recipients to obtain department approval before creating single-sex programming,[105] suggesting that a school district's decision to create such programming should be considered presumptively valid. In this regard, the proposed amendments send school districts the green light to try single-sex education with little consideration given to the implications for gender equality in schools. The department suggests that such a message is appropriate based on its view that sex discrimination is a problem of the past and that sex segregation is not only benign but also beneficial. Thus, the Office for Civil Rights can now turn its attentions to promoting "flexibility"[106] through the proposed regulations.

This proposal is at odds with long-established law and has serious implications for the children who supposedly will benefit from this approach, who primarily are students of color.[107] As the next part demonstrates, segregated education—race-based and sex-based—has played a major role in the subordination of white women and people of color, in different but overlapping ways. This history suggests that sex segregation in education has the very real potential to retrench raced and gendered stereotypes, to the detriment of the very students these policies purport to serve. Here, it makes sense to examine the history of educating Blacks, white men, and white women in the United States to comprehend fully what is at stake with today's versions of single-sex schooling.

II. Looking Backward to Look Ahead: Race- and Sex-Based Segregation in Education

Without question, educational institutions inform the social roles that young people will assume as adults.[108] In this connection, separating students based on sex takes on great importance as a means of constructing masculinity and femininity in this society.[109] When further examined within the context of state-sanctioned, state-enforced racial segregation, separating the sexes for educational purposes takes on additional significance as a means of constructing the social meaning of race. History suggests that sex segregation has promoted a raced and gendered hierarchy that identifies white males and white females as the prototypes of masculinity and femininity and relegates Black men and Black women to a subordinated position because they fail to

---

bard eds., 2002) (noting that "there has been no national comprehensive controlled study of academic performance for U.S. students in public and private K–12 single-sex and coed schooling"). In fact, two weeks after the department released the proposed regulations, *Education Week* reported that department officials had commissioned Providence College Professor Cornelius Riordan to study single-sex education in the nation's public elementary and secondary schools. Michelle R. Davis, *Federal Study Examining Single-Sex Public Schools*, Educ. Week, Mar. 24, 2004, at 24.

105. 69 Fed. Reg. at 11,277.

106. "The benefit of the proposed regulations is the expanded flexibility to provide single sex schools or classes." *Id.* at 11,283.

107. *See supra* note 31.

108. Among the lessons that children learn in school is about their proper place in society. *See, e.g.*, Cynthia Hudley, *Schools as Contexts for Socialization, in* Race and Education: The Roles of History and Society in Educating African American Students 225–29 (William Watkins et al. eds., 2001).

109. An examination of women's colleges might suggest otherwise; however, a full examination of those institutions is beyond the scope of this chapter.

conform to those norms.[110] As a result, sex segregation historically has been a key element of the hidden curriculum,[111] which reinforces gendered and raced expectations for students, limits their educational opportunities, and ultimately constrains their life opportunities.

Though the past does not necessarily predict the future, examining the history of sex segregation with respect to sex and race provides a strong foundation for understanding current efforts to resuscitate single-sex schooling. As Reva Siegel has observed, examining the past demonstrates how the legal system has supported racial and gender-based hierarchies.[112] With this understanding, Siegel argues we can also determine whether reforms in the law actually dismantle such subordination or whether they merely allow it to take another form.[113] In this context, then, one must ask the following: if we acknowledge that the rationales justifying sex segregation may have evolved over the past 100 years or so, will single-sex schooling, in its "new" form, deliver the promised reforms so necessary for students of color, or will it merely perpetuate racial and gender-based subordination?[114] Guided by this inquiry, the next section examines sex segregation within the context of the nation's history of racial segregation.[115]

A. The History of Educating African Americans: Segregation Constructing Race and Gender

For much of its history, the nation's system of educating its young excluded African Americans. Because of slavery, questions persisted regarding the propriety and wisdom of educating Blacks. Prior to 1835, ad hoc efforts to educate Blacks existed, promoted by "masters who desired to increase the economic efficiency of their labor supply; ... sympathetic persons who wished to help the oppressed; and ... zealous missionaries who ... taught slaves the English language that they might learn the principles of the Christian religion."[116] As slavery became the engine propelling the nation's economy, however, op-

---

110. *See, e.g.*, Crenshaw, *supra* note 57, at 156 n.43 ("Women, who often fail to conform to 'appropriate' sex roles, have been pictured as, and made to feel, inadequate—even though as women, they possess traits recognized as positive when held by men in the wider society. Such women are stigmatized because their lack of adherence to expected gender roles is seen as a threat to the value system." (internal quotes omitted)).

111. *See, e.g.*, Hudley, *supra* note 108, at 226–27.

112. *See* Reva Siegel, *Why Equal Protection No Longer Protects: The Evolving Forms of Status-Enforcing State Action*, 49 Stan. L. Rev. 1111, 1116, 1119 (1997) ("In gender, race, and class relationships, the legal system continued to allocate privileges and entitlements in a manner that perpetuated former systems of express hierarchy ... [in this respect] the process of dismantling an entrenched system of status relations may well transform the regime without abolishing it." Siegel terms this "reform dynamic ... 'preservation-through-transformation.'" (footnote omitted)).

113. *Id.*

114. *Id.* at 1116; *see also* Jill Elaine Hasday, *The Principle and Practice of Women's "Full Citizenship": A Case Study of Sex-Segregated Public Education*, 101 Mich. L. Rev. 755, 779 (2002) (positing that "even a brief review of the historical record of sex-segregated public education demonstrates that a practice's role in promoting unequal citizenship and legalized inferiority can evolve and shift"). In other words, will the new sex segregation "be used as [it] once [was] to create or perpetuate the legal, social, and economic inferiority" of students of color? *See VMI*, 518 U.S. at 534 (citation omitted).

115. The history that follows is abbreviated because a full exploration of the history of race- and sex-based segregation clearly is beyond the scope of this chapter.

116. Carter G. Woodson, *The Education of the African-Americans Prior to 1861*, *in* Foundations of African-American Education 5 (Julie Kehrwald ed., 1998).

position to educating Blacks grew, particularly in the South. Historian Carter G. Woodson explained that this hostility was rooted in the desire to increase that region's ability to compete in

> the worldwide industrial movement. It so revolutionized spinning and weaving that the resulting increased demand for cotton fiber gave rise to the plantation system of the South, which required a larger number of slaves. Becoming too numerous to be considered as included in the body politic ... the slaves were generally doomed to live without any enlightenment whatsoever. Thereafter, rich planters not only thought it unwise to educate men thus destined to live on a plane with beasts, but considered it more profitable to work a slave to death during seven years and buy another in his stead, than to teach and humanize him with a view to increasing his efficiency.[117]

Accordingly, states passed laws prohibiting the education of slaves as early as 1740. The majority of such laws appeared, however, in the first half of the nineteenth century.[118] Woodson reports that in a few instances, slave masters ignored these laws because they had valuable slaves capable of "bookkeeping [and] printing." However,

> The majority of the people in the South [believed] that, as intellectual elevation unfits men for servitude and renders it impossible to retain them in this condition, it should be interdicted. In other words, the more you cultivate the minds of slaves, the more unserviceable you make them; you give them a higher relish for those privileges which they cannot attain and turn what you intend for a blessing into a curse. If they are to remain in slavery, then they should be kept in the lowest state of ignorance and degradation. The nearer you bring them to the condition of brutes, the better chance they have to retain their apathy.[119]

A literate slave was dangerous to the institution of slavery. Recognizing the important role schooling could play in their lives, however, some slaves risked being sold away from their families or worse to learn to read and write.[120]

With the approach of the Civil War, more Northerners took up the cause of education for African Americans as a way of dismantling the Confederacy:[121]

> The logic was simple: an educated ex-slave would be forever "ruined" for any future slavocracy usage. To facilitate this ruination, the government of Abraham Lincoln immediately arranged to transport hundreds of abolitionist educators, both Black and White, from the north to these areas for the purpose of setting up and staffing ... schools [for Blacks].[122]

---

117. *Id.* at 6–7.

118. *Id.* at 7.

119. *Id.*

120. Historians estimate that about 5 percent of the slave population surreptitiously learned to read before the end of the Civil War. *See* Remembering Slavery: African Americans Talk About Their Personal Experiences of Slavery and Freedom 206 (Ira Berlin et al. eds., 1998). For example, Mandy Jones, who was a slave in Mississippi, explained how slaves received a rudimentary education in "pit schools" from other slaves who had been taught secretly by white children. *Id.* She stated:

> Slaves would slip out o' de Quarters at night, an go to dese pits [holes dug in the ground by other slaves], an some niggah dat had some learnin' would have a school. De way de cullud folks would learn to read was from de white chilluns ... [who would] slip off somewhere an' learns de culled chilluns ... what deir teacher has jes' learned dem.

Id.

121. *See* Darryle J. Gatlin, *The Education of African Americans Since 1861, in* Foundations of African-American Education 15 (1998).

122. *Id.*

After the Civil War and the abolition of slavery, doors to educational opportunities slowly began to open for Blacks. The Freedmen's Bureau, which Congress established in 1866 to help the newly freed slaves,[123] provided the first public schooling for Blacks as well as for whites in the South.[124] However, a serious question arose as to what sort of education was most appropriate for the newly freed slaves, given the "political realities"[125] of the day: classical or industrial education.

1. Racialized Realities: Determining the Best Educational Fit for Blacks

Central to this debate was the issue of the role free Blacks should have in society: specifically, whether Blacks should be free to pursue educational paths that would allow them to determine their own destinies and attain rights and privileges equal to those of whites, or whether Blacks should acquire training to permit continued service to whites, which would lead to white approbation and, as a consequence, peaceful coexistence between the races. W. E. B. Du Bois, Anna Julia Cooper,[126] missionary philanthropists, and others[127] advocated educating Blacks to facilitate their struggle for equal rights.[128] For example, Du Bois argued that in order for African Americans to progress, a "talented tenth" of the Black population should receive higher education to "rise and pull all that are worth

---

123. With passage of the Civil Rights Act of 1866, codified at 42 U.S.C. § 1981, Congress created the Freedmen's Bureau and granted it the authority (albeit without any appropriations) to establish — among other things — public schools for the newly freed slaves. *See, e.g.,* W. E. B. Du Bois, *The Freedman's Bureau* (1901), *reprinted in* DuBois on Education 102 (Eugene F. Provenzo Jr. ed., 2002).

124. *See id.* at 105; *see also* Beverly Guy-Sheftall, Daughters of Sorrow: Attitudes Toward Black Women, 1880–1920, at 94 (1990). The Freedmen's Bureau's educational efforts added to existing schools created by missionaries, churches, and other private parties. *See* William H. Watkins, *Blacks and the Curriculum: From Accommodation to Contestation and Beyond, in* Race and Education: The Roles of History and Society in Educating African American Students 41–42 (William Watkins et al. eds., 2001) [hereafter Watkins, *Blacks and the Curriculum*].

125. Watkins, *Blacks and the Curriculum, supra* note 124, at 42.

126. Cooper has been called "a foundational figure among black feminists in America." Charles Lemert, *Anna Julia Cooper: The Colored Woman's Office, in* The Voice of Anna Julia Cooper 1 (Charles Lemert & Esme Bhan eds., 1998). She believed strongly in Du Bois's notions of the "talented tenth." As a principal of the all-Black M Street High School in Washington, D.C., from 1901 to 1906, she put those ideas to work by "strengthen[ing] its curriculum in classical subjects [so much] that a markedly greater number of its graduates were accepted to elite colleges like Harvard." *Id.* at 9. Her loyalty to Du Bois ultimately cost her that position; the school board fired her after she completed her fifth year of service. "[Booker T.] Washington's Tuskegee Machine, as it was known by its opponents, worked hard to exercise its control wherever in the nation the industrial education strategy was opposed." *Id.* at 10. Tuskegee targeted Cooper with hostility, not only because of her strong commitments to the industrial education program at M Street but "because she was herself so obviously well educated and [provided an] effective a model to her pupils." *Id.*

127. Southern Black leaders and educators associated attainment of quality education with progress for African Americans after the Civil War:

> The quest for self-determination ... demanded knowledge of society, citizenship, and vocation. The cultivation of teachers, leaders, ministers, managers, and skilled tradesmen were objectives of early black education. Many black educators were attracted to the New England-styled classical liberal curriculum ... as it promised participation in the social life of the new America.

Watkins, *Blacks and the Curriculum, supra* note 124, at 41.

128. Gatlin, *supra* note 121, at 21.

the saving up to their vantage ground."[129] Du Bois urged that this "best and most capable [group should] be schooled in the colleges and universities of the land," so they, in turn, might teach other Blacks formally in the classroom and informally as role models in their communities.[130] Similarly, "missionary philanthropists basically egalitarian in their views of civil rights and race relations [considered and supported] black higher education as a means to produce a college-bred black leadership that would lead the black masses in their struggle for equal rights."[131] Under this view, higher education was key to Black liberation after the Civil War.

In contrast, Northern industrial philanthropists believed that Blacks should be educated in a manner consistent with "the existing racial and social class structure of the South.... The tasks of the northern hegemonists and their southern supporters were to reconcile the growing black demand for education with the political realities of peonage and oppression."[132] This group was willing to accommodate Blacks' interest in education, but only to the extent that it did not create a large educated elite class that might foment rebellion. "Containment and subjugation became the objective of imposed Negro education."[133]

One of the proponents of industrial education, which was consistent with the "containment" strategy, was Booker T. Washington, a former slave and a chief architect of Tuskegee Institute's industrial education program. Washington believed that the true ticket to emancipation and white acceptance for African Americans lay in developing practical skills:

> Some time ago, when we decided to make tailoring a part of our training at the Tuskegee Institute, I was amazed to find that it was almost impossible to find in the whole country an educated coloured man who could teach the making of clothing. We could find them by the score who could teach astronomy, theology, grammar, or Latin, but almost none who could instruct in the making of clothing, something that has to be used by every one of us every day in the year....

---

129. W. E. B. Du Bois, *The Talented Tenth* (1903), *reprinted in* DuBois on Education 80 (Eugene F. Provenzo Jr. ed., 2002) [hereafter DuBois, *The Talented Tenth*]. It should be noted, however that Du Bois's vision was gender-specific:

> The Negro race, like all races, is going to be saved by its exceptional men.... Men we shall have only as we make manhood the object of the work of the schools—intelligence, broad sympathy, knowledge of the world that was and is, and of the relation of men to it— this is the curriculum of that Higher Education which must underlie true life.

Id. at 76. Du Bois also recognized that Black women played an important role in the African American struggle for equality and argued specifically for their liberation from constraining stereotypes. He stated:

> The future woman must have a life work and economic independence. She must have knowledge. She must have the right of motherhood at her own discretion.
>
> ....
>
> To no modern race does its women mean so much as to the Negro nor come so near to the fulfilment of its meaning.
>
> ....
>
> As I look about me today in this veiled world of mine, despite the noisier and more spectacular advance of my brothers, I instinctively feel and know that it is the five million women of my race who really count.

W. E. B. Du Bois, *The Damnation of Women, in* Darkwater: Voices from Within the Veil 164, 173, 179 (1920).

130. DuBois, *The Talented Tenth, supra* note 129, at 80, 86.

131. Watkins, *Blacks and the Curriculum, supra* note 124, at 42 (citation omitted).

132. *See id.*

133. *Id.* at 43.

> It is time to make up, as soon as possible, for this mistake ... time for both races
> to acknowledge it and go forth on the course that, it seems to me, all must now
> see to be the right one ... industrial education.[134]

In Washington's view, industrial education would impart practical skills that were sorely
needed among Blacks. With such training, African Americans would prove they could
contribute to society, which in turn would reduce the racial animosity that existed between Blacks and Whites. Washington posited that:

> the history of the world proves that trade, commerce, is the forerunner of peace
> and civilisation as between races and nations. The Jew, who was once in about
> the same position that the Negro is today, has now recognition, because he has
> entwined himself about America in a business and industrial sense. Say or think
> what we will, it is the tangible or visible element that is going to tell largely dur-
> ing the next twenty years in the solution of the race problem.[135]

Thus, according to Washington, industrial education would enable Blacks to obtain the
few opportunities available to them within the racist infrastructure, while simultaneously
casting doubt on the racist ideology that constrained African Americans.

Despite their differences, Washington and Du Bois both struggled against the prevalent
view that limited educational opportunities for Blacks simply made sense because of their
purportedly limited capacity to learn. At this time, the popular and scientific discourse
concerning African Americans was decidedly negative. For example, Columbia University
published a report that provided ample "evidence" of the intellectual deficiencies of Blacks:

> In both boys and girls among the Negroes the highest brightness seems to be
> thirteen years; the highest ability for boys was found to be eight years and for the
> girls nine years. With white children ability increases and brightness decreases with
> age. As a rule, after Negro children become older than ten or twelve years, their
> development is physical rather than mental.[136]

In addition, this report claimed that Blacks were morally deficient and weak of character:

> The Negro has few ideals and perhaps no lasting adherence to an aspiration to-
> ward real worth. He has little conception of the meaning of virtue, truth, honor,
> manhood, integrity. He is shiftless, untidy, and indolent.... The Negro shirks
> details and difficult tasks.... The Negro is improvident and extravagant; lazy
> rather than industrious.[137]

According to this report, these failings of intellect and character meant that African Americans had a limited capacity to succeed educationally; therefore, schooling for Blacks
should be focused in "agricultural and mechanical schools," military schools, and other
settings that would facilitate "manual dexterity" as early as possible.[138] Any additional
schooling was not only unnecessary but ill-advised as a policy matter:

> It seems that the whole current of mental improvement has reached unhappy
> results.

---

134. BOOKER T. WASHINGTON, THE FUTURE OF THE AMERICAN NEGRO 50, 57 (Haskell House
1968) (1899).
135. *Id.* at 65–66.
136. HOWARD W. ODUM, SOCIAL AND MENTAL TRAITS OF THE NEGRO: RESEARCH INTO THE CON-
DITIONS OF THE NEGRO RACE IN SOUTHERN TOWNS: A STUDY IN RACE TRAITS, TENDENCIES AND
PROSPECTS 38 (1910).
137. *Id.* at 39.
138. *Id.* at 44.

> The young educated Negroes are not a force for good in the community but for evil. The Negro quickly outgrows the influence and control of his instructors.... These young Negroes are not in sympathy with their parents; they appear to neglect them more than those who are not 'educated.' They feel that manual labor is beneath their dignity; they are fitted to do no other. They sneer at the idea of work, and they thus spread dissatisfaction among the members of their race.[139]

These notions of intellectual and moral inferiority, and the desire to keep Blacks satisfied with their subordinate status informed the public debate concerning education for African Americans. For example, Samuel Armstrong, founder of Hampton University, the model for Tuskegee Institute, believed that "the Negro could acquire knowledge but not digest it"; therefore, "the Negro could best be morally and socially uplifted though labor and character training."[140] Armed with this racist assessment of Black Americans, Armstrong met with other prominent white educators of the time at the Lake Mohonk Conferences in the Negro Question in Lake Mohonk, New York, in 1890 and 1891 to carve out a "suitable" educational strategy for Blacks. A majority agreed that industrial education was the best course of action for Black men *and* Black women alike because "Blacks were genetically inferior, capable of rudimentary vocational education, and urgently in need of 'character building.'"[141] Significantly, as educators determined what type of education was most appropriate for Blacks, there was little discussion regarding whether training should be limited to Black men or whether to separate African Americans by sex. The tenor of these discussions would shift, however, as gender conformity—and conformity to the patriarchal order—gained status as a strategy for Black assimilation.[142]

2. Gender Realities: An Evolving Role for Sex

When considered in light of the nation's recent experience with slavery, the lack of concern regarding Black males and Black females learning together in the post-Reconstruction era is not surprising. During slavery, Black women and Black men routinely worked side by side, performing tasks that ordinarily would be considered "man's work." Jacqueline Jones explains that males and females shared many of the same difficult jobs:

> Together with their fathers, husbands, brothers, and sons, black women spent up to fourteen hours a day toiling out of doors, often under a blazing sun. In the Cotton Belt they plowed fields; dropped seed; and hoed, picked, ginned, sorted, and moted cotton. On farms in Virginia, North Carolina, Kentucky, and Tennessee, women hoed tobacco; laid worm fences; and threshed, raked, and bound wheat....

> Stated simply, most women spent a good deal of their lives plowing, hoeing, and picking cotton. In the fields the notion of a distinctive "women's work" vanished as slaveholders realized that "women can do plowing very well [and] full well with the hoes and [are] equal to men at picking."[143]

---

139. *Id.* at 41.

140. Watkins, *Blacks and the Curriculum, supra* note 124, at 43.

141. *Id.* at 44.

142. *See infra* notes 161–80 and accompanying text.

143. Jacqueline Jones, Labor of Love, Labor of Sorrow: Black Women, Work, and the Family from Slavery to the Present 15–16 (1985) (footnote omitted). It is important to note, however, that female slaves differed from their male counterparts in one very significant aspect: the ability to procreate. As a result, female slaves were valued not only for their ability to work in the fields but also for their reproductive capacity, which would increase the slave population and thus

The absence of gendered roles was apparent even among Black slave children, who dressed alike in "'split-tail shirt[s]'... knee-length smock[s] slit up the sides," handled similar chores on the plantation,[144] and played in non–gender-specific ways.[145] Starting from a young age, Black females could not aspire—nor were expected—to become "true women."[146] Similarly, Black males were not true men.[147]

Still, even without being considered "true women," Black women confronted gendered and raced expectations about their role in society as females, which in turn informed the educational opportunities available to them. For example, with the success of the Freedmen's Bureau in providing educational opportunities in the post-Reconstruction period came a growing demand for schooling. With this demand for schooling came an increased need for teachers to provide the most basic level of education to illiterate former slaves. Black women, by virtue of their sex, were deemed the likeliest of candidates to do the teaching,[148] in light of the fact that they held significant child care responsibilities for their masters' and their own families.

The confluence of raced and gendered stereotypes about Black women also resulted in the creation of educational opportunities that addressed their perceived intellectual and moral shortcomings. For instance, because many Southerners thought Black women were unintelligent, they argued that education should be limited to teaching Black women to serve white people.[149] Northerners, on the other hand, believed that Black women were educable but lacking in morality and virtues; therefore, their schooling should emphasize character development.[150] Beverly Guy-Sheftall presents a compelling example of how white stereotypes of Black women informed their educational opportunities in her description of the founding of Spelman College.[151]

---

enhance their master's wealth. Significantly, however, this distinction did not exempt Black women from plantation work. Pregnant women still were expected to pick cotton, albeit a reduced amount. On giving birth, nursing mothers carried their babies to work with them, as described by a former slave: "'When [the baby] get hungry, she just slip it around in front and feed it and go right on picking or hoeing.'" *Id.* at 14; *see also* DEBORAH GRAY WHITE, AR'N'T I A WOMAN? FEMALE SLAVES IN THE PLANTATION SOUTH 67–69 (1985).

144. *See* JONES, *supra* note 143, at 23 (noting that "on smaller holdings especially, the demands of housework, like cotton cultivation, admitted no finely honed division of labor").

145. WHITE, *supra* note 143, at 92–93.

146. The term "true women" refers to the prototype of white femininity that emerged during the industrial revolution. BARBARA WELTER, DIMITY CONVICTIONS: THE AMERICAN WOMAN IN THE NINE-TEENTH CENTURY 21 (1976). Specifically, the "true" woman's place was in the home and on a pedestal:

> The attributes of True Womanhood, by which a woman judged herself and was judged by her husband, her neighbors and society, could be divided into four cardinal virtues—piety, purity, submissiveness and domesticity. Put them all together and they spelled mother, daughter, sister, wife—woman. Without them, no matter whether there was fame, achievement or wealth, all was ashes. With them she was promised happiness and power.

Id. But see Crenshaw, *supra* note 57, at 156 (observing that true womanhood was not available to Black women).

147. *See, e.g.*, Derrick Bell, *The Sexual Diversion: The Black Man/Black Woman Debate in Context*, *in* BLACK MEN ON RACE, GENDER, AND SEXUALITY: A CRITICAL READER 239–40 (Devon Carbado ed., 1999) (arguing that slavery controlled and humiliated Black men by limiting access to their wives and "forc[ing them] to stand by powerless and unable to protect black women from sexual access by white men," among other things).

148. WHITE, *supra* note 143, at 94.

149. GUY-SHEFTALL, *supra* note 124, at 130.

150. *Id.* at 131.

151. *Id.* at 132–37. It should be noted that despite origins based on raced and gendered stereotypes, Spelman College and its historically Black counterparts have emerged as leading institutions for educating African Americans:

In 1883, Sophia Packard and Harriet Giles, two white female missionaries from New England, ventured south on learning that Dr. Henry Morehouse, a field secretary of the American Baptist Home Missionary Society, had planned to establish a coeducational institution for Blacks in Atlanta.[152] Not unlike many white educators of the time, Giles and Packard believed in separate schooling for women;[153] they were unique in promoting this form of education for Black women. Accordingly, Giles and Packard approached Morehouse and the Missionary Society and urged that some property in Atlanta be set aside to establish an institution dedicated to educating Black women and preparing them to assume their appropriate role in the post-Reconstruction society.[154] Giles and Packard were

> preoccup[ied] with industrial and practical education ... set[ting Spelman] apart from the white female seminary tradition that concentrated, for the most part, on academic subjects.... Ever mindful of the peculiar history of black women in America and the realities of their everyday lives, Packard and Giles' primary aim was to provide training for teachers, nurses, missionaries, and church workers— areas of employment open to black women.[155]

Giles and Packard believed in "true womanhood";[156] and part of their mission was to inculcate Black women with this norm—but in a modified fashion. They recognized that the traditional "separate spheres"[157] ideology informing the "classical" education that white women received[158] did not apply to Black women. Accordingly, Giles and Packard designed a curriculum that would prepare Black women to work outside their own homes and support their families by "imparting ... practical skills that would make black women good homemakers and mothers" and provide them with the training to go into domestic service.[159] In addition, because Giles and Packard were not immune to the stereotypes regarding Black women, particularly their purported lack of morals, a key part of Spelman's training included "molding of Christian character and the eradication of those traits that were a carryover from slavery—dishonesty, tardiness, drunkenness, idleness, immorality, and irresponsibility."[160] Thus, Giles and Packard sought to provide Black women with a unique learning opportunity, informed by the intersection of racial and gender stereotypes.

> Despite a shameful history of state-enforced segregation, [historically black colleges] have survived and flourished. Indeed, they have expanded as opportunities for blacks to enter historically white institutions have expanded....
>
> The colleges founded for Negroes are both a source of pride to blacks who have attended them and a source of hope to black families who want the benefits of higher learning for their children. They have exercised leadership in developing educational opportunities for young blacks at all levels of instruction, and especially in the South, they are still regarded as key institutions for enhancing the general quality of the lives of black Americans.

United States v. Fordice, 505 U.S. 717, 748 (1992) (Thomas, J. concurring) (citations omitted) (quotations omitted). In this regard, historically Black colleges and universities might be seen as transcending their histories as agents of state-sanctioned and state-enforced subordination to become sources of empowerment for African Americans. This chapter questions whether the current versions of single-sex education will be able to do the same, particularly lacking an emphasis on gender equality. *See infra* Part III.

152. GUY-SHEFTALL, *supra* note 124, at 132.

153. *See infra* notes 194–218 and accompanying text.

154. GUY-SHEFTALL, *supra* note 124, at 132–33.

155. *Id.* at 133.

156. *See supra* note 146.

157. *See infra* notes 180–94 and accompanying text.

158. *See infra* notes 206–08 and accompanying text.

159. GUY-SHEFTALL, *supra* note 124, at 134.

160. *Id.* at 136.

Black educators also adopted a strategy of providing African American women with training that had both moral and practical aims. For example, educator Mary McCleod Bethune believed that industrial training was necessary to assist African American efforts to become fully integrated into the nation's fabric. Bethune focused her initial efforts on young women in founding the Daytona Literary and Industrial Training School for Negro Girls (the Daytona School) in 1904.[161] The Daytona School provided students with a mix of academic and vocational coursework to "develop Christian character, to send forth women who [would] be rounded homemakers and Christian leaders ... a trained mind, heart and hand being [Bethune's and her supporters'] idea of a complete education."[162] Separate education for Black girls was necessary because

> of the unique responsibilities of Black girls in the world today. The challenge to the Negro home is one which dares the Negro to develop the initiative to solve his own problems, to work out his own problems, to work out his difficulties in a superior fashion, and to finally come into his right as an American Citizen because he is tolerated. This is the moral responsibility of the education of the Negro girl; It must become a part of her thinking; her activities must lead her into such endeavors early in her educational life; this training must be inculcated into the school curricula so that the result may be a natural expression born into her children. Such is the natural endowment when her education must make it possible for her to bequeath to the future of the Negro race.[163]

Bethune's educational mission was to prepare Black women to participate in the larger effort to uplift the race. In this connection, because Black women were to be the primary caregivers of children, they, in turn, would be responsible for passing down to the next generation the tools necessary to realize the promise of national citizenship implicit in emancipation. Bethune eventually expanded her efforts to include Black males in 1924 when in her words, "the circumstances of growth and maintenance within the prevalent pattern of our young Negro institutions dictated union with Cookman Institute."[164] Thus, the all-female Daytona School evolved into the coeducational Bethune-Cookman College,[165] which remains in existence today.

Another leading educator who focused on educating young African American women to fulfill their particular roles in a constrained society was Nannie Helen Burroughs, founder of the National Training School for Women and Girls (NTS) in 1909. NTS's mission was:

1. To train women for missionary work in this and other lands,

2. To prepare women as teachers of the Word of God in our Sunday Schools,

3. To train women to become better homemakers, and

---

161. Mary McLeod Bethune, *Sixth Annual Catalogue and Industrial Training School for Negro Girls [abridged] (1910–1911), in* MARY MCLEOD BETHUNE: BUILDING A BETTER WORLD 67 (Audrey Thomas McCluskey & Elaine M. Smith eds., 1999).

162. *Id.* at 77–78.

163. *Id.* at 85.

164. *Id.* at 118.

165. It should be noted, however, that even with this development, Bethune apparently continued to believe that single-sex education was important for Black girls and their particular educational needs — that is, educating them to fulfill their obligation to promote the advancement of Black families. Additionally, sex segregation, in Bethune's view, also allowed for "the development of a morale and fellow-feeling among [those] students unconfused by the disturbances of adolescence." *Id.* at 120.

4.   To train women to give better domestic service.[166]

Nicknamed the "School of the Three Bs," for its emphasis on the Bible, bathtub, and broom,[167] NTS sought to assure its students of a firm moral foundation, along with the skills necessary to maintain a household, just as was true for Spelman College and the Daytona School.

> The aim of the School is to give a training of head, hand, and heart and develop a definite and active social interest in the spiritual and moral forces that make for human welfare.

> To accomplish this purpose we have: An atmosphere that is Christian; a spirit that is aggressive, unostentatious but happy; surroundings that are clean; personal ideals that are simple; academic and trade courses that are of high standards.[168]

Students at NTS received training in academic subjects, such as Latin and English literature, and domestic matters, such as dressmaking and housekeeping. In addition, NTS provided training in various trades, such as typesetting and salvaging.[169] Burroughs believed that the trades were of especial importance to Black women—even those with a college education—to enable them to find employment in the likely event of discrimination. As an NTS brochure explained:

> Not many of the colored graduates from normal schools or colleges are accepted in the public school system, as teachers, in the North.... A Trade School will open new avenues of employment to girls who are shut out of teaching in public schools because they live in sections where colored teacher[s] are not generally employed.[170]

Educating women to enter the trades made NTS unique by providing its students training that most assuredly was nontraditional for females and deviating far from the "true woman" construct, which proved to be very risky. Specifically, prominent members of the National Baptist Convention (NBC), a primarily male organization that supported NTS economically "were concerned that the women and girls enrolled in the trades were being trained as 'breadwinners.' For these reasons, the men of the NBC neglected to support the School"[171] and successfully persuaded the organization to withdraw its financial support.[172]

The controversy sparked by the addition of the trades to the curriculum at the NTS suggests that sex segregation for Black women was acceptable as long as it conformed with the program of reconstructing Black femininity and Black masculinity consistent with prevailing societal norms. By replicating white patriarchy, African Americans arguably could overcome the legacy of slavery that had rendered them less than true men and true women and stigmatized them as inadequate. In this regard, by providing Black female students with the opportunity to enter professions that would enable them to support their future families even without a mate, NTS subverted efforts to

---

166. *OPAL V. EASTER*, NANNIE HELEN BURROUGHS 58 (1995) (citation omitted).
167. *Id.* at 63.
168. *Id.* at 64 (citations omitted).
169. *See id.* at 64–66.
170. *Id.* at 66 (citation omitted).
171. *Id.* at 68.
172. *Id.* at 68–69.

construct the Black family as patriarchal and had thus to be corrected, in the view of its backers.

Examination of other efforts to educate Black women further demonstrates how sex segregation sought to replicate gendered norms as a strategy for gaining white respect, and presumably greater opportunities for African Americans. For example, Samuel Harris, principal of the Athens Colored High School in Georgia and advocate for industrial education, believed that increasing training in domestic services was particularly important for Black female students.[173] As a result, Harris worked in concert with other Black men in his community to establish an evening industrial school that "would train young blacks in domestic skills and moral attitudes that were generally associated with 'old black mammy' in the south."[174] Harris justified his school by asserting that there was a need for a new generation of Blacks who represented, in his view, the exemplary characteristics of the Black mammy: "unselfishness, honesty, personal affection, industrial stability and skills."[175] Harris and his supporters decided to work with whites to "establish 'The Black Mammy Memorial Institute,'" of which Harris became the principal.[176] Through this institute, Harris reportedly sought to capitalize on white nostalgia for the Black mammy and advance his own agenda to create additional opportunities for Black students to obtain industrial training.[177]

Booker T. Washington similarly justified Tuskegee's efforts to train Black women for domestic service. Washington asserted that creation of a skilled cadre of domestic workers was essential for improving race relations:

> In the average white family of the South … the white child spends a large proportion of his life in the arms … of a Negro woman.… It is mighty important … for the civilization, for the happiness, for the health of the Southern white people that the colored nurse shall be intelligent, that she shall be clean, that she shall be morally fit to come in contact with that pure and innocent child.[178]

With this appeal to whites to support the Tuskegee Institute, Washington suggested that well-trained domestic servants might help improve relationships between African Americans and whites. In addition, Washington believed domestic skills would enhance African American women's ability to help support their families and demonstrate their usefulness to society, which would in turn reduce racial animosity. These rationales supported Tuskegee's program of "Industries for Girls," which trained women in "dress making, millinery, horticulture, printing, broom making, mattress making, upholstery, cooking (required) and basketry. Like girls at Spelman, they were taught housekeeping and other aspects of domestic science, such as shopping and the planning of meals."[179] This gender-specific education was linked to improving Black self-sufficiency and, in so doing, proving that African Americans could be valuable members of society.

---

173. June O. Patton, *Moonlight and Magnolias in Southern Education: The Black Mammy Memorial Institute*, 65 J. Negro Hist. 149, 149–50 (1980).

174. *Id.* at 150.

175. *Id.* at 154 n.7.

176. *Id.* at 150.

177. *Id.*

178. Guy-Sheftall, *supra* note 124, at 147 (citing Selected Speeches of Booker T. Washington 174 (E. Davidson Washington ed., 1932)).

179. *Id.* at 148.

B. Sex Segregation and White Students: Preparing for Different Life Paths

Similar to African American women, white women were subjected to limited educational opportunities under the guise of preparing for them to enter their separate sphere in society.[180] Sex segregation was one way of readying white females for that path, which, as will be discussed in this section, stood in stark contrast to the world that would await Black women. In this connection, white femininity was constructed through the separate spheres ideology, separate schooling for females, and the separate world that was carved out for these students on account of their race and sex.

1. *Separate Spheres*

Industrialization propelled the notion that there were two spheres to which white men and white women belonged: the cold, hard workplace was for men, while the warmth of home and hearth was for women.[181] The expectation that "a woman's place is in the home" was so ingrained that even the Supreme Court took judicial notice of that "fact." For example, in *Mueller v. Oregon*,[182] the Court upheld an Oregon statute that prohibited women from working more than ten hours in a day.[183] Starting from the premise that the differences between the sexes could support distinctions in labor laws, the Court cited approvingly to other state and foreign statutes that had similar proscriptions.[184] In this connection, the Court noted that these authorities were "significant of a widespread belief that woman's physical structure, and the functions she performs in consequence thereof, justify special legislation restricting or qualifying the conditions under which she should be permitted to toil."[185] The Court detailed those characteristics of women, which it deemed "obvious," that made protective legislation a matter of common sense, a legitimate exercise of police power, and thus constitutional:

---

180. *See, e.g., Bradwell v. State*, 83 U.S. 130, 141 (1872) (Bradley, J., concurring) (upholding denial of a license to practice law for a female applicant, and explaining that part of the justification of keeping women out of the legal profession was based on the notion that "the constitution of the family organization, which is founded in the divine ordinance, as well as in the nature of things, indicates the domestic sphere as that which properly belongs to the domain and functions of womanhood").

181. Barbara Welter vividly describes the concept of separate spheres based on materials in popular culture during the early nineteenth century.

> The nineteenth-century American man was a busy builder of bridges and railroads, at work long hours in a materialistic society. The religious values of his forebears were neglected in practice if not in intent, and he occasionally felt some guilt that he had turned his new land, this temple of the chosen people, into one vast countinghouse. But he could salve his conscience by reflecting that he had left behind a hostage, not only to fortune, but to all the values which he held so dear and treated so lightly. Woman, in the cult of True Womanhood ... was the hostage in the home.... If anyone, male or female, dared to tamper with the complex virtues which made up True Womanhood, he was damned immediately as an enemy of God, of civilization and of the Republic. It was a fearful obligation, a solemn responsibility, the nineteenth-century American woman had—*to uphold the pillars of the temple with her frail white hand.*

WELTER, *supra* note 146, at 21 (emphasis added) (footnotes omitted).

182. 208 U.S. 412 (1908).

183. The statute applied to women working in "any mechanical establishment, or factory, or laundry" in Oregon. *Id.* at 416.

184. *Id.* at 419 n.1 (citing brief filed by Louis Brandeis, who was then counsel for the defendant).

185. *Id.* at 420.

by abundant testimony of the medical fraternity continuance for a long time on her feet at work, repeating this from day to day, tends to injurious effects upon the body, and as healthy mothers are essential to vigorous offspring, the physical well-being of woman becomes an object of public interest and care in order to preserve the strength and vigor of the race.[186]

Protective legislation thus was essential to assuring the health of women, their offspring, and the well-being of "the race," likely a deliberate word because this law and others like it typically excluded work performed primarily by women of color, such as domestic service.[187]

Domestic work generally was considered to be the preserve of Black women: "domestic service bore an indelible badge of racial inferiority. It was stigmatized as 'nigger's work,' a form of voluntary slavery or wage slavery that was incompatible with the values of democracy."[188] The white women who were domestic servants typically were newly arrived immigrants who worked until they could secure jobs in the developing industrial arena, positions that were off-limits to Blacks.[189]

Unlike the women working in the Oregon laundries at issue in *Mueller* and other similar locales,[190] domestic workers typically spent thirteen hours a day and upward of seventy to eighty hours a week on the job.[191] Efforts to reduce hours for these workers only commenced out of a concern that the pool of white workers was diminishing, not to protect the health and well-being of the workers or their offspring.[192] Black women, who historically had proven to be sufficiently sturdy to take on tasks normally deemed as men's work,[193] did not need protectionist laws, were not subject to them, and were expected to work in conditions that would be considered risky for white women. Not surprisingly, educational institutions reflected these norms through the manner in which they trained students. Accordingly, white female students received training to prepare them to take their rightful places as the lady of the house. Sex segregation was one of the tools used to construct this gendered and raced identity.[194]

---

186. *Id.* at 421; *see also Bradwell*, 83 U.S. at 141 (Bradley, J., concurring) (noting that the "natural and proper timidity and delicacy which belongs to the female sex evidently unfits it for many of the occupations of civil life").

187. *See generally* Peggie R. Smith, *Regulating Paid Household Work: Class, Gender, Race and Agendas of Reform*, 48 Am. U. L. Rev. 851 (1999). *See also Ritchie v. People*, 40 N.E. 454, 457 (Ill. 1895) (noting that domestic work was excluded from protectionist legislation).

188. Smith, *supra* note 187, at 877 (footnotes omitted).

189. *Id.* at 866.

190. *See Mueller*, 208 U.S. at 419 n.1 (citing similar statutes).

191. Smith, *supra* note 187, at 870.

192. *Id.* at 881–82. Peggie Smith notes that:

resolution of the servant problem depended upon the transformation of the relationship between maid and mistress from 'a position of status to one of contract.'... For reformers, such a shift was about restructuring domestic service in explicitly economic terms that conformed with modern industry, thus enabling middle-class households to compete successfully for workers.

Id. (footnotes omitted).

193. *See supra* notes 143–46 and accompanying text.

194. *See, e.g.*, Hasday, *supra* note 114, at 779–80 (arguing that sex segregation in schools and courses played a significant role in subordinating women). Schools long have been in the business of enforcing gender and racial stratification in society by constructing maleness and femaleness. For example, athletics appeared in public schools "out of a desire to inculcate masculinity in males. Schools created athletic programs in response to concerns that boys were becoming 'feminized' by the increasing absence of fathers from the home during the industrial revolution." Deborah Brake, *The Struggle for Sex Equality in Sport and the Theory Behind Title IX*, 34 U. Mich. J.L. Reform 13, 92 (2001) (footnotes omitted).

In fact, proponents of sex segregation frequently argued that separating the sexes was necessary to preserve the differences between males and females, and in doing so to ensure the perpetuation of "the race." Coeducation was problematic because it would "in some way destroy feminine sensibility" and more specifically, the feminine ability to reproduce. For example, Thomas Woody, in his scholarship examining the history of women's education, cites an 1885 publication that warns that the "'greatest evil in the [coeducational] high school was the risk of injury to the health of girls.'"[195] Woody continues, noting that experts have found that:

> coeducation in the middle teens tends to sexual precocity. This is very bad; in fact, it is one of the subtlest dangers that can befall civilization. There are momentous changes in boys at the age of fourteen. Adolescence is a crisis in their lives. The first danger to a woman is over-brainwork. It affects that part of her organism which is sacred to heredity. This danger is seen in the diminishing number of marriages. The postponement of marriage is very unfortunate in its influence upon civilization.[196]

Thus, by exposing young women to adolescent males and at the same time to the rigors of intellectual pursuits best suited to males,[197] coeducation would impede women's ability to procreate, and in so doing, destabilize the institution of marriage. Woody's report reflected long-held views on education for women. Fifty years before, Dr. E. H. Clarke, a professor at Harvard University, elaborated on the physical harms of coeducation to women in his book, *Sex in Education*. He stated:

> Identical education, or identical co-education, of the sexes defrauds one sex or the other, or perhaps both.... A combination of the two methods of education, a compromise between them, would probably yield an average result, excluding the best of both. It would give a fair chance neither to a boy nor a girl. Of all compromises, such a physiological one is the worst. It cultivates mediocrity, and cheats the future of its rightful legacy of lofty manhood and womanhood. It emasculates boys [and] stunts girls.[198]

Other scientists asserted that women who pursued education would not be able to nurse their children, or would develop a "'nervous temperament.'"[199] In fact, some argued, that the push to educate women left them "'physically unfit for her duties as woman.... She is not fairly up to what Nature asks from her as a wife and mother.'"[200]

There was no similar concern for Black women's fertility, which was rooted in stereotypes about their fecundity and lack of morality. Scholars such as Kimberlé Williams Crenshaw have noted "there has been absolutely no institutional effort to regulate Black female chastity."[201] Thus, for example, the legal system failed to recognize the rape of female slaves.[202] Similarly, Black motherhood has not been revered; instead, it has been condemned as evidence of Black women's uncontrollable sexuality or irresponsibility.[203] Dorothy Roberts explains that

---

195. Thomas Woody, A History of Women's Education in the United States 273 (1929).

196. *Id.* at 274 (footnote omitted).

197. A related argument against coeducation or otherwise limiting women's educational opportunities was that the presence of women would lower the intellectual quality of the institutions "since [the] woman was the 'weaker vessel.'" *Id.* at 271 (footnote omitted).

198. *Id.* at 275–76 (quoting E. H. Clarke, Sex in Education 127–29 (1874)).

199. *Id.* at 278.

200. *Id.*

201. Crenshaw, *supra* note 57, at 157.

202. *Id.* at 158 n.49.

203. Roberts, *supra* note 47, at 11–12.

"our society views childbearing by white women as desireable.... Procreation by Black mothers, on the other hand, is devalued and discouraged."[204] This devaluation is evidenced by the "welfare system's disproportionate denial of Black mothers' parental rights,"[205] among other things. The disparity in the social construct of Black and white womanhood was stark. The distinctions and normative judgments concerning each filtered into the educational opportunities made available. Thus, unlike Black women, who learned to work and support their families, white females received education to prepare them for becoming "true women."

2. Training for "True Womanhood"

Protectionist ideology justified limiting white female students' access to education and supported steering them to sex-segregated institutions and courses that would prepare them for the separate sphere of the home, even in coeducational settings.[206] For example, girls from working-class families who were expected to work before marriage attended schools that prepared them for female-dominated occupations such as

> public school teaching.... lunch-room management, [and] catering.
>
> Sometimes, moreover, women's public schools just trained women for marriage itself. [For example,] Louisville's Female High School ... did not offer the college preparatory classes available to the city's white male high school students. But it did supplement its class in vocational cooking with courses in household cooking, drawing, sewing, and millinery.[207]

Several states established institutions to provide white females with this type of training.[208]

Courts typically upheld admissions policies at such institutions because the coursework they provided was deemed appropriate for white women because it would presumably fulfill their educational needs and desires. Thus, for example, a court asked to strike down the admissions policy at the all-male Agricultural and Mechanical College of Texas refused to do so, in part because it doubted that any women in the entire state, absent the plaintiffs, would have a sincere interest in the college's curriculum, which in-

---

204. *Id.* at 11.

205. *Id.* at 13.

206. *See* Hasday, *supra* note 114, at 803 (noting that "coeducational public schools formally segregated a portion of their classes or programs along sex lines as a way of directing students to life paths associated with their sex (or their sex and race)").

207. *Id.* at 796–97 (footnotes omitted).

208. *See, e.g.,* 1893 Ala. Acts 1002, 1004 (establishing an "industrial school for the education of white girls in Alabama" to provide training in "kindergarten instruction and music; also a knowledge of telegraphy, stenography, photography and phonography, type-writing ... drawing, sewing, dressmaking, millinery, cooking, laundry, house, sign and fresco painting"); 1889 Ga. Laws 10, 10, 13 ("An Act to establish a Normal and Industrial College as a branch of the State University, for the education of white girls"; the training included courses in "domestic economy, cutting and making dresses, printing, industrial and decorative art in its practical application, and such other practical industries as may tend to fit and prepare girls for occupations which are consistent with feminine refinement and modesty"); 1884 Miss. Laws 50, 52 (creating the Mississippi "Industrial Institute and College for the education of white girls of the State of Mississippi in the arts and sciences," which would train students in "telegraphy, stenography and photography; also a knowledge of drawing, painting, designing and engraving in their industrial application; also a knowledge of fancy, practical and general needle-work"); 1891 N.C. Session Laws 126, 126–127 ("An act to establish a normal and industrial school for white girls" that would "fit them for teaching ... instruct[] young women in drawing, telegraphy, type-writing, stenography, and such other industrial arts as may be suitable to their sex and conducive to their support and usefulness").

cluded such subjects as history, government, and architecture.[209] The court noted that "there is no proof that any other woman in Texas, save and except [the plaintiff], desires to obtain a degree ... in [another course available at the institution]."[210]

Similarly, an appeals court upheld the single-sex policy at all-female Winthrop College in South Carolina in *Williams v. McNair*.[211] Several male students sued the state of South Carolina to enjoin enforcement of the statute barring their admission to Winthrop, which, according to the court, was the all-female counterpart to the Citadel, the all-male military college.[212] The court held that with respect to these institutions, sex segregation was based on historical reasons: by designating the Citadel as a military school, "apparently, the Legislature deemed it appropriate for that reason to provide for an all-male student body."[213] On the other hand, the legislature established Winthrop expressly as a school for white "young ladies."[214]

The South Carolina statute authorizing the college's founding called for "'the establishment, conduct and maintenance of a first-class institution for the thorough education of the white girls of this State.'"[215] As such, Winthrop offered courses that would be "specially helpful to female students,"[216] such as "'teaching ... stenography, typewriting, telegraphy, bookkeeping, drawing, ... designing, engraving, sewing, dressmaking, millinery, art, needlework, cooking, housekeeping and such other industrial arts as may be suitable to their sex and conducive to their support and usefulness.'"[217] Using this circular reasoning, the court concluded that excluding males from Winthrop was permissible because the institution was established for women only to prepare them for their particular sphere in life. The Supreme Court affirmed this ruling without an opinion.[218]

3. Sex Segregation to Safeguard "True" Womanhood

Sex segregation also "protected" white femininity during the struggle to desegregate Southern schools[219] in the wake of the Supreme Court's decision in *Brown v. Board of Education*, which declared racial segregation in public schools to be unconstitutional.[220] To remedy the violation, the Court remanded the underlying cases to district courts, ordering them to "require that the defendants make a prompt and reasonable start toward full compliance"[221] with the original *Brown* ruling and to proceed "with all deliberate speed"[222]

---

209. *Allred v. Heaton*, 336 S.W.2d 251, 259 (Tex. App. 1960).

210. *Id.*

211. 316 F. Supp. 134, 138 (D.S.C. 1970).

212. *Id.* at 135–36.

213. *Id.* at 136.

214. *Id.*

215. *Id.* at 136 n.3.

216. *Id.* at 136.

217. *Id.* at 136 n.3.

218. *Williams v. McNair*, 401 U.S. 951 (1971).

219. *See, e.g.,* Gunnar Myrdal, An American Dilemma: The Negro Problem and Modern Democracy 586 (Harper & Row 1962) (1942) (observing that segregation in education, as well in other areas, supported the notion of "'no social equality,'" which embodied a concern for "preserv[ing] 'the purity of the white race'"). Myrdal notes that the effort to preserve white purity "is focused on white women," as represented by the response of the typical "southern [white] man ... to any plea for social equality: 'Would you like to have your daughter marry a Negro?'" *Id.* at 586–87. Thus, as Myrdal describes it, protection of white women is a cover for preserving white supremacy. *See id.* at 586.

220. 347 U.S. 483, 495 (1954).

221. *Brown v. Board of Education* (Brown II), 349 U.S. 294, 300 (1955).

222. *Id.* at 301.

to integrate their school districts. Fifteen years later, after steadfast resistance on the part of defendant school districts to dismantling dual educational systems,[223] the Court concluded that the "standard of allowing 'all deliberate speed' for desegregation is no longer constitutionally permissible.... The obligation of every school district is to terminate dual school systems *at once* and to operate *now and hereafter* only unitary schools."[224] To comply with this mandate, several Southern school districts turned to sex segregation as a way of easing into racial desegregation.

Leading the way in this effort was the Tennessee, which enacted legislation in 1957[225] that allowed for separating the sexes to "dull the edge"[226] of the Court's ruling. Seven years later, Mississippi enacted a similar law that authorized the trustees of the state's school boards to separate students on the basis of sex in schools or classes "when such board, in its discretion, determines such separation will promote or preserve the public peace, order, or tranquility of the school district, or the health morals or education of the students."[227] Pupil assignment laws, which were designed to slow down the pace of desegregation,[228] also allowed school districts to take sex into consideration when determining whether a student, usually African American, could transfer to a white school. Under these laws, rather than assigning students to school districts based on their residence (which had been the custom even under a dual system in which there were two sets of zoning laws),[229] school officials had the discretion to examine a variety of factors before deciding whether the transfer should take place. Thus, a student seeking a transfer would petition the local school board, which could consider factors such as

> the sociological, psychological and like intangible social scientific factors as will prevent, as nearly as possible, a condition of socioeconomic class consciousness among the pupils ... the sex, morals, conduct, health and personal standards of the pupil ... together with any and all other factors which the board may consider pertinent.[230]

Sex was a factor to be considered in the pupil assignment laws for Alabama, Louisiana, Tennessee, and Texas.[231] By allowing school boards to decide the mix of Black and white males and females, among other things, pupil enrollment laws succeeded in delaying the integration of Southern schools. Eight years after *Brown*, "only 7.6 percent of the Negro pupils in 17 Southern and Border states and the District of Columbia were attending de-

---

223. *See, e.g., Griffin v. County Sch. Bd. of Prince Edward County*, 377 U.S. 218, 255 (1964) (holding that shutting down the public school system rather than integrating the schools violated the equal protection clause).

224. *Alexander v. Holmes County Bd. of Educ.*, 396 U.S. 19, 20 (1969) (emphasis added).

225. Act of March 5, 1957, ch. 98, § 1, 1957 Tenn. Acts 323 (codified at TENN. CODE ANN. § 49-2-108 (2002)). This measure authorized

> school boards of the counties, municipalities and special school districts of the State ... to provide separate schools for persons of the male sex and persons of the female sex; the determination of the necessity for such separate schools is hereby vested in the exclusive discretion of the school board of each county, municipality and special school district.

Id.

226. Patrick E. McCauley, *"Be It Enacted": The Legislative Record, in* WITH ALL DELIBERATE SPEED: SEGREGATION-DESEGREGATION IN SOUTHERN SCHOOLS 141 (Don Shoemaker ed., 1957).

227. 1964 Miss. Laws 57, ch. 25 § 1.

228. McCauley, *supra* note 226, at 132 (noting that three years after the Court decided *Brown*, at least eight states enacted pupil enrollment laws to "control, if not to restrain, desegregation").

229. *Id.*

230. McCauley, *supra* note 226, at 137.

231. *See* Notes, *The Federal Courts and Integration of Southern Schools: Troubled Status of the Pupil Placement Acts*, 62 COLUM. L. REV. 1448, 1478 (1962).

segregated schools,"[232] the majority of whom were located in states that did not have pupil enrollment laws.[233]

Still other school districts used sex segregation as part of their efforts to comply in "all deliberate speed,"[234] with the mandate of *Brown*, even without their legislature's assistance. For example, the Amite County School District in Mississippi included separate boys' and girls' schools as part of its desegregation plan created in response to court order in 1969.[235] The court approved this aspect of the plan, understanding it to be an "interim emergency measure to stabilize the education process,"[236] suggesting that separating the sexes was imperative to helping alleviate the discomfort of the district's students and parents with integration. The next year, the district sought to continue with the sex-segregated aspect of the plan, which the court approved and "conclud[ed] that 'the separation by sex plan stems from sound educational purposes as distinguished from racially discriminatory purposes.'"[237] Black parents in the district opposed the plan, unsuccessfully seeking review by the U.S. Court of Appeals for the Fifth Circuit.[238]

Four years later, when the "temporary" sex separation plan was still in force, the United States challenged this plan under the then-newly passed EEOA,[239] which seeks to ensure that children are able to attend schools in their own neighborhoods.[240] By the time the court addressed this issue, Black parents had boycotted the Amite County schools to protest sex segregation because, in the words of the only Black member of the school board at that time, "[the board] never had any idea of changing the [sex segregation plan]. 'The idea is to keep the black boys from having any contact with the white girls — pure and simple.'"[241] In fact, the board itself admitted as much, arguing in defense of sex segregation that "whites will leave the public school system if sex-desegregation is implemented."[242] The president of the board stated that before 1969, when the district finally desegregated the schools, "boys and girls could attend school together ... because 'we had one school for whites and another school for coloreds.'"[243] The court rejected this rationale as "impermissible"[244] and agreed with the United States that it violated the EEOA as a practice the act specifically proscribed.[245] In so holding, the court noted that the EEOA

> goes beyond the rights guaranteed to school children under the Fourteenth Amendment prior to the EEOA's adoption and incorporates a judgment that a sex-segregated school district is a dual rather than a unitary school system and

---

232. *Id.* at 1453 n.28.

233. *See id.*

234. *See supra* notes 220–21 and accompanying text.

235. *See United States v. Hinds County Sch. Bd.*, 560 F.2d 619, 621 (5th Cir. 1977).

236. *Id.*

237. *Id.*

238. *Id.* at 621 & n.4.

239. 20 U.S.C. §§ 1701–1758; *see also supra* note 63 (explaining the act's purpose and relevant provisions).

240. *Hinds County*, 560 F.2d at 623.

241. Merrill Sheils, *Segregation by Sex*, Newsweek, Sept. 19, 1977, at 97.

242. *Hinds County*, 560 F.2d at 624.

243. Sheils, *supra* note 241, at 97.

244. *Hinds County*, 560 F.2d at 624.

245. *Id.* at 624 (noting that "by Congressional definition 'segregation' means 'the operation of a school system in which students are wholly or substantially separated among the schools ... on the basis of race, color, sex, or national origin'").

results in a similar if not equivalent injury to school children as would occur if a racially segregated school system were imposed.[246]

Other school districts were not as transparent regarding their decisions to segregate students based on sex. Faced with the order to integrate, these districts typically argued that separate schooling based on sex was best as a pedagogical matter, without accounting for the fact that sex segregation had not been among the educational options available in the public school system prior to the Supreme Court's mandate that they desegregate immediately. For example, Concordia Parish in Louisiana proposed separate schools for boys and girls apparently under court-ordered pressure to desegregate.[247] During a hearing on the plan, the superintendent of schools testified "that the coeducational system in effect in Concordia was educationally sound as long as the schools are racially segregated," but sex segregation is "'most educationally sound'" under an integrated system,[248] providing a more politic—but remarkably similar—explanation as that offered by the Amite County School Board president, already discussed.[249]

Similarly, officials in Louisiana's Ascension Parish turned to separate schools based on sex under orders to dismantle its racially segregated school system.[250] In support of this plan, the school board submitted an article by the superintendent of St. Bernard Parish, which had adopted single-sex schools. The superintendent wrote that "it would

---

246. *Id.* at 623. The court of appeals came to this conclusion because among the findings of the EEOA is the statement "that the maintenance of dual school systems in which students are assigned to schools solely on the basis of race, color, sex, or national origin denies to those students the equal protection of the laws guaranteed by the fourteenth amendment." *Id.* (internal quotations omitted). Recent Supreme Court decisions suggest that the Fifth Circuit's assessment of the reach of the EEOA may be erroneous. *See City of Boerne v. Flores*, 521 U.S. 507, 515, 519 (1997) (invalidating the Religious Freedom Restoration Act of 1993 (RFRA), 42 U.S.C. § 2000bb, which prohibited the "government from 'substantially burden[ing]' a person's exercise of religion even if the burden results from a rule of general applicability"). The Court held that Congress exceeded its authority under § 5 of the Fourteenth Amendment in passing the RFRA because the act substantively redefined the scope of protection afforded by the amendment:

Congress' power under § 5 ... extends only to "enforc[ing]" the provisions of the Fourteenth Amendment.... Legislation which alters the meaning of the Free Exercise Clause cannot be said to be enforcing the Clause. Congress does not enforce a constitutional right by changing what the right is. It has been given the power "to enforce," not the power to determine what constitutes a constitutional violation.

Id. at 519. This reasoning suggests that the Fifth Circuit's holding is likely erroneous because Congress does not have the power to declare all sex-based classifications in education unconstitutional. *See VMI*, 518 U.S. at 533–34 (noting that "sex classifications may be used to compensate women 'for particular economic disability [they have] suffered'... to 'promot[e] equal employment opportunity'... to advance full development of the talent and capacities of our Nation's people").

247. *See Singleton v. Jackson Mun. Separate Sch. Dist.*, 419 F.2d 1211, 1220 (5th Cir. 1969). The *Singleton* decision litigation consolidated numerous appeals and incorporated the appeals into this single litigation, but the court provided independent decisions for each case. In this instance, I cite the *Singleton* decision to discuss several decisions included in the matter, *Singleton*, such as *Smith v. Concordia Parish School Board*, 419 F.2d 1211, 1220 (5th Cir. 1969).

248. Brief for Appellants at 9, *Smith*, 419 F.2d 1211 (No. 28342) (on file with author). For its part, the school board argued that considering sex segregation for the first time made sense because under *forced integration* the district was going to make many changes to all the schools. *Id.* at 6–7. The court did not decide whether the sex segregation aspect of the plan violated the Constitution because the plan as a whole failed to create a unitary system. *See Smith*, 419 F.2d at 1220.

249. *See supra* note 243 and accompanying text.

250. *See Charles v. Ascension Parish Sch. Bd.*, 421 F.2d 656, 656–57 (5th Cir. 1969).

be less than honest not to add that … we felt that certain problems which might arise in newly integrated schools would be lessened if the sexes were separated."[251] Similarly, a school board in Georgia[252] argued that sex segregation was necessary to avoid disciplinary problems:

> It is common knowledge that disciplinary problems ordinarily increase in the racially integrated school. Many black citizens question the ability of any white teacher to relate to, discipline, or properly teach black children who are the product [*sic*] of black rather than white middle class culture. Is it not reasonable to assume that local school officials, faced with massive racial integration, *desiring that it work* and that meaningful public education be maintained, seize upon the device of separation by sex as a means of reducing disciplinary problems?[253]

In this respect, the state admitted that race played a part in its decision to segregate based on sex and responded to such charges leveled by the United States with a terse, "so what!"[254] For its part, the United States argued that sex segregation perpetuated racial segregation.

> Despite this conversion to sex-separation in the schools, Taylor County continued to racially segregate students on buses with white boys and girls being transported by white drivers and black boys and girls being transported by black drivers.… In some instances, black girls were assigned to separate seats within a bus by the white drivers.[255]

Confronted with this aspect of the county's plan, which the district court had approved without even holding hearings concerning its validity, the Fifth Circuit reversed the ruling below and ordered the district court to hold a full hearing to determine whether the planned sex segregation was, in fact, racially motivated.[256]

As the foregoing demonstrates, the confluence of sex and racial segregation supported racial and gender hierarchies and the attendant subordination of African Americans and white women. By separating students based on sex and race, the nation's educational system constructed a gendered and raced hierarchy that privileged white masculinity and white femininity. To the extent that sex segregation was deemed appropriate and necessary for Black students, it was for purposes of replicating and thus reinforcing white patriarchy, thereby ensuring that African Americans would remain at the bottom rungs of the social strata. Needless to say, these hierarchies persist in our society. Accordingly, the question for today's versions of single-sex education is whether they will provide the needed reforms to begin dismantling ingrained patterns of discrimination that limit opportunities for inner-city children or merely provide cover for continued subjugation of these students. Part III demonstrates how an intersectional analysis can assist in that inquiry.

---

251. Brief for Appellant at 105, *Charles*, 421 F.2d 656 (No. 28573) (on file with author). Here again, the court did not rule on the constitutionality of sex segregation, because the rest of the plan failed to create a unitary school district. *Charles*, 421 F.2d at 657.

252. *See United States v. Georgia*, 466 F.2d 197, 199–200 (5th Cir. 1972).

253. Brief for the State of Georgia et al. at 17, *Georgia*, 466 F.2d 197 (No. 71-2563).

254. *See id.* ("Even assuming … that the separation by sex was 'racially motivated,' the proper response is so what! This is what the federal courts require.").

255. Brief for the United States at 19, *Georgia*, 466 F.2d 197 (No. 71-2563).

256. *Georgia*, 466 F.2d at 200.

III. What the Past Means for Today's Single-Sex Schools

For much of its history, single-sex schooling has occurred within a larger context of racial segregation in the schools, working to reinforce the racial and gender hierarchies that permitted and indeed sanctioned continued subordination of African Americans.[257] Today's versions of sex segregation similarly occur against a backdrop of racially segregated urban schools—albeit de facto rather than de jure.[258] As a result, and given the nation's history, any analysis of proposed single-sex education must consider, at the bare minimum, the interaction of race and gender. Under such an intersectional analysis, we can determine whether new efforts will in fact provide for new and expanded life paths for Black students or whether these new schools merely will support the retrenchment of racist and sexist norms.

A. Through an Intersectional Looking Glass: Raced and Gendered Social Roles

Examining single-sex education relationally—that is, as it relates to racial segregation—demonstrates how integral sex segregation has been to racializing gender roles and sexualizing race.[259] The first step necessary to understanding current single-sex schooling proposals' potential for perpetuating gender and racial stratification is to explain how sex segregation's past supported racism and patriarchy.

Under a single-sex schooling regime, white females learned that they were destined to become "true women," the keeper of home, hearth, and the holder of the future for the race. Schools for "white girls"[260] protected their charges' weak constitutions and trained them to take their *rightful* places in their husband's castles, through acquiring such *useful* skills as cooking, sewing, and millinery.[261] White males, on the other hand, expected to become providers for their families, obtained the rigorous education necessary to prepare them for this role and thus had access to a wide range of educational opportunities.[262] This framework stood in stark contrast to the education provided to African Americans.

The education system prepared Blacks—male and female alike—to work, consistent with the almost genderless manner in which slavery constructed African Americans—from dressing boys and girls alike to requiring men and women to perform virtually identical physical labor.[263] After slavery and Reconstruction, some gendered distinctions emerged that only further constrained African Americans. Thus, for example, the educational system ensured that Black women could take care of white families, rather than

---

257. *See supra* Part II.
258. *See* Gary Orfield, *Schools More Separate: Consequences of a Decade of Resegregation* (Harvard Civil Rights Project, July 2001), *at* www.civilrightsproject.harvard.edu/research/deseg/-Schools_More_Separate.pdf.
259. *Supra* Part II.
260. *See supra* note 208 and accompanying text.
261. *See supra* notes 206–18 and accompanying text.
262. *See supra* note 194 and accompanying text.
263. *See supra* notes 143–47 and accompanying text.

or at the expense of their own,[264] and provided them with training to compensate for their perceived moral failings.[265]

The primary mission of sex-separate education was to prepare Black females to take their *rightful* positions in the workplace, often in the homes of white people, or in other low-paying occupations,[266] which, in turn, constructed Black women as "true workers." In so doing, the educational system also supported the construction of Black men as "true laborers." As a result, rather than provide and preside over the household as "true men," Black men were expected to need help supporting their families financially, largely because they were denied access to the educational opportunities that would guarantee economic independence.[267] In this sense, sex segregation among whites contributed to consigning Black males and females to raced and gendered roles that diverged from those of the majority, which in turn were held up as proof of Black inferiority.

African American efforts at self-help sought to combat these images and constraints, with the hope of demonstrating that Blacks deserved equal rights in society. However, the manner in which some of these efforts were carried out relied overtly on patriarchy to privilege Black males, holding them out to be the hope for racial equality. Thus, for example, Du Bois's vision of a "talented tenth" would have constructed a class of classically educated elite African American men. These men, through their superior education, would uplift the entire Black race, facilitating their agency and liberation from discrimination.[268] In Du Bois's view, Black women — though hugely important to the Black race — did not have the central role with respect to this plan. Therefore, he advocated "knowledge" for African American women but did not count them as making up a large percentage of the talented tenth.[269] Booker T. Washington, for his part, used the Tuskegee Machine to replicate traditional gender roles, providing a separate program of "Industries for Girls," to assure white society that African Americans were capable of assimilation.[270] Thus, even according to the leading schools of thought regarding Black education, allegiance to patriarchy played a role in strategies for improving the lot of Black people.

As a result, when Nannie Helen Burroughs provided her female students with training in the trades — nontraditional work for women — she was met with great opposition.[271] The specter of young women attaining the skills that would enable them to provide for their families threatened the notion of the Black male as the provider that Washington and others were trying so carefully to establish.[272] Burroughs was forced to abandon that program for lack of financial and political support.[273] Thus, even in the context of Black-provided education, the construction of a gendered hierarchy that identified Black males as protectors for the race emerged as a key strategy.

In today's world, the discourse around single sex focuses once again on making sure Black males learn how to become men,[274] and, in a less direct way, to ensure that Black

---

264. *See supra* notes 149–54 and accompanying text.
265. *See supra* note 160 and accompanying text.
266. *See supra* note 159 and accompanying text.
267. *See supra* note 165 and accompanying text.
268. *See supra* notes 129–31 and accompanying text.
269. *See supra* note 129 and accompanying text.
270. *See supra* notes 178–79 and accompanying text.
271. *See supra* notes 170–72 and accompanying text.
272. *See supra* notes 171–72 and accompanying text.
273. *See supra* note 172 and accompanying text.
274. *See supra* notes 34–38 and accompanying text.

females grow into "real women" who support their men.[275] The goal essentially is to replicate the roles exemplified by whites and, in so doing, establish the "proper patriarchal balance"[276] between Black women and Black men, without determining whether that goal is workable or desirable for African Americans.[277]

Thus, in the rhetoric, Black females continue to stand apart from their white counterparts. For example, single-sex education helps white females become more confident and empowered, more likely to engage in the fields of science and mathematics.[278] For Black girls, on the other hand, single-sex education means they are less likely to get pregnant or engage in sexual activity at "dangerous proportions."[279] White femininity remains prized for its virtue and its delicacy; single-sex education is a means of empowering their flagging confidence. Black femininity, on the other hand, is marked by hypersexuality and fecundity.

The deviance of Black femininity is further underscored in the larger debates regarding the justifications for sex segregation in the nation's inner cities. Specifically, by suggesting that single-sex education will compensate for the proliferation of female-headed households among Black families, current single-sex efforts support the construction of Black motherhood as abnormal and blameworthy for social problems as broad and divergent as juvenile delinquency and poverty.[280]

These depictions of Black femininity also have implications for the construction of Black masculinity. Here again, Black males are posited as irresponsible and undependable—that is, if they were "true men" they would take care of their own families and not expect the government to do so. Similarly, the trope of the oversexed Black male, which supported racially segregated schools,[281] persists. In this connection, single-sex education will help stop Black males from impregnating so many females. The discourse further posits Black males as dangerous and threatening, just as was true in the post-*Brown* era, when proponents for single-sex education argued that just having African American males in the classroom would disrupt the environment and make desegregation less likely to work.[282] In the present day, the absence of Black males is enough to proclaim a school a safe haven for girls.[283]

A brief examination of California's recent experiment in single-sex education[284] is illustrative. In 1997, California provided funding to create single-sex academies for boys and girls, with an eye toward, in the words of former Governor Pete Wilson, helping "at-risk boys"—that is, low-income, African American and Latino boys.[285] With this goal in

---

275. *See supra* note 36 and accompanying text.

276. Paulette M. Caldwell, *A Hair Piece: Perspectives on the Intersection of Race and Gender*, 1991 Duke L.J. 365, 395 (1991).

277. *Cf.* bell hooks, Black Looks: Race and Representation 113 (1992) (urging Black men and Black women to "break the life-threatening choke-hold patriarchal masculinity imposes on black men and create life sustaining visions of a reconstructed black masculinity that can provide black men ways to save their lives and the lives of their brothers and sisters in struggle").

278. *See supra* note 44 and accompanying text.

279. *See* Salomone, *supra* note 11, at 18.

280. *See supra* note 40 and accompanying text.

281. *See supra* notes 219–56 and accompanying text.

282. *See supra* note 253 and accompanying text.

283. *See supra* notes 51–53 and accompanying text.

284. *See generally* Amanda Datnow et al., Is Single Gender Schooling Viable in the Public Sector? Lessons from California's Pilot Program (2001), *available at* www.oise.utoronto.ca/depts/tps/adatnow/final.pdf (on file with author).

285. One commentator has explained the troubling "significance" of the "at-risk" label as follows:
    It was no coincidence that the at-risk-boys targeted for the academies were primarily lower-class, African-American and Latin-American students.... The modal category for African

mind, six districts—four of which were predominately minority—established single-sex academies that were either schools on their own, or single-sex schools within a coed school.[286] Researchers studied these academies, in part to determine whether they would provide some insight into the potential for sex segregation to reform public education, particularly in light of the lack of "systematic research" in this area.[287] Among the many findings, the researchers noted that because the state had established the schools with an emphasis on helping "at-risk boys," there was a concomitant emphasis on gender, which manifested itself in preconceived notions regarding what type of curriculum was most appropriate, among other things. Thus, the schooling emphasized "discipline for boys and curriculum opportunities for girls."[288] For instance, at one academy, researchers "found that the boys' classes were in a 'lock down' status and no one was allowed to enter or leave the classroom."[289] The terminology used suggests a penal institution, rather than an educational one. Indeed, some educators believed that the academies could not provide the "at-risk" boys with enough discipline,[290]

> express[ing] the belief that their at-risk population of boys were difficult and would have in retrospect benefited more from an "academic boot camp," which would ideally be taught by male teachers.... The tone and approach of discipline for boys was often quite harsh and usually meant that their classes were "very regimented."[291]

Girls, in contrast, were not subject to the same level or degree of discipline as were the boys, prompting students to "talk about discipline as a gendered practice.... [where] boys felt they were singled out and presumed to behave poorly."[292]

Girls had their own curricular choices that were deemed suitable. For example:

> In [one district's] girls' academy, the students chose to read *Pride and Prejudice*. In the boys' academy, the students chose to read *All Quiet on the Western Front*. One teacher explained: "[t]he girls tend to choose the romantic spiel ... and the guys tend to go for the action."

> When students in [another] district's academies were studying the early history of the United States and the migration of settlers to the West, boys took a survival skills class from a young male teacher and the girls studied quilting and sewing, taught by middle-aged women teachers.... At another school, a male teacher said he used sports to clarify or simplify ideas for his male students because "guys can kind of relate to that." ... In sum it appears that when teachers geared the curriculum to respond to students' interest, they perhaps uninten-

American boys is at-risk.... The concept of at-riskness is central to a discourse about the contemporary crisis in urban schools in America that explains children's failure as largely the consequence of their attitudes and behaviors.

Elisabeth L. Woody, *Constructions of Masculinity in California's Single-Gender Academies, in* GENDER IN POLICY AND PRACTICE: PERSPECTIVES ON SINGLE-SEX AND COEDUCATIONAL SCHOOLING 286 (Amanda Datnow, Lea Hubbard eds., 2002) [hereafter Woody, *Constructions of Masculinity*] (quotations omitted).

286. DATNOW, *supra* note 284, at 20.

287. *Id.* at 5 (noting that "little is known about [the schools'] motivations, design, or outcomes with respect to students, teachers, and school systems").

288. *Id.* at 41.

289. *Id.* at 42.

290. *Id.* Significantly, however, the researchers noted that as the level of discipline increased, so did the problems. For example, by the last time they visited one of the schools, "police were on campus because students had written gang graffiti on the walls." *Id.*

291. *Id.* at 42.

292. *Id.* at 43.

tionally reinforced traditional gender roles. Significantly, in most cases, teachers did little to change student choices by suggesting alternative book choices or topics that might potentially challenge gendered dispositions.[293]

Researchers found that even with a stated concern for "neutrality,"[294] teachers approached students with gendered expectations and that gendered curricula resulted even when students were allowed to *choose*[295] for themselves.

The overt and covert curricula in California's experiment reinforced existing social constructions of femininity and masculinity based on race, sex, and class. For girls of color, that meant focusing on romance and developing practical skills for the home, rather than on building capacity in academic subjects. Similarly, for males, the academies reinforced a vision of masculinity that focused on disruptive behavior, athleticism, and being "bad," such that when confronted with disciplinary action, the boys would proclaim, "Ooh, I'm the man."[296]

Significantly, while these raced and gendered lessons were occurring, there was much less emphasis on the preparation that would truly advance life opportunities for these students. For example, none of the single-sex academies offered students Advanced Placement courses,[297] which suggests that for all the talk about reform and increasing educational opportunity for "at-risk" students, these schools were not deemed college preparatory in function. In fact, the researchers concluded that based on California's experience, single-sex schooling has great potential to create a new low-educational track for students labeled as "at risk."[298]

In addition, by supporting traditional gender roles, with all the concomitant racial implications, the academies fostered an environment that reinforced existing limiting conceptions of gender roles for students. For example, in some instances, the academies fostered a hypermasculinized environment that led

> girls [at one] academy [where discipline of males was particularly harsh] … to express fears and frustration about persistent sexual harassment from their male peers. Likewise, as researchers, we experienced discomfort and disrespect, including foul language and sexual innuendos, in interviews with boys at this school that were never experienced anywhere else throughout the project. If anything, strict discipline at this school instilled a strong sense of male privilege and authority. Men were either positioned as the protector and provider or as the predator, and women were either in need of assistance or in a position of sexual objectification.[299]

---

293. *Id.* at 40.

294. *See id.* at 39 (noting that the teachers "attempted to make the curriculum 'gender neutral.' In practice, this sometimes meant that the curriculum was oriented toward the males, as teachers were very concerned about maintaining order in the all boys classes"); *cf.* CATHARINE A. MACKINNON, TOWARD A FEMINIST THEORY OF THE STATE 163 (1989) (observing that the "foundation for [the law's] neutrality is the pervasive assumption that conditions that pertain among men on the basis of gender apply to women as well"). As MacKinnon argues, if neutrality assumes masculinity as the norm, then it is hardly surprising that with an unexamined emphasis on "gender neutrality," the California educators unwittingly took an approach to learning that was geared toward the boys.

295. *Cf.* Vicki Shultz, *Telling Stories About Women and Work: Judicial Interpretations of Sex Segregation in the Workplace in Title VII Cases Raising the Lack of Interest Argument*, 103 HARV. L. REV. 1749, 1756 (1990) (arguing that women's choices in employment are shaped in large part by employers' cultural expectations, among other things).

296. Woody, *Constructions of Masculinity*, *supra* note 285, at 290 (internal quotations omitted).

297. DATNOW, *supra* note 284, at 67.

298. *Id.* at 73 (cautioning that single-sex schooling could become "a new form of tracking or resegregation").

299. Woody, *Constructions of Masculinity*, *supra* note 285, at 288.

Researchers also found that although there was some flexibility for the girls to go beyond traditional gender roles notwithstanding the other messages they received,[300] there was little if any flexibility concerning what it meant to be "male."[301] The researchers found that as a result, the boys enforced the gender code in a variety of ways, including through the use of insults:

> Boys set the rules of masculinity through the uses of insults such as sissy or fag to describe peers who did not fit their norm of boyhood. Crossing the lines of gender, as in acting like a girl, or sexuality was considered suspect. Students used homophobic teasing as a means to enforce the rules of masculinity and femininity.[302]

In this connection, the intersection of race, gender, and class combined to reinforce a construct of femininity and masculinity that was limiting for students and perpetuated subordination based on those characteristics. California's experience is likely to be replicated under the current Bush proposal, which would establish few constraints on the creation of single-sex schools and classes.[303]

Just as in California, the Bush effort is not motivated by or rooted in a desire to promote gender equality,[304] which necessarily would entail questioning and challenging traditional gendered and raced norms. Instead, as articulated in the notice, the proposal is intended to enhance public education agencies' flexibility[305] to experiment in this way, based on the misinformed assumption that single-sex education is benign.[306] Moreover, the notice indicates that no consideration will be given to the fact that students of color likely will be most affected if Title IX regulations are modified to permit the spread of sex segregation. Lacking even the basic understanding of gender, much less the racial implications of the proposed policy, the department fails to conduct the searching inquiry necessary to ensure that single-sex education really improves educational outcomes for students of color. The next section demonstrates how an intersectional approach might be used in cases to make that determination.

B. Intersectionality Applied

Garrett[307] illustrates the importance of considering sex and race. In *Garrett*, the court assumed erroneously that race was not an issue because all the students involved were Black, as were the parents and the school board that ultimately decided to create the all-male academies.[308] However, as this section demonstrates, consideration of race is essential to determining the plan's validity as a legal matter and advisability as a public policy matter.

---

300. *Id.* at 295 (observing that "girls were well-versed in the notion that they could 'do anything'").

301. *Id.* (noting that "boys expressed stricter expectations to be strong and support a family, upheld in part by institutional messages that boys should be more disciplined").

302. *Id.* at 295–96 (internal quotations omitted).

303. *See supra* notes 84–106 and accompanying text.

304. DATNOW, *supra* note 284, at 5 ("Instead of seeing the single gender academies as primarily an opportunity to address gender inequities for girls and boys (as one might predict) most educators saw the $500,000 state grant as a way to help address the more pressing educational and social problems of low achieving students.").

305. *See supra* note 81 and accompanying text.

306. *See supra* Part II.

307. 775 F. Supp. at 1004; *see supra* notes 5–20 and accompanying text.

308. *Nightline, supra* note 4.

Garrett became emblematic of certain aspects of school reform in the inner cities, which were characterized by parents who were fed up with the failure of public schools to educate their children, sympathetic educators who were willing to experiment to find something that works, and civil rights advocates who were fearful of losing the little ground that has been attained post-*Brown.* These conflicting interests came to a head before a federal judge, who at the urging of advocates seen as interlopers,[309] invalidated the academies.[310] The decision itself, though not a final determination on the merits after a trial,[311] became the authoritative word on the impermissibility of single-sex education in the public schools,[312] and sparked a series of national efforts to *fix* the situation.[313] Now the legal landscape apparently is about to shift[314] to provide school districts such as Detroit greater flexibility[315] to segregate students based on sex, if the Bush administration has its way. But as the foregoing demonstrates, the history of sex segregation demands more questions, not fewer, and greater protection not less, to ensure that the new single-sex schools and classes do not create yet another dead-end academic track for Black children.[316]

The primary plaintiff in *Garrett* challenged her daughter's exclusion from three planned all-male academies, alleging that the admissions policy violated the federal Constitution, Title IX and other laws.[317] The Detroit Board of Education created these academies for Black males, who, in the board's estimation, were in need of particular assistance because of their high dropout rates, involvement in the drug trade, and incarceration.[318] In this regard, the academies were to offer special programs designed to meet these boys' needs, including "Rites of Passage"; preparation for twenty-first-century careers; mentors; and "male responsibility."[319] The board also recognized that Black females faced a crisis of their own, which the board argued it already was addressing through pregnancy-related programs.[320]

Assuming that the case presented only the issue of sex-based exclusion, the court applied heightened scrutiny,[321] concluding that although the stated purpose of assisting troubled African American males was an important governmental purpose, the means proposed were not closely related to that purpose.[322] Specifically, the court found that "there [was] no showing that it [was] the co-educational factor that result[ed] in failure" of the schools to serve Black males appropriately.[323] The court also suggested that had the board established a similar program for Black females, the academies might have survived,[324] indi-

---

309. *See supra* note 11 and accompanying text.
310. *Garrett,* 775 F. Supp. at 1008.
311. The matter came before the court on a motion for a preliminary injunction. *Id.* at 1006.
312. Salomone, *supra* note 11, at 131.
313. *See supra* note 60.
314. *See supra* note 84 and accompanying text.
315. *See supra* note 84 and accompanying text.
316. *See supra* note 298 and accompanying text.
317. *Garrett,* 775 F. Supp. at 1005.
318. *Id.* at 1007.
319. *Id.* at 1006–07.
320. *Id.* at 1007.
321. *See id.* at 1006–07; *see also Hogan,* 458 U.S. at 723–24 (discussing heightened levels of scrutiny applicable in gender cases).
322. *Garrett,* 775 F. Supp. at 1007.
323. *Id.*
324. *See id.* at 1009 (noting that the "plaintiffs' claims ... do not rest solely on the denial of admission; [they also seek to vindicate] their right to the same benefits and services"); *id.* at 1006 n.4 (noting that the court was "not presented with the question of whether the Board can provide separate but equal public school institutions for boys and girls").

cating that a formal equality approach might have remedied the violations of equal protection and Title IX. But this reasoning is inadequate.

The question for courts, as well as policy makers for that matter, is whether sex segregation will perpetuate race- *and* gender-based subordination of African American students, irrespective of whether *equal* resources are available. Though advocating for an antisubordination inquiry is not a new approach,[325] this chapter suggests that the inquiry should focus not only on the students who would benefit from sex segregation but also on the students who are excluded. Thus, *Garrett* raises the issue of whether the proposed academies would subordinate the Black boys who attend them as well as the Black girls who cannot. Specifically, based on the potential for single-sex education to perpetuate racism and patriarchy, at a minimum, the following questions should be addressed: Do the academies perpetuate racialized gender roles, and do they contribute to sexualizing race? When applied to *Garrett*, the inquiry demonstrates that rather than representing a progressive reform strategy, the proposed academies actually supported retrenchment of the very subordination that its proponents wanted to attack.

1. Perpetuating Racialized Gender Roles

As proposed, the academies at issue in *Garrett* would have constructed masculinity in a traditional manner and thus supported white patriarchy.[326] Consider the rhetoric justifying their creation. Namely, the academies were going to help Black males overcome the handicap of being raised in female-headed households by providing them with role models.[327] Though it is well documented that households that are headed by single women, including single Black women, are more likely to be poor,[328] it is doubtful that providing masculine role models for boys will improve the economic status of their families or create a plethora of two-parent households. In fact, suggesting that the problems of African Americans can be solved by teaching Black boys to be men is precisely the same racist and sexist rhetoric that has cast Black women as deviant and Black families as matriarchal, and therefore pathological.[329]

Additionally, in proposing to emphasize traditional male behavior and coping strategies,[330] the academies would have reinforced a construct of "hegemonic masculinit[y]"[331] that is both limiting to the boys who seek to replicate it and threatening to those who fail to conform to its standards.[332] As the California example illustrated, the emphasis on traditional "male" behavior, particularly in the context of educating "at-risk boys," resulted in the belief that strict discipline was necessary. This emphasis in turn resulted in the boys acting out with overly aggressive, or "stereotypically male" behavior.[333] In addition, this vision of maleness excludes and alienates students who do not conform to the tradi-

---

325. *See generally* Morgan, *supra* note 80.

326. *See supra* notes 34–38 and accompanying text.

327. *See supra* note 40.

328. Bernadette D. Proctor & Joseph Dalaker, *U.S. Census Bureau, Current Population Reports, P60-219, Poverty in the United States*: 2001, at 16 (2002) (noting that the poverty rate for female-headed households is 28.6 percent).

329. *See generally* Ryan, *supra* note 39.

330. *Garrett*, 775 F. Supp. at 1006–07 (outlining proposed programs, including programs designed to help boys control their emotions).

331. *See* Woody, *Constructions of Masculinity, supra* note 285, at 296; *see also supra* notes 268–87 and accompanying text.

332. *See supra* note 302 and accompanying text.

333. *See* DATNOW, *supra* note 284, at 50; *see also supra* notes 268–76 and accompanying text.

tional gender stereotype,[334] which typically leads to physical and psychological violence intended to force the boys to become *men*, for example.[335] In this connection, the emphasis on the traditional gender roles has the potential to subordinate students who identify themselves as gay, lesbian, bisexual, transgendered, or undecided.

Finally, the Detroit Board of Education's emphasis on saving boys in this context privileged Black males as the racial victims,[336] which is a limiting strategy upon which to build a liberation movement.[337] As the court correctly noted, the focus on Black boys rendered the problems affecting Black females invisible and perpetuated the myth that females are doing just fine[338] without addressing their problems meaningfully. Indeed, any student of color who did not match the profile of Black males was excluded from this effort, which sent the message that those students were not worth saving.

2. Sexualizing Race

Similarly, the plan in *Garrett* was flawed because it contributed to sexualizing Blacks. Specifically, when confronted with its failure to provide any special programming for Black girls, the board responded that such programming was available in the form of pregnancy-related courses.[339] Although there is no doubt that the rate of teen pregnancy for Black girls is too high,[340] the board's strategy fed into the construction of Black females as overly fecund and hypersexual by suggesting that the only program they needed was one focusing on child-bearing, not on math or science, for example, which have been characterized as fostering a sense of competence, at least with respect to middle-income white females.[341] In this context, emphasizing the development of essential academic skills likely would prove more effective at discouraging teen pregnancy by providing the tools for higher education or meaningful employment—true disincentives for premature child-bearing.[342] Such an alternative was unavailable and not even under consideration.

---

334. *See, e.g.*, Deborah Brake, *The Cruelest of the Gender Police: Student-to-Student Sexual Harassment and Anti-Gay Peer Harassment Under Title IX*, 1 Geo. J. Gender & L. 37, 92 (1999) ("Students can be the cruelest of the gender police. Gender role conformity is particularly important as a source of security and confidence in childhood and adolescence."). In light of Black Americans' perceived failure to conform to traditional gender norms, the pressure for young African Americans to do so may be particularly intense. *Cf.* Benoit Denizet-Lewis, *Double Lives on the Down Low*, N.Y. Times Mag., Aug. 3, 2003, at 28, 31 (describing cultural strictures that discourage Black gay men from being open about their sexuality). One interview subject noted, "'if you're white, you can come out as an openly gay skier or actor or whatever. It might hurt you some, but it's not like if you're black and gay, because then it's like you've let down the whole black community, black women, black history, black pride.'" *Id.* at 31.

335. *See* Brake, *supra* note 334, at 92–93 (noting that sexual harassment frequently is the means used "to punish gender outliers ... and to reinforce the boundaries of gender by bolstering the sex stereotypes associated with maleness and femaleness").

336. *See* Carbado, *supra* note 38, at 434.

337. *See id.* at 434–35.

338. *See Garrett*, 775 F. Supp. at 1007–08.

339. *See id.* at 1007.

340. *See* Annie E. Casey Found., *supra* note 49.

341. *See* Stabiner, *supra* note 43, at B1 (contrasting white females at a suburban, private, single-sex institution with Black females attending TYWLS).

342. *See* Austin, *supra* note 48, at 558 (arguing that "blame for black teenage pregnancy must be shared by an educational system that fails to provide black youngsters with either the desire or the chance to attend college").

Thus, by according primacy to Black males and reinforcing the construction of traditional masculinity with the end of replicating patriarchy, the board's plan in *Garrett* was, in fact, regressive. The effect of the plan would be to support the very systems that have subordinated African Americans since the nation's founding.

IV. Conclusion

It cannot be denied that the wisest plan of education for any people should take cognizance of past and present environment, should note the forces against which they must contend, or in unison with which they must labor in the civilization of which they form a part.[343]

As we evaluate strategies designed to reform today's inner-city schools, we must examine and comprehend fully the past. Thus, as the debate concerning single-sex education moves forward, we must first recognize the role sex segregation in schools has played in reifying limiting race and gender roles that have contributed to the subordination of African-Americans and women. Only by reckoning with the past can we fully evaluate the potential for sex segregation to provide the academic reform so necessary for students to succeed in the future. Such an analysis requires examining the intersection of race and sex, at a minimum, to assess the likely effect of single-sex education on students of color today. Unfortunately, that history and its legacy suggest that single-sex schools may not be the progressive reform strategies for public schools its proponents hope.

When viewed within the context of race- and sex-based discrimination in education, sex segregation emerges as a means of supporting patriarchy and white supremacy. Single-sex schools helped construct "true" masculinity and femininity as white,[344] while constructing Black masculinity and femininity as deviant.[345] History also shows that at times, African Americans have adopted single-sex schooling as a strategy to gain white acceptance and equal access to opportunities in society. However, even in this context, single-sex education continued to reinforce raced and gendered norms to support the patriarchal framework that has subordinated Blacks.[346]

The legacy of this history is evident in today's discourse regarding single-sex education. Arguments that separating the sexes in inner-city schools will promote safety and prevent pregnancy echo long-standing, constraining stereotypes concerning students of color. For example, the California experiment with single-sex education, which was not grounded in efforts to achieve equality, reflected those stereotypes[347] by subjecting male students of color primarily to discipline,[348] while exposing female students of color to romance and homemaking skills.[349] Significantly, sex segregation in that setting did not provide the promised academic opportunities and lead researchers to conclude that single-sex edu-

---

343. Anna Julia Cooper, *On Education, in* THE VOICE OF ANNA JULIA COOPER 248, 250 (Charles Lemer & Esme Bhan eds., 1998).

344. *See supra* notes 194–206 and accompanying text.

345. *See supra* notes 138–47 and accompanying text.

346. *See supra* notes 170–79 and accompanying text.

347. *See supra* notes 288–302 and accompanying text.

348. *See supra* note 288 and accompanying text.

349. *See supra* notes 293–96 and accompanying text.

cation had the potential to be a new dead-end track for low-income students of color.[350] It is worth noting that, just as was true in the case of California, the department of Education's current proposal lacks a focus on gender equality. In fact, the Department has gone so far as to suggest that such an emphasis is unnecessary.[351] Given the lessons of the past, the failure to consider the race and gender norming likely to occur means the proposed policy changes will probably result in no reform whatsoever. Real change in our public schools will come only when we recognize the manner in which educational institutions have entrenched race- and sex-based subordination in the past and the implications of that past for today. Then we must commit our best efforts to devising new strategies to dismantle that legacy and establish a new track of equality of opportunity for all our sons and daughters.

---

350. *See supra* note 298 and accompanying text.
351. *See supra* notes 87–88 and accompanying text.

13

Constitutional Remedies for Latino Educational Neglect

Lupe S. Salinas[*]

I. Introduction

On one hand, Latino parents see more concerted efforts in schools from both the state and the national levels of government. On the other hand, they see insufficient, inadequate results in their own children. Latino parents are generally not well equipped to address this problem because many did not receive formal education in the United States.[1] Like others, Latino parents send their children to school so that teachers and other experts in the public schools can address their children's needs. The purpose of this chapter is to address the unique educational needs of the Latino/a[2] child. I also seek to determine if cases like *Westminster School District v. Mendez*,[3] *Brown v. Board of Education*,[4] *Her-*

---

[*] Professor of Law, Thurgood Marshall School of Law, Texas Southern University. Judge Lupe Salinas teaches a course titled "Latinos and the Law." A retired state district judge for Harris County, Texas, Salinas also served as an Adjunct Professor and Visiting Professor of Law at the University of Houston Law Center, where he first began teaching the Latino civil rights course in 1975. His writings include articles concerning Latino school segregation, unequal educational opportunities, the administration of justice, language rights, undocumented Mexican immigration and the punitive and ex post facto consequences of the 1996 Immigration Acts. In addition, he served as a civil rights attorney, litigating educational equality issues for the Mexican American Legal Defense and Education Fund, prosecuting violations of civil rights for the U.S. Attorney's Office in Houston, Texas, and defending civil rights claims against Harris County, Texas, peace officers and officials.

1. Interview with Arnulfo Garcia Salinas, author's father, in Galveston, Texas (May 18, 2005). The author dedicates his efforts in the educational field to his mother, Benita Lopez Salinas (1922–2005) and to his eighty-six-year-old father who, notwithstanding the devastating effects of age on his memory, still recalls the bitterness caused by his exclusion from a public school education in Texas from 1927 through 1933 in spite of being an American citizen and notwithstanding the mandates of the Texas Compulsory Attendance legislation.

2. The term "Latino/a" generically refers to all persons, regardless of gender, who identify themselves as of Latin American or Hispanic descent. More specifically, this group includes persons of Mexican, Puerto Rican, Cuban, Colombian, Dominican, Salvadoran, Guatemalan or other South or Central American descent. The author hereafter uses the term "Latino" to refer to any and all of these ethnicities.

3. 161 F.2d 774, 780 (9th Cir. 1947).

4. *Brown v. Board of Education*, 347 U.S. 483 (1954).

nandez v. Texas,[5] and several other authorities possess any vitality in the battle for educational equity for Latino children. These principles should continue to provide a foundation for the prospect of a race-neutral America, free of debilitating discrimination.[6] This vision remains not only a worthy goal but also a challenging undertaking.

To resuscitate the remedies found in the authorities listed above, I urge the Supreme Court and the lower federal courts to adjust to the realities of the subtle and sometimes ingenuous acts of discrimination that plague our society. In other words, evidence of continued and persistent Latino educational neglect should alone prompt the Court to alleviate the burdens imposed by current constitutional principles that fail to address the issues in the field of public education. I recommend in educational equality cases the application of the foreseeable consequences test described in early school desegregation cases, the "result bespeaks discrimination" standard found in *Hernandez* and the deliberate or callous indifference standard announced by the Court in *Estelle v. Gamble*,[7] a case involving an inmate claiming a violation of his Eighth Amendment rights.

II. The History and Demographics of the Latino Population

The development and growth of the Latino American population should assist in an understanding of the issues covered in this chapter. The United States began as a confederation of colonies in the 1600s, primarily comprised of English settlers and African slaves. The closest geographic influence of Latinos (Spaniards)[8] existed in Florida[9] and Louisiana, but that population did not yet affect the original thirteen colonies. Approximately two-thirds of New Spain, later known as the Mexican Empire, continued north of the Rio Grande into the current states of Texas, New Mexico, Colorado, Arizona and California. This is the area that Spanish conquistadors visited and inhabited in the name of the Spanish Crown.[10] These explorers provided the Latino names to the cities and rivers and valleys in California and throughout the Southwest United States.[11]

---

5. *Hernandez v. Texas*, 347 U.S. 475 (1954).

6. The principles discussed in this chapter may be found in detail in the following law journal articles: Lupe S. Salinas & Dr. Robert H. Kimball, *The Equal Treatment of Unequals: Barriers Facing Latinos and the Poor in Texas Public Schools*, 14 GEO. J. ON POVERTY L. & POL'Y 215 (2007); Lupe S. Salinas, *Latino Educational Neglect: The Result Bespeaks Discrimination*, 5 MD. L.J. RACE, REL., GENDER & CLASS 269 (2005).

7. 429 U.S. 97 (1976).

8. Few are aware of the role played by Spaniards under General Bernardo De Galvez, as allies to the colonists, in the defeat of British forces at sea during the American Revolution. *See* DAVID J. WEBER, THE SPANISH FRONTIER IN NORTH AMERICA 267–70 (1992).

9. Susana H. O'Mara, *The Hispanic Presence*, BALTIMORE SUN, Nov. 8, 1979, at A23 (referring to the Spanish as the first colonizers of what is today the territory of the United States).

10. *See* THE WORLD ALMANAC AND BOOK OF FACTS 538 (Erik C. Gopel ed., World Almanac 2005) [hereafter 2005 WORLD ALMANAC]. In 1540, Francisco Vasquez de Coronado explored the Southwest United States north of the Rio Grande River.

11. For example, Juan Ponce de Leon explored the Florida coast in 1513, and then Hernando de Soto landed in Florida in 1539, setting the stage for the founding of St. Augustine. 2005 WORLD ALMANAC, *supra* note 10, at 538.

The real test of Anglo-Latino relations began in the 1820s when Mexico began to allow and encourage the migration of Anglos to Mexican Texas. In a relatively short period of time, the racial-cultural conflict began to surface in Mexican Texas.[12] Anglos encountered a group of Mexicans comprised in small part of European-Spaniard blood but in larger part of pure Indian and *mestizo* blood.[13] Another major conflict resulted from language differences. The newly adopted Mexican nation frustrated English-speaking Anglos by not only governing but also educating Anglo and Mexican children in Spanish.[14]

These conflicts led to the call for Texas independence and bloodshed. During battles at the Alamo and at Goliad, Mexican troops slaughtered all rebels, both Anglo and Mexican, who took up the fight for independence.[15] The battle cry, "Remember the Alamo," became symbolic of the stereotypical view of all Mexicans as a vicious and savage group of people and became symbolic of anti-Latino racial prejudice.[16]

In April 1836, with the loss of the Mexican army at San Jacinto, located near Houston, General Sam Houston negotiated a treaty allowing Texas to become an independent nation. The U.S. leadership in the Congress decided to manifest their destiny in 1845 into what is now the U.S. Southwest.[17] Over the vociferous protests of South Carolina Senator John C. Calhoun that America was adding a "colored race," Mexicans became an integral part of the post-1848 United States.[18] In the resulting Mexican-American War of 1846–48, the United States obtained half of Mexico's national domain.[19] Approximately 75,000 persons of Mexican descent opted to remain in the territory they had lived on and harvested and ranched for several generations and become American citizens.[20]

At the time of the passage of the Fourteenth Amendment in the 1860s, Latinos, primarily of Mexican descent, suffered discriminatory treatment in various phases of life. When Mexicans became Americans officially in 1848, they came in as a conquered people.[21]

---

12. *See* Samuel Harman Lowrie, Culture Conflict in Texas, 1821–1835 59–60 (1967).

13. The Mexican population is currently listed as being 60 percent *mestizo* and 30 percent Indian. 2005 World Almanac, *supra* note 10, at 802. *See generally, In re Rodriguez*, 81 F. 337 (W.D. Tex. 1897) (The applicant for citizenship had a "chocolate brown" skin color, but he qualified for "white" under the naturalization law).

14. *See id.* at 120–21, 123–24.

15. *See* Hubert Herring, A History of Latin America 317 (1966).

16. *Id.* Racial restrictive covenants in Texas, discovered during litigation in school desegregation and real estate cases, often read, "This property shall not be conveyed to any person of the African or Mexican Race." *See generally, Matthews v. Andrade*, 198 P.2d 66 (Cal. 1948) ("No person or persons of the Mexican race or other than the Caucasian race shall use or occupy any buildings or any lot."); *Clifton v. Puente*, 218 S.W.2d 272 (Tex. Civ. App.-San Antonio 1948) (pursuant to *Shelley v. Kraemer*, 334 U.S. 1 (1948), a state court unconstitutionally engages in state action when it seeks to enforce racially discriminatory deeds or covenants).

17. *Id.* at 320, 322.

18. David J. Weber, Foreigners in Their Native Land: Historical Roots of the Mexican Americans 137 (1973) [hereafter Foreigners In Their Native Land], quoting Cong. Globe, 30th Cong., 1st Sess. 98–99 (1847). The highly respected Calhoun stated, "Ours, sir, is the Government of a white race. The greatest misfortunes of Spanish America are to be traced to the fatal error of placing *these colored races* on an equality with the white race." *Id.* at 135 (emphasis added).

19. Herring, *supra* note 15, at 323. The Treaty of Guadalupe Hidalgo, U.S.-Mex., Feb. 2, 1848, 9 Stat. 922 [hereafter Treaty of Guadalupe Hidalgo] formally ended the war. The United States paid $15,000,000 to Mexico and obtained Texas and the territory that later became California, New Mexico, Arizona, Nevada, Utah and part of Colorado. *Id.*

20. Carey McWilliams, North from Mexico 52 (1948).

21. *See* Rodolfo Acuna, Occupied America: The Chicano's Struggle Toward Liberation 9 (1972) [hereafter cited as Acuna].

Latinos in Texas and other parts of the Southwest suffered abuses in the criminal justice system during the 1850s and 1860s.[22]

This type of disrespect of Latino rights also carried over into a person's right not to be deprived of liberty without due process of law.[23] In 1854, in California, "the Spanish-speaking of Los Angeles felt oppressed by a double standard of justice."[24] In addition, "every important lynch-law episode and most minor ones involved the Spanish-speaking."[25] In Texas, early tales of Anglo-Mexican relations reveal horrific violence against persons of Mexican descent.[26] The controversies often centered on Anglo desires to acquire land, cattle and other livestock.[27] Other controversies focused on law enforcement brutality. Known derogatorily among Mexican Latinos as *rinches*, the Texas Rangers developed a reputation for shooting first and determining later if the Mexican was armed.[28] At times, the Rangers, in an apparent effort to terrorize the Latino population, eliminated innocent people in what became known as "revenge by proxy."[29]

Conditions for Latino workers in the 1860s compared to slavery and involuntary servitude. Even though slavery involving African Americans was barred by the Thirteenth Amendment,[30] the practice continued de facto as to both the newly emancipated slaves and others, like Mexican and Chinese workers, who were victims of labor abuses.[31] The condition known as Mexican peonage was of such concern that it was mentioned by the U.S. Supreme Court as a reality[32] and was addressed by the League of United Latin American Citizens (LULAC) in 1929, at its founding, as a major concern.[33] Peonage allowed an

---

22. For example, in 1859 in Brownsville, Texas, Juan Nepumeceno "Cheno" Cortina, a man of means, observed the town constable pistol-whipping an intoxicated Latino. On recognizing the Latino as one of his mother's workers, Cortina offered to assume responsibility for the man. The constable replied: "What is it to you, you damned Mexican." ACUNA, *supra* note 21, at 47. Around the same time that Cortina fought his battles, the murder case of the State of Texas versus Chipita Rodriguez occurred in San Patricio County. *See* VERNON SMYLIE, A NOOSE FOR CHIPITA (1970). The first woman ever executed in Texas, *Id.* at 3, faced the following due process: the grand jury returned an indictment on October 7; the trial began and ended on October 9; the judge ordered that the death sentence by hanging be carried out on November 13, 1863. *id.* at 25–26, 28–29.

23. U.S. CONST. amend. XIV.

24. LEONARD PITT, THE DECLINE OF THE CALIFORNIOS: A SOCIAL HISTORY OF THE SPANISH SPEAKING CALIFORNIANS, 1846–1890, at 160 (1968).

25. *Id.* at 154.

26. *See, e.g.,* DAVID MONTEJANO, ANGLOS AND MEXICANS IN THE MAKING OF TEXAS, 1836–1986, at 26–37 (1999).

27. Latinos lost nearly four million acres of land. Valdez, *Insurrection in New Mexico*, 1 EL GRITO 14 (1967). Article VIII of the Treaty of Guadalupe Hidalgo provides, "The present owners, the heirs of these, and all Mexicans who may hereafter acquire said property by contract, shall enjoy with respect to it guaranties equally ample as if the same belonged to citizens of the United States." Treaty of Guadalupe Hidalgo, *supra* note 19, at 929–30. It has obviously become another ignored treaty provision.

28. *See generally* AMERICO PAREDES, WITH HIS PISTOL IN HIS HAND 23–32 (1958).

29. *Id.* at 26. The lynchings continued to such an extent that in 1919, Texas State Representative J. T. Canales filed a complaint and commenced hearings in the Texas Legislature on how to modernize and train the Texas Rangers. *See* David McLemore, *The Forgotten Carnage Between Hispanics, Rangers*, DALLAS MORNING NEWS, Nov. 25, 2004, at A5. For more documentation of the violence against Latinos, see *Mexican Rights in the United States,* 115 THE NATION 51–53 (1922).

30. U.S. CONST. amend. XIII.

31. ACUNA, *supra* note 21, at 86; *see generally Plessy v. Ferguson,* 163 U.S. 537, 542 (1896).

32. *Plessy,* 163 U.S. at 542.

33. *See* discussion of the LULAC Charter, *infra,* at Part III.A.

Anglo creditor to bind a Latino debtor until the debt was satisfied.[34] The other facet of this new form of servitude involved the differential pay scales for Latinos. The double wage standard providing for a much lower pay for Latinos became known as "peon's wages."[35] The company store extended credit, but the store also marked up items as much as 300 percent.[36] Over 100 years later, the plight of some Latino workers continues to convey vestiges of the days of slavery.[37]

The Latino population in the United States reached 39.9 million by 2003.[38] This growth resulted from many events, including two Mexican revolutions, an open border through the 1930s, a higher than average birth rate, economic troubles in Mexico and economic needs in the United States. These last two factors — the economic problems in Mexico and the American economic needs — operate as push-pull dynamics between the United States and Mexico and the other Latin American countries.[39]

To put this growth in perspective, data released by the Census Bureau showed that the total U.S. population roughly doubled (a 2.2 increase) from 131.7 million in 1940 to 290.8 million in 2003.[40] During this same time period, the Latino population increased from about 1.4 million to 39.9 million (an increase of 28.5).[41] This population growth has occurred in spite of the Washington-sanctioned efforts known respectively as Operation Repatriation and Operation Wetback in the 1930s and the 1950s,[42] as well as the Minuteman Project along the Arizona–Mexico border in 2005.[43] The growth has continued notwithstanding similar efforts to rid the country of "illegals" during the 1974 recession and the 1994 and 2006 congressional elections in which issues involving aliens accented the political landscape.[44] Census demographers predict that by 2050 Latinos will increase to 67 million, or 24 percent of the population of the United States.[45]

Historically, other events involving Puerto Rico, Cuba, Central America and more recently South America, resulted in an increase in the ethnic and linguistic diversity of the United States. Pursuant to the Treaty of Paris, which ended the Spanish-American War

---

34. Professor Paul Taylor's study in Nueces County, Texas, documented Latino labor and peonage-type conditions in 1929. *See* Paul S. Taylor, An American Mexican Frontier 147–57 (1934) [hereafter cited as Taylor].

35. Acuna, *supra* note 21, at 87.

36. *Id.* at 88.

37. The Latino worker continues to lead the nation in occupational deaths. L. M. Sixel, *Hispanics Suffer More Deaths on Job*, Hous. Chron., Mar. 26, 2002, at B1 (Hispanics accounted for a disproportionate number of workplace fatalities in 2000).

38. Louis Kincannon, *U.S. Census Bureau Takes the Nation's Socioeconomic Pulse*, *in* 2005 World Almanac, *supra* note 10, at 619.

39. *See generally* Julian Samora, Los Mojados: The Wetback Story 33–34, 38–40 (1971) [hereafter cited as Samora]; U.S. Comm'n on Civil Rights, The Tarnished Door: Civil Rights Issues in Immigration 10–12 (1980).

40. 2005 World Almanac, *supra* note 10, at 8.

41. *Id.*

42. *See* Samora, *supra* note 39, at 51–53.

43. *See* Ioan Grillo, *Minutemen Aside, Some Migrants Undeterred*, Hous. Chron., Apr. 3, 2005, at A29.

44. For example, in 1996 Congress enacted harsh legislation aimed at ridding the country of aliens who had committed so-called aggravated felonies at any time, even prior to the effective date of the new legislation. *See* 8 U.S.C. § 1101(a)(43)(F) (2000) (defining an aggravated felony). *See* Lupe S. Salinas, *Deportations, Removals and the 1996 Immigration Acts: A Modern Look at the Ex Post Facto Clause*, 22 B.U. Int'l L.J. 251 (2004) (critically assessing the constitutionality of this extremely punitive legislation).

45. 2005 World Almanac, *supra* note 10, at 629.

of 1898, Spain ceded the territory today known as Puerto Rico to the United States.[46] Congress later enacted a law that Puerto Ricans, even if born outside the continental United States—for example, in Puerto Rico—would be U.S. citizens.[47]

The Cuban migrations of the 1960s and the 1980s brought more Latinos. The United States attracted and welcomed refugees from Fidel Castro's communist regime beginning in 1959. Humanitarian concerns then forced the United States to accept thousands of Cubans who left the Port of Mariel in June 1980. The Castro regime released *Los Marielitos,* as they became known in the Spanish-language media, because these Cubanos allegedly suffered from mental and psychopathic problems.[48] Cubans continue to come, albeit more slowly, taking advantage of their special legislative status that allows them to seek asylum if they reach American soil.[49]

In addition to the Cuban refugee migration, the United States, through the exercise of its foreign policy, aided, abetted, enticed and otherwise encouraged Latinos from Central America to migrate to Mexico and then to the United States to avoid tyrannical abuses of leaders supported by different factions of our government from the State Department to the Central Intelligence Agency.[50] During the 1980s, this foreign policy thus magnetically brought more Spanish-speaking peoples to large urban centers like New York, Los Angeles, Houston, Chicago and Washington, D.C. Additionally, the Narco Wars in Colombia forced thousands of Colombianos to seek a new and safe life in America.[51]

III. The Educational History of the Latino Population

A. Unequal Educational Opportunities for Latino Students

"Education is our freedom and freedom should be everybody's business." With that slogan, Dr. Hector P. Garcia founded the American GI Forum, a Latino civil rights organization, in 1948. Dr. Garcia heard complaints of and witnessed the school segrega-

---

46. *Id.* at 442.

47. Congress declared that persons born in Puerto Rico between 1899 and 1941, and residing in Puerto Rico or other U.S. territory, would be citizens of the United States, adding that all others born after January 13, 1941, would be citizens at birth. 8 U.S.C. § 1402 (2005).

48. *See Benitez v. Wallis,* 337 F.3d 1289, 1290 (11th Cir. 2003) (many of these refugees were dissidents, criminals or individuals with mental illness). *See generally Clark v. Martinez,* 543 U.S. 371 (2005); *Fernandez-Roque v. Smith,* 599 F. Supp. 1103, 1106 (N.D. Ga. 1984) (the Cubans who left the Port of Mariel were considered scum by their government).

49. *See* Thomas Alexander Aleinkoff, Immigration and Citizenship: Process and Policy 1173 (4th ed. 1998).

50. The United States was deeply involved in armed conflicts in El Salvador, Guatemala and Nicaragua, usually supporting the military governments in those countries. *See* Thomas Kleven, *Why International Law Favors Emigration over Immigration,* 33 U. Miami Inter-Am. L. Rev. 69, 85 n.49 (2002); Howard Zinn, A People's History of the United States: 1492–Present 572 (Perennial Ed. 2005) (references to the financial support that President Jimmy Carter extended to back the military junta in El Salvador and the support for the Somoza family dictatorship in Nicaragua); Kenneth C. Davis, Don't Know Much About History 520 (Perennial Ed. 2004) (reference to CIA Chief Casey's encouragement for Nicaragua's military).

51. 2005 World Almanac, *supra* note 10, at 765, 850 (as of December 31, 2003, approximately 233,600 Colombians sought refuge in other countries).

tion of Latino children and the mistreatment of Latino veterans returning from World War II.[52] The earliest battles that Latino political and social groups fought centered on education.[53] In 1929, Latinos formed LULAC, their first civil rights group, as a result of educational deficits in public education.[54] From the 1930s through the 1950s, LULAC assisted in the fight to end school segregation and grand jury exclusions in *Independent Sch. Dist. v. Salvatierra* (Del Rio),[55] *Delgado v. Bastrop Independent School District*[56] and *Hernandez v. Texas*.[57]

Census figures report that our nation's schools have failed Latinos. A 2003 study of the educational attainment of Americans twenty-five years of age or older reveals that Latinos find themselves at the bottom of the educational ladder.[58] Non-Hispanic whites (Anglos) have the following educational attainments: 30 percent have a college degree or beyond and over 89 percent have a high school education.[59] On the other hand, Latinos average only 11 percent with a college degree, and only 57 percent have a high school education.[60]

Dr. Angela Valenzuela, an educational expert who conducted an ethnographic study of an inner-city high school in Houston, Texas,[61] found that Mexican-descent students feel uncared for by teachers and other personnel who uphold an approach to schooling, pedagogy and caring that subtracts students' cultural resources and identities, thereby compromising students' abilities and desires to enter into productive learning relationships with adults.[62] Dr. Valenzuela criticizes current schooling methods because "it's more like trying to make all children into replicas of Anglo children. It's a process that doesn't value what a student can offer in terms of a dual culture or bilingualism."[63]

---

52. *See* Patrick J. Carroll, Felix Longoria's Wake 54–65 (2003) (describing Three Rivers, Texas, funeral home's refusal to handle the services for Felix Longoria, an army private killed in action in the Pacific Theater during World War II).

53. *E.g., Independent Sch. Dist. v. Salvatierra*, 33 S.W.2d 790 (Tex. Civ. App. 1930), *cert. denied*, 284 U.S. 580 (1931). One should not be surprised that the Court did not see a legal problem with the *Salvatierra* ruling when it denied the petition for certiorari. A few years earlier, the Court decided that the exclusion of a Chinese-descent American was appropriate under the edict of the Mississippi constitution that provided for separate schools for the "colored" students of the state. The message was that if one were not Caucasian, he was "colored." *Gong Lum v. Rice*, 275 U.S. 78, 86–87 (1927).

54. *See* Taylor, *supra* note 36, at 243–44. The newest civil rights group in the fight for Latino educational equality came into existence in 1968. Aided by a Ford Foundation grant, a group of Latino civil rights leaders formed the Mexican American Legal Defense and Educational Fund (MALDEF). *See* Guadalupe Salinas, Comment, *Mexican Americans and the Desegregation of Schools in the Southwest*, 8 Hous. L. Rev. 929, 932–33 (1971). MALDEF's battles have concentrated on educational equality on behalf of Latinos. *See, e.g., Zamora v. New Braunfels Ind. School Dist.*, 519 F.2d 1084 (5th Cir. 1975), *rev'g* 362 F. Supp. 552 (W.D. Tex. 1973); *Arvizu v. Waco Ind. School Dist.*, 495 F.2d 499 (5th Cir. 1974), *rev'g in part and remanding in part*, 373 F. Supp. 1264 (W.D. Tex. 1973); *Ross v. Eckels*, 434 F.2d 1140 (5th Cir. 1970); *Keyes v. School Dist. No. One, Denver*, 413 U.S. 189 (1973). The Puerto Rican Legal Defense and Educational Fund (PRLDF) serves a similar role in the Northeast.

55. 33 S.W.2d 790 (Tex. Civ. App. 1930), *cert. denied*, 284 U.S. 580 (1931).

56. Civil No. 388 (W.D. Tex. June 15, 1948).

57. 347 U.S. 475 (1954).

58. 2005 World Almanac, *supra* note 10, at 10.

59. *Id.*

60. *Id.*

61. Angela Valenzuela, Subtractive Schooling: U.S.-Mexican Youth and the Politics of Caring 3 (1999).

62. Henry T. Trubea, *Pushing Boundaries: Language and Culture in a Mexicano Community*, 27 Anthropology & Educ. Q. 3 (1996) (book review).

63. Ivan Chavez, *Paving the Way for the Equality and Justice in Education*, Hisp. J. (May–June 2003), *available at* www.hispanicjournal.com/journal/2003/may_june/angela_valenzuela.htm.

A professor at the University of Texas, Dr. Valenzuela firmly believes that dual-language education programs hold the most promise in the success of Latino education.[64] Furthermore, dual-language programs benefit not only the student but also the nation, because globalization is the future. Expanded business with Mexico and Latin America will necessitate that all professions, whether in education, public health, science or computer technology, incorporate a greater demand for bilingual, bicultural and biliterate language skills.[65]

Another concern in Dr. Valenzuela's studies involves the Texas Assessment of Knowledge and Skills (TAKS) reading test.[66] Texas third-graders have to pass this test to be promoted. Failure by even one point retains the child. She argues against placing all the emphasis on this one test because it is not a complete picture of the child's competency: "What we should do is implement multiple criteria. It's not just the test, but also grades, teacher recommendations, even other test information that really tells the story about a child's competency. Some children just can't show it on an exam."[67]

According to Dr. Valenzuela, "retaining a child once in grade results in a 50 percent chance that they will be dropouts. Retain them twice and it's a virtual certainty (90 percent)."[68] She sees a sinister and devious twist by lawmakers to promote standardized tests:

> When you attach standards that can't possibly be met, the public school system gets discredited and the path to vouchers get[s] paved. For certain powerful business and economic interests, I think that's the ultimate goal. There is a hidden agenda to discredit public school systems.[69]

The general view is that education correlates to employment opportunities and to income. In the first quarter of 2004, the unemployment rate for Latinos was 8.1 percent, whereas that for non-Hispanic whites reached only 5.8 percent.[70] That meant that Latinos took home weekly wages of $502 while Anglos averaged $702.[71] It should not shock the public to find that the Latinos' share of the poverty level exceeds 21 percent of the population as opposed to only less than 8 percent of non-Hispanic whites.[72] The statistics support the sad thesis of educational neglect.[73]

---

64. *Id.* (proposing that dual-language programs turn immigrant children into assets rather than liabilities).

65. *Id.*

66. In a related matter, a federal district court in Texas ruled that the Texas Assessment of Academic Skills examination does not unconstitutionally discriminate against minority students or perpetuate prior educational discrimination. *G I Forum v. Texas Educ. Agency*, 87 F. Supp. 2d 667, 684 (W.D. Tex. 2000).

67. Chavez, *supra* note 63.

68. *Id.* (describing the test process as abusive to the children who struggle with their fear of failure or the threat of retention as they take the exam).

69. *Id. See also Zelman v. Simmons-Harris*, 536 U.S. 639 (2002) (holding that the establishment clause does not bar a Cleveland, Ohio, financial assistance program, sometimes called vouchers, which would allow public school students to transfer to a private school, whether it is religious or not).

70. Trubea, *supra* note 62.

71. *Id.*

72. *Id.*

73. *See generally* Thomas P. Carter, A History of Educational Neglect (1970) (documenting discriminatory practices against Latino students). Dr. Carter served as one of the experts on Latino educational needs that the author and his co-counsel presented in *Arvizu v. Waco Ind. Sch. Dist.*, 373 F. Supp. 1264 (W.D. Tex. 1973).

How we educate our children will determine our economic future. Businesses and growth depend on an educated population, and a primary portion of that population that must be educated is Latino. According to Dr. Stephen Klineberg of Rice University, who has studied the economy of Houston, Texas, for over twenty years, Houston will not attain a successful status unless it offers its Latino community special educational programs and scholarships for the children of immigrants.[74] By 2030, nearly one-fourth of the U.S. labor workforce will be children of Latino immigrants.[75] Due to the large number of Latino immigrants and their high birth rate, there is now a new generation of Latino youth with a median age of thirteen.[76] In 2003, the Census Bureau reported that Latinos had surpassed African Americans as the nation's largest minority group.[77] The population growth of Latinos can only continue in numbers that exceed that of other racial groups.[78] The largest impact of this growth will first be felt in the nation's schools and then in the economy.[79]

In the late 1960s, the U.S. Commission on Civil Rights conducted research on the crisis of Latino educational attainment. Known as the Mexican American Education Study, the particular account most pertinent is *The Excluded Student* report on the educational neglect that describes the Latino experience.[80] The report examines the way the public school systems deal with the unique linguistic and cultural background of Latino students.[81] The basic finding is that public school systems of the Southwest have not recognized the rich culture and tradition among Latino students and have not adopted policies that would enable them to participate fully in the benefits of the educational process.[82] The report also criticized the exclusionary practices that deny Latinos the use of the Spanish language and a pride in their heritage.[83] The commission found that a significant number of the school districts enforced a "no Spanish rule" by either discouraging the speaking of Spanish on school grounds or actually imposing discipline on the offender.[84] Finally, the report addressed the exclusion of the Latino history and heritage of the Southwest, noting that only slightly more than 7 percent of the surveyed schools included a Latino history course in their curricula.[85]

To assimilate Latinos, the school system must recognize the history of the Latino population in the United States and the geographic proximity of Mexico, Central America

---

74. Galia Garcia-Palafox, *Urge Educar a Inmigrantes Hispanos [Urgent that Latino Immigrants Be Educated]*, Rumbo De Houston, 9 May 2005, at 3.

75. Robert Suro, *A Growing Minority*, in 2005 World Almanac, *supra* note 10, at 7.

76. *Id.*

77. *Id.*

78. *See id.*

79. *Id.*

80. U.S. Comm'n on Civil Rights, Report III: The Excluded Student 3 (1972) (hereafter The Excluded Student) (examining the denial of equal opportunity by exclusionary practices).

81. *Id.* at 5. The focus of the study primarily concerned Mexican American students.

82. *Id.* at 48.

83. *Id.*

84. *Id.* One-third of the school districts admitted to the harsh measure of castigating Spanish speakers at school.

85. The Excluded Student, *supra* note 80, at 49 (finding almost a quarter of a century of educational efforts did not provide any improvement in the state of Latino education). Another governmental report found the lack of adequate responses to the educational needs of Latino children. President's Adv. Comm'n on Educ'l Excellence for Hispanic Americans, Our Nation on the Fault Line: Hispanic American Education (1996), *available at* www.ed.gov/pubs/FaultLine/cover.html.

and other nations where Spanish is the predominant language. First, the United States went into Mexico and conquered Texas and other parts of the Southwest. Thus, many Latinos, even generations later, were made to feel like strangers in their own land.[86] Second, the mother country for many Latino immigrants is quite close, in contrast to the European immigrants who cut off ties with their homelands. In addition, the more recent Latino immigrants find so much cultural support when they arrive, particularly in cities like Los Angeles and Houston.[87] Finally, due to Latinos having a substantial amount of Indian blood, the darker skin features prompt Anglos to think of Latinos as "colored" people[88] and to label Mexican Latinos as being members of the "Mexican race."[89]

The greatest damage to the Latino student probably occurs when school administrators and teachers degrade his culture, particularly his Spanish language. That in itself is an attack on the student's ethnicity. Language is an integral part of an ethnic minority's being.[90] It is the means of communication with family and friends. It is an area where schools should be rewarding rather than ridiculing the child. The so-called no Spanish rule castigated innocent children who merely carried out a family value.[91] If the child is in fact not speaking either language correctly, then where is the school's responsibility for this fact? The Commission on Civil Rights states, "The Mexican culture and the Spanish language were native to the country for hundreds of years before the Anglo's arrival. They are not easy to uproot."[92]

One of the primary missions of a school district is to serve as a means to assimilate children of diverse ethnic backgrounds into the American melting pot. A school's actions, however, should never result in the following, all-too-common emotion among Latinos: "Schools try to brainwash Chicanos. They try to make us forget our history, to be ashamed of being Chicanos Mexicans, of speaking Spanish. They succeed in making us feel empty, and angry inside."[93]

---

86. *See* U.S. Comm'n on Civil Rights, Stranger in One's Land 3 (1970) (an account prepared by journalist Ruben Salazar, formerly of the *Los Angeles Times*, of a hearing held by the Civil Rights Commission in San Antonio, Texas).

87. Both cities have Latino leadership. On May 17, 2005, Los Angeles elected its first Latino mayor in over 133 years. In early 2004, Mayor Bill White appointed Arturo Michel as City Attorney for Houston. In addition, each city has extensive culinary, entertainment and media avenues to make Latinos feel as if they were "at home."

88. Foreigners in their Native Land, *supra* note 18, at 137.

89. *See, e.g., Clifton v. Puente*, 218 S.W.2d 272, 273 (Tex. Civ. App.-San Antonio 1948) (prohibiting deed through a restrictive covenant the sale or lease of real property to persons of "Mexican descent"); *Hernandez v. Driscoll Consol. Sch. Dist.*, 2 Race Rel. L. Rep. 329 (S.D. Tex. 1957) (holding that using the inability to speak English as a pretext is unreasonable race discrimination where the segregated child could speak not a word of Spanish). *See also In re Rodriguez*, 81 F. 337 (W.D. Tex. 1897) (struggling with the question whether the applicant for citizenship was a white person and thus eligible; the applicant had "chocolate brown skin").

90. Theodore Eisenberg, Civil Rights and Employment Discrimination Law 58 (1996) ("The primary language of an individual is often an essential national origin characteristic.").

91. Violation of the Spanish prohibition usually led to scolding, detention or punishment, e.g., by having to write 500 times "I will not speak Spanish on school grounds." The author's brother earned this writing assignment after being caught speaking our parent's primary language at Sam Houston Elementary in McAllen, Texas, in the 1950s. Interview with Reynol Salinas, Houston, Texas, May 30, 2005. The rule probably derived from Tex. Laws 1933, ch. 125, section 1, at 325 (repealed 1969), which required all school business to be conducted in English. Violation could result in criminal prosecution and loss of the teacher's certification. For other forms of punishment, see The Excluded Student, *supra* note 80, at 18–20.

92. The Excluded Student, *supra* note 80, at 11.

93. *Id.* (citing a statement by Maggie Alvarado, a student at St. Mary's University, San Antonio, Texas).

B. Compulsory School Attendance and the Exclusion of Latino Scholastics

Proof that the Latino child has been a victim of exclusion from public education can be traced to the early 1920s, when the Latino population in Texas began to grow in correlation with the practice of farmers who cultivated more crops. In the early twentieth century, Texas joined many other states in the enactment of compulsory school attendance legislation, the statute in Texas taking effect as early as 1915.[94] The current statute provides that "a child who is at least six years of age ... and who has not completed the academic year in which the child's 17th birthday occurred shall attend school."[95]

The critical focus should be on the actual practice of the state of Texas and other Southwestern border states with regard to the children of these workers. The answer to educational neglect might actually be found in the concerted state-imposed policy of immunizing Latino kids from the mandatory compulsory school attendance law.[96] Field studies conducted in 1929 in Texas demonstrate that Latino students received exemptions not authorized by the statute.[97] When Latino children did go to school, they often encountered segregated schooling.[98] Whether the exemptions resulted from "legislative" or from "executive" decisions at the school board level, the end result fails to differ: Latino children suffer educational inequity. Both legislative and executive decisions possess the force of law for purposes of the Fourteenth Amendment's equal protection clause.[99]

Historically, white men who owned the ranches and had an interest in the crops being picked in timely fashion comprised the school boards in Texas. An "American farmer" gave his opinion on the best worker for his crops:

> If I wanted a [Mexican] I would want one of the more ignorant ones—possibly one who could read and write and weigh his own cotton. The educated Mexicans are the hardest to handle. Educate them? We have to do that under the law of the state. It is right; they pay taxes. It is all right to educate them no higher than we educate them here in these little towns. I will be frank; they would make more desirable citizens if they would stop about the seventh grade. *The*

---

94. TEX. EDUC. CODE ANN. §25.085 (1995). Attendance laws generally mandate that a child who is at least six years of age and who has not completed the academic year in which the child's seventeenth birthday occurs shall attend school. *Id.* The statute lists certain exemptions, such as the child attending a private or parochial school, having a physical or mental impediment, being expelled, or attending a high school equivalency program. TEX. EDUC. CODE §25.086 (1995).

95. *Id.*

96. *See* TAYLOR, *supra* note 34, at 194–200.

97. *Id.*

98. *E.g., Hernandez v. Driscoll Consol. Ind. Sch. Dist.*, 2 Race Rel. L. Rep. 329 (S. D. Tex. 1957) (school district claimed language needs of Latino children required their separation in classes for Spanish-dominant children; plaintiff child did not speak any Spanish). In 2006 history repeated itself in a Dallas public school where the principal maintained segregated classes for Latino children to please the Anglo parents. *See Santamaria v. Dallas Ind. Sch. Dist.*, Civ. Action No. 3:06-CV-692-L, 2007 U.S. Dist. LEXIS 26821, at 6–7 (N.D. Tex. Apr. 10, 2007); Cary Clack, *Lasting Legacy*, SAN ANTONIO EX-PRESS-NEWS, Sept. 23, 2007, at A1, A22.

99. U.S. CONST. amend. XIV. *E.g., Shelley v. Kraemer*, 334 U.S. 1 (1948) (holding that state judicial enforcement of agreements that bar persons from ownership of real property on racial grounds constitutes state action and violates the equal protection clause).

Mexican parents don't send their children. Some children near here have never been to school.[100]

Another reason for nonenforcement of the Compulsory School Attendance Act seems to center on the financial impact. The farmers needed all the labor, even children. LULAC's concern with the employment of underage children[101] proves it was a serious problem in 1929, the same year that Berkeley Professor Paul S. Taylor conducted his study of Nueces County, where Corpus Christi and Robstown are located.[102] Taylor quoted an unnamed school superintendent about the Nueces County educational system:

> A man from the University of Texas came here with the idea of doing something for the Mexicans. He said after his experience: "But they don't appreciate it, and the more you do for them, the less they do for themselves...." To run the Mexican school longer is a waste of money. I have run a Mexican school two months with only two children, with a teacher at $90 a month. *As long as the attitude of the people who control Mexican labor controls the schools, little will be done, not until a few generations come and then demand it.... White folks don't want the Mexicans to do anything but ignorant common labor. They are not going to do what they think is not to their interest [i.e., to educate the Mexicans].*[103]

During the 1920s there was no attempt to enforce the compulsory attendance requirements on persons of Mexican descent, including citizens. The superintendent of Public Instruction, in his 1928–29 report, acknowledged this fact when he questioned the payment of funds to local districts for students who do not attend school and who "are not really wanted since there are practically no efforts being made in such districts to enforce the compulsory attendance law."[104] Superintendents in four small towns explained that "the board won't let me enforce compulsory attendance. When I come to a new school I always ask the board if they want the Mexicans in school. Here they told me to leave them alone.... If I got 150 Mexicans ready for school I would be out of a job." Another one stated, "The trustees say ... don't build up any more Mexican enrollment. We have more than we can handle now; we would have to have a new building and three or four teachers."

However, the most prominent reason for nonenforcement outside of Corpus Christi was the attitude of the farmers, many of whom are themselves on the boards of education.[105] "In general, the farmers of Nueces County, and the rural townsfolk do not want the Mexicans to receive much education ... the danger [being] that if educated they will advance economically and migrate to the cities."[106] A school official added, "It would seriously jeopardize the entire system and particularly the American [Anglo] part of it if I

---

100. TAYLOR, *supra* note 34, at 310–11 (emphasis added).

101. *Id.* at 244.

102. *See id.* at 1, 3, 4, 143, 213–14.

103. *Id.* at 214 (emphasis added). Professor Taylor from an unnamed "professional man" also learned, "Reasons for the inferiority of Mexicans? In the first place there's color — color and race; a Negro even as white as you couldn't get social recognition. He's different inside. So is a Mexican. He's a mixture of Latin and Indian. A white man just naturally looks down on those who are not white." *Id.* at 303. The 1930 census defined "Mexicans" for its purposes as "all persons born in Mexico, or having parents born in Mexico, who are not definitely white, Negro, Indian, Chinese, or Japanese." *Id.*

104. *Id.* at 201 n.14.

105. TAYLOR, *supra* note 34, at 195.

106. *Id.*

enforced the compulsory attendance law."[107] Another concern associated with educating Latinos was that school authorities feared the Latino kids would become educated—and worse, in the Anglos' minds, than leaving the agricultural work—would get sociable with the white girls.[108]

Others, clearly the minority, supported the education of the Latino children, explaining, "Schooling Mexicans won't ruin the country. If they go to school, the machine is coming. There is no question it is coming."[109] However, those districts that registered Latinos in their schools and received additional money from the state took "the money out of the Mexican allotment and use[d] it for the whites."[110] Is this discriminatory treatment or is it discriminatory impact? Either way, it constitutes state-sponsored denial of equal protection.

C. The Separate Classes for the Language "Challenged"

Another early educational policy as to Latinos involved segregation into "language handicap" schools or classrooms within an Anglo-dominated school.[111] In *Independent School District v. Salvatierra*,[112] the Latino plaintiffs complained of the school district's practice of segregation of the Latino children from the Anglos.[113] The court agreed that the school officials did not have the power to segregate Latino students "merely or solely because they are Mexican."[114] But the court concluded that the children's language deficiencies justified their separate schooling for educational purposes.[115]

Was the alleged Spanish-language dominance of the Latino student a subterfuge for racial discrimination? In *Hernandez v. Driscoll Consolidated School District*,[116] a federal court judge determined that the language justification was in fact a pretext for segregation. School officials in Driscoll, Texas, abandoned the racially based separate schools for Mexicans and Anglos and required that a majority of Latino children spend three years in the first grade to learn English well.[117] However, the segregated student in *Driscoll* could speak only English. As a result, the district court judge criticized the district for engaging in "unreasonable race discrimination."[118]

---

107. *Id.* at 200.

108. *Id.* at 195, 219.

109. *Id.* at 199.

110. *Id.* at 200; Jorge C. Rangel & Carlos Alcala, *Project Report: De Jure Segregation of Chicanos in Texas Schools*, 7 Harv. C.R.-C.L. L. Rev. 307, 317 (1972) [hereafter cited as Rangel & Alcala].

111. *See Independent Sch. Dist. v. Salvatierra*, 33 S.W.2d 790 (Tex. Civ. App. 1930) (involving the schools in Del Rio, Texas), *cert. denied*, 284 U.S. 580 (1931).

112. *Id.*

113. *Id.* LULAC fought a citizen-approved bond that included an addition to the two-room "Mexican school." *Id.* at 791.

114. *Id.* at 795.

115. *Id.* The superintendent admitted that "generally the best way to learn a language is to be associated with the people who speak that language." *Id.* at 793. A Nueces County study revealed that Latino students wanted to go to school with Anglos so they could learn English more quickly. Taylor, *supra* note 34, at 223.

116. 2 Race Rel. L. Rep. 329 (S.D. Tex. 1957).

117. *Id.* at 331. The three-year separation requirement violated a federal court consent decree that provided for only one year for language needs. *See Delgado v. Bastrop Ind. Sch. Dist.*, Civil No. 388 (W.D. Tex. June 15, 1948).

118. 2 Race Rel. L. Rep. 329, 331–32 (S.D. Tex. 1957). The district justified the separation of the Latino students because they could not speak English; the child plaintiff spoke English only and no Spanish. *Id.* Further proof that the Mexican language handicap was a deceptive means to segregate the

The Driscoll schools were bound by state educational policy. Prior to the litigation in *Driscoll*, a federal court issued a consent decree in *Delgado v. Bastrop Independent School District*.[119] The 1948 consent decree in *Delgado* permanently enjoined not only Bastrop and the several other named school districts from "segregating pupils of Mexican or other Latin-American descent in separate schools or classes within the respective school districts," but also the state superintendent of Public Instruction "from in any manner, directly or indirectly, participating in the custom, usage or practice of segregating pupils of Mexican or other Latin-American descent in separate schools or classes."[120] By including the state superintendent in the litigation, the decree had the potential of statewide relief for the impermissible segregation of Latinos.[121] However, the final judgment lacked a directive that the court would retain jurisdiction to enforce the decree. In addition, the judgment lacked notice to offending districts as to what sanctions, such as contempt or loss of accreditation, the superintendents of the named districts or other future offending districts could expect if prohibited segregation were proved. Aggravating matters and setting the stage for a *Driscoll* language abuse, the decree continued by providing that "this injunction shall not prevent said defendant school districts or their trustees, officers and agents from providing for, and maintaining, *separate classes on the same campus in the first grade only*, and solely for instructional purposes, *for pupils* in their initial scholastic year in the first grade … who … clearly demonstrate … that they *do not possess a sufficient familiarity with the English language* to understand substantially classroom instruction in the first-grade subject matter."[122]

As late as 2006, Latino parents unfortunately had to complain that Teresa Parker, an elementary school principal in the Dallas Independent School District, racially segregated students by routing English-speaking Hispanic children into the school's English as a second language program.[123] After finding that white students formed the majority of mainstream general education classes in the school, which was 66 percent Latino, federal judge Sam Lindsay ruled that the principal in effect operated "at taxpayer's expense, a private school for Anglo children within a public school that was predominantly minority."[124]

As to amendment of conclusions of law, lawyers for the school district requested that the court remove its reference to a "separate but equal" argument, claiming the district never made such an argument. The court acknowledged that school counsel never used the words "separate but equal," but the judge noted that the record was replete with instances of such thinly masked arguments. The defense counsel elicited testimony that

---

Latino kids can be found in the fact that "Bohemian and German and other non-English speaking children go to the American school, and some Mexicans want their children to go there." Taylor, *supra* note 34, at 224.

119. *Delgado*, Civil No. 388. For a review of the full consent decree, *see* Lupe S. Salinas, *Gus Garcia and Thurgood Marshall: Two Legal Giants Fighting for Justice*, 28 T. Marshall L. Rev. 145, 166–68 (2003) [hereafter cited as Salinas].

120. *Id.*

121. Contrary to the Texas constitution's specific provision requiring the segregation of colored children, Tex. Const. art. 7, § 7 (1876), the Bastrop Independent School District segregation of Latinos was based on "regulations, customs, usages, and practices." *Delgado*, Civ. No. 388.

122. *Delgado v. Bastrop Ind. Sch. Dist.*, Civil No. 388 (W.D. Tex. June 15, 1948).

123. *Santamaria v. Dallas Ind. Sch. Dist.*, Civ. Action No. 3:06-CV-692-L, 2007 U.S. Dist. LEXIS 26821, at 6 (N.D. Tex. Apr. 10, 2007).

124. Cary Clack, *Lasting Legacy*, San Antonio Express-News, Sept. 23, 2007, at A1, A22. The judge ordered the principal to pay $20,200 to Lucrecia M. Santamaria, the lone named plaintiff, who sued on behalf of her three children; but he did not find the Dallas Independent School District liable. *Santamaria v. Dallas Ind. Sch. Dist.*, Civ. Action No. 3:06-CV-692-L, 2007 U.S. Dist. LEXIS 26821, at 6–7 (N.D. Tex. Apr. 10, 2007).

promoted the argument that limited English proficient minority students were receiving an equal education as their Anglo counterparts, albeit in a separate classroom.[125]

D. The Mexican School: De Jure, State-Imposed Segregated Schools

Assuming that a school district in Texas chose to obey the Compulsory School Attendance Act, that district faced a dilemma. Once the board decided to accept the Latino child, the conflict arose: integrate them into the existing schools or construct a separate school for Latino children. The Latino segregation practices were rampant.[126] For example, one Nueces County school had a cornerstone that read, "Public school for Mexicans."[127] Other districts blatantly labeled the separate facilities as "Mexican Schools."[128] As in *Salvatierra*, the primary rationale for segregation was the Spanish language of the Latino child.[129] However, an explanation other than language concerns might be found in the following quote from a rural superintendent: "Some Mexicans are very bright, but you can't compare their brightest with the *average* white children. They are an inferior race."[130]

Anglo leadership in the schools worried that the Latino children would slow the learning process of their children[131] and believed that separation of the Latino children would be advantageous.[132] In addition, the color superiority complex played a major factor in the decisions to segregate. The farmers and ranchers used the following terminology in referring to Latinos: "The white class of people wants to stay white, and the brown to stay brown. It is human nature. I have raised two children with the idea they they [*sic*] are above the doggone Mexican nationality and I believe a man should."[133] In addition, another school executive stated, "It is desirable to carry segregation further for reasons of social equality. Then you will eliminate the *greaser*.[134] The Spanish will get up, and you can equalize yourself with them.... Those [Spanish Latinos] who get up in school are blond with clear skin."[135]

---

125. *See Santamaria v. Dallas Ind. Sch. Dist.*, Civ. Action No. 3:06-CV-692-L, 2007 U.S. Dist. LEXIS 26821, at 14–20 (N.D. Tex. Apr. 10, 2007).

126. *See generally* Rangel & Alcala, *supra* note 110, at 313–15, 333–42 (discussing the operation of Mexican schools). The statistics of poor performance speak powerfully about inadequacies in Latino education. *See, e.g.*, 2005 WORLD ALMANAC, *supra* note 10, at 10. A 2002 study posted positive news about an increase in the number of Latino immigrants completing high school and going to college, but it recognized that the education gap with native-born Americans remained wide. *More Latinos Completing College*, CNN, Dec. 5, 2002, *available at* www.cnn.com/2002/EDUCATION/12/05/hispanic. education.ap/index.html.

127. TAYLOR, *supra* note 54, at 246.

128. *See, e.g.*, Rangel & Alcala, *supra* note 110, at 313–15, 333–42.

129. Interestingly, the Salvatierra language issue is the same one that surfaced again over seventy-five years later in *Santamaria v. Dallas Ind. Sch. Dist.*, Civ. Action No. 3:06-CV-692-L, 2007 U.S. Dist. LEXIS 26821 (N.D. Tex. Apr. 10, 2007).

130. TAYLOR, *supra* note 34, at 203.

131. *Id.* at 220 ("The problem of protecting the educational progress of the American children from the lagging Mexicans.").

132. *See generally* TAYLOR, *supra* note 34, at 217 (stating that many who supported separation of Americans and Mexicans in schools asserted that separation would be advantageous to the Mexicans).

133. *Id.* at 219.

134. The term *greaser* derogatorily refers to persons of Mexican descent. WEBSTER'S NEW COLLEGIATE DICTIONARY 362 (1958).

135. TAYLOR, *supra* note 34, at 219.

E. The Kimball Report on the "Pushout" Rate in an Urban School System

Although this chapter discusses a national concern, the discussion includes quite an extensive number of cases and educational statistics from Texas, a state with a large Latino population.[136] Texas has been the scene of many battles for quality education.[137] Many educational opportunity encounters, such as equitable school financing, continue in Texas.[138] The question in this chapter centers on whether decisions and policies by public school systems incorporate the serious educational needs of all the students in the state. Society needs an objective answer or explanation for the poor educational attainment of Latino children in Texas and the rest of America.[139]

According to a Texas educator, Dr. Robert H. Kimball,[140] Latino students are victims of a public education system that does not recognize their culture, language or goals.[141] Consequently, many Latinos become disillusioned and are forced to leave public schools. Dr. Kimball noted that several states reported to the Department of Education that the dropout rate for minorities was over 50 percent in 1998.[142] However, Dr. Kimball notes that in 2003, the Houston Independent School District (HISD) reported a dropout rate for Latino students at only 1.2 percent.[143] School board members, the superintendent and

---

136. Latinos comprise 32 percent of the Texas population, making them the largest minority group. Latinos also rank first in the states of California and New Mexico. James Pinkerton, *More Than Half of Texans Are Minorities,* HOUS. CHRON., Aug. 11, 2005, B1.

137. *See, e.g., United States v. State of Texas,* 509 F.2d 192 (5th Cir. 1975); *Delgado v. Bastrop Ind. Sch. Dist.,* Civ. No. 388 (W.D. Tex. June 15, 1948). For a full reading of the consent order in Delgado, see Salinas, *supra* note 119, at 166–68 (2003).

138. The Texas legislature tackled, once again, the school financing issue during the session that began in January 2005. The effort, overcome with political bickering over lower taxes and higher educational costs, resulted in no education plan for Texas public school children. The Republican leadership did not appoint a single Democrat or minority to the conference committee charged with fine-tuning the bill. Jane Elliott, *Craddick Partisan on Conferee Picks,* HOUS. CHRON., May 14, 2005, at B1.

139. The statistics for those who experience educational failure tell an incredible but real story: a higher incidence of prison confinement, low self-image, functional illiteracy, unskilled, lower-paying jobs, drug and alcohol abuse and early death. *See* Brief for the Mexican American Bar Association of Houston as Amicus Curiae at 3–11, *Plyler v. Doe,* 457 U.S. 202 (1982).

140. Interview with Robert Kimball *in* CATHERINE CAPELLARO, BLOWING THE WHISTLE ON THE TEXAS MIRACLE, RETHINKING SCHOOLS (2004), *available at* www.rethinkingschools.org/special_ reports/bushplan/tex191.shtml [hereafter Kimball Interview]. Kimball is a former Houston Independent School District (HISD) vice principal at Sharpstown High School. After HISD reported a 1.5 percent dropout rate for the 2001–2002 school year and a 0 percent dropout for his high school, he wrote his principal and exclaimed in disbelief, "We go from 1,000 freshmen to 300 seniors without no [*sic*] dropouts. Amazing!" Kimball, himself a dropout, prompted a state investigation that confirmed that the miraculous dropout rates were falsified by underreporting 2,999 students. He was removed from the high school and eventually ended up in a closet-type office. His whistleblower lawsuit resulted in a settlement in his favor.

141. Dr. Robert H. Kimball, University of Houston/Clear-Lake, How Hispanics Are Pushed out of Public Education (Feb. 16, 2005) (unpublished report, on file with author) [hereafter Kimball Report].

142. *Id.* The Intercultural Development Research Association (2003) reported that the attrition rate for Latinos in public education was 50 percent in Texas. *Id.*

143. *Id.*

community groups agreed that the dropout rate could not realistically be that low, but the district nevertheless sent a report to the state using those deflated, improbable figures.[144]

Dr. Kimball cites the language barrier as a reason for a high dropout rate.[145] Many public schools have no Spanish-speaking members on the staff, and the non-Latino school counselors and administrators have preconceived attitudes that Latino students are not interested in obtaining an education.[146] In addition, many school staff members are not making an effort to learn Spanish or study Latino culture.[147] Dr. Kimball reports that 40 percent of Latino students who are pushed out of school are not proficient in English, confirming a high correlation between language proficiency and school success.[148]

HISD has elementary schools classified as bilingual programs that in reality only provide instruction in Spanish. As a school administrator, Dr. Kimball was assigned to an elementary school in HISD where every student was Latino and fluent in Spanish. The teachers taught only in Spanish.[149] On a daily basis, Dr. Kimball visited these classrooms and never observed lessons being taught in English. This Spanish-only teaching method does not help students succeed and will only result in a higher dropout rate because of a lack of English proficiency.

Dr. Kimball asserts that Latino students are being pushed out by the policies and behavior of school administrators, teachers and board trustees. In many Texas schools, Latino students are being targeted by educational leaders for elimination because they are not likely to pass the state examinations that are used to rate schools and provide financial incentives to all employees.[150] In Texas, the school rating system thus discriminates against those school districts with large Latino populations. One side calls it a plan to hold schools accountable, but others label it a plan that encourages schools to push out low-performing students and, in some cases, to help them cheat on state-mandated tests.[151] As a result, students are being systematically pushed out of the educational system.

Several strategies are being used by school districts to push out Latino students. In 2002, the HISD School Board adopted a policy of retaining students who did not pass one core course in high school. This policy had been in effect since 2000 at many of the high schools in Houston, because these schools had asked for a waiver on course requirements. When the waiver policy significantly increased scores on state-mandated tests, the board made it a district policy.[152] By making this policy change, they were able to keep low-performing Latino students from taking the Texas examinations at the tenth-grade level where it counted for the school's rating. Under this policy, over 20,000 Latino youth in Houston were kept in the ninth grade for up to three years.[153] Latino youth became disillusioned at being retained and often quit. Statistically, students have a 50 per-

---

144. Kimball Interview, *supra* note 140. *See* Joshua Benton & Holly K. Hacker, *Poor Schools' TAKS Surges Raise Cheating Questions*, DALLAS MORNING NEWS, Dec. 30, 2004 [hereafter Benton & Hacker] *available at* www.dallasnews.com/sharedcontent/dws/dn/education/stories/121904dnmet cheating.

145. Kimball Report, *supra* note 141.

146. *Id.*

147. *Id.*

148. *Id.*

149. *Id.*

150. *Id.*

151. *See* Benton & Hacker, *supra* note 144.

152. Kimball Report, *supra* note 141.

153. *Id.*

cent chance of dropping out if they are retained one year and 90 percent if they are retained two years.[154] After the national media addressed this issue, Houston changed its policy of requiring that students pass all subjects before being moved to the next grade level.[155]

IV. The Latino Quest for Equitable Educational Opportunity

A. Litigation Prior to *Brown*

Assessing responsibility as to who or what is responsible for low educational attainment
among Latinos probably depends on a person's political and/or social ideology. Repub-
licans and Democrats differ on the means to the end. Rich and poor disagree as to the relevance of financial support insofar as the educational ladder one can climb.[156] Many claim
that the major responsibility rests with the family. Although family can make a difference, a very small percentage of Latino families have a college-educated head of the household to guide the student with college potential. While Latino families strongly support
the value of an education, they encounter limits to the promotion of a quality education.[157] Many students have to drop out of school to satisfy their debts and help the family with finances. Some parents can afford and do enroll their children in private schools.
Those are admirable sacrifices. However, the major educational hope for Latinos rests
with the public school systems. The large and growing Latino population pays taxes and
expects a fair, equitable and effective public education for its children.[158]

Attaining equal or equitable educational opportunity for Latino children who are socially, culturally and linguistically different from Anglo children has been an almost insurmountable goal. The parents of Latino children merely ask for a fair chance. These
parents do not desire a situation where their children face the educational competition
with one hand tied behind their backs. The struggle against segregation and unequal educational opportunity in the public schools has not been easy.

---

154. *Id.* Kimball notes that there are many high schools that begin with a freshman class of over
1,000 students and in four years graduate fewer than 200 of them. *Id.*

155. *Id.*

156. *See generally San Antonio Ind. Sch. Dist. v. Rodriguez*, 411 U.S. 1 (1973) (holding that education is not an implicit fundamental right and the poor do not constitute a suspect class).

157. *See* Katherine S. Mangan, *Professor's Comments on Affirmative Action Inflame a Campus*,
Chronicle of Higher Education, 1997, *available at* chronicle.com/che-data/articles.dir/art-
44.dir/issue-05.dir/05a03301.htm; The Sociology of Race and Ethnicity, *available at*
www.trinity.edu/~mkearl/race.html. The article refers to University of Texas Law Professor Lino
Graglia, who gratuitously declared himself a sociological expert and stated that black and Latino students perform poorly in college because they come from cultures that do not value education and
that accept failure more readily than Caucasians.

158. Aaron Zitner, *Census Shows Illegal Immigrants Filled Need for Workers*, L.A. Times, Mar. 10,
2001, at A2. This statement does not include undocumented Latino children and their educational needs.
However, it should be noted that experts recognize that the undocumented worker contributes to the
American economy. In addition, in some circumstances, undocumented children have protected constitutional rights. *See Plyler v. Doe*, 457 U.S. 202 (1982) (holding that heightened scrutiny protected
undocumented children because they, unlike their parents, lacked responsibility for their presence).

Chronologically, the official battles for a nondiscriminatory educational opportunity began in the mid-1920s in Arizona and in the early 1930s in California and Texas. In 1925, in *Romo v. Laird*,[159] a Mexican American rancher near Phoenix, Arizona, sued to have his four children attend a school with certified teachers. The Tempe board of trustees had designated the Tenth Street School for "children of the white race" and the Eighth Street School for children of Spanish American or Mexican American descent.[160] The board had designated the Eighth Street School as a student teacher training facility.[161] Tempe considered Latinos so culturally different as to require separate placement. The court rationalized the segregation on the basis of the *Plessy v. Ferguson*[162] "separate but equal" doctrine.[163] In an odd twist, the court granted the Romo children the relief they sought—attendance at the school with certified teachers. However, as to all other Latino children, the board of trustees ordered the hiring of certified teachers in the "Mexican school," a decision that allowed Latino segregation to continue until the 1950s.[164]

California was the setting for *Alvarez v. Owen*,[165] known more popularly as the Lemon Grove incident. The all-white Lemon Grove school board decided in July 1930 to build a separate school for Latino students. The principal of the grammar school stood at the door and directed the Latino children to go to a new facility, a wooden two-room structure. The parents organized a boycott and hired lawyers to sue the district and enjoin the segregation. The school defended the separate school as a good Americanization process where the Latino kids could be instructed more to their capabilities.[166]

Independent School District v. Salvatierra,[167] the first Latino school case that sought to end segregation in Texas public schools, involved a setback to equal educational opportunity when the school officials successfully asserted that the children's language deficiencies warranted their separate education.[168] When LULAC and the Salvatierra family petitioned the Supreme Court to give meaning to the equal protection clause, the Court denied the petition for certiorari.[169] One should not be surprised that the Court did not see a legal problem with the *Salvatierra* ruling. A few years earlier, the Court decided in *Gong Lum v. Rice* that the exclusion of a Chinese-descent American was appropriate under the edict of the Mississippi constitution that provided for separate schools for the "colored" students of the state.[170] The message was that if one were not Caucasian, then he

---

159. James A. Ferg-Cadima, *Black, White and Brown: Latino School Desegregation in the Pre- and Post-*Brown v. Board of Education *Era*, MALDEF, May 2004, App. A at 35, citing No. 21617 (Maricopa County Super. Ct. 1925) (on file with author).

160. *Id.*

161. *Id.*

162. 163 U.S. 537 (1896).

163. *Id.* at 540. The Court addressed a Louisiana statute that provided "equal but separate" accommodations for the white and colored races. *Id.*

164. Ferg-Cadima, *supra* note 159. *See also Gonzales v. Sheeley*, 96 F. Supp. 1004, 1009 (D. Ariz. 1951) (stating that segregation created a stamp of inferiority on Latinos).

165. Ferg-Cadima, *supra* note 159, at App. C at 39, citing No. 66625 (San Diego County Super. Ct. Mar. 30, 1931) (on file with author).

166. *Id.*

167. 33 S.W.2d 790 (Tex. Civ. App. 1930), *cert. denied*, 284 US 580 (1931).

168. *Id.* at 793. The Texas attorney general later added legal support for this policy by issuing an opinion allowing the separation of linguistically challenged Latinos. Tex. Att'y Gen. Op., No. V-128 (1947).

169. *Salvatierra v. Independent Sch. Dist.*, 284 US 580 (1931).

170. *Gong Lum v. Rice*, 275 U.S. 78, 87 (1927).

was "colored," even though in the United States the term "colored" socially and histori-cally described persons of African descent.[171]

Other eventful litigation occurred in California, where a large number of Latino fam-ilies sued the Westminster schools in Orange County. In *Mendez v. Westminster School District*,[172] a suit brought under the civil rights statute,[173] the district court held that equal protection is not met by providing "separate schools [with] the same technical facili-ties."[174] The court added that segregation fosters "antagonisms in the children and suggest[s] inferiority among them where none exists."[175] These words sound strikingly similar to the U.S. Supreme Court holding in *Brown v. Board of Education* eight years later that "separate educational facilities are inherently unequal."[176]

The school district appealed *Mendez*. The Ninth Circuit Court of Appeals affirmed the lower court, concluding that the segregation cases, which authorized schools to justify segregation so long as they provided equal facilities for black children, did not apply.[177] The appellate court noted that the California statute limited segregation to Indians and certain Asiatics.[178] The judge further reasoned that California law did not specifically in-clude the segregation of schoolchildren because of their Mexican blood and that the state, by legislative action, allowed Mexican children, citizens of a foreign country, to attend pub-lic schools.[179] The judge then stated;

> It follows that the acts of [the school district] were and are entirely without au-thority of California law, notwithstanding their performance has been and is under color or pretense of California law.... By enforcing the segregation of school children of Mexican descent against their will and contrary to the laws of California, [the district has] violated the federal law as provided in the Four-teenth Amendment to the Federal Constitution by depriving them of liberty and property without due process of law and by denying to them the equal protec-tion of the laws.[180]

---

171. Taylor, *supra* note 34, at 202. Recall that the 1930 census defined "Mexicans" for its purposes as: "all persons born in Mexico, or having parents born in Mexico, who are not definitely white, Negro, Indian, Chinese, or Japanese." *Id.*

172. 64. F. Supp. 544 (S.D. Cal. 1946).

173. 42 U.S.C. § 1983 provides:

Every person who, under color of any statute, ordinance, regulation, custom, or usage, of any State or Territory, subjects, or causes to be subjected, any citizen of the United States or other person within the jurisdiction thereof to the deprivation of any rights, privileges, or immunities secured by the Constitution and laws, shall be liable to the party injured in an action at law, suit in equity, or other proper proceeding for redress.

174. *Mendez*, 64. F. Supp. at 549.

175. *Id.*

176. *Brown v. Bd. of Educ.*, 347 U.S. 483, 495 (1954).

177. See *Plessy v. Ferguson*, 163 U.S. 537 (1896).

178. *Westminster Sch. Dist. v. Mendez*, 161 F.2d 774, 780 (9th Cir. 1947). The court held that Eng-lish language deficiencies of some children as they enter elementary public school may justify differ-entiation by public school authorities as to the pedagogical methods of instruction to be pursued with different pupils, and foreign language handicaps may be to such a degree among elementary stu-dents as to require separate treatment in separate classrooms. *Id.* at 784 (Denman, J., concurring).

179. *Id.* at 780.

180. *Id.* at 780–81. The Ninth Circuit opinion also resorts to the use of a Latin maxim, *expressio unius est exclusio alterius,* that which is not expressly stated is implicitly not intended. *Id.* at 781. This term is a canon of construction holding that to express or include one thing implies the exclusion of the other, or of the alternative. For example, if the law states that a citizen is entitled to vote, then it means that a noncitizen is not entitled to vote. Reed Dickerson, The Interpretation and Appli-cation of Statutes 234–35 (1975).

In other words, because the California segregation statute did not expressly include Latinos, their segregation violated due process and equal protection of the laws.[181]

Following the major victory expressly on behalf of Latinos, and implicitly on behalf of African Americans in *Mendez*, the legal battle moved to Texas. In April 1947, Texas Attorney General Price Daniel issued an opinion in which he expressed that segregation or linguistic classification could not be based solely on "Latin-American or Mexican descent."[182] Latinos thereafter filed *Delgado v. Bastrop Independent School District*.[183] *Delgado* gave the Latino community hope that segregated education would end, but the forces of segregation prevailed.[184] In response to *Delgado*, the Texas superintendent of Public Instruction advised public school districts that there had never been any requirement or authority to segregate Latino children. However, he did not present a plan for the integration of Latino students into the more modern and better equipped white schools.[185] Thus, the *Delgado* consent decree provided hope, but the lack of specificity allowed school districts to continue their segregation practices. One superficial victory involved the fact that the 1948–49 public school directory listed only one Mexican school for the entire state of Texas.[186] In reality, however, hundreds continued to exist.

B. *Brown v. Board of Education*

In *Brown v. Board of Education* the Supreme Court described the issue before it as follows: "Does segregation of children in public schools solely on the basis of race, even though the physical facilities and other 'tangible' factors may be equal, deprive the children of the minority group of equal educational opportunities?"[187] The Court held that such segregation violates the equal protection clause even though the physical and other facilities may be equal, concluding that in the field of public education "separate educational facilities are inherently unequal."[188] Chief Justice Warren elaborated:

> Today, education is perhaps the most important function of state and local governments. *Compulsory school attendance laws and the great expenditures for education both demonstrate our recognition of the importance of education to our democratic society.* It is required in the performance of our most basic public responsibilities, even service in the armed forces. It is the very foundation of good citizenship. Today it is a principal instrument in awakening the child to cultural values, in preparing him for later professional training, and in helping him to adjust normally to his environment. In these days, it is doubtful that any child may

---

181. *Westminster Sch. Dist.*, 161 F.2d at 781.

182. *Independent Sch. Dist. v. Salvatierra*, 33 S.W.2d 790 (Tex. Civ. App. 1930), *cert. denied*, 284 U.S. 580 (1931); Tex. Att'y Gen. Op. No. V-128 (1947).

183. *See* Lupe S. Salinas, *Gus Garcia and Thurgood Marshall: Two Legal Giants Fighting for Justice*, 28 T. Marshall L. Rev. 145, 166–68 (2003).

184. *See, e.g., Hernandez v. Driscoll Consol. Ind. Sch. Dist.*, 2 Race Rel. L. Rep. 329 (S. D. Tex. 1957).

185. *See* Rangel & Alcala, *supra* note 110, at 312 n.35, 316 n.52. In 1949, Supt. Woods canceled Del Rio's accreditation (the same district as in *Salvatierra* in 1930) because they continued to segregate Latino children and the district declined to assign Latino teachers to the Anglo school. *Id.* at 338 nn.183–84. Incredibly, this same school district reappears for sanctions in *United States v. Texas*, 342 F.Supp. 24 (E.D. Tex. 1971).

186. Rangel & Alcala, *supra* note 110, at 316 n.57.

187. *Brown v. Bd. of Educ.*, 347 U.S. 483, 493 (1954).

188. *Id.* at 495.

reasonably be expected to succeed in life if he is denied the opportunity of an education. *Such an opportunity, where the state has undertaken to provide it, is a right which must be made available to all on equal terms.*[189]

C. *Hernandez v. Texas*

In *Hernandez v. Texas*,[190] the Supreme Court declared that certain groups other than African Americans qualified for coverage under the equal protection clause of the Fourteenth Amendment.[191] The Texas Court of Criminal Appeals had taken an opposite position.[192] The state's highest court for criminal matters labeled Hernandez as a "Mexican, or Latin American."[193] Hernandez alleged that he was discriminated against because members of the Mexican nationality were deliberately, systematically and willfully excluded from the grand jury that found and returned the indictment and from the petit jury that tried the case, thus depriving him of equal protection.[194] Hernandez took the position that the so-called rule of exclusion applied to him.[195] The Court ruled that the long and continued failure to call African Americans for jury service, where it is shown that members of that race were available and qualified for jury service, grand or petit, constitutes a violation of due process and equal protection against members of that race.[196] Texas cases historically classified Latinos as members of the white race[197] and reasoned that the Fourteenth Amendment equal protection clause knew only two classes: one white and one black.[198]

Hernandez emanated from Edna, Jackson County, Texas, about 100 miles south of Houston. The accused believed he had a better chance at justice if some members of his community participated in hearing the evidence. No Latino served on any jury, grand or petit, in the twenty-five years prior to the trial.[199] To prove Latinos were treated as other than whites, counsel proved at the trial court that the dominant attitude in Jackson County

---

189. *Id.* at 493 (emphasis added). This language led several civil rights attorneys in the early 1970s to conclude erroneously that the fundamental rights concept implicitly included education. *See Rodriguez*, 411 U.S. at 35.

190. *Hernandez v. Texas*, 347 U.S. 475 (1954), *rev'g Hernandez v. State*, 160 Tex. Crim. 72, 251 S. W. 2d 531 (Tex. Crim. App. 1952*)*.

191. U.S. CONST. amend. XIV, after initially referring to the rights of citizens of the United States, provides, "Nor shall any State deprive any *person* of life, liberty, or property, without due process of law; nor deny to any *person* within its jurisdiction the equal protection of the laws" (emphasis added). One does not have to be a U.S. citizen to receive constitutional protections.

192. *See Hernandez*, 347 U.S. at 475.

193. *Id.* at 532.

194. *Id.* The state stipulated that "for the last twenty-five years there is no record of any person with a Mexican or Latin American name having served on a jury commission, grand jury or petit jury in Jackson County." *Id.* at 533. A witness estimated that 15 percent of the county population was "Mexican." *Id.*

195. The rule appears to have been first announced in *Norris v. Alabama*, 294 U.S. 587 (1935).

196. *Hernandez*, 347 U.S. at 532.

197. "Mexicans are white people, and are entitled at the hands of the state to all the rights, privileges, and immunities guaranteed under the Fourteenth Amendment." *Id. See also Sanchez v. Texas*, 243 S.W.2d 700 (Tex. Crim. App. 1951) ("Mexican people are not a separate race but are white people of Spanish descent.").

198. *See e.g., Hernandez*, 347 U.S. at 475; *Sanchez*, 243 S.W.2d at 700; *Bustillos v. State*, 213 S.W.2d 837 (Tex. Crim. App. 1948); *Salazar v. State*, 193 S.W.2d 211 (Tex. Crim. App. 1946); *Sanchez v. State*, 181 S.W.2d 87, 90 (Tex. Crim. App. 1944).

199. *Hernandez*, 347 U.S. at 482.

was that Latinos are "Mexican" and not white. The Court specifically noted that the Latino's initial burden in substantiating the claim of group discrimination was to prove that persons of Mexican descent constitute a separate class in Jackson County, distinct from "whites." The lawyers offered proof at the trial level that residents of the community distinguished between "white" and "Mexican." The participation of persons of Mexican descent in business and community groups was shown to be slight. Until shortly before the trial, children of Mexican descent were assigned to a segregated school for the first four grades.[200] At least one restaurant in town prominently displayed a sign announcing "No Mexicans Served." On the courthouse grounds at the time of the hearing, there were two men's toilets, one unmarked, and the other marked "Colored Men" and "Hombres Aqui" (Spanish for "Men Here").[201] Thus, the Court had little trouble concluding that Latinos received separate treatment socially, educationally and politically.

Chief Justice Earl Warren authored the unanimous opinion recognizing Latinos as a unique group distinct from other whites. The Court stated:

> Throughout our history differences in race and color have defined easily identifiable groups which have at times required the aid of the courts in securing equal treatment under the laws. But community prejudices are not static, and from time to time other differences from the community norm may define other groups which need the same protection. Whether such a group exists within a community is a question of fact. When the existence of a distinct class is demonstrated, and it is further shown that the laws, as written or as applied, single out that class for different treatment not based on some reasonable classification, the guarantees of the Constitution have been violated.[202]

Chief Justice Warren then expressed doubts that it was unintentional that no Latino in 6,000 had been selected for jury participation in a twenty-five year period, stating, "The result bespeaks discrimination, whether or not it was a conscious decision on the part of any individual jury commissioner."[203]

V. Equal Protection Standards in Educational Discrimination Settings

A. Discriminatory Purpose or Effect?: It Really Does Not Matter When It Comes to Educational Equality and Success

One of the earliest cases to hold that failing to address the unique educational needs of Latino students could be a constitutional violation was *Arvizu v. Waco Independent School District*.[204] U.S. District Court Judge Jack Roberts, who also presided over *United*

---

200. *See* Taylor, *supra* note 34, at 203, 215–25 (Mexicans are an inferior race; section on school separation, i.e., the Mexican schools).

201. *Hernandez*, 347 U.S. at 479–80.

202. *Id.* at 478.

203. *Id.* at 482.

204. 373 F.Supp. 1264 (W.D. Tex. 1973), *rev'd in part*, 495 F.2d 499 (5th Cir. 1974). At the time of the *Arvizu* litigation, the author served as a staff attorney for MALDEF. He participated as one of

States v. Texas Education Agency[205] (Austin I), found de jure segregation of blacks in Waco.[206] Among other inadequate remedies, Judge Roberts found that a "neighborhood school" system, appearing on its face to be neutral, is unacceptable where it fails to "counteract the continuing effects of past school segregation resulting from discriminatory location of school sites or distortion of school size in order to achieve or maintain an artificial racial separation."[207]

As to the Latino students, Judge Roberts recognized that the formulation of an appropriate legal framework for analyzing their status is a task not free of difficulty.[208] Five schools in the Waco school system had disproportionately large numbers of Mexican American students. Indisputably, this concentration of Mexican Americans in certain schools resulted from residential housing patterns. Arvizu did not seriously contend that state action created the pattern of residential concentration of Mexican Americans.[209] In addition, Arvizu conceded that no history of statutorily imposed segregation of Mexican Americans could be shown.

However, this did not cause Judge Roberts to stop the inquiry into the educational needs of Latino students. Absent a Waco history of state-imposed Latino segregation, the presumption of discrimination disappears, and each case involving alleged discrimination against Latinos must be determined on an ad hoc basis. The court in *Arvizu* emphasized that *Brown*'s declaration that "separate educational facilities are inherently unequal"[210] was made in the context of a history of decades of official discrimination against blacks.[211] Although Judge Roberts found that the concentration of Mexican American students in certain schools was not the result of state action, he declared,

> Our obligation to assure to the Mexican American Plaintiffs in this case the equal protection of the laws does not end with our finding that such segregation of Mexican Americans as does exist in Waco is not the result of state action. Mexican Americans in Waco constitute an identifiable ethnic minority, recognizable by their numbers, concentration, cultural uniqueness, and common special needs and problems. We find that Mexican American students in Waco constitute "an identifiable, ethnic-minority class entitled to the equal protection guarantee of the Fourteenth Amendment." As such, Mexican American students are entitled to proper implementation of steps necessary to assure them the equal protection of the laws and an equal educational opportunity.[212]

The court noted that because Mexican Americans in Waco are an identifiable ethnic class with special educational needs, the district had an affirmative obligation to assure that Latino students are assured the equal protection of the laws in the future.[213] The court

the two trial lawyers for Pedro Arvizu and the other Latino parents and children in W-71-CA-56. The black plaintiffs litigated their action under *Baisey v. Board of Trustees of the Waco Ind. School Dist.*, No. W-71-CA-72.

205. 467 F.2d 848 (5th Cir. 1972).
206. *Arvizu*, 373 F.Supp. at 1266, 1268.
207. *Swann v. Charlotte-Mecklenburg Board of Educ.*, 402 U.S. 1, 28 (1971).
208. *Arvizu*, 373 F.Supp. at 1268.
209. This comment, applicable to Waco, should not suggest that residential segregation of Latinos in Texas and other parts of the Southwest did not result from official state action. *See Clifton v. Puente*, 218 S.W.2d 272, 273 (Tex. Civ. App.-San Antonio 1948) (deed prohibited, through a restrictive covenant, the sale or lease of real property to persons of "Mexican descent").
210. *Brown v. Bd. of Educ.*, 347 U.S. 483, 495 (1954).
211. *Arvizu*, 373 F.Supp. at 1269.
212. *Id.*
213. *Id.*

specifically noted that, among other remedies, Latinos in the district are entitled to "implementation of a curriculum and special educational programs, such as bilingual education, necessary to provide equal educational opportunities for Mexican American students as a group."[214] The judge reasoned that this approach would protect Latinos against future discrimination occurring after recognition of their new legal status in *Cisneros* as an identifiable ethnic minority group.[215]

Judge Roberts further found that the future failure of school officials to provide the required affirmative relief "should be regarded as *state action with a foreseeable discriminatory effect*."[216] Applying the teachings of *Brown*, the court concluded,

> In these days, it is doubtful that any child may reasonably be expected to succeed in life if he is denied the opportunity of an education. Such an opportunity, where the state has undertaken to provide it, is a right which must be made available to all on equal terms.... Development of a curriculum and special programs to assure that Mexican-American students will receive an equal opportunity for a quality education is both an educational and a legal obligation of the school district.[217]

Notwithstanding the sensible conclusion of Judge Roberts's discriminatory impact approach in *Arvizu*, later cases appear to cast some doubt on his reasoning. For example, in 1976 the Supreme Court announced an extremely inflexible equal protection standard of proof in *Washington v. Davis*.[218] *Davis* involved a suit by African American police officers and applicants who were denied promotion or hiring on the basis of the results of a written personnel test that was applied across the board to all. A disproportionately large number of African Americans failed the test administered by the District of Columbia's police department. The plaintiffs alleged that the examination violated the equal protection aspect of the due process clause of the Fifth Amendment.[219] Because the litigation involved an employment discrimination issue, the District of Columbia Circuit Court of Appeals utilized the discriminatory impact test announced in *Griggs v. Duke Power Co.*[220]

Griggs involved a private employer whose actions were reviewed under Title VII of the 1964 Civil Rights Act.[221] The Court held that proof of disproportionate impact sufficed to establish a rebuttable case of race discrimination.[222] Consequently, the *Davis* appellate

---

214. *Id.* at 1269–70.

215. *See generally* Guadalupe Salinas, Comment, *Mexican Americans and the Desegregation of Schools in the Southwest*, 8 Hous. L. Rev. 929, 932–33 (1971).

216. *Arvizu*, 373 F.Supp. at 1270 (emphasis added).

217. *Id.* (citing *Brown v. Bd. of Educ.*, 347 U.S. 483, 493 (1954)). The trial court ordered that for the 1973–74 school year, Waco will implement a more sophisticated bilingual, bicultural program, utilizing available Mexican American educational consultants and continually reevaluating the bilingual program. *Id.* at 1280. Based on the author's personal knowledge of the trial evidence, the classes for the educable mentally retarded (EMR) disproportionately included 85 percent black and Latino students in a school district that had slightly over 40 percent minority. When the author's co-counsel repeatedly asked the director of elementary education to explain the incredible imbalance, after initially stating she did not know, she startled everyone and stated, "Well, maybe that's the way God made them!" The Latino plaintiffs made their point; like any good lawyer should do, co-counsel passed the witness.

218. *Washington v. Davis*, 426 U.S. 229 (1976); *see also Personnel Administrator v. Feeney*, 442 U.S. 256 (1979).

219. *See Bolling v. Sharpe*, 347 U.S. 497 (1954) (the discriminatory actions of the District of Columbia school system are subject to the equal protection component of the due process clause of the Fifth Amendment.).

220. 401 U.S. 424 (1971).

221. 42 U.S.C. § 2000e.

222. *Griggs*, 401 U.S. at 432.

court held that the police department, by using an examination that had not been shown to be an adequate measure of job performance as a police officer, engaged in unconstitutional discrimination.[223]

However, the Supreme Court reversed the D.C. Circuit, holding that it had erroneously applied standards developed for Title VII of the 1964 Civil Rights Act to the Constitution.[224] The Court discarded the disproportionate impact avenue as sufficient alone to make a case of unconstitutional racial discrimination. Instead, the Court held that only actions involving purposeful intent to discriminate on the basis of race reach the requirements of the equal protection clause.[225]

The Court nonetheless left the door open to circumstances where proof of discriminatory impact would be relevant by holding that proof of discriminatory or purposeful intent could be inferred from the totality of the pertinent facts, including the very fact of the disproportionate impact.[226] As to the fact that many more African Americans than whites failed the test, the Court found the test neutral on its face and rationally related to a legitimate governmental purpose, that is, the modest improvement of the communicative skills of the police officers.[227] Therefore, under the totality of the circumstances, which included affirmative efforts to recruit officers of color and the improved minority numbers in the recruit classes, the Court determined that the evidence negated any inference of intentional racial discrimination.[228]

B. Application of the Davis Standard to Latino Educational Neglect

A problem in attaining Latino educational equity could result if the Supreme Court were to consider the implementation of dual and bilingual programs as efforts that negate any inference of intentional racial discrimination. Under the totality of the circumstances, public schools have failed miserably in the efforts to educate Latino children. Many school districts have programs for limited English learners. They run the gamut from total immersion into the English language curriculum (the sink or swim model), to English as a second language (ESL) projects (the make-it-across-the-bridge model) to bilingual education and finally to dual-language programs. The first three serve as "bridges" to the attainment of a working knowledge of English and then leave the limited English learner to either remain on or cross over the bridge or possibly fall into the waters and "drown," being pulled further downward by the undercurrent and thus obstructing the path to graduation.

These comments find support in the studies conducted by Dr. Angela Valenzuela.[229] She found that "no Spanish" rules commonly found their way into American schooling involving Mexican-descent children.[230] These pro-English policies seemed to have emanated from

---

223. *Davis*, 426 U.S. at 238–39.
224. *Id.*
225. *Id.* at 241–42.
226. *Id.* at 242; *see also Personnel Administrator v. Feeney*, 442 U.S. 256 (1979).
227. *Davis*, 426 U.S. at 245–46.
228. *Id.* at 246.
229. *See* Angela Valenzuela, Subtractive Schooling: U.S.-Mexican Youth and the Politics of Caring 172–81 (1999).
230. *Id.* at 172. The relevant Texas statute threatened to strip the teacher or administrator of his or her educational certificate for violating the "no Spanish rule." That law prohibited any teacher or school administrator from conducting school business, including teaching, in a language other than

the flurry of statutes that state legislatures enacted in the World War I era when Germany threatened American interests by seeking an alliance with Mexico if the United States gave up its neutrality once the United States learned of Germany's plan to begin unlimited submarine warfare.[231] Once World War I ended, the anti-German attitudes diminished and animosity against Mexicans in Texas increased. For example, "Bohemian and German and other non-English speaking children [went] to the American school," but Latino children were assigned to Mexican schools.[232]

Meyer v. Nebraska[233] not only represents one of the first cases to address the issue of governmentally sponsored restrictions on language but also epitomizes the emergence of a new concept of liberty protected by the due process clause of the Fourteenth Amendment.[234] In *Meyer* the Supreme Court reviewed a state conviction of an instructor of a private religious school for teaching German to a child of ten years who had not attained and successfully passed the eighth grade.[235] The Nebraska Supreme Court, in affirming the conviction, held that the statute forbidding this foreign language teaching was a valid exercise of the state's police power.[236] The state court observed that the legislature had seen the negative effects of permitting resident foreigners to rear and educate their children in the language of their native land.[237] The U.S. Supreme Court noted that it had to determine whether the Nebraska statute as construed and applied unreasonably infringed on the liberty guaranteed by the Fourteenth Amendment.[238] In seeking to define this liberty, the Court stated,

> Without doubt, it denotes not merely freedom from bodily restraint but also the right of the individual to contract, to engage in any of the common occupations of life, to acquire useful knowledge, to marry, establish a home and bring up children, to worship God according to the dictates of his own conscience, and generally to enjoy those privileges long recognized at common law as essential to the orderly pursuit of happiness by free men.[239]

The Court further observed that this liberty may not be interfered with, under the guise of protecting the public interest, by legislative action that is arbitrary or without reasonable relation to some purpose within the competency of the state to effect.[240]

English, excepting foreign language classes. The Texas version, now repealed, was found at TEX. LAWS 1933, ch. 125, § 1, at 325 (repealed 1969).

231. 29 ENCYCLOPEDIA AMERICANA 777 (1967); *see, e.g., Meyer v. Nebraska*, 262 U.S. 390 (1923).

232. *See generally* PAUL S. TAYLOR, AN AMERICAN MEXICAN FRONTIER 224 (1934). *See Hernandez v. Driscoll Consol. Sch. Dist.*, 2 RACE REL. L. RPTR 329, 331–32 (S.D. Tex. 1957) (Judge Allred found this separation practice to constitute racial discrimination.).

233. 262 U.S. 390 (1923).

234. *See* Meyer v. Nebraska, 262 U.S. 390, 399–400 (1923).

235. *Id.* at 397–98. The Nebraska statute barred any person from teaching in any school, private or public, any subject in any language other than English; the law punished that conduct as a misdemeanor by fine of not less than $25 and not more than $100 or by confinement in the county jail for any period not exceeding thirty days for each offense. *Id.* at 397. A similar Texas statute went even further by threatening to strip the teacher or administrator of his or her educational certificate for violating the "no Spanish rule." That law prohibited any teacher or school administrator from conducting school business, including teaching, in a language other than English, excepting foreign language classes. The Texas version, now repealed, was found at TEX. LAWS 1933, ch. 125, § 1, at 325 (repealed 1969).

236. *Id.* at 397.

237. *Id.* at 397–98.

238. U.S. CONST. amend. XIV.

239. *Meyer v. Nebraska*, 262 U.S. 390, 399 (1923).

240. *Id.* at 399–400.

The Supreme Court held that the teacher's right to teach a foreign language and the right of the parents to engage him to instruct their children are within the liberty concept of the Fourteenth Amendment,[241] emphasizing that the protection of the Constitution extends to all, "to those who speak other languages as well as to those born with English on the tongue. Perhaps it would be highly advantageous if all had ready understanding of our ordinary speech, but this cannot be coerced by methods which conflict with the Constitution—a desirable end cannot be promoted by prohibited means."[242]

Another avenue for possible relief on behalf of Latinos and other suspect classes in public educational disputes can be found in a principle that is firmly rooted in the common law of torts: An actor is held to intend the reasonably foreseeable results of his actions.[243] The Supreme Court, in settings that had a history of state-imposed racial segregation, has barred practices that have "the foreseeable and anticipated effect of maintaining the racial separation of the schools."[244] Although stated in the context of a de jure school segregation setting, the Fifth Circuit declared in the Austin school case,

> It is difficult—and often futile—to obtain direct evidence of the official's intentions. Rather than announce his intention of violating antidiscrimination laws, it is far more likely that the state official "will pursue his discriminatory practices in ways that are devious, by methods subtle and illusive—for we deal with an area in which subtleties of conduct ... play no small part."[245]

The most probative evidence of intent will usually be objective evidence of what actually happened rather than evidence describing the subjective state of mind of the actor who is normally presumed to have intended the natural consequences of his deeds.[246] This principle more particularly applies in cases of governmental action in which one frequently encounters the products of compromise, of collective decision making and of mixed motivation.[247]

The Supreme Court also addressed the tort concepts in *Monroe v. Pape*[248] when it held that specific intent is not a necessary element of a cause of action under the civil rights statute,[249] the statute under which school desegregation cases are litigated. The Court stated that civil rights actions involving schools "should be read against the background of tort liability that makes a man responsible for the natural consequences of his actions."[250]

---

241. *Id.* The Court further noted that mere knowledge of the German language cannot reasonably be regarded as harmful, adding that knowledge of a foreign language has commonly been looked on as helpful and desirable. *Id.*

242. *Id.* The Court recognized the legislative desire to foster a homogeneous people with American ideals prepared readily to understand current discussions of civic matters. The Court also noted that the unfortunate experiences during the late war (World War I) and aversion toward the adversaries (Germans) were certainly enough to quicken the aspiration to make all American residents more homogeneous and loyal. *Id.* at 402.

243. *See, e. g.,* W. PROSSER, THE LAW OF TORTS § 8 (4th ed. 1971); Restatement (Second) of Torts § 8A, Comment b (1965), cited in *United States v. Texas Education Agency* (*Austin III*), 564 F.2d 162, 167 (5th Cir. 1977).

244. *Columbus Bd. of Educ. v. Penick*, 443 U.S. 449, 462 (1979).

245. *United States v. Texas Education Agency* (*Austin III*), 564 F.2d 162, 168 (5th Cir. 1977) (citing *United States v. Texas Education Agency* (*Austin II*), 532 F.2d 380, 388 (5th Cir. 1976)).

246. *Austin III*, 564 F.2d at 168.

247. *Id.*

248. 365 U.S. 167, 187 (1961).

249. 42 U.S.C. § 1983 (2005).

250. 365 U.S. 167, 187 (1961).

The Fifth Circuit in the Austin school case declared that "the disproportionate racial impact of the neutral application of a long-standing neutral policy, by itself, will rarely constitute a constitutional violation."[251] *Washington v. Davis* had previously stated, "Disproportionate impact is not irrelevant, but it is not the sole touchstone of an invidious racial discrimination forbidden by the Constitution."[252] Historically, school officials have engaged in decisions "motivated by racially and ethnically neutral *bona fide* concerns."[253] In those circumstances, the natural and foreseeable consequence of a discriminatory result is insufficient to infuse the challenged acts with the type of discriminatory intent required by *Washington v. Davis*.[254] Additionally, the uneven consequences of governmental action claimed to be racially discriminatory must be traced to a racially discriminatory purpose.[255]

According to the Fifth Circuit, *Washington v. Davis* did not banish from the law of racial and ethnic discrimination the principle that a person intends the natural and foreseeable consequences of his actions.[256] The Fifth Circuit stated in *Austin III*, "When the official actions challenged as discriminatory include acts and decisions that do not have a firm basis in well accepted and historically sound non-discriminatory social policy, discriminatory intent may be inferred from the fact that those acts had foreseeable discriminatory consequences."[257] Consequently, the court in the Austin school case found the school district's claim less than convincing when the school officials argued that to meet the special educational needs of Mexican American children, the district had to "keep these children in separate schools, isolate them in Mexican American neighborhoods, or prevent them from sharing in the educational, social, and psychological benefits of an integrated education.... A benign motive will not excuse the discriminatory effects of the school board's actions."[258]

Shortly after *Davis,* the Court decided *Castaneda v. Partida,*[259] a grand jury discrimination case. The Court reviewed proof that although Latinos accounted for 79.1 percent of the population, over an eleven-year period Latinos included only 39 percent of those summoned for grand jury service.[260] Where a disparity is sufficiently large, it is unlikely that it is due solely to chance or accident; in the absence of evidence to the contrary, one must conclude that racial or other class-related factors entered into the selection process.[261] Recent cases have established that an official act is not unconstitutional *solely* because it has a racially disproportionate impact.[262] Nevertheless, the Court recognizes that "sometimes a clear pattern, unexplainable on grounds other than race, emerges from the effect of the state action even when the governing legislation appears neutral on its face."[263]

---

251. *Austin III*, 564 F.2d at 168.
252. *Davis*, 426 U.S. at 242.
253. *Austin III*, 564 F.2d at 168.
254. *Id.*
255. *See Davis*, 426 U.S. at 239–46 (1976) (public employment); *Keyes v. School Dist. No. 1, Denver, Colo.*, 413 U.S. 189, 208 (1973) (public schools).
256. *Austin III*, 564 F.2d at 168.
257. *Id.*
258. *Id.* at 172.
259. 430 U.S. 482 (1977).
260. *Id.* at 495.
261. *Id.* at 496, 501.
262. *See, e.g., Davis*, 426 U.S. at 239; *Arlington Heights v. Metropolitan Housing Dev. Corp.*, 429 U.S. 252, 264–65 (1977).
263. *Arlington Heights*, 429 U.S. at 266.

In *Personnel Administrator of Massachusetts v. Feeney*,[264] a nonveteran female with high test scores alleged denial of equal protection where veterans received preference by a state employment statute.[265] The Court rejected the claim, following the teachings of *Washington v. Davis*.[266] The Court concluded instead that "the disproportionate impact must be *traced to a purpose to discriminate on the basis of race*."[267] The Court repeated this standard later in the opinion, stating that "even if a neutral law has a disproportionately adverse effect upon a racial minority, it is unconstitutional under the Equal Protection Clause *only if that impact can be traced to a discriminatory purpose*."[268] Our history, involving discrimination against certain nationality groups, includes cases in which impact alone can unmask an invidious classification.[269]

Feeney recognized that it would be disingenuous to say that the adverse consequences of this legislation for women were unintended, in the sense that the consequences were not the result of volitional acts or in the sense that they were not foreseeable.[270] However, the Court stressed that the discriminatory purpose concept implies more than intent as volition or intent as awareness of consequences.[271] Instead, it implies that the decision maker, a state legislature in *Feeney*, selected or reaffirmed a particular course of action at least in part "because of," not merely "in spite of," its adverse effects on an identifiable group.[272] This is not to say that the inevitability or foreseeability of consequences of a neutral rule has no bearing on the existence of discriminatory intent. Certainly, when the adverse consequences of a law on an identifiable group are as inevitable as the gender-based consequences of the state law, a strong inference that the adverse effects were desired can reasonably be drawn.[273]

---

264. *Personnel Administrator v. Feeney*, 442 U.S. 256, 259 (1979) (preference operates overwhelmingly to the advantage of males).

265. On the 1973 examination, Ms. Feeney was placed in a position on the list for appointment behind twelve male veterans, eleven of whom had lower scores. *Id.* at 264.

266. The distinction made by the Massachusetts statute is between veterans and nonveterans, not between men and women. *Feeney*, 442 U.S. at 275.

267. *Feeney*, 442 U.S. at 260. *See Davis*, 426 U.S. at 238–44. A central theme of this chapter is precisely that the discrimination is *traced to a purpose to discriminate on the basis of race*. The states of Arizona, California and Texas, particularly, have engaged in de jure segregation and in other discriminatory practices against persons of Latino descent. As a result, these school districts are not in position to argue de facto or inadvertent segregation or disparate impact issues as a defense to state action under the Fourteenth Amendment. *See, e.g., Romo v. Laird*, No. 21617 (Maricopa Co. Super. Ct. 1925); *Mendez v. Westminster Sch. Dist.*, 64 F.Supp. 544 (S.D. Cal. 1946); *Delgado v. Bastrop Ind. Sch. Dist.*, Civil No. 388 (W.D. Tex June 15, 1948); *Cisneros v. Corpus Christi Ind. Sch. Dist.*, 324 F.Supp. 599 (S.D. Tex. 1970).

268. *Feeney*, 442 U.S. at 272 (emphasis added).

269. *See, e.g., Yick Wo v. Hopkins*, 118 U.S. 356 (1886) (a facially neutral policy unfairly and disproportionately impacted the Chinese community).

270. *Id.*

271. *Id.* at 279.

272. *Id. Feeney* further stated that when "the impact is essentially an unavoidable consequence of a legislative policy that has historically been deemed to be legitimate, the inference of discrimination simply fails to ripen into proof." *Id.* The same cannot be said of the historical policy involving Latino education where the courts have found educational discrimination. *See, e.g., Keyes v. School Dist. No. One, Denver*, 413 U.S. 189 (1973); *Arvizu v. Waco Ind. Sch. Dist.*, 373 F.Supp. 1264 (W.D. Tex. 1973); *Cisneros v. Corpus Christi Ind. Sch. Dist.*, 324 F.Supp. 599 (S.D. Tex. 1970); *Hernandez v. Driscoll Consol. Sch. Dist.*, 2 Race Rel. L. Rep. 329 (S.D. Tex. 1957); *Delgado v. Bastrop Ind. Sch. Dist.*, Civil No. 388 (W.D. Tex June 15, 1948); *Mendez v. Westminster Sch. Dist.*, 64 F.Supp. 544 (S.D. Cal. 1946); *Romo v. Laird*, No. 21617 (Maricopa Co. Super. Ct. 1925).

273. *Feeney*, 442 U.S. at 279 n.25.

VI. An Appropriate Standard for Proving Unequal Educational Opportunity

A. The Need for an Equal Protection Standard That Is Not Unequal or Arbitrary

Gone are the days when racists will document with impunity that they need to build another Mexican school to contain the growing Latino population.[274] Or that they do not serve Mexicans in the restaurant intended for whites only.[275] Or include in their restrictive covenants that this property shall not be conveyed to persons of the "African or Mexican Race."[276] Or that the business community wants to continue to have a workforce that will do the dirty, dangerous jobs at dismally low wages.[277] The equal protection clause provides, "No State shall ... deny to any person within its jurisdiction the equal protection of the laws."[278] The language is simple; but the courts, including the Supreme Court, have complicated matters by superimposing a burden of proof that as a practical matter defeats the promise of equal protection.

The language of the equal protection clause does not explicitly or implicitly provide that the discriminatory action has to be consciously taken, that is, to deprive one of equal treatment because the person is African American or Latino. In that regard, the language lacks guidance. If the action or policy discriminates, and the burden of the action or policy falls more on the Latino community, then why can that not be classified as a violation of "equal protection?" The Court needs to adopt a true historical interpretation that provides the ammunition to make the purpose of the equal protection clause meaningful.

When it passed the Fourteenth Amendment, the nation took the drastic action to eradicate the discrimination previously practiced against African Americans. However, the justices who controlled the majority provided their own reading of history behind the amendment.[279] Supreme Court historian Leonard W. Levy has stated,

> Two centuries of Court history should bring us to understand what really is a notorious fact: the Court has flunked history. The Justices stand censured for abusing historical evidence in a way that reflects adversely on their intellectual rectitude as well as on their historical competence.... The Court artfully selects

---

274. Rangel & Alcala, *supra* note 110, at 313 n.41.

275. This happened to Sgt. Macario Garcia in Richmond, Texas, while in uniform, two months after being awarded the Congressional Medal of Honor by President Harry S Truman. *See* Alonso S. Perales, Are We Good Neighbors? 156–57 (1948).

276. *See generally Matthews v. Andrade*, 198 P.2d 66 (Cal. Dist. Ct. App. 1948) ("No person or persons of the Mexican race, or other than the Caucasian race shall use or occupy any buildings or any lot, except that this covenant shall not prevent occupying by domestic servants of a different race domiciled with an owner, tenant, or occupant thereof."); *Clifton v. Puente*, 218 S.W.2d 272 (Tex. Civ. App.—San Antonio 1948). *See also* Taylor, *supra* note 34, at 226.

277. *See* Taylor, *supra* note 34, at 195.

278. U.S. Const. amend. XIV.

279. Justices on the Supreme Court have read the Fourteenth Amendment and other parts of the Constitution to conclude disputes in fashions that have shocked historians in the justices' misuse of history. *See, e.g.,* Leonard W. Levy, Original Intent and the Framers' Constitution 310–21 (1988) [hereafter cited as Levy]. Some of the cases Levy mentions include *Scott v. Sanford*, 60 U.S. 393 (1857), the *Slaughterhouse Cases*, 83 U.S. 36 (1873), the *Civil Rights Cases*, 109 U.S. 3 (1883) and *Plessy v. Ferguson*, 163 U.S. 537 (1896).

historical facts from one side only, ignoring contrary data, in order to support, rationalize, or give the appearance of respectability to judgments resting on other grounds.[280]

Levy emphasizes the words of George Orwell: "Who controls the past controls the future; who controls the present, controls the past."[281] Levy concludes, "We might be better off if judges were cabined and contained by those words [of the U.S. Constitution], rather than deciding on the basis of their own agendas."[282]

The jurisprudence of original intent relies completely on history.[283] The problem arises when Justices of the Court "think along lines that members of the bench and bar tend to share as people trained in the adversarial process."[284] A "scholar who has no stake in the outcome of a question is more likely to answer it correctly ... than [is] the advocate. The adversarial system ... invites the manipulation of evidence and distorted interpretations."[285]

Pointing to *Brown v. Board of Education*, Levy criticized the Court for allowing distorted perspectives to be promoted from both the NAACP and the school districts and thus avoiding an ultimate decision based on original intent.[286] He concludes that the Supreme Court in *Brown* "could have easily held, in conformance with the preponderance of evidence, that the framers of the Fourteenth Amendment and the state legislatures that ratified it, intended the amendment to establish the principle of racial equality before the law."[287] I recognize that the segregation factors in *Brown* explicitly established an equal protection violation. On the other hand, I argue that practices and policies that inevitably result (discriminatory impact) in inequality implicitly violate the principle of racial equality that the Fourteenth Amendment intended to promote as a means of ending discrimination.

The case that *Brown* effectively reversed, *Plessy v. Ferguson*,[288] displays the Court's disastrous use of history.[289] In *Plessy*, the Court upheld the constitutionality of state Jim Crow laws that provided for "equal but separate accommodations for the white and colored races" in railroad cars.[290] The *Plessy* Court shockingly concluded that the amendment could not have intended to eliminate distinctions based on color[291] and that laws requiring segregation "do not necessarily imply the inferiority of either race to the other."[292] "The Court ignored massive evidence heard in the trumpetings of white racists from the pulpits, the press and public platforms, that the purpose of Jim Crow laws was to uphold white supremacy and keep the blacks in their places of inferiority."[293]

The same message prevails from the halls of Harvard when a scholar warns that America faces a "clash of civilizations" with the increase in the Latino population. Samuel

---

280. Levy, *supra* note 279, at 300.
281. *Id.* at 320, citing George Orwell, 1984, at 35 (1949).
282. *Id.*
283. Levy, *supra* note 279, at 310.
284. *Id.* at 310–11.
285. *Id.* at 311.
286. *Id.* at 312.
287. *Id.*
288. *Plessy v. Ferguson*, 163 U.S. 537 (1896).
289. Levy, *supra* note 279, at 317.
290. *Plessy*, 163 U.S. at 550–51.
291. *Id.* at 544.
292. *Id.*
293. Levy, *supra* note 279, at 318.

P. Huntington, a Harvard professor, stirred much controversy several years ago with his book on the changing face of America and the "clash of civilizations."[294] Huntington concedes that the "central elements of any culture or civilization are language and religion."[295] He seems concerned that American civilization is changing too radically in that the number of Latinos is growing so rapidly. He specifically states, "While Muslims pose the immigration problem to Europe, Mexicans pose the problem for the United States.... The American population will ... change dramatically in the first half of the twenty-first century, becoming almost 50 percent white and 25 percent Hispanic."[296] Huntington makes the following additional warning about the American Latino growth:

> The area settled by Mexican immigrants was annexed by the United States after it defeated Mexico in the mid-nineteenth century. Mexican economic development will almost certainly generate Mexican *revanchist* sentiments. In due course, the results of American military expansion in the nineteenth century could be threatened and possibly reversed by Mexican demographic expansion in the twenty-first century.[297]

The question as to whether this is serious academic work or an effort to sell books or mere xenophobia is left to the educated mind.

B. The Inadequacy of the Purposeful Intent Test

The purposeful intent test[298] is unreasonable in that it requires litigants to prove almost the impossible to make the equal protection clause a constitutional reality. The standard effectively prevents jurors from drawing conclusions from evidence and actions as we all do on a daily basis. The purposeful intent test requires a burden of proof[299] that effectively adds the element of specific intent.[300] The purposeful intent standard forces the victim of ethnic discrimination to play the role of a prosecutor and establish that the accused acted with the specific intent to put the Latino "in his place."[301] Racism in American law and society has caused substantial damage to victims. As a result, efforts to ameliorate that damage and heal the psychological wounds are critical to healthy present-day racial interactions.[302]

---

294. Samuel P. Huntington, Clash of Civilizations and the Remaking of World Order 8 (Paperback ed., Simon & Schuster 2003) (1996).

295. *Id.* at 59.

296. *Id.* at 204.

297. *Id.* at 206 (emphasis added).

298. This test refers to the requirement found in *Washington v. Davis*, 426 U.S. 229, 239 (1976). *Davis* held that only actions involving *purposeful intent* to discriminate on the basis of race reach the requirements of the equal protection clause. *Id.* (emphasis added).

299. The burden of proof includes the burden of persuasion (e.g., beyond a reasonable doubt) and the burden of production. Bryan A. Garner, A Handbook of Criminal Law Terms 79 (2000) [hereafter cited as Garner].

300. Specific intent is the "intent to accomplish the *precise* criminal act that one is later charged with." General intent is the state of mind required for other than specific intent crimes and usually takes the form of recklessness (involving *actual awareness* of a risk and the culpable taking of that risk). *Id.* at 354.

301. An example of a specific intent crime is burglary, traditionally proved by alleging the entry (general intent) of a habitation with the intent to commit theft or a felony (specific intent).

302. *See* Eric Yamamoto, Interracial Justice: Conflict and Reconciliation in Post-Civil Rights America 83 (1999).

Prosecutors often establish the concept of "intent" even where there was no eyewitness who heard the defendant say, for example, "I am going to kill you."[303] Whether the accused acted with specific intent to kill or with the intent to commit an act clearly dangerous to human life does not really matter. A high awareness of an outcome can also establish a general intent. These methods of proof are allowed in criminal cases where the burden of proof is beyond a reasonable doubt.[304] However, in constitutional civil rights cases, where the standard is theoretically by a preponderance of the evidence, the requirements imposed by *Davis* and *Feeney* seem to have commandeered the civil preponderance of the evidence[305] test and substituted the criminal case standard of beyond a reasonable doubt. There is no logical explanation other than "judicial legislation" for this outcome.[306]

C. Latinos Qualify for Application of the Totality of the Circumstances Foreseeable Consequences Test in Public Education

As previously discussed, the Supreme Court held that proof of discriminatory or purposeful intent could be inferred from the totality of the pertinent facts, including the very fact of the disproportionate impact.[307] In *Washington v. Davis*, the Court concluded that affirmative recruitment efforts and the improved minority numbers in the police force negated any inference of intentional racial discrimination.[308] Generally, an actor is held to intend the reasonably foreseeable results of his actions.[309] The Supreme Court, in settings that had a history of state-imposed racial segregation, has barred practices that

---

303. Civil rights litigants rarely possess the admission of a racist attitude in seeking to prove their case. Seldom will they have the frank comment of one's racist thoughts as that made by William Bennett, former secretary of Education for the United States. Bennett suggested that aborting black children would reduce crime, but he immediately stated such a policy would be an "impossible, ridiculous and morally reprehensible thing to do." Michael A. Fletcher & Brian Faler, *Bennett Defends Abortion Comment as 'Thought Experiment,'* Hous. Chron., Oct. 1, 2005, at A3. If Bennett is being honest, then why utter such racially insensitive words?

304. Garner, *supra* note 299, at 574.

305. *Id.* at 78.

306. For example, when Title VI of the 1964 Civil Rights Act, 42 U.S.C. § 2000d, was first interpreted, the courts concluded that Congress created a results test. *E.g., Lau v. Nichols*, 414 U.S. 563 (1974). The federal regulations provided, "Discrimination is barred which has that effect even though no purposeful design is present." 45 C.F.R. § 80.3(b)(2). However, the Court later ruled that compensatory relief should not be awarded to private plaintiffs in the absence of discriminatory intent, while primarily holding declaratory and limited injunctive relief is available where a disparate impact can be shown by a private party. *Guardians Ass'n v. Civil Serv. Comm'n*, 463 U.S. 582, 584 (1983). Congress had a chance to change the administrative interpretation of Title VI, but the House in 1966 defeated a proposal to bar only intentional discrimination. It never received action in the Senate. *Id.* at 620 (Marshall, J., dissenting). More recently, the Supreme Court concluded that there is no private cause of action to enforce regulations promulgated under Title VI. *Alexander v. Sandoval*, 532 U.S. 275, 293 (2001).

307. *Id.* at 242; *see also Personnel Administrator v. Feeney*, 442 U.S. 256 (1979).

308. *Id.* at 246.

309. *See, e.g.,* W. Prosser, The Law of Torts § 8 (4th ed. 1971); Restatement (Second) of Torts § 8A, Comment b (1965), cited in *United States v. Texas Educ. Agency (Austin III)*, 564 F.2d 162, 167 (5th Cir. 1977).

have had "the foreseeable and anticipated effect of maintaining the racial separation of the schools."[310]

As noted earlier, a state official operating from a discriminatory purpose is apt to "pursue his discriminatory practices in ways that are devious, by methods subtle and illusive."[311] In some cases, school officials engage in decisions "motivated by racially and ethnically neutral *bona fide* concerns."[312] In those circumstances, the uneven consequences of governmental action claimed to be racially discriminatory must be traced to a racially discriminatory purpose.[313]

Latinos, an ethnic language minority, have established that a particular rule, such as a "no Spanish rule," has a disproportionately adverse impact. By the same token, an English immersion school language policy will provide equality—that is, the same language for all students—but it will sacrifice the limited English learner. Some Latinos might succeed, but an excessive number will fall behind. Even a dual-language policy that is staffed by teachers with limited Spanish language abilities falls short of an equitable education.

Such language policies, even if seen as benign by school administrators, capriciously negate the cultural and linguistic world in which Latinos live. It defies reality to conclude that the discriminatory outcome is acceptable if the action was allegedly taken with the benevolent motive of improving the English language abilities of Latinos. Opponents will undoubtedly counter that protesting English language immersion programs will delay the English language skills of Latino children. An equal or greater number of people will vigorously counter that the immersion programs themselves delay the English language skills of the Latino children.[314]

Legal standards traditionally allow the fact-finder the opportunity to draw certain conclusions as to an awareness or high probability of a result. The mental state required for this effort can be either knowledge or recklessness. One who acts knowingly acts consciously or deliberately; the circumstances indicate that the actor is aware and well-informed.[315] A person acts recklessly if his conduct is "characterized by the creation of a substantial and unjustifiable risk of harm to others and by a conscious (and sometimes deliberate) disregard for or indifference to that risk."[316]

Regardless of whether a person, agency or school district acted purposely, knowingly, or recklessly, the result is the same: the target of the disparate treatment or disparate impact knowingly suffers unequal educational opportunity or recklessly ends up in a life of inadequate educational attainment. Where the state continuously applies an unsuccessful practice or policy that has continuously been shown to be ineffective, the state proceeds knowingly in reckless disregard or callous indifference to the student's serious educational needs. In other words, to continue providing the same futile remedy to the ailment in full awareness of its ineffectiveness constitutes poor, inadequate educational med-

---

310. *Columbus Bd. of Educ. v. Penick*, 443 U.S. 449, 462 (1979).

311. *Austin III*, 564 F.2d at 168 (citing *United States v. Texas Educ. Agency (Austin II)*, 532 F.2d 380, 388 (5th Cir. 1976)).

312. *Austin III*, 564 F.2d at 168.

313. *See Washington v. Davis*, 426 U.S. 229, 239–46 (1976) (public employment); *Keyes v. School Dist. No. 1*, Denver, Colo., 413 U.S. 189, 208 (1973) (public schools).

314. *See Indep. Sch. Dist. v. Salvatierra*, 33 S.W.2d 790, 793 (Tex. Civ. App. 1930) (concession by superintendent that the best way for a child to learn another language is to be in the company of the children who speak the other language).

315. GARNER, *supra* note 299, at 395–96.

316. *Id.* at 576. The mental state of recklessness also connotes a circumstance where one foresees the harmful consequence and consciously takes the risk. *Id.* at 577.

icine. In summary, the state's actions can only be described as constituting a knowingly callous, insensitive disregard to the serious educational needs of Latinos, America's largest and still growing language minority group.[317]

How can discriminatory purpose or intent be shown? Though the days of overt racism have in great part disappeared into the history books, proof of individual prejudice continues to surface.[318] Private discrimination, of course, does not become a federal constitutional issue until private conduct creeps into the governmental domain; but we must recognize that private individuals run for office, get elected and then exercise their judgment, even if it is covertly racist, in official governmental matters.

In a very few circumstances, a statute will clearly create a suspect classification and target the group for adverse action.[319] Another circumstance involves a facially neutral statute or ordinance that discriminates in its application.[320] The Court in *Davis* even stated that disparate impact could be relevant to determine if, in the totality of the circumstances, illegal discrimination exists.[321] Based on this standard, a school district practices discrimination on the basis of ethnicity if, knowing the totality of the circumstances, that district makes or enforces a decision that has an outcome that disadvantages or harms a suspect class.[322]

D. Awareness of Latino Educational Neglect by Public School Administrators

How long do public education officials have to be aware of, for example, the educational crisis involving Latino children? Texas school officials received "actual" notice certainly when the Superintendent of Public Instruction signed the 1948 consent decree in *Delgado v. Bastrop Ind. School District*.[323] Beginning in 1968, the U.S. Commission on Civil Rights conducted hearings and published through 1974 a series of studies that exposed the dismal history of discrimination and educational neglect involving the Mexican American/Latino community.[324] The Civil Rights Commission published an additional

---

317. Not every single Latino speaks Spanish. However, the article addresses the needs of those Latinos whose educational opportunities are impacted by their cultural characteristics, which include the use of the Spanish language.

318. A recent and notable example is the racial epithet used by former Senator George Allen of Virginia; many attribute his 2006 electoral defeat to his use of a derogatory term. E.g., Brendan O'Shaughnessy, *GOP Rethinks Parker After Remarks on Jews*, Indianapolis Star, Feb. 23, 2007, at Local 1; Umang Varma, Opinion, *Why 'Macaca' Was Worse*, Wash. Post, Feb. 17, 2007, at A29; Tim Craig, *Offensive GOP Words Might Speak Louder Than Va. Transit Deal*, Wash. Post, Jan. 22, 2007, at B01.

319. *E.g., Plyler v. Doe*, 457 U.S. 202 (1982).

320. *E.g., Yick Wo v. Hopkins*, 118 U.S. 356 (1886).

321. *Washington v. Davis*, 426 U.S. 229, 242 (1976). Justice John Paul Stevens, concurring, stated that "the line between discriminatory purpose and discriminatory impact is not nearly as bright, and perhaps not quite as critical, as the reader of the Court's opinion might assume." *Id.* at 254 (Stevens, J., concurring).

322. The Court has concluded that Latinos constitute a suspect class under the equal protection clause. *Hernandez v. Texas*, 347 U.S. 475 (1954); *see Keyes v. School Dist. No. One, Denver, Colorado*, 413 U.S. 189 (1973).

323. *Delgado v. Bastrop Ind. Sch. Dist.*, Civil No. 388 (W.D. Tex. June 15, 1948).

324. The six reports in the Mexican American Education Study include Ethnic Isolation of Mexican Americans in the Public Schools of the Southwest (1971); The Unfinished Education: Outcomes for Minorities in the Five Southwestern States (1971); The Excluded Student: Educational Practices Affecting Mexican Americans in the Southwest (1972); Mexican American Education in Texas: A Function of Wealth (1973); Teachers and Students: Classroom Interaction in the Schools of the Southwest (1973); and Toward Qual-

report in 1975 that proposed ideas for improving the educational opportunities for Latinos.[325] In 1980, the U.S. Department of Health, Education, and Welfare (DHEW) sponsored a report on the condition of Latino education.[326]

If these official notices proved insufficient, in 1983 the National Commission on Excellence in Education alerted the entire nation with the following statement: "If an unfriendly foreign power had attempted to impose on America the mediocre educational performance that exists today, we might well have viewed it as an act of war."[327] Sadly, the wheels of legislative and judicial justice proceeded slowly, not even observing any "deliberate speed." The executive branch followed with a 1996 report on the crisis in the field of Latino education.[328] Utilizing earthquake imagery in the title ("Our Nation on the Fault Line"), the appointed commission apparently hoped to wake the national leadership and the educational community. More than a decade has come and gone, however, and Latino and other underserved children continue to either drop out or receive an education characterized by mediocre results.

The 1996 report first points to the national need to prepare a workforce that possesses cognitive, rather than manual, skills.[329] It also reiterates a common theme, that is, that Latino children will benefit from a quality pre–primary school experience where they will be taught skills for learning and socialization.[330] In addition, the report notes the similarities between race and poverty, observing that "both African American and Latino students are much more likely than white students to be in schools that are segregated and poorly funded."[331] The presidential agency designated for the development of national educational policy specifically recommends that "effective educational models must incorporate high-quality standards, equitable financial support, and diverse language and cultural knowledge."[332] After concluding that the Latino educational dilemma is rooted in a "refusal to accept, to recognize, and to value the central role of Hispanics in the past, present, and future of this nation," and characterizing the history of Latino education as "a history of neglect, oppression, and periods of wanton denial of opportunity,"[333] the commission's report ends with the plea, "The United States should not tolerate the loss to our society of any more generations of children of any cultural, racial, or linguistic background. Excellence and equity must be inseparable benchmarks for the education of all of our nation's children."[334]

ITY EDUCATION FOR MEXICAN AMERICANS (1974). U.S. COMM'N ON CIVIL RIGHTS, TOWARD QUALITY EDUCATION FOR MEXICAN AMERICANS ix (1974), *available at* www.marclink.com/ pdf_thurgood.pdf.

325. *See* U.S. COMM'N ON CIVIL RIGHTS, A BETTER CHANCE TO LEARN: BILINGUAL-BICULTURAL EDUCATION (1975).

326. *See* GEORGE BROWN ET AL., NAT'L CTR. FOR EDUC. STATISTICS, THE CONDITION OF EDUCATION FOR HISPANIC AMERICANS (1980).

327. NAT'L COMM'N ON EXCELLENCE IN EDUC., A NATION AT RISK: THE IMPERATIVE FOR EDUCATION REFORM 5 (1983). The report did not directly focus on Latinos, but the message is the same: public education must be improved.

328. *See* PRESIDENT'S ADVISORY COMM'N ON EDUC. EXCELLENCE FOR HISPANIC AM., OUR NATION ON THE FAULT LINE: HISPANIC AMERICAN EDUCATION (1996).

329. *Id.* at 27.

330. *Id.* at 33.

331. *Id.* at 44.

332. *Id.* at 59.

333. *Id.* at 65.

334. *Id.* at 66.

E. The *Hernandez* "Result Bespeaks Discrimination" Test

The *Hernandez* and *Brown* cases send different signals as to the Court's rationale for finding a Fourteenth Amendment violation. *Brown* epitomizes the disparate treatment case. *Hernandez*, on the other hand, appears to represent the disparate impact case. The school districts in *Brown* overtly classified black students for segregated education. On the other hand, in *Hernandez*, Jackson County, Texas, covertly justified the exclusion of Latinos from grand and petit juries by suggesting that the number of qualified venire candidates from the Latino community was low.[335]

Hernandez lacks the smoking gun direct proof of racism that *Brown* abundantly possesses. However, the *Hernandez* Court found the circumstantial evidence to be quite compelling. In *Hernandez*, the state argued that the exclusion of Latinos from juries occurred not on the basis of Latino ancestry but on the fact that few Latinos qualified for jury duty. The Court found something strangely wrong when, during a period of twenty-five years, a county with a 14 percent Latino population could not find even one Latino to serve on a jury. The statistics alone seem to pave the road to the Court's language that the "result bespeaks discrimination."[336]

However, the evidence in *Hernandez* additionally indicated a community animosity against Latinos in schools and restaurants; the courthouse restroom even had the notorious sign that read "Colored Men" and "Hombres Aqui."[337] While *Hernandez* leaves room to argue that discriminatory impact evidence suffices to prove a violation of equal protection, precedents like *Davis* and *Feeney* bring civil rights attorneys and their clients back to a pessimistic reality that as a practical matter, they need the smoking gun of an overtly racist act to prove their equal protection claim.[338]

F. The Deliberate or Callous Indifference to Serious Educational Needs Test

Why should the equal protection clause be restricted to circumstances where only overt racism is proved? This should not be the case. Professor Levy has taken issue with the twisted nature of Supreme Court reasoning.[339] Since the Court is not likely to change the equal protection precedents previously discussed, lower courts need to assess another avenue for relief. *Estelle v. Gamble*[340] provides optimism for those who feel "excluded" from the American dream of equal opportunity.

Estelle holds that a prison official violates one's civil rights when that official engages in deliberate indifference to a prisoner's serious medical needs.[341] Gamble, an inmate in

---

335. *See generally Hernandez v. Texas*, 347 U.S. 475, 480–81(1954).
336. *Hernandez*, 347 U.S. at 482.
337. *Hernandez*, 347 U.S. at 479–80. The Spanish term "Hombres Aqui" obviously conveyed the message that the "colored" restroom was to be shared with Latinos in that community.
338. *See, e.g.*, *Feeney*, 442 U.S. at 279.
339. *See, e.g.*, Levy, *supra* note 279, at 310–21.
340. 429 U.S. 97 (1976).
341. *Id.* at 104 (finding that such indifference constitutes the unnecessary and wanton infliction of pain proscribed by the Eighth Amendment).

the Texas prison system, sued the prison doctor and other officials and alleged cruel and unusual punishment in violation of the Eighth Amendment's provision that "excessive bail shall not be required, nor excessive fines imposed, nor cruel and unusual punishments inflicted."[342] The Court concluded that these elementary principles establish the government's obligation to provide medical care for those whom it is punishing by incarceration. The inmate has no choice but to rely on prison authorities to treat his medical needs.[343] If the authorities fail to respond to his medical problems, those needs will not be met. The Court noted that a failure to react may actually produce physical "torture or a lingering death," the evils of most immediate concern to the drafters of the Eighth Amendment.[344] The infliction of such unnecessary suffering is inconsistent with contemporary standards of decency as manifested in modern legislation codifying the common law view that "it is but just that the public be required to care for the prisoner, who cannot by reason of the deprivation of his liberty, care for himself."[345]

By analogy, a school system violates a student's civil rights when that system, operated by school boards, principals and teachers, is consciously and thus deliberately indifferent to a student's serious educational needs. The purposeful intent test is too unyielding and obstructive to a full enforcement of the goals of the Fourteenth Amendment. The *Hernandez* results test constitutes a practical and enforceable standard for the Fourteenth Amendment.[346] The public school student depends on the state to provide an education, and compulsory attendance school laws mandate that the child appear in the school. The untrained student, like the inmate in *Gamble*, has no choice but to rely on school authorities to meet his serious educational needs. If the authorities fail to do so, those scholastic needs will not be met. In the worst cases, such a failure to meet these academic needs may actually produce an illiterate population of Latinos or at least one that is barely capable of competing in our highly competitive and technological world.

The Latino student in the public school system is akin to the inmate in prison: "It is but just that the public be required to care for the prisoner, who cannot by reason of the deprivation of his liberty, care for himself."[347] Students who are linguistically or educationally disadvantaged are not at liberty and do not have the means to care for their serious educational needs. Those students need trained instructors to pave the way to educational freedom.

VII. Conclusion

This chapter seeks to address the unique educational needs of the Latino child and to determine if *Brown* and *Hernandez* continue to possess legal relevance in this millennium. The equal protection purposeful intent test as set forth in *Washington v. Davis* and its progeny must give way to a more realistic test that recognizes the devious forms in which discrimination can surface. *Brown* and *Hernandez* present continuing avenues for

---

342. U.S. CONST. amend. VIII.

343. *Estelle*, 429 U.S. at 103.

344. *Id.* at 103.

345. *Id.* at 104.

346. As an alternative, the Eighth Amendment's deliberate indifference standard would aid in the assessment of the equal educational opportunity needs of the Latino child.

347. *Estelle*, 429 U.S. at 104.

relief from discriminatory practices. The promise of *Brown* and *Hernandez* for a race-neutral America, free of debilitating discrimination, remains not only a worthy goal but also a challenging undertaking. Will twenty-five years suffice to remove these vestiges of discrimination, as Justice O'Connor targeted in *Grutter v. Bollinger*?[348] The Court must adjust to the realities of the covert and ingenious acts of intolerance that our society experiences.[349] In other words, the Court should alleviate the burdens imposed by the *Davis* purposeful intent principle, particularly in the public school system.

The state acts in the educational arena when a governmental agent (principal, superintendent) or authority (school board) decides a course of action that will lead to a burdensome, harmful or an unequal result. In the case of the Latino child with racial, ethnic, cultural and/or linguistic differences from the majority Anglo population, the imposition of a pedagogical approach that clashes with or excludes the Latino child can only be described as being the product of state action in violation of the due process[350] or Eequal protection clauses of the Fourteenth Amendment[351] (state matters) or of governmental action in violation of the due process clause of the Fifth Amendment (federal matters).[352] Justice Powell closed his opinion in *Keyes* with the following words:

> It is well to remember that the course we are running is a long one and the goal sought in the end — so often overlooked — is the best possible educational opportunity for all children. Communities deserve the freedom and the incentive to turn their attention and energies to this goal of quality education, free from protracted and debilitating battles over court-ordered student transportation.[353]

By the same token, parents of all students, regardless of ethnic ancestry, deserve to have a school leadership focused on programs that deliver a quality and effective education, one free from the need to find purposeful intent to discriminate before remedial action can be taken by school officials. Although education is not considered a fundamental constitutional right, it is nonetheless critical to society in meeting its members' basic needs.

Where a Latino child's educational program is one that has been failing for years, the continued utilization of those failed programs is egregious and capricious. One ignores reality to argue that the results are not the product of state action. Whether the policy is purposefully implemented at the expense of the Latino child or is callously indifferent to the serious educational needs of the Latino children, the result of educational neglect is the same: it is unfair, unjust, inequitable, unreasonable, undeserved, arbitrary, capricious, dishonorable, biased and just plain wrong. We must remember the words of wisdom expressed over half a century ago by Justice Felix Frankfurter, one of our leading

---

348. 539 U.S. 306, 343 (2003). "We expect that 25 years from now, the use of racial preferences will no longer be necessary to further the interest approved today." *Id.*

349. "A strict focus on intent permits racial discrimination to go unpunished in the absence of evidence of overt bigotry. As overtly bigoted behavior has become more unfashionable, evidence of intent has become harder to find. But this does not mean that racial discrimination has disappeared. We cannot agree that Congress in enacting the Fair Housing Act intended to permit municipalities to systematically deprive minorities of housing opportunities simply because those municipalities act discreetly." *Metro. Hous. Dev. Corp. v. Village of Arlington Heights*, 558 F.2d 1283, 1290 (7th Cir. 1977).

350. *Westminster Sch. Dist. v. Mendez*, 161 F.2d 774 (9th Cir. 1947), *rev'g* 64 F. Supp. 544 (S.D. Cal. 1946).

351. *Brown*, 347 U.S. 483.

352. *Bolling v. Sharpe*, 347 U.S. 497 (1954) (holding that the District of Columbia school segregation violated the Fifth Amendment due process clause).

353. *Keyes v. School Dist. No. One, Denver*, 413 U.S. 189, 253 (Burger, J., concurring).

jurists: "It was a wise man who said that there is no greater inequality than the equal treatment of unequals."[354]

More has to be done to level the playing field of educational opportunity. We should heed the words of wisdom expressed in *Plyler v. Doe*,[355] where the Court, almost ten years after declaring that education is neither an explicit nor an implicit fundamental constitutional right,[356] made the following comments regarding the need for fair and equitable educational opportunities in our society:

> Public education is not a "right" granted to individuals by the Constitution.... But neither is it merely some governmental "benefit" indistinguishable from other forms of social welfare legislation. Both the importance of education in maintaining our basic institutions, and the lasting impact of its deprivation on the life of the child, mark the distinction.... [As] ... pointed out early in our history, ... some degree of education is necessary to prepare citizens to participate effectively and intelligently in our open political system if we are to preserve freedom and independence. ... In addition, education provides the basic tools by which individuals might lead economically productive lives to the benefit of us all. In sum, education has a fundamental role in maintaining the fabric of our society. We cannot ignore the significant social costs borne by our Nation when select groups are denied the means to absorb the values and skills upon which our social order rests.[357]

In addition to the pivotal role of education in sustaining our political and cultural heritage, denial of education to some isolated group of children poses an affront to one of the goals of the equal protection clause: the abolition of governmental barriers presenting unreasonable obstacles to advancement on the basis of individual merit.[358]

The Court must clear the air to save another generation of innocent students whose unique educational needs are not being addressed. The fact that Latinos constitute our nation's largest ethnic minority group alone warrants drastic action from all three branches of our government. Otherwise, a substantial portion of the American population will be left in a state of educational distress. Do the arguments presented by ranchers in 1929 to keep the Latino population uneducated still have vitality today? Unless legislatures and courts take immediate action to address the educational neglect of America's Latino population, the answer to this question appears to be "yes."

The federal courts must be in position to apply flexible equal protection principles in the fight for true educational equality. Latinos live in practically every state in the nation. They will be found in certainly the most populous states where economic opportunities beckon. Each state applies different models of education. Some politicians engineer voter propositions, as occurred in California, that dictate what professionals (educators) should be deciding.

The principles apply to other settings where state involvement raises questions of equal protection or of unequal application. Equality in the field of public education qualifies for this type of assessment. The fact that the Supreme Court held in *San Antonio Independent School District v. Rodriguez* that education is not a fundamental right[359] should

---

354. *Dennis v. United States*, 339 U.S. 162, 184 (1950) (Frankfurter, J., dissenting). *See* Lupe S. Salinas & Robert H. Kimball, *The Equal Treatment of Unequals: Barriers Facing Latinos and the Poor in Texas Public Schools*, 14 Geo. J. On Poverty L. & Pol'y 215 (2007).

355. *Plyler v. Doe*, 457 U.S. 202 (1982).

356. *San Antonio Ind. Sch. Dist. v. Rodriguez*, 411 U.S. 1 (1973).

357. 328 *Plyler*, 457 U.S. at 221.

358. *Id.* at 221–22.

359. 411 U.S. 1, 35 (1973).

not excuse the continued racial and ethnic disparities in educational achievements that result from public educational policies and practices. Latinos can establish the following in the educational context:

- Latinos have been held to be a group that is a recognizable, distinct class, singled out for different treatment under the laws, as written or as applied.[360]

- Latinos can unfortunately establish a substantial degree of under-representation in the categories of educational success and of over-representation in the attrition or dropout rate when compared to the white Caucasian population.

- Latinos can prove that public educational systems in the United States have been aware, since the early part of the twentieth century,[361] of conflicts in the handling by the dominant white Caucasian population of Latinos' unique educational needs.

- Furthermore, Latinos can establish that the pedagogical procedures implemented by school administrators have been "susceptible of abuse," or at least support the presumption of discrimination that is raised by the abysmal statistical showings.[362]

Once Latino plaintiffs show substantial under-representation in the positive results and an over-representation in the negative categories, they have made out a prima facie case of discriminatory purpose, and the burden then shifts to the state or public entity to rebut that case.[363] Because Latinos constitute a suspect class, the state must establish at least a compelling governmental objective for why it must adhere to the enforcement of policies that continuously produce disparate outcomes and deprive Latinos of an equitable educational opportunity.[364] A policy of complete equality in facilities, books and expenditures does not suffice.[365] Practices such as the retention of students to enhance the outcome of test results and the failure to incorporate the linguistic characteristics and needs of a child are "susceptible of abuse" or at least support the presumption of discrimination. In addition, as applied to the Houston setting, even though HISD has a Latino superintendent, under the *Castaneda* principle, that does not result in a rebuttal based on the presumption that Latinos will not "discriminate" against their own.[366]

In short, it will be a sad day for America's national interest to have such a large population of its citizenry operating at levels of minimal education. Our nation has the human resources necessary to provide for our future economic and security needs. America does

---

360. *Hernandez*, 347 U.S. at 480; *White v. Regester*, 412 U.S. 755, 767 (1973); *Cisneros v. Corpus Christi Ind. Sch. Dist.*, 324 F. Supp. 599, 606 (S.D. Tex. 1970).

361. *See, e.g.*, *Salvatierra*, 33 S.W.2d at 793 (Tex. Civ. App. 1930). The reports by the Commission on Civil Rights illustrate the official awareness of Latino educational neglect. *See*, *supra* notes 323–34 and accompanying text.

362. *Partida*, 430 U.S. at 494 (*citing Davis*, 426 U.S. at 241).

363. *Id.* at 495.

364. Where an identifiable ethnic group, or suspect class, is involved in a benefit or program that does not involve a fundamental right, such as education, then the second tier of review controls. *See Rodriguez*, 411 U.S. at 28.

365. *Lau v. Nichols*, 414 U.S. 563 (1974) (holding that the Civil Rights Act of 1964, 42 U.S.C. § 2000d (2005), prohibits any program that receives federal funding from excluding participants on the basis of race, color or national origin).

366. "Because of the many facets of human motivation, it would be unwise to presume as a matter of law that human beings of one definable group will not discriminate against other members of their group." *Partida*, 430 U.S. at 499 (Blackmun, J., majority opinion). Justice Marshall observed, "Social scientists agree that members of minority groups frequently respond to discrimination and prejudice by attempting to disassociate themselves from the group, even to the point of adopting the majority's negative attitudes towards the minority." *Id.* at 503 (Marshall, J. concurring).

not need to "subtract"[367] the positives that Latino children bring to the classroom. The language foundation in Spanish that many bring to school can only serve them as a plus in job opportunities if the public school system does not eradicate this talent. America has a gold mine of opportunities that she is squandering. We should incorporate the cultural and linguistic talents minority children bring to the classroom.

---

367. *See* Angela Valenzuela, Subtractive Schooling: U.S.-Mexican Youth and the Politics of Caring 172–81(1999).

14

Untold Stories: College Persistence for First-Generation Students: Family Roots of Inspiration and Burden to Accomplish the Family Dream

Kate E. Bueler

The study of college persistence—the study of if and why college students drop out before finishing their degrees—is particularly timely given recent demographic trends in college attendance and completion rates, as well as economic changes, and historical and political transformations occurring within our society. The number of students attending college is at its highest point in U.S. history, and as a result this trend will likely continue due to a number of factors.[1] Although it is promising to see the increase in college attendees nationally, there are other contradictory phenomena occurring within postsecondary education trends. Students who enroll do not necessarily graduate from college. College students most sensitive to attrition are from under-represented groups, particularly lower socioeconomic status (SES), minorities, and first-generation students who are the first in their immediate families to complete postsecondary four year institutions.[2] Most important, even if first-generation students are admitted to and attend universi-

---

1. H. B. Shin, U.S. Census Bureau, Student Enrollment—Social and Economic Characteristics of Students: October 2003. (2005). First, population trends of baby boomers having their own children who are now college age and an increase in immigration has created a large K–12 school and college-age populations. *Id.* Second, there has been a growth in access, based on court cases, legislation, and affirmative action, for women and minority students historically denied admission to universities. Although increased access is not a recent phenomenon, its legacy affects college's acceptance rates today. Access for students was also targeted by political initiatives in the 1960s and 1970s, leading to increased financial accessibility through the availability of financial aid provided via the Higher Education Act of 1965 and reauthorizations that have followed (Nora and Horvath 1989 and Stampen and Fenske 1988). Third, economic changes affecting the demand of increased skills and knowledge in the workforce required improved rates of educational attainment. Y. Lin & W. P. Vogt, U.S. Department of Educ., Condition of Education (1999); L. Leslie & P. Brinkman, The Economic Value of Higher Education (1988). {**Query to author:** Please provide full citations for Nora & Horvath 1989 and Stampen & Fenske 1988 in this note.}

2. D. Brooks, *The Education Gap*, New York Times, Sept. 25, 2005, at 41; D. Brooks, *Pillars of Cultural Capital*, New York Times, Oct. 6, 2005, at 37; D. Leonhardt, *The College Dropout Boom; Class Matters*: New York Times, May 24, 2005, at A.1.

ties, they are less likely to persist until graduation (58 percent) compared to students whose parents had completed a four-year degree (77 percent).[3]

Currently, the research on social class and the family's ability to affect students' college persistence is not the foremost focus of college persistence research. The perspective of the students themselves who persist successfully through college, particularly first-generation students, is also missing from the current literature. College persistence research illustrates that one of the strongest effects on the intent to persist among students is encouragement from family and friends.[4] Reasons for *how* and *why* this occurs are needed to increase an understanding of the role of the family in college persistence, especially important for first-generation students.

For the future of the American economy to successfully compete globally, it is imperative to increase the number of well-prepared and college-educated workers, as well as the need for them to assist in supporting the retiring baby boomers.[5] In addition, degree completion is becoming increasingly necessary for economic opportunity and yields the greatest benefits.[6]

Researchers have identified numerous factors that contribute to college persistence. The majority of psychological research is based on Tinto's Student Integration Model and Bean's Student Attrition Model, used together or separately as models. Tinto's theory maintains that students' persistence is reflective of the student and institutional match,[7] the student's commitment to an educational goal, and commitment to remain within the institution.[8] Bean's model accounts for outside forces, such as a student's background, academic variables, environmental variables (such as employment and finances), and social integration, simultaneously highlighting the intent to persist, attitudes, institutional fit, external factors: friends and family.[9]

To address these issues in depth — the role of the family and social class in college persistence for first-generation students — I conducted qualitative interviews with eleven college graduates[10] rom elite universities.[11] y goal was to become aware of *how* graduates

---

3. E. C. Warburton et al., U.S. Department of Education, Bridging the Gap: Academic Preparation and Postsecondary Success of First-Generation Students (2001).

4. A. F. Cabrera et al., *College Persistence: Structural Equations Modeling Test of an Integrated Model of Student Retention.*, 64 Journal of Higher Education 123–39 (1993).

5. S. Dynarski, Harvard University & National Bureau of Economic Research, Building the Stock of College-Educated Labor (2005); A. Dohm, *Gauging the Labor Force Effects of Retiring Baby-Boomers.* Monthly Labor Review (2000).

6. Y. Lin & W. P. Vogt, *supra* note 1; *Occupational Outcomes for Students Earning Two-Year College Degrees: Income, Status, and Equity,* 67 Journal of Higher Education 446–75 (1996); Leslie & Brinkman, *supra* note 1.

7. Institutional match is defined by Tinto as a match between a student's motivation and the institution's academic and social characteristics.

8. 8. J. P. Bean, *Dropouts and Turnover: The Synthesis of a Causal Model of Student Attrition,* 12 Research in Higher Education 155–87 (1980); A. F Cabrera et al, *College persistence: Structural Equations Modeling Test of an Integrated Model of Student Retention,* 64 Journal of Higher Education 123–39 (1993).

9. V. Tinto, *Dropout from Higher Education: A Theoretical Synthesis of Recent Research,* 45 Review of Educational Research 89–127 (1975).

10. Recent college graduates represent graduates of classes 1995 to 2006.

11. Elite institutions are defined based on multiple sources. *US News and World Report* served as a guide for determining elite status. *Barron's Guide to the Most Competitive Colleges* (2005), another source of determining elite status, measures schools by most selective, highly selective, very selective, and less and nonselective. Another source of determining elite status, Dale and Krueger, measures schools via top twenty-five "gotta get in at this moment" as elite, the second echelon of elite status as may be only slightly less good than the "original" elites, and the third echelon as many other schools

understand their families' and social class roles in their success and persistence. The purpose of this study is to determine how first-generation students successfully graduate college at elite institutions and what factors contributed to their college persistence that can be applied to other students who are historically under-represented at elite schools.

Investigating elite colleges is very significant because first-generation students can benefit largely from increased accessibility to important social networks there. Accessibility can contribute positively to future economic opportunities as well as additional monetary value placed on a degree received from an elite school. The choice of elite institutions is based on its historically highly selective nature and current demographics of serving mostly upper SES students.[12] This environment creates challenges for first-generation students who do not reflect these ideals or social class. I chose college graduates as opposed to current college students because they have, in fact, persisted, and I wanted to examine the factors that contributed to their successful completion. I framed my study around one central question: *how do first-generation college graduates understand the role of their family and family's social class in their college persistence at an elite institution?*

Qualitative Research Design

Given, this apparent gap in persistence research focusing on first-generation students, the best way to answer my question is through a qualitative research design based on in-depth interviews of participants (the average interview lasted one and a half hours). I collected data for this study from February 2006 until March 2006, interviewing a total of eleven people. The people I interviewed consisted of mostly women (nine out of eleven), reflective of recent trends of women college attendance surpassing their male counterparts. Nearly half of the participants are of black descent (five out of eleven), and the largest group attended UC Berkeley (four out of eleven).

> **Racial Breakdown**: black (5); Latino (2); white (2); Asian (1); mixed descent, Mexican and black (1).

> **Institution Breakdown:** University of California at Berkeley (Cal) (4); Cornell (2); Barnard (1); Sarah Lawrence (1); Grinnell (1); Dartmouth (1); New York University (NYU) (1).

For all the participants, family backgrounds were reflective of a two-parent home, either traditional mother and father or a mother and grandmother. Three participants were either immigrants themselves or had parents who immigrated to the United States. Many participants had only one sibling (six out eleven), and most were the eldest or acting as the eldest (eight out of eleven). Almost all the participants were raised with religion; four reported a strong presence of religion in their lives in their childhood and translating to their adult lives. The participants' ages ranged from twenty-two to thirty-one. Many of

---

that may lack the *je ne sais quoi* of the top elite schools but are estimable. S. Dale & A. Krueger, *Estimating the Payoff to Attending A More Selective College: An Application of Selection on Observables and Unobservables.*, 117 QUARTERLY JOURNAL OF ECONOMICS 1491–527 (2002). Last, Dominic Brewer and Ronald Ehrenberg (1996) breakdown elite status of schools by Top Private, Middle Private, Top Public, and Middle Public. {AU: please provide full title of Brewer & Ehrenberg reference.]

12. ANNETTE LAREAU, UNEQUAL CHILDHOODS: CLASS, RACE, AND FAMILY (2003); J. KARABEL, THE CHOSEN: THE HIDDEN HISTORY OF ADMISSION AND EXCLUSION AT HARVARD, YALE, AND PRINCETON (2005).

them attended elite postsecondary institutions for graduate study, such as Columbia Law, Harvard Law, University of Pennsylvania Law, Teachers College at Columbia University, and Georgetown University.

Welcome to the Two Worlds Concept

A major finding from my research is that many of the individuals I interviewed starkly described their familial/home lives as one particular sphere or world and their lives at the educational institutions as a separate world. I will explain the qualities of both the "old world"—the families and home communities—and the "new world"—the college environment. This is in no way a comparison of the two worlds; instead, it is an explanation of a tension that is unique to first-generation students, and learning how these students reconcile these tensions can assist with other students' persistence to graduation. Unlike other research, the old and new worlds that I explain as my major finding is a new concept in that it transcends race and affects all first-generation students based primarily on class effects. The concept of balancing two worlds has been presented within literature, particularly international literature that involves issues of race and experiences of people of color, people of mixed descent, and children of immigrants.[13] In addition, U.S. history reveals a legacy of navigating worlds revolving around race, class, and the immigrant experience. Through understanding the complexities of the old and new worlds and the challenges each presents for first-generation students, we can better understand the tensions between these worlds and how the students must move between them.

First, the concept of freedom permeates both worlds. The participants talked about the freedom they had within their family unit and increased autonomy, particularly in decision making in activities. This was reflected in the freedom to pursue a postsecondary education free from parental constraints. Furthermore, the choice of college major within the new-found freedom provided them with a freedom in their lives and within their professions unlike the experience of their families. This freedom, however, created challenges for the students because they had to determine on for themselves how to prepare and apply to college, as well as how to be successful within the college environment. By illuminating the challenges the students have faced while navigating the new world and maintaining connections with the old, I expose how these eleven students reconciled these differences and persisted successfully through the elite college experience.

Another characteristic existing within both worlds was the participants' strong sense of self and identity that assisted them through the process of life in both the old and new worlds and ultimately college persistence. The road to successful college persistence is indicative of the participants' strong sense of self, values of hard work, having pride in self, and never giving up, all of which were transmitted primarily through their family units and experience. This strong identity enabled them to gain admittance to elite institutions,

---

13. E. G. Karpinski, *Negotiating the Self: Eva Hoffman's Lost in Translation and the Question of Immigrant Autobiography,* 28 Canadian Ethnic Studies 127–35 (1996); N. Karakayali, *Metamorphoses of the Stranger: Jews in Europe, Polish Peasants in America, and Turks in Germany,* 28–29 New Perspectives on Turkey, 37–59 (2003); L. Soysal, *Diversity of Experience, Experience of Diversity: Turkish Migrant Youth Culture in Berlin,* 13 Cultural Dynamics 5–28 (2001); Negotiating Identities: Essays on Immigration and Culture in Present-Day Europe (A. Alund & R. Granqvist eds., 1995); S. C. Berrol, Growing Up American: Immigrant Children in America Then and Now (1995); W. Proefridt, *The Education of Eva Hoffman,* 18 Journal of Ethnic Studies, 123–34 (1991).

to be the first in their families to have this experience, and in the end assisted them in their successful college persistence.

Old World

Parent Involvement: A Different Perspective, More Complex than Previously Thought

Overall, most participants had somewhat to very strong family relationships with not only their immediate but also their extended families, common of most "working-class" families.[14] At one point, a grandparent served as an additional caretaker for ten out of eleven participants; many of the grandparents lived with the participants during part of their childhood. All participants reported a two-parent household; either the participants had an intact family[15] or a grandmother who served as a parent as well, replacing the role of the father. In addition, the extended family served as a part of the immediate family, with a strong involvement in the participants' lives.

Largely there was an emphasis on education, its importance, and what future possibilities the participant would have access to because of pursuing college. This is particularly important because most research has long argued that the level of parental involvement in education occurs at a lesser rate within homes of lower SES and within families where parents have less formal education.[16] It is imperative to understand that within the participants' childhood homes, education was ultimately valued, encouraged, and supported primarily through moral support in ways previous literature (such as Lareau and Rothstein) ultimately underestimated.

The value of education was exhibited in many ways, with parents taking an active role in making sure their child was appropriately placed within programs and schools. Similar to other literature findings, active parental involvement does make a difference in a child's education. Parents petitioned to have their children appropriately placed out of English as second language into gifted programs and charter and magnet schools. Furthermore, many participants discussed their parents' active role in the schools they attended mainly when the neighborhood schools were unsatisfactory and parents took action by registering for another school.

Live Our Dream: Heavy Burden and Inspiration Both Leading to Persistence

The discussion of college in the family was primarily the focus when study participants told stories of regrets and missed opportunities of their family members, parents

---

14. Annette Lareau, Home advantage: Social Class and Parental Intervention in Elementary Education (1989); M. D. Lanham et al., Unequal Childhoods: Class, Race, and Family (2003).

15. An intact family refers here to a two-parent household.

16. Lareau, *supra* note 15; Lanham et al., *supra* note 15; R. Rothstein, Class and Schools: Using Social, Economic, and Educational Reform to Close the Black/White Achievement Gap (2004).

and grandparents, coupled with the emphasis on the college endeavor as part of their family's collective dream. Some participants reported one or more parent(s) attending some college, ranging from one to three years (five out of eleven). The heavy burden originated from many of the lessons learned from family members of their personal regrets of attending but not completing college. These regrets included opting for marriage or children as opposed to schooling, not being able to go to college because of financial constraints due to social class effects, and the reality of immigration and the sacrifices made to come to America. The focus on both family regrets and attending college as the family dream simultaneously occurs while one or more parent is making sacrifices of both time and personal fulfillment through their occupation(s). These occurrences contribute to the concept of the heavy burden and inspiration. There is a duality to this concept because it is *both* a burden and an inspiration to these participants.

More than one participant actually used the words "heavy burden," enlightening me to a name for the phenomenon occurring within first-generation students leading to both motivation and persistence through college. Jacqueline,[17] a Latina child of immigrants who grew up in Queens and attended Cornell University, discussed how she became aware of her motivation to continue her studies: "It got to the point I was not only doing it for me, I (was) doing this for my family, my brother so he (could) see what possibilities are there for him."

There is a strong responsibility to aspire to the family dream and complete college not only for one's parents but for those to follow. The value of hard work that the participants experienced in their upbringing resonated with them and strengthened their ability to pursue postsecondary education. All participants discussed having a responsibility to a younger generation, including siblings and cousins, to assist in them attending college, from providing information to giving moral and financial support.

Lessons Learned, Motivation Outside of Self

Having a motivation outside of oneself and a responsibility to others were both strong factors assisting these first-generation students in persistence through college. The participants could also have benefited from the feeling that they were not alone in attaining their goals because their families were behind them. Janneh, who attended University of California at Berkeley (Cal), a black female whose mother and grandmother raised her in a diverse suburb of Los Angeles, remembers how her mother quitting school affected her: "It actually pushed me more to go to college. It was always the family dream, not only for my mother but my grandmother, to have one of us finish and go to college. It was definitely a huge motivating factor for me." As shown in previous research, the encouragement of friends and family was one of the strongest predictors affecting students' intent to persist.[18] Given the attrition among first-generation students occurring in postsecondary at a higher rate than any other groups, motivation factors among those who complete is imperative to understand. Motivation assists with entrance into the college environment; however, it is not the only component for the students to successfully persist through college.

The stories of their families and the importance of the family dream resonated with all of the participants and instilled the responsibility to pursue the dream of college (both attending and graduating). All participants attended elite institutions, which could have

---

17. All participants' names have been changed to protect anonymity.
18. Cabrera, *supra* note 4, at 123–39.

contributed to their successful persistence; not only did they have the family dream as an incentive, they were also going to obtain a degree from an elite university that no doubt would positively affect their future options.[19] Additionally, given the elite environment, the interventions to assist to persistence could have been more readily available if needed, as opposed to such opportunities in a public state school.

Most of the participants (nine out of eleven) were first-borns, or inherited the role of first-born in their families, which could have attributed to resonation of this ideal as well. The strongest difference in academic grades between siblings is based on birth order, not gender, with older siblings doing better than younger siblings in school.[20] Older siblings tend to excel in school regardless of SES, whereas younger siblings are more affected by their family's economic class level.[21]

The Motivation to Go Is Not "Who You Will Be": Freedom Strengthens Motivation, but Obstacles Remain

Although this pressure of college completion and responsibility for one's entire family can be overwhelming, other students of a higher social class or from more formally educated parents often face parental expectations regarding which college to attend or which profession to enter. The participants did not experience the affects of the overinvolved parent dictating what they will do in their lives, a characteristic consistent with Lareau's[22] findings regarding parent involvement and the upper and middle classes. Education is seen as freedom in and of itself.

This freedom is somewhat similar to the freedom they were provided in their childhoods, such as decisions over their schoolwork and activities. The freedom contributed to an increase in ownership over their educations, assisting their persistence. Participants recognized this difference among their parents as opposed to peers and had an appreciation for this freedom. Christina, a white female who grew up in a predominately white working-class community in Vestal, New York, with her father, mother, and sister, explains the freedom her parents allowed her in her educational choices attending college: "I think they were happy [about my attending college], but I think I had the impression it was my [choice], if I wanted to do it. I never felt pressured." Thus, this sense of ownership over their decisions, combined with a sense of familial burden and inspiration, led most participants to feel that they were highly driven by both intrinsic and extrinsic motivations.

Difficulty Understanding My Experience: No One to Help Me Navigate This World

Tanisha, a black female raised by her mother and her extended family, grew up in Crown Heights, New York, and attended New York University; she explained, "It helps you

---

19. Lareau, *supra* note 13; Karabel, *supra* note 13; Dale & Krueger, *supra* note 12.

20. J. Teachman, *Gender of Siblings, Cognitive Achievement, and Academic Performance: Familial and Nonfamilial Influences on Children,* 59 Journal of Marriage and the Family 363–74 (1996).

21. *Id.*

22. Lareau, *supra* note 13.

when your parents had already gone to college, because you don't think about school, it is second nature. You are expected to go, if that is not your life, it is sort of harder to conceptualize going through it. I definitely think there are exceptions to the rule, including myself." Family members' attendance alleviates the anxiety and burden placed on the participant to envision being able to go and persist through college successfully, as well as the burden of understanding the actual steps involved in the process. First-generation students essentially make their own way and lack the permanence that others attain.

This struggle, being able to relate to family in this way, is a unique experience for first-generation students, given they are the first in the family to attend college. Janneh explains the frustration:

> There came a time when I would call about what I was going through and experiencing at Cal, and they could not understand, it wasn't from a lack of want, but a lack of experience. They couldn't fathom what I was going through because they had never been there themselves. For me it was frustrating because they couldn't be what I needed them to be for me, because they didn't know what I was going through.

It was particularly complex for study participants during times of academic stress, such as midterms and finals; when students called home to express their feelings and elicit advice, they usually did not receive the support. This is not to underestimate the support families provided to the participants because there was strong moral support and sentiments, such as "you can do it" and "we believe in you." Consistently with findings reported in the literature,[23] a participant's family's ability to support the student and acknowledge the importance of earning the degree affects persistence. The ability to relate with family members, a key point, was lacking in a way that made it difficult for the participants to feel supported and share the challenges of college.

Entering the New World of College: Opening the Door to New Opportunities, but Do I Belong Here?

All participants believed college opened up a new world to them and increased opportunities and access. Many felt for the first time in their lives that they could be or do anything. This entrance into the new world is not unique to first-generation students but occurs for all incoming freshman; however, the entrance into the new world is distinctive for first-generation students.

Similar to Lareau's[24] findings for working-class families, many students were given freedom to choose activities; however, it was within a limited scope. This new freedom provided the students with a real feeling of independence to make their own choices without the confines of social class, which is a unique experience for first-generation students. The access to this new world provided the students with not only access to information but also entry to the professional world with key social and professional networks. This

---

23. A. Nora, *The Depiction of Significant Other in Tinto's "Rites of Passage": A Reconceptualization of the Influence of Family and Community in the Persistence Process*, 3 Journal of College Student Retention: Research, Theory & Practice 41–56 (2001–2002).

24. Lareau, *supra* note 13.

new world provided first-generation students opportunities to a world that many of the families would not have been able to provide.

Entrance to the New World: An Avenue to Transcend Social Class: Freedom to Choose Profession

Entrance into this new world of academia was for many a conscious and unconscious departure from their former world of family, particularly the family's social class, home community, and the economic limitations that they both held. This is not only a desire for upward mobility; it is much more complicated than attaining a higher social class. Instead, it is a desire for freedom to choose one's profession and the freedom to enjoy life without the same economic limitations and strains one's parents may have experienced. For almost all the participants, a college education was the only way to gain access to a professional and academically focused social world that many of their family members did not have a chance to be a part of before.

Janneh remembers, "I think my experiences at Cal opened me up to all that I could do. My family is in Azusa,[25] they have been there since 1962. My grandmother has the same number (telephone) since 1962, my mom and my aunt live across the street from her; that is where they are going to be. I realized I don't have to be in just Azusa."

College provided participants an avenue to depart from their home community to seek other opportunities that existed for them. Another participant, Nicole, a white women who grew up in a working-class community in Long Island with her father, mother, and sister and attended Sarah Lawrence,[26] realized her departure from her former world was much more an intentional escape. "I think underlying, I always knew it was my out, and it was a way to gain freedom that no one had in our family. It was a way to be an individual to figure out what I loved and cared about. I think in my family it hasn't happened for many people," she said. This is not to say the departure is the participants' denial or shame concerning their families, their social class, or their parents' professions; instead, it is an entrance into a world that all of their families desired for them.

New World Exposure: Expansion of Aspirations

The new culture of academia was also an introduction to a different academic culture that many of the participants had either consciously or unconsciously longed for before attending college. The entrance into the new world exposed the participants to a connection to academia and assisted in expanding their aspirations. Many described themselves as young intellectuals, indicating that a strong part of their identities revolves around books, school, education, and feeling safe or at home within the realm of education. One male participant, Will, a graduate of Dartmouth and an immigrant who grew up in a predominately Asian suburb in southern California with his father, mother, and brother—his parents are currently separated—describes his experience: "Going to college felt like

---

25. The name of the participant's hometown has been changed to protect anonymity.

26. Nicole attended Sarah Lawrence, considered tier one (in the top fifty schools) according to *US World News and Report.*

I entered a new world, a new way of people talking, learning [that] people read certain newspapers. It felt like I was being introduced to and connected to American society in ways that I had not before." He exposes the isolation from elite, academic society he felt during his childhood.

Jacqueline explains her college experience: "It has changed my aspirations, I would [have] never thought I would be capable to go on to a doctorate, aspire to it, if I had not had this [college] experience." Without entrance into this new world, life aspirations would not have been the same for these students; I argue that this is particularly important for firs-generation students because they do not have the ability to rely on their families' capital, both financial and social, in helping them transition into the workforce.

The participants' ownership of their education and their own lives might surpass that of their more affluent peers, given their freedom in pursuing college. This freedom is closely related to the value of hard work, pursuing goals, and never giving up—values transmitted by one or more parent or grandparent. Nicole explains the difference in her classmates' dedication based on first-generation and social class distinctions:

> It was different, it was easier because those students knew that it didn't matter if they excelled academically or not because they would have a place to go (professionally). We knew we had to prove ourselves. There are no connections. There is no daddy to get me a job, there isn't a network, I was going to prove myself here, and go out and make something or I was going to go home to Long Island.

Many participants expressed the conviction that one of the main reasons for their persistence is the alternative of returning home, which would not offer as many professional opportunities if they were not to complete their undergraduate educations. The feeling of not having financial and job security was exacerbated by the pressure of the family dream and the fear of disappointing their families if they did not complete college. Essentially, this drove them to strive harder than the average student.

This empowerment also provided a sense of purpose for participants in their future aspirations and allowed them to negotiate between the two worlds of their lives. Nicole remembers, "For the first time I could reconcile going to college and my personal background. For me it was a way to find meaning in work in what I was doing. I could come home and say [that] what I am doing with that is fighting for my family and all people who are struggling in the class system."

Can I Make It in This New World and Why Do I Have to Justify My Presence Within It to Others?

The majority of the participants (eight out of eleven) initially questioned their attendance at their colleges—and aspects of separation, transition, and incorporation phases.[27] Additionally, there is a direct relationship between parents' influence on the student's college aspiration and persistence.[28] Those who experienced support from family and friends

---

27. Nora, *supra* note 24; Nora & Lang, *Pre-College Psychosocial Factors Related to Persistence,* AIR Annual Forum (2001).

28. Nora, *supra* note 24, at 41–56; Nora & Lang, *supra* note 28.

have an easier transition to college and incorporation into the college environment.[29] These phases were exacerbated for participants because they experienced challenges to fitting into the new world both academically and socially because of race and class (or both). Fitting into a new world, however, was not completely new for all the participants. Many, particularly students of color, had been navigating the family and cultural worlds and the realm of school for many years. Additionally, this new world was a struggle across racial lines, distinctive to first-generation students.

Academic Realms: Within the College Environment: Questioning of Self

The feelings participants chose to express about their college experiences are imperative in understanding the psyche of first-generation students at elite institutions in their first year (if not years) at college. Participants used phrases such as "being scared out of my mind," "how long is this ride going to last?" and "when are they going to realize I am not smart enough to be here?" These expressions expose the uncertainty the students felt in their future at their institutions, an uncertainty embedded in being the first in their families to attend college, particularly an elite university that predominately serves white and economically privileged students. These feelings exemplify the lack of permanence the students felt, in part because they do not have the security of following in a family member's footsteps. They had to lead the way on their own, while experiencing intense feelings of being alone within the academic setting. This sense of not belonging is very strong and could be a contributing factor for the high attrition rate for first-generation students. Research[30] illuminates this challenge: students are highly affected by the "personal and social fit" persisting within the institution. A student's decision to re-enroll is established if he or she feels personally accepted at the college. Many participants felt that they did not belong in the elite institutions, as if they were accepted into this new academic world by mistake.

Will explains his feelings regarding the background of his peers in his undergraduate tenure at Dartmouth, culminating at Harvard Law: "It became complicated, it is strange going to college and yet all these people have gone to all these prep schools and have lineage years and years of upper degrees, elite colleges, if not PhDs." The feeling of academic inadequacy relative to their college peers was not exclusively about education; rather, it included a sense that these first-generation students did not compare to peers' backgrounds, making it hard to compete with them in school. These feelings of being an "outsider" were felt by a majority of the participants across racial lines.

Academic Realms: Questioning Academic Competitiveness in the Classroom: Less Academic Preparedness

Most of the students' feelings of being less academically competent compared to their peers originated from academic struggles. For instance, Felicia, a Barnard graduate of

---

29. Nora, *supra* note 24, at 41–56.
30. Nora, *supra* note 24, at 41–56.

black and Mexican descent and one of two participants who were raised their mothers and grandmothers, explained she felt other students were smarter than her because they knew literary references made by the professor. Similar to findings in the previous research conducted by Horn and Kojaku[31] and by Nora and Kojaku and Warburton, Bugarin, and Nunez,[32] the participants who were less prepared academically were more sensitive to attrition. Students struggled academically, predominantly because they felt their previous education (K–12) insufficiently prepared them for college. However, most did not feel this way until they arrived at the elite institution. Most participants (ten out of eleven) attended schools were they were not in the minority either racially or socioeconomically.

It was particularly difficult because all of the students' intelligence was a strong aspect of their identities. One participant, Christina, recalls lack of preparedness based on her high school experience: "I didn't have to work that hard because I didn't have to try [in high school]. I could pass by looking over three pages, in college you have to read five to seven books and you can't go in there — I think without that level of preparedness — I had to learn." The lack of preparedness of the students could be attributed to less rigorous schools they attended as opposed to their counterparts who attended mostly private and some preparatory schools.

Academic Realms: Academia: Not Always Welcoming

The feelings of being unprepared academically, discussed earlier, were internally occurring within the participants. Other assessments occurring externally from people in positions of authority and peers increased the students' feelings of being outsiders in the new world of academia. These experiences affected the students' ability to navigate academically and socially. Some participants reported negative interactions with teachers' assistants; alternatively, no participants reported this negative interaction with professors.[33] This type of negative interaction is particularly troubling because a student's commitment to persist increases when he or she believes the faculty and staff care, which is exhibited by their supportive words.[34] Additionally, research highlights the apprehension students of color feel in approaching staff when they feel unaccepted on campus.[35]

The two examples of negative interactions with teachers' assistants (TAs) occurred at the same university, UC Berkeley, to two black women participants. Janneh explained her experience with a TA who recommended she reconsider taking a class and changing her major after reading the first draft of her paper for a literature class. Janneh remembered, "I went to her and told her my ideas and she saw what I wrote, and she looked at it and said to me 'I am not really sure how it is that you got into Berkeley but your writ-

---

31. L. Horn & L. K. Kojaku, U.S. Dep't of Educ., High School Academic Curriculum and the Persistence Path Through College: Persistence and Transfer Behavior of Undergraduates 3 Years After Entering 4-Year Institutions (2001).

32. E. C. Warburton et al., U.S. Department of Education. Bridging the Gap: Academic Preparation and Postsecondary Success of First-Generation Students (2001).

33. Participants' higher education institution size varied; for instance, students at smaller institutions had more accessibility to direct contact with professors, which could affect their interactions with professors, both positively and negatively.

34. Nora, *supra* note 24, at 41–56.

35. A.Cabrera et al, *Campus Racial Climate and the Adjustment of Students to College: A Comparison Between White Students and African-American Students.* 70 Journal of Higher Education 134–60 (1999).

ing skills are far below par, I don't anticipate you graduating from this school in a degree in English, so I would just drop this class because I don't think you are going to make it.'"

This experience highlights this individual's lack of experience in dealing with students different from herself. This is not only my interpretation; Janneh herself felt this: "I honestly can say it largely was racial, being a black student at Cal was one of the most difficult things that anyone could do. I think that by me being a black student in the English department, no less. It was like automatic defeat, she had probably seen it a hundred times. She felt she was giving it to me real, to save me some time, and money." Regardless of the rationale behind this behavior, research has consistently shown that university staff interactions affect persistence,[36] and it is noteworthy that this did not negatively affect Janneh. This type of experience can be one of the many factors affecting attrition.

Instead, with the help of a friend from her social network, Janneh excelled beyond this bleak prediction. The most valuable piece of this story is that she not only passed the class, she accomplished all the endeavors the TA told her she could not accomplish, graduating with a degree in English in a timely manner. Today, she is a published author. In understanding how she accomplished these goals and persisted against adversity, she explained that she was very discouraged and about to quit school after this experience, but support from someone in her social network enabled her to continue on.

> She was like "you are one of six black people at this school, you can't quit, you can't, you have something to prove to yourself and your family, they accepted you here—there is a reason that you are here. You can't give you up, just take a C in the class, you came here for a reason to get a degree, get your degree." From that moment on it took me out of the competition that was Cal, for me I did take a C in that class, for me it was a proud because, um, I passed the class, and she told me I couldn't for that moment on, I was in it for myself. I wound up getting my degree in English in two years. Everything she said I wasn't going to do, I wound up doing it. It was a proud moment for me.

In addition to having a supportive network, this was not Janneh's first challenge, and many other participants shared the challenge. They were well equipped to handle these challenges given past experiences with adversity, their ability to work hard, and the strong incentive to complete college.

Social Realms: Informal Interactions with Peers, Snubbed in Elite Liberal Settings: Justify Our Existence

Within the social realm of interacting with peers, there seemed to be a need for justification to peers for the students' presence at the elite school, especially for students of color. I argue that the two white female study participants, despite the internal and external struggles, were able to blend in with the predominant makeup of the elite institutions; the frequency of verbal justification of belonging in the institution was minimal.

Students of color shared experiences that were very telling as to how others were trying to make sense of them as their peers. Most participants were surprised by the reac-

---

36. Nora, *supra* note 24, at 41–56.

tion from peers because they felt they were attending elite schools where everyone should be intelligent, critical thinkers not subscribing to racial stereotypes.

One participant, Derrick, a black male raised in a large single-parent family and the youngest of five children who attended Grinnell College, describes such an experience:

> We are at a liberal arts school, and people would come up to me, "are you on the football team?" It made me realize, I am not going to be that part of the school [athletics]. The whole idea, "did you come in [to college] because of affirmative action?" I think it was interesting, people always have to address those issues. I actually transferred here with a [GPA of] 3.5. Why did I need to affirm, validate my position when no one else does? It was hard to constantly having to justify.

Due to the expectations of their peers based on racial stereotypes, many participants went out of their way to avoid situations such as playing on sports teams, where they would confronted with this stereotype. The challenge of justifying one's existence can be one of the factors leading to attrition. An unintended consequence of this justification became participants' sense of self, and the desire to prove themselves to others was strengthened.

A similar experience was described by Amanda, a first-generation El Salvadorian raised by her father and mother in south central Los Angeles who attended UC Berkeley. She remembered, "'Do you speak Mexican?' was one of the questions—it is not even a language and I am not even Mexican to begin with. Wow, I thought people who came to college were smart but obviously they aren't. You know everyone throwing around their numbers around, 'what is your SAT score?' You don't need to know, I am here right."

Consistent with findings in other research, prejudice and discrimination were unique psychological stressors affecting minorities, intensifying feelings of not belonging and affecting performance and persistence.[37] Still, all participants were able to persist through these stressors successfully. This type of interaction with peers may have strengthened belief in self, and social networks proved key in successful persistence.

The peers who interacted with the participants were not always the anomaly. Some of the participants discussed a volatile racial environment within their colleges and provided examples of incidents of racially based hate crimes and other incidents (e.g., the school newspaper, the *Daily Californian,* writing articles on why black students cannot succeed; "affirmative action bake sales").[38] One school in particular, UC Berkeley, was an institution where students of color, mostly black and Latino, began to attend college at a lower rate than in previous years.[39] Although this is not to generalize the whole college environment for all participants, negative peer interaction can be reflective of the greater college environment at these elite schools.

One white participant explains her isolation within the classroom based primarily on class. Christina describes an instance at Columbia Law School when she admitted that her parents had once been on welfare, and the reaction she experienced from peers was quite negative. "I felt like, wait, should I feel embarrassed? I wasn't embarrassed about it, but I felt like I should be. There has always been a weird dynamic because I came from a different class than my peers, especially at Columbia and Cornell. I don't feel bad about it; it is just how it is."

---

37. Cabrera, *supra* note 36.

38. Affirmative action bake sales are campus bake sales sponsored by conservative groups charging different prices based on race in an effort to expose the "unfairness" of affirmative action.

39. Demographic changes in the student body are based on public policies such as Proposition 209 and those students choosing not to apply, given the change in demographics in the student body.

This type of questioning from peers resulted in participants' striving harder to be successful. This dedication to working hard originated from family values, and I found it assisted the participants' persistence in college and in their professional lives. Tanisha, a graduate of NYU, explained her experience in college, in law school (Penn), and now in her professional life at a law firm:

> I felt like and still do because I am a black woman, I feel I have to work a little bit harder. I can't graduate with a 3.0 [GPA], I have to do better because someone is going to think I am there because someone else isn't, so if you think that, I am also going to prove to you that I deserve to be there, and that is always on my mind even at this job [that] I am on at work on President's Day. How can I work harder in everything I do?

Most of the participants cite hard work as one of the most important values they learned from a close family member or from the most influential persons of their lives and college careers, ultimately having the greatest effect on persistence.

Social Realms, Social Networks: Mirrors Self Assist in Persistence in College, Common Experience Is Imperative

Almost all participants found maintaining a social network and creating connections with students similar to themselves based on class and racial background to be essential factors in their persistence in college to graduation. The necessity for a strong social network has been exposed in previous literature as one of the main factors in successful persistence for all students.[40] Arguably, it is more difficult for first-generation students at elite institutions, where they are in the minority based on class and racial differences. This is particularly important for first-generation students given the intricacies of creating connections with peers when the students are grappling with issues of being an outsider and a minority within an institution.

Amanda explains a social network that benefited her: "Las Hermanas Unidas, Sisters United, it is a female Hispanic organization where a lot of the girls come from similar backgrounds. They are trying to create a network, for support, financial support, and trying to help each other." Social networks for participants served as a place to be understood, to be able to relate to others, and to discuss the challenges they face. Based on common experience, networks supplemented what participants lacked from both their families and most of their peers at college.

Social networks also impacted confidence among participants within the academic environment. Amanda explains how she reached out to social networks comprised of people similar to her, which ultimately positively affected her confidence in the classroom and her college experience: "So it wasn't until the end of my sophomore year, when I actually was speaking up and asking questions and finally accepting that I couldn't do it alone, just because I couldn't do it alone didn't mean I was stupid, I just needed help."

Participants finding avenues to social networks based on racial identity was a more straightforward process because many racially centered organizations were already in place. Some students reported that they founded similar organizations if they were not

---

40. Nora, *supra* note, at 41–56.

sufficient. Nevertheless, the two white female participants found that navigating a social network was more difficult, given that there was not an organization for them to belong to based on racial identity. In addition, there were no class-based or first-generation organizations across racial lines at the participants' universities.[41]

Social Realms, Work: Another Avenue to Social Connections

Social networks ranged in their ability to provide additional social capital required for the participants' entrance to the professional world. Social connections created at work provided this avenue for many participants. Much previous research debates the benefit of working while in college;[42] most students needing to work are from middle and lower SES backgrounds. I found students overwhelmingly stated that work was a benefit because it forced them to balance their time. In fact, some jobs allowed them to study while at work. Most important, either the experience or the connections they made at work increased their personal social capital.

Elizabeth, a black female raised in a diverse suburb of predominately black and white students outside of Sacramento and the eldest of three children raised by her father and mother, describes how a job at the chancellor's office at UC Berkeley assisted her in applying to Hass Business School: "I got to do a few projects because he [the chancellor] was big on giving people projects and challenging them. A project I worked on one of his assistant wrote a letter of recommendation about it for the business school. I really got a lot more out of it than a recommendation from one of the chancellors."

The participants' need to work translated into benefits that they otherwise would not have been available to them. I learned that work connection and connections with professors supplemented the participants' social capital in ways their families could not. Additionally, all participants reported working two or more jobs at one time. The hard work value learned during their childhood was transferred with them to the college environment, increasing their personal success.

Balancing New and Old Worlds: Education Can Create Distance from Families

The participants and the families were not aware of how entrance into the new world of academia would affect their family dynamics. The participants were not free from the

---

41. Based on all eleven participants' knowledge, there were no such organizations at the universities they attended.

42. K. Anderson, *Post-high School Experiences and College Attrition*, 54 SOCIOLOGY OF EDUCATION 1–15 (1981); A. ASTIN, PREVENTING STUDENTS FROM DROPPING OUT (1975); R. Ehrenberg & D. Sherman, *Employment While in College, Academic Achievement, and Post College Outcomes: A Summary of Results*, 11 JOURNAL OF HUMAN RESOURCES 1–23 (1987); A. Kohen et al., *Factors Affecting Individual Persistence Rates in Undergraduate College Programs*, 15 AMERICAN EDUCATIONAL RESEARCH JOURNAL 233–52 (1978); E. Pascarella et al., *Does Work Inhibit Cognitive Development During College?*, 20 EDUCATIONAL EVALUATION AND POLICY ANALYSIS 75–93 (1998).

tensions they experienced within the college environment or within their family unit. This tension of belonging in the most pertinent aspects of the participants' lives can be a factor leading to attrition with first-generation students.

Some participants reported not being able to communicate about politics, race, poverty, and religion the way they could before education had created distance from their family. Both white participants (Christina and Nicole) noted that the feelings of not belonging resulted from the impression felt by their families that the students felt they were superior to everyone else. The other way participants reported distance from their families was difficulty in the families' ability to understand their daily lives in college. Additionally, they lacked their families' support or knowledge to assist in navigating the new world of college.

I Don't Belong, They Don't Understand: Speaking Different Languages

Education has the ability to open new doors of opportunity, but it can also make familiar realms difficult to navigate. For first-generation students, returning home to their former world of family was a complicated process. This is not to underplay the difficulty any college students encounter when returning home. The tension existing within the first-generation home, however, is distinct because it can create distance from family and exacerbates the feelings of not belonging in college or at home—the two vital aspects of the students' lives.

First-generation students must deal with this tension, some more intensely than others. "I think sometimes my family thinks I am too good for anybody. My dad says 'Christina you shouldn't act so smart, you act like you are better than everyone else.' They have never been openly resentful about that. I think subtly that comes into play."

I found returning home and feeling judged by one's family could be a unique stressor, especially when the family has served as a support network throughout one's life. Given these experiences, I can see how the distance created within one's family could be a contributing factor to attrition. Additionally, first-generation students must be able to balance and negotiate the two worlds of their lives to successfully have relationships with their families and successfully continue with their studies.

A common experience among the participants was a transformation in the conversations they had with family members. Given the change in perspective, participants felt their education had created distance in their ability to communicate and a feeling they were creating strain in their home due to these conversations. Brianne explains, "I sometimes felt like coming home just sort of stirring up trouble because I am bringing up all these issues." It is a complicated experience for the participants to feel as if they cannot express themselves completely when returning home. This may not be unique to first-generation students, but the feeling of belonging in neither the college nor the family environment can contribute to attrition. These complexities are a window into the real challenges of first-generation students.

The feelings of tension were not entirely internal; another experience was explicit expression from family members of dismay about the way the participants discussed contentious issues with their families. Tanisha remembers her uncle's reaction to her discussion of the Bible: "I can't believe you are doing this, I can't believe you are talking about this from an academic perspective, this is the Bible, you aren't suppose[d] to look at in this way."

Reconcile Worlds: Embrace Difference

There were multiple isolations occurring for participants within the new world of college and the old world of their families. In spite of all this, the participants were able to persist successfully through undergraduate, and most went on to postsecondary elite institutions. The ability for the participants to successfully reconcile these tensions within the realms of their lives is crucial to understanding their persistence.

Reconciling My Place in College

One of the greatest challenges of being a first-generation student is to reconcile who one is, one's background, and one's place within the new college environment. This is the case not only for first-generation students but for all undergraduates. The challenges for first-generation students are unique in that they are attending an elite institution where they are in the minority, either racially or socioeconomically, compounded with the necessity to make sense of their place in the old world of their family and the new world of college.

In understanding how they overcame this challenge, most participants reported embracing their difference and deciding to seek avenues where they felt most comfortable (usually within social networks of people similar to themselves). The feeling of support from peers proved imperative for all of the participants; most felt they would not have finished college without a social network of people like themselves.

Lessons Learned: Actions to Take

Educators

There are many actions that individuals at all levels of a student's life and education can take to improve college persistence. During students' K–12 education, it is imperative for counselors and teachers to discuss college and the logistics of planning and applying. They should also use techniques to encourage not only applying but persisting as well. Many of the participants relied on social networks and outside interventions to receive this information. Thus, I recommend either strengthening outside interventions—government, privately funded, and university-sponsored—or increase the interventions within the public school system. Within education, given the reaction of many peers to first-generation students, private and preparatory schools do bear some of the responsibility in creating diverse schools and creating critical thinkers who do not subscribe to racial, ethnic, and class assumptions.

Education for families is another essential piece to assist first-generation students through the process of applying, attending, and graduating from college. Given parents' lack of knowledge, education must be provided throughout K–12 education for parents to better support their children through the college application process and attendance, alleviating the distance created in being a first-generation student.

The Family

Families themselves can learn that they can provide effective moral support for their children to attend college by stressing the importance of education in the home and placing value on attending college. The families can also become aware of the challenges the students face while in college and when returning home, to ease the transition for the students. The best ways to transmit this knowledge is through the K–12 school, the universities, and advocacy organizations.

College Institutions

College institutions also bear a significant burden. Given that much of the findings pointed to students feeling as if they did not belong in the institutions—particularly the elite schools—colleges must address this problem. First and foremost, providing programs and additional support for first-generation students across racial lines could be beneficial in creating social networks for all first-generation students. Second, institutions should not tolerate a culture that accepts teacher assistants' and peers' questioning the presence of students who do not reflect the majority population. This is not entirely the fault of the university, but the university should bear partial responsibility for addressing this problem.

Federal and State Government/Legal Field

Federal and state intervention should include programming to assist students in the application process to college and in persistence to graduation. Government agencies should provide additional funding for individual financial aid and for groups on campus supporting first-generation students. Federal or state government should provide matching funds to institutions that set up these types of programs. Congress should expand the Higher Education Act and TRIO and CAMP programs. Lawyers and counsel can create and recommend these types of legislation changes.

15

My Only Ticket to a Better Tomorrow: Immigrant and Refugee Student Determinants and Strategies to Academic Success in American Schools

Jerono Phyllis Rotich*

Although immigrant and refugee children constitute the fastest-growing sector of the American child population, no other American institution has felt the effect of this influx more forcefully than the nation's public school system. Noteworthy is the fact that despite their high-stakes educational goals and their awareness of the relationship between academic achievements and their future success, many are confronted by unprecedented challenges. As they acculturate and integrate into American schools, their academic achievement determinants seem to go beyond language and cultural barriers. It is therefore evident that unless educators and administrators become more aware of their challenges and unless they implement culturally appropriate interventions and strategies across the school system, immigrant and refugee children will continue to face the possibility of being undereducated, underemployed, and unprepared to be productive workers and full-fledged participants in U.S. society. This chapter gives an overview of the trends of at-risk immigrant and refugee students, determinants of academic achievement, and possible strategies that would enhance equal opportunities and educational equity. The determinants are categorized into seven U's, namely: underachievement, unequal educational opportunities, underresourced, undereducated, underinsured, underrepresented, and undocumented.

Immigrant and Refugees in American Schools

Equal opportunities and equity-minded environments in a multicultural, cross-cultural, and the ever diverse America are all an essential springboard to the academic success and a better tomorrow for all students. Over the past decades, America has continued to ex-

---

* Dr. Rotich is an assistant professor at North Carolina Agricultural & Technical State University, in the Human Performance and Leisure Studies Department. She teaches health and wellness, activity courses, pedagogy, and health and safety.

perience a dramatic influx of multiethnic immigrant and refugee youth and children. According to Friedlander (1991), approximately two million school-age immigrants migrated to the United States in the 1980s and over five million entered the U.S. public schools in the 1990s. Friedlander also reported that these children speak over 150 different languages and the majority have difficulty communicating in English. Recent statistics indicate that the immigrant and refugee student population in the United States is over 30 million and has a projected growth of 3.8 percent per year (Friedlander, 1991). Similar statistics from the U.S. Bureau of Census (1998) indicate that out of the total 72.3 million youths under eighteen years in the United States, 2.8 million were immigrants or foreign born. It has also been reported that nearly one in every five youth in American schools today is an immigrant or a refugee (Jensen, 2001).

Guilford County in North Carolina, for exampl,e has consistently continued to witness an increase in numbers of diverse immigrants and refugees (i.e., Africans, Latinos/Hispanic, Montagnards, Vietnamese, Cambodians, and Eastern Europeans, etc.). It has over 50,000 immigrants and refugees and almost 50 percent of these are under the age of thirty (Bailey, 2002). Demographic data indicate that Guilford County and North Carolina are more diverse, both culturally and linguistically, than at any other time since the early decades of this century. It is also important to take note of the fact that North Carolina has a very diverse population of refugees because it has several refugee resettlement agencies. Recognized nationally is the fact that the state of North Carolina houses the largest numbers of Montagnard refugees in the world outside of Vietnam (Kaleidoscope, 2003; Bailey, 2002). Similar statistics from Guilford County Schools indicate that there are over 3,050 students who are from different cultures and ethnicities and speak one of the ninety-seven languages represented at the school other than English. According to the chairman of the school board, immigrant and refugee students continue to increase, and in 2002, Guilford County had 600 more students than 2001. A breakdown of students from one of the local high schools indicates that there are over ninety different countries and twenty different languages represented.

Regardless of where they are, all immigrants and refugees have come and continue to come to the United States with myriad hopes and expectations (Bailey 2002; Balgopal, 2000). They are fleeing poverty and persecution, pursuing athletic or educational glory, and are seeking better and healthier ways of life than that of their countries of origin. Most of them see America as a beacon of hope. The refugees and asylees, for example, are a special category of immigrants who are admitted into the United States because they are fleeing extreme persecution, war, or natural disaster (Bailey, 2002; Balgopal, 2000). Immigrants, on the other hand, are in America voluntarily and are here to seek better ways of life and education, among others. Noteworthy is the fact that some immigrant children, especially those who are in America voluntarily, do not encounter as many challenges, if any, because of their social economic status.

What Is Going Well with Schooling in America

According to Nyaro, a refugee student from Sudan, coming to America is the greatest thing that has happened to her. She emphasized the fact that there is so much peace in her life. She narrated all the horrifying experiences and encounters that she went through after the war broke out in southern Sudan. She described her journey from Sudan all the way to the Kakuma refugee camp in Kenya and finally their long-awaited arrival in America. When asked to describe her schooling experiences in American schools, she said,

American schools are the greatest so far. They bring me to school and take me back home in a big yellow bus every day, give me good food, books and have lots of great things to offer. The schools are so big with lots of buses, students, classrooms, food, computers, books and even their own sports stadium. I just love the big and clean school environment because going to school in my country and village was not fun.

The free access to education in America was an unbelievable surprise and a blessing to all the children and their families. H'Yat, a refugee child from Vietnam, was so excited and was in disbelief at first. She said, "I am was so happy because I did not know how my parents were going to pay my school fees. I worried so much about them, but I am so glad because they do not have to sell buffalos, elephants or cows so that my sisters and I can go to school."

H'Yat explained that for her and her sister to go to school in Vietnam, her parents had to sell their buffalos or elephants to raise money. However, this would not be the case in America. She indicated that she was determined to work hard in school because she wanted to get a good-paying job that would enable her to take care of her aging parents who had worked so hard to sustain her life in the war-torn Vietnam. She ascertained the fact that nothing in life could be compared with their past pains and hardship and emphasized that likewise, nothing in life is as fulfilling as the opportunity to go to school in America.

Having free access to education, numerous facilities (i.e., big buildings with electricity, clean running water, indoor toilets, playground, swimming pools, etc.) and equipment (i.e., computers, own desk, books, lockers, etc.) has motivated most immigrant and refugee students to place greater value on their academic achievement. Most of them came from countries and origins that had limited or no resources for education. Those who went to school in the rural areas prior to coming to America reported that they did not have electricity or running water, among many other basics necessities. They therefore acknowledged the fact that their access to education in America was indeed a lifetime golden opportunity. To most, their education in America is "their only ticket to a better tomorrow, an opportunity to make an upward economic and social mobility and a way out of the vicious circle of poverty."

Naliaka, a refugee student from Rwanda, noted that coming to America is the best thing that has happened in her life. When asked why she felt this way, she said,

> "I do not have to go to the farm, take care of the cattle nor go to the river and forest to search for water and firewood before coming to school, during lunch time and after school. Though I may struggle with language, I think I have everything I need to do well in school here."

Alonzo, an immigrant student from Mexico, indicated that he liked the free food that they always eat at school, the playgrounds and the fact that he did not have to wear uniforms anymore. He said, "I love it because I do not have to wear the same clothes all week. I like the fact that I get to decide what I want to wear every day. I get new clothes, shoes and a new bag back every school year and not just on Christmas."

On the contrary, the students reported that they loved the social freedoms and some of their new roles. They enjoyed the fact that they are in control of most decisions at home (i.e., shopping, balancing checkbooks, driving, and translating and interpretational needs) because they learn English faster than their parents. Due to the immediate and free educational access that is available to all immigrants and refugee children, they end up being the first ones to learn English, and they acculturate into the American culture much faster than their parents. Most students, especially at middle and high school, perceived their schooling in America to be liberating. This, however, did not resonate well with most immigrant and refugee parents. Those who could not speak and write English were devastated because of the reality of coming to America. They indicated that though they sincerely appreciate the fact that they are in America, they are unhappy because it has literally robbed them of their parenting responsibilities. One parent narrated a very unfortunate incident where his son attempted to kick him and his wife out of their apartment. He explained that because of his language limitations and transportation challenges, it was difficult for him and his wife to get a job that would enable them to provide for their family as well as pay the bills. As a result, their two high school sons were forced to work after school and during weekends so as to sustain the family.

Because this situation caused the family to be totally dependent on their children, they had limited control over their children's activities. Mr. Aloung said that he was in shock and disbelief when his two older sons asked him and his wife to leave the apartment because they were always questioning their children's activities and behaviors.

My older son came home drunk one evening and started screaming at me saying,"Dad I am fed up with your rules in this house. I am tired of you telling us who we should bring to the house, when we should be home and what we should do or not do yet you do not pay or provide anything in this house. Dad, get it right, this is America, and because we are paying all the bills and therefore I suggest that if you cannot live with this, then I am sorry but you and your wife might want to move out because we are not the little boys that you knew back home anymore."

Though Mr. Aloung was in shock and almost ended up in the emergency room, it is especially unfortunate because this kind of defiant behavior is becoming more prevalent over time. Additionally, it is important to take note of the fact that an experience like Mr. Aloung's further curtails parental participation in the education of their children.

The immigrant and refugee students also loved the fact that it was illegal to spank kids at school and at home. Mariana, a refugee student from Haiti had this to say, "No more spankings! I cannot imagine a day without a beating from my teacher or Parents. I love it because all they do is put me in a time out corner."

Though it is evident that though most immigrant and refugee children have great attitudes and are motivated to achieve highly in education, most of them have not experienced significant success due to the following determinants.

Underachievement

Language and culture has played a pivotal and instrumental role in determining the academic achievements of the immigrant and refugee child in America. English language proficiency, which is a key indicator of successful acculturation and academic achievement, has been the most formidable obstacle (Balgolpal, 2000). Most immigrant and refugee children have limited English proficiency skills; therefore, they have not done as well as they would have liked to do in academics. They have struggled in most academic areas and have been made the scapegoat for low test scores in some schools.

Their ability to learn English is further limited because most of them live in linguistically isolated households. It has also been pointed out that most of them are poor, have poor health, have high school dropout rates, are over age for their grade levels, have low rates of participation in postsecondary education, are from low-income families, and give more priority to work (Portes & Rumbant, 1996). Because of the power of "word of mouth," the financial strains, and the fears of settling in a new land, most immigrants and refugees tend to gravitate toward areas and neighborhoods that have people who "look like them" and "speak like them." Pertinent to this barrier is the fact that they come from countries where English is not commonly spoken and from families and neighborhoods where English is not the main language of communication. This makes it difficult to practice English after school or during nonschool hours.

Limited time allocated to learning English and the limited number of English as second language teachers is another determinant of their academic success. The students elaborated on their struggles, and they pointed out the fact that they wished they had more English teachers and more time to practice reading and writing during and out of class hours. They indicated that most of their parents worked two or three jobs because of the financial shortcomings. Though some reported that their parents were home, they lamented that their parents did not help them because they did not have the ability to read or write English. This limited exposure, therefore, makes it harder for the children to speak up in class, participate in class discussions, and do assignments. This inability to communicate ideas and feelings confidently has been overwhelming and has resulted in confusion, frustration, anger, and feelings of alienation among most immigrant and refugee students. One high school student pointed out that "It is a no wonder we are always targeted as potential recruits for gangs."

Roxana, an immigrant student from Mexico, had this to say about her English language experience in the American classroom. She noted that

> coming to school and being laughed at because of incorrect English, and always being teased because of my heavy accent has been the most painful thing I had ever experienced in America. I hated myself and my parents for bringing me to America to suffer.

Experiences like Roxana's further complicate their educational challenges and makes it less likely for them to participate in academic or any extracurricular programs that are offered before or after school.

The English language barrier is further exacerbated by test-driven assessment and curricula that are prevalent in American schools. This pressure tends to limit the time that should be devoted to the specific needs of the at-risk immigrant and refugee students. They ascertained that though they received English language classes, the time allocated to them is not sufficient to enable them to compete on the same level as their American peers. However, anecdotal reports indicate that though most programs have made tremendous efforts to hire interpreters and to have most documents translated into various languages, most languages (with the exception) of Spanish have not been translated. It is also important to note that some immigrants and refugees are illiterate even in their own languages. Another challenge with translating documents is that among the different communities, language terminologies differ even if individuals are from the same country.

The converse, however, is a difficult reality to most parents. Anecdotal evidence indicates that though these children may struggle to learn the language, the moment they learn it, they fall in love with it so much that they shy away from their parents' ethnic language. They lose their home language and culture because they are eager to become Americanized. It is therefore evident that because of the language limitations, immigrant and refugee students have a high probability of not receiving sufficient education to enable them to become independent, successful, and productive adults.

Anecdotal reports from agencies that work with immigrants and refugees in Guilford County, just like other agencies across the country, have alluded to the notion that cultural differences are another major determinant of acculturation and academic success among students. It is evident that as the children acculturate and integrate into their new school environment, they are confronted by two different cultures (Bailey, 2002). This often puts them at a crossroads because they struggle to balance the two cultures, which seem to be on two extreme ends. They leave behind familiar language, culture, role models, community, and a social system and are forced to adjust to totally new ways of life. In addition to the school environment, the students must balance the value systems of their native culture, ever present at home, with those of the dominant peer culture, which prevail at school. Once again, these pressures and the time devoted to balancing them jeopardizes the time and effort that is devoted to their academics.

The cultural conflict between the students, especially teenagers, seems to affect academic achievement levels. Over time, immigrant youth reject the traditions of their parents and try to adopt the practices and cultures of their new American peers. Most immigrant and refugee parents are concerned and fearful because they feel as though they are losing control over their children. All these fears, conflicts, and limitations keep many immigrant and refugee children from making education a priority.

Adolescent youth in particular are very quick to conform to the peer pressure. Most of them indicated that they were so torn that they resorted to lying to their family members as way of coping with pressures and stress. Zenaibu, a Muslim student who has been in the United States for two years, reported that she was eager to be Americanized. She pointed out, however, that American and Muslim cultures were two extremes and that the only way to cope with this culture shock was to adopt a "dual identity." She had this to say:

> The pressure to conform was too much and I could not take it anymore so I decided to lie to my parents and to my Muslim culture. I would leave home and get on the bus dressed as a Muslim, but changed to "American" clothes as soon as I got to school. I would go straight to the bathroom, where I would put on tight jeans, tight top and makeup because I wanted to fit in the American youth culture. I would then change back to my Muslim regalia just before I got on the bus home in the evening.

Over time she became a stranger to her culture and to herself. She and her friends did this for a while, but she finally confessed that despite all the efforts that she made to "fit" she became even more frustrated. As much as she had focused all her energy on herself and not on her academics, she became "a misfit" to both cultures. She still remained a Muslim to her American peers because she did not really fit in. On the other hand, her parents would not give her peace because they accused her of trying to be too "American." She was often in trouble with her parents because she was failing all her subjects in school and she was not following the rules that were required of her as Muslim girl.

Mohammed is another Muslim student who also faced challenges at school because he did not give in to the peer pressure. Mohammed indicated that it was a struggle to remain a faithful Muslim in school, especially during Ramadan. He indicated that "it was not easy to get a quiet place to pray five times a day and over time I got extremely frustrated and I started to question my values and religion because other students laughed at me and made fun of me anytime I kneeled down to pray."

The immigrant and refugee students also reported that though technology and all the facilities across the school were great, too many destructive behaviors and activities made it difficult for them to concentrate on their schoolwork. They specifically indicated that the whole school culture and routine was a nightmare. The mode of dressing, use of cell phones, students' behavior, inappropriate language, and frequent fights, among other things, were cultural shocks to most of the immigrant and refugee students.

Cultural ignorance on the part of the teachers and other student peers was another deterrent to academic success. According to Y'bihm (from Vietnam) and Abu-Bakar (from Kenya), the teachers and students are not informed of the immigrant students' cultural values and practices. They indicated that they were often in trouble with their teachers because the teacher interpreted their cultural differences, values, and behaviors as discipline problems. They were sent to the principal's office and got in trouble for raising their hands when a teacher asked a question in class, for standing up to answer a question, and for looking at the floor to avoid eye contact when addressing the teacher. Though these behaviors were gestures of respect in their culture, they were misinterpreted as disruptive, and the students were often sent to in-school suspension (ISS). This created great fear among the students, and some of them vowed never to participate in class or out of class activities.

Unequal Educational Opportunities

Limited access to equal opportunities has to a great extent affected the academic achievement rates of most immigrant and refugee children. Because most immigrants and refugees students settle in poor neighborhood, most of them do not have equal access to educational services and programs. Those children in more affluent neighborhoods tend to get more as compared to those in low social economic neighborhoods. The immigrant and refugee children feel as though they do not deserve much educational resources because they have little to offer to society. A significant number of Latino children in California receive a substantially inequitable education as compared to their peers (Gutiérrez et al., 2004). Guriérrez also points out the fact that English learners tend to enroll in schools that have inadequate facilities as well as curricular materials.

It is also important to note the fact that most immigrant and refugee children have not had equal or comparable education opportunities compared to their American counterparts. Living in environments with unequal educational opportunities is not new to most of these students. They came from countries where their education system was interrupted by economic hardship, civil wars, and political instability. Due to this instability, some of them are either over age for their grade level or had dropped out of school prior to enrolling in school in America. According to the 1992 Census Bureau, roughly 50 percent of Hispanics ages sixteen to twenty-four dropped out of high school. Thus, the increase in dropout rates among immigrant adolescent students is cause for a growing concern. Many of these changes render them vulnerable to leading unhealthy lifestyles (i.e., gangs, drug use, obesity, participation in youth violence, and teen pregnancies) (Maat, 1997; Kaleidoscope, 2003).

Though ESL classes are beneficial, they tend to isolate participants from the rest of the school activities; hence, the participants do not get exposed to the equal opportunities (i.e., extracurricular activities such as sports and performing arts). Due to the substantial pecuniary and psychological effects of war, most of the refugees have experienced post-traumatic related stress that has set them back in their academics. In addition, most of them feel that the school system has not given them time to recover. Throughout their entire school day, most ESL students feel different and separated from the rest of the school community. Alonzo, an immigrant student from Colombia, alluded to the fact that he felt he was perceived to be more of a burden than a significant member of the school. He indicated that he felt that his American peers did not appreciate him and other children from his culture because they held everybody back in class. He gave an example of an American peer who said, "I get so tired of these Mexicans because we always have to go at a slow pace in everything so as to accommodate them."

Statements and perceptions like this often tend to result in unhealthy tensions between different cultural groups (e.g., Latinos and African Americans), making the school environment unhealthy for meaningful learning.

Underresourced

The impact of the increase in income inequality on the education of immigrant and refugee children continues to be significant. Due to low incomes, manual jobs, and parents with limited or no formal education, most such children are raised in poorer neighborhoods that do not offer schools with the greatest resources. Immigrant and refugees tend to gravitate toward low social economic neighborhoods that have people who look like them or speak like them. They form enclaves that over time help contribute to the ever occurring segregation.

They are also under-resourced when it comes to parental support and mentoring. According to Portes and Rumbant (1996), most immigrant and refugee youth come from low income families who tend to give more priority to work. Therefore, they are more likely to live in poor neighborhoods that have schools with minimum resources and few posteducational opportunities (McLaren, 2000). This lack of resources gets even more overwhelming because the children have limited access to other public services, such as libraries and computers labs. Regardless of how hard they try, it is difficult for them to complete projects and assignments because they do not have their own computers, calculators, and so on, at home. Compounded with this are the limited technology skills. When asked to comment on this, Bernardino, an immigrant student from the Dominican Republic, said,

> It is tough for me to do any homework that requires the use of a computer because we do not have one at home; I do not have transportation to the library where I can use a computer. And even if I get to a computer, I do not even know how to type anything on a computer.

Undereducated/Underschooled

Because some immigrant and refugee children arrive from their home countries with minimal or no formal educational experiences, it is difficult for them to do well academically. Most immigrants and refugees have had limited or no formal education prior to migrating to America. This problem is especially prevalent among those who grew up in rural areas and those who were displaced by war.

Others come from families where parents have low levels of education and do not motivate or encourage their children to focus more on their academics. In most cases, a parental academic accomplishment is a key indicator of how well the kids perform in academics. Some high school students indicated that they were always being referred to or ended up in GED classes, unlike their American counterparts, who are encouraged and mentored to pursue sciences and engineering. Despite their past experiences and the paths they have come through, they tend to receive less academic-related counseling and guidance services. Amelia, a high school student from Nigeria, and another student Manuel from Mexico noted that on different occasions, their counselor discouraged them from applying to science colleges and universities. Instead, they were encouraged to apply to community colleges and pursue degrees in child care, liberal studies, and other service careers. They were informed that they would struggle academically and financially if they applied to go to a university.

Because of the perception and stereotype that immigrant children do not speak English, these groups of students are not recognized. Few teachers take time to identify their potentials, therefore they often run the risk of being underchallenged. Some students have reported that they were placed in ESL classes despite their strong language skills. They indicated that their names (just because they sound and look foreign) warranted them to be placed in these ELSL classes. Stacy, a middle school student from Ghana, had a similar experience:

> I was shocked to find myself in ESL classes instead of advanced learner classes. I was in advanced learner classes in all my grades in elementary school and was always a straight A student. I was awarded a trophy for attaining the highest points in accelerator reading program and after all this, someone thinks I cannot read.

Underinsured

Most immigrant and refugee students do not attend school regularly due to health insurance–related challenges. Most of them come from families that are poor and have poor health due to lifestyle and health insurance–related barriers. Due to limited or lack of health insurance, most immigrant children reported getting to school late because of lack of vaccination records. The notion of vaccination records and accessing health care has been a nightmare to most immigrant and refugee students and their families. Others reported missing school significantly due to illness and limited access to health care. These particular students reported that they would stay home and miss school anytime they became sick because their parents did not have immediate access to a doctor due to lack of health insurance. They noted, however, that though they were aware of programs in the community that would provide care to those who did not have insurance, the intake and appointments process was very long, and some had to wait for over two weeks to get an appointment. As a result, they ended up staying home and taking over-the-counter medications or other traditional medicine or home remedies. Thus, they would have to stay home longer and would miss out on the academics.

It was also evident that most refugee and immigrant students are underinsured (do not have all the necessary components, i.e., vision and dental insurance) and therefore cannot participate in extracurricular activities such as sports. It has also been reported that most students do not participate or belong to any school sports teams due to lack of insurance. Students who are part of school sports teams are often required to provide proof of health insurance before they are allowed to be part of the team. Malik, a student from Morocco, reported that he was terribly disappointed because he could not join the soccer team due to lack of insurance. Sonya, a student from Colombia, had a similar experience. She was outraged that she could not participate in the volleyball team because she could not afford her vision examination. When asked to describe her experience she said,

> I felt so bad and I was in tears after I found out that I could not attend the volleyball tryouts because I was unable to get my vision exam. When I found out that the school was offering physical examinations for only five dollars, I took my only allowance that I had saved and on the day of the physicals, I stood on line for over two hours because there were so many other students. But when the doctor gave me a note saying that I need to get a specialist to check my eyes, I knew that this was the end of my volleyball dreams because I knew my mother did not have the money to do all this.

Sonya felt that her hopes in academics and health had been shattered because she indicated that she was hoping to play so hard she could get a volleyball scholarship to put her through college because her mother could not afford to pay. Furthermore, Sonya emphasized that she really wanted to play sports because it helped her relieve all the stress related to acculturation and academics. Studies have indicated that a positive relationship exists between participation in physical activity and academic performance (Dwyer, Sallis, Blizzard, Lazarus, & Dean, 2001). These studies indicate that students who participate in physical activity tend to perform better in academics than those who do not participate.

Underrepresented

Immigrants and refugees are underrepresented in advanced academic programs, and are overrepresented in remedial and special programs. When Alicia first went to school in North Carolina, she was shocked and wanted to run away because she did not see a student, teacher, or administrator who looked like her or spoke a language like hers. She wondered where everybody was because she did not see many French-speaking students or anyone from Congo in her class. She did not see any teacher, administrator, social workers, or counselors from any African country or even the Caribbean. She indicated that she wished they had even one out of all the many staff and faculty so that she could have someone to ask questions and explain to her teachers about her culture. She said,

> "I get tired of these students and teachers shouting and screaming at my ears because when I don't talk, they think I have a hearing problem."

Compounding this lack of mentors or roles models is the parents' inability to represent their children and actively monitor their educational progress. Some parents may not be in a position to attend school meetings (i.e., PTA, teacher conference, games, etc.) due to lack of time, economic survival demands, lack of transportation, and limited English proficiency skills. The children have parents or guardians who have limited or non English proficiency skills and are unfamiliar with parental advocacy roles in America; hence, it is difficult for them to be proactive. Most of the students indicated that their parents do not come to school because *everything* is in English and some Spanish, and none of the other fifty-plus languages are included. Nonetheless, it is evident that due to underrepresentation, most immigrant and refugee parents and students do not have a voice in any decision making that pertains to academics.

Similar reports from immigrant youth indicated that due to limited representation, most of them feel insecure and isolated around natives not only in class but also during sports and other physical activities. They are not motivated to participate in anything that is out of class because they do not see someone like them.

Undocumented

Lack of legal documents makes it hard for these children to transition easily. Families and children who are not documented are constantly living in fear of deportation. They are afraid to question or ask for help from teachers and the school system in general. Modulo, an undocumented student from West Africa, reported that he was always afraid to ask questions in class because his parents cautioned him to be very careful due to their immigration status. Jesus, an undocumented student from Mexico, told a similar story. He indicated that his parents do not sign any of his school papers and the address that they use for school is not their own. He said that he is always quiet, and even if other students pick on him and called him racist names, he never complains because he does not want to put his family and himself in any trouble. He said, "Sometimes they hit me, call me names and even spit on me, but I have never said a word to them. All I do is go to the bathroom and cry and when I get home we pray with my parents and hope that this fear and treatment will come to an end one day."

Some immigrants, especially the undocumented, fear that seeking services from the community or schools may create problems with Immigration and Naturalization Services (INS) and may subject them to deportation (Bailey, 2002). Others (mostly refugees) have to wait for a period of five years before they can become eligible for most public benefits. Others also fear that using public benefits or even seeking education-related services may affect their chances of obtaining permanent residency or citizenship.

These fears continue to be compounded by the contentious politics that surround immigration and immigrant education. According to Ramirez,

> I was only nine when my mother brought me to this country. I like school and I am doing my very best because I want to be a medical doctor, but it may difficult to achieve my dream because I am undocumented. I have no Social Security number, nor permission to work, no driving license, and I am not eligible for tuition assistance. It is tough because I was hoping that they would pass the DREAM Act.

Another student, Amina, had this to say:

> I really wanted to be an engineer so I registered for an intensive summer math class. I was so excited, but when they asked me for my Social Security card, I almost collapsed and it was then that it dawned to me that I could not be what I want to be because I was undocumented.

Amina's and Ramirez's words illustrate the complexities and the consequences of immigration status for academic achievement and advancement.

Alternative Strategies to Academic Achievement

It is evident that the determinants of academic achievement among immigrant and refugee students go way beyond language and cultural barriers. Due to the ever increasing numbers of immigrant and refugee children in America, it is paramount that equal opportunities and equitable environments be created in the school system. According to Crosland (2004), *equity* refers to the elimination of disparities by providing equal opportunities (i.e., incorporating a cross-cultural curriculum, utilizing culturally sensitive pedagogical strategies and environments).

It is also clear that unless immigrant and refugee children in American schools receive appropriate intervention, they will continue to face the possibility of being undereducated, underemployed, and unprepared to participate fully in society.

According to Carmona (1996), the social setting, the teacher, and the educational approaches are different in the United States. Therefore, unless schools and other agencies work together and unless teachers and the community develop a clear understanding of the acculturation process of their diverse students, both the society and the immigrant and refugee community may be forced to pay the costs of inadequate schooling and services.

Because it is evident that education is a critical acculturation and integration asset for all immigrants and refugees, it is paramount that all stakeholders bring their resources and ideas to the table. They should work collaboratively to develop programs, strategies, infrastructure, and policies that would enhance academic achievements for all diverse immigrant and refugee children. Some of these interventions and strategies could include (but are not limited to) the following:

a. Encourage and train educators and administrators who will provide culturally and linguistically appropriate education to all immigrant and refugee children regardless of their country of origin, language, immigration, or SES.

b. Incorporate cross-cultural trainings as part of staff development trainings. These trainings will inform educators, administrators and all school staff (i.e,. bus drivers, cafeteria workers, housekeeping, etc.) on the acculturation challenges that affect academic achievement. This will help everyone better understand the cultures, specific needs, and culturally appropriate interventions of diverse immigrant and refugee children.

c. Create school environments that are responsive to the specific needs of diverse immigrants and refugee students, as well as to their families. School and classroom environments should nurture positive attitudes and motivate the students to aim higher.

d. Provide and identify other resources that the students and families can utilize during class and nonschool hours (i.e., libraries, community programs, mentoring and tutoring programs).

e. Provide infrastructure in the schools that will effectively serve non-native English speakers as well as their parents/families.

f. Explore opportunities to incorporate collaborative activities between newcomers or newcomer schools with established immigrants and refugees or between immigrant and refugee students and mainstream American students.

g. Create programs that demonstrate respect and appreciation for students' differences and cultures (e.g., by sponsoring or co-sponsoring on-campus or community cultural events).

h. Increase funding for ESL programs, especially at the elementary level (e.g., increase teachers and provide staff development trainings).

i. Increase the number of teachers who are trained to teach English language learners.

j. Provide interpreters and translators to foster parental involvement during meetings, ongoing school activities, and other school visits. They could help translate all documents that are sent home into all relevant languages.

k. Provide transportation where needed to parents for school meetings (e.g., PTA or open house).

l. Work with parents, teachers, and the immigrant and refugee community to implement a culturally appropriate dropout prevention program.

m. Communicate high expectations to immigrant students and provide explicit step-by-step directions on how to succeed (e.g., career orientation and tutoring).

n. Provide orientation to U.S. society and the school system, provide access to extracurricular activities, including transportation, and effectively communicate school expectations.

o. Provide resources or a roadmap on how to access health care in the community. If possible, sponsor health fairs that offer immunization, physicals, and other health services on site.

p. Continuously recruit diverse candidates for all positions across the school and not just in housekeeping. On this same note, seek ways to attract and retain diverse workers.

q. Work closely with professional development and preservice and in-service teacher and administrator preparation entities, such as local colleges and universities, to ensure that they prepare students effectively to meet the needs of all students and to conduct research and document best practices.

Working with an awareness of these determinants and having an open mind to other interventions and strategies will allow the school system in general to develop effective environments, policies, skills, knowledge, and dispositions that can nurture academic achievement for all immigrant and refugee children in American schools. This will not only help them successfully acculturate, it will enhance their ability to contribute to the American economy and culture more quickly and effectively.

References

Bailey, R. (2002). Demographics of Immigrants in Guilford County, NC. Retrieved December 10, 2003, from the CNNC Web: cnnc.uncg.edu/information/pop_ demgraphics.html.

Balgopal, R. P., (2000). *Social Work Practice with Immigrants and Refugees*. Columbia University Press: New York.

Carmona, A. (1996). Dispelling Myths about Immigrant Students. IDRA Newsletter.

Crosland, K. (2004). *Color-Blind Fesegregation: Race Neutral Remedies as the New "Equal Opportunity."* Paper presented at the annual meeting of the American Educational Research Association, San Diego, California.

Dwyer, T., Sallis, J. F., Blizzard, L., Lazarus, R., & Dean, K. (2001). Relation of Academic Performance to Physical Activity and Fitness in Children. *Pediatric Exercise Science,* 13, 225–238.

Friedlander, M. (1991). The Newcomer Program: Helping Immigrant Students Succeed in U.S. Schools. NCBE program Information Guide No. 8. Washington, DC: National Clearinghouse on Bilingual Education. Retrieved June 15, 2006, from www.ncbe.gwe.edu/ncbepubs/pigs/pig8.html.

Gutierrez, K. (2004). Literacy as Laminated Activity: Rethinking Literacy for English Learners. In C. M. Fairbanks, J. Worthy, B. Maloch, J. V. Hoffman, & D. L. Schallert (Eds.), *National Reading Conference Yearbook* (pp. 101–114). Chicago, IL: National Reading Conference.

Jensen, L. (2001). The Demographic Diversity of Immigrants and Their Children. In A. Portes & R. G. Rumbaut (Eds.), *Ethnicities: Children of Immigrants in America* (pp. 21–56). Berkeley: University of California Press.

Kaleidoscope (2003). *Cultural Diversity in Guilford County.* A Training Handbook for Health and Human Service Providers.

Maat, M. B. (1997). A Group Art Therapy Experience for Immigrant Adolescents. *American Journal of Arts Therapy* 36: 11–19.

McLaren, P. (2000), Democracy Sabotaged by Democracy: Immigration under Neoliberalism. In L. Bartolome & E. Truebe (Eds.), *Immigrant Voices: In Search of Educational Equity* (pp. 1-16). Lanham: Rowman and Littlefield.

Portes, A., & Rumbaut, R. G. (1996). *Immigrant America.* Berkeley: University of California Press.

U.S. Bureau of the Census (1998). United States of America Census Report.

V
Disability and Delinquency: Stereotype Tracking and Bullying in the Classroom

16

A Coordinated Public Response to School Bullying

Douglas E. Abrams[*]

January 2, 2002, was the first day back to classes for students in the Meriden, Connecticut school district. Twelve-year-old Daniel Scruggs stayed home from the Washington Middle School, as he had for forty-four of the prior seventy-eight school days, to escape relentless bullying by classmates that left him humiliated and fearful to attend.[1] Daniel stayed up late that night and watched a movie with his older sister. Shortly after midnight, he went alone to his bedroom, entered the walk-in closet, wrapped his dark blue necktie around the overhead bar, tied it around his neck and hanged himself.[2]

Pediatric professionals recognize bullying as a form of child abuse, perpetrated by other children rather than by adults.[3] Bullying in school occurs when a student or group of students repeatedly cause intentional physical or emotional harm to another student in a relationship marked by imbalance in physical or emotional power. The harm may come from physical assault, words, ostracism, teasing or some combination.[4] Repetition and power

---

 * Douglas E. Abrams is a law professor at the University of Missouri, where he teaches family law, children and the law, constitutional law and American legal history. He holds a B.A. from Wesleyan University and a J.D. from the Columbia University School of Law. He has written or coauthored five books, including *Children and the Law: Doctrine, Policy and Practice* (3d ed. 2007), *Contemporary Family Law* (2006) and *Children and the Law in a Nutshell* (3d ed. 2008). He recently received the Meritorious Service to the Children of America Award, presented by the National Council of Juvenile and Family Court Judges.

I thank James R. Devine, Sarah H. Ramsey and Peter Randall for their valuable comments on earlier drafts of this chapter.

1. Office of the Child Advocate and the Child Fatality Review Panel, Investigation of the Death of Joseph Daniel S. 11 (Jan. 2003).

2. Helen O'Neill, *No Heroes for Suicidal Schoolboy*, Times Union (Albany, N.Y.), Jan. 18, 2004, at A2.

3. *See, e.g.*, Richard Goldbloom, *Children's Inhumanity to Children*, 144 J. Pediatrics 3, 3 (2004); Susan P. Limber, *Addressing Youth Bullying Behaviors*, in Am. Med. Ass'n, Educ. Forum on Adolescent Health: Youth Bullying 5, 6 (May 3, 2002); Kirsti Kumpulainen et al., *Bullying and Psychiatric Symptoms Among Elementary School-Age Children*, 22 Child Abuse & Neglect 705, 706 (1998); Dan Olweus, *Bullying at School: Basic Facts and Effects of a School Based Intervention Program*, 35 J. Child Psychol. & Psychiatry 1171, 1173 (1994).

4. *See, e.g.*, Wendy M. Craig, The Relationship Among Bullying Victimization, Depression, Anxiety, and Aggression in Elementary School Children, 24 Personal Individual Differences 123, 123 (1998); Susan P. Limber, *Addressing Youth Bullying Behaviors, supra* note 3, at 6; Dan Olweus, *Bullying at School: Basic Facts, supra* note 3, at 1172; Jan P. Piek et al., *The Relationship between Bullying and Self-Worth in Children With Movement Coordination Problems*, 75 Brit. J. Educ. Psychol. 453, 454 (2005); Rana Sampson, Bullying in Schools 2–3 (U.S. Justice Dep't. 2002).

imbalance distinguish bullying from isolated disagreements between students or even from isolated acts of violence or intimidation.

The peer abuse Daniel Scruggs endured in school qualified as bullying on all counts. "Children would push him off the bleachers, yell at him, treat him like dirt," a classmate said after his death. "They put 'kick me' signs on his back and spit on his chair. He was easy to pick on — they knew he wouldn't do anything back."[5]

Daniel was "different," indeed an easy target. At only sixty-three pounds, he was small for his age.[6] His IQ had tested in the "very superior range" at 139 when he was a sixth grader, but he also had an identified learning disability.[7] The family apartment was filthy, and he soon stopped bathing and brushing his teeth. He resisted his mother's entreaties to go to school, and he often wore dirty, mismatched clothes when he did attend. He would defecate and urinate on himself during the day, hoping that school authorities would send him home.[8] Daniel, the state Office of the Child Advocate concluded after his death, did not fit in socially, emotionally or academically.[9]

Daniel's single mother, Judith Scruggs, was raising her two children alone while working sixty hours a week at two jobs, at Wal-Mart and as a teacher's aide at Daniel's school. The prosecutor responded to Daniel's death by indicting her for risk of injury to the boy arising largely from the family's squalid living conditions. After a jury convicted her of the felony count, the trial court denied her motion for acquittal but chronicled the state's inaction. "Many people," the court began, "knew that ... Daniel was in great distress."[10]

> School officials knew that Daniel missed a lot of school and was often tardy, knew that he had severe personal hygiene problems, and did nothing to protect him from constant bullying. The Department of Children and Families was aware of Daniel's truancy, knew that [his mother] wanted him placed in a different school, had been in the house during the period that the state claims the home living conditions endangered the child's health, but closed its case on the family six days before the suicide.[11]

Citing the "relentless bullying that [Daniel] endured at school and his inherently fragile psyche," the Connecticut Supreme Court reversed Judith Scruggs's conviction on the ground that the felony statute was unconstitutionally vague as applied to her conduct.[12] The state's most sustained effort to intervene in the Scruggs family had failed.

Bullying in the nation's elementary and secondary schools calls for a coordinated public response by the "pediatric safety system," the network that failed Daniel Scruggs long before the prosecutor ever entered the picture. The pediatric safety system begins with the child's parents, but extends in appropriate cases primarily to the school district (for public school students), the juvenile and criminal courts, the state child protective agency and perhaps the mental health agency and law enforcement.

---

5. J. D. Heyman et al., *Did Bullying — Or a Mother's Neglect — Drive a 12-Year-Old Boy to Suicide?*, People, Oct. 20, 2003, at 117.

6. Office of the Child Advocate, *supra* note 1, at i; Linda D. Voss & Jean Mulligan, *Bullying In School: Are Short Pupils at Risk? Questionnaire Study in a Cohort*, 320 Brit. Med. J. 612 (2000).

7. Office of the Child Advocate, *supra* note 1, at 7.

8. *Id.* at 10.

9. *Id.* at 17.

10. *State v. Scruggs*, 2004 WL 1245557 *1 (Conn. Super. Ct. Mar. 8, 2004), *rev'd on other grounds*, 905 A.2d 24 (Conn. 2006) (parenthetical omitted).

11. *Id.*

12. *State v. Scruggs*, 905 A.2d 24, 38 (Conn. 2006).

After measuring the epidemic of bullying in the nation's schools, this chapter describes the emerging national consensus supporting a coordinated public response. The consensus is grounded in growing public sensitivity to the devastating immediate and lasting damage that bullying can inflict on its participants. The chapter then describes the reported effectiveness of time-tested and rigorously evaluated school-based bullying prevention programs. The chapter concludes by exploring the central roles that the various members of the pediatric safety system play, consistent with constitutional constraints, in the effort to prevent bullying and react firmly to incidents that occur.

Bullying in America's Schools

Bullying in public elementary and secondary schools, America's most pervasive form of school violence, has reached epidemic proportions. The nation has seventy-three million children under eighteen, nearly forty-three million of whom attended grades one through twelve in the public schools in 2003, the latest year for which census figures are available.[13] Studies estimate that 20 percent to 30 percent of these students are frequently involved in bullying as perpetrators, victims or both in urban, suburban and rural districts.[14] More than 3.2 million victims suffer each year in the sixth through tenth grades alone, nearly one in six children in these grades.[15] Half of all students suffer bullying at some time before they leave high school.[16]

Students like Daniel Scruggs, socially isolated or with special mental health needs, may offer particular targets.[17] So may children who draw attention for such reasons as race, ethnicity, gender or perceived sexual orientation, physical or emotional disability, obesity, small size or lack of social skills.[18] Researchers have identified a link between bullying and children with special physical health needs such as speech or language impairment, vision problems, cancer, cerebral palsy, diabetes or muscular dystrophy.[19]

Bullying has increased dramatically in the past few years, thanks to "cyber bullying" on the Internet, "the bully's new playground."[20] Cyber bullies can repeatedly target victims

---

13. Forum on Child and Family Statistics, America's Children in Brief: Key National Indicators of Well-Being, 2006, www.childstats.gov/americaschildren/pop.asp; U.S. Census Bureau, Statistical Abstract of the United States: 2006, tbl. 225, at 153 (2005).

14. *See, e.g.,* Jaana Juvonen, *Bullying Among Young Adolescents: The Strong, the Weak, and the Troubled,* 115 Pediatrics 1231 (Dec. 2003); Susan P. Limber, *Addressing Youth Bullying Behaviors, supra* note 3, at 6; Susan P. Limber, *Peer Victimization: The Nature and Prevalence of Bullying Among Children and Youth,* in Handbook of Children, Culture, and Violence 313 (Nancy E. Dowd, Dorothy G. Singer & Robin Fretwell Wilson eds., 2006).

15. James Alan Fox et al., Bullying Prevention *Is* Crime Prevention 2 (2003).

16. Am. Med. Ass'n, Featured CSA Report: Bullying Behaviors Among Children and Adolescents (2002), ama-assn.org/ama/category/14312.html.

17. Jeanne Van Cleve & Matthew M. Davis, *Bullying and Peer Victimization Among Children With Special Health Care Needs,* 118 Pediatrics 1212 (2006).

18. *See, e.g.,* Am. Ass'n of Univ. Women Educ. Found., Hostile Hallways: Bullying, Teasing, and Sexual Harassment in School (2001); Ian Janssen et al., *Associations Between Overweight and Obesity With Bullying Behaviors in School-Aged Children,* 113 Pediatrics 1187 (2004); Kirsti Kumpulainen et al., *supra* note 3, at 712; Jan P. Piek et al., *supra* note 4, at 454; Young Shin Kim et al., *School Bullying and Youth Violence,* 63 Arch. Gen. Psychiatry 1035, 1039–40 (2006).

19. *See, e.g.,* Susan P. Limber, *Addressing Youth Bullying Behaviors, supra* note 3, at 9–10; Jeanne Van Cleve & Matthew M. Davis, *supra* note 17, at 1212.

20. Bob Meadows et al., *The Web: The Bully's New Playground,* People, Mar. 14, 2005, at 152.

with threats, "rumors," gossip or insults through email, instant messaging, blogs, cell phones, social networking sites, and even Web sites featuring the victim. With bravado cloaked in virtual anonymity, bullies no longer need to be stronger physically than their victims. A few keystrokes can inflict hurt sometimes even more severe than fists or playground confrontations because Internet postings can hound the victim around the clock far beyond the confines of the campus.

A 2006 national survey found that one-third of all students between twelve and seventeen, and one-sixth of all younger preteens, have suffered cyber bullying, which can leave victims feeling "tethered to their tormenters."[21] "Rather than just some people, say 30 in a cafeteria, hearing them all yell insults at you," said one teenage victim, cyber bullying is "there for six billion people to see" on their computer screens.[22] "If someone is picking on you in the school yard, you can go home," added the mother of a thirteen-year-old Virginia boy who committed suicide with a shotgun in 2005 after cyber bullies had taunted him about his small size and dared him to kill himself for more than a month. "When it's on the computer at home, you have nowhere to go."[23]

"It's so much easier to be mean online," explained one sophomore, because the bullies "don't see your reaction."[24] Thirteen-year-old Vermont middle schooler Ryan Halligan hanged himself at home after two years of cyber bullying by students who urged him to take his own life. In his final instant message, Ryan typed, "Tonight's the night," and the reply came back, "It's about time."[25] Ryan's father says his son's tormentors may not have realized they were driving the boy to suicide: "The kids could have thought Ryan was joking, but ... they didn't see him, ... they didn't hear the tone of his voice, they didn't see the body language that was going along with the words."[26]

Cyber bullies have posted classmates' photographs on Web sites to conduct "Who's the Ugliest?" contests or similar interactive insults.[27] Students with camera phones have posted photographs of classmates undressed in locker rooms or partially exposed in lavatories or at slumber parties.[28] Innocent photos of classmates have been morphed to make the target appear in degrading, yet realistic, positions.[29] Students have beaten up weaker classmates, videotaped the beatings and posted the tapes for ridicule on a Web site; one such

---

21. Opinion Res. Corp., Cyber Bully—Teen 3 (July 6, 2006), www.fightcrime.org/cyber bullying/cyberbullyingteen.pdf; Opinion Res. Corp., Cyber Bully—Pre-Teen 3 (July 6, 2006), www.fightcrime.org/cyberbullying/cyberbullyingpreteen.pdf; Darby Dickerson, *Cyberbullies on Campus*, 37 U. Tol. L. Rev. 51–56 n.44 (2005) (quoting Glenn R. Stutsky, school violence expert, Michigan State Univ.) ("tethered").

22. Cyber-bullying (CBC News Online, Mar. 2005 www.cbc.ca/news/background/bullying/cyber_bullying.html).

23. Bob Meadows et al., *supra* note 20, at 152.

24. Pat Ferguson, *Fight "Cyberbullying," But How to Enforce?*, Oregonian (Portland, Or.), May 17, 2007, at 8.

25. M. Mindy Moretti, Playground Bullying Heads to Cyberspace, www.naco.org/Printer Template.cfm?Section=Issues&template=/ContentManagement/ContentDisplay.cfm&ContentID=15014 (Nat'l Ass'n of Counties Web site).

26. Cyber-Bullying Growing (CBS News, Mar. 21, 2005), cbsnews.com/stories/2005/03/21/earlyshow/living/caught/printable681867.shtml.

27. *See, e.g.*, Norman Draper, *House Approves "Cyberbullying" Bill*, Star Tribune (Minneapolis, Minn.), May 5, 2007, at 2B; Amanda Paulson, *Internet Bullying*, Christian Sci. Mon., Dec. 30, 2003, at 11.

28. Chris Kenning, *Many Students Face Cyber-Bullying*, Courier-J. (Louisville, Ky.), Dec. 28, 2006, at 1A.

29. Amanda Paulson, *supra* note 27, at 11.

posted beating, a four-minute film of a bloodied thirteen-year-old girl, gained such a large audience in early 2007 that it became a "worldwide symbol of cyberbullying."[30]

The potential lifelong damage to photographed or filmed bullying victims recalls the potential lifelong damage that led the Supreme Court, in *New York v. Ferber* in 1982, to create an exception to First Amendment freedom of expression and permit states to criminalize production or dissemination of child pornography, "photographs and films depicting sexual activity by juveniles."[31] Creating exceptions to free speech rights is serious business, but *Ferber* took the extraordinary step to protect "the physiological, emotional, and mental health of the child."[32] Photographs and films of sexual activity, the Court explained, create "a permanent record of the children's participation and the harm to the child is exacerbated by their circulation."[33]

Reaffirming *Ferber*'s aim to prevent the "exploitative use of children," the Court went a significant step further in *Osborne v. Ohio* in 1990.[34] Over a First Amendment objection, *Osborne* upheld state authority to criminalize private possession of child pornography, even in one's home.

Child exploitation is child exploitation, regardless of whether the exploiter is an adult or another child. Indeed, the photographs and films produced, disseminated and possessed by cyber bullies and their audiences carry risks of permanency and harm even more widespread than the risks that accompanied the manually transmitted pre-Internet images that underlay *Ferber* and *Osborne*. The two Supreme Court decisions thus provide strong child protective rationales for a coordinated public response to cyber bullying, even though the Internet postings normally fall outside the decisions' First Amendment doctrine because they do not depict sexual activity.

Emerging National Values About Bullying

Daniel Scruggs was victimized not only by his classmates but also by teachers and other school personnel who failed to respond to the open and notorious bullying, except to suspend Daniel at least twice for fighting when he tried unsuccessfully to resist.[35] One suspension ignored classmates' reports that he had been "choked, put up against the wall, stomped on, kicked, and punched across the face."[36] At least one teacher said that Daniel should fend for himself because bullying is "typical behavior of children" and "kids will be kids."[37]

Like many bullying victims, Daniel did try to resist for a while, though he often left physical confrontations in tears.[38] Once when his older sister offered her help resisting his classmates' taunts, he protested, "No.... I can take care of myself."[39] For most bully-

---

30. Corey Kilgannon, *Teenagers Misbehaving, for All Online to Watch*, NEWSDAY, Feb. 13, 2007, at B1; Zachary R. Dowdy, *Teen Charged for Allegedly Taping Attack*, NEWSDAY, Jan. 30, 2007, at A15.
31. 458 U.S. 747, 759 (1982).
32. *Id.* at 758 (footnote omitted).
33. *Id.* (footnote omitted).
34. 495 U.S. 103 (1990).
35. OFFICE OF THE CHILD ADVOCATE, *supra* note 1, at 7–8.
36. *Id.* at 8.
37. *Id.* at 25 (italics omitted).
38. Helen O'Neill, *supra* note 2, at 2.
39. *Id.*

ing victims, however, self-help is wishful thinking because without intervention by adults or peers, resistance can fan the flames. Most victims are no match physically or emotionally for the bullies. If the playing field were level, chances are that the victim would not be bullied in the first place.

The first step in the pediatric safety system's coordinated public response is to shuck the timeworn excuse that bullying is an inevitable and ultimately benign rite of passage that children and adolescents outgrow after "toughing it out." Some observers have even argued that bullying can be a positive experience by helping prepare victims for the rough-and-tumble of the "real world."[40] The argument recalls Johnny Cash's hit song, "A Boy Named Sue." The father said this about why he named his son so oddly and thus targeted him for incessant bullying: "Son, this world is rough/And if a man's gonna make it, he's gotta be tough/And I knew I wouldn't be there to help ya along."[41] In the real world, adults do not breed toughness by naming their sons Sue. Nor should adults tolerate bullying of other people's children as a crude down payment for rugged individualism.

Until the past decade or so, America's tolerance of school bullying had proved remarkably resistant to meaningful change. Death or serious injuries to a particular student might provoke an arrest or other temporary public response to media coverage, but sustained public antibullying initiatives did not gain traction. Researchers first paid serious attention in Scandinavia in the early 1970s, and the pace accelerated in 1982 when three Norwegian boys between ten and fourteen committed suicide, probably in reaction to persistent bullying.[42] Most Americans, however, did not take notice until after April 20, 1999, when two seniors turned bombs and semiautomatic weapons on classmates at Columbine High School in Littleton, Colorado. The commando-style raid left twelve classmates, a teacher and the two killers dead and two dozen other victims wounded.[43]

Columbine was a watershed event in the history of American public education because it focused unprecedented attention on school violence, including bullying. As the bewildered nation cast about for explanations, Americans learned that bullies had teased and taunted the two killers in school for years, without intervention by the school or other agencies in the pediatric safety system. After the killers' pent-up rage became public, more than three dozen parents and students told the Colorado governor's Columbine Review Commission that "a significant amount of bullying had occurred (especially from athletes)," but that "it would have been futile to report bullying to the school administration because no one there would have done anything about it."[44] The commission called bullying a "risk factor" for school violence and recommended that schools "adopt one or more of the bullying-prevention programs that have already been tested and proven effective."[45]

The U.S. Secret Service and the U.S. Department of Education studied Columbine and thirty-six other incidents of targeted school violence involving forty-one attackers since 1974. In 2002, the agencies reported that "almost three quarters of the attackers felt

---

40. *See, e.g.,* Ronald Oliver et al., *The Perceived Roles of Bullying in Small-Town Midwestern Schools,* 72 J. COUNSELING & DEV. 416 (1994) (quoting observers); Peter K. Smith, *The Silent Nightmare: Bullying and Victimisation in School Peer Groups,* 4 PSYCHOLOGIST 243, 245 (1991) (same).

41. JOHNNY CASH, *A Boy Named Sue,* www.azlyrics.com/lyrics/johnnycash/aboynamedsue.html.

42. DAN OLWEUS, BULLYING AT SCHOOL: WHAT WE KNOW AND WHAT WE CAN DO 1–2 (1993).

43. REPORT OF GOVERNOR BILL OWENS' COLUMBINE REVIEW COMMISSION xxi (May 2001), www.state.co.us/columbine/Columbine_20Report_WEB.pdf.

44. *Id.* at 98 n.211.

45. *Id.* at xvi, 98.

persecuted, bullied, threatened, attacked or injured prior to the incident."[46] "In several cases, individual attackers had experienced bullying and harassment that was long-standing and severe."[47] Several attackers "described being bullied in terms that suggested that these experiences approached torment. These attackers told of behaviors that, if they occurred in the workplace, likely would meet legal definitions of harassment and/or assault."[48]

As of this writing, the last major school shooting in the United States was the carnage at Virginia Tech on April 16, 2007. By the end of the week, the media reported that the obviously deranged shooter had been bullied in high school for his shyness, ethnicity and unusual speech.[49]

The nation's traditional tolerance of school bullying—the cavalier "kids will be kids" attitude—provides no excuse for continued tolerance in the twenty-first century. The nation's values have changed with greater contemporary knowledge and sensitivity about bullying's prevalence and harmful effects. Statutes in at least thirty states (most enacted since Columbine) now require state and local school boards to adopt written policies specifically prohibiting bullying in the schools.[50] In these and other states, generally applicable safe-schools acts require school administrators to inform law enforcement authorities about criminal conduct characteristic of much bullying (such as peer assault, harassment, sexual or racial intimidation, stalking or intimidation). With or without using the term "bullying," schools have strengthened written policies prohibiting such conduct. Federal agencies have recommended creative antibullying strategies, and Congress has appropriated block grants to states and localities for bullying and cyber bullying prevention programs in the schools.[51]

The accelerated state and federal response since Columbine demonstrates an emerging public policy consensus. The unpalatable choices Daniel Scruggs and millions of other schoolchildren have faced for years—to stay home from school, or risk emotional or physical injury from attendance—compromise educational equity, the aspiration that should underlie every state's guarantee of a free public education. "Freedom from fear of bullying is not enough to ensure successful learning but it is a necessary condition for effective learning."[52]

The emerging legislative focus on bullying resembles Congress's earlier, belated focus on educational equity for children with physical or mental disabilities. For most of our

---

46. Bryan Vossekuil et al., The Final Report and Findings of the Safe School Initiative: Implications for the Prevention of School Attacks in the United States 21 (U.S. Secret Serv. & U.S. Dep't of Educ. 2002). *See also Mind of the Assassin* (CBS "60 Minutes" Apr. 22, 2007), www.cbsnews/ stories/2007/04/22/60minutes/printable2714959.shtml (following the Virginia Tech shootings, interview with two of the report's authors).

47. Bryan Vossekuil et al., *supra* note 46, at 21.

48. *Id.* at 35–36.

49. *High School Classmates Say Gunman Was Bullied*, Apr. 19, 2007, www.msnbc.msn.com/ id/18169776/.

50. Nat'l Conf. of State Legislatures, School Bullying (2007), www.ncsl.org/programs/educ/ bullyingoverview.htm.

51. *See, e.g.*, U.S. Dep't of Educ., Exploring the Nature and Prevention of Bullying, www.ed.gov/admins/lead/safety/training/bullying/index.html (2007); U.S. Dep't of Health & Human Servs., What We Know About Bullying, mentalhealth.samhsa.gov/publications/allpubs/bullying/ SBN_Tip_9.pdf (2007); 42 U.S.C. §§ 3796ee(b)(13), 14043c-3(i)(4) (2007); Dan Olweus, Bullying is NOT a Fact of Life 8–9 (U.S. Dep't of Health & Hum. Servs. 2003).

52. Kris Bosworth et al., *Factors Associated With Bullying Behavior in Middle School Students*, 19 J. Early Adolescence 341, 342 (1999).

history, courts upheld cruel statutes that closed schoolhouse doors to deaf, blind and mentally challenged students deemed "ineducable."[53] In 1970, more than half the nation's eight million children with disabilities were still "either totally excluded from schools or sitting idly in regular classrooms awaiting the time when they were old enough to 'drop out.'"[54] As late as 1974, the educational needs of 82 percent of the nation's emotionally disturbed children went unmet.[55]

Congress responded by enacting the Education for All Handicapped Children Act in 1975, which the lawmakers renamed the Individuals with Disabilities Education Act (IDEA) in 1990.[56] Today the IDEA guarantees "full educational opportunity to all children with disabilities" in every state.[57] The guarantee of special education and related services remains quite expensive for the federal government and states alike, but extending educational opportunity to children with disabilities has become a national priority designed (in the Supreme Court's words) to "reverse [a] history of neglect."[58]

The recent state bullying legislation and federal funding initiatives similarly demonstrate a national priority to reverse a history of neglect. Bullying might contribute to depression or other emotional disturbance that would entitle victims to rights under the IDEA, but state and federal action now require public intervention even when no disability covered by the federal act appears.[59] Elementary and secondary school educators can no longer dismiss bullying as the victim's personal predicament and not a transcendent public concern.

School antibullying strategies will not necessarily prevent thankfully rare Columbine-style massacres, but turning back the clock—perpetuating yesterday's shortsightedness that left bullying victims, like children with disabilities, to their own devices—is simply no longer acceptable public policy in light of today's national values grounded in understanding about the harms of bullying.

A Legacy of Harm

The American Medical Association recognizes three groups of participants in school bullying: "We are all ... bullies, bullied, or bystanders."[60] With research showing the profound immediate and lasting harm that bullying can wreak on all three groups, the AMA and the National Institutes of Health correctly recognize bullying as a public health crisis.[61]

---

53. Douglas E. Abrams & Sarah H. Ramsey, Children and the Law: Doctrine, Policy and Practice 91–92 (3d ed. 2007).

54. H.R. Rep. No. 94-332, at 2 (1975).

55. S. Rep. No. 94-168, at 8 (1975).

56. Douglas E. Abrams & Sarah H. Ramsey, *supra* note 53, at 91–92.

57. 20 U.S.C. § 1412(a)(2) (2007).

58. *Schaffer v. Weast*, 546 U.S. 49, 52 (2005).

59. *See, e.g.*, *Shore Reg'l H.S. Bd. of Educ.*, 381 F.3d 194, 195 (3d Cir. 2004) (applying IDEA to bullying victim diagnosed with depression and perceptual impairment); 20 U.S.C. § 1401(3)(a) (2007).

60. Am. Med. Ass'n, Educ. Forum on Adolescent Health: Youth Bullying 2 (May 3, 2002); AMA, Featured CSA Report: Bullying Behaviors Among Children and Adolescents (2002), ama-assn.org/ama/category/14312.html.

61. *See, e.g.*, Am. Med. Ass'n, Educ. Forum on Adolescent Health: Youth Bullying (May 3, 2002); Victoria Stagg Elliott, *AMA Recognizes Bullying as Public Health Problem*, AMNews, July 16, 2001, www.ama-assn.org/amednews/2001/07/09/hlsa0709.htm; Nat'l Insts. of Health, Nat'l Inst. of Child Health & Human Dev., Bullying Widespread in U.S. Schools, Survey Finds (Apr. 24, 2001), www.nichd.nih.gov/news/releases/bullying.cfm.

The Bullies

Bullies "may need as much help as their victims."[62] Bullies unchallenged by the pediatric safety system "experience poor psychosocial and emotional adjustment, difficulty making friends, and increased loneliness."[63] Bullying may signal generally antisocial, aggressive and even delinquent and criminal conduct that can escalate throughout adolescence and adulthood.[64] "Bullies have a more positive attitude towards violence than students in general," often have "a strong need to dominate others," and "seem to enjoy ... subdu[ing] others."[65] Bullies may sense that violence, intimidation or degradation are acceptable, or at least tolerable, ways to impose their will on others, including future dating partners, spouses, children, neighbors or co-workers.[66]

Some studies have shown that one in four boys who bully will have a criminal record before they turn thirty.[67] At least one researcher has even reported that bullying can be intergenerational: "Adolescent bullies tend to become adult bullies, and then tend to have children who are bullies."[68]

The Bullied

Status, acceptance and friendships determine the social networking that characterizes childhood and adolescence. When bullying short-circuits the network, victims may display psychosomatic symptoms resembling ones suffered by many child abuse victims, including sleep disturbances, bedwetting, abdominal pain, high levels of anxiety and depression, loneliness, low self-esteem and heightened fear for personal safety.[69]

As Daniel Scruggs demonstrated, bullying can also induce school phobia, increase truancy or impair the victim's concentration and classroom achievement.[70] Victims seeking escape from torment may be at greater risk of dropping out of high school before graduation.[71] Research also indicates that persistent bullying leaves many victims with life-

---

62. Richard Goldbloom, *supra* note 3, at 3.

63. Gitanjali Saluja et al., *Prevalence and Risk Factors for Depressive Symptoms Among Young Adolescents*, 158 Arch. Ped. Adolescent Med. 760, 761 (2004).

64. Am. Med. Ass'n, Featured CSA Report: Bullying Behaviors Among Children and Adolescents (2002), ama-assn.org/ama/category/14312.html. *See also, e.g.,* Dan Olweus, Bullying at School: What We Know, *supra* note 42, at 35–36; Marcel F. van der Wal et al., *Psychosocial Health Among Young Victims and Offenders of Direct and Indirect Bullying*, 111 Pediatrics 1312 (2003).

65. Dan Olweus, *Bullying at School*, *supra* note 3, at 1180, 1181.

66. *See, e.g.,* Kirsti Kumpulainen et al., *supra* note 3, at 706; Rolf Loeber & Dale Hay, *Key Issues in the Development of Aggression and Violence From Childhood to Early Adulthood*, 48 Ann. Rev. Psychol. 371 (1997); Peter K. Smith, *supra* note 40, at 245.

67. Am. Med. Ass'n, Educ. Forum on Adolescent Health, *supra* note 60, at I.

68. David P. Farrington, *Understanding and Preventing Bullying, in* Michael Tonry (ed.), 17 Crime and Justice: A Review of Research 381, 383 (1993).

69. *See, e.g.,* Louise Arseneault, *Bullying Victimization Uniquely Contributes to Adjustment Problems in Young Children: A Nationally Representative Cohort Study*, 118 Pediatrics 130 (2006); Minne Fekkes et al., *Bullying Behavior and Associations With Psychosomatic Complaints and Depression*, 144 J. Pediatrics 17, 21 (2004); Gwen M. Glew et al., *Bullying, Psychosocial Adjustment, and Academic Performance in Elementary School*, 159 Arch. Pediatr. Adolescent Med. 1026, 1030–31 (2005); Gitanjali Saluja et al., *supra* note 63, at 764.

70. *See, e.g.,* Gwen M. Glew et al., *supra* note 69, at 1030; Kirsti Kumpulainen et al., *supra* note 3, at 715.

71. Kris Bosworth et al., *supra* note 52, at 341.

long emotional scars, including difficulty maintaining meaningful relationships with the opposite sex.[72]

The suicides of Daniel Scruggs in Connecticut and Ryan Halligan in Vermont may not have been typical, but they were also not unique. Leading Norwegian researcher Dan Olweus found that "victims' devaluation of themselves sometimes becomes so overwhelming that they see suicide as the only possible solution" to bullying.[73] Other bullying victims may harbor suicidal thoughts that diminish enjoyment of childhood even when they do not ripen into suicide attempts.[74] A recent study found depression and suicide ideation common among nine- to thirteen-year-old boys and girls victimized by bullying.[75] A recent book coined a new term: "bullycide."[76]

We do not know the precise number of victims driven by bullying to contemplate or attempt suicide, but what we do know reinforces numerous studies that find "compelling reasons to associate at least some of the child and adolescent risk for suicidal thoughts and actions to school bullying."[77] We know, for example, that half the nation's forty-three million elementary and secondary students suffer face-to-face or cyber bullying at some time before leaving high school; that a victim may endure bullying for weeks, months or even years;[78] and that suicide is the third leading cause of death among American adolescents.[79] As researchers intimate, the lines likely cross more often than we would wish to imagine.

"Bullying is not the only risk factor for suicidal thoughts and behaviors, but it surely now must be added to the list."[80] The numbers are daunting. In a 2005 nationwide survey by the U.S. Centers for Disease Control and Prevention, 28.5 percent of high school students said they felt so sad or hopeless every day for two consecutive weeks in the prior month that they stopped doing some usual activities. During the twelve months preced-

---

72. *See, e.g.*, Lyndal Bond et al., *Does Bullying Cause Emotional Problems? A Prospective Study of Young Teenagers*, 323 Brit. Med. J. 480 (2001); Wendy M. Craig, *supra* note 4, at 128–29; Riitakerttu Kaltiala-Heino et al., *Bullying at School—An Indicator of Adolescents at Risk for Mental Disorders*, 23 J. Adolescence 661, 668 (2000); Kirsti Kumpulainen et al., *supra* note 3, at 706; Dan Olweus, *Bullying at School, supra* note 3, at 1179; Andre Sourander et al., *Persistence of Bullying From Childhood to Adolescence—A Longitudinal 8-Year Follow-up Study*, 24 Child Abuse & Neglect 873, 874 (2000); Dieter Wolke et al., *Bullying Involvement in Primary School and Common Health Problems*, 85 Arch. Dis. Child. 197, 197 (2001).

73. Dan Olweus, *Bullying at School, supra* note 3, at 1182–83. *See also, e.g.*, Maria Elana Baca, *Technology Gives Teens Myriad Ways to Torment Their Peers*, Buffalo (N.Y.) News, Mar. 26, 2007, at C1; Daarel Burnett, *Bullitt East Group Fights Suicide and Cyber-Bullies*, Courier-J. (Louisville, Ky.), May 9, 2007, at 5H; Gretchen Voss, *Mean-Kids.com*, Boston Mag., Jan. 2006.

74. *See, e.g.*, Minne Fekkes et al., *supra* note 69, at 17; Peter K. Smith, *supra* note 40, at 245.

75. Marcel F. van der Wal et al., *supra* note 64, at 1312.

76. Neil Marr & Tim Field, Bullycide: Death at Playtime (2001).

77. Young Shin Kim et al., *School Bullying and Suicidal Risk in Korean Middle School Students*, 115 Pediatrics 357 (2005) (presenting U.S. findings and citing other studies reaching similar conclusions). *See also, e.g.*, Anat Brunstein Klomek, *Bullying, Depression, and Suicidality in Adolescents*, 46 J. Am. Acad. of Child & Adolescent Psychiatry 40, 47 (Jan. 2007) (finding depression, serious suicidal ideation and suicide attempts "significantly associated with" bullying behavior among high school students in and away from school).

78. *See, e.g.*, Amie E. Grills & Thomas H. Ollendick, *Peer Victimization, Global Self-Worth, and Anxiety in Middle School Children*, 31 J. Clin. Child & Adolescent Psychol. 59 (2002); Susan P. Limber, *Bullying Among Children and Youth*, Juvenile Justice Bulletin (OJJDP Apr. 1998); Dan Olweus, *Bullying at School, supra* note 3, at 1182.

79. U.S. Centers for Disease Control & Prevention, Suicide: Fact Sheet, www.cdc.gov/ncipc/factsheets/suifacts.htm (2007).

80. Young Shin Kim et al., *supra* note 77, at 357 (presenting U.S. findings and citing other studies reaching similar conclusions).

ing the survey, 13.0 percent of students had planned how they would attempt suicide, 8.4 percent of students had actually attempted suicide one or more times, and 2.3 percent of students had made a suicide attempt that resulted in an injury, poisoning, or overdose that required treatment by a physician or nurse.[81] These alarming predictors may be underestimates because medical experts believe that many child and adolescent deaths reported as "accidental" are actually suicides.[82]

The Bystanders

Bystanders have been called "secondary victims" of bullying.[83] Most bullies operate alone or in small groups, but crave onlookers, who are also exposed to serious risks.[84] "There isn't much satisfaction in bullying unless the bully has an audience to see what he is doing and give him some of the gratification he seeks."[85] The audience may be physical or virtual, but bystanders may suffer regardless of whether they remain on the sidelines, join the bullying or defend the victim.

For one thing, bullying can infect the school culture by encouraging violence, interrupting teaching, distracting teachers and administrators, and scaring other students.[86] Researchers have found that "both bullying and being bullied are associated with higher rates of weapons carrying, fighting, and fighting injuries" on and off campus, and that rates of overall school violence consistently increase with increased bullying.[87] The post-Columbine report by the Secret Service and the Education Department stressed that bullies may not be the sole targets of victims bent on revenge,[88] and some researchers conclude that bullying can breed hate crimes against students who are not direct targets of the bullying itself.[89]

Meekness may weaken bystanders' empathy for the distress of others, and may damage bystanders' self-esteem and schoolwork by inducing guilt about timidity and lack of resolve in face of a classmate's overt victimization. Students watched the bullying of Daniel Scruggs day in and day out, but no classmate ever rose to his defense. Most student bystanders do not intervene on a victim's behalf or report the bullying to an adult; the normal response is to avoid associating with the victim, or even to join the bully in an effort to boost the bystander's own social position or to avoid being targeted.[90] One study found

---

81. U.S. Centers for Disease Control and Prevention, Youth Risk Behavior Surveillance — United States 2005 (2006).

82. Leon Eisenberg, *The Epidemiology of Suicide in Adolescents*, 13 Pediatr. Ann. 47 (1984).

83. Linda R. Jeffrey, *Bullying Bystanders*, 11 Prevention Researcher 7, 7 (2004).

84. Susan P. Limber, *Addressing Youth Bullying Behaviors*, *supra* note 3, at 7.

85. Richard L. Gross, Panelist Remarks, in Am. Med. Ass'n, Educ. Forum on Adolescent Health: Youth Bullying, *supra* note 3, at 20.

86. *See, e.g.*, Dorothy L. Espelage et al., *Examining the Social Context of Bullying Behaviors in Early Adolescence*, 78 J. Counseling & Dev. 326, 326 (2000); Gwen Glew et al., *Bullying: Children Hurting Children*, 21 Pediatrics in Rev. 183 (2000).

87. Tonja R. Nansel et al., *Relationships Between Bullying and Violence Among U.S. Youth*, 157 Arch. Pediatr. Med. 348, 353 (2003).

88. Bryan Vossekuil et al., *supra* note 46, at 16. *See also, e.g.*, Richard L. Gross, Panelist Remarks, in Am. Med. Ass'n, Educ. Forum on Adolescent Health: Youth Bullying, *supra* note 3, at 19.

89. John H. Hoover et al., *Perceived Victimization by School Bullies: New Research and Future Directions*, J. Humanistic Educ. & Dev. 76 (1993).

90. Amelia Kohn et al., What Do Bystanders Do When Children Are Being Bullied ... And Why Do They Do It? 1–2 (2006), www.chapinhall.org.

that 85 percent of bullying incidents had student bystanders, but that bystanders intervened for the victim in only 10 percent of the incidents.[91] Bullies wield real or perceived power, and (as we know from incidents of adults who recoiled from aiding crime victims) public confrontation takes courage.

When bullying drives victims like Daniel Scruggs and Ryan Halligan to suicide, bystanders may suffer enduring guilt from knowledge that their inaction contributed to the classmate's senseless, avoidable death. Nearly five months after Daniel's burial, a classmate publicly lamented his suicide in a letter to the editor of a local newspaper, an unusual step for a preteen. "I am really sorry," said the young writer, that Daniel was "verbally picked on or physically picked on..., and I watch [sic] it happen numerous times. I was in his classes." The writer despaired that "a child of the age of twelve hated his life enough to decide it wasn't worth living."[92] The letter came from the heart, but it came too late.

Bullying Prevention

The Central Role of Prevention

The pediatric safety system's coordinated response to bullying begins with prevention, both at home and in the schools. "Fairly consistent evidence suggests that children's bullying behavior can be significantly reduced by well-planned interventions."[93]

The role of public prevention efforts in the lives of youths prone to antisocial conduct is hotly debated these days. Much of the heat concerns public responses to delinquency, misconduct by a youth that would be a felony or misdemeanor if committed by an adult. The delinquency debate offers a useful framework for discussing public initiatives to prevent bullying in the schools.

Researchers have demonstrated the capacity of carefully conceived and rigorously evaluated prevention programs to reduce delinquency. Some delinquency prevention programs are "universal" (designed for the entire student population), and others are "selective" (designed to identify and intervene with youths at higher risk than their peers of antisocial conduct, including youths previously adjudicated for delinquency). The most effective programs are geared to the developmental level of the audience, stressing general skill building for elementary school students before targeting alcohol, tobacco, drugs and other critical choices faced in middle school and high school.[94]

Convincing evidence also shows the cost-effectiveness of carefully conceived and rigorously evaluated delinquency prevention programs. Juvenile confinement facilities incur operating costs that typically exceed $60,000 per cell each year; but community options such as drug treatment or counseling, including wrap-around services to assure that youths get to school or work on time, rarely exceed $15,000 annually and often cost less

---

91. Debra J. Pepler, *Observations of Bullying in the Classroom*, 92 J. Educ. Res. 1 (1998); Linda R. Jeffrey, *supra* note 83, at 7.

92. Office of the Child Advocate, *supra* note 1, at 25–26.

93. Rachel C. Vreeman & Aaron E. Carroll, *A Systematic Review of School-Based Interventions to Prevent Bullying*, 161 Arch. Pediatr. Adolescent Med. 78, 87 (Jan. 2007).

94. Peter W. Greenwood, Changing Lives: Delinquency Prevention as Crime-Control Policy 49–83 (2006).

than $5,000.[95] A 1998 study estimated that the nation saves between $1.7 million and $2.3 million for every youth prevented from following a life of juvenile or adult crime.[96]

Carefully conceived and rigorously evaluated school-based bullying prevention programs have also combined success with cost-effectiveness. A school district's bullying prevention expenses—perhaps no more than a few thousand dollars—"more than pay for themselves" because bullying has been shown "very responsive to community intervention," with reductions of between 25 percent and 50 percent reported in some schools.[97] A school's bullying prevention program costs initial and ongoing training time for school personnel; one-time or at most periodic payments for videos and similar materials; instruction time while the children are already in class; and expenses for ongoing supervision and program refinement. Existing revenue sources may provide much of the necessary funding when schools integrate bullying prevention in an existing life skills, antiviolence or antidrug curriculum.

Bullying prevention can also reduce intervention costs by the pediatric safety system described below. "Special education classes for 12 years for one child with emotional problems can cost $100,000 more than regular schooling,"[98] and the 1998 study already cited demonstrates the cost-effectiveness of preventing youth crime, including crime apparently associated with many students who bully.

Human savings also factor into the equation. Bullying prevention at a particular school can prevent devastating short-term and long-term damage to many members of the American Medical Association's triad—the bullies, the bullied and the bystanders. The students and families spared this damage are much better off, even though they may never know of their good fortune.

Goals, of course, must remain realistic. Delinquency or bullying prevention efforts cannot eliminate all incidents of the targeted antisocial conduct, any more than criminal statutes can eliminate all incidents of the conduct they target. A criminal statute stems from hope that proscription reduces the number of such acts committed. Reduction, the most realistic outcome of prevention efforts, remains a worthwhile goal when the alternative is tolerating unacceptably high rates of injury to person or property. Bullying prevention belongs at the head of the table because reaction occurs only after victims have suffered emotional or physical damage.

What about taxpayer hostility to prevention efforts aimed at juveniles? Effective prevention programs cost money, and their results—acts that do not occur—are not readily apparent. Many taxpayers have traditionally resisted delinquency prevention as a state-imposed obligation to raise and support other people's crime-prone children,[99]

---

95. Jasmine S. Tyler et al., Cost Effective Corrections: The Fiscal Architecture of Rational Juvenile Justice Systems (2006).

96. Mark A. Cohen, *The Monetary Value of Saving a High Risk Youth*, 14 J. Qualitative Criminol. 5 (1998).

97. *See, e.g.*, Am. Psychol. Ass'n, School Bullying Is Nothing New, but Psychologists Identify New Ways to Prevent It, www.psychologymatters.org/bullying.html; Minne Fekkes et al., *Effects of Antibullying School Program on Bullying and Health Complaints*, 160 Arch. Pediatr. Adolescent Med. (June 2006) (25 percent reduction in one year); James Alan Fox et al., *supra* note 15, at 2–3; Dan Olweus, Bullying at School, *supra* note 3, at 1173 (50 percent or more in Norway); Young Shin Kim et al., *supra* note 77, at 357 (presenting U.S. findings and citing other studies reaching similar conclusions) ("very responsive").

98. James Alan Fox et al., *supra* note 15, at 3.

99. *See, e.g.*, Ariz. Republic, Mar. 3, 1996, at H5 (letter to the editor) ("I am tired of hearing that I should be doing my part in cleaning up society to protect children that aren't even mine.... The bleeding-heart socialists will insist that we should protect our children. Excuse me! It should be the parents that protect the children—not society!").

though recent polls do show greater public approval for prevention as one element of a coordinated strategy to combat delinquency, perhaps because falling violent juvenile crime rates for most of the past decade have diminished insistence on "get tough" measures.[100]

Sound reasons exist for believing that school-based bullying prevention programs will continue to win even greater public support than delinquency prevention efforts frequently enjoy. Delinquency prevention and bullying prevention each target antisocial behavior, but with at least one significant distinction. Delinquency prevention sometimes raises taxpayers' hackles because public spotlight inevitably focuses on youths prone to committing crimes, sometimes serious and even vicious crimes. Bullying prevention focuses more naturally on victims. Like abused and neglected children, bullied children usually have done nothing wrong, have not provoked their victimization and remain vulnerable to physical or emotional pain for reasons beyond their control.[101] Taxpayers can much more easily imagine their own children as victims of bullying than as criminals.

The Scorecard in the States

Most of the recent state antibullying statutes fall short because they emphasize reaction without assuring a role for prevention, and indeed because their emphasis on reaction does not require state or local school boards to assert the full range of disciplinary authority that courts have permitted.

The antibullying statutes generally require state or local boards to adopt and publish in the student handbook policies prohibiting bullying in the schools, on buses or other school vehicles and at school-sponsored events on or off campus.[102] The statutes do not require boards to assert disciplinary authority over physical or virtual bullying that takes place off campus. Where the student handbook prohibits off-campus bullying, however, most courts uphold disciplinary authority over acts, such as written or Internet communications, that occur away from school but materially and substantially interfere with the school environment or impinge on the rights of other students, including the right to feel safe and secure in school.[103]

Reaction claimed the lion's share of the state legislatures' attention. Written antibullying policies generally must establish protocols for reporting bullying; for receiving, investigating and responding to these reports; and for punishing bullies with suspension, expulsion or referral to law enforcement.[104] Most statutes protect reporters, whether school personnel or parents or students, against reprisals and confer immunity from civil or criminal liability for good faith reports.[105]

State antibullying legislation generally gives prevention efforts shorter shrift. Most statutes "encourage" state and local boards to adopt bullying prevention programs in the

---

100. Douglas E. Abrams, *Reforming Juvenile Delinquency Treatment to Enhance Rehabilitation, Personal Accountability and Public Safety*, 84 Or. L. Rev. 1001, 1071–74 (2005).
101. *See, e.g.*, Dan Olweus, Bullying is NOT a Fact of Life, *supra* note 51, at 8–9 (estimating that only about 10–20 percent of victims provoke the bullies).
102. *See, e.g.*, Ariz. Rev. Stat. § 15-341(A)(40) (2007); N.J. Stat. Ann. § 18A:37-15 (2007).
103. *See infra* note 154 and accompanying text.
104. *See, e.g.*, Conn. Gen. Stat. § 10-222d (2007); N.H. Rev. Stat. § 193-F:3 (2007).
105. *See, e.g.*, Ohio Rev. Code Ann. § 3301.22 (2007).

schools, but only a few states actually require adoption.[106] Legislation normally does not appropriate funds for creating and maintaining the programs,[107] and some statutes remain silent about prevention altogether.

These legislative shortcomings should not discourage schools, in the best interests of the children they educate, from stressing prevention while responding to acts of bullying in cooperation with other actors in the pediatric safety system.

The Pediatric Safety System

Research and commentary tend to emphasize antibullying initiatives within the schools, which belong on the front lines but cannot always shoulder the entire burden. For one thing, parents play a central role in disciplining and protecting their own children. In particularly serious bullying cases, effective intervention may also depend on cooperation among other agencies in the public pediatric safety system—the juvenile court, the state child protective agency and perhaps the state mental health agency, and law enforcement. Differences in professional training and objectives may affect approaches and perceptions, but coordination can help avoid the systemic breakdown that left Daniel Scruggs vulnerable and unprotected.

Parents

Bullying prevention and reaction begin with parents. "The custody, care and nurture of the child," the Supreme Court recognized more than sixty years ago in *Prince v. Massachusetts* (1944), "reside first in the parents, whose primary function and freedom include preparation for obligations the state can neither supply nor hinder."[108] Parents, the Court added in *Wisconsin v. Yoder* (1972), hold both opportunity and responsibility for "inculcation of moral standards ... and elements of good citizenship."[109] Peers, teachers and other adults exert influence during childhood and adolescence, but parents remain prime role models for their own sons and daughters.

The home environment is central to antibullying initiatives because psychologists agree that children are not born as bullies. Bullying is learned behavior. The corollary is that bullying can also be unlearned, and most of the child's early socialization happens within the family.[110]

Researchers have found that parents can help prevent bullying by raising their sons and daughters from their youngest years in a household that rejects intimidation and

---

106. *See, e.g.*, ILL. COMP. STAT. ANN. § 5/27-23.7 (2007) (encouraging bullying prevention programs); Or. Rev. Stat. § 339.359 (2007) (same); VERNON'S TEX. STAT. & CODES ANN. § 37.083 (2007) (requiring bullying prevention programs).

107. *See, e.g.*, N.J. STAT. ANN. § 18A:37-17 (2007).

108. 321 U.S. 158, 166 (1944), *quoted in Troxel v. Granville*, 530 U.S. 57, 65–66 (2000) (plurality opinion).

109. 406 U.S. 205, 233 (1972).

110. *See, e.g.*, *Hearing on Understanding Violent Children before the Early Childhood, Youth and Families Subcomm. of the House Educ. and the Workforce Comm.*, Apr. 28, 1998 (statement of Dr. Ronald D. Stephens, Exec. Dir., Nat'l School Safety Center); Frederick J. Zimmerman et al., *Early Cognitive Stimulation, Emotional Support, and Television Watching as Predictors of Subsequent Bullying Among Grade-School Children*, 159 ARCH. PEDIATR. ADOLESCENT MED. 384, 384–85 (2005).

urges nonviolent conflict management while stressing civility, tolerance for individual differences and empathy for others.[111] Studies have also shown increased propensity for bullying by children raised in homes marked by physical or sexual abuse, domestic violence, lack of clear disciplinary rules for children or lack of parental supervision.[112] Parents also help stem future bullying by intervening firmly and teaching mutual respect whenever they learn that their child has sought to intimidate other children.[113]

Victims' parents may initially be unaware of the bullying, either because their child is embarrassed to confide in them, or (in the case of cyber bullying) because the parents do not understand the Internet's intricacies. Researchers urge parents to play active roles in their children's lives, maintain open lines of communication with the children and their physician and remain alert for early telltale signs of bullying. Something is likely wrong, for example, when the child demonstrates such abnormal behavior as bedwetting, chronic sleepless nights, sudden plunges in academic performance, or periodic stomachaches or other physical complaints whenever it is time to leave for school.[114]

Parents may be unable to protect their bullied child without cooperation from the school and other members of the public pediatric safety system. Connecticut's Office of the Child Advocate found that Judith Scruggs brought Daniel's predicament to the school's attention and tried unsuccessfully to get him to attend.[115] When the school denied effective help, she once confronted her son's chief tormenter, leaving Daniel frantic. "Mom," he told her, "You've only made things worse."[116]

The Schools

Prevention

Schools can choose from an array of bullying prevention programs, some more time-tested and rigorously evaluated than others. The paragon is the Olweus Bullying Prevention Program, developed in the 1980s by pioneering Norwegian researcher Dan Olweus and now embraced in the United States by federal and state agencies for its success in reducing bullying in European and American schools.[117] The comprehensive Olweus program proceeds from the core premise that bullying prevention requires changing the overall school environment, and not merely reacting to individual acts of bullying. Schools and other institutions develop distinctive cultures over time, and systemic change stim-

---

111. *See, e.g.*, Dorothy L. Espelage et al., *supra* note 86, at 331; Riitakerttu Kaltiala-Heino et al., *supra* note 72, at 670.

112. *See, e.g.*, Louise Bowers et al., *Perceived Family Relationships of Bullies, Victims, and Bully/Victims in Middle Childhood*, 11 J. Social & Personal Relationships 215 (1994); Minne Fekkes et al., *supra* note 69, at 21; Richard L. Gross, Panelist Remarks, in Am. Med. Ass'n, Educ. Forum on Adolescent Health: Youth Bullying, *supra* note 3, at 20; Susan P. Limber, *Addressing Youth Bullying Behaviors*, *supra* note 3, at 8; Peter K. Smith, *supra* note 40, at 246.

113. Dan Olweus, *Bullying at School, supra* note 3, at 1181–82.

114. *See, e.g.*, Ontario (Canada) Safe Schools Action Team, Shaping Safer Schools: A Bullying Prevention Action Plan 20 (2005); Minne Fekkes et al., *supra* note 69, at 21; Dan Olweus, Bullying is NOT a Fact of Life, *supra* note 51, at 14–16; Dieter Wolke et al., *supra* note 72, at 200.

115. Office of the Child Advocate, *supra* note 1, at 9, 13, 25, 26.

116. Helen O'Neill, *supra* note 2, at 2.

117. *See* Dan Olweus, Bullying at School: What We Know, *supra* note 42. *See also, e.g.*, Nat'l Middle School Ass'n, Bullying 2 (Feb. 2006), www.nmsa.org/Research/ResearchSummaries/ Bullying/tabid/709/Default.aspx (citing other programs that "have been used to decrease bullying incidents and improve the social climate of schools").

ulates individual behavioral change. Researchers recommend that antibullying efforts begin early in elementary school, with yearly reinforcement through high school.[118]

The Olweus program operates simultaneously at three levels—the school level, the class level and the individual level.

The school level.[119] All students complete an anonymous survey asking whether they have bullied others, have been bullied or know of prior acts of bullying. The survey provides context that enables school authorities to frame the prevention program, justify its costs to external constituencies and carefully monitor the program's later performance with periodic followup surveys. Anonymity helps overcome the reluctance of bullied students, like victims of rape and other antisocial conduct that induces humiliation and fear, to report victimization to family members or authorities.[120] Overcoming reluctance is central because bullying remains "perhaps the most underreported safety problem on American school campuses."[121]

Early in the process, school administrators appoint an antibullying coordinator and schedule a conference day, when teachers and staff (including custodians, cafeteria workers and crossing guards) join with selected parents and students to commit to the prevention program. The training session stresses, among other things, that adults must set a positive example by respecting and not bullying students and must remain vigilant for acts of bullying (because school personnel "dramatically overestimate their effectiveness in identifying and intervening in bullying situations").[122] Parental input continues during later conference days, individual parent-teacher conferences, and Parent-Teacher Association meetings.

The next step is to ensure adult supervision throughout the school day because most in-school bullying occurs in areas where teachers and staff do not closely monitor, such as playgrounds, lavatories, and isolated hallways and stairwells.[123] Adults must react "quickly and decidedly" to protect victims because children may be reluctant to report bullying if they lose confidence in the school's handling of prior incidents and reports.[124]

The class level.[125] Teachers set concrete antibullying rules for their students. By formulating these rules with student input, teachers give students a stake in the process, and thus greater incentive to comply. Films and literature can help instruct students about bullying's harms, while encouraging empathy for classmates and support for a healthier school environment free from fear and intimidation. Praise for students who heed the antibullying rules, and sanctions swiftly and firmly imposed on bullies, also help foster a positive school environment.

Classroom curricula remain central but insufficient by themselves. In one 2007 study, "whole-school interventions, which included multiple disciplines and complementary components directed at different levels of school organization, more often reduced victimization and bullying than the interventions that only included classroom-level curricula or social skills groups."[126]

---

118. *See, e.g.*, Minne Fekkes et al., *supra* note 69, at 21; Gwen M. Glew et al., *supra* note 69, at 1029.

119. Dan Olweus, Bullying at School: What We Know, *supra* note 42.

120. *See, e.g.*, Gwen Glew et al., *supra* note 86, at 183; Marcel F. van der Wal et al., *supra* note 64, at 1312.

121. Rana Simpson, *supra* note 4, at 1.

122. Susan P. Limber, *Addressing Youth Bullying Behaviors*, *supra* note 3, at 12.

123. Dan Olweus, Bullying is NOT a Fact of Life, *supra* note 51, at 6.

124. Susan P. Limber, *Addressing Youth Bullying Behaviors*, *supra* note 3, at 11.

125. Dan Olweus, Bullying at School: What We Know, *supra* note 42, at 81–95.

126. Rachel C. Vreeman & Aaron E. Carroll, *supra* note 93, at 86.

The individual level.[127] When bullying occurs, the teacher quickly initiates talks with the bully and the victim. The clear message to the bully is that the school will not tolerate intimidation; with the victim's consent to proceed, the message to the victim is "efficient protection." One or more meetings with the parents follow. Changing the victim's class or school may be the final outcome.

Reaction

As the Olweus program contemplates, the school must respond firmly to acts of bullying not prevented. Teachers and other school personnel (such as administrators, guidance counselors and the school nurse or physician) are the public pediatric safety system's members closest to students daily during the academic year. State law charges these professionals with monitoring attendance, observing students and reporting reasonably suspected acts of abuse or neglect by parents or other caretakers to the child protective agency or law enforcement. Safe-schools acts or antibullying legislation may also require reports to law enforcement of bullying that constitutes assaults or other crimes. Connecticut did not have antibullying legislation in 2002, but Daniel Scruggs's school waited more than a year to report signs of neglect marked by truancy and poor hygiene.[128] Thereafter the school barely communicated with the child protective agency and did not communicate at all with the juvenile court.[129]

Discipline

Prevention and reaction each depend on the school's willingness to impose disciplinary sanctions on bullies in accordance with guidelines stated in the student handbook, actions that the Washington Middle School did not take before Daniel Scruggs's suicide.

The school's disciplinary authority may implicate First Amendment free speech protections because physical or virtual bullying typically includes at least some spoken or written words such as taunts or threats. These constitutional protections, however, do not disable elementary and secondary schools from imposing sanctions on bullies. The Supreme Court permits schools to sanction students for speech that would "materially and substantially disrupt the work and discipline of the school,"[130] or that would "impinge upon the rights of other students."[131] In *Morse v. Frederick* in 2007, the Court confirmed that a school's reasonable disciplinary decisions are entitled to deference.[132] "The education of the nation's youth," the Court has said, "is primarily the responsibility of parents, teachers, and state and local school officials, and not of federal judges."[133]

Bullying may combine physical assault with words or may be entirely verbal. In either circumstance, the First Amendment permits schools considerable latitude where deci-

---

127. Dan Olweus, Bullying at School: What We Know, *supra* note 42, at 97–107.

128. Office of the Child Advocate, *supra* note 1, at I.

129. *Id.*

130. *Tinker v. Des Moines Ind. Cmty. Sch. Dist.*, 393 U.S. 503, 513 (1969), *quoted in Morse v. Frederick*, 127 S. Ct. 2618, 2626 (2007).

131. *Id.* at 509.

132. 127 S. Ct. 2618, 2625–29 (2007). *See also Hazelwood Sch. Dist. v. Kuhlmeier*, 484 U.S. 260, 267 (1988) ("the determination of what manner of speech ... is appropriate properly rests with the school board," *quoting Bethel Sch. Dist. v. Fraser*, 478 U.S. 675, 683 (1986)).

133. *Hazelwood*, 484 U.S. at 273.

sion makers base disciplinary sanction not on the content or viewpoint of the bully's words, but on the bully's intent to inflict emotional maltreatment and the victim's reasonable reactions of embarrassment, intimidation or fear.[134]

The first circumstance—physical assault plus words—implicates the balance struck by the Supreme Court between conduct and speech. In *United States v. O'Brien* in 1968, the Court held that where conduct involves elements of speech, the First Amendment permits the state to punish the conduct if punishment "is within the constitutional power of the Government; if it furthers an important or substantial governmental interest; if the governmental interest is unrelated to the suppression of free expression; and if the incidental restriction on alleged First Amendment freedoms is no greater than is essential to the furtherance of that interest."[135]

Where the bully's conduct involves physical assault, *O'Brien* permits schools to discipline the assault without regard for any words the bully may have uttered. The Supreme Court has held that "a physical assault is not by any stretch of the imagination expressive conduct protected by the First Amendment.... 'Violence or other types of potentially expressive activities that produce special harms distinct from their communicative impact ... are entitled to no constitutional protection.'"[136] Because schools have the "obligation to protect pupils from mistreatment by other children,"[137] *O'Brien* means that bullies gain no First Amendment sanctuary when words accompany a punch in the nose.

In schools or elsewhere, the First Amendment also offers no protection for speech that constitutes "fighting words" or "true threats." Fighting words are "personally abusive epithets which, when addressed to the ordinary citizen, are, as a matter of common knowledge, inherently likely to provoke violent reaction."[138] True threats "encompass those statements where the speaker means to communicate a serious expression of an intent to commit an act of unlawful violence to a particular individual or group of individuals."[139] "The speaker need not actually intend to carry out the threat" because "a prohibition on true threats 'protect[s] individuals from the fear of violence' and 'from the disruption that fear engenders,' in addition to protecting people 'from the possibility that the threatened violence will occur.'"[140]

These two categories of unprotected speech characterize much physical or virtual bullying, including face-to-face confrontations and Internet communications such as the one that led a seventeen-year-old Louisville, Kentucky, junior to commit suicide three weeks after telling her parents that an anonymous posting on MySpace.com warned, "I am going to beat you up. Oh, and by the way, I'm not going to put you in the hospital. I'm going to put you in the morgue."[141]

---

134. *Cf. Test Masters Educ. Servs. v. Singh*, 428 F.3d 559, 580 (5th Cir. 2005) (harassment); *Commonwealth v. Welch*, 825 N.E.2d 1005, 1008 n.1, 1016–20 (Mass. 2005) (same); *Trummel v. Mitchell*, 131 P.3d 305, 311–12 (Wash. 2006) (same).

135. 391 U.S. 367, 377 (1968).

136. *Wisconsin v. Mitchell*, 508 U.S. 476, 484–85 (1993), *quoting Roberts v. U.S. Jaycees*, 468 U.S. 609, 628 (1984).

137. *New Jersey v. T.L.O.*, 469 U.S. 325, 350 (1985) (Powell & O'Connor, JJ., concurring). *See also, e.g., Butler v. Rio Rancho Public Sch. Bd. of Educ.*, 341 F.3d 1197, 1201 (10th Cir. 2003); *Bogle-Assegai v. Bloomfield Bd. of Educ.*, 467 F. Supp. 2d 236, 244 n.5 (D. Conn. 2006) ("legitimate interest in providing a safe environment for students and staff").

138. *Virginia v. Black*, 538 U.S. 343, 359 (2003), *citing* Cohen v. California, 403 U.S. 15, 20 (1971), and *Chaplinsky v. New Hampshire*, 315 U.S. 568, 572 (1942).

139. *Virginia v. Black*, 538 U.S. 343, 359 (2003) (citations omitted).

140. *Id.* at 359–60 (citation omitted).

141. Daarel Burnette, *supra* note 73, at 5H.

The Supreme Court's decision in *Tinker v. Des Moines Independent Community School District* (1969) authorizes schools to discipline verbal bullying not amounting to fighting words or true threats.[142] *Tinker* stated that students do not "shed their constitutional rights to freedom of speech or expression at the schoolhouse gate."[143] The Court specified, however, that students' rights (including their First Amendment free expression rights) must be "applied in light of the special characteristics of the school environment,"[144] including the obligation of school officials to "prescribe and control conduct in the schools,"[145] and to meet "interference, actual or nascent, with the schools' work or … collision with the rights of other students to be secure and to be let alone."[146]

The Supreme Court's post-*Tinker* speech decisions have strengthened the schools' hand in disciplinary proceedings arising from bullying. Because of "the schools' custodial and tutelary responsibility for children … for their own good and that of their classmates,"[147] the Court has specified that the constitutional rights of public school students "are not automatically coextensive with the rights of adults in other settings."[148] Schools remain "responsible for maintaining discipline, health, and safety" for students compelled to attend by compulsory education acts, and "securing order in the school environment sometimes requires that students be subjected to greater controls than those appropriate for adults."[149]

The Supreme Court also recognizes that in elementary and secondary schools, the "basic educational mission" emphasizes "teaching students the boundaries of socially appropriate behavior"[150] and "the shared values of a civilized social order."[151] Schools remain "a principal instrument in awakening the child to cultural values, in preparing him for later professional training, and in helping him to adjust normally to his environment."[152]

In the exercise of reasonable disciplinary authority approved by the Supreme Court, schools may discipline bullies because bullying produces "interference with schools' work" and "collision with the rights of other students to be secure and to be let alone." Regardless of any speech associated with individual acts of bullying, disciplinary sanctions fulfill the schools' responsibility for "maintaining discipline, health, and safety." Sanctions also enable schools to teach that bullying and similar physical or emotional coercion remain inconsistent with "socially appropriate behavior" and "the shared values of a civilized social order."

As a practical matter, what do these constitutional principles mean for daily discipline in the public schools? Bullies may be suspended or expelled for violating student handbook provisions proscribing such peer abuse as assault, threats, harassment, disruptive behavior or disorderly conduct in school, on school buses or during school-sanctioned or school-supervised events.[153] In accordance with these provisions, most courts uphold

---

142. *Tinker v. Des Moines Ind. Cmty. Sch. Dist.*, 393 U.S. 503 (1969).

143. *Id.* at 506.

144. *Id.*, *quoted in Morse v. Frederick*, 127 S. Ct. 2618, 2625, 2626–27 (2007).

145. 393 U.S. at 507.

146. *Id.* at 508.

147. *Vernonia Sch. Dist. 47J v. Acton*, 515 U.S. 646, 656 (1995).

148. *Bethel Sch. Dist. v. Fraser*, 478 U.S. 675, 682 (1986), *quoted in Morse v. Frederick*, 127 S. Ct. 2618, 2626 (2007).

149. *Board of Educ. v. Earls*, 536 U.S. 822, 830–31 (2002).

150. *Bethel Sch. Dist. v. Fraser*, 478 U.S. 675, 681, 685 (1986).

151. *Id.* at 683.

152. *Hazelwood Sch. Dist. v. Kuhlmeier*, 484 U.S. 260, 272 (1988), *quoting Brown v. Board of Educ.*, 347 U.S. 483, 493 (1954).

153. *Cf. Morse v. Frederick*, 127 S. Ct. 2618 (2007) (upholding suspension of high school student for misconduct committed during off-campus, school-sanctioned and school-supervised school ac-

school disciplinary authority over acts, such as written or Internet communications, that occur off campus but materially and substantially interfere with the school environment or impinge on the rights of other students, including the right to feel safe and secure in school.[154] Cyber bullies present special challenges because anonymity may permit them to evade detection, but these tormenters often seek an audience and brag to their friends. "You just have to use good old-fashioned sleuthing to find out," says one researcher.[155]

The Juvenile Court, the Child Protective Agency and Law Enforcement

Parents can prevent or resolve some and indeed, perhaps many bullying cases. The school can resolve other cases that resist prevention or parental resolution. Particularly serious cases, however, may require invocation of the juvenile court's truancy, delinquency, or abuse or neglect jurisdiction. With or without juvenile court intervention, these serious cases may also summon involvement by a child protective agency, mental health agency or law enforcement.

Truancy

Daniel Scruggs was a truant, and teachers and administrators in the Washington Middle School knew it. Truancy (a child's wrongful refusal to attend school) is a "status offense," misconduct by a youth that the juvenile court may adjudicate even though the misconduct would not be a crime if committed by an adult. A child habitually absent from school is truant only where the fault for absence lies with the child and not with the parents.[156] Truancy petitions present opportunities for creative child protection because much truancy stems from underlying personal or family stresses beyond the student's

---

tivity); *Kolesnick v. Omaha Pub. Sch. Dist.*, 558 N.W.2d 807 (Neb. 1997) (affirming expulsion of student for bringing knife on school bus).

154. *Compare, e.g., Wisniewski v. Bd. of Educ.*, 494 F.3d 34, 35 (2d Cir. 2007) (affirming eighth-grader's suspension for sharing with friends on the Internet a drawing, which he sent from his parents' home computer, suggesting that a named teacher should be shot and killed; held that it was "reasonably foreseeable that [the drawing] would cause a disruption within the school environment"), *with Layshock v. Hermitage Sch. Dist*, 496 F. Supp. 2d 587 (W.D. Pa. 2007) (school violated high school senior's First Amendment free expression rights by disciplining him for an Internet parody of the principal, created outside school, because no substantial disruption of the school environment was shown). *See also, e.g., Doe v. Pulaski County Special Sch. Dist.*, 306 F.3d 616, 621–28 (8th Cir. 2002) (en banc) (upholding junior high school student's expulsion for writing a threatening letter at home about a classmate); *Flaherty v. Keystone Oaks Sch. Dist.*, 247 F. Supp. 2d 698, 702 (W.D. Pa. 2003) (reversing discipline imposed on high school student arising from Internet posting made at home because student handbook did not limit school's authority over off-campus activity to that which causes a material and substantial disruption to the school day); *Killion v. Franklin Reg'l Sch. Dist.*, 136 F. Supp. 2d 446 (W.D. Pa. 2001) (suspension of high school student for writing, at home, an email document that ridiculed a teacher violated First Amendment because the district failed to adduce evidence that the email disrupted school activities or interfered with the rights of others); *J.S. v. Bethlehem Area Sch. Dist.*, 807 A.2d 847, 864–69 (Pa. 2002) (affirming school district's decision to expel student based on his creation, at home, of an Internet Web site containing threatening and derogatory comments about his teacher and the school's principal).

155. Amanda Paulson, *supra* note 27, at 11.

156. *See, e.g., In re Whittekind*, 2004 WL 3090246 (Ohio Ct. App. Dec. 17, 2004) (child was not truant because his absence from school was due to his father's refusal to allow him to attend).

control, and indeed sometimes beyond remedy by only a coercive juvenile court order to attend school.

Chronic absenteeism from school frequently stems from embarrassment and anxiety characteristic of bullying.[157] In one survey, truants were teased in the hallways, ridiculed in gym class or otherwise harassed for their shyness or peculiar behavior.[158] Many of the truants were depressed, angry or both, and some had attempted suicide or had expressed homicidal thoughts.[159] The researchers called truancy "a useful marker for identifying adolescents with … substantial psychological and social difficulties," and advised authorities to make "a thorough assessment of the surrounding circumstances at home, at school, and in the peer group."[160] Such an assessment might have spared Daniel Scruggs misery in school and saved his life.

Truants with undiagnosed learning disabilities and attention deficit disorders may be labeled as discipline problems without receiving needed special education.[161] A truancy petition may provide an opportunity for testing and diagnosis, and perhaps also for preventing or responding to bullying that frequently accompanies manifestations of such disorders. Daniel Scruggs was suspended for resisting bullies after special educational services for his learning disability, provided in elementary school, were discontinued in middle school without testing to determine his needs.[162]

To help assure the truant's return to the classroom, the juvenile court may need to confront underlying personal or family stresses in cooperation with the schools, the child protective agency, other social agencies such as mental health or private providers. To enhance coordination in truancy cases, many juvenile courts hold "truancy court" in the schools themselves, often early in the morning so parents can attend without taking time off work. The aim is to enable parents, school authorities and other care providers to help the court fashion remedies responsive to stresses on the family or child.[163] Where bullying is apparent, however, the court must also remain sensitive to the child's resistance to appearing in proceedings at school, the scene of the bullying and a location that may be within the bully's view.

The Coalition for Juvenile Justice states the widely accepted view that juvenile courts should balance firmness with restraint in truancy cases: "Generally, other agencies, such as social services or mental health, should have the principal responsibility for developing and providing services," and "court intervention should be reserved for those cases where services have been offered but not utilized or where a youth's behaviors pose a significant threat to his or her own safety."[164] The juvenile court remains the quarterback, helping ensure that the bullied truant receives services and protection.

---

157. Arthur Neilson & Dan Gerbner, *Psychosocial Aspects of Truancy in Early Adolescence*, 14 Adolescence 313 (1979).

158. *Id.* at 323.

159. *Id.* at 316.

160. *Id.* at 323.

161. *See, e.g.*, Robin Russel et al., *Status Offenders: Attitudes of Child Welfare Practitioners Toward Practice and Policy Issues*, 72 Child Welfare 13, 19 (1993 No. 1).

162. Office of the Child Advocate, *supra* note 1, at I.

163. *See, e.g.*, *Truancy Court Good First Step of Keeping Kids in School*, Green Bay (Wis.) Press-Gazette, Aug. 30, 2007, at 7A.; Brian Lewis, *Going Before the Judge*, Springfield (Mo.) News-Leader, Apr. 24, 2007, at 1B; *Judgment Day: Truancy Court Aids Families*, Oklahoman (Oklahoma City), Apr. 6, 2007, at 10A (editorial); John Norton, *Truancy Court Goes to School*, Pueblo (Colo.) Chieftain, Mar. 21, 2007.

164. Coalition for Juvenile Justice, A Celebration or a Wake?: The Juvenile Court After 100 Years 48 (1998).

Delinquency

Bullies may fall within juvenile court delinquency jurisdiction or, in serious cases, criminal court jurisdiction under statutes that permit some youths to be tried and sentenced as adults. Delinquency referrals may come from school resource officers or other law enforcement officials, public agencies or private persons.

Face-to-face or cyber bullying may violate criminal statutes proscribing such acts as assault, battery, extortion, threats or terroristic threats.[165] These statutes would be implicated, for example, by pushing, shoving or beating the victim; stealing or destroying the victim's property; or, under some statutes, even stealing the victim's identity.

Even without the latitude the Supreme Court accords schools in the reasonable exercise of their disciplinary authority, delinquency or criminal petitions may overcome any First Amendment free speech defenses raised by the bully. Isolated instances of taunting or name calling may be constitutionally protected speech, making delinquency adjudication or criminal conviction more difficult to secure than school discipline.[166] Fighting words and true threats characteristic of bullying, however, remain unprotected by the First Amendment and thus subject to prosecution. Bullying's persistence may also permit content-neutral prosecution of speech or conduct under harassment, stalking or similar statutes that criminalize the bully's intent to inflict emotional maltreatment and the victim's reasonable reactions of embarrassment, intimidation or fear.[167]

Abuse and Neglect

The juvenile court's abuse jurisdiction reaches physical abuse, emotional abuse or sexual abuse inflicted by a parent or other caretaker. The court's neglect jurisdiction reaches failure by these adults to provide the child support, education, nutrition or medical, surgical or other necessary care.[168] Because the facts of individual cases so often manifest both abuse and neglect, some authorities combine the two concepts under the inclusive term "maltreatment."

Where bullying triggers maltreatment charges, the subjects are usually the child victim and his or her family. In light of the studies discussed showing increased propensity for bullying by children raised in homes marked by abuse or domestic violence, however, authorities should also remain alert for maltreatment plaguing bullies' families.[169]

---

165. *See, e.g., Bowman v. Williamson County Bd. of Educ.*, 488 F. Supp. 2d 679, 680 (M.D. Tenn. 2007) (student who threatened classmate on school bus and committed a battery on school grounds was arrested for assault, suspended from school, and sent to alternative learning center); *Doe v. Ennis Ind. Sch. Dist.*, 2007 WL 273550 *1 (N.D. Tex. Jan. 31, 2007) (bullies criminally prosecuted for assault of classmate); *Miller v. State*, 571 S.E.2d 788 (Ga. 2002) (affirming fifteen-year-old bully's convictions for aggravated battery, aggravated assault, and felony murder of bullying victim); *In re Jeffrey K.*, 728 N.W.2d 606 (Neb. 2007) (affirming bully's delinquency adjudication for violating criminal stalking statute). *Cf. State v. Kuhia*, 96 P.3d 590, 600 n.15 (Hawaii 2004) (terroristic threat against public servant); *People v. Feldman*, 791 N.Y.S.2d 361 (S. Ct. 2005) (extortion in primary election campaign).

166. *See, e.g., In re Douglas D.*, 626 N.W.2d 725 (Wis. 2001) (eighth-grader in creative writing class wrote story expressing hostility toward his teacher and depicted a student beheading her with a machete; court reversed delinquency adjudication on First Amendment grounds, but upheld school's suspension of the boy).

167. *See supra* note 134 and accompanying text.

168. Mo. Rev. Stat. § 210.110(1), (12) (2007).

169. *See supra* note 112 and accompanying text.

In the case of bullied children, a parent or custodian might be neglectful where underlying family dysfunction appears related to absenteeism from school, or to the child's victimization. Informal response may remain central. After the child protective agency or law enforcement investigates potential neglect underlying reported bullying, the matter may be closed because authorities turn the matter over to the school or find the parent's voluntary acceptance of services sufficient. Where more intensive intervention and oversight are warranted, or where the parent refuses to accept services voluntarily, the agency may refer the case to the juvenile court for an order mandating services. The child protective agency or the juvenile court may coordinate public efforts, and the case may end up involving not only social workers, physicians and psychologists but also service providers in such fields as health care, housing assistance and drug and alcohol counseling.[170]

Juvenile courts should tread carefully before invoking their expansive neglect jurisdiction against the families of bullying victims. Most bullying does not stem from failures directly or indirectly attributable to the bullied child's parents, and a neglect petition may only worsen the situation by appearing to blame the victim's family. The black letter rule is that the juvenile court's civil neglect jurisdiction focuses on the child's condition, leaving it to the criminal courts to determine the parent's culpability if authorities choose to prosecute.[171] Reality is frequently at odds with the rule, however, because civil neglect orders inevitably tar the parents as wrongdoers and may invite remedies punitive in fact if not in law, including the child's removal from the home in extreme cases. Such civil orders may also impose harsh collateral consequences on the parents, such as loss of tenuous employment or diminished respect in the eyes of the child and siblings.

When nonperpetrator parents face maltreatment proceedings, the petition normally charges failure to protect the child from a known or readily apparent danger, such as physical or sexual abuse by an adult companion residing in the household.[172] Most bullying cases implicating conduct of the victim's parents, however, stem not from the parents' failure to protect their child but from their ability to protect. Indeed, the parents typically appear as blameless as their bullied child, and may even remain reasonably unaware of the bullying for some period. Judith Scruggs's filthy apartment and her inattention to Daniel's personal hygiene might have supported a neglect petition, but even she reported the bullying to school authorities and sought their assistance.

Carelessly invoked neglect jurisdiction may also be unduly harsh on the bullied child. Children frequently blame themselves for divorces and other domestic difficulties that land their parents in court or before a child protective agency. Targeting the victim's parents as neglectful may only weaken the already emotionally fragile child, who now suffers from both the bully's torment and perceived responsibility for trapping the parents in the child protection system.

On the other hand, neglect proceedings may protect some bullied children where juvenile court jurisdiction does not otherwise attach in the absence of truancy. For one thing, circumstances at home may contribute to bullying at school, as they apparently did in Daniel Scruggs's case. Without a court order, the school district may also remain unable or unwilling to provide the child effective services, including services unavailable outside the child protective system.

---

170. SARAH H. RAMSEY & DOUGLAS E. ABRAMS, CHILDREN AND THE LAW IN A NUTSHELL 94–95 (2d ed. 2003).

171. *See, e.g., K.D. v. People*, 139 P.3d 695, 699 (Colo. 2006); *In re Alexander C.*, 843 N.E.2d 211, 221 (Ohio Ct. App. 2006).

172. *See, e.g., In re T.G.*, 578 N.W.2d 921 (S.D. 1998).

Where the juvenile court finds the child neglected, it may order the child protective agency or mental health agency to make reasonable efforts to work with the family to remedy the neglect. The Scruggs's filthy apartment and its effect on Daniel's personal hygiene may have made Daniel's bullying case unusual, but timely intervention by the juvenile court and these public agencies might have saved the boy's life and avoided the mother's indictment soon after his burial.

Conclusion: Looking Toward the Future

Recent state bullying legislation and federal funding initiatives arouse both optimism and concern—optimism because the measures demonstrate public support for meaningful action to spare millions of today's schoolchildren the pain endured by their parents and grandparents, but concern because the measures also suggest perennial unwillingness to apply civil and criminal statutes that have long authorized schools and others in the pediatric safety system to respond to conduct characteristic of bullying.

In our nation whose educational policy strives to "leave no child behind,"[173] Dan Olweus states the core aspiration: "It is a fundamental democratic right for a child to feel safe in school and to be spared the oppression and repeated, intentional humiliation implied in bullying. No student should be afraid of going to school for fear of being harassed or degraded, and no parent should need to worry about such things happening to his or her child."[174] The leap from aspiration to reality remains a challenge because legislation, schools' written bullying policies and public agency protocols depend on inspired application to achieve their child protective goals.

---

173. No Child Left Behind Act of 2001, Pub. L. No. 107-110, 115 Stat. 1425 (codified in scattered sections of 20 U.S.C.).

174. Dan Olweus, *Bullying at School*, *supra* note 3, at 1183 (italics and exclamation point omitted).

17

Brutality and Blindness: Bullying in Schools and Negligent Supervision by School Officials

Daniel B. Weddle

Normally, when we think of equity in educational opportunity, we think in terms of equality of treatment toward racial, ethnic, religious, gender, or other groups with specific characteristics that mark individual members as part of such groups. Such an emphasis makes sense because many such groups have been the historical targets of discrimination by majority populations not only in the provision of education but in numerous other arenas. Another pervasive and insidious inequity in educational opportunity exists, however, in nearly every school in the nation, an inequity that has received little systematic attention among those who run the nation's schools or those who define what schools should be legally required to do about that inequity. It is an inequity easily overlooked because it takes place largely out of the view of teachers and administrators and because it does not target some easily identified group with common identity characteristics. Nevertheless, it is as damaging and long-lasting as any created by traditionally recognized inequities. That inequity in educational opportunity springs from the damage caused by students bullying their peers.

It may seem a stretch to group the effects of students bullying peers with the effects of unequal treatment of racial minorities, the poor, and others we traditionally recognize as disadvantaged by our educational system.[1] Bullying, however, shares important characteristics with traditionally recognized sources of educational inequity. It affects anywhere from 15 percent to 30 percent of all students who attend school in the United States.[2] It is a major force behind dropout rates among high school children, and it is among the chief causes of chronic absences among students of all ages.[3] It results in serious emotional problems for its victims, problems that include severe depression and suicide;[4] and

---

1. See Nan Stein, *Bullying or Sexual Harassment? The Missing Discourse of Rights in an Era of Zero Tolerance*, 45 ARIZ. L. REV. 783 (2003) for her discussion of potential detriments to civil rights discourse if the focus on bullying is allowed to swallow up efforts to protect children from discrimination; see also, Daniel B. Weddle, *Bullying in Schools: The Disconnect Between Empirical Research and Constitutional, Statutory, and Tort Duties to Supervise*, 77 TEMP. L. REV. 641, 645 n.20 (2004), for a discussion of Stein's objections to grouping traditional discrimination concerns under the umbrella of "bullying."
2. *See infra* notes 36–37 and accompanying text.
3. *See infra* notes 23–28, 154, and accompanying text.
4. *See infra* notes 23–28 and accompanying text.

it is a consistent predictor of later criminal behavior among its perpetrators.[5] For those who are not completely driven away from schooling, it serves as a constant and crippling interference with learning.[6] It coarsens the cultures of the schools in which it operates, and it often serves as the forerunner of traditionally recognized forms of harassment.[7] In short, it is among the most detrimental and pervasive threats to educational equity in our schools.

It is in some ways unfortunate for U.S. students that the empirical research into bullying began in Europe, because the term "bullying" is for most adults in the United States an innocuous term that conjures images of a child occasionally picked on by a larger, stronger classmate who will one day be faced down by his peers. Had the research begun in the United States, perhaps the phenomenon would have been termed something that to U.S. ears would be more evocative of its true nature. Bullying, as it has been studied over the past two decades or so, is more akin to torment and brutalization than run-of-the-mill childhood power struggles and jockeying for position on the social hierarchy among schoolchildren. It is instead a targeted, ongoing, and severe attack on a particular child that leaves the child isolated, legitimately afraid, and far too often emotionally debilitated and dangerously depressed.[8] Viewed in that light, bullying is more difficult to dismiss and its pervasiveness in American schools much more disturbing.

Bullying nevertheless does not typically command the moral and legal attention that other forms of harassment often receive for some understandable reasons. Majority populations rightly recognize a moral responsibility, often explicitly undergirded by legal compulsion, to ameliorate the effects of past and ongoing discrimination against racial, ethnic, and other groups defined by identity characteristics, because majority populations have been the genesis of that discrimination and often benefit significantly from its continuation at the expense of victims. The perpetuation of unequal educational opportunities for minorities continues to ensure that members of majority populations enjoy unfair access to the rewards that education provides, while those who are targets of discrimination are largely cut off from enjoyment of those rewards. In addition, the deep-seated nature of discriminatory attitudes demands specific attention from those in positions of power if inequity in education on the basis of identity characteristics is ever going to become a relic of an unenlightened and unjust past.

The moral case for holding schools responsible for protecting victims of bullying from the torment they endure at school rests on different grounds and tends to defy the legal theories most often employed to combat traditionally recognized types of discrimination.[9] Victims share no common identity traits that would make them easily identifiable and therefore subject to protection under the equal protection clause as the victims of an "invidious classification of persons" that has inspired disparate treatment by the state.[10] Similarly, antidiscrimination statutes such as Title VI and Title IX are helpful only if the lack of protection from school officials is based on race or gender, respectively; and even

---

5. *See infra* notes 29–32 and accompanying text.

6. *See infra* notes 23–28 and accompanying text.

7. Weddle, *supra* note 1, at 649.

8. *See infra* notes 18–28 and accompanying text.

9. For a detailed discussion of the inadequacy of current legal approaches to the problem of bullying, see generally Weddle, *supra* note 1, at 641.

10. *Nabozny v. Podlesny*, 92 F.3d 446, 453–54 (7th Cir. 1996) (explaining that "[t]he gravamen of equal protection lies not in the fact of deprivation of a right but in the invidious classification of persons aggrieved by the state's action.... A plaintiff must demonstrate.... that a decisionmaker singled out a particular group for disparate treatment and selected his course of action at least in part for the purpose of causing its adverse effects on the identifiable group").

then the threshold for school liability is very high.[11] Theories rooted in the due process clause succeed only where school officials' action is so deliberately indifferent to the torment that the inaction "shocks the conscience of the court."[12] Few situations have been judged to rise to that level.

A cause of action based on the tort of negligent supervision would seem the most natural because the elements of negligence do not require that the victim be the member of an identifiable minority group. That cause of action, however, breaks down quickly for several reasons. First, many states shield schools and school officials from liability for negligence unless the officials' negligence rises to a level of recklessness or gross negligence.[13] Second, because the injuries inflicted by bullies, when they rise to some actionable level, are the results of third-party acts, courts usually will not find liability unless school officials were aware of a specific threat and did nothing to prevent injury or school officials were simply absent altogether from an area where supervision was required.[14] Even in the latter case, courts are often reluctant to second-guess school officials' judgments about whether supervision was actually required. In other words, because it is the bully who actually causes the injury, the injury is generally deemed unforeseeable to school officials, so either school officials have no duty to provide supervision to prevent the injury in the first place;[15] or if they have a duty, the school's breach cannot be the proximate cause of the injury because the bully's actions constitute an unforeseeable intervening or superseding cause.[16]

The problems with foreseeability are not surprising when one considers the nature of schooling. Teachers must supervise large numbers of children and cannot be expected to anticipate every malicious action and prevent its occurrence. If a child decides to strike out against another child, there may be little or no warning that would alert a teacher to the need to take action. It seems hardly fair that school officials should be required to educate children and then be held liable for failing to read a child's mind. Even when some warning arguably exists, the harm may take place in a moment in which the teacher's attention is directed elsewhere; it would simply be unrealistic to then blame the teacher because a child is smart enough to attempt his misconduct when the teacher is distracted.

Yet we are left with the reality that some children are subject daily to ongoing, severely damaging bullying in their schools. Because state law requires that they attend those schools or attend private schools generally suffering from the same problems, these children and their parents are often trapped in an untenable position that forces them to send their children off each morning to the mercies of bullies who operate largely free of adult interference. It does them no good to hear that legal theories do not address such torment and that teachers cannot be expected to protect children from every harm.

---

11. Under the standard enunciated in *Davis v. Monroe County Bd. of Educ.*, 526 U.S. 629 (1999), Title IX liability will attach only if plaintiff demonstrates that school officials had actual knowledge of the alleged sexual harassment and were deliberately indifferent to the plaintiff's plight.

12. *Castaldo v. Stone*, 192 F. Supp. 2d 1124, 1173 (D. Colo. 2001) (holding, in a case springing from the shootings at Columbine High School, that school officials' "alleged toleration of bullying, teasing, and intimidation on the part of the Columbine student body, while reprehensible if true, is not conscience shocking in a Fourteenth Amendment substantive due process sense").

13. *E.g., Duncan v. Hampton County Sch. Dist. No. 2*, 517 S.E.2d 449, 453 (S.C. App. 1999) (explaining that for liability to attach, school officials' supervision of students must be shown to have been grossly negligent under the state's Tort Claims Act).

14. *See infra* notes 55–59 and accompanying text.

15. *Id.*

16. *See infra* notes 118–20 and accompanying text.

The Problem of Bullying

One of the first difficulties in talking about bullying in the United States is that the term itself engenders little concern among those unfamiliar with the research into the phenomenon because in this country's common usage *bullying* evokes images of the common encounters all schoolchildren experience at one point or another. The term, as it is used in educational research, however, comes from work done initially in Norway in response to the suicides of three teenagers from different schools who found they could not endure any more of the torment they had been receiving at school.[17] Norway began an intensive study of the bullying phenomenon, and that research sparked research around the world, spurred in part in this country by the shootings at Columbine and other U.S. schools.

From that initial research, led by Dan Olweus, came the term *bullying*; as Olweus defined the term, it applied when a student "is exposed, repeatedly and over time, to negative actions on the part of one or more other students."[18] Olweus considered "negative actions" to be similar to the what the social sciences would regard as "aggressive behavior."[19] Perhaps a more evocative definition is one that often animates U.S. research: "longstanding violence, physical or mental, conducted by an individual or group and directed against an individual who is not able to defend himself in the actual situation."[20] Bullying, as it is understood by researchers, always occurs where there is an imbalance of power, either physical or otherwise, between the victim and the bully or the group of bullies.[21] Such aggression is likened by two researchers to child abuse perpetrated by a child's peers.[22]

The gravity of the phenomenon comes home more clearly when one considers its effects.[23] The damage to victims is primarily emotional in nature, but it is not at all trivial. Victims suffer from suicidal tendencies, psychiatric problems, depression, chronic anxiety, eating disorders, increased absenteeism, and lack of motivation at school.[24] Relational aggression, a form of bullying especially common among girls, targets the victim's friendships and inclusion in the social group,[25] and produces isolation that leads to long-term mental health problems for girls who fall victim to such bullying.[26] In fact, irrespective of whether bullying consists of direct threats and harassment or relational aggression, the emotional problems that stem from bullying often continue for years after the bullying

---

17. D.L. Espelage, *Research on School Bullying and Victimization: What Have We Learned and Where Do We Go from Here?* 32 Sch. Psychol. Rev. 365, 365 (2003).

18. Joseph A. Drake et al., *The Nature and Extent of Bullying at School*, 73 J. Sch. Health 173, 173 (2003).

19. Dan Olweus, *A Profile of Bullying at School*, Educ. Leadership., March 2003, at 12.

20. Espelage, *supra* note 17, at 368.

21. Drake et al., *supra* note 18, at 173.

22. Sue Ellen Fried & Paula Fried, Bullies, Targets, & Witnesses: Helping Children Break the Pain Chain 3–4 (1989).

23. For a more detailed discussion of the implications of current empirical research concerning the effects and prevention of bullying in schools, see Weddle, *supra* note 1, at 641.

24. *See* Drake et al., *supra* note 18, *at* 174; *see also* Jill Packman, et al., *We're Not Gonna Take It: A Student Driven Anti-Bullying Approach*, 125 Educ. 546, 548 (2005).

25. Espelage, *supra* note 17, at 371.

26. Nancy Mullin-Rindler, *Relational Aggression: A Different Kind of Bullying*, 82 Principal 60, May–June 2003, at 60.

has ended.[27] One Australian study found that these effects even in the short term had demonstrable physical consequences in that victims of bullying taking place in "early high school suffered significantly poorer physical health later in high school."[28]

Allowing bullying to continue unabated can severely damage even the bullies themselves. A study by the National Institute of Child Health and Human Development revealed that by the time boys who have been identified as bullies reach age twenty-four, 60 percent will have at least one criminal conviction, and nearly 40 percent will have three or more convictions.[29] Those figures make some sense when one considers the characteristics of bullies themselves and what ignoring those characteristics can mean. In one study, fewer than one half of the bullies studied showed any remorse for their behavior, and more than 20 percent were actually happy about what they had done to other children.[30] As one commentator noted, an FBI study of schools, many of which had experienced school shootings, found that school shooters shared a significant number of traits and behaviors

> that are chillingly characteristic of school bullies or their victims, including poor coping skills, lack of resiliency, alienation, dehumanization of others, lack of empathy, intolerance, exaggerated sense of entitlement, low self-esteem,[31] and anger management problems.[32]

Even bystanders are often deeply affected by bullying that occurs in their presence. They tend to become desensitized over time to the pain endured by the victims and to develop rationalizations for the bullying rather than seeing it as clearly wrong or undeserved.[33] In fact, when witnessing bullying incidents, bystanders spend as much as 75 percent of that time reinforcing the bullies' behavior.[34] The result can only be the coarsening of school culture and the further isolation and victimization of the bullies' targets.

What usually surprises many parents and educators is that severe bullying is prevalent in schools across the country and across socioeconomic lines. Whether urban, rural, or suburban, schools tend to be equally afflicted by bullying. In fact, a school's location, size, and ethnic makeup are not significant factors in predicting the prevalence of bullying.[35] Nevertheless, despite the wealth of research that has been done with regard to its effects and its prevention, bullying continues to be a problem that is global in scope and is on the rise in this country[36]. A study published in the *Journal of the American Medical Association* found that of over 15,000 Midwestern students surveyed, 29.9 percent admitted to "frequent involvement in bullying," either as victim or bully.[37]

---

27. Jill Packman et al., *supra* note 24, at 547.

28. Drake et al., *supra* note 18, at 176.

29. Weddle, *supra* note 1, at 649.

30. Drake et al., *supra* note 18, at 177.

31. Bullies actually tend to have high self-esteem, while victims develop low self-esteem. Kathy Christie, *Chasing the Bullies Away*, 86 Phi Delta Kappan 725, 725 (2005). Victims, however, according to a study by the U.S. Centers of Disease Control and Prevention, are at high risk for resorting to the type of retaliation played out in school shootings. Kathleen Conn, Bullying and Harassment: A Legal Guide for Educators 4 (2004).

32. Conn, *supra* note 31, at 4.

33. Mullin-Rindler, *supra* note 26, at 60.

34. Packman et al., *supra* note 24, at 550.

35. Weddle, *supra* note 1, at 652.

36. Packman et al., *supra* note 24, at 547.

37. Espelage, *supra* note 17, at 367.

The Educational Solution to Bullying

The news is not all bad, however. It turns out that bullying can be dramatically reduced in a very short time if school officials are willing to do the hard work to change the school culture. For example, a program developed by Dan Olweus based on the work he began in Norway typically reduces bullying by 50 percent or more in the first year it is implemented.[38] What programs like Olweus's have tapped is what research has demonstrated as the single most important factor influencing whether a school does or does not have a bullying culture: whether the administration and faculty have engaged in a deliberate, informed, and sustained effort to create a culture where bullying is not tolerated by students, staff, or parents.[39] When properly implemented, comprehensive, school-wide approaches involving all levels of the school community have been consistently shown to be the most effective approach to reducing bullying.[40] Therefore, school officials who wish to save their students from what has been shown to affect virtually every type of school in the country must adopt a school-wide approach that involves staff, students, and parents in developing a strategy and policies for preventing bullying.[41] If, on the other hand, the school does not engage in a deliberate, whole-school effort to both determine whether a problem exists and turn the school culture around, the school almost certainly will perpetuate a bullying culture that already exists and that is hidden from the eyes of the administration and faculty.[42]

These programs, to be effective, must involve education and training for administrators, teachers, maintenance staff, bus drivers, as well as parents—in short, every adult who is a part of the school community.[43] Strikingly, "nearly 25% of teachers report that they do not think it is necessary to intervene in bullying,"[44] and though bullying has been demonstrated to be pervasive in American schools, teachers intervene in fewer than 5 percent of the bullying situations that occur.[45] The children know what is happening around them; it is the adults who need to be educated.

The first step in that education is to conduct an assessment, through anonymous questionnaires completed by the students, to determine the level of bullying in the school.[46] Once that data is shared with the school community, along with data regarding the profoundly damaging effects bullying behavior inflicts on children throughout the school, the community tends to wake up and determine to turn the culture around.[47] If school officials then initiate a serious, school-wide effort to learn about and respond to bullying over the following year, the culture of the school changes.[48]

This school-wide process seems to lie at the heart of the change. A short-lived focus will not do it; a new policy against bullying, posted around the school will not do it; a

---

38. Olweus, *supra* note 19, at 15.

39. Weddle, *supra* note 1, at 652–56.

40. Packman et al., *supra* note 24, at 548–49.

41. Ted Feinberg, *Bullying Prevention and Intervention*, PRINCIPAL LEADERSHIP, Summer 2003, at 10.

42. Jina S. Yoon, *Predicting Teacher Interventions in Bullying* Situations, EDUCATION AND TREATMENT OF CHILDREN, Fall 2004 at 38.

43. *See* Doug Cooper and Jennie L. Snell, *Bullying—Not Just a Kid Thing*, EDUC. LEADERSHIP, March 2003, at 22, 24.

44. Feinberg, *supra* note 41, at 10.

45. Packman et al., *supra* note 24, at 551.

46. Olweus, *supra* note 19, at 16.

47. Weddle, *supra* note 1, at 655.

48. Olweus, *supra* note 19, at 15.

series of promises to get serious about bullying will not do it; a handful of in-services for teachers will not do it. What is required is a sustained, serious discussion that changes the outlook of the members of the school community about the seriousness of bullying and the need to stop it. If students find that adults will back them up when they report bullying, and if adults begin to supervise with an eye to spotting the symptoms of bullying among the students, the mentality of the student body changes; and bullying becomes something to stop, not something merely to witness or encourage.

Redefining the Tort of Negligent Supervision

The legal requirements governing school officials' duty to supervise their students need to be realigned to reflect these realities about bullying, its prevalence, its effects, and its prevention. That realignment is long overdue, but it is ironically neither radical nor even particularly new. Nearly a century of legal precedent and well-accepted doctrine support refining the definition of negligent supervision to require a duty on the part of school officials to initiate serious, research-based reform to combat the torment and brutality large numbers of their students daily endure or daily inflict. That same precedent and doctrine support finding a failure to do so to be a breach of the duty to supervise and to be the proximate cause of compensable physical and emotional damages inflicted by bullies on their peers.

That change can begin with and incorporate the generally accepted definition of negligent supervision. The tort is typically defined as containing three elements:

(1) The existence of a teacher-student relationship giving rise to a legal duty to supervise; (2) the negligent breach of that duty by the teacher; and (3) proximate causation of the student's injury by the teacher's negligence.[49]

The third element can actually be broken into three parts, consistent with the general definition of negligence: factual causation, proximate causation, and the existence of actual, legally recognized harm.[50] Of course, the definition is not limited to teachers but is applicable to all school officials.[51] Each of these elements is readily adaptable to alignment with current empirical research about bullying if courts are willing to abandon a number of unnecessary theoretical obstacles that have been constructed over the years and that have served mainly to obscure and confuse longstanding, perfectly serviceable tort doctrines.

---

49. *Broward County Sch. Bd. v. Ruiz*, 493 So. 2d 474, 476 (Fla. Dist. Ct. App. 1986); *see also, e.g.,* *Roberson v. Duval County Sch. Bd.*, 618 So. 2d 360, 362 (Fla. Dist. Ct. App. 1993).
50. *See* DAN B. DOBBS, THE LAW OF TORTS §114, at 269. Dobbs characterizes the elements of negligence as follows:
1. The defendant owed the plaintiff a duty of care, for instance, not to engage in unreasonably risky conduct.
2. the defendant breached that duty by his unreasonably risky conduct;
3. the defendant's conduct in fact caused harm to the plaintiff;
4. the defendant's conduct was not only a cause in fact of the plaintiff's harm but also a proximate cause, meaning that the defendant's conduct is perceived to have a significant relationship to the harm suffered by the plaintiff;
5. the existence and amount of damages, based on actual harm of a legally recognized kind such as physical injury to person or property.
51. *Doe v. DeSoto Parish Sch. Bd.*, 907 So. 2d 275, 281 (La. Ct. App. 2005) (explaining that "school board employees have a duty to provide reasonable supervision commensurate with the age of the children and the attendant circumstances").

The Existence of a Duty to Supervise

Schools have long been held to have a duty to supervise the children in their care. Courts have been quite willing to recognize such a duty to supervise schoolchildren for their safety, at least during the school day and on school grounds.[52] That duty is generally seen to vary in scope with the age and maturity of the children being supervised,[53] but it nevertheless exists.

The duty is also circumscribed by general concerns for the safety of all the children at a given time and the practical constraints that exist in the day-to-day management of a school. For example, no duty to supervise a particular student would generally exist where such a duty would require a teacher to abandon supervision of a class to accompany a child to the restroom.[54]

The more difficult question for courts has been whether that duty includes protecting children from the tortious or criminal acts of other children. It is a fundamental rule in American tort law that no duty exists to control the conduct of third persons, absent a special relationship between the actor and the tort victim.[55] While the drafters of the Restatement (Third) of Torts clearly contemplate such a special relationship,[56] its recognition among courts has not consistently required school officials to anticipate the violent acts of students against one another. The Kansas Supreme Court, for example, has explicitly rejected such a requirement as beyond the bounds of what should be expected by school officials regarding their charges.[57]

More common is the requirement that there be some prior alert to the specific danger before a school is deemed to have a duty to protect students from each other.[58] Courts

---

52. *Dailey v. Los Angeles Unified Sch. Dist.*, 470 P.2d 360, 363 (Cal. 1970).

53. *Id.* at 363; *see also Broward County Sch. Bd.*, 493 So. 2d at 477.

54. *Broward County Sch. Bd.*, 493 So. 2d at 477.

55. The Restatement (Second) of Torts provides that
There is no duty so to control the conduct of a third person as to prevent him from causing physical harm to anther unless
a) a special relation exists between the actor and the third person which imposes a duty upon the actor to control the third person's conduct, or
b) a special relation exists between the actor and the other which gives to the other a right to protection.
Restatement (Second) of Torts § 315 (1965).

56. Draft versions of the Restatement (Third) of Torts continue the recognition of the school's duty to supervise its students for their safety:
(a) An actor in a special relationship with another owes the other a duty of reasonable care with regard to risks that arise within the scope of that relationship.
(b) Special relationships giving rise to the duty provided in Subsection (a) include ... a school with its students.
Restatement (Third) of Torts: Liability for Physical Harm § 40 (Proposed Final Draft No. 1, 2005). In explaining the explicit recognition of this duty, the drafters note that the "relationship of the school and its students parallels aspects of several other special relationships—it is a custodian of students, it is a land possessor who opens the premises to a significant public population, and it acts partially in place of parents." *Id.* This draft version has received final approval but has yet to be published in final form at the time of this writing.

57. *Sly v. Bd. of Educ.*, 515 P.2d 895 (Kan. 1973). While the court's conclusion is couched in terms of proximate cause rather than duty, it is arguably limiting the duty itself. See Dobbs, *supra* note 50, § 182, at 450 (explaining that such categorical rejections of foreseeability are more appropriately viewed as limitations on the duty itself).

58. *Agnes Scott College, Inc. v. Clark*, 616 S.E.2d 468 (Ga. Ct. App. 2005).

often stress that schools are not the "insurers of their students' safety"[59] and that requiring them to foresee criminal and tortious acts would cast them in precisely that role. In addition, there is a long-standing concern that schools should not be responsible for the "sudden, unanticipated acts of school children"[60]—acts that even the physical presence of a teacher may not be able to thwart.

The latter justification certainly makes sense. If two middle schoolers become embroiled in a rivalry for the affections of the same girl, a simmering anger unknown to school officials could boil over into throwing punches in a hallway before anyone could realistically react. Such are the hazards of bringing school-age children together in a building every weekday for nine months out of the year, and it is unreasonable to expect school officials to magically see such situations develop.

On the other hand, the flat rejection of any duty to anticipate students' tortious or even criminal acts is extreme, given what educators now know about the prevalence and dynamics of bullying and retaliation. In addition, many courts and both the First and Second Restatements have recognized that such behavior is to be expected and planned for. As the drafters of the Restatement (Third) have pointed out in a comment to § 320, the Second Restatement's obligation of custodians to control third persons from injuring those in the custodians' care is explicitly applied to schools for their students.[61] The duty explained in that comment stems, in turn, from the 1934 First Restatement of Torts:

> One who is required by law to take or who voluntarily takes the custody of another under circumstances such as to deprive the other of his normal power of self-protection or to subject him to association with persons likely to harm him, is under a duty of exercising reasonable care so to control the conduct of third persons as to prevent them from intentionally harming the other ... if the actor
>
> (a) knows or has reason to know that he has the ability to control the conduct of the third persons, and
>
> (b) knows or should know of the necessity and opportunity for exercising such control.[62]

Comment (a) to that section states that "the rule in this Section is applicable to ... teachers or other persons in charge of a public school [as well as] to persons conducting ... a private school."[63] The Second Restatement employed the same material language thirty years later.[64] Likewise, courts had explicitly considered § 320 to apply to schools under the First Restatement.[65]

Significantly, the duty recognized by the restaters contemplated not only the anticipation of and protection against third-party tortious acts generally but also the acts of bullies specifically, even if no specific danger is apparent. Comment (d) to § 320 in both the First and Second Restatements provides,

---

59. *E.g.*, *Calabrese v. Baldwin Union Free Sch. Dist.*, 741 N.Y.S.2d 569, 570 (N.Y. App. Div. 2002).

60. *See, e.g.*, *Calabrese*, 741 N.Y.S.2d at 570.

61. RESTATEMENT (THIRD) OF TORTS: LIABILITY FOR PHYSICAL HARM § 40 cmt. l (Proposed Final Draft No. 1, 2005).

62. RESTATEMENT (FIRST) OF TORTS § 320 (1934).

63. *Id.*

64. RESTATEMENT (SECOND) OF TORTS § 320 (1965).

65. *See, e.g.*, *McLeod v. Grant County Sch. Dist. No. 128*, 255 P.2d 360, 362–63 (Wash. 1953) (holding that such custody existed in a school setting so as to raise a duty of care to control the conduct of third persons if the school knew it had the ability to control those persons and knew that the control was necessary).

> One who has taken custody of another may not only be required to exercise reasonable care for the other's protection when he knows or has reason to know that the other is in immediate need thereof, but also to make careful preparations to enable him to give effective protection when the need arises, and to exercise reasonable vigilance to ascertain the need of giving it.... *So too, a schoolmaster who knows that a group of older boys are in the habit of bullying the younger pupils to an extent likely to do them actual harm, is not only required to interfere when he sees the bullying going on, but also to be reasonably vigilant in his supervision of his pupils so as to ascertain when such conduct is about to occur.*[66]

The restatements justify this requirement on the theory that a child "who has been deprived of the protection of his parents or guardian" is necessarily dependent on the protection of the adult in whose care he has been placed.[67] It is especially important to note that both restatements use both actual and constructive knowledge formulations ("knows or should know") regarding the "necessity and opportunity for exercising" control over third persons to prevent them harming one who is under the actor's custody.[68] Thus, the restatements contain no requirement that actual knowledge of the specific threats exist before the school official is under a duty to remain vigilant in ascertaining and preventing such behavior.

In discharging this duty to students, school officials must recognize that they live "in an actual world, and not in Utopia" and must realize that "third persons may act in a variety of ways, all of which are not only morally but legally wrong."[69] They must know the "qualities and habits of human beings ... so far as they are matters of common knowledge at the time and in the community."[70] As one court put it, supervision of school children is necessary "precisely because of the commonly known tendency of students to engage in aggressive and impulsive behavior which exposes them and their peers to the risk of serious physical harm."[71] In fact, even if those third-party acts are criminal in nature, an actor may be liable for acts or omissions if he either does or should realize that his acts or omissions involve an unreasonable risk of harm from a third party's intentionally harmful criminal conduct.[72]

Beyond recognizing the commonly known fact that some children will engage in tortious or even criminal conduct toward one another even in school, some courts have considered school officials to be governed by a higher standard of conduct than the reasonable person standard adopted by the restatement. For example, where a student was injured

---

66. RESTATEMENT (FIRST) OF TORTS § 320 (1934); RESTATEMENT (SECOND) OF TORTS § 320 cmt. d. (1965) (emphasis added).

67. Comment b to § 320 of both the First and Second Restatements provides that "a child while in school is deprived of the protection of his parents or guardian. Therefore, the actor who takes custody ... of a child is properly required to give him the protection which the custody or the manner in which it is taken has deprived him." RESTATEMENT (FIRST) OF TORTS § 320 (1934); RESTATEMENT (SECOND) OF TORTS § 320 cmt. d. (1965).

68. RESTATEMENT (FIRST) OF TORTS § 320 cmt. b (1934); RESTATEMENT (SECOND) OF TORTS § 320 cmt. b (1965).

69. RESTATEMENT (SECOND) OF TORTS § 290 cmt. m (1965).

70. RESTATEMENT (SECOND) OF TORTS § 290 (1965).

71. *Dailey*, 470 P.2d at 364.

72. Section 302B of the Second Restatement provides that "an act or omission may be negligent if the actor realizes or should realize that it involves an unreasonable risk of harm to another through the conduct of the other or a third person which is intended to cause harm, even though such conduct is criminal." RESTATEMENT (SECOND) OF TORTS § 302B (1965).

while participating in a football program, the Nebraska Supreme Court held the appropriate standard for determining the liability of a school football coach was "that of a reasonably prudent person holding a Nebraska teaching certificate with a coaching endorsement."[73] In doing so, the court turned to § 290 of the Restatement (Second) of Torts, which requires actors to utilize special knowledge if they possess special knowledge, hold themselves out as possessing that knowledge, or "undertake a course of conduct which a reasonable man would recognize as requiring it."[74]

Given state requirements for ongoing professional development of teachers and administrators, it strains credulity to claim that elementary and secondary school officials should continue to be unaware of the wealth of empirical data concerning bullying in schools. Schools of education are aware of that research; school districts are aware of that research; and both novice and veteran teachers and administrators should be aware of that research if they have kept up with the professional literature of their fields at all. For courts to hold that school officials should not be required to anticipate severe and pervasive bullying among their students and become vigilant in their efforts to confront and prevent it flies in the face of legal precedent dating at least to the First Restatement in 1934 and continuing to the date of this writing, over seventy years later,[75] and ignores two decades of empirical research in the field of education.

Courts should therefore reject the temptation to state categorically that today's teachers and administrators should not be required to foresee what is patently evident, according to twenty-five years of educational research. Instead, courts should state very plainly and directly that school officials already know or should know that bullying is prevalent in every virtually every school and that the special relationship created by taking custody of school children for the school day imposes on those officials an affirmative duty to employ proven strategies to combat bullying on behalf of the children in their charge.

Negligent Breach of the Duty to Supervise

Once a duty to supervise is found to exist, the question becomes what conduct constitutes a breach of that duty. The question of duty and the question of breach are significantly interrelated because to some extent the parameters of the duty define the parameters of the acceptable conduct. For example, where a court refuses to require school officials to anticipate the tortious or criminal actions of third persons, failing to prevent harms from such persons cannot constitute negligence, absent actual knowledge of the specific threat. As discussed earlier, however, no such limitation on the duty need be recognized.[76] Therefore, because, according to §302 the Second Restatement, negligent conduct—that is, unreasonably risky behavior—may include a "negligent act or omission ... which involves an unreasonable risk of harm to another through ... the foreseeable action of a ... third person,"[77] a failure to identify and address a bullying school culture should be held to be negligent conduct.

---

73. *Cerny v. Cedar Bluffs Junior/Senior Public Sch.*, 628 N.W.2d 697, 706 (Neb. 2001).

74. *Id.* at 704.

75. *See supra* note 61 and accompanying text.

76. *See supra* notes 52–74 and accompanying text.

77. Restatement (Second) of Torts §302 (1965). In a comment to the section, the drafters note that the section goes only to the question of negligence and not to liability, because there may be no relationship between the actor and the other that would give rise to a duty to act. Thus, it is

Unfortunately, courts have generally required something akin to complete and unwarranted absence of supervision before considering supervision to be negligent in peer-on-peer injury cases,[78] and that tendency makes bullying cases particularly hard to prosecute under a theory of negligent supervision because bullying usually happens underground, deliberately out of view of school officials.[79] Limiting breach to the complete absence of supervision, however, seems unnecessary and runs contrary to the better reasoned cases.

In *Doe v. DeSoto Parish School Board*,[80] for example, the Louisiana Court of Appeals held that a failure simply to supervise competently could sustain a claim of negligent supervision even though the teacher was physically present.[81] Jane Doe, a minor, was assaulted by five male members of a basketball team on a bus trip (the defendants alleged that Jane Doe had voluntarily participated in the sex), despite the fact that coaches were on the bus.[82] The jury found against the school officials, and the court of appeals upheld the verdict, concluding that a teacher is liable under the Louisiana Civil Code if the teacher is able to prevent the damage and does not do so.[83]

Similarly, a Florida court refused to accept the notion that liability could be imposed only if the teacher was absent at the time of the incident.[84] In that case, a girl was struck by another student while walking in a line led by a teacher.[85] The teacher was not enforcing a policy that required students to walk single file without talking; in addition, the teacher was walking at the head of the line yet did not respond when the girl twice told her attacker in a loud voice to stop trying to push her.[86] When the girl resorted to pushing the boy away, he broke her jaw.[87] Because the jury could reasonably have concluded that the teacher heard the disturbance but negligently failed to respond in a timely manner, the court held that a directed verdict for the board was error.[88]

What is significant about these cases is that the negligent officials were present but were simply inattentive. They were unaware of the misconduct occurring among their students, but the reason was self-imposed ignorance through inattention. In the same way, school officials who ignore what educational research has demonstrated concerning the prevalence of bullying among schoolchildren are simply inattentive. They are inattentive

---

theoretically possible that an actor's failure to act, despite his knowledge of a third person's criminal propensities, would be negligence — that is, unreasonably risky behavior — yet he would not be held liable because no duty existed. In the school setting, however, the special relationship between school officials and their students should provide the necessary duty. *Id.* at cmt. a. Nevertheless, many courts persistently miss that connection in refusing to hold that school officials should foresee tortious behavior among students. See, for example, *James v. Charlotte-Mecklenburg Bd. of Educ.*, 300 S.E.2d 21 (N.C. Ct. App. 1983), where a child was injured when two other children engaged in pencil fight while the teacher ate lunch in the cafeteria, leaving the students unsupervised in another location; the teacher was held to have no duty to "remain with her class at all times or to provide other adult supervision at all times while she was absent." 300 S.E.2d at 24. The court concluded that the students' propensity to engage in such conduct was unforeseeable, despite the fact that on an earlier occasion, the students had engaged in an "orange fight" in her absence. *Id.* at 24–25.

78. Weddle, *supra* note 1, at 692–93.

79. Weddle, *supra* note 1, at 651.

80. *Doe v. DeSoto Parish Sch. Bd.*, 907 So. 2d 275, 277–79 (La. Ct. App. 2005).

81. *See generally id.*

82. *Id.* at 277–79.

83. *See generally id.*

84. *Roberson v. Duval County Sch. Bd.*, 618 So. 2d 360, 362 (Fla. Dist. Ct. App. 1993).

85. *Id.* at 361.

86. *Id.*

87. *Id.*

88. *Id.* at 362.

to the research, and as a result they are inattentive to the dynamics plaguing their schools' cultures. It seems completely consistent to define such inattentiveness as negligence — as a breach of the duty to supervise — regardless of whether specific acts among their students would necessarily have forewarned them had they been more attentive and had they mounted an affirmative whole-school effort to transform the school culture.

Educational researchers' calls for whole-school approaches apparently have found sympathy in a federal court in Kansas, where failure to implement such approaches may have been the foundation for a jury verdict under Title IX. The district court, in a denial of summary judgment on a plaintiff's Title IX claims, noted that an expert had testified that "the administration [of a school district] should have brought teachers and students together to try to develop a school culture that sends the message that sexual harassment will not be tolerated."[89] The court viewed the testimony as evidence that the district's responses to the harassment were inadequate under Title IX.[90] The court reasoned that while

> responses to various discrete incidents of known harassment might not have been clearly unreasonable ... [given several years of severe and continuous harassment], a reasonable jury certainly could conclude that at some point during the four-year period of harassment the school district's standard and ineffective response became clearly unreasonable."[91]

The jury later returned a verdict against the district and awarded the plaintiff $250,000.[92]

These cases are beginning to reflect what educational research has been demonstrating for two decades: when students are left to the mercy of bullying peers by school officials too professionally ignorant or too personally indifferent to the existence of a bullying culture to take steps to change that culture, students become victims and have little recourse to save themselves from the torment. Courts that have been timid about holding schools liable for injuries inflicted by their peers should take a cue from their colleagues on the state and federal benches and begin to treat such ignorance and indifference among school officials as a breach of the duty to supervise the children in their care.

Factual and Proximate Causation

Although the inquiry into factual causation is fairly straightforward, the concept of proximate cause is a source of considerable confusion for courts. Therefore, it should not be surprising that the case law is often inconsistent in its treatment of the causation element of negligent supervision. The confusion often unnecessarily prevents plaintiffs' success in peer-on-peer abuse cases because it creates artificial barriers to liability that ignore the realities of schooling and the dynamics of school cultures in which bullying flourishes.

The primary difficulty with proximate cause lies in the term itself: it suggests that the inquiry is about cause and effect when, in reality, the inquiry is about scope of lia-

---

89. *Theno v. Tonganoxie Unified Sch. Dist. No. 464*, 377 F. Supp. 2d 952, 961–62 (D. Kan. 2005).

90. *Id*. at 966.

91. *Id*.

92. Robert A. Cronkleton, *Taunted Teenager Wins Federal Suit*, KAN. CITY STAR, Aug. 12, 2005, at B1.

bility for harms caused. In other words, under the causation prongs of the negligent supervision definition, a negligent act or omission must first be a true causal factor in the sequence of events that led to the injury; but it must also be conceptually related to the harm in a way that society, as a matter of fairness, is willing to recognize as justifying the imposition of liability. Courts therefore often speak in terms of "factual causation" or "cause in fact" to refer to the first step in the analysis and speak in terms of "legal cause" or "proximate cause" to refer to the second. Unfortunately, the terms *proximate cause* and *legal cause* have little actual relationship to the notion of cause, so they foster confusion even when courts clearly separate the inquiries. Compounding the problem, many courts blend that two-step analysis under the single "proximate cause" rubric.

Factual Causation

The first concept, cause in fact, is not particularly difficult to understand or to apply. The term means, in essence, that the negligent conduct "played a role in the history leading to the plaintiff's injury."[93] Although many factors may have led to the plaintiff's injury, the defendant's conduct must be among them in a straightforward, historical, or scientific sense.[94] In addition, it must be a factor that contributed in some significant way to the injury rather than a trivial occurrence among other, more influential causes.[95]

One can argue, perhaps, that the injury to a bullying victim is caused by the bully, independently of any conduct by school officials. After all, school officials did not bully the child or intend to encourage such behavior. The school officials may have failed to prevent it, but they did not actively set out to cause it to happen. Therefore, one might argue, the school officials' inaction was not a causal role in the history of the victim's injury.

The empirical research belies such a conclusion, however. School culture is a consequence of school officials' leadership, and failure to act cultivates the conditions necessary to sustain bullying behavior.[96] In that sense, passivity toward bullying is a direct causal factor in the creation of the school culture that is necessary for bullying to flourish and consequently to injure a child in the school. In fact, as one researcher put it, research has shown that

> lack of appropriate consequences would reinforce students' bullying behaviors and would indirectly contribute to repeated victimization by allowing the continued success of the bully exerting control over a victim. Furthermore, a teacher's permissive attitude toward a perpetrator (i.e., not following through with the consequences of bullying or blaming a victim) are more likely to perpetuate victims' feeling of being alienated and helpless.[97]

---

93. Jean Stapleton, *Legal Cause: Cause-in-Fact and the Scope of Liability for Consequences*, 54 Vand. L. Rev. 941, 977–78 (2001).

94. *Id.* at 978.

95. Restatement (Third) of torts: Liability for Physical harm § 36 (Proposed Final Draft No. 1, 2005) This draft version has received final approval but has yet to be published in final form at the time of this writing.

96. *See supra* notes 38–48 and accompanying text.

97. Yoon, *supra* note 42, at 38 (citations omitted).

Notably, under a federal theory of recovery that has traditionally required an affirmative act on the part of school officials to support liability, a federal court has concluded that school officials' passivity in the face of bullying behavior could be shown to have significantly heightened the dangerousness of the school environment.[98] Under the "state-created danger theory," a person can maintain a claim for damages if she is denied the right to bodily integrity guaranteed by the due process clause of the Fourteenth Amendment and that deprivation is the result of a danger created by the state.[99] Courts have typically required some affirmative act on the part of state officials[100] that either creates the danger or enhances the vulnerability of the plaintiff to an existing danger.[101] Even where the affirmative act exists, it must rise to the level of behavior that "shocks the conscience" of the court before liability will attach.[102] In other words, a mere failure to render aid to a student who is being severely harassed cannot usually trigger liability because a failure to act does not constitute the creation or enhancement of a danger.[103]

The U.S. District Court for the Eastern District of Pennsylvania, however, was willing to retreat from that position in the face of egregious indifference toward schoolchildren's plights. In denying a motion to dismiss a section 1983 claim, the court concluded that the Philadelphia School District's inattention to violent attacks on its students by a gang of other students could be shown to have enhanced the risk of injury to the plaintiff by encouraging the bullies to continue their attacks.[104]

A group of fifteen students had been routinely attacking other students in unmonitored areas of the school.[105] They typically pulled a garment over a random target's head and then beat him severely.[106] Amazingly, even though school officials knew the identities of the fifteen students who were engaging in these assaults, they never made any coordinated effort to discipline the students, monitor the common areas where the assaults typically took place, report the incidents to police, or even record the incidents.[107]

When plaintiff Matthew Gremo was attacked, he was injured so badly that he had to be helped to the nurse's office because he could not walk.[108] After the nurse "performed

---

98. *Gremo v. Karlin*, 363 F.Supp. 2d 771 (E.D. Pa. 2005).

99. Under § 1983, a person may assert a private right of action for deprivation of rights secured by the Constitution or other federal law:

> Every person who, under color of any statute, ordinance, regulation, custom, or usage, of any State ... subjects, or causes to be subjected, any citizen of the United States or other person within the jurisdiction thereof to the deprivation of any rights, privileges, or immunities secured by the Constitution and laws, shall be liable to the party injured in an action at law.

42 U.S.C. § 1983 (2000).

100. Jeff Horner and Wade Norman, *Student Violence and Harassment*, 182 EDUC. L. REP. 371, 378 (2004).

101. *O'Hayre v. Board of Educ. for Jefferson County Sch. Dist. R-1*, 109 F. Supp. 1284, 1289 (D. Colo. 2000).

102. *Gremo*, 363 F. Supp. 2d at 789.

103. *See, e.g.*, *Nabozny v. Podlesny*, 92 F.3d 446, 460 (7th Cir. 1996) (holding that a mere failure to render aid to a student who is being harassed on the basis of sexual orientation or gender is insufficient to support liability under the "state-created-danger" theory).

104. *See generally Gremo*, 363 F.Supp. 2d 771.

105. *Id*. at 778–79.

106. *Id*.

107. *Id*.

108. *Id*. at 778.

a cursory examination of Gremo without conducting a routine nursing vital assessment, or summoning an ambulance, [the nurse] maintained that he was not injured and released him to his mother."[109] Gremo suffered permanent brain damage from the attack.[110]

Two years prior to the attack on Gremo, a state legislative investigation of the school district had uncovered "rampant, unabated, unfettered, ongoing violence" throughout the district, including the school in which Gremo was injured.[111] The investigation also found that throughout the district, school officials had engaged in a pattern of denying the existence of violence in the schools and had impliedly threatened retaliation against teachers or administrators who broke the silence.[112] The pattern included affirmative efforts to conceal incidents of violence.[113]

The court concluded that "the knowledge of violence in the school was so widespread as to create an atmosphere that made a certain level of violence acceptable."[114] As a result, the school officials' passivity placed Gremo in a more vulnerable position because their "failure to act in these circumstances may have informed the perpetrators that, even though the defendants knew of the violent incidents, they would not interfere."[115] While the court went on to conclude that the acts of concealment may have added to the attackers' boldness,[116] it is striking that the court noted an enhanced danger existed simply as a result of the failure to intervene.

The court's reasoning seems to echo the conclusions of bullying research that suggest a school culture left to itself is a breeding ground of peer-on-peer bullying. Admittedly, the facts in *Gremo* are outrageous and certainly "conscience shocking," but the dynamics are precisely the same as those in all schools where teachers and administrators turn a blind eye to bullying. By failing to address bullying in a coordinated and sustained fashion, as the research repeatedly reveals must be done if bullying is to be reduced, school officials send a message that bullying will not be taken seriously—at least not seriously enough to spend energy and resources combating it. Bullying will flourish unabated, its perpetuation encouraged by school officials' inaction.

Importantly, the theory of negligent supervision, to support liability, does not actually require an affirmative act on the part of school officials. Omissions, where a special relationship exists, can be found to be unreasonable risks of harm where those omissions create an opportunity for third-person tortious or criminal behavior.[117] Where school officials ignore a culture of bullying and students find themselves harmed in the midst of that indifference, courts should feel perfectly comfortable allowing juries to find that the indifference caused the injury.

---

109. *Id.*

110. *Id.*

111. *Id.* at 778–79.

112. *Id.*

113. *Id.*

114. *Id.* at 790.

115. *Id.* at 789. The court began its analysis of Gremo's state-created danger claim by laying out the four prongs that in the Third Circuit must be satisfied to avoid the general rule that the state owes its citizens no duty to protect them from private violent acts:

> (1) the harm ultimately caused was foreseeable and fairly direct; (2) the state actor acted in willful disregard for the safety of the plaintiff; (3) there existed some relationship between the state and the plaintiff; [and] (4) the state actors used their authority to create an opportunity that otherwise would not have existed for the third party's crime to occur.

In a lengthy analysis, it then found that all of the first three prongs had been satisfied. *Id.* at 782–89.

116. *Id.* at 789.

117. *Supra* note 77 and accompanying text.

Proximate or Legal Causation

The second concept, legal or proximate cause, creates confusion because rather than an inquiry into whether the conduct actually "caused" the harm, it is really an inquiry into "the proper limits on liability for harm [that has been determined to have been] actually caused by the defendant's conduct."[118] The cause-in-fact inquiry assumes that a defendant should not be liable for harms either which he did not cause or to which he did not contribute in any significant way. The legal cause inquiry assumes, on the other hand, that a defendant should not necessarily be liable for all harms to which he actually contributed. It assumes that an actor should be liable only for those harms that were foreseeable risks of his conduct at the time he acted because an actor can reasonably be expected to take care to avoid only those harms he understands or should understand may flow from his acts.

The scope of liability question often turns on whether a third person's tortious conduct should be viewed as a superseding cause that cuts off the liability of the original actor for harm that in fact flows from both actors. Although it sounds similar to the question of whether a duty exists at all in such situations, it is actually a somewhat different question. It begins with an assumption that a duty of due care was owed the plaintiff and that the defendant breached that duty, but it then asks as a factual matter whether the particular actions by the third person were within the scope of the risks the standard of care was intended to avoid. Its justification is often described in terms reminiscent of physics: a force has put in motion a chain of events that will lead to a particular harm, but another independent force has broken that chain and replaced it with a new chain of causation; thus, the first actor may have been negligent, but a new actor's intentional act has broken the original chain of events and has created a new series of events leading to the harm.[119] In that sense, the second force is a superseding cause, and the actor who began the second chain should bear the responsibility of the harm.

For example, suppose a person painting his house leaves a long extension ladder leaning unattended against the edge of the roof of his two-story house on a windy day.[120] That night the wind blows the ladder down, and the ladder lands on his neighbor's fence, damaging the fence. The court may hold that the actor had a duty to be careful that in his use of the ladder he not do anything with it that would foreseeably endanger his neighbor's property. A jury might then be asked whether it was foreseeable that the ladder would fall and land on the fence, given the windy conditions; if so, the actor has breached his duty of care, and that breach is the proximate cause of the damage to the fence.

Suppose instead that a third person steals the ladder in the night, uses it to climb in through an upper window in the neighbor's house and burglarize his house, and while hurrying from the ladder to make his escape carelessly causes it to fall on the same fence. A court might well hold that the actor had no duty to lock up his ladder to prevent its use by a third person in a burglary because such a use is not within the foreseeable risks encompassed by the duty to use

---

118. Patrick J. Kelley, *Restating Duty, Breach, and Proximate Cause in Negligence Law: Descriptive Theory and the Rule of Law*, 54 Vand. L. Rev. 1039, 1053 (2001).

119. *E.g.*, *Rupp v. Bryant*, 417 So. 2d 658, 669 (Fla. 1982) (holding that "rough-housing or hazing at a high school club is not so extraordinary as to break the chain of causation between the school's failure to supervise and the injury to the student").

120. *See* Prosser & Keeton on the Law of Torts § 44, at 304 (W. Page Keeton, ed., 5th ed. 1984) (explaining that defendants may be held "to anticipate the usual weather of the vicinity"). "If the defendant's conduct has created an unreasonable risk of harm," given the conditions, he will be liable for the resulting harm. *Id.* at 305.

the ladder carefully.[121] In that case, no question of proximate cause arises because no duty existed in the first place, even though the same fence is damaged by the same ladder.[122]

A closer question arises, however, if a vandal pushes the ladder from its place against the first person's roof down onto the neighbor's fence. There, a court, having recognized a duty to store the ladder in a way that it would not fall and damage the neighbor's property, might leave it to the jury to decide whether, under the circumstances of the place in which the neighbors live, such vandalism was within the foreseeable risks of leaving the ladder perched against the roof in that manner.[123] The jury, having heard evidence that vandals routinely take advantage in that neighborhood of any opportunity to do damage, might conclude that leaving the ladder up was a temptation likely to be acted on by vandals and therefore within the foreseeable risks of the actor's negligent conduct. If, on the other hand, the jury instead heard evidence that no vandalism had taken place in that neighborhood for years, the jury might conclude that the vandalism was unforeseeable and therefore outside the risks associated with the otherwise negligent conduct of leaving the ladder unattended against the roof.

Using the term "proximate cause" to describe the result in that final scenario, of course, suggests that leaving the ladder unattended against the roof was not a cause of the damage, that the true and therefore superseding cause was the vandal's actions. On closer inspection, however, cause and effect are not really so scientifically simple.[124] A harm may arise from multiple causes, each contributing more or less than others to the ultimate harmful result, and among those causes may be conduct that was negligent and conduct that was intentional or even criminal. When jurors conclude that liability should fall on the second, intentional actor rather than on the first, merely negligent actor, they are not really applying a scientific notion of cause and effect so much as making a value judgment about relative culpability among actors. They are saying that, as between a negligent actor who begins a chain of events leading to a harm and an unforeseen intentional actor who makes certain the harm results, the intentional actor is sufficiently more culpable that he should shoulder all of the blame and the liability.

When that moral judgment is described in terms of physical cause and effect, however, it tends to overreach. It treats intentional and criminal acts as if they serve to obliterate the effect of the original negligent conduct. The real inquiry should focus on what harms were reasonably foreseeable as consequences of the negligent behavior and, as a result, risks to be avoided by a reasonable actor. Even if some of those reasonably foresee-

---

121. See Prosser & Keeton, *supra* note 120, §44, at 312, for a similar illustration concerning a thief who steals an unlocked car and negligently runs down the plaintiff. In such a case, the defendant will not be held liable by most courts because, while the theft might be considered likely enough, the later negligence by the thief is generally considered not so likely as to require the defendant to guard against it.

122. Some courts might see the question as whether a duty existed, but others may treat the question as one of proximate cause. *Id.* at 314. *See also id.* at 316 (citing *Moore v. Townsend*, 78 N.W. 880 (Minn. 1899) (holding that even where an "unusual blast of wind" knocked a forty-foot ladder down, injuring the plaintiff, the defendant's negligent act of leaving the ladder leaning over a crosswalk and against a building "was the efficient cause of the injury to plaintiff")).

123. As Professor Keeton explains, "In any case where there might be reasonable difference of opinion as to the foreseeability of a particular risk, the defendant's conduct with respect to it, or the normal character of an intervening cause, the question is for the jury." Prosser & Keeton, *supra* note 120, §44, at 321.

124. For a discussion of proximate cause theory's roots in "scientism," see Restatement (Third) of torts: Liability for Physical harm §34 cmt. a (Proposed Final Draft No. 1, 2005) This draft version has received final approval but has yet to be published in final form at the time of this writing.

able harms would result only from another's intentional act, they should be considered among the risks for which the negligent actor should have taken precaution if the actor's negligence makes those intentional acts more likely.

From its inception, the restatement has recognized that intentional and even criminal acts may be foreseeable and therefore not superseding causes:

> The act of a third person in committing an intentional tort or crime is a superseding cause of harm to another resulting therefrom, although the actor's negligent conduct created a situation which afforded an opportunity to the third person to commit such a tort or crime, *unless the actor at the time of his negligent conduct should have realized the likelihood that such a situation might be created thereby and that a third person might avail himself of the opportunity to commit such a tort or crime.*[125]

The Second Restatement repeats that language verbatim,[126] and the drafters of the proposed Third Restatement carry the concept forward into the latest version.[127]

Under the restatement's logic, a case like *Sly v. Board of Education*[128] is problematic because it seems to take the superseding cause logic too far and to ignore the real risks that the school officials' conduct created. In *Sly*, racial tensions had been running high at a school, yet the school allowed students to congregate unsupervised outside locked school doors in the mornings before the school day officially began.[129] Eventually, the tensions resulted in an assault by two black students on a white student.[130] The court held that school officials' conduct in failing to supervise the congregating students could not have been the proximate cause of the injuries because the officials had not received sufficient warning that the two attackers were likely to attack.[131] Absent a warning, said the court, such behavior was unforeseeable as matter of law, for school officials should not be required to anticipate the malicious and criminal acts of their students.[132]

As other courts have recognized, such logic flies in the face of what we know about schooling and about adolescents. The Minnesota Supreme Court, for example, explicitly rejected the requirement of notice of prior conduct in *Sly* on the grounds that some adolescent misconduct, including tortious or criminal physical attacks, is foreseeable absent appropriate supervision.[133] Therefore, according to the court, the Minnesota school's awareness of racial tension and its lack of supervision supported a jury's finding of breach and causation.[134] The court explained that

> although the school district might not be liable for sudden, unanticipated misconduct of fellow students, it is liable for sudden, foreseeable misconduct which could have been prevented by the exercise of ordinary care. The reason is that fore-

---

125. RESTATEMENT (FIRST) OF TORTS § 448 (1934) (emphasis added).

126. RESTATEMENT (SECOND) OF TORTS § 448 (1965).

127. In the notes to the proposed draft of § 34, the drafters explain that when the intervening act is the very harm the plaintiff was to guard against, the third-party act does not create a "scope of liability limitation" on the negligent actor's liability. RESTATEMENT (THIRD) OF TORTS: LIABILITY FOR PHYSICAL HARM § 34 (Proposed Final Draft No. 1, 2005).

128. *Sly v. Bd. of Educ.*, 515 P.2d 895 (Kan. 1973).

129. *Id.* at 897–98.

130. *Id.* at 898.

131. *Id.* at 903–04.

132. *Id.*

133. *Raleigh v. Indep. Sch. Dist. No. 625*, 275 N.W.2d 572, 575–76 (Minn. 1978).

134. *Id.* at 576.

seeability creates a duty of ordinary care and proximate causation is established by showing the likelihood that the misconduct would have been prevented had the duty been discharged.[135]

As the reader may have noticed, the preceding explanation sounds suspiciously like the explanation of duty given earlier. The difficulty arises in the treatment of foreseeability by the courts. As one commentator has noted, the concept of foreseeability has caused considerable confusion in the courts: "Sometimes foreseeability is treated as an issue of law [and thus a decision for the court as to the existence and scope of a duty], sometimes as an issue of fact [and thus a decision for the jury as to whether the particular type of harm that occurred was foreseeable, given the negligent behavior].... Foreseeability is in the language of duty, the language of breach, and the language of proximate cause."[136] Further complicating the analyses is the fact that, as one commentator colorfully put it, "'There are clear judicial days on which a court can foresee forever'[;] conversely, on a cloudy judicial day you can't foresee for schmatz."[137]

Whether attacking the problem from the perspective of duty or from the perspective of proximate cause, courts and juries ought at least to employ a clear-eyed approach to the foreseeability of bullying behavior among students. Empirical research in the field of education ought to help push some of the clouds out of the way if common sense cannot. When school officials fail to foresee bullying in their own schools and fail to employ serious, proven, research-based strategies to combat it, they should be held to have breached the duty to supervise; that breach should be found to have been the proximate cause of injuries sustained by children left to the mercy of more powerful or more numerous peers.

The Existence of Actual, Legally Recognized Harm

While those who have been physically injured by bullies face all of the obstacles already addressed in this chapter, those who have suffered serious emotional harms rather than physical harms face an additional hurdle because of a general reluctance on the part of courts to regard emotional harms, standing on their own, as legally cognizable. Courts often manifest a deep distrust of the legitimacy of emotional harm, characterizing it as "trivial," potentially nothing more than neurosis that ought not to be compensated.[138] As a result, even those who have succumbed to severe depression, have become suicidal, have dropped precipitously in their academic performanc, or have finally left school as a result of their inability to endure the ongoing torment of threats, ridicule, and isolation also face the prospect that a court will not recognize their injuries without proof of some sort of physical contact or some physical manifestation of their emotional harms. Standing before such courts, children who have been seriously emotionally damaged find that because they have no observable physical injuries, they cannot maintain a cause of action against inattentive school officials despite the fact

---

135. *Id.*
136. John C. P. Goldberg and Benjamin C. Zipursky, *The Restatement (Third) and the Place of Duty in Negligence Law*, 54 Vand. L. Rev. 657, 727 (2001).
137. Kelley, *supra* note 118, at 1046.
138. Nancy Levit, *Ethereal Torts*, 61 Geo. Wash. L. Rev. 136, 172 (1992).

that their very real and serious emotional injuries are a direct result of the officials' negligent supervision.

A number of the objections to recognizing emotional harms revolve around problems of proof.[139] In other words, courts worry that such harms may be faked, are hard to quantify, and may be more imagined than real.[140] There also exists a persistent fear that a flood of lawsuits will overwhelm courts if plaintiffs are able to bring actions for emotional harms, absent some physical harm or some evidence of extraordinarily bad conduct on the part of the defendant.[141] Further, because emotional harms often build over time rather than result from a single incident, as physical harms generally do, they present special problems of foreseeability, proof of causation, and exposure to unpredictable and even potentially "limitless" liability.[142]

As a result, courts have tried to reign in the potential of frivolous claims of emotional harm with a "tangled array of rules" and "arbitrary bright lines."[143] Although society and even courts have been less reticent in recent decades about recognizing emotional harms, many courts still require some sort of physical manifestation of alleged emotional damage to ensure that the harm is severe enough to justify compensation.[144] Other courts still require some sort of physical contact before mental distress damages can be assessed, even though this "physical impact" test has largely been abandoned in most jurisdictions.[145] For example, the same court that allowed a student's case to go forward under Title IX granted summary judgment against the plaintiff on his negligent supervision claim because every Kansas case recognizing a duty of proper supervision involved "physical bodily harm to the student."[146]

A significant part of the resistance to readily compensating emotional harms is a pervasive societal attitude that views emotional injuries as evidence of emotional weakness, "a self-inflicted—and, in a strange sense perhaps a deserved—disability."[147] Such trivialization of real harms should be rejected by the courts as a "hopelessly inauthentic account of humanity"[148] and an outdated and scientifically unjustified approach to injuries to emotional well-being. After all, it is not as if psychology and psychiatry are any longer in their infancy or the existence of severe emotional trauma is any longer seriously debated in those fields or impossible to document. In fact, it is now recognized among health care professionals that emotional injuries can be some of the most profound and most damaging injuries of all.[149]

---

139. Dobbs, *supra* note 50, § 308, at 836–39.

140. *Id.* at 836.

141. *See, e.g., Theno v. Tonganoxie Unified Sch. Dist. No. 464*, 377 F. Supp. 2d 952, 970 (D. Kan. 2005) (granting summary judgment against a plaintiff's negligent supervision claim for emotional harm because "as a practical matter, imposing upon public schools the duty to supervise students in such a manner as to prevent emotional harm to other students would undoubtedly subject Kansas schools to an enormous number of lawsuits").

142. *See* Robert J. Rhee, *A Principled Solution for Negligent Infliction of Emotional Distress Claims*, 36 Ariz. St. L. J. 805, 807–09 (2004).

143. *Id.* at 806–07.

144. Dobbs, *supra* note 50, § 308, at 836, 837–38.

145. Rhee, *supra* note 142, at 815–16.

146. *Theno*, 377 F. Supp. 2d at 968–69; *see also, Burrow v. Postville Comm. Sch. Dist.*, 929 F. Supp 1193, 1211 (N.D. Iowa 1996) (holding that a claim of negligent infliction of emotional distress could go forward because there were allegations that the plaintiff student had been subjected to physical assaults in the hallways of the school).

147. Levit, *supra* note 138, at 175.

148. *Id.* at 179.

149. *Id.* at 191.

Propping up the myth that physical injuries are real and that emotional injuries are trivial[150] does nothing to advance the interests of justice and, in fact, may foster the underlying causes of bullying. Though evidence increasingly suggests that compensating emotional injury actually helps in healing it, evidence also suggests that refusing to acknowledge its legitimacy teaches children to devalue such pain.[151] Desensitizing children to the reality of emotional pain is especially wrongheaded because it is precisely that inability to feel compassion for others' pain that is the one characteristic most common to bullies.[152] Further, courts' refusals to recognize the legitimacy of severe emotional distress at the hands of bullies help legitimize school officials ignoring not only the pain itself but the infliction of that pain as well.

Such a result is especially ironic, given the pervasiveness of awards for emotional suffering in a host of other causes of action. As Professor Keeton points out, long before the present era, "courts were quite willing to allow very substantial sums as damages for ... 'mental anguish' itself, where it accompanied a slight physical injury. And it is well recognized that mental anguish may be a substantial element in an award for a severe injury."[153] In fact, a number of traditional torts—libel, slander, assault, invasions of privacy— have at their core not physical injury but mental and emotional harm.[154]

An especially instructive development has been the importance that emotional harms have played in causes of action based on antidiscrimination statutes. While federal and state antidiscrimination statutes are certainly intended primarily to remedy the denial of economic and other rights, they are also designed to remedy the emotional distress that the denial of civil rights inflicts.[155] In fact, the recognition of the effects of a hostile educational environment is central to peer-on-peer discrimination claims. In *Davis v. Monroe County Board of Education*,[156] the Supreme Court held that peer-on-peer sexual harassment to be actionable under Title IX must be "so severe, pervasive, and objectively offensive that it can be said to deprive the victims of access to the educational opportunities or benefits provided by the school."[157] Such a definition explicitly accepts the reality that severe harassment can have emotional effects so severe that the child is no longer able to participate meaningfully in some or all of the educational services to which she is entitled. One need only read the emotional effects commonly detailed in Title IX opinions to see the courts' acceptance of their legitimacy:

> [The plaintiff] began suffering from stomach problems that required prescription medication and depression so severe that his physician prescribed medication and he sought counseling. He was diagnosed with post-traumatic stress disorder, anxiety disorder, and avoidant personality disorder that likely stemmed from the harassment. The harassment was so humiliating that he eventually left school.... The school district's argument that the harassment is not actionable because it involved only name-calling and crude gestures, not physical harassment, [is] without merit."[158]

---

150. As Levit points out, "The diminishment of emotional injuries creates a mythology about what qualifies as valid injuries. Injuries—to be considered 'real'—must be physical, visible, or discernible." *Id.* at 174.

151. *Id.* at 187.

152. *Supra* notes 29–34 and accompanying text.

153. Prosser & Keeton, §12, at 55.

154. Dobbs, *supra* note 50, §302, at 821.

155. *Id.*, at 821–22.

156. *Davis v. Monroe County Bd. of Educ.*, 526 U.S. 629 (1999).

157. *Id.* at 650.

158. *Theno*, 377 F. Supp. 2d at 968.

While the award of damages in a Title IX action is based on the denial of educational services and not on the emotional harms themselves,[159] the emotional harms are critical to the award because without them there can be no credible denial of educational services based on harassment.

Perhaps the better interpretation of such cases, of course, is that the denial of educational services in essence functions, in a roundabout way, as a proxy for a physical manifestation test or other mechanism for screening frivolous claims. In other words, until the denial of educational services is shown to be the result of the harassment, the harassment—and the consequent emotional distress—cannot be viewed as rising to the requisite severity to support the claim. This is not to say that the denial of services is intended to be such a test—for it is the denial itself that Title IX prohibits—but it does have the effect of screening for severity of emotional harm.

Even so, Title IX cases serve as a recognition that the emotional effects of harassment, which is itself simply a form of bullying based on identity characteristics,[160] are nevertheless real and damaging in important ways. The entire claim for Title IX discrimination in the context of peer-on-peer harassment rests on the same principle that empirical educational research into bullying has repeatedly confirmed to be valid: severe, targeted bullying has profoundly debilitating emotional and psychological effects on its victims.

Fortunately, some courts have recognized that emotional harms, in and of themselves, are legitimate, provable, and therefore compensable. These courts have rejected the various physical harm and physical contact requirements as unnecessary and unreliable means for screening frivolous claims.[161] According to these courts, such requirements (1) unjustifiably deny recovery where the emotional harm is severe and long-lasting despite the lack of physical manifestations of injury and (2) unjustifiably allow trivial claims of harm simply because a minor physical contact or symptom can be shown.[162] Instead, these courts require only that mental harm be proven by a preponderance of the evidence.[163] As one commentator has suggested, there is no reason that the claims of direct victims of a defendant's negligence—as opposed to the claims of indirect victims such as bystanders who allege emotional injuries as a result of witnessing harm to a third person—should be resolved under anything other than traditional tort doctrines of duty, proximate cause, and damages.[164] Because the class of victims is limited, the scope of liability is similarly limited and is no different from that of physical injury claims.[165]

Although it is encouraging that some courts have indeed adopted a traditional foreseeability test with regard to such emotional harms, it may be some time before it is clear whether such an approach will overtake the more restrictive tests that are still common[166] and longer still before it is common that such damages are cognizable in negligent supervision claims.

---

159. *Id.* at 966–67.

160. Weddle, *supra* note 1, at 645 n. 20, 659–60.

161. Dobbs, *supra* note 50, § 328, at 838.

162. *Id.*

163. *Id.*

164. Rhee, *supra* note 142, at 865–66 (explaining that indirect victims may require a different treatment because of the practically unlimited number of people who might witness, for example, a horrific event unfold live on television).

165. *Id.*

166. Dobbs, *supra* note 50, § 312, at 850–51.

One court, however, has explicitly recognized such damages in that context. New York's highest court held that children's claims for emotional damage resulting from the school's negligent supervision of bullying students were cognizable. Those claims, said the court, were

> predicated on well-recognized principles: first, that if there is a duty owed by a defendant to a plaintiff, a breach of that duty resulting directly in emotional harm is compensable even though physical harm is lacking, and second that a school district is obliged to adequately supervise the activities of students within its charge.... [Therefore], it will be held liable in damages for a foreseeable injury proximately related to the absence of supervision.[167]

The court's approach is imminently reasonable; whether an injury is genuine and severe as opposed to fraudulent or trivial should not be considered beyond the ability of courts and juries to determine on the basis of competent evidence.[168]

The final element of negligent supervision, therefore, should present no obstacle to plaintiffs who have been injured by the torment of peers left to prey on them by school officials who have not taken seriously what the literature in their own field has told them. Whether the harms caused by that failure to supervise competently are physical or emotional, if they are real and provable under ordinary evidentiary standards, they should be legally sufficient to justify damage awards.

Conclusion

Children of both genders and all races in this country are daily subjected to indignities, threats, and abuse that most adults would never tolerate in their own workplaces; yet those same children have little recourse but to endure as best they can what their elders do not wish to see. While schools remain blind to the problem in their own hallways and classrooms, too many children face a daily brutality that will permanently scar some, will drive others to suicidal desperation, and will drive still others to what used to be unthinkable retaliation.

Plaintiffs' attorneys and school attorneys should shake schools out of their slumber and demand that they align their educational practices with what educational researchers have long been telling them about bullying and its debilitating damage. Courts should shake off their own timidity about holding schools accountable for ignoring those voices and turning a blind eye to the torment of children in their care. Doing so requires no new theories of liability, no excursions into uncharted legal territory. It requires no radical reorganization of schools, no radical revision of the nation's laws. There is nothing radical about calling inattentiveness and professional blindness what it is: it is negligence. When children are subjected to brutality because of that negligence, there is nothing radical about holding schools accountable to those children.

---

167. *Cavello v. Sherburne-Earlville Central Sch. Dist.*, 494 N.Y.S.2d 466, 467–68 (N.Y. App. Div. 1985).

168. Rhee, *supra* note 142, at 832–34.

18

The New IDEA:
Shifting Educational Paradigms
to Achieve Racial Equality in
Special Education

Robert A. Garda Jr.[*]

Introduction

Since the landmark decision of *Brown v. Board of Education* mandated desegregation in public schools, African American students have been resegregated within public schools through their overplacement in special education classes.[1] The enforcement of *Brown* coincided with schools classifying African American students as disabled and placing them in special education classes as a pretense for discrimination.[2] The disproportionate identification of African American children with disabilities for special education under the Individuals with Disabilities Education Act [hereafter IDEA][3] persists today to the extent that IDEA is viewed as a tool of racial discrimination and a dumping ground for minor-

***

[*] Reprinted with permission of the Alabama Law Review. First published at 56 Ala L. Rev 1071 (2005). Assistant Professor, Loyola University of New Orleans School of Law. The author wishes to express his appreciation to Professor Mark Weber of DePaul University College of Law, Professor Theresa Glennon of Temple University Beasley Schoool of Law, and Dr. Quaisar Sultana, Professor of Special Education at Eastern Kentucky University, for their invaluable insights and comments on earlier drafts of this chapter.

1. Edward Garcia Fierros and James W. Conroy, *Double Jeopordy: An Exploration of Restrictiveness and Race in Special Education*, in Daniel J. Losen and Gary Orfield, Racial Inequity in Special Education 39 (2002) [hereinafter Racial Inequity]; Lauren Katzman, *Minority Students in Special and Gifted Education,* 7/1/03 Harv. Educ. Rev. 225239, located at 2003 WL 55851225 (2003) (noting that as early as 1965, certain California school districts allegedly used special education classes as a cover for segregation within schools). *See also United States v. Yonkers Bd. of Educ.*, 624 F.Supp. 1276, 1453–62 (S.D.N.Y. 1985) (holding that "the historically discriminatory operation of the Special Education program continued to have discriminatory effects.").

2. Daniel J. Losen and Kevin G. Welner, *Disabling Discrimination in our Public Schools: Comprehensive Legal Challenges to Inappropriate and Inadequate Special Education Services for Minority Children*, 36 Harv. C.R.-C.L. L. Rev. 407, 434 (2001) ("Once desegregation began in earnest ... schools experienced a wave of second discrimination taking the form of ... special education placements in substantially separate classrooms"); Weinstein, Note, *Equal Educational Opportunities for Learning Deficient Students*, 68 Geo. Wash. L. Rev. 500, 517 (1999–2000).

3. 20 U.S.C. §§ 1400 *et. seq.* (1997).

ity students.[4] African American students are identified as disabled under IDEA in numbers that so exceed their proportion in the general population that the Department of Education considers it a "national problem"[5] and experts proclaim it a "crisis."[6]

The long history of African American overrepresentation in special education is now accompanied by a recent explosion in the overall number of children identified as IDEA-eligible.[7] The last decade witnessed a 35 percent increase in the number of children served under IDEA, while school enrollment grew only 14 percent.[8] Currently, over six million children are served under IDEA, or 11.5 percent of the school-age population.[9] Many of these students are merely "instructional casualties" rather than students with genuine disabilities.[10] As former Secretary of Education Rod Paige explains, "our educational system fails to teach many children fundamental skills like reading, then inappropriately identifies some of them as having disabilities, thus harming the educational future of those children who are misidentified and reducing resources available to serve children with disabilities."[11]

---

4. *See e.g.,* Theresa Glennon, *Race, Education, and the Construction of a Disabled Class,* 1995 Wis. L. Rev. 1237, 1242 (1995) [hereafter Glennon, *The Construction of a Disabled Class*]; Patrick Linehan, *Guarding the Dumping Ground: Equal Protection, Title VII and Justifying the Use of Race in Hiring Special Educators,* 2001 BYU Educ. & L.J. 179 (2001); Stanley S. Herr, *Special Education Law and Children With Reading and Other Disabilities,* 28 J.L. & Educ. 337, 347 (1999) (discussing that special education classes often become holding operations for minority students and others found intractable in regular classes); Joseph A. Patella, Note, *Missing the "IDEA": New York's Segregated Special Education System,* 4 J.L. & Pol'y 239, 256 (1995) (stating that teachers use special education as dumping ground for poor readers and unruly students); H.R. Rep. No. 108-77, at 153 (2002).

5. Jane Burnette, *Reducing the Disproportionate Representation of Minority Students in Special Education,* ERIC/OSEP Digest #E566 (1998).

6. Marilyn Milloy, *Truth in Labeling,* NEA Today (January 2003) (stating that minority disproportionality in special education is a "crisis"); Donald P. Oswald et al., *Community and School Predictors of Overrepresentation of Minority Children in Special Education,* in Racial Inequity, *supra* note 1, at 1 (identifying the "crisis in minority student education."); Shapiro et al., *Separate and Unequal,* U.S. News & World Report, Dec. 13, 1993.

7. Senator James Jeffords, *Foreword, in* Racial Inequity, *supra* note 1, at xi (stating that "special education enrollments have spiraled in the last decade"); Tara L. Eyer, Comment, *Greater Expectations: How the 1997 IDEA Amendments Raise the Basic Floor of Opportunity for Children with Disabilities,* 103 Dick L. Rev. 613, 627 (1998) ("overidentificaiton of children has become a significant problem in recent years").

8. Committee on Minority Representation in Special Education of the National Research Council, Minority Students in Special and Gifted Education 1–2, 18 (2002) [hereafter NRC Report]; Elena Gallegos, *Thirty Years of Special Education Law: The Long and Winding Road,* 10 No. 6. Special Educ. L. Update 1 (2002); Herr, *supra* note 4, at 376.

9. Lynn Olson, *Enveloping Expectations,* 23 Educ. Wk. 8 (2004) (indicating that there are 6.6 million children in special education); United States Dep't. of Educ., Annual Report to Congress on the Implementation of the Individuals with Disabilities Education Act, xxiii, II-21 (2002) (noting the figures of the 2000–01 school year) [hereafter 24th Annual Report]. Special education expenditures are estimated at $50 billion or roughly 14 percent of public education spending. Katzman, *supra* note 1, at 225239; Thomas Parrish, *Racial Disparities in the Identification, Funding and Provision of Special Education,* in Racial Inequity, *supra* note 1, at 15.

10. President's Commission on Excellence in Special Educ., A New Era: Revitalizing Special Education for Children and their Families 26 (July 1, 2002) [hereafter President's Commission], available at www.ed.gov/inits/commissionsboards/whspecialeducation/; H.R. Rep. No. 105-95, at 89 ("Today, the growing problem is over identifying children with disabilities when they might not be truly disabled").

11. H.R. Rep. No. 108-79 at 7 (2003). *See also, id.* at 137 ("The overidentification of children as disabled and placing them in special education where they do not belong hinders the academic development of these students. Worse, the misidentification takes valuable resources away from students who are truly disabled").

In short, IDEA is suffering an eligibility crisis on two intersecting fronts: African American overrepresentation and an overall eligibility increase resulting from special education sweeping up students from a broken general education system. Congress's new IDEA, the Individuals with Disabilities Education Improvement Act of 2004 [hereafter IDEIA],[12] embodies a dramatic educational paradigm shift to resolve these problems. For the first time, Congress recognizes that special education eligibility is directly linked to the general education system. Through the IDEIA, Congress reaches into the general education system to remedy the overidentification crises by legislating a certain level of individualized instruction. This model of individualized instruction in general education departs significantly from the one-size-fits-all educational model embodied in the old IDEA, wherein specialized instruction is exclusively the domain of special education that is provided only to disabled children. The IDEIA favors the individualization model almost out of necessity, as today's increasingly diverse students require a certain level of individualized instruction in the general classroom. It is better to address diverse needs in the general education classroom than to classify children as disabled and rely on special education to address their unique learning styles, cultural backgrounds and different abilities. Special education's swelling rolls and the disproportionate representation of African Americans reveal particular shortcomings of the general education system that the IDEIA seeks to reform.

The IDEIA will inevitably fall far short of solving the dual eligibility crisis, however, primarily because its incremental reforms merely adopt, but do not embrace, its new pedagogy. It will not ensure a low level of individualized instruction to all students, as opposed to merely IDEIA-eligible students, and it will not ensure that students will receive appropriate services in regular education before placement into special education. The IDEIA simply cannot redefine regular education without first redefining "special education" and who "needs" it in the stagnant thirty-year-old eligibility criteria that the IDEIA employs.[13]

Eligibility under the IDEIA and all of its predecessor statutes hinges on finding that the child has an enumerated disability and "needs special education."[14] The broad definition of "special education"—the adaptation of instructional content, methodology or delivery—permits some decision makers to find that children requiring *any* adaptation to the general education environment need "special education" and are eligible, while other decision makers limit "special education" to significant and unique adaptations. The nonexistent definition of "need" leads to diverging views as to what level of services a child must be provided in general education before a "need" for special education is found. With little statutory guidance, decision makers apply their own pedagogical beliefs about what constitutes "special education" and who "needs" it—resulting in subjective eligibility determinations influenced by bias rather than uniform application of eligibility criteria.

This chapter proposes that without fundamental changes to—and a proper understanding of—the "needs special education" eligibility criteria, the educational paradigm

---

12. IDEIA, H.R. 1350, 108th Cong (2004). The IDEIA was signed by President Bush on December 3, 2004. thomas.loc.gov/cgi-bin/bdquery.

13. NRC Report, *supra* note 8, at 18, 20.

14. IDEIA, H.R. 1350, § 101 amending § 602(3). 20 U.S.C. § 1401(3) (1997); 34 C.F.R. 300.7(a) (2003). The progenitor of special education law, the Education for All Handicapped Children Act of 1975, defined an eligible child as one with an enumerated disability that "requires special education." Pub. Law 94-142 § 602(a) (1975). The language remained until the 1990 reauthorization of IDEA, which only changed "requires" to "needs." Pub. Law 101-476 § 101(a) (1990). For discussion of the legislative history of the "needs special education" requirement, *see* Robert A. Garda, *Untangling Eligibility Requirements Under the Individuals with Disabilities Education Act*, 69 Mo. L. Rev. 441, 491–93 (2004).

adopted in the IDEIA cannot take root, and the eligibility problems will persist. Reclaiming special education from overrepresented African Americans and instructional casualties and placing it back in the hands of the genuinely disabled cannot occur until "special education" relinquishes its exclusive grip on individualized instruction, thus allowing certain unique student needs to be served in regular education without IDEIA eligibility attaching. To do so, the definition of "special education" must be limited to only significant instructional adaptations that are not provided all students, regardless of disability. A child should also not be found in "need" of special education until all available accommodations and regular education interventions have proven to be unsuccessful. These circumscribed definitions prohibit the placement of students into special education if their individual needs can properly be served through general education. The result will be consistent eligibility decisions. It is only by limiting the definition of "special education" and when it is "needed" that general education can be redefined to embrace the paradigm of individualized instruction, and uniformity can be brought to eligibility determinations.

Though changing the eligibility criteria alone cannot remedy minority disproportionality and rising special education rolls, it is a necessary first step. Part I of this chapter explores the nature of African American overrepresentation in special education, its negative effects and its controversial causes. Part II critiques the IDEIA's solutions to its dual eligibility crisis. Part III explores the division in authority interpreting the term "special education" that will persist under the IDEIA and proposes a new definition. Part IV discusses the division in authority interpreting when a child "needs" special education that will continue under IDEIA and proposes that a child should not be found in "need" of special education until all available regular education interventions and supports have proven ineffective.

I. The Nature, Harm and Causes of the Disproportionate Representation of African American Students in Special Education

It is beyond dispute that African Americans are represented in special education disproportionately to their representation in general education.[15] But solutions to African American overrepresentation cannot be developed without knowing its causes, and its causes cannot be ascertained without understanding its nature. Before assessing the propriety of the IDEIA solutions, it is therefore necessary to explore these issues.

A. The History and Nature of Disproportionate Representation

African Americans have long been overrepresented in special education. Researchers in the 1960s recognized that African Americans were disproportionately represented in pro-

---

15. Congress explicitly found that minority overrepresentaiton exists when reauthorizing the IDEA in 1997, 20 U.S.C. § 1400(c)(7) (1997), and in the IDEIA. H.R. 1350 § 601(c)(9). *See also* Katzman, *supra* note 1, at 225239.

grams for the mentally retarded, emotionally disturbed and learning disabled.[16] Children in these programs were segregated from the general education population and placed in separate special education classrooms. Minority overrepresentation in these segregated programs persisted through 1975, when Congress passed the IDEIA's progenitor, the Education of All Handicapped Children Act [hereafter EAHCA].[17] At that time, the mislabeling of students was considered "the major controversy in special education."[18] In response, Congress mandated that the National Academy of Sciences conduct a study on the factors accounting for the overrepresentation of minorities in special education programs for the mentally retarded.[19] The resulting 1982 study by the National Research Council [hereafter NRC] concluded that African Americans were represented in the mentally retarded category disproportionate to their numbers in general education.[20] Between 1978 and 1992, there was no significant change in the statistics establishing disproportional representation of African Americans in special education.[21] By 1992, African Americans were twice as likely to be classified as mentally retarded as their white peers, and 1.46 times more likely to be classified as emotionally disturbed.[22]

African American overrepresentation did no go unnoticed by federal courts during this time period. In the landmark case of *Hobson v. Hansen*, Judge Wright found that African American students were disproportionately represented in the mentally retarded education track, which denied them equal educational opportunity.[23] In *Larry P. v. Riles*, the court enjoined the use of Intelligence Quotient [hereafter IQ] tests as part of special education eligibility determinations because IQ tests led to the overidentification of minority students as mentally retarded.[24]

Congress took note of African American overrepresentation in special education when it reauthorized the EAHCA as IDEA in 1990.[25] But Congress did not formally recognize African Americans' disproportionate representation until 1997, when it amended IDEA to expressly provide that "more minority children continue to be served in special edu-

---

16. Marie E. Arnold, *Overrepresentation of Minority Students in Special Education*, 124 EDUCATION 230 (2003); John L. Hosp and Daniel J. Reschly, *Referral Rates for Intervention or Assessment: a Meta-Analysis of Racial Differences*, 37 J. SPECIAL ED. 67 (2003); Theresa Glennon, *The Stuart Rome Lecture Knocking Against the Rocks: Evaluating Institutional Practices and the African American Boy*, 5 J. HEALTH CARE L. & POL'Y 10, 38 (2002) [hereafter Glennon, *The Stuart Rome Lecture*]; David L. Kirp, *Schools as Sorters: The Constitutional and Policy Implications of Student Classification*, 121 U.PENN. L.R. 705, 760–61 (1973); NRC REPORT, *supra* note 8, at 22–23.

17. Pub L. No. 94-142 (1975). NRC REPORT, *supra* note 8, at 18; Thomas Hehir, *IDEA and Disproportionality: Federal Enforcement, Effective Advocacy, and Strategies for Change, in* RACIAL INEQUITY, *supra* note 1, at 219. The EAHCA has been amended and renamed numerous times, including 1977, 1983, 1986, 1988, 1990, 1991, 1994 and 1997. 20 U.S.C. § 1400 (1997).

18. H. Goldstein et al., *Issues in Classification of Children: Volume* 2, Schools 4–61 (N. Jobbs ed., 1975).

19. NRC REPORT, *supra* note 8, at 18.

20. NRC REPORT, *supra* note 8, at 1; Losen and Welner, *supra* note 2, at 41.

21. Glennon, *The Construction of a Disabled Class, supra* note 4, at 1251; Shapiro et al., *supra* note 2.

22. Glennon, *The Construction of a Disabled Class, supra* note 4, at 1252. *See also* Donald Lash and Jennifer Weiser, *Disproportional Representation*, 96 PLY/NY 299, 320–22 (2001).

23. 269 F.Supp. 401, 442, 448, 456–57, 514 (D.D.C. 1967), *cert. dismissed* 393 US 801, *aff'd sub nom.*

24. 495 F.Supp. 926, 942–44, 955–56 (N.D. Cal. 1979), *aff'd in part and rev'd in part*, 793 F.2d 969 (9th Cir. 1984). *See also Diana v. State Bd. of Educ.*, C-70-37 RFP (N.D. Cal. 1970); *Covarrubias v. San Diego Unified Sch. Dist.*, No. 70-304-T (S.D. Cal. July 31, 1972).

25. *See, e.g., Reauthorization of Discretionary Programs—Education of the Handicapped Act: Hearing Before the Subcomm. on Select Education of the House Comm. on Education & Labor*, 101st Cong., 1st Sess. 9, 33 (1989); H.R. REP. No. 101-544 (1990), reprinted in 1990 U.S.C.C.A.N. 1723, 1737.

cation than would be expected from the percentage of minority students in the general school population."[26] Congress also recognized that "poor African American children are 2.3 times more likely to be identified by their teacher as having mental retardation than their white counterparts … Although African Americans represent 16 percent of elementary and secondary enrollments, they constitute 21 percent of total enrollments in special education."[27] Congress responded by, among other things, mandating that the NRC again study minority children in special education.[28]

In its 2002 study, the NRC verified that African Americans are disproportionately represented in special education.[29] Over 14 percent of African American children were identified for special education, compared to only 12 percent of whites.[30] Furthermore, while African American students constitute 15 percent of the school population, they represent over 20 percent of the students referred for special education eligibility.[31]

The nature of African American overrepresentation sheds light on its causes, as overrepresentation is not uniform throughout the IDEIA's disability categories. To be eligible, a child must have one of the following qualifying disabilities: "mental retardation, hearing impairments (including deafness), speech or language impairments, visual impairments (including blindness), serious emotional disturbance, orthopedic impairments, autism, traumatic brain injury, other health impairments, or specific learning disabilities."[32] For children between the ages of three and nine, states may ignore the enumerated disabilities and find children eligible that experience "developmental delays" in physical, cognitive, communication, social, emotional or adaptive development.[33]

These qualifying disabilities can be divided into high-incidence and low-incidence categories. Students with low-incidence disabilities—hearing impairments, visual impairments, orthopedic impairments, autism, traumatic brain injury and other health impairment—constitute only 12 percent of the IDEA-eligible population.[34] These medical model or "nonjudgment" disabilities are "clearly identifiable disorders of the central nervous system, sensory status or neuromotor capabilities that can be said to cause the

---

26. 20 U.S.C. § 1401(8)(A) and (B) (1997). *See also* Hehir, *supra* note 17, at 219 (stating that it was not until the 1997 reauthorization process that IDEA directly addressed racial disporportionality).

27. 20 U.S.C. § 1401(8)(C) and (D) (1997).

28. NRC Report, *supra* note 8, at vi.

29. NRC Report, *supra* note 8, at 1–2, 357. Numerous scholars and researchers reach this same conclusion. *See e.g.,* Racial Inequity, *supra* note 1, at 219, xviii–xxi; Arnold, *supra* note 16; Glennon, *The Stuart Rome Lecture, supra* note 16, at 17–18 (African American males are grossly overrepresented in special education).

30. NRC Report, *supra* note 8, at 1–2, 61. *See also* Alfredo J Artiles, *Special Education's Changing Identity: Paradoxes and Dilemmas in Views of Cultures and Spaces,* 7/1/03 Harv. Educ. Rev 247, 2003 WL 55851226 (2003).

31. IDEIA, H.R. 1350, § 101 amending § 601(c)(12)(D). *See also* Dierdre Glenn Paul, *The Train has Left: The No Child Left Behind Act Leaves Black and Latino Literacy Learners Waiting at the Station,* 47 Journal of Adolescent and Adult Literacy 648 (2004).

32. IDEIA, H.R. § 1350, § 101 amending § 602(3)(A)(i); 20 U.S.C. § 1401(3)(A)(i) (2002).

33. IDEIA, H.R. § 1350, § 101 amending § 602(3)(B)(i); 20 U.S.C. 1401(3)(B)(i) (2002); 34 C.F.R. § 300.7(b) (2003). The "developmental delay" category allows states increased flexibility for this age group by eliminating the need for finding that the child has a particular disability before eligibility attaches because "it is sometimes difficult to pinpoint a child's disability during the early developmental years." Terry Overton, Assessment in Special Education: An Applied Approach 37 (2d ed. 1996).

34. 24th Annual Report, *supra* note 9, at II-22; President's Commission, *supra* note 10 at 3, 30; Lynn Olson, *Enveloping Expectations,* 23 Educ. Wk. 8 (2004); NRC Report, *supra* note 8, at 220.

disability."[35] Diagnosing a child with low-incidence disabilities is typically an objective determination, and "few would question the accuracy of a diagnosis in these cases."[36]

African American students are not overrepresented in these low-incidence or non-judgmental categories in which the problem is observable outside of the school context.[37] Rather, African American overrepresentation occurs in the high-incidence categories of mental retardation [hereafter MR], severe emotional disturbance [hereafter SED] and to some extent in specific learning disability [hereafter SLD] — "categories in which the problem is often identified first in the school context and the disability is typically given without confirmation of an organic cause."[38] Children with these disabilities constitute roughly 88 percent of IDEA-eligible students.[39] These "social system" or "judgmental" disabilities are not biologically based; there is no uniform test to determine their presence or agreement on how to diagnose them; and their definitions are open to discretion in application.[40] Unlike the low-incidence disabilities, diagnosing a child with a high-incidence disability is a subjective clinical judgment that merely reflects social and cultural beliefs about appropriate learning and behavior in the school setting.[41]

The recent findings that African American children are overrepresented in the MR and SED classifications are to be expected considering the long-standing overrepresentation

---

35. NRC Report, *supra* note 8, at 220. Congress defines "low-incidence disability" in the IDEIA as "a visual or hearing impairment, or simultaneous visual and hearing impairments; a significant cognitive impairment; or any impairments for which a small number of personnel with highly specialized skills and knowledge are needed in order for children with that impairment to receive ... a free appropriate public education." H.R. 1350 § 401, amending § 662(c)(3)(A)-(C).

36. NRC Report, *supra* note 8, at 55. *See also* Parrish, *supra* note 9, at 24–25.

37. NRC Report, *supra* note 8, at 1–2, 54–61. *See also* Parrish, *supra* note 9, at 16; Paul, *supra* note 31; Arnold, *supra* note 16. Not surprisingly, these disability categories have not been at issue in court cases regarding minority overrepresentation. NRC Report, *supra* note 8, at 55.

38. NRC Report, *supra* note 8, at 1, 20, 222. *See also* Paul, *supra* note 31; Arnold, *supra* note 16; IDEIA, H.R. 1350, § 101 amending § 601(c)(12)(C); H.R. Rep. No. 108-77 at 137 (2002) (the "proportion of minority students identified in some disability categories is dramatically greater than their share of the overall population"); A Position Statement of the International Reading Association, *The Role of Reading Instruction in Addressing the Overrepresentation of Minority Children in Special Education in the United States,* located at www.reading.org/positions/1063.html.

39. NRC Report, *supra* note 8, at 55, 220; 24th Annual Report, *supra* note 9, at II-22 (mental retardation accounts for 10 percent of all IDEA eligible children and severe emotional disturbance accounts for 8 percent). Specific learning disability and speech language impairments alone account for roughly 70 percent of IDEA eligible children. A Position Statement of the International Reading Association, *supra* note 38; NRC Report, *supra* note 8, at 1–2, 19, 47–48. The specific learning disability category has also seen the largest growth rate over the last decade. *Id.* There has been a 28.5 percent increase in children classified as severely learning disabled since 1992. 24th Annual Report, *supra* note 9, at II-24.

40. Parrish, *supra* note 9, at 24–25; Beth Harry et al., *Of Rocks and Soft Places: Using Qualitative Methods to Investigate Disproportionality, in* Racial Inequity, *supra* note 1, at 76–77; Glennon, *The Construction of a Disabled Class, supra* note 4, at 1259, 1302–03 (noting that MR, LD and SED are not biologically based and their definitions are vague and changeable); Laura E. Naistadt, *Understanding Learning Disabilities,* 42 S. Tex. L. Rev. 97, 100 (Winter 2000); Herr, *supra* note 4, at 387; Mark Kelman and Gillian Lester, Jumping the Queue: An Inquiry into the Treatment of Students with Learning Disabilities 17–20, 29 (Cambridge: Harvard University Press 1997); Pamela Smith, *Our Children's Burden: The Many-Headed Hydra of the Educational Disenfranchisement of Black Children,* 42 How. L.R. 133, 190, 194–97 (1999).

41. Glennon, *The Construction of a Disabled Class, supra* note 4, at 1302–03. *See also* Harry et al., *supra* note 40, at 71–72, 77 ("the point at which differences result in one child being labeled disabled and another not are matters of social decisionmaking."); Arnold, *supra* note 16; Glennon, *The Stuart Rome Lecture, supra* note 16, at 18 (MR, SED and SLD open to subjective decision making); Linehan, *supra* note 4, at 183; Parrish, *supra* note 9, at 24–25.

of African Americans in these categories. School districts historically overclassify African American students as MR in comparison to their white peers.[42] The most recent data shows that African American children are nearly three times more likely to be identified as MR than are white children.[43] While only 1 percent of white students are designated MR, a remarkable 2.6 percent of African American students receive the MR designation.[44] Overall, African Americans account for 33 percent of MR enrollment but only 15 percent of the student population.[45] The MR category far and away represents the greatest degree of African American disproportionality.[46]

The statistics are similarly stark for African Americans in the SED category. African Americans are historically and currently at higher risk of SED classification than any other group.[47] They are 1.59 times more likely to be identified as SED than their white counterparts.[48] Only 0.91 percent of white students are identified as SED, compared to 1.56 percent of African American students.[49] African Americans constitute 27 percent of the SED population, but only 15 percent of the overall school population, firmly establishing their disproportionate representation in the SED category.[50]

African Americans are also disproportionately represented in the broad developmental delay [hereafter DD] category for three- to nine-year-olds. While DD is not found in a high incidence of the population,[51] it shares the subjective diagnosis hallmark of high-incidence disabilities. Diagnosing DD does not require the finding of a specific disability; instead, the child's development needs only to be below expectation. African Americans are 2.06 times more likely than whites to be classified as DD.[52] While there is only a 0.05 percent chance that an African American will be classified DD, whites are only classified as DD at a rate of .02 percent.[53] Despite the low numbers of children served under the DD category, African American students' disproportionate representation in this category is dramatic.

There is disagreement as to whether African Americans are disproportionately represented in the SLD category—the most populated disability category. The NRC concluded

---

42. NRC Report, *supra* note 8, at 45–46. *See also* Glennon, *The Stuart Rome Lecture, supra* note 16, at 18.

43. NRC Report, *supra* note 8, at 44, 82; H.R. Rep. No. 108-77 at 137, 147, 154, 169–70 (2002); Parrish, *supra* note 9, at 21–23; Milloy, *supra* note 6 (stating that African Americans are three times more likely to be found MR than whites); A Position Statement of the International Reading Association, *supra* note 38 (stating that African Americans are 2.8 times more likely to be found MR than whites); Losen and Welner, *supra* note 2, at 413.

44. NRC Report, *supra* note 8, at 2.

45. *Id.* at 44; Mathhew Ladner, *Minorities Overrepresented in Special-Ed,* Patriot News, 2/27/04 p. A13.

46. NRC Report, *supra* note 8, at 251; Parrish, *supra* note 9, at 15, 21.

47. NRC Report, *supra* note 8, at 48–49, 51, 82, 261. *See also* H.R. Rep. No. 108-77 at 137, 154 (2002) (noting that African Americans are overrepresented in the SED category); David Osher et al., *Schools Make a Difference: The Overrepresentation of African America Youth in Special Education and Juvenile Justice System, in* Racial Inequity, *supra* note 1, at 100.

48. NRC Report, *supra* note 8, at 57; H.R. Rep. No. 108-77 at 147, 169–70 (2002); A Position Statement of the International Reading Association, *supra* note 38 (stating that African Americans are 1.92 times more likely to be found SED than whites); Paul, *supra* note 31 (concluding that African Americans are identified as SED at over 1.5 times the rate of white students).

49. NRC Report, *supra* note 8, at 57.

50. *Id.* at 42. The rate at which risk of identification for SED has increased is more rapid for African Americans than for whites. *Id.* at 51.

51. 24th Annual Report, *supra* note 9, at II-24 (children classified with developmental delay comprise only 0.5 percent of the IDEA population).

52. NRC Report, *supra* note 8, at 59, 61.

53. *Id.*

that African Americans are identified at 1.08 times the rates that whites are identified — or roughly the same — and that no national overrepresentation exists.[54] Other researchers disagree, finding that African Americans are significantly more likely to be classified as SLD than whites.[55] Even assuming the NRC to be correct on a national scale, it is undisputed that African Americans are vastly overrepresented in the SLD category in certain states. For example, African Americans in Delaware have a 12.19 percent chance if being identified as SLD, but only a 2.33 percent chance in Georgia.[56] Similar state disparities exist between the states in the SED and MR classifications.[57]

Disparities exist among the states in the total number of children found IDEA eligible, and in the number of children identified under each disability category, because the states employ significantly different eligibility standards.[58] The IDEIA continues the practice of establishing only broad definitions of the qualifying disabilities, allowing states to provide the precise criteria for their application.[59] For example, the regulations define mental retardation as "significantly subaverage general intellectual functioning, existing concurrently with deficits in adaptive behavior."[60] One state may require that a child's IQ fall below eighty to establish subaverage intellectual functioning, another state may require an IQ below seventy, and yet another state may not employ any IQ cut-off.[61] State variations in defining the enumerated disabilities is one significant cause of the discrepancy among states as to which children they identify as IDEIA eligible and under which category.

The incongruity also results from states employing varied definitions of the second eligibility criterion — that the child with an enumerated disability "needs special education." As will be discussed in detail, the IDEIA continues the practice of only broadly defining "special education" — which states can alter — and provides no definition of "need." This leads to a significant division among the states, courts and hearing officers as to what constitutes "special education" and when a child "needs" it. Differing eligibility and identification practices, coupled with the highly subjective nature of eligibility determinations, compound the variability in minority representation across the states.

Despite state variability, particularly for the SLD category, it is certain that African Americans historically and currently are disproportionately represented only in the high-incidence or judgmental disabilities of SED, MR, DD and likely SLD, on a national level. This begs the critical question — is overplacement into special education harmful?

---

54. *Id.* at 47–48, 83.

55. *See e.g.,* Fierros and Conroy, *supra* note 1, at 41; Daniel J. Losen and Gary Orfield, Racial Inequity in Special Education xvi, xx (2002); Smith, *supra* note 40, at 194–97 (concluding that African Americans are disproportionately represented in the SLD category); A Position Statement of the International Reading Association, *supra* note 38 (determining that African Americans are 1.32 times more likely to be classified SLD than whites).

56. NRC Report, *supra* note 8, at 67. *See also* Statement of Dr. Douglas Carnine, Subcommittee on Education Reform Committee on House Education and the Workforce, March 13, 2003, located at 2003 WL 11716331.

57. NRC Report, *supra* note 8, at 37, 39–41, 62–70 (identifying significant variability among states in identification of African American students in the SED and MR categories), 270–71.

58. Losen and Welner, *supra* note 2; Lynn Olson, *Enveloping Expectations*, 23 Educ. Wk. 8 (2004).

59. IDEIA, H.R. 1350 § 101, amending § 602(3)(A)(i). The statute defines only "specific learning disability." H.R. 1350 § 101, amending § 602(30). The regulations broadly define the remaining disabilities. 34 C.F.R. § 300.7(c) (2003). While the states define the disabilities differently, most require a medical diagnosis or certification before finding that a child has a specific disability. President's Commission, *supra* note 10, at 23.

60. 34 C.F.R. § 300.7(c)(6) (2003).

61. NRC Report, *supra* note 8, at 38.

B. The Harm of Misplacement in Special Education

Calling African American overrepresentation a crisis appears contradictory, as eligibility for special education is intended to yield educational benefit.[62] The impetus for enacting the EAHCA in 1975 was to ensure that disabled children accessed appropriate education.[63] The EAHCA and its successors, including the IDEIA, entitle eligible children to a "free appropriate public education," which means special education and related services that confers educational benefit.[64] Because IDEA, and now the IDEIA, entitles eligible children to more benefits than general education students, some question whether African American overrepresentation is actually a problem.[65] But courts,[66] scholars[67] and the NRC[68] conclude that significant harm results from misidentifying African Americans for special education eligibility.

Congress finds in the IDEIA that "greater efforts are needed to prevent the intensification of problems connected with mislabeling and high dropout rates among minority children with disabilities."[69] The House Report regarding the IDEIA stated that the overidentification of minorities as eligible for special education is a primary concern.[70] It concluded that the mislabeling of minority students has "significant adverse consequences"

---

62. Glennon, *The Construction of a Disabled Class*, *supra* note 4, at 1311 ("classification as disabled is widely viewed as a two-edged sword, bringing both benefit and stigma"); NRC Report, *supra* note 8, at 20 ("we recognize the paradox inherent in a charge that posits disproportionate placement of minority students in special education as a problem").

63. Pub L. No. 94-142, § 1, 89 Stat. 773 (1975). The historical underpinnings of the EAHCA are extensively discussed in the scholarship and case law. *See e.g., Bd. of Education of Hendrick Hudson Central Sch. Dist. v. Rowley*, 458 U.S. 176, 189–204 (1982); Blakely, *Judicial and Legislative Attitudes Toward the Right to an Equal Education for the Handicapped*, 40 Ohio St. L.J. 603, 606–13 (1979).

64. IDEIA, H.R. 1350, 108th Cong. § 101, amending § 602(8); 20 U.S.C. § 1401(8) (1997); *Rowley*, 458 U.S. at 200. For a general discussion of the educational and procedural benefits IDEA provides eligible children and their parents, *see* Garda, *supra* note 14, at 441–51.

65. A.J. Artiles et al., *Culturally Diverse Students in Special Education: Legacies and Prospects* in J.A. Banks & C.M. Banks (Eds.), in Handbook of Research on Multicultural Education (2nd ed. 2004); Artiles, *supra* note 30.

66. *See e.g., Hobson v. Hansen*, 269 F. Supp. 401, 443, 514–15 (D.D.C. 1967) (holding that the racially disproportionate placement of African American students in special education denied them equal educational opportunity); *Larry P. v. Riles*, 495 F.Supp. 926 (N.D.Cal. 1979, *aff'd in part and rev'd in part*, 793 F.2d 969 (9th Cir. 1984); *P.A.S.E. v. Hannon*, 506 F.Supp. 831, 834 (N.D. Ill. 1980) (concluding that improperly placed students suffer severe harm and "educational tragedy"). More recently, in *Lee v. Macon County Bd. of Educ.*, 267 F.Supp. 458 (M.D. Ala. 1967), the court entered a consent decree addressing Alabama's persistent problem of minority student overrepresentation in special education. *Lee v. Phoenix City Bd. of Educ.*, C.A. No. 70-T-854 (M.D. Ala. August 30, 2000). For a discussion of courts considering minority overrepresentation, see Losen and Welner, *supra* note 2, at 434–35.

67. *See e.g.,* Losen and Welner, *supra* note 2, at 412; Kirp, *supra* note 16, at 761–62; Hosp and Reschly, *supra* note 16.

68. NRC Report, *supra* note 8, at 20.

69. H.R. 1350 § 101, amending § 601(c)(12)(A). *See also* 20 U.S.C. § 1400(c)(8)(A) (1997).

70. H.R. Rep. No. 108-77 at 143 (2002) ("The Committee is concerned that there continues to be a problem with the overidentification of children, particularly minority children, as having disabilities"), 137 (one purpose of the reauthorized IDEA is "reducing the overidentification or misidentification of nondisabled children, including minority youth"), 142 (the bill adds provisions "to address the over and under-inclusion of students in special education"), and 149–50 (the committee is "very concerned about the problem of overidentification and disproportionate representation of minority children in special education"), 169 (Committee wants to see "the problem of overidentification of minority children strongly addressed").

because of the stigma attached to labeling a child with a disability, the decreased self-perception of the labeled child, and the reduced curriculum that eligible children often receive.[71]

The negative stigma attached to being labeled disabled can be traumatic. As noted by the Third Circuit, "stigma, mistrust and hostility ... have traditionally been harbored against persons with disabilities."[72] Researchers and scholars have long recognized the isolating consequences that result from special education eligibility.[73] Once labeled, the child's value in the eyes of others is reduced.[74] Peers and teachers significantly lower their expectations for labeled students.[75] For example, teachers will often focus on the negative behaviors of students who are considered to have behavior problems even if the behaviors are not significantly different from other students in the same classroom.[76]

Labeled students also lower their own expectations, as they understand what their disability label means.[77] In the end, the children often fulfill their own and others' low expectations, making the disability label a self-fulfilling prophecy.[78] The stigmatizing effect of the label alone is so great that Professor Smith, himself diagnosed with SLD, believes that shedding the outsider status of being disabled, and not the actual disability, is the most "daunting barrier."[79]

The negative labeling effects on children identified for special education are compounded by their placement in classes separate from their peers with less demanding curriculums.[80] The result is further performance disparities between eligible students and

---

71. H.R. Rep. No. 108-77 at 137, 147, 149 (2002) ("the misplacement of students in special education stigmatizes and denies students the opportunity of a high quality education").

72. *Oberti v. Bd. of Educ.*, 995 F.2d 1204, 1217 n.24 (3d. Cir. 1993). *See also Larry P. v. Riles*, 495 F.Supp. 926, 979–80 (N.D.Cal. 1979), *aff'd in part and rev'd in part*, 793 F.2d 969 (9th Cir. 1984) (finding that the stigma resulting from placement in MR classes results in feelings of racial inferiority).

73. *See e.g.,* Martha Minow, *Learning to Live with the Dilemma of Difference: Bilingual and Special Education*, 48 Law & Contemp. Problems 157, 181 (1985) ("identification as handicapped ... labels the child as handicapped and may expose the child to attributions of inferiority for this labeling with the attendant risks of stigma, isolation, and reduced self-esteem."); Artiles, *supra* note 30 (showing that "special education placement is a highly consequential decision, as disability labels carry visible stigma and have other high cost repercussions"); Andrew Weis, *Jumping to Conclusions in "Jumping the Queue,"* 51 Stan. L.R. 183, 199–200 (1998) (stating that people with specific learning disability suffer social rejection and isolation); Linehan, *supra* note 4, at 187; Glennon, *The Construction of a Disabled Class*, *supra* note 4, at 1240 (concluding that "IDEA eligibility stigmatizes and severely limits educational opportunities"), 1315–17; Losen and Welner, *supra* note 2 (noting that mislabeled children feel "unnecessarily isolated, stigmatized, and confronted with fear and prejudice").

74. Linehan, *supra* note 4, at 187; Kirp, *supra* note 16, at 733–37; Weis, *Jumping to Conclusions in "Jumping the Queue,"* *supra* note 73, at 183, 200–01 (teachers consider children with LD to have negative and bothersome characteristics).

75. Glennon, *The Construction of a Disabled Class*, *supra* note 4, at 1311; NRC Report, *supra* note 8, at 2, 20; Shapiro et al, *supra* note 6.

76. Hosp and Reschly, *supra* note 16.

77. Armantine M. Smith, *Persons with Disabilities as a Social and Economic Underclass*, 12 Ka. J.L. & Pub. Pol'y 13, 19 (Fall 2002); Linehan, *supra* note 4, at 187; Kirp, *supra* note 16, at 733–37; NRC Report, *supra* note 8, at 2, 20.

78. Glennon, *The Construction of a Disabled Class*, *supra* note 4, at 1311; Linehan, *supra* note 4, at 187.

79. Smith, *supra* note 77, at 24.

80. NRC Report, *supra* note 8, at 20; Linehan, *supra* note 4, at 187. *See also Larry P. v. Riles*, 495 F.Supp. 926, 945 (N.D. Cal. 1979), *aff'd in part and rev'd in part*, 793 F.2d 969 (9th Cir. 1984) (concluding that mentally retarded classes were dead-end classes).

their general education peers, as many IDEA-eligible children are left behind academically.[81] This is particularly true for students with high-incidence disabilities. While eligibility has proven effective for severely disabled children, it has often had negative consequences for children with mild disabilities such as SLD, SED and MR.[82] This problem is exacerbated by the fact that once children are inappropriately placed in self-contained special education programs, it is difficult for them to return to the regular classroom.[83]

While IDEIA eligibility negatively impacts all misidentified students, the effects are particularly damaging to African Americans. Minorities in general do not have positive outcomes from special education,[84] and special education programs do not help African Americans in particular.[85] Professor Artiles summarized the negative effects of improper identification: "It adds another layer of difference to racial minorities, restricts their access to high-currency educational programs and opportunities, and further limits their long-term educational outcomes, as special education populations have lower graduation, higher dropout, and lower academic achievement rates than their general education counterparts."[86]

African American students are more likely to have poor outcomes from special education for several reasons. First, eligible black students are typically instructed by lower-quality special education teachers.[87] Poor schools, where African Americans are concentrated, have less-qualified special education teachers and fewer resources, leading to poor results from eligibility.[88]

Second, parent advocacy—critical to the success of eligible children—is less likely to occur in high-poverty school districts where African American children are concentrated.[89] The IDEIA and its predecessors rely heavily on parental advocacy to ensure that eligible children receive appropriate educational services and placements.[90] But African Americans are less likely than whites to avail themselves of the IDEIA's protections and are less likely to prevail if they do.[91] They are less likely to contest a finding that their child is eligible and the educational services provided to their child. They are often ostracized from the

---

81. H.R. Rep. No. 108-77 at 136 (2002). The academic progress of IDEA eligible children often ceases and sometimes regresses. Patella, *supra* note 4, at 259; Herr, *supra* note 4, at 346. Arguably, the No Child Left Behind Act [NCLB] solves this problem by requiring equal standards for special education and regular education students. In essence, it eliminates the two-track system and requires equal performance. Lynn Olson, *Enveloping Expectations*, Ed. Wk. 8, Vol 23, Issue 17 (1/18/04); Daniel J. Losen and Kevin G. Welner, *Legal Challeneges to Inapprorpiate and Inadequate Special Education for Minority Children*, *in* Racial Inequity, *supra* note 1, at 187. It remains to be seen how the NCLB is implemented and its effects on special education.

82. Mark Kelman and Gillian Lester, Jumping the Queue: An Inquiry into the Treatment of Students with Learning Disabilities, 138–57 (1997) (special education is not effective for LD students); Linehan, *supra* note 4, at 187–88; Arnold, *supra* note 16; Kirp, *supra* note 16, at 728 (demonstrating that special education classes help severely disabled but not moderately disabled).

83. Patella, *supra* note 4, at 243.

84. Arnold, *supra* note 16; Losen and Welner, *supra* note 2, at 418–19 (concluding that the benefit of special education to minorities is "meager").

85. *See generally,* J.M. Patton, *The Disproportionate Representation of African Americans in Special Education: Looking Behind the Curtain for Understanding and Solutions*, 32 J. Special Ed. 25–31 (1998) (special ed programs for African Americans are ineffective); Losen and Welner, *supra* note 2, at 420; Glennon, *The Stuart Rome Lecture*, *supra* note 16, at 20; Osher et al., *supra* note 47, at 101.

86. Artiles, *supra* note 30. *See also* Donald P. Oswald et al., *Community and School Predictors of Overrepresentation of Minority Children in Special Education*, *in* Racial Inequity, *supra* note 1, at 1.

87. NRC Report, *supra* note 8, at 6.

88. NRC Report, *supra* note 8, at 339–40; Osher et al., *supra* note 47, at 102–3.

89. NRC Report, *supra* note 8, at 6.

90. Herr, *supra* note 4, at 351, 359; Losen and Welner, *supra* note 2, at 429.

91. Losen and Welner, *supra* note 2, at 430; NRC Report, *supra* note 8, at 186–88.

advocacy process, leaving their children ineffectively represented and with inappropriate placements and services.[92]

One final explanation for African Americans students' poor outcomes from special education is that eligible African American children are more likely than their white counterparts to be placed in restrictive, segregated settings apart from general education students and the general curriculum.[93] Such segregated special education classes are less likely to provide a rigorous and appropriate education.[94] Moreover, African American students find it particularly difficult to extricate themselves from these special education placements.[95]

In summary, African American children experience poor educational results from special education placements because they receive "inadequate services, low quality curriculum and instruction, and unnecessary isolation from their nondisabled peers."[96] Irrespective of the reason, it is clear African American children improperly identified as eligible for special education do not receive its guaranteed educational benefits but instead suffer poor outcomes. African American overrepresentation in special education is undoubtedly a problem requiring a solution, but solutions can only be judged once the causes are examined.

C. The Causes of African American Disproportionality

Although there is general agreement as to the existence and nature of African American overrepresentation in special education, there is great controversy about its causes.[97] Some conclude that African Americans need special education more than their peers because of biological and socioeconomic differences. In other words, African Americans are not "over"-represented, because they have a higher incidence of actual disability. Yet others conclude that racial and cultural biases are the roots of special education's racial imbalance, and once bias is eliminated, equity will be restored.[98] These theories are not mutually exclusive, as socio-economic differences, biological differences, educational differences and bias all combine to cause the disproportionate representation of African American students in special education.

The cause of the racial imbalance is certainly not biological or genetic differences based on race alone, as there is no correlation between race and disability.[99] But there is a strong

---

92. NRC Report, *supra* note 8, at 338–39; Herr, *supra* note 4, at 366–67; Losen and Orfield, *supra* note 55, at xxvi.

93. Parrish, *supra* note 9, at 26–28; Fierros and Conroy, *supra* note 1, at 40–42; Losen and Orfield, *supra* note 55, at xxi; Glennon, *The Stuart Rome Lecture*, *supra* note 16, at 20; Glennon, *The Construction of a Disabled Class*, *supra* note 4, at 1255; Smith, *supra* note 40, at 197–98; Losen and Welner, *supra* note 2, at 418, 427.

94. Glennon, *The Stuart Rome Lecture*, *supra* note 16, at 20; Hosp and Reschly, *supra* note 16; Fierros and Conroy, *supra* note 1, at 42; Losen and Welner, *supra* note 81, at 171; Hehir, *supra* note 17, at 219.

95. Paul, *supra* note 31.

96. Racial Inequity, *supra* note 1, at xv, xxi.

97. Artiles, *supra* note 30 ("Although few question whether overrepresentation exist, there is some disagreement about the causes and magnitude of the problem"); Losen and Orfield, *supra* note 55, at xvi.

98. Oswald et al., *supra* note 47, at 1–4 (explaining competing hypotheses as to the causes of minority overrepresentation).

99. H.R. Rep. No. 108-77 at 147 (2002).

correlation between race and poverty, and poverty and disability.[100] Socioeconomic status is closely tied to race and correlates directly with educational outcomes.[101] Poverty leads to biological and social deficits, which in turn lead to a higher need for special education in African Americans who are disproportionately underprivileged.

The biological effects of poverty that contribute to an achievement gap in cognition and behavior include lower birthweight, poor nutrition and increased exposure to toxins (i.e., lead, alcohol, tobacco, drugs), all of which correlate to educational performance.[102] Some of these risk factors disproportionately affect African Americans beyond the poverty effect. Specifically, African American students are more likely to have low birthweight and to be exposed to harmful levels of lead across all income groups, both of which lead to achievement gaps on entering school.[103]

The social and environmental effects of poverty also contribute to African American students' greater need for special education. Low socioeconomic status homes display less optimal educational environments, as they have less language stimulation, less direct teaching, higher incidences of maternal depression, lower quality child care and less stimulating parenting practices.[104] The result is a further separation between the socioeconomic classes in behavior and achievement on entering school.

The most dramatic concept to emerge from the recent focus on IDEA's racial imbalance is that the inadequate education received by children from low socioeconomic status homes contributes to eligibility.[105] More African Americans attend substandard schools, and such schools create students that need special education.[106] African Americans attend schools with larger classes, less funding and less qualified teachers, so their overplacement in special education necessarily follows.[107] The factor of teacher quality is telling. The quality of instruction and behavior management in the classroom are both important contributors to student behavior and achievement.[108] Children referred for special education eligibility assessments often come from classrooms in which teachers exhibit poor behavior management and instructional skills.[109] The teachers that are unable to teach or control their students dump poor performers and unruly students into special education, as they cannot make the improvements necessary to serve these children.[110]

---

100. Oswald et al., *supra* note 47, at 7 (stating that the general consensus "is that increased poverty is associated with increased risk of disability.").

101. Fifteen percent of whites live in poverty while up to 45 percent of African Americans live in poverty. NRC Report, *supra* note 8, at 30, 118–32.

102. *Id.* at 4, 97–117, 162.

103. *Id.* at 4.

104. *Id.* at 118–40, 163.

105. Glennon, *The Construction of a Disabled Class*, *supra* note 4, at 1285; NRC Report, *supra* note 8, at 4–6, 27; Losen and Welner, *supra* note 55, at xvi, xxv (concluding that special education overidentification is tied to general education).

106. Glennon, *The Construction of a Disabled Class*, *supra* note 4, at 1285. *See also* NRC Report, *supra* note 8, at 6, 27 (noting that "key aspects of the context of schooling itself" contribute to the identification of students as disabled); Osher et al., *supra* note 47, at 96–97.

107. NRC Report, *supra* note 8, at 173–80; Losen and Orfield, *supra* note 55, at xxvii (determining that overrepresentation stems from shortcomings in general education).

108. NRC Report, *supra* note 8, at 170; Harry et al., *supra* note 40, at 88 (noting that the quality of instruction and classroom management are "crucial variables").

109. NRC Report, *supra* note 8, at 170–71.

110. Fierros and Conroy, *supra* note 1, at 40; Patella, *supra* note 4, at 256; Linehan, *supra* note 4, at 191.

Because African Americans are twice as likely as whites to have ineffective teachers, they are misidentified as IDEIA eligible simply because they do not receive effective instruction in the general education classroom.[111]

Poor reading instruction is of particular note, because it leads not only to the overidentification of African American students but also to the recent spiraling special education rolls. Many children are referred to special education because of reading difficulty.[112] Eighty percent of children classified as learning disabled are classified because of reading difficulties, meaning that 40 percent of the overall IDEIA population is eligible due to reading deficits.[113] As the House Report recognized, there is a "practice of overidentifying children as having disabilities, especially minority students, largely because the children do not have appropriate reading skills. Special education is not intended to serve as an alternative place to serve children if the local educational agency has failed to teach these children how to read."[114]

In summary, the low socioeconomic status of many African American students leads to biological and social differences that result in their needing special education at a higher incidence than their white counterparts.[115] But their unequal representation in IDEA cannot be explained by socioeconomic factors alone.[116] In fact, there is a stronger relationship between race and special education placement than poverty and special education placement.[117] Recent studies show that overrepresentation persists even when poverty is taken into account and, alarmingly, African American students are in fact more likely to be identified as eligible in upper- and high-income schools.[118] These recent studies verify court findings from the 1960s and 1970s. The court in *Larry P. v. Riles* expressly rejected the argument that African American children were properly overrepresented in special education courses because of their low poverty levels and genetically lower IQ results.[119] A similar argument was rejected in *Hobson v. Hanson*, wherein Judge Wright held

---

111. Lynn Olson, *Enveloping Expectations*, 23 Educ. Wk. 8 (2004); NRC Report, *supra* note 8, at 174.

112. A Position Statement of the International Reading Association, *supra* note 38.

113. Lynn Olson, *Enveloping Expectations*, 23 Educ. Wk. 8 (2004); President's Commission, *supra* note 9, at 3.

114. H.R. Rep. No. 108-77 at 156 (2002). *See also* Lois Maharg, *Special Ed: Keeping the Numbers Down*, Lancaster New Era (6/9/03) (stating that children who do not know how to read are inappropriately identified as SLD).

115. NRC Report, *supra* note 8, at 93–140, 167 (concluding that African American children "are more likely to experience multiple biological and environmental correlates of disability and low achievement"); Lois Maharg, *Special Ed: Keeping the Numbers Down*, Lancaster New Era, 6/9/03 (discussing how African Americans' higher incidence of need for special education "stem from being culturally and economically deprived"); Oswald et al., *supra* note 6, at 6, 10; Osher et al., *supra* note 47, at 94.

116. Oswald et al., *supra* note 6, at 6–7, 11; Losen and Orfield, *supra* note 55, at xxii–xxiii ("The studies, however, do uncover correlations that cannot be explained by factors such as poverty or exposure to hazardous substances"); Hehir, *supra* note 17, at 219; Shapiro, *supra* note 6; Paul, *supra* note 31.

117. Parrish, *supra* note 9 at 16, 25, 32–33.

118. The IDEIA finds that "schools with predominantly Caucasian students and teachers have placed disproportionately high numbers of their minority students into special education." IDEIA, H.R. 1350 § 101, amending § 601(c)(12)(E). *See also* Oswald et al., *supra* note 6, at 8–9; Losen and Orfield, *supra* note 55, at xxiv; Milloy, *supra* note 6; Mathhew Ladner, *Minorities Overrepresented in Special-Ed*, Patriot News, 2/27/04 p A13; Shapiro et al., *supra* note 6.

119. 495 F.Supp. 926, 955–56 (N.D. Cal. 1979), *aff'd in part and rev'd in part*, 793 F.2d 969 (9th Cir. 1984).

that the placement of African American students in special education courses was the result of discrimination and not actual disabilities within the students themselves.[120]

The nature of African American overrepresentation also belies the conclusion that the negative biological, environmental and educational effects of poverty account for the entire imbalance in special education. African American students' overrepresentation in the high-incidence or judgmental disabilities but not in any of the low-incidence or nonjudgmental disabilities, indicates that factors independent of socioeconomic status affect the eligibility process.[121] The most evident factor is that bias, whether intentional or unconscious, enters the highly subjective eligibility determinations. Bias permeates both the diagnosis of high-incidence disabilities as well as the determination that a child "needs special education."

The mere mention of bias in special education referral and assessment invites controversy. The NRC circumnavigated the storm by finding that there were insufficient data to determine if discrimination or bias occurs in eligibility decisions.[122] It simply did not consider how race influenced eligibility decisions.[123] Though the NRC is unwilling to enter the fray, most scholars and researchers dive headlong into it, finding that bias, whether conscious or unconscious, intentional or benign, dramatically affects minority representation in special education.[124]

It is difficult to conclude any longer that African American children are intentionally and systematically segregated into special education classrooms. Desegregation lawsuits are on the wane, and teachers and administrators have proven to be among the least prejudiced professionals in the United States.[125] But the remnants of intentional discrimination continue to affect classrooms, and a cultural divide exists between today's predominantly white teachers and the increasingly diverse student body, particularly African American students. While one-third of the students in public schools are minorities (15 percent African American),[126] only 13 percent of teachers are minorities (7.5 percent African American) and 60 percent of teachers are white females.[127] The trend over the last decade showing an increase in the proportion of minority students but a decrease in the proportion of minority teachers promises that the cultural gap in the classroom will widen in the future.[128]

---

120. 269 F.Supp. 401, 443, 514–15 (D.D.C. 1967). *See also P.A.S.E. v. Hannon*, 506 F.Supp. 831, 834 (N.D.Ill. 1984).

121. *See e.g.,* Parrish, *supra* note 9, at 16, 25.

122. NRC REPORT, *supra* note 8, at 5, 78.

123. Katzman, *supra* note 1, at 225239.

124. *See e.g.,* Smith, *supra* note 40, at 196–97; Linehan, *supra* note 4, at 212; Milloy, *supra* note 6; Glennon, *The Stuart Rome Lecture, supra* note 16, at 35–41; Glennon, *The Construction of a Disabled Class, supra* note 4, at 1317–25; Losen and Welner, *supra* note 2, at 413–16 (2001) (arguing that statistics establish systemic discrimination).

125. NRC REPORT, *supra* note 8, at 185. *But see* Katzman, *supra* note 1, at 225239 (stating that teachers are biased against minority youth).

126. 20 U.S.C. § 1401(c)(9)(E) (2002).

127. Linehan, *supra* note 4, at 189; Hosp and Reschly, *supra* note 16; MINI-DIGEST OF EDUCATIONAL STATISTICS 2003 Table 17.

128. "Ten years ago, 12 percent of the United States teaching force in public elementary and secondary schools were members of a minority group. Minorities comprised 21 percent of the national population at that time, and were clearly underrepresented then among employed teachers. Today, the elementary and secondary teaching force is 13 percent minority, while one-third of the students in public schools are minority children." 20 U.S.C. § 1401(c)(9)(E) (1997). The IDEIA recognizes that "minority children comprise an increasing percentage of public school children." H.R. 1350 § 101, amending § 601(c)(9)(C). *See also* NRC REPORT, *supra* note 8, at 175.

The racial imbalance in today's classrooms leads to a "lack of cultural synchronization" between students and teachers of different races, particularly black students.[129] The cultural mismatch leads to teachers' "spiraling misunderstanding" of their diverse students, and to misidentification of black students as eligible for special education.[130] Professor Glennon explains:

> Teachers and administrators usually do not perceive themselves to be racially prejudiced or engaged in overtly racist actions. Since overt racial hostility is the only definition of racism readily available to them, they would not see racial meaning in their actions. Unnoticed are the pervasive but more insidious effects of unconscious and structural racism, which are not limited to one moment, such as the use of culturally biased IQ tests, but pervade the school lives of African American students in all aspects of their identification as disabled.[131]

She concludes that the cultural disconnect between white teachers and black students leads to unintentional bias is in eligibility determinations.[132] Social scientists agree, as the "most commonly cited factor" for the disproportionate placement of black students into special education is the cultural differences between white teachers and African American students.[133]

Bias initially plays a role in who is referred for IDEIA eligibility. The eligibility process usually begins when the general education teacher refers a student for evaluation to determine eligibility.[134] Bias rarely enters the referral process for children with low-incidence disabilities, because these children typically enter school with the disability already identified and eligibility established.[135] For high-incidence disabilities, however, where African American overrepresentation is significant, teacher referral is a critical aspect of the eligibility process as such children rarely enter school with a disability determination. Instead, these children are typically identified as disabled after school begins by a referral from their teacher.[136] The teacher's decision to refer a child for IDEIA eligibility virtually

---

129. Linehan, *supra* note 4, at 180, 188–89; Paul, *supra* note 31.

130. NRC REPORT, *supra* note 8, at 185 (2002).

131. Glennon, *The Construction of a Disabled Class*, *supra* note 4, at 1317. *See also* Jacqueline J. Irvine, BLACK STUDENTS AND SCHOOL FAILURE: POLICIES, PRACTICES AND PRESCRIPTIONS 63–79 (1991) (even well-meaning teachers respond less favorably to contributions from African American students than white students).

132. Glennon, *The Stuart Rome Lecture*, *supra* note 16, at 35–41; Glennon, *The Construction of a Disabled Class*, *supra* note 4, at 1317–25.

133. Hosp and Reschly, *supra* note 16; *See also* Oswald et al., *supra* note 6, at 2 ("a significant portion of the overrepresentation problem may be a function of inappropriate interpretation of ethnic and cultural differences as disabilities."); Losen and Orfield, *supra* note 55, at xviii, xxii–xxiii ("The research does suggest that unconscious racial bias, stereotypes and other race linked factors have a significant impact on the patterns of identification … particularly for African American children"); Osher et al., *supra* note 47, at 106 ("cultural discontinuity within classroom learning environments has been identified as a significant contributing factor in the overclassification of children of color as disabled").

134. 20 U.S.C. § 1414(a), (b) and (c); 20 U.S.C. § 1412(a) (1997); 34 C.F.R. §§ 300.320 and 125(a)(1) (2002). The statutory procedures schools must follow to find a child eligible are clear-cut. 20 U.S.C. § 1414(a)–(c) (2003); 34 C.F.R. §§ 300.530–543 (2003). The LEA must provide full and individualized evaluation and assessment of each child suspected of a disability. 20 U.S.C. § 1414(a)(1) (2002); 34 C.F.R. § 300.531 (2003). Once the evaluations are complete, an eligibility team determines whether the child has an enumerated disability and needs special education and is therefore eligible. 20 U.S.C. § 1414(b)(4) (1997); 34 C.F.R. § 300.534 (2003).

135. NRC REPORT, *supra* note 8, at 224.

136. *Id.* at 209, 224.

seals the child's educational fate, as 90 percent of students referred by teachers are found eligible for special education.[137]

But which students a teacher decides to refer for special education is a subjective determination infused with bias.[138] Teachers exercise vast discretion in determining which students to refer for special education evaluation.[139] "The referral is a signal that the teacher has reached the limits of his or her tolerance of individual differences, is no longer optimistic about his or her capacity to deal effectively with a particular student in the context of the larger group, and perceives that the student is no longer teachable by him- or herself."[140] Bias inherently enters these highly subjective referral determinations.

Teachers, like all of us, are simply less understanding of behaviors that are not part of their cultural experience.[142] White teachers, therefore, view the traditional socialization practices of African American students to be incongruent with classrooms permeated with white culture.[143] African Americans are viewed as unruly and more hyperactive than whites, instead of merely employing different learning styles.[144]

For example, white teachers perceive certain conduct by African Americans to indicate behavior problems—one of the most common reasons for special education referral.[145] African American students display "verve" or a propensity to "accompany their cognitive involvement with affective and physical involvement," which some white teachers view as disruptive or distracting.[146] African Americans also devote significant time to "stage setting" that precedes performance of a task, yet white teachers perceive this to be

137. B. Algozzine, S. Christenson, and J. Ysseldyke, *Probabilities Associated with the Referral to Placement Process*, Teacher Education and Special Education, 5, 19–23 (1982); Linehan, *supra* note 4, at 184, 188; NRC Report, *supra* note 8, at 4 (finding that teachers refer a majority of children in special education), 167–68, 226; Harry et al., *supra* note 40, at 77–78.

138. Linehan, *supra* note 4, at 184; NRC Report, *supra* note 8, at 5, 227; Osher et al., *supra* note 47, at 100; Harry et al., *supra* note 40, at 78 (demonstrating that teacher referral judgments display gender and ethnicity bias).

139. Glennon, *The Construction of a Disabled Class*, *supra* note 4, at 1324–25; NRC Report, *supra* note 8, at 5; Patella, *supra* note 4.

140. N. Zigmond, *Learning Disabilities from an Educational Perspective*, in G.R. Lyon et al., Better Understanding Learning Disabilities: New Views from Research and Their Implications for Education and Public Policy, 262–63 (1993). "The general education teacher makes the determination that the child's academic progress or behavior is unacceptable." NRC Report, *supra* note 8, at 226.

142. Hosp and Reschly, *supra* note 16.

143. Artiles, *supra* note 30; A.W. Boykin, *The Triple Quandary and the Schooling of Afro-American Children*, in The School Achievement of Minority Children, 57–92 (Ulrich Neisser ed. 1986); M.E. Franklin, *Culturally Sensitive Instructional Practices for African American Learners With Disabilities*, 59(2) Exceptional Children, 115–22 (1992); S.E. Gilbert and G. Gay, Improving the Success in School of Black Children in Culture, Style and the Educative Process 275–91 (Robinson Shade ed. 1989); J.J. Irvine, Black Students and School Failure: Policies, Practices, and Prescriptions (Greenwood, 1990).

144. NRC Report, *supra* note 8, at 197.

145. Glennon, *The Construction of a Disabled Class*, *supra* note 4, at 1318–20; NRC Report, *supra* note 8, at 7. The public school classroom adopts the white culture that often leads to a perception of African American scholastic underachievement as well. NRC Report, *supra* note 8, at 183–85. It not only leads to the perception of African American underachievement but also undermines their achievement. *Id.* at 184.

146. S.E. Gilbert and G. Gay, Improving the Success in School of Black Children in Culture, Style and the Educative Process, 279 (Robinson Shade ed. 1989); A.W. Boykin, *The Triple Quandary and the Schooling of Afro-American children*, in The School Achievement of Minority Children, 57–92 (Ulrich Neisser ed. 1986); Linehan, *supra* note 4, at 189–90.

lack of attention or wasting time.[147] These behaviors can be built on productively, but instead are viewed as a hindrance to the child and the class.

Even more alarming is the fact that teachers view the exact same behavior by white and black students differently. Teachers judge behavioral transgressions as more severe when committed by a black male student than a white student.[148] These cultural misperceptions become self-fulfilling prophecies as students achieve in a manner consistent with their teachers' expectations.[149] The result is a referral for special education assessment, and almost certainly placement to remove the culturally different—or "disruptive"—behavior from the classroom.[150]

The cultural disconnect is manifested by the fact that white teachers are more likely than nonwhite teachers to refer black students for special education evaluation.[151] Even before school begins, teachers are more likely to believe that an African American will be referred for special education in the future.[152] They not only believe it, they are also more likely to refer African American students to special education than white students.[153] African Americans are referred for assessment as MR at 2.23 times the rate for whites, for SED at 1.68 times the rate for whites, and for SLD at 1.11 times the rate for whites.[154] The statistics are so compelling that even the NRC concludes that referral bias is "a crucial influence in the disproportionate minority representation."[155]

Prejudice also permeates the assessment phase of eligibility. The eligibility team to which the student is referred must determine first that the child has an enumerated disability, and second that the child needs special education. As discussed, diagnosing high-incidence disability is a subjective judgment that reflects social and cultural beliefs about appropriate learning and behavior in school, thus opening the door to cultural bias. The assessment tools used to determine the existence of a disability are often culturally and racially biased, leading to overrepresentation of minorities.[156] For example, most states employ culturally and racially biased IQ tests to determine eligibility for MR and SLD.[157]

---

147. Sonia Nieto, Affirming Diversity: The Sociopolitical Context of Multicultural Education 115–16 (1991). Another example is disciplinary practices, which in African American families is explicit and directive compared to the classroom, where authority is camouflaged in a style that invites rather than directs students to participate in the rules. As a result, teachers assume that children know the rules and deem them socially incompetent when they do not. L.D. Delpit, *The Silenced Dialogue: Power and Pedagogy in Educating Other People's Children*, 58(3) Harv. Educ. Rev. 280–98 (1988).

148. Herbert Grossman, Ending Discrimination in Special Education 70 (1998).

149. Nieto, *supra* note 147, at 182. *See also* Osher et al., *supra* note 47, at 96–97.

150. Weinstein, *supra* note 2, at 517; Shapiro et al., *supra* note 6.

151. Linehan, *supra* note 4, at 190.

152. *Id.* at 181 (illustrating that teachers have negative judgments based on perceptions of race and are more likely to believe that a minority student will be referred for special education in the future). Teachers have differing opinions of their students based on their race, which reflect racial stereotypes, particularly with respect to behavior. *Id.* at 197–98 *See also* Jacqueline J. Irvine, Black Students and School Failure: Policies, Practices and Prescriptions 63–79 (1991) (even well-meaning teachers respond less favorably to contributions from African American students than white students).

153. NRC Report, *supra* note 8, at 227–30.

154. Hosp and Reschly, *supra* note 16.

155. NRC Report, *supra* note 8, at 234.

156. Linehan, *supra* note 4, at 181; Milloy, *supra* note 6; Shapiro et al., *supra* note 6; J.M. Patton, *The Disproportionate Representation of African Americans in Special Education: Looking Behind the Curtain for Understanding and Solutions*, 32 J. Special Educ. 25–31 (1998).

157. *Id.*; Harry et al., *supra* note 40, at 82–84. *See also, Larry P. v. Riles*, 495 F.Supp. 926, 942–44, 955–56 (N.D. Cal. 1979), *aff'd in part and rev'd in part*, 793 F.2d 969 (9th Cir. 1984) (enjoined the

Moreover, many of the evaluators are white and lack training in culturally sensitive assessment techniques, resulting in improperly applied assessment and evaluation tools to diagnose disabilities.[158]

Determining that a child "needs special education" is also a subjective determination fraught with the potential for prejudice. While subjectivity is inherent in the diagnosis of high-incidence disabilities, the subjectivity in determining that a child "needs special education" is the result of scant legislative guidance and ignorance on behalf of decision makers of the importance of this eligibility limitation. As discussed in detail in Sections III and IV, the open-ended definition of "special education" combined with absolutely no federal guidance as to who "needs" it does little to limit an eligibility teams' discretion in deciding these matters. Decision makers' ignorance of these eligibility limitations eliminates any vestige of objectivity.[159]

In summary, cultural bias flourishes in an eligibility landscape overgrown with subjective judgments as to who is referred for special education, who is diagnosed with a disability and who is found in need of special education.[160] The bias permitted in these subjective determinations leads directly to over referring African American children for eligibility assessment and, consequently, overrepresentation in special education.[161] To curb the bias in eligibility decisions, the unchecked subjectivity of the process must be curtailed. The House Report recognized this and concluded that minority overrepresentation can only be remedied if eligibility "procedures provide consistent results rather than subjective decisions"[162] and called for identification processes that are "clear, consistent and not subject to abuse."[163]

The causes of African Americans' disproportionate representation in special education are numerous and controversial. Yet any viable solution must address the negative biological and environmental effects of low socioeconomic status, particularly ineffective general education, and bias in referral, diagnosis and assessment that a child "needs special education." The IDEIA does not adequately address each of these underlying causes, particularly that of subjectivity and its attendant bias, and will ultimately fail at achieving both racial equality in special education and reducing the overall number of students served.

---

use of IQ tests as part of special education eligibility determinations because they led to the overidentification of minority students as mentally retarded); *Hobson v. Hansen*, 269 F.Supp. 401, 442, 448, 456–57, 514 (D.D.C. 1967), *cert. dismissed* 393 US 801, *aff'd sub nom.* Ironically, these "objective" tests were used to avoid the bias inherent in the subjective diagnosis of these disabilities, which has clearly backfired.

158. Patella, *supra* note 4, at 257; Glennon, *The Construction of a Disabled Class*, *supra* note 4, at 1262.

159. Patella, *supra* note 4, at 245.

160. Glennon, *The Construction of a Disabled Class*, *supra* note 4, at 1324–25; NRC REPORT, *supra* note 8, at 5; Patella, *supra* note 4; Losen and Orfield, *supra* note 55, at xxv (noting that eligibility is "inescapably subjective in nature."); Harry et al., *supra* note 40, at 86 (concluding that eligibility "is subjective, if not capricious."); Losen and Welner, *supra* note 81, at 168 (stating that eligibility involves many subjective decisions).

161. Losen and Welner, *supra* note 2, at 419–20, 440; NRC REPORT, *supra* note 8, at 5; Linehan, *supra* note 4, at 185, 189–90; William H. Clune and Mark H. Van Pelt, *A Political Method of Evaluating the Education for All Handicapped Children Act of 1975 and Several Gaps of Gap Analysis*, 58 LAW & CONTEMP. PROBLEMS 7, 24 (1985).

162. H.R. REP. NO. 108-77 at 150. *See also* Parrish, *supra* note 9, at 33 (identifying "subjective identification and inconsistency in the identification process" as causes of minority overrepresentation).

163. H.R. REP. NO. 108-77 at 169.

II. The IDEIA's Response to African American Overrepresentation in Special Education and the Eligibility Explosion

No matter the cause of minority overrepresentation and the recent rise in special education rolls, it is certain that policy change is needed.[164] Scholars have made few suggestions to curb the eligibility boom but suggest numerous changes to address overrepresenation, ranging from the hiring of more minority teachers,[165] to improving enforcement efforts by the Office of Civil Rights,[166] to allowing class action lawsuits under Title VI of the Civil Rights Act of 1964 based on the disparate impact school policies have on special education eligibility.[167] Another solution may be not to prevent African American disproportionality but to ameliorate its harms by strictly enforcing the IDEIA's least restrictive environment (LRE) requirement, which compels schools to educate eligible children in the general education environment to the maximum extent appropriate rather than in segregated settings.[168] Proper application of the LRE requirement would prevent much, but not all, of the harm of identification for special education because mainstreamed children would not suffer the additional stigma of separate classes and the attendant watered-down curriculum. The IDEIA and its progenitors, however, are drafted as strictly as possible in favor of mainstreaming — "to the maximum extent appropriate" — but the harms of African American disproportionality persist. In other words, the LRE requirements alone cannot prevent the negative effects of overrepresentation. Rather, students should not be found eligible, and put at risk of segregated settings, in the first instance. Proper application of the LRE requirement also does not address the recent explosion in eligibility that has led to decreased resources for the truly disabled.

Each of these proposed remedies should be pursued, as there is no one simple solution or quick fix to the dual eligibility crisis.[169] Yet the researchers agree that legislative change is needed as a necessary first step toward a remedy.[170] The past alterations to IDEA, discussed in this section, failed to resolve the racial inequality and the dramatic rise in children served in special education.[171] The current alterations in the IDEIA will also fail to resolve the dual eligibility crisis.

---

164. NRC Report, *supra* note 8, at 78.

165. *See e.g.,* Linehan, *supra* note 4.

166. *See e.g.,* Theresa Glennon, *Evaluating the Office of Civil Rights' Minority and Special Education Project, in* Racial Inequity, *supra* note 1, at 195.

167. *See e.g.,* Glennon, *The Stuart Rome Lecture, supra* note 16 (arguing that the regulations to Title VI permit direct disparate impact claims); Losen and Welner, *supra* note 2 (arguing that disparate impact claims under Title VI should be combined with disability laws and brought through 42 U.S.C. § 1983 because direct disparate impact claims have been disallowed under Title VI); Losen and Welner, *supra* note 81, at 167. For an overview of potential legal challenges to overrepresentation, *see* Glennon, *The Construction of a Disabled Class, supra* note 4, at 1263–85, Losen and Welner, *supra* note 81, at 180–89.

168. IDEIA, H.R. 1350, 108th Cong. § 101 amending § 612(a)(5)(A)); 20 U.S.C. § 1412(a)(5) (1997); 34 C.F.R. § 300.550 (2003).

169. Glennon, *The Construction of a Disabled Class, supra* note 4, at 1334 (stating that "no single lawsuit or legislative tinkering will provide a remedy"); Losen and Orfield, *supra* note 55, at xxxi.

170. Losen and Orfield, *supra* note 55, at xxix.

171. Lash and Weiser, *supra* note 22, at 327; Oswald et al., *supra* note 6, at 2; Losen and Orfield, *supra* note 55, at xv–xvi.

A. Additional Grants to Study Disproportionality

The IDEIA augments grants to study the disproportionate representation of minorities in special education. In 1997, Congress authorized grants to study minority over-representation and mandated the NRC study.[172] The IDEIA bolsters the research grants and creates a National Center for Special Education Research to examine overidentification and its causes.[173] The secretary of Education is also required to study the effectiveness of states in "reducing the inappropriate overidentification of children, especially minority and limited English proficient children, as having a disability."[174] While more study is needed, particularly on the causes and potential solutions to overrepresentation, the existing body of research is more than sufficient to enact policy changes immediately.

B. Curbing Bias in the Diagnosis of Disabilities

Congress also addressed the fundamental causes of African American disproportionality in special education. Congress made minor changes in the IDEIA to curb bias in the diagnosis of disabilities. The IDEIA maintains the thirty-year-old requirement that tests and other evaluation materials used to diagnose a disability "are selected and administered so as not to be discriminatory on a racial or cultural basis."[175] It also continues the trend of diagnosing children based more on classroom performance than potentially biased standardized tests. The 1997 reauthorization moved away from diagnosing disabilities based on standardized testing to a more functional assessment approach that relies on how well the child performs in the classroom.[176] This movement continues in the IDEIA, which changes the eligibility requirements for SLD by eliminating the need to find a severe discrepancy between achievement and intellectual ability, which is often measured by biased IQ tests.[177] Though these are necessary steps, eliminating bias from the diagnosis of high-incidence disabilities is virtually impossible as such disabilities are intrinsically judgmental and merely reflect the social and cultural beliefs of the assessors.

C. Curbing Referral and Assessment Bias

While the IDEIA addresses the bias inherent in diagnosing disabilities, it does little to address referral bias and the bias attendant in finding that a child needs special education. The IDEIA continues the fourteen-year-old practice of supporting the hiring of more minority general and special education teachers.[178] Congress expects that with more mi-

---

172. 20 U.S.C. § 1472(a)(3) and (b)(2)(A) (2003); NRC Report, *supra* note 8, at vi.

173. H.R. 1350, § 201, amending § 177(a)(8).

174. H.R. 1350, § 101, amending §664(b)(2)(D)(vii).

175. *Id.* at §101, amending §614(b)(3)(A)(i). *See also* 20 U.S.C. §§ 1412(a)(6)(B); 1414(b)(3)(A)(i); 34 C.F.R. §543(a)(1)(I).

176. 34 C.F.R. §300.532(b); NRC Report, *supra* note 8, at 218.

177. H.R. 1350 § 101, amending §614(b)(6).

178. H.R. 1350 § 101, amending § 601(c)(10)(D) (suggesting that "recruitment efforts for special education personnel should focus on increasing the participation of minorities in the teaching profession in order to provide appropriate role models with sufficient knowledge to address the special education needs of these students"); 20 U.S.C. § 1453(c)(3)(D)(viii); 34 C.F.R. §300.382(h) (2003) (requiring states to "recruit, prepare, and retain qualified personnel, including ... personnel from groups that are under-represented in the fields of regular education, special education, and related ser-

nority teachers in the classroom, myriad behavioral and learning styles will be viewed as cultural learning differences rather than disabilities.[179] Yet this approach has failed to resolve disproportionality in the past—and will continue to do so in the future—it is impossible to place a minority teacher in front of every minority student and on every eligibility team.

Congress also hopes to stem the referral and assessment bias which emanates from educators' ignorance of the eligibility criteria. Eligibility criteria are the most complex requirements in special education law.[180] The IDEIA requires professional development to train teachers and evaluators in understanding the identification process.[181] The IDEIA adds funding to train teachers to "ensure appropriate placement and services for all students and to reduce disproportionality in eligibility ... for minorities."[182] Funding is also provided to train teachers on how to "teach and address the needs of children with different learning styles."[183] This is certainly a necessary step, as eligibility teams and teachers referring students must understand and apply the "needs special education" limitation. While training can lead decision makers to recognize the eligibility limitations, it cannot help them understand the vague criteria. With no clear standards as to what constitutes "special education" and when a child "needs" it, no amount of training will eliminate subjective determinations that a child needs special education.

D. "Early Intervening Services"

While these small measures address the dual eligibility crisis, the IDEIA's primary solution is altering the concept of general education. Total racial equality in special education is not possible without either eliminating the disproportionate representation of minorities in poverty or eliminating poverty, as factors related to poverty lead to African Americans genuinely needing special education more often than their white counterparts. Resolving these intractable problems is well beyond the scope of special education law, and apparently beyond the capabilities of Congress. But the IDEIA addresses one particular negative consequence of poverty—ineffective schools—to solve both the racial imbalance in special education and its swelling rolls.

---

vices"). The congressional push for hiring minority special educators began in the 1990 reauthorization process. *Reauthorization of Discretionary Programs—Education of the Handicapped Act: Hearing Before the Subcomm. on Select Education of the House Comm. on Education & Labor*, 101st Cong., 1st Sess. 9, 33 (1989); H.R. Rep. No. 101-544, 101st Cong., 2d Sess. 15–17 (1990), reprinted in 1990 U.S.C.C.A.N. 1723, 1737–39.

179. *See also* Linehan, *supra* note 4 (arguing that hiring more minority teachers in general education is necessary to remove bias in the eligibility process that leads to the disproportionate representation of African Americans in special education).

180. President's Commission, *supra* note 10, at 21 (finding the eligibility requirements among the most "complex" requirements in IDEA).

181. H.R. Rep. No. 108-77 at 150 (2002).

182. IDEIA, H.R. 1350 § 101, amending § 663(c)(9) and (10). Grants are also authorized to assist in "implementing effective teaching strategies, classroom-based techniques, and interventions to ensure appropriate identification of students who may be eligible for special education services, and to prevent the misidentification, inappropriate overidentification, or underidentification of children as having a disability, especially minority and limited English proficient children." H.R. 1350, § 101, amending § 662(b)(2)(A)(3). In awarding grants, priority is to be given to "projects to reduce inappropriate identification of children as children with disabilities, particularly among minority children." *Id.*, amending § 681(d)(4).

183. H.R. 1350 § 101, amending § 654(a)(3)(B)(I).

Scholars have long advocated that solving minority disproportionality requires addressing the entire educational system, because substandard education creates children who need special education.[184] Minority overrepresentation and growing eligibility rolls are inevitable if special education is resigned to cleaning up the pieces of a broken general education system. Congress recognizes this problem in the IDEIA, which emphasizes improving regular education to prevent referral of mere instructional casualties to special education.[185] But rather than simply prohibit eligibility based on lack of instruction in reading or math or limited English proficiency—as is the long-standing yet ineffective practice under IDEA[186]—the IDEIA attempts to level the educational playing field by encouraging schools to provide children appropriate specialized instruction prior to finding them eligible.

To achieve this goal, the IDEIA introduces the "important new concept" of "early intervening educational services" or pre-referral services.[187] The IDEIA, for the first time, requires all states to have in effect "policies and procedures designed to prevent the inappropriate overidentification or disproportionate representation by race and ethnicity of children as children with disabilities."[188] The IDEIA does not identify acceptable "policies and procedures," but anticipates states will employ "early intervening services."

Congress finds in the IDEIA that the education of children with disabilities can be made more effective by "providing incentives for whole-school approaches, scientifically based early reading programs, positive behavioral interventions and supports, and early intervening services to reduce the need to label children as disabled in order to address the learning and behavioral needs of such children."[189] Accordingly, the IDEIA permits states and local educational agencies to use 15 percent of the federal funds they receive "to develop and implement coordinated, early intervening services ... for students in kindergarten through grade 12 who have not been identified as needing special education or related services but who need additional academic and behavioral support to succeed in a general education environment."[190] "Early intervening services" are not specifically defined in the IDEIA, but Congress allows these funds to be spent on training teachers to deliver scientifically based academic instruction and behavioral interventions, including scientifically based literacy instruction and behavioral supports.[191] In essence, the IDEIA

---

184. *See e.g.,* Glennon, *The Construction of a Disabled Class, supra* note 4, at 1335 ("It is through effective regular education, not special education, that we may begin to see the racial disparities reduced."); Milloy, *supra* note 6; Losen and Orfield, *supra* note 55, at xxviii; Losen and Welner, *supra* note 81, at 187 ("The most effective remedies will go beyond the special education evaluation process and entail regular education reforms"); NRC REPORT, *supra* note 8, at 28. The NRC concluded that examination of the regular education classroom is critical to any effort to address race-linked disproportion in IDEA eligibility. *Id.* at 171.

185. H.R. REP. No. 108-77 at 150.

186. 20 U.S.C. § 1414(b)(5) (2003); 300.534(a)(2)(B)(1)(i) (2003). The IDEIA continues this prohibition. H.R. 1350 § 101, amending § 614(b)(5). The existence of SLD also cannot be the result of cultural or economic disadvantage. 34 C.F.R. § 300.541(b).

187. H.R. REP. No. 108-77 at 153 (2002). The House version of the IDEIA called the services "pre-referral services" but the name was changed to "intervening educational services" in the final bill. The concept of pre-referral services is not new. 20 U.S.C. § 1400(c)(5)(F) (1997) (Congress found that "providing incentives for whole-school approaches and pre-referral intervention to reduce the need to label children as disabled in order to address their learning needs"). But the IDEIA includes it in the substantive provisions of the act for the first time.

188. IDEIA, H.R. 1350 §101, amending §612(a)(24); H.R. REP. No. 108-77 at 149 (2002).

189. H.R. 1350 § 101, amending § 601(c)(5)(F). Congress intended to encourage the use of pre-referral services before eligibility attaches. H.R. REP. No. 108-77 at 150 (2002).

190. H.R. 1350 §101, amending §613(f) and §613(a)(4)(A)(ii); H.R. REP. No. 108-77 at 137, 153 (2002).

191. H.R. 1350 § 101, amending §613(f)(2)(A) and (B).

encourages schools to provide a certain level of individualized instruction to children to avoid finding them eligible for special education.[192]

By reaching into general education to resolve special education problems, the IDEIA departs significantly from past legislation which left general education untouched. Congress essentially recognized that today's increasingly diverse students with myriad cultural backgrounds, varied learning styles and differing needs require individualized, rather than standardized, instruction and interventions. Congress acknowledged that it is only by individualizing general education that schools "will be able to differentiate between children that have different learning styles and children that have disabilities."[193] But because such specialized instruction has long been the exclusive realm of "special education," today's diverse learners are diagnosed with judgmental disabilities and found to be eligible. Congress intends to curb this trend by encouraging individualized services to be provided in general education to children who need additional academic and behavioral support.[194] As the Presidential Commission on Special Education aptly concluded, "Students struggle in a one-size-fits-all educational setting that may not fit their learning needs. It is time for educational systems to [apply] research-based and culturally competent practices to educating diverse students in their classrooms."[195]

By improving general education through the use of pre-referral measures, Congress expects to end both the racial imbalances of special education and also its growing rolls.[196] As one example, Congress expects to reduce the large number of children that are eligible because of reading problems, which can often be addressed without eligibility attaching. By funding pre-referral measures and requiring them in limited instances, Congress anticipates that children will receive appropriate individualized reading instruction in the first instance, obviating the need for special education placement. African Americans should see the most dramatic effect, as they are more likely to be subject to an inadequate reading instruction.

But the IDEIA's pre-referral services are not mandatory unless a state finds that it or its local educational agencies have "significant disproportionality."[197] Since 1997, IDEA required states to provide data on special education eligibility broken down by race and ethnicity.[198] Based on these data, Congress directed that any state that determines it has "significant disproportionality with respect to the identification of children as children with disabilities ... shall provide for the review, and if appropriate, revision of the policies, procedures, and practices used in such identification or placement."[199] The IDEIA adds

---

192. This new educational model of individualized instruction in general education works in conjunction with NCLB, which attempts to improve educational results for all children. While the NCLB promotes a high level of scientifically based instruction to all children, the IDEIA encourages that the instruction be individualized through intervention services prior to referral for special education.

193. H.R. Rep. No. 108-77 at 157.

194. H.R. Rep. No. 108-77 at 137, 153.

195. President's Commission, *supra* note 10, at 57.

196. H.R. Rep. No. 108-77 at 137, 150, 153, 156.

197. H.R. 1350 § 101, amending §618(d)(2); *id.*, amending § 664(b)(2)(D)(vii) (requiring a national assessment of the effectiveness of schools in achieving the purposes of the act by "reducing the inappropriate overidentification of children, especially minority and limited English proficient children, as having a disability"). *See also* H.R. Rep 108-77 at 138, 169.

198. 20 U.S.C. § 1418(a)(1)(A)(i)–(viii) and (c) (2003); 34 C.F.R. § 300.755(a) (2003).

199. 20 U.S.C. § 1418(c)(2) (2003); 34 C.F.R. 300.755(b) (2003); NRC Report, *supra* note 8, at 217. *See also* Hehir, *supra* note 17, at 219 (stating that IDEA imposes "an affirmative responsibility [on states] to monitor and intervene where overrepresentation occurs. If a state does not do this, it runs the risk of losing its eligibility to receive funds under IDEA").

that if significant disproportionality exists, then the state or secretary of the Interior shall require that the maximum 15 percent of funds reserved for pre-referral intervention services are used, particularly for the benefit of the overidentified group.[200] In short, the IDEIA permits states and districts to use federal funds to develop early intervening services services, but only mandates their provision in states with "significant disproportionality."[201]

E. The Shortcomings of the IDEIA

The permissive nature of the IDEIA's pre-referral measures shows that while Congress prefers an individualized general education paradigm over a generic, one-size-fits-all educational model, it is not committed to its new pedagogy. The IDEIA's half-measures will continue to allow bias and competing pedagogies to influence eligibility decisions to the detriment of African American students and those genuinely in need of special education. Congress acknowledged that altering general education to include a certain level of individualized instruction is necessary to solve the dual eligibility crisis. But instead of redefining general education directly by redefining "special education" and who "needs" it, Congress "back-doors" its pedagogy through complex and permissive early intervening services, and mandates unspecified policies and procedures to prohibit minority overidentification. In short, the IDEIA attempts to remedy its eligibility crisis without reconsidering its eligibility criteria — an impossible task.

The IDEIA leaves unchanged the definition of an eligible child with a disability as well as the definition of "special education."[202] The IDEIA also leaves unchanged the assessment provisions determining who "needs" special education.[203] This same broad eligibility requirement has been misinterpreted for years, thwarting its consistent application and opening the door for overrepresentation that the IDEIA does not shut.[204] The IDEIA cannot effectively reduce minority overrepresentation because it does not limit the bias that accompanies highly subjective identification practices. While subjectivity cannot be eliminated from the diagnosis of high-incidence or judgmental disabilities no matter how their definitions are modified, it can be reduced in referral and in the determination that a child "needs special education."

To resolve the misidentification of students as eligible, particularly minorities, the antiquated eligibility criteria must be revisited as a necessary first step. Schools cannot fully embrace the individualized general education paradigm unless "special education" relinquishes its firm grasp on all individualized instruction. So long as minor instructional modifications are considered "special education" and not simply sound general education practices, today's diverse learners remain at risk of being diagnosed

---

200. H.R. 1350 § 101, amending § 618(d)(2)(B); H.R. Rep. No. 108-77 at 138, 169.

201. States are given complete discretion to determine if "significant disproportionality" exists in their school districts Losen and Orfield, *supra* note 55, at xxx; Lash and Weiser, *supra* note 2, at 328–29.

202. H.R. 1350 101, amending § 602(3) and (29).

203. *Id.* at § 204, amending §614(b). The IDEIA continues to provide that "a child shall not be determined to be a child with a disability if the determinant factor for such a determination is (A) lack of scientifically based instruction practices and programs that contain the essential components of reading instruction … ; (B) lack of instruction in math; or (C) limited English proficiency." *Id.* at § 614(b)(5).

204. Herr, *supra* note 4, at 352.

with a high-incidence, or judgmental, disability and found in need of special education. Although the cultural divide in the classroom and resulting bias cannot be eliminated in the short term, the bias inherent in subjective determinations can be curbed, and racial balance brought to the IDEIA, by objectifying certain aspects of the eligibility process. Because imprecise eligibility standards lead to discretionary error and bias in finding children eligible, this discretion must be limited through precise definitions.[205]

To reclaim eligibility for the truly disabled in "need" of "special education," Congress must restrict these definitions. "Special education" should be limited to significant adaptations to the content, method or delivery of instruction that are not provided to all general education students. Further, a child should not be found to "need" special education until all accommodations and pre-referral interventions available in the district are attempted and proven unsuccessful. These restrictive definitions are necessary to limit cultural bias in eligibility assessments and implement the individualization paradigm envisioned in the IDEIA.

III. "Special Education" Redefined

The IDEIA and its predecessor statutes hinge eligibility on a finding that a child not only has an enumerated disability, but also needs "special education and related services."[206] The definition of "special education" is often determinative of eligibility, as not all services provided by schools to disabled students are "special education." A child with cystic fibrosis may need respiratory therapy; a child with spina bifida may need catheterization services; and a child with diabetes may need monitoring of meals; but these services are not "special education" and these children are not eligible under IDEA or the new IDEIA.[207]

Rather, these children typically receive services under Section 504 of the Rehabilitation Act of 1973 [hereafter Section 504],[208] a nondiscrimination statute that works in tandem with IDEA.[209] While eligibility under Section 504 entitles children to a "free appropriate public education," such eligibility entitles students to a different level of services than under IDEA with significantly fewer procedural safeguards.[210] In a nutshell, states are required to "do more" for IDEA-eligible students than for students that are merely eligible

---

205. Linehan, *supra* note 4, at 183.

206. H.R. 1350 § 101, amending § 602(3); 20 U.S.C. § 1401(3)(A)(ii).

207. Bonnie Tucker & Bruce Goldstein, Legal Rights of Persons with Disabilities: An Analysis of Federal Law II.A (LRP 2003). *See also* President's Commission, *supra* note 10, at 48 ("Not every student with a disability in elementary, middle of high school receives special education services because his or her disability does not impair their ability to learn to such a degree that special education services are necessary"); Garda, *supra* note 14, at 486–87.

208. 29 U.S.C.A. § 794 (1998); 34 C.F.R. § 104.4 (2002).

209. 34 C.F.R. § 104.33 (2002); Robert T. Stafford, *Education for the Handicapped: A Senator's Perspective*, 3 Vt. L. Rev. 71, 82 (1978) ("The two laws and their regulations reinforce and reciprocate each other"). For a discussion of Section 504 protections, see Judith Welch Wegner, *Educational Rights of Handicapped Children: Three Federal Statutes and an Evolving Jurisprudence, Part I: The Statutory Maze*, 17 J. of Law & Educ. 387, 395–404 (Summer 1998); Laura F. Rothstein, Disabilities and the Law 84–86 (1984).

210. Some scholars assert that the free appropriate public education under Section 504 requires a higher level of educational benefit than IDEA, but no court has so held. *See* Daniel and Coriell, *supra* note 17, at 576.

under Section 504.[211] Typically, students eligible under Section 504 receive "accommodations" or "related services," whereas children eligible under IDEA receive "special education."[212]

Indeed, the need for "special education" is the critical distinction between eligibility under Section 504 and IDEA.[213] Section 504 covers significantly more students than IDEA because it does not consider the child's need for "special education"; rather, it only considers whether the child's disability impairs a major life function such as learning.[214] Accordingly, many IDEA eligibility decisions hinge on whether the services the child requires are in fact "special education."[215] It is for this reason that the First Circuit found that

211. Hehir, *supra* note 17, at 225.

212. Mark Weber, Special Education Law and Litigation Treatise §§ 2.3, 8.1 (LRP 2002); Bonnie P. Tucker & Bruce A. Goldstein, Legal Rights of Persons with Disabilities: An Analysis of Federal Law Chapter 5 (LRP 2003).

213. Bonnie P. Tucker & Bruce A. Goldstein, Legal Rights of Persons with Disabilities: An Analysis of Federal Law (LRP 2003) ("IDEA only protects children who, by virtue of their disabilities, require special educational services. Section 504, however, prohibits discrimination against all school-age children with disabilities, regardless of whether they require special educational services") (footnotes omitted); Mark Weber, Special Education Law and Litigation Treatise § 2.1 (LRP 2002) ("Nevertheless, some children with physical limitations or other conditions have no unique needs that call for special instruction, but cannot receive an equal education without services that IDEA classes as related services. If such a child meets the definition of an individual with handicaps found in the Rehabilitation Act of 1973, the school district must provide the services to the child").

214. Letter to Honorable Wayne Teague, 20 IDELR 1462, 1463 (1994). *See also* Mark Weber, Special Education Law and Litigation Treatise § 8.1; Thomas F. Guernsey, *The Education for All Handicapped Children Act, 42 U.S.C. § 1983 and Section 504 of the Rehabilitation Act of 1973: Statutory Interaction Following the Handicapped Children's Protection Act of 1986*, 68 Neb. L. Rev. 564, 566 (1989) ("Section 504 is broad and general in coverage, while EAHCA is narrow and specific"). Children eligible under Section 504 often seek IDEA eligibility because IDEA specifies additional services and rights. *See e.g., Yankton Sch. Dist. v. Schramm*, 93 F.3d 1369 (8th Cir. 1996) (child eligible under Section 504 sought IDEA eligibility because only IDEA required the school to provide transition services such as instruction in driver's education, self-advocacy and independent living skills); *In re Laura H.*, 509 EHLR 242 (Mass. SEA 1988) (child sought IDEA eligibility because desired closed circuit television for chemistry lab rather than mere provision of alternative biology class that was provided as a Section 504 accommodation).

215. *See e.g., Delaware County Intermediate Unit v. Jonathan S.*, 809 A.2d 1051, 1054 (Pa. Commw. Ct. 2002) (child ineligible despite orthopedic impairment because "the record ... is bereft of any evidence that Student's gross and fine motor development delays require the adapting of content, methodology, or delivery of instruction to address Student's unique needs. Because there is no evidence of record that Student requires such specially designed instruction, he does not meet the controlling definition of a child with a disability"); *West Chester Area Sch. Dist.*, 32 IDELR 275, 278 (Pa. SEA 2000) ("the Panel concludes that Nicole is not eligible as emotionally disturbed due to the lack of preponderant evidence of the need for special education attributable to her emotional state"); *In re Wayne Highlands Sch. Dist.*, 24 IDELR 476, 484 (Pa.SEA 1996) ("The parents contend that Laura is in need of specially designed instruction and asserts that Laura has been receiving just such instruction.... The District counters that Laura simply requires accommodations to her regular education program and that these accommodations do not qualify as specially designed instruction.... Despite the parents' assertion to the contrary, these accommodations do not rise to the level of specially designed instruction"); *Smithtown Cent. Sch. Dist.*, 29 IDELR 293, 300 (N.Y.SEA 1998) ("I am unable to determine whether these accommodations employed by the child's teachers to address the boy's [disabilities] amounted to [special education]" and therefore whether child needs special education and is eligible); *Rochester City Sch. Dist.*, 31 IDELR 178, 185 (N.Y. SEA 1999) ("Though his IQ scores place him in the superior range of intellectual functioning, and his academic performance is in the average range, it is not clear that the child requires special education services. The child's health concerns provide an explanation for his frequent absences, but there is little explanation in the record for his failure to complete homework. These issues could be addressed without the need for special education services"); *Old Orchard Beach Sch. Dep't.*, 21 IDELR 1084, 1090 (Me. SEA 1994) ("AG is now in a per-

the definition of "special education" is an "extremely important and nuanced question."[216] Yet there is a significant divide in the authority as to what constitutes "special education," a divide that will continue under the IDEIA. This section explores the confusion in the authority and propose a definition of "special education" that addresses the dual eligibility crisis.

A. The Statutory Definition

The IDEIA and its predecessors define an "eligible child with a disability" as a child that is diagnosed with an enumerated disability, and by reason thereof "needs special education and related services."[217] "Special education" is defined as "specially designed instruction, at no cost to parents, to meet the unique needs of a child with a disability."[218] Accordingly, the definition of an eligible "child with a disability" is circular: a child is only eligible if he needs special education, but a child does not need special education unless he has the unique needs of an eligible child.[219] Until 1999, decision makers were provided no further guidance than this circular definition, and generally held that "special education" means specialized or individualized instruction.[220]

Regulations were added in 1999 explaining that the term "specially designed instruction" means "adapting ... the content, methodology, or delivery of instruction (i) to address the unique needs of the child that result from the child's disability; and (ii) to ensure access of the child to the general curriculum, so that he or she can meet the educational

---

sonalized program with a low teacher/student ratio, lots of accountability, a case manager to communicate with home on a regular basis and deal with social skills issues, and taking one course at the high school by her choice. If she were labeled, nothing would change as this program is the one described by the psychologists to meet her needs and the program serves both special education and regular education students"); *Wayne Westland Comm. Schools*, 37 IDELR 150 (Mich. SEA 2002) ("Even if this hearing officer were to assume, for the sake of argument only, the presence of a severe discrepancy between [ ]'s ability and achievement in the areas of Basic Reading Skill and Mathematics Calculation, there is a complete lack of evidence to support a finding that the purported discrepancy is not correctable without special education").

216. *Greenland Sch. Dist. v. Amy N.*, 358 F.3d 150, 162 (1st Cir. 2004).

217. H.R. 1350 §101, amending §602(3); 20 U.S.C. §1401(3)(A)(ii). A technical reading of the statute and regulations requires that for IDEIA eligibility to attach, the child must need both "special education *and* related services." IDEIA, 1350 §101, amending §602(3); 20 U.S.C. §1401(3)(A)(ii); 34 C.F.R. §300.7(a)(1). In other words, if a child needs only "special education," he or she is not eligible under a literal reading of the statute and regulations. Courts and hearing officers do not literally apply the "and" requirement, however, as no reported decision denies a child eligibility because he or she only needs "special education" but not "related services." Such a literal reading is outright rejected without discussion, because the many children who need only "special education" and not "related services" would be ineligible and not receive appropriate specialized instruction.

218. H.R. 1350 §101, amending §602(29); 20 U.S.C. §1401(25) (1997); 34 C.F.R. §300.26(a)(2)(i)–(iii) (2002).

219. *See e.g.,* Jeffrey Champagne, Commentary, *Special Education Law—Sometimes its Simple: An Examination of* Honig v. Doe, Timothy W. v. Rochester, New Hampshire, Sch. Dist. Dellmuth v. Muth, and Moore v. Dist. of Columbia, 59 ED. LAW REP. 587, 588 (1990) (eligibility standards are circular); MARK WEBER, SPECIAL EDUCATION LAW AND LITIGATION TREATISE (LRP 2002) ("The definition of children covered under IDEA is doubly circular").

220. *See e.g., Bd. of Educ. v. Rowley*, 458 U.S. 176, 189 (1982); Letter to Smith, 18 IDELR 683 (OSEP 1992) (OSEP defined "special education" as "education planned for a particular individual or 'individualized instruction'"). *See also Grkman v. Scanlon*, 563 F.Supp. 793, 794 (W.D. Pa. 1983) ("specially designed personalized instruction, deviating from the normal routine program offered to pupils generally, and geared to the particular needs of a handicapped child").

standards within the jurisdiction of the public agency that apply to all children."[221] There is no reason to believe these regulations will change with the passage of the IDEIA, which does not alter the statutory definition of "special education." "Special education," therefore, is the adaptation of the content, methodology or delivery of instruction to address a child's unique needs and to ensure access to the general curriculum.

"Related services," on the other hand, are "transportation, and such developmental, corrective, and other supportive services … as may be required to assist a child with a disability to benefit from special education."[222] Specific examples include "speech-language pathology and audiology services, psychological services, physical and occupational therapy, recreation, including therapeutic recreation, social work services, counseling services, including rehabilitation counseling, orientation and mobility services, and medical services."[223]

"Related services" are provided to eligible children only if the services are necessary to assist a child with a disability to benefit from "special education."[224] If a child needs only "related services" and not "special education," then the child is not eligible.[225] The Supreme Court explains that "to be entitled to related services, a child must be handicapped so as to require special education. In the absence of a handicap that requires special education, the need for what otherwise might qualify as a related service does not create [eligibility]."[226] In short, the enumerated "related services" are necessarily not "special education."[227]

But there is one major caveat to this general rule: states are permitted to include any of the enumerated "related services" that are also "special education" within their definition of "special education."[228] But the regulations do not identify which of the enumerated "related services" constitute "special education" and can be appropriately classified as such. Some states employ the narrow federal definition of "special education" that ex-

---

221. 34 C.F.R. § 300.26(b)(3) (2003). *See e.g., Katherine S. v. Umbach*, 2002 WL 226697 at *10 (M.D. Ala. 2002) ("Therefore, in order to qualify as a 'student with a disability' pursuant to the IDEA, Katherine must require 'specially designed instruction' in order to have access to, and benefit from, the general educational curriculum").

222. H.R. 1350 § 101, amending § 602(26); 20 U.S.C. § 1401(22); 34 C.F.R. § 300.24(a).

223. *Id.* The regulations add school health services, social work services in schools and parent counseling and training to the list of related services, 34 C.F.R. § 300.24(a), and provide specific definitions of each of the enumerated related services. 34 C.F.R. § 300.24(b).

224. H.R. 1350 § 101, amending § 602(26); 20 U.S.C. § 1401(a)(22); 34 C.F.R. § 300.24(a). It is not possible for an IDEA-eligible child to need only related services and not special education, as related services are provided only as "required to assist a child with a disability to benefit from special education." 20 U.S.C. § 1401(22); 34 C.F.R. § 300.24(a).

225. 34 C.F.R. § 300.7(a)(2)(i) (2003).

226. *Irving Indep. Sch. Dist. v. Tatro*, 468 U.S. 883, 894 (1984) (citations omitted). *See also Katherine S. v. Umbach*, 2002 WL 226697 at *10 (M.D. Ala. 2002) ("a student who has an impairment, but who only needs a related service and not special education, is not a 'student with a disability' within the meaning of the law").

227. *See e.g., Corvallis Sch. Dist.* 509J, 28 IDELR 1026, 12 (Or. SEA 1998) ("Related services are not 'special education'"); *Katherine S.*, 2002 WL 226697 at *10 ("a student who has an impairment, but who only needs a related service and not special education, is not a 'student with a disability' within the meaning of the law."); *A.A. v. Cooperman*, 526 A.2d 1103, 1106 (N.J. Super. Ct. App. Div. 1987) (an orthopedically impaired child needed only transportation and was therefore "not educationally handicapped because he had not been found to require special education"); *Hackensack Bd. of Educ.*, 18 IDELR 988 (N.J. SEA 1992) (asthmatic child that needed only related service of transportation was not IDEA eligible because she did not need special education).

228. 34 C.F.R. § 300.26(a)(2)(i) (2003). *See also* Letter to Tucker, 1 ECLPR ¶ 67 (OSEP 1990) (holding that states may include within their definition of "special education" any of the related services which are specially designed instruction and giving the example of a physical therapy program teaching positioning which could be considered special education if the state defines it as such).

cludes the enumerated "related services,"[229] whereas others broadly define "special education" by including many, if not all, of the enumerated "related services."[230] IDEIA eligibility is greatly expanded in these latter states. For example, a child who requires only speech-language pathology is not IDEIA eligible in New Jersey, which employs the federal definition of "special education" excluding the related service of speech-language pathology, but the same child is IDEIA eligible in Nebraska, which includes speech-language pathology within its definition of "special education." Accordingly, states control eligibility standards not only by defining the enumerated disabilities, as noted, but also by controlling the definition of "special education," potentially enlarging the group of eligible children.

In summary, to be eligible under the IDEIA a child with a qualifying disability must need "adapting" of the "content, methodology or delivery of instruction" to "address the unique needs of the child" and "ensure access of the child to the general curriculum."[231] This broad definition is hopelessly ambiguous, however, and permits decision maker to employ his own pedagogical ideology when interpreting "special education."[232] There are essentially two competing pedagogies underlying the decisions that deal with the definition of "special education": the general education paradigm embodying individualized instruction versus the generic or one-size-fits-all general education model. Decision makers operating under the former model find that only children requiring significant modifications in general education need "special education," while decision makers employing the latter model find that diverse or differing student needs are the exclusive jurisdiction of "special education" and general educators need not modify instruction to accommodate such children. The broad definition of "special education" encompasses either pedagogical model, leading decision makers to often ignore the limitation or provide vastly divergent interpretations.

---

229. *See e.g.,* 14 Del.C. §3101(2) (2003); D.C ST §38-2901(11) (2003); F.S.A. §1003.01 (3)(b) (2002); GA Comp. R. & Regs §160-4-7-.01(1) (2003); Ka. St. Ann. §72-962(i) (2003); K.R.S. §157.200(2) (2003); 707 KAR 1:280(49) (2003); Md. Code, Education, §8-401(4) (2003); Miss. Code. Ann §37-23-133(i) (2003); M.C.A. §20-7-401(4) (2003); N.H. Rev. Stat. §186-C:2(IV) (2003); N.J. Admin. Code Title 6, §14-1.3 (2004); Tx. St. Ann. §29.002(1) (2004); Va. Ann.Code §22.1-213 (2004).

230. *See e.g.,* Conn. Stat. Ann. §10-76a (West 2003) (special education includes all related services); Cal. Educ. Code §56031 (2003); Id.C. §33-2001(5) (2003); Ind. Code §20-1-6-1(7) (2003); Io. Code Ann. §256B(2) (2003); 20-A M.R.S.A. §7001(5); M.G.L.A. 71B §1 (2003); Minn. R. Stat. 3525.0200(20a) (West 2003); Mo. Ann. St. §162.675(4) (including certain related services in definition of special education); Neb. Rev. St. §79-1125 (special education includes speech-language pathology, occupational therapy, and physical therapy); N.M. Rev. St. §22-13-6(A) (West 2004); N.Y. §4401(2) (West 2003); N.C.G.S.A. §115C-108 (special education includes speech-language pathology, occupational therapy, and physical therapy); N.D.D.C. §15.1-32-01(2) (West 2004); Or. R. St. §343.035(18) (West 2004); S.D.C.L. §13-37-2 (2004); Tenn. C. Ann. §49-10-102(4); Vt. St. Ann. §2942(2) (2004).

231. *See e.g., Delaware County Intermediate Unit v. Jonathan S.,* 809 A.2d 1051, 1056 (Pa. Commw. Ct. 2002) ("the record in this case, however, is bereft of any evidence that Student's gross and fine motor development delays require the adapting of content, methodology, or delivery of instruction to address Student's unique needs. Because there is no evidence of record that Student requires such specially designed instruction, he does not meet the controlling definition of a child with a disability … and is therefore ineligible for a FAPE"); *see also id.* at 1057 ("The special needs of the child are what determines his entitlement to funded services, but neither the hearing officer, the Panel, nor Student have cited to any actual substantive evidence that Student requires specially designed instruction, i.e. the adaptation of the content, methodology, or delivery of instruction to address the unique needs of the child that result from the child's disability").

232. Minow, *supra* note 73, at 179–80 ("the statute is unclear about which children shall be included within the reach of its guarantees … The substantive dimensions of the program remain ambiguous, however, especially regarding what kind of special needs should entitle the child to special placements or services").

B. "Special Education" Ignored

The most extreme example of decision makers employing the generic general education model are decisions that entirely ignore the "special education" limitation. These decision-makers presume that if a child is diagnosed with a disability, then the child automatically needs "special education." Professor Zirkel concludes that such oversight "is not to be faulted; these subtle distinctions are not generally recognized."[233] But in failing to recognize this subtle yet critical distinction, decision makers are implicitly concluding that disabled children necessarily cannot fit into the general education system, no matter their needs, and resign them to "special education."

For example, in *Muller v. East Islip Union Free School District*, a child was denied IDEA eligibility by the school district, the hearing officer and the state review panel because, among other things, there was no evidence " 'that the child requires special education and related services to benefit from instruction.' "[234] The Second Circuit disagreed, finding the child eligible merely because her disability adversely affected her educational development.[235] The court did not discuss the "need special education" requirement. Instead it presumed that a child with an enumerated disability could not be served in general education, and requires remediation through "special education."[236] Similarly, in *Elida Local Sch. Dist. Bd. of Educ. v. Erickson*, a child with a health impairment needed small group tutoring, extended time to complete tests and assignments, use of a computer and teacher notes.[237] The school district declassified the child as IDEA eligible, arguing that these services were not "special education." The court never addressed this issue, instead finding the child IDEA eligible because her disability adversely affected her educational performance.[238] Many other courts and hearing officers likewise presume that children with disabilities cannot be served through general education and necessarily need "special education."[239]

---

233. *West Chester Area Sch. Dist.*, 18 IDELR 802, 803 n.31 (Pa.SEA 1992).

234. 145 F.3d 95, 100 (2nd Cir. 1998).

235. *Id.* at 103. *See also id.* at 104, n.6 ("The IHO's apparent belief that Treena's emotional problems were unrelated to school is of little if any relevance, so long as those problems had a significant effect on her ability to learn").

236. The Second Circuit's conclusion may well be correct, as the child may in fact have needed special education, but it employed an incomplete analysis by failing to expressly consider this eligibility requirement and finding by the lower review officers.

237. 252 F. Supp. 2d 476, 488 fn.7 (N.D.Oh. 2003).

238. *Id.* at 491.

239. *See e.g., Greenland Sch. Dist. v. Amy N.*, 2003 WL 1343023 (D.N.H. 2003), *overruled on other grounds*, 358 F.3d 150 (1st Cir. 2004) (finding IDEA eligibility without addressing whether services child required were special education); *Corchado v. Rochester City Sch. Dist.*, 86 F. Supp. 2d 168, 171–72, 176 (W.D.N.Y. 2000) (court found eligibility without discussing need for special education merely because child had documented impairments); *George West Indep. Sch. Dist.*, 35 IDELR 287, 290 (Tx. SEA 2001) ("the legal issue is whether that impairment adversely affects her educational performance and thus whether she 'needs' special education and related services"); *In re Kristopher H.*, 507 EHLR 183 (Wash. SEA 1985) (hearing officer did not consider the district's argument that the child did not need special education, finding rather that the child was IDEA eligible because his disability adversely affected his educational performance); *Benjamin R.*, 508 EHLR 183, 187–88 (Mass. SEA 1986) (child found IDEA eligible despite being "gifted ... with very superior cognitive abilities" and performing well socially and academically in kindergarten because "perceptual deficits exist which impact on educational progress."); *Philadelphia Sch. Dist.*, 27 IDELR 447 (Pa. SEA 1997) (without discussing the "need" requirement, the hearing officer found a gifted child who received D's in Spanish was IDEA eligible as learning disabled).

This presumption is incorrect because a child's disability may often be appropriately addressed by something other than "special education."[240] Professor Zirkel explains that it is a "circular conclusion that in light of the adverse effect [of a disability], [a student] needs special education" as the existence of a disability and the need for "special education" are simply not coterminous.[241] Children with enumerated disabilities often need only "related services" or "accommodations" to address their needs. Such children should not be eligible yet are assigned to "special education" by decision makers subscribing to the idea that general education should not serve disabled students, no matter what their needs may be.

The failure of courts, hearing officers and review panels—the bodies charged with interpreting IDEA—to consider the "special education" limitation trickles down to eligibility teams that also fail to consider what "special education" the child needs before finding eligibility. This disregard for the "special education" limitation has slowly transformed IDEA into a repository for LD students, especially those struggling with reading.[242] These students' reading deficits may be addressed through something other than "special education," such as regular education modifications or simply better reading instruction.[243] The Committee on Education and Workforce reported to the House of Representatives that it was "discouraged by the practice of over-identifying children as having disabilities, especially minority students, largely because the children do not have appropriate reading skills."[244] This has led to the overrepresentation of African American students identified as SLD, at least in some states, and to the general rise in "special education" rolls. Recognizing the "special education" limitation as well as comprehending exactly what services are and are not "special education," therefore, is necessary to prevent African American overrepresentation and the eligibility explosion.

A similar and equally harmful practice by courts and hearing officers is acknowledging the "special education" limitation, yet failing to identify the "special education" the child requires. For example, in *West Chester Area Sch. Dist. v. Bruce,* the court found the child IDEA eligible and in need of "special education"—overturning the state review panel decision—without identifying the "special education" the child required.[245] In *Blazejewski v. Allegany Central Sch. Dist.,* the court made the same omission, ruling the child needed "special education" without identifying the services required by the child.[246] In *In re An-*

---

240. *See e.g.,* Dixie Snow Huefner, *Judicial Review of the Special Education Program Requirements Under the Education for All Handicapped Children Act: Where Have We Been and Where Should we be Going?,* 14 HARV. J.L. & PUB. POL'Y 483, n.63 (1991) ("The reason that the IDEA-B requires a student evaluated as disabled to need special education is that some students with disabilities can be educated successfully in the regular classroom without special education and related services.").

241. *West Chester Area Sch. Dist.,* 18 IDELR 802, 803 (Pa. SEA 1992) (Professor Zirkel found that the child needed only family therapy, which is not "special education").

242. PRESIDENT'S COMMISSION, *supra* note 10, at 3, 30 (50 percent of children served under the IDEA are learning disabled, and overall, 40 percent of children identified under the IDEA are identified because of their inability to read).

243. Herr, *supra* note 4, at 338, 340 (strong incentives exist to place children that could benefit from good reading instruction into special education. Many children placed in special education just need a good reading teacher); H.R. REP. No. 108-77 at 137 (2002). For this reason the IDEIA encourages educationally sound methods in literacy and reading instruction. *Id.* at 153, 156. Congress recognizes the difference between reading difficulty and reading-based learning disabilities and hopes that the use of proper literacy instruction and speech therapy will help eligibility teams differentiate between children with different learning styles and students with genuine disabilities. *Id.* at 154.

244. H.R. REP. No. 108-77, at 156 (2002). *See also id.* at 153 (children "are being inappropriately referred to special education primarily because of reading difficulties").

245. 194 F. Supp. 2d 417, 420 (E.D.Pa. 2002).

246. 560 F. Supp. 701, 703 (W.D.N.Y. 1983).

thony F., the court found that a child with speech and language deficits needed more than merely the "related service" of speech therapy, and was thus IDEA eligible, but the court never specifically identified the "special education" the student needed.[247] These decisions leave eligibility teams with no guidance as to what services are and are not "special education," allowing bias and diverging pedagogies to influence eligibility decisions.

The first step to resolving the dual eligibility crisis is a simple acknowledgment of the "special education" limitation and a push for decision makers to specifically identify the "special education" the child requires when finding eligibility. Recognition of the "special education" limitation by courts, hearing officers and state review panels can only be accomplished by advocates properly identifying the limitation to these decision makers. Once advocates press for the finding of a need for "special education," courts, hearing officers and state review panels will be forced to address the issue in their opinions. The trickle-down should lead to greater consideration of the "special education" limitation by eligibility teams.

Congress hopes to accomplish this directly in the IDEIA by requiring funds to be expended on professional development to train teachers and evaluators in understanding the identification process.[248] Training, however, is necessary but insufficient to solve the overidentification problem. Though it is possible to instruct eligibility teams that "special education" is needed before eligibility attaches, it is almost impossible to train them as to what constitutes "special education," as there are no clear standards in the statute, regulations or caselaw. This is best demonstrated in the great divide in authority interpreting "special education."

C. Varied Interpretations of "Special Education"

Decision makers' reticence to tackle the "special education" limitation is understandable in light of the difficult nature of concretely identifying what is and is not "special education" (i.e., what constitutes an adaptation of content, methodology or delivery of instruction to meet the unique needs of the child). Decision makers ignoring the "special education" limitation are the most extreme example of the generic or one-size-fits-all educational paradigm. But even decision makers who acknowledge the limitation find enough wiggle room within the definition of "special education" to employ the ideology that children needing any modification to the generic curriculum, content and methodology, no matter how minor, are the responsibility of "special education." On the other hand, decision makers adopting the individualized general education paradigm recognize that certain modifications should not be considered "special education," and that the general education system—not special education—should be primarily responsible for diverse learning styles. This paradigm blurs the line between "special education" and best educational practices in the general classroom, because it propounds that all children need individualized instruction, but not all children need "special education."

---

247. 216 A.2d 564 (Sp. Ct. N.Y. 1995). *See also Bd. of Educ. of the City Sch. Dist.*, 34 IDELR 216, 219 (N.Y.SEA 2000) ("the boy's emotional problems significantly interfered with his ability to benefit from his regular education program" and his failure to attend school was caused by his disability; therefore he needed special education, but the hearing officer did not identify the special education that was needed); *Maine Sch. Admin. Dist.* 49, 35 IDELR 174 (Mn. SEA 2001) (hearing officer finds child eligible as SED and in need of special education yet fails to identify what special education was required).

248. H.R. REP. No. 108-77 at 150 (2002).

Some decision makers recognize this dichotomy and draw a line between merely good teaching techniques for all general education students and a specific program of instruction for a particular child, while others steadfastly maintain that children needing any modifications need "special education." The result is a patchwork of decisional authority interpreting "special education" that provides no firm guidance to eligibility teams. Without firm authority or certain definitions, eligibility teams are permitted vast discretion to insert their own pedagogical beliefs. Bias inevitably influences their eligibility decisions.

1. Adaptation of Content as "Special Education"

Children with enumerated disabilities that require adaptation to the content of instruction to meet their unique needs are IDEIA eligible. If a child needs to learn different skills or information than his or her general education counterparts, that child needs "special education." Yet decision makers do not draw such a precise line, and often find children in need of minor curriculum modifications to be ineligible.

One seemingly clear-cut area of agreement is that instructing a child in a unique skill set is "special education." A long line of decisions holds that children requiring habilitative services or training in basic life skills—skills significantly different than those taught to the general education population—require "special education" and are eligible.[249] In *Yankton Sch. Dist. v. Schramm*, one of the most cited opinions on the issue, Tracy had weakened hand strength and dexterity as a result of cerebral palsy.[250] Tracy was classified under IDEA between kindergarten and eighth grade because she needed adaptive physical education (PE), mobility assistance, copies of teacher notes, separate textbooks for home and school and modified assignments.[251] The district declassified her in ninth grade, reasoning that the only "special education" she received was adaptive PE—which no longer needed to be provided because she had fulfilled her PE requirements. The district continued to offer all the other assistance it previously provided under a new Section 504 plan. The parents contested the declassification because they wanted the district to provide Tracy with transition planning (i.e., teaching her to drive and certain independent living skills) that are available under IDEA but not under Section 504.[252]

The parties agreed that Tracy needed the offered services, and "the legal question thus [was] whether those services constitute 'special education and related services' under

---

249. *See e.g., Padilla v. Dep't of Educ.*, 30 IDELR 503, 505 (Puerto Rico Cir. Ct. App. 1998) (teaching a severely disabled child basic communication is "special education" because "education for disabled children should be afforded a broader scope, to include not only traditional academic skills, but also the basic functional skills of daily living.... After all, a person's development as a human being is the ultimate purpose of education"); *In re Contra Costa County Consortium*, 507:300 EHLR (Cal. SEA 1985) (teaching severely disabled child basic communication skills is special education which child needs and is therefore IDEA eligible); *Jenkins v. Florida*, 1984–85 EHLR 556:471 (M.D. Fla. 1985), *vacated and remanded in part on other grounds*, 815 F.2d 629 (11th Cir. 1987) (habilitative services provided severely disabled is special education); *Polk v. Central Susquehanna Intermediate Unit No. 16*, 853 F.2d 171, 182–83 (3rd Cir. 1988), *cert. den.*, 488 U.S. 1030 (1989) (physical therapy and training in basic life skills are special education); *Gladys J. v. Pearland Independent Sch. Dist.*, 520 F.Supp. 869, 879 (S.D. Tex. 1981); *Campbell v. Talladega County Bd. of Educ.*, 518 F.Supp. 47 (N.D. Ala. 1981).

250. 93 F. 3d 1369 (8th Cir. 1996).

251. *Id.* at 1371.

252. This case would be easily decided today as the regulations currently provide that "travel training," teaching the skills necessary to move safely from place to place—are defined as "special education." 34 C.F.R. § 300.25(a)(2)(ii) and (b)(4)(ii).

IDEA."[253] The Eighth Circuit held that modifying the length and nature Tracy's assignments, providing teacher notes and teaching her to type using only her left hand and the first finger of her right hand were "individualized instruction" and, therefore, "special education." The mobility assistance and provision of multiple sets of books, on the other hand, were found to be "related services."[254] Because Tracy needed special education and related services she was IDEA eligible.[255]

The holding that modified typing instruction was "special education" was facially correct, because Tracy was taught an entirely different typing skill set than was being taught her general education peers. Yet not all teaching of unique skill sets is "special education." Speech-language pathology, audiology services, physical and occupational therapy, counseling services and orientation and mobility services, all of which teach different skills than are being taught in general education, are defined as "related services" and not "special education."[256] It is too simple to conclude, therefore, that the mere teaching of a different skill than is being taught the rest of the students is "special education," as much depends on whether the state has included any related services in its "special education" definition.[257] The *Yankton* court did not consult the relevant state law to determine if Tracy's typing instruction—likely occupational therapy—was defined as a "related service" and not "special education," possibly making her ineligible. Many courts and hearing officers make this same error.[258]

The Eight Circuit also held in *Yankton* that modifying the length and nature of assignments was also "special education" the child required. The court did not discuss the extent of the modifications to the assignments or whether modified assignments were available to general education students as well. Instead, the Eight Circuit employed a strict view, finding that any content modification constituted "special education." While the content of instruction is modified when the nature of assignments is altered for a particular student, the deviation may be quantitative rather than qualitative, or minor rather than significant, and may be provided to all general education students irrespective of disability. In fact, best educational practices mandate individualizing assignments to fit the abilities of the child.[259] By holding that any modification to content is special education, the Eighth Circuit implicitly adopts the one-size-fits-all general education paradigm and reserves all individualized instruction, no matter how slight, exclusively for eligible children.

---

253. *Id.* at 1374 fn. 4.

254. *Id.* at 1374. The court also identified the related services the child received: transportation to school on lift bus, mobility assistance in school, assistance with lunch tray, assistance in setting up her saxophone and provision of separate textbooks for home and school. *Id.*

255. *Id.* at 1376.

256. These terms are specifically defined in 34 C.F.R. § 300.24(b) (2003).

257. *See e.g., Pittsburgh Sch. Dist.*, 24 IDELR 1119 (Pa. SEA 1996) (child requiring Life Skills Program, which was counseling to teach organization and responsibility, did not need special education and was not IDEA eligible); *Radnor Township Sch. Dist.*, 25 IDELR 1229, 1231 (Pa. SEA 1997) (drug and alcohol counseling does not "constitute specialized instruction").

258. *See e.g., Michael P. v. Illinois State Board of Education*, 919 F. Supp. 1173, 1180 (N.D. Ill. 1996), *amended by* 934 F.Supp. 989 (1996) (court held that child needing speech therapy needed "special education" but failed to examine state standards to see if speech therapy was included in definition of "special education."); *Natchez-Adams Sch. Dist. v. Searing*, 918 F. Supp. 1028, 1037–38 (S.D. Miss. 1996) (court held that child needing occupational therapy needed "special education" but failed to examine state standards to see if occupational therapy was included in definition of "special education.").

259. *See infra* notes 315 through 326 and accompanying text.

Hearing officers and state review panels—typically education experts and not legal experts—more willingly reject the static general education paradigm and hold that minor curriculum modifications, which are provided to nondisabled general education students, do not constitute "special education," and deny eligibility to children requiring only limited services. For example, in *Mountain Empire Unified Sch. Dist.*, an LD child required small group and individualized instruction, preferential seating, curriculum one year below grade level, tutoring, pull-out assistance in language arts, additional teacher time and assistance from the special education aide in the classroom.[260] The hearing officer denied eligibility because these services were not "special education," but rather "services offered within the regular instructional program."[261] Similarly, in *Howard County Public School*, the school district provided the student with an adjusted spelling list, corrective reading instruction and a unique reading/spelling program and allowed the parents to use alternative methods to complete assignments.[262] It was agreed that the child needed these services, yet she was denied IDEA eligibility because these modifications were "alternative teaching methods" and not "special education methods necessary for the child to receive educational opportunity, within the meaning of IDEA."[263] Finally, in *Avon Public Schools* the child received phonological awareness training and direct instruction in the Wilson reading program, but was denied eligibility because these were deemed to be only "supplemental services."[264]

In each of these cases, the child required modification of the curriculum or the teaching of unique skills, yet the decision makers refused to find that the child required adaptation of instructional content, that is, "special education." These decision makers implicitly recognized that the modern classroom should, and does, make many accommodations and changes for all students, and reserved eligibility only for those requiring significant modifications not provided to all students.

The prevalent use of behavior management plans [hereafter BMPs] is illustrative. BMPs are plans designed to modify a child's behavior—they essentially teach a child proper behavior through specified methods. Despite the fact that BMPs adapt the content of instruction, they are consistently found not to constitute "special education."[265] The implicit justification is that BMPs are simply good teaching techniques that should be applied

---

260. 36 IDELR 29 (Cal. SEA 2001).

261. *Id.* However, because the child did not do well with these regular education services she required special education. *Id.*

262. 25 IDELR 771, 14 (Md. SEA 1997).

263. *Id.* at 14.

264. 25 IDELR 778 (Mass. SEA 1997). *See also Corvallis Sch. Dist.* 509J, 28 IDELR 1026 (Or. SEA 1998) ("social skills training" is not special education); *Metro. Nashville Pub. Sch. Sys.*, 27 IDELR 756 (Tenn. SEA 1997) (court found child not get special education at private school despite finding that he received individualized instruction); *Smithtown Central Sch. Dist.*, 32 IDELR 46 (N.Y. SEA 1999) ("The Section 504 accommodations designed to address the child's hearing impairment included ... encouraging the child to maintain appropriate physical aspects necessary for communication, such as eye contact; ... I am unable to find that any of these accommodations constitute specially designed instruction.").

265. *See e.g., Metropolitan Nashville Pub. Sch. Systems*, 27 IDELR 756 (Tenn. SEA 1997) (provision of behavior management plan at private school was not special education); *Corvallis Sch. Dist.* 509J, 28 IDELR 1026 (Or. SEA 1998) (a "strategy for managing outbursts" is not special education); *In re K.M.*, 29 IDELR 1027 (Vt. SEA 1999) (crisis management is an accommodation and not special education); *Ludington Sch. Dist.*, 35 IDELR 137 (Mich. SEA 2001) (child with behavior management plan "is able to profit from regular learning experiences without special education support."); *Radnor Township Sch. Dist.*, 25 IDELR 1229, 1231 (Pa. SEA 1997) (a behavior management plan "does not constitute specialized instruction.); *Gregory-Portland Ind. Sch. Dist.*, 38 IDELR 168 (Tx. SEA 2002) (discipline plan was Section 504 accommodation and not special education).

to all students and not merely those with disabilities.[266] Teachers must use many tech-niques to manage a classroom, and BMPs are just one tool in their chest.[267]

The tension between the old and new pedagogical paradigms leaves decision makers divided as to how much modification of content is needed to constitute "special educa-tion" and ample room ample room for differing pedagogical beliefs and bias to pervade the ultimate eligibility decision.

2. Adaptation of Method as "Special Education"

It is not necessary that the content of instruction be modified to find that a child needs "special education." The use of general education materials to meet a disabled child's needs may appropriately be labeled "special education," so long as the method of instruction is adapted.[268] But decision makers disagree as to what constitutes mere "accommodations" or "related services" provided to students that are not "special education," as opposed to mod-ifications teachers make to their teaching method and content that is "special education."

The difficulty distinguishing mere accommodations from content adaptation was ev-ident in *Troy Area School District*, wherein a child with physical difficulties affecting her balance and strength required significant modifications to her PE class.[269] The district contended that the child needed only accommodations in PE, but the hearing officer con-cluded that "what Laura [needed] clearly [qualified] as 'specially designed instruction.' ... [T]here is no lingering doubt that what Laura [needed] because of those challenges [was] well beyond that which is provided in the regular education curriculum.... Equally ob-vious is that the level of intervention that Laura will need to participate in most of them far [exceeded] the regular PE curriculum."[270] In essence, the child's accommodations were so significant that the child was actually learning a different skill set than her peers. There-fore, accommodations, when significant and taken in toto, can constitute adaptation in content or methodology.[271]

Distinguishing accommodations from adaptations to teaching method, procedures or technique is more difficult. There is general agreement that children needing the accom-

---

266. *See e.g.,* Robert J. Marzanno et al., WHAT WORKS IN SCHOOLS, 88 (Association for Supervi-sion and Curriculum Development, 2003) ("the most effective classroom managers tended to em-ploy different types of strategies with different types of students, whereas ineffective managers did not.... Where some students need encouragement, other students need a gentle reminder, and still others might require a firm reprimand").

267. NEA-NH, I CAN DO IT! CLASSROOM MANAGEMENT 25–27, 80.

268. 34 C.F.R. § 300.26(b)(3) (2003); OSEP Policy Letter 19 IDELR 494 (1992).

269. 30 IDELR 551, 552 (Pa. SEA 1999). For example, to learn how to kick a ball "significant strengthening of various muscles would be necessary as well as a breaking down of the task into dis-crete elements" and she would have to either substitute certain movements to meet the balance cur-riculum or not participate at all in certain activities. *Id.* at 2.

270. *Id.* at 8.

271. *See also Bristol Township Sch. Dist.*, 28 IDELR 330 (Pa. SEA 1998) (holding that preferential seating, additional time to complete written work, oral testing; special modifications to classroom texts, workbooks and worksheets to eliminate visual complexity; an assistive communication device for writing, adaption of school materials, assistance with organizational skills, use of information on tape and a full integration of all the services "are, in fact, special education and related services as de-fined by the IDEA and the PA Code" and that the issue "was not even close"); *Tucson Unified Sch. Dist.*, 30 IDELR 1000 (Az. SEA 1999) (the child received "special individualized instruction, attention and guidance in the classroom efforts" and was therefore IDEA eligible because "without these ac-commodations and individualized instruction ... student would not receive educational benefit in a regular classroom").

modations of oral tests or longer time periods to complete tests are not IDEA eligible because they do not need "special education."[272] Accommodating students with additional time to complete assignments is also not considered adapting the method of instruction.[273] Decision makers also find that the provision of aides to assist students with mobility, handwriting, organization or behavior is also not "special education."[274] Furthermore, children that need additional organizational assistance or systems are not considered in need of "special education,"[275] and neither is the provision of notetakers or interpreters.[276] Likewise, the provision of technology to students, such as tape recorders and laptop computers is also not "special education."[277] Rather, laptops, computers and other techno-

272. *See e.g., Santa Ana Unif. Sch. Dist.*, 21 IDELR 1189 (Cal. SEA) (despite need for oral instead of written tests, learning-disabled child not IDEA eligible because she did not need special education); *In re Wayne Highlands Sch. Dist.*, 24 IDELR 476 (Pa. SEA 1996) (child with chronic fatigue syndrome that needed techniques which minimized the time she had to spend in completing assigned tasks, including oral testing was ineligible because "these accommodations do not rise to the level of specially designed instruction."); *Petaluma Joint Unified Sch. Dist.*, 25 IDELR 262 (Cal. SEA 1996) (allowing student extra time to take tests is a modification which did not help student, therefore he needed special education and was IDEA eligible).

273. *See e.g., Gregory-Portland Indep. Sch. Dist.*, 38 IDELR 168 (Tx. SEA 2002); *Pennsbury Sch. Dist.*, 26 IDELR 1208 (Pa. SEA 1997) (visually impaired student that required more time to complete written assignments was not IDEA eligible because she did not require special education); *Howard County Pub. Sch.*, 25 IDELR 771, 14 (Md. SEA 1997) (allowing use of additional time to complete assignments is an "alternative teaching method" and not "special education methods necessary for the child to receive educational opportunity, within the meaning of IDEA"); *Arlington Central Sch. Dist.*, 35 IDELR 205 (N.Y. SEA 2001) (child that needed more time to complete assignments did not need special education).

274. *See e.g., Mountain Empire Unified Sch. Dist.*, 36 IDELR 29 (Cal. SEA 2001) (assistance from special education aide in classroom was not special education but rather a "service offered within regular instructional program"); *Radnor Township Sch. Dist.*, 25 IDELR 1229, 1231 (Pa. SEA 1997) (a 1:1 aide to assist with behavior problems does not "constitute specialized instruction."); *St. Clair County Bd. of Educ.*, 29 IDELR 688 (Ala. SEA 1998) (child with orthopedic impairment needed aid to assist load and unload from school bus, carry books and materials, carry lunch and assist in restroom use was not IDEA eligible because she did not need special education); *Norton v. Orinda Union Sch. Dist.*, 168 F.3d 500, 1999 WL 97288, 29 IDELR 1068 (9th Cir. 1999) (use of aide to assist in handwriting which child required was a "modification to the regular school program" and not special education therefore child not IDEA eligible); *Monrovia Unified Sch. Dist.*, 38 IDELR 84 (Cal. SEA 2002) (Section 504 accommodation of providing child with aides to remind student to stay on task and help him with writing assignments were not enough to help student therefore he needed special education).

275. *See e.g., Conrad Weiser Area Sch. Dist.*, 27 IDELR 100 (Pa. SEA 1997) (child with SLD and ADD needed accommodation of organizational system to address missed work assignments, but he was not IDEA eligible because he did not need special education); *Howard County Pub. Sch.*, 25 IDELR 771, 14 (Md. SEA 1997) (allowing use of "graphic organizers" is an "alternative teaching method" and not "special education methods necessary for the child to receive educational opportunity, within the meaning of IDEA"); *Corvallis Sch. Dist.* 509J, 28 IDELR 1026 (Or.SEA 1998) ("accommodations" of verbal reminders, a portable file and visual cues to address organizational problems are related services and not special education); *Long Beach Unified Sch. Dist.*, 33 IDELR 113 (Cal. SEA 2000) (use of daily planner is an accommodation in the regular education program and not special education).

276. Letter to Pollo, 21 IDELR 1132 (OSEP 1994).

277. *See e.g., Norton v. Orinda Union Sch. Dist.*, 168 F.3d 500, 1999 WL 97288, 29 IDELR 1068 (9th Cir. 1999) (use of notebook computer which child required was a "modification to the regular school program" and not special education; therefore child not IDEA eligible); *Petaluma Joint Unified Sch. Dist.*, 25 IDELR 262 (Cal. SEA 1996) (child required more than mere "modification" allowing use of notebook computer for homework and was therefore eligible for special education); *Conrad Weiser Area Sch. Dist.*, 27 IDELR 100 (Pa. SEA 1997) (child with SLD and ADD needed accommodation of "technological assist" but he was not IDEA eligible because he did not need special education); *Pennsbury Sch. Dist.*, 26 IDELR 1208 (Pa. SEA 1997) (visually impaired student that required use of com-

logical devices are considered "assistive technology devices" and are not considered "special education."[278] Finally, decision makers often agree that preferential seating is an accommodation and not "special education."[279]

These accommodations provided students to assist them in receipt or use of instruction are properly not considered "special education," because the teacher is not adapting instructional methodology. Rather, the student is adapting how he or she receives or employs the instruction. Accommodations merely allow the child to access instruction and demonstrate her learning—they are not modifications in methodology by the teacher, and are therefore properly excluded from the definition of "special education."[280]

But the line separating accommodations from "special education" is uncertain, especially for modifications in method such as modified assignments or the coordination of accommodations.[281] Providing modified assignments is not only an adaptation in content,

---

puter was not IDEA eligible because she did not require special education); *Howard County Pub. Sch.*, 25 IDELR 771, 14 (Md. SEA 1997) (allowing use of computer to assist in spelling is an "alternative teaching method" and not "special education methods necessary for the child to receive educational opportunity, within the meaning of IDEA"); *Aransas County Indep. Sch. Dist.*, 29 IDELR 141 (Tx. SEA 1998) (child with ADD and LD required "instructional modification" of computer assistance but was not IDEA eligible because he did not need special education); *Long Beach Unified Sch. Dist.*, 33 IDELR 113 (Cal. SEA 2000) ("Appropriate modifications such as a tape recorder ... are available through regular education. Implementing the types of accommodations previously written into STUDENT's intervention plan will allow him to sustain his academic progress without placing unreasonable demands on him. As a result, the Petitioner fails to satisfy the second prong of the severe leaning disability eligibility requirement because his disability can be accommodated in the regular education program"); *George West Independent Sch. Dist.*, 35 IDELR 287 (Tx. SEA 2001) ("although she needs the amplification device to assist her in the classroom environment, these facts alone do not rise to the level of an educational 'need' for special education for IDEA eligibility purposes"); *Santa Ana Unif. Sch. Dist.*, 21 IDELR 1189 (Cal. SEA) (child required use of a spell check in classroom because of learning disability in spelling, but child not IDEA eligibile because he did not need special education).

278. 20 U.S.C. § 1401(1) (2003); 34 C.F.R. § 300.5 (2003).

279. *See e.g., Norton v. Orinda Union Sch. Dist.*, 168 F.3d 500, 1999 WL 97288 (9th Cir. 1999) (the Ninth Circuit held in that a child who required preferential seating did not need special education because preferential seating is merely a "modification to the regular school program"). *See also Gregory-Portland Independent Sch. Dist.*, 38 IDELR 168 (Tx. SEA 2002); *Mountain Empire Unified Sch. Dist.*, 36 IDELR 29 (Cal. SEA 2001) (preferential seating is a modification of the regular education curriculum and not special education); *Howard County Pub. Sch.*, 25 IDELR 771, 14 (Md. SEA 1997) (allowing preferential seating is an "alternative teaching method" and not "special education methods necessary for the child to receive educational opportunity, within the meaning of IDEA."); *Corvallis Sch. Dist. 509J*, 28 IDELR 1026 (Or. SEA 1998) ("The recommendations in her report ... include various accommodations and supportive services (... seating preference ...), but not specially designed instruction."); *Smithtown Central Sch. Dist.*, 32 IDELR 46 (N.Y. SEA 1999) ("The Section 504 accommodations designed to address the child's hearing impairment included seating the child close to the teacher; directing the child to move his seat at any time to insure hearing ... I am unable to find that any of these accommodations constitute specially designed instruction"); *Bd. of Education of the East Syracuse-Minoa Central Sch. Dist.*, 21 IDELR 1024, 8 (N.Y. SEA 1994) (child required preferential seating to address auditory processing deficit but not eligible for special education).

280. OSEP concludes that certain accommodations furnished to students in the regular classroom, such as provision of an interpreter for hearing-impaired students or the use of modified materials for students with visual or physical impairments, may constitute "specially designed instruction." OSEP Policy Letter, 20 IDELR 1462 (1994). OSEP does not state that such accommodations are specially designed instruction but rather that they may be specially designed instruction.

281. *Compare Bristol Township Sch. Dist.*, 28 IDELR 330 (Pa. SEA 1998) (coordination of related services is special education) to *In re K.M.*, 29 IDELR 1027 (Vt. SEA 1999) (case management to coordinate plan is an accommodation and not special education) and Ellen A. Callegary, *The IDEA's*

as discussed, but is more so an adaptation in teaching method. Similar to the Eighth Circuit's holding in *Yankton*,[282] the court in *Greenland Sch. Dist. v. Amy N.,* held that a child requiring modified assignments needed "special education."[283] While modifying the length and nature of assignments is an adaptation of teaching method, many decision makers find it is not "special education." They reason that modified assignments are minor modifications to the regular education setting that are available to all children.[284]

Similar reasoning is employed to find that other minor teaching modifications children need are not "special education" and therefore deny eligibility. The analysis in *Smithtown Central School District* is typical:

> The Section 504 accommodations designed to address the child's hearing impairment included seating the child close to the teacher; directing the child to move his seat at any time to insure hearing; encouraging the child to maintain appropriate physical aspects necessary for communication, such as eye contact; requesting the child to repeat directions before beginning independent activities when necessary; monitoring the child during initial practice of activities; and encouraging the child to inform the speaker of his auditory needs on an ongoing basis. I am unable to find that any of these accommodations constitute specially designed instruction. The child is not in a special class, nor does he have special education teachers .... The accommodations set forth in the child's Section 504 plan are common strategies that apply to students in general, not just students with disabilities.[285]

Using similar analysis, decision makers often hold that many minor modifications to the method of instruction are not "special education." For example, children that need tasks broken down into manageable pieces,[286] written or concrete visual instructions[287] or vi-

---

Promise Unfulfilled: A Second Look at Special Education & Related Services for Children with Mental Health Needs after Garret F., 5 J. HEALTH CARE L. & POL'Y 164, 170–72 (2002) (service coordination is a related service).

282. 93 F.3d 1369, 1373 (8th Cir. 1996).

283. 2003 WL 1343023 at *8 (D.N.H. 2003), *aff'd on other grounds* 358 F.3d 150 (1st Cir. 2004) (a child with ADHD and Asperger's syndrome required modified assignments, parent checklists and contacts, behavior modification techniques, ability grouping, significant parental assistance with homework, preferential seating in the front of the class and a tutor).

284. *See e.g., Mountain Empire Unified Sch. Dist.*, 36 IDELR 29 (Cal. SEA 2001) (allowing take-home tests and assignments is not special education); *Conrad Weiser Area Sch. Dist.*, 27 IDELR 100 (Pa. SEA 1997) (child with SLD and ADD needed accommodation of shortened assignments but not IDEA eligible because does not need special education); *Pennsbury Sch. Dist.*, 26 IDELR 1208 (Pa. SEA 1997) (visually impaired student that required shortened written assignments was not IDEA-eligible because she did not require special education); *Long Beach Unified Sch. Dist.*, 33 IDELR 113 (Cal. SEA 2000) ("Appropriate modifications such as ... reduced reading assignments, and modified class and homework demands are available through regular education. Implementing the types of accommodations previously written into STUDENT's intervention plan will allow him to sustain his academic progress without placing unreasonable demands on him. As a result, the Petitioner fails to satisfy the second prong of the severe leaning disability eligibility requirement because his disability can be accommodated in the regular education program"); *Monrovia Unified Sch. Dist.*, 38 IDELR 84 (Cal. SEA 2002) (accommodation of modified assignments did not assist student therefore he needed special education).

285. *Smithtown Central Sch. Dist.*, 32 IDELR 46 (N.Y. SEA 1999) (citations omitted).

286. *Corvallis Sch. Dist. 509J*, 28 IDELR 1026 (Or. SEA 1998) ("The recommendations in her report ... include various accommodations and supportive services (... tasks broken down into manageable pieces ...), but not specially designed instruction").

287. *Gregory-Portland Independent Sch. Dist.*, 38 IDELR 168 (Tx. SEA 2002); *Corvallis Sch. Dist. 509J*, 28 IDELR 1026 (Or. SEA 1998) ("The recommendations in her report ... include various ac-

sual cues[288] are often not found in need of "special education." The same is true for students that require additional monitoring of attendance, behavior or homework[289] and additional communication between parents and the school.[290] Even students that require small classes are often not deemed in need of "special education."[291] Finally, the provision of a tutor or special small groups, a clear adaptation of method of instruction, is often not considered "special education."[292]

commodations and supportive services (… written instructions …), but not specially designed instruction").

288. *Id.* ("The recommendations in her report … include various accommodations and supportive services (… visual cues …), but not specially designed instruction").

289. *Gregory-Portland Independent Sch. Dist.*, 38 IDELR 168 (Tx. SEA 2002); *Pittsburgh Sch. Dist.*, 24 IDELR 1119 (Pa. SEA 1996) (child requiring plans to track and encourage homework and attendance did not need special education); *Metropolitan Nashville Pub. Sch. Systems*, 27 IDELR 756 (Tenn. SEA 1997) (provision of constant monitoring of behavior at private school was not special education); *St. Clair County Bd. of Education*, 29 IDELR 688 (Ala. SEA 1998) (orthopedically impaired child that needed adult chaperon to monitor band activity was not IDEA eligible because she did not need special education); *Corvallis Sch. Dist. 509J*, 28 IDELR 1026 (Or. SEA 1998) (teacher "follow-up to be sure assignments are turned in" is not special education); *In re K.M.*, 29 IDELR 1027 (Vt. SEA 1999) (daily check-ins and monitoring of academics and behavior are accommodations and not special education); *Smithtown Central Sch. Dist.*, 32 IDELR 46 (N.Y. SEA 1999) ("The Section 504 accommodations designed to address the child's hearing impairment included … monitoring the child during initial practice of activities … I am unable to find that any of these accommodations constitute specially designed instruction"); *Long Beach Unified Sch. Dist.*, 33 IDELR 113 (Cal. SEA 2000) (nightly homework checks were accommodations to the general education program and not special education). *But see, Bristol Township Sch. Dist.*, 28 IDELR 330, 8–9 (Pa. SEA 1998) (finding that mom's monitoring of child's needs, in addition to numerous other services, constituted special education).

290. *Corvallis Sch. Dist. 509J*, 28 IDELR 1026 (Or. SEA 1998) ("The recommendations in her report … include various accommodations and supportive services (… consistent communication between school and parent …), but not specially designed instruction."); *In re K.M.*, 29 IDELR 1027 (Vt. SEA 1999) (communication with school counselor is an accommodation and not special education); *West Haven Bd. of Educ*, 36 IDELR 221 (Conn. SEA 2002) (increased parental contact is not special education).

291. *Metropolitan Nashville Pub. Sch. Systems*, 27 IDELR 756 (Tenn. SEA 1997) (provision of small classes at private school was not special education but rather a "service offered within regular instructional program."); *In re K.M.*, 29 IDELR 1027 (Vt. SEA 1999) (provision of small classes is an accommodation and not special education).

292. *Mountain Empire Unified Sch. Dist.*, 36 IDELR 29 (Cal. SEA 2001) (small group placement and individualized instruction was not special education); *Howard County Pub. Sch.*, 25 IDELR 771, 14 (Md. SEA 1997) (district permitted tutor to come into school once a week to assist student in production of written documents, but the court found this to be a mere "alternative teaching method" and not "special education methods necessary for the child to receive educational opportunity, within the meaning of IDEA"); *Los Alamitos Unified Sch. Dist.*, 26 IDELR 1053 (Cal. SEA 1997) (student with a reading problem was provided a tutor, but the hearing officer found this to be services offered within the regular instructional program and not special education); *Aransas County Indep. Sch. Dist.*, 29 IDELR 141 (Tx. SEA 1998) (child with ADD and LD required "instructional modification" of an after-school tutor and counseling but was not IDEA eligible because he "has not demonstrated a need for special education services"); *In re K.M.*, 29 IDELR 1027 (Vt. SEA 1999) ("academic support as needed" and "supported study" are accommodations and not special education); *Bellflower Unified Sch. Dist.*, 33 IDELR 262 (Cal. SEA 2000) (child with reading learning disability required small group reading sessions with a reading specialist and later a reading tutoring program yet not IDEA eligible because "STUDENT'S recent academic progress indicates that, at this point, he remains able to learn and remediate his severe discrepancy within the regular education system"); Ludington Sch. Dist., 35 IDELR 137 (Mich. SEA 2001) (child that received "extra help in school" is not IDEA eligible because he was "able to profit from regular learning experiences without special education support"); *Northshore Sch. Dist.*, 35 IDELR 144, 10 (Wash. SEA 2001) (child that required special reading group did not "need[] specially designed instruction"); *Arlington Central Sch. Dist.*, 35 IDELR 205 (N.Y. SEA 2001) (child

The tension is palpable between the individualized education paradigm underlying the above decisions, and the one-size-fits-all paradigm underlying the *Greenland* and *Yankton* line of decisions. Any child requiring modification to the generic educational method needs "special education" according to the generic educational model, while the individualized model anticipates that minor adaptations are available to all children and reserves "special education" for those needing significant modifications to methodology. Again, this pedagogical divide in the authority leaves eligibility teams with significant discretion to determine when a child needs "special education" in the form of modified methodology.

3. Adaptation of Delivery as Special Education

The authority is also divided as to what constitutes adaptation of delivery of instruction. The first point of disagreement is whether modifying *who* delivers the instruction is itself "special education." Some states require that only certified special education teachers can provide "special education."[293] In other words, any adaptation by the regular classroom teacher, no matter how significant, cannot be considered "special education" in these states—the child must need modifications provided by a certified special education teacher.[294] IDEA and the IDEIA contain no such mandate, instead leaving personnel decisions to the states.[295] But IDEA and the IDEIA imply that only appropriately trained personnel will provide "special education" and related services.[296] Despite the implication, many decision-makers ignore who is providing the education to determine if it is "special education," holding that assistance from a special education teacher is not necessarily "special education," or that "special education" can be provided by general educators.[297]

---

in "reading recovery program" and later a private tutor was not IDEA eligible because he did not need special education); *Pennsbury Sch. Dist.*, 37 IDELR 267 (Pa. SEA 2002) (child performed well when he received "extra services in reading" including small group and individual reading services; therefore, he did not need special education). *But see, Toledo Pub. Sch. Dist.*, EHLR 401:335 (Oh. SEA 1989) (child IDEA-eligible because he needed special education in the form of tutoring); *Greenland Sch. Dist. v. Amy N.*, 2003 WL 1343023 (D.N.H. 2003) (child succeeded in school because provided a tutor, which was special education).

293. Bonnie Tucker & Bruce Goldstein, Legal Rights of Persons With Disabilities: An Analysis of Federal Law Chapter 3B (LRP 2003).

294. *See, e.g., Smithtown Central Sch. Dist.*, 32 IDELR 46 (N.Y. SEA 1999) ("I am unable to find that any of these accommodations constitute specially designed instruction. The child is not in a special class, nor does he have special education teachers").

295. 34 C.F.R. §§ 300.136(b)(2)(i) (2003) ("Each State may determine the specific occupational categories required to provide special education and related services within the State"); 34 C.F.R. § 300.136(b)(3) ("nothing in [IDEA] requires a State to establish a specified training standard (e.g., a master's degree) for personnel who provide special education and related services").

296. *See, e.g.,* 20 U.S.C. § 1412(a)(14) (2003) (requiring states to implement a comprehensive system of personnel development "to ensure an adequate supply of qualified special education, regular education, and related services personnel"; 20 U.S.C. § 1412(15)(C) (permitting states to require LEAS to "make an ongoing good faith effort to recruit and hire appropriately and adequately trained personnel to provide special education and related services to children with disabilities"); 34 C.F.R. § 300.135(a)(1) (2003); 34 C.F.R. § 300.380(a)(2) (2003). *See also* 20 U.S.C. § 1435(a)(8); 34 C.F.R. § 300.380–82 (2003). IDEA specifically requires that early intervention services provided to infants and toddlers must be provided by qualified special educators or related service providers. 20 U.S.C. § 1432(4)(F) (2003).

297. *See, e.g., Bristol Township Sch. Dist.*, 28 IDELR 330 (Pa. SEA 1998) (fact that special education teacher is not required does not mean the child does not need special education); *Ashland Sch. Dist.*, 28 IDELR 630 (Or. SEA 1998) (child moved to Learning Center and taught by special education teacher was not IDEA eligible because she succeeded without special education); *Weston Pub.*

There is also disagreement on the parallel issue of whether parents delivering instruction, typically through assistance with homework, constitutes "special education." Some courts find that parental assistance, particularly if substantial, is an adaptation in delivery that qualifies as "special education" while other courts do not.[298]

Finally, there is disagreement as to whether delivery of instruction in a unique setting alone is special education. In *Weixel v. Board of Education of the City of New York*, a child with chronic fatigue syndrome and fibromyalgia could not consistently attend school.[299] The district acknowledged her qualifying disability, but denied IDEA eligibility on the grounds the child did not need "special education"—she merely needed provision of the general curriculum outside of the school. The Second Circuit disagreed, holding that the child's impairment "made it impossible for her to attend school. As a result of her inability to attend classes, she required 'special education' in the form of home instruction."[300]

In contrast, in *Katherine S. v. Umbach*, the child needed homebound instruction and residential placement, but the court denied eligibility, finding that instruction in alternative settings does not constitute "special education."[301] Similarly, in *In re Wayne Highlands Sch. Dist.*, the hearing officer found that homebound instruction of the regular education curriculum is not "special education," and therefore a child with chronic fatigue syndrome that required homebound instruction was not IDEA eligible.[302]

The division again arises from the differing pedagogies underlying the decisions. The individualized model entrusts the general educators to provide the standard curriculum to children in alternate settings, while the one-size-fits-all model resigns the duties and the children to "special education."

D. "Special Education" Redefined

The division in authority as to what constitutes "special education" is a product of its vague statutory and regulatory definition. Those subscribing to the educational model

---

Sch. Dist., 34 IDELR 75, 8 (Mass. SEA 2001) ("Although he is receiving support from the third grade special education teacher, he does not require specialized instruction or modifications to the general curriculum and would not have difficulty accessing the curriculum without her support").

298. *See, e.g., Conrad Weiser Area Sch. Dist. v. Dep't of Educ.*, 603 A.2d 701, 705 (Pa. 1992) (the child needed special education because he needed parental assistance with homework); *Greenland Sch. Dist. v. Amy N.*, 2003 WL 1343023 at *8 (D.N.H. 2003), *aff'd on other grounds* 358 F.3d 150 (1st Cir. 2004) (significant parental assistance constituted special education); *Toledo Pub. Sch. Dist.*, EHLR 401:335 (Oh. SEA 1989) (child IDEA eligible because he needed special education in the form of substantial parental help). *But see, e.g., West Haven Bd. of Educ*, 36 IDELR 221 (Conn. SEA 2002) (additional homework assistance was not deemed special education).

299. 287 F.3d 138, 141–42 (2d Cir. 2002).

300. *Id.* at 150.

301. 2002 WL 226697 at *12, (M.D.Ala. 2002).

302. 24 IDELR 476 (Pa. SEA 1996). *See also Pocono Mountain Sch. Dist.*, 36 IDELR 224 (Pa. SEA 2002) ("Tiber's physical condition required homebound instruction beginning in January 1998 and continuing through the 1998–1999 school year. This accommodation and support was clearly not an adaptation in content, methodology or delivery. 34 C.F.R. §300.26 (b) (3)—definition of specially designed instruction. Homebound instruction is not a special education placement; it is a temporary excusal from school, under general education compulsory attendance regulations, for physical, mental or other urgent reasons. Homebound instruction is distinct from the special education placement known as 'instruction in the home.' Instruction in the home is a particular placement for students who require full time special education services and programs outside of the regular school").

that children who do not benefit from the generic one-size-fits-all education are the responsibility of "special education" alone find support in the definition of "special education" which implies that children requiring *any* adaptation of content, method or delivery need special education. Decision makers adopting the individualized general education model find support in the definition of "special education" which requires that the adaptations be made to meet the unique needs of the child, as opposed to the generic needs of all students.[303] Reducing the vast discretion in eligibility determinations and the inevitable resulting bias requires a more certain definition of "special education," one that yields consistent rather than subjective results.

The best means to address these problems is to adopt the emerging educational pedagogy by redefining "special education" to mean significant adaptations in content, method and delivery that are not provided to all general education students, irrespective of disability. In other words, children with enumerated disabilities should only be eligible if they need significant individualized instruction beyond that provided to all students.[304] This circumscribed definition acknowledges that minor modifications to content, delivery and instruction are not "special education" but good pedagogy for all students. Good teaching requires adjustment to classroom instruction to meet the varying individual needs of all students.[305] Educators cannot "be enmeshed in a system geared up to treat all first graders as though they were essentially the same, or all Algebra I students as though they were alike."[306] Rather, educators must "acknowledge that students learn in varied ways—some by hearing, others by doing, some alone, others in the company of peers, some in rapid fire fashion, others reflectively ... To teach well is to attend to all of these things."[307]

Best educational practices, for example, mandate that teachers should provide certain students and parents feedback on the students' performance (i.e., adapt their method of instruction). The use of checklists and parental contact "is the most powerful thing that a classroom teacher can do to enhance student achievement.' The most powerful single modification that enhances achievement is feedback. The simplest prescription for improving education must be dollops of feedback.'"[308] Similarly, the use of small groups "accom-

---

303. 20 U.S.C. §1401(25); *Letter to Smith*, 18 IDELR 683 (OSEP 1992) ("'specially designed instruction' is education planned for a particular individual or 'individualized instruction.'"). *See also* Theresa N. Willard, Note, *Economics and the Individuals with Disabilities Education Act: The Influence of Funding Formulas on the Identification and Placement of Disabled Students*, 31 IND. L. REV. 1167 ("specialized services are those offered to the disabled child to address needs which cannot be served in the regular education program").

304. This limited definition does not infringe on state sovereignty to select educational programming because it does not require any level of individualized instruction in the general education classroom. Rather, by defining "special education" as significant modifications not provided in the general classroom, states and school districts are still free to select the amount of individualized instruction they will provide all students. The new definition does not compel states to individualize general education; it merely permits schools to embrace the new model by eliminating such instruction from the definition of "special education." For an in-depth discussion of Congress's reticence to intrude on state sovereignty over education, *see* Garda, *supra* note 14, at 451–55.

305. ENHANCING PROFESSIONAL PRACTICE, A FRAMEWORK FOR TEACHING, 49–50 (Association for Supervision and Curriculum Development, 1996).

306. CAROL ANN TOMLINSON ET AL., LEADERSHIP FOR DIFFERENTIATING SCHOOLS AND CLASSROOMS, Chapter 1 (Association for Supervision and Curriculum Development, 2d ed. 2000).

307. CAROL ANN TOMLINSON, HOW TO DIFFERENTIATE INSTRUCTION IN MIXED ABILITY CLASSROOMS, Chapter V (Association for Supervision and Curriculum Development, 2d ed. 2001).

308. ROBERT MARZANO ET AL., A HANDBOOK FOR CLASSROOM INSTRUCTION THAT WORKS, 185 (Association for Supervision and Curriculum Development, 2001).

modates students who are strong in some areas and weaker in others.... . This teacher knows that sometimes she needs to assign students to groups so that assignments are tailored to student need."[309] In addition, many regular education students receive tutoring. In fact, the NCLB requires that schools in need or improvement provide "supplemental educational services," including tutoring.[310]

Despite the fact that provision of certain minor modifications is the best educational practice for all students, many decision makers find such modifications to be "special education" reserved for students with disabilities, as noted. The limited view of general education propounded by certain courts and hearing officers inevitably influences teams determining a particular child's eligibility. Dr. Sultana randomly sampled over 200 Individualized Education Plans, or IEPs, which delineate the services to be provided eligible students. Dr. Sultana found that the "special education" provided on a majority of these IEPs included only modeling, examples, feedback, encouragement, advance organizers, verbal praise, clear instruction, clear directions, verbal/visual cues, reviews and guided practice.[311] Dr. Sultana further noted that such specially designed instruction methods are also accepted indicators of effective instruction for all children, not just disabled children.[312] In short, Dr. Sultana discovered that many IDEA-eligible students receive "special education" that should be provided to all students.

All children require certain adaptations in the regular classroom—not just children with disabilities. These modifications should be encouraged in regular education and not resigned exclusively to "special education." Children are often referred for IDEA eligibility despite needing only extra support or intensified instruction.[313] Such extra support and intensified instruction must be carved out of the definition of "special education"; otherwise instructional casualties, particularly minorities, will be found in need of "special education." There simply must be "alternatives to special education. If special education is the only place where students with learning difficulties can receive supplemental help, the greater the attraction of this program will be."[314] Children who need only the minor modifications available to all should not be resigned to "special education" with its attendant harms. Rather, only significant adaptations in instructional content, unavailable to other all children irrespective of disability, should be considered "special education." As noted, many decision makers already employ a similar unwritten standard, finding that generic programs available to all or minor modifications are not special education.[315]

---

309. CAROL ANN TOMLINSON, HOW TO DIFFERENTIATE INSTRUCTION IN A MIXED ABILITY CLASSROOM, 3 (Association for Supervision and Curriculum Development, 2d ed. 2001).

310. 20 U.S.C. §§6316(b)(6) and (e)(12)(c).

311. Quaisar Sultana, "SDI: What Is It and How Well Do We Provide It," May 5, 2004 presentation at the LRP Special Education Conference.

312. *Id.*

313. H.R. REP. No. 108-77 at 153 (2002).

314. Parrish, *supra* note 9, at 34.

315. *See also Old Orchard Beach Sch. Department*, 21 IDELR 1084, 1086, 1088 (Me. SEA 1994) (emotionally disturbed child placed in a personalized program that was available to all at-risk kids, whether suffering from a disability or not, did not need special education); *Ashland Sch. Dist.*, 28 IDELR 630 (Or. SEA 1998) (child placed in Learning Center which was available to all students was not IDEA eligible because she progressed with related services); *Smithtown Central Sch. Dist.*, 29 IDELR 293 (N.Y. SEA 1998) ("Teaching techniques and modifications which the child's teacher used with all of the children in her classroom would obviously not fall within the definition of special education under either Federal or State law"); *West Haven Bd. of Educ.*, 37 IDELR 56, 8 (Conn. SEA 2001) (child that needed help with homework and meeting deadlines did not need special education because "these types of needs can be met in the regular education program through the progress reports and after school assistance from teachers, which is available to all students at the high school, including this one");

Though limiting "special education" to only significant adaptations not provided to all students finds support in the IDEIA and certain decisions, it cannot be uniformly applied without redefining "special education." Without such change, sufficient latitude exists within the IDEIA for decision makers to continue to insert their diverging pedagogies, and eligibility decisions will continue to be divided, subjective, and influenced by bias. Circumscribing the definition of "special education" will limit the discretion of referring teachers and eligibility teams. Under the new definition, eligibility teams will have to determine if regular education interventions are sufficient to assist the student, rather than presuming that broadly defined "special education" is needed. Referring teacher subjectivity will also be reduced, as they will become aware that children will not be found eligible if regular education interventions will succeed. The circumscribed definition of "special education" promotes the best educational practice of regular education with ancillary services, instead of the current default of "special education" placement.[316]

IV. Defining When a Child "Needs" Special Education

With a more certain definition of "special education," bias is reduced in part of the eligibility process, and special education law will not impede the individualization model in general education. Narrowing the definition of "special education," however, is not enough to prevent minority overrepresentation and ensure that only those truly in "need" of special education are found eligible. A general education teacher, without attempting any general education interventions for a child, may refer a child to special education merely because the child does not fit the generic educational model of the classroom, and the eligibility team could conclude the same and classify the child. Strictly defining "special education" addresses only half of the problem — the other half is defining who "needs" special education.

While the IDEIA and its predecessors at least broadly define "special education," the IDEIA "contains no explicit guidelines for determining whether a student with an impairment *needs* special education."[317] Instead, states are left to determine who "needs" special education and who does not.[318] The only limitation is that a state's criteria may not "operate to exclude any student who, in the absence of the state's criteria, would be eligible for services under [IDEA]."[319]

Very few states define when a child "needs" special education. For example, Massachusetts provides that there is a "need" for special education when the child is "unable to progress effectively in a regular education program."[320] Similarly, Colorado pronounces

---

Long Beach Unified Sch. Dist., 33 IDELR 113 (Cal. SEA 2000) ("Appropriate modifications such as ... modified class and homework demands are available through regular education.... As a result, the Petitioner fails to satisfy the second prong of the severe leaning disability eligibility requirement because his disability can be accommodated in the regular education program").

316. Herr, *supra* note 4, at 374 (special education is promoted over regular education with supportive services).

317. Letter to Pawlisch, 24 IDELR 959, 964 (OSEP 1995). *See also J.D. v. Pawlett Sch. Dist.*, 224 F.3d 60, 66 (2nd Cir. 2000).

318. Letter to Pawlish, 24 IDELR 959, 963 (OSEP 1995).

319. *Id.*

320. M.G.L. c.71B, 1; 603 C.M.R. § 28.02(9). To "progress effectively" in regular education means to "make documented growth in the acquisition of knowledge and skills, including social/emotional

that a child only "needs" special education if the child cannot receive "reasonable bene-fit from regular education,"[321] and Tennessee articulates that a child "needs" special edu-cation when the child is "unable ... to be educated appropriately in the regular school program."[322]

These standards, though better than nothing, are still vague and subject to bias. As a result, determining who "needs" special education has historically plagued decision mak-ers.[323] The "need" for special education is clear for the severely disabled at the far end of the continuum of cognitive and behavioral competence.[324] It is difficult to draw eligibil-ity lines, however, once one moves away from the extremes of ability.[325] Some find that a child "needs" special education merely because the child can benefit from it. Others find that the fact a child can benefit from special education does not establish a "need," and instead require that a child be failing or performing below average before finding a need for special education.[326] The division in authority results in an artificial and variable line between those who do and do not require special education.[327]

The effect is a wholly subjective standard by which eligibility teams determine "need." With the attendant bias inherent in such a subjective decision, minority children become over-represented in special education, and the floodgates of eligibility are opened to all. What is needed, therefore, to limit overall eligibility to those truly in "need" and to reduce the sub-jectivity when deciding who needs special education, is a more concrete definition of "need."

In considering the IDEIA, Congress received numerous recommendations that children should not be considered for special education until scientifically based pre-referral mea-sures in the regular education classroom were tried and shown unsuccessful. The Presi-dential Commission reported to Congress that "children should not be identified for special education without documenting what methods have been used to facilitate the child's learning and adaptation to the general education classroom."[328] The Presidential Commission recommended that interventions should be attempted before a referral for special education is made.[329]

The NRC also strongly recommended that pre-referral interventions be provided be-fore children are referred or considered for eligibility. It found that "early intervention should be essential prerequisites to any consideration of student referral to special educa-tion."[330] The NRC concluded that it should be "the responsibility of the teachers in the reg-

---

development, within the general education program, with or without accommodations, according to chronological age and developmental expectations, the individual educational potential of the child, and the learning standards set forth in the Massachusetts Curriculum Frameworks and the curricu-lum of the district." 603 CMR § 28.02(18). Indicators of a student's inability to make effective progress include not performing up to expected levels on standardized, criterion-referenced or curriculum based assessments, or failing to earn promotion to the next grade level at the end of the school year (Massachusetts Department of Education Eligibility Guidelines for Special Education, 1994).

321. C.C.R. § 220-R-2.02(1)(a).

322. *Tennessee Rules, Regulations, and Minimum Standards.*

323. NRC REPORT, *supra* note 8, at 3 ("Who requires special education? Answering that question has always posed a challenge.").

324. *Id.* at 25–26.

325. *Id.* at 26.

326. *See* Garda, *supra* note 14, at 491–507.

327. NRC REPORT, *supra* note 8, at 25, 27.

328. PRESIDENT'S COMMISSION, *supra* note 10, at 26.

329. *Id.* at 21.

330. NRC REPORT, *supra* note 8, at 299. The NRC recommended numerous regular education interventions that should be attempted before referral. *Id.* at 296–99. *See also id.* at 303 ("We reiter-

ular classroom to engage in multiple educational interventions ... before referring the child for special education assessment."[331] The NRC recommended a system "in which no child is judged by the school to have a learning or emotional disability ... until efforts to provide high quality instructional and behavioral support in the general education context have been tried without success."[332] The NRC specifically recommends that eligibility ensues only when there is evidence of insufficient response to high-quality interventions in the relevant domains of functioning in the school setting.[333] It concluded that "future practices are likely to place additional emphasis on the special education need component of eligibility. This may be done by (1) strengthening interventions prior to referral and (2) determining empirically that well designed and properly implemented interventions in general education are not sufficient to enable the student to receive an appropriate education."[334]

The Committee on Workforce and Education agreed with these recommendations and reported to Congress that "a disproportional number of minority students are wrongly placed in special education rather than being provided positive behavioral interventions and supports and intensive educational interventions."[335] The report recognized that many minority children are inappropriately referred to special education, primarily because of reading difficulties or behavioral problems that could be remedied through appropriate regular education interventions and that such measures have worked in some states.[336]

The success of mandatory pre-referral intervention services in Alabama is of particular note. In reviewing a consent decree from a long-standing desegregation suit, the court in *Lee v. Macon County Board of Education*[337] found that African American students in Alabama were three times more likely to be found mentally retarded than their white peers, and entered a consent decree to address the problem.[338] The court ordered, among other measures, a new pre-referral process requiring teachers to use a host of intervention strategies for at least six weeks before considering special education referral.[339] Since the order, the number of special education students overall has dropped, and African American disproportionality has significantly decreased.[340] The teachers' use of multiple teaching strategies, particularly in reading and math, and specialized attention to struggling students, including flexible grouping, led to zero referrals of African American students in 2003. More important, the at-risk children are doing better academically.[341]

In summary, there is a broad consensus in the literature that pre-referral interventions should be applied prior to considering special education eligibility.[342] Some states follow

---

ate that special education should not be considered unless there are effective general education programs ... and early high-quality interventions prior to referral").

331. *Id.* at 299 (citing to 1982 NRC STUDY).

332. *Id.* at 6.

333. *Id.* at 7–8.

334. *Id.* at 220.

335. H.R. REP. No. 108-77 at 137, 147.

336. *Id. at* 153, 157.

337. 267 F. Supp. 458 (M.D. Ala. 1967).

338. *Lee v. Phoenix City Bd. of Educ.*, C.A. No. 70-T-854 (M.D. Ala. August 30, 2000).

339. *Id. See also* Milloy, *supra* note 6 (explaining the *Lee v. Macon County* decision).

340. Milloy, *supra* note 6.

341. *Id.*

342. NRC REPORT, *supra* note 8, at 302. *See also* A Position Statement of the International Reading Association, *supra* note 38 (recommending that referral for special education should not be made until the child is first put in a high-quality reading program and moderate classroom interventions are employed); Losen and Welner, *supra* note 81, at 187–88.

this consensus and require that children not be found eligible until non–special education interventions are shown to fail.[343] Hearing officers and courts, without any legislative guidance, also often hold that children whose needs can be addressed through non–special education services should not be eligible. Many decision makers find that a child's "need" for special education should be ascertained by taking into account the non-special education services the child receives, typically under Section 504.[344] In other words, children are

---

343. California defines an eligible "individual with exceptional needs" as a student with an impairment that "requires instruction, services, or both which cannot be provided with modification of the regular school program." Calif. Educ. Code § 56026(b). *See also* Calif. Educ. Code § 56337 (learning disability requires a severe discrepancy between ability and "that discrepancy cannot be corrected through other regular or categorical services offered within the regular instructional program."). Decision makers applying California law consistently find that schools must provide tutoring, reading and academic assistance, handwriting assistance, preferential seating, use of a word processor for taking notes, careful teacher selection, teacher planning to increase participation, counseling, support systems, clarification of school rules and increased communication with parents all within general education before a child is found in "need" of special education. *See, e.g., Norton v. Orinda Union Sch. Dist.*, 168 F.3d 500, 1999 WL 97288, 29 IDELR 1068 (9th Cir. 1999) (child benefited from handwriting assistance, preferential seating and use of a word processor in general education and therefore was not eligible for special education); *Berkeley Unified Sch. Dist.*, 507:436 (Cal. SEA 1986) (The hearing officer found the child ineligible because the modifications to the regular education program such as careful teacher selection, teacher planning to increase participation, counseling, identification to the child of a support system, clarification of school rules, increased communication with parents and assistance to promote attitude change by the student had not yet been tried); *Los Alamitos Unified Sch. Dist.*, 26 IDELR 1053 (Cal. SEA 1997) (child requiring the regular education supports of tutoring and reading and academic assistance did not need special education).

344. *See, e.g., In re West Chester Area Sch. Dist.*, 35 IDELR 235, 239 (Pa. SEA 2001) (child ineligible because child performed well with supports); *Arlington Central Sch. Dist.*, 35 IDELR 205, 213 (N.Y. SEA 2001) (examined child's performance with non–special education services to determine if the child needed special education); *George West Independent Sch. Dist.*, 35 IDELR 287, 293 (Tx. SEA 2001) ("Instead, the evidence showed that she is successful in the regular mainstream classroom with the assistance of the amplification device already being provided to her by the school district. She has been and will continue to be served under the school district's 504 program.... There is no educational need for special education and related services under these circumstances"); *Ludington Sch. Dist.*, 35 IDELR 137, 140 (Mich. SEA 2001) (child not eligible because his "needs can be met in the regular education setting with some modifications, and cooperation and consistency from his parent"); *In re K.M.*, 29 IDELR 1027, 1035 (Vt. SEA 1999) ("the student does not require a special program of instruction in order to obtain an appropriate education despite her handicaps. She has succeeded in a regular program of instruction, but she needs considerable accommodations to her handicap in order to do so. As was pointed out by several witnesses, including the parent's own consultant, this is a distinction between 504 and special education eligibility that is often confused or misunderstood"); *Corvallis Sch. Dist. 509J*, 28 IDELR 1026, 1038 (Or. SEA 1998) ("Thus, when related services and accommodations allow a student to make progress in the regular education program, as indicated by grades or performance on academic achievement test, there is no need for special education and therefore no eligibility under IDEA"); *Old Orchard Beach Sch. Department*, 21 IDELR 1084, 1090 (Me. SEA 1994) ("Special education and related services are only for those children who need assistance in order to benefit from their education. AG is now in a personalized program with a low teacher/student ratio, lots of accountability, a case manager to communicate with home on a regular basis and deal with social skills issues, and taking one course at the high school by her choice. If she were labeled, nothing would change as this program is the one described by the psychologists to meet her needs and the program serves both special education and regular education students"); *Academy Sch. Dist. #20*, 21 IDELR 965 (Colo. SEA 1994) (concluding child did not need special education based on child's performance taking into account behavior management strategies); *Toledo Pub. Sch. Dist.*, 401 EHLR 335, 338 (Oh. SEA 1989) ("In this case the evidence is clear that without substantial tutoring and parental help he received, he would not have passed to the next grade, for the second time. So for this child, special education is required for him to benefit from his education"); *In re Laura H.*, 509 EHLR 242, 248 (Mass. SEA 1988) (child not eligible because "there is no current indication that she cannot continue to make effective educational progress

not eligible if their needs are adequately addressed through non–special education services.[345] Other decision-makers, however, find that children "need" special education if they can benefit from it, irrespective of the child's success with regular education interventions.[346]

Despite the recommendations of the Presidential Commission and the NRC and the success of pre-referral interventions in some states, Congress only incrementally adopted pre-referral measures in the IDEIA. It permits but does not mandate districts to use federal funds to provide pre-referral services to students before they are identified as needing special education.[347] Pre-referral measures are only mandatory once a state determines that significant minority overrepresentation exists, which is after the harm of misidentification attaches. Congress's reticence to compel schools to provide individualized interventions prior to referral likely stems from its strong unwillingness to impede on state sovereignty over instructional methodologies. Congress felt justified in mandating pre-refferal intervention services where significant disproportionality exists but not elsewhere. But the definition of "need" can be altered to limit subjectivity and bias in referral and assessment, while maintaining state hegemony over educational methodology.

I have argued elsewhere that a child should not be found in "need" of special education merely because the child can benefit from it—a standard many decision makers employ due to the lack of federal or state guidance. Rather, a child should not be considered in "need" of special education unless his or her educational performance is below average.[348] But this conclusion begs the question of what services a district must provide in regular education before a child's performance is deemed below average. A child in one school may perform below average, despite receiving numerous general education supports, and a child in another school may perform below average without any such services.

To bring uniformity to "need" determinations, a child's educational performance should not be considered below average until all regular education interventions and services available in the district have been proven unsuccessful for the child. The IDEIA should provide that a child with a disability does not "need" special education until all services, accommodations and pre-referral interventions available in the school district have been tried and proven unsuccessful. In short, "teachers should attempt a variety of educational strategies to reach students who are struggling academically or socially before referring them for special education evaluation."[349] Requiring districts and teachers to employ all available services, interventions and pre-referral measures will force districts to maximize regular education interventions before relying on potentially damaging special education placements.

---

in the regular education program, particularly with the modifications (including continued regular education guidance services) offered by Wellesley").

345. 34 C.F.R. Part 300, App. A at 106 (2002) ("Because many students receiving services under IDEA will also receive services under the Rehabilitation Act, it is important, in planning for their future, to consider the impact of both statutes"); Letter to Lillie/Felton, 23 IDELR 714, 719 (OSEP 1994) ("Generally, it would be appropriate for the evaluation team to consider information about outside or extra learning support provided to the child … as such information may indicate that the child's current educational achievement reflects the service augmentation, not what the child's achievement would be without such help").

346. For a discussion of these cases, *see* Garda, *supra* note 14, at 493–98.

347. IDEIA, H.R. 1350, 108th Cong § 203(a)(2)(4) and (f) (2003); H.R. Rep. No. 108-77 at 137 and 157 (2002) ("The eligibility for special education services would focus on the children who, even with these services, are not able to be successful").

348. *See* Garda, *supra* note 14, at 491–512.

349. Parrish, *supra* note 9, at 16.

The advantages to requiring exhaustion of regular education interventions before eligibility attaches are significant. It will assist in reducing African American overrepresentation in special education by ensuring that these students get all the educational
supports the district has to offer prior to referral. It will also reduce bias, particularly referral bias, by prohibiting teachers from dumping African American students into special
education without first providing all accommodations and supports that are available to
general education students. Teachers will be required to exhaust all available proper instructional methods for "problem" children, leading to improved general education for
all. By using a variety of teaching measures in the general education classroom, rather
than a one-size-fits-all approach, referral to special education will be prevented.[350]

State hegemony over educational methodology is maintained because districts are not
forced to develop and create pre-referral intervention services (except in the case of significant disproportionality); rather, only all *available* services must be provided. The proposed definition of "need" does not alter the general education model; it merely ensures
that districts essentially "try their best" with what they have available before referring a
child to special education, which is not the current practice.

The IDEIA's provisions permitting federal funds to be used to develop pre-referral
intervention services and to train teachers should certainly be retained because much
more is known about effective interventions than is implemented in classrooms, and
this disparity negatively impacts minorities.[351] The most prevalent reasons African
Americans are referred to special education are for behavior and reading. The lack of
appropriate reading instruction and early reading interventions contributes to the
overrepresentation of African Americans in high-incidence disability categories of MR,
ED, and, in some states, SLD.[352] Appropriate general education interventions have been
shown to significantly raise African Americans' achievement.[353] Indeed, "a key factor
in addressing disproportion in special education is support for minority student achievement in general education," and mandatory pre-referral measures ensure appropriate
support.[354] One example is the use of the Rightstart method of math instruction, a
general education intervention that has shown to assist disadvantaged students.[355]

Supplemental reading instruction has also been shown to assist minorities with reading
difficulty. Proper reading instruction can solve a continuum of reading problems present in
regular education, and minority students will be the most benefited.[356] Tutoring also has
been found to have a major impact on reading ability.[357] With the appropriate reading instruction
tailored to each child provided in the general classroom, minority overrepresentation should
be dramatically curbed.[358] The International Reading Association summarized the solution:

> If quality instruction combined with timely and appropriately intense reading in-
> terventions does not solve the reading problem that is the source of the referral,
> then it is time to consider alternative programs such as special education. If edu-
> cators deliver excellent reading instruction to children before considering a special

---

350. Milloy, *supra* note 6.

351. NRC Report, *supra* note 8, at 337.

352. A Position Statement of the International Reading Association, *supra* note 38.

353. NRC Report, *supra* note 8, at 188.

354. *Id.* at 5.

355. *Id.* at 190.

356. *Id.* at 191.

357. *Id.* at 193–94.

358. A Position Statement of the International Reading Association, *supra* note 38; NRC Report,
supra note 8, at 194, 324–25.

education placement, they will identify more of the children for whom special education is truly appropriate. If children are identified correctly, the proportions of minority children in special education in the United States most likely will reflect the proportions of minority children in the general school population, and the risk of being placed in special education will be similar for children of all racial and ethnic categories.

Many pre-referral regular interventions are also effective for children with behavior problems. Social skills instruction, classroom reinforcement systems, peer tutoring and parent support are known to significantly decrease problem behaviors in the classroom and prevent referral for emotional disturbances.[359] The use of technical assistance teams that assist general education teachers deal with behavior problems also have been shown to reduce referral based on poor behavior.[360] However, "the generally inappropriate application of regular education support services to students of color" results in African American overrepresentation in the SED disability category.[361]

In sum, general education interventions in reading and behavior management reduce the number of children who fail at reading or are later identified with behavior disorders.[362] There are numerous general education interventions available for children that could prevent their referral for eligibility.[363] These interventions are the accommodations and minor modifications that should be excluded from the definition of "special education." Yet these modifications are not always employed before referring a child to special education.

These interventions, if available within the school district, must be mandatory rather than permissive and must be included in the IDEIA's eligibility criteria.[364] Requiring all available in-class supports will not only decrease referral for special education but improve the performance of all students.[365]

In summary, requiring schools and teachers to exhaust all available general education services, supports and accommodations prior to finding a child in "need" of special education will ensure that IDEIA eligibility and special education is reserved to "those who truly require them and can benefit from them."[366] The strict definition will reserve eligibility for high-need children, the primary concern of the IDEIA, and prevent low-need children from displacing or draining resources from those truly in need.[367]

Conclusion

Congress should be applauded for seriously addressing for the first time the overrepresentation of African Americans in special education and its spiraling eligibility rolls. But a standing ovation is not warranted, as the piecemeal and incremental solutions pro-

---

359. NRC REPORT, *supra* note 8, at 201–204; Osher et al., *supra* note 47, at 105–106.

360. NRC REPORT, *supra* note 8, at 199.

361. Osher et al., *supra* note 47, at 108–109.

362. NRC REPORT, *supra* note 8, at 7.

363. NRC REPORT, *supra* note 8, at 142–44, 329–33.

364. *See, e.g.,* Osher et al., *supra* note 47, at 105–106 (arguing that schools should provide necessary supports in general education to prevent overidentification in the SED category).

365. Hehir, *supra* note 17, at 236.

366. COMMITTEE ON MINORITY REPRESENTATION IN SPECIAL EDUCATION OF THE NATIONAL RESEARCH COUNCIL, MINORITY STUDENTS IN SPECIAL AND GIFTED EDUCATION, 3 (2002).

367. PRESIDENT'S COMMISSION, *supra* note 10, at 30.

posed in the IDEIA will prove inadequate. The revolutionary concept embodied in the IDEIA of essentially "fixing" special education by reaching into general education is the inevitable and necessary future of American schools. The IDEIA recognizes that general education's identity must be changed to remedy special education's dual eligibility crisis, yet Congress incompletely adopts its new educational paradigm, and minority overrepresentation and the rise in overall eligible children will persist.

Altering special education eligibility requirements as proposed in this chapter is not the sole solution to minority overrepresentation and the rise in overall eligibility, but it is a prerequisite to any viable solution. Professor Artiles was not exaggerating when he concluded that African American overrepresentation is one "of the most important developments in special education's contemporary history" and will transform its identity.[368] The transformation must entail carving out certain specialized instruction from the definition of "special education" so that all students, not just eligible students, can have their diverse and individualized needs met in the general education classroom without suffering the harms of misidentification as IDEIA eligible. The emerging educational paradigm of specialized instruction for all students cannot entrench itself in today's schools until special education relinquishes its stranglehold on individualized instruction.

Yet merely changing the IDEIA's eligibility criteria alone will not resolve the dual eligibility crisis. Mandating action does not guarantee its implementation, as best exemplified by fifty-year-old struggle to fulfill the desegregation mandate of *Brown v. Board of Education.* It is one thing to legislatively reserve IDEIA eligibility only for children who need significant modification to content, method or delivery and who have been provided all available pre-referral interventions, yet quite another for the standard to be applied in all eligibility determinations. Mere legislative change cannot, by itself, remove engrained cultural bias. But changing the eligibility criteria would have a "vast influence on how disabilities are conceptualized and assessed for special education eligibility."[369]

For the changes suggested in this chapter to be effective, the funding formula of the IDEIA likely needs to be revisited. The IDEIA and its successors are funding statutes wherein the federal government essentially covers a portion of the state's costs to educate eligible children.[370] Because the amount of special education funds a state receives from the federal government hinges on the number of eligible children within the state,[371] there is an incentive to overidentify students as eligible.[372] There is also a strong disincentive to provide students with pre-referral intervention services because there is no separate fund-

---

368. Alfredo J. Artiles, *Special Education's Changing Identity: Paradoxes and Dilemmas in Views of Cultures and Spaces*, 7/1/03 Harv. Educ. Rev. 247, 2003 WL 55851226 (2003).

369. NRC Report, *supra* note 8, at 224. *See also id.* at 270 (legal eligibility standards "heavily influence" eligibility determinations).

370. IDEIA, H.R. 1350, 108th Cong. § 101, amending § 611; 20 U.S.C. § 1411(a)(2) (1997). The maximum state grant is determined by multiplying the number of eligible children served by the state times 40 percent of the national average per pupil expenditure. For an explanation of the funding formula, see Theresa M. Willard, Note, *Economics and the Individuals with Disabilities Education Act: The Influence of Funding Formulas on the Identification and Placement of Disabled Students*, 31 Ind. L. Rev. 1167, 1179–81 (1998).

371. IDEIA, H.R. 1350 § 201(a), amending § 611; 20 U.S.C. § 1411(a) (1997). Most states also divide IDEA monies among its school districts based on how many IDEA eligible children they are serving. Willard, *supra* note 372, at 1179–81.

372. Parrish, *supra* note 9, at 28–31; Mark Weber, Special Education Law and Litigation Treatise, Chapter 18 (LRP 2002); H.R. Rep. No. 105-95 at 89 (1997) (concluding that many problems of overidentification result from IDEA's current child-count based funding system that "reduces the proactive scrutiny that such referrals would receive if they did not have the additional monetary benefit"); Marc S. Krass, *The Right to Public Education for Handicapped Children: A Primer for the New*

ing for such services. The financial incentive is for districts to classify a child as IDEIA el-igible—which brings funding to the district—rather than provide unfunded pre-refer-ral interventions to prevent eligibility. To eliminate this incentive and encourage the use of early intervention services in general education, state and district funding should hinge on the overall number of children in public schools rather than on the number of eligi-ble children. With this funding division, states and districts will more willingly apply the 15 percent of IDEIA funds to pre-referral intervention services rather than find children eligible to increase their funding.

Furthermore, Congress must continue to encourage, and fund, effective scientifi-cally based pre-referral intervention strategies. All schools must be provided the neces-sary resources to train general education teachers to effectively instruct today's diverse learners, using sound, scientifically based methods. School districts and teachers will not be able to implement appropriate pre-referral measures without knowledge of such measures, and training on how they are implemented. Neither can occur without full funding of the IDEIA, which has yet to occur.[373] As Senator Jeffords concluded, suc-cessfully addressing special education's eligibility problems "will require an infusion of funding for higher quality teaching in both general and special education."[374] Congress and the president have refused full funding of the IDEIA, however, until the eligibility problems identified in this chapter are resolved.[375] Congress must recognize that it is only with full funding that African American disproportionality and the overall eligibility increase can be remedied.

Advocate, 1976 U. Ill. L.F. 1016, 1066 (describing how the funding formula creates incentives to serve more children); Tara L. Eyer, Comment, *Greater Expectations: How the 1997 IDEA Amendments Raise the Basic Floor of Opportunity for Children with Disabilities,* 103 Dick L. Rev. 613, 627 (1998). *But see* H.R. Rep. No. 108-77 at 143 (2002) (stating that "the Committee does not believe that individual ed-ucators identify children in order to maximize the level of funds that flow to the school, district, or state").

373. Jeffords, *supra* note 7, at x (the federal government funds only 17 percent of special educa-tion costs); Hehir, *supra* note 17, at 228 (the federal government funds only 13 percent of the excess costs to educate an eligible child).

374. Jeffords, *Foreword, supra* note 7, at ix.

375. Losen and Orfield, *supra* note 55, at xviii.

19

Achieving the Promise: The Significant Role of Highly Qualified Teachers in Transforming Children's Mental Health in America

Deann Lechtenberger and Frank Mullins

According to the U.S. Department of Education, during the 2001–2002 school year, 476,908 American children and youth attending public schools received special services under the category of serious emotional disturbance (SED), which is also referred to as emotional behavioral disorders (EBD).[1] It has been estimated that there are as many as nine million children across the United States who have been labeled SED.[2] According to the Surgeon General's Office of the United States, this estimate is destined to rise sharply within the next fifty years as the number of children and youth with mental health disorders climbs from 20 percent to nearly 50 percent.[3]

Recent high school graduation rates for students with disabilities point to improvement for most students with disabilities; however, students identified with EBD still rank among the lowest in graduation rates and highest in dropout rates across disability groups.[4] Without appropriate interventions that support the development of the academic and social skills necessary for successful transition into adulthood, many students with EBD who drop out will eventually become statistical data in the correctional or welfare systems.[5] It has been reported that over 20 percent of youth in juvenile correctional facili-

---

1. U.S. Dep't of Educ., Twenty-fifth Annual Report to Congress on the Implementation of the Individuals with Disabilities Education Act (2003).

2. Robert M. Friedman et al., *Prevalence of Serious Emotional Disturbance in Children and Adolescence, in* Mental Health, United States, 1996, at 71–88 (Robert W. Manderscheid & M.A. Sonnerschein eds., Center for Mental Health Services 1996).

3. U.S. Dep't of Health & Human Services, Mental Health: A Report of the Surgeon General-Executive Summary (1999).

4. U.S. Dep't of Educ., No Child Left Behind: A Toolkit for Teachers (2004); U.S. Dep't of Educ., Twenty-third Annual Report to Congress on the Implementation of the Individuals with Disabilities Act (2001); U.S. Dep't of Educ., National Agenda for Achieving Better Results for Children and Youth with Serious Emotional Disturbance (1994).

5. Jay & Padilla, Special Education Dropouts (SRI International 1987); U.S. Dep't of Educ., National Agenda for Achieving Better Results for Children and Youth with Serious Emotional Disturbance (1994).

Table 1. Disease Burden by Selected Illness Categories in Established Market Economies

Percent of Total DALYs*

All cardiovascular conditions	18.6
All mental illness**	15.4
All malignant disease (cancer)	15.0
All respiratory conditions	4.8
All alcohol use	4.7
All infectious and parasitic disease	2.8
All drug use	1.5

Source: The U.S. Surgeon General's Report on Mental Health, 1999.
 * Disability-adjusted life year (DALY) is a measure that expresses years of life lost to premature death and years lived with a disability of specified severity and duration. Murray, C and Lopez, A. (1996) *The Global Burden of Disease*, Cambridge, MA: Harvard University Press.
** Disease burden associated with mental illness includes suicide.

ties have been identified as having EBD.[6] Youth with EBD are almost four times as likely to be arrested before completing school as their peers. Reports estimate that these young people have a 58 percent chance of being arrested within five years of high school graduation; however, this number escalates to a 73 percent chance if they drop out of school.[7]

In 1999, the U.S. Surgeon General's Report on Mental Health reported that in economically developed countries, such as the United States, mental illness is the second leading cause of disability and premature death. According to this same report, mental health disorders are collectively responsible for more than 15 percent of the burden of disease from *all* causes and slightly more than the burden associated with all forms of cancer (see Table 1).

A year later, the U.S. Surgeon General's Report on Children's Mental Health (2000) reported that during any given year, one out of five children and adolescents in the United States experience the signs and symptoms of a diagnosable mental health disorder.[8] This translates to roughly four million American young people with significant emotional and behavioral disorders that severely disrupt their daily lives and the lives of their families. This same report noted that two-thirds of these young people do not receive the appropriate supports and services they need to address their mental health needs to lead healthy, productive lives in their communities.

On review of this dismal data, educators must face the fact that today's public school classrooms need to provide positive learning environments and other emotional supports for all students to ensure that they receive a quality education, especially students with emotional and behavioral disorders (EBD). With the passage and implementation of recent legislation (i.e., No Child Left Behind Act of 2001(NCLB) and the Individuals with Dis-

---

6. Open Society Institute's Center for Crime, Communities and Culture & The National Gains Center for People in Contact with the Justice System (SAMHSA Cooperative Agreement), The Courage to Change: A Guide for Communities to Create Integrated Services for People with Co-occuring Disorders in the Justice System (2000).

7. U.S. Dep't of Educ., National Agenda for Achieving Better Results for Children and Youth with Serious Emotional Disturbance (1994).

8. U.S. Dep't of Health & Human Services, Report of the Surgeon General on Children's Mental Health: A National Action Agenda (2000).

abilities Education Improvement Act of 2004 (IDEIA)), increased academic standards, and the accompanying challenges of high stakes testing requirements, highly pressurized learning environments have resulted in today's public schools for most students as well as their teachers.[9] Standardized state testing and reported outcome scores have become the priorities of school districts across the nation due to the passage of the NCLB, a federal initiative to improve academic outcomes for all students in U.S. public schools.[10]

The IDEIA Amendments of 2004 amend the Individuals with Disabilities Education Act (IDEA) and add a reference to NCLB[11] that requires all students with disabilities be included in all general state- and district-wide assessment programs with appropriate accommodations and alternate assessments where necessary and as indicated in their respective individualized education programs (IEPs).[12] NCLB and IDEIA require that educational leaders—including teachers and administrators from local, state, and federal education agencies—step up and be held accountable for students who are not typically held to higher standards and are often less successful in academic settings.[13]

Efforts to address these priorities by school personnel are ultimately designed to decrease student drop-out rates, improve school discipline and classroom behavior management, as well as to meet Annual Yearly Performance (AYP) requirements for student progress. Unfortunately, the additional pressure on students may lead to more acting out behavior and an increase in some students becoming depressed or overwhelmed as they work to keep pace with these current educational demands. These stressors may be especially taxing for students with EBD and can cause other students to become more susceptible to being at risk for emotional or behavioral problems.

In addition to the students feeling overwhelmed by the increase of high stakes testing, school personnel also feel the strains of these increased accountability measures. Teachers, principals, and other school staff spend inordinate amounts of time drilling and practicing for these standardized tests due to the highly publicized results of testing on individual school campuses and the pressure that this public scrutiny imposes. Often, school subjects such as art, music, physical education, science, and other more interactive courses are dismissed and replaced with practice tests and computerized worksheets in an effort to boost school test scores. School administrators sponsor pep rallies, free McDonald's breakfasts, and other gimmicks or prizes to invigorate faculty and the student body to work hard on these exams. High stakes testing takes on a whole new meaning once all these activities are taken into account. The emotional stress on teachers, administrators, and students is evident if one visits most local public school campuses during these testing periods each year.

University preservice teacher education programs provide little, if any, training for preservice teachers and administrators in the area of children's mental health, much less in how to recognize the early symptoms of a mental health disorder in children or adolescents. An

---

9. See Individuals with Disabilities Education Improvement Act of 2004, Pub. L. No. 108-446, 118 Stat. 2647 (codified as amended at 20 U.S.C. §§ 1400 to 1482, 9567 to 9567b (Supp. I 2004)) (amending Individuals with Disabilities Education Act, Pub. L. No. 110-131, 84 Stat. 175, 175–88 (1970) (codified as amended at 20 U.S.C. §§ 1400 to 1482 (2000)); No Child Left Behind Act of 2001, Pub. L. No. 107-110, 15 Stat. 1425 (codified as amended in scattered sections of 20 U.S.C.).

10. *See, e.g.,* U.S. Dep't of Educ., No Child Left Behind: A Toolkit for Teachers (2004).

11. Individuals with Disabilities Education Improvement Act of 2004, Pub. L. No. 108-446, § 101, 118 Stat. 2647 (codified as amended at 20 U.S.C. § 1412 (Supp. I 2004)).

12. 20 U.S.C. § 1412(a)(3)–(4) (Supp. I 2004).

13. Margaret E. Goertz, *Implementing the No Child Left Behind Act: Challenges for the States*, 80 Peabody J. Educ. 73, 76–77 n.2 (2005).

urgent need exists for all teachers and school administrators to become more informed about children's mental health, as well as the treatment resources available in local communities to support students with EBD and their families. University teacher preparation programs must take the lead in working to produce highly qualified personnel who will graduate with the skills and knowledge base to recognize and understand the importance of children's mental health for all students. With appropriate training, these highly qualified and trained educators can create positive, stable learning environments that promote better mental health for all students and reduce the number of students who may become at risk for exhibiting emotional and behavioral problems. As educators become more collaborative partners with families and communities to support children's mental health, fewer students should have to wait until they have a crisis to receive the services and supports they will need. Hopefully, as a result, schools, families, and communities can become more proactive with all students and less reactive to those students who may develop emotional or behavioral problems.

A number of effective behavioral, psychosocial, and pharmacological treatments exist for many mental health disorders such as attention deficit/hyperactivity disorder, depression, and anxiety disorders; however, families and school personnel are often unaware of or skeptical of these treatments. Many families fear dispensing psychotropic medications to their children because of the possible side effects as well as the lack of empirical evidence examining the long-term effects of these drugs on physical and emotional development in children. Many of these pharmacological treatments have not been adjusted for children because they were developed for the adult population.

Early intervention with children at risk for EBD provides promising results if treatment is provided to these children and if their families are engaged and supported during treatment. Primary health care facilities and schools are prime settings for possible early screening, early identification, and early mental health interventions for children with EBD. Because families frequent such facilities with their young children—especially primary care physicians, pediatricians, child care facilities, and elementary schools—young children could be easily screened for early warning signs of emotional and behavioral concerns. Unfortunately, there is a shortage of competently trained personnel, especially on school campuses and child care centers where these assessments would be the most beneficial.

Addressing Current Issues

In 2003, the President's New Freedom Commission on Mental Health released a report titled, *Achieving the Promise: Transforming Mental Health Care in America* as a response to the 1999 U.S. Surgeon General's Report on Mental Health and the 2000 U.S. Surgeon General's Report on Children's Mental Health.[14] This new report set forth six goals to promote American citizens' living happy, healthy lives in their communities (see Table 2). These six goals address the mental health needs of all children and adolescents as well as their families. Only as these recommendations become reality throughout state and

---

14. New Freedom Commission on Mental Health, Achieving the Promise: Transforming Mental Health Care in America, Final Report (2003); *see also* U.S. Dep't of Health & Human Services, Report of the Surgeon General on Children's Mental Health: A National Action Agenda (2000); U.S. Dep't of Health & Human Services, Mental Health: A Report of the Surgeon General—Executive Summary (1999).

Table 2. The President's New Freedom Commission on Mental Health: Goals and Recommendations

Goal 1: Americans Understand that Mental Health Is Essential to Overall Health.
- Advance and implement a national campaign to reduce the stigma of seeking care and a national strategy for suicide prevention.
- Address mental health with the same urgency as physical health.

Goal 2: Mental Health Care Is Consumer and Family Driven.
- Develop an individualized plan of care for every adult with a serious mental illness and child with a serious emotional disturbance.
- Involve consumers and families fully in orienting the mental health system toward recovery.
- Align relevant federal programs to improve access and accountability for mental health services.
- Create comprehensive state mental health plans.
- Protect and enhance the rights of people with mental illnesses.

Goal 3: Disparities in Mental Health Services Are Eliminated.
- Improve access to quality care that is culturally competent.
- Improve access to quality care in rural and geographically remote areas.

Goal 4: Early Mental Health Screening, Assessment, and Referral to Services Are Common Practice.
- Promote the mental health of young children.
- Improve and expand school mental health programs.
- Screen for co-occurring mental and substance use disorders and link with integrated treatment strategies.
- Screen for mental disorders in primary health care, across the life span, and connect to treatment and supports.

Goal 5: Excellent Mental Health Care Is Delivered and Research Is Accelerated.
- Accelerate research to promote recovery and resilience, and ultimately to cure and prevent mental illnesses.
- Advance evidence-based practices using dissemination and demonstration projects and create a public-private partnership to guide their implementation.
- Improve and expand the workforce providing evidence-based mental health services and supports.
- Develop the knowledge base in four understudied areas: mental health disparities, long-term effects of medications, trauma, and acute care.

Goal 6: Technology Is Used to Access Mental Health Care and Information.
- Use health technology and telehealth to improve access and coordination of mental health care, especially for Americans in remote areas or in underserved populations.
- Develop and implement integrated electronic health record and personal health information systems.

---

federal human service systems, including the nation's educational systems, can our country fulfill the promise of a transformed mental health care delivery system that can proactively support healthy children, families, and communities. Too often schools, universities, and other systems are reactive in nature and wait for a wake-up call such as the highly publicized campus shootings at Virginia Tech and Columbine High School before they begin to address the mental health needs of students and their communities. If teacher education programs would study and teach students how to implement and support these six goals in our local school campuses and in our communities, they could provide the leadership and guidance that could lead to better academic outcomes as well as emotional development for all children and adolescents, thereby reducing the need for more costly and intensive interventions (i.e., out-of-home placements, incarceration, and foster care).

The goals of the New Freedom Commission on Mental Health provide guiding principles that could be easily incorporated into preservice teacher and school administrator training programs and used to address and outline the skills that highly qualified teachers will need to teach America's students. Schools are an obvious venue to address child and adolescent mental health needs, in as much as young people spend a majority of their waking hours at school or involved in school-related activities. State education agencies and local school districts are working to incorporate the major provisions of NCLB.[15] It is imperative that university teacher preparation programs partner with state and local education agencies to address the training, recruitment, and retention of highly qualified teachers for every American classroom, which should include information on children's mental health as a part of teacher training curricula.

The significant question for teacher educators now becomes, "How could teacher preparation programs take a leadership role in this vital mission to support the mental health of all students, their families, and the professionals who serve and support them?" Teacher preparation programs can play an essential role in disseminating information on children's mental health and designing curricula that teach the skills necessary for promoting good mental health in schools to preservice and in-service professionals from diverse backgrounds and disciplines. Our system of public education is responsible for educating all students, including students with disabilities. Only when special education and general education work together can we be confident that *no child will be left behind* and that all of America's children and youth will have the equal opportunity to receive a quality education that prepares them for a productive and happy future.

Guidelines for Achieving the Promise

The following guidelines provide a roadmap for redesigning coursework and training preservice teacher and school administrator preparation programs for future school faculty and administrators. These guidelines can strengthen the skills of educators to work within education systems as they partner with other community agencies and human service organizations who can provide the expertise, skills, and mental health resources and linkages for children and families to be healthy and successful.

Guideline 1: Strengthen and Expand the Role of Schools in Promoting Social and Emotional Well-Being for All Students

Preservice teacher education programs need to build into their curricula an awareness of children's mental health and its impact on student social emotional development and academic achievement. Schools have a definitive role in promoting social and emotional well-being for all students, faculty, and staff. Teachers, administrators, school staff, and families need to be well informed about children's mental health and about why it is important to the overall healthy development of children. Most in our society think of mental illness only when they see dramatic headlines in the paper or

---

15. U.S. Dep't of Educ., No Child Left Behind: A Toolkit for Teachers (2004).

on the news; however, school personnel need training that will assist them in identifying the early warning signs of emotional and behavioral problems, know how to make appropriate referrals for assessment and services, and promote safe and supportive learning environments at school for all children and adolescents, as well as the school faculty and staff.

Positive Behavior Supports (PBS) is a scientifically based approach that promotes building a safe and secure "host" environment for all students and school personnel.[16] PBS provides interventions resulting from social, behavioral, and biomedical sciences that can be applied at the individual, classroom, and school level to achieve reductions in problem student behavior and improved quality of life.[17] PBS works to change both adult and student behaviors to support a positive learning environment where students can connect, contribute, and be successful. Such a positive learning environment provides the foundation for more instructional time for teachers to teach and students to learn, and supports good mental health outcomes aligned with the report from the President's New Freedom Commission on Mental Health.[18] As more educators are trained and become implementers of this evidence-based practice, schools can take the lead in meeting the needs of students with EBD and their families.

Guideline 2: Expand Prevention and Early Intervention Programs in Schools

School personnel need to understand how to proactively design, develop, and expand prevention and early intervention guidelines that address student behavior through the use of PBS. In the three-tiered PBS model, behavior is addressed at the school-wide level, in the classroom, and on an individual student basis (see Figure 1). Implementation of this model promotes a school-based leadership team approach that supports school personnel in a problem-solving process to create healthy and supportive school environments for all students and their families, as well as school personnel. This model promotes a proactive response that includes partnering with families, mental health professionals, and other community resources as central elements in redesigning school environments.

PBS has demonstrated its effectiveness in reducing discipline problems in schools across the country. Schools implementing this three-tiered PBS model have reported

- decreases in the number of expulsions, suspensions, and detentions throughout the school year, decreases that have been correlated with an increase in standardized achievement test scores;[19]

---

16. *See generally* George Sugai & Robert H. Horner, *The Evolution of Discipline Practices: School-Wide Positive Behavior Supports*, 24 CHILD & FAMILY BEHAVIOR THERAPY 23, 23–50 (2002); George Sugai & Robert H. Horner, *Features of Effective Behavior Support at the District Level*, 11(1) BEYOND BEHAVIOR 16, 16–19 (2001); Robert H. Horner & George Sugai, *School-Wide Behavior Support: An Emerging Initiative*, 2 JOURNAL OF POSITIVE BEHAVIORAL INTERVENTIONS 231, 231–33 (2000); George Sugai & Robert H. Horner, *Discipline and Behavioral Support: Preferred Processes and Practices*, 17(4) EFFECTIVE SCHOOL PRACTICES 10, 10–22 (1999).

17. Tim Knoster et al., *Emerging Challenges and Opportunities: Introducing the Association for Positive Behavior Support*, 5(3) JOURNAL OF POSITIVE BEHAVIOR INTERVENTIONS 183, 183–86 (2003).

18. NEW FREEDOM COMMISSION ON MENTAL HEALTH, ACHIEVING THE PROMISE: TRANSFORMING MENTAL HEALTH CARE IN AMERICA, FINAL REPORT (2003).

19. Terrance M. Scott, *Positive Behavioral Support: A School-Wide Example*, 3(2) JOURNAL OF POSITIVE BEHAVIORAL INTERVENTIONS 88, 88–94 (2001).

Figure 1. Designing a Community School-Wide System for Student Success

Academic Systems		Behavioral Systems

Intensive Individual ↔ **Intensive** ↔ **Intensive Individual**
Individual students (High-Risk Social skills teaching
Assessment-based Students) Individual behavior intervention plans
High intensity Individual Parent training and collaboration
Interventions Multiagency collaboration
(1–5% Students) (wraparound)

Targeted Group Intervention ↔ **Targeted Group** ↔ **Targeted Group Intervention**
Some students (at risk) **Interventions** Intensive social skills teaching
High efficiency (At-Risk Students) Self-management programs
Rapid response Classroom and Small Group Adult mentors (check in)
Strategies Increased academic support
(5–10% Students) Classroom management
strategies

Universal ↔ **Universal** ↔ **Universal**
Interventions (All Students) **Interventions**
School-wide School-Wide Systems of Support Social skills teaching
All students (80–90% of Students) Positive discipline
Preventive Teaching school
Proactive behavior
expectations

FAMILIES AT EACH LEVEL

System of Care and School-Based Wraparound Planning
Mary Margaret Salls
May 2003

- increases in standardized achievement test scores as a result of a decrease in the number of behavior problems;[20]
- reductions in the number of office referrals for behavior problems, with lower levels maintaining across school years;[21]
- reductions in the number of observed behavior problems on playgrounds.[22]

Although PBS training is commonly delivered through in-service and other professional development opportunities for existing school personnel, many university preservice teacher education programs have identified PBS as an evidence-based practice

20. Susan J. Taylor-Green & Douglas T. Kartub, *Durable Implementation of School-Wide Behavior Support: The High Five Program*, 2(4) Journal of Positive Behavior Interventions 233, 233–45 (2000); Susan J. Taylor-Green et al., *School-Wide Behavioral Support: Starting the Year Off Right*, 7 Journal of Behavioral Education 99, 99–112 (1997).

21. Susan J. Taylor-Green & Douglas T. Kartub, *Durable Implementation of School-Wide Behavior Support: The High Five Program*, 2(4) Journal of Positive Behavior Interventions 233, 233–45 (2000); Susan J. Taylor-Green et al., *School-Wide Behavioral Support: Starting the Year Off Right*, 7 Journal of Behavioral Education 99, 99–112 (1997).

22. Timothy J. Lewis, Lisa J. Powers, Michele J. Kely, & Lori L. Newcomer, *Reducing Problem Behaviors on the Playground: An Investigation of the Application of School-Wide Positive Behavior Supports*, 39 Psychology in the Schools 181, 181–90 (2002).

and have begun to provide this training to preservice educators to prepare new teachers in using PBS to address behavior in their future classrooms. The South Plains region of West Texas is providing an example of how this approach can work. Through the combined efforts of the College of Education at Texas Tech University; local school districts; and the Education Service Center, Region XVII, a collaborative PBS implementation model has been developed that includes partners such as the Texas Education Agency, the Texas Council for Developmental Disabilities, local school districts, human services providers, as well as families of children with disabilities. To date, over 500 pre-service teachers have been introduced to the PBS model through the preservice teacher education program at Texas Tech University. Additional professional development training offered through the Education Service Center, Region XVII, has also reached teachers and school administrators through in-service training in over thirty school campuses in west Texas. Although this collaborative PBS implementation model is still in its infancy, it builds on the expertise and experiences of families and community-based service providers, along with local business and community leaders who can mentor, coach, and provide other supports to students and school leadership teams as they begin to implement PBS on individual school campuses.

Just as educators have begun to learn how to work collaboratively with families, mental health professionals, and other human services staff who traditionally have not worked on school campuses, these outside resource personnel will also need to become more familiar with how to work in schools. University preservice teacher education programs can build this type of preparation into their curricula to produce graduates that are ready to work collaboratively with a variety of human service personnel and families. Additional orientation and training on how to collaborate with school-based personnel will also need to be made available to human services personnel such as social workers, mental health counselors, health providers, and juvenile probation officers.

Guideline 3: Support School-Based Mental Health Resources for Students, Families, and Professionals

The establishment of school-based mental health programs as well as other community collaboratives can also bring a wealth of resources to local school campuses. Preservice teacher education programs can prepare future teachers to work in true collaborative arrangements with a variety of community stakeholders and families by helping teachers and school administrators understand the mandates, timelines, and overall missions of other public human service agencies. This type of information is critical and could be easily incorporated into the general and special education teacher preparation curricula, including field experiences in schools as well as in community human services agencies (such as mental health centers, juvenile). Furthermore, curricula that address families as equal partners in child and adolescent academic and social/emotional development are consistent with the goals of the New Freedom Commission on Mental Health report and will strengthen any school plans to address children's emotional and academic development.[23] These collaborations would produce essential skills that preservice preparation

---

23. New Freedom Commission on Mental Health, Achieving the Promise: Transforming Mental Health Care in America, Final Report (2003).

programs need to address in their efforts to prepare highly qualified teachers and school administrators as mandated by NCLB and IDEIA.[24]

School-based mental health settings can provide students and their families access to mental health resources in a familiar, emotionally safe environment. These on-campus settings also promote a better understanding between school and mental health personnel by allowing mental health professionals to work with children and families in a more natural context. For example, on-campus mental health facilities would be especially helpful when monitoring the effects of specific drug or behavioral therapies and can provide immediate feedback to parents, teachers, and clinicians as changes do or do not occur in a student's ability to successfully navigate the school and the extended community. Having such facilities available would also allow students, teachers, and families to have more access to mental health services and supports without the usual stigma of going to a traditional mental health clinic or provider's office.

As schools incorporate mental health professionals into local schools, more resources can become available to students who might not otherwise have access behavioral health services and supports. The school faculty and staff would also benefit from school-based mental health resources. Teaching in today's public schools is often extremely stressful due to lack of fiscal resources, increased academic accountability, excessive high-stakes testing, ever-changing curriculum demands, overcrowded classrooms, shifting demographics, and student misbehavior. Having mental health professionals located on school campuses would provide valuable supports to school staff and teachers. Professional development delivered by mental health professionals would also provide skill training on a variety of topics for school personnel, including how to distinguish between typical and problematic social-emotional development in students as well as what actions to take with students from either category.

Mental health personnel can also provide referrals that link families to other community programs and resources. Some mental health service providers have developed creative billing guidelines that can support their participation in parent conferences and student IEP meetings. This type of partnership can create a problem-solving team who can get a more holistic view of what is going on with a student who is experiencing difficulties in school, in the community, or at home. Utilizing this team approach can also enhance the recruitment and retention of quality teachers by providing supports and services that will help newly certified teachers survive their first years on the job and aid veteran teachers in avoiding professional burnout from working with students who are at risk for or who have been identified as EBD.

Guideline 4: Promote Partnerships Between School Personnel, Community Agencies, and Families

As a result of ongoing reauthorization of the IDEIA, schools have been challenged to develop partnerships with families of children with disabilities as well as with local com-

---

24. *See* No Child Left Behind Act of 2001, Pub. L. No. 107-110, 15 Stat. 1425 (codified as amended in scattered sections of 20 U.S.C.); Individuals with Disabilities Education Improvement Act of 2004, Pub. L. No. 108-446, 118 Stat. 2647 (codified as amended at 20 U.S.C. §§ 1400 to 1482, 9567 to 9567b (Supp. I 2004)).

munity organizations that serve children, youth, and families (such as public health and mental health agencies, Boys and Girls Clubs, 4-H Clubs, YMCAs/YWCAs). Such partnerships have become a necessity because current school and stand-alone community programs have historically fallen short of meeting the mental health needs of today's students. It has become increasingly apparent that no one system or program alone can meet these children's needs. To complicate matters further, students with EBD have historically received services that are often too little, too late, and too fragmented.[25] Collaborative community partnerships encourage better communication between the most important people in the lives of children and youth—family members, schools, and the community—thereby providing greater opportunities for better student outcomes.[26]

Family-school-community partnerships have been promoted through mental health and education systems through a number of federal legislative and policy reform movements. Federal legislative and policy changes clearly point to the intent of governmental leadership over the past thirty years to support and guarantee partnerships between the home, community, and school environments for students with disabilities. It is imperative that state education agencies and local district policies model the federal efforts to be more inclusive of families in their children's education.[27]

The New Freedom Commission and NCLB, as well as the 2004 reauthorization of IDEIA, all continue to promote, mandate, and ensure partnerships between families, schools, and community organizations and agencies on behalf of all children and youth.[28] Even with all of these efforts, families, school personnel, and others in the community must understand their roles and collective responsibilities to promote and ensure student success at school, at home, and in the community.

Partnering with families is an essential and mandated element for improving educational outcomes for children with disabilities. As the 21st Report to Congress on Implementation of Individuals with Disabilities Education Act emphasized, involving families in their children's education is a formidable factor that affects student learning and school

25. See Jo Webber & Brenda Scheuermann, *A Challenging Future: Current Barriers and Recommended Action for Our Field,* 22(3) BEHAVIORAL DISORDERS 167, 167–78 (1997); Jane Knitzer, Zina Steinberg, & Brahm Fleisch, AT THE SCHOOLHOUSE DOOR: AN EXAMINATION OF PROGRAMS AND POLICIES FOR CHILDREN WITH BEHAVIORAL AND EMOTIONAL PROBLEMS (Bank Street College of Education 1990); Jane Knitzer, UNCLAIMED CHILDREN (Children's Defense Fund 1990).

26. See DeAnn Lechtenberger & Frank E. Mullins, *Promoting Better Family-School-Community Partnerships for All of America's Children,* 14(1) BEYOND BEHAVIOR 17, 17–22 (2004);*see also* Susan Hodges, Teresa M. Nesman, & Mario Hernandez, *Promising Practices: Building Collaboration: Systems of Care, in* SYSTEMS OF CARE: PROMISING PRACTICES IN CHILDREN'S MENTAL HEALTH, 1998 Series, VOL. VI. (Center for Effective Collaboration and Practice, American Institutes for Research 1998); W.G. Anderson, FINDING HELP FINDING HOPE: A GUIDEBOOK TO SCHOOL SERVICES FOR FAMILIES WITH A CHILD WHO HAS EMOTIONAL, BEHAVIORAL, OR MENTAL DISORDERS (Federation of Families for Children's Mental Health 1994).

27. Diana B. Hiatt-Michael ed., PROMISING PRACTICES FOR FAMILY INVOLVEMENT IN SCHOOL (Information Age Publishing 2001); Joyce L. Epstein, SCHOOL, FAMILY AND COMMUNITY PARTNERSHIPS: PREPARING EDUCATORS AND IMPROVING SCHOOLS (Westview Press 2001); Darren W. Woodruff et al., *The Role of Education in Systems of Care: Effectively Serving Children with Emotional or Behavioral Disorders, in* SYSTEMS OF CARE: PROMISING PRACTICES IN CHILDREN'S MENTAL HEALTH, 1998 Series, VOL. III (Center for Effective Collaboration and Practice, American Institutes for Research 1998).

28. See No Child Left Behind Act of 2001, Pub. L. No. 107-110, 15 Stat. 1425 (codified as amended in scattered sections of 20 U.S.C.); Individuals with Disabilities Education Improvement Act of 2004, Pub. L. No. 108-446, 118 Stat. 2647 (codified as amended at 20 U.S.C. §§ 1400 to 1482, 9567 to 9567b (Supp. I 2004)); NEW FREEDOM COMMISSION ON MENTAL HEALTH, ACHIEVING THE PROMISE: TRANSFORMING MENTAL HEALTH CARE IN AMERICA, FINAL REPORT (2003).

performance.[29] Basic guidelines must be implemented through proven evidence-based practices to address the question we all need to ask ourselves: How can families, educators, and community leaders build and establish practical, everyday activities that make family partnerships with schools and communities less a matter of political rhetoric and more a matter of reality?

Guideline 5: Ensure State Special Education and Related Services Are Accessible for Children with Disabilities and Their Families Under IDEA

State educational agencies, universities, local school districts, and other policy-making entities need to improve existing services for all students, especially those students with the poorest academic outcomes (i.e., students with disabilities, students at risk of school failure, children from diverse backgrounds). In addition to strengthening existing programs and support, creative policy makers and program developers will need to identify the gaps in community-based services according to such variables as socioeconomic needs, diverse cultural identities and preferences, and equity across geographic regions.

Students with EBD have mental health needs and require a multidisciplinary team approach to support their success. Such an example exists with the Comprehensive Community Mental Health Services Program for Children and Their Families. This federally funded program provides grants and cooperative agreements to local communities from the U.S. Department of Health and Human Services, Substance Abuse and Mental Health Services Administration, Center for Mental Health Services, to meet the needs of an estimated 4.5 to 6.3 million American children identified as having serious mental health needs and their families.[30] This grant program supports the development of comprehensive, coordinated, community-based, and culturally competent systems of care for families who have children and adolescents with EBD.

The Comprehensive Community Mental Health Services Program for Children and Their Families was first authorized to provide funding support to states, communities, territories, Indian tribes, and tribal organizations in fiscal year 1993 by sections 561–565 of the Public Health Service Act.[31] In 2006, this grant program has funded a total of ninety-two grantees across the country and currently supports sixty-four active Systems of Care communities.[32]

---

29. U.S. Dept' of Educ., Twenty-First Annual Report to Congress on the Implementation of the Individuals with Disabilities Act (1994); *see also* DeAnn Lechtenberger & Frank E. Mullins, *Promoting Better Family-School-Community Partnerships for All of America's Children*, 14(1) Beyond Behavior 17, 17–22 (2004); Mary Margaret Salls, DeAnn Lechtenberger, & Laura Atkins, *Revolutionizing Education Through Positive Behavior Supports and the System of Care in Travis County, in* Newsletter of the Technical Assistance Partnership for Child and Family Mental Health (Feb. 2004).

30. U.S. Dep't of Health & Human Services, Comprehensive Community Mental Health Service Programs for Children and their Families, systemsofcare.gov/ResourceDir/ Comprehensivehom.aspx (last visited Jan. 28, 2008).

31. An Act to Amend the Public Health Services Act, Pub. L. No. 102-321, ch. 373, sec. 119, §§ 561–65, 106 Stat. 323, 329 (1992) (codified as amended at 42 U.S.C. §§ 290ff–290ff-5 (2000)).

32. U.S. Dep't of Health & Human Services, Comprehensive Community Mental Health Service Programs for Children and their Families, systemsofcare.gov/ResourceDir/ Comprehensivehom.aspx (last visited Jan. 28, 2008).

A system of care is defined as a partnership of service providers, families, teachers, and others who are associated with or care for children and adolescents with serious mental health issues. By bringing together these entities, a child and family team is created to develop an individualized service plan that builds on the unique strengths of each child and family. This multidisciplinary plan, also known as the wraparound planning process, is uniquely tailored for the targeted child and implemented in a way that is consistent with the family's culture and language.[33] The natural connection between Systems of Care and PBS is through the local community schools; therefore, interagency and cross-disciplinary training efforts can bridge these two strength-based reform initiatives to create communities and schools who can work together to support better outcomes for students with EBD.[34]

The wraparound planning process has proven to be an effective process for designing individualized service plans for children with EBD and their families. In the three-tiered PBS model (see Figure 1), the wraparound planning process is one guideline that can address the complex needs of students who fall into the top of the PBS triangle, which denotes the 3 to 5 percent of students who need intensive and individualized behavioral interventions. Wraparound is designed to support children and youth with complex needs and their families by (a) identifying what families really need, (b) building on child and family strengths, (c) utilizing both formal and informal supports, and (d) providing services that are flexible and individualized. Most students who fall within the top tier of the PBS triangle have exhausted traditional school programs and behavioral interventions. By bringing together the significant people in a student's life, the wraparound planning process can provide a multidisciplinary approach that will enhance the traditional school program for students who fall within the top tier of the PBS model.

Schools offer a more natural environment for implementing the wraparound planning process than other child serving systems (i.e., juvenile justice, child welfare) for a number of reasons. Schools were designed to serve children on average six to eight hours a day, five days a week; they are legally mandated to provide a free public education to all children in America, regardless of the children's abilities. Most important, schools are located in local communities and are organized to utilize public and private resources to promote academic achievement of children for their success in later life. A quality Wraparound plan can ensure the safety of the identified child and family, as well as school personnel and other students, by providing opportunities for the child to be successfully maintained at home, in school, and in the child's community. Schools cannot provide this level of intervention alone; but with this type of planning, additional human services providers and community agencies can support schools as they work to help these students have better academic outcomes and become more successful in life.

Final Thoughts

With strong community involvement and support, local schools provide a logical venue and a unique opportunity to bring students, families, educators, and other community

---

33. Sheila A. Pires, Building Systems of Care: A Primer (Georgetown University 2002); Beth A. Stroul & Robert Friedman, A System of Care for Children and Youth with Severe Emotional Disturbances (Georgetown University 1994).

34. Bazelon Center for Mental Health Law, Way to Go: School Success for Children with Mental Health Care Needs (2006).

members together to build collaborative partnerships that support equal opportunities for quality educational, recreational, and social opportunities for all children and their families. These kinds of partnerships provide the safety net that children need to feel safe and valued at home, in school, and in the community. Furthermore, this safety net can provide all children the opportunity to learn, live, and reach their potentials to lead happy, healthy, and productive lives. This safety net can assist in intervening early in a child's life and, therefore, also decrease the number of children who have or will become at risk for mental health issues and eventually be labeled EBD. A true transformation of service delivery systems would promote better outcomes for children through strengthened partnerships between families, education, mental health, and other human service providers.

The information provided in this chapter should encourage more conversations between leadership in higher education, state education agencies, local schools, families, and communities to achieve the promise—the promise to help all Americans live happy, healthy lives within their communities. It will take the entire community, including local school districts, to transform society's view and increase its understanding of mental health and its impact on all children and their families.

Voices from the Bottom of the Well: No Child Left Behind and the Allegory of Equitable Education as a Gateway to Crime and Delinquency

Geneva Brown and Susan Stuart

Introduction

One of the fundamental problems with the No Child Left Behind Act (NCLB) is its facade of equity that does not translate to equality. This aperture between equity and equality can have devastating outcomes for minority juveniles. The inherent weakness in NCLB is its one-size-fits-all theory of accountability and its reliance on high-stakes testing, neither of which addresses the true educational needs of minority groups. When this one-size-fits-all theory does not and cannot adapt to the needs of high-risk youth, it pushes them out of school and becomes the gateway to crime and delinquency. The contradiction between the intended impact of NCLB and the reality of educating African American males is just one example of how politically disconnected NCLB is from educational needs, and that contradiction serves as an allegory for the intended equities yet actual inequalities of minority education created by NCLB.

The impetus for this failure is that children drop out of school if they find the NCLB school environment does not meet their needs or are being pushed to drop out if they are low academic performers and would hurt a school district's educational performance. When a child drops out of school, however, he is leaving a safe haven and is at risk for more dangerous influences leading to delinquency. Because social networks shape youth perceptions of the opportunities available to them and, therefore, influence a youth's decision making, a continuing attachment to school can be a powerful protection against juvenile substance abuse and crime. High-risk children who are not involved in juvenile crime or drug use are more likely to be committed to school and the importance of education. However, poor academic achievement and failure are strongly linked with juvenile crime because once children opt out of the educational system, the rates of delinquency rise.

Unfortunately, NCLB is proving to be the antithesis of a successful educational model for minority children in general and has had a profound negative impact on African American males in particular. Through its emphasis on high-stakes testing and the extrinsic pressures schools put on these children to perform well on behalf of the school district, NCLB has fostered a policy that pushes — sometimes deliberately — poorly performing juveniles out of the education system and onto the streets. Thus, the avenue to delinquency begins in the sad allegory of NCLB and African American juvenile males.

NCLB and the Promise of Equity

The explicit motivation for NCLB was the improvement of educational opportunities for minority students. Broadly conceived as a means for transforming the Elementary and Secondary Education Act,[1] NCLB was designed to enhance the teaching and education achievement in schools receiving Title I funds.[2] Particularly targeted are "low-achieving children in our Nation's highest-poverty schools, limited English proficient children, migratory children, children with disabilities, Indian children, neglected or delinquent children, and young children in need of reading assistance."[3] One of the premier goals of NCLB is to close the "achievement gap" between minority and nonminority students.[4]

The two most notable features to close that gap are nationwide standardized testing and school district accountability. The first NCLB prescription — nationwide standardized testing — includes the implementation of annual assessments for math, reading and, as of academic year 2007–08, science. These assessments are conducted in grades three through eight and in one of grades ten through twelve. By academic year 2013–14, a statewide "minimum percentage" of tested students should demonstrate 100 percent academic proficiency in these three subjects. "Academic proficiency" is generally considered grade-level proficiency in the skills and knowledge for that particular subject. Each state is charged with setting academic standards to achieve proficiency in these subjects, although the typically recognized norm is the National Assessment of Educational Progress (NAEP).[5]

Congruent with the adoption of these standards is the states' adoption of instruments to assess that proficiency. These instruments are standardized tests that typically rely on multiple-choice questions to test content proficiency. Although some states have adopted writing tests, the scores on those tests tend to be much less reliable than the scores on multiple-choice tests, which also have the virtues of being easily replicable and portable. Because they are multiple-choice tests, standardized tests have necessarily narrow learn-

---

1. 20 U.S.C. §§ 6301–7941 (Supp. 2004).

2. *E.g.*, Charles R. Lawrence III, *Who Is the Child Left Behind?: The Racial Meaning of the New School Reform*, 39 SUFFOLK U. L. REV. 699, 702 (2005–06); Gershon M. Ratner, *Why the No Child Left Behind Act Needs to Be Restructured to Accomplish Its Goals and How to Do It*, 9 UDC/DCSL L. REV. 1, 8 (2007).

3. 20 U.S.C. § 6301(2) (Supp. 2004).

4. 20 U.S.C. § 6301(3) (Supp. 2004).

5. Ratner, *supra* note 2, at 3–5, 8–9; SHARON L. NICHOLS, GENE V. GLASS, & DAVID C. BERLINER, EDUCATION POLICY STUDIES LABORATORY, HIGH-STAKES TESTING AND STUDENT ACHIEVEMENT: PROBLEMS FOR THE NO CHILD LEFT BEHIND ACT (2005), www.asu.edu/educ/epsl/EPRU/documents/ EPSL-0509-105-EPRU.pdf.

ing goals for the test takers and tend not to test higher level analytical or complex thinking skills.[6]

In tandem with NCLB's standardized testing plan for proficiency, many states have adopted these or similar standardized tests for retention-promotion decisions and graduation decisions. Thus, standardized tests have a value-added aspect when school districts use tests not only to assess proficiency and achievement but also to influence the students' continuing education.[7] Approximately nineteen states require graduation testing so that students must pass a competency test before they can receive their diplomas. Although graduation tests previously required *minimum* competency, post-NCLB graduation tests require *grade-level* competencies of tenth grade or above.[8] Contemporaneous with this rising reliance on higher-level exit testing is the increasingly widespread use of standardized tests for promotion and retention decisions. Promotion tests are required in approximately seventeen states and many urban school districts. Often administered at both the elementary and middle-school level, these tests are considered a "cure" for social promotion by conditioning grade advancement on satisfactory test scores. NCLB's requirement has encouraged such end-of-year testing, and it is speculated that most states will use the NCLB achievement test as a proxy for promotion.[9] Therefore, standardized testing has not only become the norm for its own purposes but encouraged the additional use of such tests for other goals.

Second, in addition to reliance on standardized testing to close minority achievement gaps, NCLB makes school districts publicly accountable for their students' progress. This accountability system incorporates both rewards and sanctions to prod higher school district achievement. Each state must adopt a plan that will ensure adequate yearly progress (AYP) so that by academic year 2014–15 each district will have 100 perecent proficiency. Among such plans' requirements is the publication of report cards of progress in academic achievement. In those report cards, the school districts must disaggregate test scores to show the achievement levels of targeted subgroups, specifically segregated by race, ethnicity, limited English proficiency, special education, and poverty. This disaggregation requirement is designed to measure improvements in achievement gaps. To achieve its AYP goals, a school district's disaggregated subgroups must reach a minimal proficiency in 95 percent of the students in each subgroup.[10]

Accountability goes both ways in these plans. Rewards flow to those school districts that accomplish the state's goals, including academic achievement awards and financial rewards to teachers. However, failure to meet those goals results in sanctions for those schools receiving Title I funds.[11] Sanctions include a school being designated as needing improvement (failure to reach AYP for two consecutive years); being required to offer supplemental services to low-income students (three consecutive years); being forced to take "corrective action" (four consecutive years); and restructuring (five consecutive years). The

---

6. *See generally* ANN OWENS & GAIL L. SUNDERMAN, CIVIL RIGHTS PROJECT AT HARVARD UNIVERSITY, POLICY BRIEF: SCHOOL ACCOUNTABILITY UNDER NCLB: AID OR OBSTACLE FOR MEASURING RACIAL EQUITY? (2006), www.civilrightsproject.ucla.edu/research/esea/NCLB_Policy_Brief_Final.pdf.

7. NICHOLS ET AL., *supra* note 5, at 16–17.

8. Jay P. Heubert, *High-Stakes Testing, Nationally and in the South: Disparate Impact, Opportunity to Learn, and Current Legal Protections, in* 4 RACE, ETHNICITY, AND EDUCATION: RACISM AND ANTIRACISM IN EDUCATION 115, 116–17 (E. Wayne Ross ed., 2006); *see also* NICHOLS ET AL., *supra* note 5, at 3–4.

9. Heubert, *supra* note 8, at 118.

10. NICHOLS ET AL., *supra* note 5, at 6; Ratner, *supra* note 2, at 8–9.

11. Ratner, *supra* note 2, at 9–10.

last entails unsavory options such as a private management company or state takeover.[12] Thus, NCLB requires that the equivalent of a corporate annual report be given to its "shareholders" based on the results of this standardized testing.

NCLB's standardized testing regime therefore not only serves as the individual student's litmus test of continuing educational success or failure but also serves as public evidence that a school district is improving overall student achievement. The rewards are rather ordinary—promotion or graduation for students and achievement awards for schools. The sanctions, however, are onerous, especially in psychic costs to students. It isn't called "high-stakes testing" for nothing.

Standardized Testing and Inequity

The Wrong Strategy

Although promoted as a method for closing the achievement gap between white students and minority students, NCLB is wholly unsuited to do so and has been since its inception. NCLB, because of its sole focus on standardized testing, has been roundly criticized on numerous grounds, but two in particular relate to educational equity for minority students. First, standardized testing is an ineffective method of improving school achievement as a pedagogical strategy. Second, standardized testing's pedagogy is especially ineffective for improving individual achievement in minority students.

There are several pedagogical flaws in relying on standardized testing as a measure of an effective education. First, as a practical matter, the validity and reliability of the tests themselves are questionable.[13] Second, some students are just naturally better at taking standardized tests than others, even accounting for similar grades. More important, when standardized testing is the sole method of measuring school achievement, a school district does not and cannot incorporate the best of learning theory and teaching techniques into the curriculum.

Unfortunately, a school district held financially accountable for progress based on standardized test scores has little choice but to adapt to that reality. In so doing, the schools often— and perhaps must—abandon other valid and highly reliable teaching methods. Instead, school districts teach to the test by resorting to "drill and kill" exercises to raise test scores.[14] The outcome rather than the learning process becomes paramount. Perhaps most important, the NCLB's focus on testing diverts attention from the true problems facing schools that must narrow achievement gaps or face murderous sanctions. Instead, NCLB creates a disincentive to make more effective improvements in minority education.[15]

---

12. Nichols et al., *supra* note 5, at 6–7; Ratner, *supra* note 2, at 9–11.

13. National Organization for Fair and Open Testing (FairTest), *Joint Organizational Statement on No Child Left Behind (NCLB) Act* (2004), www.fairtest.org/joint%20statement%20civil%20rights%20grps%2010-21-04.html. FairTest questions whether NCLB's strategy is a valid method of accurately measuring achievement and further questions the quality of the tests themselves and their inherent inability to diagnose problems so that remediation, and thus achievement, can occur. *Id.* at 2.

14. *E.g.*, Ratner, *supra* note 2, at 2.

15. Linda Darling-Hammond, *Evaluating 'No Child Left Behind*,' The Nation, May 21, 2007, www.thenation.com/doc/20070521/darling-hammond (last visited Sept. 13, 2007). In the absence of structural change in NCLB's limited focus, it neglects such structural concerns as teacher development, curriculum development, high-quality preschool education and healthcare for poor students. *Id.* at 3. The business interests that heavily promoted NCLB as the panacea for school reform and a

Standardized testing simply does not address the lack of money and the necessity of investing in minority education. Nearly all authorities agree that school improvements require money, not sanctions, especially in the poorer school districts where most minority populations reside. Furthermore, NCLB is a famously underfunded mandate,[16] asking school districts to do more with little or even decreasing resources. Sanctions just make matters worse.[17]

In addition, NCLB's standardized testing regime is not working. Instead of promoting achievement, the emphasis on standardized testing has promoted "widespread manipulations of test standards, scores and schedules to produce artificial compliance with AYP and postpone sanctions as long as possible."[18] The numbers themselves do not bode well: The 2005 *High-Stakes Testing and Student Achievement* study indicates that there were no gains posted in reading scores at fourth-grade level and reading and math scores at the eighth-grade levels as a result of NCLB, with only a weak positive link to fourth-grade math improvement.[19] The Civil Rights Project's *Tracking Achievement Gaps and Assessing the Impact of NCLB on the Gaps*[20] documented trends in fourth- and eighth-grade math and reading achievement scores pre- and post-NCLB, using one consistent assessment of NAEP. That report compared trends from 1990–2001 to those from 2002–05 and found little if any gains in math and reading in either of the grade levels measured. Reading achievement remained flat, whereas math achievement, after an initial jump, reverted to pre-NCLB growth.[21] So the underlying promise of achievement and proficiency, in general, is not being met.

When examined in light of minority achievement, the results of the standardized testing regime are even more discouraging. Preliminarily, testing problems are magnified for minority students because they enter the playing field with fewer educational resources. If their school districts have inadequate AYP reports, minority students will have progressively fewer resources as a result of sanctions. Add the failure to provide adequate funds, and NCLB fails "to give all students an equal opportunity to learn—the same access to well-trained teachers, appropriate curricula, and up-to-date learning material."[22] The research is unequivocal that lack of funding has a direct impact on achievement.[23]

NCLB's failure to address this resource problem was a glaring omission in light of the extensive "history of segregation, of inadequate funding, of white flight, of neglect, of

---

better prepared workforce apparently wanted to do it on the cheap without regard to whether it would work or not.

16. Lawrence, *supra* note 2, at 704–05.

17. Darling-Hammond, supra note 15, at 2–4.

18. Ratner, *supra* note 2, at 14.

19. Nichols, et al., *supra* note 5, at ii, 109–10.

20. Jaekyung Lee, Civil Rights Project at Harvard University, Tracking Achievement Gaps and Assessing the Impact of NCLB on the Gaps: An In-depth Look into National and State Reading and Math Outcome Trends (2006), www.civilrightsproject.ucla.edu/research/esea/nclb_naep_lee.pdf.

21. *Id.* at 10–11. The newly published results 2007 Nation's Report Cards are not much more encouraging. See National Center for Education Statistics, National Assessment of Education Progress, The Nation's Report Card: Mathematics 2007 (2007), nces.ed.gov/nationsreportcard/pdf/main2007/2007494.pdf; National Center for Education Statistics, National Assessment of Education Progress, The Nation's Report Card: Reading 2007 (2007), nces.ed.gov/nations reportcard/pdf/main2007/2007496.pdf.

22. Lawrence, *supra* note 2, at 705.

23. National Research Council Committee on Minority Representation in Special Education, Minority Students in Special and Gifted Education 179–80 (M. Suzanne Donovan & Christopher T. Cross eds. 2002). "If minority students are to have an equal opportunity to achieve, they must have access to the educational experience provided in more affluent neighborhoods." *Id.* at 180.

eyes averted and uncaring while the savage inequalities of American education [grow] ever wider."[24] As a consequence, predominately minority schools have difficulty attracting quality faculty and resources to raise achievement. Without new resources, they are caught in a vicious circle and destined for failure.[25] Thus, NCLB's "superficial-deficit model ... focus[es] on outputs (racial achievement gaps) instead of inputs (resources, accessibility, and quality of instruction)."[26]

In addition to funding problems, minority students and school districts face systemic problems with standardized testing plans that nonminority populations and schools do not face. For instance, states with larger populations and states with higher minority populations tend to have NCLB accountability plans with greater pressure built into them.[27] This problem is especially true of Southern states, which placed significant emphasis on graduation and promotion standardized tests even before NCLB.[28] In addition, NCLB's strategy adds more burdens to minority populations because those populations started at lower proficiency levels when NCLB was implemented. As a consequence, their AYPs began at a deficit. Last, these school districts have multiple targets to meet and report when they disaggregate their scores for multiple subgroups of race, poverty, and ethnicity.[29] As a consequence, NCLB is an ill-fitting solution to closing the achievement gaps.

In actual experience, minority test results are not encouraging either. The empirical analysis of pre- and post-NCLB tests from NAEP indicate that the minority achievement gap has not diminished under NCLB. The gaps in reading and math proficiency are relatively unchanged among racial and socioeconomic groups. There have been slight improvements in fourth-grade math between whites and African Americans and in both reading scores in the poor-nonpoor groups. Otherwise, the gaps have remained stagnant.[30] Thus, systemically and in application, NCLB has proved a failure in its standardized testing aim to improve equality for minority students.

The Wrong Pedagogy

The basic impediment to closing achievement gaps is that NCLB's testing focus is not designed to address appropriate teaching methods for minority populations. A threshold issue, of course, is that standardized testing has historically been biased against minority groups.[31] Worse, however, is that NCLB ignores the learning differences in children, a basic institutional component understood and acknowledged by educators but woefully misunderstood and ignored by Congress.

---

24. Lawrence, *supra* note 2, at 706.

25. Darling-Hammond, *supra* note 15, at 4–5.

26. Monique McMillian, *Is No Child Left Behind 'Wise Schooling' for African American Male Students?*, Dec. 2003/Jan. 2004 HIGH SCHOOL JOURNAL 25, 26 (2004). NCLB is also not designed to address the disproportionality of minorities assigned to nonacademic or lower track classes in multiracial schools or to lower level courses that predominate in single-race schools. Ratner, *supra* note 2, at 20.

27. NICHOLS ET AL., *supra* note 5, at 101.

28. Heubert, *supra* note 8, at 117–18.

29. OWENS & SUNDERMAN, *supra* note 6, at 1–2, 18–19.

30. LEE, *supra* note 30, at 42; *see also* NATIONAL CENTER FOR EDUCATION STATISTICS, NATIONAL ASSESSMENT OF EDUCATION PROGRESS, THE NATION'S REPORT CARD: TRIAL URBAN DISTRICT ASSESSMENT, READING 2005 (2006), nces.ed.gov/nationsreportcard.gov/pdf/dst2005/2006455r.pdf.

31. *See generally* Walter Haney, *Testing and Minorities, in* BEYOND SILENCED VOICES: CLASS, RACE, AND GENDER IN UNITED STATES SCHOOLS 45, 56–60 (Lois Weis & Michelle Fine eds., 1993).

NCLB's emphasis on ends testing engages a teaching method that focuses on repetition and rote memorization to remember the details necessary to recall facts and concepts sufficiently to recognize the right answer (or the best answer) from a menu listed on a multiple-choice question. Because the outcome is so important to the school district's accountability reports, the teaching method impressed on teachers teaching to succeed on the tests is "drill and kill," a monotonous and highly regimented litany of exercises designed to make students remember facts and perform well only for a multiple-choice test. The teacher tends to follow a regimented list of subject matter content and questions that emphasize repetition so that facts and skills become automatic.[32] Schoolchildren endure daily grinds that resemble months-long preparation for the SAT. This teacher-directed instruction is clearly not a learning and teaching model designed to teach students "analytical, problem-solving and other higher-order thinking skills."[33] It is especially not a model for closing the gaps in African American achievement.

African American students flourish with a more child-centered educational model, one that relies on more student participation than the NCLB approach allows. Studies reveal that the African American population has greater difficulty than the dominant culture in working with abstract visual cues, which are fundamental to reading proficiency. Instead, African Americans rely on tactile or kinesthetic experiences for learning. Consequently, teaching methods that require active student involvement, rather than rote activities, are better suited to teaching African American students. African Americans are also proficient in the oral-aural learning modality and learn more successfully when they practice their lessons rhythmically and even nonverbally.[34]

In addition, an ethnographic study determined African American students' language experiences at home are distinctly different from the dominant culture's: whereas the white parent will pose learning experiences through inauthentic questions, such as "What color is that car?" the African American parent will engage the child through authentic questions, such as "What is your favorite book?"[35] The inauthentic questions better mirror the multiple-choice testing paradigm and thus the "drill and kill" method of teaching than do authentic questions. As a result, the teaching method encouraged by NCLB tends to teach to the dominant culture.[36] The African American learning style is ill-suited to the NCLB environment while different teaching methods necessary to educate minority children are discouraged by NCLB's requirements.[37]

Furthermore, the competitive atmosphere engendered by standardized testing places particular pressure on African American students. There is, of course, the implicit (if not

---

32. *E.g.*, Lawrence, *supra* note 2, at 711–12.

33. Ratner, *supra* note 2, at 16.

34. Olivia N. Saracho & Cynthia Koren Gerstl, *Learning Differences Among At-Risk Minority Students, in* Students at Risk in At-Risk Schools: Improving Environments for Learning 105, 114–15 (Hersholt C. Waxman et al. eds. 1992).

35. National Research Council, *supra* note 23, at 183–84. When teachers were asked to alter their teaching methods to accommodate this cultural difference, achievement among African American students increased.

36. *Id.* at 185. This conclusion is not to suggest that teachers and school administrators are explicitly biased against minority students. Indeed, research shows that educators are among the least prejudiced members of the American workforce. However, to the extent that educators are uninformed about more culturally diverse pedagogies but instead are encouraged to teach to the dominant culture, they are unable to serve minority children adequately. *Id.*; *see also* Na'ilah Suad Nasir, Ann S. Rosebery, Beth Warren, & Carol D. Lee, *Learning as a Cultural Process Achieving Equity Through Diversity, in* The Cambridge Handbook of the Learning Sciences 489 (R. Keith Sawyer ed. 2006).

37. Saracho & Gerstl, *supra* note 34, at 116–17.

explicit) pressure they feel from the cultural stereotype that they will not do as well on standardized tests as will white students.[38] In addition, school-imposed pressures exist in the competition for the district's AYP reports. These students also feel the pressures of their personal lives where they often are dealing with instability in their families and the impact their poverty has on their educational futures.[39] Such pressures only add to the pedagogical problems experienced by African American students.

With all of these difficulties, minority students too often become disengaged from the educational process under NCLB. First, they become disengaged because school is "boring" and simply not relevant to them.[40] Second, minority students are also being actively disengaged by the school districts to increase test scores and AYP reports, In other words, NCLB is becoming instrumental in students dropping out of school.

NCLB and Dropouts

It is ironic that NCLB is creating its own dropout clientele because it has a Dropout Prevention Act[41] and includes a further provision "to prevent at-risk youth from dropping out of school."[42] The Dropout Prevention Act states that

> the purpose of this part is to provide for school dropout prevention and reentry and to raise academic achievement levels by providing grants that—
>
> (1) challenge all children to attain their highest academic potential; and
>
> (2) ensure that all students have substantial and ongoing opportunities to attain their highest academic potential through schoolwide programs proven effective in school dropout prevention and reentry.[43]

Instead, the evidence indicates that NCLB has become a significant factor in causing minority students to drop out.

---

38. *See, e.g.,* Tyrone C. Howard & Ifeoma A. Amah, *Bridging the Gap: Effective Practice and Research to Improve African American Student Achievement, in* 3 RACE, ETHNICITY, AND EDUCATION: RACIAL IDENTITY IN EDUCATION 219, 222–23 (H. Richard Milner & E. Wayne Ross eds., 2006); *see also* McMillian, *supra* note 26, at 28; Ratner, *supra* note 2, at 19–20. "With regard to black students, [one researcher] found that teachers quickly formed lasting impressions of students' academic abilities that were often inaccurate, particularly with regard to black males." NATIONAL RESEARCH COUNCIL, *supra* note 23, at 182.

39. *See, e.g.,* Carl Grant & Anthony L. Brown, *Listening to African American Males' Conceptions of High-Stakes Tests, in* 1 RACE, ETHNICITY, AND EDUCATION: PRINCIPLES AND PRACTICES OF MULTICULTURAL EDUCATION 103, 103–05 (Valerie Ooka Pang ed., 2006).

40. For African American males, even the standardized tests themselves are somewhat irrelevant, albeit important, because the students cannot connect those tests with their future success. *Id.* at 117–18.

41. 20 U.C.S. §§ 6551–6578 (Supp. 2004). The highest of ironies is that Congress may eliminate funding for this dropout prevention program. *See, e.g., Statement of Rebecca Pringle, Submitted by NEA to the Aspen Institute's Commission on No Child Left Behind* (National Education Ass'n, Aug. 4, 2006), www.nea.ort/lac/esea/080406testi.html:mode=print (last visited Sept. 13, 2007).

42. 20 U.S.C. § 6421(a)(3) (Supp. 2004).

43. 20 U.S.C. § 6552.

Disengagement and fear of failure in school are the biggest factors propelling students out the door.[44] Congruent with both factors is research that reveals that high-stakes testing, such as that required by NCLB, has a direct influence on a state's dropout rate. In a pre-NCLB study of minimum competency testing, a direct statistical link existed between the dropout rate and the stakes linked to testing. Of the ten states with the *highest* dropout rates, nine of them used the tests as a condition for graduation and were less flexible in the use of the test scores. On the other hand, the ten states with the *lowest* dropout rates had either no minimum competency tests or tests involving low stakes. The empirical evidence was especially startling in its direct correlation between eighth-grade minimum competency tests and early high school dropout rates.[45]

The numbers are important when one considers the dropout rate in the United States is nearing epidemic proportions, with the graduation rate hovering around 68 to 71 percent.[46] Despite the accountability imposed by NCLB,[47] the graduation rate has continued to decline since 1990. Males have a lower graduation rate than females—65 percent compared to 72 percent[48]—but the hardest hit are minority students, particularly African American males, whose graduation rate is below 50 percent.[49]

Rather than correcting this problem, NCLB seems to be encouraging it. If disengagement is the reason the majority of dropouts leave school, then an educational system that emphasizes rote memorization and standardized testing will not cure that disengagement. This is especially true when the pressure to improve proficiency and close achievement gaps redounds to the minority population, which is already experiencing dropout problems. Unfortunately, NCLB's effect is even more insidious because school districts are actively forcing students to drop out of school to increase scores on the AYP reports.

These activities are deliberately designed to effect the withdrawal from school of students in those subgroups whose scores will negatively affect AYP. One trend, which began before NCLB, is for schools to retain students in ninth grade rather than to pass them

---

44. JOHN M. BRIDGELAND, JOHN J. DILULIO JR., & KAREN BURKE MORISON, CIVIC ENTERPRISES, THE SILENT EPIDEMIC: PERSPECTIVES OF HIGH SCHOOL DROPOUTS 3–8 (2006), www.civicenterpises.net/pdfs/thesilentepidemic3-06.pdf. A focus group analysis revealed that three of the top five reasons students gave for dropping out were that classes are not interesting (47 percent); attendance problems (43 percent); and failing in school (35 percent). The other reasons were closely connected to attendance problems: peer pressure (42 percent) and too little discipline in life (38 percent). *See also* PEW PARTNERSHIP FOR CIVIC CHANGE, THE SCHOOL DROPOUT CRISIS: WHY ONE-THIRD OF ALL HIGH SCHOOL STUDENTS DON'T GRADUATE, WHAT YOUR COMMUNITY CAN DO ABOUT IT 7–8 (2006), www.pew-partnership.org/pdf/dropout_overview.pdf; *see generally* Robert B. Stevenson & Jeanne Ellsworth, *Dropouts and the Silencing of Critical Voices, in* BEYOND SILENCED VOICES: CLASS, RACE, AND GENDER IN UNITED STATES SCHOOLS 259 (Lois Weis & Michelle Fine eds. 1993).

45. MARGUERITE CLARKE, WALTER HANEY, & GEORGE MADAUS, NATIONAL BOARD ON EDUCATION TESTING & PUBLIC POLICY, HIGH STAKES TESTING AND HIGH SCHOOL COMPLETION 2 (2000) www.bc.edu/research/nbetpp/publications/v1n3.html.

46. BRIDGELAND ET AL., *supra* note 44, at 1.

47. THE SCHOOL DROPOUT CRISIS, *supra* note 44, at 5.

48. JAY P. GREENE & MARCUS WINTERS, CENTER FOR CIVIC INNOVATION AT THE MANHATTAN INSTITUTE, LEAVING BOYS BEHIND: PUBLIC HIGH SCHOOL GRADUATION RATES (Executive Summary) (2006), www.manhattan-institute.org/pdf/cr_48.pdf.

49. One study puts the African American male graduation rate at 48 percent, *id.* at 3, 7, while another puts it as low as 43 percent. GARY ORFIELD, DANIEL LOSEN, JOHANN WALD, & CHRISTOPHER B. SWANSON, CIVIL RIGHTS PROJECT AT HARVARD UNIVERSITY, LOSING OUR FUTURE: HOW MINORITY YOUTH ARE BEING LEFT BEHIND BY THE GRADUATION RATE CRISIS 2 (2004), www.urban.org/UploadedPDF/410936_LosingOurFuture.pdf.

along. Passing them along would put those students (and the school district) in jeopardy of failing high-pressure minimum competency tests. This trend has had a huge impact on minority students, whose ninth-grade enrollment was at least 23 percent higher than their comparable eighth-grade population, indicating that they were not being passed to higher grades with their peers.[50] Consequently, they have a higher incidence of early high school dropouts.

Another trend is for school districts to fiddle with their graduation rates because there is no national norm for accounting for dropouts and dropout rates.[51] This lack of data is driven in large part because—unless a school district is getting funding through the Dropout Prevention Act[52]—NCLB regulations do not require that dropout data be published in the AYP reports, only graduation rates. As states are allowed some flexibility in this regard,[53] school districts are reporting faulty and incomplete graduation data with little or no consequence[54] while members of certain subgroups are vanishing from the average daily attendance rolls. At least one state has been accused of systematic efforts to encourage students to leave school before critical testing so as to not affect both the proficiency scores and graduation rates.[55] Anecdotal evidence supports the accusation in other states:

> Student narratives from states as diverse as Alabama, Florida, New York, Illinois, and Mississippi include reports of being encouraged … to drop out with little regard for their future prospects. There are, for instance, accounts of students with low test scores but otherwise respectable school records who are actively discouraged from and, in many cases, literally barred by school officials from reenrolling—and then officially categorized as having withdrawn from school because of lack of interest.[56]

As a consequence, some states are reporting a 5 percent dropout rate for African Americans when it is actually 50 percent.[57]

States also have little incentive to correct the reporting of minority dropout rates because, unlike proficiency test scores, NCLB regulations do not require states to report disaggregated graduation rates.[58] Thus, there is no incentive to keep track of (much less report) minority student dropouts; it is anticipated the increased pressures of NCLB will only exacerbate this "dropout/push-out syndrome."[59] Hence, NCLB's promise of equity has actually stimulated greater inequality, as demonstrated by its impact on African American male dropout rates and the delinquency problem that it creates.

---

50. David Shriberg & Amy Burke Shriberg, *High-Stakes Testing & Dropout Rates*, Fall 2006 Dissent, www.dissentmagazine.org/article/?article=702&print=1 (last visited Sept. 13, 2007).

51. *E.g.*, Lyndsay Pinkus, Alliance for Excellent Education, Who's Counted? Who's Counting? Understanding High School Graduation Rates 5–6 (2006), www.all4ed.org/publications/WhosCounting/WhosCounting.pdf.

52. 20 U.S.C. §6577 (Supp. 2004).

53. Christopher B. Swanson, Urban Institute, Ten Questions (and Answers) about Graduates, Dropouts, and NCLB Accountability 3 (2003).

54. Daria Hall, The Education Trust, Getting Honest About Grad Rates: How States Play the Numbers and Students Lose 2 (June 2005), www2.edtrust.org/NR/rdonlyres/ C5A6974D-6C04-4FB1-A9FC-05938CB0744D/0/GettingHonest.pdf.

55. Texas has been increasingly criticized for publishing numbers that bear no relationship to reality. *See* Shriberg & Shriberg, *supra* note 50, at 3.

56. *Id.* at 4; *see also* Orfield et al., *supra* note 49, at 11.

57. *Id.* at 7.

58. *Id.* at 13.

59. *Id.* at 14.

Delinquency and Dropouts

The gateway to delinquency begins with poor academic performance and low school commitment. Low school commitment creates a culture of young people who eventually drop out of school and become delinquent. Nearly a half-million youth dropped out of high school in 2000.[60] The Annie E. Casey Foundation estimates that 3.8 million eighteen- to twenty-four-year-olds do not have high school diplomas.[61] From 2000–2004, the number grew by 700,000.[62] The rates of crime and delinquency in this population are alarming. Over 400,000 men between eighteen and twenty-four-years-old are in federal and state prisons.[63] Over 60 percent of young men under the age of twenty-four who are in federal and state prison have not graduated high school.[64] The long-term effects of not having a high school diploma are devastating. African American males are particularly vulnerable because of the disproportionate impact of poverty and unemployment has on their population.

Low academic performance has consistently been the precursor delinquency. Experts have shown that students who dropout of high school have a greater chance of becoming delinquent.

Academic Performance and Delinquency

The poorer a young person performs academically, the greater the likelihood of delinquency.[65] The odds of delinquent behavior in poor academic performers are 2.1 times higher than for high academic performers.[66] In other words, 35 percent of poor academic performing youth become delinquent versus 20 percent of high academic performing youth.[67]

Researchers Eugene Maguin and Rolf Loeber conducted a study to measure when delinquency begins and the effect of delinquency on academic performance.[68] They measured delinquency in three phases: onset, escalation, and desistance. For the onset of delinquency, a relationship was found between poor academic performing youth fourteen years old and older and delinquency.[69] They found that academic performance could be

---

60. Howard Snyder & Melissa Sickmund, *Juvenile Offenders and Victims: 2006 National Report*, NATIONAL CENTER FOR JUVENILE JUSTICE, OFFICE OF JUSTICE PROGRAMS MARCH 2006 at 14 [hereafter Snyder and Sickmund].

61. Nancy Martin & Samuel Halperin, *Whatever It Takes: How Twelve Communities Are Reconnecting Out-of-School Youth, The Drop Out Problem in Numbers*, American Youth Policy Forum (2006) at vii [hereafter Twelve Communities], available at www.aypf.org/publications/WhateverItTakes/WITfull.pdf.

62. *Id.*

63. Paige Harrison & Jennifer Karlberg, *Prison and Jail Inmates at Midyear 2003*, U.S. Dept. of Justice, Bureau of Justice Statistics, May 2004, Table 13 [hereafter *Prison and Jail Inmates*].

64. See *infra* notes 85–95 and accompanying text.

65. Eugene Maguin & Rolf Loeber, *Academic Performance and Delinquency*, 20 CRIME & JUST. 145, 247.

66. *Id.*

67. *Id.*

68. *Id.*

69. *Id.*

used as a predictor for earlier delinquent behavior.[70] In measuring escalation of delinquent behavior, low academic performance was found to be significantly linked to delinquent behavior.[71] Youth were found to deescalate their delinquent behavior if they had high academic performance.[72] The strongest correlation for delinquency was found in older adolescent males who were poor academic performers.[73]

One of the actions that push poor academic performers into becoming delinquent is the decision to drop out of high school. Students who perform poorly in high school are more likely to drop out of school at an earlier age.[74] Students who drop out of high school at an earlier age are more likely to engage in crime and delinquency.[75] A student's own dissatisfaction with school and lowered expectations for academic achievement leads to the decision to drop out.[76] Academic performance is not an exclusive variable in determining why students drop out. Absenteeism, truancy, and discipline problems are also associated with the decision to drop out.[77] However, Michael Newcomb established that delinquency is a unique risk factor to high school failure.[78] He found that African American males had strong correlations between school problems, delinquency, and high school failure.[79] Newcomb found an inimitable relationship between high school failure and low academic competence.[80]

Academic performance can predict high school success, high school completion, as well as avenues to deviance and delinquency. Academic ability is the strongest predictor of high school success.[81] Academic incompetence is a strong indicator of future delinquent behavior.[82]

African American Males

The overrepresentation of African American males in the juvenile court and adult criminal system is the trademark of the tragedy of an inequitable system. If African American males exempt themselves from completing a high school education, the pathways to delinquency and criminality increase exponentially. High school dropouts are three and

---

70. *Id.*

71. *Id.*

72. Michael Newcomb, Richard Abbott, Richard Catalano, et al., *Mediational and Deviance Theories of Late High School Failure: Process Roles of Structural Strains, Academic Competence and General Versus Specific Problem Behavior*, 49 JOURNAL OF COUNSELING PSYCHOLOGY (2002) 172, 173. The researchers used race, academic performance, and socioeconomic status as variables in conducting their study.

73. *Id.*

74. *Id.*

75. See Snyder and Sickmund, supra note 60, at 24.

76. *Id.*

77. *Id.*

78. *Id.*

79. *Id.* Both variables were influenced by family socioeconomic status. African American ethnicity significantly correlated with lower family socioeconomic status. Newcomb deduced that family socioeconomic status had a direct impact on high school failure. Higher family socioeconomic status reduced high school failure and general deviance. Newcomb summarized his findings: "General deviance and family socioeconomic status was a strong predictor contributed to high school failure with equal force and academic competence was clearly the most important unique predictor for high school failure." Academic competence was the strongest influence on high school outcomes.

80. *Id.* at 181.

81. *Id.*

82. *Id.*

a half times more likely to be incarcerated than high school graduates,[83] and African American males are disproportionately incarcerated. Of all African American males in their thirties, 52 percent have been imprisoned.[84] Racial disparities occur through each critical stage in the criminal justice system that processes African American males. From 2002–2004, African American youth represented 16 percent of all youth under eighteen but made up 28 percent of all juvenile arrests, 30 percent of court referrals, 37 percent of the pretrial detained population, 30 percent of youth judged delinquent, 38 percent of youth in residential facilities, 35 percent of youth waived into adult courts, and 58 percent of youth incarcerated in adult prisons.[85]

In 2003, of the 1.6 million juvenile cases referred to the nation's juvenile courts, 480,000 involved African American adolescents.[86] Of the 332,000 juveniles detained, over 122,000 were African Americans.

If African American males discontinue their education prior to graduating from high school, delinquency and criminality are more likely to occur. Over one third of jail inmates cite academic problems as their reason for quitting school,[87] and three quarters of state prison inmates are high school dropouts.[88] Significantly, African American inmates were less educated their white counterparts.[89]

Unemployment statistics for dropouts are staggering. The employment rate for African American males who did not obtain a high school graduation have dropped precipitously in the last thirty years. In 1979, the rate employment rate for males sixteen to twenty-four years old was 53 percent, but by 1999 only 37 percent of African American high school dropouts were employed.[90] Future employment forecasts for African American high school dropouts are just as bleak. After the economic boom that peaked in 2000, the economy has not been able to absorb or employ 213,000 African American males.[91] An increase in unemployment rates for the general population will affect young African American males sixfold.[92]

Ex-offenders will have an especially hard time finding employment. Crime and incarceration, of course, have a significantly negative effect on actual employment and earnings;[93] approximately 600,000 to 700,000 are in the criminal justice system each year. Additionally, 500,000 young African American males are on felony probation.[94] In addition, a large number of young men are released from prison and sent back into their com-

---

83. Lilli Allen, Cheryl Almeida, & Adria Steinberg, *From Prison Track to the College Track: Pathways to Postsecondary Success for Out-of-School Youth, Jobs For the Future* (2004) at 5, available at www.eric.ed.gov/ERICDocs/data/ericdocs2sql/content_storage_01/0000019b/80/30/b1/01.pdf.

84. Twelve Communities, *supra* note 2, at 2.

85. *And Justice For Some: Differential Treatment of Youth of Color in the Justice System*, National Council on Crime and Delinquency, January 2007 at 37, available at www.nccd-crc.org/nccd/pubs/2007jan_justice_for_some.pdf.

86. *Id.* at 10.

87. Caroline Wolf Harlow, EDUCATION AND CORRECTIONAL POPULATIONS, BUREAU OF JUSTICE STATISTICS SPECIAL REPORT, OFFICE OF JUSTICE PROGRAMS, U.S. DEPT. OF JUSTICE (2003) at 3.

88. *Id.*

89. *Id.*

90. Harry Holzer & Paul Hoffner, *Trends in the Employment Outcome of Young Black Men 1979–2000* in BLACK MALES LEFT BEHIND (Ronald B. Mincy ed. 2006) at 22–23 [hereafter BLACK MALES].

91. William Rogers III, *Forecasting Labor Market Prospects* in BLACK MALES, supra note 12, at 58.

92. *Id.* at 53.

93. Harry Holzer, Stephen Raphael, & Michael Stoll, *How Do Employer Perceptions Affect Employer?* in BLACK MALES at 69.

94. *Id.*

munities each year. In total, nearly half of all noninstitutional African American men will have some contact with the criminal justice system,[95] with all of the negative implications of that contact for their future employment.

Social Disorganization

This mass incarceration of African American males has a calamitous effect on neighborhoods and communities. Neighborhoods that are unable to self-regulate because of the damaging environment of crime and poverty suffer social disorganization,[96] and the disrupted neighborhood organizational structure attenuates residents' ties to each other and to the community.[97] As a result, some residents no longer submit to normative social controls.[98]

Neighborhoods need the normative social controls that spring from the kind of supervision and surveillance that occur naturally within healthy communities as people interact in normal day-to-day routines.[99] These controls operate within the broader local, interpersonal networks, including the relationship among local institutions, such as stores, schools, and churches.[100] Exercising informal community control tactics means having the willingness to intervene to prevent truancy or street-corner loitering by teenagers or confrontation of individuals who are damaging public property or disturbing the neighborhood.[101] Stronger communities produce fewer offenders because they suffer from fewer of the environmental conditions conducive to crime.[102] Stronger communities also have larger supplies of human and social capital; they have stronger foundational structures and, as a result, suffer from less crime.[103]

Researchers Robert Sampson and W. Byron Groves have shown that individual residents who are integrated and tied to the neighborhood improve its capacity to self-regulate.[104] Conversely, when residents' ties are attenuated, when they feel anonymous and isolated, local control is difficult to achieve.[105] Social control becomes compromised because there is a lack of community interaction and shared obligation.[106] As a result, the community is weakened, and individuals can no longer intervene effectively on behalf of the neighborhood.[107]

Mass incarceration of African American males undermines the social, political, and economic systems already weakened by the low levels of human and social capital produced

---

95. *Id.* at 70.

96. Dina Rose & Todd Clear, *Incarceration, Social Capital and Crime: Implications for Social Disorganization Theory*, 36 Criminology 441 at 443.

97. *Id.*

98. *Id.* at 445.

99. *Id.*

100. *Id.*

101. *Id.*

102. *Id.* at 467.

103. *Id.*

104. *Id.* quoting Robert Sampson & W. Byron Groves, *Community Structure and Crime: Testing Social Disorganization Theory*, 94 American Journal of Sociology 744.

105. *Id.*

106. *Id.*

107. *Id.*

under conditions such as high rates of poverty, unemployment, and crime.[108] This continued erosion of healthy normative social controls means that communities with already scarce supplies of human and social capital are unable to produce the resources they so greatly need.[109]

Social Capital and Social Development

Because commitment to school is a fundamental component in retaining African American males in school and attachment to school is a powerful inhibitor against delinquent behavior, cultivating in African American males a commitment to school is especially important to the creation of social capital in the communities The connection a student feels with his school is linked to a variety to positive life outcomes and is particularly important for promoting academic achievement[110] and the healthy development of the student's social capital.

Social capital—the sum of a person's actual and potential resources associated with his social network[111]—includes social assets that reflect an adolescent's integration within social networks.[112] Social capital can make a difference in academic attainment and strengthen identity, commitment, and relationship development for at-risk African American males.[113] The greater the level of a young African American male's of interpersonal competence, the greater the social capital quality in the future.

In the social development model, which expands on the social capital construct, an individual's level of bonding to a social unit is determined by the amount of opportunity for involvement available in that social unit, by the skills in the individual applies in the social unit and by the reinforcement provided by the unit for the individual's behavior.[114] The social development model proposes that positive social bonds to school and family and belief in school and family values develop when students have opportunities for active involvement in the classroom and family. Classroom and family experiences lead to successful participation when there is consistent reinforcement for productive involvement.[115] Teaching and family practices that maximize positive learning conditions enhance social bonding and when paired with risk reduction activity, lessen the involvement in problem behaviors such as academic failure and delinquency.[116]

---

108. *Id.*

109. *Id.*

110. Debra Zand & Nicole Renick Thomson, *Academic Achievement Among African American Adolescents: Direct and Indirect Effects of Demographic, Individual and Contextual Variables*, 31 JOURNAL OF BLACK PSYCHOLOGY (2005) 352, 355.

111. Jennifer Kerpelman & Lloyd White, *Interpersonal Identity and Social Capital: The Importance of Commitment for Low Income, Rural, African American Adolescents*, 32 JOURNAL OF BLACK PSYCHOLOGY (2005) 219, 220.

112. *Id.*

113. *Id.*

114. Julie O'Donnell et al., *Preventing School Failure, Drug Use, and Delinquency Among Low-Income Children: Long Term Intervention in Elementary Schools*, 65 JOURNAL OF AMERICAN ORTHOPSYCHIATRY (1995) 87, 89.

115. *Id.*

116. *Id.*

School activities that take advantage of these dynamics serve to attenuate delinquency in African American youth.[117] For example, the Seattle Social Development Project (SSDP) developed and implemented a successful intervention classroom program that engaged students and reduced delinquency.[118] The teachers from SSDP were trained in instruction methods that engaged students. Classroom intervention had three major components: proactive classroom management, interactive teaching, and cooperative learning.[119] Proactive classroom management established an environment conducive to learning, promotion of appropriate student behavior, and minimization of classroom disruption.[120] Teachers gave clear and explicit instructions, rewarded attempts to comply, and used encouragement and praise to reinforce positive behavior.[121] Interactive teaching required that student master learning objectives before proceeding with more advanced work.[122] The teaching method required frequent monitoring of students to assess their comprehension of material.[123] Cooperative learning paired students with different abilities to compose a team and receive recognition as a team for academic performance.[124] Incorporating team rewards and individual accountability proved more effective than traditional instruction methods.[125]

Researchers Julie O'Donnell and Michael Newcomb studied the effects of the project in several schools and determined that classroom intervention was an essential component in keeping academically challenged students engaged and bonded to school.[126] The researchers found that

> among low income boys, the pattern of findings suggests that the intervention affected both the social competencies and academic skills and efforts. The latter appear to have yielded higher scores at the end of the sixth grade on standardized achievement test in math, reading, and language arts for low-income boys in the intervention condition. Intervention-group boys also perceived slightly greater reinforcements for classroom involvement than did their control-group counterparts and exhibited more attachment and significantly greater commitment to school. They tended to initiate delinquency at significantly lower rates than was the case for their control-group counterparts.[127]

---

117. John Hoffman & Jiangmin Xu, *School Activities, Community Service and Delinquency*, 48 Crime and Delinquency (2002) 568, 583 [hereafter Hoffman and Xu].

118. O'Donnell et al., *supra* note 63, at 90.

119. *Id.*

120. *Id.*

121. *Id.*

122. *Id.*

123. *Id.*

124. *Id.* at 91.

125. *Id.*

126. O'Connell et al. reviewed the Seattle Social Development Project, a long-term intervention program that utilized risk reductions strategies based on the premise that academic failure, delinquency, and drug abuse can be prevented by reducing, eliminating, or mitigating the effects of the precursors or risk factors. The program identified and established intervention schools and classrooms in eighteen Seattle elementary schools. Students were randomly assigned from the first to fourth grades. The project tested intervention aimed at reducing primary risk factors of school failure, early conduct disorders, family management problems, and involvement with antisocial others by combining modified teaching skills in mainstream classrooms, child social skills training, and developmentally adjusted parent training. The strategies were designed to enhance opportunities, skills, and reinforcements for children, both in the classroom and in family settings. *Id.* at 90.

127. *Id.* at 97.

O'Donnell found that intervention programs such as the SSDP also lowered the initiation into delinquency.[128] There was a negative correlation between bonding-to-school measures and delinquency initiation.[129]

Social bonding and school activities operate as an important deterrent against poor academic achievement and are the key components for keeping African American youth involved in their schools and assisting with them in completion of high school. Students must exhibit an emotional attachment, attain high achievement, and be involved in school activities.[130] Involvement in school activities not only provides a time-consuming alternative to delinquent behavior, it also socializes students to adhere to conventional values such as teamwork, fair play, and cooperation.[131]

NCLB

The application of NCLB requirements on public schools can have demoralizing effects for students who are in the most vulnerable status in education hierarchy because the requirements too often cut against the very dynamics necessary to retaining at-risk African American students. The erosion of the education process and the financial penalties tied to poor academic performance have transformed public education into a system where schools must gamble on their most vulnerable students' exiting school early to maintain academic status and funding. NCLB also requires teachers narrow the goals of the educational process to rote test-taking skills that leave little room for integrating classroom techniques that are geared to challenge academically marginal students. Both processes create an attrition that have direct and indirect pathways to juvenile delinquency and adult prison.

Conflating academic performance with Title I funding places academically vulnerable schools in survivalist mode. If a school fails its AYP for a second year, the school faces financial sanctions. Students who erode the academic performance of a school are discouraged from to continuing their education at that school.[132] African American males have disastrous dropout rates because of the discouragement by schools to continue to educate them.

Students need to have a stake in their own education and positive feelings of self-worth and school bonding to continue their education. NCLB reduces the social capital of academically challenged students. If students are not in school, they are left to the streets. Neighborhoods have an established link to delinquency as well. Neighborhood disorganization has been found to have some indirect influence on educational behavior through perceived levels of supportive parenting and parental educational support.[133] However, if neighborhoods are permeated with poverty, crime, undereducation, and unemployment, parental support must compete with a socially disorganized neighborhood. The values that build the foundation for positive school behavior have been found to decrease as the neighborhood social disorganization increases.[134]

---

128. O'Connell et al., *supra* note 63, at 98.

129. *Id.*

130. Hoffman and Xu, *supra* note 66, at 570.

131. *Id.*

132. *See supra* notes 39–53 and accompanying text.

133. Natasha Bowen, Gary Bowen, & William Ware, *Neighborhood Social Disorganization, Families and the Educational Behavior of Adolescents*, 17 JOURNAL OF ADOLESCENT RESEARCH (2002) 468, 483.

134. *Id.*

Conclusion

The original concept for the NCLB was to enhance teaching and educational achievement for minority students. The NCLB was designed to close the achievement gap between minority and nonminority students through nationwide standardized testing and school district accountability. However, the rising reliance on standardized tests for promotion and retention has eroded the educational process. The drive to make school districts directly accountable for the achievement of their students has led to academically low achieving students' being driven from schools and increasing the dropout rate. High school dropouts, especially African American males, are particularly vulnerable to pathways to crime and juvenile delinquency.

Delinquency is the red flag that exists in the juvenile justice system that a youth that is delinquent has a presumption of educational and familial dysfunction. Academic achievement is one of the bulwarks against a youth engaging in delinquent conduct. Youth who are considered high risk for delinquency and violence have academic failure and poor commitment to school. Unless a young person is bonded to his school and has social capital, academic failure is strong likelihood.

The statistics for African American dropouts who are unemployed are grim—hovering at 63 percent. Because undereducated African American males are also over-represented in the criminal justice system and the juvenile system is a feeder the adult system, in the prevention of crime and delinquency, schools are where desistance and intervention can take place. High academic achievement does counter delinquency, stabilize neighborhoods, and increase employment opportunities. NCLB has eroded public education and undermined the future of a generation of African American males.

21

Ability Grouping and Tracking and No Child Left Behind: Stratification in the Accountability Era

Donna M. Harris

The stratification of students via ability grouping and tracking has been an issue of continuing significance to educational researchers. There have been concerns about how race and socioeconomic status affect the assignment of students into learning groups (Rist 1970; Oakes 1985; Gamoran and Mare 1989) and how ability group and track placement affect student outcomes (Slavin 1987). This research has focused on comparing the relative learning opportunities and outcomes of students in high and low ability groups in elementary and middle schools (Rist 1970) and college preparatory and non–college preparatory tracks or subjects in high schools (Rosenbaum 1976; Oakes 1985; Gamoran and Mare 1989; Lucas 1999).

The majority of research about ability grouping and tracking was conducted prior to the implementation of current state and federal accountability policies that attempt to equalize educational experiences and outcomes via standards-based education and high-stakes testing. In this accountability environment, all students are expected to be exposed to state-level educational standards and master them. As a result, schools are supposed to provide students within and between schools similar learning experiences. In light of this policy's focus on promoting more equitable educational experiences for students who vary in academic skills, it is necessary to conceptualize a different understanding about how schools organize learning opportunities, given the assumption that most (if not all) students are exposed to challenging academic knowledge. What is less obvious is how schools will meet the needs of students that vary academically, culturally, and linguistically. There have been no clear provisions with No Child Left Behind (and with the implementation of state standards) regarding how schools should organize learning opportunities across grade levels.

Public schools confront a significant challenge because these institutions have the task of educating a student population that has become more racially, ethnically, and socioeconomically diverse (Zhou 2003). These students tend to have the lowest academic outcomes among those educated in public schools. As a result, many students come to school with varying skill levels and academic needs. These needs include addressing below grade-level literacy of both native English speakers and English language learners. Public schools also function within an educational policy context of accountability promoted by academic standards and testing.

With this diversity comes a tension that has yet to be resolved because schools are now expected to meet students' individual needs and at the same time assist them to achieve high academic standards via state assessments. Despite efforts to promote equity by requiring states to align their curriculum to standards and requiring students to attain proficiency on state tests, we cannot ignore the fact that schools and teachers must possess the resources, skills, and expectations to successfully operate within their classrooms.

This chapter discusses the demographic and academic challenges confronted in public schools and how standards and accountability via No Child Left Behind are intended to address these inequalities. It then discusses how ability grouping and tracking are manifested in the contemporary reform environment, focusing on the organization and function of these learning groups. The chapter concludes by examining how the differentiation of learning opportunities exists in school-level collective beliefs about students—beliefs that reflect entrenched expectations and influence the modification of standards.

Demographic Diversity

In the twenty-first century, public schools are confronting a more demographically diverse student population. Using 2000 census data, Zhou (2003) shows that there has been an overall increase in the U.S. population, where the biggest growth was experienced among Hispanics and Asians. Between 1990 and 2000, Hispanics went from representing 9 percent of the U.S. population to 12.5 percent. During the same time, Asians went from representing 2.9 percent to 4.4 percent of the population. The African American population has remained stagnant at 12.6 percent, and the white population has decreased to 69 percent. African Americans, Hispanics, and Asians are concentrated in various regions of the country. Over 50 percent of African Americans reside in the South, 43 percent of Hispanics in the West, and almost 50 percent of Asians in the West.

The changes in general population demographics are also reflected in public school trends. Between 1972 and 2003, the percentage of white students has substantially decreased, whereas the enrollment of African American students has remained relatively the same. As a result, data from 2003 show that 58 percent of public school population was white, 16 percent African American, 19 percent Hispanic, and 7 percent Asian (Zhou 2003). In addition, by 2003 19 percent of the public school population was comprised of language minority students whose primary language at home was not English (Wirt et al. 2005). Many of these diverse student populations attended schools in large urban cities (Zhou 2003). Schools serving this increasingly diverse student population also confront high concentrations of poverty. Among the 100 largest public schools in the United States in 2001–2002, 94.8 percent of their students qualified for free or reduced lunch (Sable and Young 2003).

Academic Diversity

Given the demographic diversity of the public school population, schools confront serious challenges regarding the promotion of high levels of achievement for all students.

Many public schools have struggled with promoting high academic outcomes among African American and Hispanic students. Schools serving these populations confront a unique problem because many students leave elementary schools without achieving proficiency in reading and math. Therefore, these students confront the greatest challenge in being able to meet the goals of state standards and assessments as they move on to secondary schools. The 2005 National Assessment of Educational Progress (NAEP) data show that among all fourth graders, 64 percent were at or above the basic reading level and 31 percent were at or above proficient. By eighth grade, 73 percent were at or above the basic reading level and 31 percent were at or above proficient.

For African Americans and Hispanics, these reading results were less promising because their performance in fourth and eighth grades lagged behind both white and Asian students. In eighth grade, African Americans scored twenty-eight points and Hispanics scored twenty-five points lower than their white and Asian peers on the 2005 NAEP reading test. Fifty-two percent of African Americans and 56 percent of Hispanics obtained reading scores at or above basic, compared to 81 percent of white and 80 percent of Asian eighth graders. Only 12 percent of African Americans and 15 percent of Hispanics achieved reading scores at or above proficient, compared to 39 percent of white and 40 percent of Asian students (NCES 2005b). The NAEP trends were similar in math (NCES 2005a).

A disproportionate number of public schools are confronted by the fact that the academic playing field is not level when many poor, African American, and Hispanic students enter and continue through schools with lower academic outcomes.

Federal and State Policy Responses to Student Diversity

School administrators, teachers, and students currently function within an educational policy environment of standards-based accountability where academic standards and high-stakes testing directly influence the focus of curricula, instruction, and outcomes. The implementation of academic standards and state testing reflect federal and state policy responses to student diversity by attempting to provide more equitable educational experiences.

State Standards

The promotion of academic standards in the early 1990s was the result of efforts to foster national educational goals under George H.W. Bush's administration. It was with the passage of the 1994 Improving Schools Act (the reauthorization of the Elementary and Secondary Education Act) that the Clinton administration was able to require states to develop subject-specific standards (Cross 2004). These academic standards provide explicit goals that teachers must help students achieve. They also provide the criteria to determine whether these goals have been met. As Finn and Kanstoroom assert, "Standards are the target that gives people a place to aim their arrows and a means by which to gauge how hard they must pull on the bowstring" (2001, 131).

All states have academic standards in the core academic subjects, including reading, English language arts, and mathematics. Most states have also established similar goals in history, science, and foreign language. For example, Florida has Sunshine State Standards in core academic subjects such as language arts, mathematics, science and social studies for the middle grades (six through eight). There are also standards for the performing and visual arts, foreign language, physical education, and health. Although standards are state-specific, they require that local districts and schools align their teaching to these educational goals. It is expected that this alignment will promote common expectations, experiences, and outcomes for students.

An underlying assumption is that standards will eliminate the disparities in educational access because teachers will expose all students to subject-specific goals, regardless of the schools they attend or ability groups and track placements. As a result, the educational experiences of students should be less idiosyncratic because common expectations have been established.

In the past, schools and their teachers developed a curricular focus that often varied within schools and across classrooms. This variation in access to curriculum and instruction has had significant consequences regarding the educational experiences for the poor and students of color. "Absent standards, it was too easy to ignore the millions of youngsters who were learning very little—many of them poor and minority students from troubled communities—or settle for providing them with extra services that, all too often, turned out to have little to do with academic achievement. This is far harder to do in the standards era" (Finn and Kanstoroom 2001). Because African American, Hispanic, and poor students are more likely to attend schools with fewer academic resources and lower expectations (Kozol 1991), standards may offer the greatest hope for equalizing educational opportunities.

No Child Left Behind

Whereas the Clinton administration promoted educational standards, the George W. Bush administration fostered accountability regarding student outcomes with the No Child Left Behind (NCLB) Act of 2001. This legislation uses standardized testing as a means of promoting equity among diverse students by requiring state departments of education to establish common levels of educational outcomes in reading and mathematics for grades three through eight. The pressure to meet these outcomes is intended to promote the improvement of teaching and learning. Schools must meet adequate yearly progress (AYP) targets that show proficiency on predetermined benchmarks. State departments of education must analyze assessment data for disaggregated student subgroups (i.e., race, socioeconomic, and limited English proficiency status) to monitor their progress in relation to AYP (Goertz and Duffy 2003; Cross 2004). Schools that have not met AYP for multiple years may be subject to sanctions, including state-level intervention. Chronic underperformance by schools can lead to reconstitution. Students attending chronically failing schools have the option of receiving supplemental tutoring services or attending another school of choice in their districts (Fusarelli 2004).

Testing advocates assume that the pressure associated with requirements for student outcomes will motivate teachers and students to work harder (Kornhaber and Orfield 2001; Fuhrman 2004). Because NCLB assumes that the problem is the lack of motivation to change, it is believed that the consequences associated with testing provide teachers and students with the appropriate incentives to achieve the required educational standards. As a result of state standards and testing, public schools are under tremendous pressure to meet the needs of individual students at the same time that they are required to create academic parity by exposing most to common academic content. State assessments certify whether students have attained subject-specific proficiency. Despite the goals of state standards and high-stakes testing, it is unlikely that these strategies will equalize the learning experiences of students in schools because placement in lower ability groups and tracks often puts a ceiling on what students learn (Oakes 1985).

A new conceptualization of ability grouping and tracking in the accountability era must consider how schools respond to student diversity at the school level in two ways. First, it must consider how schools continue to accommodate student differences through the formal school structures and how accountability may influence the character of learning groups based on ability. Second, it must also consider how the differentiation of learning opportunities is reflected in the collective beliefs and practices of school personnel (Diamond, Randolph, and Spillane 2004).

Ability Grouping in the Accountability Era

Given the demographic and academic diversity of students, how should we presume that schools respond to these demands on an organizational level or on a level of expectations about standards? Despite efforts to improve the quality of teaching and learning within schools, the disparate academic and cultural backgrounds of students pose formidable challenges to overcome. Schools are confronted with the dilemma of how to best address the needs of a diverse student body. Although research shows that ability grouping should be eliminated or limited, it is difficult to dismantle such rigid structures when schools and teachers may believe they lack other practical options. In addition, the pressures from federal and state accountability foster new manifestations of learning groups that further differentiate and may limit student learning.

Formal School-Level Organizational Reponses to Student Diversity

Despite efforts among educational reformers to limit this type of stratification of students, there has been consistent evidence that ability grouping continues to exist. The grouping of students starts as soon as students enter school. Elementary school data from the Early Childhood Longitudinal Study (ECLS) show that during spring 1999, 26 percent of public school kindergarten teachers who taught in full-day programs and 14 percent of those teaching in half-day programs reported using achievement grouping for reading. However, 48 percent of the full-day kindergarten teachers and 42 percent of half day teachers also indicated using mixed-level groups for reading (U.S. Department of Education, 2003a). Research shows that students' prior group placements continue as they move through elementary school (Rist 1970).

ECLS survey responses from school administrators show that testing begins to play a role in placement decisions as early as kindergarten. Over two-thirds of public school administrators (69 percent) reported that entrance exams and placement tests were used at kindergarten. Although only 18 percent of these administrators indicated that they used this information for class placement decisions, 55 percent used the information to target students needing other assessments, 54 percent used the data to individualize instruction, and 24 percent used it to suggest delaying kindergarten entry (U.S. Department of Education, 2003b).

The use of ability grouping continues as students move through elementary schools. There has been long-standing concern regarding whether students' race, socioeconomic status, and gender affect placement in these learning groups. Condron's (2007) analysis focused on first grade reading group placement using ECLS data and found that relative ranking of students by race, socioeconomic status, and gender. Asian students have the highest ranking in reading groups, followed by students who are identified as white, other, Hispanic, and black. Girls have a higher reading group ranking then boys, and those with the highest socioeconomic status are ranked higher in reading groups than those with the lowest socioeconomic status. To explain these differences in relative reading group ranking, Condron (2007) found that after controlling for student prior achievement, classroom and school characteristics, teacher evaluation of student effort, and eagerness for learning and externalizing problem behaviors, the statistical differences in reading group ranking for black students were no longer significant but still negative. It must be noted that teacher evaluations were the lowest for black students compared to other students in the sample; however, there was no additional information provided to determine whether these teacher evaluations were fair and not biased.

Ability grouping continues in middle grades, and one reason this occurs is that teachers in these grades confront the challenge of addressing the needs of students leaving elementary schools and preparing them for the rigors of high school curricula. Data from the late 1980s set the context for understanding how schools serving middle grades continue to sort students into learning groups. Mac Iver and Epstein (1993) found that 60 percent of middle schools from the National Education Longitudinal Study of 1988 (NELS: 88) reported that students were assigned to between-class ability groups or attended all classes based on ability.

Data at the turn of the twenty-first century show the prevalence of ability grouping. Principal respondents from the 2000 National Study of Leadership in Middle Level Schools (NSLMLS) show that more than 80 percent of the 1,400 middle schools included in the study reported using some form of between- or within-classroom ability groups (Petzko 2004). In addition, Harris's (2004) data from a sample of middle schools involved with the standards-based, whole-school reform model America's Choice show that 60 percent of schools surveyed used ability grouping despite this program's aspiration to limit such practices. Principal survey data from a subsample of 109 America's Choice middle schools indicated that 13 percent of these schools had all core subjects differentiated by student ability, and 47 percent had some subjects differentiated by student ability.

Tracking among high school students is more complex because all students have to fulfill an academic core of courses to graduate. High school transcript studies show that between 1982 and 2004 there was an overall increase in the number of academic courses (i.e., English, history/social studies, mathematics, and the physical and biological sciences) taken among graduates, and a decrease in vocational course credits (U.S. Department of Education 2007a). These increases have been brought on by the increase in the number of academic courses required for high school graduation. The majority of states in 2005 required that students take either three to four credits of English. Thirty-six states mandated that students take three mathematics courses, and fifteen states required two years of mathematics. What is surprising is that in 2005 only four states required four years of mathematics, and seven states (Colorado, Iowa, Massachusetts, Minnesota, Nebraska, North Dakota, and Pennsylvania) indicated that such requirements were not applicable. However, in Pennsylvania, local school districts determine graduation course requirements (U.S. Department of Education 2007). The increase in academic course requirements has been supported by state policies, including those in Massachusetts, where the general education track was eliminated by a 1993 educational reform act.

Data from the NAEP transcript study show that increased academic course enrollment can be found among all racial groups. In 2005, 10 percent of all high school graduates had completed a rigorous academic curriculum, including four years of English; three years of social studies; four years of mathematics, including precalculus or higher; three years of science, including biology, chemistry, and physics; and three years of foreign language. There has also been an increase by racial groups in students taking mid-level courses or higher. Sixty-three percent of Asian/Pacific Islander, 52 percent of white, 51 percent black, and 44% of Hispanic students take a mid-level curriculum or higher. In the same report, data show that 32 percent of all high school graduates in 2005 took a program of study that was less than a standard curriculum. That is, these students had less than four years of English, three years of mathematics, three years of social studies, three years of science, and no foreign language. Thirty-one percent of white, 27 percent of black, 46 percent of Hispanic, and 27 percent of Asian high school graduates completed a less than standard program of study in 2005 (U.S. Department of Education 2007b). Despite the gains in overall academic course enrollment, there were a number of students taking a nonrigorous program of study.

When the course enrollment data are disaggregated by subject, we see big racial disparities in mathematics courses taken by 2005 high school graduates participating in NAEP. Most black and Latino students who graduated in 2005 took mid-level mathematics courses. Seventy-one percent of black and 72 percent of Hispanic students took Algebra II, Geometry, or Algebra I or below before graduating from high school. In contrast, 63 percent of Asian/Pacific Islanders and 46 percent of white high school graduates in the same year took advanced math and calculus (U.S. Department of Education 2007b). As a result, Asian and white students enrolled in the most rigorous mathematics available to high school students, which provided them with the prerequisite knowledge to be prepared for college-level mathematics and majors that require a strong foundation in advanced mathematics. Despite efforts to increase access to academic courses, federal data show that access to advanced courses is not readily available to all students. This fact can limit access to colleges, influence the preparation to fulfill college-level core requirements, and limit access to mathematics-related majors.

Ability Groupings and the Influence of Accountability

Ability grouping as a school-level response, especially in the elementary and middle schools, is not surprising, because research shows that eliminating these organizational structures is very difficult (Oakes, Wells, Jones, and Datnow 1997). Recent research in Chicago and Texas, however, provides examples of how accountability can foster additional learning groups designed to promote learning, while in reality limiting student attainment. Remedial classrooms and test preparation groups are two examples of past practices that take on a new role with high-stakes testing.

Harris et al. (2005) found that remedial courses were found in 58 percent of forty-eight high schools involved with the Study of High School Strategies of Instructional

Practices.[1] These courses assisted students with obtaining content knowledge. Most of these remedial courses were focused on students who had not met proficiency on a state assessment. Depending on the state accountability system, the focus of remedial courses was on ninth- through twelfth-grade students. For example, in some North Carolina schools, students who had not achieved reading proficiency on the eighth-grade test were placed in a ninth-grade reading course. Because North Carolina has a requirement that all high school students pass Algebra I to graduate, schools have created courses to assist students in fulfilling this mandate.

Lipman (2004) shows that remedial programs can reflect ability grouping at its worst when learning needs are poorly served in these academic settings. Districts and schools that are on probation or experiencing chronic low achievement are contexts in which remedial programs may be put into place to address academic outcomes. Schools encountering intense accountability pressure may offer only low-level curriculum and instruction by focusing on basic skills related to state testing. Such programs instituted in Chicago did not adequately serve the academic needs of students because of the mismatch between lessons and the district test. Despite district subject area frameworks, transition high schools in Chicago provided students with a basic skills curriculum with rote seat work. In addition, participants of summer remedial programs in the city often experienced classes with unqualified teachers who were not certified in the subject area taught.

Schools on probation or at risk of being sanctioned by their local accountability systems may also respond to this pressure by employing educational triage—that is, targeting instructional resources toward students who are most likely to attain the required threshold that removes schools from probation. Booher-Jennings found that one Texas school district responded to the threat of state accountability sanctions by having school staff use test data to label elementary school students as passers, "bubble kids," and foundation/remedial kids (2005, 232). Students labeled as bubble kids were provided the majority of resources necessary to pass the state test. They were given test preparation assistance during the school day by nonelective teachers (e.g., music and physical education), during after-school hours by tutors, and during the summer. Those classified as remedial were ignored, with little to or no academic resources provided to them. The practice of educational triage exists outside of Texas, and Lipman (2004) and Diamond and Spillane (2004) found these practices were fostered by district and school administrators in Chicago. The existence of remedial learning groups, coupled with the strategy of selecting a subset of students to participate in them, creates a low-level ability group that focuses on basic skills in response to district or state tests.

The biggest travesty is that there are students in these schools who are neglected and denied remedial resources. These remedial test prep groups are not the learning structures typically associated with ability grouping; nevertheless, assignment to such groups has an impact on students' learning opportunities. Being placed in a remedial learning group is not the most desirable learning environment for students, but it does serve the short-term purpose of meeting the demands of accountability systems. However, that some are not being targeted for such services shows that there is a population of students being written off in low-performing schools. In fact, Booher-Jennings (2005) found that teachers in her study made deliberate attempts to have students they believed to have little chance of passing the state assessment be classified as special education so that their scores would not count for accountability purposes.

---

1. The Study of High School Strategies of Instructional Improvement was conducted between 2001 and 2007 of forty-eight high schools in California, Florida, Michigan, North Carolina, New York, and Pennsylvania to understand their responses to high-stakes accountability.

In addition, these remedial programs and test prep groups in a school or district on probation represent a low-level academic track because there is a ceiling placed on student learning fostered by a narrow focus on basic skills. Diamond and Spillane (2004) and Lipman (2004) found that teachers committed to innovative curriculum and instruction were often forced to abandon these strategies when they recognized their practices could not guarantee student proficiency on required assessments. As a result, the low-level practices fostered by these schools contradict the intentions of accountability policy.

Collective School-Level Beliefs About Students: A New Dimension of Curriculum Differentiation

Although it is important to understand how curriculum and learning experiences are differentiated by the creation of formal learning groups in schools and classrooms, it is also necessary to understand how this differentiation is manifested in collective beliefs among teachers and administrators about students. These beliefs shape the instructional strategies used with students and the effort made to help them succeed. Beliefs about students are a significant barrier to any significant educational change proposed based on standards.

Diamond, Randolph, and Spillane (2004) examined how Chicago elementary school-teachers' collective responsibility for student learning affected the instructional strategies used with students. Their data show that teacher expectations were related to the racial and socioeconomic composition of schools. The schools with large African American and low-income student populations had low expectations, and teacher comments focused on student deficits rather than assets. For example, less than a quarter of teachers in predominantly African American schools and only 10 percent of teachers in poor schools[2] emphasized students' academic assets versus deficits. Therefore, we must also pay close attention to alternative ways that differentiation continues to be perpetuated beyond formal ability grouping and tracking.

When deeply entrenched beliefs interact with the implementation of standards, they are adjusted to fit beliefs about students. Standholtz, Ogawa, and Scribner (2004) found in a California school district that school officials modified state standards by developing less rigorous benchmarks. Because many believed that the state's standards were unrealistic for their students, the district modified them to align with perceptions about student ability. As a result, this district established three levels of standards: minimal, essential, and accelerated. The authors suggest that differentiation of standards is analogous to academic tracking because they were associated with perceptions about student ability. Teachers in this district used the accelerated standards with students identified as possessing the highest abilities, and the minimal standards were implemented with those with the lowest abilities. In mixed-ability classrooms, teachers tended to focus on basic skills with the intention of meeting the needs of their lowest-performing students.

At the very least, we can assume that accountability has fostered increased access to the academic curriculum. Research shows that the implementation of standards and testing has provided some students with better access to core curricula often neglected in the

---

2. Poor schools represented those with 90 percent or more identified as low income.

past. Hamilton, Berends, and Stecher (2005) found in their study of standards-based accountability that most mathematics and science teachers in California, Georgia, and Pennsylvania reported it had a positive impact on instruction. For example, 67 percent of middle school mathematics teachers in California, 73 percent in Georgia, and 64 percent in Pennsylvania indicated that their instruction was different as a result of mathematics assessments during the 2003–2004 academic year. It is important to recognize, however, that the modification of standards and expectations according to student ability leads to many students not attaining mastery.

Although there are many factors that affect student mastery, including time (Harris 2004), we must seriously consider how teachers' collective responsibility for students limits the extent to which students achieve and the extent to which the implementation of accountability fulfills its goal of promoting educational equality. Teachers' expectations regarding standards intersect with the demographic and academic diversity of students and reveal the inherent conflict that exists between implementing a common academic curriculum and meeting individual instructional needs. As a result, teachers respond to differences by showing a commitment to exposing students to standards, but there is less agreement among them about whether mastery could be attained by all. Harris (2004) found that although some America's Choice middle school teachers held a general belief that most of their students could achieve standards, they did not expect all of them to attain mastery. Petzko's (2004) study also found that approximately 50 percent of teachers surveyed for the NSLMLS did not work to ensure content mastery. If the goal of standards is limited to increasing curriculum exposure without mastery for most students, then we will not see the radical changes in academic outcomes, especially for students of color and the poor located in racially isolated and low-performing schools.

Conclusion

The demographic and academic diversity in public schools poses considerable challenges because students arrive at schools with varying skills. The implementation of standards and testing reflects federal and state policy responses to diversity with an objective to promote equality of educational opportunity by mandating common educational goals and outcomes. Equity-based reform efforts can be thwarted, however, by structural responses to student differences (i.e., ability groups and tracks) and teachers' collective beliefs. Schools at the greatest risk of being sanctioned at district and state levels provide fertile ground for remediation that narrowly focuses on basic skills. These schools may also be more likely to ration educational resources to those students most likely to help schools evade probation, while neglecting those students with the greatest educational needs.

In addition to structural responses to student academic diversity, collective beliefs about students influence curriculum differentiation. The fact that districts, schools, and teachers may modify standards and have different expectations regarding their attainment reveals the realities associated with providing all students with common standards-based curricula. It is questionable whether reform efforts alone can drastically change teacher practices without deeply embedded beliefs about students being addressed first to effectively deal with the variation in student skills (Oakes 1992; Weinstein 1996).

As Weinstein suggests,

> Calls for the raising of standards (however meaningful) fail to grapple with the complexity of what is currently in place in schools and the systemic changes needed to fix the problem. Attention must be paid to changing limiting beliefs about differential ability to learn and self-defeating teaching methods that follow from such beliefs. These have led to the inappropriate adjustment of standards (lower expectations) and the inappropriate adjustment of teaching methods (watered-down treatment) for certain groups of children, thereby creating enormous inequities in conditions for learning. (1996, 16)

We must recognize that without high goals, we will not equalize educational outcomes. Standards in and of themselves are irrelevant if expectations are not aligned with the goals of this reform. These goals cannot be accomplished, however, without schools and teachers possessing strategies and belief systems that oppose the tendency to impose limits for the lowest-performing students, many of whom are African American, Hispanic. and poor.

References

Booher-Jennings, J. "Below the Bubble: 'Educational Triage' and the Texas Accountability System." *American Educational Research Journal* 42(2) (2005): 231–68.

Braddock, J.H. and Dawkins, M.P. "Ability Grouping, Aspirations, and Attainments: Evidence from the National Educational Longitudinal Study of 1988." *Journal of Negro Education* 62(3) (1993): 324–36.

Braddock, J.H. and McPartland, J.M. "Education of Early Adolescents." *Review of Research in Education* 19 (1993): 135–70.

Condron, D.J. "Stratification and Educational Sorting: Explaining Ascriptive Inequalities in Early Childhood Reading Group Placement." *Social Problems* 54(1) (2007): 139–60.

Cross, C.T. *Political Education: National Policy Comes of Age.* New York: Teachers College Press, 2004.

Diamond, J., Randolph, A., and Spillane, J. "Teachers' Expectations and Sense of Responsibility for Student Learning: The Importance of Race, Class, and Organizational Habitus." *Anthropology and Education Quarterly* 35(1) (2004): 75–98.

Diamond, J. and Spillane, J. "High-Stakes Accountability in Urban Elementary Schools: Challenging of Reproducing Inequality." *Teachers College Record* 106(6) (2004): 145–76.

Finn, C.E. and Kanstoroom, M. *Brookings Papers on Educational Policy 2001.* Ed. D. Ravitch. Washington: Brookings Institution, 2001. 131–79.

Fuhrman, S.H. Introduction. *Redesigning Accountability Systems for Education* Eds. S.H. Fuhrman and R.F. Elmore. New York: Teachers College Press, 2004. 3–14.

Fusarelli, L.D. "The Potential Impact of the No Child Left Behind Act on Equity and Diversity in American Education." *Educational Policy* 18(1) (2004): 71–94.

Gamoran, A. and Mare, R.D. "Secondary School Tracking and Educational Inequality: Compensation, Reinforcement, or Neutrality?" *American Journal of Sociology* 94 (1989): 1146–83.

Goertz, M. and Duffy, M. "Mapping the Landscape of High-Stakes Testing and Accountability Programs." *Theory into Practice* 42(1) (2003): 4–11.

Good, T.L., Grouw, D.A., and Mason, D.A. "Teachers' Beliefs about Small-Group Instruction in Elementary School Mathematics." *Journal of Research in Mathematics Education* 21(1) (1990): 2–15.

Hamilton, L., Berends, M., and Stecher, B. *Teachers' Responses to Standards-Based Accountability*. RAND Report No. WR-259-EDU. Santa Monica: RAND, 2005.

Harris, D.M. "Curriculum Differentiation and School Reform: Contradictions in Providing Educational Opportunity." American Educational Research Association Meeting. San Diego, April 2004.

Harris, D.M., Prosky, M., Bach, A., Heilig, J., and Hussar, K. "Overview of Actions Taken by High Schools to Improve Instruction." *Holding High Hopes: How High Schools Respond to State Accountability Policies*. Eds. Betheny Gross and Margaret E. Geortz. Philadelphia: Consortium for Policy Research in Education, 2005.

Kornhaber, M.L. and Orfield, G. "High-Stakes Testing Policies: Examining Their Assumptions and Consequences." *Raising Standards or Raising Barriers?: Inequality and High-Stakes Testing in Public Education*. Eds. G. Orfield and M.L. Kornhaber. New York: Century Foundation Press, 2001. 1–18.

Kozol, J. *Savage Inequalities*. New York: Crown, 1991.

Lipman, P. *High Stakes Education: Inequality, Globalization, and School Reform*. New York: Routledge Falmer, 2004.

Lucas, S.R. *Tracking Inequality: Stratification and Mobility in American High Schools*. New York: Teachers College Press, 1999.

Mac Iver, D.J. and Epstein, J.L. "Middle Grades Research: Not Yet Mature, but No Longer a Child." *Elementary School Journal* 93(5) (1993): 519–33.

Oakes, J. *Keeping Track: How Schools Structure Inequality*. New Haven: Yale University Press, 1985.

———. "Can Tracking Research Inform Practice?: Technical, Normative, and Political Considerations." *Educational Researcher* 21(4) (1992): 12–21.

Oakes, J., Wells, A.S., Jones, M., and Datnow, A. "Detracking: The Social Construction of Ability, Cultural Politics, and Resistance to Reform." *Teachers College Record* 98(3) (1997): 482–510.

Page, R. *Lower-Track Classrooms: A Curricular and Cultural Perspective*. New York: Teachers College Press, 1991.

Petzko, V.N. "Findings and Implications of the NASSP National Study of Leadership in Middle Level Schools, Volumes I and II: Teachers in Middle Level Schools." *NASSP Bulletin* 88(638) (2004): 69–88.

Rist, R. "Student Social Class and Teachers' Expectations: The Self-Fulfilling Prophecy in Ghetto Education." *Harvard Educational Review* 40 (1970): 411–50.

Rosenbaum, J.E. *Making Inequality: The Hidden Curriculum of High School Tracking*. New York: Wiley, 1976.

Sable, J. and Young, Beth A. *Characteristics of 1000 Largest Public Elementary and Secondary School Districts in the United States: 2001–2002 Report* (NCES Report No. 2003-353). U.S. Dep't of Education, National Center for Education Statistics. Washington: Institute of Education Sciences, 2003.

Slavin, R. "Ability Grouping and Student Achievement in Elementary Schools: A Best-Evidence Synthesis." *Review of Educational Research* 57(3) (1987): 293–336.

——. "Achievement Effects of Ability Grouping in Secondary Schools: A Best-Evidence Synthesis." *Review of Educational Research* 60(3) (1990): 471–99.

Standholtz, J.H., Ogawa, R.T., and Scribner S.P. "Standards Gaps: Unintended Consequences of Local Standards-Based Reform." *Teachers College Record* 106(6) (2004): 177–202.

U.S. Dept. of Education, National Center for Education Statistics. *The Condition of Education* (NCES Report No. 2007-64). Washington: GPO, 2007a.

——. *The Nation's Report Card—America's High School Graduates: Results from the 2005 NAEP High School Transcript Study* (NCES Report No. 2007-467). Washington: GPO, 2007b.

——. *The Nation's Report Card: Mathematics 2005* (NCES Report No. 2006-453). Washington: Institute of Education Sciences, 2005a.

——. *The Nation's Report Card: Reading 2005* (NCES Report No. 2006-451). Washington: Institute of Education Sciences, 2005b.

——. *Reading—Young Children's Achievement and Classroom Experiences* (NCES Report No. 2003-070). Washington: GPO, 2003a.

——. *Schools' Use of Assessments for Kindergarten Entrance and Placement 1998-1999* (NCES Report No. 2003-004). Washington: GPO, 2003b.

Weinstein, R.S. "High Standards in a Tracked System of Schooling: For Which Students and with What Educational Supports." *Educational Researcher* 25(8) (2006): 16–19.

Welner, K.G. "They Retard What They Cannot Repel: Examining the Role Teachers Sometimes Play in Subverting Equity-Minded Reform." *Journal of Negro Education* 68(2) (1999): 200–12.

Wirt, J., Choy, S., Rooney, P., Hussar, W., Provasnik, S., and Hampden-Thompson, G. *The Condition of Education 2005* (NCES Report No. 2005-094). U.S. Dep't of Education. Washington: Institute of Education Sciences, 2005.

Zhou, M. "Urban Education: Challenges in Educating Culturally Diverse Children." *Teachers College Record* 105(2) (2003): 208–25.

VI
Creating Learner-Centered Communities

22

Examining the Connection of NCLB to Educational Equity: Smaller Learning Communities (SLC) Program

Na'im H. Madyun and Moosung Lee

Introduction

Since the enactment of No Child Left Behind (NCLB), closing the racial achievement gap has become the core of educational policy. Schools across the country are feverishly seeking ways to achieve educational equity. Amid such reform, smaller learning communities—a smaller subunit within a larger high school such as an academy, house plan, school-within-in-a school or other structural unit—have emerged as a promising federal program for raising student achievement.[1] Over the last decade, smaller learning communities (SLC) have been widely implemented as a policy intervention under Title V, part D, subpart 4 of the Elementary and Secondary Education Act of 1965, as reauthorized by NCLB.[2] The federal government provided approximately $275 million across the country from 2000 to 2004 in implementing this ambitious initiative. Additionally, SLC has been substantially supported by wealthy foundations (e.g., the Gates Foundation, the Annenberg Foundation, the Carnegie Foundation, the Joyce Foundation, the Pew Charitable Trust, the Annie E. Casey Foundation, etc.). For example, the Gates Foundation has funded this program with more than $650 million,[3] and the Annenberg Foundation has also allocated $500 million to the reform of urban schools, including the SLC program.[4] By virtue of this substantial funding, as of 2006, there are 1,076 SLC schools from 480 school

---

1. DEP'T OF EDUC., AN OVERVIEW OF SMALLER LEARNING COMMUNITIES IN HIGH SCHOOLS (2001), *at* www.ed.gov/programs/slcp/resources.html#PUBLICATIONS.

2. Department of Education, *Smaller Learning Communities Program: Notices* (2004) *at* a257.g.akamaitech.net/7/257/2422/14mar20010800/edocket.access.gpo.gov/2004/pdf/04-5818.pdf.

3. Todd J. Sparger, *An Investigation of Implementations of Smaller Learning Communities in Florida High Schools* (2005) (unpublished doctoral dissertation, University of Central Florida).

4. Valerie E. Lee et al., *Educational Equity and School Structure: School Size, School Overcrowding and Alternative Organizational Structures* (2002) *at* www.idea.gseis.ucla.edu/publications/williams/reports/pdfs/wws15-LeeReadyWelner.pdf.

districts across the country. In addition, most recently awarded SLC high schools, including 145 schools from 57 school districts, will be financially supported until 2010.[5]

Why is the SLC program, buttressed by such immense financial viability, gaining popularity and becoming the buzzword in the arena of high school reform? Why the large push for SLC schools among policy makers? One of the pivotal assumptions associated with the SLC program is that "small is better" in improving student achievement and narrowing the achievement gap.[6] This assumption has been shaped by many school-size studies that overwhelmingly affirm small schools' effectiveness vis-à-vis large schools in terms of educational attainments such as student achievement,[7] academic equity,[8] graduation rate[9] and safety schools.[10] Moreover, small school environments have shown some evidence that the racial achievement gap between whites and people of color has been reduced in many smaller schools, which are mostly located in large cities such as New York, Chicago, Los Angeles, Philadelphia and others.[11] The positive relationship between small schools and equitable student achievement across race has been particularly compelling. As such, under the policy framework of NCLB, small schools have received broad attention by policy makers and educators for high school reform.

The literature supports the effectiveness of small schools in promoting educational equity. Unfortunately, there is yet not enough empirical support to argue for substituting SLCs for small schools. Some research findings from inherently small high schools are restricted in their application to the larger high schools. Consequently, the consistency between SLCs and small schools is unknown. This is critical because larger high schools have tried to capture the small school benefits by implementing the SLC program. This unknown quite naturally invites scholarly criticism in some circles that view SLCs as very problematic, criticism which in turn threatens sustainability. It is only a matter of time before the enormous amount of foundational and governmental support behind the SLC program begins to fade due to lack of direct empirical evidence for promoting educational equity. This will affect not only future resource allocations into similar interventions but also policy. In brief, as it stands now, we have only the empirical evidence drawn from an analogous setting.[12]

An attempt to establish empirical support must begin with research on which components of SLC schools contribute to academic achievement across race. Given that SLC high

---

5. Southwest Educational Development Laboratory (2006), *at* www.sedl.org/work/projects/slc.html.

6. Moosung Lee & Tom Friedrich, *The Smaller the School, the Better?: The Smaller Learning Communities (SLC) Program in U.S. High Schools*, 10 IMPROVING SCHOOLS (Oct. 2007).

7. *See e.g.*, Craig Howley, *The Academic Effectiveness of Small-scale Schooling* (1994), *at* http:www.eric.ed.gov; Lee E. Valerie & Smith B. Julia, *Effects of High School Restructuring and Size on Early Gains in Achievement and Engagement*, 68 SOCIOLOGY OF EDUCATION 241, 270 (1995); Steifel Leanna et al., *High School Size: Effects on Budgets and Performance in New York City*, 22 EDUCATIONAL EVALUATION AND POLICY ANALYSIS 27, 39 (2000).

8. Craig Howley et al., *Research about School Size and School Performance in Impoverished Communities* (2000) *at* www.eric.gov.

9. Robert B. Pittman & Perri Haughwout, *Influence of High School Size on Dropout Rate*, 9 EDUCATIONAL EVALUATION AND POLICY ANALYSIS 337, 343 (1987).

10. Susan Klonsky & Michael Klonsky, *Countering Anonymity Through Small Schools*, 57 EDUCATIONAL LEADERSHIP 38, 41 (1999).

11. Kathleen Cotton, *New Small Learning Communities: Findings from Recent Literature* (2001) *at* www.nwrel.org/scpd/sirs/nslc/pdf.

12. *See* Lee et al., *supra* note 4. They also raise the important question about whether research results on small schools can legitimately be used to validate SLC programs.

schools feature various curricular structures (twenty-one types) in their programs, it is quite unclear which structures are more effective and which combinations of those structures would be the most effective. Furthermore, the effectiveness of the SLC program in closing the racial achievement gap is likely to be affected by where the program is initiated due to demographic differences in racial composition by locale (e.g., large central city, mid-size central city, suburban area, small town and rural area).

Although there are a lot of evaluation reports of SLC schools, because all grantees (i.e., SLC schools) are asked to submit an annual evaluation report to the Department of Education, most of the evaluation reports are not accessible to the public. The department also gathers individual SLC schools' performance data, yet the data are also not accessible to the public. A handful of evaluation reports of the SLC program can be obtained from the Internet. I argue, however, that these reports are not sufficiently representative for charting the effectiveness of the SLC program because it is quite possible that only successful schools are more likely to allow the release of their evaluation data.

Because of the current dearth of widescale evaluations of the SLC program, policy makers and educators simply do not know how well SLC schools across the country are achieving their program goals. To my knowledge, three relatively large-scale studies indirectly connected to the SLC program have been found. One is an evaluation study on the Chicago High School Redesign Initiative (CHSRI), utilizing theory-based evaluation as well as a matched comparison: twelve CHSRI schools, which is another version of SLC, versus fifty-nine non-CHSRI schools.[13] This study found that SLCs contribute to improving attendance rate and cumulative dropout rate. It also revealed that instructional leadership is key to the SLC program. Still, the result is restricted to the Chicago school district.

The second study, conducted by the Manpower Demonstration Research Corporation, examined nine high schools adopting a career academy program, which is one typical type of the various SLC structures.[14] This study showed a positive, long-term effect of career academies on labor market outcomes among the participants of career academies. Yet the result is also limited to the particular SLC structure, and thus the effectiveness of other subcomponents of SLC remains unanswered.

The third study[15] provided a relatively big picture of SLC's effectiveness on school performance. However, the study did not adequately address its missing data because the repeated measures ANOVA used in the study could not cover this missing data issue in a longitudinal analysis. In brief, these three studies added more knowledge of SLC's effectiveness on educational equity, yet a big picture remains undeveloped.

Therefore, the primary purpose of this chapter is to address this research gap. Specifically, I examine whether SLC high schools contribute to both improving overall academic achievement and closing the racial achievement gap through a longitudinal analysis as well as on a larger scale. Alongside this main research question, I also explore which SLC structures are more effective for improving school performance. Further, I investigate the contribution of SLC to educational equity by focusing on how the effectiveness of the SLC is associated with location and racial proportion.

---

13. Joseph E. Kahne et al., *Small Schools on a Larger Scale: The First Three Years of the Chicago High School Redesign Initiative* (2006) at ccsr.uchicago.edu/ content/publications.php?pub_id=4.

14. James J. Kemple & Judith Scott-Clayton, *Career Academies: Impacts on Labor Market Outcomes and Educational Attainment* (2004) at www.mdrc.org/publications/366/full.pdf.

15. *See* Lee & Friedrich, *supra* note 6.

On the SLC Program

Before going further in this section, I begin with a brief introduction of SLC for readers. The primary goal of the SLC is to raise academic achievement for all students enrolled in large high schools by creating smaller learning communities within the schools.[16] Although there is no universal definition and model for capturing the whole concept of SLC, the federal government provides a comprehensive policy guideline and structural examples that are predominantly integrated into current SLC schools. According to the Department of Education,[17] "SLC" refers to smaller subunits, such as academies, house plans, schools within schools, or other structural units for creating smaller subunits in a large school. Current SLC schools thus try to create smaller subunits that fit in their schools by combining different SLC structures. Within this context, I use the term "SLC" as the organizational restructuring of high schools that seek to create smaller, more personalized, autonomous learning environments, which are more likely to provide better educational outcomes stemming from the smallness of schools.

The federal government categorizes the existing models of SLC as four main structures.[18] The four major structures include academies, house plans, schools within schools and magnet programs. *Academies* are subgroups consisting of students and teachers who focus on particular themes. For this reason, it is interchangeably used with the term of theme-based academies. Career academies, as typical instances, cover both academic and occupational areas by combining "the school-to-career movement."[19] *House plans* are designed to "divide students in a large school into groups of several hundred, either across grade levels or by grade levels."[20] Under the guidance of their house teachers, students take their core courses based on the tightly interwoven social relationships of house systems. *Schools within schools* pursue "a small, autonomous program housed within a larger school building."[21] The current SLC schools employing this structure have "different degrees of autonomy"[22] in operating the school-within-a-school structure; usually the schools represent "their own culture, program, personnel, students, budget, and school space."[23] *Magnet programs* draw students from the entire school district by highlighting an academic specialty focus (e.g., mathematics, science, arts), based on either competitive admission requirements or open enrolling systems.[24] Importantly, these SLC structures somewhat overlap in terms of their basic concepts, yet they are analytically separable in measuring their effectiveness. Current SLC schools may employ more than one SLC structure, yet there is no school adopting all of the structures. The beauty of the diversity in structure and implementation is that interventions can be designed to fit locale. Unfortunately, the accompanying beast is in developing an effective and fair method of assessment across the implementations.

---

16. *See* DEPARTMENT OF EDUCATION, *supra* note 1, at 1–5.
17. *Id.* at 4–8.
18. *Id.* at 4–8.
19. *Id.* at 6.
20. *Id.* at 6.
21. *Id.* at 6.
22. *See* Cotton, *supra* note 11, at 9.
23. *See* DEPARTMENT OF EDUCATION, *supra* note 1, at 6.
24. *See id.* at 6.

Method

Data

This study aimed to trace back one SLC cohort, which included 222 high schools from 36 states that implemented the SLC program during the 2002–2004 period. Covering 29 states, we sampled 191 out of the 222 SLC schools.[25] Primary information about SLC schools (e.g., name, district, SLC structure, racial proportion, grant period, locale, etc.) was gathered from the Southwest Educational Development Laboratory and the National Center for Education Statistics. Another data set used in this study came from the Public School Ranking Dataset, which provided substantial ranking data of those twenty-nine states. School performance data for 2002, 2003 and 2004 were constructed by changing school rankings into quantified school performance data.

Data Analysis

Because the school performance data employed in this study were incomplete , meaning that there were several missing values, I utilized hierarchical multivariate linear modeling techniques (HMLM) allowing "the estimation of multivariate normal models from incomplete data."[26] More specifically, a time-oriented predictor, called "occasion," was used as a level-1 predictor. The variable was coded 0–2 (i.e., three consecutive years) to enhance the interpretation of the school performance intercepts. I did a series of analyses based on the locale and racial proportion of SLC schools, which were used as level-2 predictors.[27] Dummy variables were employed for coding these predictors. SLC schools located in a large central city were coded as 0. SLC schools located in mid-size central city, urban fringe and small town were coded as 1, 2 and 3, respectively.[28] The 191 SLC schools were categorized into three groups by racial proportion: predominantly white, black and Hispanic schools. Predominantly white SLC schools were coded as 0. Predominantly black and Hispanic SLC schools were coded as 1 and 2, respectively. Additionally, the four SLC structures representing important institutional characteristics were also used as level-2 predictors.

While those level-1 and level-2 predictors were employed as independent variables, the ranking of each school was used as a dependent variable. The dependent variable was

---

25. Therefore, our findings would be restricted in explaining the effectiveness of 31 SLC schools in seven states (i.e., Alaska, Arkansas, Maine, New Mexico, North Carolina, Rhode Island and Utah), which were not included in this sample.

26. *See* STEPHEN RAUDENBUSH ET AL., HLM 6: HIERARCHICAL LINEAR & NONLINEAR MODELING, 140.

27. The initial plan was to do a three-level analysis (i.e., HMLM2) since individual SLC schools are nested within a particular locale type. However, as the associated intra-class correlation between level 2 and level 3 was too small, I chose a two-level analysis.

28. The locale types in this study are based on the locale definitions of the Southwest Educational Development Laboratory: large central city (population greater than or equal to 250,000), mid-size central city (population less than 250,000), urban fringe of city (suburban areas within a Metropolitan Statistical Area of a large city and a mid-size city, defined by the Census Bureau), small town (a population less than 25,000 and greater than or equal to 2,500) and rural area (place with less than 2,500, defined rural by the Census Bureau).

a composite of standardized test scores of reading, writing and mathematics, which were gathered from state departments of education. The conversion formula of school rankings into quantified dependent variables is {100 − [individual high school ranking/the total number of high schools in each state] × 100}. For example, from 2002 to 2004, the state-wide rankings of high school X in California in terms of academic achievement were as follows: 351/880 (2002), 465/1167 (2003) and 497/1863 (2004). Based on the formula, these rankings were converted into percentiles—respectively, 60.2 (2002), 60.2 (2003) and 73.4 (2004). Here, 73.4 means that high school X is ranked as the top 73.4 percent among all high schools including non-SLC schools in California in 2004. The ranking scale thus ranged from 0 to 100. From this conversion, how much progress each SLC school made on academic achievement year by year was identified.

Results

Descriptive Characteristics of the SLC Schools

As mentioned earlier, the SLC schools adopted more than one structure. As presented in Table 1, academies (88.0 percent) were the most popular structure adopted by the 2002 SLC cohort. In terms of locale, 41.4 percent of the SLC schools were located in large central cities. A relatively small percentage of the SLC schools were located in small towns or rural areas (7.3 percent). If more than 50 percent of the total proportion was from a particular ethnicity, that school was considered to be predominated by that ethnicity. According to the data, 33.5 percent, 31.9 percent and 16.8 percent were predominantly white, black and Hispanic, respectively. This suggests that most SLC schools sampled in this study were racially segregated to some extent. The racial diversity of the 191 SLC schools also reflects this aspect. The average racial diversity was 38.5, suggesting that most SLC high schools were not racially diverse or racially mixed in the sense that the mean of racial diversity was below 50 percent.[29]

Does SLC Contribute to Improving Academic Achievement?

I first examined whether SLC high schools contribute to overall academic achievement by examining the change of school ranking from 2002 to 2004. An unconditional model first fitted showed an estimated mean of initial school ranking at the entry time-point (β_{00}, 39.0). This means that the average state-wide ranking was 39.0 percent for the sample in 2002. This also means that many of SLC schools involved in this study were historically low-performing schools (i.e., below the top 50 percent of the total number of high

---

29. *See* Peter Blau, *A Macrosociological Theory of Social Structure,* 83 AMERICAN JOURNAL OF SOCIOLOGY 26, 54 (1977). Based on Blau's formula, racial diversity was calculated by summing each racial group's squared population proportion and then subtracting this sum from 1. The formula for this calculation is represented by (1 − %p2), where p is equal to the population proportion, *id.* For instance, an SLC school that is 80 percent White and 20 percent African American will have a diversity score of 0.32 {1 − (0.802 + 0.202)}. A more diverse SLC school that is 50 percent White, 25 percent African American and 25 percent Asian American will have a diversity score of 0.63 {1 − (0.52 + 0.252 + 0.252)}.

Table 1. Descriptive Statistics	
SLC Structures	**Number of Schools**
Academies	168 (88.0%)
House Plans	39 (20.4%)
Schools-Within-Schools	27 (14.1%)
Magnet Programs	17 (8.9%)
SLC Schools by Locale	**Number of Schools**
Large Central City	79 (41.4%)
Mid-Size Central City	30 (15.7%)
Urban Fringe of City	68 (35.6%)
Small Town and Rural Area	14 (7.3%)
Total	191 (100%)
SLC Schools Dominated by One Particular Racial Group	**Number of Schools**
Predominantly White Schools	64 (33.5%)
Predominantly Black Schools	61 (31.9%)
Predominantly Hispanic Schools	32 (16.8%)
Other Schools	34 (17.8%)
Total	191 (100%)

schools). However, despite these schools' below-average performance, the SLC program appeared to make slight progress in school performance year by year. That is, the estimated mean growth rate (β_{10}) was 1.34 ($p = 0.011$), meaning that the SLC schools were increasing an average 1.34 percent of their ranking per year.

The unconditional model also indicated that there were significant variations of the individual SLC schools' growth trajectories. The estimates for the variances of π_{0j} and π_{1j} were 865.5 and 42.7, respectively. As such, the null hypotheses (H_0: $\tau_{00} = 0$ and H_0: $\tau_{11} = 0$) were rejected. This reveals that school performance varied significantly across the SLC schools at the initial status (2002), and there was also significant variation in the annual academic progress. Notably, the correlation between the initial academic achievement of individual SLC schools (π_{0j}) and the change of academic progress (π_{1j}) was -0.373, meaning that low-performing SLC schools in 2002 tended to improve their school performance at a moderately faster rate than high-performing SLC schools in initial status.

Does SLC Contribute to Closing the Racial Achievement Gap?

Based on the variances of individual SLC schools' growth trajectories, level-2 predictors were added in to the unconditional model. To examine more specifically the impact of SLC schools on the racial achievement gap, three school groups defined by racial proportion were used as level-2 predictors (i.e., predominantly white, black and Hispanic SLC schools). The HMLM model was constructed as follows:

Level-1 Equation: $Y_{ti} = \pi_{0i} + \pi_{1i} a_{ti} + e_{ti}$
Level-2 Equation for Level-1 Intercept:

$\pi_i = \beta_{00} + \beta_{01}(\text{Predominantly White Schools})_I + \beta_{02}(\text{Predominantly Black Schools})_I$
$+ \beta_{03}(\text{Predominantly Hispanic Schools})_I + r_{0i}$

Table 2. HMLM Results by Racial Proportion				
Fixed Effect	Coefficient	SE	Approx. d.f.	P-Value
Intercept				
Predominantly White Schools, β_{00}	65.03***	2.80	154	0.000
Predominantly Black Schools, β_{01}	−45.54***	4.01	154	0.000
Predominantly Hispanic Schools, β_{02}	−33.46***	4.84	154	0.000
Occasion Slope				
Predominantly White Schools, β_{10}	−0.27	0.86	154	0.751
Predominantly Black Schools, β_{11}	0.38	1.23	154	0.756
Predominantly Hispanic Schools, β_{12}	4.98**	1.47	154	0.001
Note: n = 157 SLC schools (see Table 1). †$p < 0.10$, *$p < 0.05$, **$p < 0.01$, ***$p < 0.001$				

Level-2 Equation for Level-1 Slope:

$$\pi_{1i} = \beta_{10} + \beta_{11}(\text{Predominantly White Schools})_I + \beta_{12}(\text{Predominantly Black Schools})_I + \beta_{13}(\text{Predominantly Hispanic Schools})_I + r_{1i}$$

Based on the model, Table 2 presents the HMLM results. One salient finding was that predominantly white SLC schools performed significantly better than both predominantly black and Hispanic schools in the initial status: predominantly white (65.03***), black (65.03 − 45.54 = 19.49***) and Hispanic (31.57***) SLC schools. This initial gap between white SLC schools and black/Hispanic SLC schools was not just statistically significant but also practically substantive, given that the range of school ranking is from 0 to 100. This also suggests that the sample schools also mirror the persistent achievement gap facing U.S. high schools. However, amid this wide gap, predominantly Hispanic SLC schools showed significant yearly progress (the estimated coefficient β_{12} was 4.98**), whereas both predominantly white schools and predominantly black schools did not make notable yearly progress between 2002 and 2004.

Figure 1 represents the initial status and growth rate of those three SLC groups with the estimated grand mean of all SLC schools. Again, the growth rate of predominantly Hispanic SLC schools was a significant 4.71 points ($\beta_{10} + \beta_{12}$), which led those schools to reach an almost equal point (41.5) to the grand mean of the entire SLC school sample (41.7) in 2004. In contrast to the academic progress of predominantly Hispanic schools, predominantly white and black schools had not shown any significant progress in school performance during the same period.

This findings is consistent with the study of Lee and Friedrich. In providing a plausible explanation about the significant progress of predominantly Hispanic schools, they speculated that as the proportion of Hispanic students increases, so might the proportion of Hispanic adults functioning in various instruction and supportive capacities throughout the school. Lee and Friedrich went on to support their speculation by referencing previous studies (e.g., Monzo and Rueda's study).[30] According to these previous studies, a higher percentage of Hispanic teacher and para-educators improve the effectiveness of non-Hispanic teachers with Hispanic students, just as much as they help improve the ed-

---

30. *See* Pat A. Goldsmith, *Schools' Racial Mix, Students' Optimism, and the Black-White and Latino-White Achievement Gaps*, 77 SOCIOLOGY OF EDUCATION 121, 147 (2004).

ucational outcomes of Hispanic students themselves.[31] In addition, it has been found that educational experiences, aspirations and outlooks are more positive for Hispanic students when there is a large presence of people of color within the schools.[32]

To validate whether this speculation is true, I need to turn to the effect of locale on SLC. Locale is a critical factor because many Hispanic students who have a low SES and a linguistically marginalized status in academic achievement reside in large central cities. Therefore, SLC schools located in these areas should be expected to show a difference in academic achievement. To seek an answer, the next step turned to the effect of locale on SLC.

Figure 1. Initial Status and Growth Rate by Three Racial Groups

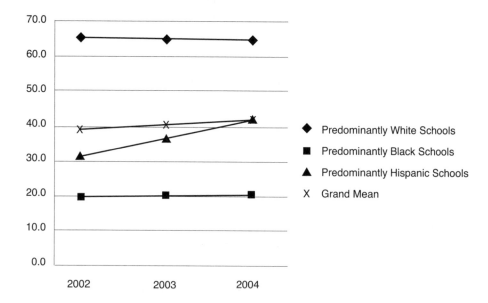

Does the Locale of SLC Matter?

Based on the four different types of locale, I added four level-2 predictors to the unconditional model. Table 3 shows the comparison the effect of the locale of SLC schools on academic achievement. In terms of initial academic performance, SLC schools located in large central cities lagged far behind their counterparts located in other areas. The estimated initial status by locale was as follows: large central city (25.93***), mid-size central city (25.93 + 16.05 = 41.98**), urban fringe of city (50.58***) and small town/rural area (48.32**). SLC schools located in large central cities were the only group left behind the estimated grand mean (39.0) in 2002. Further, the initial gap between SLC in large central cities and SLC in urban fringe of city is not just semantic but also substantive (24.65).

31. Lilia D. Monzo & Robert S. Rueda, *Professional Roles, Caring and Scaffolds: Latino Teachers' and Paraeducators' Interactions with Latino Students,* 109 AMERICAN JOURNAL OF EDUCATION 438, 471 (2001).

32. *See* Goldsmith, *supra* note 30 at 121–47.

Table 3. HMLM Results by Locale

Fixed Effect	Coefficient	SE	Approx. d.f.	P-Value
Intercept				
Large Central City, $\beta 00$	25.93***	3.08	187	0.000
Mid-Size Central City, $\beta 01$	16.05**	5.85	187	0.007
Urban Fringe of City, $\beta 02$	24.65***	4.52	187	0.000
Small Town and Rural Area, $\beta 03$	22.39**	7.95	187	0.005
Occasion Slope				
Large Central City, $\beta 10$	3.11***	0.83	187	0.000
Mid-Size Central City, $\beta 11$	−2.94†	1.55	187	0.057
Urban Fringe of City, $\beta 12$	−2.34†	1.21	187	0.053
Small Town and Rural Area, $\beta 13$	−4.95*	2.17	187	0.023

Note: n = 191 SLC schools. $†p < 0.10$, $*p < 0.05$, $**p < 0.01$, $***p < 0.001$

Figure 2. Initial Status and Growth Rate by Locale[33]

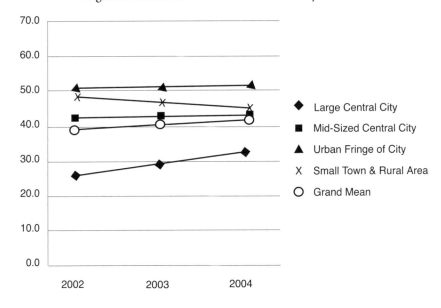

However, SLC schools located in large central cities showed continuous academic progress year by year (3.11***), although those SLC schools still lagged behind their peer SLC schools in other locales. That is, compared to the substantive academic progress of SLC schools in large central cities, both SLC schools in mid-size central cities ($\beta_{10} + \beta_{11}$ = 0.17) and SLC schools in urban fringe of city (0.77) made tiny progress. In the case of SLC schools in small towns/rural areas, the estimated growth rate interestingly declined year by year (−1.84*).

---

33. *See* Lee & Friedrich, *supra* note 6. They showed a similar pattern of the effect of SLC schools' locale on their performance. One different feature, however, is that SLC schools located in small towns and rural areas showed annual progress in their study. The reason for the different result stems from the different sample size. Although they used the same ranking data set, their final analysis utilized 168 SLC schools, while I included 191 SLC schools.

Notably, Figure 2 sheds some light on the reason why predominantly Hispanic SLC schools showed the noticeable academic progress since implementing the SLC program. That is, given the fact that Hispanic students in general and Hispanic immigrant students in particular tend to enroll in high schools in large central cities, it is speculated that major beneficiaries of the academic progress of SLC schools located in large central cities would be ethnic minority groups such as Hispanic students. Interestingly, our data indicate that 75 percent of the predominantly Hispanic schools were located in large central cities. Where Hispanic students predominated in these SLC schools in large central cities, the gains in student achievement seemed to be significant.

What Structures Are More Effective?

The final analysis focused on revealing more effective SLC structures in improving school performance. Table 4 represents the HMLM result of a conditional model that includes the four SLC structures as institutional characteristic predictors. As mentioned, binary variables were employed for coding these predictors (0 = not adopting a particular SLC structure, 1 = adopting a particular structure). The sample SLC schools combined particular structures in various ways, and no schools adopted all structures. As such, if a high school A adopted two SLC structures (e.g., academies and house plans), the predicted school ranking would be the top 37.98 percent in 2002. Also, the estimated school rankings of the school A in 2003 and 2004 would be the top 38.89 percent and 39.80 percent, respectively.[34] This suggests that the estimated school performance is determined by the combination among different structures on the condition that other latent factors are held constant. Therefore, it is important to look at which SLC structures are positively associated with academic achievement so that we can optimize the combination among those structures.

Table 4 presents the estimated school performance in the initial stage. For example, the estimated performance of SLC schools adopting academies alone was 38.84, and that of SLC schools implementing magnet programs alone was 45.15. Given that one SLC school employs more than one SLC structure, the estimated school ranking would depend on the combination of SLC structures adopted by individual SLC schools. Notably, such SLC schools adopting academies or magnet programs tended to show lower school performance at the entry time-point of the SLC program (β_{01}, -15.22^* and β_{04}, -8.91); but they were also likely to show continuous annual progress β_{11} (4.20^*) and β_{14} (5.12^*). Given that 88 percent of the sample schools adopted academies as one of their SLC structures (see Table 1), this would suggest that initially low-performing schools were more likely than initially high-achieving schools to benefit from the SLC program in general and academies in particular. Indeed, the correlation between initial status and growth rate was -0.338, meaning that lower achieving SLC schools at the entry time-point tended to show a faster growth rate than higher achieving SLC schools year by year. Finally, although the coefficient of schools within schools (β_{13}) was a significant 3.06 point, the growth rate was -0.10 ($\beta_{10} + \beta_{13}$). Therefore, academies and magnet programs are viewed as more effective subprograms of SLC, as illustrated in Figure 3.

---

34. The initial ranking was calculated by $54.06 - 15.22 - 0.86 = 37.98$. Based on this approach, the 2003 ranking was calculated by $37.98 - 3.16 + 4.20 - 0.13 = 38.89$. In the same way, the 2004 ranking was calculated by $38.89 - 3.16 + 4.20 - 0.13 = 39.80$.

Figure 3. Initial Status and Growth Rate by SLC Structures

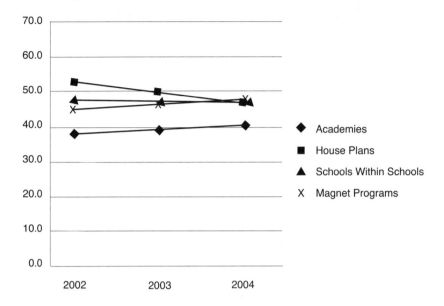

Table 4. HMLM Fixed Effects for SLC Structures				
Fixed Effect	Coefficient	SE	Approx. d.f.	P-Value
Intercept1				
Intercept2, β_{00}	54.06***	7.58	186	0.000
Academies, β_{01}	−15.22*	7.34	186	0.038
House Plans, β_{02}	−0.86	5.72	186	0.880
Schools Within Schools, β_{03}	−5.98	6.49	186	0.358
Magnet Programs, β_{04}	−8.91	7.67	186	0.246
Occasion Slope				
Intercept2, β_{10}	−3.16†	1.81	186	0.080
Academies, β_{11}	4.20*	1.75	186	0.017
House Plans, β_{12}	−0.13	1.37	186	0.924
Schools Within Schools, β_{13}	3.06*	1.55	186	0.048
Magnet Programs, β_{14}	5.12**	1.94	186	0.009

Note: n = 191 SLC schools. $†p < 0.10$, $*p < 0.05$, $**p < 0.01$, $***p < 0.001$

Discussion and Conclusion

Four main research questions were examined. (1) Does SLC contribute to improving academic achievement? (2) Does SLC contribute to closing the racial achievement gap? (3) Does the locale of SLC matter? (4) What structures are more effective?

With regard to the first question, my answer is that SLC contributes to improving academic achievement "slowly but surely." This is a particularly important finding of SLC if one considers the fact that the majority of sample schools were historically low-performing schools (below the top 50 percent of the total number of high schools). Coupled with the first question, the second and third research questions revealed that historically low-performing schools in the initial status improved their school performance at a moderately faster rate than high-performing SLC schools. Further, predominantly Hispanic SLC schools and SLC schools located in large central cities showed significant yearly progress. Given that general student populations enrolled in SLC schools in large central cities and predominantly Hispanic schools are socioeconomically or linguistically marginalized, SLC is viewed as contributing to building educational equity and thereby social justice.

In contrast to schools located in affluent neighborhoods (mainly suburban, predominantly white neighborhoods), most schools in large central cities suffer from the lack of social resources and supports, often resulting from a high degree of racial diversity, high poverty, a high number of single-parent households or a high rate of residential mobility. In this regard, the positive effect of SLC on academic progress of such marginalized schools is noticeable.

THe analyses of SLC not only revealed the positive effect of SLC but also reflected a critical educational issue facing U.S. high schools. First, the racial proportion of the sample schools mirrored the current school segregation problem afflicting schools across the nation. Of the 191 SLC schools, 157 schools were racially segregated. In other words, one particular racial group occupied more than 50 percent of the total proportion in 157 of 191 schools. Second, the unequal feature of the initial school performance of SLC schools by locale exactly reflects the educational problem facing most inner-city schools across the country. In this sense, the initial status of the 191 SLC schools is viewed as quite representative of the persistent educational inequality present in the United States.

More problematic was that this initial inequality still remained. For example, despite the significant academic progress, predominantly Hispanic schools still lagged far behind predominantly white schools at the ending point of the SLC program. Third, black students in this sample were a truly disadvantaged group. Predominantly black SLC schools lagged behind predominantly Hispanic SLC schools in the initial status, and the initial gap between the two groups was significant. In addition, predominantly black SLC schools did not appear to obtain substantive academic benefit from the SLC program during the period of program implementation.

With regard to the final question, we found that academies and magnet programs are more effective subcomponents of SLC. This finding is consistent with Kemple and Scott-Clayton's study,[35] reporting the positive and long-term effect of career academies, which are the most typical instance of academies. However, caution should be exercised in interpreting my finding. Since the SLC structures account for only 11.9 percent of the parameter variance in the growth rates of school performance, the variance of school performance growth is not so much explained by SLC structures alone. This means that there is still significant variance, which can be explained by other factors.

Based on this analyses, several implications for research and policy can be drawn. First, future research may benefit from this study by focusing on some unanswered questions. For example, it is important to further examine why both predominantly black and white schools did not obtain academic benefit from SLC. In addition, although I found that academies and magnet programs are more effective SLC structures in improving academic achievement, one still does not know why those two structures work better. This mandates some micro-level analysis exploring the struc-

---

35. *See* Kemple & Scott-Clayton, *supra* note 14, at 12–21.

tural dynamics within a particular SLC structure, including teacher–student relationship, reflective dialogue, social support, interactive communication between students and so on. This kind of micro-analysis will lead to examining other types of educational outcomes generated from SLC, such as social support, self-efficacy, school safety and positive learning culture, to name a few.

Additionally, certain policy implications can be offered from this analyses. First, I believe that policy sustainability should be secured for crystallizing the substantial potential of SLC. As mentioned, SLC showed its effectiveness in taking steps toward educational equity—slowly but surely. Due to the desire for quick results, major stakeholders may place more emphasis on the "slowly" aspect than the "surely" feature, a focus that will undoubtedly challenge the sustainability of SLC. Given that SLC aims to scaffold irrefutable common goods (i.e., closing the racial achievement gap) through various democratic designs (i.e., personalized learning environments), SLC as a policy intervention has substantive potential.[36] I have often noticed that some policy initiatives with truly "good intentions" took "the road to hell." In this regard, instead of implementing SLC as an episodic or one-time initiative, SLC needs to be treated as a long-term policy strategy.

Another important reason why I support the sustainability of SLC is that the program contributes to the achievement of socioeconomically and linguistically marginalized student groups. In other words, it is a critical merit of SLC that major beneficiaries of the academic progress generated from SLC schools are students in large central cities and are students of color. Further, given that the racial achievement gap is still wide between Whites and students of color within those SLC schools at the ending time-point of the program, SLC should be regarded as unfinished business that needs to be aggressively supported. In relation to this, it is essential to disseminate and share the best practice of SLC schools across the country.

Since the *Brown v. Board of Education*[37] decision, many negative school factors have been well identified regarding the racial achievement gap, yet relatively little is known about some facilitating mechanism that is positively associated with the academic success of students of color. Therefore, cultivating and disseminating positive, effective mechanisms embedded in SLC is important. As Fullan stated, truly applying innovation to education is so complex because too many focus on changing the structure rather than understanding and changing the culture.[38] Simply copying or transplanting structural features of SLC would not necessarily guarantee educational equity because we need more knowledge about the positive mechanisms embedded in SLC. Therefore, lessons from successful SLC designs and implementations should be shared in an accessible way to the public.

As a promising federal program among various NCLB policy strategies, SLC now stands at a crossroads. One seems to be "the road to hell with good intentions," taken by many former ambitious policy interventions, and the other an elusive, challenging path that is our right ideal, one which may in fact now be beginning to traverse. Let us let it be so.

---

36. *See* Lee & Friedrich, *supra* note 6.
37. *Brown v. Bd. of Educ.*, 347 U.S. 483 (1954).
38. MICHAEL FULLAN, THE NEW MEANING OF EDUCATIONAL CHANGE (2001) at 34.

23

Compromising Curricula: Inequity in Literacy Instruction

Caitlin McMunn Dooley and Lori Czop Assaf

Introduction

Enter two U.S. schools—just minutes apart if you were to travel by car but vastly different if you were to examine their literacy curricula. Despite similarities between the teachers, their schools are very different. Jacqueline's (all names are pseudonyms) suburban school, River Ranch Elementary, rests in the heart of a golf-course community serving a predominately white, upper-middle-class population. Based on statewide accountability records, River Ranch Elementary has been rated "Exemplary" with a 98 percent passing rate on the state-mandated standardized assessment over the five years prior to our original study. As one of two Reading Resource teachers at River Ranch, Jacqueline served about thirty children in a day, and enrollment was relatively consistent throughout the year. We observed Jacqueline daily over four months as she worked for 1.5 hours daily with a group of nine fourth-grade students identified as struggling readers (African American [3]; Mexican American [2]; and white [6]; no English language learners [ELLs]). Travel about twenty-five minutes on Highway 39 and you would find Marcia teaching at Chavez Elementary, an urban school that serves a low-income community with a majority of students (93 percent) who are Mexican and Mexican American. Test scores for Chavez Elementary had been below the state average for the five years prior to the original study with approximately 65 percent of all students passing the year of the study. As one of two Reading Resource teachers at Chavez, Marcia worked for thirty minutes daily with a group of nine fourth-grade students who had not successfully passed the state test (all Mexican American and all ELLs). Marcia served about seventy students per day and enrollment was "rolling." In other words, Marcia served students when they failed a benchmark reading test (district-based six-week test) or when they were new to the school. If a student passed the test (even marginally), he or she was pulled from Marcia's classroom and a new student took his place. We spent more than 130 hours over four months within each teacher's classroom separately conducting case studies to closely examine their literacy instruction. The differences were disturbing.

We could try to dismiss these differences as merely individual and suggest that the context of their teaching had little to do with what we saw; however, ample research suggests that inequitable differences are common between educational opportunities offered in upper-income suburbs and lower-income cities. In this chapter, we examine inequities in literacy instruction offered in K–12 U.S. public schools, as well as illustrate how two reading teachers, one working in an urban school and the other working in a suburban school, are affected by different professional development opportunities, resources, and testing pressures.

We use the term "urban school" to describe a school setting that serves historically disenfranchised minority groups (in the case of this study, Latinos and immigrants) in an urban community with few financial resources. The term "suburban school" implies one serving a predominately white community with abundant financial resources. We recognize that not all schools in urban and suburban locations share these descriptors; however, there is a growing accumulation of educational research that illustrates these descriptors of contextually determined inequities are more a rule than exception.[1] We offer our case studies as examples of what might be true in many U.S. suburban and urban districts; we contrast the cases because sometimes images are clearer when placed against contrasting backgrounds.

Literacy Curricula at the Crossroads

A recent review of literature on literacy research suggested that equity is the most pressing issue in literacy education.[2] The vast majority of this research shows that children in low-income urban communities are offered a "lesser-than" curriculum than are children in predominately white, middle- to upper-income communities.[3] Anyon[4] has summarized more than seven decades of research to show that urban schools are more likely (than suburban schools) to suffer a constellation of factors that contribute to inequity, including economic hardships, lack of community support, and racist disenfranchisement. Finding that differences exist across educational contexts is not new; however, this chapter focuses specifically on how inequity can exist between an urban classroom and a suburban classroom due to how two reading teachers respond to the pressures of high-stakes standardized testing.

Notice that our argument is not about the "achievement gap." Certainly standardized performance assessments have indicated that minority and low-income students score lower than their upper-income, majority-white counterparts. This was also true in the cases we studied with Jacqueline and Marcia. However, this "achievement gap" argument has distracted researchers from instructional issues. Research on the achievement gap has pulled apart child characteristics such as family poverty,[5] attitudes, and behaviors[6] and had, in a sense, blamed the child (and his or her family) for not learning to read and write. Though

---

1. Jean Anyon, J *What Counts as Education Policy? Notes Toward a New Paradigm*, 75 Harvard Educational Review 65 (2005); Jane Hannaway & Joan E. Talbert, *Bringing Context into Effective Schools Research: Urban–Suburban Differences*, 29 Educational Administration Quarterly 164 (1993).

2. Katherine Au & Taffy Raphael, *Equity and Literacy in the Next Millennium*, 35 Reading Research Quarterly 170 (2000).

3. *Id.*; Shirley B. Heath, Ways with Words: Language, Life, and Work in Communities and Classrooms (1983); Jabari Mahiri (Ed.), What They Don't Learn in School: Literacy in the Lives of Urban Youth (2003); Linda McNeil, *Creating New Inequalities: Contradictions of Reform*, 81 Phi Delta Kappan 729 (2000).

4. Anyon, *supra* note 1.

5. Richard Rothstein, Class and Schools: Using Social, Economic, and Educational Reform to Close the Black-White Achievement Gap (2004).

6. Karl L. Alexander & Doris R. Entwisle, *From First Grade Forward: Early Foundations of High School Dropout*, 70 Sociology of Education 87 (1997).

we do not dismiss the role of a child's background in learning, we also feel strongly that instruction plays a key role in literacy learning. Current standardized assessments might not be the best indicator of whether a child learned from high-quality instruction (more on the issue of validity of standardized testing to come). Thus, our focus is specifically on the ways *instructional opportunities for literacy learning differ inequitably* for urban schools — those most likely serve to children of color who come from low-income families.

Curricular Ideologies: Functional and Critical Literacy

Ideology refers to a framework of thought or a belief system that guides how teachers and administrators use curricular materials and how instructional processes are carried out in schools. As Auerbach stated,[7] "There can be no disinterested, objective, value-free definition of literacy: The way literacy is viewed and taught is always and inevitably ideological." Two primary ideologies seem to drive literacy curricula today: functional literacy and critical literacy. Understanding functional and critical literacy ideologies enables a more nuanced examination of popular instructional practices.

Functional Literacy

Functional literacy is an ideology supported by curricula aimed to prepare students to read and write well enough to function in society. Literacy from this perspective is viewed as a fixed inventory of skills, objectives, and basic abilities that students must master to complete their schooling and survive in the world. Most often, functional literacy is associated with knowing life skills that would enable someone to understand street signs and bus schedules, write checks, fill out a job application form, or navigate social services typically available to people who have low incomes.[8] It can also relate to school-based literacies such as writing a book report, identifying the main idea of a passage, or taking a standardized test. Students are judged on their ability to meet certain institutional and functional expectations. Functional literacy ideology adheres to teacher directed, skills-based instruction. Basic reading and writing (e.g., letter-sound correspondence, subject/verb agreement, word meanings) are taught in a lock-step fashion, regardless of individual or cultural differences, and students are tested regularly on their mastery of basic skills. Often associated with developing countries,[9] the goal of functional literacy curricula is to eliminate the evils of illiteracy that lead to poverty and ignorance and to arm individuals with the life skills needed to survive everyday life.

Critical Literacy

Critical literacy is an ideology supported by curricula that focus on helping students become critically aware of their world. Literacy from this perspective is viewed as a so-

---

7. Elsa Auerbach, *Literacy and Ideology*, in William Grabe (Ed.), ANNUAL REVIEW OF APPLIED LINGUISTICS 71 (1991), at 71.

8. Irwin Kirsch & John T. Guthrie, *The Concept and Measurement of Functional Literacy*, 13 READING RESEARCH QUARTERLY 485 (1977/8); MILES MYERS, CHANGING OUR MINDS: NEGOTIATING ENGLISH AND LITERACY (1996).

9. BRIAN STREET, SOCIAL LITERACIES (1995).

cially constructed practice and varies according to personal and social circumstances, meaning all individuals and societies are literate in some form or fashion. Critical literacy[10] has been associated historically with supporting individuals and societies with engaging in problematizing—or examining the complexities of a situation to seek alternative explanations and solutions. Embedded in critical literacy curricula is a belief that "reflection and action upon the world" will transform the world.[11] This process is not passive but active, challenging and disrupting the status quo for the purpose of relieving inequity and injustice.[12] Critical literacy integrates reading and writing with purposes such as constructing knowledge about a topic, applying knowledge to real-world situations, and challenging the status quo.[13] Students acquire critical literacy through their uses of literacy (e.g., writing letters, reading magazines, analyzing stories, synthesizing information from books and Web sites); and teachers responsively instruct and give feedback based on students' individual and cultural differences. Unlike functional literacy that focuses on helping individuals survive in the world, the goal of critical literacy curricula is to create individuals who feel a sense of agency in the world and who use their literate abilities to shape that world. Critically literate individuals are better equipped to take leadership roles, build new knowledge, and redefine the status quo.

Understanding functional and critical literacy ideologies enables a more nuanced examination of curricula, instruction, and testing in K–12 schools. Functional literacy curricula are more likely to be found in urban schools that serve children of color from low-income families, whereas critical literacy curricula are more likely to be found in schools serving children who are white and who come from upper-income families.[14] Because functional literacy ideologies assume that many families and children of color who attend schools in urban settings have not attained the necessary literacy to function in society, instruction focuses on skills and objectives that can be tested for evidence of literacy acquisition. Haberman described functional literacy instruction as the "pedagogy of poverty" characterized by skill-and-drill instruction, low-level questioning, and emphasis on remediation.[15] Macedo[16] argued that functional literacy ideologies have been used as a tool for those in power to educate oppressed citizens just enough to get by, but students who have received functional literacy instruction fail to comprehend the world outside of their immediate localities. Those who are functionally literate do not possess the understanding of others or the agency to become active change makers. Instead, they are merely able to read text at basic skill levels, making them servants to survival.

---

10. Paolo Freire, Pedagogy of the Oppressed (1970).

11. *Id.* at 36.

12. Mitzi Lewison, Amy Seely Flint, & Katie Van Sluys, *Taking on Critical Literacy: Journey of Newcomers and Novices*, 79 Language Arts 382 (2002).

13. Colin Lankshear & Peter M. Mclaren, Critical Literacy: Politics, Praxis, and the Postmodern (1993).

14. Martin Haberman, *The Pedagogy of Poverty*, 73 Phi Delta Kappan 290 (1991); Martin Haberman & L. Post, *Teachers for Multicultural Schools: The Power of Selection*, 37 Theory into Practice 96 (1998); Joyce King, *The Purpose of Schooling for African American Children: Including Cultural Knowledge*, in E. R. Hollins et al. (Eds.), Teaching Diverse Populations: Formulating a Knowledge Base (pp. 25–59) (1994); Johnathan Kozol, The Shame of the Nation (2005).

15. Haberman, *supra* note 14, at 118.

16. Donaldo Macedo, Literacies of Power: What Americans Are Not Allowed to Know (1994).

Examining Inequitable Instruction: Scripted Programs and Test Emphasis

Two practices seem to be especially influenced by a functional literacy ideology: the use of scripted reading programs and the overemphasis of testing and test practice. Unfortunately, research shows that these practices most often occur in urban schools that serve low-income communities and children of color.[17]

Scripted Curricular Programs

Instructional programs involving scripted, sequenced lessons are often marketed to urban districts; these programs focus primarily on skill building and functional literacy. These "scripted programs" include Open Court, Success for All (SFA), Direct Instruction, and America's Choice, among others. Prior to implementation, most programs require approval by at least 80 percent of the teachers at a school; however, due to high teacher attrition in urban schools as well as to disillusionment, once a program begins, teachers often lose confidence.[18] Dantow and Castellano's qualitative examinations of teacher buy-in in two urban schools show that "teachers felt pressured to adopt SFA either because an administrator was in favor ... or there was funding available."[19] If a school adopts a scripted program, it usually receives textual materials (textbooks, tests, and workbooks), a teacher training session, as well as scripted lesson plans that the teacher must carry out on subsequent days. Most schools and districts that adopt a program like this also integrate some means of oversight to ensure fidelity to the program (derisively called "the teacher police" by many teachers).

Several literacy researchers have questioned whether scripted programs reflect the demands of real-world literacy learning. Shannon[20] conducted a survey of 486 general education teachers, reading teachers, and administrators in schools using commercial reading programs. Quantitative comparisons indicated that administrators felt more inclined to trust these programs than did teachers. Teachers were skeptical about the materials because they felt they limited literacy to what could be tested by the multiple-choice assessments packaged with the program. One teacher put it this way:

> I took several tests home and asked my husband to take them. He's a vice president of his company and has a degree in engineering. I can vouch for his ability to read. Anyway, there were at least three tests on which he failed to reach mastery because he couldn't pass the sub-tests. The funny part is that our fourth grade son who goes to school in this district.... Well, the funny part is my son could pass all the tests.[21]

---

17. Haberman, *supra* note 14; Kozol, *supra* note 16.
18. Amanda Dantow & Marisa Castellano, *Teachers' Responses to Success for All: How Beliefs, Experiences, and Adaptations Shape Implementation*, 37 American Educational Research Journal 775 (2000).
19. *Id*. at 794.
20. Patrick Shannon, *Use of Commercial Reading Materials in American Elementary Schools* in Patrick Shannon & Jacqueline Edmondson (Eds.), Reading Education Policy: A Collection of Articles from the International Reading Association (pp. 298–324) (2005).
21. *Id*., as quoted by Shannon, p. 314.

More recently, Wiltz and Wilson[22] compared scripted reading programs in several urban schools with "balanced literacy" programs in higher-income, suburban schools in the same district. They found that the lower-income students of color were more likely to show gains in phonemic awareness (an early indicator of low-level, basic reading skills) but were less likely to increase in comprehension levels (an indicator of higher-level thinking) similar to that of their higher-income, mostly white peers. This comparison indicates that the reading programs influenced the children's development—promoting some students as able to perform low-level, functional skills and some to perform higher-level, critical thinking. In short, children learn what is taught: If taught functional skills, children learn to simply function in society.

Emphasis on Testing (And Only Testing)

Urban schools are more likely to be targets of accountability policies and pressures associated with high-stakes testing.[23] Simply because they serve ethnically and economically diverse populations, urban schools are more likely to show "achievement gaps" and thus become targets of sanctions related to NCLB.[24] Additionally, urban schools are more likely to have students who can be identified in multiple subcategories (such as "economically disadvantaged" and "limited English proficiency") for disaggregated score reports, causing some students to be counted twice (or more) for/against their school's accountability rating.[25] After reviewing achievement data from six states, Kim and Sunderman concluded that

> because Black and Latino students often belong to other subgroup categories defined by NCLB, including subgroups for economically disadvantaged students and limited English proficient students, schools with a minority subgroup will have to meet multiple targets, which further increases the chances of failing to make AYP [adequate yearly progress].[26]

This kind of "double jeopardy" increases the pressure felt by urban teachers and students.

Ironically, although proponents of NCLB tout high-stakes testing as the panacea for inequity that so often strikes urban schools, research suggests that pressures related to high-stakes testing do nothing to improve instruction or student achievement. Nichols, Glass, and Bereiter[27] reviewed twenty-five U.S. states' accountability policies and systems via statistical ranking of each state (using reviews of summary statements of state-level

---

22. Nancy Wiltz & Patricia Wilson, *An Inquiry into Children's Reading in One Urban School Using SRA Reading Mastery*, 37 Journal of Literacy Research 493 (2006).

23. John B. Diamond & James Spillane, *High-Stakes Accountability in Urban Elementary Schools: Challenging or Reproducing Inequality?* 106 Teacher College Record 1145 (2004); Linda McNeil, *Creating New Inequalities: Contradictions of Reform*, 81 Phi Delta Kappan 729 (2000); Michael L. Smith & P. Fey, *Validity and Accountability in High-Stakes Testing*, 51 Journal of Teacher Education 334 (2000); Angela Valenzuela, Subtractive Schooling (1999).

24. Gary Orfield & Mindy L. Kornhaber (Eds.), Rising Standards or Rising Barriers (2001). Richard Rothstein, Class and Schools: Using Social, Economic, and Educational Reform to Close the Black-White Achievement Gap (2004); James S. Kim & Gail L. Sunderman, *Measuring Academic Proficiency under the No Child Left Behind Act: Implications for Educational Equity*, 34(8) Educational Researcher 3 (2005).

25. *Id.*

26. *Id.*, at 5.

27. Sharon L. Nichols, Gene V. Glass, & David C. Berliner, *High-Stakes Testing and Student Achievement: Does Accountability Pressure Increase Student Learning?* 14(1) Education Policy Analysis Archives, available at epaa.asu.edu/epaa/v14n1/ (last viewed January 30, 2006).

policy, legislation, and media reports relating to each state's accountability systems) as well as comparisons between those rankings and student achievement data from the National Assessment of Educational Progress (NAEP). "No relationship was found between testing pressure and reading achievement ... at any grade level or for any ethnic student subgroup."[28] In other words, in states with the most severe accountability policies and implementation systems (including Texas, where the case studies analyzed in this report took place), student achievement was *not* more likely to increase.

In another recent study commissioned by the Harvard Civil Rights project, researchers found that the higher the pressures of testing, the less likely it is that students will perform well.[29] This study compared NAEP scores from two time periods (1990–2001 [pre-NCLB] and 2002–2005 [post-NCLB]) and compared NAEP to state-mandated tests. Lee found that (1) there has been no significant rise in achievement across racial and SES groups since the implementation of high-stakes testing under NCLB, and (2) in states with higher sanctions (e.g., NC, TX, and FL), score discrepancies between NAEP and state tests were greater, particularly for historically discriminated-against groups (e.g., low SES, black and Latino). These studies lead to a dilemma: if urban schools are subject to more pressure by high-stakes testing, and pressure to increase scores does not help student performance, then what *is* happening in urban schools?

Several studies have shown the detrimental effects of pressures related to accountability and high-stakes testing on instructional practice and suggest that these pressures seem to be far more deleterious in urban schools.[30] As an illustration of these inequities, a series of reports[31] conducted by the *Baltimore Sun* focused on how NCLB has affected urban schools in Maryland and New Jersey. MacGillis focused on comparative differences in resources provided to urban and suburban schools and found that urban schools are less likely to receive proper funding for teacher education (beyond "training" for mandated programs), technological resources, and other financial resources. He also noted that urban teachers are more likely to be enticed by for-profit textbook and technology companies catering to a "back to the basics" (i.e., functional) approach to instruction (e.g., Open Court) that aligns with low-level skills prevalent on multiple-choice reading tests. MacGillis quoted several urban elementary school teachers who described their own instructional practice as basic skills instruction and directly attributed this to pressures to achieve high test scores.

This finding aligns with Booher-Jennings's[32] conclusion that urban teachers and administrators subject students to "educational triage"—a term indicating intensive test-practice sessions. According to Booher-Jennings, urban teachers and administrators have a tendency to focus on the "bubble kids"—those students whose standardized tests scores were just below mandated cut scores. Her conclusion came from a qualitative case study of

---

28. *Id.* at 1–2.

29. Jaekyung Lee, *Tracking Achievement Gaps and Assessing the Impact of No Child Left Behind: An In-depth Look at National and State Reading and Math Outcome Trends*, available at www.civilrightsproject.ucla.edu/research/esea/nclb_naep_lee.pdf (last viewed Sept. 25, 2007).

30. M. Gail Jones, Brett D. Jones & Tracy Hargrove, The Unintended Consequences of High-Stakes Testing (2003); Johnathan Kozol, The Shame of the Nation (2005); Pedro A. Noguera, City Schools and the American Dream: Fulfilling the Promise of Public Education (2003); Mike Rose, Possible Lives (1999); Mike Rose, Lives on the Boundary (2004); Angela Valenzuela, *Leaving Children Behind: How Texas-style Accountability Fails Latino Youth* (2004).

31. Alex MacGillis, *Poor Schools, Rich Targets*, Baltimore Sun, September 19, 20, 21 (2004).

32. Jennifer Booher-Jennings, *Below the Bubble: "Educational Triage" and the Texas Accountability System*, 42 American Educational Research Journal 231 (2005).

one urban school. In a survey of 225 students in grades 3–6 from multiple urban and rural schools, Tripplet and Barksdale[33] found that low-income students have particularly anxious and isolated perceptions of literacy due to the increased emphasis on testing and test practice. After closely examining the history and impact of high-stakes testing in eighteen states, Amrein and Bereiter[34] concluded "high-stakes testing policies have had a disproportionately negative impact on students from racial minority and low socioeconomic backgrounds"—not surprisingly, these are the very students who are most likely to attend urban schools.

Not only has an overemphasis on testing and test practice unduly affected urban school instruction, but current standardized tests also reinforce a functional literacy ideology. The multiple-choice formats most common to reading assessments grossly oversimplify "real" reading at best and, at worst, fail to support critical thinking, problem solving, and collaboration—critical literacy skills often regarded as important attributes in a global economy.[35] Clifford Hill, professor at Teachers College, has authored several books on language and literacy assessment. He stated, "There's a huge tension between the model of literacy that the test makers are working with, which I do call a restricted one, kind of a strict information processing [or functional] model, as opposed to a constructivist [or critical] model."[36] David Pearson, dean of the College of Education at Berkeley, stated,

> formal assessments ... have attracted even more pointed criticism for their potential to corrupt early literacy curricula and teachers instructional practices.... These tests can tell teachers very little about the real literacy of young readers and writers and at best they reveal whether students have learned the skills within instructional programs geared to the tests that accompany them.[37]

Given the prevalence of research on testing and inequities in urban schooling, in the next section we illustrate how educational inequity played out in an urban and a suburban school. Specifically, we describe how two teachers shaped literacy instruction and how curricular and contextual factors contributed to inequitable experiences.

Two Teachers: Cases Illustrating Inequity

Jacqueline teaches in a suburban, predominately white community that includes students from families with abundant financial resources. Marcia teaches in a neighboring urban, predominately Latino community that includes children from families with few financial resources. Both are white, middle-aged, experienced teachers of literacy (ten and thirty years of teaching, respectively). Both have earned master's degrees in reading and literacy instruction and teach fourth graders in pull-out, resource programs for struggling readers who read below grade level and have not passed the state-mandated liter-

33. Christine F. Tripplet & Mary Anne Barksdale, *Third Through Sixth Graders' Perceptions of High-Stakes Testing*, 37 Journal of Literacy Research 237 (2005).

34. Audrey L. Amrein & David C. Bereiter, *High-Stakes Testing, Uncertainty, and Student Learning*. 10 Education Policy Analysis Archives, available at epaa.asu.edu/epaa/v10n18 (last visited July 25, 2007).

35. P. David Pearson, *Standards and Assessments: Tools for Crafting Effective Instruction?* in Jean Osborn & Fran Lehr (Eds.), Literacy for All: Issues in Teaching and Learning (pp. 264–88) (1998).

36. Clifford Hill, *Falling Short of the Standards Part 1: High Stakes Testing in American Education—the English Language Arts Test—the Reading Test*, TCRecord (Dec. 7, 2000) available at www.tcrecord.org/PrintContent.asp?ContentID=10662 (last visited April 24, 2007).

37. Pearson, *supra* note 35, at 268.

acy tests. Because of their reputation as exemplary teachers, Jacqueline had been nominated by her peers to mentor new teachers and had been selected by district-level administrators to conduct teacher education workshops on literacy instruction for students
in special education, and Marcia was nominated the year prior to the study as Teacher of
the Year for her school (a peer nomination) and was assigned by her school administrator to mentor new teachers. Marcia had also received several grants to support her literacy instruction and an after-school program that she founded and ran for several years.

Despite similarities between these teachers, their instructional practices are very different. Through the use of observational field notes and interviews, we identified how
their literacy instruction varied in response to mandated tests. Following are two snapshots of instruction within these contexts, followed by hypothesized contextual differences that contributed to inequity.

Snapshots of Instruction

Jacqueline engaged in critical literacy instruction by facilitating authentic discussions
that allowed her students to become owners of their literacy learning, whereas Marcia
spent more time directly teaching comprehension strategies with little time for application
or attention to students' responses. Her approach was decidedly more functional.

In the first snapshot, Jacqueline's students discussed the motives and actions of the
main character, Ash, in their Pokemon trade book:

> The students moved into small groups to begin stations. One group is meeting
> as a literature circle with Jacqueline at a small round table in the corner of the
> room. They've read an easy Pokémon chapter book (the group has three boys and
> a girl, all interested in Pokémon). Jacqueline, noticing that one of the students
> had not read, asked her to go back to her desk to complete the reading that the
> group had agreed to. The rest seem engrossed in discussing whether Ash should
> get another Pokémon after a successful battle. Some students point out that be-
> cause Ash already has that type of Pokémon, he might not need another. Oth-
> ers disagree, stating that Ash should collect as many as possible.

This discussion illustrates a critical literacy in action: the children engaged in a discussion
about motivation and were problem solving to determine what the character should do
next. They were making decisions collaboratively.

In contrast to Jacqueline's students' authentic discussion about character motivation
that led to critical interpretations of the text, Marcia provided more explicit, functional
instruction that focused on comprehension strategies outlined by the district-mandated
curriculum, such as identifying the main idea or summarizing. These were testable skills
that did not require students to socially construct interpretations of texts, but rather, required them to find one right answer.

In the second snapshot, Marcia used a test-like passage to guide her students to think
about the steps to making an inference.

> "Making inferences" is written on the white board. Marcia set the stage for the
> lesson by stating, "A writer doesn't always tell us everything, so we need to use the
> words and the pictures to fill in the pieces." … Marcia gave an example of a bark-
> ing dog. She asked the students, "If a dog is barking, what do you think is hap-
> pening? What inferences can you make?" The students responded with statements
> like, "someone's coming" and "a car is outside." Marcia then directed her students
> to turn to p. 6 on visual information in the *National Geographic for Kids* magazine.

Students read "making inferences guidelines," a small text box in the upper corner of the magazine.

"Read words carefully," Veronica read aloud.

"Study all of the pictures and other visuals. Look for clues," Emily read.

Marcia related these strategy tips to the test, stating, "I promise you they [the test writers] are going to ask you the meaning of unfamiliar words." Unfortunately, time ran out during the above lesson and Marcia's students did not have time to apply their inference strategy to their reading.

Marcia's instruction required students to individually reconstruct an intended meaning, much as they would have to do for the standardized test. This kind of instruction aims to create readers who can function on tests, not necessarily citizens who can work together to construct new ideas or read across multiple genres to gain information.

Differences in Professional Development Opportunities

Differences between the two teachers' practices are likely related to different professional development opportunities presented by their respective districts. The suburban district provided Jacqueline with a menu of choices, and she chose an on going, nine-week technology workshop. She immediately incorporated her learning into instruction as a means to engage students in multiple modes of expression, stating, "Right now we're working on making the kids' own Web sites. They're playing with the fonts and choosing pictures. I think they're having fun, but I'm still learning about how to really show their writing." Jacqueline used technology as yet another mode for teaching the students about themes and topics shared by other texts within her instruction.

Marcia attended district-mandated workshops that focused on explicit comprehension strategy instruction that students could apply in test situations. Taught by the urban district's instructional leaders, Marcia's workshops encouraged the use of tangible strategies such as graphic organizers and sentence starters for such things as writing main ideas. Marcia shared that the workshops she had to go to were not helping her properly address her students' individual literacy needs: "Graphic organizers, everything, you name it ... I must go to all those teacher workshops where they never talk about children's *reading*." Marcia grappled with the mixed messages she was receiving from the district and her own understanding of effective literacy instruction. Marcia explained her struggle: "I can just tell you I haven't covered or used as many books this year because they [district administrators] keep throwing all these TAKS things [prep materials for the Texas Assessment of Knowledge and Skills, the state-mandated test] at me ... The TAKS wants us to keep children reading. But we [teachers] never let them read.... they can't sit down and curl up to a passage and play like it's a book they really like. I can't ask them to curl up to a passage, can I?"

Differences in Case Load, Time, and Resources

Perhaps the most influential contextual factors contributing to the inequity in individualization of instruction within these contrasting cases were (1) the availability of instructional aides and (2) the time and number of students each teacher had to serve. With three part-time instructional aides, Jacqueline taught nine students within an hour and a half, whereas Marcia served nine students within thirty minutes with no assistance. Jacqueline differentiated instruction by regularly pulling small groups to work on specific reading, spelling, and word-work tasks. Notably, part-time assistants helped her facilitate these groups. For example, Ms. B, a paraprofessional, took individual reading assessments of student's reading in trade books, and Ms. F, another paraprofessional, sat at a table in the corner of the room calling out words to groups of two to three students from their individual spelling lists. Jacqueline led a literature circle discussion at a small table with four students. However, Marcia was not provided extra assistance; all of her instruction was full-group. Although these contextual factors certainly influenced other categories, Marcia explained that lack of time was a dire issue: "I spend all my time pulling different kids who need my help to read on grade level. My principal says I must get them reading and get them out, but there are so many kids ... and I am the only ESL [English as a second language] certified reading teacher on campus who works with them."

During one observation, Marcia guided students to choose books that "fit" their ability level—a common practice intended to help address students' various individual needs; ironically, however, the following example shows that she addressed her students as though they were all at the same level. Marcia wrote the terms "independent" and "instructional" on the board and directed the students' attention to a stack of series books she had available for them to check out. She told the students, "These are the books that you are taking home and they are on your independent level which means that you can read them at home by yourself. You don't need any help." Marcia then pointed to the book *Sideways Stories from Wayside School*[38] and stated, "This book is on your instructional level, which means that I will guide you. Instructional means you will get guidance." While Marcia attempted to help students to align texts with their abilities, she did not differentiate this lesson by individually addressing each student's instructional and independent levels, but rather, treated the group as a whole. When Lori asked Marcia why she used the same book for the whole group, Marcia explained, "In here, there is simply not enough time to have everyone work in different books. I must get them all reading on grade level as quickly as possible."

Differences in Quantity and Stakes of Tests

Both teachers questioned the validity (truthfulness) of the state-mandated literacy tests as indicators of students' abilities. Jacqueline said,

> This kind of one-day assessment [referring to the state-mandated TAKS test] doesn't really show as much in depth as that person really needs to have in a content area. I think the test isn't necessarily a true indicator. I don't really think it shows exactly what a student is doing as well as some of the competency testing we use. [Also], I think a portfolio assessment would show more of what their abilities really are.

Additionally, Jacqueline stated that she did not believe in the validity of the state-mandated test because those scores were so often higher than scores offered by informal reading inventories and other assessments. While talking about how these incongruities affect her parent conferences, she described her discomfort with explaining to parents that although their child is performing below grade level, the child needs to take the grade-level test. She sighed, "It [the state test] seems to make me lose some credibility." Similarly, in an informal interview after an observation in mid-February, Marcia explained her dismay that the test did not accurately reflect her students' reading abilities, stating, "Some [students] do pass [even though they read] below grade level, and some that are on grade level don't pass. So I don't know what that is. But it's a real struggle."

---

38. Louis Sachar (1978).

Both teachers described dire consequences of district-mandated benchmark testing, a process in which students take many multiple-choice tests throughout the school year. Under the best circumstances, benchmark testing is intended to assess a child's content knowledge in time to remediate before he or she takes a state-mandated test that could result in retention. Both Jacqueline's and Marcia's districts implemented benchmarking systems within the years that these studies took place. Fourth graders at River Ranch Elementary took ten benchmark tests; fourth graders at Chavez Elementary took more than seventeen benchmark tests.

Each teacher stated that benchmark testing took time away from instruction. Jacqueline stated that benchmark testing seemed to be draining her students' energy in their regular classrooms so that when they came to her class they were unable to focus. In one instance, one of Jacqueline's students came to the resource classroom late because he had just been given a one-hour science benchmark test. Jacqueline said, "He was pretty good about concentrating on the test. But by the time he was in the language arts session with the nine others, he had had it!" Marcia described benchmark testing, but she was more concerned that her students pass the tests so they would not miss their regular classroom instruction and be identified as "needing more help."

Both teachers noted that benchmark test scores were increasingly being used to identify students to be pulled from regular classroom instruction. Notably, the timing of the initiation of benchmark testing in both districts coincided with the legislated ending of "social promotion" for third graders (called the "Student Success Initiative [SSI]"[39]). Since benchmark testing began the year of the study, Jacqueline said that the third grade group of special education students had doubled in size (from five to ten students). By mid-February Jacqueline estimated that she had already attended six separate child study meetings spurred primarily by benchmark testing scores. All but one qualified for special education services. Marcia experienced similar referrals; however, her students did not usually go through a formal special education referral process. Rather, the majority of students were pulled from their regular classrooms and parental notification consisted of a letter stating that process. Marcia's students were selected and deselected based solely on benchmark reading test scores. For example, a student could enter her instructional program after failing one benchmark test and exit once she passed a subsequent test.

Marcia's school district used benchmark scores not only to identify individual students but also to rate schools within a tier system, with Tier 3 being the highest level and Tier 1 being the lowest (designated when 70 percent or below pass benchmark tests). At Tier 1, teachers are required to give their students additional tests at least every three weeks in every content area, and district administrators conducted classroom observations and collected data to ensure that teachers were covering the curriculum. During the time of this study, Chavez moved from Tier 3 to Tier 2 ranking, and Marcia felt the consequences. Due to this shift, Marcia and other teachers at the school had to adhere to a strict testing schedule. Benchmark tests occurred at least twice monthly and district-mandated multiple-choice tests occurred weekly (note: these tests were only for the poorly rated schools). At the same time, Marcia and the other teachers were required to turn in weekly lesson plans, be observed by an instructional specialist from the district office, and attend professional development workshops. Marcia expressed her frustration: "Being a Tier 2 school is the pits! I don't like it at all."

---

39. Texas Education Agency, available at www.tea.state.tx.us/student.assessment/resources/ssi/ (last viewed July 6, 2007).

Both teachers prepared their students to take the state-mandated assessments; however, differences in their approaches were substantial. Jacqueline did not spend as much time preparing her students for testing. She provided a short test passage each Friday as part of the "stations" and discussed open-ended questions about the passage at the end of each Friday session. However, this "test practice" time was minimal, constituting less than fifteen minutes with students each Friday. In fact, Jacqueline did not talk extensively about the state-mandated test until a week prior to the test. When she did talk about the test, she told her students that they would be taking a test in the upcoming week and they would have to be very quiet.

Marcia spent almost all of her time during the course of the study conducting whole-group lessons focused primarily on test preparation. Lori, the second author, recorded forty out of forty-eight sessions in which Marcia and her students read test-like materials and discussed test-taking strategies. For instance, one day, as Lori entered Marcia's classroom, Marcia was talking to the students:

> Each of you can pass the TAKS. Make it fun. Make fun of the little man making up the tests. If you get bored, draw a picture to give yourself a break. Governor Perry will think, "Who are those fourth graders at Chavez Elementary School? The test is not hard for them!"

The teachers experienced and coped with test-related pressures differently. For example, when Jacqueline was asked if she had heard any directives from her administrator or district about testing, she said, "The [state-mandated] writing test is coming up, for the fourth graders at least, but no, they [the administration] haven't said anything. I hadn't realized that—they haven't said a word, I don't think, all year." Whereas Jacqueline felt little administrative pressure to test her students, Marcia described feeling overwhelmed because of the pressures of testing. For example, when Marcia was guiding her students as they read a trade book she was interrupted by a phone ringing. Her principal called to inquire about particular students' test scores. Marcia felt compelled to answer the phone, but regretted the interruption. She felt that her principal and district administration were too focused on test scores. Marcia said, "I am just too overwhelmed by the testing pressures the district is placing on us. I used to have fun, but this year there is too much pressure, too many tests, and that's all we do." She coped with the pressure by providing multiple practice tests and trying to cheer her students on to pass the test in order to help them (and maybe even herself) gain a sense of efficacy. On multiple occasions, she would tell her students, "You can do this!" or "You're going to impress that little man who writes the test [referring to some imagined test writer]."

Discussion

Jacqueline's and Marcia's cases detail the differences in literacy instruction within their urban and suburban contexts. The snapshots offer a glimpse at instruction in each context; in addition, the extended description of differences show that instruction was not simply an individual teacher's choice—rather, their choices were affected by multiple contextual influences. Unfortunately, these contextualized cases are not unique. Multiple studies have shown that children in urban schools often receive instructional curricula that value functional literacy and basic skills more than critical literacy and higher-level thinking skills.[40] Although neither teacher had to deal with the scripted programs that have been

---

40. Anyon, *supra* note 1; Au & Raphael, *supra* note 2; Hannaway & Talbert, *supra* note 1; Heath, *supra* note 3.

shown to reify a functional literacy curriculum,[41] high-stakes testing in Marcia's urban context seemed to achieve a similar goal. Inequitable differences in professional development opportunities, case loads, and assistance, as well as the sheer number of tests given and stakes associated with those tests, all contributed to these teachers' instruction.

Contrasting the suburban and urban contexts reveals an overwhelming presence of high-stakes testing emphasis in Marcia's urban school. Again, her case is not unique. Marcia's struggle to maintain a case load of seventy students, offering short sessions that looked more like test prep than literacy instruction, seems grossly aligned with Booher-Jennings's[42] description of "educational triage," a short-cut effort to raise tests scores. But Marcia's triage efforts were not an individual decision; she felt pressure from school administrators as well as the district workshops and "teacher police" to focus on testing. Likewise, Kim and Sunderman[43] found that across six states, urban districts (because they are most likely to serve students from multiple subgroups [Latino, African America, ELLs, and low socioeconomic status] were more likely to be targets of test pressures. Additionally, Kozol, McNeil, and Valenzuela (among others) have described for years the deleterious effects of high-stakes testing in urban schools, suggesting that the testing movement has limited curricula to simple, basic skills that can be assessed within a multiple-choice format (e.g., only one answer is correct every problem, only test makers ask the questions, individual or unique interpretations are worthless). Ironically, even with all of these pressures, students seldom do better on the very tests for which they have been prepared.[44] Marcia's students were no different. Some passed, some failed. The overall percentage passing rate at the school did not rise significantly that year.

Possibilities for Urban Schools

That result leads one to wonder what might actually "work" when it comes to teaching children to read and write. Though we do not believe in any single panacea, we believe in a vision of literacy as a means of critical thinking. This vision can be carried out in the most germane ways: professional development for teachers, providing the required resources and assistance for individualization, and systematically reducing the emphasis on multiple-choice, high-stakes assessment. Expanding the professional development opportunities for urban teachers—beyond "training" sessions for commercial programs—could provide the intellectual stimulation that teachers desire and require for inspiration and growth. Offering choice. Offering support. Offering resources. All would move teachers forward toward achieving a more critical stance in literacy instruction. Providing resources in urban districts for more reading teachers and more paraprofessional assistants in classrooms could reduce teachers' case loads and allow for more time for students and teachers to get on with the business of learning to read and write.

Most important, testing and test emphasis need to be systemically reduced in urban districts. Educational equity involves helping students become literate in all facets of life, helping them obtain not just functional literacy used to survive in society but literacy that *critiques*, solves problems, and takes action in a global and changing world.

---

41. Shannon, *supra* note 20; Wiltz & Wilson, *supra* note 22.
42. Booher-Jennings, *supra* note 32.
43. Kim & Sunderman, *supra* note 24.
44. Lee, *supra* note 29; Nichols, Glass, & Berliner, *supra* note 27.

24

Increasing the School Year for Some, but Not All, Children: Barriers to Extending the School Year

Len Biernat*

Introduction

No real doubt exists that too many U.S. students, especially those among low socioe-conomic groups, are failing to receive an adequate education in the nation's public schools. Critics of public education are quick to list flaws in the nature of public education to explain this failure and suggest that nothing short of an overhaul will remedy the problem. Ironically, however, it may not be that these underserved students are trapped in a system that dooms them to failure; it may be that they do not spend enough time in that very system—a system that, in fact, can make them successful. An important part of the solution, in other words, may be to increase the amount of time those students spend in school.

Education is an extremely important state interest because an educated citizenry is essential to a democratic society in which citizens participate in the process. Education is also necessary for the economic and social benefit it provides for both individuals and society.[1] The U.S. Supreme Court has acknowledged that education is perhaps the most important function of state and local government.[2] For this reason, every state now has compulsory education statutes requiring that children attend school, usually between the ages of six and sixteen.[3]

The length of the school year and enforcement of compulsory education statutes vary from state to state.[4] Sanctions for noncompliance with these statutes may include misde-

---

* Professor of Law, Hamline University School of Law.

1. *See Plyler v. Doe*, 457 U.S. 202, 221 (1982); *San Antonio Indep. Sch. Dist. v. Rodriguez*, 411 U.S. 1, 30 (1973); *Brown v. Bd. of Educ.*, 347 U.S. 483, 493 (1954).

2. *Brown*, 347 U.S. at 493.

3. Homer H. Clark Jr., The Law of Domestic Relations in the United States 331 (2d ed. 1988). Forty-eight state constitutions require the creation of public school systems. Arval A. Morris, The Constitution and American Education 113 (1974).

4. See Appendix A for a listing of the length of the school year for each state.

meanor convictions of the parents and a civil proceeding in the juvenile courts against the children for their truancy.

Ironically, until recently, states were mainly concerned only that the children be in school. There were few state requirements that the students had to demonstrate what they learned. Graduation requirements were based on students meeting the requisite number of hours in certain subjects, instead of on passing grades or successful completion of a test. "Seat time," not knowledge, was the prerequisite to completing high school. In most instances, grading standards and specific curricular content were determined at the local, not state, levels. As a result, few states had uniform, statewide standards for all schools.

Nevertheless, the system worked well for the vast majority of American children. Many students performed well and went on to higher education. Other children would meet the minimal attendance standards for graduation and would complete high school. However, some students would graduate having learned very little. In addition, other students would put in the requisite amount of time before they were allowed to drop out of school without any sanctions.

In the United States, there is a growing concern about the failure of public education to reach all segments of the population. Some students are putting time in school but are not learning. Some students are graduating but do not meet basic reading and mathematic standards. At the same time, there is a growing frustration that the academic standards in the schools are too low to be competitive in a global economy.

This dissatisfaction has led to a growing involvement by the federal government in public education, an area traditionally reserved to the states. The federal No Child Left Behind Act (NCLB)[5] requires states, as a condition of receiving federal funds, to establish higher academic standards and periodic testing to measure the extent to which the standards are being met.

The NCLB served as a catalyst for states to restructure public education to improve accountability and meet higher academic standards in the schools. Virtually all states have now established state standards, and some now require passage of a standardized test as a requirement for receiving a high school diploma.[6] However, there is a fear that as standards increase, more children will be left behind, while at the same time, there is a concern that many students are well below even very low standards, and that states might drop their academic standards even further in an attempt to avoid possible sanctions under the NCLB.

The demand by the public for increased accountability has led to a more thorough examination of schools and the production of more statistical data that are available for the public. The NCLB requires that states publish test results so that parents are armed with the information needed to select a good school or identify those in need of remedial action. The Act also requires that test results be disaggregated by student demographic subgroups to identify and compare the test results. These comparisons show a clear achievement gap among students from various income groups and between white students and students of color. Not surprisingly, many of the schools with the lowest test scores are located in large urban areas where the population of children of color and poverty levels are high.

As a result, more attention is being given to students who reside in poor urban communities or who do not speak English as their primary language. This increased atten-

---

5. No Child Left Behind Act of 2001, 20 U.S.C. § 6301 (2002).

6. As an example, Minnesota requires public school students to pass a basic skills test in reading, mathematics, and written composition to receive a high school diploma. *See* Minn. Stat. § 120B.02 (2006). Washington has a similar requirement. *See* Wash. Rev. Code § 28A.655.060(3)(i)(i) (2000).

tion, however, has not translated into a significant closing of the achievement gap. Critics blame the schools for not meeting the needs of these children. In turn, the schools defend current practices, claiming that many children come to school with problems that are beyond the ability of the schools to address.[7] They claim that poverty and its associated problems are the most significant barriers to academic success, and that the schools do not have the resources to deal with the growing number of children in poverty and the associated risk factors.[8]

Although the link between poverty and low student performance is clear,[9] what remains uncertain is the causal connection between them, if any. Some individual schools in poor urban areas throughout the country are very successful. Some poor children are very successful within schools that are not performing well. At the same time, some children from moderate or wealthy families do not do well in various types of schools. Therefore, the states need to focus on the individual students who fail, not just all students who live in poverty.

Nevertheless, this distinction in student populations does create some constitutional issues because states may have to treat children who are passing differently from those who are not. Can states go beyond the compulsory education requirements set for all children to mandate that those who are having academic difficulty have a longer school day or a longer school year? Can states require that these students attend summer school or other special programs to improve student achievement?

This chapter examines some of these issues. The next section presents a brief history of compulsory education in this country, some of the legal challenges to these state requirements, and some of the barriers to extending the school year or making summer school mandatory. Then the chapter examines some current research that supports extending the school year to reach students who are having academic difficulty. Finally, this chapter makes several recommendations on how the states could improve the education of children having academic difficulty using mandatory summer school and other alternative programs funded by the federal government.

Compulsory Education

State statutes requiring the education of all children between certain ages for a fixed number of days each year, or compulsory education statutes, have long formed the background of the educational system within the United States. The power to establish these statutes is a valid exercise of the state to ensure a well-educated citizenry that is needed within a democratic form of government. The creation of an enlightened citizenry serves the welfare of the state, which leads to the general happiness of all as well as the preservation of liberty.

---

7. *See* James E. Rosenbaum, *Effective Policies to Help Youth, in* Voices from the Field: 30 Expert Opinions on American 2000, The Bush Administration Strategy to "Reinvent" America's Schools (William T. Grant Found. Comm'n on Work, Family and Citizenship and Inst. for Educ. Leadership, 1991).

8. Len Biernat & Christine Jax, *Limiting Mobility and Improving Student Achievement*, 23 Hamline L. Rev. 1, 3 (1999).

9. *See* Christopher J. McCarthy, *Rethinking Liberal and Radical Perspectives on Racial Inequality in Schooling: Making the Case for Nonsynchrony, in* Facing Racism in Education (Hidalgo et al. eds., 1990); *See* The Children's Defense Fund, The State of America's Children (1994).

Early education statutes required parents to ensure that their children were educated either by attending a school or by receiving instruction at home. Massachusetts established the first such law in 1642 and 200 years later adopted the first compulsory attendance law, requiring children between the ages of eight and fourteen to attend school for twelve weeks each year.[10]

Toward the end of the nineteenth century, because most states had made schooling compulsory, the United States had developed a vast system of public education. Nevertheless, the public hotly debated the concept of compulsory education on ideological grounds, and enforcement of attendance laws was limited.[11] The lack of enforcement caused some to refer to compulsory education during this time as the "symbolic stage."[12] Americans, however, were starting to embrace the need to compel children to attend school.

The public no longer debates the desirability of compulsory education. Moreover, the courts have consistently upheld the concept of compulsory education as a proper governmental interest.[13] The remaining debate centers on the number of days per year that should be required and on the application of certain provisions of state laws.

The U.S. Supreme Court has ruled directly on three cases that challenged a state's application of its compulsory education laws, finding against the state in all of them. In one, *Pierce v. Society Sisters*, the Court struck down an Oregon statute that required all students to attend public schools because it unconstitutionally denied parents the option of educating their children in private school.[14] In *Meyer v. Nebraska*, the Court invalidated a provision in Nebraska law that required instruction only in English and prohibited the teaching of modern foreign languages.[15] In both cases, the Supreme Court recognized the right of a state to require all students to attend school, but the Court recognized as well that parents had a constitutional right to provide education by alternative means.

In *Wisconsin v. Yoder*, the court, ruling against the state of Wisconsin, carved out a narrow exception to the state's compulsory education law, which required children to attend school until age sixteen.[16] Amish families had sought an exemption from the law based on their religious beliefs. This case did not challenge Wisconsin's right to require students to attend school; instead, it challenged Wisconsin's right to require school attendance past the age of fourteen when that attendance interfered with religious beliefs and practices, and when parents were providing the education necessary to make the children self-sufficient adults.

Most of the current challenges to compulsory education come from private schools that do not want to be regulated or by parents who wish to home-school their children.[17] The challenges center on state requirements that private schools or home-school parents provide equivalent instruction to public education that meets state standards.[18] Again,

---

10. Tyll Van Geel, The Courts and American Education Law 18 (1987).

11. David B. Tyack, *Ways of Seeing: An Essay of the History of Compulsory Schooling*, 46 Harv. Educ. Rev. 355, 359–61 (1976).

12. *Id.*

13. Ralph D. Mawdsley, *Compulsory Education Under Attack*, 30 Educ. L. Rep. 627, 627 (1986).

14. *Pierce v. Soc'y of Sisters*, 268 U.S. 510, 534–35. (1925).

15. *Meyer v. Nebraska*, 262 U.S. 390 (1923).

16. *Wisconsin v. Yoder*, 406 U.S. 205, 219 (1972).

17. *See* James C. Easterly, *Parent v. State: The Challenge to Compulsory School Attendance Laws*, 11 Hamline J. Pub. L. & Pol'y (1990); Daniel J. Rose, *Compulsory Education and Parent Rights: A Judicial Framework of Analysis*, 30 B.C. L. Rev. 861 (1989).

18. Mawdsley, *supra* note 13 at 634.

these cases challenge the application of the law and not the law itself or the valid government interest in education.

That parents today have the ability to have their children educated outside of the public school system gives them more control over the education of their children because there are fewer statutory regulations over their options. For those parents whose children stay in public schools, however, the right to direct that education has fewer protections because of laws and court decisions that give greater authority to school officials to control policies and resources.[19]

The fact that education is an important state interest gives the government the right to make reasonable laws that relate to education even though some parents might object to those laws. Thus, there are three sets of interests in actual or potential conflict: those of the parent, those of the child, and those of the state. Even though parents are given a great deal of autonomy in bringing up their children, the state still has an interest in protecting the child.

The common law doctrine of *parens patriae*, which makes the state the guardian of all those under a disability or in need of protection, provides the foundation for compulsory education laws. Under this doctrine, the state has the inherent prerogative to provide for the commonwealth and individual welfare. This prerogative gives the legislature the power to establish reasonable laws that are for the good of the state and not repugnant to the constitution.

Length of the School Year

As compulsory education evolved in this country, so did the conventional school year consisting of nine months in school followed by a three-month vacation. This model, based on agricultural needs, has remained largely unchanged. The result is that students in the United States typically attend school six or seven hours a day for approximately 180 days a year.

Appendix A provides a listing of the length of the school year for each state. Overall, the range is between 160 and 186 days, with the majority of states being close to or at the 180-day mark. Minnesota leaves the exact number of days to the local school district, but most districts are close to the norm. Despite the relative consistency between and among the states, there remains a concern that the 180-day model does not include enough time for students to reach their full potential.

In 1983, the seminal report *A Nation at Risk* noted the shortcomings of American public education and the need to improve expectations, content, and time. Specifically, the report stated that to compete effectively in the global economy, American students needed to spend considerably more time in school. The report recommended that the education system expand the school year from the 180-day norm to 200–220 days a year.[20] The call for more time raised public awareness of the issue and caused some thirty-seven states to

---

19. *See* Ralph D. Mawdsley, *Directing Children's Education: The Changing Views of Courts and Legislatures*, 171 Educ. L. Rep. 381, (2003); *see* Eric A. DeGroff, *State Regulation of Non-Public Schools: Does the Tie Still Bind?* 2003 BYU Educ. & L.J. 363 (2003).

20. The Nat'l Comm'n on Excellence in Educ., *A Nation at Risk: The Imperative for Educational Reform* (Apr. 1983), www.ed.gov/pubs/NatAtRisk/index.html (last visited Sept. 29, 2007).

consider extending the school year. Some states increased the school year to reach the norm of 180 days, but none of the states increased the year length beyond this norm.[21]

In recent years, advocates for extending the school year and school day point to international comparisons of student achievement that show American students lagging behind their counterparts in other industrialized nations. Some of the studies show that the nations that outperform the United States have significantly longer school years.[22]

The arguments for increasing the school day or year assume that more time in school will yield proportionally higher academic performance. The research, however, seems to reveal that the correlation between time and achievement is not as high as critics expected and suggests that the focus should be on the quality of time instead of the quantity of time.[23] In addition, the research hints that the costs of extending the school year are disproportionate to any expected gain in academic achievement.

There are a number of estimates of the cost of expanding the school day. One estimate is that it would cost states between $2.3 and $121.4 million for each additional day. Another study placed the overall cost for moving to a national norm of 200 days at somewhere between $34.4 and $41.9 billion annually.[24] This staggering price tag is beyond the resources of most state and local governments and leads to a continuation of the status quo of the 180-day school year.

Some states and districts have tried to alter their school calendars in a variety of ways in an attempt to improve student achievement. Other states have restructured the school day to maximize educational time.[25] Some states allow local districts to restructure the school years to save money by using buildings year-round in a more efficient manner. For example, students would still go to school for 180 days, but the summer vacation would no longer be sacrosanct.[26] Students would have more vacation breaks, but the breaks would be shorter, so there would be less learning loss.

Nonetheless, these various state efforts seem unlikely to address the needs of students who are well behind the performance of their peers. These students need more than a restructured school day; they also need an expanded summer program. In addition, they may need additional assistance before they even start elementary school to reduce the achievement gap.

Nevertheless, the focus of education critics has been on increasing the school year for all students, even those who perform at a high level and may not need the expanded year to meet minimal state standards. These students might benefit from enrichment programs if the state has the resources; however, the state needs to provide the resources so that all students can meet the basic state standards before diverting funds for enrichment.

The cost of expanding the school year only for those students who need the additional help would be far less than the cost of expanding the year for all students. In addition,

---

21. Julie Aronson et al., *Improving Student Achievement by Extending School: Is It Just a Matter of Time?* 1–10 (2005), www.wested.org/wested/papers/timeandlearning/TAL_PV.html.

22. *Id.*

23. *Id.*

24. *Id.*

25. Bill Metzker, *School Calendars* (2004), www.ericdigests.org/2003-2/calendars.html (last visited Sept. 29, 2007).

26. Harris Cooper et al., *The Effects of Summer Vacation on Test Scores: A Narrative and Meta-Analytic Review*, 66 REV. OF EDUC. RES. 228, 228 (1996). For commentary on this study, *see* Geoffrey Borman, *The Effects of Summer School: Questions Answered, Questions Raised*, 65 MONOGRAPHS OF THE SOCIETY FOR RESEARCH IN CHILD DEVELOPMENT 119 (2000).

the educational benefits that these students receive would be more in proportion to the money spent because these are the students who need it the most and who rely primarily on the schools for academic learning.

Compulsory Summer School

A state-by-state listing of regulations for summer school is contained in Appendix B, which shows considerable variation between and among the states. Summer school has been traditionally an option that is available to the local school district; most states, by statute, give local school districts the discretionary authority to operate these programs. Though some states require school districts to offer summer programs to meet the remedial needs of students, only a few states require or allow local districts to require students to attend these programs. One state, Massachusetts, allows districts to offer summer school programs but prohibits the districts from making them mandatory. Louisiana allows a local district to require students who fail state tests to attend summer school but allows parents to opt out of the requirement.

So far, there have been no direct challenges to these mandatory summer school requirements, perhaps because the requirements are of recent origin and seem to be a logical extension of a state's authority to require students to attend school and meet certain educational standards. In addition, most parents want their children to be in school during the summer if they need additional help. It is not clear, however, how rigorously the compulsory attendance during the summer is enforced. Nevertheless, because of new federal mandates under NCLB and the resulting state standards, schools are under considerable pressure to improve academic achievement to avoid remedial sanctions. Interestingly, one of the sanctions the federal government can impose on a school that does not reach adequate yearly progress for three or more years in a row can be a mandate to extend the school year or school day.[27] Ironically, to avoid these sanctions, schools are looking at a variety of ways to improve student achievement, and that search has led to an increase in the number of summer school programs, especially in larger city schools where test scores tend to be very low.[28]

The increase in the number of summer school programs may lead to legal challenges by parents who believe a summer requirement would interfere with their right to raise their children according to their wishes. Those challenge are not likely to succeed because of the state's interest in education and the related requirements that all students meet the state standards.

A recent Wisconsin case for example, dismissed a parent's claim that assigning homework during the summer violated the parent's fundamental right to direct and control the upbringing and education of his childrent under the due process clause of the Fourteenth Amendment. The parent claimed that the school had no right to claim the time of the student after the student met the compulsory attendance law. The teacher had re-

---

27. No Child Left Behind Act of 2001, 20 U.S.C. §6316(b)(7)(A)(B)(C) (Supp. I 2001). NCLB has been criticized for this remedial approach against failing schools. *See* Gershon M. Ratner, *Why The No Child Left Behind Act Needs to Be Restructured and How to Do It*, 9 UDC/DCSL L. Rev. 1 (2007); James E. Ryder, *The Perverse Incentives of the No Child Left Behind Act*, 79 N.Y.U. L. Rev. 932 (2004).

28. David R. Denton, *Summer School: Unfulfilled Promise*, Southern Regional Education Board (2002).

quired students to complete the summer assignments, which would become part of the grade during the fall semester. The student turned the assignments in late and received a reduced grade.

The Wisconsin Court of Appeals rejected the parent's claim as frivolous and remanded the case for the assessment of reasonable costs and attorneys' fees incurred by the school district. The court cited numerous federal courts of appeal that "have held that in certain circumstances the parental right to control the upbringing of a child must give way to a school's ability to control curriculum and the school environment."[29]

One issue not raised in the Wisconsin case was whether the family had received adequate notice about the summer assignments. This lack of notice could be a potential problem for schools that require summer school. Arguably, as a matter of due process, parents should know well in advance that summer school is required for those students who fall below certain standards. Minnesota, for example, allows local districts to require summer school, but mandates that the school district announce the criteria for which students will be required to attend when it acts to establish mandatory summer attendance.[30] This prior announcement, if given within a reasonable period, would give parents notice and eliminate potential due process claims.

Cost, however, is the most significant barrier to establishing any type of summer program, whether mandatory or voluntary. In most states, the costs of any summer program are borne primarily by the local district. Many school districts do not have enough resources to operate the regular school year and cannot divert any money to operate a summer program. The sagging national economy in 2002 caused many school districts to cut back or eliminate summer school.[31] To remedy this significant barrier, summer school needs to become an integral part of the overall educational system with a consistent stream of revenues that are dedicated to these programs and cannot be diverted to other programs or reduced when the economy falters.

One option would be for the school district to charge tuition for summer school. However, a tuition charge would serve as a barrier to the children living in poverty who may have the most need for the program; in fact, several school districts have faced challenges to charging tuition as a violation of equal protection. In each case, the court found no violation because summer school was separate from the regular school year and the district's lack of funding was a rational basis for the tuition requirement.[32]

If the state makes summer school attendance mandatory for failing students, however, such charges would be more problematic because then summer school would be an actual extension of the regular school year for those students, and courts would view the issue of charging tuition differently. As a result, the state and local school district would have to provide funding for these programs. Free remedial summer school should be available to the students from a reliable and predicable stream of resources. Districts should not charge students for remedial education.

Even if the state does provide enough resources for valuable programs that could help these students, the state must still ensure that the students attend. Statistics from North Carolina from 1997–2000 indicated that 76,319 students attended summer school be-

---

29. *Larson v. Burmaster*, 720 N.W.2d 134 (Wis. Ct. App. 2006).

30. MINN. STAT. § 120A.22(5)(b) (2001).

31. David R. Denton, *Summer School and Summer Learning*, Southern Regional Education Board (2002).

32. *See Moore v. Bd. of Trustees*, 344 F. Supp. 682, 685(D. S.C. 1972); *Crim v. McWhorter*, 252 S.E.2d 421, 425 (Ga. 1979); *Washington v. Salisbury*, 306 S.E.2d 600, 602 (S.C. 1983).

cause they were not performing at grade level. Of the attending students, 57,681, or 76 percent, reached grade level by the end of the summer. Unfortunately, another 165,196 students who were below grade level did not attend at all and thus were held back from a grade.[33]

Simply making summer school a mandatory requirement does not mean that students will attend, of course. After Minnesota allowed local districts to require summer school attendance in 1997, the Minneapolis school district required students who failed to meet either reading or math standards to attend summer school in 1998; but only about 50 percent of these students actually enrolled and attended.[34] Therefore, there needs to be more enforcement under truancy laws; after all, summer school cannot help students if they do not attend.

The Value of Summer School

Because of the requirements of the NCLB, states have made it a priority to identify early those students at risk of failure to provide them with help during the school year. In many cases, this additional assistance might help them meet the state standards as measured by state tests. For the lowest performing students, however, this assistance may not be enough. Summer school may help some of them pass the tests and avoid retention at the same grade level, but others may be too far behind to make up the difference in a brief summer program. Nevertheless, summer school could be a starting point for many, even if they require more assistance than a grammar program can provide.

Unfortunately, summer school has been traditionally a local option for school districts, so the quality and consistency of most of these programs has never been widely analyzed. Because summer school is normally a local option, it is often funded only from local resources with little help from the state or federal governments. Viewed as an addition to the regular school year, summer school is often one of the first things to be cut when resources are scarce. Moreover, very little research is available on the effectiveness of these programs, so school districts cannot fully understand their importance or dynamics.

Most of the current studies that examine the relationship between school time and student learning have relied on correlational data. There has never been a controlled study or a longitudinal study that directly measures extending the school year and the impact on student achievement.[35]

Clearly, however, a three-month gap in formal education does have an impact on student learning. It is "increasingly apparent that a long summer vacation does not represent just a pause in student learning, but actually causes many students to forget what they have learned."[36] Moreover, this "summer slide" has the most significant impact on poorer families, who tend to rely primarily on schools for academic learning; middle-class chil-

---

33. Denton, *supra* note 28, at 6.

34. Mark L. Davison et al., *A Few Weeks of Summer: Post-Summer School Achievement Among State Funded Students Who Do Not Initially Pass Minnesota's High School Graduation Test*, 15 (Office of Educ. Accountability, Univ. of Minn. 2001), www.education.umn.edu/oea/PDF/AFewWeeksInSummer.pdf.

35. *See* Aronson, *supra* note 21, at 2.

36. Denton, *supra* note 28, at 8; *see* Harris Cooper, *Summer School: Research-Based Recommendations for Policymakers* (Se. Reg'l Vision for Educ. 2001); Harris Cooper, *Summer Learning Loss: The Problem and Some Solutions*, 1–7 (ERIC Clearinghouse 2003).

dren, in contrast, typically rely on school for only a portion of their learning and can receive considerable educational stimulation during the summer. Thus, without summer school, the achievement gap between classes can actually widen during the summer.[37]

A recent review of the research on summer learning loss and the impact on student achievement test scores found that summer learning loss equaled at least one month of instruction; on average, achievement test scores were at least one month lower when students returned to school in the fall without having spent time in summer school.[38] The study also found that the summer loss was more pronounced for overall math skills than for reading, suggesting that the students had more opportunities to practice reading skills than to practice mathematics over the summer months.[39]

Another recent study demonstrated the impact of this phenomenon over a five-year period during the group's elementary education. During the school year, the gains between the high socioeconomic (SES) group and the low SES group were less than five points in both reading and math. During the five summers without summer school, however, the high SES group gained forty-six points in reading comprehension and about twenty-five points in math. The low SES groups essentially stood still in reading, and either gained or lost a little in math.[40]

While both SES groups made progress during the school year at a relatively close rate, the lower SES group had a much lower starting point at the beginning of the school year, so that the achievement gap actually increased at the end of the school year. Although these data do indicate that the schools were moving both groups forward and improving academic achievement, the higher SES group was moving faster during the school year. During the summer with no school, however, the lower-class children's academic growth basically stopped, while the middle-class children's growth continued to rise, so that the achievement gap was wider when the students returned to school compared to the previous spring.

Several dynamics explain why the academic achievement level of middle class students improves during the summer without summer school. First, in many instances, their parents have the time to be active participants in the learning process and understand how the process works, so they know how to encourage activities that will help students learn. Second, these families also have the income for expenditures for books, computers, travel, and tutoring that will help their children. Third, even entertaining family activities, unavailable to those with limited resources, can reinforce education.[41] Finally, because these parents are often more active in their children's educational lives, they respond quickly if their children fall behind by finding special programs and monitoring their progress.

Importantly, however, summer school is not the panacea for eliminating the achievement gap. Summer school is a short period, usually three to six weeks, and the gain for

---

37. Suzie Boss & Jennifer Railsback, *Summer School Programs: A Look at the Research, Implications for Practice, and Program Sampler* 11 (2002), www.nwrel.org/request/2002sept/summerschool.pdf.

38. Cooper *supra* note 26, at 253.

39. *Id.* at 254.

40. Karl L. Alexander & Doris R. Entwisle, *Early Schooling and Educational Inequality: Socioeconomic Disparities in Children's Learning*, JAMES S. COLEMAN (Jon Clark ed., 1996); *see* Doris R. Entwisle & Karl L. Alexander, *Summer Setback: Race, Poverty, School Composition, and Mathematics Achievement in the First Two Years of School*, 57 AM. SOC. REV. 72, 80 (1992).

41. *See* Boss & Railsback, *supra* note 37, at 12.

students of all socioeconomic levels is quite small as measured by standardized tests.[42] This small increase for lower SES students does not completely offset the greater increase the higher SES students experience during the summer even without going to summer school. By the time these sets of students reach high school, the gap becomes so large that even a significant amount of extra time in school may not ever be enough to narrow it.

For example, while a study of the Minneapolis/St. Paul summer programs involving eighth-grade students suggested that summer school helped enrolled students boost test scores by three to nine percentage points, these students were still twenty to twenty-five percentage points below the passing score.[43] Thus, at the eighth-grade level, summer school does not seem to be the only intervention needed for many of these students.

For this reason, the additional time should be provided in preschool and the early grades. Studies indicate that a relatively small gap in children's test scores exists based on family income when the students start first grade.[44] Even if a gap does exist, it is likely that it is smaller at this point than it will be later. Therefore, educators need to reach these students while the achievement gap may be still manageable. The evidence is clear that good preschools can improve the early success of disadvantaged children. The major goal of these programs is to reduce the retention rate in first grade, which is higher than in any subsequent grade.[45]

Children in poverty need high-quality preschool programs before they start first grade and must have high-quality extended day and summer school programs after they reach first grade. Moreover, students who are having academic problems in these early years must be required to attend these programs. Similarly, because many children who could benefit from kindergarten do not attend because it is not compulsory,[46] school districts should make kindergarten programs mandatory for those students who need the additional assistance and expand half-day kindergarten programs to full-day programs.

Conclusion

States have both a legal and a moral obligation to ensure that all citizens are educated and attain a standard of proficiency as set by the government. Regardless of its numerous shortcomings, NCLB has made the public more aware of the difficulty states are having in ensuring that all students are meeting state education standards.[47] Nevertheless,

---

42. Doris R. Entwisle et al., *Keep the Faucet Flowing: Summer Learning and Home Environment*, 25 AM. EDUCATOR 47, 50 (2001).

43. Davison et al., *supra* note 36, at 24.

44. *Id.* However, some researchers point out that the achievement gap is already large before children enter kindergarten. *See* Geoffrey D. Borman, *How Can Title I Improve Achievement?* 60 EDUC. LEADERSHIP 49 (2003); *see* Amy H. Tathbun et al., *The World Around Them: The Relationship Between Kindergartners' Summer Experiences and Their General Knowledge* 2 (Am. Educ. Research Ass'n 2003).

45. Borman, *supra* note 44, at 52.

46. *Id.*

47. For a critical review of the remedial sanctions of the NCLB, and a concern that states might lower their standard and focus too much on teaching to the tests, *see* Gershon M. Ratner, *Why the No Child Left Behind Act Needs to Be Restructured to Accomplish its Goals and How to Do It*, 9 UDC/DCSL L. REV. 1 (2007); Melanie Natasha Henry, Comment, *No Child Left Behind? Educational Malpractice Litigation for the 21st Century*, 92 CAL. L. REV 1117 (2004).

despite valiant efforts on behalf of some educators, many children are still falling behind. It is obvious that most states will not be able to meet the stated goal of the NCLB — namely, that all students reach the escalating targets so that they are 100 percent proficient by the year 2014.[48]

Schools that do not have all students reach the 100 percent proficiency level will face increasingly harsh sanctions set out in the NCLB. But what happens to these students? Will the students have a cause of action against the school district or the state because the state failed to fulfill its obligation to ensure that no child was left behind? Will there be an action against the federal government for devising an educational scheme without fully funding its operation?[49]

The federal government needs to provide more than sanctions against schools that do not meet the annual yearly progress targets. Schools that have a high percentage of students who do not meet standards need research and financial support, as well as flexibility to try new methods to improve student achievement. The federal government should monitor and evaluate these programs to determine their effectiveness and publish the results. State governments alone do not have the resources to accomplish these tasks.

In January 2002, as part of NCLB, Title I[50] received the largest funding increase in its history, pushing expenditures over $10 billion.[51] Title I is specifically designed to eliminate the persistent achievement gap separating low-income and more advantaged students, and students of color and white students. More of those funds need to be directed to preschool, full-day kindergarten, and summer programs when the achievement gap is still small and before the gap starts widening.[52]

State and federal governments must also provide support for preschool programs. The bulk of federal support for preschool children comes from the Head Start Program,[53] yet this program still serves only 58 percent of eligible children and has had budget cuts totaling 11 percent since 2002.[54] States are required to provide 20 percent of the overall cost of the program, but much more is needed from both federal and state governments.

Head Start may not be the only solution for reducing the achievement gap; however, it is well established and has a large structure that reaches many economically disadvantaged children. The federal government should consider fully funding this program and expanding it to reach all children. Additional federal support should also fund research to determine the effectiveness of this program and identify areas for improvement.

Some researchers should examine the use of distance learning for students who need additional assistance. These programs could reduce personnel costs, provide more course offerings, and allow increased flexibility for scheduling student time. Several states now

---

48. No Child Left Behind Act of 2001, 20 U.S.C. § 6311(b)(2)(G)(iv) (Supp. I 2001).

49. *See* Paul T. O'Neill, *High Stakes Testing and Litigation*, 2003 BYU Educ. & L.J. 623 (2003); Rebecca R. Glasgow, *Can Students Sue When They Don't Make the Grade? The Washington Assessment of Student Learning and Educational Malpractice*, 76 Wash. L. Rev. 893 (2001); Rachel F. Moran, *Sorting and Reforming: High Stakes Testing in the Public Schools*, 34 Akron L. Rev. 107 (2000); Jay P. Heubert, *Nondiscriminatory Use of High-Stakes Tests: Combining Professional Test-Use Standards with Civil Rights Enforcement*, 133 Educ. L. Rep. 17 (1999).

50. Elementary and Secondary Education Act of 1965, as amended, 20 U.S.C. § 1001 (1998).

51. *See* Borman, *supra* note 44, at 4.

52. *Id.* at 3.

53. Head Start Act, 42 U.S.C. § 9801 (1998).

54. National Head Start Association, 2007 Policy Agenda 1–2 (2007), www.nhsa.org/download/advocacy/2007_policy_agenda.pdf.

have statewide virtual schools for struggling students under a single, centralized administration.[55] These courses could be offered in the summer as well as throughout the school year.

Finally, the federal government needs to take the lead in conducting research on summer school and extended year programs and, in the meantime, fully fund these programs so that they do not fall victim to the budget problems faced by states and local school districts. Summer school programs need a consistent and continuous stream of resources so that they can be monitored over a number of years to determine their impact on student performance.

Because "research clearly shows that quality summer programs for struggling students are essential to closing the gaps" in achievement,[56] summer school should be an integral part of a year-round program structure of extra time and assistance for those students who are falling behind. It should not be viewed as an add-on program, available only when resources are available. Additionally, because an effective summer school program needs to respond to the individual needs of students, teachers need to be given special training to have the ability to help struggling students.

Summer should not be limited to the traditional academics, although there should be an emphasis on math and reading. Summer programs for disadvantaged children should include physical activity and enrichment experiences similar to the educational experiences typically available to students in higher socioeconomic classes during the summer.[57]

Summer school cannot help failing students if it is not available, nor can it provide much help if it is not of the highest quality and designed to meet the needs of individual students. In addition, summer school cannot help students if it is available but students do not attend. Therefore, states should require students who are falling behind to attend summer school and other extended day and extended year programs.

To avoid possible legal challenges, the states themselves should mandate extended day and summer school attendance instead of leaving this decision to the local school district. Such a mandate would make it clear that these programs are an integral part of the school year and a component of already existing compulsory education statutes. In addition, the states should provide to the parents and students notice of the standards that will be used to require attendance. The standards should be clear and published well in advance of the time when these extended programs would commence. The states should also develop appropriate enforcement mechanisms to ensure that the students attend. Most important, summer school and extended day programs need to receive the necessary financial assistance from state and federal authorities to make these programs work.

Extended day and extended year summer school may not solve all of the problems that contribute to achievement gaps among socioeconomic groups, but they can make significant headway against many of those problems. If the nation is serious about closing achievement gaps, it must become serious about providing students with enough uninterrupted instruction to shrink those gaps.

---

55. Alabama, Arkansas, Florida, and Kentucky have virtual schools offering summer courses. Denton, *supra* note 28, at 7.

56. *Id.* at 12.

57. Alexander & Entwisle, *supra* note 40, at 184.

Appendix A: Length of School Year — 2007

State	Minimum Length of School Year (days)	State Legislation
Alabama	175	Ala. Admin. Code r. 290-3-1-.02(2)(a)(1) (2006)
Alaska	180	Alaska Stat. § 14.03.030 (2007)
Arizona	180	Ariz. Rev. Stat. § 15-341.01(A) (2007)
Arkansas	(1)	Ark. Code § 6-10-106 (2007)
California	175	Cal. Code Regs. tit. 5, § 2(1) (2007)
Colorado	160	Colo. Rev. Stat. § 22-33-104(1)(b) (2007)
Connecticut	180	Conn. Gen. Stat. § 10-16 (2007)
Delaware	1060 hours	Del. Code Ann. tit. 14, § 1049(a)(1) (2007)
Florida	180	Fla. Stat. § 1000.01 (2007)
Georgia	180	Ga. Code Ann. § 20-2-168(c))(1) (2007)
Hawaii	180	(2)
Idaho	(3)	Idaho Code § 33-512(1)(a) (2007)
Illinois	176	105 Ill. Comp. Stat. 5/10-19 (2007)
Indiana	180	Ind. Code § 20-30-2-3 (2007)
Iowa	180	Iowa Code § 279.10 (2007)
Kansas	186	Kan. Stat. § 72-1106(a) (2006)
Kentucky	185	Ky. Rev. Stat. Ann. § 158.070(1) (2007)
Louisiana	177	La. Rev. Stat. § 17:154.1(A)(1) (2007)
Maine	175	Me. Rev. Stat. Tit. 20-A, § 4801 (2007)
Maryland	180	Md. Code Ann., Educ. § 7-103(a)(1)(i) (2007)
Massachusetts	185	603 Mass. Code Regs. 27.03(2) (2007)
Michigan	1098 hours	Mich. Comp. Laws § 388.1701(3)(a) (2007)
Minnesota	(4)	Minn. Stat. § 120A.41 (2007)
Mississippi	180	Miss. Code § 37-13-63(1) (2007)
Missouri	174	Mo. Rev. Stat. § 160.011(9) (2007)
Montana	(5)	Mont. Code § 20-1-301 (2005)
Nebraska	(6)	Neb. Rev. Stat. §79-101(7) (2007)
Nevada	180	Nev. Rev. Stat. § 388.090(1) (2007)
New Hampshire	180	N.H. Rev. Stat. § 189:1 (2007)
New Jersey	180	N.J. Stat. § 18A:7F-9 (2007)
New Mexico	(7)	N.M. Stat. § 22-13-2 (2007)
New York	180	N.Y. Educ. Law § 3204.7 (McKinney 2007)
North Carolina	180	N.C. Gen. Stat. § 115C-84.2 (2007)
North Dakota	173	N.D. Cent. Code § 15.1-06-04(1)(a) (2007)
Ohio	182	Ohio Rev. Code § 3313.48 (2007)
Oklahoma	180	Okla. Stat. tit. 70, § 1-109 (2007)

Oregon	(3)	Or. Admin. R. 581-022-1620 (2007)
Pennsylvania	180	24 Pa. Stat. 24, § 15-1501 (2007)
Rhode Island	180	R.I. Gen. Laws § 16-2-2(a) (2007)
South Carolina	180	S.C. Code § 59-1-425 (2006)
South Dakota	(8)	S.D. Codified Laws § 13-26-1 (2007)
Tennessee	180	Tenn. Code § 49-6-3004(a)(1) (2007)
Texas	180	Tex. Educ. Code § 25.081(a) (Vernon 2007)
Utah	180	Utah Admin. Code r. 277-419 (2007)
Vermont	175	Vt. Stat. tit. 16, § 1071(a)(1) (2007)
Virginia	180	Va. Code § 22.1-98 (2007)
Washington	180	Wash. Admin. Code 180-16-215(1)(a) (2007)
Washington, D.C.	180	D.C. Mun. Regs. tit. 5 § 305.6 (2007
West Virginia	180	W. Va. Code R. 18-5-45 (2007)
Wisconsin	180	Wis. Stat. § 120.12(15) (2007)
Wyoming	185	Wyo. Stat. § 21-13-307(a)(ii) (2007)

1. Uniform dates for beginning and end of school year, but no specific number of days

2. According to teachers' contracts in Hawaii, the teacher is to work no more than 190 days with 10 of those being noninstructional days

3. Eight hundred ten hours for grades one through three; 900 hours for grades four through eight; 990 hours for grades nine through twelve

4. School districts must adopt calendars with at least the number of student instruction days as the 1996–1997 year had

5. Seven hundred twenty hours for grades one through three and 1,080 hours for grades four through twelve

6. One thousand thirty two instructional hours for elementary grades other than kindergarten; 1,080 instructional hours for high school grades

7. Nine hundred ninety hours for grades one through six and 1,080 hours grades seven through twelve

8. Board of education shall promulgate rules setting the minimum number of hours for grades one through three; the number of hours in school-term for grades four through twelve may not be less than 962.5 hours, excluding recess or lunch

Appendix B; Summer School Programs—2007

State	State Legislation and Administrative Rules	Summary
Alabama	Ala. Admin. Code r. §290-3-1-.02(6)(b)(2)(i) (2007)	The public summer school shall be authorized by the local board of education.
Alaska	Alaska Admin. Code tit. 4, §06.845 (2007)	As part of a school improvement plan, a school may incorporate, as appropriate, activities for students before school, after school, during the summer, and during any extension of the school year.
Arizona	Ariz. Rev. Stat. §3-7-2-306(F)(4) (2007)	English language learners will be provided with an education outside of the regular school period to achieve state academic standards.
Arkansas	Ark. Code. §6-15-1602 (2007)	Local school districts shall identify students in all grades who have been placed at risk of academic failure and implement personal education plan, which may include summer school, Saturday school, and extended days.
	Ark. Code §6-16-701, 702, 704-706 (2007)	Public schools authorized to operate optional summer school programs. School district should be authorized to charge a fee. Those districts not offering summer program shall offer remediation program during regular school year to students kindergarten through third grade not performing to grade level.
California	Cal. Educ. Code §37252 (West 2007)	School district shall offer students in grades seven through twelve who are not demonstrating progress toward passing the high school exit exam supplemental summer instructional programs.
	Cal. Educ. Code §37252.8 (West 2007)	Public and charter schools with second through sixth grades may offer supplementary instruction, including summer school, to pupils deficient in math, reading, and writing or who are at risk of dropping out.
	Cal. Educ. Code §37252.2(a) (West 2007)	School district shall offer students who have been retained in second through ninth grades supplemental instructional programs including summer school.
	Cal. Educ. Code §37253 (West 2007)	A school district may offer summer school programs in core academic areas.
Colorado	Colo. Rev. Stat. §22-23-106 (2007)	An educational program for migrant children may be operated during the summer.

	Colo. Rev. Stat. § 22-32-118(1) (2007)	A board of education may provide summer school programs and may fix and collect a fee.
	Colo. Rev. Stat. § 22-7-801 (2007)	Summer school grants are available for public and charter schools to provide intensive reading, writing, and math to students in fourth through eighth grades who performed unsatisfactorily in standardized tests.
Connecticut	Conn. Gen. Stat. § 10-74a (2007)	Local or regional board of education may establish summer school for children on voluntary basis and may charge a reasonable fee.
Delaware	Del. Code Ann. tit. 14, § 153(d) (2007)	A third-, fifth-, or eighth-grade student who falls below the required performance on a standardized reading test will not advance grades unless their parents or guardians agree on an individual assessment program (which may include summer school). Summer school may be mandated if the student does not meet expectations the following year. Mandatory summer school may not be forgiven more than twice for extenuating circumstances.
Florida	Fla. Stat. § 1003.413 (3) (2007)	Districts shall implement policies, including summer school, for students needing intensive reading or math intervention or additional credits.
	Fla. Stat. § 1003.428(3) (2007)	School districts may develop summer school programs to aid students in graduating high school.
Georgia	Ga. Code Ann. § 20-2-168(d) (2007)	The governing board may adopt a summer school program.
	Ga. Code Ann. § 20-2-168(f) (2007)	Local boards of education must provide summer school for those in kindergarten through eighth grade who have been retained or who have failed an academic subject. The session must be six weeks and students may not be charged.
	Ga. Comp. R. & Regs. 160-4-2-.14(2) (2007)	Each school system implementing the state-funded Instructional Extension Program shall provide instructional opportunities at no cost to eligible students with low performance in academic subjects; which may include summer school.
	Ga. Comp. R. & Regs. 160-4-2-.37 (2007)	Local school board may establish a summer remedial program for the high school graduation test.
Hawaii	(—)	
Idaho	(—)	

Illinois	105 Ill. Comp. Stat. 5/10-22.33B (2007)	Summer school shall be required of any student that is academically at risk in a critical subject area.
Indiana	Ind. Code § 20-3.1-13-1 (2007)	The school city must provide summer remediation services to students who do not meet state achievement standards.
	Ind. Code § 20-3-7-3 (2007)	A school district may conduct a voluntary summer school enrichment program in which they offer classes not taught during the normal school year.
	Ind. Code § 20-30-7-5 (2007)	School districts may partner with one another to offer summer school.
Iowa	Iowa Code § 282.6 (2007)	School districts may charge tuition for summer school.
Kansas	Kan. Stat. § 72-8237 (2007)	The board of education of any school district may establish, operate, and maintain a summer program for pupils.
	Kan. Stat. § 72-7534(b) (2007)	School districts must provide intervention for students not making satisfactory progress in reading, which may include summer school.
Kentucky	704 Ky. Admin. Regs. 3:390(2)(3)(c) (2007)	The rule extends school beyond the minimum term for those students in need of additional assistance.
Louisiana	La. Rev. Stat. § 17:24.4(G)(4)(a) (2007)	The governing body must establish a summer school remediation program to all students who do not meet the minimum achievement level to be promoted to the fifth or ninth grade.
	La. Rev. Stat. § 17:24.4(G)(4)(c) (2007)	School districts may require students who fail a required test to attend summer school before advancing to the next grade. Parents may refuse after they are told the consequences of their decision.
	La. Rev. Stat. § 17:401.12(A)(1) (2007)	Each school district must have the ability to provide K–4 students with summer enrichment classes for every student who needs extra instruction, reinforcement, or time on task to be able to achieve basic skills of reading, math, and writing. Other students may attend if they pay tuition.
Maine	Me. Rev. Stat. Ann. Tit. 20-A, § 8801, (2006)	The state board and commissioner shall jointly adopt consistent rules for summer school credit for students.
Maryland	Md. Code Regs. 03.02.05 (2007)	Each local school system may provide summer school programs for original and review credit as determined by the needs of the student.

Massachu-setts	Mass. Gen. Laws ch. 71, § 28 (2007)	The school committee may maintain a summer school program but may not make it mandatory.
Michigan	(—)	
Minnesota	Minn. Stat. § 120A.22(5)(b) (2006)	A school district may require its students to attend summer school.
	Minn. Stat. § 120B.12, subd. 3 (2006)	A school district may require summer school attendance of a first-grade student who is at risk of not learning to read.
	Minn. Stat. § 123B.02(10) (2006)	A school board may establish summer sessions.
Mississippi	Miss. Code Ann. § 37-3-59 (2007)	The school boards of all school districts are authorized to establish a summer program for kindergarten through eighth grade for students making unsatisfactory progress.
Missouri	Mo. Code Regs. Ann. tit. 5, § 50-340-050 (2006)	A school board may adopt a summer school program.
	Mo. Rev. Stat. § 167.645(3) (2006)	Third graders who fall below grade reading level may be required to attend summer school.
	Mo. Rev. Stat. § 167.645(7) (2006)	Each school district is required to offer summer school reading instruction to any student with a reading improvement plan. This may be accomplished through partnering with neighboring districts.
	Mo. Rev. Stat. § 167.640(2) (2006)	School districts may require summer school as a condition of grade promotion for students who fail to master skills and competencies.
Montana	(—)	
Nebraska	Neb. Rev. Stat. § 79-536 (2006)	A school district's board of education may require children five to fifteen years of age to attend summer school if they are making unsatisfactory progress and it is believed it will help them.
Nevada	Nev. Rev. Stat. § 392.4655 (2007)	If a student is a habitual disciplinary problem, the school may develop a plan of behavior, which may include summer school if voluntarily agreed on by the student and parents/guardians.
New Hampshire	(—)	
New Jersey	N.J. Stat. Ann. § 18A:7C-6.2 (West 2007)	For eighth grade students not meeting established examination standards, the local board of education shall provide for appropriate remediation in areas of demonstrated deficiency, which may include summer programs.

New Mexico	N.M. Stat. § 22-2C-6 (2007)	Local school boards shall approve school district–developed remediation programs and academic improvement programs, which may include summer school, to provide special instructional assistance to students in grades one through eight who fail to attain adequate yearly progress. Parents or guardians must bear the cost of summer school for students in ninth through twelfth grade unless they are indigent.
New York	N.Y. Educ. Law § 1950 (4)(bb) (McKinney 2007)	Boards of cooperative educational services may provide academic and other programs and services in the school year on a cooperative basis, including summer programs and services.
	N.Y. Comp. Codes R. & Regs. Tit. 8, § 110.1 (2007)	The commissioner of education must approve a summer school program.
North Carolina	N.C. Gen. Stat § 115C-105.41 (2007)	Local school administrative units may develop a personal education plan for students at risk of academic failure, which may include summer school at no cost to the students.
	N.C. Gen. Stat. § 115C-233 (2007)	Each local school administrative unit may establish and maintain summer schools.
North Dakota	N.D. Cent. Code § 15.1-27-19 (2007)	Each school district may offer summer school.
Ohio	Ohio Rev. Code Ann. § 3317.029(J)(7)(c) (West 2007)	Districts may extend the school year either through adding regular days of instruction to the school calendar or by providing summer programs.
	Ohio Rev. Code Ann. § 3313.608(B)(2) (West 2007)	A school district shall offer a summer remediation program for students failing to achieve required test scores.
	Ohio Rev. Code Ann. § 3313.641 (West 2007)	A city's board of education may operate a summer school of their wishes and charge tuition to students choosing to attend.
Oklahoma	Okla. Stat. tit. 70, § 3-153 (2007)	The state board of education does not need to make prior approval of local summer schools.
	Okla. Stat. tit. 70, § 1210.508E (2007)	Third-grade students may be required to attend summer school to achieve the required reading level to be able to be promoted to the fourth grade.
Oregon	Or. Rev. Stat. Ann. § 343.830 (2007)	A school district may establish a summer program for migrant children.
Pennsylvania (—)		
Rhode Island (—)		

South Carolina	S.C. Code Ann. § 59-18-500 (2006)	A student may be required to attend summer school if the student, in a grade from third to eighth, lacks the skills to perform at grade level.
South Dakota	S.D. Codified Laws § 13-26-2 (2007)	A school board may operate a special term during the summer months.
	S.D. Codified Laws § 13-33-3 (2007)	A school board may maintain summer school.
Tennessee	Tenn. Code Ann. § 49-6-601 (2007)	Credits earned in a state-approved summer school program may be transferred to other approved schools in the state.
Texas	Tex. Educ. Code Ann. § 29.088 (Vernon 2007); Tex. Educ. Code Ann. § 29.090 (2007)	A school district may provide an intensive program for the summer to provide mathematics or science instruction to at-risk students.
	Tex. Educ. Code Ann. § 29.060 (2007)	A school district may establish summer school programs for students of limited English proficiency.
Utah	(—)	
Vermont	Vt. Stat. Ann. tit. 16, § 4001 (2007)	A public school may maintain summer school for its pupils.
Virginia	Va. Code Ann. § 22.1-253.13.1(C) (2007); Va. Code Ann. § 22.1-254.01 (2007)	Any student who does not pass the literacy tests of standards of learning in grades three, five, or eight shall be required to attend a summer school program, or to participate in another form of remediation. The superintendent may seek immediate compliance with this program under the compulsory school attendance laws.
Washington	Wash. Rev. Code § 28A.320.500 (2007)	Every school district board of directors is authorized to establish summer programs. Attendance is voluntary.
Washington, D.C.	(—)	
West Virginia	W. Va. Code R. 18-2E-3c (2007); W. Va. Code R. 18-2E-3d (2007)	Any county that has received a competitive grant for a reading or math program should encourage students in kindergarten through fourth grade who did not perform at grade level to attend summer school. The county may consider student attendance in this program as a factor in determining whether the child is eligible to be promoted to the next grade.
	W. Va. Code R. § 18-5-39 (2007)	Counties may charge tuition for summer school as long as families can have the fees reduced or waived if needed.

| Wisconsin | Wis. Stat. § 118.04 (2007) | Any school board may elect to operate summer classes. |
| Wyoming | (—) | |

(—) No legislation regarding summer school

Cases

A.A. v. Cooperman, 526 A.2d 1103 (N.J. Super. Ct. App. Div. 1987).

Abbott v. Burke (Abbot V), 710 A.2d 450 (N.J. 1998).

Abbott v. Burke (Abbott VI), 790 A.2d 842 (N.J. 2002).

Abbott v. Burke, 693 A.2d 417 (N.J. 1997).

Adarand v. Pena, 515 U.S. 200 (1995).

Agnes Scott College, Inc. v. Clark, 616 S.E.2d 468 (Ga. Ct. App. 2005).

Alabama Coalition for Equity v. Hunt (Ala. Circ. Ct. 1993) (published as Appendix to Opinion of the Justices, 624 So.2d 107, 110 (Ala. 1993)).

Alexander C., In re, 843 N.E.2d 211 (Ohio Ct. App. 2006).

Alexander v. Holmes County Bd. of Educ., 396 U.S. 19 (1969).

Alexander v. Sandoval, 532 U.S. 275 (2001).

Allred v. Heaton, 336 S.W.2d 251 (Tex. App. 1960).

Alston v. Sch. Bd. of City of Norfolk, 112 F.2d 992 (4th Cir. 1940).

Alvarez v. Owen, No. 66625 (San Diego County Super. Ct. Mar. 30, 1931).

Anderson v. State, 168 Vt. 641, 723 A.2d 1147 (1998).

Anthony F., In re, 216 A.2d 564 (Sp. Ct. N.Y. 1995).

Arlington Heights v. Metropolitan Housing Dev. Corp., 429 U.S. 252, 264–65 (1977).

Arvizu v. Waco Indep. Sch. Dist., 373 F.Supp. 1264 (W.D. Tex. 1973).

Arvizu v. Waco Indep. Sch. Dist., 495 F.2d 499 (5th Cir. 1974).

Ass'n of Cmty. Organizations for Reform Now v. New York City Dep't of Educ., 269 F. Supp. 2d 338 (S.D.N.Y. 2003).

Baisey v. Board of Trustees of the Waco Indep. Sch. Dist., No. W-71-CA-72, (1974).

Bd. of Educ. of City of Millville v. New Jersey Dep't of Educ., 872 A.2d 1052 (N.J. 2005).

Bd. of Educ. of City of Passaic v. New Jersey Dep't of Educ., 872 A.2d 1062 (N.J. 2005).

Bd. of Educ. of Hendrick Hudson Central Sch. Dist. v. Rowley, 458 U.S. 176 (1982).

Bd. of Educ. v. Dowell, 498 U.S. 237 (1991).

Bd. of Educ. v. Earls, 536 U.S. 822 (2002).

Bd. of Educ. v. Nyquist, 408 N.Y.S.2d 606 (1978).

Bd. of Educ. v. Nyquist, 439 N.E.2d 359 (N.Y. 1982).

Bd. of Educ. of Okla. City v. Dowell, 498 U.S. 237 (1991).

Bd. of Educ. v. Walter, 390 N.E.2d 813 (Ohio 1979).

Bd. of Regents v. Roth, 408 U.S. 564 (1972).

Benitez v. Wallis, 337 F.3d 1289 (11th Cir. 2003).

Bethel Sch. Dist. No. 403 v. Fraser, 478 U.S. 675 (1986).

Blazejewski v. Allegany Central Sch. Dist., 560 F.Supp. 701 (W.D.N.Y. 1983).

Bogle-Assegai v. Bloomfield Bd. of Educ., 467 F.Supp. 236 (D. Conn. 2006).

Bolling v. Sharpe, 347 U.S. 497 (1954).

Dailey v. Los Angeles Unified Sch. Dist., 470 P.2d 360 (Cal. 1970).

Daniels v. Williams, 474 U.S. 327 (1986).

Danson v. Casey, 399 A.2d 360 (Pa. 1979).

Davis v. Monroe County Bd. of Educ., 526 U.S. 629 (1999).

Davis, 426 U.S. at 241).

Delaware County Intermediate Unit v. Jonathan S., 809 A.2d 1051 (Pa. Commw. Ct. 2002).

Delgado v. Bastrop Indep. Sch. Dist., Civil No. 388 (W.D. Tex. June 15, 1948).

Dennis v. United States, 339 U.S. 162 (1950).

DeRolph v. State, 728 N.E.2d 993 (Ohio 2000).

Diana v. State Bd. of Educ., C-70-37 RFP (N.D.Cal. 1970).

Directors of Eastern and Western Sch. Districts of Cincinnati, Ohio ex rel. v. City of Cincinnati, 19 Ohio 178 (1850).

Doe v. DeSoto Parish Sch. Bd., 907 So.2d 275 (La. Ct. App. 2005).

Doe v. Ennis, Indep. Sch. Dist., 2007 WL 273550 (N.D. Tex. Jan. 31, 2007).

Doe v. Pulaski County Special Sch. Dist., 306 F.3d 616 (8th Cir. 2002).

Douglas D., In re, 626 N.W.2d 725 (Wis. 2001).

Duncan v. Hampton County Sch. Dist. No. 2, 517 S.E.2d 449 (S.C. App. 1999).

Duncan v. Louisiana, 391 U.S. 145 (1968).

Dupree v. Alma Sch. Dist. No. 30, 651 S.W.2d 90 (Ark. 1983).

Edgewood Indep. Sch. Dist. v. Kirby, 777 S.W.2d 391 (Tex. 1989).

Edwards v. California, 314 U.S. 160 (1941).

Eisenberg v. Montgomery County Pub. Schs., 197 F.3d 123 (4th Cir. 1999).

Elida Local Sch. Dist. Bd. of Educ. v. Erickson, 252 F.Supp.2d 476 (N.D.Oh. 2003).

Estelle v. Gamble, 429 U.S. 97 (1976).

Ex parte (see name of party).

Fair Sch. Finance Council of Okla. v. State, 746 P.2d 1135 (Okla. 1987).

Fernandez-Roque v. Smith, 599 F. Supp. 1103 (N.D. Ga. 1984).

Fisher v. Hurst, 333 U.S. 147 (1948).

Flaherty v. Keystone Oaks Sch. Dist., 247 F. Supp. 2d 698 (W.D. Pa. 2003).

Florence County Sch. Dist. Four v. Carter, 114 S. Ct. 361 (1993).

Fordice, United States v., 505 U.S. 717 (1992).

Freeman v. Pitts, 503 U.S. 467 (1992).

Gaines, Missouri ex rel. v. Canada, 305 U.S. 337 (1938).

Garrett v. Bd. of Educ., 775 F.Supp. 1004 (E.D. Mich. 1991).

Gebhart v. Belton, 144 A.2d 137 (Del. 1952).

Georgia Conference of NAACPs v. Georgia, 775 F.2d 1403 (11th Cir. 1985).

Georgia, United States v., 466 F.2d 197 (5th Cir. 1972).

GI Forum Image de Tejas v. Texas Educ. Agency, 87 F.Supp. 2d 667 (W.D.Tex. 2000).

Gladys J. v. Pearland Indep. Sch. Dist., 520 F.Supp. 869 (S.D.Tex. 1981).

Gong Lum v. Rice, 275 U.S. 78 (1927).

Gonzales v. Sheeley, 96 F.Supp. 1004 (D. Ariz. 1951).

Goss v. Bd. of Educ., 373 U.S. 683 (1963).

Gratz v. Bollinger, 539 U.S. 244 (2003).

Gray v. Univ. of Tenn., 342 U.S. 517 (1952).

Green v. County Sch. Bd. of New Kent County, 391 U.S. 430 (1968).

Greenland Sch. Dist. v. Amy N., 2003WL 1343023 (D.N.H. 2003).

Greenland Sch. Dist. v. Amy N., 358 F.3d 150 (1st Cir. 2004).

Gremo v. Karlin, 363 F.Supp.2d 771 (E.D. Pa. 2005).

Griffin v. County Sch. Bd. of Prince Edward County, 377 U.S. 218 (1964).

Griggs v. Duke Power Co., 401 U.S. 424 (1971).

Grkman v. Scanlon, 563 F.Supp. 793 (W.D.Pa. 1983).

Grutter v. Bollinger, 539 U.S. 306 (2003).

Guardians Ass'n v. Civil Serv. Comm'n, 463 U.S. 582 (1983).

Guinn v. Legislature of Nev., 71 P.3d 1269 (Nev. 2003).

Parents Involved in Community Schs. v. Seattle Dist. Schs., 551 U.S. ___, 127 S.Ct. 2738 (2007).

Parents Involved in Community Schs. v. Seattle Sch. Dist. No. 1, 137 F.Supp. 2d 1224 (W.D. Wash. 2001).

Pauley v. Bailey, 324 S.E.2d 128 (1984).

Pauley v. Kelly, 255 S.E.2d 859 (1979).

Pearson v. Murray, 182 A. 590 (Md. 1936).

People v. Feldman, 791 N.Y.S.2d 361 (S. Ct. 2005).

Personnel Administrator of Massachusetts v. Feeney, 442 U.S. 256 (1979).

Pierce v. Soc'y of Sisters, 268 U.S. 510 (1925).

Pitts v. Freeman, 887 F.2d 1438 (11th Cir. 1989).

Planned Parenthood of Southeaster Pa. v. Casey, 505 U.S. 833 (1992).

Plessy v. Ferguson, 163 U.S. 537 (1896).

Plyler v. Doe, 457 U.S. 202 (1982).

Polk v. Central Susquehanna Intermediate Unit No. 16, 853 F.2d 171 (3rd Cir. 1988).

Prince v. Massachusetts, 321 U.S. 158 (1944).

Raleigh v. Indep. Sch. Dist. No. 625, 275 N.W.2d 572 (Minn. 1978).

Regents of University of California v. Bakke, 438 U.S. 265 (1978).

Reynolds v. Board of Pub. Instruction for Dade County, Fla., 148 F.2d 754 (5th Cir. 1945).

Ritchie v. People, 40 N.E. 454 (Ill. 1895).

Roberson v. Duval County Sch. Bd., 618 So. 2d 360 (Fla. Dist. Ct. App. 1993).

Roberts v. City of Boston, 5 Cushing Reports 198 (1849).

Roberts v. U.S. Jaycees, 468 U.S. 609 (1984).

Robinson v. Cahill (Robinson I), 303 A.2d 273 (N.J. 1973).

Rodriguez, In re, 81 F. 337 (W.D. Tex. 1897).

Romer v. Evans, 517 U.S. 620 (1996).

Romo v. Laird, No. 21617 (Maricopa County Super. Ct. 1925).

Roosevelt Elem. v. State, 74 P.3d 258 (Ariz. Ct. App. 2003).

Roosevelt Elem. v. State, 877 P.2d 806 (Ariz. 1994).

Rose v. Council for Better Educ., 790 S.W.2d 186 (Ky. 1989).

Ross v. Eckels, 434 F.2d 1140 (5th Cir. 1970).

Rupp v. Bryant, 417 So. 2d 658 (Fla. 1982).

Rutan v. Republican Party of Ill., 497 U.S. 62 (1990).

Salazar v. State, 193 S.W.2d 211 (Tex. Crim. App. 1946).

Salvatierra v. Indep. Sch. Dist., 284 U.S. 580 (1931).

San Antonio Indep. Sch. Dist. v. Rodriguez, 411 U.S. 1 (1973).

Sanchez v. State, 181 S.W.2d 87 (Tex. Crim. App. 1944).

Sanchez v. Texas, 243 S.W.2d 700 (Tex. Crim. App. 1951).

Santamaria v. Dallas Indep. Sch. Dist., Civ. Action No. 3:06-CV-692-L, 2007 U.S. Dist. LEXIS 26821, at 6–7 (N.D. Tex. Apr. 10, 2007).

Schaffer v. Weast, 546 U.S. 49 (2005).

Scott v. Sanford, 60 U.S. 393 (1857).

Serrano v. Priest (Serrano I), 487 P.2d 1241 (Cal. 1971).

Serrano v. Priest (Serrano II), 557 P.2d 929 (Cal. 1976).

Shapiro v. Thompson, 394 U.S. 618 (1969).

Sheff v. O'Neill, 678 A.2d 1267 (Conn. 1996).

Shelley v. Kraemer, 334 U.S. 1 (1948).

Shofstall v. Hollins, 515 P.2d 590 (Ariz. 1973).

Singleton v. Jackson Mun. Separate Sch. Dist., 419 F.2d 1211 (5th Cir. 1969).

Sipuel v. Board of Regents of Univ. of Okla., 332 U.S. 631 (1948).

Skeen v. State, 505 N.W.2d 299 (Minn. 1993).

Slaughterhouse Cases, 83 U.S. 36 (1873).

Sly v. Bd. of Educ., 515 P.2d 895 (Kan. 1973).

Smith v. Concordia Parish Sch. Bd., 419 F.2d 1211 (5th Cir. 1969).

Smithtown Central Sch. Dist., 32 IDELR 46 (N.Y. SEA 1999).

Smuck v. Hobson, 408 F.2d 175 (D.C.Cir. 1969).

South Carolina, United States v., 445 F. Supp. 1094 (D.S.C. 1977).

Spangler v. Pasadena City Bd. of Educ., 611 F.2d 1239 (9th Cir. 1979).

State v. Bd. of Edu. of City of St. Louis, 233 S.W.2d 697 (Mo. 1950).

State v. Kuhia, 96 P.3d 590 (Hawaii 2004).

State v. Scruggs, 2004WL 1245557 (Conn. Super. Ct. Mar. 8, 2004), rev'd on other grounds, 905 A.2d 24 (Conn. 2006).

Stowe Citizens for Resp. Gov't. v. State, 730 A.2d 573 (Vt. 1999).

Swann v. City of Charlotte Mecklenburg Bd. of Educ., 402 U.S. 1 (1971).

Sweatt v. Painter, 339 U.S. 629 (1950).

Sweetwater County v. Henkle, 491 P. 2d 1234 (Wyo. 1971).

Sweezy v. New Hampshire, 354 U.S. 234 (1957).

Tenn. Small Sch. Sys. v. McWherter, 851 S.W.2d 139 (Tenn. 1993).

Tenn. Small Sch. Sys. v. McWherter, 91 S.W.3d 232 (Tenn. 2002).

Test Masters Educ. Servs. v. Singh, 428 F.3d 559 (5th Cir. 2005).

Texas Educ. Agency, United States v. (Austin II), 532 F.2d 380 (5th Cir. 1976).

Texas Educ. Agency, United States v. (Austin III), 564 F.2d 162 (5th Cir. 1977).

Texas Educ. Agency, United States v., 467 F.2d 848 (5th Cir. 1972).

Texas, United States v., 342 F.Supp. 24 (E.D. Tex. 1971).

Texas, United States v., 509 F.2d 192 (5th Cir. 1975).

Theno v. Tonganoxie Unified Sch. Dist. No. 464, 377 F. Supp. 2d 952 (D. Kan. 2005).

Thompson v. Engelking, 537 P.2d 635 (Idaho 1975).

Thompson v. Gibbes, 60 F. Supp. 872, 876 (D.C.S.C. 1945).

Tinker v. Des Moines Indep. Cmty. Sch. Dist., 393 U.S. 503 (1969).

Toliver, State ex rel. v. Board of Educ., 230 S.W.2d 724 (Mo. 1950).

Troxel v. Granville, 530 U.S. 57 (2000).

Trummel v. Mitchell, 131 P.3d 305, 311–12 (Wash. 2006).

Turner v. Keefe, 50 F.Supp. 647 (D.C.Fla. 1943).

Tuttle v. Arlington Sch. Bd., 195 F.3d 698 (4th Cir. 1999).

United States v. _____ (see opposing party).

Vernonia Sch. Dist. 47J v. Acton, 515 U.S. 646 (1995).

Vincent v. Voight, 614 N.W.2d 388 (Wis. 2000).

Virginia v. Black, 538 U.S. 343 (2003).

Virginia, United States v., 518 U.S. 515 (1996).

Vorchheimer v. Sch. Dist. of Philadelphia, 400 F.Supp. 326 (E.D. Pa. 1975).

Washington v. Davis, 426 U.S. 229 (1976).

Washington v. Salisbury, 306 S.E.2d 600 (S.C. 1983).

Washington v. Seattle Sch. Dist. No. 1, 458 U.S. 457 (1982).

Watson v. City of Memphis, 373 U.S. 526 (1963).

Wayne Highlands Sch. Dist., In re, 24 IDELR 476 (Pa. SEA 1996).

Weixel v. Board of Education of the City of New York, 287 F.3d 138 (2nd Cir. 2002).

West Chester Area Sch. Dist. v. Bruce, 194 F.Supp.2d 417, 420 (E.D.Pa. 2002).

West Chester Area Sch. Dist., In re, 35 IDELR 235 (Pa. SEA 2001).

West Orange-Cove Consol. Indep. Sch. Dist. v. Alanis, 107 S.W.3d 558 (Tex. 2003).

Westminster Sch. Dist. v. Mendez, 161 F.2d 774 (9th Cir. 1947).

White v. Regester, 412 U.S. 755 (1973).

Whittekind, In re, 2004WL 3090246 (Ohio Ct. App. Dec. 17, 2004).

Williams v. McNair, 316 F.Supp. 134 (D.S.C. 1970).

Williams v. McNair, 401 U.S. 951 (1971).

Wilson v. Bd. of Supervisors, 92 F.Supp. 986 (E.D.La. 1950).

Wisconsin v. Mitchell, 508 U.S. 476 (1993).

Wisconsin v. Yoder, 406 U.S. 205 (1972).

Wisniewski v. Bd. of Educ., 494 F.3d 34 (2nd Cir. 2007).

Wygant v. Jackson Bd. of Educ., 476 U.S. 267 (1986).

Yankton Sch. Dist. v. Schramm, 93 F.3d 1369 (8th Cir. 1996).

Yick Wo v. Hopkins, 118 U.S. 356 (1886).

Yonkers Bd. of Educ., United States v., 624 F.Supp. 1276 (S.D.N.Y. 1985).

Zamora v. New Braunfels Indep. Sch. Dist., 519 F.2d 1084 (5th Cir. 1975).

Zelman v. Simmons-Harris, 536 U.S. 639 (2002).

Zobrest v. Catalina Foothills Sch. Dist., 113 S. Ct. 2462 (1993).

About the Contributors

Douglas E. Abrams is an Associate Professor of Law at the University of Missouri school of Law. He earned his B.A. *summa cum laude* from Wesleyan University (Phi Beta Kappa) and his J.D. from Columbia University School of Law. He has written or co-authored five books, and the U.S. Supreme Court has cited his law review articles in four decisions. From 1976–78, Professor Abrams served as law clerk to Judge Hugh R. Jones of the New York Court of Appeals (New York's highest court). From 1978–81, he was in private practice with a Park Avenue firm in New York City. From 1982–89, he was an associate professor at Fordham University Law School. Professor Abrams' first book was *The Law of Civil RICO* (Aspen 1991). Thomson/West recently published the third editions of his casebook, *Children and the Law—Doctrine, Policy and Practice* (co-author), and his *Children and the Law In a Nutshell* (co-author). In 2003, he wrote *A Very Special Place in Life: The History of Juvenile Justice in Missouri*. His most recent book is *Contemporary Family Law*, a casebook published by Thomson/West in 2006 (co-author). His published works include "Missouri's Long Road to Juvenile Justice" in *Law, Society, and Politics in the Midwest* (Ohio University Press Series 2007); "An Open Letter to Communities: What Community Leaders Can Do to Improve Youth Sports" with Bob Bigelow, Bruce Svare, Richard Irving and Steve Fisher in *Learning Culture Through Sports: Exploring the Role of Sports in Society* (eds. Sandra Spikard Prettyman and Brian Lampman) (Rowman and Littlefield Education 2006); and "Child Abuse and Neglect" in *Missouri Juvenile Law* (MoBar 3rd ed. 2007).

Lori Czop Assaf is an Assistant Professor at Texas State University–San Marcos College of Education. Her published works include "Professional Identity of a Reading Teacher: Responding to High-Stakes Testing Pressures" (2008); " 'Everything They Were Giving Us Created Tension': Creating and Managing Tension in a Graduate-Level Multicultural Course Focused on Literacy Methods" (2006); "Exploring Identities in a Reading Specialization Program" (2005); "Exploring Fifth Grade Bilingual Students' Understanding of Character" (2004); "The Authoring of Self: Looking at Preservice Teachers' Professional Identities as Reflected in an Online Environment" (2003); "Fifth-Grade Bilingual Students and Precursors to 'Subtractive Schooling'" (2003); "High-Stakes Testing in Reading: Today in Texas, Tomorrow?" (2001); "One Teacher's Response to the Testing Pressures: Are Urban Schools Losing the Battle?" (2005); "Using Series Books with Your Students: Tricks to Get You Started" (2005); and " 'I Can't Ask Them to Curl Up to a Passage': Two Teachers' Responses to High-stakes Reading Tests" (2005).

Bruce D. Baker is Associate Professor in the Department of Educational Theory, Policy and Administration at Rutgers, The State University of New Jersey. Professor Baker is lead author of *Financing Education Systems* (Merrill/Prentice Hall 2008) and sits on the editorial boards of the *Journal of Education Finance* and *Education Finance and Policy*. He has participated as an expert witness in school finance litigation in Arizona, Kansas, Nebraska, and Missouri and in ongoing litigation in Pennsylvania and New Jersey and has consulted with numerous additional state legislatures and special interests. Professor Baker has published extensively on educational issues, including *The Ecology of Educational Systems: Data and Models for Improvisational Leading and Learning* (Merrill/Prentice-Hall 2007) (Morphew, C. and Baker, B.D); "On the Utility of National Data for Estimating Generalizable Price and Cost Indices in Higher Education" in the *Journal of Education Finance* (2007) (with Wolf-Wendel, L.E., Twombly, S.B.); "Exploring the Faculty Pipeline in Educational Administration: Evidence from the Survey of Earned Doctorates 1990 to 2000" in *Educational Administration Quarterly*; "Academic Drift, Institutional Production and Professional Distribution of Graduate Degrees in Educational Administration" in *Educational Administration Quarterly*; "Kansas School Finance Litigation: Judicial Activism, Legislative Defiance & Legal Innovation" in *Journal of Education Finance*; "Evaluating the Reliability, Validity and Usefulness of Education Cost Studies" in *Journal of Education Finance*; "Urban Legends, Desegregation and School Finance: Did Kansas City Really Prove That Money Doesn't Matter?" in *Mich. J. of Race and Law* (2007) (with Oluwole, J.); "Race Conscious Funding Strategies in School Finance" in *B.U. Pub. Int. L.J.*; "Charter Schools, Teacher Labor Market Regulation and Teacher Quality: Evidence from the Schools and Staffing Survey" in *Educational Policy* (2006) (Wolf-Wendel, L., Baker, B.D., Twombly, S., Tollefson, N., & Mahlios, M.); and numerous other articles.

Len Biernat is a Professor of Law at Hamline University School of Law. As a former member of the Minnesota House of Representatives, Professor Biernat links the legal curriculum he teaches with actual law making. He has served as a member of the Supreme Court Task Force on Visitation and Support and is currently a member of a Task Force on Parental Cooperation. Professor Biernat also served as a member of the Minneapolis Board of Education from 1990–97. He has authored several major bills that have become Minnesota laws. He has served on the ad hoc committee of ABA Model Rules of Professional Conduct and has chaired continuing legal education programs in family law, school law, legal education, and lawyer competency. Professor Biernat is coauthor of *Legal Ethics for Management and Their Counsel* (Lexis Law Publishing), and he wrote a chapter on the federal role in education in *Federal Administrative Practice* (West Law Publishing). He has published "The Federal Role in Education Aid and Assistance" in *West's Federal Administrative Practice* (2008 Update); "Federal Intent for State Child Support Guidelines: Income Shares, Cost Shares, and the Realities of Shared Parenting," 37 *Fam. L.Q.* 165 (2003) (with Jo Michelle Beld); "Forces Changing Family Law in Minnesota," 28 *Wm. Mitchell L. Rev.* 873 (2001); "Aid to Education" in *West's Federal Administrative Practice* (Charles McManis, et al., eds., 3rd ed. 1999; 2000–2006 supplements); "Limiting Mobility and Improving Student Achievement," 23 *Hamline L. Rev.* 1 (1999); *Legal Ethics for Management and Their Counsel* (Lexis Law Publishing, 1995–1998 eds.) (with R. Hunter Manson); "Corporate Practice: From the Model Code to the Model Rules to the States," 34 *St. Louis U. L.J.* 27 (1989); "Subjective Criteria in Faculty Employment Decisions Under Title VII: A Camouflage for Discrimination and Sexual Harassment," 20 *U.C. Davis L. Rev.* 501 (1986–1987); and "Why Not Model Rules of Conduct for Law Students."

Geneva Brown is an Assistant Professor of Law at the Valparaiso University School of Law. She earned her M.A. at the University of Illinois–Chicago. She also earned her J.D. at the University of Wisconsin Law School and her B.A. at the University of Wisconsin. She has published "Brothers Always Die First: The Failure of the Social Contract and Reinforcement of the Racial Contract that Prohibits the Rehabilitation and Reintegration of Black Male Offenders Into a Free Society" (in progress); "Little Girl Lost: Secondary Victimization of Teenaged Girls: The Las Vegas Metro and the Use of Material Witness Holds" (2007); "False Confessions and Miranda Warning" in *Encyclopedia of American Civil Lib-*

erties (Paul Finkelman ed., Routledge 2006); "When the Bough Breaks: Traumatic Paralysis: An Affirmative Defense Battered Mothers," *Wm. Mitch. L. Rev.* (2005)

Kate Bueler is the Selection and Placement Manager, Teach California Charters. She has also served as The New Teacher Project State Outreach Manager at American Board for Certification of Teacher Excellence, Literacy Educator at Say Yes to Education! and the Data Collector at National Center for Children and Families.

Victoria Dodd is a professor of law at Suffolk University School of Law. She received her B.A. from Radcliffe College and her J.D. from the University of Southern California. Her professional activities include Honorary Member, Phi Delta Phi; Member, Order of the Coif; Member, Judicial Administration Section Council, 1987–92; Member, Massachusetts Special Advisory Committee on Time Standards (Case Management Sub-Committee), 1987–88; Chair, Section on Law & Education, AALS, 1987–88, 1993–94, 2000–01; Executive Committee Member, 1986–present; Co-Chair, Court Accreditation Project, MA Bar Association, 1988–91; Trustee, Massachusetts Law Reform Institute, 1992–96; Life Member, Massachusetts Bar Foundation; Member, AALS Standing Committee on Sections and the Annual Meeting, 2002–05. Her published works include: *Practical Education Law for the Twenty-First Century* (2003); "A Critique of the Bush Education Proposal," 53 *Admin. L. Rev.* 851 (2001); "The Education Justice: The Honorable Lewis Franklin Powell, Jr.," 29 *Fordham Urb. L.J.* 683 (2001); "Student Rights: Can We Create Violence-Free Schools That Are Still Free?" 34 *New Eng. L. Rev.* 623 (2000); "Public Education and Change: Not an Oxymoron," 17 *St. Louis U. Pub. L. Rev.* 109 (1999); "Becoming Gentlemen," 4 *Mass. L. Rev.* 9 (1997); "Introduction to Symposium on Law and Education," 39 *U.S.D. L. Rev.* 233 (1994); "Toward a National System of State Court Accreditation," *Judicature* (1989); "The Non-Contractual Nature of the Student–University Contractual Relationship," 33 *Kan. L. Rev.* 701 (1985); and "*McDuffy v. Robertson*: An (Adequate) Education for All," *Advocate* (1993) (Suffolk University Law School).

Caitlin McMunn Dooley is an Assistant Professor of Law at Georgia State University Department of Early Childhood Education. She earned her Ph.D. at the University of Texas at Austin, her M.T. at the University of Virginia, and her B.A. at the University of Virginia. Dr. McMunn Dooley conducts research related to literacy development, teacher education, learning, and the value of diversity. Her research has appeared in peer-reviewed journals and books published by the National Council of Teachers of English, the International Reading Association, Sage Publishers, and the American Educational Studies Association. She teaches courses related to literacy instruction and learning to pre-service teachers and graduate students. She is the recipient of the Outstanding Dissertation Award given by the Georgia Association of Teacher Educators (as well as a Distinguished Finalist in the International Reading Association and National Reading Conference awards). Prior to joining the ECE faculty in 2005, Caitlin taught teachers and children in urban schools for more than a decade.

Maurice R. Dyson is an Associate Professor of Law at Thomas Jefferson School of Law. Following his graduation from Columbia Law School as a Harlan Fiske Stone Scholar, Professor Dyson practiced law with the firm of Simpson Thacher & Bartlett where he specialized in mergers and acquisitions, securities, and leverage buyouts valued at approximately $166 billion. Professor Dyson has also participated in landmark school finance litigation and in federal civil rights enforcement as the Special Projects team attorney for the U.S. Department of Education Office for Civil Rights (OCR) where he was recognized for his work in inter-district funding equity analysis. A member of the Bar of the U.S Supreme Court, Professor Dyson has also served as the national chairperson of the Association of American Law Schools (AALS) Section on Education Law, the national executive board member of the AALS Section of Minority Groups, a member of the board of directors of the Mildred Quinn Foundation, and the NY program coordinator of the Merrill Lynch Philanthropic Foundation. In addition, he has served as educational policy adviser to the Texas State Legislature Joint Select Committee on Public School Finance and to various elected officials, and he has taught law on the faculties of Columbia University, the City University of New York, and Southern Methodist University Dedman School of Law. Professor Dyson received his A.B. from Columbia College, Columbia University, and is the recipient of numerous awards including the prestigious King's Crown Award, the Kluge Award, the Albert Roothbert Endowment, the Lester A. and Stella Porter Russell Endowment, the Society of the Order of the Barristers, and the Taft Samuel Carpenter Award for Teaching Excellence. He has published in the fields of education law, civil rights, critical race theory, philosophy, race and economics, and psycho-sociology. His works include "When Government Is a Passive Participant in Private Discrimination: A Critical Look at White Privilege & the Tacit Return to Interposition in *PICS v. Seattle School District*," *U. of Tol. L. Rev.* (2008); "De Facto Segregation & Group Blindness: Proposals for Narrow Tailoring Under a New Viable State Interest in *PICS v. Seattle School District*," *UMKC L. Rev.* (2008); "Awakening an Empire of Liberty: Exploring the Roots of Socratic Inquiry & Political Nihilism in American Democracy," *Wash. U. L.Q.* (2005); "Towards an Establishment Clause Theory of Race-Based Allocation: Administering Race-Conscious Financial Aid After *Grutter* and *Zelman*, *S. Cal. Interdisc. L.J.* (2005); "Racial Free-Riding the Coattails of a Dream Deferred: Can I Borrow Your Social Capital?" *Wm. & Mary Bill Rts. J.* (2005); "The Death of Robin Hood?: Proposals to Overhaul Public School Finance," 11 *Geo. J. on Poverty L. & Pol'y* 1 (2004); "Putting Quality Back into Equality: The Constitutionality of Charter School Enabling Legislation in a Post-*Grutter* Era," *Rutgers L.J.* (2004); "Playing Games with Equality: A Game-Theoretic Critique of Educational Sanctions, Remedies and Strategic Noncompliance," 77 *Temp. L. Rev.* 577 (2004); "Multiracial Identity, Monoracial Authenticity & Racial Privacy: Towards an Adequate Theory of Multiracial Resistance," 9 *Mich. J. Race & L.* 387 (2004); "Safe Rules or Gay Schools: The Dilemma of Sexual Orientation Segregation in Public Education," 7 *U. Pa. J. Const. L.* 183 (2004) (with N. Harris); "In Search of the Talented Tenth: Diversity, Affirmative Access, and University-Driven Reform," 6 *Harv. Latino L. Rev.* 41 (2003); "Leave No Child Behind: Normative Proposals to Link Educational Adequacy Claims and High Stakes Assessment Due Process Challenges," 7 *Tex. J.C.L & C.R.* 1 (2002); "Finance and Educational Ultimatums: A Look at School Funding Implications for Public School Accountability," *Conn. Pub. Interest L. J.* (2002) (symposium); and "A Covenant Broken: The Crisis of Educational Remedy for New York City's Failing Schools," 44 *How. L.J.* 107 (2000).

Robeert A. Garda is an Associate Professor of Law at the University of Loyola New Orleans School of Law. Professor Garda joined the Loyola Law School faculty in 2002. Prior to joining the faculty, he graduated from Duke University Law School, where he served as Articles Editor on the *Duke Law Journal*. After externing for Justice Zimmerman of the Utah Supreme Court, Professor Garda became a partner at the Salt Lake City firm of Fabian & Clendenin, focusing primarily on the areas of commercial litigation, employment law and education law. Professor Garda's teaching and scholarly interests include contracts and education law, with an emphasis on legal issues relating to educating the disabled. He served as 2008 chair of the Education Law Section of the American Association of Law Schools. He has published "Coming Full Circle: The Journey from Separate but Equal to Separate and Unequal Schools," 2 *Duke J. Const. L. & Pub. Pol'y* 1 (2007); "Who is Eligible Under the Individuals with Disabilities Education Improvement Act?" 35

J. L. & Educ. 291 (Summer 2006); "The New IDEA: Shifting Educational Paradigms to Achieve Racial Equality in Special Education," 56 *Ala. L. Rev.* 1071 (2005); Untangling Eligibility Requirements Under the Individuals with Disabilities in Education Act, 69 **Mo. L. Rev.** 441 (Spring 2004); "If You've Received This Document in Error…," *The Young Lawyer* (April 2003); and "Lessons Learned from Due Process Hearings: How to Create 'Court-Proof' IEPs," *The Utah Special Educator* (Spring 2000).

Preston C. Green III is a professor at Pennsylvania State University. He also taught at the University of Massachusetts, where he served as an associate professor in the Department of Educational Policy, Research, and Administration and as assistant dean for pre-major advising services. Dr. Green holds an Ed. D. in educational administration from Teachers College, Columbia University, and a J.D. from the Columbia University School of Law. Professor Green's research has focused on the legal issues surrounding charter schools and the impact of the law on minority and disadvantaged students' ability to obtain a quality education. His recent publications include *Financing Education Systems* (with Craig Richards & Bruce Baker) (Merrill/Prentice Hall 2008); *Charter Schools and the Law: Establishing New Legal Relationships* (with Julie Mead) (Gordon 2004). He publishes regularly in educational journals and law reviews, including *West's Education Law Reporter*, *Brigham Young University Law & Education Journal*, and the *Texas Forum on Civil Rights & Civil Liberties*. Dr. Green has taught courses relating to the legal and policy aspects of personnel management, labor relations, and social justice issues.

Donna M. Harris is an Assistant Professor of Law at the University of Rochester Warner School of Education. She earned her Ph.D. at the University of Wisconsin at Madison and currently researches school reform, educational policy, and the social organization of public schools and classrooms. She is particularly interested in understanding how educational institutions, policies, and practices affect learning opportunities and experiences—especially for students of color. She explores how teacher expectations affect the application of educational standards and the impact race has on elementary school reading ability group placement. Harris's expertise includes ability grouping and tracking, whole school reform, standards-based education, and high-stakes testing. She teaches courses in school reform, educational policy, and race and education.

Danielle Holley-Walker is an Associate Professor of Law at the University of South Carolina School of Law. She received her J.D. from Harvard Law School and her B.A. from Yale University. Professor Holley-Walker teaches Civil Procedure I and II, Race and the Law, Administrative Law, and Federal Practice. Professor Holley-Walker has published numerous articles on issues of civil rights and education, including recent articles on No Child Left Behind, charter school policy, desegregation plans, and affirmative action in higher education. Her ongoing research agenda focuses on issues of educational equity and the governance of public schools. Before joining the University of South Carolina faculty, Professor Holley-Walker taught at Hofstra University School of Law. Prior to beginning her teaching career Professor Holley-Walker practiced civil litigation at Fulbright & Jaworski, LLP in Houston, Texas. She also clerked for Judge Carl E. Stewart of the Unites States Court of Appeals for the Fifth Circuit. Professor Holley-Walker earned a B.A. from Yale University and her law degree from Harvard University. Her published works include "The Accountability Cycle: The Recovery School District Act and New Orleans' Charter Schools," 40:1 *Conn. L. Rev.* 125 (2007); "The Importance of Negotiated Rulemaking to the No Child Left Behind Act," 85:4 *Neb. L. Rev.* 1015 (2007); "Is *Brown* Dying?: Exploring the Resegregation Trend in Our Public Schools," 49 *New York Law School L. Rev.* 1085 (2004–2005); "Narrative Highground: The Failure of Intervention as a Procedural Device in Affirmative Action Litigation," 53 *Case W. Res. L. Rev.* 103 (Fall 2003); and "The Texas Ten Percent Plan" (with D. Spencer), 34 *Harv. C.R.-C.L. Rev.* 245 (1999).

Osamudia R. James is an Associate Professor of Law at the University of Miami School of Law. Professor Osamudia James received a B.A. *cum laude* from the University of Pennsylvania in 2001; a J.D. *cum laude* from the Georgetown University Law Center in 2004; and an LL.M. from the University of Wisconsin Law School, where she also served as a William H. Hastie Fellow from 2006 to 2008. She was previously an associate with King & Spalding in Washington, D.C. She writes and teaches in the areas of education law, race and the law, administrative law, and torts. She is a member of both the Florida and D.C. Bars. She has published "Business as Usual: The Roberts Court's Continued Neglect of Adequacy and Equity Concerns in American Education," 59 *S.C. L. Rev.* 793 (2008); and "Breaking Free of Chevron's Constraints: *Zuni Public School District et al. v. U.S. Department of Justice*," 56 *U. Kan. L. Rev.* 147 (2007).

William Kaplin is a professor of law at the Catholic University of America since 1970 and has been a tenured full professor since 1978. He specializes in education law and policy, constitutional law, and civil rights law. He has also been special counsel to the university since 1981. In 1984–85, he served as founding director of the law school's Law and Public Policy Program. Professor Kaplin has been a visiting professor at Cornell University (1975), a visiting professor at Wake Forest University (1990–91), a visiting scholar at the Institute for Educational Leadership, George Washington University (1976–77), a distinguished visiting scholar at the Institute for Higher Education Law and Governance, University of Houston Law Center (1991), and a scholar-in-residence at Stetson University Law School (2000). Professor Kaplin's books include: *Cases, Problems, and Materials: An Instructional Supplement to the Law of Higher Education* (Rev. ed. 2001) (with Barbara Lee); *A Legal Guide for Student Affairs Professionals* (with Barbara A. Lee) (Jossey-Bass, Inc., 1997); *The Law of Higher Education: A Comprehensive Guide to the Legal Implications of Administrative Decisionmaking* (with Barbara A. Lee) (3rd ed., Jossey-Bass, Inc., 1995); and *The Concepts and Methods of Constitutional Law* (Carolina Academic Press, 1992). The first edition of *The Law of Higher Education* was recognized by the American Council on Education as the most outstanding book on higher education for the year 1978. The third edition of this book was recently supplemented by the *Year 2000 Cumulative Supplement* (with Barbara Lee) (National Association of College & University Attorneys, 2000). An earlier work of Professor Kaplin's, *State, School, and Family: Cases and Materials on Law Education* (Matthew Bender, 1973 & 2nd. Ed. 1979) (with Sorgen, Duffy, and Margolin) was the first law school casebook on education law in the United States. Professor Kaplin is the past chair of the Education Law Section of the Association of American Law Schools, the former editor of the *Journal of College and University Law*, and a former member of the Education Appeal Board of the U.S. Department of Education. He is currently a contributing editor for *Synfax Weekly Report on Critical Issues in Higher Education*, editorial board member for the *Journal of College and University Law*, and a mentor/leader for the biannual Houston Higher Education Law Roundtable; and since 1991 he has been a faculty member/presenter for the Annual National Conference on Law and Higher Education. He has been awarded the American Council on Education's Borden Award, the Association of Student Judicial Affairs' D. Parker Young Award, and the 20th Anniversary Scholarship Award presented by the Annual National Conference on Law and Higher Education, and he has been named a fellow of the National Association of College and University Attorneys. He has also published the *Year 2000 Cumulative Supplement to the Law of Higher Education* (third edition. Washington, D.C.: National Association of College and University Attorneys 2000) (with Barbara A. Lee); *The Importance* *of Process in Campus Administrative Decision-Making* (University of Houston: Institute for Higher Education Law and Governance 1992); *The Law of Higher Education: 1985–1990 Update* (National Association of College and University Attorneys 1991) (with Barbara A. Lee); *The Law of Higher Education: A Comprehensive Guide to Legal Implications of Administrative Decision Making* (Second edition, Jossey-Bass Inc. 1985); *Accrediting Agencies' Legal Responsibilities: In Pursuit of the Public Interest* (Council on Postsecondary Accreditation, 1982); *The Law of Higher Education* (Jossey-Bass Inc. 1980); *State, School, and Family: Cases and Materials on Law and Education* (Second edition, Matthew Bender 1979 (with others); *The Law of Higher Education: Legal Implications of Administrative Decision Making* (Jossey-Bass Publishers 1978); *Respective Roles of Federal Government, State Governments, and Private Accrediting Agencies in the Governance of Post Secondary Education* (Council on Postsecondary Accreditation 1975); *State, School, and Family: Cases and Materials on Law and Education* (with others) (Matthew Bender 1973); "The Law's View of Professional Power: Courts and the Health Professional Associations" in *SASHEP Staff Working Papers, Part II* (National Commission on Accrediting 1972); "Review of Rich Schools, Poor Schools: The Promise of Equal Educational Opportunity," 55 *Cornell Law Review* (1969); "A Typology and Critique of Title IX Sexual Harassment Law after Gebser and Davis," 26 *J.C. & U.L.* 615 (2000); "Limited Liability for Sexual Harassment by Students," 862 *Synfax Weekly Report* (June 1999); "Sexual Harassment: Law and Policy Issues in 1999," 815 *Synfax Weekly Report* (Feb. 1999); "Problem Solving and Storytelling in Constitutional Law Courses," 21 *Seattle U. L. Rev.* 101 (1998); "Case Study: Cyberspace Speech and Peer Harassment at State University" (with Gary Pavela), 9 *Synthesis: L. & Pol'y in Higher Educ.* 675 (Winter 1998); "'Hate Speech' on the College Campus: Freedom of Speech and Equality at the Crossroads," 27 *Land & Water L. Rev.* 243 (1992); "A Proposed Process for Managing the First Amendment Aspects of Campus Hate Speech," 63 *J. Higher Educ.* 517 (1992); "The Process of Constitutional Interpretation: A Synthesis of the Present and a Guide to the Future," 42 *Rutgers L. Rev.* 983 (1990); "Tributes to Mrs. Dorothy E. Lord (Secretary of the Cornell Law Review)," *Cornell L. Rev.* 72 (March 1987): IV; "Law on the Campus 1960–1985: Years of Growth and Challenge," 12 *J.C. & U.L.* 269 (1985); "Accrediting Agencies' Legal Responsibilities: In Pursuit of the Public Interest," 12 *J.L. & Educ.* 87 (1983); "An Overview of Legal Principles and Issues Affecting Postsecondary Athletics," 5 *J.L. & Educ.* 1 (1979); "Flag Salute, Patriotic Exercises, and Students' Rights," 44 *Contemp. Educ.* 84 (1972); "The Marjorie Webster Decisions on Accreditation," 52 *Educ. Record* 219 (1971); "Judicial Review of Accreditation: The Parsons College Case," 40 *J. Higher Educ.* 543 (1969); and "The Legal Status of the Educational Accrediting Agency" (with J. Philip Hunter), 52 *Cornell L. Rev.*104 (Fall 1966), *reprinted in* AACSB Bulletin 3 (1967).

DeAnn Lechtenberger is an Assistant Professor in the program area of Special Education at Texas Tech University College of Education Department of Educational Psychology & Leadership. She holds an M.S. degree in special education from the University of Texas at Dallas and a Ph.D. in special education leadership from the University of North Texas. She joined the Texas Tech faculty in 2003 and is the Principle Investigator and Program Director for Project IDEAL: Informing and Designing Education for All Learners, a grant program funded by the Texas Council for Developmental Disabilities. Dr. Lechtenberger's primary research interest involves human services reform efforts to support individuals with disabilities, specifically systems of care and mental healthcare transformation in America. Her work involves collaborating with community leaders, family members of individuals with disabilities, individuals with disabilities, and human services agencies (i.e., mental health agencies, schools, juvenile justice systems, child protective services) to enhance the ability of communities to become more inclusive of diverse individuals with a wide range of abilities. Dr. Lechtenberger's research also focuses on teacher education issues surrounding inclusive practices in schools, strengthening family–school–community partnerships, positive behavior supports in schools and communities, and transition to adulthood for individuals with developmental disabilities. Her published works include "Achieving the Promise: The Significant Role of Schools in Transforming Children's Mental Health in America," (with Mullins, F.E., & Greenwood, D.) *Teaching Exceptional Children* (in press); *Strengths-Based Planning for Transitioning Students with Sensory Impairments* (with Griffin-Shirley, N., Davidson, R., Shaunessey, M., & Laman, E.) (Linus Publications 2008); "Promoting Better Family–School–Community Partnerships for All of America's Children" (with Mullins, F.E.), *Beyond Behavior* (2004); "Communication with Families" (with Montague, M. & Warger, C. L.), *After School Extensions: Including Students with Disabilities in After School Programs* (Exceptional Innovations) (2002).

Moosung Lee is a Ph.D. candidate in the Department of Educational Policy and Administration at the University of Minnesota, funded by a Fulbright Scholarship. Currently, he is nearing completion of his Ph.D. dissertation about African-American immigrant students, funded by a Doctoral Dissertation Fellowship from the University of Minnesota. His main research areas are social mobility, social capital, and lifelong learning. His publications include "The Impact of Neighborhood Disadvantage on the Black–White Achievement Gap" (with N. Madyun), 14(2) *Journal of Education for Students Placed at Risk* (March 2009); and "Community Influences on E/BD Achievement" (with N. Madyun), 40 *Education and Urban Society* 307–328 (2008).

Na'im Madyun is an assistant professor in the Social Sciences in the College of Education and Human Development's Postsecondary Teaching and Learning Department at the University of Minnesota. His research is on social factors that influence achievement, with a special emphasis on the role of social disorganization theory, social capital, and social networks in explaining the achievement gap. His publications include "The Impact of Neighborhood Disadvantage on the Black–White Achievement Gap" (with M. Lee), 14(2) *Journal of Education for Students Placed at Risk,* (March 2009); and "Community Influences on E/BD Achievement" (with M. Lee) 40 *Education and Urban Society* 307–328 (2008).

Frank E. Mullins is an Associate Professor of Law at the University of North Texas. Dr. Mullins enjoys lifetime certifications in elementary education, secondary education, generic special education, seriously emotional disabilities, learning disabilities, and mental retardation, and is a certified Special Olympics coach. Dr. Mullins has worked as an instructor at the K–12 and university levels, and has also been a consultant and site analyst among other positions. He has given conference presentations in areas including NCLB, IDEA, student empowerment and success, and parent/teacher collaboration. Dr. Mullins has also spent countless hours serving the community as a foster parent, an AIDS counselor, and a HOST mentor, as well as working in foster care regulation, providing respite services.

Molly Townes O'Brien is a Professor of Law at the University of Wollongong. Professor O'Brien was an Associate Professor of Law at the University of Akron School of Law, where she taught Evidence, Trial Advocacy, and Criminal Law. From 1997 through 2001 she was the Director of Advocacy Skills Programs at Emory Law School. A graduate of Brown University and Northeastern University School of Law, O'Brien received her LL.M. from Temple University School of Law. She served as a judicial clerk in the United States District Court and the Georgia Supreme Court before practicing law in Pennsylvania as a civil litigator and then as an Assistant Public Defender. She later was an Honorable Abraham L. Freedman Teaching Fellow at Temple University. Proffesor O'Brien is an academic fellow to the International Society of Barristers, a fellow of Akron University's Center for Constitutional Law, and co-chair of the Clinical and Skills Education Committee of the American Bar Association Section of Legal Education and Admissions to the Bar. She also served on the Ohio Supreme Court Task Force on Jury Service and as Chair of the Association of American Law Schools Section on Education Law.

Dr. Joseph Oluwole is an Assistant Professor of Education Law at Montclair State University. His research interests include legal rights and responsibilities of teachers and public school districts, social justice and social responsibilities, educational access and equity, legal rights and responsibilities of students, and ethics in education. He is also an attorney licensed in Ohio and in Washington, D.C., and has served as Assistant Attorney General for the State of Ohio. Dr. Oluwole has published several articles analyzing laws and policies affecting education and has given conference and symposium lectures at several national venues, including the University of Iowa College of Law, Stanford Law School, the American Education Research Association, and the University Council for Educational Administration. His publications include "*Parents Involved* and Race-Conscious Measures: A Cause for Optimism" (with P. Green), 26 *Buffalo Pub. Int. L.J.* 1–38 (2008); "Charter Schools: Racial Balancing Provisions and *Parents Involved*" (with P. Green), 61 *Ark. L. Rev.* 1–52 (2008); "No Child Left Behind Act, Race and *Parents Involved*" (with P. Green), 5 *Hast. Race and Pov. L.J.* 271–308 (2008); "The *Pickering* Balancing Test and Public Employment—Free Speech Jurisprudence: The Approaches of the Federal Circuit Courts of Appeals," 46 *Duquesne L. Rev.* 133–76 (2008); "The implications of *Parents Involved* for Charter School Racial Balancing Provisions" (with P. Green), 229 *Educ. L. Rep.*, 309–32 (2008); "Eras in Public Employment-Free Speech Jurisprudence," 32 *Vermont L. Rev.* 317–47(2007); "Charter Schools Under the NCLB: Choice and Equal Educational Opportunity" (with P. Green), 22 *St. John's J. of Legal Commentary* 165–96 (2007); "Re-examining the constitutionality of prayer in school in light of the resignation of Justice O'Connor" (with J. Mead & P. Green), 36 *J.L. & Educ.* 381–406 (2007); "Hand Rule, Negligence and Public Adoption Agencies, 32 *U. Dayton L. Rev.* 32, 255–74 (2007); "Race-Conscious Funding Strategies and School Finance Litigation" (with B. Baker & P. Green), 16 *B.U. Pub. Int. L.J.* 39–71 (2006); and "An Open Question—Is There Really a Shortage of Administrators?" 24(2) *Pennsylvania Educational Leadership,* 47–52 (2005).

Angela Onwuachi-Willig graduated from Grinnell College in Grinnell, Iowa, where she majored in American Studies and was elected Phi Beta Kappa. She received her law degree from the University of Michigan Law School, where she was a Clarence Darrow Scholar, a Note Editor on the *Michigan Law Review,* and an Associate Editor of the founding issue of the *Michigan Journal of Race and Law.* After law school, Professor Onwuachi-Willig clerked for the Honorable Solomon Oliver, Jr., United States District Judge for the Northern District of Ohio, and the Honorable Karen Nelson Moore, United States Circuit Judge for the Sixth Circuit Court of Appeals. She also practiced law as a litigation and employment attorney at Jones Day in Cleveland, Ohio, and as an employment attorney with Foley Hoag LLP in Boston, Massachusetts. Professor Onwuachi-Willig joined the College of Law faculty in 2006 after three years as a professor at the University of California, Davis School of Law (King Hall). Her research and teaching interests include family law, employment discrimination, critical race theory, feminist legal theory, and evidence. Her recent publications include "Representative Government, Representative Court? The Supreme Court as a Representative Body," 90 *Minn. L. Rev.* 1252 (2006); "Undercover Other," 94 *Cal. L. Rev.* 873 (2006); "The Admission of Legacy Blacks," 60 *Vand. L. Rev.* 1141 (2007); "A Beautiful Lie: Exploring *Rhinelander v. Rhinelander* as a Formative Lesson on Race, Marriage, Identity, and Family," 95 *Cal. L. Rev.* 2393 (2007); "There's Just One

Hitch, Will Smith: Examining Title VII, Race, and Casting Discrimination on the Forti-eth Anniversary of *Loving v. Virginia*," 2007 *Wis. L. Rev.* 319; "Volunteer Discrimination," 40 *U.C. Davis L. Rev.* 1895 (2007); "Cracking the Egg: Which Came First—Stigma or Affirmative Action?" (with Emily Hough & Mary Campbell), 96 *Cal. L. Rev.* 1299 (2008). Professor Onwuachi-Willig was honored for her service by the Minority Groups Section of the Association of American Law Schools with the Derrick A. Bell Award, which is given to a junior faculty member who has made an extraordinary contribution to legal education, the legal system, or social justice.

Jerono Phyllis Rotich is an Assistant Professor at North Carolina Agricultural and Tech-nical State University. She earned her Ph.D. at the University of North Carolina Greens-boro in exercise science, health, and physical education. She also earned her M.S. in Education from SUNY Brockport and her B.S. at Kenyatta University. Professor Rotich began her teaching and coaching career in Kenya. She taught and coached at the K–12 as well as the college and university levels. While in the United States, she served as a grad-uate teaching and research assistant at the State University of New York at Brockport and at the University of North Carolina at Greensboro. In addition to her teaching, she is ac-tively involved in several community projects that focus on health and wellness. She serves on several boards and committees in Guilford County.

Jodie Roure is a first-generation college student and the daughter of Puerto Rican im-migrants. She graduated from Douglass College, Rutgers University, with a Bachelor's of Arts in English and a minor in Spanish. She is a former United States Supreme Court in-tern. She obtained her J.D from Western New England College School of Law in Massa-chusetts. She also studied International Human Rights Law Protection in San Jose, Costa Rica, at the University of Costa Rica Law School. In Costa Rica, she lived among the Bri Bri Indigenous tribe. She obtained her Ph.D. at the University at Buffalo–SUNY in Amer-ican Studies with a major in intercultural studies and international human rights and is an Arturo A. Schomburg Fellow. She has conducted extensive research in the area of human rights, including violence against women in Brazil, Puerto Rico, and the United States. Her doctoral dissertation is titled *International Human Rights Law as a Resource in Combating Domestic Violence: Transcending Legal, Social and Cultural Obstacles in Brazil and the United States.* She is currently an Assistant Professor in the Department of Latin American and Latina/o Studies at John Jay College of Criminal Justice, CUNY. She teaches in the areas of domestic violence/gender rights; criminal justice; international human rights international criminal justice; race, class, and ethnicity in the United States; and Latina/o studies. She is currently the John Jay Director of the Ronald H. Brown Summer Pre-Law Program. Prior to joining the faculty at John Jay, she worked for the Director of the Administrative Office of the New Jersey State Judiciary, the University at Buffalo–SUNY and the Center for Latino Arts and Culture at Rutgers University.

Hon. Lupe Salinas is a Professor of Law at Texas Southern University Thurgood Marshall School of Law. He earned his B.A. and J.D. at the University of Houston. He has served as Visiting District Court Judge, Houston, Texas, 1997–2006; Judge, 351st District Court, Houston, Texas, 1989–96; Chief, Federal Trial Division, Harris County Attorney's Office, Houston, Texas, 1985–88; Visiting Professor of Law, University of Houston Law Center, Houston, Texas, 1985; Chief, Civil Rights Division, U.S. Attorney's Office, Houston, Texas, 1980–83; Adjunct Professor of Law, University of Houston Law Center, 1975, 1982, 1985, 1992–93; Distinguished Lecturer, Political Science, University of Houston, 1975–83; 1992–94; Special Assistant to the U.S. Attorney General, U.S. Department of Justice, Wash-ington, D.C., 1979–1980; Assistant United States Attorney, Southern District of Texas Civil Rights Division, Houston, Texas, 1977–1979; Assistant District Attorney, Harris County,

Houston, Texas, 1974–1977; and Staff Attorney, Mexican–American Legal Defense & Educational Fund (MALDEF), San Antonio, Texas, 1972–1974. His published works include "Immigration and Language Rights: The Evolution of Private Racist Attitudes into American Public Law and Policy," 7 *Nevada L. J.* 895 (2007); "The Equal Treatment of Unequals: Barriers Facing Latinos and the Poor in Texas Public Schools" (with Dr. Robert H. Kimball), 14 *GEO. J. on POVERTY L. & POL' Y* 215 (2007); LINGUAPHOBIA, "Language Rights and the Right of Privacy," 3 Stan. *J. Civil Rts. & CIVIL LIBERTIES* 53 (2007); "Is It Time to Kill the Death Penalty?: A View from the Bench and the Bar," 34 *Am. J. Crim. L.* 39 (2006); "Latino Educational Neglect: The Results Bespeak Discrimination," 5 *U. Md. L. J.* 269 (2005); "Latinos and Criminal Justice in Texas: Has the New Millennium Brought Progress?" 30 *T. Marshall L. Rev.* 289 (2005); "Deportations, Removals and the 1996 Immigration Acts: A Modern Look at the Ex Post Facto Clause," 22 *B. U. Int'l L.J.* 245 (2004); "Gus Garcia and Thurgood Marshall: Two Legal Giants Fighting for Justice," 28 *T. Marshall L. Rev.* 145 (2003); Salinas & Hinojosa, "MABAH: The First Twenty Years," 1992 *Tex. B.J.* 365 (1992); Salinas & Torres, The Undocumented Mexican Alien: A Legal, Economic, and Social Analysis," 13 *Hous. L. Rev.* 863 (1976); *Comment*, "Mexican–Americans and the Desegregation of Schools in the Southwest," 8 *Hous. L. Rev.* 929 (1971); "Mexican–Americans and the Desegregation of Schools in the Southwest—A Supplement," 4 *El Grito* 59 (1971); "Can Chicanos Find Justice in Schools?" *Agenda*, (Fall 1973); and, prepared by Lupe Salinas & Ruben De Luna, *Notarios Publico*, a bilingual pamphlet published by the Texas Young Lawyers Association as a consumer protection service (1979).

Anita Kuykendall Stoll earned her Doctorate in Education from Teachers College, Columbia University. She serves as the Assistant Principal & Coordinator of the Extended Learning Opportunities at the Banneker Middle School. She has written in the arena of educational policy research including, "The Transfer of Scanning Probe Microscope Research to the University Classroom" and "A Study of White Flight from a Funky Suburban High School."

Susan Stuart is a Professor of Law at the Valparaiso University School of Law. She earned her J.D. at the Indiana University–Indianapolis. In addition, Professor Stuart earned her M.Ed. at Valparaiso University, and her B.A. at DePauw University. Professor Stuart practiced law for eleven years in Indianapolis after a three-year clerkship with the Indiana Court of Appeals. Her practice focused on education, labor, and employment law, but also included commercial litigation and bankruptcy matters. She left practice in 1996 to join the faculty at Indiana University School of Law–Bloomington and joined the Valparaiso University School of Law faculty on a full-time basis in 2001. She teaches legal writing, education law, and remedies, and is Director of the Academic Support Program.

Daniel B. Weddle is a Clinical Professor of Law at the University of Missouri–Kansas City School of Law, where he serves as Director of the UMKC Law School Strategies Program and teaches several courses, including Governmental and Legal Aspects of Education, Legal Aspects of Higher Education, Scholarly Writing, Litigation Drafting, Practical Skills, and Introduction to Lawyering Processes. As Director of the Law School Strategies Program, he oversees a comprehensive academic support program that includes a lecture series on effective study skills; a number of student-led structured study groups and academic enrichment workshops; a combination legal writing and law school strategies course; and individualized instruction for first, second, and third year students. He is also a contributing editor to the Law School Academic Support Blog. Professor Weddle developed and directed the first Council on Legal Education Opportunity (CLEO) Summer Institute ever held at UMKC and developed a second Institute for the summer of 1999. The six-week Institutes serve educationally and economically disadvantaged students who are planning to attend law schools around the country. He has served as a consultant to CLEO, designing and directing the annual CLEO summer Attitude Is Essential Weekend Seminar and Mid-Winter Seminar, which provide initial preparation and mid-year follow-up to disadvantaged first-year law students who are unable to attend the longer summer Institutes. A former high school teacher and administrator and former assistant dean of UMKC's School of Education, Professor Weddle has focused his research on issues in educational law, especially those concerning violence and bullying in schools. He has also been a frequent presenter at education law conferences, addressing religious issues arising in the public school context. In 2007, he served as chair of the Education Law Section of the Association of American Law Schools. His published works include "Gaming the Establishment Clause: Intelligent Design in the Public School Classroom" (in progress); "Brutality 101: Bullying in Higher Education" (in progress); "Holding Schools Accountable When Children Bully Children," *in Viewpoint: Understanding the Issues That Shape Education Today* (James V. Freemyer & Nancy Saunders, eds.) (2008); "Bullying in Schools: The Disconnect Between Empirical Research and Constitutional, Statutory, and Tort Duties to Supervise," 77 *Temp. L. Rev.* 641 (2004); "Dangerous Games: Student Hazing and Negligent Supervision," 187 *Educ. L. Rep.* 373 (2004); and "When Will Schools Take Bullying Seriously?" *Trial*, Oct. 2003, at 18. Professor Weddle graduated from the University of Kansas School of Law in 1995, serving on the staff of the Kansas Law Review and as the editor-in-chief of the Law Review's Criminal Procedure Review. Prior to joining UMKC, he practiced with the Wirken Group, P.C., in Kansas City, where he specialized in business, family law, and tort litigation.

Verna L. Williams is a Professor of Law at the University of Cincinnati College of Law. Professor Williams earned a B.S. degree from Georgetown University and her J.D. degree from Harvard Law School. Prior to joining the faculty in 2001, Professor Williams was Vice President and Director of Educational Opportunities at the National Women's Law Center, where she focused on issues of gender equity in education. During her time at the Center, Professor Williams was lead counsel and successfully argued before the United States Supreme Court *Davis v. Monroe County Board of Education*, which established that educational institutions have a duty to respond to and address complaints of student-to-student sexual harassment. Professor Williams also clerked for the Hon. David S. Nelson, U.S. District Judge for the District of Massachusetts. After the clerkship, she practiced law at the Washington, D.C., office of Sidley & Austin and at the U.S. Department of Justice. Professor Williams's current research examines the intersection of race, gender, and class in education law and policy. She has presented papers at such venues as the Latina/o Critical Race Theory Conference and meetings of the Association of Law, Culture and the Humanities. Professor Williams also has served as a consultant for the Ford Foundation; in that capacity, she chaired the convening of a national conference at the University of Cincinnati entitled "Women Coming Together: Claiming the Law for Social Change." Professor Williams received the Goldman Prize for Excellence in Teaching in 2004. She has published "Reading, Writing, and Reparations: Systemic Reform of Public Schools as a Matter of Justice," 11 *Mich. J. of Race & L.* 419 (2006); "Private Choices, Public Consequences: Public Education Reform and Feminist Legal Theory," 12 *Wm. & Mary J. Women & L.* 563 (2006); "On Being a Mentor," 22 *Harv. BlackLetter L.J.* 127 (2006); "Reform or Retrenchment: Single Sex Education and the Construction of Race and Gender," 2004 *Wis. L. Rev.* 15; and *Symposium Introduction*: "Women's Work is Never Done: Employment, Family, and Activism" (with Kristin Kalsem Brandser), 73 *U. Cin. L. Rev.* 361 (2004).

Index